The Edinburgh International Encyclopaedia of Psychoanalysis

The *Encyclopaedia* portrays psychoanalysis as a single discipline greater than any individual author including its founder, Freud. Entries are alphabetically arranged and fully cross-referenced, many with suggestions for further reading. Most importantly the book features both contributors and entries reflecting the various disciplines that have contributed to the development of psychoanalysis and a critical understanding thereof. It includes topics on psychoanalysis from psychoanalysts themselves, as well as topics that are best handled by psychiatrists, psychologists, psychotherapists, philosophers, medical researchers, historians, literary critics, anthropologists and linguists.

The *Encyclopaedia* caters for readers who require knowledge at a glance as well as those seeking a more detailed account. It includes numerous illuminating essays by distinguished contributors including: Howard Bacal, Hazel Barnes, Charles Brenner, Marcia Cavell, Morris Eagle, Peter Fonagy, Michael Eigen, James Grotstein, Thomas Ogden, Paul Roazen, Murray Stein, Allan Schore, Robert Stolorow and Robert Wallerstein.

The Edinburgh International Encyclopaedia of Psychoanalysis will stand as a major reference work for teaching, learning and researching psychoanalysis for the foreseeable future.

Features:

- Entries on all the concepts of the main psychoanalytic schools of thought including Jung
- Freud, Fairbairn, Jung, Klein, Bion, Kohut, Winnicott and Lacan are covered in detail
- Biographies of great analysts of the past are provided, as well as those of living psychoanalysts
- Existential psychoanalysis, child psychotherapy, group psychotherapy and psychiatry are dealt with extensively
- Surveys of psychoanalysis in forty-seven countries worldwide convey the extent and development of the discipline.

Ross Skelton is Senior Lecturer in Philosophy and Psychoanalysis, Trinity College, Dublin.

The Edinburgh International Encyclopaedia of Psychoanalysis

General Editor:
Ross M. Skelton, Trinity College, Dublin

Edinburgh University Press

Edinburgh University Press Ltd
22 George Square, Edinburgh

Typeset in 10/12pt Monotype Ehrhardt
by Servis Filmsetting Ltd, Manchester and
printed and bound in Great Britain by
Antony Rowe Ltd, Chippenham, Wilts

A CIP record for this book is available from the British Library

ISBN-10 0 7486 1265 3 (hardback)
ISBN-13 978 0 7486 1265 9 (hardback)

[redacted]

Contents

Acknowledgements	vi
Introduction	vii
The Edinburgh International Encyclopaedia of Psychoanalysis	1
List of Contributors	495
Index	504

Acknowledgements

In bringing *The Edinburgh International Encyclopaedia of Psychoanalysis* to completion, I owe a great debt of gratitude to psychoanalysts and scholars of psychoanalysis all over the world, in particular the *Encyclopaedia*'s 319 individual authors. In a work of some 1,000 entries it is inevitable that errors will occur, as word lengths had suddenly to be altered, resubmissions hastily arranged and perceived gaps instantly filled. But these will be no fault of my authors as they were unfailingly uncomplaining as well as quick to come to my aid. In particular I was fortunate to obtain the services of June Bernstein and Morris Eagle, assisted by Aleksandra Wagner, at short notice to complete the Freud entries. Similarly Jennifer Johns and Malcolm Pines stepped in at the eleventh hour to supply the Winnicott and Group Psychoanalysis entries respectively.

At a very early stage the late Paul Roazen was an inspiring source in suggesting contributors. However, the first inkling of how much help I would receive, and need to receive, at the editorial level was when I approached James Grotstein in Los Angeles for advice, which he gave at length and in depth. On my return to Ireland, it struck me that he himself might like to be involved more officially, so I contacted him and after a pause for thought he agreed to oversee nearly all of the Object Relations Theory entries – an enormous task in itself. With Bernard Burgoyne co-ordinating the Lacan entries and helping with a good number of the Freud entries, Murray Stein supervising Analytical Psychology and Cleo van Velsen attending to Psychiatry, these four have been an outstanding Editorial Board.

Together with the distinguished Consultant Editors (Lewis Aaron, Howard Bacal, June Bernstein, Ron Britton, Morris Eagle, John Muller, Malcolm Pines, Eric Rayner, Paul Roazen, William Richardson, Andrew Samuels, Robert Wallerstein) and the outstanding Executive Editors (Joe Aguayo, Shelley Ahanati, Betty Cannon, Rebecca Curtis, Elinor Fairbairn Birtles, Kirsty Hall, Rik Loose, Maria Rhode, David Scharff, Richard Tuch, Jane van Buren, Aleksandra Wagner) they made a magnificent team. Working with them has been not merely a pleasure for me, but an educative experience as well.

From the very start of this six-year project, my colleague, the philosopher William Lyons, gave me the benefit of his great scholarly ability at all times and this has helped me avoid many pitfalls. Jackie Jones and James Dale of Edinburgh University Press, while I suspect that they may often have wondered whether the *Encyclopaedia* would ever be completed, were unfailingly energetic and ever helpful over these long years. Fiona Barr has constructed a fine index which illuminates detail inside the alphabetically listed entries. I would also like to thank the governing board of the Arts and Social Sciences Benefactions Fund of Trinity College, Dublin, for much-needed and much-appreciated financial assistance.

In conclusion I want to express my deep gratitude for the 'hands-on' editorial assistance of Stephen Byrne, Alexandra Kohn, Dermot Moran, Joseph O'Gorman, Rachel Vaughan, Rob Weatherill and Roger Willoughby.

Introduction

At the opening of the twenty-first century, a hundred years after Freud's *Interpretation of Dreams*, hardly a country in the world remains untouched by psychoanalysis. It has adapted itself to rather than invaded the culture of many nations, even China, where the traditional 'distant' relation between doctor and patient might seem to be at the opposite pole from the intimacy of the analytic session. It is always interesting and informative to see how psychoanalysis adapts to the prevailing culture of a nation. In my own country, Ireland, deeply Christian in the first half of the twentieth century, it is doubtful if the discipline could have taken root had it not been for the linking of Freud with Jesus by Jonathan Hanaghan. Subsequent generations of Irish analysts have dropped this connection. In Japan psychoanalysis has been influenced by Buddhism by the inclusion of the *Ajase* complex and in India some analysts have been influenced by Hinduism. In Russia, surprisingly, Trotsky wanted to link Pavlov with Freud in a Marxist context. There are many such stories.

In the practice and theory of psychoanalysis there has always been a tragic tendency to split off into opposing schools and a history of mutual incomprehension; consequently there are dictionaries for individual schools but no comprehensive one for the whole subject. This encyclopaedia sets out to be a non-partisan and scholarly reference book on all schools of psychoanalysis and one that also treats all varieties of psychoanalyst (and analytical psychologist) even-handedly. Both Rycroft's *Critical Dictionary of Psychoanalysis* as well as Moore and Fine's *Psychoanalytic Terms and Concepts* were an inspiration for this enterprise, combining as they do excellence with accessibility. Unfortunately, they are both miniature, each a mere 200 pages in length. This *International Encyclopaedia* gives a more comprehensive account of all the terms of all major schools and, in addition, important disciplines not usually in existing dictionaries, such as child and group psychotherapy, are extensively covered.

The single simple idea behind the *Encyclopaedia* is that all the schools have more in common than the various historical and theoretical schisms suggest and, as an unexpected bonus, a volume such as this inevitably reveals previously unnoticed or unacknowledged overlaps and 'borrowings', lacunae and blindspots which may show the way towards a single stronger discipline. As regards overlap, it is arguable that all psychoanalytic schools conform to Freud's fundamental rule of speaking with least restraint – free association – and that most theories have something to say about the following central concepts: anxiety, defence, drive, ego, object, the Oedipus complex, self, super-ego, transference and the unconscious. Other common focus points are the concepts of complex, countertransference, death, hysteria, intersubjectivity, myth and obsessionality. However, whereas differing opinions are often juxtaposed in the *International Encyclopaedia*, they are not distortingly merged or 'summed up' in any way, but are kept separate, allowing readers to judge for themselves.

Those impatient with psychoanalytic schisms may feel vindicated by reading the entry in this encyclopaedia by Robert Wallerstein on outcome studies which, while confirming the general efficacy of psychoanalytic treatment, shows an almost alarming discrepancy between the theories of analysts and clinical results. For example, there is apparently no clear connection between the analyst's 'depth' interpretation and deep change in the patient. Nor are there marked differences in outcome as between one psychoanalytic school and another. These two insights might give analysts pause for thought in rushing to judgement about rival schools. Early in my own involvement with psychoanalysis I was fortunate to meet Masud Khan (over an extended, rather alcoholic lunch in Dublin) and he impressed on me the fact that, since sessions are private, no one knows what really happens in them. Since then I have come to learn that analysts often (and understandably) conform to theories of particular groups or schools to secure referrals and earn a living. However what analysts say when advertising their allegiances and training may be opposed to what they actually do in their analytic sessions. It has often been pointed out that even within a given 'school' the actual clinical practice of an individual analyst can be more like the practice of another 'alien' group. I am, therefore, hopeful that in private, at least, analysts are pragmatists and that when looking up a term in this work they may happen upon terms and approaches they would not have been 'taught' in training but which in practice they now recognise they have 'learnt' by doing the work. In seeing how the other half talks we may learn quite different approaches, not just in order to translate them into our own terms, but to come to sympathetic understanding and even, dare I say it, admiration for other ways of practising psychoanalysis.

The original vision of this project was a dictionary format, that is, the terms of different schools would all be given equal alphabetic status – for example, transference (Freud); transference (Jung); transference (Lacan). There have been many temptations to abandon this when faced by the strong context dependency of some psychoanalytic terms. However, it can be argued that terms only survive insofar as they are eventually able to transcend the contextual terminology and, let us be honest, jargon of their school. However, to satisfy readers who need to gather all the terms of a given school together, a list of key terms is given at the end of that school's précis. Originally, the policy on biographies for the *Encyclopaedia* was that 'the dead should prevail over the living'. However, there is great interest in living analysts too and so some contemporary analysts such as Searles, Etchegoyan and Kernberg, generally agreed to have made significant contributions, are included. Included too are creative casualties of psychoanalysis like Viktor Tausk and Wilhelm Reich as well as innovative rebels like Masud Khan and Ronnie Laing. Scholars, too, have their place and so Joseph Sandler and Jean Laplanche are included.

Recent years have seen a rapid expansion of research in psychoanalysis internationally, particularly in the universities. Numerous courses have helped broaden the scope of the discipline by linking it with other areas such as philosophy, feminism, literature, art, anthropology and many more – all of which are given substantial coverage. In fact the *Encyclopaedia* deliberately tries to broaden Freud's founding psychoanalytic vision, including as it does substantial material on how the family of psychoanalysts has spread around the world as well as how it has spawned many offspring, such as child psychotherapy, group psychotherapy and analytically informed psychiatry. It is worth pointing out that the psychiatry entries were written either by psychoanalysts who are psychiatrists or psychiatrists open to psychoanalytic approaches.

The reader will find here quite a lot of philosophy, particularly of the continental variety. This is, perhaps, due in part to the fact that the editor has been a philosophy lecturer as well as an analytic practitioner for many years. More significantly, philosophy has influenced psychoanalysts' theorising about 'lived experience' to an extent they may not readily realise.

For example, influenced by Heidegger, Binswanger started a philosophical correspondence with Freud which eventually yielded the Sartre-inspired 'existential' psychoanalysis of Laing in England and May in America. The more modern 'intersubjectivity' theory pioneered by Atwood and Stolorow, which blossomed in self psychology, though differing from the existential approach, has similar roots. Relationism, pioneered by Mitchell, is intimately linked with these modern approaches making the notion of intersubjectivity a rising influence. Surprisingly perhaps, a similar trend has taken place in Europe where the influence of Lacan's theory, underpinned by Hegel's thought as well as Heidegger's, shows how the speaking of a language shapes our (inter) subjectivity.

Researchers using the *Encyclopaedia* will find information about not only philosophy but all relevant influences on psychoanalysis, from whatever viewpoint. However, perhaps most importantly, the *International Encyclopaedia of Psychoanalysis* features not merely entries but contributors who reflect a wide variety of the schools, disciplines and backgrounds that have contributed to the development of psychoanalysis and to a critical understanding of it. The reader will find not merely the expected topics on psychoanalysis written by psychoanalysts themselves, but also topics that are best handled by, and so contributed by, psychiatrists, psychologists, psychotherapists, philosophers, medical researchers, historians, literary critics, anthropologists, sociologists and linguists. This may prompt readers of the *Encyclopaedia* to acknowledge the need for a developing relationship of psychoanalysis with other disciplines, to the benefit of all.

Since Freud's day there has in fact been an increasing contact with other disciplines. Ethology, or the study of animal life in the wild, had an influence on the psychoanalyst John Bowlby and his pioneering attachment theory. Anthropology too has made its mark with Jung via Levy Bruhl, who gives a central position to myth. Then there is Lacan who, via Lévi-Strauss, isolates the impact of language and cultural structures on the formation of the individual. Even more recently the advances in neuroscience are beginning to be felt, something Freud, trained as he was in neurology, would have welcomed, and there is now a journal on neuroscience and psychoanalysis.

Jung gave a special place to religion whereas Freud was militantly atheist. However at the present time the attitude towards religion is much more open and in this respect mainstream psychoanalysis is more open to Jungian ideas. One notable feature of our time is the level of interest in mysticism too and a number of analysts have been attracted to Buddhism – a religion 'without a God' – in the belief that psychoanalysis is best seen as humanist while not antipathetical to the religious point of view. This raises the question of psychoanalysis as a secular religion. Lacan has said 'psychoanalysis can lead you to the gates of ethics but cannot lead you in'. One might say the same about psychoanalysis and religion.

A small though significant number of analysts seem to believe that psychoanalysis is a science and there is no doubt that it has some features of the sciences. This claim is vigorously pursued in their different ways by Grünbaum the philosopher and Ahumada the analyst; the latter enlists the help of the philosopher of science Imre Lakatos to show psychoanalysis is a scientific enterprise. Although the already-mentioned influence of ethology, neuroscience and linguistics or even semiotics on psychoanalysis would seem to support this vision, the analysts themselves seem increasingly drawn towards seeing intersubjectivity theory as illuminating the analytic relationship more than any application of scientific theory. Yet recent advances in neuroscience give reason for optimism that Freud's ideal of a bridge between the psychoanalytic perspective and experimental science is becoming a reality.

Encyclopaedias aim at universality but are often written from the perspective of a single country. This *International Encyclopaedia* deliberately draws on authors from most countries of the world, thus avoiding an exclusively 'English' or 'American' bias. While the choice of section editors is admittedly limited to English speakers, two of whom are English and two American, the reader will find many authors from France and South America as well as those from Germany, Hungary, Japan and Australia, to name but a few. Some forty countries of the world where psychoanalysis is practised have an article on the development of the discipline in that country, for example 'Japan', 'Italy' and 'Brazil'.

Beginning with Freud's discovery of the unconscious, a vast family of psychoanalysts has spread around the world. They in turn have spawned many rich and fascinating theories about the unconscious whose proponents compete – often to the detriment of the whole discipline. Tempted as we may be to throw up our hands in exasperation at the sheer diversity of approaches in psychoanalysis, let us not forget that in its one hundred years, psychoanalysis has already relieved vast amounts of human suffering. It is the contention of this *Encyclopaedia* that a comparative approach to our discipline can only strengthen psychoanalysts of whatever school in their dedication to the amelioration of human suffering.

Ross M. Skelton

The Edinburgh International Encyclopaedia of Psychoanalysis

A

Abraham, Karl (1877–1925) Due to his contributions to psychoanalytic theory, as well as his commitment to the psychoanalytic movement, Karl Abraham is regarded as one of the most important early students of *Freud. He was born 3 May 1877 in Bremen, the second son of Nathan Abraham (1842–1915) and his cousin Ida Abraham (1847–1929), née Oppenheimer. His father was a merchant and for many years chairman of the city's Jewish community. From 1896 to 1901 he studied medicine in Würzburg, Berlin, and Freiburg. Following an appointment at a Berlin mental asylum he worked as assistant at the Burghölzli psychiatric clinic in Zurich, where he was introduced to psychoanalysis by *Bleuler and *Jung. In 1906 he married Hedwig Buergner. His daughter Hilda, who later became a psychoanalyst and wrote a biography of her father, was born in the same year. A son, Gerd, followed in 1910.

In the summer of 1907, he sent his first psychoanalytic publication to Freud and was soon accepted into his circle of close friends and students. At the end of 1907 he gave up the position in Zurich, his career prospects as a foreigner being meagre, and settled in Berlin as a neurologist. His attempts to attract others to psychoanalysis were initially met with rejection, especially from his medical colleagues. Nevertheless, in 1908 he succeeded in organising the first psychoanalytic group in Germany, the *Berliner Psychoanalytische Vereinigung* which two years later joined the newly founded *Internationale Psychoanalytische Vereinigung* (International Psychoanalytic Association or IPA). He led the Berlin group until his death on 25 December 1925 of septic bronchial pneumonia.

From 1913 Abraham was a member of the so-called 'secret committee'. Following the resignation of Jung from the position of president of the IPA in 1914, he was appointed provisional president (until 1918). He became secretary and in 1924 president of the IPA. In 1920 the first psychoanalytic polyclinic was founded in Berlin by *Eitingon. It was re-organised in 1923 as the Berlin psychoanalytic institute and served as a model for similar institutions the world over. Abraham played a leading role in drafting the guidelines regarding membership and training. Amongst his analysands were Boehm, *Deutsch, Glover, *Horney, *Klein, Carl Mueller-Braunschweig, Josine Mueller-Ebsen, Sándor Radó, (Theodor) Reik, Simmel, (Alice) Strachey, and Nelly Wolffheim. Abraham himself was not analysed by another analyst.

While in other cases Freud was liable to break with his students, his relationship with Abraham was comparatively steady and calm, even though shortly before Abraham's death differences emerged which could not be reconciled. Freud appears to have been less taken with Abraham than he was (at least initially) with Jung or *Ferenczi. He nevertheless valued Abraham's correctness and loyalty. Their correspondence provides the best insight into their relationship and the exchange of ideas between them.

Abraham's contributions are very much grounded in Freud's *libido theory and do not include the *ego-id-super-ego model of the mind. Many of them have become classical texts of Freudian psychoanalysis. Their influence was enormous and is prominent in Klein's early work. They deal with clinical pictures of schizophrenia, *depression, *hysteria, agoraphobia, *ejaculatio praecox*, *fetishism, tic, or *war neurosis; with character formation (*oral, *anal and *genital character); with psychoanalytic technique; with infantile trauma, infantile sexuality and infantile sexual phantasies, incest, the oral and anal stages, the scoptophilic impulse and the female castration complex; as well as with subjects like Greek mythology, the painter Segantini or King Amenhotep IV.

In contrast to Freud, Abraham was interested in the psychoanalysis of psychotic disorders. His early publication in 1908 on schizophrenia (then *dementia praecox*) and its differentiation from hysteria had been stimulated by Freud and became widely known. From the Freud-Abraham point of view schizophrenics lacked the capacity for *transference which made them refractory for psychoanalysis. This therapeutic pessimism was later criticised by other authors. Abraham studied the *depressive and manic-depressive disorders in greatest detail in papers from 1911, 1912, 1916, and 1924. Again, his views of the aetiology and the psychodynamics of these syndromes developed in exchanges and disputes with Freud. Abraham highlighted as etiologically relevant factors: constitutionally increased oral-eroticism, fixation at the oral phase, and severe frustrations of pre-Oedipal love which arouse cannibalistic-hostile impulses particularly towards the mother. According to Jones, no other author made the importance of the oral phase in both normal and pathological development as clear as Abraham did. In general, his main interest was in the pre-Oedipal stages of the development of the libido. This focus he shared with other authors of the early 1920s such as *Rank, Ferenczi and Klein.

Despite Abraham's dislike of speculative theorising (in contrast to Freud or Ferenczi), he succeeded in formulating a synthesis of his views at the height of his creative powers. His 1924 theory of libidinal development describes a progression – determined primarily by endogenous factors and less by experience – from *autoerotism through *narcissism and partial love to mature, post-ambivalent object-love. The latter includes loving as well as aggressive impulses and relates to the whole object. All these developmental stages refer both to functional modes of the partial drives and to different types of *object relations. The subdivision of the oral phase into an object-less, pre-ambivalent and oral-sucking stage on the one hand and an oral-sadistic stage on the other originates mainly from him. The latter is distinguished by the ambivalent wish to incorporate and devour the object, a lack of consideration for the object, and is connected with fear. Similarly, he divided the anal phase into an *anal-sadistic and an anal-retentive stage. Already in the former, *guilt feelings are present, the appearance of which Freud had linked to the later Oedipal phase. He distinguished, too, an early from a final genital stage. Only at the latter stage does post-ambivalent object-love become possible.

Abraham, H. (1974) 'Karl Abraham: an unfinished biography'. *International Review of Psycho-Analysis* 1: 17–72.

Abraham, K. (1927) *Selected Papers of Karl Abraham*. London: Maresfield.

Abraham, K. (1955) *Clinical Papers and Essays on Psycho-Analysis*. London: Maresfield.

Freud, S. and Abraham, K. (2002) *The Complete Correspondence of Sigmund Freud and Karl Abraham 1907–1925*. Completed edition. Transcribed and edited by Ernst Falzeder. London and New York: Karnac Books.

U. M.

ABREACTION The therapeutic discharge that occurs when repressed memories are recalled with all their attendant emotions and given verbal expression. When a forgotten experience that has precipitated a *symptom can be brought into consciousness, and its *affect discharged, the force that has maintained the symptom ceases to operate and the symptom disappears.

J. A. Ber.

ABSENCE The term absence relates to the importance of the lack of the *object in psychical structuring. For Lacan this lack acquires its psychical status through the signifier by which it becomes represented. The lack organises a structure of the drives which is centred around the problematic of the *phallus and *castration. Undifferentiated being or oneness with the body of the mother, which Lacan includes in his notion of the *'thing', is actually absent from the very beginning. For the speaking being, this creates the precondition for signifying the organisation and structuring of desire.

A. I.

ABSTINENCE Psychoanalytic treatment requires that neither the patient nor the analyst use the relationship as a means for gratification of desires. The desires of the patient for satisfaction of sexual or other needs is analysed rather than acted upon.

See also: neutrality

J. A. Ber.

ACCEPTING OBJECT The term Fairbairn first used to describe the satisfying aspect of the introjected primary caretaker, an object that could be retained in relative consciousness by the central organisation. He later called this structure the *ideal object.

See also: endopsychic structure; rejecting object

Fairbairn, W. R. D. [1944] (1952) 'Endopsychic structure considered in terms of object relationships' + Addendum (1951)' in *Psychoanalytic Studies of the Personality*. London: Routledge. Pbk 1994.

E. F. B. / D. E. S.

ACT An act changes the subject of the unconscious and involves the subject's relation to the object. There are several modalities of the act: *acting out, **passage à l'acte* and, emphasised by Lacan, the analytic act. The analytic act – cutting the session, introducing an equivocation – punctuates the treatment by isolating the subject's master signifiers with a view to producing in the subject a change of position. The position of the analyst is the sole guarantee that the act is ethical.

V. V.

ACTING OUT A form of *repetition in place of remembering. It is an expression of repressed content that arises in analysis on the basis of *resistance; here the greater the level of resistance the more extensively will acting out (repetition) replace remembering. The analytic task, therefore, is to seek to elaborate the communicative import of such *acts, which are addressed to the analyst as a *transference figure. Lacan distinguishes acting out and **passage à l'acte* in terms of different positions taken up by the subject as reactions to a puzzling question or conflict in the unconscious. Acting out is unconsciously determined impulsive behaviour that addresses the analyst, and indicates that some material has not been sufficiently interpreted. This happens in a weak moment in the treatment and is a demand for *symbolisation.

A. R. / R. M. B.

ACTIVE/PASSIVE In descriptive clinical writing, the presence versus the lack of behavioural initiative and agency. In *Rapaport's 1967 metapsychology, originally passive infants react only to external stimuli (*environmental) or internal ones (*drive). With ego development, the active mode of deliberately interposing delay and choice becomes possible (*autonomy from drives and environment).

Rapaport, D. (1967) 'Some metapsychological considerations concerning activity and passivity' in M. M. Gill (ed.) *The Collected Papers of David Rapaport*. New York: Basic Books.

R. Hol.

ACTUAL NEUROSIS see NEUROSIS, ACTUAL

ADAPTATION The processes by which the ego modifies itself or the environment to arrive at satisfactory solutions to conflicts. An *alloplastic process is one in which the environment is changed to accord with one's wishes. In an autoplastic process the ego adapts itself to the demands of the environment.

See also: Hartmann

R. T.

ADAPTIVE POINT OF VIEW One of the five metapsychological points of view that are offered to account for the psychological functioning of human beings. The adaptive point of view proposed by *Rapaport and Gill in 1959 considers the capacity of the individual to both successfully adjust oneself (autoplastic changes) to demands placed upon one by the environment and to modify the environment (alloplastic changes) in order to optimise the satisfactions the environment can offer. Successful adaptation to the environment, as measured by an individual's productivity and his capacity to enjoy life, is one measure of healthy ego functioning.

R. T.

ADDICTION In *Confessions of an English Opium Eater*, Thomas de Quincey described the most basic ingredients of the psychopathology of addiction: the search for an ideal existence, the denial of anything that might interfere with the belief that such a state exists and an intrinsic ego weakness. Addiction is complex and one should not incur the mistake of thinking of addicts as sharing a common pathology. The longstanding interest of psychoanalysts in addiction started with Freud, who linked oral eroticism in men with their desire for smoking and drinking, thus discovering the most important link in the chain of events underlying drug dependence. Some years later he noted the need to acknowledge the specific action of intoxicants. Subsequent psychoanalytical investigations (*Abraham, Simmel, *Fenichel, Little, *Kohut, Adams, Wurmser) revealed that serious addiction is also connected with disturbances in other developmental stages and with a variety of conditions, notably *perversion and manic-depressive psychosis. Radó initiated the modern psychoanalytic understanding of addictions by considering them as an effort toward adaptation, albeit one frequently leading to destruction. Glover had already described the role of addiction as a defence against aggressive impulses and as a protection against psychotic reaction. He thought of addictions as transitional states more difficult to treat than neurotics, yet not necessarily psychotic or borderline. Radó's and Glover's observations represent the origins of the influence of *ego psychology on the comprehension of addictions. Anna *Freud considered addiction as a complex structure in which the action of passive-feminine and self-destructive tendencies is added to oral wishes. Rosenfeld in his *Psychotic States* developed a Kleinian view of addiction, clinically closely related to manic-depressive illnesses (although not identical) even where underlying paranoid feelings are masked by the manic phase. He was one of the psychoanalysts who saw no need to change the traditional psychoanalytic approach for these patients. Rodríguez de la Sierra and others (Limentani, Yorke, Radford) disagree and emphasise the level of disturbance in these patients' self-esteem, and addiction as a symptom of a more profound and multidetermined disturbance. Rodríguez de la Sierra underlines the addict's failed unconscious attempts to resolve an experienced internal conflict and points out the similarities and differences to psychopaths as well as the intricacies of the addicts' complex *transferences, the intense *countertransference reactions they provoke, and he recommends modifications in their analyses.

Lacan once referred to a drug as something that allows one to break away from being 'married to the penis'. He implied that any kind of mood-altering drug-taking is possibly a sign of the attempt to escape the consequences of *castration. This means that some subjects, especially addicts, find it difficult to accept that total satisfaction (or total *jouissance) is not available to them anymore. From a Lacanian point of view addiction can be defined as the administration of jouissance via the route of the body (i.e. the toxic effects of drugs and alcohol) which, as an act, is something that takes place independently of the Other (or language) and which therefore has an immediate effect on the jouissance economy of the subject. This 'administration of jouissance' can take different forms and these different forms are dependent on the position or clinical structure of the subject. For the psychotic subject the administration of jouissance using drugs and alcohol concerns the management of an overwhelming confrontation with Real jouissance as substitute for the lack of symbolisation (*foreclosure of the name-of-the-father) in psychosis. For neurotic and perverse subjects the administration of jouissance concerns a supplying, dispensing or distribution of extra jouissance as compensation for having to give up the claim to total jouissance or satisfaction as a consequence of castration.

Abraham, K. (1926) 'The psychological relation between sexuality and alcoholism'. *International Journal of Psychoanalysis* 7: 2–10.

Glover, E. (1932) 'On the etiology of drug addiction'. *International Journal of Psycho-Analysis* 13: 298–328.

Loose, R. (2002) *The Subject of Addiction*. London: Karnac Books.

Radó, S. (1933) 'The psychoanalysis of pharmacothymia'. *Psychoanalytic Quarterly* 2: 1–23.

Rodríguez de la Sierra, L. (1995) 'Of sentiments and sensations'. *British Journal of Psychotherapy* 12 (2).

L. R. S. / R. Loo.

Adler, Alfred (1870–1937) Since Alfred Adler's break with Freud in 1911 and his formulation of individual psychology, his theory of personality and principles of psychotherapy have influenced nearly every form of contemporary psychology. The classical Adlerian approach, still solidly rooted in Adler's original teachings and style of treatment, has evolved into a uniquely coherent and creative synthesis: a philosophy of living; a model of personality; a theory of psychopathology; strategies for education and prevention; and a technique of psychotherapy. In addition to its core application in individual, depth psychotherapy, Adlerian principles are being applied to brief therapy, couple and family therapy, career counselling, parent and teacher education, and organisational consulting.

The theory of individual psychology can be summarised in six central principles that were first articulated by the Ansbachers. (1) *Unity of the individual*: The individual is not internally divided or a battleground of conflicting forces. While not always apparent, there is an underlying consistency to thoughts, feelings, and behaviours, guiding the person in one direction. (2) *Goal orientation*: The central personality dynamic is a future-oriented striving toward a fictional final goal of security and significance that promises compensation for early childhood feelings of inferiority. (3) *Self-determination and uniqueness*: The goal may be influenced by hereditary and environmental factors, but it ultimately springs from the creative power and opinion of the individual. (4) *Social context*: As an indivisible whole, a system, the human being is also part of larger wholes or systems – family, community, culture, nation, humanity, the planet, the cosmos. (5) *Feeling of community*: Each human being has the capacity to develop the feeling of interconnectedness with other living beings and to learn to live in harmony with society. The personal feeling of security is rooted in a sense of belonging and embeddedness in the stream of social evolution. (6) *Mental health*: Social usefulness and contribution are the criteria of mental health. Maladjustment is characterised by an underdeveloped feeling of community, a deeply felt sense of inferiority and an exaggerated, anti-social goal of personal superiority.

The goal of therapy is to increase the sense of community, reduce feelings of inferiority, promote a feeling of equality, and replace egocentric self-protection, self-enhancement, and self-indulgence with self-transcending, courageous, social contribution. Unlike traditional psychoanalysis, classical Adlerian psychotherapy does not emphasise *transference or *counter-transference as cornerstones of treatment. The therapist diplomatically unveils the client's transfer of perception and feeling as a long-standing habit that inhibits cooperation. Having dealt with his or her personal issues in a training analysis, the Adlerian therapist uses counter-transference primarily as a clue to the effect that the client has on other people.

Classical Adlerian psychotherapy has enhanced practice with several refinements of technique that promote change on cognitive, affective, and behavioural levels. Socratic questioning is used to elicit information and lead the client to insight. Eidetic and guided imagery are used to promote emotional breakthroughs and provide missing developmental experiences. Role-playing – playful as well as practical – prepares the client for applying new solutions to old problems. A twelve-stage model of treatment offers clear benchmarks for progress, with an inspiring potential for optimal personality development, as envisioned by Abraham Maslow.

Ansbacher, H. L. and Ansbacher, R. (eds) (1956) *The Individual Psychology of Alfred Adler*. New York: Basic Books.

Stein, H. (1988) 'Twelve stages of creative Adlerian psychotherapy'. *Individual Psychology* 44: 138–43.

Stein, H. (1990) *Classical Adlerian Psychotherapy: A Socratic Approach*. Audiotape study and consultation program. San Francisco: Alfred Adler Institute of San Francisco.

Stein, H. (1991) 'Adler and Socrates: similarities and differences'. *Individual Psychology* 47: 241–6.

Stein, H. and Edwards, M. (1998) 'Classical Adlerian Theory and Practice' in P. Marcus and A. Rosenberg (eds) *Psychoanalytic Versions of the Human Condition: Philosophies of Life and Their Impact on Practice*. New York: New York University Press.

Stein, H. and Edwards, M. (1999) 'Providing the missing developmental experience'. Alfred Adler Institute of San Francisco web site: www.go.ourworld. nu/hstein/provid.htm

H. T. S. / M. F. E.

ADULT SEXUALITY All the partial drives and *erotogenic zones become subordinated to the primacy of the genital zone. A sexual object is found in a member of the opposite gender. The affectionate and sensual currents converge and are both directed towards the sexual object and sexual aim.

J. A. Ber

AFFECT Freud gives the following definition of affect in his *Introductory Lectures on Psychoanalysis*: 'It is in any case something highly composite. An affect includes in the first place particular motor innervations or discharges and secondly certain feelings; the latter are of two kinds – perceptions of the motor actions that have occurred and the direct feelings of pleasure and unpleasure which, as we say, give the affect its keynote. But I do not think that with this enumeration we have arrived at the essence of an affect. We seem to see deeper in the case of some affects and to recognize that the core which holds the combination we have described together is the repetition of some particular significant experience. This experience could only be a very early impression of a very general nature, placed in the prehistory not of the individual but of the species.' (Lecture XXV)

These ideas are akin to modern process-oriented definitions such as that of Scherer on emotion. They also have close affinity with *Darwin's conception of human emotions. Darwin and most contemporary *ethology assume that the motor signal system expressing 'affect' has co-evolved together with the corresponding capacity to 'read' affect in others as an indicator of their internal feeling states. However, in most of his writings Freud explicitly discounts the influence of the external world upon affect. Thus a baby's cry might be deemed to tell the mother something but the questions remain – what precisely does the baby's cry represent to the mother and how does the cry affect her?

Affect is a composite term. The German term *Affekt* does not cover the experiential aspect of the corresponding word in English. The equivalent term to the latter in German would be *Gefühl* (sentiment or feeling). *Affekt* is a technical term used mainly in forensic medicine. Thus *Affekthandlung* (affective impulsive act) describes unlawful acts during which the accused loses control. Freud's distinction between quota of affect (*Affektbetrag*) and affect as a descriptive term reflects a widespread view of his time according to which the quantitive substrate of affect is an unspecified energy whilst the qualitative distinction between different states is related to the representational world. Thus Freud includes the quota of affect as part of his metapsychology, and at the same time he admits that it cannot be measured.

Freud makes use of his theory of affect to describe three distinct clinical phenomena: 1) transformation of affect into motor actions accompanied by the repression of the disturbing ideas in conversion hysteria; 2) displacement of energy onto differing representations in *obsessional neurosis; and 3) exchange of affect in the case of *anxiety neurosis and melancholia or *depression.

*Lacan challenges the distinction between the emotional (affects) and the intellectual (thought processes) in his *Seminars I*, *VII* and *X*. For him affects and words or *signifiers are inextricably interwoven in the unconscious. The Lacanian clinical approach understands affect as being capable of displacement, and as such, equally as misleading as the meaning produced by the patient. Thus, the focus in the analytic endeavour is on structure, beyond both affect and meaning. According to Lacan, anxiety is the only affect that does not deceive.

In Freud's early writings on actual neuroses, he thought that affect was directly connected to the *drives. Pleasure and unpleasure were placed at the end of the process and pleasure was the experiential correlate to a reduction in drive energy. Unpleasure occurred as a consequence of an increase in energy. High amounts of undischarged and repressed libidinal energy led to anxiety (unpleasure) and less clearly, a continually repressed investment of energy in a lost object of affection led to depression. In his later writings, Freud was unsure which came first, the chicken or the egg, anxiety or depression but he remained convinced that each of these affects was intimately bound up with the other.

Despite the modernity of Freud's thinking about affect, he underrated the communicative aspect of affect. In other words, under certain conditions affects can be perceived, for example in *projective identification, and felt by other people and as a result produce identical or complementary reactions in them.

Contemporary research focused on *attachment styles, depression and panic attacks, starts with Freud's thinking. In his pioneering work in this area, *Bowlby argued that intensity of early attachments to the primary caregiver (usually the mother) led to the making and breaking of affectional bonds. He believed that the quality of these early attachments was extremely influential in the subsequent experience of sexuality, pleasure, and love in the individual. However, he differed from Freud in that he regarded people as primarily attachment seeking rather than driven by their sexual needs. Followers of Bowlby believe that most clinical disorders can be understood as being based on maladaptive relationship patterns. If the nature of relationship patterns of interaction is changed then this has been shown to have the potential for long-term psychotherapeutic change.

Stern offers evidence that the building up of attachment patterns and internal working models of the self is predominantly moulded on the early communications of mother and baby. This means that long before developing a subjective self-reflective representational model of his or her own affects, the infant acquires very specific knowledge about both the outside world including the mother and its own internal world as a result of this early pattern of communication.

In Freud's thinking, the concept of 'primary' *identification is used to describe these phenomena without the necessity for an elaborated differentiation between self and the other. However, it is not easy to connect primary identification to the Freudian conception of a baby born in a completely undifferentiated or objectless state. However the baby identifies not with the mother as such but with the mother's projections of herself. These projections are transmitted via the affect of the mother and her affective reactions to the response of the baby. From the beginning, the baby is capable of differentiation and cannot therefore be completely undifferentiated itself.

Despite the fact that Freud discussed primary identification in the context of *suggestion as the basis of regressive social influences in groups, this way of thinking was not applied to the understanding of the analytic situation. Contemporary research has shown that patients with mental disorders unconsciously superimpose their 'standards' of affective relationship patterns on their social partners. Thus partners of people suffering from paranoid schizophrenia, or severe psychosomatic disorders, produce only half the facial signals found in the control group. Similarly it can be demonstrated that people with limited emotional capacity unconsciously superimpose their reduced and unvaried patterns on their partners. This seems part of a joint unconscious defensive pattern since both partners 'know' that the patient has a reduced capacity to peg the affective signal to their mental world, making negative affective signals potentially interactive and dangerous. However, positive signals such as smiling and concern, are also few. All this happens unconsciously since nobody taking part in the experiment is aware of the prior diagnosis.

In groups with *hysterical rather than psychotic features, increased social affective signalling can be found. These microprocesses heavily influence the affective experience of the interacting partners. *Sandler and Sandler offer a theoretical frame where they describe these phenomena as 'the present unconscious'. They believe that these relate to the dynamic unconscious of the patient's history in a manner not yet well understood.

An indicator of the efficacy of psychotherapeutic treatment can be found in the different way successful therapists react to the, often unconscious, affective enticements of patients. Whilst laymen may endorse and exacerbate existing problematic relationship patterns by reciprocal behaviour, for example, by responding with anger to an angry patient, professional therapists attempt to abstain from emotional reactions to the material brought by their patients. If they do react it may be in a complementary manner, for instance, by being curious about a patient's expression of disgust.

Bowlby, J. (1979) *The Making and Breaking of Affectional Bonds*. London: Tavistock.

Freud, S. (1916–17) *Introductory Lectures on Psycho-Analysis*. S. E. 16. London: Hogarth Press.

Krause, R. and Merten, J. (1999) 'Affects, regulation of relationships, transference and countertransference'. *International Forum of Psychoanalysis* 8: 103–14.

Sandler, J., and Sandler, A. (1994) 'The past unconscious and the present unconscious'. *Psychoanalytic Study of the Child* 49.

Scherer, K. (2000) 'Emotions as episodes of subsystem synchronization driven by nonlinear appraisal processes' in M. D. Lewis and I. Granic (eds) *Emotion, Development and Self-organization*. New York: Cambridge University Press.

Stern, D. (1995) *The Motherhood Constellation: A Unified View of Parent-Infant Psychotherapy*. New York: Basic Books.

R. Kra.

AFFECT (LACAN) One of Lacan's most significant challenges to psychoanalytic orthodoxy consisted in challenging an organising dichotomy present within of all forms of psychology; namely the distinction between the emotional (affects) and the intellectual (thought processes). For Lacan affects and signifiers are inextricably interwoven in the unconscious. Affects can be displaced and are therefore no less misleading than the meaning produced by the subject: hence the analytical treatment's focus on structure, beyond both affect and meaning. The only affect, according to Lacan (and Klein), that does not deceive is anxiety.

V. V.

AFFECTIVE SHARING The act of a patient causing his (or her) affect to be felt by the therapist. This constitutes a potential *selfobject experience that imbues the self with a sense of togetherness. There are two types of affective sharing experiences that can take place in the clinical setting. 'Descriptive sharing' occurs when patients try to share affect through evocative descriptions of their life events, both past and present. 'Active sharing' happens when patients attempt to share affect with the therapist through a specific activity or enactment. In both circumstances patients hope that their feeling states will be felt by another. The therapist's verbal or non-verbal communication that a patient's affect has been shared can function as an optimal response when a sharing selfobject transference is activated.

Herzog, B. (1998) 'Optimal responsiveness and the experience of sharing' in H. Bacal (ed.) *Optimal Responsiveness: How Therapists Heal their Patients*. New York: Jason Aronson.

See also: self psychology

H. B.

AFRICA AND PSYCHOANALYSIS Psychoanalysis has not yet taken root in Africa, except in South *Africa, some North African countries, and Senegal.

During Africa's so-called 'colonial period', roughly 1900–75, psychoanalysis did not have much impact, but traces of it can be found in the work of such people as René Laforgue and Octave Mannoni. Laforgue, a French psychoanalyst who settled in Morocco at the beginning of the 1950s, used psychoanalytic terminology to elaborate on the allegedly inferior mental status of Arabic people. Mannoni worked as a secondary school teacher in Madagascar from 1925 to 1945. In 1950, he published a book, *Prospero et Caliban: Psychologie de la Colonization* in which he uses psychoanalytic concepts in analysing the relationship between the colonist and the colonised. In *Peau Noir*, and *Masques Blancs* Frantz Fanon, the most important theoretical figure of the African anticolonial liberation struggle, criticises what he takes to be the racism of Mannoni's book.

In contrast to North and South America, the fertilisation of psychoanalysis on the African continent was hindered by colonial immigration policies. Psychoanalysts who fled from Fascism and National Socialism in Europe could not enter African countries due to the restrictive refugee and asylum policies of the colonial powers. South Africa was an exception; it was the only African country to accept a number of German-speaking (mostly Jewish) immigrants.

Some of the roots of psychoanalysis in South Africa were planted in the pre-World War II period. In the 1930s, the president of the International Psychoanalytic Association (IPA), Ernest Jones, developed a plan to found a psychoanalytic group in South Africa with the Viennese psychoanalyst Richard Sterba as its director. The French psychoanalyst Marie Bonaparte, who was a family friend of Freud, stayed in South Africa from 1941 to 1944 to help establish this group.

Fritz Perls, the founder of Gestalt therapy, trained as a psychoanalyst in Berlin and Vienna before emigrating to South Africa, and lived there from 1933 to 1946. Erich Heilbrun, a member of the Viennese Psychoanalytic Society after the Second World War, also emigrated from Berlin to South Africa. The Dutch psychoanalyst Johann H. W. van Ophuijsen worked in South Africa for some time during 1935 before settling in the US. In the same context, the Berlin-based psychoanalyst Erich Simenauer should also be mentioned. In 1933, he migrated via Cyprus to Tanganyika (today Tanzania) where he practised as a physician and undertook psychoanalytic studies from 1941 to 1957, before returning to Berlin.

Wulf Sachs, the pioneer of psychoanalysis in South Africa, lived in Johannesburg from 1922 onward. In 1929, he began his psychoanalytic training with Theodor Reik in Berlin and in 1934 became a member of the British

Psychoanalytic Society. In 1935, the South African group became affiliated with the London Psychoanalytic Society, and in 1949 Sachs founded the first South African Psychoanalytic Society. His pioneering work is documented in the book *Black Hamlet: the Mind of an African Negro Revealed by Psychoanalysis*, first published in 1937. The book is a biography of his client, the black Zimbabwean traditional healer John Chavafambira, and is the first known report of psychoanalysis conducted with an African. In writing it, Sachs was going against old prejudices and taboos characteristic of Christian European ethnocentrism and racism. Part of this racism held that blacks and 'savages' (and also children, women, and the mentally ill) were only animals and did not have a soul. This ideology informed European colonial expansion as well as the slave trade. To credit a black African with an internal world was to go against the creeds of explicit racism and of medical science. Thus the contribution by Sachs is, in this context, significant. The psychoanalytic group he founded disbanded shortly after his death in 1949. The installation of the apartheid system in South Africa prevented the further institutionalisation of psychoanalysis until a Psychoanalytic Study Group was founded in 1979.

In the phase of decolonisation, the example of Senegal shows how psychoanalytic thinking became an integral part of modern social psychiatry in collaboration with traditional healers. A pioneer of this approach, the French psychiatrist Henri Collomb, who also trained in psychoanalysis, established and directed a psychiatric center in Dakar-Fann and founded the Journal *Psychopathologie Africaine* in 1965. The Dakar-Fann clinic became a center for psychoanalytic studies such as the work of Marie-Cécile and Edmond Ortigues on *Oedipe Africain*, based on their psychoanalytic experiences there from 1962 to 1966. The Swiss psychoanalyst Lise Tripet has also reported from there on the only psychoanalytic treatments of African patients known to have occurred anywhere on the continent.

The anthropologist Vincent Crapanzano conducted two *ethnopsychoanalytic field studies in Morocco in which he combined theory and research method with psychoanalysis. Furthermore, he emphasised in his 1985 book *The Whites of South Africa* the importance of the dialogue relationship between the researcher and the subject of the study. In this view, this would lead – as part of the research process – to a better understanding of the phenomena under study.

There was also an initiative by the retired American psychoanalyst Marie Nelson to establish psychoanalysis in Nairobi, Kenya at the end of the 1980s. Some Kenyan professionals were trained in affiliation with the Philadelphia Psychoanalytic Institute, but progress came to a standstill after she left. In the area of developmental psychology, a number of researchers have undertaken studies from a psychoanalytic perspective. For example, Ainsworth wrote on attachment theories in Uganda in 1967, and in 1992 LeVine wrote on the self in African culture. But investigations of this kind belong to the following section and the interested reader will find them well covered in volume 55 of the 1998 *American Imago*, an issue devoted to Southern Africa.

If we reverse the question and ask what important traces Africa has left on psychoanalysis (besides the metaphoric usage of the term 'dark continent' by Freud), we will find an answer in the development of *ethnopsychoanalysis.

In the last decade of the twentieth century, there were several indications of the future relevance of psychoanalysis in Africa. A number of clinical psychologists and psychiatrists who trained in Europe and North America and who had been practising psychotherapy in Africa for years adopted psychoanalysis in theory and practice. Some taught psychoanalysis at academic institutions, while at the same time being familiar with those African realities of psychotherapy in which traditional forms of psychotherapy are dominant.

Rapid societal change and urbanisation in African societies seem to create the need for western forms of psychotherapy including psychoanalysis. The activities of psychotherapy societies such as those in Nigeria or the African Chapter of the World Council for Psychotherapy play a major role by exchanging and promoting experiences with traditional healers at conferences. Psychoanalysis is recognised and taught in different university departments of psychology, clinical psychology, and psychiatry.

As can be seen in the example of the refoundation of Psychoanalytic Study Groups in South Africa in the late 1970s, African-born psychoanalysts, trained in Europe and North America, have played a major role in the spread of psychoanalysis in Africa for example, Joseph Sandler, Sadie Gillespie, Anne Hayman, Malcolm Pines, Max and Wally Joffe, and Mark Solms. This has now also led to an affiliation between a South African Psychoanalytic Study Group and the British Psychoanalytic Society with a view to establishing a psychoanalytic training institute and society in South Africa.

Ainsworth, M. D. S. (1967) *Infancy in Uganda: Infant Care and the Growth of Love*. Baltimore: Johns Hopkins University Press.

Ebigbo, P. O., Oluka, J., Ezenwa, M., Obidigbo, J. and Okwaraji, F. (1995) *The Practice of Psychotherapy in Africa*. Enugu: International Federation for Psychotherapy (IFP).

LeVine, R. A. (1992) 'The self in African culture' in D. H. Spain (ed.) *Psychoanalytic Anthropology After Freud*. New York: Psyche Press, 37–48.

Madu, S. N., Baguma, P. K. and Pritz, A. (eds) (1996) *Psychotherapy in Africa: First Investigations*. Wien: World Council for Psychotherapy.

Nelson, M. C. (1987) 'Immunization factors in development of the African personality: preliminary observations'. *Psychoanalytic Review* 74: 233–7.

Peltzer, K. (1995) *Psychology and Health in African Cultures: Examples of Ethnopsychotherapeutic Practice*. Frankfurt: IKO Verlag.

Peltzer, K. (1998) 'Psychology and health in sub-Saharan Africa'. *Journal of Psychology in Africa* 8: 142–70.

Peltzer, K. and Ebigbo, P. O. (eds) (1989) *Clinical Psychology in Africa*. Frankfurt: IKO Verlag.

Rose, J. (1998) 'Wulf Sachs's Black Hamlet' in C. Lane (ed.) *The Psychoanalysis of Race*. New York: Columbia University Press, 333–52.

Sachs, W. (1947) *Black Anger*. New York: Grove.

Sterba, R. F. (1982) *Reminiscences of a Viennese Psychoanalyst*. Detroit: Wayne State University Press.

K. P. / J. R.

AFRICA, SOUTH Psychoanalysis in South Africa, although having a long history from the 1930s, has had a greater struggle in establishing itself within the country than its important export of significant analysts; its history has had three distinct phases.

The first recorded psychoanalyst in South Africa was an immigrant, Dr Wulf Sachs, who was born in St Petersburg in 1893. He worked in the Psychoneurological Institute of Pavlov and Bechterev in the period 1913–18, before taking further medical degrees in Cologne and London. He migrated to South Africa in 1922 and was the pioneer of psychoanalysis in South Africa. He had various analyses in Europe and perhaps a short analysis with Freud in Vienna. In South Africa he gathered an interested group of doctors, mental health workers, speech therapists and teachers around himself in the mid 1930s. This group became a psychoanalytical seminary and was known as the South African Psycho-Analytical Study Group. After Sachs became a training analyst in 1946, this group was formally constituted in May 1949 as the South African Psycho-Analytical Society, a branch of the British Society. However with Sachs's death in June 1949 the group dissolved. Most of that group – Wally Joffe, Hayman, Saffrey (who later returned to South Africa) Max Joffe, and Sadie Gillespie – settled in England and became psychoanalysts and training analysts.

In later waves many South Africans moved to Britain where they qualified as psychoanalysts. Their contribution has been significant; Joseph *Sandler, Edna O'Shaughnessy, Irma

Brenman-Pick, Leslie Sonn, Mervyn Glasser, Michael Feldman and Anton Obholzer have all been important. In more recent years Fakhry David, Ronnie Doktor, Cyril Couve, Mark and Karen Solms (see *neuropsychoanalysis) have settled in the UK.

From the 1950s onwards the very few remaining qualified psychoanalysts worked independently and without any organisational support: namely Dr Sam Stein, now in Australia, and Elmore Smit, now in Canada. A wealthy businessman named Sydney Press who was indebted to psychoanalysis became a patron of the discipline and sponsored many young professionals to become psychoanalysts in the USA and Britain, hoping they would return to establish an IPA presence in South Africa. Currently there is only one IPA- registered and Paris-trained psychoanalyst in South Africa, Madame Kate Aubertin-Lasch.

The third and current phase has been the establishment and development of psychoanalytic psychotherapy. In 1978 Isca Wittenberg from the Tavistock ran a workshop for psychologists and social workers in Johannesburg. This inspired the formation of a small group of psychoanalytic psychotherapists to form a study group that has met regularly ever since. This type of group was also established in Cape Town and Durban so that currently there are approximately 150 therapists in South Africa. There are small but very active psychoanalytic psychotherapy study and training groups, albeit none except that dedicated to child psychoanalytic psychotherapy training has any international recognition. These groups have been supported for over twenty years by annual visits of senior training psychoanalysts from the British Society. They have run workshops, clinical and theoretical seminars, and held public scientific meetings. A number of psychoanalytic psychotherapists trained at the Tavistock are currently in practice in South Africa. There is no psychoanalytic presence in the national health system. There has been a national journal, *The South African Psychoanalytic Psychotherapy Journal*, since 1992.

To date two major international psychoanalytic psychotherapy conferences with visiting British psychoanalysts have been successfully held – in Cape Town, during 1998, and Johannesburg, during 2001.

Dr Mark Solms took up a chair at the University of Cape Town in 2002 and, with his and his wife's return plus Aubertin-Lasch's presence, perhaps for the first time since Sachs a possibility exists for the establishment of an IPA-registered Psychoanalytic Study Group and eventual Institute.

Gillespie, S. (1992) 'Historical notes on the first South African Psycho-Analytical Society'. *Psycho-Analytic Psychotherapy in South Africa* 1: 1–6.

Hamburger, A. S. (1992) 'The Johannesburg Psycho-analytic Psychotherapy Study Group: a short history'. *Psycho-Analytic Psychotherapy in South Africa* 1: 62–71.

Rickman, J. (1950) 'Wulf Sachs, 1893–1949', Obituary. *International Journal of Psychoanalysis* 31: 288–9.

Sachs, W. (1996) *Black Hamlet*. Johannesburg: Witwatersrand University Press.

A. H.

AGALMA (Greek: a magnificent object, a statue) This term, used by Lacan, is used by Alcibiades in Plato's *Symposium* to qualify Socrates, insisting on the strong contrast between the unattractive, siren-like shape of his body and the delicacy of his soul. Alcibiades's paradoxical discourse comes at the end of the Symposium and is classically opposed to the previous discourses on love, which implied mainly idealistic and sublime relationships. Socrates refused a carnal and reciprocal relationship with Alcibiades; and his electrifying interventions and focus on the specific paradoxes of desire. Lacan has used the term *agalma* to qualify the 'analyst's desire' (he always refused to use the term *countertransference) in the handling of transference. His concept of *agalma* was developed to indicate the position of the analyst as a semblance of an object. He insists on the idea that the analyst's interventions should always imply a fundamental refusal of the demands of the patient as a means of encouraging him or her to 'take care of his or her own desire'.

See also: desire of the analyst

F. S.

AGENCY, MENTAL A theoretical (*metapsychological) mental construct such as the *id, *ego and *super-ego possessing certain functions or tendencies (see *psychic structure). Thinking in terms of mental agencies like the id, ego, etc. helps delineate some of the functional components of the psyche. However, the reification of such abstract concepts or structures can lead to oversimplification, and to the assignment of functions to one agency that are, in fact, shared between agencies. Lacan extends this notion to the structure of language in his term 'the agency of the letter'.

A. I.

AGGRESSION (GENERAL) Aggression and aggressiveness are general terms which are used to cover a range of phenomena ranging from necessary engagement with the world of objects, through assertiveness, to destructiveness, sadism and violence. The terms refer to fantasy (conscious), phantasy (unconscious) or actual behaviour. *Adler originally introduced the idea of an aggressive 'instinct' in 1908, but it is generally held that both Freud, and psychoanalysts in general, were late to acknowledge the importance of aggression in the form of an aggressive instinct. Nevertheless, an awareness of aggressiveness abounds in Freud's early writing – in the *Dora Case, in early conceptualisations of *resistance, *paranoia, the *Oedipus complex, interpretation of *dreams, and in the idea of the ambivalence of love and hate (e.g. in *Little Hans and the *Rat Man). In 'Beyond the Pleasure Principle', however, Freud described the *death drive (Thanatos) of which a derivative was outwardly directed aggression. Continuing his use of a dualistic theory he opposed the death instinct to the psychic energy manifest in the possible (unsatisfactory) term 'libido' (which may roughly be equated with 'love', 'life instinct' or 'Eros').

There is dispute, in theory, as to whether aggression and its cognate forms are expressions of a primary instinct or drive, as proposed by Freud (albeit in origin inwardly directed) and especially developed by *Klein or, rather, are secondary phenomena resulting from frustration as proposed by Glover, *Winnicott and *Fairbairn. There is dispute, too, as to whether or not this theoretical divide has pragmatic consequences for therapeutic technique and treatment. Winnicott proposed an innate aggressivity but likened this to that described by ethologists.

Klein developed the conceptualisation of the negative aspects of aggression and destructiveness, linking them to the paranoid-schizoid position, the 'death instinct' and to primary envy. Rosenfeld developed the concept of 'negative narcissism' to account for profoundly destructive and self-destructive phenomena and *Kernberg described the related concept of 'destructive narcissism'.

There is recognition, however, that aggression is a necessary, as well as an ubiquitous human characteristic: Klein herself, contrary to common belief, considered aggression and its mitigation, sublimations and transformations, to be important in the development of libido and in the development and maturing of the mind.

One especially important and (partially) obscured form of aggression and destructiveness is that contained within the perversions, where it is sexualised and masquerades as creative sexual desire and behaviour.

Freud's early preoccupations concerned self-directed aggression, for example in 'Mourning and Melancholia', 'unconscious guilt', the negative therapeutic reaction and masochism. The complex interaction of masochism and sadism is the prototype of the vicissitudes of internally and externally directed aggression and destructiveness.

The terminology in this whole area of Freudian theory is confusing and changes over time. For example, Freud's use of the term 'Nirvana principle' in relation to his coining of the term and concept of the 'death drive' is different from its meaning within the belief systems of Hinduism or the philosophy of *Schopenhauer: the conjunction of concepts is speculative and stimulating but has not helped engage the sympathies of those of a more empirical and pragmatic turn of mind.

Freud, S. (1905a) *Fragments of the Analysis of a Case of Hysteria*. S. E. 7. London: Hogarth Press.
Freud, S. (1917) *Mourning and Melancholia*. S. E. 14. London: Hogarth Press.
Freud, S. (1920) *Beyond the Pleasure Principle*. S. E. 18. London: Hogarth Press.
Kernberg, O. (1992) *Aggression in Personality Disorders and Perversions*. New Haven, CT and London: Yale University Press.
Rosenfeld, H. (1971) 'A clinical approach to the psychoanalytic theory of the life and death instincts: an investigation into the aggressive aspects of narcissism'. *International Journal of Psychoanalysis* 52.

C. C.

AGGRESSION (FAIRBAIRN) Unlike Freud and Klein who believed that aggression was a basic affect directly derived from the instincts, Fairbairn believed that aggression only arose as the result of experience of frustration – even though he considered the experience of frustration to be inevitable. He thought that reactive aggression did become a formative factor throughout life, operating under the general influence of the innate need for relationships. Klein's emphasis on the intrinsic nature of aggression is useful with patients who seem clinically to have an excess of aggression, while Fairbairn's starting point is useful in understanding the quality of aggression that arises in reaction to disappointment and rejection.

E. F. B. / D. E. S.

AGGRESSIVITY The attack of the *ego on itself as a structure presenting an Imaginary, false unity. Aggressivity, according to Lacan, is the desire to shatter this unity in order to return to a previous state of total fragmentation. As such it can be considered to be an aspect of the *death drive, often projected outwards onto objects or people.

R. Loo.

AIM The aim is one of the four constitutive components of the drive, alongside the pressure, the *source and the *object. For Freud, the aim of the drive is invariably an experience of satisfaction, which can only be achieved if the excitation at the source of the drive is neutralised. However, a drive can be *aim inhibited, which may still induce a partial satisfaction.

D. N.

AIM INHIBITED Freud uses this term to describe a *drive which does not reach its direct aim of satisfaction, owing to internal and/or external obstacles, and which develops into a more culturally productive and socially sanctioned tendency. As such, the aim inhibited sexual drive generates feelings of love and tenderness.

D. N.

AJASE COMPLEX The Ajase complex is a desire to kill one's mother because of the very love one bears for her, and is derived from oral sadistic impulses. It was defined by the Japanese psychoanalyst Kosawa in 1931, in contrast to the Oedipal desire to kill one's father because of the love for one's mother. If the internalisation of the murdered father following the Oedipal desire creates the feelings of guilt, the forgiveness from the parents for the Ajase-type desire gives birth to repentance, which is not only a consequence of this desire but also the true foundation of religious feelings.

Ajase (*Ajatasatru*), a prince in ancient India, is the protagonist of a legend written in the Buddhist sutra *Guan wuliangshou jing*. He usurped the throne from his father by imprisoning him, and murdered him when he discovered that his mother had secretly brought nourishment to the imprisoned father. He wanted to kill his mother, too, but was dissuaded by a minister. Later, he resorted to the Buddha's compassion because of gnawing feelings of remorse and was saved because he found inconceivable faith growing in him. This story was introduced to Japan and was popularised in the teachings of *Jodo-Shin* Buddhism, and it was from that tradition that Kosawa, then staying in Vienna, put forward the concept of the Ajase complex.

It is true that this concept has certain disadvantages, such as confusion of psychoanalytic unconscious guilt with religious guilt, and divergence between the concept and the legend. Nevertheless, it should be remembered in the history of the psychoanalytic movement that a concept potentially homologous to those of Klein was invented in a very different cultural context and in contemporary times. For we can see that the early Oedipus complex and the transition from the paranoid-schizoid to the depressive position are adumbrated in this concept.

Kosawa, K. 'Two kinds of guilt feelings (Ajase complex)'. *Japanese Journal of Psychoanalysis* 1: 5–9. (In Japanese)

K. Shi.

ALCHEMY A medieval forerunner of chemistry which Jung thought could be seen as an analogue of the psychological transformations usually associated with psychotherapy. It was seen by him as an operational *mythology, doing something with the psyche and the matter of life. The old alchemists sought a living relationship with substances through perceiving how elements, functions, or 'principles' of metals reacted within flasks in relation to the *prima materia*, the dregs of matter. Through psychic activity and chemical operations, their goal was transcendence. For the poor, it was gold; for the sick, it was a universal medicine for the body. For illnesses of the soul and diseases of the mind, the formation of the *lapis* or 'philosopher's stone' relieved spiritual darkness.

Alchemy was the *magnum opus* that provided historical material for Jung's comparative research on the images emerging in the psychotherapeutic and *individuation processes. It also illuminated the integration of unconscious contents by *ego consciousness through the phenomenon of *transference. The elements to be integrated produce alchemy's central *symbol, the philosopher's stone or *lapis*. The *lapis* and its synonyms correspond to Jung's concept of the psyche's organising centre, the *self. He pointed out that modern *dreams contain images of integrating elements in the form of *archetypal symbols of the self, such as quaternity, the mandala (circle), the hermaphrodite, the child. These suggest wholeness and order of the personality through a kind of 'alchemical' integration of the unconscious.

Jung saw a practical therapeutic application for alchemy's unimpeded symbol formation, free of epistemological criticism of psychic images. He presented his studies in his mature works, *Psychology and Alchemy*, *Mysterium Coniunctionis* as well as *Alchemical Studies* and 'The Psychology of the Transference'. These offered a new depth perspective and provided a broader range of meaning in associative material.

Edinger, E. F. (1985) *Anatomy of the Psyche: Alchemical Symbolism in Psychotherapy*. Chicago and La Salle: Open Court.
Von Franz, M.-L. (1980) *Alchemy: An Introduction to the Symbolism and the Psychology*. Toronto: Inner City Books.

M. K.

ALEXANDER, FRANZ (1891–1964) Hungarian-born psychoanalyst who directed the Chicago Institute of Psychoanalysis for twenty-four years. His chief contributions were in psychosomatics and brief analysis. He was the first graduate of the Berlin Institute, analysed by

Sachs and one of the prominent members of the second-generation psychoanalysts. In 1929 Freud invited him to Vienna, but Alexander left for the University of Chicago where he was nominated Professor of Psychiatry. Every summer, though, he visited Freud, who considered him as 'his best pupil in the United States'.

Alexander may be considered the founder of psychological medicine. In the area of brief analysis, he anticipated important ideas (such as the concept of 'corrective emotional experience') considered unorthodox by the psychoanalytic establishment of the time. He became leader of the 'Chicago school of psychoanalysis', characterised by an emphasis on emotional relationship rather than intellectual insight as the main curative factor. It might be no coincidence that, a generation later, *Kohut came from the Chicago Institute. Also *Ferenczi, the Budapest School's leader, emphasised the importance of emotional relationship, and that is why the Chicago school is considered linked by a *fil rouge* to the Hungarian school, its ideal prosecution.

One of the most outspoken critics of Alexander's technique was Eissler.

P. Mig.

ALIENATION In existential philosophy and psychoanalysis this is a state of separation or estrangement from others, the world, one's own self, or God. The idea of alienation from others has its basis in *Hegel's account of the master/slave relationship, which was taken up by *Marx on the one hand as the basis of his social philosophy and by the existentialists on the other as an account of the way in which we may turn or be turned by the other into an 'object' or an 'it'. Alienation may be evoked by an absurd universe, unsympathetic to human consciousness, where one must either create meaning or be lost in nihilism. *Sartre says one may be alienated from oneself through self-deception or denial of freedom and responsibility whereas *Heidegger draws our attention to getting lost in the 'they' of ordinary daily public existence. *Buber claims that one may become alienated from others through using the other instrumentally in an I–It relationship rather than relating dialogically to the other as a Thou. For religious existentialists such as Kierkegaard, alienation may occur because one has lost an immediate personal connection with God, leading to boredom, melancholy and despair.

For Lacan alienation denotes the unavoidable and essential effect of the moment at which the 'I' first comes to be constituted. The mirror stage encapsulates this alienating moment in which the I is conceived fundamentally as an other and this process of alienation is continued further by the subject finding its 'true alien self' only in the field of the Other through being represented there by the *signifier. The human subject, thus split at its origin, emerges from this alienated core, a lack-in-being coming to be at the kernel of being.

See also: aphanisis

A. M. / B. C. / H. T.

ALLOPLASTIC ADAPTATION see **ADAPTATION**

ALPHA ELEMENTS According to Bion the product of *alpha function (or dream-work-alpha). When sense impressions related to emotional experiences (beta elements) are transformed, they become alpha elements. Alpha elements are necessary for the formation of dream thoughts, unconscious waking dreaming and thinking, and the contact barrier. In infancy, the mother's capacity for reverie is directly related to the fulfilment of the baby's potential for producing alpha elements.

Bion, W. R. (1992) *Cogitations*. London: Karnac Books.

Bion, W. R. (1962) *Learning from Experience*. London: Heinemann. Also in *Seven Servants*. New York: Jason Aronson, 1977.

Bion, W. R. (1963) *Elements of Psychoanalysis*. London: Heinemann. Also in *Seven Servants*. New York: Jason Aronson, 1977.

Bion, W. R. (1965) *Transformations*. London: Karnac Books. Also in *Seven Servants*. New York: Jason Aronson, 1977.
Bion, W. R. (1970) *Attention and Interpretation*. London: Tavistock. Also in *Seven Servants*. New York: Jason Aronson, 1977.

S. A.

ALPHA FUNCTION (DREAM-WORK-ALPHA) A function for digesting emotional experiences by transforming sense data into *alpha elements and then into *dream thoughts that can then be stored as memory and used for thinking. Alpha function operates on the sense impression and emotions of which the patient is aware. In so far as the operation is successful, alpha elements are produced which are suited to storage and for dream thoughts.

In *Cogitations* we have Bion's thoughts about 'dream-work-alpha', the name he gave there to alpha function. Bion extended the meaning of the word 'dream' so as to help understand certain events in the analysis of severely disturbed patients. When he stated that all emotional experiences (either asleep or awake) had to be 'dreamt', he meant that all dream thoughts arise from an 'undigested fact'. If a person manages to 'dream' it, then the fact can be digested and this allows him/her to learn from experience. This function also makes possible differentiation between conscious and unconscious by means of the creation of the *contact barrier. 'Dreaming' is part of the process of digesting truth, which is as necessary to emotional growth as food is to the body. Bion here challenges Freud's view that a dream is a hallucinatory satisfaction of a wish, since hallucination is aimed at unburdening the psyche of what it cannot tolerate. Dream-work-alpha operates in an opposite direction, towards containment and storage. Dream-work-alpha can be reversed. This entails the dispersal of the contact barrier. Alpha elements are then stripped of all that differentiates them from beta elements, and this produces objects which resemble bizarre objects with *ego and *superego traces added to beta elements.

Bion, W. R. (1962) 'A theory of thinking'. *International Journal of Psycho-Analysis* 53. Also in *Second Thoughts*. London: Heinemann, 1967.
Bion, W. R. (1962) *Learning from Experience*. London: Heinemann.
Bion, W. R. (1992) *Cogitations*. London: Karnac Books.

E. T. B.

AMAE The Japanese word *amaeru* means 'to depend and presume upon another's benevolence', and *amae* is its noun form. Its usage was introduced in psychoanalysis by Doi in the 1950s not only to describe the Japanese people's interpersonal behaviour but also to explain what occurs in the unconscious in general by making optimal use of the semantic network of the Japanese language. Because the word *amae* has an important connotation of *amai* (sweet), it can ingeniously suggest pregenital oral need and its frustration. It is a relational concept and agrees well with object-relations theory. According to Doi, we must keep in mind that *amae*, or an urge to passively enjoy being loved, is already present from the beginning of therapy and that it becomes the kernel of *transference. This concept has the merit of enabling discussion of what would otherwise remain preverbal. As far as Doi claims to employ this word to refer to a primary human act to relate to others, it comes close to Freud's *identification and Klein's *projective identification, and shows a striking correspondence with what Kohut calls narcissistic libido.

Doi, T. (1962) '*Amae*: a key concept for understanding Japanese personality structure' in R. J. Smith and R. K. Beardsley (eds) *Japanese Culture: Its Development and Characteristics*. Chicago: Wenner-Gren Foundation for Anthropological Researches.
Doi, T. (1989) 'The concept of *amae* and its psychoanalytic implications'. *International Review of Psycho-Analysis* 16.

K. Shi.

AMBIGUITY Ambiguities are exploited by the dreamwork and other *primary processes (jokes, delusions, free association, creative intuition) to express latent thoughts and to provide *verbal bridges to the unconscious.

J. A. Ber.

AMBIVALENCE Strictly speaking, ambivalent organisation of the *drive is a term taken up by Freud as a result of his dialogue with *Abraham on the structure of the drive. Freud characterised drive ambivalence in terms of the simultaneous stress on contradictory aspects: contradiction, opposite, negation. Abraham, speaking of cannibalism, stresses an aim to spare the object, whilst also aiming to devour it. In general, the term refers to the co-existence of love and hate in someone but differs from mixed feelings in that the two halves of the ambivalent feeling are interdependent.

B. B.

AMNESIA Greek for forgetfulness; loss of *memory, an inability to recall past experiences. Can be organic, caused by head trauma or Alzheimer's disease; or psychogenic, i.e. caused by emotional stress, hypnotic suggestion, or inner *conflict. Freud and Breuer argued that such amnesia arose as a result of a splitting of consciousness which took place in the context of psychological trauma. Freud argued that when an individual was exposed to some sort of traumatic event, or the effort of suppressing a feeling, this could bring about a separation of experience from consciousness, which was then accompanied by amnesia for either the experience or the feeling.

Organic amnesia is usually related to the size and extent of causal brain damage. Classically head injuries which give rise to brain damage cause two types of organic amnesia: retrograde amnesia referring to loss of memories for the time before the head injury; and, anterograde referring to failure to establish memories for the time after the head injury. Organic amnesia may also be caused by intoxication with different types of substance.

Contemporary neuropsychological research would support Freud and Breuer's original contention that there may be aspects of conscious traumatic experience that are apparently 'forgotten', either because they are stored in a fragmented and unconscious way, or cannot be retrieved without stress to the individual. Research data is lacking on the extent to which ordinary events, or events that produce feelings such as guilt or shame, can cause this type of amnesia. The area is also a contentious one related as it is to memory and the *'memory wars'.

Freud, S. and Breuer, J. (1895) *Studies on Hysteria*. S. E. 2. London: Hogarth Press.

Van der Kolk, B. A. and Fisler, R. (1995) 'Dissociation and the fragmentary nature of traumatic memories: overview and exploratory study'. *Journal of Traumatic Stress* 8(4): 505–26.

G. A. / Z. L.

AMNESIA, INFANTILE Many recent and memorable traumas or pivotal experiences that surface in the course of an analysis are merely *screen memories that are unconsciously contrived to evoke and, simultaneously, to disguise memories of much earlier traumata and their associated conflicts, including the celebrated *primal scene. The task of interpretation is to reach behind the defensive screen memories from late childhood and adolescence, and thereby lift the infantile amnesia which presumably lies at the root of the patient's current psychosexual difficulties.

D. Bur.

AMPLIFICATION Devised by Jung, this is a method of interpretation that applies relevant analogies from diverse cultural and historical sources to psychological phenomena, especially dreams. The purpose is to enrich the personality through experiential understanding of the symbolic nature of the psyche. Jung developed this as a means of extending interpretation beyond the causal-reductive constructions of early psychoanalysis to a synthetic approach that includes the role of the collective *unconscious in psychological transformation. If, after personal associations to psychic contents have been analysed, inexplicable fascination remains, then cogent, objective associations may be judiciously introduced. Dangers in openly employing such information reside in *intellectualisation and *inflation. Contemporary views of amplification are broadening to include processes that intensify awareness of the psychological background.

J. C.

ANACLITIC The term initially derived by Freud from the Greek 'anaclitas' – to lean, rest, or depend upon – to describe an *object choice or attachment to a primary caregiver. Later used in psychoanalysis to describe a depression noted in infants and young children who, in response to psychological neglect or abandonment, became listless and apathetic. More recently, the term has been used to describe a type of depression in adults and adolescents associated with intense preoccupations and concerns about abandonment, loss, and loneliness.

See also: narcissistic object-choice

Freud, S. (1914) *On Narcissism: An Introduction*. S. E. 14. London: Hogarth Press.
Spitz, R. and Wolf, K. M. (1946) 'Anaclitic depression'. *Psychoanalytic Study of the Child* 2: 313–42.

S. J. B.

ANAL Term used to characterise behaviour (for example, stinginess, excessive orderliness (anal retentive traits) and messiness (anal expulsive traits)) presumably influenced by *fixation or *regression to a specific psychosexual stage of development – the anal stage in which conflicts around toilet training and cleanliness training are first prominent. The convergence of aggressive and eroticised tendencies in the second to third year of life has led to the designation of the 'anal-sadistic' phase.

Freud, S. (1916–17) *Introductory Lectures on Psychoanalysis*. S. E. 16. London: Hogarth Press.
Jones, E. (1918) 'Anal-erotic character traits' in *Papers on Psychoanalysis*. Boston: Beacon, 413–37.
Nunberg, H. (1955) *Principles of Psychoanalysis*. New York: International Universities Press.

D. Wol.

ANAL-SADISTIC PHASE One of the *partial drives of the pregenital sexual organisation. *Fixation at this stage is believed to play an important part in the symptomatology of the *obsessional neurosis. *Ambivalence between love and hate is understood as a regression of the libido to this phase.

Freud, S. (1913) *The Disposition to Obsessional Neurosis*. S. E. 12. London: Hogarth Press.

R. M.

ANALYTIC CONTRACT An understanding between patient and analyst, either explicitly stated or implicitly understood, that patient and analyst will engage in a psychological treatment using the psychoanalytic method at an agreed upon number of sessions per week. The aim of the treatment is to uncover the unconscious sources of the patient's difficulties and, primarily through interpretation, help that individual arrive at more satisfactory solutions. Psychoanalytic treatment is ordinarily carried out at a frequency of between three and five times per week.

Brenner, C. (1982) *The Mind in Conflict*. New York: International Universities Press.
Waelder, R. (1960) *Basic Theory of Psychoanalysis*. New York: International Universities Press.

T. J. J.

ANALYTIC RELATION Lacan conceived the analytic relation as a quaternary structure, (his L-schema) first defined as a process moving from the *Imaginary to the *Symbolic plane. Avoiding the dual relation between two egos, the analyst interprets the relationship of the subject with the *Other. Later, as he developed his concept of the *Real further, Lacan reformulated the analyst's position as a semblance of the object-cause-of-desire of the subject, which allows the traversal of phantasy beyond Imaginary identification, as such establishing a new tie with the symptom and the possibility for the subject to pass to the analytic position him- or herself.

See also: resistance; transference

R. M. W.

ANALYTIC THIRD A conception of the analytic process that views the analytic relationship as including not only the analyst and the analysand, but also a third co-created unconscious subject of analysis which Ogden terms 'the *intersubjective analytic third or simply 'the analytic third'. The (intersubjective) third subject of analysis stands in dialectical tension with the analyst and analysand as separate individuals with their own distinct subjectivities, histories, personality organisations and so on. Analyst and analysand each participate in the unconscious intersubjective construction (the analytic third), but do so asymmetrically. Specifically, the relationship of the roles of analyst and analysand structures the analytic interaction in a way that strongly privileges the exploration of the unconscious internal object world of the analysand. This is so because fundamentally the analytic relationship exists for the purpose of helping the analysand make psychological changes that will enable him to live in a more fully human way.

See also: intersubjectivity

Ogden, T. H. (1994) 'The analytic third: working with intersubjective clinical facts'. *International Journal of Psycho-Analysis* 75: 3–20.

T. O.

ANALYTICAL PSYCHOLOGY PRECIS This is the descendent of the 'Zurich School' of psychoanalysis founded by Jung while he was the first president of the *International Psychoanalytic Association from 1910 to 1914. The term 'analytical psychology' first occurs in a lecture given to the Psycho-Medical Society in London on 5 August 1913, entitled 'General Aspects of Psychoanalysis'. It officially became the name of a separate school after Jung's break with Freud in 1913. For many years there was debate over whether the more correct term for this school would be 'complex psychology'; in the end, however, analytical psychology prevailed.

By 1925 Jung had worked out the main theoretical outlines of what he conceived of as general depth psychology. Among the key factors that have characterised analytical psychology from the beginning are: a) the view that the individual personality includes an innate lifelong striving toward growth and toward seeking the fullest possible expression of the *self (*individuation); b) an understanding of psychic energy that sees it organised by a broad range of innate *instincts and *archetypes as well as by personal *complexes, including the *ego complex; and c) a synthetic/symbolic component in treatment. Frequency of sessions varies from once to four times per week, depending on the local culture and the specific training of the analyst, as well as the needs and means of patients. *Dreams play a central role both for the analysis of *transference and *countertransference as well as for use in the promotion of psychological integration and individuation.

Since the 1940s the field of analytical psychology has displayed great diversity, and debate among members pertaining to clinical and theoretical matters has been vigorous. In the 1950s and 60s a central division appeared between analysts who emphasise what Jung called reductive analysis (represented chiefly by the London school, now usually referred to as the developmental school) and those who prefer to emphasise synthetic methods (the Zurich school, sometimes called the classical school). The former tend to have close ties to Freudian circles, while the latter have become somewhat linked with such movements as psychosynthesis, Gestalt therapy, and humanistic psychology. Michael *Fordham of London was the chief proponent of the developmental school, while M. L. *von Franz of Zurich carried the banner for the classical school. While this tension continues, the dividing lines have softened and more mutual understanding and cross-fertilisation have occurred than was earlier possible. Today it is difficult to find pure types of either extreme in the wider field of analytical psychology. The diversity and debate have resulted in increased internal complexity and broader connections to the many other schools of psychoanalysis and psychotherapy.

In addition to works with a strictly clinical focus, an impressive wealth of studies on cultural subjects of all sorts from *myth, ritual and religion to the arts to popular culture have been produced by members of the field of analytical psychology. Important in these areas have been *Neumann, *Henderson and *Hillman. More recently, increasing attention has been given to a range of other disciplines that interface with analytical psychology. Some of the new areas of interest are philosophical studies, the cognitive sciences, the neurosciences, and evolutionary psychology.

Throughout the 1990s and beyond, interest in Jung's writings and in the theory and practice of analytical psychology has grown rapidly in Eastern Europe, South America, Asia, and Africa. Scientific studies testing the hypotheses of analytical psychology take place today in a wide variety of cultural contexts and in many universities and institutes throughout the world. Journals of analytical psychology exist in English, French, German, Italian, Japanese, Korean, Portuguese and Spanish. International Congresses are held every three years.

See also: alchemy; amplification; anima and animus; defences of the self; ego-self axis; energy; Eros; fairy tales; Gnosticism; group psychotherapy (analytical psychology); image; imagination; inflation; International Association for Analytical Psychology; logos; mana personality; mandala; numinosity; participation mystique; persona; psychoid; sandplay; shadow; stages of life; symbol; synchronicity; teleology; transcendent function; unconscious (collective)

Kirsch, T. (2000) *The Jungians*. London and Philadelphia: Routledge.

Samuels, A. (1985) *Jung and the Post-Jungians*. London: Routledge.

Stein, M. (ed.) (1995) *Jungian Analysis*. Chicago and LaSalle: Open Court.

M. Ste. / J. C.

ANIMA AND ANIMUS Jung's names for the feminine in a man and the masculine in a woman respectively. When these contrasexual complexes function well, they act as a bridge between *ego consciousness and the *self, the centre of the whole psyche. They help us choose a good mate, connect sexual and spiritual longings for union with another and contact creative inner resources for working and living in the world. When the bridge is not functioning well, these complexes appear in personified form in dreams or fantasy to hound us into compulsive behaviour, such as an inability to let go of a bad relationship, or into overwhelming moods of sentimentality, self-righteous indignation, or rigid convictions.

The content of these contrasexual complexes varies, influenced by childhood experiences with significant people of the opposite sex and the dominant images of masculine and feminine in our cultural, historical era. But all share the same function of anima/us connecting ego and self. Thus the impact of these complexes brings a sense of ultimate importance, even life and death, they are involved when we take a risk in a job or relationship to find our soul. We can also be impelled to go on a wild-goose chase; hence, having a conscious relationship to the anima or animus within makes a real difference in how we find our personal ways of combining passion and permanence. Critics of Jung claim anima and animus reassert essentialist categories of masculine and feminine, but they miss the radical impact of the *archetypal image at the core of the anima or animus that can overthrow cultural stereotypes. For example, we can find courage to value our actual body-type over the dictates of fashion, to find our own masculinity over the cultural icon, to express original creativity over what the culture defines as 'real' painting.

Jung, C. G. (1951) 'The syzygy: anima and animus'. *Aion* (*CW* 9: 1). New York: Pantheon.
Ulanov, A. and Ulanov, B. (1994) *Transforming Sexuality. The Archetypal World of Anima and Animus*. Boston: Shambhala.

A. U.

Anna O see **Breuer**

ANTICATHEXIS/COUNTERCATHEXIS
Investment of interest or *cathexis used to maintain a repression of another cathected object. This can be achieved through substitution. For example, *Little Hans substituted *Oedipal fear of his father with a phobia of horses. Anticathexis may also operate with the use of the defence mechanism of *reaction-formation. For example, a mother's hatred of her child may continue to be repressed if the opposite emotion of love is exaggerated, masking the aggressive aspect of her feelings.

S. Byr.

ANTI-FREUD LITERATURE Critical books on Freud, generally popularising and of doubtful scientific value. Critical writings on psychoanalysis fall into three categories. The first usually addresses a restricted readership and is at a high intellectual level. Writers such as Popper, Grünbaum, Crews, and Roustang mount sophisticated arguments that probe the status of psychoanalysis as a science and question whether the practice of psychoanalysis and the subtle art of hypnotic suggestion are one and the same.

The second consists of the many popular works opposing Freud and psychoanalysis. This anti-Freud literature is easily characterised, given that the arguments of the different authors are very much alike and fairly straightforward. Thus they usually quote from Freud's writings on sexuality pointing to some of Freud's personal faults to which he himself had courageously confessed. These authors then claim that Freud was morally deficient or even insane. The reasoning is clear: since a man like this conceived psychoanalysis, we do not need to take it seriously.

There is a third type of literature that is worthy of mention, namely critical biographies of Freud. Freud himself formulated some of the paradigms that dominate accounts of the history of psychoanalysis. He claimed (a) that his insights were essentially original, especially with regard to repression and infantile sexuality; and (b) that his theories were initially ignored, later fiercely attacked. This position was corroborated by Freud's biographer *Jones and was taken over more or less unchanged by many subsequent writers on this topic. Ellenberger was the first to cast doubt on this widely held position. In his painstaking book, *The Discovery of the Unconscious*, Ellenberger discovered that Breuer's patient, Anna O, discussed at length in *Studies in Hysteria* jointly written by *Breuer and Freud, was not relieved of her symptoms by what she herself termed 'the talking cure'. In fact she spent months in a sanatorium after the end of her treatment. Nevertheless Ellenberger's broader assertions that Freud's work lacks originality are not substantiated. He attempted to show that many Freudian concepts were formulated years before, for example, by the French psychiatrist, Janet. Janet indeed detected that a loss of memory underlies hysterical symptoms – a fact that was readily acknowledged by Freud.

However, Janet was far from attributing this to repression. Instead, he tried to explain the loss as a permanent attention deficit due to a general 'cerebral exhaustion'.

Basing his argument partially on Ellenberger's writings, Sulloway wrote a critique of Freud entitled *Freud, Biologist of the Mind: Beyond the Psychoanalytic Legend*. He pointed out that with respect to infantile sexuality, Freud was strongly influenced by contemporaries such as Moll. However there is no evidence to attribute the discovery of infantile sexuality to Moll. Indeed, he ardently asserted that up to the age of seven signs of sexual impulses should be suspected of having a pathological origin. Although Sulloway's book is interesting to read, the vast majority of his most provocative statements can be refuted. For example, Sulloway asserts that the reception of psychoanalysis was much more favourable than the accounts of other commentators would suggest. As proof, Sulloway quotes parts of contemporary reviews but completely omits critical passages.

Although, in contrast to other anti-Freud authors, Ellenberger and Sulloway do not try to disparage Freud and are far from drawing wholesale conclusions on the validity or otherwise of psychoanalysis, both are heavily biased and try to cast serious doubt on the credibility of both Freud and Jones. This is of especial importance, because other anti-Freud authors use Ellenberger's and Sulloway's unsound refutations of Freudian statements as *ad hominem* arguments.

Anti-Freud writings in many languages could already be found during Freud's lifetime and have not ceased to appear to the present day. They are bestsellers and are benevolently reviewed and promoted by the media. In America large numbers of anti-Freud books were published in the 1960s and 1970s; their titles express their intentions very clearly, for example, Jurjevich's book *The Hoax of Freudism*. As a rule, these authors are extremely conservative. Special blame is reserved for sexual liberty for which Freud is mainly held to account, despite the fact that any serious reader of Freud will know that he was opposed to sexual promiscuity.

Although he uses the same basic arguments as other anti-Freud authors, Thornton's *Freud and Cocaine: The Freudian Fallacy* is somewhat original insofar as the author tries to prove that Freud was a cocaine addict and that his theories were formulated under the influence of an intoxicating drug. Köhler offers a critique of Thornton's confused reasoning, her ignorance of psychoanalytic theory and frequent misquotation in *Anti-Freud-Literatur von ihren Anfängen bis heute*.

A few words must be said about Eysenck's famous book *The Decline and Fall of the Freudian Empire*. During his life, Eysenck was the most famous psychologist of his time and an outstanding adversary of psychoanalysis. In the aforementioned book he attempted to impugn Freud's moral integrity not only by making use of Ellenberger's and Sulloway's work, but also, like Thornton, by using the tactics of allegations of drug dependence, selective misquotation and wilful misunderstanding.

Ellenberger, H. F. (1970) *The Discovery of the Unconscious*. New York: Basic Books.

Eysenck, H. J. (1985) *The Decline and Fall of the Freudian Empire*. London: Viking Penguin.

Jurjevich, R. (1974) *The Hoax of Freudism*. Philadelphia: Dorrance.

Köhler, T. (1996) *Anti-Freud-Literatur von ihren Anfängen bis heute* [Anti-Freud-Literature from its Beginnings to the Present Day]. Stuttgart: Kohlhammer.

Sulloway, F. J. (1979) *Freud, Biologist of the Mind*. New York: Basic Books.

Thornton, E. (1983) *Freud and Cocaine: The Freudian Fallacy*. London: Blond & Briggs.

T. K.

ANTI-GROUP A concept formulated by Nitsun to describe the negative, disruptive processes in groups that can threaten the therapeutic development of the group. The concept challenges the optimism inherent in the group psychotherapeutic field, but also seeks to strengthen the group endeavour by understanding, containing and transforming potentially group destructive processes. The idea of an anti-group has applications to individuals, families, work and organisational groups, and society at large. Originating in group analysis, the concept parallels some of *Bion's thinking about the regressive potential of groups, but attempts to maintain *Foulkes' positive emphasis on the group as a creative medium.

Craib, I. (1997) 'Making sense of the anti-group'. *Group Analysis* 30: 107–18.

Nitsun, M. (1991) 'The anti-group: destructive forces in the group and their therapeutic potential'. *Group Analysis* 24: 7–20.

Nitsun, M. (1996) *The Anti-Group: Destructive Forces in the Group and their Creative Potential.* London: Routledge.

M. N.

ANTHROPOLOGY The relationship between psychoanalysis and anthropology has usually taken the form of applying psychoanalytic ideas to societies ordinarily studied by anthropologists. The situation calls for some two-way traffic but the ground for a useful dialogue remains to be established. In what follows I have preferred to look at the current situation rather than retrace the dead ends of the past.

Psychoanalysis deals with inner states and anthropology deals with collective representations, externally observable. Most schools of psychoanalysis take our constructions of the world as projections of psychic conflicts: the world, as it were, is constructed from the inside out. Only perhaps the Lacanians see the *ego as constructed from the outside in: we identify with an external view of ourselves. There is no agreed opinion on this issue or on the psychic mechanisms by which we become settled in our world. While the Lacanian view is clearly more congenial to the cultural constructionism of anthropology, in the words of Geertz, 'They [humanity], every last one of them, are cultural artefacts'. The issue can be re-stated in a different way. We may be inclined to one or other side in the ancient philosophical debate between our view of the phenomenal world as determined by our thinking (Hume) as opposed to a view of the mind as an 'empty cabinet' (Locke) to be filled with the impressions of experience. Either way, what we encounter empirically must always be a measure of congruence between man and his world. And if we assume, following Jung, that 'the psyche is part of nature', then what is found within (microcosm) is not likely to be wholly foreign to what is found without (macrocosm). In other words, we have good reason to suppose that psychoanalysis and anthropology are dealing with the same subject matter, that is, with *human nature, different only in its locale and the methods of its investigation. But it is precisely this difference in method, aims and field situation that presents an obstacle to collaboration.

Superficially a comparison can be made between the situation of the ethnographer in the field (see *ethnopsychoanalysis) and the psychoanalyst in the consulting room, both strange, exotic places, and afterwards between the two in the quite different situation of writing up. Thousands of hours of arduous fieldwork, selected, re-worked and re-assembled into an impersonal, coherent monograph. Years of patient analysis reduced and re-presented illustratively as a short case history. Although both psychoanalyst and anthropologist are changed by their experience, they are changed in different ways. The psychoanalyst, through the *countertransference, is drawn into the situation he is studying, while the anthropologist finds himself between two cultures, unable to identify completely with either; a stranger to his country and to himself. The tendency of his profession is to detach the anthropologist and to anchor the psychoanalyst.

Psychoanalysis has a therapeutic aim, while anthropology typically has not. It was Durkheim who described religion as 'science in a hurry'. There are babies to be brought up, patients to treat; we cannot wait for science to tell us how best to do this. The psychoanalyst, unlike the anthropologist, must believe in the efficacy of his method for it to work. Through his personal analysis as the critical feature of his initiation or training, he becomes subjectively committed to the approach learnt from his analyst and 'confirmed' by his patients. As a result there is a quasi-religious quality to the division into different schools, each claiming a monopoly of the 'truth'. Although quick to apply its 'findings' to other fields, psychoanalysis has been slow to recognise itself. This gives to the discipline a parochial quality, the existence of competing schools each with a particular model of the mind weakening its claims to universality.

Out of their respective trainings are created two distinct beings, the psychoanalyst and the anthropologist, working in different field situations, who see things differently. For the psychoanalyst his observations are universal: this patient, unique in himself, is at the same time a particular instance of the way all individuals are. The anthropologist, on the other hand, usually studies individuals as typical of the roles (the shaman, the mother's brother, the ascetic) they occupy within a given culture. To quote Geertz again: 'To be human here is thus not to be Everyman, it is to be a particular kind of man, and of course men differ'. Individuals, in the catch-phrase, are 'culturally constructed', although the mechanism remains unclear. And cultures themselves – this is the current trend – are seen as autonomous, diverse, and even incommensurable.

Clearly between cultures there are differences as well as similarities. From one point of view, humanity is constantly re-inventing itself, transforming its world by technological innovations unimaginable before, and thinking new thoughts which cannot be anticipated. Humanity falsifies its own predictions. But from another point of view, we are part of nature, our mentation embodied in the workings of our brains and limited, computer-like, to the design built into it. Different schools of psychoanalysis incline to one view rather than the other (for example the ego psychologists versus the Kleinians), while anthropologists are divided between the cultural relativists arguing that we are products of cultures which differ from each other and the comparativists looking for their common features. Two observations can be made here. First, that people are social animals realising themselves in and through culture, so that any radical opposition between 'nature' and 'nurture', 'individual' and 'social' must be self-contradictory. And second, that universalism, as understood in psychoanalysis, is not the same as universalism, when posited in anthropology.

By the psychoanalyst the universal is taken for granted: we are all heirs to the *Oedipus complex, it must be so. We could describe this as deductive and prescriptive. When 'universal' is used in anthropology, it may be to identify a general pattern or structure underlying the manifest diversities of cultures; and for 'universal' is substituted 'global', that is, although a given trait does not appear everywhere, it has the potential of doing so. We could describe this as empirical and enabling. The thrust of Lévi-Strauss's structuralism was to identify the permanent structures of the human mind through the kaleidoscope of seemingly contingent events, first in relation to marriage rules and then to myth. The human, in his view, is not free to think as it chooses; it must make do with what it is. Leach, also comparative in his outlook, criticised the 'radical weakness of the basic assumption of cultural anthropology, namely, that not only are cultural systems infinitely variable, but that human individuals are products of their culture rather than of their genetic predisposition'. Needham has used comparative data to identify certain innate ideas or 'primary factors of experience', as he terms them, which have a global distribution in the sense that they are found in disparate cultural traditions in far separated parts of the globe. They include colours (white-black-red), numbers (3, 7, 101), images (the half-man, shaman, witch) and formal structures such as duality (right/left, male/female, king/priest), symmetry and analogical classifications. They answer to the question, 'What is man?', and their origin, he conjectures, lies in the natural properties of the brain and its vectors of operation. To my knowledge, there is no significant comparative work of this order being carried out today. If ethnographic data are to be used to identify the constant features of human nature in the flux of events and to test the universalist claims of psychoanalysis, this is a gap that needs to be filled.

As things stand, the disciplines proceed in parallel, as it were, brushing against each other only at the margins. Psychoanalysis still looks hopefully to anthropology (as to history) to confirm its theories but, because of the time lag in moving across disciplinary boundaries, the occasional anthropologist who uses psychoanalysis in the interpretation of his data is often using some concept, selected to fit, which is on its way out in psychoanalysis itself. There are some subjects, for example, *memory or *incest, where the two can perhaps usefully engage. But we may have to await a redefinition of terms like individual/social, even an epistemological upheaval in our disciplines and their boundaries, before their insularities can yield to new connections and more radical forms of thought.

Durkheim, E. (1915) *The Elementary Forms of the Religious Life*. Translated by J. W. Swain. London: Allen & Unwin.

Geertz, C. (1993) *The Interpretation of Cultures*. London: Fontana Press.

Leach, E. (2000) *The Essential Edmund Leach*. S. Hugh-Jones and J. Laidlaw (eds). New Haven, CT and London: Yale University Press.

Lévi-Strauss, C. (1969) *The Elementary Structures of Kinship*. Translated by J. H. Bell and J. R. von Sturmer. London: Eyre & Spottiswoode.

Lévi-Strauss, C. (1970) *The Raw and the Cooked*. Translated by J. and D. Weightman. London: Jonathan Cape.

Needham, R. (1985) 'Locke in the huts of Indians'. *Exemplars*. California and London: University of California Press.

A. C.

ANTIDOTE FUNCTION Within *intersubjectivity theory, experiences that are sought in order to counteract painful states that originate in pathogenic organising principles are said to serve an antidote function. Unlike *selfobject experiences, which promote developmental transformation, antidote experiences tend to become addictive because they only counteract painful states without altering the principles of organisation that underlie them. Antidote function can be seen not only in addictions but also in patterns of sexual, aggressive, and grandiose enactment.

R. S.

ANTILIBIDINAL EGO Originally referred to by Fairbairn as the *internal saboteur, this portion of the ego is split off and attached to the *rejecting object through emotional affects of anger and sadness. This is the angry and self-destructive part of the self. Fairbairn described the dynamics of hysteria, in which the antilibidinal ego directs its aggression towards the *libidinal ego and the *exciting object in order to reduce the pain of unsatisfiable longing. The extent to which such attacks predominate determines the extent of aggression evident in the hysterical personality.

E. F. B. / D. E. S.

ANTISOCIAL TENDENCY The antisocial tendency characterises the child who is deprived as a result of not being held during the period of relative *dependence upon the mother, and becomes what may also be termed 'a nuisance as a way of life'. This may be the tendency to steal, or tell lies, or be aggressive, or cruel or perverse in varying degrees and levels. Such delinquency is also recognised as a request for help or 'sign of hope'. Winnicott distinguishes such behaviour from that of the child who has suffered *privation, that is, the failure to be held during the period of absolute dependence. The emphasis on the delicate balance of environmental provision in relation to the infant's need in this model may be distinguished from the theories of destructive behaviour in Klein's work which are related to innate *unconscious phantasy in the newborn towards the *breast.

Newman, A. (1995) *The Antisocial Tendency*. London: Free Association Books.
Segal, H. (1973) *Introduction to the Work of Melanie Klein*. London: Hogarth Press.
Winnicott, D. W. (1984) *Deprivation and Delinquency*. London: Tavistock Publications.

H. T. R.

ANXIETY Anxiety is an unpleasant affect accompanied by a myriad of physiologic manifestations (quickened heart beat, gastrointestinal distress, 'butterflies' and diarrhoea, a tightening in the chest, tremulousness, sweating, muscle tension) as well as psychological manifestations (a sense of dread and impending danger, of helplessness, of insecurity and uncertainty). Freud's first theory of anxiety (1895) mainly drew on the thermodynamic models he had worked on with *Breuer, and paid tribute to some contemporary presentations of *neurasthenia as he attempted to explain the freshly differentiated symptoms of *phobia and agoraphobia. He considered that pathological anxiety, in 'anxiety neurosis' (i.e. agoraphobia and anxious states not directly related to a single object) arose mainly as the result of an excess of sexual energy that had not been disposed of through satisfactory sexual intercourse.

By 1905, discussing the case of *Little Hans, he elaborated a second theory, claiming that the change of sexual excitation into anxiety could not simply be a mechanical phenomenon. At that point, he had differentiated 'anxiety hysteria' (i.e. phobia) from this earlier view of 'anxiety neurosis', and tended to link the issue of the surge of anxiety to *castration threats coming from the child's environment rather than to a mechanical quantitative factor.

A crucial moment in the Freudian theory of anxiety was his book *Inhibitions, Symptoms and Anxiety*, in which he assigned the origin of anxiety to a primary state of *helplessness experienced by the child overwhelmed by his drives, in the absence of the reassuring mother. Freud dismissed the hypothesis upheld by *Rank and *Ferenczi, according to whom all forms of anxiety ultimately result from a primitive birth-trauma. Helplessness, he assumed, began with the experience of undifferentiated *schreck* (*fright) that was secondarily transformed into anxiety when the child managed to differentiate hints of danger, the only way to ensure a subjectivation through a mastery of the anxiety surge. However, the elaboration of *death drive theory brought a significant change in Freud's theory of anxiety, as the evidence of unconscious *guilt and self-punitive mechanisms led him to admit the limitations of his second theory: the threat of castration appeared to be a highly limited mechanism in front of the more pervasive and technically embarrassing *negative therapeutic reactions.

See also: anxiety, signal

F. S.

ANXIETY (FAIRBAIRN) Fairbairn believed that the most basic anxiety was over loss of the primary caregiver, since it arises in response to the threat of loss of the relationship on which all else depends. This affective response to threat triggers defensive strategies, beginning with the *introjection of the caregiver and the subsequent splitting of the maternal internal object into satisfying and unsatisfying. Thus *separation anxiety and the defensive responses to it play a major role in organising the psyche. Fairbairn responded to *Jones's 1929 paper on anxiety.

Fairbairn, W. R. D. [1929] (1994) 'Some points of importance in the psychology of anxiety' in *From Instinct to Self: Volume II*. D. Scharff and E. Fairbairn Birtles (eds). Northvale, NJ: Jason Aronson.
Jones, E. (1929) 'The psychology of anxiety'. *The British Journal of Medical Psychology* 9(1): 17–25.

E. F. B. / D. E. S.

ANXIETY (EXISTENTIAL) For existential philosophy and psychology, anxiety is not just a sign of the return of the repressed, as it is for classical psychoanalysis, but a marker of the authentic human condition. Anxiety and related concepts such as anguish, fear and dread point to our fundamental freedom. Kierkegaard and *Heidegger distinguish between anxiety and fear, noting that fear takes a definite object whereas anxiety has none. For Heidegger, anxiety is an essential structure of *Dasein as Being-toward-possibility and Being-toward-death. For *Sartre, anxiety points to the threat that my freedom poses to my sense of myself as solid object and also to the threat that others pose to my freedom. The flight from anxiety is a flight from *authenticity. Existential analysts note that existential anxiety often arises as analysands approach moments of profound change in therapy.

B. C.

ANXIETY (LACAN) Lacan claimed that anxiety was the central *affect with which psychoanalysis is concerned. In contrast to Freud's mainly pathological construction of the concept, Lacan drew on the German Romantic tradition, Russian literature and Kierkegaard's concept of anxiety. Lacan considered anxiety to be an inevitable dimension of desire – incarnated by *object a, which at that time he alternately called the 'object of desire' and 'object of anxiety' – insisting that, in relation to this conflict, psychoanalysis was underpinned by a tragic concept of life. The object can be conceived of as a lack which is the result of an extraction of *jouissance brought about by language. This function of *lack allows the constitution of the *mirror stage and this confirms the ego and the body-image. Failing this, the lack brought into being by the subtraction of jouissance disappears, and the *subject in psychosis is confronted by an unlimited figure of the Other which does not allow for the secure experience of the limits of his or her body. Lacan considered that anxiety, in neurotic cases, has a limit which is determined by castration, where – like the lizards which are capable of dropping their tail in hazardous situations – the neurotic is endowed with the specific capacity of losing a part of his or her *jouissance during the analysis, opening the way to a structural concept of the end of analysis.

Lacan notes that, in general, because affects can be displaced they are no less misleading than the meanings produced by the subject: hence the analytical treatment's focus on structure, beyond both affect and meaning. For him, the only affect that does not deceive is anxiety.

For Lacan affects and *signifiers are inextricably interwoven in the unconscious and one of Lacan's most significant challenges to psychoanalytic orthodoxy consisted in challenging an organising dichotomy present within of all forms of psychology: namely the distinction between the emotional (affects) and the intellectual (thought processes).

F. S. / V. V.

ANXIETY, REALISTIC The anxiety response to a danger believed to be real. Freud originally explained neurotic anxiety as the transformation of excessive quantities of libidinal energy resulting from insufficient gratification of instinctual wishes which had been repressed. In 1926 he reversed this causal relationship claiming that false beliefs about real dangers such as castration cause anxiety which, in turn, causes the repression of sexual wishes.

See also: anxiety

Freud, S. (1926) *Inhibitions, Symptoms, and Anxiety*. S. E. 10. London: Hogarth Press.

E. Gil.

ANXIETY, SIGNAL A small dose of anxiety is generated by the ego as a signal of a threat or potential traumatic situation (e.g. loss of love, castration). A signal of anxiety is often precipitated by a forbidden wish or impulse. In adequate functioning, signal anxiety triggers a defence (e.g. repression) which removes the thought or affect associated with the forbidden wish from being consciously experienced and thus prevents signal anxiety from becoming traumatic anxiety.

E. Gil.

APHANISIS Used by *Jones to refer to the disappearance of desire, Lacan uses it to explicate the disappearance or fading of the subject. The subject reduced to being represented by the signifier in the field of the *Other is the fading or aphanisis of the subject in Lacan.

C. Owe.

APHASIA A dysfunction of language that occurs with acquired brain lesions, but is also seen in abnormal development, sleep talking and other altered states. In anterior or non-fluent aphasia, there are errors of initiation, timing and syntax, phonetic sequencing and production. In posterior or fluent aphasia, there are lexical-semantic and phonemic errors. Various subtypes occur.

Freud, S. [1891] (1953) *On Aphasia: A Critical Study*. New York: International Universities Press.

Brown, J. W. (1972) *Aphasia, Apraxia, Agnosia*. Springfield, IL: C. C. Thomas.

Brown, J. W. (1986) *Life of the Mind*. Hillsdale, NJ: Erlbaum.

J. W. B.

ARCHAIC HERITAGE Freud uses this term to designate the store of psychical experiences passed on by previous generations to each individual. He introduced it in 1919 to indicate how the analysis of dreams can give access to man's phylogenesis. In Lacan's reading the term indicates that the structure of the *Other precedes the subject.

D. N.

ARCHETYPE The basic concept of Jungian psychology. Archetypes are innate neuropsychic centres possessing the capacity to initiate, control, and mediate the common behavioural characteristics and typical experiences of all human beings irrespective of race, culture, creed, or historical epoch. An individual's entire archetypal inheritance comprises the *collective unconscious, which provides a (phylogenetic) evolutionary foundation on which (ontogenesis) individual development proceeds. The development and function of the psyche as a whole is coordinated by a central nucleus which Jung termed the *Self, or 'the archetype of archetypes'. Whereas Freud assumed that our mental equipment is acquired in the course of growing up, Jung asserted that all the essential psychic characteristics that distinguish us as human beings exist as potential when we are born. It is a mistake, Jung wrote, 'to suppose that the psyche of the newborn child is a *tabula rasa* in the sense that there is absolutely nothing in it. Insofar as the child is born with a differentiated brain that is predetermined by heredity and therefore individualised, it meets sensory stimuli coming from outside not with any aptitudes, but with specific ones'.

The intuition that there is more to the psyche than individual experience could possibly put there began in Jung's childhood when it struck him that there were things in his dreams that came from somewhere beyond himself. Confirmation of this childhood intuition came when he worked under *Bleuler at the Burghölzli Hospital in Zurich from 1901 to 1908. What impressed Jung about the delusions and hallucinations of individual schizophrenic patients was the similarity of their content to the delusions and hallucinations of other patients and to the content of myths, fairy tales and legends derived from people inhabiting widely separated parts of the world. These findings convinced him that some universal structures must exist which are common to both the mind and the brain of all men and women and that they must underlie all human experience and behaviour.

At first (in 1912), he referred to these universal structures as 'primordial images' – a term he borrowed from Jacob Burckhardt – and later (1917) as 'dominants of the collective unconscious'. His first use of the more satisfactory term 'archetype' is in his essay 'Instinct and the Unconscious' published in 1919. This change of nomenclature occurred because, with time, Jung recognised that the manifestations of these universal dominants were not restricted to images but occurred also in ideas, feelings, and experiences as well as in characteristic patterns of behaviour.

Jung's earlier identification of archetypes with 'primordial images' laid him open to the charge of Lamarckism – namely, that he believed in the genetic transmission of acquired characteristics. It was not until the publication of his 1947 essay 'The Spirit of Psychology' (revised in volume eight of the *Collected Works* as 'On the Nature of the Psyche') that he finally shed his incipient Lamarckism by making a clear distinction between the deeply unconscious and therefore unknowable 'archetype-as-such' (similar to Kant's 'thing-in-itself') and the archetypal images, ideas and behaviours that the archetypal-as-such gives rise to. It is the archetype-as-such (the predisposition to have certain experiences) that is inherited, not the experience itself. This position is fully in accord with modern biological usage and is no more Lamarckian than the statement that children are innately disposed to acquire speech or to run on two legs. The archetype-as-such possesses an inherent dynamic to seek its own realisation in actuality; and in this it resembles the 'evolved' psychological mechanisms, 'algorithms' and 'modules' of contemporary evolutionary psychology. Indeed, as Stevens points out, the value of the archetypal concept may be judged from the manner in which researchers in other disciplines keep rediscovering it and re-announcing it in their own terminologies.

Jung proposed that archetypal structures preconditioned all psychophysical events: they were not only fundamental to the existence of all living organisms but were continuous with structures controlling the behaviour of inorganic matter as well. Jung considered that the physicist's investigation of matter and the psychologist's investigation of mind were different ways of approaching the same underlying reality – a view strongly supported by the physicist and Nobel Laureate Wolfgang Pauli. Since archetypes precondition all existence, they are manifest in the spiritual achievements of art, science, and religion, as well as in the organisation of organic and inorganic matter.

See also: anthropology; Darwin

Jung, C. G. (1953–78) References are to the *Collected Works* (*CW*), by volume and paragraph number. H. Read, M. Fordham, G. Adler and W. McGuire (eds). London: Routledge; Princeton: Princeton University Press.

Stevens, A. (1982) *Archetype: A Natural History of the Self.* London: Routledge; New York: William Morrow & Co.

Stevens, A. (1999) *On Jung*. Second edition. London: Penguin; Princeton: Princeton University Press.

A. Stev.

ARGENTINA Until 1940, there were no psychoanalysts trained in Argentina; there were however some psychiatrists such as Pizarro Crespo or Jorge Thenon, who were really self-made psychoanalysts.

The Argentinean Psychoanalytic Association (APA) was formed in December 1942, in the midst of World War II, with two streams. Firstly, the European exiles: Angel Garma, Marie Langer and secondly, Argentine physicians and intellectuals: A. Rascovsky, Pichon Rivière and Cárcama, who were soon joined by M. Rascovsky, Alvarez de Toledo, Wencelblat, Scolni, Tagliaferro and Ferrari Hardoy.

During the first period from 1942 to 1953, theories about the Freudian nucleus contributed to an inspiring and creative development as the APA generated original writings: Garma's *Interpretation of Dreams*, differing from Freud, through his theory of the traumatic situation in dreams; his books and papers on psychosomatic symptoms where he emphasises his conception of masochism; Rascovsky's papers on infantile endocrinology, epilepsy and foetal psychology; Pichon Rivière's works on psychosis, and Langer's on female sexuality.

Since the 50s, with the second generation of psychoanalysts such as Arminda Aberastury and Elizabeth Garma, both pioneers of children's psychoanalysis, as well as Liberman, Grinberg, Abadi, Bleger, Racker, Cesio, Rolla, M. and W. Baranger and Rodrigué among others, the Kleinian influence took root in Argentina – where it prevailed until the 90s – and expanded throughout Latin America, thanks to Garma and Rascovsky.

From the 50s to the 70s, a great number of Latin American medical doctors were trained in the Institute of the APA. The Kleinian theories pervaded the Associations in Venezuela, Colombia, Peru, Uruguay and Brazil. Mexico was less affected, because of its North American influence. A specifically Argentian voice emerged with *Racker's papers where *countertransference became more and more important; this relationship became a feature of the Argentine school.

Side by side with this exhilaration and theoretical creativity, towards the end of the 60s and beginnings of the 70s, an antagonistic movement began to appear in the APA, corresponding to the socio-political revolutionary ideas which were greatly disturbing Latin America at the time. Two groups – Plataforma (Platform) and Documento (Document) – split from the APA and IPA and entered the political arena.

Besides the withdrawal of these two groups, in 1974 a new moderate Kleinian group emerged under the leadership of M. and W. Baranger and J. Mom. Putting forward a stimulating, revitalised and pluralistic project they won the elections that year.

This was the beginning of the division of the APA, which finally came to pass in 1977. The Psychoanalytic Association of Buenos Aires (APDEBA) was born; it was afterwards recognised by the IPA. Since 1972, as a result of Leclaire's visit, followed by André Green's arrival, the APA has opened itself up to the influence of the French school of Lacan. Klein's ideas were no longer the only ones being followed, and Lacan's thoughts began to spread, not only within the APA, but also in other Argentine psychoanalytic institutions.

In 1998, another group of psychoanalysts left the APA because of theoretical and political disagreements and, formed the Argentine Society of Psychoanalysis (SAP) which is recognised by the IPA.

Sabsay Foks, G. (1996) *Psychoanalysis in Argentina and Latin America. History of Ideas.* Buenos Aires: ALHP.

G. S. F.

Arlow, Jacob A. (1913–2004) Pioneering American psychoanalyst (ego-psychology) and author of the successful metapsychological text *Psychoanalytic Concepts and the Structural Theory* (1964), written in collaboration with Charles Brenner where they dispose of the topographical theory in favour of structural theory, and in addition to other issues, revise Freud's theory of regression in terms of ego-psychology. He was a former President of the American Psychoanalytic Institute and from 1967 to 1969 was also Vice-President of the International Psychoanalytic Institute. He was also former editor-in-chief of the *Psychoanalytic Quarterly*.

Amongst his many psychoanalytic interests was his concern with the internal conflicts within psychoanalysis both in theory and its organisations. These arise, he contended, largely from the differences of opinion as to what constitutes the etiology of the neurosis-psychosis spectrum as well as accounts of the process of normal development. He also conducted research into the interface between psychoanalysis and the neurosciences.

Arlow's central clinical insight, elaborating on theory implicit in Freud's later work, is that the ego performs a synthesising function where the aim is to integrate fantasy material manifested by drive, defence, reality and superego imperatives for the purpose of constructing a personal identity myth. However, he parts with Freud insofar as the clinical role based on these conceptions is not one of merely making the unconscious conscious, which will only elicit a renewed and reinforced defensive fantasy structure promoted into a higher hierarchical order, but one of analysing unconscious conflict and its concomitant defences into their component elements.

Arlow has been admired for his frankness, pellucid theoretical writing and his gift as a natural pedagogue on psychoanalytic issues.

S. Byr.

ARROGANCE According to Bion, references to arrogance in the psychoanalytic session are one of the three features (along with references to curiosity and stupidity) that make up a constellation that is evidence of a psychological catastrophe. Bion felt that whereas pride generally develops into self-esteem when life drives predominate, pride leads to arrogance when death drives predominate. He later modified this view to emphasise the necessity of the presence of an adequate *container and maternal *reverie for the development of healthy self-esteem. Arrogance, in his later writings, came to be viewed as being more the result of a psychological catastrophe in which the absence of an adequate container, or the presence of an anti-container, causes minute splitting and a fragmentation of the personality.

Bion, W. R. (1967) *Second Thoughts*. London: Heinemann.
Bion, W. R. (1992) *Cogitations*. London: Karnac Books.

S. A.

ART AND PSYCHOANALYSIS Kubler, an art historian, defined art as an object made for emotional experience, yet, against expectation, psychoanalysis has historically had an uneasy interface with the arts, largely due to an exclusive focus on motivation. In the universalist one-person psychology that characterised Freud's systemic thought, the emphasis was on art as a product, the product of the individual's inherently primitive and conflictual internal life. Freud thought that primitive drives and the conflicts they aroused were the sole motivator for creating works of art and for stirring responses in the viewer, who had the same drives and conflicts. Freud's originally sexual motivational theory of instinctual drives (later expanded to include aggression) had to account for activities that were not inherently sexual in aim, such as creative, intellectual and humanistic pursuits. Thus arose the notion of *sublimation, although it was never well developed. Sublimation was evocative both of the sublime (referring to the awe and exhilaration of experiencing the wonders of nature), and of the gaseous transformation of solids in chemistry. This last metaphor helps to elucidate an exchange of the original sexual aim (and, possibly, object) for another not directly sexual. But Freud was ambivalent about art and artists, and psychoanalytic metapsychology never did stretch to include considerations of aesthetics, the visual arts, and the problems of creative life. Freud's excursions into art tended toward pathobiography, which was used primarily to confirm existing theories.

Because of Freud's conviction that even sublime works of art emerge from universal primitive urges, efforts at applied psychoanalysis have often been formulaic and pathologising. Jung, in explicit disagreement, protested that a work of art is not a disease, it is a creative reorganisation of those very conditions to which a causalistic psychology must always reduce it. Many in the arts have been more drawn to Jungian *analytical psychology, with its emphasis on symbolism and its recognition of creativity as an autonomous complex, than to those who followed Freud. Glover criticised such artists as neurotic for exchanging the hard truth of unconscious conflict for the comfort of Jungian illusion, yet the artist Yayoi Kusama (among others) experienced Freudian psychoanalysis in the 1950s, with its relentless search for unconscious conflict underlying the creative impulse, as destructive.

*Kris, an art historian-turned-psychoanalyst, took a fresh look at creativity using *ego psychology's notion of a conflict-free sphere. As a distinguished curator of the Vienna *Kunsthistorisches Museum*, he was familiar with the biographies of artists, and his interest in the creativity of psychotics cast doubt on earlier assumptions about a singular artistic motive. Kris asserted that the id was not the wellspring of creativity. The complex mental processes involved were preconscious aspects of the ego. What creativity required, he proposed, was regression in the service of the ego, joining the notion of highly developed ego functions to Freud's more primitively organised drives.

Certain psychoanalytic schools continued to work within a drive-psychological system. The followers of *Klein and of *Lacan remained preoccupied with the content of artistic production. Kleinian theory emphasised the act of creativity as reparation for aggression and guilt. *Segal found the stimulus to creation in the acknowledged loss of internal objects, and located aesthetic pleasure in the unconscious communication of the artist's state of mind in the act of creation. Stokes saw the work of art as a *good object that nourishes as it repairs. Special mention should be made here of Ehrenzweig, a non-clinical scholar of the visual arts and music and of psychoanalysis and gestalt psychology, who used the tools of depth psychology, and a Kleinian language, to propose a developmental line of the perceptual functions, for the first time enlarging the psychoanalytic field to bring in the central issues of aesthetics as an external consideration separate from either drives or object relations. Lacan's notion of the structuring of the unconscious as a language has contributed to the discourse of postmodernism, opening up the communicative intent of not only art but the everyday elements of culture to critique and interpretation.

Eventually the one-person system of both drive theory and *ego psychology was challenged by a two-person psychology, in which Freud's original notion of a universal psychological substrate gave way to the acknowledgment of a common neurobiological substrate of infinite variability in its genetic penetration and interface with the human environment. Some sources of this shift were *Kohut and the self drive-free systems of motivation, and the hierarchical model of the mind originally proposed by Gedo and Goldberg, and developed by Gedo. The Kleinian world contributed *Winnicott's notion of transitional space, an area of early human experience distinctly separate from the control of drives or of object relations. The idea of a separate pathway of development for creativity owes something as well to *Ferenczi, who, as early as 1912, indicated that *narcissism had a developmental line of its own that persisted throughout the life cycle. All along, a few unique individuals have contributed their voices: *Rank, who looked at the difficulties of artists living in the real world and likened the mutative clinical encounter to a work of art; *Balint (the area of creation) and Milner (the answering activity), who refused to locate creativity in the conflictual object world; Szasz, who identified the neurotic symptom as the alternative communication of the powerless; and Stoller, who saw in perversion a creative transformation of trauma.

The (re)emergence of interpersonal (*relational) ideas of psychoanalysis, in insisting that an individual's internal state is created not solely by the operation of his internal motivational system but is instead co-constructed throughout the life cycle by interactions with significant others, changes the notion of the art object as a product to one that belongs to an interactional field, part of a process of engagement, with self and with other. Much current applied psychoanalysis draws on these developmental and relational perspectives and rejects the notion that artistic activity is either regressive or pathological. This enlightenment has been served well by the independent work of Rose and Gedo.

Gedo's important contribution is in recognising significant creativity as a separate developmental line, a matter of intrinsic temperament and talent that is not the product of conflict or of primitive drives. The major artist (or highly creative individual in any field) is differently organised, and retains (and develops, and uses, if the environment is facilitative) a unique, fluid, multifaceted perceptual apparatus long after the more ordinary versions of the open systems of childhood have closed for the rest of us. The artist may be predisposed to fall ill because of his greater sensitivities, but such illness is a matter separate from the creative impulse. Creativity is not served by illness; rather, it tends to be diminished until recovery is underway.

The term 'creativity of everyday life' was coined by Rose, to recognise the application of creative energy to the task of self-creation, for the rest of us who are not major artists. Rose's body of work is distinguished by the conceptualisation of artistic activity as a dialogue, a dialogue of the artist with his art-object and a dialogue of the art-object with the viewer. Rose's *relational approach is compatible with contemporary art practice that includes installation and performance.

Ehrenzweig, A. (1967) *The Hidden Order of Art*. Los Angeles and Berkeley: University of California Press.

Gedo, J. (1996) *The Artist and the Emotional World*. New York: Columbia University Press.

Jung, C. G. (1922/1976) 'On the relation of analytical psychology to poetry' in J. Cambell (ed.) *The Portable Jung*. Translated by R. F. C. Hull. New York: Penguin.

Rose, G. (1996) *Necessary Illusion: Art as Witness*. Madison, CT: International Universities Press.

Zelevansky, L. (1998) 'Driving image: Yayoi Kusama in New York'. *Love Forever: Yayoi Kusama, 1958–1968*. Los Angeles: Los Angeles County Museum of Art.

J. V.

AS IF PERSONALITY *Deutsch's most famous clinical concept (Freud had originally disapproved of her using the expression 'as if'; unknown to her, Freud was reminded of *Adler's use of the phrase).

In her concern with 'as if' problems she was trying to describe a false affectivity that was neither neurotic nor psychotic. The patients in question make an impression of 'complete normality'. They are intellectually intact and gifted and show great understanding in all intellectual matters. But when they try to be productive their work is formally good but totally devoid of originality. It is always an imitation of a model without the slightest personal trace. Their relations with people are also intense, in terms of friendship, love, understanding, and sympathy, but still something is chillingly absent. A key point was that the patients themselves were not aware of any impoverishment, but believe that their empty performances are the same as the feelings and experiences of others – a chameleon-like regrouping in the environment of the person's circle of acquaintances.

The origins of an 'as if' personality lies in the patient's inability to develop a normal *Oedipus complex. Such people validate their existence by identification. This tendency toward mimicry was a substitute for genuine relations with people as well as causes. To the extent that in our culture the concept of 'as if' applied primarily to women, Deutsch was being critical of the conformism associated with the traditional conception of femininity.

Deutsch, H. (1965) 'Some forms of emotional disturbance and their relationship to schizophrenia ("as if")' in *Neuroses and Character Types*. New York: International Universities Press.

P. R.

ASPERGER'S SYNDROME Asperger's syndrome is classified as a developmental disorder. It is characterised by major social interactional problems similar to those seen in *autism, though with some important differences. It was first described by Hans Asperger in 1944. He emphasised the failure of socio-emotional communication, stereotyped behaviour, resistance to change and isolated special interests.

A person with Asperger's syndrome is typically impaired in their ability to express emotion, and to recognise and respond to emotions in others. They have problems with self-reflective awareness and symbolic thought. They want to interact socially but don't know how to do it. Their problems with emotional understanding and relating have been described as an innate incapacity – basically an ego deficit state.

From the point of view of psychoanalytic treatment they require an intervention based on a major modification of classical psychoanalytic technique. The psychoanalyst needs to understand that the person with Asperger's syndrome has difficulties understanding emotions, beliefs and pre-suppositions. They may lack understanding of the psychoanalyst's mind – a so-called Theory of Mind deficit. The analysis of the relationship to the analyst is crucial because of the major deficit in the interpersonal area. The analyst's goal is to help the person to feel understood and to gain some emotional understanding of another mind, and in that way to begin to make a meaningful, understandable emotional connection to another human being. Recognising the reality of the sense of difference which the person with Asperger's syndrome often has can be crucial. So can the sensitive handling of problems with sensory overload and with the body image, and the careful monitoring of the countertransference.

Asperger, H. (1944) 'Die autistischen Psychopathen im Kindesalter'. *Archiv für Psychiatrie und Nervenkrankheiten* 117: 76–113. Translated in U. Frith (ed.) *Autism and Asperger's Syndrome*. Cambridge: Cambridge University Press.

Grotstein, J. S. (1997) 'One pilgrim's progress: notes on Frances Tustin's contributions to the psychoanalytic conception of autism' in T. Mitrani and J. L. Mitrani (eds) *Encounters with Autistic States: A Memorial Tribute to Frances Tustin*. Northvale, NJ: Jason Aronson.

Rhode, M. and Klauber, T. (eds) (2004) *The Many Faces of Asperger's Syndrome*. London: Tavistock/Karnac Books.

Shuttleworth, J. (1999) 'The suffering of Asperger children and the challenge they present to psychoanalytic thinking'. *Journal of Child Psychotherapy* 25: 239–55.

Youell, B. (1999) 'Matthew: from numbers to numeracy: from knowledge to knowing in a ten-year-old boy with Asperger's Syndrome' in A. Alvarez and S. Reid (eds) *Autism and Personality*. London and New York: Routledge.

M. F.

ASSOCIATION For Freud psychic contents relate to each other via complex pathways of association, which may be conscious or unconscious. Psychoanalysis emphasises the unconscious associations, which are governed by *primary process thinking as against rational thinking processes. Repressed unconscious associations linked to conscious ones explain aspects of a person's actions or experience that might otherwise seem puzzling.

See also: free association; verbal bridge

A. R.

AT-ONE-MENT A state of mind that *Bion felt was necessary for true psychoanalytic discovery to take place. The exercise of suspending memory and desire was felt to provide the necessary conditions to allow for a state of at-one-ment with ultimate reality. Ultimate reality, or *O, cannot be known but its presence can be recognised and felt. That is, it is possible to be at one with it.

Bion, W. R. (1970) *Attention and Interpretation*. London: Tavistock. Also in *Seven Servants*. New York: Jason Aronson, 1977.

S. A.

ATTACHMENT Attachment theory is almost unique among psychoanalytic theories in bridging the gap between general psychology and clinical psychodynamic theory. A gulf exists to this day between theories of the mind rooted in empirical social science (largely psychological research), and clinical theories that focus on the significance of individual experience in determining life course, including psychopathology. In psychoanalysis, giving meaning to experience is seen as the primary explanation of behaviour as well as the royal road to its therapeutic change. Experimental psychology emphasises parsimony, insists on reliable observation, and abhors rhetoric and speculative theory-building. Yet attachment theory straddles this gulf.

*Bowlby was among the first to recognise that the human infant enters the world predisposed to participate in social interaction. Children have the propensity to form a number of attachment relationships in early life and there appears to be a hierarchy of major caregivers with a preferred principal attachment figure. Bowlby thought that disruption of the early caregiver-child relationship should be seen as a key precursor of mental disorder. His critical contribution was his unwavering focus on the infant's need for an unbroken (secure) early attachment to the caregiver.

Like classical psychoanalysis, Bowlby's attachment theory has a biological focus. He emphasised the survival value of attachment in enhancing safety through proximity to the caregiver in addition to feeding, learning about the environment and social interaction as well as protection from predators (the biological function of attachment behaviour). Attachment behaviours were seen as part of a behavioural system. This is key to understanding the earlier controversy between psychoanalysis and attachment theory. A behavioural system involves inherent motivation. It is not reducible to another drive. This explains why feeding is not causally linked to attachment and why attachment occurs to abusive caretakers.

Bowlby's formulations and those of object relations theorists therefore differ importantly. The child's goal is not the object, but initially a physical state (maintenance of a desired degree of proximity), which is later supplanted by the more psychological goal of a feeling of closeness to the caregiver. In the first volume of his *Attachment and Loss* trilogy Bowlby was unclear about how attachment behaviour functioned beyond the termination of the system once physical proximity was ensured. In the 1970s Mary Ainsworth's work helped to refine the attachment concept. She recognised that infants' responses to separation can be explained by their appraisal or evaluation of the mother's departure in the context of her expected behaviour. The disruptions occasioned by separation from the primary caregiver are moderated by an increasingly complex set of (unconscious) evaluative processes.

Bowlby addresses the critical role of appraisal in the third volume of his trilogy, where he introduces the concept of the internal working models. The internal working model is a repository of representations of past interactions with the caregiver that helps to determine the pattern of their interaction in the present and the infant's expectations of future interactions. The caregiver's availability is central to the child's internal working model. Bowlby also envisioned a complementary working model of the child's self. The key determining factor of this is how acceptable or unacceptable the child feels in the eye of the attachment figure. A child whose internal working model of the caregiver is focused around rejection is expected to evolve a complementary working model of the self as unlovable, unworthy and flawed. Although Bowlby does not say so explicitly, these models of the attachment figure and the self are transactional, interactive models representing self-other relationships.

Positing a representational system underpinning attachment permitted a far more sophisticated consideration of individual differences. Attachment could now be understood as secure or insecure. Secure attachment implies representational systems where the attachment figure is seen as accessible and responsive when needed. Anxious attachment implies a representational system where the responsiveness of the caregiver is not assumed and the child adopts strategies for circumventing the caregiver's perceived unresponsiveness. The anxious-avoidant strategy embodies the denial of the emotional tie to the caregiver while the anxious-resistant strategy hints at the need to amplify signals of distress in order to ensure that they will be heard. There is considerable empirical support for Bowlby's assumption that caregiver responsiveness was critical in determining the security of the attachment system.

In the late 70s Alan Sroufe and Everet Waters redefined the set goal of the attachment system as 'felt security' rather than physical distance regulation. Thus internal cues such as mood, illness or even fantasy could be seen as relevant to the child's response to separation as well as external events and the social environmental context. This substantially extends the Bowlbian notion because the range of experiences that could contribute to felt security is in no way restricted to caregiver behaviour. Felt security as a concept extended the applicability of the concept of attachment from early childhood to older children and even adults. Sroufe re-conceptualised attachment theory in terms of affect regulation. Securely attached individuals, who have internalised the capacities for self-regulation are contrasted with those who precociously either down-regulate or up-regulate affect. Such individuals are classified as having 'avoidant' or 'resistant' attachment in accordance with their respective dismissal of or preoccupation with their attachment figures.

During the late 70s and 80s, attachment research was increasingly concerned with child maltreatment, physical and sexual abuse. The child's entire attachment behavioural system can potentially be undermined if the attachment figure is at once the signal of safety and of danger. When this happens the child's attachment is said to be disorganised. In such cases reappearance of the caregiver after separation is often marked by fear, freezing and disorientation in the infant. Childhood maltreatment accounts for some but not all attachment disorganisation observed in infancy. The potential reasons for the disorganisation of the attachment system have therefore been extended to include experiences which were more subtle but nevertheless deeply unsettling from an infant's point of view, such as moments of dissociation in the caregiver. A number of longitudinal investigations link infant disorganisation to later psychopathology. Research and theory on attachment disorganisation offers a more satisfactory theoretical link between early attachment experience and personality disturbance than has thus far been available and is therefore the cutting edge of current clinical attachment research.

Animal studies have revealed that the evolutionary value of staying close to and interacting with the mother goes beyond protection, providing the caregiver with an opportunity to shape both the developing physiology and the behaviour of the infant through their patterned interactions. This suggests that attachment is not an end in itself but a system adapted by evolution to fulfil key ontogenetic physiological and psychological tasks. The traditional attachment model is clearly circular: the response to separation is attributed to the disruption of a social bond, the existence of which is inferred from the presence of the separation response. More recent research suggests that what is lost in 'loss' is not the bond but the opportunity to develop a higher order regulatory mechanism for appraisal and reorganisation of mental contents. In this context attachment is conceptualised as a process that brings complex mental life into being from a multi-faceted and adaptable behavioural system. Some, but by no means all, of such mental function is unique to humans. The mechanism that generates these (the attachment relationship) has evolutionary continuity across non-human species.

Rapprochement has become possible between attachment theory and psychoanalysis because of a number of concurrent historical changes. Attachment theory has shifted its focus from infant behaviour and its determinants in the child's physical environment to broader concerns with internal representations in the infant and the parent, and has begun to recognise the limitations of a purely cognitive science approach in clinical work and a need for alternative theoretical frames of reference to enrich research and theory building of relevance to clinicians. Psychoanalysts have become more interested in systematic observation and empirical research. The theoretical hegemony that governed psychoanalysis in the United States (and to a lesser extent in Europe) has broken down, leading to more openness to the possibility of plurality in theory, where clinical usefulness and intellectual appeal are the primary criteria for the acceptability of new ideas.

Ainsworth, M. D. S., Blehar, M. C., Waters, E. and Wall, S. (1978) *Patterns of Attachment: A Psychological Study of the Strange Situation*. Hillsdale, NJ: Erlbaum.
Bowlby, J. (1988) *A Secure Base: Clinical Applications of Attachment Theory*. London: Routledge.
Main, M. and Morgan, H. (1996) 'Disorganization and disorientation in infant strange situation behaviour: phenotypic resemblance to dissociative states' in L. K. Michelson and W. J. Ray (eds) *Handbook of Dissociation: Theoretical, Empirical, and Clinical Perspectives*. New York: Plenum Press.
Polan, H. J. and Hofer, M. (1999) 'Psychobiological origins of infant attachment and separation responses' in J. Cassidy and P. R. Shaver (eds) *Handbook of Attachment: Theory, Research and Clinical Applications*. New York: Guilford.
Solomon, J. and George, C. (1999) *Attachment Disorganization*. New York: Guilford.
Sroufe, L. A. (1996) *Emotional Development: The Organization of Emotional Life in the Early Years*. New York: Cambridge University Press.

P. F.

ATTACKS ON LINKING see LINKING, ATTACKS ON

ATTENTION A function which searches the outer world to ensure that information is familiar in case an urgent inner need should arise. Attention which is evenly suspended or poised was recommended by Freud in listening to the patient. This complements the rule of *free association recommended to the patient.

R. M. S.

ATTENTION DEFICIT DISORDER Attention Deficit Hyperactivity Disorder (ADHD) is a diagnosis of children that is frequently made on both sides of the Atlantic. It describes children who, finding it difficult to focus on a task, bend their energies to irrelevant and often physical and disruptive activities: a classical 'naughty child'. Such children cannot concentrate, are overactive and act on impulse. The ICD-10 diagnosis, in particular, emphasises the hyperactive components of the 'condition', which often occurs in children together with other behaviour problems. It has been widely treated with Ritalin (methylphenidate), which can be helpful in calming children's tendencies to over-react and flattens the affect of all children. The National Institute has endorsed the use of Ritalin recently for the treatment of children over six years of age for Clinical Excellence. Perry and his co-workers have drawn attention to the similarity of the symptoms of ADHD and those experienced by people in traumatic situations – described briefly as hyper-alertness to danger. Perry et al. hypothesise that at a critical age in childhood (before the age of two) children with ADHD have experienced trauma that has caused on-going reactions, as though to trauma, to be incorporated into the nervous system. This will have consequences for the neuro-biological make-up as a whole, establishing by use a greater responsiveness to events as though they might be dangerous.

Such a hypothesis opens up the possibility of modification by psychoanalytic treatment as suggested by Emanuel. Furthermore, such an hypothesis provides an opportunity for early intervention and work with families to rework potentially traumatic interactions before they become fully established as Pozzi has shown. Shore, linking attachment theory with neurobiological findings, draws attention to the fact that reworking of trauma requires reliving of the emotional experience if neuro-biological functions are to be reorganised. Orford has shown in his psychoanalytic work with children diagnosed with ADHD that their wariness and hyperactive response to their expectations of threat can be addressed in the transference.

Given that children like this bring to the therapeutic relationship an expectation of danger, the work is likely to require considerable delicacy of technique. It is important to be alert to the child's tendency to test the therapist's capacity to protect the child's own person, to look after him/her self, and guard against attacks against the therapy itself. Only if the therapist can demonstrate his or her capacity to recognise and cope with such attacks can the child feel safe enough to work on his fears and on the developmental delay consequent on his internalisation of damaged and damaging figures. It is important that carers can have parallel intervention so that their expectations can keep pace with the therapeutic work with the child. In such a situation gains can be made of a lasting kind and without side effects.

Emanuel, R. (1995) 'Psychotherapy with children traumatized in infancy'. *Journal of Child Psychotherapy* 22: 214–39.

Orford, E. (1998) 'Wrestling with the whirlwind: an approach to the understanding of ADHD'. *Journal of Child Psychotherapy* 24: 253–66.

Pozzi, M. (2000) 'Ritalin for whom?' *Journal of Child Psychotherapy* 26: 25–43.

Perry, B. D., Pollard, R. A., Blackley, T. L., Baker, W. I. and Vigilante, D. (1995) 'Childhood trauma, the neuro-biology of adaptation and the use-dependent development of the brain: how states become traits'. *Infant Mental Health Journal* 16: 271–91.

Shore, A. (1994) *Affect Regulation and the Origin of the Self*. Hillsdale, NJ: Erlbaum.

E. O.

AUSTRALIA The new and controversial discoveries of Freud were felt in this country in the early part of the twentieth century. *Jones, in his biography of Freud, reported a number of events that accord Australia a significant place in the early history of psychoanalysis. In 1909 Freud reported having received a letter from Sydney, Australia, telling him there was a group there eagerly studying his work. A Dr Donald Cameron, about this time, had to resign his position because of his Freudian views. Jones noted 'this is the first instance, but far from being the last, of this kind of victimisation'.

In 1911 an invitation was made to Freud, Jung and Havelock Ellis to read papers to the Australian branch of the British Medical Association in Sydney. Freud was not able to come but he sent a paper entitled 'On Psychoanalysis' which was published, for the first time, in 1989 in the *Scientific Proceedings of the Australian Psychoanalytic Society*.

Dr Roy Winn was the first psychoanalyst to practise in Australia. He worked as an analyst in private practice for thirty years until 1960 when he retired. As an Honorary Assistant Physician at Sydney Hospital he published a number of articles on the relation of psychoanalysis to medical practice which did not endear him to the majority of his medical colleagues. In fact the response to his articles was highly abusive. The Professor of Medicine at the time and other senior medical men labelled his, and Freud's, ideas as 'Quackery' and the theory of *infantile sexuality was dismissed as the greatest libel that had ever been published about the human race. A few psychiatrists who were sympathetic to psychoanalysis rebutted these responses.

It is significant that the interest in psychoanalysis prior to the war was mainly intellectual whereas today the interest is mainly professional. In the period immediately before the war, keen interest was shown in psychoanalysis not only by psychiatrists but also in the wider intellectual community. Educationists, churchmen, members of the judiciary and psychologists had all been intrigued with the promise and the challenge of the new depth psychology. In Melbourne an enthusiastic group of supporters, including an Anglican bishop, and a number of psychiatrists, including the only psychoanalyst, Dr Roy Winn, actively supported the efforts made at the time by Jones to assist the migration of psychoanalysts to Australia.

Despite the efforts of an influential group in Australia working to ensure Jones' effort, considerable difficulty was encountered in obtaining Commonwealth Government support for displaced European analysts to enter the country. As events transpired Jones's efforts to encourage psychoanalysts to settle in this country resulted in only one analyst being granted an entry permit. That was Dr Clara Geroe from Budapest. The enthusiastic local group immediately formed the Melbourne Institute of Psychoanalysis and Dr Geroe commenced work in 1943. Acting in isolation her task was a difficult one and for years, until 1968, she was the only Training Analyst in Australia. Jones had named her as Training Analyst and the Melbourne Institute acted as a 'branch' of the British Society.

In 1966 there was great dissatisfaction with the training arrangements in Australia and particularly the hegemony that centred on the training in Melbourne. Professor Martin met a special meeting of the British Society to discuss this matter. As a result Australia was made a Study Group and training was no longer centred in Melbourne but Sydney also was permitted to train. The Sydney Institute for Psychoanalysis had been established since 1951 when Dr Peto from the USA came to Sydney in the hope that training would commence.

In 1970 the Australian Psychoanalytic Society was formally accredited. Professor Martin became the President and endeavoured to introduce standards of training that he had encountered in Britain. From about the early eighties growing dissatisfaction with the new methods began to emerge, which were quite different from the ones they were replacing and a Site Visiting Committee was invited in 1983. This Committee was unable to settle the demands of those who had expressed dissatisfaction and a second Site Visiting Committee comprised of Dr J. *Sandler and Dr A. Cooper was appointed. This Committee approached the problem from a different standpoint from the initial Committee. They were intent upon widening the issues from standards and training to a formula for power sharing, increasing the membership and the number of Training Analysts and of developing the scientific life of the Society. The result was a change in the culture of analysis. No longer was it possible to arrange for visiting analysts only from Britain (especially Kleinians), but also from America and elsewhere.

Australia has one important feature that distinguishes it from most other countries and which is playing an important role in the growth and use of psychoanalysis: that is the existence of a generous Commonwealth Insurance Scheme. This scheme covers the cost of analysis for patients of medically qualified analysts but it is not without its difficulties – notably that only medically qualified analysts are included, not the 40% of non-medical analysts.

Psychoanalysis is currently well established. Melbourne, Sydney and Adelaide are all training centres. In each of the centres outreach programmes designed to interest other professionals and the wider public in analytic ideas are being conducted. There are currently ninety members plus ten students of the Australian Psychoanalytic Society.

R. T. M.

AUSTRIA The history of Austrian psychoanalysis is bound to the name and work of Sigmund Freud and to the psychoanalytic movement in Vienna. The significance of Vienna for the foundation and development of psychoanalysis is evident. Psychoanalysis developed in Vienna during the Habsburg Monarchy until 1918, in the *Red Vienna* of the First Republic until 1934, and then in Vienna during Austrofacism until the *Anschluß* in 1938 under different socio-political and socio-cultural circumstances, from which various scientific and organisational developments benefited or were impeded. The 'science of the unconscious' was founded in Vienna during the Austro-Hungarian Monarchy and Viennese Modernity. Bourgeois society and European Modernity showed significant crises in *fin de siècle* Vienna. On a socio-political level, the multinational state tended to search for a renewal including different forms of living. During the period 1890 to 1910, extraordinary advancements in the areas of music, literature, art and science were achieved. These were fundamentally influential for new developments in observation and thought in the twentieth century. Freud's psychoanalysis with its topics of 'subjectivity' and the 'scientific empirical method' can be interpreted in this vein.

The first expression of the formation of the psychoanalytic movement is considered to be the weekly conferring assembly, which began in late 1902 and was known as the Wednesday Psychological Society. Sigmund Freud invited the first participants to his apartment in Vienna at Berggasse 19. These people were interested in Freud's discoveries and achievements, they attended his lectures at the University of Vienna from 1886/87 onwards and saw themselves as protagonists of a new scientific movement. Otto Rank's minutes of the Viennese Psychoanalytical Society from 1906 to 1918 illustrate how the establishment of psychoanalysis as an independent scientific discipline proceeded with Sigmund Freud in mutual exchange with this group of people.

The contact with psychiatrists from the renowned Burghölzli university clinic in Zurich in 1906 (Jung, Bleuler) signalled Freud's first international recognition. In April 1908 an international meeting took place in Salzburg, and in 1910 the Viennese Psychoanalytical Society and the International Psychoanalytic Association were officially registered. The psychoanalytic movement in Vienna was in its heyday in the years before World War I.

Many projects of Viennese modern ideas were realised in the social-democratic *Red Vienna* after the fall of the Habsburg Monarchy. The mutual understanding between psychoanalysis and Social Democracy was extended to institutional and public levels. With the activity of its publishing house (*Internationaler Psychoanalytischer Verlag*) from 1919, the work done at the outpatient clinic (*Ambulatorium*) of the Viennese Psychoanalytical Society from 1922, and the psychoanalytical Training Institute, founded in late 1924, an intensive atmosphere of research and study prevailed (e.g. child observation and analysis, education, juvenile delinquency, theory and therapy of psychoses).

With the establishment of the totalitarian state in Austria in 1933/34 psychoanalytical work lost its cultural and intellectual ground due to the proscription of Social Democracy and its institutions together with the emigration of important leftist Freudians. Austria's subsumption under the National Socialist Third Reich led to the destruction of psychoanalysis and the exodus of almost all the psychoanalysts. The history of psychoanalysis in Austria after 1933/34 must be written as the history of its emigration. Following the occupation of Austria by German troops, the board of the Viennese Psychoanalytical Society held a meeting on 13 March 1938. A consensus was soon reached and a resolution passed that urged psychoanalysts to leave the country and to move the seat of the Society to where Freud was to settle. On 4 June 1938, Freud and part of his family left for exile in London. The fleeing of more than fifty psychoanalysts and trainees to Great Britain and the United States meant the closure of the Viennese Psychoanalytical Society in September 1938.

Five of the former members of the Vienna Psychoanalytic Society stayed in Vienna. August Aichhorn, who was able to practise privately during the National Socialist rule and World War II, organised a group of analysts and individual psychologists who were concerned with keeping their independence and refused to conform as much as possible. Officially, the group was affiliated with the

Institute for Psychological Research and Psychotherapy of the German Reich. The majority of them formed the core of the new Vienna Psychoanalytic Society in 1946. Due to the difficult post-war situation, only two former members returned for a brief period to Vienna. The psychoanalytic organisations and the representation of psychoanalysis in intellectual and popular culture were only slowly and under difficult circumstances re-established after World War II. The discontinuity due to the previous exodus of the Viennese psychoanalysts had created a situation that amounted to having to begin totally anew. Scientific traditions were broken and tendencies of anti-enlightenment, especially clerical prejudices, had continued from the time of Austrofascism and National Socialism.

It was under the heading of 'depth psychology', a concept more common in post-war Austria, that it became possible once again to discuss Freudian psychoanalysis, yet theory was exposed to arbitrary revisions, simplifications, reductions and interpretations in keeping with the Christian world-view. The results of the rupture have been obvious for a long time and a factor to consider for the history of Austrian psychoanalysis after 1945. A year after the re-foundation of the Viennese Psychoanalytical Society, the *Wiener Arbeitskreis für Tiefenpsychologie* was organised by Igor A. *Caruso. This circle expanded under the title *Arbeitskreis für Psychoanalyse* on a national and later on an international level. Caruso was the first analyst to become professor of psychology at the university of Salzburg from 1972 until 1979 and encouraged research and study on an academic level. In 1971, the first International Psychoanalytical Congress took place in Vienna, and the same year saw the opening of the Sigmund Freud Museum in Freud's Berggasse 19. At the University of Vienna, the *Institut für Tiefenpsychologie und Psychotherapie* was founded in 1971 as well. These events together with the results of the student movement in the 1960s led to a wider discussion and presence of psychoanalysis in Austria again.

See also: Nazis

Berner, W. (1992) 'Austria. The Viennese Psychoanalytical Society after 1945' in P. Kutter (ed.) *Psychoanalysis International*. Stuttgart-Bad Cannstatt: Klett Cotta, 16–23.

Huber, W. (1977) *Psychoanalyse in Österreich seit 1933*. Wien and Salzburg: Geyer Edition.

Mühlleitner, E. and Reichmayr, J. (1995) 'The exodus of psychoanalysts from Vienna' in F. Stadler and P. Weibel (eds) *Vertreibung der Vernunft. The Cultural Exodus from Austria*. Second edition. Wien and New York: Springer-Verlag, 98–121.

Mühlleitner, E. and Reichmayr, J. (1997) 'Following Freud in Vienna. Development and structure of the Wednesday Psychological Society and the Viennese Psychoanalytical Society 1902–1938'. *International Forum of Psychoanalysis* 6: 73–102.

Nunberg, H. and Federn, E. (eds) (1962–75) *The Minutes of the Vienna Psychoanalytic Society*. 4 vols. New York: International Universities Press.

Reichmayr, J. (1992) *Spurensuche in der Geschichte der Psychoanalyse*. Frankfurt: Fischer Taschenbuch.

E. M. / J. R.

AUTHENTICITY/INAUTHENTICITY A term used to differentiate between a person who is genuine in his or her being and one who is prone to self-deception. In *Heidegger's usage the meaning is more subtle, as he plays on the etymology of the German *eigen* meaning to 'own' or 'one's own'. Hence to be authentic is to assume 'ownership' of oneself by taking responsibility for one's actions and states of being, as when 'owning one's feelings'. The most prevalent example of inauthenticity is when following the crowd by adopting standards of behaviour purely for the sake of gaining acceptance or furthering ambition. This does not imply, however, that a person can become 'saved' from inauthenticity by becoming authentic, a project that Heidegger would also deem inauthentic. Hence we are all inauthentic but capable of acting authentically in spite of it, exemplified by moments of sacrifice or facing death or disappointment. Clinically, authenticity may be construed as becoming self-aware of one's unacknowledged inclinations, or in psychoanalytic terms by coming to grips with 'unconscious' motives. In contradistinction to psychoanalysis which holds that one is not responsible for what is unconscious, for Heidegger one is responsible even for unconscious motives because they are a dimension of one's being and, hence, one's 'own'. Whereas psychoanalysts shy away from holding patients accountable for unconscious motives for fear of eliciting guilt, Heidegger held that existential guilt is axiomatic and, hence, an inescapable burden of behaving authentically.

*Sartre built on Heidegger's conception of authenticity with his notion of 'bad faith', the refusal to take responsibility for the existential choices that have made us who we are. According to Sartre, there are two fundamental forms of bad faith or lying to oneself about the nature of existence: overemphasising *facticity and denying freedom (as in 'my family made me what I am') on the one hand and overemphasising freedom and denying facticity (as in 'my family had no impact on me whatsoever') on the other. Contemporary practitioners of existential psychoanalysis typically mould these terms to fit their agendas, so one should be sensitive to how a given practitioner employs them.

See also: depressive position

M. G. T.

AUTHORITY Authority, in its neurotic form, is the appeal for support from the father. It is authentic when, on the contrary, an artist for example is able to do without this appeal to the father in *sublimation. Freud takes it that psychoanalysis makes better use of the father function and is thus able to go beyond the traditional appeal to the father.

J. D. M.

AUTISM, AUTISTIC (lit. self-oriented) A mental condition present from early childhood characterised by extreme self-absorption and reduced ability to communicate with others. Infantile autism, described by Kanner in 1943, and *Asperger's syndrome form part of the range of autistic spectrum disorders. This overlaps with communication disorders and some kinds of developmental delay which show some but not all of the defining characteristics of autism. For example, in *Asperger's syndrome the development of language is relatively unimpaired. According to the psychiatric classifications of the *DSM-IV*, the autistic spectrum disorders show aberrant development before the age of three, together with Kanner's classic triad of impairments – social, communicative and cognitive. Children with autism typically lack the capacity for imaginative play, resorting instead to stereotyped, ritualistic behaviour. They avoid eye-contact, and their speech may be absent or merely echo others. Psychotherapy for autistic spectrum disorders remains controversial, partly because of differences of opinion between neurological and psychodynamic theorists as to how the condition originates, and partly because of a backlash against Kanner and Bettelheim's blame of the children's parents. This attitude of blaming parents is no longer held by psychodynamic authors, some of whom give more weight to neurological factors. At the same time, research on the interplay of emotion and brain structure suggests that autism may result from the interaction of many factors. Among researchers regarding autism as due to a failure in brain development, some hold that a primary cognitive deficit leads to the autistic child's difficulty in developing a theory of mind in establishing emotional contact. Others, including Trevarthen and Hobson, emphasise the primacy of emotional relatedness between baby and caregiver, though their views on the part played by brain defects differ in emphasis.

Among pioneers in the psychoanalytic treatment of autism, *Klein held that these children had not regressed, but that their development had been inhibited through fear of their destructive feelings. *Mahler emphasised difficulties in mother-child separation while *Tustin and *Meltzer have followed *Bion in stressing the emotional components of cognitive difficulties. Tustin has described existential terrors of annihilation: of being engulfed by a black hole; of losing part of the mouth when separateness from the mother is recognised; of liquefying, spilling out, falling, burning and freezing. In her view, children with autism protect themselves from a catastrophic experience of separateness by encapsulation and by deriving illusory feelings of strength from a sensual relation to hard 'autistic objects' such as a hard metal toy car pressed into the hand. *Meltzer similarly emphasises the sensuality of children with autism, which facilitates the 'dismantling' of the mental apparatus into components associated with the separate senses. In his view, dismantling differs from *splitting in that it involves little sadism, and leads to a mindless state rather than to a destruction of the mind. However, according to *Tustin, autistic devices can sometimes serve as a 'straitjacket' which holds schizophrenic processes in check, and such interplay between characteristically autistic and schizoid ways of coping can sometimes be traced in therapy. The study of autistic processes has implications for the understanding of fundamental aspects of the development of the mind and its relation to the body, as well as for the treatment of children with autism. A development from the work with autistic children has been the possibility of addressing autistic processes in adult patients who have difficulty in making emotional contact.

See also: dyspraxia; psychosis (childhood)

Kanner, L. (1943) 'Autistic disturbances of affective contact'. *Nervous Child* 2: 217–50.

Klein, S. (1980) 'Autistic phenomena in neurotic patients'. *International Journal of Psycho-Analysis* 61: 395–402.

Edwards, J. and Lanyado, M. (1999) 'Autism: clinical and theoretical issues' in M. Lanyado and A. Horne (eds) *The Handbook of Child and Adolescent Psychotherapy*. London and New York: Routledge.

Trevarthen, C., Aitken, K., Papoudi, D. and Robarts, J. (1998) *Children with Autism: Interventions to Meet their Needs*. Second edition. London: Jessica Kingsley.

M. Rho.

AUTOEROTIC *Infantile sexuality is essentially autoerotic and finds its object in the infant's own body. The component sexual instincts are disconnected from each other in their search for pleasure. They include such activities as thumb sucking and masturbation.

J. A. Ber.

AUTOMATISATION In 1939 *Hartmann proposed that with increasing exercise the intermediate steps of an action disappear from consciousness, which explains how the ego achieves relative *autonomy from both instinctual drives and the environment. Motor behaviour, perception, and thought may come to function automatically.

E. G.

AUTOMATISM *Repetition compulsion for Lacan is (at least initially) symbolic repetition. It is the automatic and insistent return of *signifiers as effects of the unconscious that govern the very appearance of the subject. The structure of the Symbolic network in which these signifiers are organised determines their return.

See also: repetition

D. B.

AUTONOMOUS EGO FUNCTIONS see EGO FUNCTIONS, AUTONOMOUS

AUTONOMY Autonomy is a measure of the extent to which *ego functions can be maintained despite strong drives or detrimental environmental factors. It is a term generally associated with *ego psychology, a measure of the extent to which *ego functions can be maintained despite strong drives (see *intrapsychic factors) or detrimental environmental factors. However Freud himself, despite his medical training, increasingly emphasised *psychical reality as having autonomy. He insisted upon the non-reducibility of 'the psyche' to 'anatomy' despite the fact that he gave somewhat ambiguous accounts of the relationship between these two worlds. In Lacan, this separateness takes the form of the autonomy of the *Symbolic, and in particular the autonomy of the Symbolic framing of *phantasy.

R. T. / E. B.

AUTOPLASTIC ADAPTATION see **ADAPTATION**

B

BAD OBJECT (FAIRBAIRN) Both Fairbairn's exciting and rejecting internal objects are bad from the affective point of view. The *exciting internal object stimulates painfully unsatisfied desire, while the *rejecting internal object stimulates anger and sorrow. Repressed bad internal objects may return in all significant relationships such as marriage or psychoanalysis, and are likely to result in traumas in stressful situations such as war when the individual's inner security is threatened.

See also: object (Fairbairn); war neuroses

Armstrong-Perlmann, E. (1994) 'The allure of the bad object' in J. Grotstein and D. B. Rinsley (eds) *Fairbairn and the Origins of Object Relations*. London: Free Association Books.

Fairbairn, W. R. D. [1943] (1952) 'The war neuroses – their nature and significance' in *Psychoanalytic Studies of the Personality*. London: Routledge. Pbk 1994.

E. F. B. / D. E. S.

BAD OBJECT (KLEIN) The concept of the bad object is developed within Klein's theories of the *death instinct and the *paranoid schizoid position. She believed that the death instinct made itself known as annihilation anxiety. In the first few months of life, splitting and persecutory anxiety are at their height; the ego, still largely unintegrated, is liable to split itself. Disruptive experiences coming from inside (annihilation anxiety) combined with those coming from outside are projected into the mother/breast and re-introjected as the bad object. In early days the bad object is kept separate from the good object in order to preserve the needed maternal image.

Klein, M. [1957] (1975) *Envy and Gratitude*. London: Hogarth Press, 1975 (111). Also in *Love, Guilt and Reparation*. London: Hogarth Press, 1975 (1).

J. V. B.

BADNESS (CONDITIONAL AND UNCONDITIONAL) Fairbairn makes a distinction between libidinal and moral badness. He uses 'bad' primarily in the libidinal sense that a relationship feels bad. This distinction describes the situation of the *moral defence, when the abused, neglected or deprived child, nevertheless describes his parents as morally good and himself as morally bad in order to preserve a sense of morality in the objects on which he depends. Fairbairn distinguished between conditional and unconditional badness as follows. If a child is in a relationship with a punitive parent, he is likely to believe that the parent is good and he himself is bad. This is 'conditional badness', on the grounds that if the child reforms, the parent will treat him better. 'Unconditional badness' pertains to the child's belief that the parent is bad and the child good, in which case there is no hope that if the child improves his behaviour anything will get better. Fairbairn summarised this in 1943 by writing, 'It is better to be a sinner in a world ruled by God than to live in a world ruled by the devil.'

Fairbairn, W. R. D. [1943] (1952) 'The repression and return of bad objects (with special reference to the "war neuroses")' in *Psychoanalytic Studies of the Personality*. London: Routledge, 59–81.

E. F. B. / D. E. S.

Balint, Michael Maurice (1896–1970) The Hungarian-born British psychoanalyst was a highly respected representative of the line of thought first inaugurated by *Ferenczi, characterised by the central importance of *object relations, the importance of *regression in psychoanalytic treatment, and by the interplay of *transference/counter-transference in the psychoanalytic process. He introduced the notion of three areas in the psychic development (three-person = oedipal, two-person, and one-person = level of creativity), and he discarded the notion of primary narcissism in proposing the hypothesis of primary love and its counterpart, basic fault, instead. He was born in Budapest on 3 December 1896, his father, Dr Bergsmann, was a general practitioner in a neighbourhood populated by craftsmen and small shopkeepers. He changed his German name at the heights of the liberal-nationalist period in Hungary in 1913 from Bergsmann to Balint. He studied medicine, biochemistry and physics in Budapest. In 1919, he became a pupil of Ferenczi's and married Alice Székely-Kovács, later herself a famous child analyst. For political reasons (the establishment of the anti-Semitic regime of Admiral Horthy), he felt forced to emigrate to Berlin, where he underwent his first analysis with Hanns Sachs. Returning to Budapest in 1924, he continued his psychoanalytic activities, was a collaborator of the Psychoanalytic Out-Patient Clinic and finally Director of the Budapest Psychoanalytic Institute from 1935 to 1939. In 1939, he emigrated to Manchester, England, marrying Enid Albu after Alice's death and then moving to London. He was visiting professor in Cincinnati, Ohio. He held several offices in the British Psychoanalytical Society: Scientific Secretary from 1951 to 1953 and President from 1968 until his sudden death on 31 December 1970. He created discussion groups for general practitioners in a psychoanalytic spirit.

Haynel, A. (1988) *The Technique at Issue: Controversies in Psychoanalysis from Freud and Ferenczi to Michael Balint*. London: Karnac Books.
Kohon, G. (ed.) (1986) *The British School of Psycho-Analysis: The Independent Tradition*. London: Free Association Books.
Korompay, K. (2001) 'J'écris ton nom'. *L'Inactuel* 7.
Moreau Ricaud, M. (2000) *Michael Balint: Le renouveau de l'Ecole de Budapest*. Ramonville Saint-Agne: Erès.
Rayner, E. (1990) *The Independent Mind in British Psychoanalysis*. London: Free Association Books.

A. Hay.

---

basic assumptions Bion, in 1961, proposed these as primitive states of 'group mentality' that are automatically generated when people combine in groups. While leaving open how many such states there might be, he described three: 'dependence' (D: expecting solutions to be bestowed by the therapist/leader); 'fight/flight' (F/F: fleeing from or battling with adversaries, especially outside the group) and 'pairing' (P: encouraging or hoping for a coupling of individuals, which could lead to the birth of a person or idea that would provide salvation). Institutionalised respectively in church, army and aristocracy, these states usually interfere with the working capacity of ordinary groups. When arising spontaneously, and usually fleetingly, such groups 'elect' their own leaders, often not the designated members of the formal working groups. According to Bion, they might co-exist or alternate.

Bion distinguished these primitive forms of group mentality from the 'group culture' essential to human mental life, which in his view is split between the pull towards individuality and to group belonging. He held that each individual has a 'valent' tendency to contribute towards one or other basic assumption state as a result of infantile predispositions. On this basis, individuals will vary in their 'anonymous' contributions to the prevailing basic assumption state.

It has been suggested by Brown that such states are more likely to interfere with a group's work when a group or organisation is led in an autocratic or mystifying way. Others have proposed further basic assumption states: Turquet proposed 'Oneness' (O) – in which members seek union in a powerful all-encompassing group; Lawrence suggested 'Me-ness' (M) – in which individuals withdraw into isolated individuality; and Hopper speaks of 'Aggregation/Massification' (A/M) – in which groups of traumatized people oscillate intrapsychically between fusion and fragmentation.

Bion, W. R. (1961) *Experiences in Groups*. London: Tavistock.
Brown, D. G. (1985) 'Bion and Foulkes: basic assumptions and beyond' in M. Pines (ed.) *Bion and Group Psychotherapy*. London: Routledge & Kegan Paul.
Hopper, E. (1997) 'Traumatic experience in the unconscious life of groups: a fourth basic assumption'. *Group Analysis* 30(4): 439–70.
Hopper, E. (2001) *The Fourth Basic Assumption*. London: Jessica Kingsley.
Lawrence, W. G. (2000) *Tongued with Fire: Groups in Experience*. London: Karnac Books.
Turquet, P. (1975) 'Threats to identity in the large group' in L. Kreeger (ed.) *The Large Group*. London: Constable.

D. Bro.

BEATING Freud's clinical work led him to observe the ubiquity of beating phantasies in the psychical life of many of his patients. He devoted an article to the question in 1919, in which he gave special attention to the development of beating scenarios in phantasy life, and identified three basic phases of the phantasy. An analysis of these phases can shed light both on the passage through the *Oedipus complex and also on the early construction of gender identity. The beating itself can signify both hostility and love, and the phantasy scenarios map out the parameters of emergent object relations.

D. L.

BEAUTIFUL SOUL Lacan draws on *Hegel's use of the notion to expose the illusory nature of *identifications and of the idea of a consciousness transparent to itself. The beautiful soul believes itself to be the repository of truth and indulges itself in conceit and self- absorption. The *hysteric occupies this position which allows the beautiful soul to put everything that is not good out into the world and to accuse and complain about her entourage.

H. T.

BEHAVIOUR THERAPY Based on learning theory pioneered by Watson and Skinner, and developed by Eysenck in the 1950s, behavioural (or behaviour) therapy relies on treating pathological behaviour through habituation to the discomfort that occurs when the behaviours are resisted. Exposure (to discomfort or anxiety) is teamed with response prevention (most usually checking or rituals in obsessive compulsive disorder, and escape or avoidance in phobias). Such methods are generally considered most helpful in treating fears, phobias and other uncomplicated anxiety disorders.

Behavioural interventions also comprise part of cognitive behavioural therapy for other neurotic disorders, such as depression, and even more recently have been applied to psychotic illnesses and disorders of personality. Such interventions may include: scheduling tasks to induce feelings of competence and pleasure in depression; behavioural experiments to test the validity of pathological beliefs; and, distraction tasks to decrease the impact of hallucinations, and to impart a sense of control over symptoms. At the most extreme end of the range of behavioural treatments lies flooding, which involves literally 'flooding' the patient with the feared stimulus and subsequently causes intense discomfort that would usually precipitate escape and avoidance (the 'flight' response driven by the release of adrenaline caused by threat perception or fear and discomfort). The patient is prevented from avoiding the stimulus until the discomfort subsides to a manageable level, at which point treatment is complete. The patient learns that the stimulus itself is not dangerous and the fear is driven by anxiety in its presence, rather than rational and adaptive fear pathways. A more common approach is systematic desensitisation which involves graded exposure to successively more feared stimuli, usually approached hierarchically in the treatment of specific phobias.

Token economies were used to promote desirable behaviour through behaviour modification techniques such as reward, punishment, modelling and shaping based on conditioning and learning theory. Such approaches are less popular in the twenty-first century, but some of these techniques are still used in some in-patient settings and for behavioural programmes with children or people with *learning disabilities. The rationale is that the changes in contingencies, and the environment, can alter behaviour without the need to know about, or understand, the individual's mental operations. This makes behaviour therapy almost the diametric opposite of psychoanalysis, which works exclusively with the individual's subjective internal conscious and unconscious worlds.

Eysenck, H. J. (ed.) (1973) *Handbook of Abnormal Psychology*. London: Pitman Books.

Skinner, B. F. (1974) *About Behaviourism*. New York: Knopf.

Watson, J. B. (1919) *Psychology from the Standpoint of a Behaviourist*. Philadelphia: Lippincott.

J. W.

BEING For Lacan the subject's being is subordinated to the structural function of *lack introduced by the signifier. It is instituted as a 'lack-in-being' or 'want-to-be' that can only recuperate a semblance of being through Symbolic identification and fantasy. The introduction of the subject into the Symbolic order implies the alienation (or disappearance) of pure being and a 'choice' of the subject for existence.

P. D.

BELGIUM In 1933, with the agreement of the Psychoanalytical Society of Paris, the future founders of the Belgian Psychoanalytical Society, Maurice Dugautiez, Fernand Lechat and Mme Lechat-Ledoux, entered into a training analysis with Dr Ernest Hoffman, a Jew from Vienna, who was a disciple of Freud and a pupil of Ferenczi, and who established himself the same year in Antwerp, as he was fleeing from persecution by the Nazis. Dr Hoffman was arrested in 1942 and deported to a concentration camp from which he did not return.

In 1936, Dugautiez and Lechat undertook analyses which were supervised in Paris by Dr J. Leuba and Mme Marie Bonaparte.

In 1939, they were authorised to practise analysis of adults and Mme Lechat was also authorised to practise analysis of children. Up until this date they participated extensively in the activities of the Society of Paris. The war years meant they had to break off contact with their French colleagues.

On 24 December 1946 they founded the Association of Psychoanalysts in Belgium with Dr John Leuba as their honorary president and under the patronage of the Society of Paris. Dr Ernest Jones, president of the IPA, had encouraged this initiative. In 1947, the Association was accepted as a member of the IPA.

The tenth International Conference of French-speaking Psychoanalysts, which was held for the first time in Brussels in May 1948, sanctioned the official existence of this very young association. Ten years after its foundation the Association numbered eleven full members and sixteen candidates.

In 1957 a significant modification took place, with the creation of a Training Committee which was made up of titular members. This would take a vote on the acceptance of those engaged in analysis at different levels of membership in the Association; the analyst of the candidate, however, would have no say in this matter. The work of the Training Committee allowed a better assessment of the personality and the motivations of the candidates for training in analysis.

In 1960, for formal reasons, the Association changed its name to the Belgian Psychoanalytical Society. This period of change coincided with the deaths, with only an interval of a few months between them, of two of the founder members: Lechat in 1959 and Dugautiez in 1960.

Exchanges about long-term planning relating to the life of the Society have contributed to the realising of new initiatives, including, among other things: the organisation, since 1975, of a cycle of courses and seminars which are obligatory for the candidates; the creation in 1977 of a Bulletin for internal use; the organisation since 1978 of a biannual residential Scientific Conference; the setting up of seminars centred on the observation of infants and on the mother-child relationship; the birth in 1982 of the *Revue Belge de Psychanalyse*, which comes out twice a year; and the forming of a Committee for Ethics in 1988. By 2001, the Belgian Society numbered sixty-eight full members and fifty-four affiliates or candidates.

Although our country has adopted a federal structure, the Belgian Society has remained unitary and includes analysts who are both Francophone and Flemish-speaking. With regard to theoretical references, the specific features of the Belgian Psychoanalytical Society are in keeping with the national culture's own characteristic of integrating contributions from different sources in an atmosphere of tolerance and openness. The theoretical currents which are actively represented within the Society are on the one hand the 'standard' Freudian school of thought, an inheritance of the contacts which were made with French psychoanalytical thought, and on the other hand the Kleinian and post-Kleinian schools of thought which have been encouraged by contacts with analysts of the British Society. Although certain members claim clearly that they subscribe to these movements, there is, however, no group centred on a particular school of psychoanalytical thought within the Society. The differences of opinion do not hamper dialogue at all; on the contrary this is enriched by these confrontations. In Belgium several other psychoanalytical societies exist which are located essentially within the Lacanian movement. The most important of these is the Belgian School of Psychoanalysis.

J. A. D.

BETA ELEMENTS Those sense impressions related to emotional experiences that are not transformed through *alpha function. Since they have not been converted into a form that can be used by the psyche, they are not available to be thought about or dreamt about. Beta elements are therefore often evacuated through *projective identification and are influential in producing acting out since they are experienced not as thoughts and memories but as objects and undigested facts. Beta elements are, however, necessary for non-verbal communication, for the ability to use projective identification, and for the communication of emotion within a group. They bear some resemblance to Lacan's *Real.

Bion, W. R. (1962) *Learning from Experience*. London: Heinemann. Also in *Seven Servants*. New York: Jason Aronson, 1977.
Bion, W. R. (1963) *Elements of Psychoanalysis*. London: Heinemann. Also in *Seven Servants*. New York: Jason Aronson, 1977.
Bion, W. R. (1965) *Transformations*. London: Karnac Books. Also in *Seven Servants*. New York: Jason Aronson, 1977.
Bion, W. R. (1970) *Attention and Interpretation*. London: Tavistock. Also in *Seven Servants*. New York: Jason Aronson, 1977.

S. A.

BETA SCREEN (OR BETA-ELEMENT SCREEN) The beta screen, which is part of the psychotic personality, is an agglomeration (not a true composition) of *beta elements (or degraded alpha elements). It does not allow for the separation of conscious and unconscious thought. The beta screen gives the appearance of a confusional state but is actually quite coherent and purposive. The beta screen has the quality of enabling it to provoke a response from the analyst. In contrast, in the non-psychotic part of the personality, alpha elements allow for the separation of conscious and unconscious thought by coming together to form the contact barrier.

Bion, W. R. (1962) *Learning from Experience*. London: Heinemann. Also in *Seven Servants*. New York: Jason Aronson, 1977.

S. A.

Bettelheim, Bruno (1903–1990) Bruno Bettelheim was a pioneer in the use of Freudian concepts to treat infantile psychosis. Although his success rate with autistic children was not as high as he reported in *The Empty Fortress: Infantile Autism and the Birth of the Self*, that book, published in 1967, had a determining influence on the way psychotic children were viewed in psychiatric institutions worldwide. Bettelheim portrayed the most disturbed children not in terms of their deficiencies, but as full-fledged individuals, showing that even the strangest behaviour has a meaning. As the director, from 1944 to 1973, of the Orthogenic School of the University of Chicago, he was opposed to the use of straitjackets or drugs, insisting that all symptoms have to be deciphered to help the troubled child.

Born on 3 August 1903 into a Jewish family in Vienna, Bettelheim studied aesthetics and psychology before taking over his father's lumber business after the latter's death in 1926. He was in analysis with Richard Sterba when the Nazis occupied Austria in March 1938 and was sent by them to the Dachau and later Buchenwald concentration camps. Released in April 1939, he emigrated to the United States, where he became a successful academic, therapist and author within a decade.

Bettelheim was the first (and for a long time the only) thinker to apply psychoanalysis to the concentration camp universe. He analysed his fellow-inmates' behaviour and his own psyche in an article published in 1943, that was later used by US forces in Europe. He coined the notion of 'extreme situation'. In 1956, he drew up the comparison that would remain his hallmark between the imprisonment in a Nazi camp and that within one's own psychosis.

In addition to his books on the treatment of emotional disturbances, education and his camp experience, Bettelheim published a critical essay on the English translations of Freud's works, a study of kibbutz education and an analysis of circumcision and other puberty rites. His most popular book, *The Uses of Enchantment*, published in 1976, deals with the role of fairy tales in the development of a child's psyche.

Bettelheim's career was marked by numerous controversies. He was considered an outsider by both the academic and psychoanalytic establishments. An explanation can be found in his determination to deal with the darker side of 'man's soul', as he put it, coupled with an intellectual freedom which led him to pick the concepts he needed in various schools of Freudian psychology with little regard for their dogmatic differences, not to mention his Socratic teaching method and the fact that he took his own life in March 1990.

Bettelheim, B. (1974) *A Home for the Heart*. New York: Knopf.

Bettelheim, B. (1979) *Surviving and Other Essays*. New York: Knopf.

Bettelheim, B. (1982) *Freud and Man's Soul*. New York: Knopf.

Marcus, P. and Rosenberg, A. (1994) 'Bruno Bettelheim's contribution to psychoanalysis'. *The Psychoanalytic Review* (special issue) 81(3).

Sutton, N. (1995) *Bruno Bettelheim, the Other Side of Madness*. London: Duckworth.

N. S.

Bick, Esther (1901–83) Esther Bick (née Wander) was born in Poland in 1901. She completed a PhD with Charlotte Bühler, a Viennese psychologist who encouraged her to look at the complex social interactions between two-and-a-half-year-old children. At the time of *Anschluß*, Mrs Bick and her husband fled from Austria to Switzerland; she separated from her husband and came to England shortly thereafter. At this time she embarked on an analysis with *Balint. In 1948 she qualified at the Institute of Psycho-Analysis in London and was analysed by *Klein, who was to become her life-long friend.

Also in 1948, at the request of *Bowlby, Bick founded the child psychotherapy training at the Tavistock Clinic. Believing as she did that direct observation of an ordinary infant's interactions within his family context at home was essential for understanding the development of the human personality, she was responsible for incorporating one-year *infant observation seminars into the training both of child psychotherapists at the Tavistock Clinic and of psychoanalysts at the British Institute of Psycho-Analysis. She was able to affirm many of Klein's conclusions about the first year of life and also introduced new concepts which focused on the infant's primitive experiences in the first six months of life, and include:

1. *Primary skin sensation and containment by the internal mother*. Bick held that the infant lived through an early state of unintegration (as opposed to later states of disintegration) in which its primitive sensory experiences and aspects of its personality were bound together only when the mother was in close resonance emotionally, mentally and physically with her baby's experience. The baby's 'psychic skin' initially depends on the introjection of a primary external object that provides experiences of continual interaction between the surface of the infant's body as a sensory organ and the relationship with the physically, emotionally and mentally holding and containing mother. Throughout her life Bick undertook detailed observations and explorations of actual infants and of the infantile parts of the personality of analytic patients. These led to formulations concerning primitive anxieties such as the fear of falling, and the fear of unintegration and disintegration.

2. *Secondary skin phenomena*. Bick compared the newborn infant to a spaceman suddenly thrown into space without a space suit. In the absence of a firm, containing mother, he must rely on his own methods of coping with overwhelming primitive anxieties as Magagna and Briggs have spelled out. These fears can be aroused by the slightest environmental change and may be detected in the baby's frantic body movements, shivering and muscular rigidity. These intense anxieties gradually lessen as the baby comes to trust a loving, holding mother whom he can internalise. Bick described the baby's use of second-skin phenomena used by babies who do not feel contained by their mothers, and who rely instead on their own musculature, on frantic non-stop movement, on curling up motionless without breathing to prevent spilling out. As Symington shows they are 'sticking' intently with eyes, mouth, ears or nose used as suction pads for adhesion to a constant sound or surface. The majority of ordinary people may use such second-skin phenomena at times in order to deal with primitive fears of catastrophic disintegration. For example, Symington differentiates *negative therapeutic reaction from self-protective devices designed to cope with the primitive fears which may be re-awakened by the analytic relationship. Similarly, Bick has described how major life changes, such as adolescence, parenthood and old age, can stir up the fear of losing one's identity and of going to pieces. New mothers may experience a process similar to the baby's experience, and depend for their ability to contain the baby on they themselves being held externally by her husband and others and internally by a holding mother.

3. *Adhesive identification*. Bick and Meltzer have delineated the survival function for the baby of being in contact with the object in order to hold together mental and emotional contents,

as yet undifferentiated from bodily contents. Unintegrated and helpless states of being can lead to two-dimensional ways of relating, prior to developing a sense of an internal containing space created through the introjection of a containing external object. If internalisation of such an object fails or has never adequately succeeded, people may resort to 'adhesive identification' (involving mimicry and sticking to surfaces) as a mode of protection against falling apart. Bick subsequently reformulated this concept as 'adhesive identity'; it is a primitive mode of protection used prior to the mechanism of *projective identification. Bick's concept of adhesive identification (or identity) led many analysts, particularly those working with autistic and psychotic children and with young infants, to revise their framework based exclusively on projective identification.

Such considerations make subtle differentiations possible: a baby's mouth may seek the mother's nipple as a source of nourishment, or as a provider of sensations that may make it possible for the baby to hold itself together. However, as Magagna indicates, such defensive clinging to sensations leaves no room for change, the growth of knowledge, the exploration of the baby's world, or the deepening of his relationships with his parents.

Bick, E. (1968) 'The experience of the skin in early object relations'. *International Journal of Psycho-Analysis* 49.

Bick, E. (1986) 'Further considerations of the function of the skin in early object relations'. *British Journal of Psychotherapy* 2.

Briggs, A. (2002) *Surviving Space: Papers on Infant Observation*. London: Karnac Books.

Magagna, J. (1987) 'Three years of infant observation with Mrs Bick'. *Journal of Child Psychotherapy* 13(1).

Meltzer, D. (1975) 'Adhesive identification'. *Contemporary Psychoanalysis* 11.

Symington, J. (1985) 'The survival function of infantile omnipotence'. *International Journal of Psycho-Analysis* 66.

J. M.

BINDING Term originally used by Freud to denote various processes associated with curbing excitations or to the linkage of unconscious ideas, memories and feelings. An outcome of binding is to minimise anxiety thereby creating relative intrapsychic stability. Binding is most often understood as an ego function, but later Freudian theory postulates that binding occurs in the unconscious as the process by which unconscious thoughts and feelings become associated with each other. In more technical terms, binding is when stimuli are discharged according to established pathways. Binding is thus the fixation of a stable *cathexis to a *representation. This inhibits the flow of overwhelming magnitudes of stimulation and assists development of *secondary processes. Binding allows the *ego to prevent the occurrence of primary processes and infringements of the reality principle.

Freud, S. (1920) *Beyond the Pleasure Principle*. S. E. 18. London: Hogarth Press.

Freud, S. (1923) *The Ego and the Id*. S. E. 19. London: Hogarth Press.

A. P. / E. K.

BINOCULAR VISION The capacity to view an experience from two different perspectives. The ability to shift back and forth from one point of view to another is seen as a pre-requisite for the growth and development of the non-psychotic personality. Bion uses the familiar perceptual exercise of the drawing which can be seen as either two faces or a vase to illustrate this.

Bion, W. R. (1963) *Elements of Psychoanalysis*. London: Heinemann. Also in *Seven Servants*. New York: Jason Aronson, 1977.

S. A.

BINSWANGER, LUDWIG (1881–1966) Ludwig Binswanger was the founder of **Daseinsanalysis*. An early student and colleague of *Freud, Binswanger crossed the disciplinary divide between psychiatry, psychoanalysis, and philosophy with ease. He was the director of the Bellevue Sanatorium in Kreuzlingen, Switzerland from 1910 until 1956. During his tenure, Bellevue became a centre for European learning and was visited by many of the leading thinkers of the time.

Binswanger trained as a psychiatrist under *Bleuler and *Jung at the Burghölzli Hospital in Zurich, where he became acquainted with psychoanalysis. Binswanger and Freud first met in 1907 and entered into a voluminous correspondence, punctuated by personal visits, which lasted until Freud's death in 1939. Binswanger was attracted to Freud because of the insights psychoanalysis provided into human behaviour. At the same time, he was critical of Freud's conception of mind and rejected the determinism implicit in the psychoanalytic theory of drives. He sought to understand and explain human beings in the totality of their existence, not as natural objects constructed from various parts. To this end, Binswanger incorporated the findings of philosophy into his clinical work.

Husserl's project of phenomenology provided Binswanger with a method to explain the 'visual reality' of the mentally ill person, that is, how the patient appeared to him as opposed to the analyst's usual musings about the internal workings of the patient's mind taken as truth. *Heidegger's *Being and Time* influenced Binswanger's thinking most directly. Heidegger's notion of 'being-in-the-world' enabled Binswanger to develop a philosophically oriented approach to psychiatry that sought to understand the context – or world-design – in which the individual exists and discovers meaning. Following Heidegger, Binswanger used the term **daseins-analysis* to describe his new approach.

Just as Binswanger was never a follower of Freud, however, neither was he a follower of Heidegger. Instead, Binswanger turned to *Buber's philosophy of I-Thou in order to elaborate a theory of relation which he felt was missing in the work of Freud and Heidegger. Binswanger's criticism of Heidegger led to the philosopher's later rebuke and caused a split between Binswanger and his one-time colleague, *Boss. Binswanger emphasised the dialogical nature of human existence in his chief theoretical work, *Basic Forms and Knowledge of Human Existence*, in 1942. Binswanger's theory of intersubjectivity is based on the notion that the self is inherently relational – a position that parallels the work of *Sullivan and intersubjective psychoanalysis.

Frie, R. (1997) *Subjectivity and Intersubjectivity in Modern Philosophy and Psychoanalysis: A Study of Sartre, Binswanger, Lacan, and Habermas*. Lanham, MD: Rowman & Littlefield.

R. Fri.

Bion, Wilfred Ruprecht (1897–1979) Wilfred Bion was chiefly responsible for ushering in the post-Kleinian development; his own ideas linking Freud and Klein revolutionised contemporary psychoanalytic thought. Born in Muttra, in the Punjab, on 8 September 1897, the eldest child and only son of Rhoda and Frederick Bion, he left India and his parents when he was eight years old to attend Bishop's Stortford College, where he remained until 1915. Commissioned as a Second Lieutenant into the Machine Gun Corps, he served with the 5th Tank Battalion, seeing considerable fighting during the terrible carnage of the First World War. Taking part in the battle of Chambrai in 1917, the first occasion tanks were significantly employed, Bion was later awarded the Distinguished Service Order for his outstanding leadership and gallantry, to which the French added their Legion of Honour.

After demobilisation he went to Queen's College, Oxford on a scholarship to read for a compressed ordinary BA in Modern History. Enjoying his time there, Bion, in addition to playing rugby and captaining the swimming team, developed an interest in philosophy (and especially the work of Kant) through his contacts with the philosopher H. J. Paton. After graduating, he spent 1921–2 at Poitiers

University studying literature at the same time as developing what was to be a lifelong interest in art. Returning to England, Bion briefly taught at his old school, before taking a medical degree at University College Hospital, there coming under the influence of Wilfred Trotter, the author of *Instincts of the Herd in Peace and War*. Although he had gained the Gold Medal for Clinical Surgery during his time at UCH, Bion's interest was in psychiatry and psychoanalysis. Various posts followed his graduation in 1930, most substantially at the Institute for the Scientific Treatment of Delinquency and later the Tavistock Clinic, where he was consulted by Samuel Beckett during 1934–5. They attended Jung's Tavistock lectures together. Bion's own experience of psychotherapy at the hands of J. A. Hadfield was disappointing. However, in 1937 he met John Rickman with whom he went into analysis, before enrolling as a candidate at the Institute of Psychoanalysis the following year.

The outbreak of the Second World War in September 1939 interrupted his analysis and training, Bion being commissioned a Major in the Royal Army Medical Corps. In April 1940 Bion married the actress Betty Jardine, having met her at the beginning of the previous year. The war brought Bion into a close professional relationship with Rickman, the two men serving together at the Northfield Military Hospital where they employed group methods to focus attention on everyday tasks and to resurrect morale. The approach was novel and appeared effective, though the initial confusion it entailed led to Bion's (and Rickman's) rapid transfer to other duties. Although the First Northfield Experiment, as it became known, had lasted a mere six weeks, its reverberations profoundly moulded subsequent thinking on groups, particularly through what became known as the Tavistock model. Bion's initial formulation of the experience, jointly written with Rickman, appeared as 'Intra-group tensions in therapy' in the *Lancet* in 1943. Bion's other principal achievement in military psychiatry arose from his work assessing officer candidates with the War Office Selection Boards, various sections of which he was attached to before and after Northfield. In his first such attachment, in 1942, Bion devised the 'leaderless group project', which he described in an article of the same name in 1946. The approach proved efficient, highly effective and influential in tandem with Northfield. In the project a group of usually eight candidates were given a task to be completed within a set time, during which the selectors focused on each participant's capacity to negotiate the tensions between individual and group ambition, competence and fears of failure. In February 1945 Bion's first child, a daughter, Parthenope, was born, Betty tragically dying three days later. Widowed, Bion threw himself into work. At the end of the war he returned part time to the Tavistock Clinic where he remained until 1948, further developing his ideas on groups, the fruits of which he published in a groundbreaking series of articles later collected together, along with his Northfield paper, as *Experiences in Groups*.

Bion's interests at this time however were turning more towards individual psychoanalysis, spurred on by his developing private practice, his psychoanalytic training which he had resumed in November 1945, and above all his training analysis with Klein, a return to that with Rickman being inappropriate following their close wartime association. His analytic formation was complemented by supervision from Heimann and Payne. Graduating in June 1948, Bion went on to read 'The imaginary twin' as his membership paper to the British Psychoanalytical Society in November 1950. It was the start of a profound series of papers, including 'Notes on the theory of schizophrenia', 'Differentiation of the psychotic and non-psychotic personalities', 'Attacks on linking' and 'A theory of thinking', which Bion collated along with his later commentary in *Second Thoughts*. Based substantially on his pioneering work analysing psychotic and borderline patients, Bion elaborated the processes of pathological splitting and massive projective identification resorted to in primitive attempts to ward off anticipated unbearable psychic catastrophe. As part of this development Bion distinguished between pathological forms of *projective identification (characterised by the degree of hatred and omnipotence involved, the evacuatory intent and splitting which amounts to fragmentation) and more normal varieties, which carry primitive communicative intent. Bion was thus able to move from a consideration of the severe psychopathology of the psychoses to a view of normal mental development, both of which hinged upon the ways in which frustrating, painful and inchoate feelings are relocated through projective processes. In normal development the projections are contained prototypically within the infant's mother, made understandable by virtue of the operation of her developed psychic capacities on them, and are in due course reintrojected by the infant; such meaning-conferring cycles lead incrementally to the internalisation and growth of an apparatus for thinking or digesting thoughts. In developing these ideas Bion highlighted the crucial role of the interpersonal environment, thought by some to have been relatively neglected by Bion's Kleinian forebears, and at the same time offered a conceptual model for the analytic process.

In developing these ideas Bion was strongly supported by his second wife, a young widow, Francesca McCallum (née Purnell), whom he married in June 1951 following a whirlwind romance. With Francesca, Bion had two children, Julian, born in July 1952 and Nicola, born in June 1955, their nurturance perhaps feeding Bion's metaphors.

Bion was successively Director of the London Clinic of Psychoanalysis, from 1956 to 1962, and President of the British Psycho-analytical Society, from 1962 to 1965. During the latter term of office Bion consolidated the ideas outlined in 'A theory of thinking' in three major metapsychological works, *Learning from Experience* in 1962, *Elements of Psycho-Analysis* the following year and *Transformations* in 1965. His thoughts on technique now increasingly emphasised that the main concern of psychoanalysis is psychical reality, which consists primarily of non-sensuous ineffable emotions and phantasies rather than the sensuous phenomena of physical reality. Consequently, Bion argued that the analytic attitude should be one that eschews memory, desire and understanding in favour of the development of negative capability, reverie, or patience, until a selected fact is intuited, which may in turn act as an organising nexus for further conceptualisation. These views contribute to an understanding of the difficulty of conveying psychoanalytically relevant material outside of the confines of the analytic situation with our existing vocabulary and shed light on Bion's own literary style.

This emphasis on the unknown, or O, and the dangers of foreclosure due to clinging to establishment dogma may have contributed to Bion's acceptance of an invitation from the growing Californian Kleinian group to move there, which he did in 1968. The move to Los Angeles, while startling some of his British colleagues, was an increment to both his hosts and his own creativity during his final years. There he developed his thoughts on technique and the processes of psychic change in *Attention and Interpretation*, published in 1970, and demonstrated his ideas through extensive teaching and clinical seminars, famously in São Paulo in 1973, 1974, 1978 and 1979, Rio de Janeiro in 1974, Brasilia in 1975, and New York in 1977, transcripts of which seminars have been subsequently published. Looking back on his life led to a series of autobiographical studies and publication of his mammoth enigmatic three-volume *A Memoir of the Future*, a fictional evocative autobiography of a man of achievement. On 8 November 1979 Bion died of myeloid leukaemia in Oxford, shortly after returning to Britain, thus curtailing new plans he had to start yet another chapter of his life. His influence however remains indelibly impressed on psychoanalysis and group and organisational theory, sustained by the publication of stimulating posthumous works such as *Cogitations*, in 1992, and the climate his ideas have created.

Bion, W. R. (1982) *The Long Week-End 1897–1919: Part of a Life*. London: Free Association Books.
Bion, W. R. (1985) *All my Sins Remembered: Another Part of a Life* and *The Other Side of Genius: Family Letters*. Abingdon: Fleetwood.
Bléandonu, G. (1994) *Wilfred Bion: His Life and Works 1897–1979*. London: Free Association Books.
Grotstein, J. (ed.) (1981) *Do I Dare Disturb the Universe? A Memorial to W. R. Bion*. London: Karnac Books.
Symington, J. and N. (1996) *The Clinical Thinking of Wilfred Bion*. London: Routledge.

R. Wil.

Bion precis Bion's early original work pioneered *group psychotherapy, however following his analytic training he began analysing psychotic patients and studied their thought disorders. He drew on this experience in forming deep philosophical views on the nature of the mind, placing emotional experiences at the centre of mental life. He concluded that the psychotic patient may have suffered as an infant from not having a mother who could contain their potentially catastrophic internal feelings of dread. These exaggerated feelings tend to emerge whenever the infant feels all is not well. Bion further concluded that actual thinking begins in infancy when the infant can sufficiently tolerate the frustration of the mother's absence, while having access to a mother who is able to *contain the infant's normal or realistic *projections of dread. This mothering fends off any sense of catastrophe. These normal projections, or more accurately, *projective identifications, constitute a subliminal communication between infant and mother. The containing mother experiences in her *reverie, projections which may realistically correspond to what the infant feels.

From his analysis of psychotic patients he also concluded that they had a normal as well as a psychotic personality and that the same is true, to a lesser degree, of all of us. Further, he distinguished certain features in the psychotic personality such as *attacks on linking and the emergence of *bizarre objects. Adult patients with a predominantly psychotic structure had probably, he thought, experienced an emotional catastrophe in infancy.

As part of his philosophical investigation into 'how we come to know things' Bion formulated a psychoanalytic theory of epistemology which he gave a diagrammatic form as a *grid. In this theory of thinking he says that the human being is born with inherent expectations or preconceptions of, say, the breast. When the infant finds the real breast that corresponds to its personal preconception this actual realisation generates what he calls a 'conception'. On the other hand if the infant is frustrated by the breast and the realisation is negative, thought should evolve and if things go well, these thoughts will develop into concepts. Through growing processes of abstraction, such thoughts can become systems of knowledge, what Bion calls 'scientific deductive systems'. In addition he postulated the existence of 'unmentalised' mental elements of experience termed *beta elements, which normally undergo transformation by *alpha function – a notion akin to Freud's *dream work – into *alpha elements suitable for mental processing. Originally, it is the mother's empathic alpha function, recruited in a state of *reverie, which constitutes her ability to contain. Such empathy is her own emotional approximation to what her infant is experiencing. The mother's capacity for reverie and containment or understanding is then internalised by the infant, who thereby acquires his or her own capacity for emotional experience, thinking their own 'wild' thoughts and above all, learning from experience. This internalised alpha function serves as a *contact barrier between consciousness and the unconscious. Bion designates these functions of self-containment and self-knowledge the 'psychoanalytic functions of the personality'. Without adequate access to these functions, the infant who is intolerant of frustration may experience nameless dread and, unable to use normal projective identification, perhaps resort to abnormal projective identification of forceful raw emotions, thereby creating a 'beta screen'. This screen evokes strong negative feelings in the receptive mother that are intolerable for the infant to bear.

From the notion of the infant's realistic projective identifications (the contained) into the receptive mother's mind (the container) Bion formulates the model of the 'container-contained' relationship, denoting these concepts with the signs (♂/♀) respectively. The emotional relationship between container and contents can be benevolent or malevolent and Bion designates the emotional *links between the containing subject and its contained object as L (loving), H (hating) or K (knowing), and includes their negative counterparts, −L, −H, and −K, which are anti-emotional. These L, H, and K links Bion considers as primary in the human being. In this respect he differs from Freud and Klein, who considered the drive to knowledge (K) or epistemophilia, as secondary to self-preservation and sexuality. His reading of the *Oedipus, Eden, and Babel myths shows how the conflict between knowing (K) and not knowing (−K) is present in all of them, along with sexuality (L) and aggression (H). Seeking a method of notation for analysts, he also created a *grid to classify thoughts and emotions according to their genesis for Bion believed that, in the beginning, there were only feeling-thoughts (without a thinker), but that these feeling-thoughts need a 'mind' to think them. This embryonic mind is early alpha function, at first that of the mother and then that of the infant.

Bion then contemplated how the individual 'learns from experience', that is, how the mind grows and develops. He reasoned that the mind grows via 'transformations' of the 'unknowable' which he refers to as *O. This symbol represents what Kant meant by 'noumena' or 'things in themselves' – his way of referring to the ultimate nature of things beyond our ability to represent it. We must be content, Kant thinks, with 'phenomena' or the world as it appears to be. In the psychoanalytic process, O, the unknowable, is experienced as the symptom needing to be understood, and Bion terms this the *psychoanalytic object. As O evolves, the individual sense organs receptive to emotional experiences intersect with it, and the experiencing of O becomes subject to *transformations by the mother's or psychoanalyst's alpha function into knowledge (K) that is relevant for the infant or analysand.

Normal mental growth is catastrophic, and the mental attitude of the psychoanalyst, in order to access his or her intuition about what is happening during the analytic session, must remain without *memory, desire, or understanding, with an evenly suspended attention, and the 'faith' that something will evolve from the link. In this state of mind the *paranoid-schizoid (PS) oscillation from dispersed elements into integrated ones, and the discovery of a *selected fact giving coherence to dispersed elements will be favoured. Bion emphasises that the psychoanalyst's states of mind, while in session, should move from 'patience', a normal paranoid-schizoid position, to 'security', a normal depressive position. This will allow the analyst to intuit an experience of 'at-one-ment' with the analysand and then to put into words or 'publish' what Bion, following Keats, terms the 'language of achievement', which is accessed by *negative capability.

Bion also speaks about 'truth', 'falsities' and 'lies'. At the end of his life he insisted that ultimate reality or 'absolute' Truth, which he equates with the 'Godhead' and O, and in turn with noumena and the thing-in-itself, are unknowable. We can only know about them from our transformations of them from the *infinite to the finite domain. Finally he introduced the idea of the *caesura, the original prenatal parts of the personality, which allow us to conjecture about very primitive reactions of our analysands, as well as our own vestigial and as yet unborn aspects.

See also: arrogance; at-one-ment; beta screen; binocular vision; Bion, Wilfred Ruprecht; catastrophic change; emotional experience; evolution; ideogram; intuition; invariance; memory; desire; messianic idea; model;

mystic; myth; nameless dread; pre-conception; prenatal states of mind; PS-D; psychoanalytic function of the personality; reversible perspective; splitting, enforced; super-ego (Bion); thinking, theory of; thoughts without a thinker; truth

E. T. B.

BISEXUALITY Biologically, the result of the fusion of both sexes and showing organs belonging to both. Extended to mean psychological gender identity, it is now viewed as psychological *identification with each parent and a social construct, both transcending biology.

Lothane, Z. (1992) *In Defense of Schreber. Soul Murder and Psychiatry*. Hillsdale, NJ: The Analytic Press.

Z. L.

BIZARRE OBJECTS The product of the splitting attacks by the psychotic personality which are directed at the perceptual apparatus and then projected into his/her objects. Each particle is felt to consist of a real object which is encapsulated in a piece of the personality that has engulfed it. In the phantasy of the psychotic personality the expelled particles lead an independent and uncontrolled existence and function as if the ordeal to which they have been subjected served only to increase their number and hostility to the psyche that ejected them. The patient then feels him/herself to be surrounded by bizarre objects. Splitting attacks on the *super-ego lead to a mass of super-egos – which are, in effect, bizarre objects. This is the murderous super-ego.

Bion, W. R. (1962) *Learning from Experience*. London: Heinemann. Also in *Seven Servants*. New York: Jason Aronson, 1977.
Bion, W. R. (1967) *Second Thoughts*. London: Heinemann.

S. A.

BLEULER, EUGEN (1857–1939) He was one of the first psychiatrists to apply psychoanalytical methods in his research. He was an early proponent of the theories of Sigmund Freud, and he attempted to show how the various mechanisms Freud had found in neurotic patients could also be recognised in psychotic patients. Bleuler challenged the prevailing belief that psychosis was the result of organic brain damage, insisting instead that it could have psychological causes.

Bleuler attended the universities of Zurich, Bern, and Munich, becoming a licensed physician in 1881. He travelled to France and England. In 1898 Bleuler was appointed professor of psychiatry at the University of Zurich and director of the University Psychiatric Hospital, the Burghölzli Asylum. During the early 1900s Bleuler's assistant was Carl Gustav *Jung (1875–1961), and the two were early members with Freud of the Vienna Psycho-Analytical Society.

Bleuler first advanced the term 'schizophrenia' in 1908 in a paper based on a study of 647 Burghölzli patients. His 1911 *Dementia Praecox; or the Group of Schizophrenias* is regarded as a classic work of twentieth-century psychiatry. For him the term 'schizophrenia' implied that the 'splitting' of the different psychic functions is one of its most important characteristics. Bleuler is credited with the introduction of two concepts fundamental to the analysis of schizophrenia: *autism, denoting the loss of contact with reality, frequently through indulgence in bizarre fantasy, and *ambivalence, denoting the coexistence of mutually exclusive contradictions within the psyche.

He opposed the view that schizophrenia is caused by an irreversible brain damage emphasising the associative disturbances, and learned to understand and interpret schizophrenics' way of expressing themselves. Bleuler concluded that schizophrenia consisted of internal conflict and argued that it was not invariably incurable, an opinion at odds with the accepted wisdom of his time.

R. M. S.

BODY see **SOMATISATION**

BODY (LACAN) Lacan's theory of the body is situated in his conceptual triad of the *Imaginary, the *Symbolic and the *Real. His first theory emphasises the Imaginary body of the *mirror stage where it comes from the Symbolic *Other, and is imposed upon the subject. It is the first layer of Imaginary identity, introducing the process of *alienation, and providing the subject with a false sense of self and mastery. In the later Lacan, the emphasis is on *jouissance belonging to the organism (as the Real body). This jouissance is traumatic, and can be understood in terms of Freud's drive fixation, present in every symptom. The aim of the treatment is redefined by Lacan in this later phase as an identification with the Real contained within the symptom.

P. V.

BODY (RELATIONISM) The body's functions, modes and sensations, and the fantasies that emerge inseparably from these, exist in flux. It is the meaning made of these, rather than their origin, that is the element of greatest importance in *relational psychoanalysis. Freed from any specific motivational design, meaning in this arena can be constructed again and again to represent continuously changing parameters of desire and conflict as they interact in each relationship, across time.

Meaning, in this context, implies an internal world that can shift, almost kaleidoscopically, depending on the position held by the inner 'I', as it is acted upon by unconscious,*dissociated events and is simultaneously looking inward at itself and outward at the other. Implicit here is a process in which mind/body separation is minimised; instead, there is an ongoing exchange between perception of self, based on changing perceptions of the body, and of the body, based on changing perceptions of self. This exchange may be affected alternately or in combination by cultural, social, familial and more intimate personal experience. In fact, a myriad of private longings inevitably become lodged in the body's surface and these, just as inevitably, become inextricably tangled with outer demands.

In the two-person analytic setting itself, the patient's inextricable tangles may first be perceived as bodily sensations in the analyst, through perceptual mechanisms which at present are barely understood. Further exploration of these mechanisms promises increased knowledge, not only of the psychoanalytic terrain, but of human communication altogether.

See also: Mitchell

Aron, L. (1998) 'Introduction: the body in drive and relational models' in L. Aron and F. S. Anderson (eds) *Relational Perspectives on the Body*. Hillsdale, NJ: The Analytic Press.

Harris, A. (1998) 'Psychic envelopes and sonorous baths: siting the body in relational theory and clinical practice' in L. Aron and F. S. Anderson (eds) *Relational Perspectives on the Body*. Hillsdale, NJ: The Analytic Press, 39–64.

Mitchell, S. (1988) *Relational Concepts in Psychoanalysis*. Cambridge, MA: Harvard University Press.

B. E.

BODY IMAGE The image of the body is constituted as a whole in the *mirror phase. Starting from a state of motor insufficiency the child anticipates and identifies with his or her image in the mirror, which offers a corporeal image in an alienated way. This is the moment of the constitution of *narcissism, and of the *ego, which supports this *Imaginary body.

S. Ten.

BORDERLINE PERSONALITY DISORDER Borderline personality disorder is defined in the 1995 *Diagnostic and Statistical Manual of Mental Disorders*, fourth edition – *DSM-IV* – as a condition which manifests as a pervasive pattern of instability of interpersonal relationships, self-image and moods. It begins in early adulthood and is characterised by: frantic efforts to avoid real or imagined abandonment; unstable and intense relationships; identity disturbance with unstable self image or sense of self; impulsivity; recurrent suicidal or self-mutilating behaviour; mood instability; chronic feelings of emptiness; and, transient stress-related paranoid ideation or severe dissociative symptoms.

The term was first used in 1938 by Stern to describe patients on the border between neurosis and psychosis and then was developed by *Deutsch to refer to the 'as if' personality, namely those patients unable to make genuine emotional contact. Historically, the disorder was conceptualised as being a variant of schizophrenia, a view that is no longer held. Those diagnosed with borderline personality disorder are differentiated from schizotypical personality disorder, where the psychopathology is thought to be related to psychotic disorders.

Although descriptively defined as a discrete entity, there is considerable debate within psychiatry regarding its status as a diagnosis. There is also frequent comorbidity with affective disorders, anxiety disorders, *post traumatic stress disorder and substance abuse. Some are of the opinion that affective disorders and borderline personality disorder can co-exist but are probably unrelated, although others hypothesise it as a variation of an affective disorder. Berelowitz and Tarnopolsky suggest that borderline personality disorder should be regarded as a severe personality dysfunction with heterogeneous features which overlap with antisocial, histrionic narcissistic and paranoid personality disorders. *Kernberg describes borderline personality organisation as a broad concept that can encompass many different types of personality disorders. He conceptualises it as a stable state defined by four features: the excessive use of primitive defence mechanisms; ego weakness which manifests itself in inability to tolerate anxiety and poor impulse control; a tendency towards irrational dream-like thinking patterns; and, identity diffusion and pathological internal object relations, such that self and others are represented internally as fragmented. This description brings to attention another area of confusion around the term borderline, as in psychoanalysis it is used to describe intra-psychic processes rather than symptoms.

The aetiology is multi-factorial, with most theories suggesting an interaction between an innate biological vulnerability to regulating anxiety and affect and psychological and social risk factors. Childhood experiences of abuse and neglect are extremely common in borderline patients, often with impaired attachments between mother and child, and instability in the family.

Within a psychiatric population in 1989 Widigier and Frances found the incidence of borderline personality disorder to be 10% of outpatients and 20% of inpatients. It is significantly more common in women (75% of diagnoses) and is not usually diagnosed after the age of forty. There is no general consensus about treatment, which probably reflects the heterogeneity of the disorder. It is agreed that a combination of drugs and psychotherapy can be effective and a flexible approach is required. Medication is useful to help manage anxiety, unstable mood and the psychotic experiences encountered and can allow the patient to engage in psychological approaches, including psychoanalytic psychotherapy, and cognitive behavioural therapy including dialectical behavioural therapy which combines support with a problem-orientated directive approach. Supportive psychotherapy can help in crises. Batemen and Fonagy have shown that an eighteen-month programme in a psychodynamically orientated day hospital is significantly more effective than a standard psychiatric follow up.

Bateman, A. and Fonagy, P. (1999) 'Effectiveness of partial hospitalization in the treatment of borderline personality disorder: a randomised control trial'. *American Journal of Psychiatry* 156.

Berelowitz, M. and Tarnopolsky, A. (1993) 'The validity of borderline personality disorder: an updated review of recent research' in P. Tyrer and G. Stein (eds) *Personality Disorder Reviewed*. London: Gaskell.

Deutsch, H. (1942) 'Some forms of emotional disturbance and their relationship to schizophrenia'. *Psychoanalytic Quarterly* 11.
Kernberg, O. F. (1975) *Borderline Conditions and Pathological Narcissism*. New York: Aronson.
Stern, A. (1938) 'Psychoanalytical investigation and therapy in borderline group of neuroses'. *Psychoanalytic Quarterly* 7.
Widigier, T. A. and Frances, A. (1989) 'Epidemiology, diagnosis, and comorbidity of borderline personality disorder'. *American Psychiatric Press Review of Psychiatry 8*. Washington, DC: American Psychiatric Press.

A. J.

BORDERLINE PSYCHOSIS (CHILD) For decades it has been recognised that not only neurotic, but also psychotic or psychotic-like symptoms occur in childhood – in childhood schizophrenia and affective disorders, for example. Yet the area in between neurosis and psychosis, the condition of borderline psychosis (where there is impairment in, but not total absence of ego development and of reality testing), is not included in the tenth edition of the *International Classification of Diseases* (*ICD-10*). It is included in the fourth *Diagnostic and Statistical Manual* (*DSM-IV*) of the American Psychiatric Association as a sub-category of personality disorder, with its main features cited as: 'a pervasive pattern of instability of interpersonal relationships, self-image and marked impulsivity beginning in early adulthood'. Yet authors such as Pine and Lubbe describe similarly severe disturbance in children with weak egos who experience extremes of terror, despair, hatred, or dissociation. There is clearly concern on the part of the psychiatric classifiers to avoid an assumption of permanent damage in a person who is by definition still developing. But for the psychoanalytic psychotherapist, the notion of a psychotic part of the personality, or brief instances of psychotic thinking in anyone's life, is acceptable, not pejorative, and in any case treatable by methods precisely calibrated to the severity of the psychopathology. Most writers concur that, under these conditions, some degree of recovery is possible.

One word more about classification: the child psychotherapist might want to include many severely deprived, abused, traumatised children and also many of those in the 'disorganised attachment' group. Pine has offered a very helpful list of sub-classifications. It is important to note that borderline children are different from many borderline adults in that psychotic illness in children interferes with normal psychological development and therefore usually produces developmental arrest and developmental deficit (with effects on cognition).

In 1946 Geleerd and later in 1954 Ekstein and Wallerstein were the first to identify these children in the USA. In the UK, therapists in the Anna Freud (then Hampstead) Clinic's Borderline Workshop attempted to formulate the meaning of the concept 'Borderline'. Rosenfeld and Sprince concluded that the illness resided both in the 'quality and level of ego disturbance and in the precarious capacity for object relations'. In a paper on technical issues, they stated that they found that borderline children experienced interpretations as permissive, or as too overwhelming to a weak ego, and phantasy and anxiety could escalate uncontrollably. They concluded that it was necessary to facilitate the very *defence mechanisms which in a neurotic child one would attempt to undo: for example, *repression and *displacement. There were differences in the workshop as to how much ego support, reassurance and encouragement of the positive, as distinct from interpretation of the negative, should take place. This issue of the choice between the abstinence and deprivation implied in the classical psychoanalytic method developed for neurotic patients, and the gratification 'needed' by borderline patients, has been addressed by Chethnik and is a continuing source of creative controversy.

Alvarez argued that the dispute over gratification versus deprivation was a false dichotomy. An interpretation could be receptive to the child's wish to assure himself that the therapist and he had something in common, without being collusive or seductive. A too defensive interpretation could be experienced by a suspicious or deprived child as cruelly rejecting of what could be his first overture of friendliness. She saw many so-called defences as attempts to recover from, or overcome, dreadful states of *anxiety or despair. She suggested that, in borderline children, the Kleinian 'defences' of the *paranoid-schizoid position could be seen as often signalling the beginnings of developmental achievements – for example, omnipotence as potency, and manic denial as new hope or relief.

Alvarez, A. (1997) 'Projective identification as a communication: its grammar in Borderline Psychotic children'. *Psychoanalytic Dialogues 7(6) Symposium on Child Analysis, Part I.*

Chethik, M. (2000) 'Treatment of the borderline child' in *Techniques of Child Therapy: Psychodynamic Strategies*. New York: Guilford.

Ekstein, R. and Wallerstein, J. (1954) 'Observations on the psychology of borderline children'. *Psychoanalytic Study of the Child* 9.

Kut Rosenfeld, S. and Sprince, M. (1965) 'Some thoughts on the technical handling of borderline children'. *Psychoanalytic Study of the Child* 18.

Lubbe, T. (2000) *The Borderline Psychotic Child: A Selective Integration*. London: Routledge.

Pine, F. (1985) 'Borderline pathology in childhood'. *Developmental Theory and Clinical Process*. New Haven, CT: Yale University Press.

A. A.

BORROMEAN KNOT Lacan referred to *knots and the mathematical theory of knots throughout most of his work. Initially he used knot theory as a metaphor for the different relationship modalities of the subject in psychoanalysis to the *object a and the *Other. However, by 1973 Lacan had ceased to use the knot metaphorically. By then it was the *matheme which allowed him to express how the three registers of the *Symbolic, the *Imaginary, and the *Real have to hold together in order for the *subject to be able to assume their sexual and social being. A clinic of the knot could subsequently be developed, introducing eventually a fourth link, the *sinthome, which ties together the first three links.

N. C.

BOSS, MEDARD (1903–90) Medard Boss was among the first classically trained psychoanalysts to develop an existential approach to practice. Born in St Gallen, Switzerland, Boss lived in Zurich from the age of two until his death. Discouraged by his father from pursuing a career as an artist, Boss undertook medical studies in Zurich, Paris, and Vienna. While in Vienna, he embarked on his career as a psychoanalyst with a brief analysis by Freud. After receiving his medical degree from the University of Zurich in 1928, he worked as an assistant to *Bleuler at the Burghölzli psychiatric hospital and completed his personal analysis with Behn-Eschenburg. From 1932 to 1934 Boss continued his psychoanalytic training in Berlin and London. In Berlin, where his primary training and supervisory analyst was *Horney, Boss also studied with Sachs, *Fenichel, and *Reich. In London, he was supervised by *Jones. Returning to Zurich, Boss opened his own practice in psychiatry and psychoanalysis in 1935, the same year he initiated a decade-long study with *Jung.

Increasingly dissatisfied with the mechanistic and deterministic theories of human nature propounded by psychoanalysis, Boss eventually turned to the philosophically grounded works of Straus, von Gebsattel, Kunz, and *Binswanger. Binswanger introduced Boss to Heidegger's *Being and Time* and, in 1947, Boss wrote to *Heidegger, initiating a twenty-five year long personal and intellectual friendship with the philosopher. Boss was impressed by Heidegger's understanding of human existence as being-in-the-world or *dasein, which emphasised *freedom, possibility, and *care as opposed to causality, necessity, and control. Boss was also drawn to the promise of Heidegger's *phenomenology to ground its understanding of human nature not in suppositional theories of psychopathology and the unconscious, but in the inherent meaningfulness of human existence as it is actually lived. Vigorously disputing the philosophical dualisms found in psychoanalysis, Boss insisted that a human being could be adequately understood only in terms of its entire existence, that is, as a being-in-the-world, as dasein, a whole and inseparable constellation of world relationships. Like Binswanger, Boss called his approach to existential psychoanalysis *daseinsanalysis. While frequently criticised for his rejection of psychoanalytic theories of the unconscious, drives, and developmental determinants of behaviour, Boss's understanding of human existence and of the practice of analytical psychotherapy as fundamentally relational anticipated many later trends in psychoanalytic thought and practice.

Boss, M. (1963) *Psychoanalysis and Daseinsanalysis*. New York: Basic Books.

Boss, M. (1979) *Existential Foundations of Medicine and Psychology*. New York: Aronson.

E. C.

BOUNDARIES AND BOUNDARY VIOLATIONS Boundaries in psychoanalytic therapy provide the safe structure within which work can take place, and violations occur when these structures are breached. As in everyday life, there are explicit and implicit limits as to what is acceptable, and in all cultures there are those who push and break these limits.

In reference to psychoanalytic work, the patient will be expected to develop strong positive and negative feelings towards their therapist, at times feeling loving, and at others hateful. In order to explore these issues safely, two boundaries are essential: the therapist needs to know that the patient will not resort to physical violence, and the patient needs to know that the therapist will not take advantage of their transferential loving feelings by initiating or allowing intimate (sexual) contact. Similarly, during development children can have strongly eroticised feelings towards their parents, which may be very trying. Parents made vulnerable, for example by personality dysfunction or mental illness, may not be able to contain themselves. In this context, boundary violations involving sexual contact and violence are particularly traumatic and damaging, as the child is prevented from learning about the nature of boundaries, and the safety that observance of them can bring about.

Such examples of boundary violations might be seen as extreme. More common examples in analytic work can include lateness to sessions, contact with the analyst outside the session and other enactments which impinge on the structure or contract of the work. Also, some would argue that, at a very fine grain level, in the process of therapy there are continual and subtle boundary breaks and violations created by both patient and analyst – for example the analyst laughing at a patient's joke, or scolding the patient in a parental way, thereby breaking the boundary of the contract to be the patient's analyst. From this perspective, the analytic task is the exploration and understanding of the meaning of these minor boundary testings and breakings, and the examination of how they might reflect other issues in the patient's current and past life. For example the patient might chronically feel scolded and belittled, so that the occurrence of this in the treatment is highly significant.

Boundary violations can be seen as inevitable within treatment, in the same way that parental failure is inevitable. Development and growth emerges from the negotiation of such traumata.

M. Mor.

BOWLBY, JOHN (1907–90) After qualifying in psychiatry and psychoanalysis and serving in the army in World War II, Bowlby was based at the Tavistock Clinic where he was director of the Department for Children and Families; there he worked as a clinician and conducted research.

Bowlby was deeply influenced by Freud's intention that psychoanalysis should be a science, the science of unconscious mental processes. He intended to develop this science by reformulating psychoanalytic theory in terms compatible with contemporary science, so making it capable of being researched. In his reformulation he employed ethology, systems theory and cognitive psychology. His Darwinian orientation convinced him that children's development must be adapted to their environment and so more influenced by real life events than by their unconscious fantasies. The life event that he researched was the effect of separating young children from their families in hospitals or foster care. One outcome of this research was a revolution in childcare practices. The results of Bowlby's research and reformulation were published in his most influential work, the trilogy *Attachment and Loss* published in 1969, 1973 and 1980 respectively, which contained his views on attachment, separation anxiety, trauma, mourning, and sensitive periods in early life. He construed the child's tie to his mother as an instinctive attachment, as essential for survival as nutrition and reproduction. He concluded that anxiety is primarily due to the lack of a secure attachment to people who should provide a safe base.

Although Bowlby's views were very controversial, especially among psychoanalysts, by the time of his eightieth birthday he was rewarded by an increasing recognition of his contribution. Research by his followers, Mary Ainsworth and Mary Main, had provided empirical evidence of the significance of parental influence on infant development and on the intergenerational transmission of attachment styles. Bowlby's impact on child development research continues to be immense while his impact on psychoanalysis has been limited, though growing. His theorising and research continue to be developed by some psychoanalysts, most notably Peter Fonagy.

J. Hop.

BOY Psychoanalysts employ this notion to refer to the male child, yet rather than genes or sex roles they consider his psychic reactions to the presence of the penis to be the most important feature of boyhood. When the boy is confronted with sexual difference, this presence will instil *castration anxiety and expedite the dissolution of the *Oedipus complex.

D. N.

BRAZIL The first period of psychoanalysis in Brazil began in 1919, with the publication of Freud's papers and the appearance of groups interested in analytic ideas, and continued until 1936, when Adelheid Koch, from the Berlin Society, arrived in Brazil to begin the training of analysts in São Paulo. The second period runs from 1936 to the present, with the establishment of the Societies and Study Groups affiliated to the IPA and the spreading of analytic ideas throughout this huge country.

The oldest societies are the Brazilian Psychoanalytic Society of São Paulo (1951), the Psychoanalytic Society of Rio de Janeiro (1955), the Brazilian Psychoanalytic Society of Rio de Janeiro (1959) and the Porto Alegre Psychoanalytical Society (1963). The pioneers of the psychoanalytic movement were Adelheid Koch, Durval Marcondes, Flávio Dias, Virgínia Bicudo, Darci Uchoa, Frank Philips (São Paulo), Werner Kemper, Mark Burke, Luiz Dahlheim, Fábio Lobo, João Marafelli, Inaura Leão, Ines Besouchet, Zenaira Aranha, Noemy Rudolfer, Alcyon Bahia, Danilo Perestrello, Marialzira Perestrello, Walderedo Oliveira, João Barros, Luis Lyra (Rio de Janeiro), Mario Martins, José Lemmertz, Celestino Prunes, Cyro Martins and Zaira Martins (Porto Alegre).

In the following years, new societies were established in several cities, and in 1967 the Brazilian Psychoanalytic Association (ABP) was founded; its president was Mario Martins. There are currently almost a thousand IPA members in Brazil, and besides the aforementioned, there are psychoanalytic organisations in Recife, Brasilia, Pelotas, Campo Grande,

Ribeirão Preto, Porto Alegre and Rio de Janeiro. ABP organises a Brazilian Congress every two years, generally open to non-members, and including a training conference.

Apart from those institutions, there are a large number of other organisations involved in training analysts, developing analytic ideas and organising meetings – mainly Lacanian and Jungian societies active in the main Brazilian cities.

In terms of analytic ideas, Freud is the most important author. Melanie Klein was very influential in São Paulo, Rio de Janeiro, and Porto Alegre. Bion is very influential in São Paulo and in other cities. In Recife, French psychoanalysis is very influential, following the training of its Brazilian pioneer, Jose Lins, in Paris.

In recent years, there has been a growing tendency to study authors from different traditions, like the British post-Kleinians (Joseph, *Segal, Steiner) and Independents (*Winnicott), French (*Lacan, *Green, *Laplanche, Chasseguet Smirgel, MacDougall), and Americans (*Kernberg, *Wallerstein). Since the beginning of the analytic movement in Brazil, there has been a very strong tie with Argentina and the work of its authors, such as *Racker, Liberman and the Barangers. Brazilian authors are also active: for example Mezan, Freire Costa, Rocha Barros, and Herrmann.

In all analytic institutions there is a very active scientific life, both internally and in training as well as externally, in a growing interface with the surrounding culture. In the first decades, psychoanalysis was very influential on psychiatry and medicine. More recently, this influence has decreased, but there are several active university centres, where research and postgraduate programmes in psychoanalysis attract many students.

Brazil is the third largest international editorial market for analytic books. The main analytic thinkers are translated into Portuguese and several analytic journals are regularly published.

The main challenges currently faced by psychoanalysis in Brazil are: to keep its relevance as an effective treatment; to find a proper way of regulating it as a profession; to expand its presence in the university and the culture; to maintain its high standards in spite of economic difficulties; and, to make Brazilian theoretical and clinical production better known abroad.

G. Bou.

BREAKDOWN A state in which there is a failure of the defensive structures to hold the self, and a new organisation or pattern of illness has to be created. Winnicott stresses that the patient's fear of breakdown in an analysis is his/her recognition of the initial, experienced breakdown that has already occurred, and which must now be remembered and hopefully worked through to a more satisfactory outcome. Again this terminology may be alternatively represented as the patient's fantasising on the basis of the original breakdown and representing in repeated fears/phantasies aspects of the trauma.

Winnicott, D. W. (1989) *The Fear of Breakdown.* Psychoanalytic Explorations. London: Karnac Books.

H. T. R.

BREAST Dividing sexual life into *object and *aim, Freud first defines the breast as the object of a baby's *oral phase and then as the template for later sexual satisfaction: 'No one who has seen a baby sinking back satiated from the breast and falling asleep with flushed cheeks and a blissful smile can escape the reflection that this picture persists as a prototype of the expression of sexual satisfaction later in life'. The baby first reproduces the breast by sucking his thumb, thus finding satisfaction in *autoerotic activity and later in life, seeks the lips of another person: 'The finding of an object is in fact a refinding of it'. Clinically, Freud sees the satisfactions or disappointments experienced at the breast as a point of fixation for some patients. He assigns 'avidity' or an 'insatiable' quality to an infant's hunger which is carried forward into adult life as a reproach against the mother: she did not give me enough milk, she did not love me.

Freud, S. (1900) *Three Essays on the Theory of Sexuality*. S. E. 7. London: Hogarth Press.
Freud, S. [1915–17] (1916–17) *Introductory Lectures on Psychoanalysis*. S. E. 16. London: Hogarth Press.

E. S.

Brenner, Charles (1914–) Like several of his colleagues in ego-psychology Brenner's first incursions into psychoanalysis began at the doorstep of neurology. His psychiatric training was at the Boston Psychopathic Hospital and in neurology at the Boston City Hospital. From 1939 to 1945 he was simultaneously an Assistant in Neurology at Harvard and Sigmund Freud Fellow at the Boston Psychoanalytic Society and Institute.

His first book, *An Elementary Textbook of Psychoanalysis* (1955), is perhaps his most notable contribution to psychoanalysis and gained him an international reputation. With Jacob A. Arlow, he co-authored the metapsychological text *Psychoanalytic Concepts and the Structural Theory* (1964).

His work is wide-ranging: a revision of affect theory; an exploration of compromise formation as the central organising principle of psychic structure; and a thorough treatment of the fundamentals of psychoanalytic technique. These ideas were unified in two books *Psychoanalytic Technique and Psychic Conflict* (1976) and *The Mind in Conflict* (1982).

Besides faculty posts at Yale Medical School and at the Downstate Medical Centre in New York, he has been a member of the faculty of the New York Psychoanalytic Institute since 1955 and was president of the New York Society from 1961 to 1963. He chaired the Program Committee of the American Psychoanalytic Association from 1955 to 1962, and served as Counsellor-in-Large from 1959 to 1963, then was President-Elect and subsequently President of the Association from 1966 to 1968. He was also honoured as the A. A. Brill Lecturer of the New York Psychoanalytic Society in 1966 and as the Freud Anniversary Lecturer of its Institute in 1982.

S. Byr.

Breuer, Josef (1842–1925) Breuer, who was the son of a liberal Jewish teacher of religion, studied medicine in Vienna and achieved his doctoral degree in 1864. He was an assistant to the internist Theodor Oppolzer, worked on regulation of body temperature and physiology of respiration ('Hering-Breuer-reflex'), and in 1871 started as a general practitioner in Vienna. Besides his practical work he did experimental research on the function of the semicircular canals in the labyrinth of the ear ('Mach-Breuer flow theory of the vestibular apparatus'). In 1874 he qualified as a university lecturer, but ten years later retired from the university.

Breuer was a personal friend and family doctor to numerous members of the board of professors at Vienna University and to many members of the Vienna bourgeoisie. He was in correspondence with artists and authors, philosophers, psychologists and medical colleagues. In 1894 he was appointed corresponding member of the Academy of Sciences.

Breuer was trained in *philosophy and concerned himself with epistemological problems and with the theoretical foundation of *Darwinism. He was an active participant in fundamental debates on political and sociocultural matters and discussed fine arts, literature, and music with his wife and his friends. Being a well-assimilated Jew he was an adherent of a kind of pantheism referring to Goethe and Gustav Theodore Fechner. His personal motto was *suum esse conservare*, a phrase of Spinoza's meaning 'to preserve one's own character'. He felt himself bound in a kind of scepticism and spoke – referring to William Thackeray – of a 'Demon but', which forced him to call into question any insight immediately after it was gained. His exact knowledge of the cultural and social history and of the political background of his time as well as elements of his own biography made it difficult for him to act unscrupulously.

Breuer's physiological research was guided by the search for the relation between structure and function, which implies a *teleological approach. He was especially interested in mechanisms of self-regulation. In contrast to numerous physiologists of the so-called bio-physical movement around the group of Brücke, von Helmholtz and DuBois-Reymond, he was not a mechanist but an adherent to neovitalism.

From 1880 to 1882 Breuer treated a young patient named Bertha Pappenheim – Anna O – who was suffering from an intense nervous cough, and many additional symptoms like rapid changes of mood, dissociation of two states of consciousness, visual disturbances, paralyses with contractures, aphasia, and so on. During many long-lasting sessions the doctor and his patient observed that she would lose certain symptoms after remembering the very first appearance and then reproducing it with the accompanying affects, thus 'abreacting' them. This was especially successful during spontaneously appearing autohypnotic states. Referring to these accidental observations the patient and her physician developed a systematic method of treatment, during which the symptoms were recalled into consciousness one by one until the disappearance of the symptom. From time to time, artificial hypnosis was also used, in cases in which the patient did not succumb to spontaneous autohypnosis. The patient, who had temporarily 'forgotten' her mother tongue and then could only express herself in English, called her therapy 'talking cure' or 'chimney sweeping'.

In spite of the apparently surprising success of the method various severe disturbances still persisted such as temporary loss of the mother tongue and a trigeminal neuralgia, which made the use of morphine necessary. However, that led to an addiction to morphine. To cure these symptoms Breuer referred his patient for further treatment to Dr Binswanger's asylum – Bellevue in Kreuzlingen, Switzerland – in July 1882. In October she was discharged, partly but not completely recovered. She lived in Vienna until 1888, but had to be treated in a sanatorium from time to time. Later in Frankfurt she lived an active life as an author, Jewish social worker, and as a leading member of the Jewish suffragette movement in Germany.

From 1882 onwards Breuer discussed this case with his colleague Sigmund Freud, fourteen years his junior. Freud made his own attempts with Breuer's method after he had established himself as a specialist for nervous diseases. In disputing the theories of Charcot, Janet, Möbius, Bernheim and others, Freud and Breuer developed a theoretical concept explaining the function of the psychic apparatus in combination with a method of treatment, which they now called the 'cathartic method' in reference to the Aristotelian concept of the function of tragedy (catharsis, the spectator's purification of passion). In 1893 they published a *Preliminary Communication on the Psychical Mechanism of Hysterical Phenomena*. This was followed two years later by *Studies on Hysteria*, the book that was to be called the inaugural text of psychoanalysis (*Urbuch der Psychoanalyse*, Grubrich-Simitis). In this book we find five case studies (Anna O, Emmy von N, Katharina, Lucy R, Elisabeth v R) illustrating what the authors explain in a chapter on theory (Breuer) and one on therapy (Freud) about hysteria and its cure.

During the process of writing this joint book, Freud developed his theory and technique further ('The Neuro-Psychoses of Defence', of 1894; the technique of free association). Breuer questioned Freud's emphasis on sexual aetiology, and Freud took Breuer's cautious attitude for cowardice. From 1895 a growing alienation could be felt so that finally their co-operation came to an end. Breuer was still interested in the further development of psychoanalytical theory, but gave up treating patients by means of the cathartic method. Later Freud developed the hypothesis that Breuer had stopped treating his patient Anna O abruptly because of erotic transference-countertransference problems culminating in a hysterical pregnancy and childbirth. This version which was spread by Ernest Jones and others proved to be a myth rather than historic reality. In fact there is no sufficient reason to draw into question the efficiency of Breuer's treatment in general. Borch-Jacobsen's thesis about Breuer's 'mystification' is mere polemic.

Borch-Jacobson, M. (1996) *Remembering Anna O. A Century of Mystification*. London: Routledge.
Freud, S. and Breuer, J. (1895) *Studies on Hysteria*. S. E. 2. London: Hogarth Press.
Hirschmüller, A. (1989) *The Life and Work of Josef Breuer: Physiology and Psychoanalysis*. New York: New York University Press.
Porter, R. (ed.) (1970) *Breathing*: Hering-Breuer Centenary Symposium: A Ciba Foundation Symposium. London: Churchill.

A. Hir. / Ann. M.

BRIEF PSYCHOTHERAPY There are two essential elements in brief dynamic psychotherapy. First is the formulation by the therapist of the life problem or main anxiety in the patient. Second is the time limit which is set from the beginning of the therapy. Within the realm of brief psychotherapy, very brief consultations (four to six sessions) can be distinguished from brief psychotherapy (six to thirty sessions).

Brief psychotherapy is often a treatment of choice for some adolescents or young adults; for parents with infants or young children; and for parents of adolescents.

Services offering very brief consultations do not generally demand specific criteria for acceptance. However, young people with severe psychiatric problems are directed to their doctor. Self-referrals tend to be made informally over the telephone. By contrast there is an extensive literature on the criteria for formal brief psychotherapy, such as motivation, the capacity to think about interpretations and a basic resilience in the patient.

As adolescence is a period of transition, change and negotiation of separateness, a great number of young people choose such brief work because they need quick help or they are in crisis, but do not wish to make long-term commitment to therapy. They come with a whole range of problems. Some of these may be relationship difficulties, the search for sexual identity, separation from home, anxiety about exams, reactions to parental divorce, bereavement, deeply buried childhood traumas, recurring depression, breakdowns, and so on.

The psychotherapist explores, listening to the difficulties experienced by the young person and to his/her life events while observing the quality of contact between therapist and patient. The adult part of the young person is encouraged to observe and think about the more infantile feelings in their personality. However, infantile *transference is not encouraged, especially in brief consultations. Often thinking, exploring, specifically naming the anxiety and sharing an understanding of it, brings a great relief to the young person, facilitating a thrust forward towards emotional growth. Some patients may choose to pursue long-term psychotherapy after they experience brief work.

Other applications of brief psychotherapy within child and adolescent mental health include work with parents of adolescents who may be experiencing conflicts or emotional difficulties in their relationships with their children. Families with children under five can also benefit from brief work. As in adolescence, parents of infants and young children are often living through turmoil and change. They may be experiencing anxieties and self-doubts and possibly re-experiencing on an unconscious level their own childhood self and the kind of parenting they received. These bewildering anxieties in parents and the capacity for rapid change in young children make such families very receptive to brief professional help when in difficulty.

H. D.

BRUNSWICK, RUTH MACK (1897–1946) Ruth Mack Brunswick was born in Chicago, and had completed her psychiatric residency when, at the age of twenty-five, she went to Freud. She taught at the Vienna Psychoanalytic Institute; her specialty was psychoses, an area that Freud personally steered clear of. Brunswick's access to Freud seemed unique; she came to meals at his apartment, visited him in summer, and was on excellent terms with his children. She was considered a member of Freud's extended family.

Brunswick played a special role in mediating between the American analysts and Freud's circle in Vienna. She became one of the few women who received a ring from Freud. She also played a notable part in supervising Freud's precarious health. Her own patient in analysis, Dr Max Schur, became appointed Freud's personal physician.

Brunswick's central contribution had to do with her concern with the child's earliest relationship to the mother. In 1929 she was one of the first in print to use the term *preoedipal, and Freud himself adopted it two years later. *Rank deserves the credit for being the earliest to invoke the concept.

She will be remembered as the *Wolf Man's second analyst. When in 1926 Freud had referred the Wolf Man to Brunswick for treatment, he was paying her a high compliment; he knew that anything she published would become famous in the clinical literature.

By 1934 Brunswick had a serious drug problem, and by 1937 she had become an addict. Her failure to overcome her difficulties was the main reason for Freud's final disappointment in her. However she had a special talent for manipulating Freud's theoretical concepts, and used them to set forth new ideas of her own. It was left to others, such as Rank and Melanie Klein, to go on to make 'preoedipal' problems the centres of their respective systems.

Roazen, P. (1995) *How Freud Worked*. New York: Jason Aronson.

P. R.

BUBER, MARTIN (1878–1965) Buber, the Jewish theologian and existential philosopher, was born in Vienna and died in Jerusalem. When he was three, his mother left home with a lover. Buber met her again only after thirty years. His father sent him to Lemberg to live with his affluent, scholarly grandparents. He studied at the Universities of Vienna, Berlin and Zurich before receiving his doctoral degree from Vienna University in 1904. In 1898 Buber joined the Zionist movement, and in 1899 he met and married Paula Winkler with whom he had two children. Buber was Chair of Jewish Philosophy and Ethics at the University of Frankfurt from 1921 until he was fired by the Nazi regime in 1933. In 1938 he immigrated to Israel and joined the faculty of Hebrew University in Jerusalem.

Buber's major contributions were in philosophy and theology, although his ideas have also influenced existential psychoanalysis. Buber's distinction between the I-Thou and the I-It relationship and ideas on intersubjectivity are particularly important to existential analysts like *Binswanger, Frankl and *Laing. The I-Thou relationship is characterized by genuine reciprocity and openness of one's being to the other; the I-It relationship is instrumental. One of the tasks of existential analysis is to allow persons who know only the I-It relationship to rediscover the mystery of the I-Thou encounter. Buber also introduced the idea of existential guilt in which he notes that persons can be guilty without guilt feelings and have guilt feelings without being guilty – a point which is very different from Freud's account of guilt.

Buber, M. [1923] (1987) *I and Thou*. Translated by R. G. Smith. New York: Collier Books.

H. Gor.

BUDDHISM AND PSYCHOANALYSIS Nirvana, referred to in 'Beyond the pleasure principle' by Freud, is one of the seminal concepts of Buddhism, even thought the concept was also pursued by the pre-Buddhist Brahmanism. It refers to the ideal calmness of mind that Buddha entered. His death was thought to be the perfection of that calmness, and now everyone is invited to attain that level even during life.

We can understand why Freud thought this was something comparable to what he conceptualised beyond the pleasure principle. If this principle confines us in a representational system of good and bad, *samsara* (transmigration) also does so in an agonising alternation of representations of life and death; if the Freudian death instinct beyond it is what our life is destined to join, *nirvana* is the place that we should reach by the act of *satori* which ensures us an emancipation from *samsara*.

Even if Buddhism envisages the existence of something beyond this world of representation, it denies God, for Buddhism, like psychoanalysis, is atheistic. Instead of faith in God, Buddhists make the most use of reverence for the Master; it is the dialogue with him that guides them to *nirvana*. This is where psychoanalysis comes close to Buddhism, since both emphasise the transferential relationship. In Buddhism, there is a triad that denotes the unfavourable variants of the relationship: *raga* (greed-love), *dvesa* (envy-hate) and *moha* (ignorance). Bion would qualify them as '−L', 'H' and '−K'.

This structural homology of the two relationships was noted very early by Lacan, who compared his own method (variable length of the session) to Zen. Since Suzuki, a Japanese Zen Master, advocated the idea of Zen Buddhism in Western countries, Zen has become more accessible to psychoanalysts and we can read articles – such as that by De Martino – that inspire us by bringing together Zen and the Western dialectic of the self and other.

Fromm, E., Suzuki, D. and De Martino, R. (1960) *Zen Buddhism and Psychoanalysis*. New York: Harper & Brothers.

Lacan, J. [1953] (1966) 'Fonction et champ de la parole et du langage en psychanalyse' in *Ecrits*. Paris: Seuil.

K. Shi.

C

CAESURA Bion used a quotation from Freud: 'There is much more continuity between intra-uterine life and the earliest infancy than the impressive caesura of the act of birth allows us to believe'. Bion uses 'caesura' stressing two aspects: separation (barrier, pause, cut, screen) and continuity. Emotional development takes place by layers, like the skins of the onion. Between each layer there are caesuras. The mind or personality establishes a number of gaps, splits or caesuras. Birth is only one of them. Caesuras are places of separation between different mental states: being awake or asleep, pre-natal or post-natal, etc. Freud discovered the caesura between unconscious and conscious.

Bion marks a caesura with the sign '/' in order to represent the separation but also a potential dynamic change that can be established between the mental states separated by the line, without indicating the direction of the change. For mental growth and also for psychoanalytic work it is necessary to traverse caesuras but also to be able to establish some, as for the example between unconscious and conscious states of mind. When caesuras are permeable they allow contact between different aspects of the personality, which offers the possibility for establishing dialogues and for transcending the barrier of incomprehension, and for providing different vertices of observation within the personality. When this ability is achieved, an experience of continuity or totality emerges. Although establishing caesuras is necessary for development, if the gap becomes too impermeable, the personality becomes more and more split, and wilts and deteriorates. The technical approach in psychoanalysis that Bion advises is to investigate the caesura, not only the *transference or the *countertransference but also the relation of what is 'in between'.

Bion, W. R. (1970) *Attention and Interpretation*. London: Tavistock.
Bion, W. R. (1977) 'Caesura' in *Two Papers: The Grid and Caesura*. Rio de Janeiro: Imago.
Freud, S. (1926) *Inhibition, Symptom, and Anxiety*. S. E. 5. London: Hogarth Press.

L. P. C.

Canada Although Ernest *Jones lived and worked in Toronto from 1908 to 1913, interest in psychoanalysis in Canada remained sporadic and individual until after World War II. In 1945 Miguel Prados, a Spanish neuropathologist without formal psychoanalytic training but with strong psychoanalytic interests, established the Montreal Psychoanalytic Club, leadership of which was assumed in 1948 by Theodore Chentrier, a lay member of the Paris Society who had obtained an appointment to the Department of Psychology of the *Université de Montréal*. In 1950, Eric Wittkower became the first psychoanalyst to be appointed to the faculty of Montreal's McGill University.

As several members of the Montreal group received psychoanalytic training in the United States, there was an attempt to obtain official Study Group status in the International Psychoanalytic Association through sponsorship by the Detroit affiliate of the American Psychoanalytic Association. In the face of some opposition by the APA, the group decided instead to seek sponsorship from the British Society to which two of its members (Eric Wittkower and Alastair MacLeod) belonged. This led to protests by the Americans who, as they had done in the debate over lay analysis, raised the spectre of their withdrawal from the International, this time over the threat to American hegemony over psychoanalysis in North America that this autonomous application from Canada represented to them.

Attempts by the Americans to dissuade the British from supporting the rapidly expanding Canadian Psychoanalytic Society were resisted by Anna *Freud and Ernest Jones. When Clifford Scott, an expatriate Canadian, succeeded William Gillespie as President of the British Society in 1954, British sponsorship was assured. In the face of continuing American opposition the CPS initially sought to become a Branch of the British, but in 1957 it applied for and received full component society status within the IPA.

In 1959 the Canadian Psychoanalytic Society accepted its first class of students for psychoanalytic training in Montreal where, in 1961, the Canadian Institute of Psychoanalysis was established. In 1954 Alan Parkin, a Canadian psychoanalyst trained in London, had returned to Toronto where, in 1956, he established the Toronto Psychoanalytic Study Circle, the forerunner of the Toronto Psychoanalytic Society. In 1968 three branches of the Canadian Institute of Psychoanalysis were established: the Canadian Institute of Psychoanalysis (Quebec English Branch); the *Institut Canadien de Psychanalyse* (*Section française*), which later became the *Société Psychanalytique de Montréal*; and the Canadian Institute of Psychoanalysis (Ontario Branch) in Toronto, and three corresponding branches of the Canadian Psychoanalytic Society were formed. The Toronto Institute began training its first class of candidates in 1969. In 1972 a fourth branch of the Canadian Society was formed in Ottawa, Ontario. In 1978 an Ottawa Branch of the Canadian Institute initiated training in that city. A Western Canadian Branch of the CPS was also established in that year. This was followed in 1982 by the formation of the Southwestern Ontario Branch, based in London, Ontario, and in 1989 the *Société Psychanalytique de Québec* was established in Quebec City.

At present, the IPA-affiliated Canadian Institute of Psychoanalysis offers training in the Toronto Institute of Psychoanalysis, the *Institut Psychanalytique de Montréal* and the Quebec English Branch of the CIP (Montreal). The Canadian Psychoanalytic Society currently has over 400 members, with the largest concentration being in Toronto. In 1990, the CPS established its own psychoanalytic journal,

The Canadian Journal of Psychoanalysis/Revue Canadienne de Psychanalyse.

No doubt due to its ties to both the British and French psychoanalytic traditions, despite pressures from its neighbour to the south, Canadian psychoanalysis remained somewhat friendlier to lay analysis than was the case in the American Psychoanalytic Association where it was all but non-existent. But despite providing full psychoanalytic training to selected non-medical applicants, by the late 1980s there was a feeling among some psychoanalytically-oriented psychologists in Toronto that a separate training programme, outside the CIP and the IPA, was needed. The Toronto Institute of Contemporary Psychoanalysis, an offshoot of the Psychoanalytic Section of the Ontario Psychological Association, was formed and began training candidates in 1989. It has attracted both medical and non-medical candidates; at the same time the TIP has become more welcoming to non-medical applicants. In 1991 TICP became the local chapter of Division 39 (Psychoanalysis) of the American Psychological Association.

Beginning in the 1970s some members of the Toronto Psychoanalytic Society lent active support to the establishment of the Toronto Child Psychoanalytic Programme. This offers an intensive, four-year training in psychoanalytic child and adolescent psychotherapy for trainees most of whom come from backgrounds in child care, social work, psychology and related fields.

In the 1980s, the Toronto Psychoanalytic Society established a two-year Advanced Training Programme in Psychoanalytic Psychotherapy for experienced psychotherapists from a variety of backgrounds who wish to orient their psychotherapeutic work along psychoanalytic lines.

Several of the Branch Societies of the CPS have Extension Programmes that offer lectures and seminars to the wider community on various psychoanalytic topics, such as, for example, psychoanalysis and cinema. The Toronto Psychoanalytic Society has since 1990 sponsored an Annual Day in Psychoanalysis, open to both the general and the mental health communities, at which distinguished guest speakers have presented papers on various psychoanalytic topics. In addition, since the mid-1990s a group of psychoanalysts from both the TPS and the TICP, together with interested psychiatrists and academics from the humanities and social sciences, have conducted an annual Day in Applied Psychoanalysis.

Canadian psychoanalysis has suffered from the usual trials and tribulations, scandals and infighting, and pressures toward schism that have tended to characterise psychoanalytic societies and institutes the world over. In addition to the Anglo/French tensions and rivalry between Montreal and Toronto problems that mirror those of the wider Canadian federation during the 1970s and 1980s there was considerable conflict in the Toronto Society as some of its most senior members converted to Kohut's *self psychology, a uniquely American perspective that never caught on in Montreal. But despite these and other difficulties such as the decline of psychoanalysis within psychiatry Canadian psychoanalysis is alive and well. Although it has not produced anything like its own original theoretical or clinical paradigm, its uniqueness may well lie in its openness, like the mosaic of Canadian society in general, to the multiplicity of perspectives that characterise contemporary psychoanalysis.

Frayn, D. F. (2000) *Psychoanalysis in Toronto: Historical Perspectives*. Toronto: Ash Productions.

Parkin, A. (1987) *A History of Psychoanalysis in Canada*. Toronto: The Toronto Psychoanalytic Society.

D. C.

CANNIBALISM Cannibalistic organisation is, according to Freud, the earliest of the forms of unification imposed on the *partial drives. Freud refers to cannibalism as an oral sexual organisation, a term which stresses the source of the drive, while obscuring the aim of a devouring mastery of the object.

B. B.

CAPTATION A term adopted by Lacan to denote the captivating/mesmerising effect of the specular *image on the human subject. Built around an alienated core, lacking in that which would complete it, the subject tends to be lured by the imagined promise of completion that the image presents, thus lending specular images great power.

See also: imaginary; mirror stage

H. T.

CARE is the unified thrust of the human being for Heidegger, the unique concern of which is the *Being of beings* (including itself) encountered within the World. The term is used in Being and Time to signify the structure of existence (*Dasein) considered in its wholeness, i.e. in the unity of its existential components hitherto examined separately. After the analysis of how the mood of anxiety enables Dasein to experience the world as no-thing, the remaining constitutive elements of Dasein ingredient to its functioning are brought together in a single formula. Dasein as care means: to be always ahead of itself (existentiality); as already being-in-the-world (*facticity); and thrown among-other-beings (encountered within the world) on which it referentially depends (fallenness). These three existential components on further analysis imply future, past and present, so that the unity of existence (Dasein) is grounded ultimately in the unity of time. Hence, the most profound meaning of care lies in its temporality. Dasein's principal care is to be itself, i.e. to achieve its function as being the locus among beings through which the world is disclosed. This will involve care *about* (*Besorge*) other beings that are not endowed with its unique prerogative of disclosing the world, and care *for* (*Fuersorge*) other beings that are. In the later Heidegger, Dasein's care is rather for being itself, according to which it serves as the 'shepherd of being' among beings. In any case, care for Heidegger has only this ontological sense, never a purely sociological or moral one.

Heidegger, M. [1927] (1996) *Being and Time*. Translated by J. Stambaugh. Albany: State University of New York Press.
Kisiel, T. (1993) *The Genesis of Heidegger's 'Being and Time'*. Berkeley: University of California Press.

W. R.

CARUSO, IGOR A. (1914–81) As a young psychoanalyst Caruso was a Christian-existentialist. Later he became a Freudian, though remained an enemy of all orthodoxies. He developed Freud's ideas, emphasising their dialectic and socio-critical aspects in 'Psychoanalysis and Society' in *New Left Review* of 1965. Born in Tiraspol, Russia, the only child of a twenty-one-year-old mother, his father was a noble official in the Tsar's service. His childhood was surrounded by war uncertainties, and full of geographic, cultural, religious and language diversity. In 1918 the family moved to Kischinew, Romania. He went to a strict Catholic school in Belgium and obtained his degree in Psychology from the University of Louvain in 1936. He received psychoanalytical training from Von Gebsattel and Aichhorn. He was a founder of the Circle of Depth Psychology in Vienna in 1947 which was characterised by its openness to other disciplines such as: anthropology, ethology, Darwinism and sociology. Freudian texts were at its heart and those of *Marx started being welcomed. Years later he moved to Salzburg and became a professor at the university there. Perhaps his most important contribution to psychoanalysis was his 1968 book on the phenomenology of death, specifically the love life of those who have to live through a *separation despite their love. Caruso maintained that the individual unconscious reflects historical and social factors which can be questioned through the psychoanalytic method.

He asked such questions as: 'Is culture deadly? When? How?'; and, 'Is the goal of life a struggle for more life?' Those who knew him remember his personality: engaged, charming, melancholic, sceptical, passionate.

See also: death drive

Caruso, I. A. (1964) *Existential Psychology: From Analysis to Synthesis.* New York: Herder & Herder.
Caruso, I. A. (1972) *Soziale Aspekte der Psychoanalyse*. Reinbek: Rowohlt.
Englert, E. H. (1979) (ed.) *Die Verarmung der Psyche*. Igor A. Caruso zum 65. Geburtstag. Frankfurt: Campus Verlag.

R. P. O.

CASTRATION (FREUD) For Freud it is the punishment of losing the genital organ. During the Oedipal phase the young child believes that castration will result from loving the mother. Freud speculated that castration was actually practised in the primaeval human family by the jealous, cruel father; he saw the ritual of circumcision as a recognisable relic. The threat of castration is the motive for the resolution of the *Oedipus complex, for sexual *perversion and for *repression. For example, Freud suggested that the compulsion to exhibit has as its motivating force the desire to reassure the male of the presence of the penis, while it simultaneously reiterates his infantile satisfaction at the absence of the penis in the female.

See also: anxiety; penis envy; phallus; primacy of the punishment

Freud, S. (1901) *The Psychopathology of Everyday Life*. S. E. 6. London: Hogarth Press.
Freud, S. (1905) *Three Essays on the Theory of Sexuality*. S. E. 7. London: Hogarth Press.
Freud, S. (1933) *The New Introductory Lectures on Psychoanalysis*. S. E. 22. London: Hogarth Press.

R. M.

CASTRATION (LACAN) For Lacan castration represents not so much a fear of losing the penis but the Symbolic separation of the child (as Imaginary phallus) from the mother. The fact that the penis can be lacking is precisely what allows the phallus as signifier to occupy a privileged position in the Symbolic order. The phallus not only signifies sexual difference but differentiation in general. Without it, nothing means everything, or alternatively, everything could be meant. This privilege can be understood only with reference to the paternal *metaphor which is the foundation of primary *repression. In Lacan's formulation castration is a symbolic operation whose object is Imaginary and whose agent is the father or indeed a third element that intervenes between mother and child. He contrasts this both with the operation of *frustration and with that of *privation. Symbolic castration is the price to be paid for access to desire. The subject's relation to castration is what determines the major clinical categories of neurosis, perversion, and psychosis.

J. C. R

CATASTROPHIC CHANGE This term refers to a constant conjunction of facts that can be found in diverse areas: the mind, the *group, the psychoanalytic session, and society. This particular type of configuration is inherent to different structures of psychic change and *transformation. It is an unavoidable concomitant of mental growth which is timeless and catastrophic. It implies traversing different situations of crisis.

The facts that the constant conjunction refers to can be observed when a new idea appears in any of the mentioned areas. The new idea has a disruptive force that threatens a more or less violent break with the previous structure and organisation where it is expressed. The change towards growth involves the transformation of a structure or part of it, which implies necessarily moments of disorganisation, pain and frustration.

In *Attention and Interpretation*, Bion deals with the issue of catastrophic change from the point of view of the *container-contained model. This model can be used to study different vicissitudes: the new idea can be considered the contained, and the mind, the individual, or the society a container, or vice-versa. The investigation of the relation and the different kind of interactions have a clinical importance. For development to take place the relation between container and contained has to be symbiotic.

In the analytic setting psychic change is catastrophic in several ways: in a restricted sense of an event that causes a subversion of the previous order of things; it is accompanied by feelings of disaster in the participants; and, it is sudden and violent.

Catastrophic change implies violence, subversion of the system and invariance. These elements are inherent in any situation of growth: invariance – elements of the previous structure can be recognised in the new one although transformed; subversion – an alteration of the previously existing system breaks up an existing constant conjunction; and, violence – the sudden discovery of a fact that acquires and offers meaning, with the perception of feelings of disaster.

Catastrophic change does not imply an actual catastrophe in the general sense of the word, if it takes place in a K direction. The 'act of knowledge' is in itself a catastrophic change. The act of learning from emotional experience involves successive catastrophic changes. Insight in the analytic process configures catastrophic change.

When change occurs and is contained by the analytic situation, it is a controlled catastrophic change. If the change occurs in a K medium it is not a catastrophe but an evolutionary phenomenon of mental growth. If it occurs in a −K medium, it may almost be a real catastrophe for the personality.

In *transformations Bion distinguishes two stages, pre- and post-catastrophic. It may be compared to an explosion that transforms a pre-catastrophic moment into a post catastrophic one associated with a transformation. It is not a disaster, but rather a point of departure for an evolution, a radical development of a structure.

In *Attention and Interpretation*, Bion engages with the issue of catastrophic change using the container-contained model in *Attention and Interpretation*.

L. P. C.

CATHEXIS Freud's term (*besetzung*) originally meant the 'occupation' of a neuron by a quantum of excitation; later, a quantity of *libido invested in the representation, function, or part of the *psychic apparatus or of the body. It also became a synonym for psychic *energy generally, and loosely for 'value,' 'choice,' or 'investment'.

See also: object choice

R. Hol.

CAUSE The notion of cause in psychoanalysis was initially restricted to what is involved in the aetiology of neurosis. Lacan uses it in association with his *object a and with the Freudian *thing. In this way cause could be understood as an eruption in a structure, that is, as something that moves in opposition to the law. It is then no longer an explanation, but an object, in terms of which these other uses are to be understood; the cause that can only be determined by its effect, the cause to speak and be spoken for; or indeed the cause which leads to the attempt to make sense of one's life.

R. R. B.

CENSORSHIP *Dream formation takes place under the dominance of a censorship which prevents repressed wishes from achieving undisguised satisfaction. Through the censorship the meaning of the dream is distorted so that its significance is not clear to the dreamer. It is one aspect of the repressive trends which govern the ego.

J. A. Ber.

CHANCE What is usually considered as chance action – unintentional performances – prove, if psychoanalytical methods of investigation are applied to them, to have valid motives and to be determined by motions unknown to consciousness. This is not a definition of chance, but a definition of how psychoanalytic methods can significantly reduce the domain of chance in the field of human behaviour. It applies not only to the psychopathology of everyday life, but also to every unconscious derivative, particularly during the treatment.

See also: determinism

D. W.

CHAOS THEORY Chaos theory allows the representation of dynamic systems and their behaviour by mathematical formulas. The systems that have been usefully modelled by chaos theory include fluids (gases and liquids), magnetic activity, the earth's weather, and cardiac and brain electrophysiology.

These systems share a number of aspects, which together constitute central tenets of chaos theory. The first is a sensitive dependence on initial conditions, or the 'butterfly effect'; the outcome of the fluttering of a butterfly's wings in China is the production of atmospheric perturbations that result in a tornado in Texas. Psychic determinism implies an analogous sensitivity of the individual to the cumulative and multiplying effects of a lived history. The second is non-periodicity: large scale patterns of repetition (analogous to what analysts might call recognisable 'character') coexisting with an ultimate unpredictability. And the third is scaling: the appearance of embedded idiosyncratic patterns at various 'scales' or levels of magnification. One might see a patient's *neurosis within the theme of a life story (largest scale), within the theme of a dream (smaller scale), or a single *slip of the tongue (smallest scale). Chaos theory may eventually provide research models for psychoanalytic research.

See also: chaos and complexity theory (groups)

Spruiell, V. (1993) 'Deterministic chaos and the sciences of complexity: psychoanalysis in the midst of a general scientific revolution'. *Journal of the American Psychoanalytic Association* 41.

Mich. M.

CHAOS AND COMPLEXITY THEORY (GROUPS) The theories of chaos and complexity fall within the wider field of non-linear dynamics in the natural sciences and this wider field also includes theories of dissipative structures and synergetics. This field has been growing rapidly since the 1960s and is increasingly being taken up in sociology, psychology, political sciences and organisational theory. Chaos theory is a mathematical theory that explores the properties of non-linear, iterative equations, such as those that model the weather system. It demonstrates how deterministic laws can produce indeterminate outcomes over the long term because of the property of amplifying very small disturbances. It shows how apparently random movement does have pattern, which is paradoxically regular and irregular at the same time. Such patterns are known as mathematical chaos, strange attractors or fractal phenomena. The theories of dissipative structures and synergetics are concerned with phenomena operating far from equilibrium, in which state they encounter bifurcation points at which small fluctuations are amplified into symmetry-breaking changes yielding new patterns of behaviour – the phenomenon of 'order out of chaos'.

Complexity theory is primarily concerned with the computer modelling of interactions between very large numbers of agents, demonstrating how local self-organising interaction can yield emergent pattern in the absence of any global blueprint or programme.

Unpredictable novel patterns are shown to emerge 'at the edge of chaos', a paradoxical dynamic of stability and instability at the same time. This points to the intrinsic pattern-forming capacity of interaction itself. Some natural scientists question the scientific validity/usefulness of this work; others seem to regard these developments as extensions of traditional sciences; yet others talk about a paradigm shift amounting to a principle organising evolution that is more important than chance variations and natural selection and to the end of certainty.

Those taking the last named perspective call for a new dialogue with nature and a new science of qualities. Some apply these theories directly to human action seeing them as an extension of systems thinking; others use them as metaphors; and yet others regard them as a source domain for analogy with human behaviour. Taken as a source domain for analogy, the insights require interpretation through some theory of sociology and/or psychology. As analogies these sciences are of interest to a group analytic approach because of the centrality they accord to interaction.

Rubenfeld, S. (2001) 'Group therapy and complexity theory'. *International Journal of Group Psychotherapy* 51: 449–71.

Stacey, R. (2001) 'Complexity and group matrix'. *Group Analysis* 34(2): 221–39.

Stacey, R. (2003) *Complexity and Group Processes: A Radically Social Understanding of Individuals.* London: Brunner-Routledge.

M. P.

CHARACTER What we generally think of as our psychological makeup. It is based on the idea that humans have consistent ways of functioning over a broad range of areas and that these can be identified for any individual. It will be found in our overall functioning; psychoanalytically, character refers to a person's habitual mode of overcoming inner *conflict (or failure to do so) and the consequences this has for thinking, perceiving, and feeling about the world in addition to the way in which behaviour is expressed overtly.

D. K. S. / S. Byr.

CHARACTER DISORDER/PERSONALITY DISORDER The term personality disorder is used differently by different disciplines but essentially refers to enduring interpersonal dysfunction, often accompanied by behavioural disorders. Personality disorder is traditionally seen as distinct from mental illness, although many studies of individuals with personality disorder have shown that they also suffer from mood or anxiety disorders.

The concept of personality disorder has been criticised on a number of grounds. First, given the uncertainties of what constitutes a 'normal' personality, it is hard to apply conventional medical models so as to come up with a good definition of an abnormal personality. There is also considerable debate about the extent to which personality traits endure over time, and personality styles can change. Lastly the term personality disorder has been criticised because of its use as a shorthand pejorative label for patients who are difficult, and whom clinicians do not like. Despite these criticisms, there is some validity to the concept of personality disorder, for example some types can be validly, and repeatedly, described using diagnostic instruments. *The Diagnostic and Statistical Manual of Mental Disorders* fourth edition (*DSM-IV*) identified three main clusters of types of personality disorders: 'paranoid, flamboyant and avoidant'. Although the *DSM* has been criticised for emphasising behavioural criteria in diagnosing these disorders, nevertheless, the labels themselves demonstrate the interpersonal dysfunction which is characteristic of personality disorder.

Individuals with personality disorder on the paranoid spectrum tend to relate to others in mistrustful and suspicious ways. Individuals with avoidant personality disorders tend to withdraw from others, living rather solitary lives. The so-called flamboyant group have perhaps received more research attention. They include antisocial personality disorder, borderline disorder and narcissistic personality disorder. All these three personality disorders are characterised by significant difficulties in relating to others, either manifested as callous disregard for others' feelings (antisocial), intense conflicted and angry relationships with others (borderline) or grandiose egocentric relationships with others (narcissistic).

Some personality disorders are associated with frightening behavioural manifestations, including criminal lawbreaking and violence. It is for this reason that they have received most research attention in terms of diagnosis and management. Borderline personality disorder is associated with female gender, and coexisting mood disorders. There is considerable evidence that mild to moderate degrees of borderline personality disorder may be effectively treated with psychotherapy and judicious use of medication. *Narcissistic personality disorder may be buffered by the presence of social skills, intelligence and social advantage; its prevalence and management have been less well studied.

There is increasing evidence that personality disorder is a developmental condition, which is acquired during childhood as a result of the interaction between genetic vulnerability and adverse environmental experience. The genetic contribution relates primarily to temperament, and variations in individual reactivity to arousing stimuli. There may also be a genetic contribution to affect regulation, particularly in response to stress. Probably the greater influence however is environmental; replicated studies have shown that that early adverse childhood experience is associated with an increased risk of developing adult personality disorders, especially those associated with antisocial behaviour, or the borderline diagnosis.

The term 'personality disorder' should not be confused with the psychological concept of 'psychopathy', devised by Robert Hare. Psychopathy refers to a very specific constellation of interpersonal dysfunction which is characterised by extreme violence, and has only been well studied in highly selected criminal populations. Evidence does suggest however that there are degrees of personality disorder. Most clinicians and psychotherapists will tend to see individuals with mild to moderate degrees of personality disorder which may respond well to interpersonal psychotherapeutic techniques. For severe personality disorder, there is considerably less evidence about the efficacy of psychological intervention, especially if it is manifested by severe behavioural disturbance.

Amerian Psychiatric Association (1995) *Diagnostic and Statistical Manual of Mental Disorders*, (*DSM-IV*). Fourth edition. Washington, DC: American Psychiatric Association.

Lewis, G. and Appleby, L. (1988) 'Personality disorders: the patients psychiatrists dislike'. *British Journal of Psychiatry* 153: 44–9.

R. D.

Charcot, Jean Baptiste (1825–93) Charcot's contribution to psychoanalysis was primarily indirect. As medical mentor to Sigmund Freud, he had a crucial influence on the founder of psychoanalysis. He played a similar role for Pierre Janet, leader of the French school of depth psychology.

Charcot gradually shifted from general medicine to focus on the emerging speciality of neurology. His institute within the vast Salpêtrière hospice in Paris drew students from around the world. By the early 1880s, *hysteria and hypnotism came to occupy most of his attention. Here, he has been viewed, somewhat anachronistically, by Freud and his followers as a precursor of psychoanalysis.

For Charcot hysteria remained a disease of the nervous system, most often expressed by local disorders, e.g. muscle contractures and sensory anaesthesias, or by spectacular fits (*grande hystérie*) superficially resembling epilepsy. Early on Charcot had considered hysteria to be a characteristically female ailment.

But his mature formulation described a universal disorder found in both sexes, all ages, races and epochs. If Charcot eventually accepted hysteria's psychological nature, he nonetheless believed it would ultimately be localised in the cerebral cortex. Adopting the notion of disease 'by idea' or 'psychic paralysis', Charcot hypothesised that the hysteric expressed a recent traumatic episode in which the mind rather than the body had been wounded. Hysteria resulted from an involuntary mechanism of autosuggestion within the mind of the predisposed patient – a passenger involved in a railway accident who had suffered slight if any bodily injury or a working man apparently unharmed by a fall – were among the frequent victims.

Charcot used hypnotism in well-staged public lessons to demonstrate that all the signs of hysteria could be replicated by suggestions to hypnotised subjects. Hypnotism thus was equated with experimental or artificial hysteria. Unlike contemporaries, including Freud for a time, Charcot did not use hypnotism in treating patients for he considered it a potentially dangerous state and a purely experimental technique. As far as treatment, Charcot remained largely traditional in his use of chemical and physical remedies. So-called 'moral therapy' or reliance on the physician's powers of verbal persuasion and his authoritative presence was likewise a commonplace technique and not an anticipation of psychotherapy.

Nevertheless, psychoanalysts point to Charcot's expansion and legitimation of the hysteria diagnosis along with the notion of traumatic aetiology via unconscious psychological mechanisms as influential on Freud. Probably more decisive for the Viennese visitor during his brief period of several months' contact with the 'master of the Salpêtrière' was Freud's sudden appreciation of the key role non-organic conceptions and approaches might play in neuropathology, and the sheer inspiration that he derived from the charismatic role model he perceived in Charcot.

Freud began where Charcot left off with hysteria – going much deeper into the patient's life history and broadening the notion of trauma to emphasise early experiences, especially those involving sexuality, as indispensable causal factors in neurosis. Freud's anecdote that Charcot recognised necessary sexual aetiology finds scant confirmation in the Frenchman's writings.

Charcot, J. M. [1884] (1994) *Lectures on the Diseases of the Nervous System* [*Leçons sur les maladies du système nerveux*]. Translated by G. Sigerson. New York: Classics of Medicine Library.

Goetz, C. G., Bonduelle M. and Gelfand T. (1995) *Charcot. Constructing Neurology.* New York and London: Oxford University Press.

T. G.

CHILD ANALYSIS Melanie Klein was from the early 1920s among the pioneers of the psychoanalytic treatment of children. She believed that children were able to develop *transferences to the analyst, which were expressions of internal *object relations made up of the phantasies about them, characteristic of the *paranoid schizoid position. In that context she thought that the play and drawings of children could be interpreted just as in adult analysis the patient's dreams and free associations were the road to understanding the unconscious. Klein and Anna *Freud differed intensely about the transference in child analysis. The latter initially believed that young children's transferences were only to their parents. In contrast, Klein believed strongly that without attention to transferences stemming from internal phantasies projected and introjected, a successful analysis was not possible.

See also: child psychotherapy

Klein, M. (1975) *Love, Guilt and Reparation.* London: Hogarth Press.

J. V. B.

CHILDHOOD According to Freud, childhood is the period from birth to *latency (six to seven years), during which the *libido develops progressively from polymorphous perversity and *auto-erotism to object-love. This libidinal development coincides with a series of psychosexual conflicts, the most important of which is the *Oedipus complex, which conditions the advent of sexual identity.

See also: infantile sexuality

D. N.

CHILD PSYCHOTHERAPY PRECIS Psychotherapy with children and adolescents has developed substantially in the last fifty years from its early roots in psychoanalysis. There has been a parallel vigorous intellectual flowering of ideas. The interchange between this new profession and theories of child development and personality growth deriving from psychoanalysis and child psychology has proved fertile in extending clinical understanding and techniques.

Child psychotherapy is distinguished from adult psychoanalysis in particular by its necessary location within a broad context – of child health, of the child in the family and school context, of child psychotherapy as one of a range of professions concerned with the emotional health and well-being of children from early infancy to young adulthood. Multi-disciplinary collaboration is a pre-requisite for effective clinical intervention, as is careful attention to the family relationships of children and their parents. Current trainings generally include the following: experience of infant and child observation, to develop the skills of observation and self-observation which are the basis of psychoanalytic understanding; study of classical and contemporary psychoanalytic theory, with a special emphasis on the tradition of child analysis and the expanding literature of child psychotherapy; study of the child in the community context; supervised long-term psychotherapy of children and adolescents, both intensive (three to five times a week) and less intensive, and with parents; supervised broad clinical experience of assessment, short-term interventions, family work, and so on. Outstanding features of training are the emphasis on observation and the commitment to both thorough training in individual psychoanalytic work and the application of the psychoanalytic paradigm to family and community contexts. Consultation with nurseries, children's homes, and so on is often based on the use of a 'work discussion' model of training which can introduce relevant psychoanalytic concepts – transference, countertransference, infantile anxiety, primitive defences, containment – to other professionals, and thus help to sustain their work.

Theoretical developments have greatly extended the range of children who can be helped by psychotherapy. Among current debates influencing practice are the distinction that can be drawn between mental deficit and mental disturbances; the optimal balance between family-based and individual treatments; indications for long-term intensive psychotherapy; methods of initial exploration which are helpful in engaging difficult-to-treat patients; the use of infant observation in clinical intervention; effectiveness of time-limited therapies; models of early intervention. The single most important idea that has influenced clinical practice is Bion's formulation of a theory of containment, following Klein's discovery of the psychic mechanism of *projective identification. The clinical usefulness of the *container-contained model led to changes in technique which enabled child psychotherapists to treat severely deprived and traumatised children, including those who have been maltreated, and to develop methods of working with children with *autism and other *learning disabilities, and with *borderline and psychotic conditions in children and adolescents. Recently developed specialisms include work with gender identity disorders, eating disorders, and adolescent sexual abuse of younger children. The more traditional base for child psychotherapy interventions was with children's anxiety states, conduct disorders, psychosomatic problems and relationship difficulties, and it is interesting to note that, as the capability to treat more severe conditions has expanded, the referral of the more 'neurotic' children for therapy has diminished.

Current trends which tend to favour formal psychiatric diagnosis and brief behavioural interventions or medication are probably reducing the opportunity for many children to be considered for psychotherapeutically based treatment which could explore the meaning of their symptomatic behaviour within a broadly based understanding of their psychological development. This is particularly evident in the area of *attention deficit disorder, diagnoses which are now so prevalent. These conditions can usefully be linked to problems in early psychic containment, explored by *Bick in her work on 'second skin' phenomena. There is, fortunately, evidence of some growth in awareness that therapy which addresses the child's state of mind is usually needed alongside medication.

Child psychotherapy practice now encompasses a large range of treatment modalities based on the imaginative use of a psychoanalytic frame of reference. Brief interventions, particularly effective with parents and babies or pre-school children and with adolescents who eschew formal referral to mental health services, are widely in use. Skilled short-term intervention depends, however, on training in depth in the understanding of *transference and *countertransference phenomena, and is particularly supported by the grasp of non-verbal communication which is rooted in extensive observational experience. The specific contribution of child psychotherapists to the assessment of children in various contexts derives its distinctive qualities from attention to detail and the capacity to focus on what Bion called the *selected fact in the clinical encounter. *Group psychoanalytic psychotherapy with children is a relatively new growth area with potential both to help larger numbers of children and to provide therapy for some children who are resistant to individual approaches. Other significant specialisms include work with parents, which ranges from supportive casework to individual or couple psychoanalytic therapy, and school or college counselling, which is an example of work in the wider community for which child and adolescent psychotherapists are particularly well suited. Indirect work via consultation with foster parents, social workers, childcare staff in residential homes, and so on, is extensive.

As public awareness of, and interest in, child psychotherapy grows, the profession is extending itself to take account of social changes such as the multi-ethnic composition of modern cities and the forced migration of refugees; of research opportunities within a public health culture which demands that treatment is evidence-based; and of the need for and benefit of a wide range of writing and publication to support the international dissemination of ideas. The contradictory trends in health policy seem likely to leave continuing space for public provision of child psychotherapy since parents often seek treatment which deals with the child as a whole developing person, and many children, adolescents and parents respond to a model of therapy based on the growth of understanding of the mind and its depths.

See also: borderline psychosis (child); brief psychotherapy; deprived children; children, ill or dying; dyspraxia; eating disorders; groups (child and adolescent); infant observation; learning disabilities; outcome studies (child psychotherapy); psychosis (childhood); sexual abuse (child); sleep disorders (in children); trauma in chidren

Alvarez, A. (1992) *Live Company*. London and New York: Routledge.

International Journal of Infant Observation and its Applications. London: Tavistock Clinic Foundation/ Lawrence & Wishart.

Journal of Child Psychotherapy. London and New York: Routledge.

Lanyado, M. and Horne, A. (eds) (1999) *Handbook of Child and Adolescent Psychotherapy.* London and New York: Routledge.

Rustin, M. and Quagliata, E. (eds) (2000) *Assessment in Child Psychotherapy.* London: Tavistock/ Duckworth.

M. R.

CHILDREN, DEPRIVED see **DEPRIVED CHILDREN**

CHILDREN, ILL OR DYING (PSYCHOTHERAPY WITH) 'Illness', whether chronic or acute, whether the result of accident or long-term condition, affects the child in many different ways. Cognitive, cultural, medical, and socio-economic factors, age, the establishment of reliable 'inner parents', as well as the previous negotiation of traumas and losses, all influence the psychological impact and outcome. Serious illness disrupts the child's sense of continuity, security, and bodily intactness, and challenges infantile omnipotence and denial of death. Illness and possible death can push the child into a heightened awareness of these implications, or it can lead to a retreat behind denial. Some denial of the painful reality is a useful protection against being overwhelmed psychically, but if it is excessive and the child becomes emotionally frozen, their whole psychic functioning is impaired.

Research by Judd has shown that children are aware of what is happening to them and are therefore in need of adults who can help them to process the experience by hearing their concerns. Young children are less aware of the implications than are adolescents. The young child mainly fears separation from loved ones, and before the age of six may not have fully grasped all the other aspects of death, including irrevocability and universality, as Kane shows. The availability of parents who are not unduly traumatised is crucial to the child's capacity to process the experience. A child psychotherapist may be helpful in containing parents' anxieties so that they can bear the child's distress, or in working with the child, with the parents' permission, if the parents are absent or overwhelmed.

Adolescents facing a life-threatening illness have a more arduous task, because they are aware of the implications of the illness and the disruption to their developmental path towards independence. This awesome reality can either force them back to a more dependent pre-adolescent state of mind, where parents are resurrected as vital protectors, or push them into pseudo-independence and denial of the real situation. If the adolescent path has been securely achieved, they are less likely to resort to regression or omnipotent denial.

Since Robertson, there has been a more conscious awareness of the emotional and attachment needs of children in hospital. As paediatric staff may find it hard to acknowledge the child's distress, as Menzies Lyth says, a child psychotherapist is as much concerned with the medical team's functioning as with the child and his or her family.

In sequestered time, albeit adapted to a ward setting, a child psychotherapist can offer children necessary containment and understanding, less encumbered by an emphasis on 'cure'. If some of the child's emotions can be known, 'nameless dread' may be transformed into something more bearable.

Judd, D. (1995) *Give Sorrow Words: Working with a Dying Child.* Second edition. London: Whurr.

Kane, B. (1979) 'Children's concepts of death'. *Journal of Genetic Psychology* 134: 141–53.

Menzies Lyth, I. [1959] (1988) 'The functioning of social systems as a defence against anxiety' in *Containing Anxiety in Institutions.* London: Free Association Books.

Robertson, J. (1952) Film: *A Two-year-old Goes to Hospital.* London: Tavistock Child Development Research Unit.

D. J.

CHILDREN IN CARE Psychotherapy with this group of children is significantly influenced by two factors: firstly, the high level of neglect and of physical and sexual abuse; and secondly, the frequency with which children move through placements within the care system. Historically, these two factors meant that such children were often considered not to be suitable candidates for psychotherapy. Pioneering work carried out by members of the Fostering and Adoption workshop at the Tavistock Clinic published as

Psychotherapy with Severely Deprived Children in 1983 by Boston and Szur demonstrated that such work could be successful, though highly demanding of the therapists technically and emotionally. Henry describes a major feature of work with this population with her concept of 'double deprivation' whereby the defence mechanisms erected in order to protect against an initial trauma or series of events are of such magnitude that this leads to an impoverished ability to make use of new, potentially helpful relationships including that with the therapist. This difficulty is often compounded by the number of foster, adoptive, or residential placements these children experience. Indeed, there is a debate as to whether children without a solid, supportive external framework should be offered psychotherapy. (For an overview of the arguments, see Barrows.) Increasingly, child psychotherapists are selectively providing psychotherapy to children in care in transitional placements in recognition that this can help them to make better use of future placements and provide a space for thinking through children's current difficulties and what led to them. The consequences for the structuring of the internal world of children who have the experience of multiple moves and many carers is evocatively outlined in Rustin's paper 'Multiple Families in Mind'. This paper gives a lucid account of the therapeutic process with this particular patient group.

Barrows, P. (1996) 'Individual psychotherapy for children in foster care: possibilities and limitations'. *Clinical Child Psychology and Psychiatry* 1: 386–97.

Boston, M. and Szur, R. (eds) (1983) *Psychotherapy with Severely Deprived Children* London: Routledge & Kegan Paul. Reprinted. London: Karnac Books, 1990.

Henry, G. (1974) 'Doubly deprived'. *Journal of Child Psychotherapy* 7: 15–28.

Rustin, M. (1999) 'Multiple families in mind'. *Clinical Child Psychology and Psychiatry* 4: 51–62

H. C.

CHILE The pre-history begins in 1857 when Dr Manuel A. Carmona related biographical and clinical information regarding a girl who was declared 'the woman of Santiago possessed of the devil'. He suggested a mental space unknown to consciousness in which amorous and sexual desires are elaborated. As they cannot be expressed directly for fear of sin or punishment, they are converted into hysterical symptoms.

In 1925 Dr Fernando Allende Navarro returned to Chile after fifteen years in Europe. He analysed several Chilean medical leaders in the fields of psychiatry and neurology as well as some priests. This paved the way for the later flourishing of psychoanalysis with the arrival in Chile in the 1940s of Dr Ignacio *Matte Blanco from England. He was trained at the British Society of Psychoanalysis. On 3 August 1949 he became Titular Professor of Psychiatry of the University of Chile. In the same year the Chilean Psychoanalytical Association (CPA) was recognised by the International Psychoanalytical Association, initiating one of the most brilliant periods in Chilean psychoanalysis, which lasted until 1960. This period was marked by simultaneous progress in dynamic psychiatry, clinical psychology and psychoanalysis. Analysts held positions as professors of psychiatry and psychology at several universities. The Chilean Institute started with eleven candidates but soon doubled that number.

From 1960 there was a decline in the fortunes of Chilean psychoanalysis. Chairs of Psychoanalysis were lost in the universities. A Kleinian orientation, with the idea of preserving the purity of psychoanalysis through its isolation and an emphasis on technique, predominated. There followed twenty-five years of stagnation in growth and a reduction in scientific output. Later, the possibility of changing the statutes of the CPA permitted greater openness on theory, transparency in training and promotion, and a clear dependence of the Institute on the Association. As a result the number of analysts increased by more than one hundred percent. There was renewed interest in joining the CPA, and courses with more than ten candidates now begin every second year. In 1995 the Institute approved the training of child and adolescent analysts.

Since the nineties several groups akin to psychoanalysis have appeared: Lacanians of diverse origins, as well as psychoanalytically oriented institutions for psychotherapy. University qualified doctorates and masters programs have been created. This contributes to an atmosphere that is particularly stimulating for the development of psychoanalysis.

The 1999 International Congress of Psychoanalysis was held in Chile and one of the presidents of the International Psychoanalysis Association, Dr Otto Kernberg, was trained in Chile.

Gomberoff, M. (1998) 'Psychoanalysis in Chile'. *News Letter IPA International Psychoanalysis* 7 (2).

M. G.

China Writing in the 1920s in a period of significant social and political reform, Chinese intellectuals used Freudian notions of sexual tensions in families in calling for a change of attitude to the secrecy surrounding sex and to child education. But psychoanalytic practice in China has been slow to take root. This is because, it has been argued, there has been no tradition of expressiveness in the doctor-patient relationship, and the doctor in a traditional Chinese setting adopts an authoritarian attitude towards patients. Before World War II there was only one Chinese psychoanalyst, Bingham Dai, who trained under Harry Stack *Sullivan and taught psychotherapy in Peking from 1935–39.

With the political upheavals in the early years of the People's Republic of China, there were no analysts. Since 1995, the International Psychoanalytical Association has begun inviting Chinese professionals to its conferences and organising a subcommittee for Asia. The Chinese-German Academy for Psychotherapy, comprising analysts interested in and familiar with Chinese culture, has initiated a wide range of training programs covering different behavioural, systemic, and psychoanalytic trends. Dynamic psychotherapy is being practiced in a variety of psychiatric settings in Beijing, Shanghai and Wuhan, and a Chinese analyst trained in France recently founded a psychoanalytic centre in Chengdu. However, the range and complexity of Freud's ideas may not be fully appreciated until more of his works are translated, clinical psychology gets more firmly established, and the therapeutic context is expanded to encompass through education a range of treatments and the possibilities of the individual psychotherapeutic scheme.

Blowers, G. H. (1994) 'Freud in China: the variable reception of psychoanalysis' in G. Davidson (ed.) *Applying Psychology: Lessons from Asia-Oceania*. Carlton, Victoria: Australian Psychological Society, 35–49.

Dai, B. (1987) 'Psychoanalysis in China before the revolution' in R. Fine (ed.) *Psychoanalysis Around the World*. New York: Howarth Press.

Yuan, T. S. (2000) 'China in the history of psychoanalysis: a possible fate for psychoanalysis at the dawn of the millennium'. Paper read at the 8th International Meeting of the International Association for the History of Psychoanalysis. Versailles, 20–22 July 2000.

G. B.

---

choice of neurosis see **neurosis, choice of**

---

chum *Sullivan's name for the 'best friend'. The formation of this exclusive friendship marks the end of the juvenile era and the beginning of the pre-adolescent period. This need for intimacy occurs between the ages of eight and a half and ten. This friendship is very important in that it is the first time that a person wants to enhance the self-esteem of another as much as of themself. It is the first experience of being concerned about what matters to an equal and thus the beginning of a capacity for mature love. In this way, Sullivan sees it as a precursor to romantic love. The experience provides the opportunity to see oneself through another's eyes and thus a 'second chance' for previously *dissociated aspects of oneself to be brought into consciousness. It also allows one to see the peculiarities and limitations of one's parents. Peers, then, provide a great opportunity for growth. During this period 'two-groups' form larger groups or gangs and leadership patterns emerge. A supervisory pattern or aspect of the *self-system, a personification of imaginary people who are always with one evaluates what the child does, functioning in much the same way as the Freudian *super-ego.

Attachment theorists have suggested that the occurrence of such a friendship is more likely if a child were securely attached to the early caretaker. The importance of friends is neglected in much of psychoanalytic theory. Harris has also criticised the lack of attention to the role of peers in classical psychoanalytic and psychological theories.

Harris, J. R. (1998) *The Nurture Assumption*. New York: Free Press.

Sullivan, H. S. (1953) *The Interpersonal Theory of Psychiatry*. New York: Norton.

R. C.

CIVILISATION According to Freud, civilisation is a process in the service of *Eros, whose purpose is to combine single human individuals, families, races, peoples and nations into one great unity, the unity of mankind. Man's natural aggressive drive, the hostility of all against each, opposes the program of civilisation. Civilisation is the product of the achievements brought about through sublimation, education, and drive renunciation.

See also: culture; war

J. A. Ber.

CLASSIFICATION IN PSYCHIATRY Classification in psychiatry is the attempt to identify groups of patients similar in their clinical features, course of illness, outcome, and response to treatment. It serves as a means of facilitating communication among the professionals involved; as a basis for research; and, for offering a viable explanation to the patient. It lies at the heart of the medical approach to mental disorder. Always subject to revision, it represents a conceptual organisation of the spectrum of difficulties presented to psychiatrists by their patients, at a given time.

As in other branches of medicine, most recognised psychiatric classifications are categorical, rather than dimensional, attempting to demarcate groups of clinically distinct conditions, as opposed to conceptualising these as part of a spectrum.

Systematic attempts to classify mental disorder date from the 1960s, and after several revisions, the two most widely used classifications are the *International Classification of Diseases of the World Health Organisation*, tenth edition (*ICD 10*) Chapter V, and the *Diagnostic and Statistical Manual of Mental Disorders*, now in its fourth edition (*DSM IV*), of the American Psychiatric Association.

In each system, most of the syndromes are characterised by presenting symptoms and signs, rather than aetiology, thus purporting to be basically descriptive and atheoretical, and hence uncommitted to any specific theories regarding the origins of mental disorder. Recent critiques, however, have focused on the unacknowledged evaluative elements in this approach. Neither classification systematically addresses the relationships among the concepts of 'disorder', 'diagnosis', 'disease' and 'illness'. The historically influential distinction between the concepts of 'psychotic' and 'neurotic' are no longer an organising principle of these classifications, although some *ICD 10* descriptions incorporate these terms in a purely descriptive sense: psychotic being used to mean lack of insight with delusions, hallucinations or a limited number of markedly abnormal behaviours; and, neurotic, although not defined, linked with stress-related and somatoform disorders.

The major categories in each system, allowing for minor differences in terminology, are: organic disorders; psycho-active substance-related disorders; schizophrenia and related disorders; mood (affective) disorders; anxiety, somatoform and other 'neurotic' disorders; behavioural syndromes (including eating disorders); personality disorder; disorders of childhood and adolescence; and, mental retardation.

The demarcation in *ICD 10* of 'organic disorders', referring principally to forms of delirium and the dementias, departs from the general atheoretical approach, and is not to imply that the aetiology of other disorders has no organic component, but underlines the basis of 'organic' disorders in their demonstrable aetiology in terms of cerebral dysfunction.

Characteristic disadvantages of psychiatric classifications include labelling; creating the illusion of 'entities' by imposing a framework on what in fact are complex and overlapping phenomena; ignoring or obscuring problems of more importance for a given patient; demonstrating the reliability and validity of the putative categories; failure to address a basic controversy over the very concept of mental disorder; and, an emphasis on information based almost entirely on the clinician's judgement, and drawn from a restrictive domain of the patient's experience.

In addition, specific problems with the *ICD 10* and *DSM IV* include, firstly, an over-inclusiveness and overlap among the categories and, secondly, the (largely) atheoretical approach means they draw little on the basic neurosciences, social sciences or schools of psychology and psychoanalysis, and hence have few links with any recent developments in these fields.

Fulford, W. K. M. (1990) *Moral Theory and Medical Practice*. Oxford: Oxford University Press.

Radden, J. (1994) 'Recent criticisms of psychiatric nosology: a review'. *Philosophy, Psychiatry & Psychology* 2: 143–200. Baltimore: Johns Hopkins University Press.

C. V.

CLOACAL THEORY Children may make no real distinction between the vagina and the anus and thus believe that babies are delivered through the bowels like faeces. Cloacal theory also means that women are not castrated, intercourse takes place through the anus so a woman may still possess a penis.

See also: castration; penis envy

J. A. Ber.

COLLECTIVE UNCONSCIOUS see **UNCONSCIOUS COLLECTIVE**

COMBINATORY A combinatorial structure is present in Lacan's work from the early 1950s. The subject's determination by the *signifier is given by the signifying constellation that presided over his entry into the world, and by a certain number of places on the chessboard of his destiny, onto which these signifiers can be moved.

See also: automatism

N. C.

COMEDY There is no theory of comedy in Freud: still, there is the comic, of which Freud studies several genres (naivety; gesture; situation; caricature; joke; nonsense; parody). He approaches it through its difference from the witticism, which is linguistic and according to Lacan linked to the unconscious. Whereas the comic doesn't exist in the unconscious, it is the result of a difference of expenditure between another's gesture, exaggerated action (or some attenuated psychic production) and myself. The other is saved from expenditure, which I make up for by the discharge of my laughter. The comic is then according to Freud 'the economy of the expenditure (or investment) of representation'. You would suppose then that the comic would enter into comedy, but Freud interests himself only in tragedy, which is open to catharsis.

For Lacan, comedy makes us rediscover what Freud in his book on jokes showed was present in the practices of 'nonsense' and loss. Its effect depends on the presence of the phallus at its centre, which, in its function as the signifier of loss, establishes the connection with tragedy.

See also: wit

F. R.

COMMUNICATION According to Winnicott, this is the ability of the infant to present his experience to the mother by largely non-verbal means and to receive from her in return, with the proviso that this presentation is inevitably partial and the essential self would remain in some vital way incommunicable. The unknowability of all unconscious process in human intercourse is adhered to in this model and kept sacrosanct, and the fragility and delicacy of such relations between the self and the other is maintained.

Phillips, A. (1988) *Winnicott*. Fontana Modern Masters. F. Kermode (ed.). London: Fontana Press.
Winnicott, D. W. (1963) 'Communicating and not communicating leading to a study of certain opposites' in *The Maturational Processes and the Facilitating Environment*. London: Karnac Books.

H. T. R.

COMPENSATORY AND DEFENSIVE STRUCTURES According to *self psychology compensatory structures are complex psychological configurations which are an integral part of the overall self or personality of an individual. They, by definition, compensate or make up for some primary structural deficits in the self, and they do so by vitalising another structure. Thus when either the *mirroring or *idealising or twinship/alterego sectors of the self are deficient or poorly developed, another sector of these becomes the dominating force in the self functioning of the person. The deficiencies derive from early childhood failures in *selfobject experiences and thus in self development. The compensatory structures derive from the more successful selfobject relationship. Compensatory structures are to be distinguished from defensive structures in that the latter are serviceable but function solely to protect the self from further injury. Compensatory structures, on the other hand, become more or less independent of their original purpose and perform in a gratifying and vitalising manner, i.e. they become the primary orientation of the self. In this manner, they leave behind the frailty of the original structural deficit which then, in this context, becomes impervious to analytic intervention. Thus, in contrast to a defensive structure which can and should be analysed to reach and repair a structural deficit which it protects, compensatory structures no longer can or should be analysed to discover the underlying deficit. In this manner, compensatory structures can be said to fill in the deficit, while defensive structures cover it over. It is often the case that a successful analysis is one that allows for the fuller development and strengthening of a compensatory structure. One cannot and should not attempt to determine or direct how such an analysis should proceed, inasmuch as self development remains a multi-potential process that picks and chooses among available selfobjects.

See also: transferences, forward and trailing edge

A. I. G.

COMPLEX (FREUD) A nexus of unconscious and conscious ideas, feelings, emotions and symptoms acquired from the object relations of early childhood experience that continue to dictate patterns of behaviour in adulthood. Although the term is more readily welcomed within *analytical psychology it continues to have descriptive currency in classical and contemporary psychoanalysis, such as when it is used to refer to an Oedipus or castration complex.

Some commentators have noted that exclusive use of the term with a pathological connotation ignores the structuring function of complexes. The predominance of the pathological sense of the term probably derives from the fact that complexes are often repressed and in conflict with other conscious goals. Though the term is still popular in common psychological parlance Freud expressed misgivings about using it on the basis that it could engender a reductive typology and might serve to obscure the idiosyncratic nature of the individual.

S. Byr.

COMPLEX (JUNG) Jung distinguished two levels of the *unconscious: the personal unconscious and the *collective unconscious. Through his word association experiments, Jung noted the tendency to associate ideas around certain basic nuclei; he named these affectively toned associated ideas the complexes. The nucleus has an energic value that serves as a psychological magnet by attracting ideas in proportion to its *energy. The nucleus is determined by an impersonal and a personal factor. The impersonal core is an *archetype. The personal aspect of the nucleus is determined by a person's actual experiences and modes of reactions. The aetiology of a complex usually has to do with a trauma, an emotional shock that splits the psyche into compartments.

Complexes have their own energy and behave fundamentally the same as personality fragments, as if they have a consciousness of their own. Since a complex is relatively autonomous, its associated ideas and affects pass in and out of consciousness in an uncontrollable manner. The complex can take over aspects of functioning that normally belong to the ego. For example, the vocal chords are an aspect of the voluntary musculature under the control of the ego. However, when a complex is constellated its energy may supersede that of the ego, and the complex takes over the vocal chords and speaks. An example would be a *parapraxis.

One may say that a person has a complex, but in reality a complex usually has a person. A complex can force feelings and thoughts upon the individual, who then is preoccupied or behaves in an unconscious manner. Rather than experience feeling out of control, persons and groups may sometimes take responsibility for the complex and rationalise what the complex has done, i.e. claim and rationalise the complex behaviour as their own.

Jacobi, J. (1965) *Complex/Archetype/Symbol in the Psychology of C. G. Jung*. Princeton: Princeton University Press.

Jung, C. G. (1948) 'A review of the complex theory' in *Collected Works*, Vol. 8. Princeton: Princeton University Press.

W. S.

COMPLEX (LACAN) Complexes, for Freud, are groups of representations, memories and *affects, mainly unconscious. Lacan first accorded a major role to complexes in the constitution of the subject ('Family Complexes' including the weaning complex, intrusion complex and mirror-stage, and the Oedipus complex). Later, like Freud, he restricted the use of the term to the Oedipus and castration complexes. For Lacan the Oedipus complex is the frame of the inscription of the subject in the Symbolic order; later in his work, he viewed it as a 'Freudian myth' and situated the foundation of the subject 'beyond the Oedipus'. Building on Freud's work, he made the castration complex the central operator of sexuation.

M. Eyd.

COMPLIANCE For Winnicott, the pressure on the self to fall in with a given mode or way of being, usually, for the infant, that which is necessitated by the mother. Through a process of impingement by the mother the self adopts a false persona ('false' as opposed to *true self) which is at the expense of the personal way of life and an ill or compliant way of functioning comes into being. A sense of futility and hopelessness characterises this compliant existence. Again, this way of functioning may be understood as the self representing in fantasy a restricted and rigid aspect of object relating which requires the help of the analyst to resolve.

See also: false self; impingement

Winnicott, D. W. (1965) 'Morals and development' in *The Maturational Processes and the Facilitating Environment*. London: Karnac Books.

H. T. R.

COMPONENT Freud uses this term to indicate any process in the organism that leads to the *excitation present in the sexual drive. Usually he uses it in a slightly restricted sense to refer to the (component) partial drives in respect of their separate functioning before a unity is imposed on them by a *form of organisation of the drive and this has become the norm. It can be argued that Freud's very general sense of 'component' is lost sight of by Strachey when he chooses to translate 'partial drive' by 'component instinct', thereby losing the notion of the structure and mutability of the drive, while simultaneously relegating 'component' to refer only to the partial drive.

See also: partial drive

B. B.

COMPROMISE FORMATION A compromise formation is the result of an attempt to creatively resolve conflict generated by competing demands. The resulting compromise, which may manifest as a symptom, an inhibition, a character trait, and so on, is an attempt to partially satisfy the demands made either by competing tendencies, for example, super-ego restrictions versus drives, inclinations defined by opposing tendencies (e.g. passive/active, hetero/homosexual), or the need to adapt to the realities and expectations of the external world. For example, an unconscious wish may become sufficiently transformed by repressing forces as to be permitted into consciousness and permitted a degree of gratification, but only in an attenuated and unrecognisable form. In this way, a degree of satisfaction is permitted both the repressed as well as the repressing elements. A compromise formation can be a fleeting solution or an enduring aspect of *character or behaviour.

See also: defence

R. T.

COMPULSION The expression of peremptory, repetitive, typically unwanted urges that are usually experienced as driven and uncontrollable (e.g. compulsive handwashing, gambling, masturbation) and are presumed to stem from sexual and/or aggressive conflicts.

See also: drive for mastery

Freud, S. (1907) *Obsessive Actions and Religious Practices*. S. E. 12. London: Hogarth Press.

D. Wol.

COMPULSION (LACAN) An internal and pressing force by which the subject feels driven to act or think in a certain way. It is the most radical characteristic of the drive, taking the form of the compulsion to repeat. It is a necessary modality of psychical functioning. Clinically it is found extensively in the symptomatology of obsessional neurosis.

A. I.

CONCERN For Winnicott the capacity for concern is also the inverse of the capacity for *guilt and is the individual's ability to care or to mind, to feel, and to accept and take responsibility. It is also the basis of all constructive work and play. It is only possible when the infant has recognised the mother as a whole or established unit. Klein's *depressive position or depressive anxiety differs from the capacity for concern in that the phantasied destruction of the maternal object develops into the wish for *reparation, none of which takes place in the formulation of Winnicott.

Winnicott, D. W. (1984) 'The Development of the Capacity for Concern' in *Deprivation and Delinquency*. London: Routledge.
Laplanche, J. and Pontalis, J.-B. (eds) (1980) *The Language of Psychoanalysis*. London: Hogarth Press and Institute of Psycho-Analysis.

H. T. R.

CONCRETISATION A key concept in *intersubjectivity theory, concretisation is the process in which organisations of emotional experience are encapsulated in concrete, sensorimotor symbols. By casting emotional themes in powerful sensorimotor imagery, concretisation dramatises the central organising structures of a person's subjective life. The concretisation process underlies such phenomena as dreams, fantasies, symbolic objects, enactments, neurotic symptoms, delusions, and hallucinations.

R. S.

CONDENSATION First described by Freud in The *Interpretation of Dreams*, condensation is one of the essential mechanisms in dream work and in the functioning of unconscious processes through which several underlying ideas, themes or images are merged into, and then represented by, a single overt dream image or idea. This process, within thinking, is also seen in the formation of *symptoms, *slips, jokes and *transference.

For Lacan condensation is one of two primary processes; its mechanism is similar to the poetic function of *metaphor. One signifier comes to be substituted for or, better, superimposed upon another thus producing a novel sense or meaning. The condensation of dream images indicates their function as signifiers rather than images.

P. L. / A. I.

CONDENSER PHENOMENA A term used in *group analysis to describe a certain discharge of primitive material following the pooling of associated ideas in the group. It is a useful explanatory mechanism for understanding intense emotional outbursts in groups. It is as if the 'collective' unconscious acted as a condenser covertly storing up emotional charges generated by the group, and discharging them under the stimulus of some shared group event.

Foulkes, S. H., Anthony, E. J. (1957) *Group Psychotherapy: The Psychoanalytical Approach*. Harmondsworth: Penguin. Reprinted London: Karnac Books, 1984.

M. P.

CONFLICT/INTRAPSYCHIC CONFLICT Conflict confronts the individual with the impossible task of fully satisfying all of the experienced wishes, needs, restrictions, many of which are in opposition to one another. Conflict may occur between passive and active inclinations, by competing demands between say, sexual urges versus the demands of a strict *super-ego. An attempt to resolve conflict often results in *compromise formation.

The threatened emergence of memories associated with painful, even traumatic affects, as well as the emergence of repressed drive derivatives (childhood fantasies, impulses and wishes) creates conflict and sets in motion defensive attempts to keep such memories out of conscious awareness and to keep such drives from being gratified. Conflict often gives rise to *anxiety, *guilt, *shame, and other affects that motivate defensive action. The signal that sets the defences in motion was called signal anxiety by Freud.

See also: ambivalence; anxiety, signal; active/passive; defence

R. T.

CONSCIOUS (FREUD) At first Freud defined consciousness as a mental system characterised by awareness. Later he saw it as a quality of mental life rather than a system. Consciousness consisted of whatever the person was currently attending to and subjectively aware of. This could be an internal fantasy or affect. It could also be, for example, external sounds or lights and could change from moment to moment. *Rapaport and Shevrin developed these conceptions.

See also: attention; preconscious; topography; unconscious

Freud, S. (1900) *The Interpretation of Dreams.* S. E. 4. London: Hogarth Press.

Freud, S. (1923) *The Ego and the Id.* S. E. 19. London: Hogarth Press.

Shevrin, H. (1998) 'The Freud-Rapaport Theory of Consciousness' in R. F. Bornstein and J. M. Masling (eds) *Empirical Perspectives on the Psychoanalytic Unconscious.* Washington, DC: American Psychiatric Press.

J. Wei.

CONSCIOUS (JUNG) For Jung, consciousness is the mode of perception and action associated with the ego (complex). Consciousness exists when sensations and memories are associated with one another in conjunction with an embodied sense of oneself, the 'I', as the agent of behaviour. Jung did not propose an explicit theory of the origins of consciousness, but his reflections on consciousness began with his general theory of the complex that formed the foundation for his system of analytical psychology. Within the theory of the complex, the ego complex is most directly associated with the experiences of bodily and temporal continuity. To the extent that consciousness is an attribute of the ego complex, the complex often misconstrues its place in the overall psychic economy insofar as the other complexes and the archetypes are by definition unconscious. The individual's sense of agency may therefore be undermined as unconscious complexes or archetypes become active and disrupt the conscious intentions of the ego complex. By the same token, psychological development requires that the ego complex become increasingly conscious of the workings of the other complexes and archetypes leading to a more balanced and complete view of the psyche's world. In developing this point of view, Jung rejected much of Freud's theory where consciousness is in need of such defence mechanisms as the censorship of dreams. While Jung accepted the notion that some conscious contents could be forced out of consciousness by repression, this applied only to the ego complex. The rest of the psyche's contents – the complexes and archetypes – could be said to be unconscious because consciousness is not one of their attributes. Pathologies thus arise because the ego complex is unable or unwilling to recognise, i.e. be conscious of, the workings of psychic elements outside its limited range of experience or, in less common circumstances, when the ego complex itself is fragmented, each fragment carrying with it its own conscious element.

Jung, C. G. (1971) 'Definitions' in *Collected Works*, Vol. 6. Princeton: Princeton University Press.

G. H.

CONSCIOUS (LACAN) For Lacan, following Freud, consciousness is a pure, reflective, surface phenomenon. Consciousness becomes an epiphenomenon when responsibility and the question of freedom, the attributes traditionally associated with consciousness, are removed by psychoanalysis to the domain of the subject of the unconscious and desire. As Lacan topologises the Freudian schemas, the latter's perception-consciousness system becomes elaborated through the topological structure of the Klein Bottle, by means of which 'unmediated' perception and symbolised attention are identified.

Lacan by this means gives a structural resolution of some of the problems of consciousness that Freud built into his first *topography.

See also: topology

G. S.

CONSTRUCTION Refers to the analyst's task of laying before an analysand a piece of his early history that he has forgotten. A construction attempts a broader and historical picture of the patient's early life than an interpretation which applies to a specific and more current element (e.g. an association). The patient's production of new memories would tend to support the validity of the construction.

See also: interpretation; memory

Freud, S. (1937) *Construction in Analysis*. S. E. 23. London: Hogarth Press.

M. Eag.

CONTACT BARRIER Freud used this term to describe a neurophysiological synapse. Bion borrowed it to designate a structure that has both the functions of contact and of barrier. It is formed through the articulation of alpha elements that cohere as they proliferate. It is in a continuous process of formation and marks both the point of contact and separation between conscious and unconscious elements. They may cohere or agglomerate; be ordered sequentially as a narrative, as it happens in a dream; or, be ordered logically or geometrically. The contact barrier has the function of a semi-permeable membrane. It impedes phantasies from being overwhelmed by realistic facts and also protects contact with reality from being disturbed by emotions coming from inside. It acts as an articulating *caesura that makes thinking and communication possible.

Bion, W. R. (1962) *Learning from Experience*. London: Heinemann.

Freud, S. [1895] (1950) *Project for a Scientific Psychology*. S. E. 6. London: Hogarth Press.

L. P. C.

CONTAINER-CONTAINED Describes a relationship on a model of a container with receptive qualities and a content with a penetrating quality. Significantly, Bion uses for this model the masculine and feminine signs (♂♀), which have the characteristics of an abstraction but also contain the common matrix of the emotional experience from which they emerge. This model also emerges as a way of conceptualising the relation between *projective identification by the baby, a content with a capacity of penetration, and mother's reverie, a container with a receptive quality. This is also his model of the origin of thinking.

According to the quality of the emotion that impregnates the container, the relationship 'container-contained' can promote development or impede it. If it is impregnated by envy, container and contained are stripped of their essential qualities, meaning, and vitality. This relationship is the antithesis of growth. Bion represents an emotion that denudes the relation with the sign minus −(♂♀). This contrasts with a relationship towards growth represented by: +(♂♀). The main difference between them is that the latter has the possibility of a development based on tolerance of doubt and of a sense of the infinite. The −(♂♀) relationship leads to deterioration. When the psychotic part of the personality is dominated by −(♂♀), an omniscient *super-ego opposed to learning from experience takes the place of reverie.

Bion describes three basic types of container-contained relationships:

1) In a symbiotic container-contained relationship two get together to their mutual advantage and/or for the benefit of a third party. Projective identification is used in a communicative way and is detoxified by the container and transformed into meaning; thus it can become a *preconception open to new meanings.

2) In terms of groups, it is the establishment in a symbiotic relation with the messianic idea that carries out the container function, which detoxifies and attenuates the disruptive quality of the new idea, so that as a nutrient it can be accessible to the group that lacks the qualities of the genius. These characteristics of the relationship are growth factors.

3) In the commensal relationship, container-contained live together side by side to the mutual benefit of both. The *caesura is wide, thus no conflict ensues. The parasitic relationship between container and content is mutually destructive. Projective identification is explosive and destructive of the container. The container also is destructive of the content. The container denudes the contained of its quality of penetration, and the content denudes the container of its receptive quality.

Bion, W. R. (1962) *Learning from Experience*. London: Heinemann.

Bion, W. R. (1970) *Attention and Interpretation*. London: Tavistock.

L. P. C.

CONTEXTUALISM This broad-based philosophy of psychoanalytic practice evolved from the formulations of *intersubjective systems theory. It calls for relentless attentiveness to context – here-and-now-relational, developmental, cultural-historical, and so on – in the effort to grasp the meanings of personal experiencing. Such attentiveness to context, and to the differing perspectives that develop from different contexts, gives rise to a fallibilistic attitude toward the understandings achieved in the psychoanalytic situation.

Orange, D. M., Atwood, G. E. and Stolorow, R. D. (1997) *Working Intersubjectively: Contextualism in Psychoanalytic Practice*. Hillsdale, NJ: The Analytic Press.

Stolorow, R. D., Atwood, G. E. and Orange, D. M. (2002) *Experience: Interweaving Philosophical and Clinical Dimensions in Psychoanalysis*. New York: Basic Books.

R. S.

CONTIGUITY On the one hand, the notion of contiguity refers to the relation of proximity, of closeness, between signifiers. In this sense contiguity gives a real *topological structure to the synchronic organisation of the unconscious 'structured like a language'. On the other hand it refers to the mathematical continuum and to the problems of the *infinite that Lacan draws on to formulate questions of *jouissance and love.

N. C.

CONTROVERSIAL DISCUSSIONS This commonly used term describes a series of controversies in Britain between 1941 and 1945 relating to the theory, practice and teaching of psychoanalysis. The Discussions could be conceptualised in traditional British terms as a cricket match: *Klein, Isaacs, Riviere and Co. batting for the Kleinians; Anna *Freud, Glover, Schmideberg and Viennese psychoanalysts who had recently fled from the Nazis batting for the Freudians.

However, it was much more complicated and not at all gentlemanly. Some key players such as Brierley and *Sharpe occupied the middle ground between the two warring factions. Those who supported this view subsequently coalesced into what is now known as the Independent group of the British Psychoanalytical Society.

During the Discussions passions ran so high that one argument continued in the midst of an air raid. However, this 'war' produced debate of a high order and some classic papers were written as ammunition, the most well-known being 'The Nature and Function of Phantasy' by Isaacs. Perhaps the most important topics raised in the Discussions were the *unconscious, *phantasy and *developmental theory. There were (and still are) implications for practice and technique as a result of differing conceptualisations of these key ideas.

The heat generated by the Controversial Discussions was, to use a Freudian term, overdetermined. During 1942–3 salvoes were fired in the form of memoranda on technique. This argument concerned the future teaching of psychoanalysis. Glover's initial memorandum provoked sharply differing responses. Thus Brierley argued for a clear definition of the technique of psychoanalysis, whereas Sharpe maintained that technique is not taught, rather that each practitioner gradually evolves their own individual approach.

*Another reading of the Controversial Discussions suggests that they were an argument about how the British Psychoanalytical Society should relate to the outside world, for example, the British Medical Association. For some thirty years Glover and *Jones had occupied key positions on the most influential committees of the Society and, not surprisingly, many thought it was time for a change.

A 'gentlemen's' agreement was eventually signed by three women: Klein, Freud and Payne. Each faction was allowed to teach their own trainees with a minimal amount of influence by those from the other groupings.

This whole episode in the history of the British Psychoanalytical Society had a profound and lasting effect. Thus, to this day, the structure of the Society, and its approach to theory, practice and teaching, is resonant with echoes from this period.

See also: Great Britain

King, P. and Steiner, R. (eds) (1991) *The Freud-Klein Controversies 1941–45*. London: Routledge.

K. H.

CONVERSION In *hysteria, an unconscious sexual wish is replaced by a seemingly physical symptom (paralysis, hysterical blindness). However, there is no organic involvement. Such symptoms do not follow neural or anatomical pathways, but symbolically represent and defend against underlying wishes. Fairbairn studied somatic expression of emotional difficulty, following *Charcot, Janet and Freud. He concluded that mental conflict, expressed in terms of internal object relations conflict, was converted into bodily expression, thereby substituting a bodily problem for an emotional one. These conversions into bodily form, based on happenstance of vulnerability, meaning in relations between parent and child, and matters of symbolisation, generally represented irreconcilable conflict between relations to the exciting object and the rejecting object, brought on by the parent's rapid alternation between excitement and rejection of the child. Fairbairn also wrote that the Freudian psychosexual stage theory of development and pathology itself represented a conversion reaction in theory, mistaking the oral, anal and genital zones as models for mental development and difficulty. Instead, he thought, these regions of the body were particularly liable to lending themselves as staging areas for emotional issues, but that they were chosen out of similarity to the mental attitude that came first. However, he noted, any area of the body (skin, ears, hair, internal organs) can be used to stage mental issues, based on relational circumstance, organ vulnerability and matters of symbolisation.

Fairbairn, W. R. D. [1954] (1994) 'The nature of hysterical states' in D. E. Scharff and E. F. Birtles (eds) *From Instinct to Self: Selected Papers of W. R. D. Fairbairn*, Vol. 1. Northvale, NJ: Jason Aronson, 13–40.

J. A. Ber. / D. E. S.

CORRECTIVE EMOTIONAL FAMILY EXPERIENCE Based on *Alexander's concept of 'corrective emotional experience' according to which psychoanalysis provides a superior emotional environment for the patient to develop, Grotjahn extended this to the group therapy situation. Persons recapitulate disturbed family developmental processes and are able to recognise and to transcend them in a therapy group that works towards more adaptive norms.

Pines, M. (1990) 'Group analysis and the corrective emotional experience: is it relevant?' *Psychoanalytic Enquiry* 10(3): 389–408.
Grotjahn, M. (1977) *The Art and Technique of Analytic Group Therapy*. New York: Jason Aaronson Inc.

M. P.

CORRECTIVE SELFOBJECT RELATIONSHIP The concept of the corrective *selfobject relationship, introduced by Bacal, identifies the central factor in psychoanalytic treatment as selfobject experience that occurs within a particular kind of relationship. The patient's transference of needs that arise from injuries to the self sustained in prior relationships puts the analyst in the role of needed selfobject. The responsiveness of the analyst that is optimal to those needs will not only constitute selfobject experience; it will promote the experience of a different and, therefore, 'corrective' selfobject relationship insofar as the patient starts to expect responsiveness from the analyst that is specific to the complexity of his particular therapeutic needs (see *selfobject relationship and *specificity theory). When the patient experiences a sense of self (or relational) disruption in consequence of the perceived failure of the analyst's therapeutic responsiveness, the analyst's task will be to facilitate an optimal interaction through which both parties may discover what went wrong, and why. The experience of successfully working through this will restore the disrupted selfobject relationship and strengthen the patient's sense of efficacy and trust. Insofar as the successful negotiation of this process may be quite different from the patient's prior experience it can, of itself, constitute a significant corrective selfobject experience. Thus, a corrective selfobject relationship entails the internalisation of the analyst as a selfobject who is able and ready both to respond appropriately to the patient's progressive strivings and sufficiently strong and resilient to remain steady and understanding in the face of the patient's negative reactions to the analyst's failures to meet his expectations.

Bacal, H. A. (1990) 'The Elements of a Corrective Selfobject Experience'. *Psychoanalytic Inquiry* 10.
Bacal, H., and Newman, K. (1990) *Theories of Object Relations: Bridges to Self Psychology*. New York: Columbia University Press.

H. B.

COUNTERTRANSFERENCE The subjective experiences arising in the analyst as a consequence of her engagement in the analytic process. While historically there was much controversy over the sources of these subjective reactions, over time a consensus has developed that countertransference experiences are best understood as *compromise formations between a number of forces that impinge on the mind of the analyst. These include the analyst's perceptions and understanding of the patient, the projections and covert messages contained in the patient's communications, and the memories, phantasies and conflicts aroused in the analyst by these communications.

Heimann, P. (1950) 'On counter-transference'. *International Journal of Psychoanalysis* 31: 81–4.
Reich, A. (1951) 'On countertransference'. *International Journal of Psychoanalysis* 32: 25–31.

T. J. J.

COUNTERTRANSFERENCE (JUNG) Jung was, arguably, the first psychoanalyst to emphasise the positive value of countertransference in psychotherapy. He early on followed the standard perspective on countertransference, stating that analysts, like surgeons, must have 'clean hands' so as not to infect patients with their own unconscious reactions. He therefore recommended that future analysts have personal analysis ('training analysis') before practising, an idea Freud seconded. However, Jung moved beyond the issue of the analyst's 'neurotic' reactions to also view countertransference as induced, inevitable, and 'a highly important organ of information'.

According to Jung, the analyst 'literally 'takes over' the sufferings of his patient and shares them with him'; hence the analyst's personality becomes the primary instrument of cure and countertransference, broadly defined, the central factor in treatment. Modern-day Jungians have extended and specified Jung's 1929 idea that the analyst is 'as much "in the analysis" as the patient' through micro-study of countertransference and of what Jung called the 'reciprocal influence' of patient and analyst. Countertransference-oriented concepts from psychoanalysts like *Racker, *Bion, *Winnicott, Langs, *Searles, and others – projective and introjective identification, fusion and therapeutic symbiosis, therapeutic 'frame' issues – have been important to many Jungian analysts. Jungians combine these with traditional Jungian concepts like archetypes (the 'wounded healer'); synchronicity (parallel chaining of unconscious associations and emotions in analyst and patient, apparently mediated by an overarching Self); and alchemical imagery to describe transformative processes taking place at a deep, unconscious level. All these models enable contemporary Jungian analysts to follow Jung's insistence on – indeed, prescription for – the value of countertransference: 'A good half of every treatment that probes at all deeply consists of the doctor examining himself.'

Jung, C. G. (1954) 'The practice of psychotherapy' in *The Collected Works*, Vol. 16. Princeton: Princeton University Press.

D. Sed.

COUNTERTRANSFERENCE (SELF PSYCHOLOGY)
*Kohut initially described what he regarded as typical reactions of the analyst to specific 'narcissistic' transferences. Later, Wolf reframed these in terms of typical 'selfobject' *countertransferences. Generally, however, self psychologists such as Fosshage do not subscribe to narrow definitions of countertransference. Bacal and Thomson suggest that the analyst's self is ordinarily sustained in his work – consciously and unconsciously – by ongoing responses of the analysand (some of which are intrinsic to the analytic frame itself, such as the patient's attending the treatment session, paying the analyst's fee, co-operating with the task of the analysis, etc., as well as specific responses) that evoke selfobject experience in the analyst. They aver that the analyst's therapeutic function may be substantially interfered with, that is, that countertransference reactions may occur when the analyst's needs are significantly frustrated.

See also: narcissism

Bacal, H. A. and Thomson, P. G. (1996) 'The psychoanalyst's selfobject needs and the evect of their frustration on the treatment: a new view of countertransference' in A. Goldberg (ed.) *Basic Ideas Reconsidered: Progress in Self Psychology*, Vol. 12. Hillsdale, NJ: The Analytic Press, 17–35.
Fosshage, J. (1995) 'Countertransference as the analyst's experience of the analysand: the influence of listening perspectives'. *Psychoanalytic Psychology* 12(3): 375–91.
Kohut, H. (1971) *The Analysis of the Self.* New York: International Universities Press.
Wolf, E. (1979) 'Transference and countertransference in the analysis of the disorders of the self'. *Contemporary Psychoanalysis* 15: 577–94.

H. B.

COUNTERTRANSFERENCE (WINNICOTT)
Winnicott directs our attention to hate, conscious or unconscious, produced in the analyst in the relationship between analyst and patient. Winnicott differentiates the ordinary ambivalence of love and hate from the aggressive aspect of love, and saw it as a mostly unconscious part of every human relationship. In his 1947 paper, 'Hate in the Countertransference', Winnicott points out the difference between countertransference hate which has to do with

the patient's effect on the repressed aspects of the analyst, and the effect on the analyst of those patients whose very symptom is to provoke hate in those around them. In a therapeutic relationship the analyst's own analysis will have to some extent allowed the analyst to recognise and control the effects of his own hate of the patient. Winnicott states that normally, in the analysis of a neurotic patient, this hate is latent, and is controlled and expressed in the *boundaries of the analysis. Variation of those boundaries by the analyst, such as extending a session, however kindly meant consciously, is a reaction to that hate, and moreover one that the patient will recognise as a sign of it, which will disturb the analysis.

In the analysis of psychotic patients Winnicott points out that the analyst's struggle with his hate of the patient is greater and more problematic; the patient, whose own confusion regarding love and hate is such that the provision of a safe analytic environment is experienced as more concrete than symbolic, requires without knowing it an awareness in the analyst of the analyst's hate. Only thus can the analyst's hate, when it is deserved, be recognised as such, and the patient begin to feel that his own hate may be understood and tolerated.

A link is made with early life in that Winnicott states that the mother hates the baby before the baby hates the mother or knows her hatred of him. He lists many reasons for maternal hate, and sees sentimentality as a denial of hate in parents, much as he points out the damage that can be done by the analyst who denies his own hatred under an umbrella of permissiveness.

See also: aggression

Winnicott, D. W. [1947] (1958) 'Hate in the countertransference' in *Collected Papers: Through Paediatrics to Psychoanalysis*. London: Tavistock.

J. Joh.

COUNTERTRANSFERENCE (LACAN) Countertransference is a psychoanalytic concept which made its appearance as a proposed form of technique in the early 1950s. It tackles the question of the analyst experiencing feelings with regard to his patient. In the beginning it was thought that it was something to be analysed away in the analyst, but Paula Heimann and Roger Money-Kyrle amongst others also thought of countertransference as having its causes and effects in the patient. It was therefore seen as being an indication of something which, when purified by the analyst, gives a formulation of what is at work in the unconscious of the patient. Freud establishes no relation between the countertransference and the psychoanalyst's unconscious. In a letter to Binswanger – on 20 February 1913 – he invites analysts to overcome their countertransference. He indicates that it is a symptom with which it is not difficult to come to terms. In other words, countertransference is basically the result of a Freudian observation: the person of the analyst intervenes in the interpretation, which indicates that the analysis of the analyst must be carried out further. Lacan points out that the analysis of the analyst's feelings proposed by the proponents of countertransference technique relies upon the functioning of the ego of the analyst. The ego he claims is an unreliable instrument of analytical technique: he proposes instead that the analyst disengage from the grasp of the situation put forward by his ego. Accordingly, Lacan recommends that the analyst experiencing countertransference feelings question his place in the analytical relation. However, instead of Heimann's question 'Why is the patient now doing what to whom?' he proposes that the analyst ask himself the question 'Who is being addressed?'. By this means the context of the material is re-established, the countertransference feeling disappears, and, rather than the continued intervention of the present, the subject's history is re-established as the focus of the analytical work.

V. P.

COUNTERTRANSFERENCE (RELATIONISM) Like its sister concept of *transference, countertransference was originally viewed by Freud as an impediment to the psychoanalytic process, and has over the years evolved into being seen as a key factor in all productive analytic action. Originally, analysts' subjectivity, perceived as analysts' unresolved conflicts, was seen as interfering with the ability to see with objective clarity the inner world of the patient under 'scientific' scrutiny. Conceptions of analytic objectivity were challenged by Sullivan's 1953 portrayal of the analyst as a participant observer, questioning the very possibility of an absolutely neutral and objective analyst assuming the role of a blank screen to patients' projections. Influenced by Heisenberg's uncertainty principle in physics, and the field theory of social psychology, *Sullivan described an analyst who, despite every effort at neutrality and reserve, cannot help but participate with patients unwittingly (or unconsciously). From this point forward, the trend in the literature shifted from the study of the patient *in vacuo* (one-person psychology), to the examination of the interaction between both subjective parties in the analytic dyad (two-person psychology).

Heimann contributed significantly in breaking the barrier of using analysts' subjective emotional experience to benefit patients. She argued that analysts' emotional experiences of patients were among the most significant tools in providing insight into the latter's psyches. She underscored that all of analysts' feelings about patients had some relevance to understanding patients, and that these feelings should be subordinated to advancing patients' insight and growth. Racker agreed, positing that analysts and patients engaged in subtle interactions and influenced one another every moment they were together. Clarifying these interactions became the heart of analytic work, as they were reflective of the inner worlds of patients. He distinguished two broad categories of countertransference, complementary and concordant. The former refers to analysts being influenced by patients to engage with them in ways similar to patients' key internalised relational configurations. The latter term refers to analysts learning about patients through the process of identifying with the patients' internal affective states. Searles reminded his colleagues that many of our feeling states are visible to patients and have impact on patients. Examination of patients' experience of analysts' participation and scrutiny of the here and now interaction between analyst and patient have become central to the work of many contemporary analysts. The ultimate aim in all such analytic activity is to illuminate the psyche of patients in order that their world may become more flexible and expansive.

See also: interpersonal psychoanalysis; participant observation; relational psychoanalysis

Freud, S. [1912] (1959) *The Future Prospects of Psychoanalytic Therapy*. S. E. 11. London: Hogarth Press, 139–51.

Heimann, P. (1950) 'On countertransference'. *International Journal of Psychoanalysis* 31: 81–4.

Racker, H. (1968) *Transference and Countertransference*. New York: International Universities Press.

Searles, H. (1979) *Countertransference and Related Subjects*. New York: International Universities Press.

Sullivan, H. S. (1953) *The Interpersonal Theory of Psychiatry*. New York: Norton.

I. H.

CREATIVITY Creativity entails access to unconscious wishes and the capacity to sublimate (to achieve substitute gratification in the form of creative work). Defences which inhibit thought, spontaneity or intuitive awareness interfere with creativity while ability to combine the omnipotence of narcissism and the requirements of reality enhances it.

For Winnicott, the capacity of the human being to feel that he exists, or 'is', comes out of his own spontaneous and original productions or impulses. This is Winnicott's extension of the notion of the infant's initial omnipotence during absolute *dependence upon the mother, when, by the mother's ideal adaptation or attunement to the infant's needs, it is possible for the infant to experience a world he believes, in excitement, to have grown out of himself. What was wanted was created and found to be there. This *paradox is the source of *play and imagination and healthy non-compliant living. It allows for hope that the world contains creativity which can be enjoyed as cultural experience. Winnicott concerned himself with creativity in the self, only referring to the work of the creative artists as able to accomplish this without seeking to formulate a concept of *aesthetics, his own theory of creativity in the arts. Here he radically differed from Freud and Klein who both saw in *art a representation of the neurotic psyche and, in the case of the latter, put forward a theory of creativity as a form of *reparation for destructive phantasies, primarily towards the parental figures with *sublimation seen as a victory of the life instincts over the death instincts.

See also: culture

Freud, S. (1910) *Leonardo da Vinci and a Memory of his Childhood*. S. E. 24. London: Hogarth Press.

Klein, M. (1985) 'Love, guilt and reparation' in *Love, Guilt and Reparation, and other works 1921–1945*. London: Hogarth Press and Institute of Psycho-Analysis.

Winnicott, D. W. (1964) Chapter 13 in *The Child, the Family and the Outside World*. Harmondsworth: Penguin.

Winnicott, D. W. (1986) 'Living creatively' in *Home Is Where We Start From*. Harmondsworth: Penguin.

J. A. Ber. / H. T. R.

CULTURE Freud did not distinguish culture from *civilisation; however, culture may be considered to be the particular set of conditions by which civilisation influences how the instinctual drives will be expressed. The ten commandments are an example of the control of instincts, and the seven deadly sins describe the instincts to be avoided. Critics of Freud have protested that the *family romance, *castration anxiety, and the Oedipus complex applied only to Freud's Viennese society. However, every society (including that of gorillas) seems to possess an incest taboo. Initiation rites at infancy or puberty are pervasive and usually contain some form of symbolic castration (circumcision, clitoridectomy), which suggests that such expressions of instincts and unconscious wishes are not limited to a particular culture.

J. A. Ber.

CULTURE (INTERPERSONAL) A paramount consideration for *interpersonal psychoanalysts, so much so that the first interpersonal psychoanalytic Institute – founded by *Fromm, *Fromm-Reichman, *Sullivan, Clara Thompson, and David and Janet Rioch – was initially referred to as the 'Cultural School' of psychoanalysis. This emphasis on culture created a distinctive break from the Freudian schools of the time that espoused concepts of universalism in applying the theory of *drives. The interpersonal emphasis on culture followed their assertion that what went on between individuals, rather than what went on within the individual, was the crucial focus for psychoanalysis. This change in emphasis was also in keeping with an increased interest within the social sciences in non-western cultures and in the concept of cultural relativism that holds that phenomena within any given culture must be interpreted within the context of that particular culture and not simply from without.

Within interpersonal psychoanalysis there have developed at least two views of the individual's relationship to culture. Sullivan's view was that culture is a primary influence in the life of individuals and that socialisation – a process of being filled with culture – is that which makes people human and thus characterises their essential nature. A differing perspective put forward by Fromm is that the socialising effect of culture takes place over and across from the true nature of individuals. In this view, culture is not only a force that links people together, thereby forming a key element of their identities, but it is also that which can prevent people from achieving our full potential as human beings.

Derivatives of these diverging views of culture have continued to evolve in clinical practice within the interpersonal tradition, with Levenson emphasising 'what's going on around here', that is, the unattended and mystified aspects of the interaction between patient and analyst, while Wolstein emphasised the analysts' disclosure of their authentic experience as a way modelling this for patients.

See also: symbolic

Lionells, M., Fiscalini, J., Mann, C. H. and Stern, D. B. (eds) (1995) *Handbook of Interpersonal Psychoanalysis*. Hillsdale, NJ: The Analytic Press.

E. M. W.

CURATIVE FANTASY (SELF PSYCHOLOGY) Patients enter psychoanalytic treatment with some definite, albeit often unarticulated expectations for cure. It is important to discern what these fantasies are, and not to reject them as unrealistic (deliberately or inadvertently) since that would make the engagement of the patient in his or her treatment process difficult at best and impossible at worst. The idea of the curative fantasy – offered by Paul and Anna Ornstein – can be viewed as an aspect of any selfobject transference in which the patient's 'thwarted need to grow' is mobilised. Within the selfobject transference the curative fantasy reflects the patient's concrete expectations of how his/her 'cure' will be achieved.

See also: phantasy; selfobject; subject supposed to know

P. O. / A. O.

CZECH REPUBLIC The fact that Sigmund Freud was, in 1856, born at Příbor (now in the Czech Republic) has had no influence on the history of the Czech psychoanalytic movement. Czech psychoanalysis started later in comparison with other countries and its history has been shaped to an extent by the history of Europe. The development of the psychoanalytic movement took place and still takes place in Prague.

Until the 1980s it was mostly influenced by outsiders. The first paper published in the Czech language with psychoanalytical aspects was written by a psychiatrist who knew Freud personally – Stuchlíks who published 'Some Statistical and Psychological Observations during Vaccinating' in 1915. In 1918 after the establishment of the Czechoslovak Republic, psychoanalysis was still unknown at any of the Czech universities. However in 1921 an emigrant from Moscow, N. J. Ossipow, founder of the Russian Psychoanalytic Association, came to Prague. Ossipow and Freud knew each other and exchanged letters till Ossipow's death in 1934. He was commissioned to give lectures on psychoanalysis at Charles University in Prague.

The first person in Czechoslovakia to receive psychoanalytic training (in Bedin) was Emanuel Windholz, a psychiatrist of Jewish origin. In 1931 Windholz and Ossipow organised an international academic celebration in Příbor on the occasion of Freud's seventy-fifth birthday. Freud could not attend for health reasons and was represented by his daughter Anna.

Hitler's rise to power in Germany influenced the development of Czech psychoanalysis deeply. Several psychoanalysts emigrated to Prague and in 1933 the Prague Psychoanalytical Working Group came into being. In 1935 *Fenichel came to Prague, his foremost pupils being Karpe, Bondy and Dosuzkov, and in 1936 the Society for the Study of Psychoanalysis was established as a member of the *International Psychoanalytic Association. Windholz was the first president.

The political events of 1938 had a disastrous influence on the movement in Czechoslovakia.

Some members emigrated to the USA (Fenichel, A. Reich, Windholz); the rest of the group continued working during the German occupation until 1945. Only Dosuzkov survived; all other members died in concentration camps. In 1946 the Society was re-established and Dosuzkov became the president; he Fenichel and A. Reich had the strongest influence on the development of psychoanalysis in Czechoslovakia after 1945.

The popularity of psychoanalysis rose after 1945 and the Society got a very good response academically. However, in 1948, after the Communist takeover, the psychoanalytical movement was forbidden. Dosuzkov's decision to work and teach underground ensured that the psychoanalytic movement in Czechoslovakia was not lost and developed further. His pupils Kučera and Ladislav Haas became training analysts too. The IPA was informed about the underground activities of the PSA group and tried to help as much as possible. Colleagues from Holland, Vienna and Italy came for supervision and lectures to Prague.

In the short period of greater political liberty in 1968 the group prepared several papers, but this period was too short for the papers to be published.

In 1969 on the occasion of the thirtieth anniversary of Freud's death, Dosuzkov and Kučera succeeded in placing another commemorative plaque on the house where Freud was born. (The first plaque from 1931 had been removed by the Nazis and had disappeared.)

The PSA education continued in the eighties after Dosuzkov's and Kučera's death without any training analysts. The political changes in Eastern Europe in 1989 brought freedom to the movement.

Borecki, one of Dosuzkov's pupils, was the first president of the legal 'Group for studying the PSA'. Nowadays Czech psychoanalysts are organised as the Czech Psychoanalytical (Provisional) Society, which is a member of the IPA.

E. F. / R. F.

D

Darwin, Charles Robert (1809–82) and Alfred Russell Wallace (1823–1913) announced the origin of species by natural selection to the Linnean Society of London July 1858 when Freud was two. Darwin, born 12 February to Susannah Wedgwood, daughter of the potter Josiah, and to Dr Robert Waring, son of Dr Erasmus whose *Zoonomia* (1794–6) contained evolutionary predictions, established history as a scientific method. The genetic (Darwinian) viewpoint is basic to psycho-analysis. Darwin and Freud recognised that the minutest detail must have meaning; if it could not be found in terms of the present, it had to be sought in the past. Freud referred to Darwin twenty-one times between 1875 and 1939. Darwin's three principles of *The Expression of Emotions* appear in Freud and Breuer's 1895 *Studies on Hysteria*: associated serviceable habit, antithesis, and overflow of excess excitation. In fleeing Nazi Vienna in 1938 Freud brought to England nine Darwin volumes he had signed and/or dated between 1875 and 1883. Darwin was the source of Freud's neo-Lamarckianism. 'Great weight must be attributed to the inherited effects of use and disuse, with respect both to body and mind,' Darwin wrote in his 1871 *Descent of Man*, a paradigm that also required what Freud characterised in 'The Ego and the Id' as 'repetition often enough and with sufficient strength by many individuals in successive generations'. The mechanism of inheritance was unknown in Darwin's day. To account for use-inheritance Darwin designed pangenesis in his 1859 *The Variation of Plants and Animals under Domestication*. By 1914 advances made germ plasm the new paradigm and use-inheritance was derided as Lamarckian. Darwin, in an 1844 letter to Hooker, says Lamarck was the 'nonsense of "will" and "volition"'. Developing the concept of the ego as the organ of adaptation capable of will and volition, Freud proposed to Ferenczi a project on Lamarckism's relation to psycho-analysis. His 1916 reading of Lamarck's *Philosophie Zoologique* provided no evolutionary support and Freud abandoned the project. Freud's only other reference was in his 1884 pre-analytic 'Ueber Coca' to Lamarck's 1783 paper on the subject. Darwin criticised 'Lamarck's law of progressive development'. Natural selection encompasses regression and fixation as well as progression.

Ritvo, L. B. (1965) 'Darwin as the source of Freud's neo-Lamarckianism'. *Journal of the American Psychoanalytic Association* 13.
Ritvo, L. B. (1990) *Darwin's Influence on Freud.* New Haven, CT and London: Yale University Press.

L. B. R.

DASEIN A German word often used by existential analysts to designate the individual human being as well as humanity in general. Originally appropriated by *Heidegger to refer exclusively to human existence, the word Dasein is comprised of the common German words *Da*, which means either 'here' or 'there', and *Sein*, which means 'being'. In everyday German use, Dasein means presence or existence, i.e. the circumstance that something (e.g. God) is here or there. Heidegger and existential analysts following him employ Dasein to show that the human being exists as an openness in the world. The term Dasein emphasises the circumstance that the human being is a special kind of being for whom all being, including its own being, matters in a deeply personal way. In other words, Dasein is a being who is capable of perceiving, understanding, and caring for its own being as well as the beings of the world. For this reason, Heidegger called Dasein the 'shepherd of being'.

The term Dasein proposes radically to overcome Cartesian subject/object dualism by highlighting the perspective that the human individual exists, not as an encapsulated ego, but, rather, as a realm of world openness, a 'being-in-the-world', a being who stands forth (literally, exists) in the world. For example, existential analysts suggest that when human beings meet, they do not experience each other as separate monads of consciousness which must then find some way to interact, but, rather, they immediately find one another existing out in the world together. Although existential analysts are often criticised for their use of arcane terms such as Dasein, these analysts believe that, however difficult and obscure such words might seem initially, it is important to develop language and discourse which are faithful to human experience as it is actually lived.

See also: philosophy, continental

E. C.

DASEINSANALYSIS A term used by various existential analysts to designate their approach to clinical research or their approach to clinical practice in psychoanalysis. The term's precedent, *Daseinsanalytik*, was used by *Heidegger to denote his philosophical method for analysing the fundamental structures of human existence or *Dasein. His phenomenological philosophical analysis, which was originally presented in *Being and Time*, sought to delineate the fundamental composition of the existing human. According to Heidegger's phenomenological method, human being-in-the-world, or Dasein, is disclosed in such features of human existence as time (temporality/*Zeitlichkeit*), space (spatiality/*Räumlichkeit*), mood (attunement/*Befindlichkeit*), and body (corporeality/*Leiblichkeit*). Furthermore, Dasein is also shown as always concerned with being (*care/*Sorge*) as well as being mortal (being-towards-death/*Sein zum Tode*).

*Binswanger, one of the earliest advocates of psychiatric phenomenology, first appropriated the term *daseinsanalysis* in psychiatry, using it to designate an existential orientation to research in that field. The English anthology *Existence*, edited by *May, referred to Binswanger's appropriation of Heidegger's

Daseinsanalytik as existential analysis. Binswanger's research-oriented *daseinsanalysis* was especially concerned with basic forms of clinical-psychopathological phenomena such as schizophrenia and manic-depressive illness.

*Boss, another Swiss psychiatrist, also appropriated the term *daseinsanalysis*. Although his *daseinsanalysis* addressed psychoanalytic concerns such as *anxiety, *guilt, and psychosomatic phenomena, it especially emphasised the development of an existential approach to the practice of psychotherapy and psychoanalysis. In particular, Boss's psychotherapeutic *daseinsanalysis* focused on the phenomenological interpretation of such psychoanalytic techniques as the use of the couch and free association as well as such clinical phenomenon as transference, resistance, and dreams.

E. C.

DAYDREAMS Freud moved from emphasising similarities between daydreams and dreams, towards noticing their differences. Repressing the daydream turns it into an unconscious *phantasy, a source of neurotic symptoms, but it can transform childhood play into a springboard for artistic creativity. *Winnicott differentiated dissociated, repetitive fantasying from lively imagination.

Freud, S. (1900) *The Interpretation of Dreams*. S. E. 5. London: Hogarth Press.
Freud, S. (1908a) *Creative Writers and Daydreaming*. S. E. 9. London: Hogarth Press.
Winnicott, D. W. (1971) 'Dreaming, fantasying, and living' in *Playing and Reality*. London: Penguin.

E. Ber.

DAY['S] RESIDUE A seemingly innocuous experience from the previous day is often used in the construction of a *dream. Such a 'day's residue' is used as a cover by an unconscious wish in order to gain access to expression in the dream. The day's residue can also serve as a vehicle for the kind of wish Freud describes as a *transference.

B. B.

DEATH Lacan indicates that it is language which provides us with the experience of limits: in this sense it brings an awareness of death, as well as providing us with the means not to think about it. Human being, in its tragic dimension, is situated between-two-deaths, between the death brought by language and the prospect of the annihilation of the subject, which may be the aim of the death drive.

B. O. D

DEATH DRIVE (FREUD) The concept emerged from Freud's observation of the tendency of patients to repeat situations which they did not enjoy, offered no pleasure or mastery (as did children's stories or play) and did not help them to prepare for traumatic situations (as did repetitive dreams of trauma). He concluded that the conservative nature of the instincts led to a compulsion to repeat which was 'beyond the pleasure principle'. Since non-existence precedes life, the organism tries to return to its original non-living, inorganic state. However, once life comes into being, there is a tendency to continue living. Hence the opposition between the desire to live, to make connections, to enjoy stimulation and the desire to cease to exist, to lower stimulation, reach nirvana, and achieve peace through death. Freud suggested that aggression was the result of the death drive directed outward. He believed that in health there was a *fusion of life and death drives. The absence of aggression might lead to impotence, and the absence of libido (the life drive) might lead to a sex murder. A later theorist (Oscar Sternbach) suggested that aggression really belonged to the life drive, since it was active. The death drive leads only to the reduction of tension, and is therefore never active. He noted that in the sex act, increases and decreases of tension alternate until complete release of tension occurs ('the little death') and that this was an example of fusion of the drives.

In general the death drive is placed in opposition to life drive (*Eros), which tends towards the persistence of life, thanks to reproduction and sexuality; the death drive summons up the forces which tend towards a return towards the inanimate. The concept emerged from numerous clinical facts (traumatic dreams, play, and *negative therapeutic reaction) which are governed by the compulsion of *repetition.

This concept, held from the outset to be quite speculative, has given rise to various interpretations. We can connect it to aggressiveness, a destructive drive (*destrudo*), and more broadly to a desire for death directed at oneself or at another. Whereas *ego psychology has held it more at arm's length, considering aggressiveness as a response to frustration, the Kleinian school of thought allows it to play a determining role in the formation of personality: a process of introjection and projection which enables, through successive phases (schizo-paranoid and depressive), a regulation of life drive and the overtaking of the initial splitting.

Other psychoanalytic theorists recognise in it the biological source of repetition drive, a place of conflict between the active seeking of the object and the narcissistic withdrawal into a return on oneself. Certain theorists see in it the simple destructive aspect of the driving release.

Finally, other writers remain extremely sceptical with regard to the interest of the concept, judging it to be too speculative and a source of confusion. For them, all of the processes which could be considered as possible expressions of the existence of a death drive can be explained by other mechanisms known elsewhere.

It is true that whereas in the classical model of the neurotic conflict the concept of the death instinct is only called upon to play a secondary role, the same does not apply in psychopathology, psychotic states, borderline and narcissistic disorders.

See also: drive

D. W. / J. A. Ber.

DEATH DRIVE/INSTINCT (KLEIN) Drawing on Freud's concept of death-instinct as a metapsychological representation of its derivatives (e.g. aggression, hostility or sadism) as manifested in infantile life, Klein used this concept to account for the presence of phantastic imagos of parents as threatening *internal objects. The derivatives of the death instinct were said by Klein to be projected into the parental objects. If these phantasies were not modulated by experience with the parents, they were in turn re-introjected in an exacerbated retaliatory or persecutory form, thus leading to the formation of a harsh, primitive *super-ego.

Under the impact of external reality, the infantile ego is labile and initially capable of only a limited amount of integration of good/satisfying and bad/frustrating external experiences as prototypically represented in the breast-feeding situation. Under adverse circumstances, such as when the infantile ego is under the sway of omnipotent phantasies, it can feel bombarded by deadly anxieties which threaten disintegration and annihilation.

Hatred is felt to be more powerful than love. However, the life-instinct, particularly when bolstered by good experiences, tends to lessen the anger, modifies the persecutory experience and mobilises the baby's belief in a good external world and his own goodness. The infant's aim is to identify and keep inside the life-giving and protective good objects, while keeping out the bad object or those aspects of the self which contain the death instinct.

One of Klein's last amendments to these views related to *envy, a special element of the death instinct, which attacks the good object as the source of life. The interplay between good and bad experiences can be complicated by good experiences which produce bad effects (e.g. the recognition of another's superior talents which can lead to feelings of humiliation and smallness, which may in turn precipitate attacks on the good object).

G. Gor.

DEATH DRIVE (FAIRBAIRN) Fairbairn wrote that all drives are geared to maintain life and relationship. Drives are potentials that develop into specific types of response. Human aggression, which Freud connected to the death drive, Fairbairn believed began as a reaction to the inevitable *frustration the infant experienced in its primary relationships, but may thereafter operate to achieve libidinal aims, to remove obstacles, or to establish distance and limits, and therefore, paradoxically to regain love and security. Fairbairn thought Freud's concept of the death instinct expresses the localisation of aggression within *internal reality of infantile aggression that originally arose in response to neglect and rejection by primary caregivers.

Fairbairn, W. R. D. (1958) 'The nature and aims of psychoanalytical treatment'. *International Journal of Psycho-Analysis* 44.

Fairbairn, W. R. D. [1930] (1994) 'Libido: the theory of the pleasure principle reinterpreted in terms of appetite' in D. Scharff and E. Fairbairn Birtles (eds) *From Instinct to Self*, Vols I and II. Northvale, NJ: Jason Aronson Inc.

E. F. B. / D. E. S.

DE CLERAMBAULT'S SYNDROME A psychotic condition, also known as erotomania, in which the sufferer develops the delusional belief that they are loved by another person. First described as *psychose passionelle* by the French psychiatrist Gatain de Clerambault, the condition is now thought to comprise distinct features, for example: the subject is convinced despite evidence to the contrary; amorous communication with another person; the object of the delusional belief fell in love first; the object was the first to make advances; the object is of higher rank; the delusion is directed towards the same person throughout; the delusion has a sudden onset; the subject rationalises the incongruent behaviour of the object; the course of the condition is chronic; hallucinations are absent.

Although erotomania can present as a symptom of other illnesses, including schizophrenia, mania, or organic conditions, when it occurs alone as a persistent delusional disorder it can be conceptualised in psychodynamic terms as the projection of denied narcissistic self-love. The syndrome has been a frequent media topic, with delusions of erotomania being present in celebrity stalkers, including John Hinckley Jr, who tried to assassinate President Reagan.

De Clerambault, G. [1921] (1942) 'Les psychoses passionelles' in *Oeuvres Psychiatriques*. Paris: Presses Universitaires de France.

A. F.

DEFENCE (FREUD) As a general concept, defence designates a variety of operations initiated by the ego that share the aim of protecting the integrity of the individual. These operations are known as mechanisms of defence.

In his early work, Freud conceives primary defence as a byproduct of the experience of pain. This mechanism is generated by the *ego in order to prevent the activation of a memory of a painful experience that would result in the release of affect. Primary defence is a normal psychic process that prevents the occurrence of a *primary process. Unlike innate biological reflex action, primary defence is the result of learning through experience.

Freud postulated in 1894 that some psychoneuroses were the product of pathological defence. The compulsive and hyperintensive nature of the symptoms of these neuroses was attributed to a process aimed at impeding the activation of a painful memory.

*Repression was the first form of secondary defence postulated by Freud. This form of defence acts by severing the link between *affect and *representation, thus divesting the conflicting representation of its cathexes and making it unavailable to conscious consideration.

Although initiated by the ego, pathological defence has all the characteristics of primary processes.

E. K.

DEFENCE (EGO PSYCHOLOGY) Defences are unconscious psychological devices employed by the patient when jeopardised by the emergence into consciousness of repressed drive derivatives (fantasies, wishes, ideas, affects), repressed memories and their associated affects, or confrontation with intolerable aspects of reality. They protect the ego from being overwhelmed and traumatised by intolerably intense affects; pressing drives; super-ego demands; unbearable reality; or psychic *conflict. Drive derivatives, memories, or realities that have been repressed but threaten to become conscious give rise to signal affects (anxiety, guilt, shame, etc.). These signal affects set defences in motion that reinforce repression and quell the unpleasurable signal affects. Defence 'mechanisms' include repression, displacements, reaction formation, projection, isolation, undoing and regression. *Repression proper can be considered to be the most effective defence mechanism insofar as it directly acts to keep the offending drive derivatives or memory-associated affects from becoming conscious. All other defence mechanisms exert their effects in a roundabout way. *Displacement acts by finding a substitute satisfaction more acceptable to the ego, thereby diverting attention away from the original wishes, fantasies, etc. that are being kept out of consciousness. *Reaction formation heightens opposite tendencies, for example, overdone expressions of love to hide one's hateful feelings. *Projection externalises the unacceptable wishes, thoughts, etc., leading the ego to believe these unacceptable psychical contents lie outside of oneself. *Isolation robs an idea or memory of its associated affect, thus rendering the memory emotionally innocuous, of little psychological consequence. *Undoing negates threatening ideas or impulses by performing an act designed to erase them. While displacement, reaction formation, projection, isolation and undoing are examples of classical types of defence mechanisms, any ego function can be enlisted to function as a defence mechanism (e.g. reality testing, intellectual activity, sublimation, etc.). *Regression also serves as a defence when it causes the ego to retreat to more primitive levels in order to avoid the wishes and fantasies associated with a later developmental stage.

See also: compromise formation; conflict/intrapsychic conflict; defence analysis

R. T.

DEFENCE ANALYSIS (SURFACE TO DEPTH) This is the clinical approach of *ego psychology and focuses on the defences and resistances of the surface before underlying unconscious fantasies, wishes and anxieties. A complete interpretation may be thought to include: 1) the fact that one is defending; 2) the way in which one is defending; 3) the wishes, impulses, and fantasies that are being defended against; and, 4) the danger to which the ego is potentially exposed by such wishes, impulses and fantasies (the ultimate reason the defences were needed in the first place). An ego psychological approach focuses on the first two of these: demonstrating the fact that, and the way in which, the individual defends. Dealing with the unconscious wishes/drives is left for later in the treatment, once the surface has been dealt with and the ego has developed sufficiently.

R. T.

DEFENCE (LACAN) As early as the late 1940s Lacan strongly questioned the use of the concept of defence made by the *ego psychology school and its supporters. He opposed the debasement of the notion of defence based on its identification with resistance, presented in terms of what does not give way within the ego in response to the interventions of the analyst. Lacan proposed the notion that if resistance was related to the structural difficulty of saying, then defence had to be read as defence against the drive. He later refined the notion into that of the subject's relation to the Real. In taking this step, he was being faithful to Freud who, from his first formulations on the drive in the

1890s, had constructed primary defence as the initial relation that the subject establishes with the Real.

V. D.

DEFENCES OF THE SELF (JUNG) A total defence exhibited by patients in a transference psychosis when the patient persistently attacks the analyst, treating the analyst as the patient and playing on the weak points perceived in the analyst. Whatever the analyst says is reinterpreted by the patient's *projective identification. If undetected, a malignant form of *countertransference is established within which the analyst may become masochistic and confused.

Fordham, M. (1974) 'Defences of the self'. *Journal of Analytical Psychology* 19(2).
Fordham, M. (1985) *Explorations into the Self.* London: Academic Press.

J. A.

DEFENCE AND RESISTANCE (SELF PSYCHOLOGY) The self psychological view of defence and resistance arises from the recognition that what the self – viewed not as a component of a mental apparatus, but as the core of the personality – needs to protect itself from is not the emergence of dangerous drives and wishes, but rather the repetition of significant psychological injury. This relates in particular to traumatic assaults on its self-esteem incurred in childhood to which it might be seriously vulnerable. The patient's anxiety that the analyst may not provide him with conditions under which he may feel safe to establish a selfobject relationship with the analyst as well as his actual experience of the specific faultiness of the analyst's attunement that affects his particular vulnerabilities, will occasion the patient's defensiveness, or 'resistance' to the analysis. Protracted resistance to the analytic work, or *negative therapeutic reaction may be due to the patient's ongoing experience of the analyst's being out of tune with the patient's primary self-disorder or selfobject needs. As Kohut and Wolf have indicated, the analyst's accurate understanding of the patient's need for defence against the mobilisation of the selfobject transferences to him or to the establishment of a selfobject relationship with him, as well as the analysis of the respective contributions of analyst and patient to their disruption, constitute important ingredients of the analyst's therapeutic responsiveness.

Bacal, H. (1979) 'Empathic lag in the analyst and its relation to negative therapeutic reaction'. Presented to the 31st International Psychoanalytic Congress, New York.
Brandchaft, B. (1986) 'The negativism of the negative therapeutic reaction and the psychology of the self' in A. Goldberg (ed.) *The Future of Psychoanalysis*. New York: International Universities Press.
Kohut, H. (1984) *How Does Analysis Cure?* A. Goldberg and P. Stepansky (eds). Chicago: University of Chicago Press.
Wolf, E. (1988) *Treating the Self.* New York: Guilford.

H. B.

DEFENCE, MORAL Fairbairn's experience of disturbed, neglected and abused children who described their parent(s) as good and themselves as bad gave him insight into the bizarre situation in which the child attempts to gain security by convincing itself that its parents are good and that their love will be secured by changing its own behaviour. If the child thinks the parent bad, then no behaviour on the child's part will bring love or approval. Thus guilt arises in order to maintain the existence of a good object. If the object is bad the child has no hope; it is preferable to be bad oneself. This formulation often underlies the dynamics in psychotherapy with people who have been abused.

E. F. B.

DEFENSIVE STRATEGIES According to Fairbairn, these are techniques relative to the arrangement and relationship adopted by the ego towards accepted and rejected internal objects to diminish *anxiety. In Fairbairn, *hysterical, *paranoid, *phobic and *obsessional symptoms are techniques used during the transitional period between infantile and mature dependence, and are not therefore, pathological syndromes derived from specific developmental stages.

See also: transitional techniques

E. F. B / D. E. S.

DEFERRED ACTION / NACHTRAEGLICHKEIT Strachey translated Freud's term 'Nachtraeglichkeit', introduced in the 1895 'project', as deferred action or delayed effects. Freud, in his 'History of an Infantile Neurosis', explained how his patient, the *Wolf Man, was exposed to the *primal scene trauma of sexual intercourse between the parents at age one and a half, but responded to it pathologically only at age four when he was psychologically capable of reacting to it. Thoma and Cheshire found Strachey's translation as deferred action unsatisfactory, because Freud often combined the meanings of delayed effect with retrospective reconstruction of the psychological significance of that trauma. Turo and Wilson have explicitly distinguished deferred action, a forward-looking activity by which the past influences the present at a later time, from *Nachtraeglichkeit*, a backward-looking activity in which a present retroactive revision transforms the past by giving it new meaning.

See also: memory; time; trauma

Freud, S. (1895) *The Project for a Scientific Psychology*. S. E. 1. London: Hogarth Press.

Freud, S. [1914] (1918) *From the History of an Infantile Neurosis*. S. E. 17. London: Hogarth Press.

Thoma, H. and Cheshire, N. (1991) 'Freud's Nachtraeglichkeit and Strachey's Deferred Action: Trauma, Constructions and the Direction of Causality'. *International Review of Psycho-analysis* 18: 407–27.

Turo, J. K. and Wilson, L. (2003) 'An essay on Freudian temporality: deferred action of memory and Nachtraeglichkeit'. *Journal of Clinical Psychoanalysis*.

H. G.

DELINQUENCY The word literally means 'defaulting' or 'offending'. It is usually applied to younger age groups, as in 'juvenile delinquency', although that is a product of usage. In fantasy and phantasy, as well as in milder behavioural forms, it refers to activities that are common to us all at some stage, for example stealing, or to interpersonal acts of a violent or sexual kind.

'Antisocial' or 'criminal' behaviour are the preferred terms for similar behaviour in older people. Like crime, delinquency is a social construct which varies across cultures and historical periods; to that extent there can strictly be no psychoanalytic theory of delinquency per se, but there can be one of transgression and failure to fulfil developmental norms of behaviour.

Freud's early psychoanalytic views of 1908 emphasised the instinctual or constitutional basis of criminality, and of so-called 'outlaws' of society. Later, in 1925, he wrote 'of children, young delinquents and, as a rule, criminals dominated by their instincts' for whom 'the psychoanalytic method must be adapted to meet the need.'

*Winnicott, in his 1956 classic paper 'The Antisocial Tendency', emphasised, by contrast, the object relatedness of the antisocial or delinquent act. For Winnicott the delinquent act was an expression of hope, although misdirected, since the subject could be seen to still be engaging with the world; he contrasted this situation with that of despair – and apparent compliance – engendered by responses of non-understanding or excessively repressive regimes. However, Winnicott also emphasised the need first for 'management', sometimes by physical containment of the delinquent, before psychoanalytically informed work can proceed: he remarked – graphically – in a footnote in

Playing and Reality: 'When the analyst knows that the patient carries a revolver, then, it seems to me, this work cannot be done.'

Williams, following Melanie Klein, has emphasised the defensive function of much delinquent behaviour. The delinquent act is seen as the vehicle of expression, by projection, of unbearable and unwanted states of mind. He writes of evacuation by 'projective identification,' for example of persecutory or depressive guilt, into the 'object' – whether victim, parental or authority figure or others. One problem with this conceptualisation, however, is that other authorities regard the delinquent or criminal act as the product of a 'failure' to be able to achieve psychological projection or projective identification, thereby necessitating the use of actual physical violence.

Delinquency is frequently also a manifestation of other defence mechanisms such as identification with the aggressor (as for example in 'the bullied one becoming the bullying one' or 'the abused the abuser'), denial, splitting or reaction formation. Campbell describes two separate aims of delinquent behaviour – either self-preservation or sadism; this distinction is applied to aggressive and violent acts generally and relates to theories of aggression as of primary or secondary origin.

The issues of establishing a working alliance, and of the complexities and provocations of countertransference in working with delinquents are crucial but are part of a far larger subject.

See also: aggression

Campbell, D. (1994) 'A violent adolescent's ego ideal'. Paper. Read at Anna Freud Centre, London.
Freud, S. (1908) *'Civilised' Sexual Morality and Modern Nervous Illness*. S. E. 7. London: Hogarth Press.
Freud, S. (1925b) 'Foreword, A. Aichorn's, *Wayward Youth*'. S. E. 19. London: Hogarth Press.
Williams, A. (1982) 'Adolescence, violence and crime'. *Journal of Adolescence* 5: 125–34.
Winnicott, D. W. [1956] (1958) 'The anti social tendency' in *Collected Papers. Through Paediatrics to Psychoanalysis*. London: Tavistock.
Winnicott. D. W. (1971) *Playing and Reality*. London: Tavistock.

C. C.

DELUSION One of the ways of reconstructing reality after a psychotic breakdown. When there is *regression in the ego and *foreclosure of a part of the experience of reality, Freud says that what was foreclosed from the *psychic reality of the subject returns from the outside. Delusion is created in the second place as a kind of *defence against the horror of confronting the senseless void. It is a kind of substitute, private world which is not open to communication with others or to discussion.

For Lacan delusion is one of the main symptoms in psychosis. It represents the expression of *foreclosed *signifiers in the Real at the moment of the activation of the psychosis. Freud had raised delusion from a pathological process to being an element of an attempt at recovery. Lacan continues this emphasis on the content of the delusion being a bridge between psychotic process and external reality.

D. Cre. / R. Gol.

DEMAND The utter helplessness (*Hilflosigkeit*) of the infant institutes the fundamental dependency of the subject on the primal *Other: demand is the articulation of physical *need in speech. All speech has the Other for its addressee. By virtue of its mediation through speech, demand becomes a demand for more than the object of need: it becomes a demand for love. Speech, since it is structured through demand, is always also a demand for love, responded to by the Other's desire. Likewise, a demand for analysis is a demand for love, a dimension of transference to be handled carefully by the analyst.

V. V.

DENEGATION Lacan's (de)negation is situated at the intersection of Symbolic and Real, where Imaginary mediation is decided by the subject's structure. Lacan located neurosis and psychosis in the moment when the Real is constituted as an expulsion from the original Symbolic, which in terms of Freudian *negation, indicates a response to a primordial mythological moment. In neurosis, the symbol of negation, of a signifier as the return of the repressed, being the inter-said, is essential to thought. For the psychotic, the paternal signifier cannot be negated, since it was never present at any original time within the Symbolic. Lacking the bar of negation, instead of unconscious formations, a return of the Real, as hallucination, will occur.

R. M. W

DENIAL Whereas *affects are repressed, ideas on the other hand are said to be subject to denial. According to Klein, denial of aspects of the self leads to *splitting and *projective identification.

See also: negation

R. M. S.

DENMARK In Denmark as in other western countries psychoanalysis has had a significant influence on both cultural life and views of human nature as well as psychology and psychiatry.

In 1957 the Danish Psychoanalytical Society became a Component Society of the International Psychoanalytical Association (IPA) and has since then trained an increasing number of Danish and – from the mid-1970s – also Swedish psychoanalysts.

Psychoanalytic theory has for many years been part of the education at the University of Copenhagen and the psychological and medical faculties have accepted several psychoanalytical dissertations by the society's members.

However, psychoanalysis has never been officially recognised and for this reason all clinical psychoanalysis takes place solely in the private sector.

In co-operation with the other Scandinavian psychoanalytical societies the Danish Psychoanalytical Society has since 1978 published and contributed to the English-language journal *The Scandinavian Psychoanalytic Review*.

Theoretically the Danish society is just as pluralistic as most other psychoanalytical societies within the IPA. However, the British Psychoanalytical Society has had an appreciable influence because the Danish society since 1987 has had a continuous postgraduate programme with participation of mostly British analysts.

Paikin, H. (1992) 'Denmark' in P. Kutter (ed.) *Psychoanalysis International*, Vol. 1. Stuttgart-Bad Cannestadt: Frogmann-Holzboog.
Paikin, H. (1998) 'A letter from Denmark'. *Journal of the American Psychoanalytic Association* 46.

H. P.

DEPENDENCE (FAIRBAIRN) Fairbairn identified two kinds of dependence: infantile dependence that arises in the relationship of the infant to its mother; and mature dependence, the life-long need for interdependent relationships. The path from infantile to mature dependence is traversed during a long *transitional period through social interactions which slowly establish personal identity, while at the same time acknowledging other persons' separate identities and establishing interpersonal mutuality.

Bowlby, J. (1969) *Attachment*. New York: Basic Books.
Macmurray, J. [1961] (1995) *Persons in Relation*. London: Faber & Faber.
Murray, L. and Andrews, L. (2000) *The Social Baby*. Richmond: CP Publishing.

E. F. B. / D. E. S.

DEPENDENCE (WINNICOTT) The infant's condition of physical and emotional helplessness in relation to the mother, in the first place, and thereafter, in relation to all of those who subsequently come to symbolise her. Winnicott places emphasis on the fact of dependence for the newborn infant. He identifies three developmental stages of dependence: absolute dependence, in the first months of life, when the infant has no means of knowing about maternal care, and tends to think he is creating what he desires, whilst in fact being subject to good and bad features of maternal provision; relative dependence, usually after weaning and after the first six months of life, when he does realise another is involved, and can begin to relate the details of maternal care to his own impulses; and towards independence, where he begins to learn ways of coping without actual care, by accumulating memories of care, and by intellectual development which arises directly out of bodily experience.

These stages of dependence will also be replicated in the patient's *transference to the analyst over the course of treatment. Klein's concept of the infant's helplessness in relation to the mother and her breast as the source of life and *creativity, unlike Winnicott's, is schematised as producing innate *envy, independent of the nature of actual maternal care, and this is a fundamental difference in theory between them, despite some common ground.

Dependence, also related to maternal and psychoanalytic *holding, is a keynote term in Winnicott's thinking and can be related to Freud's notion that it is the characteristic of the human infant with its lengthy period of dependence upon the parents that gives rise to psychological life.

Klein, M. (1957) 'Envy and gratitude' in *Envy and Gratitude and other Works*. London: Hogarth Press.

Winnicott, D. W. (1965) 'The theory of the parent-infant relationship'; 'From dependence towards independence in the development of the individual' in *The Maturational Processes and the Facilitating Environment: Studies in the Theory of Emotional Development*. London: Hogarth Press.

H. T. R.

DEPERSONALISATION A subjective sense of unreality regarding various aspects of the self, experienced as disconnectedness from one's own body, mentations, feelings, or actions. It occurs transiently in normal subjects under conditions of heightened stress, as a symptom of some psychiatric disorders, and as a disorder in its own right. Ackner stressed its unpleasant quality. Insight is preserved but individuals strain for analogies that will convey their experiences to the listener. Schilder stressed the importance of excessive self-observation as a characteristic of patients with depersonalisation and considered it to be a form of *narcissistic neurosis. There are no commonly accepted psychoanalytic theories of depersonalisation and critics point out that many of these theories explain content, not form or aetiology of depersonalisation. Stamm, for example, suggested that depersonalisation involves a regression for shorter or longer periods to a primitive undifferentiated oral state, in which the individual yearns for symbiotic union with the mother.

Mellor, C. S. (1988) 'Depersonalisation and self perception'. *British Journal of Psychiatry* 153 (2).

Sedman, G. (1970) 'Theories of depersonalisation: a re-appraisal'. *British Journal of Psychiatry* 117.

Simeon, D., Stein, D., and Hollander, E. (1995) 'Depersonalisation disorder and self injurious behaviour'. *Journal of Clinical Psychiatry* 56 (4).

S. Mik.

DEPRESSION (FREUD) Although Freud commented on depression in general, his main focus was on *melancholia which he viewed as the gravest form of depression. In Freud's view, extreme *ambivalence is a precondition for melancholia. Characteristics of melancholia include extreme dejection, inhibition, loss of interest in the world and a loss of capacity to love, as well as ensuing loss of self-esteem, often expressed in severe self-reproach. Freud interpreted these self-reproaches as a displacement from the reproaches toward the loved one. This displacement is made possible by the individual's narcissistic identification with, and introjection of, the loved object – a state of affairs facilitated by the individual's narcissistic object-choice. Like normal grief, melancholia often occurs following the loss of a love object, or of a valued ideal. In contrast to normal *mourning, where the world becomes 'poor and empty', in melancholia it is the ego that is impoverished. Freud expressed doubt as to whether deeply rooted depression was treatable by psychoanalysis. In anticipation of a self-psychological formulation, he raised the question of whether a narcissistic injury itself could produce a clinical picture of melancholia.

See also: anaclitic

Freud, S. [1915] (1917) *Mourning and Melancholia*. S. E. 14. London: Hogarth Press.
Jacobson, E. (1971) *Depression: Comparative Studies of Normal, Neurotic, and Psychotic Conditions*. New York: International Universities Press.

A. W. / M. Eag.

DEPRESSION (PSYCHIATRY) The delineation of either a depressive order, or depressed mood. The latter may be a feature of everyday life, or a symptom of several disorders, chiefly depressive disorders, but also schizophrenia, delusional disorders, drug dependence, certain personality disorders, alcohol dependence, or certain general medical conditions, and hence has a differential diagnosis. In what follows, the emphasis will be on depressive disorder.

There are several recognised definitions and classifications of depressive disorder. Central to the concept is the combination of low mood, of an intensity and/or frequency judged greater than would be expected for the individual in his/her circumstances; together with one or more of certain characteristic symptoms, that include loss of the usual capacity for enjoyment (anhedonia) and disturbance of physiological functions such as sleep, appetite, weight regulation and sex drive; and providing the combination of these features cannot be accounted for by another psychiatric disorder or general medical condition. Hence depressive disorder is in a sense a diagnosis by exclusion. It is sometimes referred to in everyday clinical practice by loosely defined terms such as 'depressive illness' or 'clinical depression'.

The aetiology is thought to be multi-factorial. There is evidence for a strong genetic predisposition, but life events precede the onset of a depressive episode in the majority of cases, and often include an experience of loss. Vulnerability factors include loss of either parent in childhood, and the lack of a confiding relationship in adulthood. Freud first linked mourning and melancholia in 1917.

There are several theories concerning the origins of depressive disorders in the brain, but the most enduring remain those implicating dysfunction of monoamine neurotransmitter systems, particularly those of noradrenaline and 5-hydroxytryptamine (5HT or serotonin). Most of these theories originate from the pharmacology of antidepressant drugs.

Choices of treatments include psychological, social and biological measures, or often a combination of these, depending on severity of symptoms, patient preference, resources, and the judgement and particular training of the professionals consulted. Research indicates that biological treatments and certain psychological treatments are probably of equal efficacy for moderately severe depressive episodes. The comparative efficacies for mild and severe episodes are less clear, but for severe episodes it is generally accepted that a biological treatment will be required, the main ones being medication and electroconvulsive therapy (ECT). The latter is generally reserved for severe depressive disorders with features of psychosis, inadequate fluid intake and suicidal ideation.

Among psychological treatments, cognitive-behaviour therapy and interpersonal therapy in particular have been reviewed favourably. Psycho-dynamically informed therapies are also frequently used, so as to address problems in addition to that of the depressive disorder itself.

Freud, S. [1915] (1917) *Mourning and Melancholia*. S. E. 14. London: Hogarth Press.

C. V.

DEPRESSIVE POSITION With the introjection of the whole object in the second quarter of the first year, certain marked steps in integration are made which imply important changes in the infant's relationship to objects. The loved and hated aspects of the mother are no longer felt to be so widely separated, and the result is an increased fear of object loss, states akin to mourning and a strong feeling of guilt, because the aggressive impulses are felt to have been directed against the loved object. Destructive impulses are now felt to be a great danger to the loved object, which is increasingly perceived as a whole person. The mother who is hated is also the mother who is loved.

The anxiety relating to the formerly attacked internalised mother leads to a stronger identification with the injured object. This identification reinforces both the drive to make reparation and the ego's attempts to inhibit aggressive impulses. The ego may also make repeated use of manic defences.

When the infant is faced with the conflicts, guilt and sorrow inherent in the depressive position, its capacity for dealing with anxiety is to some degree determined by the vicissitudes of earlier development. For example, if persecutory anxiety and splitting were not excessive and a measure of integration has come about, the ego is able to more easily introject and establish a whole object and move with greater confidence towards the depressive position.

See also: reparation

Klein, M. (1946) 'Notes on some schizoid mechanisms'. *International Journal of Psychoanalysis* 27. Also in *Envy and Gratitude*. New York: Free Press, 1975.

Klein, M. (1952) 'Some theoretical conclusions regarding the emotional life of the infant' in *Developments in Psycho-Analysis*. With P. Heimann, S. Isaacs and J. Riviere. London: Hogarth Press. Also in *Envy and Gratitude*. London: Hogarth Press, 1975.

J. A.

DEPRIVED CHILDREN Deprived children who have lacked continuity of loving care in their early years, and often suffered additional traumas, were at one time thought to be unsuitable for psychoanalytic psychotherapy. Disturbances in *attachment make for difficulties in engagement in psychotherapy as well as in placement in substitute families.

Nevertheless these are the children who most urgently need help if the cycle of deprivation is to be broken. The Boston and Szur 1983 study showed that treatment was in general an arduous task for the therapists. The children tended to be more difficult to engage and slow to trust, as might be expected. However nearly all the children studied were able to use the opportunity for therapy to project their feelings of being discarded, useless, helpless and sometimes cruelly treated. All the children were different but there were common themes, such as falling, being dropped or having to leap over a terrifying abyss. Providing the therapists could tolerate being denigrated and made to feel useless, and could stay with the pain and withstand the onslaughts, some hopeful progress occurred in many cases, even though most children were only able to have once or twice weekly treatment for practical reasons. Support for therapy by carers and social workers was essential.

Some technical lessons were learned during this study. It proved important to understand the reversal of roles, which many of the children were unconsciously enacting. Direct interpretation of aggression was often counterproductive or provocative. Aggressive and cruel behaviour which made the therapist feel like a victim needed to be understood as a way of making the therapist know by experience what it felt like to be on the receiving end of the 'care' system. It was essential to hold these projections for a while until greater trust was established.

The crucial deprivation suffered by such children is of continuity of attentive, receptive loving care. They have introjected instead abandoning, neglectful or cruel parental figures, with whom they unconsciously identify and whom they also project onto would-be substitute parents, making for breakdown of placement. Offering a space in the therapist's mind was an important step towards facilitating the internalisation of caring, helpful figures from which self-esteem could grow.

Boston, M. and Szur, R. (eds) (1983) *Psychotherapy with Severely Deprived Children*. London: Routledge & Kegan Paul. Reprinted London: Karnac Books, 1990.

Emanuel, R. (1996), 'Psychotherapy with children traumatized in infancy'. *Journal of Child Psychotherapy* 22: 214–39.

Hindle, D. (1994) 'Learning to think in a "war zone"'. *Journal of Child Psychotherapy* 20: 341–57.

Lush, D., Boston, M., Morgan, J. and Kolvin, I. (1998) 'Psychoanalytic psychotherapy with disturbed adopted and foster children: a single case follow-up study'. *Clinical Child Psychology and Psychiatry* 3.

M. Bos.

DESIRE A pivotal concept in the Lacanian structuring of the subject, Lacan's term *desir* is a translation of the terms that Freud uses to establish the dynamics of the unconscious: *begierde* and *wunsch*. Desire implies a continuous force rather than an individual act of wishing or longing; for Lacan, it is around the continuity, the unstoppability, the pure insistence of desire that the human subject's trope of existence is mobilised. When we speak of desire however, it is unconscious desire that is significant in terms of psychoanalysis. Desire, for Lacan, is entirely caught up with the concepts of *need and *demand that he introduces in the 1950s. As the human being is an entity with biological needs, and these needs are expressed as demands, the other to whom these needs are addressed will supply a range of objects that may satisfy or gratify biological needs. As such, the Other's response to the demand within which needs are inherent comes to take on a Symbolic function: that of love. Now while needs may be sated by an array of objects, expressed as they are within language, addressed as they are to the Other, a gap opens up between the original need and the demand. While conveying the need, demand also ingenuously directs itself to the Other in the form of a demand for unconditional love. Therefore, even after the need has been satisfied, the subject is left with something else, which is by its very nature unsatisfiable, since the subject will never truly experience unconditional love. This something else that is left over is desire. Desire is not therefore something which is addressed to, or which can be satisfied by an object; indeed Lacan says that what a person enjoys (i.e. his or her jouissance) is his or her relationship to desire, that is desiring itself. Desire is, rather, caused by the subject's unconscious experience of lack which in Lacan is symbolised by the object a. The aim of a Lacanian psychoanalysis is that the subject should come to recognise and name this desire.

J. P. K.

DESIRE, GRAPH OF Developed by Lacan in 1957 as part of his seminar on the Formations of the Unconscious as a teaching device, and appearing in its fullest form in his essay entitled 'The Subversion of the Subject and the Dialectic of Desire in the Freudian Unconscious', the graph as such was intended to represent the structure of desire. What Lacan elucidates in the graph of desire consists of an elaboration of the two functions of speech deployed by the subject: as that which is addressed to the Other in terms of what is enunciated along the Imaginary axis of ego-ego, and as speech within which the subject unconsciously attempts to enunciate something of his/her desire ('want-to-be'). A truth of the subject emerges at the point where these two functions of speech intersect: first at that point which Lacan calls the Code, the Other (as 'companion of language'), and second, at that point which Lacan calls the Message, or meaning. The trajectory of being then speaks its way through the code of (what may be said, heard, and understood by) the Other, and because of its retroactive movement through the signifying chain and the constituting effects in terms of the Code, a meaning is 'born'. If there is any truth of the subject, Lacan says, this is where it will be enunciated.

C. Owe.

DESIRE OF THE ANALYST Lacan's concept of the desire of the analyst concerns the function of unconscious desire as an enigma. It is considered the driving force of the analytic treatment, for the analyst. This desire (of the analyst) has as its object desire itself. The analytic process is directed towards a destitution of the subject, in the form of the analysand's acceptance of the fundamental *lack. As such analysis not only touches upon the subject as subject of desire – the acceptance of desire being fundamentally alienated – but also its relation to the drive (and its objects). The latter is situated 'beyond' the process of separation, for the drive only needs the object (and not the other) to run its course. Hence, the desire of the analyst is to install and maintain the position of the cause of desire, and as such 'enable' the analysand to work through the processes of alienation and of separation, as well as affect the subject of the drive.

K. Lib.

DESTITUTION For Lacan, analysis is terminable. It does not finish on an identification with the analyst but upon a subjective destitution that implies both the end of Imaginary and Symbolic identifications and the dissolution of the transferential relation. The destitution of the analysand occurs as an effect of the verification of the inexistence of the Other achieved in the treatment, that is to say, the patient is confronted with a lack in the Other, which demonstrates that there is no response from the Other concerning the fundamental question of existence.

V. V.

DETERMINISM After Descartes, traditional dualist views held that the mind or soul, occupying a separate ontological realm from that of matter, was not subject to laws of cause and effect that determined all events in the material world. That implied *freedom, thought to be necessary to morality. Believing that psychoanalysis must be a *science, Freud asserted that all mental events were strictly determined. Sometimes freedom was an illusion, when choices were unconsciously determined, but he believed that psychoanalysis could enable patients to attain genuine freedom. Less tenably, psychic determinism is interpreted to mean that psychic events must have psychic causes only.

According to Lacan the subject is determined by the *signifier. The structure of unconscious phantasy, for instance, is established by its being represented by a phrase. In being confronted with his or her fate, a person cannot escape this destiny, but he or she can analyse its elements after the event, and in so doing, avoid repetition.

Rubinstein, B. B. (1997) 'Person, organism, and self' in R. R. Holt (ed.) *Psychoanalysis and the Philosophy of Science: Collected Papers of Benjamin B. Rubinstein*. Madison, CT: International Universities Press.

R. Hol. / R. M. B.

DEUTSCH, HELENE (1884–1982) In 1925 Hélène Deutsch became the first psychoanalyst to publish a book about feminine psychology. Her interest in the subject, along with that of *Horney, helped push Freud into writing articles about women. Other analysts such as Rank, *Ferenczi, and *Groddeck were also intrigued by the neglected role of mothering, but Deutsch insisted on its special significance for female psychology.

She was born in Przemyl, Poland; her parents were Jewish but she also grew up a Polish nationalist. In 1918 she went into personal analysis with Freud for a year, then in 1923–4 she went for a second analysis with *Abraham. Throughout the 1920s she made notable clinical contributions, which resulted in the publication in 1930 of her *Psychoanalysis of the Neuroses*.

Eventually settling in Boston she functioned as president of the Boston Psychoanalytic Society from 1939 until 1941. During World War II she wrote her two-volume *The Psychology of Women*. She wrote, for example, about the conflict in women between motherliness and eroticism. Deutsch argued that a woman's intensified inner life becomes a unique source of human superiority. Perhaps her most famous clinical concept was that of the *'as if' personality, where she highlights the sources of a woman's capacity to identify with others. For Deutsch, victimisation was a central danger of feminine masochism, while intensified self-love can be a self-preservative counter-weight, protecting a woman from her masochistic potential. Horney had ridiculed some of Deutsch's writings in technical papers, but she only answered Horney with some mild footnotes to *The Psychology of Women*.

After her husband Felix died in 1964, *Neuroses and Character Types* appeared in 1965, and two monographs came out as books. Her autobiography *Confrontations with Myself* was released in 1973.

Deutsch retained her intellectual vitality to the end – it was typical of her to question whether the generations of analysed people were any happier.

P. R.

DEVELOPMENT Psychoanalysis believes that psychological disturbance and normal adult functioning can be viewed developmentally. Since its inception, psychoanalytic thinking has consistently assumed that psychopathology is 'developmental' in that early experience is formative and that symptoms can be understood as the re-emergence of early, prototypically infantile modes of thinking and feeling. Freud's classical *libido theory enshrined this idea. Later traditions have extended the same developmental assumptions of cumulative progression and regression under internal or external stressful experience to the theories of *ego functions, *object relations, self-structures, *intersubjectivity, etc. However, these developmental theories are not based on developmental observations. Assumptions are made about development and aspects of childhood based on experience with adults seen in treatment for a variety of different forms of psychological disturbance. These speculative assumptions use development only in a metaphorical sense as a heuristic device, the validity of which cannot be subject to scrutiny.

The metaphoric use of developmental ideas in psychoanalysis is widespread. However, a number of analysts' contributions to the developmental tradition have been based on actual observations of infants and children. Anna *Freud was the first to advance a comprehensive model of psychopathology as abnormal development. Her comprehensive developmental theory used the metaphor of developmental lines to stress the continuity and cumulative character of childhood development. Her formulation stresses the interactions and interdependencies between maturational and environmental determinants in developmental steps.

Unevenness of development is a risk factor for psychiatric disturbance: thus, developmental lines have aetiological significance. A child's problem may be understood as an arrest or regression in a particular line of development. Developmentally acquired discrepancies between the relative strength of the psychic agencies result from constitutional and environmental factors and may be critical for a predisposition to psychopathology. For example, normal development is threatened if parental support is withdrawn too early, leaving the child to face archaic fears of being alone or in darkness, which require the adult's participation as an auxiliary ego. If the ego matures too late, or if the parents are neglectful, the child may regress to earlier, more intense forms of anxiety. Anna Freud's formulation implies that in addressing a child's disturbance the psychoanalytic clinician should focus not only on the determinants of symptomatic aspects of the disorder, but also on offering 'developmental help' to the child and restoring him/her to the 'path of normal development'. The clinician must address the phase-appropriate developmental issues and the meaning of the behaviour in the context of the phase.

Spitz proposed that major shifts in psychological organisation, marked by the emergence of new behaviours and new forms of affective expression (e.g. social smiling), occur when functions are brought into new relation with one another and linked into a coherent unit. He drew attention to the significance of new forms of emotional expression such as the smiling response (two–three months), initial differentiation of self and object, eight month anxiety which indicates differentiation amongst objects, especially of the 'libidinal object proper' and the assertion of self in the 'no' gesture between ten–eighteen months. He suggested that these psychic organisers reflected underlying advances in mental structure formation, indicating the integration of earlier behaviours into a new organisation. Spitz saw self-regulation as an important function of the ego. In particular, psychoanalysts have highlighted the role of affect in the development of self-regulation: the mother's emotional expression at first serves a 'soothing' or 'containing' function which facilitates the restoration of emotional equilibrium. Later, the infant uses the mother's emotional response as a signalling device to indicate safety. Later still, the infant internalises the affective response and uses his own emotional reaction as a signal of safety or danger.

In *Mahler's developmental model the biological birth of the human infant and the psychological birth of the individual do not coincide in time. She focuses on the dimension of psychological development that traces the passage from the unity of 'I' and 'not-I' to eventual separation and individuation. Separation refers to the child's emergence from a symbiotic fusion with the mother, whereas individuation consists of those achievements marking the child's assumption of his own individual characteristics. Mahler's model assumes that the child develops from normal autism through a symbiotic period to the four sequentially unfolding subphases of the separation-individuation process. Each step is strongly influenced by the nature of the mother-infant interaction. Mahler sought to enable clinicians treating adults to reconstruct the pre-verbal period more accurately, thereby making patients more accessible to analytic interventions. Several psychoanalytic workers have built on her conclusions, modifying therapeutic technique to address developmental deficits relatively directly through the relationship with the therapist. Mahlerians see the rapprochement subphase as the critical period of character formation. Its crucial conflict between separateness and closeness, autonomy and dependency, is repeated throughout development. This part of her theory has been used extensively in work with individuals with borderline personality disorder.

More recent experimental research-based psychoanalytic views of infant behaviour have led to dramatic revisions of Mahlerian views. The work of a group of psychoanalytic developmentalists (Tronick, Stern, Beebe, Murray, Emde, Mayes) has revealed that infants come into the world with cognitive, emotional and social capacities that enable them actively to seek stimulation and regulate their own behaviour through environmental interactions. They have pre-wired knowledge of both the physical and the social world. So, for example, they can integrate information across the senses as well as detect and remember unchanging aspects of the environment. Thus they can recognise their mother, imitate facial expressions and manifest at least three affect states: distress, contentment and interest. At two to three months a range of developments enhance the infant's appeal to others. For example, their cooing becomes responsive, and they develop an ability to engage adults in synchronous, reciprocal social interchanges. The nature of the caregiver's responsiveness in these interchanges has far-reaching implications for child development. At seven to nine months children develop focused attachment, acting as if they understand that another person can understand their thoughts, feelings and actions. They thus signal for parental intervention at night, show preferred attachment for a small number of care giving adults and adjust their reaction to unfamiliar stimuli on the basis of the responses of their primary caregiver. At around eighteen months, the acquisition of language and other indicators of enhancing body capacity (e.g. symbolic play) enable complex negotiations with the caregiver, true interactive play with peers and the development of moral emotions such as embarrassment and empathy and a few months later *guilt, pride and *shame. Throughout this period, individual differences arise in consequence of complex interplay of constitutional and environmental factors, with genes acting as biological regulators and cultural, familial and parental characteristics acting as social regulators. For example, most caretakers, however sensitive and positively disposed, are likely to respond negatively to so-called difficult infants (irritable, hard to soothe, fearful of novelty), which is likely to compound their constitutional problems.

Most psychoanalytic developmental theories take a surprisingly narrow view of the developmental process. Their confidence in mapping particular forms of psychopathology to specific developmental epochs (e.g. *borderline disorder and the rapprochement sub-phase of *separation and individuation) is unjustified. Their over-emphasis on early experience is frequently at odds with developmental data. It seems that pathological processes of self-representation and object relationships characterise developmental phases far later than those which have traditionally concerned psychoanalytic theoreticians. The emphasis on deficits in preverbal periods is a particular problem for psychoanalytic theory because it renders so many of the hypotheses untestable.

A major challenge for psychoanalysis is a proper expansion of the notion of 'the past and the present' and a more comprehensive tracing of developmental continuities between infancy and old age. The metaphorical 'baby' of psychoanalytic theory which stands for 'the past' will probably have to be abandoned and replaced by more appropriate neuropsychologically informed notions consistent with what we now understand about the development of the central nervous system. Yet a unique advantage of the psychoanalytic model over *neuropsychoanalytic-based developmental views is its vision of development as a series of *compromise formations. Both unconscious and conscious representations of the self are helpfully viewed as the product of competing environmental pressures and intrapsychic processes in an effort to regulate positive and negative affect. These compromises may have involved defensive distortion of mental representations; where the competing pressures have occurred particularly early or intensely, wholesale distortion or disabling of some of the mental processes which generate representations may also have occurred, leading to far more pervasive and extensive abnormalities of development.

Beebe, B., Lachmann, F. and Jaffe, J. (1997) 'Mother–infant interaction structures and presymbolic self and object representations'. *Psychoanalytic Dialogues* 7.

Emde, R., Kubicek, L., and Oppenheim, D. (1997) 'Imaginative reality observed during early language development'. *International Journal of Psycho-Analysis* 78(1): 115–33.

Freud, A. (1965) *Normality and Pathology in Childhood*. Harmondsworth: Penguin.

Spitz, R. (1965) *The First Year of Life*. New York: International Universities Press.

Mahler, M. S., Pine, F. and Bergman, A. (1975) *The Psychological Birth of the Human Infant: Symbiosis and Individuation*. New York: Basic Books.

Stern, D. N. (1985) *The Interpersonal World of the Infant: A View from Psychoanalysis and Developmental Psychology*. New York: Basic Books.

P. F.

DEVELOPMENTAL DELAY Children's development may be delayed globally, or in respect of individual milestones such as motor development, the achievement of sphincter control, or language acquisition. Global delay may be a consequence of neurological damage, following on for instance from oxygen deprivation at birth, or it can follow from severe early problems in emotional functioning which mean that the child is unable to spend enough developmental time in a frame of mind that makes it possible to take in experiences and learn from them. Organic and emotional factors can interact with each other in complex ways, and one of the positive results of psychotherapy can be to address the emotional ramifications of the impairment, and in this way to free the child to reach whatever his or her ceiling may be.

The cognitive aspect of developmental delay overlaps with *learning disability. However, the term applies also to motor capacities (where it overlaps with *dyspraxia), to language development, and to age-appropriate emotional maturity with particular reference to the sense of self and the ability to relate to other people. Children characterised as PDD (suffering from Pervasive Developmental Delay) show many, though not all, of the difficulties associated with *autistic spectrum disorders. Psychoanalytic writers such as *Klein, *Winnicott and Mannoni long ago pointed out the contribution of *childhood psychosis to states of apparent mental insufficiency. *Bion's contribution in linking emotional and cognitive development has been central to work in this area, while Haag's work on the body image provides a conceptual framework for linking problems in the motor, emotional and cognitive spheres. Therapeutic work with such children points up the central importance of fears of unintegration, fragmentation, and other severe anxieties characteristic of childhood psychosis and autism, and can lead to substantial improvement.

Rustin, M., Rhode, M., Dubinsky, A. and Dubinsky, H. (eds) (1997) *Psychotic States in Children*. Tavistock Clinic Book Series: London: Duckworth.

M. Rho.

DEVELOPMENTAL STAGES (FAIRBAIRN) Fairbairn described three developmental stages. The first, infantile *dependence characterised by an attitude of early oral incorporation (sucking or rejecting the preambivalent object); and, late oral incorporation (accepting alternating with biting the *ambivalent object). The second, transitional relating, occurring between infantile and mature dependence. In this stage, the incorporated object is related to as good or bad contents. The third, mature dependence, normally characterised by an attitude of giving, in which the *exciting and rejecting objects are exteriorised and combined within the character of the real external object. Mature dependence is characterised by a relationship to a whole object that also has genitals, not by a predominance of focus on the genital aspect of the person.

E. F. B. / D. E. S.

DIAGNOSIS The term does not appear in the General Subject Index of Freud's writings. More of a central concern in traditional psychiatry, diagnosis has been especially important in psychopharmacology, insofar as the particular medication to be prescribed is presumably dictated by the diagnosis of the patient. By contrast, at least for the general diagnostic category of psychoneurosis, whether obsessional, phobic, or hysteric, the general psychoanalytic treatment approach was pretty much the same – e.g. the use of the couch, free association, interpretation; subtle differences in treatment have to do the dynamics of the individual patient. To the extent that there was any emphasis on diagnosis, it included broad distinctions such as neurotic versus borderline versus psychotic. Within each broad category, the implicit diagnostic focus, corresponding to a development and of psychopathology, was on formulating the patient's central conflicts, predominant defences, points of developmental fixation, and degree of intactness of various ego functions.

More recently, psychoanalytic writing has appeared characterized by implicit and explicit greater emphasis on diagnosis and the accompanying suggestion that treatment approach should follow from the diagnosis. In 1971, *Kohut distinguished between self defects (narcissistic personality disorders) and intrapsychic conflict and suggested that somewhat different therapeutic approaches were differentially appropriate for each type of pathology. The clearest expression of a recent psychoanalytic emphasis on diagnosis, combined with a corresponding recommendation for treatment approach, is found in *Kernberg's writings on borderline pathology. As for the diagnostic aspect, borderline pathology is defined by, among other things, the patient's developmental history of object relations, affect expression, the kind of transference formed, and the predominant type of defenses employed. As for treatment, according to Kernberg, Clarkin and Yeoman's 2002 *A Primer of Transference Focused Psychotherapy with Borderline Patients*, a transference focused psychotherapy (TFP) is the appropriate treatment for borderline patients. Whereas traditional diagnostic categories, such as neurosis, have been dropped from the Diagnostic Statistical Manuals (DSM), the diagnostic categories most heavily emphasized by Kohut and Kernberg – namely, narcissistic personality disorder and borderline personality disorder – are included in the DSM.

Kernberg, O. (1985) *Borderline Conditions and Pathological Narcissism*. Northvale, NJ: Jason Aronson.

Kernberg, O., Clarkin, J. and Yeomans, F. E. (2002) *A Primer of Transference Focused Psychotherapy with Borderline Patients*. Northvale, NJ: Jason Aronson.

Kohut, H. (1971) *Analysis of the Self: Systematic Approach to Treatment of Narcissistic Personality Disorders*. New York: International Universities Press.

McWilliams, N. (1994) *Psychoanalytic Diagnosis: Understanding Personality Structure in the Clinical Process*. New York: Guilford.

M. Eag.

DIAGNOSIS (LACAN) Lacan's ideas on diagnosis are generally based on the central diagnostic principles within Freudian theory, yet he also developed Freud's insights along two distinct axes. First, he distinguished between three separate structures (*neurosis, *psychosis, *perversion), thus adding a third category to Freud's basic differentiation between psychoneurosis and *narcissistic neurosis. Second, he argued that each of these three structures epitomises a specific position of the *subject vis-à-vis the Symbolic order of language and the law. To Freud's approach to diagnosis Lacan added the criterion of speech. Unlike Freud, Lacan did not exclude psychotics from psychoanalysis, but investigated the technical implications of these structures for analytic interpretation, the handling of the *transference, and the general position of the analyst during the treatment.

See also: diagnosis; other

D. N.

DIALECTIC Lacan interprets analysis as a 'talking cure' in the light of the Platonic tradition of dialectic, where the truth emerges through conversation and questioning. Correlatively, the logical structure of analysis is interpreted through Hegel, with a primordial *Bejahung* subtending the psychically structuring negations of *Verneinung* (*denial), *Verleugnung* (*disavowal) and *Verwerfung* (*foreclosure), as thesis to antithesis. The outcome of analysis (and of any process which creatively produces new signifiers) would then function as synthesis.

G. S.

DIRECTION OF THE TREATMENT Lacan says the analyst directs the treatment, not the patient. The movement associated with this direction is distilled by Lacan in his work from the early 1950s where he relates the phases of the treatment, that is, beginning, middle and end, to the uncovering of the reality of the subject and the cause of the symptom. He isolates three conceptually distinct, yet practically intricate phases. Firstly, there are the preliminary sessions during which a properly analytic symptom may crystallise, but which will culminate in a 'rectification of the subject's relation to the *Real', implicating the subject in his own story, as a question. This will trigger the next phase, through installing a *signifier of transference. This latter phase introduces the role of the analyst, as a *'subject supposed to know', in relation to the unconscious dynamics of the analysand. The third phase involves the elaboration of the unconscious *phantasy, and its reduction to a grammatical phrase; correlatively, there is the emergence of an object of enjoyment (*jouissance), tied to the person of the analyst, in the eclipse of the latter's role as 'subject supposed to know' the truth of the analysand's being, in the symptom. The coherent exiting from analysis involves the reduction of the symptom to a signifying scar, and the draining from the fantasy of imaginarised enjoyment.

G. S.

DISAVOWAL Disavowal is used by Freud to describe the flight from the perception that the female does not possess a penis and that therefore *castration is possible. The *fetish is a sign that a disavowal of this kind has taken place. A pervasive disavowal and remodelling of reality takes place in psychosis. Lacan demonstrates the paradoxical rapport of the fetishist with an object which is not an object, i.e. with the Symbolic phallus which is there as absent. The fetish commemorates the moment an image (of an object) was fixed, as in a freeze-frame from a movie.

See also: perversion

J. A. Ber. / R. M. W.

DISCHARGE Defined, by Freud, as the reduction of internal excitation generated by drive demands. *Pleasure is thus attained by reducing internal stimulation to its lowest level. This concept of pleasure is analogised to the sexual orgasm. Impulsive action and *primary process thought are considered to be manifestations of rapid discharge.

S. E.

DISCOURSE Lacan's use of the term discourse implies that language is transindividual and that speech implies a social bond with an other. Any Lacanian reference to discourse immediately calls up his early formulation that 'the unconscious is the discourse of the Other'. This designates the unconscious as effect of the Other's speech and so stresses the intersubjective nature of psychical reality. This in turn carries with it the basis for other Lacanian concepts – the subject divided by language, the unconscious as language, the subject inhabited by the Other – so that discourse becomes the stage for all possible permutations of the social bond. Later, his enquiry into the various discourses constituting different social bonds will develop into the theory of his four discourses: the discourse of the Master, the University, the Hysteric and the Analyst.

H. T.

DISPLACEMENT The re-direction of an aggressive or sexual impulse toward an *object, person, belief, pre-occupation, or anxiety from its original, primary focus (e.g. the expression of concern about the intactness of one's brain functioning as a defensive avoidance of awareness of castration anxiety, referred to as displacement upward) that is, from a more threatening to a less threatening idea. For Lacan it is one of two primary processes, its mechanism being similar to the poetic function of *metonymy. The linguistic connection between *signifiers includes a semantic link that enables the displacement of meaning along the signifying chain from one element to another. This accounts, for instance, for the displacement of psychic investment onto an otherwise insignificant element.

D. W. / A. I.

DISILLUSION The experience of what Freud has also termed the *reality principle. It is the capacity of the infant who has sustained the illusion (created by the good-enough maternal figure), that all that is desired is able to be created; to accept (through maternal intervention) that this is not so; that what is desired at all times may not be created or found; and that lack, loss and ultimately death are part of reality. This is achieved by appropriate, small doses of maternal failure – the not *good-enough mother. Its success is dependent on the establishment of *illusion and the capacity to create the good mother, good experience, successfully. Disillusion is the precursor of Winnicott's 'capacity to be alone'.

Freud, S. (1911) *Formulations on the Two Principles of Mental Functioning*. S. E. 12. London: Hogarth Press.

Winnicott, D. W. (1971) 'Transitional objects and transitional phenomena' in *Playing and Reality*. London: Tavistock.

Winnicott, D. W. (1984) 'The capacity to be alone' in *The Maturational Processes and the Facilitating Environment*. London: Karnac Books.

H. T. R.

DISSOCIATION The subject of dissociated or divided consciousness has been of interest in psychopathology from the time of *Charcot and Janet. Dissociation of parts of experience is a normal process, but its excessive use figures in the pathology of dissociative disorders, including multiple personality, or 'dissociative identity disorder', states which are often the result of trauma. Fairbairn was interested in the comparative study of dissociation and repression throughout his academic career. In his MD thesis he argued that *repression was a special case of dissociation, being the dissociation of unpleasant mental content. Though he did not address the issue directly in his later writings, Fairbairn regretted the lack of analytic study of dissociation, aware that the concept was crucial to the study of the multiplicity of internalised ego-object interactions that characterize his endopsychic theory.

Fairbairn, W. R. D. [1929] (1994) 'The relationship of dissociation and repression: considered from the point of view of medical psychology' (MD thesis submitted to Edinburgh University, 30 March 1929) in D. Scharff and E. Fairbairn Birtles (eds) *From Instinct to Self: Selected papers of W. R. D. Fairbairn*, Vol. 2. Northvale, NJ: Jason Aronson.

E. F. B. / D. E. S.

DISTORTION (FREUD) In classical dream theory, the latent dream thoughts, in order to bypass *censorship, are transformed, through the dream work, into a manifest dream in which the unconscious elements are not easily recognisable. Dream interpretation reverses this effort at disguise and attempts to restore coherence. In *Jung and in other more modern psychoanalytic conceptions, the significance of distortion and disguise is disputed.

Lacan approached the question as follows: consciousness gives a formulation to the reality of an event, it subjects the event to distortion; the reason for this lies in the existence of *conflict in the unconscious. For Freud this process is apparent in *false connection, and in the construction of a dream. Lacan refuses the assumption that such distortion can be controlled by the ego, and instead takes it that the ego is characterised by misrepresentations of this kind. In order to escape the effect of such illusions, Lacan proposes the solution put forward by Freud: distortion is undone only by gaining access to the unconscious.

B. B. / P. L.

DIVISION While Freud spoke of the splitting of the ego, Lacan radicalises this split by grasping it as the basic condition of the subject. The subject is identical to the division which marks his *alienation in language. It is instituted by a repetition which effectively bars the subject, causing him to fade beneath the signifying chain. In speech the subject is split between enunciation and statement, truth and knowledge, thinking and being, signifier and jouissance.

P. D.

DORA Soubriquet for Ida Bauer (1882–1945), whom Freud analysed from October to December 1900. Diagnosed an hysteric by Freud, she is classified as a *borderline by contemporary analysts. Besides being an impressive narrative achievement in its own right, the case history is known for its observations about orality, bisexuality, psychosomatics, the interrelation between dreams and pathology, and the nature of transference and its interpretation. Feminists have complained that Freud's treatment of Dora, and his theories about female sexuality exposed how the clinical deficiencies of the case, along with showing Freud's own pathology, were glibly accepted for too long by the psychological community.

See also: feminism and psychoanalysis

Freud, S. (1905) *Fragment of an Analysis of a Case of Hysteria*. S. E. 7. London: Hogarth Press.
Mahony, P. (1996) *Freud's Dora: A Psychoanalytic, Historical, and Textual Study*. New Haven, CT: Yale University Press.

P. M.

DOUBLE BIND A communication consisting of two simultaneous messages or orders, one of which contradicts the other. Both orders carry a threat of punishment. Haley and Bateson suggested that repeated subjugation to this type of communication in an intense situation which prohibits pointing out the contradictory messages will lead to schizophrenic symptoms. *Laing called this form of prohibition 'mystification'. A parent might consciously instruct the child to be independent whilst simultaneously and unconsciously communicating to the child that the parent might disintegrate if they became independent. Both instructions carry the threat of the loss of the parent, their love and the child's place in the world, leaving the child in a maddening no-win situation.

Bateson, G. et al. (1956) 'Toward a theory of schizophrenia'. *Behavioural Science X*.

H. O.

DOUBT The inability to decide between two alternatives can invade thought and impede action. Freud identified doubt as a defence mechanism and a central feature of *obsessional neurosis. It paralyses the patient and prevents him from enjoying a love object as well as from taking some hostile action against the (ambivalent) love object.

D. L.

DREAMING/DREAM The mental activity, within sleep, of the experience of images, sensations and ideas often formed into coherent, often ambiguous, and usually forgotten, narratives. In the early development of psychoanalysis, in both Freud and Jung, the dream served as the basic experience for information about the workings of the unconscious mind. The central text of early psychoanalysis was Freud's *The Interpretation of Dreams*, published in 1900.

P. L.

DREAMS (FAIRBAIRN) Freud viewed dreams as expressions of fulfilment of wishes for infantile instincts, stirred by events of the day. Fairbairn viewed dreams as 'shorts' of object relations structure and the dynamics of the inner world. The interrelationships between the dreamer and his internal objects forms the structure of the dream and expresses its emotional content, showing, for instance, the relationship of the *central ego to *exciting and *rejecting objects. In the dream, present situations in external life are related to inner organisation, imparting psychic meaning by making connections between past and present, inside and outside, conscious and unconscious.

Fairbairn, W. R. D. [1944] (1994) 'Endopsychic structure considered in terms of object-relationships'. *Psychoanalytic Studies of the Personality*. London: Routledge.
Fairbairn, W. R. D. [1954] (1994) 'The nature of hysterical states' in D. E. Scharff and E. F. Birtles (eds) *From Instinct to Self*, Vol. 1. Northvale, NJ: Jason Aronson.
Freud, S. (1900) *The Interpretation of Dreams*. S. E. 4 and 5.

E. F. B. / D. E. S.

DREAM (JUNG) Exploration of dreams in Jungian analysis has been and remains a cornerstone for experiential grounding in the reality of the psyche. In pithy contradistinction to Freud, Jung succinctly asserted 'that the dream is a spontaneous self-portrayal, in symbolic form, of the actual situation in the unconscious'. Hence, a phenomenological-hermeneutic approach focused on – *symbolic and metaphoric readings derived from the context of the representations of objects and situations in dreams, without predetermined meaning is emphasised – rather than the search for *latent content. The fabric of dreams is articulated in terms of activated *complexes, psychosomatic splinter psyches composed of linked affects and images around an *archetypal core, i.e. layers of associations and defences accrued around primal potentials. Unconscious processes manifesting in dreams are seen as constellated in response to the attitudes of consciousness in a manner that is self-regulatory for the whole of the personality. The compensatory function of dreams is primary, with varying degrees of alteration being elicited in response to the stance of consciousness. While restoration of psychological equilibrium is the goal of compensations, consciousness retains the burden of ethical and moral responsibility for the implementation of change. Taken longitudinally over a series of dreams, the compensations resemble the successive steps in a planned and orderly process of development which Jung went on to articulate in his concept of *individuation. He therefore attributes a transformative potential to dreams as 'our most effective aid in building up the personality'. Of special note is Jung's delineation of a prospective function of dreams. This includes prognostic insight into pathological conditions, physiological and/or psychological, as well as maturational processes. Initial dreams in analysis, the first ones to capture the essence of a person's dilemma, often supply a prognostic view. As preparatory to working with dreams clinically, Jung insisted on a training analysis in order to gain experiential competency working with the multiple psychological domains. The classical methods used to work with dreams include interpretation, *amplification, and active *imagination. Interpretation includes causal- reductive analysis of the personal history of the dreamer together with exploration of the ontological components of the *transference. When warranted, however, dream interpretation can be employed to facilitate a synthetic-teleological unfolding of the whole personality. In this the ego is relativised as a second centre, the *self, is circumambulated. Free association is not employed for this latter purpose but a closer adherence to the specificity of the dream images with their symbolic, cultural and evolutionary histories used for amplification. The archetypal underpinnings of the transference/countertransference field are examined throughout. A flexible selection of intrapsychic, interpersonal, transpersonal and historical contributions that are contextually valid can be used throughout to formulate subjective and objective levels of interpretation. Contemporary Jungians have elaborated Jung's insights on dreams such as his recognition of the intersubjective origins of dreams (as exemplified in a letter to James Kirsch where Jung stated: 'In the deepest sense we all dream not out of ourselves but out of what lies between us and the other' (letter, 29 September 1934)). They have more fully articulated the differentiation, and intermingling, of personal, cultural and archetypal aspects of dreams, and have applied the findings of evolutionary psychology to Jungian views on dreams. In addition dreamwork with groups has been developed using non-interpretative as well as interpretative methods. Integration of the findings from the cognitive neurosciences with the theory of dreams in analytical psychology is in its infancy.

J. C.

DREAM (LACAN) As a formation of the unconscious, the dream expresses something of desire via the signifying material which gets press-ganged into service: constituted out of a range of forms of the subject's history/experiences and emptied of their original meaning, these signifiers become reorganised such that the desire which is unconscious finds a means of expression.

C. Owe.

DREAM, MEANING OF see **MEANING OF DREAM**

DRIVE (FREUD) Freud conceived of a drive as an internally generated stimulus that is a prime motivational factor in mammalian development. In his first formal drive theory, Freud distinguished between two drives that he labelled the survival of the self (ego libido), and the survival of the species (object or sexual libido). Early in development, survival of the self is the drive that predominantly motivates the infant. In Freud's terminology there is primarily ego libido present. The infant's first libidinal *object is the self (really a conglomerate of the mother and self) and this is the first object cathexis that occurs in development (*narcissism). At this point in Freud's theorising (1910–17), ego libido and object libido are seen as conflicting tendencies, while aggression is seen as a part of the concept of survival of the self. Despite the idea of conflicting drives, in ideal development the drives combine at various points and, eventually, object libidinal tendencies predominate over ego libidinal tendencies. Concepts like sadism and *masochism are complicated amalgams of ego and object libido.

After World War I, Freud's ideas about sadism and masochism changed dramatically and he presented a new drive theory. He posited a primary masochism which he explained in terms of a drive towards death or dissolution – Thanatos. Primary masochistic tendencies had to be countered by another drive, Eros. Eros is the drive towards life: both survival of the self and the species were seen as part of it.

Many of Freud's colleagues rejected the idea of a death instinct and instead conceived of drives in terms of sex and *aggression. Aggression is then seen as innate, while masochism is a tendency that is acquired. Melanie Klein is one of the few analysts who included the idea of the death instinct in her theoretical writings.

See also: form of organisation of the drive; partial drive; pressure of the drive

Freud, S. (1905) *Three Essays on the Theory of Sexuality*. S. E. 7. London: Hogarth Press.
Freud, S. (1915) 'Instincts and their vicissitudes'. S. E. 14. London: Hogarth Press.

S. E.

DRIVE (FAIRBAIRN) Following Drever's research, Fairbairn argued that 'instincts' were more correctly labelled 'instinctual tendencies', or drives and consisted of two types. Life-preserving tendencies are instigated by internal and external circumstances and designed to form and maintain relationships; he grouped these as the libidinal tendency. Reactive tendencies operate in response to external situations, each instance of which acquires an emotional content or affect in the form of thought, *dream or *fantasy. Thus frustration leads to anger and sorrow. *Aggression is therefore secondary to libidinal aims, although it exists as an organising factor throughout life. Fairbairn argued that all *drives are designed to promote and preserve life. The *death drive has no place in his work. He believed that behaviour organised as if by a death instinct was symptomatic of aggression operating in a closed inner world system.

Drever, James (1917) *Instinct in Man*. Cambridge: Cambridge University Press.

Fairbairn, W. R. D. [1930] (1994) 'The libido theory and the pleasure principle interpreted in terms of appetite' in E. Fairbairn Birtles and D. Scharff (eds) *From Instinct to Self*, Vol. 2. Northvale, NJ: Jason Aronson.

Fairbairn, W. R. D. [1958] (1994) 'On the nature and aims of psychoanalytic treatment' in D. Scharff and E. Fairbairn Birtles (eds) *From Instinct to Self*, Vol. 1. Northvale, NJ: Jason Aronson.

E. F. B. / D. E. S.

DRIVE (JUNG) A source of psychic *energy that is body-based, whose aim and form are affected by the *archetypal images which the psyche produces. *Jung, like *Freud, believed that the origins of mental life and psychic activity are to be found in the biological body and that the instincts or drives are the fundamental link between biology and psychological development.

However, unlike Freud, who restricted his concept of the drives to sexuality and aggression, Jung described five main groups of instinctive factors: hunger, sexuality, activity, reflection, and creativity. In his seminal essay 'Instinct and Unconscious', Jung discussed the universality of these five instinct groups and their subtle relationship with archetypal patterns of images produced by the psyche.

Instincts, or drives, and archetypes together form the *collective unconscious, and they are inextricably linked at all points. Both drives and archetypes are aspects of the same vital activity. Jung and many post-Jungians conceive of instinct and archetype along a spectrum, with instinct at the infra-red end and its counterpart, the archetype, at the ultraviolet end.

Contemporary analytical psychologists study the dynamics of interpersonal relationships as well as intrapsychic phenomena, and their more refined understanding of early developmental processes together with data from the fields of infant research by Schore and child analysis led them to speak of motivational systems rather than of instincts.

Lichtenberg describes the five basic, innate survival mechanisms: psychic regulation of physiological requirements; attachment and later, affiliation; exploration and assertion; antagonism or withdrawal, or both; and, sexual enjoyment and sexual excitement.

Jung, C. G. [1919] (1960; 1969) 'Instinct and unconscious' in *The Structure and Dynamics of the Psyche*. Princeton: Princeton University Press.

Lichtenberg, J. D. (1989) *Psychoanalysis and Motivation*. Hillsdale, NJ: The Analytic Press.

Samuels, A. [1985] (1986) *Jung and the Post-Jungians*. London: Routledge & Kegan Paul.

Schore, A. N. (1994) *Affect Regulation and the Origin of the Self*. Hillsdale, NJ and Hove: Erlbaum.

Stein, M. (1998) *Jung's Map of the Soul*. Chicago: Open Court.

Jan W.

DRIVE (LACAN) The drive in humans is fundamentally different from animal instinct. For Lacan there is no genital drive as such, there are only partial drives operating through a mixture of life and death drives. These partial drives are based on pregenital objects (oral, anal, scopic, invocative) that receive a phallic meaning through the oedipal structure.

The drive has no final goal (in the sense of genital satisfaction), but aims at satisfaction through the repetition of a looping movement aiming to catch the object situated in the Other, and trying to return it to its own body. Thus every drive is both autoerotic and active. Lacan's interpretation of Freud's original dualism accentuates the fusion between death and life drives, thereby subverting the original meaning of life and death. The aim of the life drive is to return to the original symbiotic state of being through which the subject disappears, resulting in the death of the subject.

At the same time, the opposite aim is also present, namely, separation from the symbiotic state with the other, through which the subject acquires an identity of its own. This opposition explains the unsatisfying nature of satisfaction in the drive.

P. V.

DRIVE FOR MASTERY Freud sees the drive for mastery as connected to the active part played by the male in sexuality. The wish to gain mastery over the object is seen in sadism and aggressiveness. Repetitions of traumatic events in dreams or children's play are attempts to achieve mastery over events which were passively endured. In the development of the ego, progressive trends toward greater autonomy are opposed by regressive trends and wishes for dependence. *Ego psychology posits the existence of a 'neutral energy', leading toward ego mastery, unconnected to sex or aggression.

E. B.

DUAL RELATION The ego and the other, or image of the other, are coeval and mutually dependent. This dual relation Lacan also calls the *Imaginary relationship. It is characterised by the ego's Imaginary identification and *alienation, and marked by an ambivalent relationship of aggressive rivalry and erotic attachment to the other.

See also: aggressivity mirror phase; narcissism;

A. I.

DYNAMIC According to Freud, every mental process should be examined from dynamic, topographic and *economic viewpoints. A dynamic perspective in psychoanalysis refers to the interplay of forces in the mind. The demand of an drive for satisfaction is an example of such a force. From the clinical point of view, understanding of mind in terms of inner conflict is an expression of psychodynamic perspective.

See also: metapsychology; topography

M. Eag.

DYSPRAXIA Inadequacy or clumsiness in the carrying out of gross or fine motor skills. Dyspraxia in children is often associated with *developmental delay. It may be the outcome of neurological impairment, caused for instance by oxygen deprivation at birth, and may realistically heighten those fantasies of bodily fragmentation which are often encountered in children who do not suffer from actual physical difficulties. Conversely, addressing the emotional experience of these fantasies in psychotherapy can free the child to reach whatever his physical ceiling may be. Recent work on the development of an emotional sense of bodily integration, largely derived from the interface between *infant observation and the psychotherapy of children with *autism, provides a fruitful perspective on childhood dyspraxia, as well as on the subjective experience of children and adults who experience parts of their body as being insecurely attached to each other.

Haag, G. (2000) 'In the footsteps of Frances Tustin: further reflections on the development of the body ego'. *International Journal of Infant Observation* 3: 7–22.

M. Rho.

E

EATING DISORDERS Obsessive-compulsive behaviour described either as anorexia nervosa (compulsive self-starvation) or bulimia nervosa (over-eating followed by self-induced vomiting or laxative use).

Although these conditions were not defined until comparatively recently, one encounters a clearly anorexic pattern in the description of thirteenth- and fourteenth-century saints, for example St Catherine of Siena, and of bulimic patterns in the ancient Roman practice of binging and then vomiting. Up until the twentieth century, anorexia and bulimia were understood in terms of physical illness.

Psychoanalysis has gradually shifted the focus of interest from a search for a cause to a search for meaning. In a letter to *Fliess in 1889, Freud describes anorexia as a form of melancholia due to a loss of libido. Later, in *Three Essays on the Theory of Sexuality*, he linked anorexic and bulimic behaviour to the female sexual development and oral phantasy whereby starvation or vomiting constituted defensive behaviours against an Oedipal wish for impregnation. This development was already adumbrated in a letter to Fliess in 1899.

*Abraham in his 1924 'Development of the Libido' initiates a shift from interest in drives to unconscious phantasy underlying anorexia nervosa. He argues that the body, because of its thinness, is perceived as a penis. Klein modifies previous views in so far as she sees an intense relationship to food as primary and not as a defensive regression from genitality. From a Kleinian perspective, eating disorders are seen within the context of the patient's relationship to internal objects. Klein's later 1957 references to envy are particularly significant for the understanding of eating disorders. A phantasy of fusion with the mother can be seen as a defence against envious feelings and this theme returns in a number of Kleinian writings. Rhode has described an anorexic girl whose central phantasy was totally quantitative – goodness, food, sexuality were seen as part of a pool she shared with the mother. Her phantasy was one of complete fusion with the mother in a relationship without boundaries.

Following the theories of *ego psychology as well as *self psychology, Goodsitt takes a very different view: the refusal of food in anorexia nervosa is seen as a desperate attempt to escape from a confused and undifferentiated relationship with the mother in order to reach autonomy and develop oneself.

The lack of a transitional space, described by Winnicott in 1953, has been regarded as a central aspect of eating disorders. Birksted-Breen expands on this theme, suggesting that the fantasy of fusion can only be disrupted by the presence of the father as Other and equates this with the presence of a 'transitional space'.

More recently, Williams has linked anorexic and bulimic symptoms to a phantasy, or at times an experience, of inimical input. This can be defended against by the development of a 'No Entry' system of defences which includes anorexia. It can otherwise be met by a 'porosity' which is at the core of some forms of bulimia. She suggests that in these cases the terms *container/contained relationship should be replaced by 'receptacle/foreign body' relationship.

Abraham, K. [1924] (1979) 'Development of the libido' in *Selected Papers of Karl Abraham*. London: Karnac Books.

Birksted-Breen, D. (1989) 'Working with an anorexic patient'. *International Journal of Psycho-Analysis* 70.

Goodsitt, A. (1988) 'Narcissistic disturbance in anorexia nervosa' in Schwartz, H. J. (ed.) *Bulimia: Psychoanalytic Treatment and Theory*. Madison, CT: International University Press.

Klein, M. [1957] (1975) *Envy and Gratitude in The Writings of Melanie Klein*, Vol. 3: *Envy and Gratitude and Other Works*. London: Hogarth Press.

Rhode, M. (1979) 'One life between two people: themes from the analysis of a nine-to-fifteen-year-old anorexic girl'. *Journal of Child Psychotherapy* 5.

Williams, G. (1997) *Internal Landscapes and Foreign Bodies: Eating Disorders and Other Pathologies.* Tavistock Clinic Book Series. London: Duckworth.

G. Wil.

ECONOMIC One of the five metapsychological perspectives (along with *dynamic, *topographic, structural and later, *adaptive) from which every mental process can be understood. The economic standpoint refers to hypothetical quantities of energy (*cathexis), associated with mental processes and contents. Freud equated unpleasure with dammed up energy or excitation, and pleasure with its diminution or discharge.

See also: metapsychology

Freud, S. [1925] (1926) *Psychoanalysis.* S. E. 20. London: Hogarth Press.

M. Eag.

EDINGER, EDWARD F. (1922–98) Edward Edinger was a prominent psychiatrist and Jungian analyst. He was widely considered the Dean of Jungian analysis in the United States. He was born in Cedar Rapids, Iowa, grew up in Indiana, and secured a medical degree from Yale University in 1946. He analysed with Esther Harding and eventually collaborated with her as a colleague to solidify Jung's psychology in the United States. He was a founding member of the C. G. Jung Foundation and the C. G. Jung Institute of New York where he practised and then served as president of the Institute from 1968 to 1979. In 1979 Dr Edinger moved to Los Angeles where he continued to practise, teach and write until his death on 7 July 1998; His career spanned more than forty years. Edward Edinger was a deeply introverted man whose passion for the psychology of C. G. Jung led him to devote his life to the creative amplification of Jung's vision. He was a highly regarded analyst, teacher and writer who wrote nineteen books, many of which have become classics in the field of Jungian studies.

S. M.

EFFICACY EXPERIENCES In addition to the experience of *selfobject responsiveness, the experience of one's self as an effective agent is essential to feeling cohesive and vital. Efficacy pleasure may derive from the experience of achieving a goal or from the sense of being capable of eliciting a selfobject response.

Broucek, F. (1979) 'Efficacy in infancy: a review of some experimental studies and their possible implications for clinical theory'. *International Journal of Psychoanalysis* 60.
Hendrick, I. (1942) 'Instinct and the ego during infancy'. *Psychoanalytic Quarterly* 11: 33–58.
Wolf, E. (1988) *Treating the Self.* New York: Guilford.

H. B.

EGO (FREUD) 'I' is the literal translation, but this unavoidably conveys only our felt self. 'Ego' is the term meant to refer to the identity-organisation or self-system, the way we make our inner life coherent. Ego effectiveness is the extent to which we are able to avoid the anxiety created by alien experience by making it consistent with our self-image. Originally, Freud conceived of us as intrinsically in *conflict with ourselves, having to rely on antisocial and even anti-self instincts as our ultimate source of motivation. In that frame, the ego was envisioned as able to manage instincts in the service of '*civilisation'. Recognising that this conception could hardly account for everyday functioning, the ego psychologists in the United States, in the 1950s, attempted its modification by postulating a variety of mechanisms by which we are impelled toward social relations by antisocial motives without disruption. The necessary conceptual abstractions were so removed from clinical experience, and irrelevant to it, that in less than two decades they fell into disuse. The consequent discouragement with theorising on this level has led to the general demise of such 'metapsychological' speculation and may in part be responsible for a dramatic shift in the literature toward lower-level, more concretely clinical conceptualising. As a result, the term 'ego' itself is now rarely used. In its stead we see references to specific conflicts and defense-patterns and to internal object relations. The disadvantage of the term 'ego' is that it perpetuates the vision of a pathological organisation in which separation between wishes and the self is a given, rather than being taken as a developmental failure, or as the breakdown of a previously integrated self-system.

See also: ego psychology

Freud, S. (1923) *The Ego and the Id.* S. E. 19. London: Hogarth Press.
Hartmann, H. (1958) *Ego Psychology and the Problem of Adaptation.* New York: International Universities Press.

B. A.

EGO (FAIRBAIRN) (CENTRAL EGO) According to Fairbairn, the core of the original ego, some of which is associated with conscious and preconscious functioning and with reasonable, verbal thought. The central ego is the part of the ego that remains after the formation of the *endopsychic structure by *introjection of objects, *splitting, and *repression. Fairbairn's central ego has its own *ideal object, just as the repressed parts of the ego have theirs, and it has conscious and preconscious aspects. The central ego is in active exchange with the external world and external objects, and functions as both as the agent that represses the *rejected bad objects and the parts of the ego repressed along with them. It functions as an agent of change through its interactions with the other endopsychic structures. *Guntrip reported that Fairbairn agreed with Guntrip's suggestion that this component of endopsychic structure could more accurately be called the 'central self'.

See also antilibidinal ego; libidinal ego; pristine unitary ego

Guntrip, H. (1969) *Schizoid Phenomena, Object Relations and the Self.* New York: International Universities Press.

E. F. B. / D. E. S.

EGO (JUNG) For Jung the ego is the centre of consciousness but incomplete. It is originally part of the *self, the ordering principle of the entire personality which is holistic in nature. The self is the mover and the ego the moved. However it is the function of the ego to oppose or execute the will of the self. This confrontation is especially seen in the second half of life.

See also: ego-self axis

S. M.

EGO (KLEIN) For Klein the *death drive and ambivalence are innate in the ego. By projection* of the destructive part of *ambivalence and *introjection of good experiences the infant's ego grows. Ego development takes place by introjection and projection of objects and not as progress through a number of stages in which defences are used. Therefore failures in development are not seen as *regression to *fixation points but rather as failures of *depressive activity – that is failures to neutralise destructiveness.

J. A.

EGO (KOHUT) see **EGO (SELF PSYCHOLOGY)**

EGO (LACAN) With his introduction of the *mirror phase, Lacan subdivided the Freudian *Ich* into two agencies: the subject and the ego. In this he made a frontal attack on what he saw as the mistake introduced by *ego-psychology in taking Freud's ego to be that of general psychology. The subject, responsible for its formations of the unconscious, links with Freud's first topography, while the ego links to Freud's second topography, and to *narcissism. Because the child sees an *Other whom he knows and who recognises him by his side in the mirror, he jubilantly takes on his body image, even though his corporeal schema is not yet neurologically constituted. This deceptive experience cuts him off completely from the place of the unconscious. Two axes are thus set up: an Imaginary axis that links the ego to the ego-image, and a Symbolic axis that connects the subject to the Other. The ego is the seat of resistance: only the desire of the analyst can bring about the crossing of the Imaginary axis, and thereby gain access to the subject of the unconscious.

See also: ego to ego

J. C. R.

EGO (SARTRE) (EXISTENTIAL EGO) Existential psychoanalysis has a different perspective on the ego than classical psychoanalysis. The ego for Sartre is not a psychic structure or seat of reality-orientation, but the product of impure reflection and the appraisals of others. By experiencing the dynamic, temporal flow of consciousness, one attempts to create a solid sense of self in the ego. This phenomenon undermines spontaneous interaction with the environment since all experience becomes mediated through imposed events or categories connected with the ego. The ego becomes a substantive support for a series of qualities and states which one may take to be real but which are actually reflective characterisations of nonreflective activity on the world, usually contaminated by the perspectives of others.

In his biography of *Flaubert, Sartre distinguishes between true ego and false ego. True ego is based on genuine self-awareness and acceptance of one's freedom and responsibility. False ego is based on passively accepting the appraisals of others. In analysis, a patient might move toward more authentic characterisation of the self or ego, as when one re-examines the impact one's family has had on one's reflective view of self. Also, from a Sartrean perspective, the authentic person, while pragmatically adopting a social identity, must constantly fight the tendency to allow the ego to become set or entrenched. The Sartrean ego, like the Lacanian ego, is illusory in the sense that one is not one's ego, and existential analysis requires a kind of 'deconstruction' of the neurotic ego. However, unlike the Lacanian ego, the Sartrean ego is not wholly illusory since it may be checked through pure reflection against the nonreflective experience which is its source.

Sartre, J.-P. [1937] (1957) *The Transcendence of the Ego*. Translated by R. Kirkpatrick and F. Williams. New York: Farrar, Strauss & Giroux.

Sartre, J.-P. (1981) *The Family Idiot*, Vol. 1. Translated by C. Cosman. London and Chicago: University of Chicago.

A. M. / B. C.

EGO DRIVES The problem that has plagued the tripartite model of *id, *ego and *super-ego is how to account for what is usually referred to as our drive toward mastery or, in commonsense terms, strength of will, if our motivational energies all derive from selfish, antisocial instincts. Although Freud at times tried out the notion of primary ego energies, he recognised that this could lead to an incoherent array of arbitrarily invoked energies. At bottom has been the conflict between nineteenth-century theorising, in which it made sense to think in terms of 'psychic energy', and the more modern style, in which one stays on the level of clinical data and simply endeavours to explain it without reaching for final causes.

See also: mastery, drive for

B. A.

EGO FUNCTION, CHANGE OF An ego function that has changed from primarily serving a defensive function to one that is adaptive.

See also: ego functions, autonomous

B. A.

EGO FUNCTIONS, AUTONOMOUS In *ego psychology these are ego functions that operate independently of instinctual pressures and are typically not involved in *conflict. Autonomous ego functions exhibit primary autonomy when they develop as innate potentials of the ego unrelated to libido and aggression. These ego functions resist becoming drawn into conflict, though they may, under certain circumstances, undergo instinctualisation such as sexualisation, in which case they may secondarily become embroiled in conflict. Primary autonomous functions include: perception, motility, intention, anticipation, rational thought, intelligence, thinking, speech and language. Autonomous ego functions exhibit secondary autonomy when such functions, originally involved either in ensuring, or preventing (defending against), the satisfaction of drives, subsequently come to serve non-defensive functions, thus becoming independent of their original instinctual and/or defensive roots. Such changes of function can be seen as the bases of sublimation. Autonomous ego functions are part of the conflict-free ego.

See also: ego function, change of

R. T.

EGO IDEAL/IDEAL EGO 'Negative conscience' prohibits and punishes anti-social behaviour, resulting in guilt feelings, while 'positive conscience' inspires pro-social behaviour and ethical integrity, and provokes *shame when we fall short of its lofty precepts. The former is punitive, the latter, normative. In Freudian theory, negative conscience is the province of the *super-ego, while positive conscience is the province of the *ego ideal. The ego ideal is generally more accessible to conscious introspection than the super-ego, and tied to the phenomenon of narcissism.

For Lacan the ego-ideal is a Symbolic introjection which is an identification with something of the father, enabling the subject to take up a sexual position as man or as woman. A mythological reference to this ideal is conveyed in Freud's *Totem and Taboo* by the sons' incorporation of some piece of their murdered father, acknowledging the institution of the law and love of/identification with the father. The ideal ego, on the other hand, is an Imaginary construct which emerges in the early mirror stage and which is the root of Imaginary projection, *aggressivity, *alienation and *transitivism. In sum, this ideal of the ego is a constant companion of the ego – I as an other – both promising and withholding the longed for illusory unity which drives the first and all subsequent ego-identifications.

See also: fragmented body; identification; image

Freud, S. (1914) *On Narcissism: An Introduction*. S. E. 14. London: Hogarth Press.

D. Bur. / H. T.

EGO PSYCHOLOGY PRECIS Ego psychology is a development within mainstream psychoanalysis based on the structural model introduced by Freud in his 1923 'The Ego and the Id', and his 1926 'Symptoms and Anxiety' which were subsequently elaborated upon by *Reich, *Anna Freud, *Hartmann and his colleagues, *Kris, Lowenstein, and *Rapaport, amongst others. Conflict, defences, adaptations and, in particular, resistances are ego psychology's special object of study. More recent contributors to the development of ego psychology include Gray and Busch.

Ego psychology emphasises the development of the ego, including: the role of the ego in *conflict (employing defences, arranging *compromise formations, adapting to the environment, etc.); the structure of the ego (e.g. the developing of a conflict-free sphere within the ego that remains relatively uninfluenced by instinctual pressures, as well as the ego's ability to synthesise a meaningful whole out of seemingly disparate parts); the energy available to the ego (neutral as well as neutralised energy) to accomplish the ego's goals; and, the strength of the ego (e.g. capacity of the ego to observe itself, to resist regression, etc.).

Clinically, an ego psychological approach to treatment focuses on the demonstration of *resistances (defence analysis) in order to enlist the patient's conflict-free ego, and observing capacities in an exploration of the reasons why particular material is actively being avoided – the nature of its threat to the ego. This surface approach shuns a premature interpretation of the unconscious forces (wishes, impulses and traumatic memories) being defended against in favour of exploration of resistances and an expansion of the patient's capacity for self-observation and self-reflection. Such manoeuvres help strengthen the ego, thus preparing the patient for a deeper exploration of unconscious drive derivatives. At a later time in treatment, when there is more of an observing ego even in the midst of conflict, the analyst can make deeper interpretations and know there is an ego there to listen.

Ego psychology's departure from the *id-based psychology that preceded it, is well illustrated by the concept of an autonomous dimension of the ego that is relatively uninfluenced by the dual instincts of libido or aggression. Hartmann proposed that the ego possesses an innate (inherited) potential to develop *ego functions that remain independent of the drives. The resulting 'apparatus of primary autonomy' is invested or cathected with non-instinctual (neutral) energy, and typically remains unaffected by instinctual pressure or intrapsychic conflict. The neutral energy associated with autonomous ego functions is neither derived from, nor is employed defensively against the instinctual drives, save for times when these autonomous functions become instinctualised (e.g. when motility of perception becomes sexualised or invested with aggression). Ego functions associated with neutral energy contribute to the *conflict-free sphere of the ego.

Another contribution comes from ego functions originally associated with instinctual drives that secondarily undergo a process of de-instinctualisation. Thereafter, these ego functions exhibit 'secondary autonomy' insofar as they operate independently of the drives and of intrapsychic conflict. Ego functions that originally derive their energy from libidinal or aggressive drives undergo a change of function, which results in their ceasing to be used either to help satisfy, or defend against, the satisfaction of the instincts. Ego functions that demonstrate secondary autonomy may, under conditions that promote regression or a weakening of the ego, become re-instinctualised.

Optimal ego functioning (ego strength) depends, in part, on the conflict-free sphere of the ego. An employee who is too conflicted by her projected rivalry to comfortably and competently present her work to bosses may perform other professional tasks well, ones that rely on the conflict-free part of her ego. A patient's capacity to think somewhat independently of conflict is something all analysts count on in offering interpretations, without necessarily recognising that they are assuming the existence of a conflict-free sphere of the ego. For ego psychologists these autonomous or conflict-free areas of functioning within the ego are the basis for the establishment of a working alliance with the patient.

Another evolution in Freud's thinking that proved crucial for ego psychology was his second theory of *anxiety. Originally Freud believed that anxiety was the product of instances when repression blocked the discharge of libidinal energy. The accumulating libidinal energy, Freud posited, became converted into anxiety, the treatment of which required releasing the discharge of the libido by uncovering the unconscious fantasies responsible for the blockage. According to Freud's second theory, anxiety was not so much a result of repression, but its cause. Anxiety was a signal to the ego that a threat requiring defensive action was impending. This may be seen clinically in the inhibition of *free association that develops when certain ideas, memories, affects or drive derivatives, unconsciously perceived as intolerable or dangerous, threaten to surface. It may also manifest in defensive behaviour, when the analyst is about to talk to or interact with the patient in a manner that betrays the patient's unconscious yearnings for the analyst. For example, when a very independent patient feels a longing to be taken care of by the analyst, he or she may conceal such wishes for dependency by becoming angry with the analyst, a manoeuvre that obscures the dependency needs while simultaneously expressing anger toward the analyst's emotional availability, which is experienced by the patient as stimulating his longings for the analyst.

Through the work of Gray, Busch, and others, a contemporary ego psychological approach has developed. This consists in a careful and detailed account of the analysis of resistance and a fuller role for consciousness. Gray pointed out that although a theory of resistances mediated by the unconscious ego has long existed within psychoanalysis, it is often not implemented in technique. Busch documented that from Freud on, analysts were too inclined to attempt to overcome, rather than analyse, resistances.

Gray developed a technique for bringing unconscious resistances to the analysand's attention. By closely following the patients' associations, Gray could demonstrate an unconscious resistance in action. For example, a patient angrily complaining about some recent behaviour of his mother, may interrupt to talk of a pleasant time he had with friends recently. The analyst points out how the patient was freely talking of his anger toward his mother, suddenly stopped, and then described something pleasant. It is at such moments when the patient displays discomfort with his anger, that analysis of resistance pays off.

Some analysts believe that analysing resistances means getting the patient to talk about a particular unknown wish that is being held back by the defence. This is a remnant of Freud's early thinking that the aim of psychoanalysis is to make the unconscious conscious. In accordance with the ego psychological principles, effective resistance analysis involves an exploration and working through of the nature of the threat to the ego rather than the contents of the resistance believed to underlie the patient's need to portray his mother in a more positive light. A systematic analysis of resistances is a long-term process.

Busch's work is also an effort to correct the tendency of analysts to make interpretations based on their understanding rather than on the patient's capacity to hear, understand, and fully integrate at an emotionally deep level. Thus he finds it necessary for the analyst to recognise that the patient's mind at the point of intense conflict is highly concrete. At such times, patients are no longer able to function within the conflict-free area of the ego, to think back on a train of thought to see how they've come to be so angry with the analyst. Effective treatment requires that the analyst give a succinct summary of the patient's thoughts before presenting an interpretation. The analyst has to help the patient understand, to demonstrate concretely, how this particular understanding was arrived at. The conclusion alone might be accepted by the patient, but such acceptance would depend on the analyst's authority rather than recognition by the patient's conscious ego. If the capacity to think more freely is a goal of analysis, then inclusion of all parts of the patient's mind is a necessary first step. We could say that at any one moment there are three surfaces working in the analytic process: the patient surface is what the patient believes he or she is talking about; the analyst surface is what the analyst believes the patient is talking about; and the workable surface is that intersection between patient and analyst surface that allows for a meaningful and understandable intervention to be made. An ego psychological approach attempts to work with all three surfaces.

See also: adaptive point of view; adaptation; anxiety; anxiety, signal; autonomous ego functions; autonomy; compromise formation; conflict/intrapsychic conflict; defence; defence analysis; drives; ego; ego function; ego psychology précis; ego strength and weakness; energy (Freud); fixation; regression; representation; repression; structure, psychic; symptoms/symptom formation

Busch, F. (1995) *The Ego at the Center of Clinical Technique*. Northvale, NJ: Jason Aronson.
Freud, A. [1936] (1946) *The Ego and the Mechanisms of Defence*. New York: International Universities Press.
Gray, P. (1994) *The Ego and the Analysis of Defense*. Northvale, NJ: Jason Aronson.
Hartmann, H. [1939] (1958) *Ego Psychology and the Problem of Adaptation*. Translated by David Rapaport. New York: International Universities Press.
Hartmann, H., Kris, E. and Loewenstein, R. (1947) 'Comments on the formation of the psychic structure'. *Psychoanalytic Study of the Child* 2: 11–38.
Rapaport, D. (1959) *The Structure of Psychoanalytic Theory*. New York: International Universities Press.

R. T.

EGO-SELF AXIS (JUNG) A term used by *Neumann to help differentiate Jung's psychology from that of Freud's. On the basis of Jung's understanding of the relationship between the conscious and unconscious and his distinction between ego and self, the term ego-self axis was used to describe the essential relationship between these two interacting systems of psychic life. For Neumann, the ego-self axis comes into being when the ego is established as a derivative of the self and then continues to reflect the processes of differentiation and integration of these separate but related centres of the personality. The idea was further developed by *Edinger who stated that the process of ego-self separateness and union develops as an alternating cycle throughout life reflecting the fundamental experiences of alienation and identity that shape the whole development of psychic life.

S. M.

EGO STRENGTH AND WEAKNESS (EGO PSYCHOLOGY) In the perspective of *ego psychology, the ego is the 'reasonable' mediating psychic structure responsible for effecting compromises whenever intrapsychic *conflict arises. The ego works to ensure that the primary instinctual urges emanating from the id are gratified to the extent that such gratifications are not in conflict with other intrapsychic and environmental factors. The ego contends with the multiple pressures placed upon the individual: by the super-ego's demands to adhere to a particular internal code (live up to expectations one has of oneself by forgoing certain prohibited activities in order to avoid guilt or be permitted to maintain a particular self-image); by the ego's need to find ways of satisfying competing instinctual urges and tendencies; by the need to protect the intactness of the ego by preventing the emergence of intolerable, traumatic affect; by the ego's need for synthesis – to weave all of the competing demands, identifications, etc., into a meaningful, coherent whole; and, by external ('realistic') concerns that the gratification of certain urges risks placing that individual in conflict with society or with the physical laws or limitations of reality. Many, but not all, of the operations of the ego are conscious. Those that are not conscious include the mechanisms of *defence as well as the generation of signal *anxiety when the ego feels threatened. Were these defences to become conscious, the ego's attempts to keep conflicted material from emerging into consciousness would be compromised and could not act autonomously. The *autonomous ego functions include: perception, motility, intention, anticipation, rational thought, intelligence, thinking, speech and language. The combined functioning of the various ego functions is responsible for one's ego strength: reality testing (the ability to distinguish internal stimuli, such as fantasies, memories, dreams, etc., from external reality), the maintenance of a sense of reality (versus experiencing feelings of unreality as occurs with derealisation/depersonalisation), and adaptation to reality; the maintenance of ego boundaries (being able to discern self from other) as well as the capacity for *object relations; impulse control (a combined effect of the strength of the ego relative to the strength of the impulses in question) resulting in the ability to delay gratification; frustration tolerance (the ability to withstand delays in the gratification of certain needs or urges); and, affect tolerance. The failure to attain these five achievements can be thought to either reflect ego weakness or an ego defect. Above and beyond the ego being an organisation of varying functions, it is also a product of multiple identifications with important objects in the developing individual's life.

See also: adaptation; structure, psychic

R. T.

EGO TO EGO Lacan distinguishes what he calls ego-to-ego forms of analytical technique, where the analytical relation is taken to hold between the ego of the analyst and the ego of the analysand, from what he considers to be the proper functioning of analytical technique, which is a reconstructing of the subjective history of the analysand. For Lacan the relation of ego to ego involves both misrecognition and aggressivity. He notes the diverse forms of this in infantile *transitivism, *envy, *jealousy and paranoia. Lacan has demonstrated the structure of the psychoanalytic situation on the basis of what he called his Schema-L. In this schema he indicates that an analysis should move from the defensive axis of ego-to-ego with its empty speech, to the axis which represents the unconscious subject of the analysand in relation to the position of the analyst which is the axis that is to provoke *full speech.

G. S.

EGO TRAINING IN ACTION (GROUPS) Foulkes used this phrase to describe how the central adaptive part of the personality described by Freud adapts to external reality as well as to the individual's instinctual drives (*id) and internalised social standards (*super-ego). In contrast to the 'vertical' analysis by an invisible analyst through exploration of the patient's *transference to the analyst and the analyst's *countertransference, *Foulkes privileged 'horizontal' analysis. This is carried out within a circle of visible interacting equals, including the conductor, with multiple transferences, including sibling reactions, and many non-transference interactions.

'Action' here does not mean doing or, literally, acting or role-playing: nor is it the equivalent of 'acting out' in psychoanalysis. The group provides a stage for actions, reactions and interactions within the therapeutic situation, which are denied to the psychoanalytic patient on the couch. However, the ego to which we refer is the *ego in the psychoanalytic sense, the inner ego as a metapsychological concept, which is activated and reformed.

In addition to analysis of individual and group anxieties and defences, among the processes that promote reformation and modification of personal patterns of adaptation ('ego functions') are mirroring, resonance and socialisation. These involve a recognition of oneself through the responses of others, the withdrawal of projections, and finding the courage to be at the same time honest and trusting – seeing oneself in others and others in oneself. Individual ego boundaries can be redrawn towards a more mature acceptance of oneself as well as others. The effects of early family patterns of relating can be mitigated, and the self developed through movement towards a fuller lifestyle.

See also: intersubjectivity (group)

Brown, D. G. (1994) 'Self-development through subjective interaction: a fresh look at "ego training in action"' in D. Brown and L. Zinkin (eds) *The Psyche and the Social World*. London: Routledge.
Foulkes, S. H. (1964) *Therapeutic Group Analysis*. London: Allen & Unwin.

D. Bro.

EGOISM This term belongs to Freud's earlier dual instinct theory prior to his fusion of the 'ego' or self-preservative instincts and the 'libido' or sexual instincts in the 1920s into one life-instinct, Eros. In Freud's pre-1920 thinking, when the ego is invested with interest driven by the self-preservative instinct he denotes the process as egoism. On the other hand, if the ego is invested with interest driven by the sexual instinct the process is denoted as *narcissism. Thus these terms (narcissism and egoism) while often confused are quite distinct metapsychologically. The distinction can be made in a different though related way by saying that the narcissist generally does not form object-relations whereas the egoist does.

S. Byr.

EIGENWELT This is a mode of being-in-the-world used by *Binswanger to refer to the private world of self-awareness and individual experience.

See also *mitwelt*; *umwelt*

R. Fri.

EITINGON, MAX (1881–1943) Max Eitingon was the distinguished administrator of the Freudian movement. In 1924 he founded the Berlin Psychoanalytic Institute which he continued to finance with funds derived from his family's fur business. This was the first psychoanalytic training institute and the model of later ones everywhere, introducing, for example, the set-up of treatment under supervision. From 1926 until 1932 Eitingon served as president of the International Psycho-analytical Association. He was committed to the idea of 'thorough training' which at that time, symbolised by the issue of lay analysis, threatened the unity of the IPA. In all his different functions Eitingon faithfully acted as Freud's right-hand man. In 1933 he left Nazi Germany for Jerusalem where he instituted the Palestine Psychoanalytic Society.

Freud, S. and Eitingon, M. (2004) *Briefwechsel 1906–1939*. M. Schröter (ed.) Tübingen: edition diskord.
Neiser, E. M. J. (1978) *Max Eitingon*. Diss. med. Mainz.

M. Sch.

ELECTROCONVULSIVE THERAPY (ECT) Technique of inducing therapeutic seizures by electrical stimulation of the brain. Cerletti and Bini induced the first electroconvulsion in a schizophrenic patient in 1938. ECT was administered in the 1940s and 1950s without anaesthetic – so-called unmodified or straight ECT – creating its long-standing and frightening reputation. The development of short-acting anaesthetic agents and drugs capable of briefly paralysing muscles led to the introduction of modified ECT. This resulted in the elimination of one of the main side effects of early treatment, namely, bone fractures, caused by muscle spasms at the time of the seizure. ECT is effective in the treatment of a wide range of psychiatric disorders, including major depressive illness, mania, and acute schizophrenia. Although its exact mechanism of action is unclear, the induction of a bilateral *grand mal* epileptic seizure is essential for ECT to exert its full effect. Post-treatment impairment of memory, and other cognitive functions, is related to the amount of electricity used to induce that convulsion. Although generally accepted in the UK as a safe and effective treatment, its status worldwide is more variable.

Freeman, C. P. L. (1995) 'ECT and other physical therapies' in *Companion to Psychiatric Studies*. Edinburgh: Churchill Livingstone.
Lock, Toni (1994) 'Advances in the practice of electroconvulsive therapy'. *Advances in Psychiatric Treatment* 1: 47–56.

S. Mik.

ELEMENTARY PHENOMENON Phrase used by Lacan to designate discrete psychotic symptoms which are able to sum up the structure of the final delusional system. The elementary phenomena initially described by Lacan were delusional ideas of reference, or auditory *hallucinations. Subsequently, he added the feeling of 'letting go', of dropping one's own body, as a sensation specific to schizophrenia.

F. S.

ELIAS, NORBERT (1897–1990) Born into a prosperous Jewish family in Breslau, now Wroclaw, in 1897, Elias had a classical German education. During World War I he served in the German army in a communications unit, laying and repairing telegraph wiring in the front line in France. After the war, he studied both medicine and philosophy at Breslau, but eventually gave up medicine for philosophy. In 1925 he moved to Heidelberg where he became assistant to the sociologist Karl Mannheim, who was assistant to Alfred Weber, a brother of Max Weber. Elias moved with Mannheim to Frankfurt where he encountered psychoanalysis and Gestalt psychology together with the Marxist economics of the Frankfurt School. Elias and S. H. *Foulkes met in Frankfurt and clearly influenced each other. Elias left Germany in 1933, eventually arriving in England where he was able to work on his magnum opus, *The Civilising Process*. In this Elias was able to show the changing social and economic forces that mould the personality and affect the psychoanalytic functions of *super-ego, *ego and *id. For instance, the gradual monopolisation of violence by the state imposes restraints upon the individual, who is now protected from the violence of others by the force of the state, but is himself subject to punishment if he violates the social norms. Elias came to recognise the human situation of interdependency in functional chains. He opposed the concept of 'closed man' with that of 'open man' and challenged the notion of 'economic man'. Elias emphasised the relationship of sociogenesis to psychogenesis. He accepted the importance of Freud's psychoanalysis, but pointed out that it lacked the historical dimension. Elias and Foulkes worked together on the theoretical foundation of group analysis.

After many years of neglect, the importance of Elias's work was recognised. He left the Department of Sociology at the University of Leicester for a chair at the University of Ghana. His latter years were spent in Holland and Germany where his work has been widely acclaimed.

Dalal, F. (1998) *Taking the Group Seriously*. London: Jessica Kingsley.
Elias, N. (1994) *The Civilising Process*. Oxford: Blackwell.
Elias, N. (1994) *Reflections on a Life*. Cambridge: Polity Press.
Elias, N. and Scotson, J. (1994) *The Established and the Outsiders*. London: Sage.
Mennell, S. (1992) *Norbert Elias – An Introduction*. Dublin: University College Dublin Press.
Van Krieken, R. (1998) *Norbert Elias*. London: Routledge.

M. P.

EMOTIONAL EXPERIENCE Bion places emotional experience at the very core of his theory. It is the first step, the heart of the matter. In the link between two minds (and also of two aspects of the same mind), the key word for Bion is experience, learning from experience, transformations in *O, and then becoming O. Emotional experience, if not transformed, results in an accretion of stimuli which must then be evacuated. Hallucinations, psychosomatic states, beta screens, and basic assumption group behaviour ensue.

Bion, W. R. (1962) *Learning from Experience*. London: Heinemann. Also in *Seven Servants*. New York: Jason Aronson, 1977.
Bion, W. R. (1963) *Elements of Psychoanalysis*. London: Heinemann. Also in *Seven Servants*. New York: Jason Aronson, 1977.
Bion, W. R. (1965) *Transformations*. London: Karnac Books. Also in *Seven Servants*. New York: Jason Aronson, 1977.

S. A.

EMPATHIC VANTAGE POINT OF OBSERVATION Kohut placed empathy (as vicarious introspection) at the centre of his psychoanalytic observational method (without excluding other modes of observation). Some self-psychologically informed analysts have favoured speaking of the 'empathic vantage point of observation' to underscore that they are using the term 'empathy' with its specific meaning of placing themselves imaginatively into the inner world of the other, feeling themselves and thinking themselves into the experiences of the other, and describing their observations from the other's perspective. The empathic vantage point of observation aims at capturing (as much as possible) the subjective experiences of the other. It also aims at separating the method from the everyday meaning of empathy as a caring, nurturing, kind and giving attitude, which should always be a baseline attitude without becoming a 'technique' of analysis. Furthermore, by speaking of the empathic vantage point of observation we simply describe what we actually do, without subscribing to any of the various hypotheses of what process or mechanism constitutes 'empathy'. The terms 'empathic inquiry' or 'empathic attentiveness' are used by many self psychologists who emphasise that empathy – as implied by the idea of vicarious introspection – is inevitably filtered through the subjectivity of the observer.

Kohut, H. (1959) 'Introspection, empathy, and psychoanalysis' *Journal of the American Psychoanalytic Association* 7.

P. O.

ENANTIODROMIA From Heraclitus, the regulatory function of psychical opposites, as everything runs into its opposite. In *analytical psychology, it refers to unconscious opposites, which compensate a one-sidedness of the conscious. Without the balance of opposites, we are driven by enantiodromia. 'The only person who escapes the grim law of enantiodromia is [one] who knows how to separate himself from the unconscious', Jung wrote in 1943. Through awareness of *ego and non-ego, we dis-identify with psychical enantiodromia, and participate in the *individuation process.

C. G. Jung [1943] (1966) 'On the psychology of the unconscious' in *Two Essays on Analytical Psychology*. Princeton: Princeton University Press.

S. J.

END OF ANALYSIS The end of analysis is a logical conclusion, phrased as the moment the analysand is able to testify to his/her unconscious desire at work and has been mapped in relation to the object a. The first implies that the narcissistic image of the ego has been stripped from the various forms of desire and that the subject acknowledges his/her desire as subordinate to the law of the Symbolic. The second refers to the 'traversing' of the fundamental fantasy, i.e. the subject's position vis-à-vis jouissance and desire. The traversing of this fundamental fantasy, which organises and supports the subject's psychic reality, can ultimately affect the subject's (subsequent) contingent encounter(s) with the Real.

K. Lib.

ENDOPSYCHIC STRUCTURE AND DYNAMICS Endopsychic structure, a term due to Fairbairn, is comprised of the conscious, preconscious, and repressed or dissociated representations of the self and objects resulting from the ego-splitting used as a *defensive strategy to reduce anxiety in infancy. Fairbairn described the endopsychic situation as being a dynamic one, in which the elements of mental structure acted on one another in a changing dynamic pattern. The *central ego was the prime mover in initiating splitting of the ego and its objects, but in secondary repression, one aspect of the ego could act on another. (His illustration was the attack of the antilibidinal ego on the libidinal ego and exciting object in hysteria.) His introduction of the fundamental principle that internal object relations were dynamic represents a new adaptive principle consistent with modern information processing theory and chaos theory.

Fairbairn, W. R. D. [1944] (1994) 'Endopsychic structure considered in terms of object relations' in *Psychoanalytic Studies of the Personality*. London: Routledge.

Fairbairn, W. R. D. (1954) 'The nature of hysterical states' in D. E. Scharff and E. F. Birtles (eds) *From Instinct to Self*, Vol. 1. Northvale, NJ: Jason Aronson.

Grotstein, J. (1994) 'Notes on Fairbairn's metapsychology' in *Fairbairn and the Origins of Object Relations*. London: Free Association Books. New York: Guilford.

Scharff, D. E. (2002) 'Fairbairn and the self as an organized system: chaos theory as a new paradigm' in Pereira, F. and Scharff, D. E. (eds) *Fairbairn and Relational Theory*. London: Karnac Books, 197–211.

See also: Fairbairn précis

E. F. B. / D. E. S.

ENERGY (FREUD) The motivational force that is hypothesised to drive the operations of the mental apparatus. Originally Freud believed that all psychical energy emanated from *libido. Later, he found that *aggression was an equally important role in driving the mental apparatus. Taken together, libidinal and aggressive forces constitute Freud's dual drive theory. *Ego psychology went beyond the dual drive theory by introducing a third 'neutral energy' that is associated with the ego; unrelated to aggression or libido; and, the source of such primary *autonomous ego functions as perception, motility, intention, anticipation, rational thought, speech and language.

According to the dual drive theory, at birth, drive energy is 'unbound' and seeks immediate unrestricted discharge. With maturation, in order to better meet drive needs, libidinal and aggressive energy is 'bound' within the psychical apparatus providing the power for the growth of the ego and its higher mental functions. The fusion of libidinal (building) and aggressive (tearing apart) drives has a modulating effect on the intensity of each of the drives, and further contributes to the development of ego strength. Under conditions of *regression, previously fused instincts may become unfused. Drive theorists would attribute the need to master the elements in one's environment to the binding and constructive (because fused with libido) use of aggression.

By contrast, ego psychologists would view the urge for mastery as a motivational force in its own right, the product of autonomous ego functions. In addition ego psychologists find that libidinal and aggressive energy can become neutralised (de-instinctualised), leaving 'neutralised energy'. This is another way of referring to bound energy – energy whose discharge is checked, controlled and channelled. Although energy concepts have been challenged as too mechanistic, they cannot be completely dismissed as motivational explanations for emotional investments in objects, in one's body and in various mental processes.

See also: cathexis; drives

V. D. / R. T.

ENERGY (JUNG) In *analytical psychology, the intensity of psychical processes. Jung uses the term as an equivalent to *libido, without implying an exclusively sexual source. Energy is the intensity and psychological value of the life-process, subjectively experienced as either push or pull.

Psychical energy is an analogue of physical energy – the ability to apply a force through a distance over time. Yet 'the analogy is itself an older intuitive idea from which the concept of physical energy originally developed', as Jung wrote in 1954.

By calling energy the psychological value of a life process, Jung does not mean consciously assigning moral, aesthetic or intellectual values. He means that psychical process inherently has the ability to affect *psychical reality: the greater the energetic intensity, the greater that ability. We cannot measure psychical energy quantitatively. Through the function of feeling, we can 'get a feel for' the intensity of psychical process. This is a natural and universal human capacity. Psychical intensity encompasses a spectrum from voluntary will and wish, through quasi-voluntary desire and need, to involuntary fascination, impulsion, compulsion and addiction. Energy is shaped by the possibilities for expression of any process. These possibilities structure the flow and development of energetic processes.

The potentials and limitations may be *archetypal, as well as cultural, familial or personal. Archetypal structuring may have to do with intrinsic somatic, spiritual or moral aspects of psyche. The tendency of psyche to maintain balance, through compensation of conscious one-sidedness by the unconscious, is central to the transformation of energy, mediated by the living *symbol. Jung calls this transformative tendency the *transcendent function.

C. G. Jung [1948] (1960) 'On psychic energy' in *The Structure and Dynamics of the Psyche*. Princeton: Princeton University Press.

C. G. Jung [1954] (1960) 'On the nature of the psyche' in *The Structure and Dynamics of the Psyche*. Princeton: Princeton University Press.

S. J.

ENVIRONMENT (EXISTENTIAL) Generally the world external to an animal or a person. However existential analysts do not speak of the environment in the natural science sense but of the world, *umwelt* or situation in the human sense. For Husserl, items in the world are pure phenomena, that is, they are that which appear to our consciousness. *Heidegger's *umwelt* is the 'around world' to which human beings bring *presence. It includes, but is not reducible to, the objective natural world of the scientist. It is that which 'shines forth' to consciousness. Introduced by *Jaspers, who placed transcendence back at the core of human experience, the term 'situation' was taken up by *Sartre to mean that peculiar combination of what the world brings and the meaning I give it which is human reality. For Sartre, we are neither free in a world without facts nor a fact in a world without freedom, nor are we able to separate the two, since they are intertwined. To deny either and overemphasise the other is to fall into bad faith or to lie to oneself about the nature of existence. From this perspective, the emphasis on environment as causal found in traditional psychology is in bad faith. Instead existential analysts propose a world in which consciousness and its objects are inextricably interlinked.

Variously contesting the positions of (Anna) *Freud, *Balint and the *ego psychology strand within psychoanalysis, Lacan held that the psyche is not derivative from, or adaptive to, its environment. He viewed the structure of its linguistic and cultural procedure as traumatic for the subject/psyche, akin to the thrown-ness of Heidegger's *Dasein.

B. C. / G. S.

ENVY A feeling of resentful longing aroused by belief in another's better fortune. It is within this meaning that Freud refers to *penis envy in women but womb, vagina and breast envy are sometimes mentioned by other authors. Klein gives this notion more the flavour of desirous malice emphasising the spoiling aspect ('biting the hand that feeds') because envy attacks a good object for its goodness alone. The infant, dependent for survival on the mother, has hostile feelings towards her breast as creative source of food and comfort. This spoiling attack on the goodness of the breast is drawn into the *super-ego as a harsh, attacking demonic *internal object. The envious super-ego thereafter subverts the infant's good relationships and accomplishments. Klein believed that envy was inborn (although its intensity could vary from one person to another) and incorporated a mental manifestation of the *death drive. However, critics such as Joffe see envy as a more diverse and less primitive emotion than Klein.

See also: gratitude; Klein précis; negative therapeutic reaction

J. S. G.

EPILEPSY A disorder of brain function characterised by recurring fits. Derived from the Greek, it literally means 'to be seized by forces from without'. It can be caused by diverse disease processes, the final common pathway of expression being an intermittent, paroxysmal, excessive and disorderly discharge of cerebral neurones. The International Classification of Epileptic Seizures (ICES) 1981 distinguishes generalised epilepsies in which both hemispheres of the brain are involved at the onset of the seizure and localisation-related (focal, local, partial) epilepsies which start in a circumscribed region of the brain. Patients may experience brief premonitory feelings known as 'auras' prior to certain seizures and any combination of motor, sensory, autonomic, or psychic phenomena may occur during a seizure. A number of psychiatric disorders develop in epilepsy, such as personality changes (including undue religiosity and altered sexual behaviour), mood disturbances, and delusions and hallucinations, usually of mystical or religious themes. Treatment is mainly pharmacological although behavioural and surgical approaches are also used.

Fenton, G. W. (1995) 'Epilepsy and psychiatric disorder' in *Companion to Psychiatric Studies.* Edinburgh: Churchill Livingstone.
Trimble, M. R., Ring, H., Howard, A. and Schmitz, B. (1996) *Neuropsychiatric Aspects of Epilepsy in NeuroPsychiatry.* Maryland: Maple Press.

S. Mik.

EQUIVOCATION Lacan recommends the use of equivocal terms in the formulation of an interpretation. The aim of interpretation is to go against the ego's interest in maintaining repression; it therefore seeks strategies and techniques which allow associations to progress towards the unconscious, rather than being blocked. A single such thread is fairly easily blocked by the ego; so the introduction of more than one meaning attached to a single phrase is conducive to weakening the *resistance that the ego seeks to maintain. While the first meaning is blocked, the second can develop, and vice versa. In introducing such a recommendation for technique, Lacan is extending a notion found in Freud's account of dream-work: where Lacan talks of equivocation, Freud talks of *overdetermination.

B. B.

ERIKSON, ERIK HOMBURGER (1902–94) Erik Homburger Erikson trained in child psychoanalysis under Anna Freud in Vienna. His first book *Childhood and Society*, published in 1950, essentially inaugurated the fields of psychobiography and psychoanalytic anthropology, even as it made crucial contributions to *ego psychology. Erikson extended libido theory beyond a narrow formulation of erogenous zones into a description of modes of interaction between the developing infant and the caretaking environment. Thus, the anal phase becomes intimately connected to actions of holding on to what is inside or letting go into what is outside, further structuring categories of good and bad, the definition and management of aggression, the child's experience of autonomy, etc.

Erikson elaborated his epigenetic description of the human lifecycle beyond the phases of early childhood into later childhood, adolescence, young adulthood, maturity and old age, outlining eight developmental tasks, each with its own specific 'biopsychosocial' configuration, climactic difficulty and positive or negative personality outcome. His conceptualisation of the task of identity formation ('Identity and the Life Cycle' in his 1959 *Psychological Issues*) broke new ground in the developmental and clinical understanding of adolescence, describing a complex process of assimilation, repudiation and integration of childhood identifications, conflict-free capacities and the roles offered or needed by one's larger community.

The identity concept brought into clinical work such experience-near concepts as identity crisis, identity diffusion, premature foreclosure of identity and negative identity. Individual development within any phase of the lifecycle is shaped by (and shapes) the social environment. Hence there is a 'mutuality' and 'cogwheeling' of lifecycles between one generation and the next, which makes possible the transmission of culture. Erikson thus introduced into psychoanalysis a more nuanced theory of the social reality with which the ego is always in negotiation and, necessarily then, the question of intergenerational ethics.

From his early involvement with the visual arts, Erikson's 'configurational' approach built upon play as the medium of growth. In his two major clinical papers, he illuminated the meanings within the manifest content of Freud's Irma dream in 'The Dream Specimen of Psychoanalysis' through an imaginative yet systematic study of its various configurations (sensory, verbal, interpersonal, etc.), and he proposed, in 'The Nature of Clinical Evidence' (*Insight and Responsibility*, published in 1964) the concept of 'disciplined subjectivity' as describing the analyst's ego activity of inner 'leeway' and synthesis through which evolving hypotheses are tested against each other and immediate clinical experience.

Erikson's conviction that individual development was inextricably linked to historical moments and cultural forces eventuated in major works of psychobiography, most notably *Young Man Luther* and *Gandhi's Truth*. Within the 'great man' tradition of history, Erikson argued that certain gifted individuals may be charged by their development, itself charged by unconscious cultural forces acting on their families, to represent powerful psychosocial issues which resonate collectively. The identity struggle crystallises in the assumption of leadership through which the individual actualises a creative integration of personal urgencies with the forces and opportunities provided by the historical moment. Erikson's own life embodies this interplay of the personal and the historical.

Erikson, E. (1954) 'The dream specimen of psychoanalysis'. *Journal of the American Psychoanalytic Association*.

Erikson, E. (1964) 'The nature of clinical evidence' in *Insight and Responsibility*. New York: Norton.

Erikson, E. (1970) 'Autobiographical notes on the identity crisis'. *Daedalus* 99: 730–59.

Friedman, L. (1999) *Identity's Architect: A Biography of Erik Erikson*. New York: Scribner.

M. G. F.

EROS see LIFE DRIVE

EROS (JUNG) 'Eros is a superhuman power,' wrote Jung of the mythological god of Love. Enlisting this image to describe man's or woman's animal instinctual nature, he also viewed Eros as an archetypal pattern of spiritual nature in its highest form. When the two are in harmony, Eros thrives. In later writings Jung used the term Eros to designate the feminine principle, the ability of relatedness. Eros, as a psychic function in males and females, is active and associated with facilitating, mediating, empowering, reaching out and receiving. Eros is also subjective, representing feeling. Whereas Logos, the masculine principle, communicates objective interest of the mind, Eros is the voice of the soul.

N. Q. C.

EROTOGENIC ZONE Any zone of the body which is susceptible to sexual excitation. Although any portion of the skin, or indeed the internal organs, can become cathected in such a way, the mucous membranes of the mouth and of the anus, as well as the genitals, serve as the prime examples. These areas correspond to activities (feeding, defectation, masturbation) and their related pleasures which structure *infantile sexuality.

J. B.

ERROR Accidents, bungled actions, slips of the tongue, and other seemingly unintended events are determined by unconscious wishes. In Freud's system, true accidents do not occur. *Free association will always lead to some unconscious motive which is satisfied or expressed through the error.

Mistakes such as slips of the tongue represent the best access to unconscious desire. They are therefore not in opposition to truth, but reveal it. In this way, error seen as an 'inexact' interpretation of reality can reveal a truth.

See also: parapraxis

J. A. Ber. / M. B.

ETCHEGOYEN, R. HORACIO (1919–) An analysand of Heinrich Racker and later of Donald Meltzer, Horacio Etchegoyen has had a long and distinguished career as analyst, teacher, writer and administrator. Professor of Psychiatry at Mendoza, Argentina (1957–67), he was a member of the Argentine Psychoanalytic Association, and in 1978 was a founding member and first president of the Buenos Aires Psychoanalytic Society. From 1993 to 1997 he was president of the International Psychoanalytic Association, the first Latin American elected to the post; here he was deeply involved in improving democratic procedure. His prolific output as a writer has centred on the challenging issues attending psychoanalytic method and technique, in the idea that improvement of our perforce imprecise and loose conceptual apparatus depends in the main on improvements in analytic technique (an idea that also inspired Strachey and Racker) and that close study of our method demands detailed attention to the historical changes and development of its concepts. His monumental work, *Fundamentals of Psychoanalytic Technique* appeared first in Spanish in 1986, was published in English in 1991 and expanded in 1999; it is currently also available in Portuguese, German, Italian, and Romanian.

Etchegoyen, R. H. (1999) *Fundamentals of Psychoanalytic Technique*. London: Karnac Books.

J. Ahu.

ETHICS IN PSYCHOANALYSIS In view of his professional background in medicine and science it is understandable that Freud presented his startling new ideas in terms that would be respected by these disciplines. He was, therefore, determined to dissociate himself from any practice that might be thought scientifically suspect, as, for example, imaginative literature, philosophy and morality. He insisted that his work was a technique that eliminated the vicissitudes of human bias. The psychoanalyst's emotional attitudes and ethical outlook should play no part in an exercise that was comparable to that of a scientist in the laboratory.

We now know, from the research of Paul Roazen and many others, that neither Freud nor his early followers came anywhere near to this ideal in their actual practice. It is clear that Freud made vigorous attempts to control his patients' lives, sometimes giving direct advice on major decisions even, on occasion, when his own personal agenda clearly affected his opinion.

The fact that psychoanalysts' ethical behaviour fell lamentably short of their public pronouncements did not, however, discourage subsequent practitioners from maintaining the belief that a strictly detached and objective approach was not only desirable but also possible; students of psychoanalysis and psychoanalytical psychotherapy are still widely taught the classical technique.

In recent years the matter of ethics has been given greater attention in the literature. Holmes and Lindley, for example, have covered a wide area in their discussion of the moral aspects of psychoanalysis and the need for ethical codes of conduct. The study of the moral nature of the day-to-day interaction between the two participants has not however been studied with any significant degree of rigour. There appears to be little recognition of the fact that almost any statement made by the analyst is a function of his view as to how people should live nor that the analyst cannot help unwittingly revealing it by tone of voice and posture and even the way he selects interpretations thought to be appropriate to the patient's behaviour. That these moral connotations are little noticed and largely unexplored is a measure of the hold which the technical approach retains in contemporary psychoanalysis. A notable exception is Lacan who criticises ethical theories of philosophers who equate the subject's satisfaction and his well-being. Lacan, on the other hand, suggests via Freud that *satisfaction and well-being (drive-satisfaction and the pleasure principle) are two conflicting demands on the subject. As such, both Kant's moral law that you should 'treat others as you would wish to be treated' and its opposite, de Sade's 'right to enjoy the other's body' are fundamentally misguided. They both rely upon an idea of the universal good, which rests upon the premise of a possible (utopian) solution to the 'discontents of civilisation' at a universal level. For psychoanalysis, on the contrary, it is up to each subject to find his own way to conciliate satisfaction and well-being. Lacan draws the consequences of his teaching with regards to the ethics of the analyst: there can be no prescriptive dimension to the analyst's activity. As he remarks: 'psychoanalysis can lead you to the gates of ethics but it can not lead you in'.

A recognition of the moral nature of practice need not detract from an estimation of the value of interpretation nor of the fact that one of the greatest boons of Freud's work was to provide a setting in which a suffering and vulnerable person is not condemned.

Many writers including Rieff have attempted to draw a parallel between Freud's ethical outlook and his theory and method. Freud believed in rectitude, self-restriction and hard work as opposed to easy, impulsive and short-term satisfaction. One of the many paradoxes of Freud's work is that, in spite of his leanings towards discipline and abstention, he has enabled many people to free themselves from the grip of a restrictive and tyrannical conscience. There appears to be one moral thrust common to most theories of psychoanalytic treatment: the reduction of narcissism. This aim, however, is articulated in terms of developmental process rather than considered to be a moral issue.

Holmes, J. and Lindley, R. (1989) *The Values of Psychotherapy*. Oxford: Oxford University Press.
Lacan, J. [1959–60] (1992) *The Ethics of Psychoanalysis*. J.-A. Miller (ed.). Translated by D. Porter. New York: Norton.
Lomas, P. (1999) *Doing Good? Psychotherapy out of its Depth*. Oxford: Oxford University Press.
Rieff, P. (1989) *The Mind of the Moralist*. London: Methuen.
Roazen, P. (1975) *Freud and his Followers*. New York: Knopf.

P. Lom. / V. V.

ETHNOPSYCHOANALYSIS The application of psychoanalysis to anthropology and the use of the psychoanalytic technique as a field research method. It has its own methods and research technique. By this approach deeper investigations of the social processes in one's own culture can be made and integrated within psychoanalytic theory and practice.

The combination of psychoanalysis and anthropology created the new field of psychoanalytic anthropology. Freud, in *Totem and Taboo*, indicated theoretical applications of psychoanalysis to anthropology but he did not imagine practising psychoanalysis with people from so-called primitive cultures. Even Geza Roheim's psychoanalytic field research between 1928 and 1931 could not change Freud's opinion. However, from the mid-30s until the 60s, links grew in the United States with the rise of 'culture and personality' research. The following period saw the increasing impact of psychoanalytic method on anthropology. *Psychoanalysis and the Social Sciences* edited by Roheim and later Muensterberger became the forum for many innovative studies, and was followed by *The Psychoanalytic Study of Society* edited by Muensterberger from 1960 until 1984, as well as *The Journal of Psychological Anthropology* and *The Journal of Psychoanalytic Anthropology*. From 1970 onwards, discussions were held at the annual meetings of the *Colloquium on Psychoanalytic Questions and Methods in Anthropological Fieldwork*.

Georges Devereux's combination of anthropology and psychoanalysis was based on complementary frames of reference. In his book *From Anxiety to Method in the Behavioral Sciences* he focused on the role and anxiety of the researcher in field work and showed how 'objective' methods could be used in order to protect the researcher from – what he diagnosed as – fears of *countertransference. In the 1950s a paradigm shift took place with the development of ethnopsychoanalysis. The Swiss psychoanalysts Paul Parin, Goldy Parin-Matthèy and Fritz Morgenthaler were the first to use the psychoanalytic technique as a tool in anthropological fieldwork. They evaluated their psychoanalytical experiences in foreign cultures by contrasting their findings with psychoanalytic observations in their own culture and tried to find ways of expanding, supplementing and criticising psychoanalytic concepts. In France, ethnopsychoanalytic discussion was concentrated on Georges Devereux and led by Tobie Nathan and his collaborators in their *Nouvelle Revue d'Ethnopsychiatrie* from 1983 to 1998 followed by the transcultural journal *L'Autre*. For the German-speaking countries, six volumes of *Ethnopsychoanalyse* appeared between 1983 and 2001.

Paul Parin, Goldy Parin-Matthèy and Fritz Morgenthaler are regarded as pioneers and founders of ethnopsychoanalysis. On their expeditions to West Africa during the 1950s and 1960s, they applied Freudian insights and psychoanalytic technique to their anthropological research as they worked with the Dogon in the Republic of Mali and the Anyi in the Ivory Coast in two large-scale ethnopsychoanalytic field research projects. In their two books, *Die Wissen denken zu viel* and *Fear thy Neighbour as Thyself*, they proved that psychoanalysis – in theory and practice – was well suited to study and understand the unconscious conflicts and dynamics of people who had grown up and lived in non-European traditional societal formations.

Ethnopsychoanalytic observations and research led to new insights into the relations between social institutions and unconscious processes. The ethnopsychoanalytic observations and studies made between 1954 and 1971 in West Africa led to insights into hitherto unrecognised and very revealing relationships between social institutions and unconscious processes. One major finding was that the primary influences at work on the individual are societal, with biological determinants being only secondary. Further findings were as follows: (1) normality is dependent on culture; (2) every defence mechanism (including the pathological) is most likely ego-syntonic; (3) not only early childhood experiences but also, to a large extent, adolescence and society strongly determine the personality and behaviour of the adult; (4) the analyst's own expectations and projections have to be taken into account so that transference can unfold and develop optimally in analysis; and, (5) sufficient emotional openness only develops if the analyst observes the above factors.

Parin, P. (1988) 'The Ego and the mechanisms of adaptation' in B. Boyer and S. A. Grolnik (eds) *The Psychoanalytic Study of Society*, Vol. 12. Hillsdale, NJ: The Analytic Press, 97–130.

Parin, P., Morgenthaler, F. and Parin-Matthèy, G. (1980) *Fear Thy Neighbor as Thyself: Psychoanalysis and Society among the Anyi of West Africa*. Chicago and London: The University of Chicago Press.

Parin, P., Morgenthaler, F. and Parin-Matthèy, G. (1993) *Die Weissen denken zuviel. Psychoanalytische Untersuchungen bei den Dogon in Westafrika*. 4. Auflage. With a new foreword by Paul Parin and Goldy Parin-Matthèy. Hamburg: Europäische Verlagsanstalt.

Reichmayr, J. (1995) *Einführung in die Ethnopsychoanalyse. Geschichte Theorien und Methoden*. Frankfurt: Fischer Taschenbuch Verlag.

Spain, D. H. (ed.) (1992) *Psychoanalytic Anthropology after Freud*. New York: Psyche Press.

J. R.

ETHOLOGY AND PSYCHOANALYSIS Ethology is the study of the behaviour of animals in their natural setting in the wild. In contrast with behaviourism it studies an animal's behaviour as a whole, is evolutionary in perspective and makes an effort to see how the animal views its own world. Pioneered by Lorenz and others it has produced substantial theories of the interplay between genetic and environmental factors in the formation of animal behaviour. Bowlby, in his studies on *attachment, was among the first to use ethology in psychoanalysis and showed how careseeker and caregiver are aware of each other and seek each other out when the careseeker is in danger due to physical separation, illness or tiredness. He also shows how separation or loss of mother brings about *mourning processes at an age when the child is too immature to deal with them leaving it stuck in despair, depression and anger as well as emotional detachment.

More recent ethological research on humans and their ape ancestors (hominidae) have further implications for psychoanalysis. Hominidae have three subspecies: human beings, chimpanzees and the bonobo. Man has been called a third kind of chimpanzee, being as genetically close to the chimpanzee and the bonobo as they are to each other.

The notion that speech is unique to humans receives a blow if we follow Fouts who trained the chimpanzee Washoe to 'speak' American Sign Language. (So-called ASL, American Sign Language, is not a variant of English but a language of its own, a codification of sign languages emerging in East Europe during the Middle Ages in the deaf-mutes' own closed communities; phonologists consider it a 'common' or 'natural' language.) What follows is some recorded dialogue.

Kate, a long-time woman volunteer with whom Washoe was friendly, got pregnant, and Washoe doted over her belly, asking her in sign language about her baby. Then Kate miscarried and was gone for some days. On coming back Washoe greeted her warmly, and then let her know (by signing) that she was upset about her absence. Knowing Washoe had lost two children of her own, Kate went on to tell the truth: 'my baby died', she signed to Washoe, who looked down to the ground. Then she looked into Kate's eyes and signed 'cry', touching her cheek just below her eye.

The childless Washoe was eventually brought a male baby chimpanzee called Loulis for adoption. After her careful openings were completely rejected by him on their first day together, Washoe woke up next morning, stood up and vigorously called Loulis with a loud slapping sound, while signing 'come baby'. Jolted awake, Loulis jumped straight into her arms and, engulfed in her hairy pillow, fell back asleep; the success of this move was the start of ongoing mother-child bonding. Bypassing traumatised Loulis's wary defences in half-sleep, Washoe accessed and rescued his longings for a maternal 'base', to use Money-Kyrle's term. In the process, Washoe got the baby she wanted.

Washoe's adoption strategy points to a theory of the other's mind. This theory is sophisticated enough to be able to plan surprise discovery and takeover of central, up-to-then inaccessible, emotive aspects. Washoe's signalling 'come baby' shows us she knew what she was attempting; sleeping Loulis responded not to the ASL signal but to the vocal demand and slapping. This description strongly suggests an intuitive grasp on the part of Washoe of the necessary behaviour toward Loulis akin to that needed by the psychoanalyst for interpretation.

After successful bonding with Washoe, little Loulis would only learn his ASL language signals from Washoe's signalling to him or to other chimpanzees, not from the signs which the human observers used to communicate among themselves. This shows the precedence, and dependence, of language learning on emotional relationship. Interestingly the baby chimpanzees learns 'whats' and 'hows' before 'whys', which closely parallels development in children.

On the emergence of human communication, language and thought, ethological evidence runs against the linguistics of Saussure and Chomsky who retroactively construct their whole theory of language acquisition from the latest of human linguistic developments – the written word. They also equate language and thought, unlike Freud, who, from 1895 on, held thinking to be originally wordless and unconscious. The role of consciousness is to pick up and order the results of prelinguistic thought. On the other hand the Lacanian distinction derived from Saussure between *signs (as used by chimpanzees) and *signifiers (as used by humans) seeks to restore the divide between animals and humans. However on the available ethological evidence, the early preoccupation with intersubjective loving and aggressive relationships generates a language of relationship which is articulated by gestures and bodily signs. This appears much earlier than and prepares the way for the upsurge of verbal languages, followed much later by written ones. For instance doing something to someone else already provides a recognisable model for the subject-verb-object pattern. Evidence suggests that complex chimpanzee gestures show a sentence-like structure rather than a word-like structure.

Ethology also speculates on the origins of human intersubjectivity. In contrast to linguists who ground intersubjectivity in language use, the ethologist Kano offers an alternative account. Consider the following observations about the bonobo. It has been argued that face-to-face sexual intercourse is the basis for intersubjectivity with the awareness of and sensitivity to the (sexual) partner's state of mind. It is generally assumed that human frontal coitus allows amorous intersubjectivity whereas animal coitus from behind does not. However bonobos have about a third of their coitus frontally and some sexual intersubjectivity can be glimpsed. For, in coitus if the female glances away or shows disinterest by yawning, the male often interrupts coitus and withdraws. Though not all bonobo sexual intersubjectivity follows such lines of courtesy, these observations of Kano do suggest that intersubjectivity is not uniquely human.

Infantile sexuality too has a central role in the chimpanzee and long and involved battles of weaning essential to sound emotional evolution of the breed as well as the neat incest barrier to mother-son incest in infancy, which turns absolute as the boy grows (though more so to the mother than to the son himself) is described by Goodall. Interestingly the incest taboo's pervasiveness in the chimpanzee and bonobo gives short shrift to the *Lévi-Straussian notion that the incest taboo is imposed by the father which opens the way to culture.

In general the findings of ethology act as a corrective to an overly mechanistic account of animal (or human) mentality. Jane Goodall recounts that when she started her research, respectable scientific journals stringently demanded that chimps be referred to as 'it', not as 'she' or 'he'. Neuroscience too reduces emotion to anatomical, biochemical, and molecular levels. Ethology can help restrain overly mechanistic accounts, and transcendental ones as well. Of *Darwin who pioneered ethology,

*Nietzsche said in *Dawn of Day*: 'We wished to awaken the feeling of man's sovereignty by showing his divine birth: this path is now forbidden, since a monkey stands at the entrance'. But the monkey was swiftly bypassed by most parties concerned, including Nietzsche, in the search for the transcendental. Ethology can provide a corrective to overly transcendental as well as overly mechanistic accounts of human nature.

See also: linguistics

Fouts, R., with Mills, S. T. (1997) *Next of Kin*. New York: Morrow.

Goodall, J. (1986) *The Chimpanzees of Gombe*. Boston, MA: Houghton Mifflin.

Kano, T. [1986] (1990) *The Last Ape*. Stanford: Stanford University Press.

Lorenz, K. (1952) *King Solomon's Ring*. London: Methuen.

Money-Kyrle, R. [1968] (1978) 'Cognitive development' in *The Collected Papers of Roger Money-Kyrle*. Strathtay: Clunie Press.

J. Ahu.

EVIDENCE-BASED MEDICINE AND EVALUATION The use and application of factual information, established by rigorous medical and scientific research methods, in the practice of clinical medicine. Although evidence-based medicine is now advanced as a modern way to optimise clinical practice, medicine and psychiatry have actually had evaluative practice at their core for many years. Historically, the recognised literature in each field has provided a vehicle for learning and the advancement of medical ideas, but more recently evidence-based medicine has evolved through the application of both epidemiological and statistical methods to clinical practice. In the nineteenth and early twentieth centuries, anecdotal and clinical experience had a prominent place in day-to-day decision-making, and individual case reports were an important part of the literature, particularly in psychiatry. In recent decades, the balance has changed. Anecdotes are now largely discounted for the purpose of clinical decision-making, having been replaced with a requirement for research designs that take account of potential confounding variables. Therefore, case control and cohort studies have taken over, and the concept of scientific randomisation has come to prominence. Despite the advance of evidence-based medicine, and particularly the randomised control trial, it is recognised that interpretation difficulties often persist with even the best-conducted studies when the time comes for clinical application.

The pendulum may be swinging again as the limitations of evidence-based medicine are more widely recognised, and the death of anecdotes and clinical case reports start to be lamented.

The use of evidence-based methods present particular difficulties in psychoanalytical research, to the extent that the methodological problems have been largely insurmountable. Confounding variables, including patient and therapist characteristics, techniques used, and difficulties measuring outcomes, have resulted in the failure of several multi-centre trials. However, meta-analytical studies of research outcomes have been published, and may provide a way forward.

Farmer, A. (1999) 'The demise of the published case report – is resuscitation necessary?'. *British Journal of Psychiatry* 174: 93–4.

Proileau, L., Murdoch, M. and Brody, N. (1983) 'An analysis of psychotherapy versus placebo'. *Behavioural and Brain Sciences* 6: 275.

A. F.

EVOLUTION According to Bion, when an analyst suspends memory and desire in the session, s/he is in a position to be at-one with *O (becoming O). O can never be known but being in the process of 'becoming O' allows the analyst to know events that are evolutions (the development) of O. Psychoanalysis takes place when the evolution of O in the analyst intersects with the evolution of O in the patient. Evolutions of O are perceived not by the senses, but by intuition.

Bion, W. R. (1965) *Transformations*. London: Karnac Books. Also in *Seven Servants*. New York: Jason Aronson, 1977.
Bion, W. R. (1970) *Attention and Interpretation*. London: Tavistock. Also in *Seven Servants*. New York: Jason Aronson, 1977.

L. P. C.

EXCITATION According to Freud, every experience and every stimulus, internal or external, that impinges on us increases the 'sum of excitation' in the nervous system. Excitation can be understood, in psychological terms, as roughly equivalent to 'psychical intensity' and, in physiological terms, as a level of neural activation or arousal.

See also: principle of constancy

Freud, S. (1894) *The Neuro-Psychoses of Defense*. S. E. 3. London: Hogarth Press.

M. Eag.

EXCITING OBJECT For Fairbairn, the object that incites hope and desire but fails to satisfy the needs it arouses. This object is split-off and repressed. In terms of infantile evaluation it is a *bad object because it fails to satisfy, but continues to exert an irresistible attraction. The existence of the exciting object is revealed by unrequited and anxious longing.

See also: endopsychic structure; object internal

D. E. S.

EXISTENCE For Lacan the introduction of the human being into language relativises existence to what can be constructed within language. Thus human reality finds its home within the framework of language. The Real is outside of language and is said to 'exist'. From there it has its effect on what exists.

B. O. D.

EXISTENTIAL PSYCHOANALYSIS PRECIS A branch of psychoanalysis deeply influenced by the writings of *Heidegger, *Sartre, *Buber and other existential philosophers which however follows *Freud's basic tenets: the impact of childhood on adult development, *resistance and *defence patterns, *transference and *countertransference. Acceptance of Freud's doctrine of the *unconscious is not necessary because existential thinkers reject or rethink the unconscious to account in a different way for the phenomena of self-deception noted by Freud.

European psychoanalysts, like *Binswanger and *Boss, refashioned their analytic principles and techniques in accord with the principles of Heidegger and, in the case of Binswanger, also Buber. Frankl, under Buber's influence, developed a version of existential analysis he called logotherapy or meaning therapy. *Laing, in England, was most heavily influenced by Sartre, Heidegger, Nietzsche, Kierkegaard, and Buber. Van den Berg relied on a combination of existential philosophers as did May, whose epochal book *Existence*, published in 1958, introduced existential analysis to the English-speaking world. Existential analysts have drawn on authors as diverse as Husserl, *Jaspers, *Nietzsche, Kierkegaard, Tillich, Marcel, Camus, de Beauvoir, Berdyaev, Unamuno, Ricoeur, and Merleau-Ponty. Yalom and Bugental's versions of existential psychology, also eclectic, look to a combination of psychoanalytic and humanistic principles for their inspiration.

Traditional analysts are also sometimes influenced by existential philosophy. Freud himself expressed a reluctance to read Nietzsche for fear his own ideas would have been pre-empted there. *Fromm and *Fromm-Reichmann, who were friends of Buber, include clear existential themes in their work. *Loewald and Leavy both acknowledge the influence of Heidegger. Schafer, who trained with Loewald and Leavy, introduced a new, action-oriented language for psychoanalysis, which moved strongly in the direction of existential thought. Cannon suggests that contemporary *ego psychology, *object relations theory, and *self psychology, with their emphasis on relationship and mirroring in the formation of the self, effectively integrate existentialist and Freudian principles. Thompson argues that many of Freud's technical principles are compatible with existentialist themes despite Freud's positivistic theories. There is also some crossover between existential and Jungian analysis. Boss and Binswanger studied with *Jung, and Binswanger's daughter, Hilde, became a Jungian analyst. Two contemporary Jungians with roots in existential philosophy are Leonard, who wrote a dissertation on Heidegger and did analyses with both Boss and Hilde Binswanger, and Hollis, who also acknowledges the influence of Heidegger. *Lacan, who was influenced by Sartre in his idea of the 'mirror stage' of development and the importance of the 'gaze' or the 'look', is often claimed by postmodern thinkers because of his disparagement not only of the *ego as subject but of subjectivity itself, which of course is retained by existentialist thinkers. Nonetheless, the idea prominent among Lacanian analysts that the self is not a fixed entity has its roots in Sartre and other existential thinkers.

The rejection or reframing of the Freudian unconscious in existential analysis is based on a fundamental principle of *phenomenology: there is no inwardly existing psyche confronting an objective external world. Consciousness is always 'intentional' – that is, always consciousness of this or that object. It is always world-consciousness. The subject-object dichotomy of traditional western philosophy disappears from this perspective and with it the traditional view of the unconscious. The phenomena of self-deception which Freud regarded as manifestations of the dynamic unconscious are re-explained as indications of world-consciousness and divided consciousness. Sartre says that the Freudian unconscious is really a 'mystery in broad daylight' rather than an 'unsolved riddle'. Thompson adds that the unconscious is not inside in the psyche but outside in the world. Furthermore, since reflectivity necessarily differs from raw experience, I may misname my experience and hence deceive myself about it. Analysis does not make the unconscious conscious in the classical sense but rather gives a more accurate name to, or removes the reflective distortions from, that which was known all along to gut-level awareness.

Transference is not the mechanical superimposition of the past on the present, nor is it unconscious in the usual sense. Since I am free, I may also re-choose, though this will be difficult because my way of seeing and being in the world are inextricably intertwined. To change, I must experience the existential *anxiety of standing over the abyss in which self and world, past and future, change together. In this respect, the future is as important as the past to changing transference patterns, a point which Jungian analysts also make. Exploration of the past may help to choose a different future. And the willingness to have a different future may lead to a re-characterisation of the past. The existential analyst is as careful as the Freudian analyst to investigate the impact of childhood on the present, including the transference relationship between patient and therapist. It is just that transference is regarded as something I am doing, a way I am living present relationships that is based on past interpersonal choices implying a particular future, rather than as something which unconsciously happens to me. Analysing transference will not of itself necessarily lead to change, whereas experiencing a different kind of relationship in the present may. The task of the analyst and analysand in existential analysis is to redo the analysand's interpersonal world in the context of their present relationship, a task which interpersonal analysts also recognise. Obviously, this may impact the analyst as well.

Similarly, resistance and defences are recast in existential psychoanalysis as ways of being in the world rather than as mechanisms for keeping unconscious material out of conscious awareness. The defences are not 'mechanisms' in the classical sense but nonreflective strategies for living through difficulties, usually strategies learned in early childhood. Laing points out that the term 'defence mechanisms' in some way describes the patient's experience of his problems, but that the defences have this mechanical quality because the person as he experiences himself is dissociated from them and appears to suffer from them rather than to be their author. It is the task of existential analysis to return to the analysand this sense of agency which has been lost through the assumption of illness, or, as Keen puts the matter, to change one's experience from being determined to being free.

According to Laing, the basic thrust of any effort to situate psychoanalysis in existential principles has to be rooted in the dialectic between truth and falsehood and the way in which the conflict between them accounts for a split in the self that engenders forms of human suffering typically labelled as psychopathology. Thompson adds that experience plays a far more explicit role in existential analysis than conventional psychoanalysis, so that the basic thrust of existential psychoanalysis involves understanding that knowledge about ourselves is anchored in personal experience, and that the weight of our experience is so difficult to bear that we seek to evade it through self-deception.

The existential analyst, unlike Freud, assumes that human beings are free rather than determined. This does not mean that we are free out of context, free to do or be anything whatever or to make of the world anything at all, but rather that we are the authors of our experience in the sense of being world-relating rather than environmentally determined beings. From this perspective, the ego is an object constructed by reflective consciousness, a part of the world rather than an opaque psychic structure. Hence existential analysis, unlike Freudian analysis and to some extent more like postmodern approaches, attempts a deconstruction of the ego in the interest of a return to more authentic living, a principal theme in Heidegger's philosophy.

See also: alienation; authenticity/inauthenticity; being; care; Dasein; daseinanalysis; double bind; facticity; Flaubert; freedom; group psychotherapy (existential); hermeneutics; intentionality; intersubjectivity; look; nothingness; object relations; ontological insecurity; presence; subjectivity; temporality; ultimate concerns

Cannon, B. (1991) *Sartre and Psychoanalysis: An Existentialist Challenge to Clinical Metatheory*. Lawrence: University Press of Kansas.

Keen, E. (1970) *Three Faces of Being: Toward and Existential Clinical Psychology*. New York: Meredith Corp.

May, R., Angel, E. and Ellenberger, H. F. (eds) (1958) *Existence*. New York: Simon & Schuster.

Spinelli, E. (1989) *The Interpreted World: An Introduction to Phenomenological Psychology*. Bristol: Sage Publications.

Thompson, M. G. (1994) *The Truth about Freud's Technique: The Encounter with the Real*. New York and London: New York University Press.

B. C.

EXPRESSIVE RELATING Refers to the analyst's authentic expression of feelings and perceptions arising out of the immediacy of the patient/analyst interaction and conveyed in a conscious and responsive way. It is the expression of the unique personness of the therapist that facilitates the cocreation of selfobject experience in that particular analyst/patient pair.

Preston, L. (1998) 'Expressive relating: the intentional use of the analyst's subjectivity' in A. Goldberg (ed.) *The World of Self Psychology: Progress in Self Psychology*. Hillsdale, NJ: The Analytic Press, 203–18.

H. B.

EXTERNAL OBJECT For Fairbairn, a primary person in a person's life. The term 'object' does not refer to an aim or 'thing' but to a person. It is not intended as a term that depersonalises objects, but is used to indicate the person's roles in mental function and the lifelong process of mental structuring.

D. E. S.

EXTERNAL WORLD Refers to the actuality of other people and groups. Contrasts with *internal world, which refers to innate or experientially generated representations of other people or groups. Some contemporary psychoanalytic thinking seeks to transcend the Cartesian split between internal and external with language that represents their inseparability.

Freud's belief was that external reality along with the child's constitutional factors formed a 'complemental series'. The ego and the reality principle develop out of the need to attempt to satisfy the demands of the drives while also considering the existence of reality and the external world. Distorted beliefs about the external world, called *'psychical reality', were claimed by Freud to play a major role in neurosis. Thus, a child's false memory of sexual abuse by a parent might have the same pathogenic significance as a true memory, a claim later heavily criticised.

See also: reality

E. Gil.

EXTIMACY Extimacy is a portmanteau word coined by Lacan to conjoin two places of the subject's experience: exteriority and intimacy. It is in line with Freud's *unheimlich* which united the most familiar with the most strange and sinister. Extimacy is defined as interior exclusion, an enclave or central void within the subject. For example, sexuality, the most intimate part of the subject, is precisely that which is experienced as an alien trauma, a situation to which the subject can only respond with a symptom.

R. M. W.

EZRIEL, HENRY (1909–85) A member of the British Psychoanalytic Society, Ezriel evolved the theory of the 'required', the 'avoided', and the 'calamitous' relationship. He hypothesised that the group develops a common group tension based upon unconscious transference towards the therapist. The contributions from all the group members become pooled in this underlying avoided theme, avoided because of the calamitous consequences of recognising libidinal destructive drives. Because of these fantasised consequences the group develops defences, each member contributing on the basis of their own internal object relations. The material of the group can be interpreted as if it had come from a single entity. Ezriel viewed peer transferences as displacements by group members from the leader onto other group members.

Ezriel's approach has been recognised as rigid and over-theoretical. Horwitz criticised Ezriel, pointing out the undesirable rigidity and exclusive focus on transference relationship to the group therapist. Horwitz advocates attention to and recognition of individual patient contributions leading to linking the dynamics of these individual contributions to the shared group level.

Malan reviewed the influence of Ezriel's approach on group psychotherapy at the Tavistock Clinic. Generally unfavourable responses by patients to their group therapy experience was noted; a much smaller number who appreciated and benefited had previous psychotherapy and had a greater understanding of the treatment situation.

Ezriel, H. (1973) 'Psychoanalytic group therapy' in L. R. Walberg and E. K. Schwartz (eds) *Group Therapy*. New York: Intercontinental Medical Books, 183–210.

Horwitz, L. (1977) 'A group-centred approach to psychotherapy'. *International Journal of Group Psychotherapy* 27: 423.

Malan, D. H., Balfour, F. H. F., Hood V. G., and Shooter A. (1976) 'Group psychotherapy: a long-term study'. *Archives Journal of Psychiatry* 33: 1303–5.

Whitaker, D. W. (2001) *Using Groups to Help People*. Second edition. London: Routledge.

M. P.

F

FACILITATION A concept Freud introduced in his *Project for a Scientific Psychology*. Refers to the increased permeability between psi-neurons as a result of learning and experience. Such facilitation is a neural substrate of *memory. Remarkably, Freud here anticipates the idea of synapses.

See also: Project for a Scientific Psychology

Freud, S. (1895) *The Project for a Scientific Psychology*. S. E. 1. London: Hogarth Press.

M. Eag.

FACTICITY A term utilised by Heidegger to characterise the matter-of-fact, concretely individual aspect of human life as it is experientially lived. In *Being and Time*, facticity is disclosed through the existential component of *Dasein that Heidegger calls 'attunement'. More precisely, attunement discloses Dasein's 'thrownness' (*Geworfenheit*): the sheer fact that it finds itself in-the-world without any awareness of its origin, as if simply thrown there. Simultaneously, attunement reveals Dasein to have been thrown into, and as, its existence, that is, given the charge to be what it is-in-the-world as the locus among beings through which the world is disclosed. *Sartre, influenced by Heidegger, also uses the term 'facticity' but more loosely, to designate the matter-of-fact situatedness of being-for-itself, with its own individual past, in a contingent world it did not create.

W. R.

FAIRBAIRN, W. R. D. (RONALD) Ronald Fairbairn was born on 11 August 1889. He was the son, and only child, of Thomas and Cecilia Fairbairn. While he belonged to extended families in Edinburgh, London and Yorkshire, with frequent contact, his position as an only child meant that he was thrown onto his own mental resources. Fortunately these were considerable and this childhood isolation stood him in good stead in the 1930s and 1940s when he was developing his theory of object relations.

He was educated at Merchiston Castle School in Edinburgh. In 1907 he entered the Faculty of Philosophy at the University of Edinburgh. His degree course was in Mental Philosophy, the syllabus of which was wide-ranging and included Psychology and the philosophies of Law, Education and Ethics. He graduated in 1911.

Fairbairn was undecided as to what profession to adopt. Should he become a lawyer or go into the Church? He therefore undertook short courses in Divinity and Hellenic Studies at the Universities of Manchester and Strasbourg. At this time, prior to World War I, Strasbourg was in Germany. This was a bonus as his fluency in German enabled him to read Freud in the original. In 1915 he enlisted in the Royal Artillery and was subsequently stationed on the Forth Defences. On 16 November 1916, he visited Craiglockhart Hospital for 'shell-shocked combatants' and met W. H. R. Rivers. Rivers was using Freud's ideas in his treatment of his patients. Later Fairbairn wrote that it was during the war that he decided to become a psychotherapist. So this meeting, in conjunction with his personal experience in combat in Egypt and Palestine, was of immense importance to his later life.

In 1919 Fairbairn undertook a degree in Medicine, graduating in 1923. With his eyes set upon his aim, he underwent an analysis with an Australian, Dr Ernest Connell from 1920 to 1922. He began to practise as a psychoanalyst in 1923. At the same time he held various house physician jobs in hospitals for mental conditions, geriatrics and general medicine. He was a lecturer in Psychology at Edinburgh University from 1927 to 1935, and in Psychiatry 1931–2. Between 1927 and 1935 his work at the University Psychological Clinic led to the development in 1933 of a Clinic for Children and Juveniles. This was an innovation, and it evolved as the result of Fairbairn's personal contribution. In 1927 or 1928 in his capacity as a medical witness, Fairbairn introduced the concept of 'diminished responsibility' in a Court of Law.

In 1926 Ronald Fairbairn married Mary More Gordon. His daughter was born in 1927 and his sons, Cosmo and Nicholas, were born in 1930 and 1933 respectively.

His first published papers in 1929 covered the principles of psychoanalysis and anxiety, the latter being a response to Ernest Jones. In 1929 and 1930 Fairbairn wrote three seminal papers, which were intended for a book on psychology, but were not actually published until 1994 in *From Instinct to Self.* In 1933 Fairbairn was elected an associate of the British Psycho-Analytical Society and became a full member in 1936. Fairbairn's importance was recognised by Ernest Jones, in spite of Jones's theoretical reservations. So although, after the 1929 International Congress of Psychoanalysis, Fairbairn was internationally respected and recognised, the events of 1943–5, known as the 'Freud–Klein *Controversial Discussions', meant that his ideas went unheard. At this time the British Society was riven with strife and the so-called Independents, of which Fairbairn was one, were isolated and their views became sidelined. The result of the antagonism between Anna Freud and Melanie Klein had the unfortunate effect that new psychoanalytic ideas and developments were never theoretically assessed. This has been to the detriment of the discipline of psychoanalysis itself and continues to this day.

From 1927 to 1940 Fairbairn contributed widely to current debates on art, when he put forward a projected psychology of art and discussed surrealism. His papers on education proposed radical changes in psychoanalysis and psychology, as did those on child development. In these he demonstrated that symptoms exhibited by children should be understood in terms of their actual experience of frustration and deprivation rather than as the result of disallowed instinctual desires. In his 1935 groundbreaking paper on child sexual abuse, he categorised the pathogenic effects of assault in terms of the relationship which the abuser held to the victim. In his 1939 paper he addressed the psychology of the abuser. His work with children led to his later formulation of the *moral defence, which can lead to the acceptance of the role of the victim by the assaulted individual.

During World War II, Fairbairn was Consultant Psychiatrist at Carstairs Hospital from 1940 to 1941, and occupied the same position at the Ministry of Pensions until 1954. During the whole period from 1924 till the early 1960s, Fairbairn continued his private practice of psychoanalysis.

It was during the 1940s that Fairbairn developed his mature theory of object relations, published in his 1952 *Psychoanalytic Studies of the Personality*. In this he reoriented psychoanalytic theory and practice upon a view of human nature derived from Aristotle, Hegel and Einstein, in which mind and body are an interactive whole and in which the integral human individual is programmed to develop interhuman relationships. It is through the development of such relationships that human potential is nurtured. From 1951 to 1958 Fairbairn's major contributions were his clinical paper on hysteria and his three methodical papers which changed practice. In these he focused upon his observation of the actual ways in which the analysand related to the analyst as a person. From his observations, he would work with the patient to free up their patterned responses within relationships. Fairbairn felt that interpretation had to be used with discretion.

Fairbairn's personal life was circumscribed by his practice and writings; time was short. However, he always had daily time for his children. He was fascinated by art and literature; he thoroughly enjoyed the theatre and cinema. Plays and films always provoked lively discussions. He loved antique furniture, an interest inherited from his father. He revelled in his house in Gifford, and later in Duddingston (Edinburgh), which overlooked the loch, and his gardens; his particular love was his shrub roses. Above all he was fun, making lots of silly jokes. Fairbairn died on 31 December 1964.

Fairbairn, W. R. D. (1952) *Psycho-Analytic Studies of the Personality*. London: Tavistock, Routledge & Kegan Paul. Pbk London: Routledge.
Fairbairn, W. R. D. (1994) *From Instinct to Self: Selected papers of W. R. D. Fairbairn in 2 Volumes*. D. Scharff and E. Fairbairn Birtles (eds). Northvale, NJ: Jason Aronson.

E. F. B.

FAIRBAIRN PRECIS W. R. D. Fairbairn's contribution to psychoanalysis took as its starting point the fundamental need of each individual to be in relationships throughout life, rather than Freud's starting point that assumed the need for pleasure. According to Fairbairn, the infant's need for a relationship with its mother (or primary caretaker) inevitably meets with dissatisfaction, not because the mother is necessarily depriving, but because she can never provide unfailing satisfaction. Fairbairn thought that the process of building mental structure (which he called *endopsychic structure) began with the experience of dissatisfaction, and the first defence against it is the taking in of an image of the mother; this becomes an *internal object. At first this internal object derived from experience with the mother is of her as a totality (the internal whole object), but the infant still has a painfully depriving experience of her, albeit now inside its mind. So the infant now splits the unsatisfying object into two aspects of the mother, each of which represents the mother in a particular reified affective relationship with the infant: an accepting, satisfying *object that remains mostly available to conscious and reasonable function, and an unsatisfying object that is rejected or *repressed out of central, conscious experience. (This is what Fairbairn meant in describing the *schizoid process.) This *rejected object is 'bad' in the sense that relations with it feel affectively bad to the child. There are two categories of bad internal object: the *exciting object that is excessively exciting of unsatisfiable need (analogous to the mother who is seductive, overfeeding, anxiously arousing); and the rejecting object that rejects the child's needs (the mother who is experienced as persecuting, depriving or rejecting). However, an object cannot exist alone. It is half of a relationship between this part object and a part of the ego (or self), and each of these *internal object relationships are characterised by telltale affects that organise the relationship and give it emotional meaning. The exciting object is bound to the *libidinal ego through affects of anxious and unrequited longing, teasing and frustration. The rejecting object is bound to the *internal saboteur or *antilibidinal ego by affects of anger and sorrow. The *central ego then relates with a wide and fluid range of affects to the *ideal object, the representative of the accepted object that was not subject to repression by the central ego in the first place.

These elements form the six-part organisation of personality that Fairbairn called endopsychic structure. Because they are formed from experience with the outer world with primary figures in the child's life, they install that experience in the mind as they structure it. However, once they are inside, they are subject to modification by many internal factors: the immature understanding of the child; the distortions introduced by developments in the child (for instance the sexualisation at certain developmental stages); or the way early experience teaches the growing child to interpret new experience. For these reasons, internal object relations are never perfect representatives of external experience, but a blend of lived experience and internal shaping. The structure that results mediates between the child's internal world and its external one, enabling the child to use prior experience to interpret and adapt to external experience.

Internal organisation of the mind is not static. Fairbairn described the way that internal object relations not only resonate with external experience, but also constitute an internally dynamic system. For instance, *hysterical persons have grown up experiencing some form of painful alternation of overly exciting and overly rejecting experiences. They develop a magnification of exciting (or libidinal) and rejecting (or antilibidinal) internal object sets which may alternate in seeking exciting and rejecting external objects. In consequence, central ego/ideal object relations are depleted, and the only ideal object that feels safe to the hysteric is a one depleted of excitement and threat of rejection – a bare-bones relationship. Finally, the hysteric may cover the extremely painful experience of unsatisfied longing for elusive love by substituting an angry antilibidinal object relationship for the longing, and moving to anger in external relations to avoid the greater pain of unrequited love. This is a dynamic relationship between internal object organisations. Another example is the goody-two-shoes who uses excessive goodness to cover any vestige of hostility, which is more painful. The dynamics of the healthy personality include a fluid movement among the internal categories of organisation, and an overall psychic organisation that is in open interaction with the external world. In pathology, not only do the repressed bad object relations dominate, but the person attempts to keep the mind as a closed system, relatively cut off from external influence.

Two points round out the description of Fairbairn's model of the mind. Internal objects are not simply images or representatives of primary people in a person's life. They are mental organisations – parts of the ego, formed in identification with external figures. Because they are parts of the ego, they are capable of all aspects of ego function, just like those parts of the ego that represent the self. Therefore, they can generate fantasy and action, as we see when a patient acts in a way he can later identify as being like a critical parent.

Lastly, Fairbairn thought that Freud's *super-ego was not so much a single internal structure as it was a dynamic group of functions capable of different patterns of action, sometimes harsh when derived from antilibidinal function, and sometimes more guiding and benign when derived from the ego ideal.

Fairbairn's revolutionary model of endopsychic structure moved psychoanalysis into the realm of thought characterised by modern physics and Hegelian philosophy, presenting an open systems, cybernetic model of mental function that has formed the basis of modern theories that put the need for relationships in the central role of development and therapy, and that enables the application of psychoanalysis to family, couple, and group therapy, and to organisational functioning.

Clinically Fairbairn believed that it is the actual relationship between therapist and patient that is the overarching therapeutic factor, within which elements of analytic technique play roles. *Transference or mutative interpretation, genetic reconstruction, empathy, *play with children, etc., are elements of effective analytic therapy, but no one of them is the key; rather it is the relationship itself that organises and gives meaning to the other elements. In his view interpretations given by an objective, detached analyst could be felt to usurp the patient's own voice, engendering an alienating situation in which the patient's own voice was stifled. But he also realised that in other instances when the patient was unable to speak, it did not necessarily mean rejection of the analyst, but that the experience was preverbal. Fairbairn, therefore, advocated the possibility of a more interactive model for psychotherapy. In this it is the interpretation of the actual relationship between the patient and the analyst that is crucial.

See also: accepted object aggression; antilibidinal ego; anxiety; bad object; death drive; defensive strategies; dependence; developmental stages; dissociation; dreams; external object; fantasy; good objects; hysteria; ideal object; identification; internal reality; libidinal, ego; libido; moral defence; external objects; pre-ambivalent object; object relations; Oedipus complex; oral attitude; pristine unifary ego resistance; schizoid personality; self; separation anxiety; transitional techniques

Fairbairn, W. R. D. [1952] (1994) 'Theoretical and experimental aspects of psycho-analysis' in D. Scharff and E. Fairbairn Birtles (eds) *From Instinct to Self: Volume I.* Northvale, NJ: Jason Aronson.
Fairbairn, W. R. D. [1958] (1994) 'The nature and aims of psychoanalytical treatment' in D. Scharff and E. Fairbairn Birtles (eds) *From Instinct to Self,* Vol. 1. Northvale, NJ: Jason Aronson. 1994.
Padel, J. (1973) 'The contributions of W. R. D. Fairbairn (1889–1964) to psychoanalytic theory and practice'. *Bulletin of the European Psycho-Analytic Federation* 2.

E. F. B. / D. E. S.

FAIRY TALES These are short 'once upon a time' narratives existing paradoxically concurrent with, yet removed from, the present and possessing qualities of entertainment and cautionary instruction, e.g., rites of passage, quests, awakenings, abandonment, etc. Fairy tales have been interpreted sociologically as reflections of social and political structures, but, since the influence of Freud and Jung, they have been interpreted primarily as narratives of inner psychological import. Characters are thus defined psychological attributes. Of prime importance is the first sentence, delineating 'the situation', e.g. 'There was once a miller who had fallen upon hard times' (the failed father), or 'There was once a childless king and queen' (the childless couple), and from this first sentence inevitable consequences follow.

Bettelheim, B. (1977) *The Uses of Enchantment: The Meaning and Importance of Fairy Tales.* New York: Random House, Vintage Books.
Von Franz, M. L. (1982) *The Interpretation of Fairy Tales.* Zurich: Spring Publications.

L. R.

FALSE CONNECTION *Repression renders certain representations inaccessible, and so places a neurotic individual in a state of negative hallucination. Freud's claim is that the ego cannot tolerate the gaps in consciousness brought about by this situation, and compulsively constructs fabricated realities that cover over this gap in consciousness. These fictions are ubiquitous wherever there are effects of repression in the field of consciousness. Freud calls these constructions of reality 'false connections'. Reality is constructed as a result of repression, and in the form of a misrepresentation of what is real. This is the conclusion of Freud's theory of false connection. Latin and Anglo-Saxon schools of psychoanalysis make different wagers in relation to the scope of this conclusion. Anglo-Saxon schools have generally argued for the restriction of the ubiquity of these distortions of consciousness by claiming some field to be exempt from them – that of common sense, or a region where the ego has autonomy, as for example in *ego psychology. European schools on the other hand have generally taken such misrepresentation to be inescapable, and a characteristic of the ego's organisation of consciousness. For this reason Lacan claims that the ego is not a reliable ally in analytical work, and that the direction of analysis is oriented towards gaining access to unconscious structure.

See also: scotomisation

Freud, S. (1895) *The Case of Emmy von N.* S. E. 2. London: Hogarth Press.

B. B.

FALSE SELF The concept of the false self is used by Winnicott in two ways. First it is referred to as a stable continuous working structure in the personality. 'False' does not here refer to the absence of honesty or integrity in the person. Rather it describes the adaptation that the subject has to make in order to live within his social context. In this sense each person to some extent develops a false self, and Winnicott sees the false self as the caretaker and protector of the true self, mediating between the true self and the outside world. He sees the false self, for instance, as the agency that could recognise that the true self might need the help of psychoanalysis and therefore bring the patient into treatment, a vigilant caretaker.

Second, he recognised that certain individuals could experience false self disorder, when for instance in a severe schizoid illness, the sense of a true self was all but lost so that the personality was thereby seriously depleted and the opportunity for spontaneous living was compromised.

See also: true self

Winnicott, D. W. (1965) 'True and false self' in *The Maturational Processes and the Facilitating Environment*. London: Hogarth Press.

M. Twy.

FAMILY ROMANCE A variety of fantasies in which the disenchanted child doubts that his humble lowly parents are his true progenitors. In the most familiar famous version of the fantasy, the child believes or fantasises himself to be the offspring of an exalted or noble couple with whom he will be eventually be re-united.

Freud, S. (1909) *Family Romances*. S. E. 9. London: Hogarth Press.

P. M.

FANTASY (FAIRBAIRN) Fairbairn believed that fantasy and imagination are important, infancy is not dominated by *unconscious phantasy as described by *Klein and Isaacs, for whom it was the primary expression of the drives and the foundation of unconscious organisation. Fairbairn saw the term 'psychical' or 'inner reality' as more accurate than unconscious phantasy. His short paper given in 1943, in his absence, was seen as a valuable scientific contribution to the Scientific Debates held in London in the 1940s.

King, P. and Steiner, R. (eds) (1991) *The Freud Klein Controversies 1941–45*. London and New York: Tavistock and Routledge. (For his paper and the Kleinian reply by Isaacs)

E. F. B.

FATHER Freud's discovery of the 'paternal complex' in the nucleus of neurosis made the *Oedipus complex the paradigmatic structure that accounts for the generation of symptoms, as well as for the construction of the masculine and feminine positions. The place of the father in the Oedipal triangle is in the prohibition of the *mother as a sexual object. The person in the place of the father needs to have the libidinal attention of the mother, and to use their position to introduce a 'no' into the child's claims to the continuation of the primary love bonds to the mother.

For Lacan too, the father is the central figure in his account of the formation of *subjectivity. Lacan distinguishes between several father figures, all of them to be clearly distinguished from the actual father of the child's everyday life. Freud's notion of the Oedipal father (a figure to be conceived within the Oedipal triangle, and within its relation to the castration complex) has been elaborated further by Lacan as the Symbolic father, namely, the *name-of-the-father. Freud's notion of the primal father of the primal tribe has been re-conceptualised by Lacan as the Real father, the father of *jouissance. In Lacan's early works, the father is the signifier which introduces negation into the desire of the mother. In Lacan's later works, the father is conceived as 'the *knot', namely, as the crossing point, or the intersection of the three basic dimensions: the *Imaginary, the *Symbolic, and the *Real.

D. N. / E. B.

FEMININITY The state that the little girl eventually accedes to, through her negotiation of the *Oedipus complex. In early works, Freud argued for a fundamental psychic bisexuality in everyone, whilst maintaining the phallic or masculine nature of the *libido. For Freud, notoriously, the little girl was a little man. Femininity entails giving up the active phallic role (which she has, until then, shared with her male counterpart), relinquishing the mother as the primary love object and turning toward the father. Because they do not fear castration, women do not achieve the moral level of the male *super-ego. In two late papers Freud addressed the problem of sexual difference, and described how, in women, an early masculinity, associated with activity, is replaced by femininity, a primarily passive and receptive state. These views which seem to confine femininity to a reactive and inferior position, have been criticised by feminist critics such as *Juliet Mitchell, Sarah Kofman, Luce Irigaray and many others who have found an inherent denial of the power and fear of women, unthinking patriarchy and a narcissistic over-valuation of the penis in Freud's views.

See also: masculinity; penis envy

Freud, S. (1931) *Female Sexuality*. S. E. 21. London: Hogarth Press.

Freud, S. (1933) *Femininity*. S. E. 22. London: Hogarth Press.

J. B.

FEMINISM AND PSYCHOANALYSIS Of the varieties of feminism that flowered in the twentieth century only one developed close links to Freudian psychoanalysis and contributed to its core theory: Lacanian feminism. It retained Freud's focus on the unconscious formation of sexual difference and viewed woman as a conceptual figure with its own psychic profile. *Object-relations feminism (the principal alternative orientation in psychoanalytic feminism) responded differently to Freud, preferring Klein and Winnicott. It emphasised gender (a social construction influenced by infantile nurturing) over sexual difference. To Freudo-Lacanian feminists sexual difference has an unconscious cause; to object-relations, perceptible infantile patterns of connecting to the mother shape gender-styles.

Arch-feminist Virginia Woolf's husband owned the press that printed Freud's works in English as quickly as they were written. Yet non-psychoanalytic feminism never deemed Freud its friend, even though his revolution in man's self-view opened a field that granted women greater standing than any previous scientific endeavour. Freud's dedication to knowing about something (the unconscious) formerly unknown to man and woman alike encouraged an unprecedented collaboration between the sexes. Women became psychoanalytic practitioners and those closest to Freud frequently made major theoretical contributions: Lou Andreas-Salomé (narcissism), Sabina Spielrein (death drive), Princess Marie Bonaparte (literature and analysis), Melanie *Klein (super-ego, guilt, mother-child dialectic), Anna *Freud (child psychology, ego defences), and Joan Riviere (femininity). Others (*Deutsch, *Horney, Mack *Brunswick) wrote classic case analyses. Yet these women would not now be considered feminists, simply because they subscribed to Freud's theory that the cause of woman-ness is unconscious.

Freud insisted the male sexual organ had primacy in the psychical distinguishing of sexes: sexual identification begins with a scene of *castration – the child's unconscious hypothesis about why boys have what girls do not. Freud's 'bedrock' (castration) decides all sexual difference; the anatomical absence of male genital attains inordinate command over the psychic destinies of male and female. In men, castration resolves their Oedipal complex; in women, it inaugurates a crippling envy that stunts development of their higher judgmental and reasoning powers. The emergence in woman of femininity is due to penis envy, her unconscious response to castration. The psychic cause of woman is thus not biological; it is an unconscious answer to a biological fact, re-inscribed on her body.

Historically, the represented *phallus indeed symbolises man's cultural priority over nature (and social dominion over women). Freud was not, however, historically relativist about his claims: the organisation of the body under the phallus is psychically immutable. The prestige in the psyche of the conceptual (imagined or symbolic) penis is set long before the child grasps social values. Woman's penis envy is not attributable to her lesser social evaluation; it is the unconscious significance she assigns to her body's privation. Feminism, struggling to overturn the phallic model, thus thought Freud no ally, and rejected his sexual identification inscribed unconsciously on the body. Before castration, psychical 'phallic equality' reigned between the sexes; disavowing castration hence became a feminist imperative.

Freud paid detailed attention to woman's great psychical complexity. She faced three conflicting imperatives resulting from the castration complex: femininity, the masquerade that cloaks her penis envy; female sexuality, not organised under phallic centrality and constrained only by social (not inner Oedipal) norms; and, maternity. Once she becomes a mother, woman encounters how restrictive a role it is that Oedipus concedes her (Freud says it demands the freezing of her libido). All three components arise from the way castration stamps her body.

Karen Horney fully subscribed to Freud's idea of the unconscious, but expressed feminist reservations: it was the vagina that decided the girl's psychic fate. Yet Horney reduced woman to a sub-function of her eventual maternity, and maternity could not alone account for female sexuality outside reproduction nor femininity's odd emergence.

The 1960s mantra, 'the personal is the political', epitomised the feminist strategy against the unjust after effects of the anatomical distinction between the sexes (socio-economic, legal, and political). No professions or women professionals (including psychoanalysts) were exempt from scrutiny for gender bias. Feminist Nancy Chodorow felt the need to apologize for the absence of feminist activism among early women analysts by invoking their dire political circumstances, which left them little time for the 'personal'. Feminist apologies for Freudians are however rare and psychoanalytic feminism has looked rather to Melanie Klein than to Freud. Klein provided a significant modification to Freudian theory and a corresponding revaluing of woman. Her followers rejected castration as the unconscious determinant of sexual identification in favour of Klein's powerful maternal super-ego.

Klein located infantile sexual development in the mother's body (sexed female, equipped with 'good' and 'bad' breasts); Chodorow linked gendered personality traits to the gender styles infants developed in response to a mothering provided primarily by females. Infant sons develop rigid egos; daughters, less able to detach themselves, form uncertain ego-boundaries. Freudians would judge a girl's incomplete detachment from her mother negatively; Chodorow views it as *attachment, a model even boys should emulate.

In stressing the mother's importance, object-relations feminism hoped to raise the low psychoanalytic esteem for woman and to ally themselves with non-psychoanalytic feminists who reject gender establishment in infancy. Chodorow now pleads that gender, though formed in infancy, is not binary but a continuum, and urges psychoanalytic openness to the 'differently gendered' (lesbian, gay, bi- and transsexuals). Such moves blunt feminist antipathy to psychoanalysis, but they also widen object-relations' divide from Freudo-Lacanian feminism. To the latter, object-relations' refusal to engage unconscious drives voids the very psychoanalytic definition of sexuality and loses sight of the specificity of woman: hers becomes merely one of many 'gender troubles'. Freudo-Lacanian feminism engages the critique of patriarchy but argues that the unconscious is its best resource.

Post-structural and Freudo-Lacanian feminists have thus regrouped under the banner of sexual difference. For them, the Woman Question cannot be dealt away by subordinating it to gender reform; gender merely burgeons into Grosz's 'thousand tiny sexes' that drop the radical difference in Freud's human sexuation. Juliet *Mitchell was Lacanian feminism's first major representative. She reproved feminist critics for attributing to the messenger (Freud) the ills of his message (patriarchal domination). Mitchell deemed Freudian sexual difference equally crucial to psychoanalysis and to the feminist cultural campaign to dismantle patriarchy. *Psychoanalysis and Feminism* upheld Freud's claim that sexual difference is not a fashion to be discarded at will but an old phallic root whose operations require systematic analysis. Mitchell maintained Freud's castration as the keystone of psychical architecture, insisting that the ideological success of patriarchy cannot be accounted for without a theory of the phallocentric unconscious and drives.

To non-analytic feminists Mitchell's work seemed paradoxical: she advocated cultural revolution but adhered to the castration complex that they saw as the source of phallocratic conservatism. Mitchell saw phallocentrism instead as standing in need of a revolution, but failed to specify how to alter politically something brought about through indelible, unconscious markings on the body. In the years since Mitchell first wrote, certain psychoanalytic feminists have responded by viewing sexual difference through an advanced Lacanian lens.

Psychoanalysis poses the problematic of castration as: 'How is the natural body inserted into the cultural one?' Lacan nuances castration differently: 'How does the body cope with unsupported meanings inaugurated by the signifier?' For Lacan, castration is the universal effect of the impact of language on the human organism, whose body is vexed by a linguistic logic that overthrows its original organic logic. Language carves the body up neatly, but what it carves off (*jouissance) returns to the body, inscribing it phantasmatically with 'letters' (*object a) marking the advent of drive. Drives are the after-image of a natural instinct lost to the signifier. Castration-by-language is a universal, but its solution is not single; it has two faces, masculine and feminine. In *Encore*, Lacan proposed that masculinity furnished only one possible solution to the drives.

Encore questioned the historic and psychoanalytic promotion of the phallic-masculine over the feminine solution, and feminists now saw Lacan less as espousing phallic ideology than as seizing for women the revolutionary potential of the signifier. Women were to be granted the same flexibility ('the signifier-ness of the signifier') the signifier offers men. The phallocentric ideal of a 'stable' order (Lacan cites Aristotelian-Thomist ideals) is a fiction created at women's expense; it puts the enormous energy of the signifier only at men's disposal, and makes woman representatives of the irrational Thing it diffuses. Women are made to stand outside or else serve the phallic order. But the signifier can free woman from being a mere *differentia specifica* (a biological, social or economic class member – Lacan writes 'Woman', not 'The Woman'). To Lacan, Freud was thus no apologist of patriarchy, but was driven by two questions: 'What is a Father?' and 'What does a Woman want?' These twinned questions permanently alter the phallocentric paradigm for gender relations. Freud rendered the pretensions of phallocracy imaginary. Freudo-Lacanian feminists, such as Copjec and MacCannell, thus consider Lacan's *Encore* inaugural to going beyond phallocentrism.

Freudian feminism was important to French artist Hélène Cixous (who worked for two years with Lacan) and philosopher Luce Irigaray. Cixous originally titled her institute for Feminine Studies 'Sexual Difference Studies'; Irigaray, battling Lacan, still found his linguistic framing of the sexual divide had feminist potential.

Chodorow, N. (1989) *Feminism and Psychoanalytic Theory*. New Haven, CT: Yale University Press.

Copjec, J. (1994) 'Sex and the euthanasia of reason' in *Read My Desire: Lacan Against the Historicists*. Cambridge, MA: MIT Press.

Freud, S. (1931) *Femininity*. S. E. 21. London: Hogarth Press.

Freud, S. (1933). *Female Sexuality*. S. E. 21. London: Hogarth Press.
Lacan, J. (1975) *Encore: Seminar XX*. Paris: Seuil.
MacCannell, J. F. (1991) *The Regime of the Brother: After the Patriarchy*. London: Routledge.
Mitchell, J. (1974) *Psychoanalysis and Feminism*. New York: Pantheon.

J. F. M.

Fenichel, Otto (1897–1946) Otto Fenichel had the reputation of being the 'encyclopaedia of psychoanalysis' based largely on his being the author of the exhaustive 1945 *Psychoanalytic Theory of Neurosis*. He was also the author of the secret circular letters, the *Rundbriefe*. Fenichel's priority was the establishment of the requirements and the fundamentals for the 'correct application of psychoanalysis' which he based on a 'scientific' Freudian psychoanalysis.

Fenichel was born in Vienna on 2 December 1897 to a bourgeois Jewish family, and studied medicine at the Vienna Medical School. He was active in the Vienna youth movement which championed sexual, cultural and educational reforms, and from 1915 onwards he attended Freud's lectures at the University of Vienna. In 1919, Fenichel founded the Vienna Seminar for Sexology, and in 1920, he became a member of the Vienna Psychoanalytical Society. He began analysis with Paul Federn and continued it, after relocating to Berlin in 1922, with Sándor Radó at the Berlin Psychoanalytic Institute. Fenichel became a member of the teaching staff of the Berlin Institute and transferred his membership to the German Psychoanalytic Society in 1926. He co-organised a seminar for younger colleagues, the so-called 'Kinderseminar' (Children's Seminar) – an open discussion group on psychoanalytic issues apart from the meetings of the Institute, and he led this seminar from 1924 until 1933. Apart from that, Fenichel sympathised with the views of Marxism, and organised Marxist discussion groups in Berlin. In 1933, Fenichel immigrated to Oslo, Norway, and became secretary of the Danish-Norwegian Psychoanalytic Society. In 1934, he began writing his secret circulars, the *Rundbriefe*, a continuation in written form of the discussion group in Berlin. He wrote a total of 119 circular letters which spanned a period of more than eleven years. In 1935, Fenichel moved to Prague and took over the local Psychoanalytic Study Group, and he once again became a member of the Vienna Society. In 1938, after the *Anschluß*, Fenichel moved to Los Angeles. He became a member of the Los Angeles Psychoanalytic Study Group, and was elected a training analyst. By 1942, he was one of the founding members of the San Francisco Psychoanalytic Society and, in 1944, elected vice-president. Fenichel died in Los Angeles on 22 January 1946.

Fenichel, O. (1998) *119 Rundbriefe* (*1934–1945*). Vol. 1, Europa (1934–1938). J. Reichmayr, and E. Mühlleitner (eds); Vol. 2, Amerika (1938–1945). E. Mühlleitner, and J. Reichmayr (eds). Frankfurt and Basel: Stroemfeld Verlag.
Greenson, R. (1966) 'Otto Fenichel 1898–1946. The Encyclopedia of Psychoanalysis' in F. Alexander et al. (eds) *Psychoanalytic Pioneers*. New York and London: Basic Books, 439–49.
Jacoby, R. (1983) *The Repression of Psychoanalysis. Otto Fenichel and the Political Freudians*. New York: Basic Books.
Mühlleitner, E. and Reichmayr, J. (1998) 'Otto Fenichel – historian of the psychoanalytic movement'. *The Psychohistory Review, Studies of Motivation in History and Culture* 26: 159–74.

E. M.

Ferenczi, Sandor (1873–1933) The founder of all relationship-based psychoanalysis was born on 7 July 1873, in Miskolc, Hungary, the son of Alexander Fraenkel (born Baruch Fränkel) and Rosa Eibenschütz. The family was multilingual, speaking Hungarian, German and Polish. Ferenczi himself was bilingual (speaking Hungarian and German) and would come to know English and French. He grew up in a middle-class liberal Jewish atmosphere among ten brothers and sisters. The family's bookstore and home became a meeting place for artists and intellectuals from Hungary and abroad. After completing secondary school, Ferenczi went to Vienna to study medicine. He received his medical degree in 1894. During the Viennese years, Ferenczi was influenced by Darwinism and the sexology of Krafft-Ebing. He read Freud and Breuer's paper on *hysterical phenomena but considered it artificial.

Ferenczi's pre-psychoanalytic works, original papers, essays, case reports and book reviews, written between 1897 and 1908, dealt with psychic disturbances, the psychological questions of sexuality, dreams and hypnosis and the indispensability of human co-equality in the doctor-patient relationship during treatment. He was interested in the phenomenon of spiritism and recognised the manifestation of the unconscious or semi-conscious in psychic functioning and the existence of *splits in the psyche. Having described the subjective truth of a person as early as 1899, he was still focused on the experiences of patients in his work with *Rank in 1924. These early themes, joined with the need for liberal thinking and tolerant behaviour as well as his criticism of models of hierarchical relatedness and authoritarianism, all form the core of Ferenczi's later psychoanalytic thinking (see *Ferenczi Sándor a pszichoanalízis felé. Korai írások 1897–1908)*. The majority of his earlier writing appeared in *Gyógyászat* (Therapy), a weekly medical journal whose owner and editor-in-chief was Schächter the famous surgeon, an early supporter and friend of Ferenczi. From the outset, this journal made ideas on psychoanalysis available to open-minded physicians. Even literary and political journals opened their doors to psychoanalysis, e.g. *Nyugat* (The West), founded by Ignotus, who was Ferenczi's friend and a leading figure of modern literature.

After Ferenczi met Freud in 1908, an intense lifelong relationship formed between them (see *The Correspondence of Freud and Ferenczi*, Vols 1–3). The emphasis in Ferenczi's papers had been on radical social criticism. Then in 1909, he became the first to publish writing that reflected the perspective of object relations. In addition to *projection, Ferenczi described *introjection, the other characteristic functioning of the ego ('Introjection and Transference').

At the Weimar Congress in 1911, Ferenczi proposed to establish the *International Psychoanalytical Association. He founded the Hungarian Psychoanalytic Society in 1913 and remained its president until his death. It was through Ferenczi's interdisciplinary openness and his efforts to popularise psychoanalysis – finding its way into the ranks of physicians, social scientists and other inquiring minds – that this discipline became tied to the fields of literature, pedagogy, ethnography and the arts as well as intertwining with Hungary's progressive intellectual and bourgeois radical movements.

He was elected president of the International Psychoanalytic Association in 1918. The following year, he became the first professor of psychoanalysis to be appointed at the Medical School of the Budapest University. Psychoanalysis was integrated into the medical curriculum. However, this lasted only a few months due to the turbulent political changes in Hungary.

Ferenczi resigned from the IPA presidency in 1919. In the same year he married Gizella Pálos.

In the 1920s, the psychoanalytic technique and the growing effectiveness of psychoanalysis became Ferenczi's top priorities. Ferenczi recognised *countertransference as an indispensable tool in psychoanalysis. He experimented with 'active' therapy as much as he did with mutual analysis. He eventually set aside both techniques, but these experiments greatly contributed to the development of psychoanalytic theory and practice. He recognised that an analyst's work depended on participation in an appropriate training analysis lest his/her own unresolved problems hinder work with the patient. Ferenczi initiated the establishment of a systematic training programme. He drew attention to the significance of the early mother-child relationship in character development. He placed traumatisation within a dynamic system in which interpersonal and *intrapsychic processes affect one another and in which real events and not fantasies lie at the centre of trauma (see his 'Confusion of tongues between adults and the child'). Ferenczi found Freud's first trauma theory valid and tied it to the perspective of object relations. This represented a paradigm shift. Ferenczi placed great importance on the patient reliving traumas within the context of psychoanalysis. This required the analyst to create a trusting and safe atmosphere and avoid the myth of infallibility tied to authority (see his 'The elasticity of psychoanalytical technique').

At the invitation of the New School for Social Research, Ferenczi held lectures on psychoanalysis in the United States between 1926 and 1927. His lectures in Washington and New York had an influence on early interpersonal psychoanalysis, key figures of which, *Sullivan and Thompson, maintained personal contact with him. Ferenczi's advocacy of lay analysis, however, drew strong criticism from members of the New York Psychoanalytical Society. After his return to Budapest, he continued analysing difficult cases (see *The Clinical Diary of Sándor Ferenczi*) and in so doing contributed a great deal to the development of modern psychoanalysis. Ferenczi's initiatives can also be recognised in the attitude of Budapest School. The 1920s and 30s were marked by the use of countertransference, the child-parent relationship (see *Balint), psychosomatic approaches (see also Lévy, Balint) and interdisciplinarity, e.g. in the creation of psychoanalytic anthropology (see also Roheim), as well as the establishment of the fundamental principles of psychoanalytic training. His relationship with Freud deteriorated during these years. Conflicts developed which were painful for both of them and led to a distancing between them. Ferenczi died of pernicious anaemia prior to his sixtieth birthday.

The rumour of Ferenczi's mental illness spread by *Jones prevented Ferenczi's ideas from taking their rightful place in the history of psychoanalysis. His contributions make him the most significant forerunner to post-Freudian, post-modern psychoanalysis. His students and colleagues carried with them the creative spirit of the Budapest School when they emigrated. Kindred spirits included Michael and Alice *Balint, Lorand, *Mahler, and Benedek, as well as Thompson, from among the contemporary American psychoanalysts. Several decades after the publication of three volumes of his work *First, Further* and *Final Contributions*, both *The Clinical Diary* and his correspondence with Freud and Groddeck were published, as was much of the writing which had been omitted from the earlier collections.

Brabant, E., Falzeder, E., Giampieri-Deutsch, P. and Haynal, A. (eds) (1993) *The Correspondence of Sigmund Freud and Sándor Ferenczi*, Vols 1–3. Cambridge, MA and London: The Belknap Press.

Ferenczi, S. (1980) *First/Further/Final Contributions to Psycho-Analysis.* New York: Brunner/Mazel.

Ferenczi, S. (1985) *The Clinical Diary of Sándor Ferenczi.* Cambridge, MA: Harvard University Press.

Haynal, A. [1987] (1991) *The Technique at Issue. Controversies in Psychoanalysis from Freud and Ferenczi to Michael Balint.* London: Karnac Books.

Haynal, A. (2002) *Disappearing and Reviving. Sándor Ferenczi in the History of Psychoanalysis.* London and New York: Karnac Books.

Mészáros, J. (ed.) (1999) *Ferenczi Sándor a pszichoanalízis felé. Korai írások 1897–1908.* Budapest: Osiris.

J. Mes.

FETISH Inanimate object or part of the body necessary for sexual arousal by a 'fetishist'. Most fetishists are men and their most common interests are: feet, hair, women's underwear and shoes. Freud discovered in the fetish a defence against unconscious knowledge that a woman (usually the mother) has no penis. Splitting of the *ego ensures the unconscious meaning of the fetish remains repressed thus allowing sexual fulfilment. Greenacre links fetishism to *transitional objects.

For Lacan a fetish is an object whose function is that of veiling castration – in particular, that of the mother. It emerges as an image constructed by the signifiers which disavow castration. The presence of the fetish object becomes the necessary condition for obtaining sexual satisfaction.

See also: paraphilias; perversion

Freud, S. (1927) *Fetishism*. S. E. 21. London: Hogarth Press.

Greenacre, P. (1970) 'The Transitional Object and the Fetish' in *Emotional Growth*. New York: International Universities Press.

R. M. S. / S. T.

FILM AND PSYCHOANALYSIS An important application of psychoanalytic theories to extra-clinical fields concerns the arts. Cinema, among these, has a privileged relationship with psychoanalysis and even shares its birthday with it, the screening in 1895 of the Lumière brothers' first films in Paris coinciding with the publication of Breuer and Freud's *Studies on Hysteria*.

The language of cinema is in many respects analogous to that of the unconscious. For instance, the analytic notion of *screen memories might also be used to define films. The concept of *projection is obviously crucial to both cinema and psychoanalysis. *Free associations (mostly visual in the former, verbal in the latter) have in both idioms the purpose to encourage the exploration of deep emotional meanings and of the often uncertain boundaries between reality and fantasy. Dreams, the interpretation of which constitutes a 'royal road' to the unconscious, use for the purpose of circumventing censorship, mechanisms comparable to those of many movies, including condensation, displacement, symbolic expression and editorial cuts leading to distortions of time and space. Cinema was often described as a 'dream factory'.

Given this common ground, it is not surprising that film directors and screenplay writers should have adopted in their works (and frequently abused) psychoanalytic ideas about the human mind and interpersonal relationships. At times films have attempted to represent, with an either fictional or documentary approach, the psychoanalytic profession itself. This has often been portrayed in its oversimplified version of being merely engaged in the recovery of repressed traumas for the explanation of current events, with much use of flashbacks (as the filmic device equivalent to memory), and symbolic decoding of dream sequences such as the famous one designed by Dalí for Hitchcock's 1945 *Spellbound*. Freud was himself the subject of Huston's 1962 biopic *Freud. The Secret Passion*. However Freud was sceptical; having been asked to cooperate on the first major film about psychoanalysis, namely Pabst's 1926 *Secrets of a Soul*. He wrote in a letter to Abraham: 'I do not believe that satisfactory plastic representation of our abstractions is at all possible'.

On the other hand, psychoanalytic theories, especially those originating from the ideas of Lacan, have been since the 1960s influential in academic film criticism, for instance in the prestigious journals *Cahiers du Cinéma* and *Screen*. Prominent among the analytically-oriented authors who have concentrated on the psychological meaning of cinema is Metz who observed that what unfolds on the screen is real, but what we perceive on it from a distance (through the senses of sight and hearing) is not the object itself but its projected shade. The silver screen is, in other words, a peculiar kind of distorting mirror.

Many psychoanalytically oriented critics have focused their attention on textual analysis, that is on the interpretation of the content of a film – its subject, its themes, the treatment of its characters – as if it corresponded to the 'material' brought to their sessions by analytic patients, noticing for instance the defensive mechanisms displayed by the protagonists, or some associative links between past events and present experiences. Articles of textual psychoanalytic criticism can be found regularly in professional journals. They are sometimes concerned with movies using a cinematic language deliberately reminiscent of unconscious functioning and even conveying a disturbing sense of the *uncanny such as are found in the works of Buñuel, Fellini, Surrealism, and German Expressionism. Sometimes authors display a special sensitivity to the psychological factors contributing to their characters' behaviour such as Truffaut or French New Wave; at other times they deal with powerful feelings of fear and terror often associated with a realistic or paranoid sense of being persecuted as are found for example in the films of Hitchcock.

Many films – either within the comic or, more often, the dramatic tradition – are of special interest to analysts primarily because they deal with themes also familiar to psychoanalytic enquiries: different forms of mental pathology, such as neurotic or narcissistic disturbances typified in the work of Woody Allen; psychotic disintegration such as in the work of Polanski; sexual perversions, gender and identity confusion found in Almodóvar's films; crises in subjectivity related to developmental stages (films seen from the perspective of children; dealing with the adolescence trauma of coming of age; or with the anxieties of illness, old age and death); incestuous or other conflictual family constellations, often with an emphasis on *Oedipal themes as found in Bertolucci; acute existential and moral dilemmas in the films of Bergman, Antonioni, Kurosawa and Kieslowski.

Some psychoanalytic authors have focused, more controversially, on the analysis of the personal and social history, the character, or even the psychopathology of the filmmakers as they manifest themselves in their cinematic work. In this psychohistorical or pathographical perspective, a film – or indeed any other product of creativity – is studied as if it were the symptom of its author's individual or interpersonal problems.

Finally, psychoanalysis has made a major contribution to our understanding of film spectatorship, that is, to the complexity of psychological, socio-economic and more generally cultural phenomena which affect filmmakers in their construction (and audiences in their reception) of cinematic products and the mythologies associated with them; for instance exploring the relationship between spectators and Hollywood stars. Psychoanalytic writers with a feminist orientation such as Mulvey have been particularly active in providing original perspectives on issues of gender and sexuality in films, such as male and female stereotyping and the role of women as fetishes or as objects of voyeuristic gaze.

Gabbard, G. O. (1997) 'Guest Editorial: The psychoanalyst at the movies'. *International Journal of Psycho-Analysis* 78(3): 429–34.

Metz, C. [1974] (1982) *The Imaginary Signifier. Psychoanalysis and the Cinema*. Bloomington: Indiana University Press.

Mulvey, L. (1975) 'Visual pleasure and narrative cinema'. *Screen*, 16(1).

A. S.

FINLAND Sigmund Freud's name was first mentioned in a Finnish medical journal in 1984. Psychoanalysis then began to attract attention in academic and literary circles. The most influential was Dr Yrjö Kulovesi (1887–1943), who paid his first visit to Freud in 1924 and underwent two separate analyses (with Edward Hitschmann and Paul Federn). He was elected a full member of the Viennese Psychoanalytical Society in 1931 and a training analyst in 1936. Otto *Fenichel mentioned three of his papers in his book *The Psychoanalytic Theory of Neurosis* (1945). Together with the Swede Alfhild Tamm (1876–1959) he founded the Finnish-Swedish Psychoanalytical Society in 1933 in Stockholm under the auspices of the IPA. It was accepted into the *IPA in Luzern in 1934. One can say that Kulovesi saved psychoanalysis in the Nordic countries, because he did not accept Wilhelm *Reich as a member. On Freud's recommendation Ludwig Jekels travelled to

Stockholm to support the newly-founded society, along with Otto Fenichel.

After World War II there was also another Finnish physician, Benjamin Rubinstein (1905–89), who had been in analysis in the late 1930s in London. He introduced psychoanalytic ideas to his Finnish colleagues in Helsinki in the 1940s. David *Rapaport invited him to the USA in 1948. He became a member of the New York Psychoanalytic Association in 1954.

In post-war Finland there developed an increasing interest in psychoanalysis among young colleagues. But those who wanted psychoanalytic training had to go abroad. Stig Björk was the first to go to Stockholm, in 1948, and was followed by Pentti Ikonen, Carl Lesche, Tapio Nousiainen, and Veikko Tähkä. All of them became members of the Swedish Psychoanalytical Society in the middle fifties. More followed in their footsteps to Sweden, including Eero Rechardt, Gunvor Vuoristo, Reijo Holmström, Mikael Enckell, and Matti Tuovinen. Three of them (Henrik Carpelan, Lars-Johan Schalin and Leena-Maija Jokipaltio) went to Switzerland for training, and became members of the Swiss Psychoanalytical Society in the 1960s.

The origins of organised psychoanalysis in Finland date back to 1964, when many Finnish analysts returned to Finland and were granted the status of a Study Group by the Executive Council of the IPA. Tähkä was elected the Chairman, and Carpelan the Secretary. The President of the IPA elected the Sponsoring Committee under the chairmanship of Donald Winnicott, its Secretary being Pearl King. In Copenhagen in 1967 the Finnish Study Group was elevated to the status of a Provisional Society. The Society was accepted two years later as a Component Society of the IPA, in Rome. At the end of 2002 members included fifteen child analysts and twenty-nine training analysts, with thirty-eight candidates in training.

Finnish analysts have published many articles and books. They have also contributed actively to the Nordic psychoanalytic publication, *The Scandinavian Psychoanalytic Review*, founded in 1978. Nordic orientation has played a highly important part in the work of the Society. Many of its members have published books about psychoanalysis and related topics. The thirty-second International Psychoanalytic Congress of the IPA was held in Helsinki in 1981 at Finlandia House designed by the world famous Alvar Aalto. Dr Eero Rechardt was the host and the chairman of the Finnish organizing committee, and was elected the Vice-President of the IPA. The fifth Scientific Symposium of the European Psychoanalytical Federation was held in Helsinki in 1992. The main conference of the EPF on the Unconscious was held in Helsinki in April of 2004.

Organised training began in 1965. The first training course in child analysis, with Leena-Maija Jokipaltio as teacher and supervisor, was established in 1978. The members of the society have been active in promoting psychoanalysis in Eastern Europe. In 1990, five Lithuanians began their psychoanalytic training in Helsinki and graduated in 1996. Two Estonians are also currently in training.

The growing activities of the Society encourage a positive assessment of the current state of Finnish psychoanalysis.

Kulovesi, Y. (1927) 'Der Raumfaktor in der Traumdeutung'. *International Zeitschrift fur Psychoanalyse* 13: 56–8.

Laine, A., Parland, H. and Roos, E. (1997) *Psykoanalyysin uranuurtajat Suomessa* (The Pioneers of Psychoanalysis in Finland). Kemijärvi: LPT.

Roos, E. (1992) 'Psychoanalysis in Finland'. *Psychoanalysis International*, Vol. I, in P. Kutter (ed.). Stuttgart: Fromman Verlag.

E. R.

FIXATION Perseverance with, or regression to, an early state of drive satisfaction, which interferes with the achievement of a more mature level of *development. Persons fixated on *oral, *anal, or phallic gratifications may be unable to give up eating, cruelty or exhibitionistic display in order to achieve *genital sexuality.

As a result of fixation, one or more of the following features of development persists: 1) a focus on a particular type of interpersonal interaction that is sought out metaphorically in an effort to satisfy particular needs or drives (for example passively taking in nourishment when breastfed); 2) a way of relating to objects that is treating them as *part objects; 3) the utilisation of old ways of adapting to the environment, handling *conflict, or averting psychic trauma when confronted with internal conflict; and 4) the employment of more primitive functioning of the *super-ego. Fixation may be manifest or latent (only manifesting during regression). Fixation occurs when the ego has experienced insufficient or excessive gratification or *trauma during a particular stage of development. Constitutional factors can also contribute to fixations, as can a non-specific factor referred to as 'adhesiveness of the libido', which is said to account for the ego's disinclination to give up libidinal attachments. When the ego undergoes *regression the ego reverts back to a fixation point.

R. T. / J. A. Ber.

Flaubert, Gustave The nineteenth-century novelist is the subject of Sartre's mammoth biography *The Family Idiot*, which, among other things, may serve as an illustrative case history for *existential psychoanalysis. Sartre wanted to show that psychoanalysis and Marxism (his own version of each) could be effectively combined. Tracing Flaubert's responses to his immediate family, economic and social structures, political events, and the *Zeitgeist* of the period, Sartre holds that Flaubert as a child chose the imaginary over the real, skirted the perils of madness, and 'made himself the author of *Madame Bovary*'.

Sartre finds the origins of Flaubert's neurosis in early infancy. Flaubert's mother's overprotective but unloving care for the infant failed to develop in him any sense of agency. His sense of helplessness put him out of touch with the real. A basic passivity manifested itself in Flaubert's sexuality, in his feeling that his ego was bestowed upon him by others, and in his attitude to language. He felt that he 'was spoken by language'. Later he developed a case of hysterico-epilepsy, which was intentional but not the result of reflective deliberation, in order to avoid the law career for which his father had destined him. Flaubert's childhood resentment became misanthropy. His purpose in literature was to demoralise his readers by using the imaginary to mock received ideas about the real.

Barnes, H. (1981) *Sartre and Flaubert*. London and Chicago: University of Chicago.

Sartre, J.-P. (5 vols, 1981–93) *The Family Idiot*. Translated by Carol Cosman. London and Chicago: University of Chicago.

H. E. B.

Fliess, Wilhelm (1858–1928) Wilhelm Fliess was a general practitioner in Berlin with an emphasis on rhinology and was Freud's confidential correspondent in the formative years of psychoanalysis. The research of Fliess, as reflected by his major books (*Die Beziehungen zwischen Nase und weiblichen Geschlechtsorganen*, 1897; *Der Ablauf des Lebens, 1906*), focused on connections between the nose and other bodily spheres, especially the female genitals, and then, stimulated by the first pregnancy of his wife in 1895, on periodic processes in human and non-human life. Fliess established two fundamental periods, of twenty-eight and twenty-three days, which he defined as female and male, respectively. At the outset, he conceived them as being produced by the recurring discharge of some 'toxins' (sexual hormones *avant la lettre*). Since he found both periods in either sex, he went on to postulate the bisexual make-up of all men and women. The range of phenomena he tried to explain with his ideas included the blossoming of flowers, the teething of babies, creative spurts, mood swings, the choice of a mate and the day of death.

Freud and Fliess met in 1887. Both men shared an interest in the differential diagnosis of neuroses and particularly in sexuality. It became their common scientific daydream to create a new sexual theory, developed in its relevance for biology, psychology and neuropathology – with Fliess attending to the physiological and Freud to the clinical-psychological aspects. Freud's adoption of the idea of bisexuality was the most important result of this project. After the heyday of their friendship (1893–97), each of them elaborated his own approach. While Freud fostered a psychological type of theory formation, leading to *The Interpretation of Dreams*, Fliess recast his theory of periodicity in mathematical instead of chemical terms. He thereby expected to revolutionise biology, but Freud remained doubtful of this step. Basically, Freud and Fliess had achieved a kind of scientific community *à deux* which provided mutual support for two ambitious outsiders doing medical research in private practice, isolated from academia. But rather than cooperating in a substantial way, each one used the other as a mirror for his own grandiosity. When confronted with this fact, their friendship dissolved in the period 1900–2.

In 1904, Fliess thought that Freud had promoted a double plagiarism committed against him by two Viennese philosophers, Otto Weininger and Hermann Swoboda. He published his accusations in 1906. Freud considered his behaviour paranoid and derived a general notion from it: paranoia arising from homosexual tendencies. Fliess maintained some interest in psychoanalysis, was in contact with Karl Abraham and his son, Robert Fliess became an analyst. His medical practice is said to have been very successful. After the publication of *Der Ablauf des Lebens*, Fliess continued to propagate his ideas on periodicity and bisexuality in lectures which were collected in several volumes. But he had no lasting impact on future research, apart from his influence on Freud.

The Complete Letters of Sigmund Freud to Wilhelm Fliess, 1887–1904 J. M. Masson (ed.). Cambridge, MA and London: Belknap-Harvard, 1985. Revised and enlarged German edition, ed. M. Schröter. Frankfurt: Fischer, 1986.

Porge, E. (1994) *Vol d'idées? Wilhelm Fließ, son plagiat et Freud*. Paris: Editions Denoël.

Schröter, M. (1988) 'Freud und Fließ im wissenschaftlichen Gespräch'. *Jahrbuch der Psychoanalyse* 22.

Sulloway, F. (1979) *Freud – Biologist of the Mind.* New York: Basic Books.

M. Sch.

FLIGHT INTO ILLNESS As in the somatic compliance of hysteria, or in the case of war neuroses, neurotics often choose the secondary gain of their symptom, while giving up on *compromise formation. In face of the conflicts of life, they abandon themselves to their symptoms, and give up supporting a desire which could win out over these symptoms.

J. D. M.

FORDHAM, MICHAEL (1905–95) Fordham was the most prominent *analytical psychologist in Great Britain after the Second World War. He was the pivotal figure behind the formation of the Society of Analytical Psychology in 1946, and the founder of the Child Analytical Training there. He was co-editor of the *Collected Works of C. G. Jung*, and founding editor of the *Journal of Analytical Psychology*. Along with critical expositions of *Jung's work, his research focused on child analysis, child development and autism, and the study of the analyst-patient interaction. He was the first to integrate *analytical psychology theory with elements from *object-relations theorists in an original synthesis.

Astor, J. (1995) *Michael Fordham: Innovations in Analytical Psychology*. London: Routledge.

Fordham, M. (1957) *New Developments in Analytical Psychology*. London: Routledge & Kegan Paul.

Fordham, M. (1958) *The Objective Psyche*, London: Routledge & Kegan Paul.

Fordham, M. (1969) *Children as Individuals*. London: Hodder & Stoughton.
Fordham, M. (1976) *The Self and Autism*, London: Academic Press.
Fordham, M. (1993) *The Making of an Analyst*. London: Free Association Books.

S. S.

FORECLOSURE Foreclosure was put forward by Freud – as early as 1894 – as a defence mechanism appropriate to *psychosis. It is a more radical *defence than the repression operative in neurosis. It consists of an elimination, a cutting out, and a rejection of an intolerable representation. Certain kings in Ancient Egypt chiselled out – from public monuments – the records of the achievements of their fathers. Psychosis works in a similar way in implementing foreclosure. This term was used by Lacan to designate a defence mechanism specific to psychosis: the rejection of the *name-of-the-father which provides forms of limitation to the functioning of the Symbolic order. The term was a direct translation of Freud's concept of *Verwerfung*. Later, Lacan was to generalise its meaning to the rejection of separation from the mother's desire – to its effect at the level of the *castration complex – and ultimately to the absence of knotting between the *Imaginary, the *Symbolic and the *Real, as evidenced by the most severe cases of schizophrenia.

B. B. / F. R.

FORENSIC PSYCHIATRY involves itself with those people who suffer from mental disorder who are also offenders, either against the law or against the behavioural norms of society. The Latin word 'forensics' referred to the forum or public place in ancient Rome where justice was administered: Thus, literally, forensic psychiatry is psychiatry related to the courts and encompasses cases in criminal, civil and family law.

It is also concerned (necessarily) with victims and victimisation, and one (albeit idiosyncratic) definition, by acknowledged leaders in the field, is that forensic psychiatry is the prevention, amelioration and treatment of victimisation which is associated with mental disorder. Offender patients met within forensic psychiatry are often victims of deprivations and different abuses in early life and/or of later mental illnesses. They are also 'victims' of their own self-defeating, offending behaviour, e.g. damage to their loved and family members – as well as more obviously victimisers of others.

Forensic psychiatry addresses itself to the clinical assessment and treatment of mentally disordered offenders in a variety of settings and circumstances: the circumstances may include assessment prior to the court process, involvement in the court process itself and then management and treatment thereafter (*medico-legal interface): The setting may be the community and outpatients or locked, medium-secure, or maximum-secure hospital.

Broadly speaking, services are directed at those suffering from 'functional mental illness', e.g. the schizophrenias or manic depressive illness, and, separately, the character or 'personality disorders' and sexual offenders. However, there is much diagnostic overlap and frequently an individual is said to have 'co-morbidity', signifying that our diagnostic labels will not pigeonhole him or her into a single category. Substance and alcohol abuse is a frequent co-morbid factor.

Butler Report (1975) *The Report of the Committee on Mentally Abnormal Offenders*. London: HMSO.
Gunn, J. and Taylor, P. (1993) *Forensic Psychiatry: Clinical, Legal and Ethical Issues*. Oxford: Butterworth Heinemann.

C. C.

FORGETTING see **AMNESIA**; see also **MEMORY**

FORM OF ORGANISATION OF THE DRIVE Freud claims that the originally 'polymorphously' perverse structure of the sexual drive originates from the functioning of independently acting and anarchically functioning *partial drives. More usually called the 'component drives', the partial drive is less well defined.

B. B.

FORMATION OF THE UNCONSCIOUS A term used by Lacan: the unconscious is not known directly, but is accessible via its 'formations' for example: dreams, bungled actions, slips of the tongue, jokes and symptoms. These are privileged routes to the unconscious. Any phenomenon – act, action or creation – in which the laws of the unconscious, *metaphor and *metonymy, can be detected is a formation of the unconscious.

H. T.

FORMALISATION Formalisation in Lacan is linked to the notion of the *matheme, the aim of which is to allow the teaching and transmission of whatever can be transmitted in psychoanalysis. With this aim, Lacan in 1957 developed the Saussurian formula relating the signifier to the signified (S/s) by producing his mathemes for metaphor and metonymy. These take the letter under the bar to designate a signifier just as is the case with the one above the bar. The same fractional bar allowed him to formulate in 1969 his matheme for the four *discourses (the Master, the Hysteric, the Analyst and the University), with four places and four letters. A second step beyond the system set up by Saussure was his introduction of the *object a, which designates an object, and not a signifier. Meanwhile he took notions from the theory of graphs and networks to construct his graph of desire in 1959. His study of the quadrant of Charles Sanders Peirce, together with an apparatus taken from mathematical *logic, allowed him to construct the formulae of sexuation in 1972. In this formulation clinical consequences stemming from the lack of sexual rapport between men and women are given a formalisation.

See also: sexual relations

N. C.

FORT-DA (FREUD) Freud's description of a game played by a one-and-a-half-year-old boy in which the child throws an object on a string out of sight, uttering his version of 'fort' (the German word for 'gone') and then pulls the object into sight, uttering a joyful 'da' (German, 'there'). This repeated game of disappearance and return is interpreted by Freud as the child's attempt at mastering the mother's disappearance by turning a passively endured situation into an active mastery.

Lacan finds in the speech game played by Freud's grandson ('gone/back again') an indicator of the structure of the shifting elements of the child's relation to the mother. In doing this, Lacan takes it that the child is introduced into the *Symbolic dimension by the game: the object that the child plays with – whether a ball, a bobbin, or a piece of blanket – has a role of allowing the child to bear witness to an absence. The Symbolic structure that surrounds the child is thus being taken up in a way that places the pairs yes/no, more/less, presence/absence at the centre of the child's relations to others. The game in this way represents a fundamental distress, where being only arises as presence against a background of absence. Desire – or lack – is present in the game, as is a relation to the *Real in the form of the basic rhythm of the fort/da. The Symbolic is explicit in the game, so the fort/da gives access to the text that underlies the subjectivity of the child. Because of this the game represents a moment favourable to interpretation, rather than being resistant to it. The child engages in such an action in response to its experience of frustration, of the retraction of promise.

See also: drive for mastery; repetition

Freud, S. (1920) *Beyond the Pleasure Principle*. S. E. 18. London: Hogarth Press.

M. Eag. / B. B.

FOULKES (FORMERLY FUCHS), SIGMUND HEINRICH (1898–1976) Group analysis is the name given to the theory and method originated by S. H. Foulkes. Born in Karlsruhe to an assimilated, middle-class Jewish family, Foulkes had a classical German education. During World War I he served as a telephone operator. After the war he had to choose between becoming a theatre director and a doctor. Though he chose the latter, his interest in the theatre is reflected in some of his ideas of the group process. Sophocles, Chekhov and Pirandello had shown the interconnectedness of protagonist chorus: the distribution of roles to individuals in a group whose significance can only be understood against the background of the whole group. Foulkes studied in Heidelberg, Munich and Frankfurt. He spent two years as assistant to the neurologist Kurt Goldstein from whom he learnt about the functional integrity of the central nervous system and how principles of Gestalt psychology could be applied to understanding the function of a brain-damaged individual. Foulkes trained as a psychoanalyst in Vienna in the mid-1920s; he was analysed by Deutsch and supervised by Nunberg and Hitschmann. He greatly admired the work of Schilder. After Vienna Foulkes worked in Frankfurt at the newly founded Institute of Psychoanalysis. The Frankfurt psychoanalysts met with and were influenced by the Frankfurt School of Social Research which linked Marxist economic theory with Freud's psychoanalysis. Erich Fromm and Frieda Fromm-Reichmann were Foulkes's contemporaries amongst the psychoanalysts; Horkheimer, Adorno and *Elias amongst the sociologists. Foulkes's friendship with Elias led later to a fruitful collaboration which has been reviewed by Dalal. He left Germany in 1933 for England. His first paper to the Psychoanalytic Society in 1937 was 'On Introjection', his response to his encounter with the English School of Psychoanalysis which under the influence of Melanie Klein gave primacy to projection over introjection. In 1939 Foulkes began his first groups in Exeter. His reading of the American pioneer psychoanalyst Trigant Burrow had influenced him. His activities greatly expanded in the Royal Army Medical Corps where he took a leading part in the second Northfield experiment (the first was led by *Bion and Rickman). Work at Northfield with Main and Bridger led to the concept of the therapeutic community and viewing an organisation as a whole. In 1948 he published his seminal work *Introduction to Group Analytic Psychotherapy*. As consultant psychotherapist for the Maudsley Hospital, Foulkes taught and influenced generations of psychiatrists who developed group analysis in Britain and overseas. Foulkes founded the Group Analytic Society in collaboration with Elias and de Maré and later took part in the newly-formed Institute of Group Analysis. The journal *Group Analysis* continues to develop his work.

Foulkes thought that as the human being is essentially social, the group is the natural locus for the treatment of emotional disorders. The healthy organism functions as a whole and can be described as a system in dynamic equilibrium that constantly adapts through its circumstances. Analogously the group functions as a whole in an ever-changing figure ground relationship. The socio-dynamic of the group is analogous to the network of the central nervous system; each individual represents a nodal point engaged in communication with others. Emotional disturbances will show up as disturbance in the communicative network. According to Foulkes sentences represent isolated autistic parts of the person, unsuitable for sharing; only when they are translated into socially understood articulate language do they cease to exercise mental pressure. The group-analytic method gives primacy to communication between group members over interpretation from the therapist. This is in contrast to both *Wolf, Bion and *Ezriel who give primacy to the group therapist's interpretative function. In Foulkesian group analysis the therapist has an important function as dynamic administrator, with the responsibility to create and maintain optimal conditions for the setting in which therapy takes place.

Foulkes, S. H. (1964) *Therapeutic Group Analysis.* London: Allen & Unwin. Reprinted (1984) London: Karnac Books.

Foulkes, S. H. (1990) *Selected Papers.* London: Karnac Books.

Foulkes, S. H. and Anthony E. J. (1957) *Group Psychotherapy. The Psychoanalytic Approach.* Harmondsworth: Penguin. Reprinted (1984) London: Karnac Books.

Nitsun, M. R. (1996) *The Anti-Group. Destructive Forces in the Group and their Creative Potential.* London: Routledge.

Pines, M. (1983) 'The contribution of S. H. Foulkes to group therapy' in M. Pines (ed.) *The Evolution of Group Analysis.* London: Routledge. Reprinted (2000) London: Jessica Kingsley.

M. P.

FRAGMENTED BODY Lacan's idea of the fragmented body concerns the relation between the narcissistic image which the subject has of itself, for example, a body and its mirror-image, which do not match. Experiencing the difference between the image and its body, the subject can feel as though its body is fragmented. In early Lacan the idea of the fragmented body also related to the presumed state of fragmentation prior to the constitution of the body image and ego as a unit in the *mirror phase.

R. R.

FRANCE If France was the origin of Freud's interest in psychopathology during his period at Salpêtrière in 1885–6, under Professor Jean-Martin Charcot, both the French public and doctors long remained indifferent, if not hostile, to the discoveries of psychoanalysis. Unlike in other countries, there has been no 'pioneering figure' and the first work on the subject by Dr Angélo Hesnard and Professeur E. Régis in 1914 was rapidly forgotten on account of the Great War, as well as on account of the rejection of all things German and their allies.

From 1921 on, literary people such as the Surrealists became interested in the works of Freud, translations of whom were starting to appear in French. In November 1926, Princess Marie Bonaparte, who had been analysed by Freud and had become a close friend, helped to found the first French psychoanalytical body, the *Société Psychanalytique de Paris*. The following year saw the creation of the *French Psychoanalytical Review (Revue Française de Psychanalyse)*. However, opposition to psychoanalysis was rife: people objected to Freud's 'pansexualism' and the over-systematic aspect of metapsychology. Rudolf Loewenstein, who had trained in Berlin and was the teaching analyst of the future leaders of the SPP represented the orthodox Freud; others, like René Laforgue, were intent on creating a psychoanalysis less linked to Vienna and to 'German' thought, seen as incompatible with French Cartesianism.

During World War II, given the ban in Nazi-occupied France on what was seen as a 'Jewish' science, there was no psychoanalytical activity at the official level. It was only from 1946 on that the Paris Psychoanalytical Society resurfaced under the direction of three well-known figures soon to be at loggerheads: Jacques *Lacan, Daniel Lagache and Sacha Nacht. Following the liberation a need was felt to found a Psychoanalytical Institute to train candidates, who were becoming steadily more numerous, on the lines of the American model; what was at stake was who would control this body. In June 1953 Daniel Lagache, followed by Jacques Lacan, led a breakaway group to form the French Psychoanalytical Society (*Société Française de Psychanalyse*). For a decade this group strove to rejoin the international community whose leaders were opposed to the training of candidates as conducted by Jacques Lacan, with its variably timed sessions and the dependency it created among patients, and Françoise Dolto who was more involved in the psychoanalysis of children.

It was from within the French Psychoanalytical Society that the second split in the French psychoanalytical movement was to come, with the formation in 1964, by opponents of Lacan, of the French Psychoanalytical Association (*Association Psychanalytique de France*), recognised as a official part of the IPA in 1965. For his part, Lacan went on to found the Paris Freudian School (*Ecole Freudienne de Paris*) destined to have unprecedented repercussions among the public.

His weekly seminar became a focal point for Paris intellectuals in the wake of the structuralists, Lacan himself becoming a celebrity with a host of followers. There followed an explosion of those styling themselves 'psychoanalysts' and psychoanalysis became a media event; however this also meant a rebirth of interest in the works of Freud, given Lacan's 1955 slogan: 'back to Freud'. From this stemmed, in part, the work of two former pupils, Jean *Laplanche and Jean-Bertrand Pontalis, who brought out in 1967 their *Vocabulaire de la Psychanalyse,* illustrating how partial we are in France to the study of and commentary on Freudian concepts.

Not all Freud psychoanalysts are Lacanians. Between 1950 and 1970 the Paris Psychoanalytical Society witnessed the publication of works by Sacha Nacht, Serge Lebovici, René Diatkine, Maurice Bouvet, Pierre Marty in psychosomatics, Joyce McDougall and André *Green, among others. From the French Psychoanalytical Society and the Psychoanalytical Society of France works appeared by Didier Anzieu, Jean Laplanche, Jean Clavreul, Wladimir Granoff, Serge Leclaire, Octave Mannoni, François Perrier and Jenny Aubry. A certain number of these followed Lacan into the Freudian School where conflicts arose, before long leading, in 1961, to a split giving rise to the Fourth OPLF (*IVème Groupe OPLF*) under Piera Aulagnier, François Perrier and Jean-Paul Valabrega. Opposition intensified as Lacan aged, with Lacan himself causing a sensation, in January 1980, by announcing the closure of his school. Several of his pupils protested his decision and opposed the formation of a Freudian School (*Ecole de la Cause Freudienne*) under the control of his son-in-law Jacques-Alain *Miller. Lacan's death on 9 September 1982 saw the dispersal of his followers into a loose alliance of more or less insubstantial or ephemeral groups. Maud Mannoni's Centre for Training and Research in Psychoanalysis (*Centre de Formation et de Recherche Psychanalytique*) was to prove more long-lived and was followed, after a split in 1994, by Psychoanalytical Space (*Espace Analytique*).

The French Psychoanalytical scene is thus composed essentially of Freudian psychoanalysts within the Paris Psychoanalytical Society, the oldest, most important and most 'orthodox' of its institutions, despite a number of internal currents; and the Freudian Psychoanalytical Association, much less numerous and more intellectual by reputation. On the other hand, Lacanian analysts are to be defined essentially in relation to Jacques-Alain Miller, who runs the Freudian School, (gaining it world wide renown, especially in South America) but strenuously disowned by most of Lacan's former pupils composed of several groups all claiming loyalty to their master. Between these two, but still Lacanian in origin, are the Fourth OPLF Group and *Espace Analytique*.

As a whole, having torn itself to shreds for decades, French psychoanalysis is now attempting to regroup through discussion groups – here meetings of the International Association of the History of Psychoanalysis (*l'Association Internationale d'Histoire de la Psychanalyse*) provide an opportunity; this has given rise to an approach to psychoanalysis that is particular to France. Of course, all theoretical construction arises from clinical experience but practice, as such, has never distanced itself from reflection upon Freudian themes and repeated examination of their application as they evolve within their socio-economic and political environment. From the traditional psychoanalytical cure to psychoanalytical therapy, from Klein's or Winnicott's theoretical propositions to Kohut's thesis, nothing involving psychoanalytical thought and activity has occurred in France without giving rise to reflection or critical examination. This specific approach, more often than not closer to philosophy, is sometimes surprising to foreign psychoanalysts, but it should not be allowed to obscure the deep-rooted nature of a discourse that is often abstract but conducted within rigorous clinical practice by most of its practitioners.

A. D. M.

FREE ASSOCIATION The patient's attempt to follow the so-called 'fundamental rule' of spontaneously verbalising whatever comes to mind in the psychoanalytic situation without selective editing or suppression of what is presumed to be irrelevant or important or is felt to be distressing. Freud believed that due to psychic determinism, free association would reveal unconscious repressed material.

Freud, S. (1917) *The Manifest Content of Dreams and the Latent-content of Dream Thoughts.* S. E. 15. London: Hogarth Press.

D. Wol.

FREE/BOUND ENERGY Energy available to be rapidly discharged. Bound energy is discharged at slow rates. Free energy can attach to any thought or action to attain immediate discharge (*primary process). Bound energy implies a more permanent attachment and a mode of thought that involves more stable cognitive structures (*secondary process).

S. E.

FREEDOM, EXISTENTIAL Perhaps the most fundamental tenet of existential-phenomenological psychotherapists is the insistence upon the freedom of human beings to choose not merely what to do on a particular occasion, but what to value and how to live their lives. Warnock has noted that the existentialists, uniquely among philosophers, have grasped the problem of freedom as a practical problem about how we live our lives. As Sartre asserts, existence precedes essence – which is to say that human beings do not have a fixed essential nature, as a chair or a tree can be said to have a specific set of qualities which entirely encapsulate their possibilities. Rather, they create themselves by the choices they make. They are free to choose their own destiny, though it is important to remember that this freedom exists in the context of certain 'givens' or facts of existence. A baby is not free to choose to be born into one family, with its concomitant circumstances, rather than another, or to be born with particular physical attributes and genetic make-up. Similarly, as we are all born so shall we all die; as Heidegger terms it, 'our being is a being unto death'.

Although we cannot choose the givens of our existence, we are free to choose our response to them, and in doing so we create our own values and our own life. As Sartre expresses it, human beings are condemned to be free. Many clients (indeed all of us at certain points in our lives) resist the responsibility that such a view of their place in the world entails, preferring instead to blame the shape of their life on fate, chance, economics, childhood influences, or a hundred other 'external' factors which can be pressed into service. *In extremis* almost anything can be taken up by clients and used as an explanation for their current misery or dilemma. It is in part the task of existential analysis to explode such explanations.

Heidegger, M. (1962) *Being and Time.* Translated by J. Macquarrie and E. S. Robinson. New York: Harper & Row.

Sartre, J.-P. [1943] (1956) *Being and Nothingness: An Essay on Phenomenological Ontology.* Translated by H. Barnes. New York: Philosophical Library.

Warnock, M. (1989) *Existentialism.* Oxford: Oxford University Press.

S. P.

FREUD, ANNA (1895–1982) Anna Freud was the youngest daughter of *Sigmund Freud and the only child to pursue a career as a psychoanalyst. Born in Vienna, A. Freud began reading psychoanalysis at eighteen, became a certified teacher at twenty-two, and began her psychoanalytic training at twenty-three. Her interest in education found a new focus in the development of a psychoanalytic treatment for children, and she began her practice in 1923. In 1927 she published *Four Lectures on Psychoanalysis*, a book widely criticised by *Klein and her followers in Great Britain. Anna Freud's emphasis on the multiple interacting strands of development, as well as a child's real relationships, stood in contrast to Klein's emphasis on fantasy in earliest childhood. Disagreement between these two leaders in the development of child analysis only grew more significant as each gathered a large following.

A. Freud's first major contribution to psychoanalysis, *The Ego and The Mechanisms of Defence*, published in 1936, was presented as a birthday present to her father. It remains today a basic text on defences. It reflected her interest in Freud's structural model and heralded a life's work on the elaboration of the structuralisation of the ego through its interaction with id, super-ego, and environment.

When Nazi power came to Vienna in 1938, the Freud family fled to England and were welcomed into the British Psychoanalytical Society along with other Viennese colleagues. After Freud's death in 1939, significant disagreement between followers of Klein and A. Freud culminated in the *Controversial Discussions. These meetings were unable to resolve theoretical differences, and separate training tracks were created. A. Freud, though continuing her membership in the British Society, withdrew from active leadership in order to avoid continued argument with a group whose generous efforts had provided her family's escape from the Nazis.

World War II offered an opportunity for A. Freud and her colleagues to continue study of developmental processes while contributing greatly to the war effort. The Hampstead War Nurseries were established to provide care for children who were separated from parents. Monthly reports were made to the Nursery benefactors, resulting in a book, *Infants Without Families*, published in 1974. A. Freud and her colleague Dorothy Burlingham began an informal training programme which later became part of her lifelong work, the Hampstead Child Therapy Course and Clinic. It was in the training course, the research, and the educational/observational component of a nursery school, toddler groups, and a well-baby clinic that A. Freud's theoretical contributions to psychoanalysis found fertile ground over the next thirty years.

Eight volumes known as *The Writings of Anna Freud* spanning the time period 1922–80 comprise the papers and books written during her lifetime. *Normality and Pathology in Childhood*, published in 1965, brought together A. Freud's theoretical contributions to that time. A. Freud remained grounded in *drive theory as the primary motivation for behaviour. She emphasised the importance of early experiences of satisfaction as a basis for development of *object relations. Object relations played a large part in her theory as a result of her view of libido as object-seeking. Towards the end of her life she elaborated views of *developmental psychopathology in which interactions between the young child and the external world have adversely affected the structuralisation of the ego. She, along with Hampstead colleagues, were studying the technical implications for psychoanalytic treatment of children whose ego structuralisation had gone awry prior to the development of the capacity for neurotic conflict.

Having struggled for years with anaemia, A. Freud suffered a stroke in early 1982 and died on 9 October. Her leadership had inspired generations of psychoanalysts who took from her dedication to careful, thoughtful observation and study a model for scientific inquiry.

Coles, R. (1992) *Anna Freud: The Dream of Psychoanalysis*. New York: Addison-Wesley.

Dyer, R. (1983) *Her Father's Daughter: The Work of Anna Freud*. New York: Jason Aronson.

Edgcumbe, R. (2000) *Anna Freud: A View of Development, Disturbance, and Therapeutic Techniques*. London: Routledge.

Peters, U. (1985) *Anna Freud: A Life Dedicated to Children*. New York: Schocken Books.

Young-Bruehl, E. (1988) *Anna Freud: A Biography*. New York: Summit Books.

C. E. N.

FREUD, SIGMUND (1856–1939) Biographical accounts of Freud have often been unusual vehicles of partisanship. Freud did expect that psychoanalysis would constitute a shock to intellectual history, and he came to liken his achievement of psychoanalysis to what Copernicus and Darwin had accomplished; even if Freud's contribution comes to be evaluated in more modest terms, it is incontestably true that even after all these years controversy about what he accomplished has continued to be heated. Vested interests have added to this acrimony, for rival groups of interested parties have used observations about Freud's life for the sake of promoting their own points of view.

In his 1935 'Postscript' to his *Autobiographical Study*, Freud expressed regret about how his biography had been used in connection with his work: 'The public has no claim to learn any more of my personal affairs – of my struggles, my disappointments, and my successes. I have in any case been more open and frank in some of my writings (such as *The Interpretation of Dreams* and *The Psychopathology of Everyday Life*) than people usually are who describe their lives for their contemporaries or for posterity. I have had small thanks for it, and from my experience I cannot recommend anyone to follow my example'.

We have known for some time now that Freud could also disguise his autobiography, for example in his paper on 'Screen Memories'. And Freud watched over the first biography written about him, by Fritz Wittels, sending all his comments and corrections for the sake of the future. Students of Freud need to be alert not just to the spin he could put on his life, but to the variety of biases that inevitably enter into accounts of Freud's life.

Freud was born on 6 May 1856 in Freiberg, Moravia, which was then an outlying part of the Austro-Hungarian Empire but which is now within the Czech Republic. His father had been married before, and had two grown sons at the time of Freud's birth; ultimately Freud would also have five younger sisters as well as a brother. Both Freud's parents were Jews, part of a small local minority. Freud's father (Jakob) was a wool merchant who chose to ruin himself bailing out his older sons who had improvidently invested in South African ostrich feathers; while Freud's half-brothers moved to England in 1859, Freud's own immediate family moved first to Leipzig and shortly thereafter to Vienna. Although the Hapsburg monarchy was overwhelmingly Roman Catholic, Jews had full rights of citizenship, and by the turn of the twentieth century Vienna had the largest Jewish population of any city in Western Europe.

It has never been clear what financial sources the Freud family lived on after moving to Vienna; assistance presumably came from Jakob's older sons in England among other family members, but Jakob was no longer gainfully employed. Despite the poverty of Freud's youth we know that in his school he was an unusually good student, ranking at the top of his class for seven years; he was rather less outstanding at the University of Vienna, where he originally intended to get degrees both in philosophy and medicine. He dragged out his stay for eight years, and it appears that his many interests prevented him from going forward more quickly. Early on Freud had a sense of himself as a mighty warrior; to express this on a spiritual level was no doubt part of his opposition to the hostile Gentile world. For a while he toyed with becoming a lawyer but settled on confining himself to medicine. In the end, after giving up the idea of physiological research, he settled on neurology, at that time a field separate from psychiatry.

For a time in 1885 he studied in Paris under Jean-Baptiste Charcot; he was intrigued by hysteria, and also inspired by the example of the Viennese internist Josef Breuer who, among his other medical activities, had made use of a cathartic technique as a means of using patients' memories to alleviate nervous symptoms. In the meantime Freud in 1886 had married Martha Bernays, after a four-year engagement, and before long the couple had six children – three sons and three daughters.

Much of what is known about the beginnings of psychoanalysis come from the documents that survive from his friendship with Wilhelm Fliess, a Berlin physician; Freud's letters to Fliess, during the period 1897–1904, record an intimate account of his early efforts to understand and treat psychopathology. For a time Freud believed that his patients' troubles arose from their having been sexually abused in early childhood; from 1897, however, Freud abandoned this seduction theory, and engaged in a considerable degree of self-analysis, concluding that neurosis arose from patients' longings and wishes of an infantile sexual nature.

At the end of 1899 Freud published *The Interpretation of Dreams*; for the rest of his life Freud thought that this ranked as his most enduring contribution. Not only did Freud interpret dreams in terms of their conflictual nature, arising primarily from unconscious sexual conflicts associated with early childhood, but in *The Psychopathology of Everyday Life*, 1902, he extended his theory to include such phenomena as slips of the tongue and the pen; bungled actions as well as forgetting became part of what Freud thought his system could explain. Freud was aiming not just to account for and treat abnormal psychology, as he also thought that his theories could embrace general mental functioning as well. Moreover, by now Freud had devised a specific treatment setting; he had adopted 'the talking cure' which meant that patients came to his office six days a week for hourly sessions in which, while reclining on a couch, they free-associated to whatever went through their minds.

In 1902, by which time Freud had attained his nominal standing as a professor at the University of Vienna, he started to assemble a professional following by means of holding weekly meetings at his apartment. Throughout the next decade he began acquiring disciples from abroad as well, most notably Carl G. Jung from the Burghölzli Clinic in Zurich, Switzerland. In the meantime Freud published papers like his case history of 'Dora' in 1901 as well as his *Three Essays on the Theory of Sexuality* in 1905. Besides concentrating on questions of the psychopathology of neurosis Freud extended his more general theory in the publication of *Jokes and Their Relation to the Unconscious* in 1905.

By 1910 Freud had founded the International Psychoanalytic Association with Jung as President. Freud had been eager to have Jung as a successor since he came from such a prestigious centre of psychiatric research. But his anointing Jung in this way served to alienate Freud's Viennese following, and helped cause rivalry with Alfred Adler. The difficulties with Adler were ideological as well as personal, and in 1911 Freud decided to bring his difficulties with Adler to a head. Adler presented his viewpoint at two meetings of the Vienna Psychoanalytic Society, and Freud was unsparing in his criticism. Although at the outset Adler had not had many real adherents, by the end of the battle the Society was almost split in half. Adler had initially left with a few colleagues to found his own Society; Freud decreed that members of his group could not also attend Adler's, which resulted in a number of more resignations from the Vienna Psychoanalytic Society. Despite how important the organisation might sound, or how legendary a battle it later became, this feud only concerned a tiny number of Viennese intellectuals. Adler was a Social Democrat, and his differences with Freud were subsequently to extend along a broad front; but at the time the central source of the resignations were what members perceived to be Freud's intolerance of dissent.

No sooner had Freud rid himself of Adler – and also the Viennese Wilhelm Stekel – than Freud decided that Jung was 'deviating' too. Jung's differences with Freud had been there all along, but only came to a head in 1913. Freud had written *Totem and Taboo* in 1913, to underline the differences between himself and Jung; and in 1912–13 Freud had written a series of papers on technique in order to help establish psychoanalysis as a unique discipline. Then in 1914 Freud also wrote a polemic against both Adler and Jung, 'On the History of the Psychoanalytic Movement', which provoked not only Jung's formal withdrawal from the International Psychoanalytic Association but also the resignation of almost the entire body of Swiss analysts.

World War I was inevitably a quiet period organisationally for the movement Freud had created; but he used his spare time not only to deliver and then publish his *Introductory Lectures on Psychoanalysis* but also a series of metapsychological papers. The problems of military psychiatry stimulated a broad interest in psychoanalysis, and after the war was over Freud found he was internationally famous, with students from around the world wanting to come to him for training.

In 1920 the Berlin Psychoanalytic Society opened its Training Institute, which became – until the Nazis – the most important single source of psychoanalytic apprenticeship. Freud had remained sceptical of the suggestion, first put forward by Jung before the war, that all future analysts needed themselves to have undergone training analyses, but in 1923, when Freud fell ill with jaw cancer, the need to institutionalise psychoanalysis became acute. Subsequently, other training institutes – in Vienna, London, and Budapest, for example – besides the one in Berlin were set up.

Freud's illness is also intimately associated with one other famous problem in the history of psychoanalysis – the exit of Otto Rank from Freud's circle. Rank had for years been functioning not only as Freud's personal secretary, but also as virtually an adopted son; once Freud's lifetime seemed limited, Rank prepared himself to take over, and published his pamphlet on the significance of the trauma of birth, emphasising the hitherto neglected role of mothering and the significance of separation anxiety. Rank's innovations were enough to give a licence to his rivals in psychoanalysis like Karl Abraham in Berlin and Ernest Jones in London to declare that Rank was unfaithfully following in the 'dissident' footsteps of Jung. Although Freud struggled to keep Rank, in the end Rank's need to grow up and be independent combined with the organisational hostilities of Abraham and Jones to ensure that one more quarrel in Freud's lifetime became legendary. Freud's *Inhibitions, Symptoms and Anxiety*, of 1920, was designed, by means of a new theory of the nature of anxiety, to deal with Rank's theoretical proposals.

In the meantime Freud had come to rely more and more on the help and assistance of his youngest daughter Anna, whom he had analysed. Her special field became that of child analysis, and Freud was immensely proud of what she accomplished. However she had no medical qualifications, and, in 1926, Freud undertook to make his convictions clear, by means of his *Question of Lay Analysis*, that medical qualifications for becoming an analyst were not necessary. Anna Freud's rival in the field of child analysis was Melanie Klein, who had moved to England and started to become immensely influential there. Although in public Freud tried to avoid making any more martyrs in psychoanalysis, and withheld polemical fire about Klein, in private he made plain how distasteful, and heretical, he found her work.

Once Karen *Horney and Hélène *Deutsch began publishing on female psychology in the 1920s, Freud felt that he had to establish himself on the subject by publishing his 'Some Psychical Consequences of the Anatomical Distinction Between the Sexes', in 1925, as well as 'Female Sexuality' in 1931. Freud never felt at ease when it came to the problem of priorities, and he felt driven to make sure that he left his own imprint on the subject of feminine psychology. Even though his writings on women were later to be dismissed as expressions of male chauvinism, however his theoretical convictions might appear, he did succeed in encouraging women professionally so that no profession in the twentieth century was to be more open to female talent than psychoanalysis.

(Before World War I he had been in the minority in the Vienna Psychoanalytic Society on the issue of allowing women to become full members; men a generation younger than him voted against the innovation.)

Wilhelm *Reich became the occasion for further trouble in psychoanalytic waters, first because of his recommendations about the significance of negative transference, character, and non-verbal communications, and then because of his interest in *Marxism. Reich proposed that the *Oedipus complex was a product of Western bourgeois culture, and that by making major changes in family life it would be possible to eliminate neurosis. Freud not only objected to Reich's politics, as well as his appeal for sexual emancipation, but also thought Reich was endangering psychoanalysis in countries like Russia. Therefore in 1930 Freud published his *Civilisation and its Discontents* as a way of making plain his own convictions about the inevitability of aggression and the need for civilised restraints. Reich's firm anti-Nazism was thought to be endangering psychoanalysis in Germany, and by 1934 the IPA had excluded him.

One more quarrel, associated with Sándor Ferenczi, dogged Freud's old age. For some time Ferenczi had been convinced that patients require more sympathetic empathy than is implied by Freud's technical injunctions concerning the psychoanalytic reliance on 'neutrality' and 'abstinence'. In Budapest Ferenczi had become a haven for cases psychoanalysts' elsewhere considered impossible or 'unanalysable'. Ferenczi also thought that Freud's focus on the internal world was too narrow, and that severely disturbed patients had been realistically traumatised in early childhood. Freud, however, thought that Ferenczi was proposing that psychoanalysis regress to his previous non-analytic interest in 'seduction', and that Ferenczi's need to cure was too subjectively motivated. When, in 1933, Ferenczi wrote his brilliant paper on the 'Confusion of Tongues between Adults and the Child', Freud felt scandalised, and advised Ferenczi against presenting it publicly. Ferenczi's death in 1933 deprived Freud of one of his most longstanding and faithful supporters, and Jones later spread the slander that Ferenczi's innovations were the product of mental illness.

These various intellectual difficulties were central to Freud's biography, since, as he put it in the 1935 'Postscript' to his *An Autobiographical Study*, 'psychoanalysis came to be the whole content of my life and [...] no personal experiences of mine are of any interest in comparison to my relations with that science'. All the same, it is worthy of note how much Freud suffered not only from the effects of the initial operations for his jaw cancer, but from the prosthesis it was subsequently necessary for him to wear; in all Freud underwent some sixteen operations, as cancerous tissue had repeatedly to be removed. Freud necessarily grew more distant from human contacts, which affected his attitudes toward patients in therapy.

Despite all the political turmoil in Central Europe which followed from the Great Depression, and partially because of how isolated Freud felt as various of his adherents left for the lure of America, Freud still not only stayed in Vienna but thought he could create a new international centre of psychoanalytic training there. To someone like the Hungarian Sándor Radó, already established in New York City, Freud was being wholly unrealistic about what could be done in Vienna.

Freud stayed in Vienna so long, despite the urgings of some of his closest pupils, partly because his Viennese doctors knew his case; but, also, the question remained as to where he should go apart from the city of his early youth. Freud had doubtless been counting on support from his powerful political connections, people like Ambassador William C. Bullitt, Marie Bonaparte, the Princess George, as well as Ruth Mack *Brunswick whose father was well established within New Deal circles. Once the *Nazis seized Austria in March 1938, it was only a question of time; by early June the arrangements were finally made for Freud to leave with his entourage, and England was the chosen haven.

Freud was publicly welcomed in London, but his stature there meant that his doctors treated him as a celebrity, and were inhibited about operating until it was too late. Freud went on with his psychoanalytic treatment of patients until the end of July 1939. But the final several weeks of his life were full of such immense torment that the founder of psychoanalysis could no longer maintain his profession, and disbanded his practice. Toward the end, his cheek, when the jaw was otherwise inoperable, had to be cut from outside, and he smelled so bad that his favourite dog would not go near him. A mosquito net had to be put around his sickbay so that the flies would not be attracted to the wound. When he could no longer read, he asked his personal physician, Dr Max Schur, for an easy death.

Freud finally died on 23 September 1939, and, although contrary to Jewish custom, his remains were cremated and put in a ancient Greek vase given to him by the Princess George. When his wife died in 1951, her ashes were added to his; but, unlike his funeral, a rabbi was asked to speak at hers.

Breger, L. (2000) *Freud: Darkness in the Midst of Vision*. New York: John Wiley.

Clark, R. (1980) *Freud: The Man and the Cause*. New York: Random House.

Gay, P. (1988) *Freud: A Life For Our Time*. New York: Norton.

Jones, E. (1953–57) *The Life and Work of Sigmund Freud*. 3 vols. New York: Basic Books.

Roazen, P. (1975) *Freud and His Followers*. New York: Knopf.

Schur, M. (1972) *Freud: Living and Dying*. New York: International Universities Press.

Wittels, F. (1924) *Sigmund Freud*. New York: Dodd. Mead.

P. R.

FREUD, INFLUENCES ON The various influences which played on the mind of Freud as he grew from infancy to manhood had a powerful impact on the thoughts and emotions that pointed him toward the development of psychoanalytic theory. Born on 6 May 1856, to Jewish Orthodox parents, Freud's religious background and its relationship to the emerging culture of Austrian liberalism shaped the values and expectations of his early years. Almost all of Freud's biographers, including Jones, Schur and Gay, have tended to emphasise and exaggerate the assimilationist character of his family home, but as Rice and Yerushalmi have shown, traditional Jewish beliefs and practices retained a significant role in Freud's early family environment. While valuing the new ideas of the German enlightenment, Freud's father continued to honour the religious traditions of his youth, and he tried to instil similar interests and values in his son. For example, the earliest reading material he provided his son was the Philippson Bible, which supplemented the Hebrew text and a German translation with a commentary rich in the philosophic, scientific, and anthropological insights of the German Enlightenment. Philippson used the Enlightenment faith in reason and science to support traditional religious belief and feeling. The result was a biblical commentary with a strongly psychological tone, and this was one of the earliest sources of Freud's interest in psychology.

During Freud's childhood and adolescence, Austrian liberalism appeared to be in ascendancy, and the new, modernising values it represented created strong tensions between traditional religious beliefs and liberalism's faith in reason and science. Freud was deeply affected by this tension. Turning with some embarrassment from the remnants of Jewish Orthodox tradition in his family home, he eagerly embraced the liberal outlook and the hope of assimilation it seemed to offer. Austrian liberalism advocated an end to the traditional restrictions on Jews, and seemed to offer them a world of new opportunities. That Austrian liberals saw Roman Catholicism as a powerful and well-entrenched enemy, and launched an anti-clerical campaign to curb its political and cultural influence, further aroused Freud's sympathies. Jews had long associated Roman Catholicism with a strong and enduring tradition of anti-Semitism, so Freud made this aspect of the liberal cause fully his own. The intensity of the feelings these issues stirred in Freud is revealed in the way he identified with the Carthaginian general Hannibal in his adolescent fantasies. Freud's Gymnasium education included an intense study of classical culture, and Freud has revealed that when studying the wars between the Romans and the Carthaginians he identified strongly with Hannibal and the Carthaginians (a Semitic people) while associating Rome with Roman Catholicism. So even after abandoning any sort of Jewish religious belief, he continued to see himself as a Jew in the historical sense, while also coming increasingly to regard himself as a fully assimilated German. He even embraced the strong German nationalism so popular among students of that era.

During his adolescence Freud felt such enthusiasm for the liberal assault on established authority that he considered a career in politics, and even after he abandoned that idea to enrol as a medical student at the University of Vienna, in 1873, his political views continued to influence the direction of his interests. This is seen most clearly and importantly in the way his interests in politics, religion and philosophy converged to point him toward the study of psychology. Austrian liberalism espoused not only a political program of reform but also more generally a modernising world view that sought to establish a rational, scientific way of thinking in place of what it saw as the superstition of religion and the divine right of the monarchy. So the corollary to its anti-clerical campaign against the political power of the Roman Catholic Church was a philosophical and scientific assault on the foundations of religious faith. As a college student Freud participated eagerly in this assault. His enthusiasm for the ideas of *Darwin is an obvious example. Darwin offered a scientific explanation of human origins as an alternative to the religious explanation. Similarly, Feuerbach, whose philosophy Freud read and espoused during his first years in college, offered a psychological and anthropological explanation of religion that seemed to undermine religious faith. The philosophy courses Freud took from Brentano dealt with issues such as the existence of God, and the reality of miracles, and although Brentano himself was a believer, Freud sought to find materialistic, psychological explanations as an alternative to religious faith. It was by this route that he arrived at his first interest in hysteria. While still in his first years in college he began to learn about the work of *Charcot and his followers who sought to explain a wide variety of apparently religious phenomena as misunderstood examples of hysteria.

After completing his doctorate, Freud went on in 1885 to study with Charcot in Paris. Here he was able to pursue much further the interest in hysteria he had developed earlier. Charcot elaborated a detailed analysis of medieval religious culture which argued that such things as miracles, saintly visions, stigmata, and demonic possession were actually symptoms of different hysterical disorders; Freud adopted this analytic framework as his own. In the medical practice he began in 1886 Freud used the study of medieval religious culture as a primitive road map to help understand the mental disorders exhibited by his patients, and the book he co-authored with Breuer in 1895, *Studies on Hysteria*, has many medieval analogies and examples. These references to medieval culture provide a telling clue to the way the religious and political conflicts of Freud's early years influenced the most important of his achievements, for it was his work on hysteria, and eventually his observation of hysterical symptoms in himself, that led him to undertake the self-analysis out of which psychoanalytic theory emerged.

See also: religion

Ellenberger, H. F. (1970) *The Discovery of the Unconscious*. New York: Basic Books.

McGrath, W. J. (1986) *Freud's Discovery of Psychoanalysis*. Ithaca and London: Cornell University Press.
Rice, E. (1990) *Freud and Moses*. Albany: State University of New York Press.

W. M.

FRIGHT A state into which a person falls when they encounter a danger for which they were not prepared. A nightmare can give some idea of this – it evades the protection brought about by fear or anxiety.

J. D. M.

FROMM, ERICH PINCHAS (1900–80) Fromm was born in Frankfurt and educated as a sociologist in Heidelberg. He received his psychoanalytic training from Sachs in Berlin and was for some years a member of the Institute for Social Research (the so-called 'Frankfurt School'). In 1934 he emigrated to the United States, where he was close to *Horney and *Sullivan. Although he divorced his first wife, Frieda *Fromm-Reichmann, Fromm's own therapeutic ideas are very similar to Fromm-Reichmann's *Principles of Intensive Psychotherapy*. After his split from the Horney group in 1943, Fromm – together with Sullivan and Fromm-Reichmann – became co-founder of the New York William Alanson White Institute. From 1950 through 1974 Fromm lived in Mexico, where he established his own psychoanalytic institute. His last years were spent in Locarno, Switzerland.

Fromm is often ranked among the neo-Freudians and proponents of humanist psychology. But Fromm himself consistently rejected such attributions. In the 30s he developed his own highly fruitful psychoanalytic approach to the interpretation of conscious and unconscious strivings both in the individual and in society.

Moulded by his Jewish origins and influenced by *Marx's *Early Writings*, his scientific interest was focused on the economic and social constraints that make individuals and society (and also social groups) behave in a specific way. In contrast to Freud's theory, Fromm claims that in regard to most psychic strivings we are not driven by an intrinsic *drive, or even by *partial drives; rather we are driven to satisfy psychic needs (for instance, to be related to others) which stem from our existential situation as human beings and which are not rooted in an inherent drive. By satisfying these existential or psychic needs we are driven to react in ways conditioned by those economic and social requirements that determine our social practice of life.

Hence it is that we establish by the formation of our psychic structure (or as Fromm puts it, by the formation of our *social character) the specific conscious and unconscious strivings by means of which we finally wish to think, feel and act as we are expected to do. According to Fromm, the individual develops not only an individual character but also a social counterpart. (Using this concept of a social character, Fromm goes on to explain psychoanalytically why and how a society is dynamically integrated.)

Fromm illustrates his socio-psychoanalytic approach in terms of various socially moulded orientations of social character, to wit the authoritarian character (in his 1941 *Escape from Freedom*), the marketing character (in the 1947 *Man for Himself*), the narcissistic character (in his 1964 *Heart of Man*), and the necrophilic character (in the 1964 *Heart of Man*, and in the 1973 *Anatomy of Human Destructiveness*).

Much more than for these socio-psychoanalytic concepts, Fromm is usually known for his humanistic concept of psychoanalysis. Eschewing Freud's instinctivist and (from 1920 on) dualist *drive theory, Fromm became convinced that there is a primary potentiality (or tendency) in all human beings for growth, love, reason, freedom, autonomy, creativity – i.e. for 'productivity', as he came to call it after 1947 in *Man for Himself*. Destructiveness, sadism, masochism, hate of life, etc., are only a secondary potentiality – namely the result of a severe inhibition, or thwarting, of the primary tendency to develop human productivity (or a 'productive character orientation'). Hence Fromm came to stress the human capacity for love (in *The Art of Loving*) and the ability to overcome alienation by strengthening one's own humane powers (in *To Have or to Be*? and in *The Art of Being*).

For the impact of Fromm's humanist socio-psychoanalytic approach on psychoanalytic theory and on psychotherapy, the reader is referred to Fromm's *Greatness and Limitations of Freud's Thought*, as also to the posthumously published works *The Revision of Psychoanalysis* and *The Art of Listening*.

Burston, D. (1991) *The Legacy of Erich Fromm*. Cambridge, MA and London: Harvard University Press.

Funk, R. (2000) *Erich Fromm. His Life and Ideas. An Illustrated Biography*. New York: Continuum International. Also published in German (*Erich Fromm – Liebe zum Leben*. Stuttgart: Deutsche Verlags-Anstalt, 1999) and Spanish (*Erich Fromm: El amor a la vida. Una biografía illustrate*. Barcélona: Paidós, 1999).

International Erich Fromm Society web site: www.erich-fromm.de

Knapp, G. P. (1989) *The Art of Living. Erich Fromm's Life and Works*. New York: Peter Lang.

Maccoby, M. and Cortina, M. (eds) (1996) *A Prophetic Analyst. Erich Fromm's Contribution to Psychoanalysis*. Northvale, NJ and London: Jason Aronson.

R. Fun.

Fromm-Reichmann, Frieda (1889–1957) Born in Karlsruhe, Germany, to a middle-class family with deep ties to both Judaism and Germany. The eldest of three daughters, high intellectual aspirations were instilled by her family.

She entered medical school in 1908, the first year women were admitted. There, she learned skills later useful to her: indirection, pleasant reasonableness, and making her wishes be convenient. Her size rendered her unsuitable for obstetrics; she entered the new field of psychiatry, which at that time was attempting to differentiate between conditions caused by trauma, organic causes like syphilis, and functional ones like schizophrenia.

World War I offered a rich field of study: otherwise healthy young men with head wounds. The only doctors studying such injuries were Army medics, all men. She joined the Army and became a hospital supervisor, making herself essential and leaving as a major.

She was a practical, keen observer, reading clues from patients' actions and speech, and interacting with them. Post-war, she turned her attention to the seriously mentally ill. She felt the skills needed to treat psychotics were only subtler than those used with the less profoundly involved. 'Hard and exacting work', she called it.

In the mid-1930s she opened her own sanitarium in Heidelberg, but the rise of Nazism made an exile of her. She accepted a temporary post at Chestnut Lodge, a psychotherapeutically-based mental hospital in Rockville, Maryland, and spent the war years seeing patients in and out of the hospital, writing, and caring for other refugees.

In a series of important papers published between 1939 and 1948, she reasserted her belief that schizophrenic symptoms had meaning and could be used to establish trust and contact between patient and doctor. The 'contrived neutrality' of analytic therapy did not work with her patients. Her prime work was not publication but one-on-one therapy with psychotic patients, at which she was eminently successful. She gave no name to a treatment and founded no school, but inspired large numbers of therapists.

Among many other works on aspects of psychosis is her major work, *Principles of Intensive Psychotherapy* (1950). She died in Rockville, Maryland, on 28 April 1957.

J. G.

FRUSTRATION This term is often used in a biological sense, meaning a deprivation of an object satisfying a need. Lacan noted that this was a mistranslation of the Freudian term *Versagung* which has the meaning of refusing, 'saying no' (as he finally translated it). In 1956–7, he opposed (Imaginary) frustration to (Real) *privation and (Symbolic) *castration as three different modes of *lack of an object. Frustration, as Imaginary deprivation of a real object, is experienced by the child in his or her primary relation to the mother as if he or she had been denied an object which is due him or her, opening the way to later claims. Lacan's perspective allowed him, in his commentary on *Winnicott and Ernest *Jones, to distinguish privation from frustration in the construction of *object relations.

M. Eyd. / B. B.

FULL SPEECH Freud proposed a distinction between empty and full speech; empty speech is stereotypical, bland, and disconnected, whereas full speech allows connection to other meanings, acquiring allusiveness, equivocation, and effects of surprise. A form of full speech is therefore presupposed by the ability to interpret symptoms and to associate to dreams. For Freud and Lacan, the connections of full speech reach far enough to grasp the castrating elements of oedipal love. Full speech for Lacan is a prerequisite to the analysis of desire; a movement towards full speech is, he says, necessary for the 'realisation of the subject'.

B. B

FUNCTIONAL PHENOMENON A process explored by Herbert Silberer whereby a *dream gives representation not simply to dream-thoughts, but to the subjective state and mode of activity of the dreamer. This notion was taken up in a critical way by Freud, who reworked it within his own theory of dream formation, giving it a more complex formulation than that proposed by Silberer.

D. L.

FUNDAMENTAL RULE The analyst's instruction or suggestion that the patient suspend the ordinary tendency to edit and suppress expressions of thoughts and feelings that might be embarrassing or anxiety arousing, or deemed irrelevant, and try to verbalise whatever thoughts and feelings come to mind without censorship.

See: free association

Freud, S. (1913) *On Beginning the Treatment*. S. E. 12. London: Hogarth Press.

D. Wol.

FUSION/DEFUSION The two drives, sex and aggression, or life and death, are rarely seen in pure form. Each is usually fused with, and supports the other. A modicum of aggression is required for a man to perform the sexual act. In defusion, there is a return to archaic, primitive drive states in which self-destructive aims predominate.

J. A. Ber.

G

GAP Insofar as there are stumblings, failures and mistakes in a sentence, there is a gap, and in this gap the *subject is located. In privileging the gaps, what is not said, half-said, or missaid, Lacan warns against tendencies to stitch up the gap.

C. Owe.

GENDER The concept of gender (though not yet the term itself) emerged as a site of critical awareness only with the publication of Simone de Beauvoir's *The Second Sex* in 1949. It was not until John Money's empirical work on hermaphroditic children in the 1950s that gender was formally conceived as separate and distinct from sexuality as a theoretical category. While gender was obviously central in and to

Freud's thinking, it is not to be found in the *Standard Edition*. Gender does not emerge as a psychoanalytic category in its own right until Robert Stoller, elaborating and extending Money's research into the clinical domain, conceptualised it as a central dimension of self-organisation, a move that launched the contemporary field of empirically grounded, psychoanalytic gender studies.

With the advent of psychoanalytic *feminism, Dinnerstein, Chodorow and Benjamin complicated psychoanalytic gender theory by conceptualising gender as an analytic and social category, not merely a psychological one. With this move, the psychoanalytic study of gender became increasingly multidisciplinary, as cultural, philosophical, historical, literary/linguistic and socio-political theories intersected with those being developed in clinical psychoanalysis. Feminist theories conceptualise gender as a culturally instituted, normative ideal that sexes the body and genders the mind. But sex and gender are not historically and culturally stable categories, and vary in terms of their cultural salience. In some cultures, age seniority is privileged over gender as a social organiser, as Fausto-Sterling has shown, while the notion of gender as a mutually exclusive opposition (male/female, masculine/feminine) did not develop until the late eighteenth century. By the modern period, sex and gender dimorphism had become established as normative via science and medicine.

The postmodern theorist Judith Butler has demonstrated that gender actually *creates* subjectivity itself, since persons only become intelligible through becoming gendered, and thus, that gender and sexual identities that fail to conform to norms of cultural intelligibility appear only as developmental failures or logical impossibilities. One of the core projects and accomplishments of psychoanalytic feminism has been to articulate the pathogenic implications of this regulatory regime.

See also: feminism

Benjamin, J. (1988) *The Bonds of Love*. New York: Pantheon.

Butler, J. (1990) *Gender Trouble*. New York: Routledge.

Chodorow, N. J. (1999) *The Reproduction of Mothering*. Second edition. Berkeley: University of California Press.

De Beauvoir, S. [1949] (1974) *The Second Sex*. Translated by H. M. Parshley. New York: Vintage Books.

Dinnerstein, D. (1976) *The Mermaid and the Minotaur*. New York: Harper Colophon.

Fausto-Sterling, A. (2000) *Sexing the Body*. New York: Basic Books.

Money, J., Hampson, J. G. and Hampson, J. I. (1955) 'An examination of basic sexual concepts'. *Bulletin of the Johns Hopkins University Hospital* 97.

Stoller, R. J. (1968) 'The sense of femaleness'. *Psychoanalytic Quarterly* 37.

V. G.

GENITAL ATTITUDE In maturity the genital attitude supersedes the original oral attitude. The *oral attitude of infancy describes the early state of mind based on incorporation of objects. But Fairbairn thought that in maturity object relations are characterised by relationship to whole objects that have genitals, but not primarily by a genitally-directed attitude. When adults relate to others in an excessively sexual way, there has been a sexualising *conversion reaction in the realm of relating.

E. F. B. / D. E. S.

GENITAL SEXUALITY The attainment of genital sexuality is an achievement of maturity. The component sexual drives and *erotogenic zones come under the primacy of the genitals, which have reached their mature states. For women this means giving up the external genitalia (the clitoris) in favour of the vagina.

However, neither genital sexuality nor genital love are terms used by Freud who writes instead of genital primacy through which the component drives are compelled to take their place. As used by later theorists such as Fairbairn (*genital attitude) the term genital sexuality refers to a final integration (or maturation) of the partial *drives resulting in a complementary relation between the sexes. Lacan radically disagrees with this notion, arguing, firstly, that the drives are always partial; secondly, that sexual development (e.g. from oral to anal stage) is not a question of maturation, but operates via the *demand of the *Other; and thirdly, the phallus as *signifier establishes sexual difference as two fundamentally different enunciative positions between which there is no sexual rapport.

Freud, S. (1917) *Introductory Lectures on Psychoanalysis*. S. E. 16. London: Hogarth Press.

A. R. / J. A. Ber.

GERMANY The first official appearance of psychoanalysis in Germany dates back to the year 1908 when Karl *Abraham organised a first working meeting for psychoanalysts in Berlin. This was followed in 1910 by the foundation of the first psychoanalytic association, the *Berliner Psychoanalytische Vereinigung* (BPV), which was renamed the *Deutsche Psychoanalytische Gesellschaft* (DPG) in 1926. The first German congresses on the subject of psychoanalysis took place in September 1911 in Weimar and in September 1913 in Munich.

Apart from Karl Abraham the following persons were also teaching or receiving their education in Berlin during the period of 1910 to 1933: Franz Alexander, Michael and Alice Balint, Therese Benedek, Siegfried Bernfeld, Hélène Deutsch, Max *Eitingon, Anna *Freud, Otto *Fenichel, Robert Fliess, Frieda *Fromm-Reichmann, Angel Garma, Georg *Groddeck, Karen *Horney, Edith *Jacobson, Melanie *Klein, Jeanne Lampl-de Groot, Sandor Radó, Anni Reich, Wilhelm *Reich, Theodor Reik, Gezá Roheim, Hanns Sachs and Ernst Simmel. In 1920 a psychoanalytic clinic was founded in collaboration with the Berlin Institute, which became the first institutionalised institute, with a curricular structure and examinations, for training/education and research in the field of psychoanalysis.

The twelveth International Congress on Psychoanalysis took place in Wiesbaden in 1932 under the chairmanship of Max Eitingon. After that, fifty-three years passed before the next International Congress took place in Germany, in Hamburg in 1985. Adolf Hitler's assumption of power in 1933 led to an order to exclude Jewish citizens from the boards of scientific associations. This was the same year Sigmund Freud's books were burned. In 1933 Eitingon renounced the chairmanship of the DPG. The DPG was forced to transform the Institute into a training centre for psychotherapists under state control. Also in the same year Ernst Kretschmer renounced his office and Carl Gustav *Jung became his successor. Erich *Fromm, Frieda Fromm-Reichmann, Siegmund Heinrich Fuchs (who later called himself Foulkes) and Heinrich Meng emigrated to the USA, England and Switzerland respectively. Fearing the national socialistic regime Schultz-Hencke suggested that Psychoanalysis be renamed 'Desmology' and to call its method 'Desmolysis'. Sexuality was not to have the central importance it had to Freud and his followers. Aggression and the yearning for possession was said to be decisive for the emergence of neuroses. In 1936 the DPG was pressured to step out of the *International Psychoanalytic Association and to join an institute planned by Mathias Göring (a cousin of the Reichsmarschall Herrmann Göring), which was to comprise all therapeutic schools. This Göring-Institute became an institution in Germany's national socialistic era. The essentials of Freud's psychoanalysis, for instance libido theory, the unconscious and the Oedipus complex were given up by Schultz-Hencke in order to adapt to the national socialistic regime; partly these changes coincided with his own scientific convictions and partly he was thereby able to elude the prevailing censorship, in which Mrs Göring was especially feared as a potential informer.

The DPG at first continued its existence under the covert name of Arbeitsgruppe A (Workgroup A) and then under the designation *Referatenabend für Kasuistik und Therapie* (Lectures on Casuistry and Therapy). Even so genuine psychoanalysis had been utterly destroyed in Germany. In its stead Schultz-Hencke's Neo-Psychoanalysis and its concoction of the views of Depth Psychology were trend-setting during the war and even after its end. By this unification of psychoanalysis, individual psychology and analytic psychology, Schultz-Hencke also intended to create a unitary psychotherapeutic language. During this period of time, casuistry was taught in the Threefold Seminars (Freud, Jung, Adler).

In 1942 John Rittmeister, a psychoanalyst who collaborated with the resistance organisation *Rote Kapelle* ('Red Chapel') was arrested and later executed by the *Nazis in Plötzensee in May 1943. After the German capitulation the *Berliner Psychoanalytische Gesellschaft* was founded in 1945 (and registered as an association one year later under the name of DPG). It was formed by members of the neo-psychoanalytic line like Schultz-Hencke as well as by representatives of Freud's teachings, such as Boehm, Kemper and Müller-Braunschweig. In the year 1947 the journal *Psyche* was founded; its contents at first were oriented on a model of 'synoptical' psychoanalysis in the line of Schultz-Hencke. In 1949 the various perspectives of Depth Psychology united to form the *Deutsche Gesellschaft für Psychotherapie und Tiefenpsychologie* (DGPT – German Psychotherapy and Depth Psychology Association) as an umbrella organisation meant to protect their political interests. In 1949 the DPG, just recently refounded in Berlin, attempted to join the IPV but its application was refused. In order to gain reacceptance by the IPV a small group (Hans Müller-Braunschweig, Gerhard Scheunert) refused to become members of the recently founded DPG after Schultz-Hencke had, on his part, refused to withdraw from the DPG. In 1950 the *Deutsche Psychoanalytische Vereinigung* (DPV) was founded by Müller-Branschweig as a clear representative of the Freudian line of thought. From that point on there have been two Psychoanalytic Associations in Germany, the DPG and the DPV. In the year 1951 the DPV was approved by the IPV (*Internationale Psychoanalytische Vereinigung*).

In 1956 Franz Alexander, Erik H. *Erikson, René A. Spitz and several other psychoanalysts residing in foreign countries were invited by Alexander Mitscherlich to join a cycle of lectures at Heidelberg University, in celebration of the hundredth anniversary of Freud's birth. Mitscherlich also founded an Institute for Psychoanalysis and Psychosomatics in Frankfurt in the year 1960, which four years later became the *Sigmund-Freud-Institute* (SFI). In 1985 Regine Lockots published her book *Erinnern und Durcharbeiten. Zur Geschichte der Psychoanalyse im Nationalsozialismus* (*To Remember and to Elaborate. On the History of Psychoanalysis and Psychotherapy during the National Socialistic Regime*) on the occasion of the first International Psychoanalytic Congress taking place on German soil (Hamburg) since the 30s.

Nowadays there are approximately 12,000 to 13,000 practising psychoanalysts in Germany. Thanks to Annemarie Dührssen's psychotherapy research conducted in 1967, psychoanalytic therapy (240 sessions) and psychotherapy based on depth psychology (80 sessions) are currently being financed by medical health insurance. Apart from the *Psyche. Zeitschrift für Psychoanalyse und ihre Anwendungne*, there are several psychoanalytic publications of great renown, for instance the *Forum für Psychoanalyse*, *Zeitschrift für psychoanalytische Theorie und Praxis*, *Zeitschrift für psychosomatische Medizin und Psychotherapie* and *Zeitschrift für Kinderanalyse*.

W. M.

GILL, MERTON (1914–94) After an initial internship at Michael Reese Hospital Gill took up residency in the (then) little known

Menniger Clinic. After a period as lecturer in the Menniger School of Psychiatry he took up a post at the department of psychiatry in Yale Medical School. Gill continued to take up various posts throughout his long productive career including ones in Berkeley, Palo Alto, and New York. (Downstate Medical Center of the State University of New York and then NYU) finally settling in Chicago (Abraham Lincoln School of Medicine).

In spite of the many attacks from philosophical quarters on its status Gill spent his life upholding Freud's view that psychoanalysis was a legitimate science. Gill's capacity as a unrelenting empirical researcher was formidable and he had an especial gift for collaborative work with a other well known psychoanalytic metapsychologists including David Rapaport (his mentor – see especially Rapaport and Gill 1959), Margaret Brenman-Gibson, Robert R. Holt, Roy Schafer and George Klein to name just a few.

Amongst Gill's many ideas of experimental approach was the use of tape-recorded group sessions which involved deliberately 'off-target' interpretations followed by accurate ones with a sufficient hiatus in between to evaluate and compare the respective responses elicited.

Robert Holt (Silverman and Wolitzky 2000) suggests that Gill is generally associated with seven tenets: (1) Psychic structure is a continuum – a continuum of ego and id, impulse and defence. (2) Psychoanalysis is distinguished from psychotherapy by the induction of regression and the resolution of the transference by interpretation alone. (3) Metapsychology is pseudo-biology. (4) The resistance is mainly fear of plausible transference. (5) The analyst is never a blank screen. (6) Psychoanalysis is not distinguished from psychotherapy by its use of regression; but rather by its fearless scrutiny, especially of transference. (6) [With Hoffman] The analyst lacks authority on the relationship, and should enjoy a freer but more tentative expressiveness.

Merton Gill died in November 1994.

Rapaport and Gill [1959] (2000) 'The points of view and assumptions of metapsychology' in D. K. Silverman and D. L. Wolitzky (eds) *Changing Conceptions of Psychoanalysis: The Legacy of Merton M. Gill.* Hillsdale, NJ: The Analytic Press.

S. Byr.

GIRL In Freudian theory, the girl is the female child who is troubled by the anatomical absence of a penis, and who experiences more psychic difficulties than the boy when it comes to resolving the *Oedipus complex and attaining femininity. Freud's ideas on girlhood and femininity have been challenged from the 1920s onwards and continue to spark vehement debate.

D. N.

GNOSTICISM One of three major Near Eastern religions, it flourished between 80 and 200 CE, along with Judaism and Christianity. More a philosophy than a religion, Gnosticism insists that self-knowledge is knowledge of God; thus the self and God are identical. Knowing God is experiencing the divine presence within oneself. Declaring it a heresy, the Catholic Church nearly destroyed all traces of Gnosticism. In 1945, the discovery of fifty-two Gnostic books at Nag Hammadi, Egypt, brought to light the original words of the Gnostics. Some of texts speak of the feminine element in the divine. *Jung understood Gnostic ideas as symbols arising spontaneously from the collective unconscious.

J. S.

GOOD AND BAD OBJECTS Klein believed that in normal development the infant is able to separate bad experiences from good under the auspices of the *paranoid schizoid position. This allows healthy discrimination, the development of ego strength and the growth of thought. Splitting, projective identification, idealisation and omnipotence protect the infant's vulnerable ego from overwhelming experiences, particularly those connected to frustration.

However, the differentiation between good and bad is compromised by excessive splitting, which leads to the fragmentation of both the ego and the good and bad *internal objects, or by rigid splitting in which only one aspect is known at a time while the other one is disavowed.

Klein, M. (1952) 'Some theoretical conclusions regarding the emotional life of the infant' in *Developments in Psycho-Analysis* with P. Heimann, S. Isaacs and J. Riviere. London: Hogarth Press. Also in *Envy and Gratitude*. London: Hogarth Press, 1975 (111).

J. V. B.

GOOD-ENOUGH MOTHER see **MOTHER (WINNICOTT)**

GOOD OBJECT (FAIRBAIRN) Those objects with whom one has satisfactory interactions internally and externally are good objects, also called *accepted objects because they do not need to be split off and repressed. Fairbairn argued that good objects are only internalised to compensate for the prior internalisation of bad objects. The affect towards the 'goodness' of the *ideal object (the core of the accepted object) is also suffused throughout the central ego – the core of personality. In contrast, *Klein argued that good objects are internalised from the beginning under the influence of the *life instinct. Life instinct means nothing in Fairbairn, who thought that a libidinal tendency – the need for relationships – was the organising principle of most importance in life.

Klein, M. [1957] (1988) 'Envy and gratitude' in *Envy and Gratitude*. Introduced by Hanna Segal. London: Virago Press.

E. F. B. / D. E. S.

GRANDIOSITY, DEFENSIVE OR EXPANSIVE *Intersubjectivity theory holds that it is important to distinguish traumatically deflated archaic expansiveness from a defensive grandiosity that serves to counteract unwanted and unbearable painful affect states. When a patient seeks mirroring from the analyst, it is crucial to determine whether such mirroring is for archaic expansiveness or defensive grandiosity. Whereas mirroring of the former can promote development, mirroring of the latter fosters addiction to the analyst.

R. S.

GRATITUDE One major derivative of the capacity for love is the feeling of gratitude. It is essential in building up the relation to the good object and underlies also the appreciation of goodness in others and in the self. Gratitude is rooted in the emotions and attitudes that arise in the earliest stage of infancy when the mother is the baby's primary object.

With a full gratification at the breast, the infant feels s/he has received from the loved primary object a unique gift which the infant wants to keep. This is the basis of gratitude. Gratitude is closely linked with trust in good figures. When the enjoyment and gratitude is felt repeatedly, the introjection of the good breast comes about with relative security and is the basis for trust in one's own goodness. The more often satisfaction and gratitude are experienced, the more often the wish to return the pleasure is felt. This recurrent experience plays an important role in the capacity to make reparation and in all sublimations.

Gratitude is closely bound up with generosity. Inner wealth derives from having assimilated the good object so that the individual becomes able to share its gifts with others. This makes it possible to introject a more benign outer world and a feeling of enrichment ensues.

*Envy is the most potent factor in undermining feelings of love and gratitude, and can result in the impulse towards generosity being experienced as exposing the subject to the risk of being robbed by others.

Klein, M. (1952) 'Some theoretical conclusions regarding the emotional life of the infant' in *Developments in Psycho-Analysis* with P. Heimann, S. Isaacs and J. Riviere, London: Hogarth. Also in *Envy and Gratitude*. London: Hogarth Press, 1975.

Klein, M. (1957) *Envy and Gratitude*. London: Tavistock. Also in *Envy and Gratitude*. London: Hogarth Press, 1975.

J. A. / J. S.

Great Britain The origins of psychoanalysis in Britain can be traced to a few people, most notably, Jones, the brothers James and Edward Glover, and James Strachey with the help of his wife Alix. In 1916 *Jones and Edward Glover were responsible for founding the British Psycho-Analytical Society and setting up its organisational structure. However, Strachey had what could be deemed a more profound effect on the course of psychoanalysis in the whole of the English-speaking world. It became his task in life to translate the major corpus of Freud's writing into English.

The resulting *Standard Edition* is a model of precise dating, footnotes and referencing and is of use even to scholars who can read Freud in the original German. However, Strachey has been widely criticised for his translation from the German of *Das Es*, *Das Ich*, *Besetzung* and *Trieb* into formal quasi-scientific terms derived from classical literature such as *'ego', *'id', *'cathexis' and 'instinct', rather than the much more obvious 'the I', 'the It', 'investment' and 'drive'. Some of these terms have led to conceptual confusions in the English-speaking world and, in the case of the word 'instinct', have been partially responsible for spawning theories that are believed by their exponents to be derived from ideas that Freud never supported.

Britain has had a separate tradition of analytical philosophy compared to the activities on the continent. The scientific terms of Freud's translators and the empirical approach it encouraged had a further consequence of heavily influencing the growth of *ego psychology in the United States.

The 1930s were a time when interest in psychoanalysis in Britain was limited to a small group of intellectually able people. It was further invigorated when *Klein came to live in Britain encouraged by both Jones and the Stracheys. At first her pioneering work in connection with *child psychoanalysis was greeted with interest and enthusiasm. However, with the arrival in the 1930s of Anna *Freud and other Viennese analysts such as the Hoffers fleeing Hitler, her much disputed views regarding both theory and practice provoked the furious and bitter *Controversial Discussions between 1941 and 1945.

The Controversial Discussions ended with the 'gentlemen's agreement' signed by three women, Klein, Freud and Payne. It meant that British psychoanalysis proceeded along three separate strands: the Kleinian group, the Contemporary Freudian group and, somewhat later, the Independent group. All of these schools have a distinctively British cast. It is notable that each have been prominent in the debates surrounding child psychoanalysis.

The war and its aftermath produced work by *Winnicott and *Bowlby. They were involved in demonstrating to the authorities that the separation of mothers from their babies and young children, whether as the result of evacuation or of hospitalisation, was psychologically damaging and could have lasting effects. They evolved psychoanalytic theories which supported their claims. Winnicott argued that it was vital for future psychoanalytic health that the mother/infant relationship should be 'good enough'. Bowlby focused on the importance not of early mother/infant relationships but on what he saw as the crucial period when a young child becomes attached to its mother. This led him to argue that children under the age of three should, if at all possible, be securely attached to a person he described as 'the primary caregiver'. The current emphasis on the importance of the mother/infant bond has its roots in the post war period of the 1950s.

A separate strand in the development of psychoanalysis in Britain originated with the Northfields hospital experiment during the Second World War and the promotion of the ideas of *Bion and Rickman. Bion's early work concentrated upon analysing the intrapsychic dynamics of members of a group whereas his contemporary *Foulkes concentrated on the interpsychic phenomena of groups as expressed in matrices. These ideas have since been applied in related areas such as social work. Bion's later work concentrated on the formalisation of the structures of the unconscious.

The 1960s were notable for the radical contribution of *Laing. *The Divided Self* is a book steeped in the French tradition of existentialism and *phenomenology and Laing used this work to introduce the British public to some of the problems of subjectivity. The idea that one person in the family might become the scapegoat for the ills of the others was fresh and new. The founding of Kingsley Hall and the attempt to treat mentally ill people as victims of the emotions of others rather than 'ill' was a radical departure from the prevailing practice in both psychiatry and psychoanalysis.

Other post war developments concerned the influence of psychoanalytic thinking in the areas of family therapy and couple therapy. Skynner is the best known of those in Britain who developed the theoretical ideas underpinning group therapy and then applied them both to families and couples.

Today, psychoanalytic ideas and activity are no longer centred solely on the work of the British Psychoanalytical Society. The work of Fonagy builds upon that of Bowlby and attempts to bind attachment theory more closely to an empirical study of psychology. In Britain as in the USA, there is a continuing preoccupation represented by the work of Solms concerning the relationship between psychoanalysis and *psychology and its most fashionable offspring, evolutionary psychology. Significantly, whilst both Fonagy and Solms are members of the Society, they also work in the context of the University. French psychoanalysis, particularly the work of *Lacan, is growing in influence in British universities in such diverse fields as *anthropology, *feminism, cultural studies and gender studies.

No portrait of British psychoanalysis would be complete without some reference to current clinical practice and teaching of psychoanalysis and its close relative, psychoanalytic psychotherapy. The British Confederation of Psychotherapy represents one grouping of psychoanalysts and psychotherapists and the United Kingdom Council for Psychotherapy another. A recent addition to the field is signalled by the new name of the British Association of Counselling *and Psychotherapy* (my italics). Within the organisations there are continuing differences of opinion between the groups established at the time of the *Controversial Discussions. In addition, psychoanalysts who trained in the Lacanian tradition are becoming increasingly vocal. The fastest growing area of psychotherapy is represented by the humanistic orientation who have a very distant relationship with the main body of psychoanalytic theory. There is intense argument and rivalry among all the above, the real issues at stake being, as ever, money and power, ostensibly in the service of theoretical and political correctness.

K. H.

Greece Freud and psychoanalysis were first introduced into Greece in 1915 when they began to be discussed by a group of educationists who were interested mainly in the application of psychoanalysis to education. In 1927 the psychiatrist Kouretas was the first person in medicine to speak about psychoanalysis in public in Greece. Kouretas continued to be actively involved with psychoanalysis, studying in particular the psychoanalytic interpretation of ancient Greek mythology, and he ultimately became Professor of Psychiatry at the Athens University Medical School. However, it was not until the late 1940s that psychoanalysis began to gain a certain respect in Greek medical and academic circles. At that time the first concerted attempt to establish the practice of psychoanalysis in Greece was made by the French psychoanalyst Bonaparte, who was married to a Greek prince. As a result of her support, the International Psychoanalytic Association approved the formation of a Greek group under the auspices of the Paris Society. The members of the group were the psychoanalysts Kouretas and Zavitsianos and the great Greek surrealist poet Empirikos. The activities of the group did not continue for long. Empirikos left for Paris because he was accused by the medical establishment of treating patients without being a doctor. Zavitsianos, probably because he perceived that the climate was not favourable for psychoanalysis, went to *Canada. In spite of the setback, interest in the development of psychoanalysis persisted. Increasing numbers of Greeks were studying psychoanalysis outside Greece and a few of them, mainly psychoanalysts and a small number of psychoanalytic psychotherapists, started to return in the 1970s. They began to work in university departments (medicine, psychology), in organisations and mental health services and also in private practice.

In 1982 the Hellenic Study Group under the auspices of the International Psychoanalytic Association was founded, and became later a provisional society and in 2001 a component society. The first president of the Hellenic Psychoanalytic Association was Hartocollis. In 1978 the Hellenic Association of Psychoanalytic Psychotherapy was founded, with the cooperation of psychoanalytic psychotherapists and psychoanalysts. In 1991 the Hellenic Association of Child and Adolescent Psychoanalytic Psychotherapy – a member of the European Federation of Psychoanalytic Psychotherapy in the Public Health Services – was founded. The above three organisations with the training they provide have helped to disseminate psychoanalytic thought and to promote the clinical practice of psychoanalysis and psychoanalytic psychotherapy based on a unified body of psychoanalytic thought. Finally, psychoanalytic thought and its application in clinical practice, in spite of all the difficulties, have achieved recognition in medical and psychiatric circles, among mental health professionals and also by the general public.

Hartocollis, P. (1998) 'A letter from Greece'. *The Journal of the American Psychoanalytic Association* 48 (2).

Tzavaras, Th. (1984) *Psychoanalysis and Greece*. Athens: Society of the Studies of Modern Greek Civilization and General Education. (In Greek)

J. Ts.

Green, Andre (1927–) André Green was born in Cairo, Egypt. He undertook medical studies at the Faculty of Paris, where he graduated in 1957. He took residency in Sainte Anne's Hospital in Paris, and received a psychiatric training from 1953 to 1957. From 1958 to 1959, he was Chief of the Clinic of Mental Diseases. He then established a private practice as psychoanalyst, and is now retired.

Among his titles, Green has been a Member of the Paris Psychoanalytic Society since 1963 and training analyst for this Society since 1965. He is a former Director (1970–3) of the Paris Psychoanalytic Society, and was President of this Society from 1986 to 1988. He was also Vice President of the International Psychoanalytic Association from 1970 to 1973. He was the Freud Memorial Chair Professor at University College in London from 1979 to 1980 and has been Honorary Professor at the Buenos Aires University since 1996, as well as a Member of the Moscow Academy of Humanities Research since 1996.

Green travels throughout the world in order to give conferences and is the author of seventeen books and more than 400 papers. Among his books that have been translated into English are: *The Tragic Effect*; *On Private Madness*; *The Work of the Negative*; *The Fabric of Affect in the Psychoanalytic Discourse*; *Chain of Eros*; *Life Narcissism. Death Narcissism*; and *André Green at the Squiggle Foundation*.

C. N.

GRID A sophisticated and deeply complex psychoanalytic instrument designed by Bion to record and classify statements expressed in the analytic session. It records linguistic formulations together with the emotional experiences that occur in the session. It is a tool that helps the psychoanalyst think post-session about problems that arise in daily clinical practice and elaborate on different observations made during the session. The grid is constructed on the basis of theories, but it is not a theory in itself. It belongs to the field of clinical observation or of psychoanalytic practice and as such it does not add to nor modify psychoanalytic theories.

The formulations that it categorises progress from apparently simple elements like gestures and exclamations, to complex formulations, like ideas, thoughts, concepts, etc. It may also be used to classify thoughts and interpretations of the analyst. It applies to everything that is a part of the communication between analyst and analysand.

In its formal aspects it consists of coordinates with two axes:

1) Vertical (genetic axis): The rows categorise the development of thoughts. Progression from 'A' to 'H' nominates formulations which are categorised in accordance with their state of development in grades of abstraction or complexity.

Row A: *Beta elements*: Simple statements or experiences of an evacuative character.

Row B: *Alpha elements*

Row C: *Dreams*: Dream thoughts, dreams, and myths.

Row D: *Pre-conceptions*: formulations that have a non-saturated component that anticipates its mating with realisations and provides a capacity to evolve to conceptions by transformation.

Row E: *Conceptions*: Formulations that originate in the mating of a pre-conception with a positive realisation.

Row F: *Concepts*: Abstract formulations that have the possibility of being articulated on the basis of logical considerations in a scientific deductive system.

Row G: *Scientific Deductive Systems*: A combination of concepts and hypotheses logically related to each other. This relation enhances the meaning of concepts thus linked and expresses a meaning that stems from this kind of relation.

Row H: *Algebraic Calculus*: Empty row since it has no realisation in psychoanalytic practice.

2) Horizontal (columns): The columns categorise the development of the mind as it processes thoughts. They are numbered 1 to 6, and Bion leaves one column marked as 'n', to indicate the possibility of future expansions when clinical requirements demand them. The same statement can be classified in any of its uses without varying its formulation:

Column 1: Definitory Hypotheses

Column 2: Resistance

Column 3: Notation

Column 4: Attention

Column 5: Attention directed to inquiry of a specific point of the psychoanalytic material.

Column 6: Action, including both thoughtful action *and* enactment.

Bion left empty categories to be filled in the future with the elucidation of new psychoanalytic elements.

Bion, W. R. (1977) *Two Papers: The Grid and Caesura*. Rio de Janeiro: Imago.

L. P. C.

GRODDECK, GEORG (1866–1934) Groddeck is one of the founders of psychoanalytic psychosomatics and invented the term *Es* or 'It' adopted by Freud but rendered as the *id in the English translation. He stood in the tradition of romantic medicine, vitalism and *Nietzsche's philosophy. In running his famous sanatorium in the German spa town of Baden-Baden, he developed a holistic view of the psychosomatic nature of man, rooted in the unconscious energies of the It. His most prominent works are *The Book of the It*, a psychoanalytic novel entitled *The Soul Seeker*, his 115 clinical lectures given between 1916 and 1919 and his correspondence with *Freud and *Ferenczi.

A controversial figure, a mixture of open-mindedness and grandiosity, his understanding of psychoanalysis was existential, seeing a person's involvement in the life of the It as central. Unsurprisingly perhaps, he was antagonistic to *ego psychology and science. Some called him a 'self presentation of the unconscious' but others in France, where he has been highly regarded, referred to his work as 'psychanalittérature'. He had considerable influence on his close friend Ferenczi, the development of interpersonal psychoanalysis and the *Balint tradition. He influenced authors like Lawrence Durrell, Miller, Dénes, Bachmann and Lewinter.

Chemouni, J. (1984) *Georg Groddeck. Psychanalyste de l'imaginaire*. Paris: Payot.

Will, H. (1987) *Georg Groddeck. Die Geburt der Psychosomatik*. Munich: Deutscher Taschenbuch Verlag.

H. W.

GROTSTEIN, JAMES S. (1925–) A prominent Kleinian/Bionian psychoanalyst in the United States and a pioneer in that school there. He was trained in orthodox classical Freudian analysis at the Los Angeles Psychoanalytic Institute and was a member of a post-graduate group there which studied British object relations. Because of his interest in the psychoanalytic treatment of psychotic and borderline patients and others suffering from primitive and mental disorders, he sought further analysis and supervision from an analyst and supervisor, both of whom introduced him to the work of W. R. D. *Fairbairn. He subsequently became interested in the works of Klein and Bion, and he and his study group arranged to bring *Bion and Albert Mason from London to Los Angeles, following which he entered analysis with the former and supervision with the latter. Grotstein's earlier published works apply psychoanalytic theory and technique to psychotic and borderline conditions. He has written extensively about schizophrenia, and suggested the concept of the applicability of 'rehabilitative psychoanalysis' for that condition which is explained in his 'Rationale for the Psychoanalytically-Informed Psychotherapy of Schizophrenia and Other Psychoses' in the 1999 *A Language for Psychosis*. He has also written extensively about Kleinian and Bionian theory. He has published seven books either as author, editor, and/or co-author. His first book, *Splitting and Projective Identification* (1981), was a definitive work on the subject. His second book, *Do I Dare Disturb the Universe*, which was a memorial to Bion, was an edited work. His third was a co-edited 1987 work titled *The Borderline Patient* which was an in-depth survey of the literature of the borderline and contained many new ideas, particularly Grotstein's concept of the borderline condition which represents it as a disorder of self-regulation. He co-edited a book in 1994 on W. R. D. Fairbairn entitled *Fairbairn and the Origins of Object Relations*. His 1998 monograph on *The Black Hole* was published in Portugal. His latest book in 2000, *Who Is the Dreamer Who Dreams the Dream?: A Study of Psychic Presences* represents a radical shift in his thinking. There he imparts numinous subjectivity to the unconscious. Dr Grotstein practises psychoanalysis in West Los Angeles.

R. M. S.

GROUP (FREUD) Group members are united by bonds of attachment to the same leader. They may also be united by hatred and murderous impulses. Freud postulated that in the primeval horde, a band of brothers killed a despotic father, and then agreed to observe rules that would allow them to live together.

See also: ego ideal; super-ego

J. A. Ber.

GROUPS (CHILD AND ADOLESCENT) The idea that social life begins at birth has long been accepted. Freud himself used the family group, and the patterns established therein, as the foundations for individual and group relationships. Whilst all child psychotherapists do some group work, this primarily takes place within the natural group of the family. However some psychoanalytic group psychotherapy with children and adolescents developed in the Children and Family Department at the Tavistock Clinic, London in the early 1970s.

The psychoanalytic psychotherapy group explores relationships as they appear in the here and now of the group setting between members of the group, between individuals and the group leader or leaders, and between the group as a whole with the leaders. These are explored as indicative of other levels of relating for each member of the group. An interest in meaning by all members of the group is its aspiration. There are many advantages to group psychotherapy for groups can be run in non-clinical settings; within the group children have an opportunity to understand the consequences of their behaviour – to see not only the impact of their projections, but also how they may be vulnerable to the projections of others. A sense of loneliness and isolation, experienced by many children needing help, is counteracted by the experience of being accepted by the child's group and therapists. Group therapy can also enable children and adolescents, either in homogenous or heterogeneous groups, to discover at first hand the impact they have on one another and how other people function. Being together with their peers, within the safe setting of the therapy group, creates a 'laboratory' for experimentation with new ways of thinking, feeling and behaving which can give the child the confidence to approach people outside the group in a new way.

Flynn, D. (1992) 'Adolescent group work in a hospital in-patient setting with Spina Bifida patients and others'. *Journal of Child Psychotherapy* 18: 87–107.

Reid, S. (1987) 'The use of groups for therapeutic interventions'. *Educational and Child Psychology* 4(3/4): 171–9. Special issue, J. Thacker and R. Williams (eds) *Working with Groups*.

Reid, S. (1999) 'The group as a healing whole: group psychotherapy with children and adolescents' in M. Lanyado and A. Horne (eds) *The Handbook of Child and Adolescent Psychotherapy: Psychoanalytic Approaches*. London: Routledge.

Reid, S., Fry, E. and Rhode, M. (1977) 'Working with small groups of children in primary schools' in D. Daws and M. Boston (eds) *The Child Psychotherapist and Problems of Young People*. London: Wildwood House.

Woods, J. (1993) 'Limits and structure in child group psychotherapy'. *Journal of Child Psychotherapy* 19: 63–78.

S. R.

GROUP-AS-A-WHOLE The expression 'group as a whole' first appeared as a clinical term in Burrow's 1928 rationale for the 'analysis of the immediate group in the immediate moment'. *Foulkes later credited Burrow for having 'put the idea of group analysis as a form of treatment in my mind'. Foulkes and Anthony – influenced by Gestalt psychology – suggested that the whole is more elementary than the parts. With this insight we have arrived at one of the basic concepts in group psychotherapy without which all other observations are misinterpreted or insufficiently described, namely that what we experience in the first place is 'the group as a whole'. This was identified as a 'psychological entity', 'psyche group' or 'group matrix' – associated with a variety of dynamic configurations, a network of constructive communications and a focal point for the location of a therapeutic disturbance.

The group-as-a-whole perspective – as a specialised form of systems theory (see *functional subgroups) gained momentum in the mid-twentieth century in response to the collectivism that contributed to two world wars. 'Total group' phenomena studied in experiential process settings included: *basic assumption mentality due to *Bion, 'common group tensions' due to *Ezriel, 'mother-group' dynamics from Scheidlinger, and focal conflicts explained by Whitaker and Liebermann. These concepts and later modifications due to Agazarian,

Anzieu and others attempted to explain the interaction of individual, interpersonal and group-level dynamics. Their aim was to better treat psychological problems and resolve socio-cultural impasses by considering the meaning of behaviour within its psychosocial context. Clinical theories and practices evolved further to redress criticisms about the impersonal nature of the so-called 'Tavistock' model. The aim was to reconcile the paradox of treating individuals (patients) within collective settings (psychotherapy groups).

Recent group-as-a-whole practices recognise the ambivalent struggle to balance autonomy (individuality and agency) with affiliation (collectivity and communion). The nature of group relations within a social system must also, as Rioch indicates, account for reciprocal relationships between leaders and the members who would follow. While there is no universally accepted group-as-a-whole theory, working assumptions and guiding principles of a generic model would emphasise: the analogue between the group and its members and the self and its parts; the change in psychotherapeutic attentions from primarily interpretative reconstructions of members' formative experiences toward collaborative formulations about the essence of the prevailing group process to account for how participants represent, contribute and are affected by it; and, the shift from a member-centred or therapist-centred focus to a group-centred concentration on the interrelationship between self-transformation and group transformation.

Ettin, M. F. (1999) *Foundations and applications of group psychotherapy: A sphere of influence*. London: Jessica Kingsley.

Ettin, M. F. (2000) 'From identified patient to identifiable group: The alchemy of the group as a whole'. *International Journal of Group Psychotherapy* 50: 137–62.

Ettin, M. F., Cohen, B. D. and Fidler, J. W. (1997) 'Group-as-a-whole theory reviewed in its 20th century context'. *Group Dynamics: Theory, Research and Practice* 1: 329–40.

Foulkes, S. H. (1964) *Therapeutic Group Analysis*. New York: International Universities Press.

Foulkes, S. H. and Anthony, E. J. (1957) *Group Psychotherapy: The Psychoanalytic Approach*. Harmondsworth: Penguin. Reprinted, London: Karnac Books, 1984.

M. F. E.

GROUP COHESION The attractiveness of the group to its members. First emphasised by Yalom as an important therapeutic factor, a necessary precondition for affective therapy, it is the group equivalent of Winnicott's *holding and Bion's *containing.

The powerful, basic force of group cohesion, an inner force that holds the group together, limits group development and contributes to Bion's basic assumption mentality. The move from primitive, basic forms of group solidarity and group cohesion to acceptance of differentiation, the developing capacity of the group to contain and to work with differences represents a move from unity in cohesion to unity in diversity, a move from group cohesion to group coherency.

James, C. (1984) 'Bion's "Containing" and Winnicott's "Holding" in a context of the group matrix'. *International Journal of Group Psychotherapy* 34 (2): 201–13.

Pines, M. (1996) 'Coherency and Disruption in the Sense of Self' in *Circular Reflections*. London: Jessica Kingsley.

M. P.

GROUP FOCAL CONFLICT THEORY Group focal conflict theory conceptualises individual and group dynamics in similar terms. It assists in understanding relationships between the two, and points to routes towards personal gain and to useful interventions on the part of the therapist.

Individual dynamics: 'Nuclear conflicts' develop early in life, arising within an individual's significant early human environment, usually the family. A nuclear conflict consists of a 'disturbing motive' (some impulse or wish), which is in conflict in the first instance with some reality that thwarts expression or satisfaction of the impulse. For instance, a child's yearning for closeness is thwarted by a mother who is depressed and preoccupied. This reality factor is soon replaced by an internalised 'reactive motive' (some fear or guilt), such as a fear of being unworthy of the mother's care. A young child develops solutions to early nuclear conflicts, which are behaviours or beliefs which ameliorate reactive fears/guilt and may achieve a degree of gratification of the disturbing impulse or wish. For instance, a child may behave in an attention-getting way, which breaks through the mother's preoccupations.

Nuclear conflict(s) persist in later life, but take on the form of 'derived focal conflicts', experienced in contemporary situations, and coloured by them. A person's favoured solutions also persist and, when exercised, may be personally advantageous or disadvantageous.

Group dynamics: Through associative processes in the group, individual contributions build up and combine into 'group focal conflicts'. Shared solutions emerge. The group focal conflict (plus one or more related solutions) prevails in the group for a time. They are expressed and revealed in behaviour or speech, and constitute group themes. For instance, members who share the fear that if they reveal angry, hostile feelings towards the therapist (a disturbing motive), they will be abandoned by the therapist (a reactive motive), may displace their anger onto someone or something else (a shared solution).

A solution may be either 'restrictive' or 'enabling'. Restrictive solutions deal with fears/guilt, but do not allow for explorations of the associated impulse or wish. Enabling solutions deal with fears/guilt and also allow for exploration of the associated impulse or wish.

A shared group solution could be supported by all or most members in much the same way; for instance, all or most deny certain feelings, or construct a metaphor which both expresses and conceals feelings. Sometimes role differentiation occurs: for instance, one person acts as a patient while others act as therapists, or one person becomes the *scapegoat whom others attack.

'Solutional conflicts' sometimes occur, where the majority of the group press for some particular solution and one or more of the others resist it.

Connections between group and individual dynamics: Individual and group-level disturbing motives and reactive motives tend to connect and resonate. This occurs because group-level dynamics are created by and through the interaction of the members, through associational processes, and because the group is one of the contemporary situations in which earlier individual conflicts are re-experienced and expressed. Individuals attempt to establish their own favoured personal solutions and are sometimes supported by others, sometimes not.

A therapist who monitors a therapeutic group with group focal conflict theory in mind will support the emergence of enabling solutions, thus helping to establish conditions under which beneficial exchanges are most likely to occur. The therapist will encourage explorations within prevailing themes, so that a number of members can benefit at the same time through sharing, comparing, commenting on their own and others' experiences, and giving and receiving feedback. The therapist will assist individuals to take advantage of opportunities for *corrective emotional experiences when they arise.

Whitaker, D. S. (2001) *Using Groups to Help People*. Second edition. London: Brunner-Routledge.

D. S. W.

GROUP, LARGE Large analytic groups, containing between 35 and 450 people, have been used in hospital or training contexts and integrated into organisational development work. Group analysts agree that in large groups we can learn about primitive defence mechanisms, the fear of psychotic fragmentation, the fragility of communication and the 'foundation matrix' of culture which forms the common ground for the analytic setting between patient and analyst. The split between *Foulkes and *Bion that determined the way small groups are seen also shaped our understanding of large groups. Nitsun has argued that Foulkes's 'pro-group' perspective has been dominant, but the 'negative group' perspective of Bion has been the dominant paradigm in relation to the large group.

Foulkes overcame the opposition between the individual and the group implicit in the work of Freudians and Kleinians who conceptualised the large group as a dyadic process in which the predominant dynamic is between fusion and separation, incorporation and individuation. For Turquet, the individual arrives as a socially competent person and then regresses and struggles always against the large group, as attempts at integration and relatedness tend to get attacked because they undermine the illusion of cohesiveness. Therapy is impossible in the large group setting, but the training group analyst can gain first-hand experience of the fear of annihilation and fragmentation and the group members can work through the unconscious material they carry for their parents' generation, the society they were born into, or the organisation they have chosen to belong to. For example, in the UK the issue of race is often focused on due to the undigested psychic consequences of the British Empire; in Germany, the issue of collective guilt is tangible in most large group settings.

The large group's task is to understand itself in the here and now. Its individual members seek, according to Turquet, to accomplish a psychic journey from an integrated person with a role at the start, to a regressed non-role position, to a silent 'singleton status', to a group role with a voice and finally into 'individual group membership', when a person feels re-connected and re-integrated in a holding relationship. The transformations which need to be worked through within the mind of a large group member are: loss of security, fear of speaking, a feeling of social isolation and a sense of mental fragmentation. Many of the large group members give up in the face of this list and stay in the withdrawn 'singleton' state; the minority join the chaotic communication process and go through the uncomfortable change of moving from a withdrawn into an active state of being. Survival is the name of the large group game in this vision; individual membership is reached only by those who are prepared to stand up to the group.

This dyadic view of the individual and the group in opposition is only half the story. De Maré claims that the large group frustrates the satisfaction of libidinal needs and causes hate. Resentment finds a channel for expression in sub-groups that contain the hate and turn it into the desire to speak. Through a dialogue between the sub-groups, hate is transformed into frustration, which in turn is the pre-condition for thinking and linking. He concludes that large groups can build a matrix between differing sub-groups and develop the capacity for fellowship (*koinonia*). It therefore provides an ideal setting for working through historical trauma and inter-group conflict.

Wilke has argued that Bion and Turquet help the large group practitioner understand the defences of the group and Foulkes offers a flexible way of conducting it. The conductor of the large group needs to embrace three roles: the analyst, the translator and the dynamic administrator. The conductor's work is to widen and deepen the communication at the level of the individual, the sub-group, the group as a whole and the cultural and historic context. Symptoms of disease are not an expression of individual pathology or collective fusion, but result from lost connections and disturbed communication patterns. By trusting the large group, the analyst can help it find its own way of overcoming the 'disease' between the speaker, the listener, the silent bystander(s) and the chorus within it and make dialogue, exchange and interdependence possible. The large group will then, in interaction with its individual members, like society itself, create a matrix that will hold and facilitate working through collective mourning and re-creation.

De Maré P. et al. (1991) *Koinonia: From Hate, through Dialogue to Culture in the Large Group*. London: Karnac Books.
Foulkes, S. H. (1948) *Introduction to Group-Analytic Psychotherapy*. London: Heinemann.
Kreeger, L. (ed.) (1975) *The Large Group, Dynamics and Therapy*. London: Constable.
Nitsun, M. (1996) *The Anti-Group, Destructive Forces in the Group and their Creative Potential*. London: Routledge.
Turquet, P. (1975) 'Threats to identity in the large group' in L. Kreeger (ed.) *The Large Group, Dynamics and Therapy*. London: Constable, 87–144.
Wilke, G. (2002) 'The large group and its conductor' in M. Pines and R. Lipgar (eds) *Building on Bion*. London: Jessica Kingsley.

G. W.

GROUP, MEDIAN Although many people identify a median group by its size, fifteen to forty people, median does not mean medium. What is attended to in a median group is more important than its size. Patrick de Maré defined the Median Group to differentiate a group that is small enough for everyone to have their say yet large enough to evoke those often overwhelming experiences that arise from living in a society. It is this 'in between realm' that makes the median group so important. The combination of the intimacy of the small group and the often overwhelming social forces of the large group, makes it possible to face and critically think about the society we live in. In the median group new meanings can be found that link the personal, social and political.

Historically groups like median groups have been an important method of survival for well over 60,000 years. Two examples are the Hui of the New Zealand Maori and the Native American Medicine Wheel. These societies have always been concerned to understand their collective dilemmas as a group in a way that has been lost to our more 'modern' societies.

According to de Maré, the small group is mainly concerned with kinship or blood relationship issues arising from the family where the main task is acquiring insight and learning to feel. In contrast, the median group, and any larger group, evoke issues of kith or non-blood, social relationships. Here the main task is learning to think, despite the powerful anxieties that inevitably arise, and gain 'outsight' into the cultural structures that shape society. Learning to think and to hold thoughts in a social setting is a prerequisite for living and working in the complex modern world.

High levels of anxiety usually exist resulting in a search for the familiar. To withstand the inevitable discomfort, a leap of faith is needed to resist the desire to make the median group into a small group either by symbolically excluding people or by actually pushing them out. It is then that the phenomenon of 'transposition' makes itself felt. Where *transference refers to a relationship cluster emerging, transposition refers to whole cultural contexts emerging from the past. When unacknowledged, as they often are, these usually traumatic experiences recreated in the present can lead to the belief that it is impossible to effectively use any larger group. To compound an already fragile situation, a dynamic similar to Klein's *paranoid/schizoid position usually emerges. With time and patience the need to polarise gives way to a depression, often equally unbearable, which in turn has to be worked through.

As in the large group, the currency of the median group is the intention to use dialogue. *Buber described dialogue as a true turning to another in full appreciation, not as an object in a social function but as a genuine being. Members can watch the 'climate' or 'atmosphere' change as their collective understanding of each other changes it. One aim of the median group is to humanise an increasingly depersonalised world.

De Maré's description of the median group process is the structuring of hate, arising from the frustration inherent in any larger group setting, through dialogue. The group moves from initial *chaos to a place of *koinonia*, which he describes as a new micro culture of friendliness. This process is transformative. A consciousness or 'knowing with others' develops and an unexpected creativity becomes possible.

The median group approach has many applications. It can be particularly helpful whenever the size and dynamics of a setting match those of a median group. One example is a much-needed bearing witness to catastrophic experiences. Another is working with organisational dilemmas. The opportunity to assemble everybody affected together to sit in a circle 'just talk to each other' should never be missed particularly at times of change, trauma and loss.

Bohm, D. (1985) *Unfolding Meaning: A Weekend of Dialogue with David Bohm*. London and New York: Ark Books.

De Maré, P., Thompson, S. and Piper, R. (1991) *Koinonia: From Hate, through Dialogue to Culture in the Large Group*. London: Karnac Books.

Howard, T. (1995) 'Resisting the resistance to change' in *What Makes Consultancy Work?*. London: University of South Bank.

Howard, T. (1996) 'Using median groups in academic settings'. *Journal of Therapeutic Communities* 17(4).

Howard, T. (1998) 'Learning in the Experiental Group' in A. Ward and L. McMahon (eds) *Intuition is not Enough*. London and New York: Routledge.

T. H.

GROUP PSYCHOTHERAPY (HISTORY) In the aftermath of the French revolution the power of the mass was described by Gustav Lebon in his influential book *The Crowd*. In his mass psychology and the analysis of the ego, Freud borrowed Lebon's thesis that large groups are characterised by: contagion of affect, so that feelings spread rapidly throughout the crowd; and the falling of the separate rational level of mental functioning of each individual to a lower common denominator, that of the crowd. Freud used group psychology to elucidate mechanisms of *identification. He did not practise, nor did he advocate, the use of group psychotherapy. However, he did observe that neuroses may diminish and temporarily disappear when a powerful impetus has been given to group formation. ('Justifiable attempts have been made to turn this antagonism to therapeutic account'.) Freud outlined how in large organisations such as the church and the army each individual feels himself to be in an equal relationship to the head of the organisation, the Pope, the General, the Deity. By this means there is a mutual identification between all the group members. Thus, Freud postulated, each individual has substituted the leader of the group for that part of himself that Freud later named the super-ego. If the psychological forces that maintain the organisation cease to operate, the group disintegrates; the army panics. The forces that protect the structure from disintegration are fear and love; fear of punishment, love for the substitute father shared and through whom comradeship develops. As Freud remarks: 'The essence of group formation consists in new kinds of libidinal ties among members of the group'. Freud's concept of the dynamics of groups is summed up as 'a number of individuals have put one and the same object in the place of the *ego ideal and have consequently identified with each other in their ego'.

Freud rejected the efforts of Trigant Burrow, the American psychoanalyst, to interest him in group analysis, a term coined by Burrow. Burrow wanted to show that the psychoanalytic situation is a social group situation and that the dynamics of the *transference are intimately and powerfully influenced by the social situation. Burrow, a one-time president of the American Psychoanalytic Association, was eventually removed from membership of that organisation because of his advocacy of group analysis and his thesis that the psychoanalytic organisation itself is a neurotic attempt to disregard the social basis of neurosis.

In the 1920s and 30s interest in group phenomena increased. Social psychologists studied organisations, mental hospital psychiatrists began to explore methods of influencing hospitalised patients through exhortation, persuasion and psycho-educational methods. In this they followed in the footsteps of Joseph Pratt, a Boston internist who at the beginning of this century was the first to use the 'classroom method' to educate tuberculous patients in the necessary restrictions in their activities outside of sanatoria. He encouraged his patients to regard themselves as fellow students of their illness and to regard Pratt as the respected authority whom they all shared.

There is a gap in the psychoanalytic study of groups until 1942, when Fritz Redl published his influential paper on 'Group emotion and leadership'. Redl studied groups of children in classrooms and holiday camps. He showed how the personality and activity of a leader produces different patterns of group behaviour and that the group itself makes unconscious use of the situation that develops towards the leader, the 'central person'. Redl showed how different types of groups form around different types of central persons. Around a greatly admired and loved elderly teacher a group of students become hardworking and respectful. They fear to lose his love and this causes an underlying group tension. By contrast the younger teacher, less remote, generates an atmosphere of greater freedom and less fear of disapproval.

Redl worked in North America where the 'neo-Freudians' (*Fromm, *Horney), stressed the importance of a person's relationship to the whole environment not only to the infantile past. *Sullivan's emphasis on inter-personal processes in the formation and deformation of personality considerably influenced American psychiatry.

Paul Schilder, the great psychoanalyst/neuropsychiatrist began group therapy in the 1930s in the USA. Though he only worked with single-sex groups, he found that group therapy overcomes neurotic isolation, that patients can learn through identification with one another and that transference issues can be worked with. The work of Schilder and Burrow encouraged *Foulkes to begin his first essay in group therapy in Exeter in 1940.

In 1939 in New York, *Wolf began his first essay in group therapy. Wolf was convinced that it is possible to continue with individual psychoanalysis in a group setting and his work has been categorised as 'psychoanalysis in groups' in contrast to Foulkes' 'psychoanalysis by the group' and *Bion and *Ezriel as 'psychoanalysis of the group'. Wolf strongly opposes the use of group dynamic concepts in the group, asserting that these are defences against working with the individual. Wolf emphasises therapist activity, and instruction in the use of *free association in the group, as well as alternate sessions when patients meet without the therapist and thereby can strengthen peer relationships and work through transferences to the authority figure of the leader. Foulkes's view was that these techniques complicate and interfere with the natural evolution of the group.

Kurt Lewin, an academic Gestalt psychologist, came as a refugee to the USA in the early 1930s. As a dedicated anti-Nazi, he was deeply impressed by the need to understand how social attitudes are required and influenced. He noted that attitudes are more easily changed in group situations and from this went on to explore the dynamics of personal change in a group situation. Like Redl he worked with groups of boys studying the effect of different styles of leadership on the group, such as *laissez-faire*, democratic and authoritarian styles. It was his investigations of group behaviour in the laboratory situation that led to the T-group movement, which led to much significant research into the dynamics of groups at the laboratory at Bethel Main. His concept of a person's 'life-space' is a mathematically constructed graphic representation of the psychic forces within a person. Changes within the person affect the perception of the group; changes in the group affect the person's perception of it and of his relationship to it. No change occurs that does not affect all its members in some way. Out of this movement came the significant Chicago laboratory of Herbert Feelan, who researched into psychoanalytic theories of group functioning, particularly those of Bion. Lewin's work is nowadays represented through his influence on Yvonne Agazarian.

The needs of military psychiatry during the course of World War II led to the greatly increased use of group methods. Bion initiated the group situation tests at the War Office Selection Board. Here leaderless groups were observed so as to see how its members took up roles within the group and so that qualities of leadership could be assessed. Wilfred Bion and John Rickman organised the first Northfield experiment at the military psychiatric rehabilitation hospital. In this first experiment through large group meetings soldiers were eventually confronted with their own individual and group neurotic behaviour and thereby understand factors which led to loss and restoration of morale and fighting spirit. Terminated after only six weeks because of the opposition from the surrounding environment, this led in 1943 to the second Northfield experiment in which the noticeable figures were S. H. Foulkes, T. F. Main and H. Bridger. Through the combination of small and large group work important observations were made as to how wartime stress had affected soldiers and how through organising the whole institution as what Main calls a 'therapeutic community' significant improvements in the functioning of both individuals and groups could be achieved. In 1948 S. H. Foulkes published his *Introduction to Group-analytic Psychotherapy*, a very significant work in the literature.

Bion's *Experiences in Groups*, obtained at the Tavistock Clinic after the war, is one of the most influential books on group psychotherapy. Bion revised his initial ideas under the influence of Kleinian psychoanalytic thinking, whereas Foulkes emphasised the need to differentiate group analysis from psychoanalysis and to regard it as a powerful therapeutic instrument in its own right. Bion's work has had considerable influence in the United States of America through the A. K. Rice Institute, which studies organisational dynamics.

Psychoanalytic object relations theory has a considerable influence on contemporary group psychotherapeutic approaches, particularly in North America. Moves to integrate *object relations theory and Foulkes' group analysis have been made in the United Kingdom.

Ettin, M. (1999) *Foundations and Applications of Group Psychotherapy*. London: Jessica Kingsley.
Foulkes, S. H. (1948) *Introduction to Group-Analytic Psychotherapy*. London: Heinemann. Reprinted (1983) London: Maresfield.
Harrison, T. (2000) *Bion, Rickman, Foulkes and the Northfield Experiment. Advancing on Another Front*. London: Routledge.
Neri, C. (1998) *Group*. London: Jessica Kingsley.
Pines, M. (ed.) (1985) *Bion and Group Psychotherapy*. London: Routledge.

M. P.

GROUP MATRIX A notion due to *Foulkes, the matrix concept is one of his unique contributions to psychotherapeutic science. Foulkes defined the matrix on a number of occasions and for a full appreciation it is worth becoming familiar with Foulkes' own attempts to clarify his concept.

In 1965 Foulkes said that the matrix is the 'network of all individual mental processes, the psychological medium in which they meet, communicate and interact ... This is, of course, a construct in the same way as is, for example, the concept of traffic, or, for that matter, of mind'.

In 1964 he said: 'The matrix is the hypothetical web of communication and relationship in a given group. It is the common, shared ground, which ultimately determines the meaning and significance of all events and upon which all communications, verbal and nonverbal, rest'. He goes on to say that the social matrix can be thought of as a network in the same way as the brain is a network of fibres and cells, which together form a complex unit. Within this group network, all the processes take place and in it they can be defined with regard to their meaning, their extension in time and place and their intensity.

Repeatedly, the word 'network' occurs, so that it becomes almost synonymous with matrix, and Foulkes enlarges on this, when he says that the group matrix is the operational basis of all relationships and communications. Inside this network, the individual is conceived as a nodal point. The individual, in other words, is not conceived as a closed, but as an open system. An analogy can be made with the neuron in anatomy and physiology, the neuron being the nodal point in the total network of the nervous system, which always reacts and responds as a whole. As in the case of the neuron in the nervous system, so is the individual suspended in the group matrix.

Looked at in this way it becomes easier to understand our claims that the group associates, responds and reacts as a whole. The group, as it were, avails itself now of one speaker, now of another, but it is always the transpersonal network which is sensitised and gives utterance or responds. In this sense, we can postulate the existence of a group mind in the same way as we postulate the existence of an individual mind.

There are other meanings of matrix; a generic holding device is one such. Another meaning suggests matrix as a background phenomenon. Through this aspect of matrix, Foulkes was able to underpin his introduction of concepts of Gestalt psychology to group analysis. From this we move to one of his more esoteric and less well explained concepts – that of 'location'.

In brief the mind is dependent for its existence and health on the neurophysiological matrix of the body. It is equally and paradoxically dependent on a complex 'psychosocial matrix'. There is a truly telling analogy between the brain and a complex social network, which may be likened to 'Indra's net' (from the Mahayana Buddhist tradition) which is a net with a jewel at each intersection, each jewel reflecting all the other jewels of the net.

Foulkes, S. H. (1964) *Therapeutic Group Analysis*. London: George Allen & Unwin.

Foulkes, S. H. (1967) 'The group as matrix of the individual's mental life'. *Group Analysis* 1(1): 32.

Foulkes, S. H. (1973) 'The group as matrix of the individual's mental life' in L. R. Wolberg and E. K. Schwartz (eds) *Group Therapy, an Overview*. New York: Intercontinental Medical Books.

Foulkes, S. H. and Anthony, E. J. (1957) *Group Psychotherapy, the Psychoanalytic Approach*. Harmondsworth: Penguin (New editions, 1965, 1968, 1971, 1973. Reprinted London: Karnac Books, 1984).

Roberts, J. P. (1982) 'Foulkes' concept of the matrix'. *Group Analysis* (2): 111–26.

J. Rob.

GROUP PSYCHOTHERAPY PRECIS *Basic principles*: in a properly constituted group, though each person in their unique position represents a deviant from the social norm, collectively they constitute the norm from which each is deviant. The norm of more healthy adaptation for each individual and for the group as a whole can be slowly achieved. All events in the group are seen to occur within the developing *group matrix; individual contributions are understood and analysed in the context of a transpersonal network: as if the members of the groups are the words of a sentence, none of which can express their meaning, except as objects, unless belonging to each other. It is due to the gradually developing group matrix that the analytic group has the capacity to receive, contain, integrate, and eventually, transform to a higher level of functioning the individual patient's input. In that capacity and fulfilling that task, the group becomes the maternal *container of infancy, who in *Bion's terminology, transforms the unmetabolised *beta elements into alpha elements available to the mind. When that happens, the group as a whole functions with a maturity exceeding that of its members.

Dialogue within the group opens the way for change, opening intra-psychic and intrapersonal links which can produce change in stagnating systems.

Therapeutic factors: universality, group members recognising that they share much in common, brings individuals out of neurotic isolation.

Mirroring: patients see aspects of themselves reflected in others in the group, thus confronting rejected and split-off elements of their social, psychological and body images. Through mirroring the self can become re-integrated. Resonance refers to the process whereby each individual responds in a particular fashion to a common stimulus. The individual responses indicate the dynamics of the person's internal world now externalised in the group processes.

The group is conceived of as a *transference group. Transference is universal and is conceived of as operating on several levels: current – the personal reactions to events in the person's social and emotional life without the group as well as within; projective – rejected, split-off whole and *part object relations are mobilised with group members evoking and receiving these projections; this allows for the working through and re-ownership of the discarded elements on the archetypal level. *Foulkes incorporated elements of *Jung's concept of the *collective unconscious and also referred to the concept of the 'social unconscious', a concept that originates with *Fromm, subsequently developed by Hopper and others. The social unconscious refers to those deep social processes that go towards structuring the inner world of all the members of a particular culture at a particular socio-economic and political stage.

The powerful and basic force of group cohesion, an inner force that holds the group together, limits group development and contributes to Bion's basic assumption mentality. The move from primitive and basic forms of group solidarity and group cohesion to acceptance of differentiation, the capacity of the group to contain and to work with these differences represents a move from cohesion in unity to unity in diversity.

See also: anti-group; basic assumptions; chaos; corrective emotional family experience; subgroups, functional; group-as-a-whole; group cohesion; group focal conflict theory; group, large; group matrix; group, median; group psychotherapy (history); scapegoat, group psychotherapy (self-psychology); group resonance; group therapist function; group; intersubjectivity (group); object relations theory (group); unconscious, social

Dalal, F. (1998) *Taking the Group Seriously*. London: Jessica Kingsley.

Foulkes, S. H. (1937) 'On Introjection'. *International Journal of Psycho-Analysis* 18: 269–93.

Foulkes, S. H. and Anthony, E. J. [1957] (1984) *Group Psychotherapy: The Psychoanalytical Approach*. London: Karnac Books.

Pines, M. (ed.) (1983) *The Evolution of Group Analysis*. London: Routledge.

Pines, M. and Hearst, L. E. (1993) 'Group Analysis' in H. I. Kaplan and B. J. Sadock (eds) *Comprehensive Group Psychotherapy*. Philadelphia: Williams & Wilkins.

M. P.

GROUP PSYCHOTHERAPY (ANALYTICAL PSYCHOLOGY) As early as 1916 Jung recognised the importance of groups and began a 'silent experiment' in group psychology. This he did through observation of the Psychological Club in Zurich with the aid of Toni Wolfe over a forty year period. His views on groups were expressed most directly towards the end of his life in response to the questions of Illing's 1957 study.

He maintained that group therapy could never replace individual therapy, which was essentially a dialectic process between two individuals. Jung thought that groups promoted *regressive traits and encouraged dependence on the group conductor as mother or father. He felt groups did not promote *individuation but instead increased suggestibility and an emphasis on the collective that denied the individual's uniqueness. He thought the group increased the ego, making the individual more assertive and secure, but at the expense of the *self which was reduced and pushed towards conformity with the norm.

These views remained with Jung's followers until the early 1960s when Hobson rigorously reviewed group dynamics and analytic psychology. He pointed out that Jung's observations were of a group founded by himself and that did not have a psychotherapeutic intention. The group also consisted of thirty to seventy members and so had more in common with what we would now refer to as a *median or *large group. As such it had similarities to organisations of which Jung was scathing: 'when a hundred clever heads join a group one big nincompoop is the result'.

Hobson was more optimistic about the application of Jungian ideas and regarded the group as a system with self-regulating mechanisms that move towards development and integration. In his model the analyst's task was to facilitate conscious and unconscious communication utilising the archetypal images created in the group.

Globally there have been many attempts to integrate Jung's ideas into group analytic practice. In Europe Fiumara (1976) pointed out the similarity between the ideas of Foulkes and Jung. He felt that the group provided its own archetypal matrix, which he considered a valid complement to individual analysis. In South America, Usandivaras has written both about archetypal images in the group, particularly the notion of Foulkes' primordial level, which he connects, as others do, to the Jungian concept of the *collective unconscious. In America Boyd (1991) and his colleagues have researched the expansion of consciousness and the process of personal transformation in groups by identifying consistent archetypal themes in terms of group development. In Britain Zinkin has been the most prolific writer in connecting group analytic and Jungian concepts. Amongst other things he emphasised a process of dialogue in a group which results in more sophisticated internal dialogues which does, indeed, correlate with Jung's view of individuation.

Fiumara, R. (1976) 'Therapeutic group analysis and analytical psychology'. *Journal of Analytical Psychology* 21(1): 1–24.

Hobson, R. F. (1964) 'Group dynamics and analytical psychology'. *Journal of Analytical Psychology* 9(1): 23–49.

Illing, H. A. (1957) 'C. G. Jung on the recent trends in group psychotherapy'. *Journal of Human Relations* 10(1).

Jung, C. G. (1959) 'Introduction to Wolfe's *Studies In Jungian Psychology*' in *Collected Works* 10. London: Routledge & Kegan Paul.

Usandivaras, R. J. (1986) 'Foulkes' primordial level in clinical practice'. *Journal of Group Analysis* 19(2): 113–24.

Zinkin, L. (1998) *Dialogue in the Analytic Setting: Selected Papers of Louis Zinkin on Jung and on Group Analysis*. London: Jessica Kingsley.

A. Pro.

GROUP PSYCHOTHERAPY (EXISTENTIAL) The existential view emphasises that human life is always relational before it is individual and can only be understood in its context – this context is always the world and others. *Heidegger, has called human life a 'Being-in-the-world', and defined the world as one we share with others, a 'with-world'. This view has become the foundation of many forms of existential psychotherapy and its method is existential *phenomenology – the observation and understanding of whatever encounters us. It is surprising that the existential dimension of group therapy has so far not been explored in sufficient depth, particularly since the existential concern with individuals in their contexts seems so central to group psychotherapy.

There are papers on existential group therapy, but they appear to be insufficiently familiar with their subject, or too tightly packed with unfamiliar thoughts and information. Yalom admits that he added existential factors as an 'afterthought' to his exploration of group therapy – the recognition of existential givens like mortality, isolation, responsibility and meaninglessness. He points out that these are of particular importance to group members, but they remain a thin strand in the eclectic fabric of his monumental book.

Strangely enough, it was *Foulkes, the psychoanalyst and creator of group analysis, who over the years in his books and papers developed phenomenological and existential aspects – though he did not call them that. In his first book he stated that 'the individual' was an abstraction and he rejected dualistic notions like the split between mind and body, constitution and environment, and an inside and outside world. At a congress in Milan he denounced the Cartesian subject/object split as the source of many modern 'pseudo problems'. Goldstein's holistic view of the nervous system is reflected in Foulkes' way of seeing human life as an intersubjective event that he called a network or *matrix. These are essentially existential-phenomenological views, perhaps inspired by members of the Frankfurt School who were neighbours in the early days of his psychoanalytic practice. At the same time Foulkes remained rooted in his psychoanalytic ideas, for example, a belief in unconscious processes and concern with a strict therapeutic frame. There is no reconciliation between what seemed to be opposing points of view. This inevitably led to some confusion and contradiction in his theoretical stance, but also to the creative impulse apparent throughout his work. For the practice of an existential therapy with groups the following points are worth considering: 1) Any kind of communication is important and valid; 2) Instead of reductive interpretation, a hermeneutic broadening of the context of what is said; 3) Past and future need to be experienced as aspects of the present; 4) The main therapist of a group is the group; 5) The task of the 'convening' therapist is to maintain and guard the therapeutic space of the group; 6) Foulkes' definition of therapy as an 'ever more articulate form of communication' is existential if it is not restricted to the merely verbal.

Cohn, H. W. (1997) *Existential Thought and Therapeutic Practice*. London: Sage Publications.

Foulkes, S. H. (1948) *Introduction to Group-Analytic Psychotherapy*. London: Karnac Books.

Yalom, I. D. (1985) *Theory and Practice of Group Psychotherapy*. Third edition. New York: Basic Books.

H. W. C.

GROUP PSYCHOTHERAPY (SELF-PSYCHOLOGY) The influences on group psychotherapy from *self-psychology can be summarised as follows:

1) The *selection and composition* of groups is influenced by considerations of what functions each person may need from other group members to resume emotional development: idealised parental imago; mirroring; twinship; benign opposition.

2) The *awareness* of sequences of rupture and repair of empathic bonds, regarded as essential for developing new psychic structures.

3) The *growth* of self is enhanced through the process described by Foulkes as *ego-training in action.

The self psychology approach has been fostered by the A. K. Rice Institute (AKRI) founded in the United States by Margaret Rioch in 1970 as a non-profit-making educational institution to carry forward the study of groups and organisations with a particular emphasis on the effect of covert processes and issues of authority and leadership. This way of studying authority, leadership and organisational effectiveness makes use of open systems and psychoanalytic theories. This study of groups and organisations continues the work of A. K. Rice at the Tavistock Institute of Human Relations who, together with other colleagues from Great Britain (Sutherland, Turquet and others), was brought to the United States in 1965 to conduct a residential group relations conference in what has become widely known as the 'Tavistock' or 'Leicester' model. These 'working conferences' have been conducted annually for thirty-seven years.

AKRI has published *Group Relations Reader 1, 2* and *3*.

Harwood, I. (1986) 'The need for optimal, available self-object caretakers: moving towards extended self-object experiences'. *Group Analysis* 19: 291–302.

Harwood, I. (1996) 'Towards optimum group placement from the perspective of self and group experience'. *Group Analysis* 29(2): 199–218.

Harwood, I. and Pines, M. (1998) *Self-experiences in Group: Intersubjective and Self-psychological Pathways to Human Understanding*. London: Jessica Kingsley and Philadelphia: Taylor and Francis.

M. P.

GROUP RESONANCE Each individual group member picks out of the common pool what is relevant to him, responding on a specific level of regression, fixation or developmental arrest at which the main disturbances and conflicts operate.

Foulkes, S. H. (1990) 'Notes on the concept of resonance' in *Selected Papers*. London: Karnac Books.

M. P.

GROUP SELF The first publication which contained this concept was Kohut's essay 'Creativeness, Charisma, Group Psychology'. However, it was conceived somewhat earlier. It appears in the essay 'On Courage' which was written around 1970, but not published until 1985. Kohut was not particularly interested in group psychotherapy. He sought a concept suitable for explanations of societal and historical group processes and used the relationship between Freud and the psychoanalytic community as a paradigm. He suggested the existence of a certain psychological configuration with regard to the group – the 'group self' – analogous to the self of the individual. This 'group self' dips into the deepest reaches of the psyche and accounts not only for the continuity and the cohesion of the group but also determines its most important actions. Since Kohut introduced the concept in the realm of applied psychoanalysis, it was lost for many years in clinical self psychology. A renewed interest developed in the 1990s among group psychotherapists who tried to develop a self psychological theory of group dynamics. The group self does not imply any group mind, but refers to supra-individual forces embedded in the project which unites the group members and to which they lend their individual bodies and psyche.

S. Kar.

GROUP THERAPIST FUNCTION To be a dynamic administrator creating and maintaining optimal conditions for psychotherapy as well as a group conductor functioning through sustained empathic attention, aiding the group to understand their situations and interactions, directing interpretations both towards the individual and towards the group as a whole.

M. P.

GUGGENBUHL-CRAIG, ADOLF (1923–) A psychiatrist from a family with a long and deep connection to Switzerland. Born in Zurich in 1923, he has lived there ever since except for a short stay in the United States when he did his psychiatric training. He carved out his own Jungian training in Zurich in the early 1950s before Institute training was required. He was the Honorary Secretary for Franz Riklin Jr., the second president of the *International Association for Analytical Psychology. In that capacity he edited the *Proceedings of the Second International Congress* in 1962 (*Der Archetyp*). Upon Riklin's death in 1969, he took over as president of the Curatorium of the Jung

Institut in Zurich, a position he held for over a decade. In 1977 he was elected president of the IAAP, a position he held for six years. Although not a prolific writer, his books had a great impact on *analytical psychology. His first book, *Power in the Healing Professions*, outlines in a practical manner the power *shadow of being a therapist. It demonstrates the destructive aspect of always trying to be helpful. His other books continued in the same manner, as he writes about marriage, psychopathy, and old age. Guggenbühl-Craig is known for taking controversial stands on many matters, and it is often difficult to predict his point of view. At the present time he has retired from all positions of influence, and is seen as the *éminence grise* of the Zurich community.

T. B. K.

GUILT (FREUD) The province of the super-ego. Follows when certain forbidden wishes and urges, usually sexual or aggressive, are experienced. Guilt frequently involves a fear of external *punishment (e.g. fear), and follows when certain wishes that we fear will incur punishment are considered or enacted. There are danger situations in childhood and later on in which anxiety can be stirred such as loss of the object or of the object's love or castration. When a wish is experienced as dangerous, for example an Oedipal wish with its accompanying death wishes, guilt ensues accompanied by punitive castration fears.

Following Freud, Lacan says that in obsessional neurosis, the symptom manifests itself most frequently in the form of guilt, the aggressive tendency that has undergone displacement. The symptom of obsessional guilt along with other aspects of 'obsessional thinking' is an attempt to mystify and thereby defend against anxiety.

See also: shame

D. K. S. / C. Owe.

GUILT (KLEIN) In *Studies in Hysteria* Freud had placed importance on persecutory feelings, a significance which increased with his development of the structural model wherein conscious and unconscious guilt marked one effect on the ego of super-ego criticism. Elaborating on Freud's work, Klein in 'Criminal tendencies in normal children' sought to show how primitive unbearable guilt feelings may be externalised and then enacted, the external substitute scenario feeling more manageable than its internal correlate. This type of movement – from scenario to scenario, object to object, in both internal and external worlds – Klein came to see as fuelled by epistemophilic, aggressive and omnipotent impulses on the one hand and guilt on the other. Thus, as the primary object and its early substitutes each became successively encumbered with a burden of guilt over the subject's aggressive phantasies, 'new lands' could be sought out for freer exploration. In this way guilt contributes to symbol formation and representational processes in general. Klein's seminal ideas from 'The importance of symbol-formation in the development of the ego' were later developed by Segal.

As Klein's thinking evolved with her key notions of the paranoid-schizoid and depressive positions and the interplay between these, she catalogued more precisely the very early developmental and 'positional' vicissitudes of affects including guilt. In the paranoid-schizoid state talion law prevails and guilt tends to be more primitive and persecutory, associated with terrors about the torture and destruction of the ego or self. Primitive defences such as splitting, fragmentation, externalisation or projective identification are here mobilised in attempts to manage what otherwise feels unmanageable.

With increasing psychic integration and the recognition of whole objects, guilt shifts away from anxieties about the ego's survival towards concern for the survival of the good object, the formerly split-off shadow of which is increasingly recognised. Klein sees the essence of guilt existing in the feeling that the loved object has been damaged by the self's aggressivity.

Depressive position guilt occurs in tandem with a more robust sense of self and respect for psychic truth, reparative impulses towards damaged yet evidently surviving objects bolstering the perception of the object as a whole object and ego integration. Thus for Klein, guilt in the *depressive position promotes empathy and creative and reparative object relations, supported by the hegemony of the life instinct over the death instinct. Guilt is here more bearable and by-and-large more accessible to consciousness.

Klein, M. [1948] (1975) 'On the theory of anxiety and guilt' in *Envy and Gratitude and Other Works 1946–1963*. London: Hogarth Press, 25–42.

R. Wil.

GUNTRIP, HARRY (1901–74) Former Congregational Minister, and lecturer in psychotherapy in the department of Psychiatry, Leeds University, where work with severely schizoid patients, reflecting his own psychopathology, prompted him to enter analysis with Fairbairn (1949–60) and Winnicott (1962–9). Despite important gains at the Oedipal level, Fairbairn's analysis failed to resolve Guntrip's core problem, namely a persisting underlying experience of ego-weakness, and even of non-existence (ego-loss) associated with early maternal failure. As the analysis ended in 1960, Guntrip formulated a development of Fairbairn's theory of endopsychic structure to account for the experience of patients like himself, whose sense of relatedness, and therefore of selfhood, was always vacillating and uncertain. Guntrip suggested that under the influence of anxiety (especially separation anxiety) the infant undergoes a two-stage withdrawal: first into an unhappy inner psychic world where an active part of the self (Fairbairn's libidinal ego) continues the struggle with rejecting figures; and secondly, into the deepest unconscious where the exhausted and traumatised core (Guntrip's regressed libidinal ego), seeks the safety of an earlier security.

Although, due to its extreme weakness, this deeply withdrawn core is feared and repressed by the rest of the personality, it nevertheless retains a latent capacity for personal growth, requiring of the psychotherapist a maturely parental quality for its realisation. Guntrip's clearly written book *Schizoid Phenomena, Object Relations and the Self* contains much clinical evidence to support this theory, which Fairbairn later endorsed.

The high degree of correspondence between Guntrip's concept of the regressed ego and Winnicott's true self in cold storage, both published in 1960, constituted an important element in the second analysis when Winnicott's profound understanding of Guntrip's devitalised core and manic defence yielded a decisive therapeutic gain. In his posthumous paper published in 1975 ('My Experience of Analysis with Fairbairn and Winnicott', *International Review of Psycho-Analysis* 2) Guntrip gave an account of his experience with each of his analysts and gratefully acknowledged his wife's support. Although outside main-stream psychoanalysis, Guntrip established an international reputation as a clinician and writer in the field. His work provides a bridge between that of his two analysts, and also between object relations theory and the self psychology of Kohut.

J. H.

H

HALLUCINATION (FREUD) A *primary process means of attempting to fulfil a wish entirely through fantasy and perception, without interaction with actual objects. Freud speculated that, when hungry, the infant attempts to gain immediate satisfaction through hallucinating the breast. As this does not succeed in reducing hunger, the infant is forced to turn to real objects in the external world. During sleep, adults function much like the infant when producing the vivid hallucinatory wish-fulfilling imagery of dreams.

M. Eag.

HALLUCINATION (LACAN) Hallucination is usually defined as a false perception but Lacan defines it in terms of *signifier and meaning (its sensory or psychic nature has no real importance). It is closely related to *foreclosure in psychosis: what has been rejected, foreclosed, from the *Symbolic returns in the *Real as an hallucination. It is viewed as a direct consequence of the main mechanism of psychosis (delusions are indirect consequences, attempts at recovery). That is why foreclosure in verbal hallucinations has an important, paradigmatic place in the clinical approach to psychosis.

M. Eyd.

HANNAH, BARBARA (1891–1986) Barbara Hannah was born in England in 1891 and died in Zurich, Switzerland in 1986. After reading *Jung's early works, she met him and never left his close inner circle. She knew him first as an analysand, then as a trusted colleague. She was a popular training analyst and lecturer at the Jung Institut in Zurich. In 1967 she presented the first memorial lecture after Jung's death. There were lecture tours to America in 1952 and 1968, the latter featuring the widely acclaimed *The Beyond*. Her published works include: *Striving Toward Wholeness* (1971); *Jung: His Life and Work* (1976); and *Encounters with the Soul: Active Imagination* (1981).

D. L. F.

HAPPINESS For Lacan, lack, even when it presents itself as an excess – of words or of anxiety – is at the centre of psychoanalytical work. There is no happiness therefore that is experienced as a durable fulfilment or as an accumulation of brief pleasures, but rather only through being open to an encounter. It is experienced as an increased power to love, and as the augmentation of desire when it is less fixated on objects that are pre-determined.

M. V.

HARDING, M. ESTHER (1888–1971) The noted author and analyst was born in Shrewsbury, England in 1888, trained at the London School of Medicine and practised at Plaistow Hospital. After World War I, she worked with *Jung in Zurich before coming to New York City in 1923 to open her analytic practice. She practised there and on Bailey Island, Maine, until her death in 1971. With colleagues, she founded the C. G. Jung Foundation and the C. G. Jung Institute of New York. Through her lectures, and books, she influenced many. Her *Women's Mysteries* and *Way of All Women* were vital to women's deeper understanding of themselves.

R. C. W.

HARTMANN, HEINZ (1894–1970) Hartmann was pre-eminent as a psychoanalytic teacher and theoretician for more than four decades from the publication of his first psychoanalytic paper in 1924 till his death. He lived in Vienna until Austria's annexation by Germany and subsequently in New York. His monograph, *Grundrisse der Psychoanalyse* (*Fundamentals of Psychoanalysis*, never translated into English) appeared in 1927 and established his reputation. *Das Ich und das Anpassungsproblem* (*The Ego And The Problem Of Adaptation*) followed in 1939. It did appear in English translation, but many years later. He was a professional intimate of Freud and an editor of Freud's major psychoanalytic journal, the *Internationale Zeitschrift für Psychoanalyse*. He was a founding editor of The *Psychoanalytic Study Of The Child*, in 1945, and was president, first of the American Psychoanalytic Association and then of the International Psycho-Analytical Association. From 1945 on he authored a score or more articles of outstanding calibre, most of which were reprinted in a volume called *Studies in Ego Psychology*. Along with A. *Freud, *Fenichel, and *Kris he was one of the early advocates of the importance of analysing defences (ego analysis) in addition to analysis of drive derivatives (id analysis). He wrote, very aptly, that the analysis of defences is the systematic study of self-deception.

Hartmann contributed substantially to every aspect of psychoanalytic theory. During his later years he became identified in most analysts' eyes with certain views he elaborated on ego development and functioning. He suggested that mental health is distinguished by the fact that certain aspects of ego functioning have become substantially independent of the drives. In his words, they have become autonomous, whereas in mental illness they are no longer so. Psychogenic illness, he proposed, can be understood as loss of ego autonomy. In this connection, following Freud, he believed that the psychic energy at the disposal of the ego is id energy that has become de-instinctualised – in Hartmann's term, neutralised.

Hartmann, H. (1964) *Essays in Ego Psychology*. London: Hogarth Press.

C. B.

HATE An affective state characterised by aggression and the impulse to destroy often accompanied by feelings of isolation, *jealousy, *envy and *paranoia. A synthesis of different psychoanalytic perspectives would suggest that hate is the general term for destructive impulses and the experience of existing in isolation. Hate must be viewed as the reciprocal affective state to the state of love, or to the impulse to preserve, protect, and nurture. Hate and love often exist in ambivalent relationship with each other.

See also: ambivalence; countertransference

A. P.

HEGEL, G. W. F. (1770–1831) Hegel is arguably the most influential German Idealist in the history of philosophy. He systematically articulated the nature and structure of mind (*Geist*), consciousness, world history, ethics, aesthetics, and religion through his dialectical logic. Best known for his *Phenomenology of Spirit*, which traces the historical development of Western culture and human self-consciousness, and the *Philosophy of Right*, he profoundly influenced Marx and later the Frankfurt School of political philosophy. Hegel's mature system was formalised in his *Science of Logic* and further advanced in his *Encyclopaedia of the Philosophical Sciences* where he offered a metaphysical treatise on rational thought, the natural world, human psychology and collective social life.

Hegel's philosophy rests on his logic of the dialectic, which entails a simultaneous, threefold, progressive evolutionary process that at once enters into opposition, annuls such opposition as it elevates itself over its previous moment, while at the same time preserving such opposition within its internal structure. Hegel's dialectic is often misattributed to Fichte's depiction of the transcendental acts of judgement characterised by a process of thesis-antithesis-synthesis, thus failing to capture the nuances and complexity of Hegel's system.

Within psychoanalysis, Hegel greatly influenced *Lacan's notion of *desire, largely due to Kojève's influential lectures, and is now being recognised in contemporary psychoanalytic circles for his theory of intersubjectivity. There have furthermore been attempts to apply Hegel's dialectic to theoretical, clinical, and applied psychoanalysis through an approach called dialectical psychoanalysis or process psychology.

While Freud was acquainted with Hegel's philosophy, it is not known whether he studied his texts with any precision. What remains largely unknown to psychoanalysis is that Hegel postulated a dynamic unconscious, offered a cryptic theory of mental illness, and anticipated many key concepts that Freud made more intelligible nearly a century later.

Berthold-Bond, D. (1995) *Hegel's Theory of Madness*. Albany: State University of New York Press.
Hegel, G. W. F. [1807] (1977) *Phenomenology of Spirit*. Translated by A. V. Miller. Oxford: Oxford University Press.

Hegel, G. W. F. [1812] (1969) *Science of Logic*. Translated by A. V. Miller. London: George, Allen & Unwin.
Hegel, G. W. F. [1817] (1971) *Philosophy of Mind*. Vol. 3 of the *Encyclopaedia of the Philosophical Sciences*. Translated by William Wallace and A. V. Miller. Oxford: Clarendon Press.
Hegel, G. W. F. [1821] (1967) *Philosophy of Right*. Translated by T. M. Knox. Oxford: Oxford University Press.
Mills, J. (2002) *The Unconscious Abyss: Hegel's Anticipation of Psychoanalysis*. Albany: State University of New York Press.

J. Mil.

HEIDEGGER, MARTIN (1889–1976) German philosopher; one of the major forces of twentieth century European thought. Born in Messkirch, Germany in 1889, he received his philosophical training at the University of Freiburg (Germany) where he began teaching in 1919. After serving as Research Assistant to Husserl, he moved to Marburg in 1923, where he published his major work, *Being and Time*, in 1927. In 1928 he returned to Freiburg to succeed Husserl in the chair of philosophy. In 1933, he became the first rector of the University to be elected after the assumption of power by the Nazi regime, a post he resigned before the end of his tenure, retaining his membership in the Nazi party, however, until this was dissolved in 1945. The Allies prohibited him from returning to his teaching position until he formally retired in 1951. He continued to lecture, publish and hold occasional seminars almost until his death in Messkirch in 1976.

Heidegger's analysis of the 'essence' of human being (*Dasein), under the guise of what he called 'existence' (later written 'ek-sistence'), exerted a deep influence on Sartre and subsequent existentialists, but he insisted that such an application of his thought was utterly foreign to his intention. From the very beginning, he claimed, he had sought to understand the meaning of being, which allegedly had been overlooked by philosophers since the time of Plato. The analysis of 'existence' in *Being and Time* was merely a first attempt to approach the question through a phenomenological analysis of what Dasein experientially understands by this term in everyday life as being-in-the-world. In addition to existentiality, the analysis included such intriguing themes as thrownness, *facticity, *anxiety, being-unto-death and *authenticity, all integrated into a unity under the name *'care'. It is understandable how existentialist thinkers found such terminology a very tempting menu.

After 1930, the focus of attention shifted from Dasein to being itself, experienced as revealing itself in beings as beings, i.e., in making it possible for beings to manifest themselves as what they are. Accordingly, being is thought of as a process of non-concealment (*a-lethei-a*: privation of concealment), hence a process of both revealing and concealing. Understood thus, being reveals itself in many ways, e.g. in the epochs of history, in the creativity of art and especially in language. When being is thought of in the context of Heraclitus's *Logos*, it is interpreted as language in its very origins. Despite the obvious change in focus and tone from the project of *Being and Time*, Heidegger never disclaimed the earlier effort, declaring in the preface to the seventh edition that 'its path still remains a necessary one even today [well into the later period], if the question of being is to move our Dasein'.

Heidegger, M. [1927] (1996) *Being and Time*. Translated by J. Stambaugh. Albany: State University of New York Press.

W. R.

HELPLESSNESS State of powerlessness related to a failure to reach or give up unrealistic goals; it can also be a passive expression of unconscious rage.

See also: depression; introjection; oral sadism

Cooper, P. (2002) 'The pervasion of the object: depression and unitive experience'. *The Psychoanalytic Review* 89(3).

Coyne, J. (1986) *Essential Papers on Depression*. New York: New York University Press.

P. C.

HENDERSON, JOSEPH LEWIS (1902–) One of the leading Jungian analysts in the world for the past sixty years. He was born in Elko, Nevada, matriculated at Lawrenceville under Thornton Wilder, received his BA from Princeton in 1925 and met and began his analysis with *Jung in 1929. He graduated from St Bartholomew Medical School in London in 1938 and returned to New York where he began a private practice. In 1934 he married Helena Darwin Cornford of Cambridge; they have one daughter. In 1940 the Hendersons moved to San Francisco, where he became a co-founder of the Society of Jungian Analysts of Northern California. Throughout his work at the Mt Zion Clinic during the war, he was on friendly terms with many of the early Freudians in San Francisco. In addition, he was on the faculty of the Stanford Medical School where he taught until 1959.

In 1960 Henderson contributed a chapter entitled 'Ancient Myths and Modern Man' for Jung's *Man and His Symbols*. In 1967 he published *Thresholds of Initiation*, a classic work on the *archetype of initiation. In 1984 he published *Cultural Attitudes in Perspective*. He is the author of over two hundred articles, book and film reviews, and the author/editor of five books.

He has twice been president of the San Francisco Jung Institute and has served on numerous committees. He has also been actively involved in the promotion of a national archive of pictures and their psychological meaning – the Archive for Research in Archetypal Symbolism – serving at different times as national and honorary chairman. At the age of ninety-eight he continued to have an active private practice.

T. B. K.

HERMENEUTICS Originally indicative of that part of Christian theology concerned with the interpretation of Biblical texts, hermeneutics is now understood more generally as a method of interpreting, first, texts, and second, in large part due to the work of the philosopher Dilthey, the whole social, historical and psychological world. In existential-phenomenological analysis, hermeneutics becomes important because perception and interpretation are inextricably bound together. According to this perspective, human beings each experience the world from their own unique position in it, and none are able to divorce themselves from their experiential, relational and sociocultural position in order to act as a mirror to reflect the world.

*Heidegger provides an important example of the relevance of hermeneutic method in his approach to *Being. He argues that human beings are generally forgetful of their being: while it is certainly possible for us to experience the wonder and mystery of the fact that things exist, we are generally immersed in the business of our quotidian existence and do not think of it as something which is open to interpretation. Heidegger treats the world as a code or set of symbols. By approaching Being via the method of 'hermeneutical phenomenology' he returns it to us as meaningful and as of concern to us rather than as simply given.

Heidegger's use of hermeneutical interpretation can be contrasted with the more restricted notion of interpretation employed by traditional psychoanalysis. This has been described by Walrond-Skinner as 'a communication from therapist to patient designed to elucidate the unconscious meaning and repressed wishes which lie beneath his dreams, free associations, use of symbolism and/or feelings towards the therapist expressed through the transference'. Such reductive interpretation may lose the original experience of the client or patient. This can be contrasted with a hermeneutical phenomenological mode of interpretation which seeks to uncover the fuller meaning of the symbol, symptom or dream – a fuller meaning which can in Ricoeur's phrase 'be unfolded' by the mutual exploration of client and therapist.

Heidegger, M. [1927] (1962) *Being and Time*. Translated by J. Macquarrie and E. S. Robinson. New York: Harper & Row.
Ricoeur, P. (1974) *The Conflict of Interpretations*. Evanston, IL: Northwestern University Press.
Walrond-Skinner, S. (1986) *Dictionary of Psychotherapy*. London: Routledge & Kegan Paul.

S. P.

HETEROSEXUALITY For Lacan, subjection of the subject to *castration in a way which implies the attraction towards a subject of the opposite sex. It is the consequence of a libidinal organisation and of an object choice resulting from a process of identification. It is dependent on a logic that corresponds to the later stages of the *Oedipus complex, which culminate in the formation of the ego ideal.

A. I.

HILLMAN, JAMES (1926–) Best known as the originator of archetypal psychology, a post-Jungian school with an emphasis on the primacy of the imagination in psychic and cultural life, James Hillman trained in Zurich (1953–9) and later became the first Director of Studies at the Zurich Jung Institut (1959–69). He has written over twenty books and is one of the most original and prolific analysts to come out of the classical Jungian tradition. Early work focused on analyses of mythic and imaginal structures unconsciously informing analytic theory, psychopathology and clinical practice. Later publications shifted focus to cultural, civic and political concerns, extending the analysis of archetypal dimensions of human existence to cities, architecture, family, aging and everyday life.

P. K.

HISTORY The recovery of the patient's history was a goal of Freud's early treatment. Later, the emphasis was on how significant events of the past were revived in the *transference relationship. The *repetition compulsion and the dual drive theory meant that the patient would repeat everything of significance in the relationship with the analyst. The understanding of the past as it bears upon the present is vital. Clinically, this involves the recovery of the analysand's life-story from *infantile amnesia and *repression. According to Lacan, the aim of analysis involves a reconstruction of the subjective history of the analysand. He thus presents the axis of analytical work as one which links the present to the past – in opposition to forms of analytical technique that stress the here-and-now. Lacan subsumes under what he calls *ego-to-ego forms of technique those proposals for analytical technique which locate the analytical encounter primarily in the present. Where Freud had described the construction and reconstruction of history in his late work on *Moses and Monotheism*, Lacan develops this theme in the formulation that he gives to the analytical construction of knowledge, and its place in the transference.

J. B. / H. T.

HOLDING Used by Winnicott to describe the physical and emotional care (empathy) provided in health by a young infant's mother. Emphasising the necessity of actual good environmental care for psychological and psychosomatic development, Winnicott describes a state of early psychological unintegration in the baby, requiring a degree of sensitive maternal care he called 'holding' for the *integration of the ego and the establishment of psychosomatic existence, awareness of inside and outside, leading to an awareness of self and other, and eventually to the capacity to make *object-relationships. He describes the phases of *dependence as 'absolute', when the infant has no concept of maternal care, 'relative', with some awareness on the infant's part, and 'towards independence', when the infant has internalised both memories and techniques of care, with projection of needs. Development of personality, and sense of self, as characterised by Greenacre, also begin at this stage.

The characteristics of 'holding' are that it should reliably, and at first unnoticeably from the infant's point of view, meet physiological needs and protect from physiological insult. It should involve total bodily and emotional care, and adapt to the microscopic changes in the infant's state. The mother's *identification with her baby allows her this sensitivity, and Winnicott also points out that a mother who is so sensitive that such care is prolonged beyond the point at which her baby is capable of tolerating some frustration may be depriving her infant of needed frustration. He also states that the *splitting defence mechanisms together with *projection and *introjection described by *Klein, are a result of failure of early environmental provision.

Winnicott derives this understanding of early infantile needs results from the study of the *transference itself as it develops, and makes a parallel link to sensitivity in the care of the regressed patient by the analyst who provides the physical parameters of the analytic session, emphasising the quality of the analyst's attention. The term 'holding' is used by other analysts, notably *Bion, to describe the physical element (only) of child care. The term is also often confused with Bion's concept of *containment, belonging to a different developmental framework.

Bion, W. R. (1962) *Learning from Experience*. London: Heinemann.

Greenacre, P. [1958] (1971) 'Early physical determinants in the sense of identity' in P. Greenacre (ed.) *Emotional Growth*, New York: International Universities Press.

Klein, M. (1946) 'Notes on some schizoid mechanisms'. *International Journal of Psycho-Analysis* 27: 111.

Winnicott, D. W. [1960] (1965) 'On the theory of the parent-infant relationship' in *The Maturational Processes and the Facilitating Environment*. London: Hogarth Press.

J. Joh.

HOMOSEXUALITY Coined on the margins of science, combining a Greek (*homo*: same) and a Latin word (*sexus*: sex, gender), the term was first used publicly in 1869 in a plea for tolerance written by the Hungarian physician and poet Karoly Maria Benkert, who signed it as 'Kertbeny'. It marks the emergence of a movement in Germany (with Austria and Hungary) that nearly succeeded in making what the word described, love and sexuality between persons of the same sex, an acceptable alternative, before the Nazis wiped it out, from which it did not recover until the 1970s. A major figure in the movement was the sexologist and homosexual activist Magnus Hirschfeld (1868–1935), who was also a founding member of the Berlin Psychoanalytical Society in 1908 but resigned in 1911. Freud supported Hirschfeld's petition against Paragraph 175, which criminalised homosexuality in the German Penal Code, but he sharply criticised Hirschfeld's theory, for example, without mentioning his name, in Hirschfeld's essay on Leonardo.

The most persistent amongst the many contradictions in the scientific discourse on homosexuality has been that about its origin. Hirschfeld belonged to the camp of scholars who thought homosexuality was innate, constituting the third, 'intermediate' sex, marked by the somatic characters of the other sex, and he tried to prove it by measuring these.

Freud rejected this theory without simply subscribing to the opposite view. He believed there was a play of innate and acquired elements, of which the first, 'physical hermaphroditism', only sets the possibility – the bisexual disposition. There are always both sexual apparatuses present in humans, he reasoned, which makes their 'sex' on principle somewhat uncertain, even though one of them is usually atrophied; somatic characters of the other sex may thus occur in anybody, not only 'homosexuals', and they certainly do not occur in all of the latter.

Wholly independent from this disposition is the subject's attitude towards the *object, which may be *passive or *active – this is what 'feminine' and 'masculine' seemed to signify, respectively. The sex of the object – and with it, 'homosexuality' in the ordinary sense – is now only the third and quite coincidental element in the combinatory of the sexual instinct and the Oedipal triangle.

In the same year as 'homosexuality', a more technical term appeared in medical literature: 'contrary sexual feeling' or 'sexual inversion'. Freud used it extensively in the *Three Essays on the Theory of Sexuality* of 1905, and it enabled him later to postulate the 'inverted' (or 'negative') version of the *Oedipus complex. But no simple formula could cover the observed diversity, and it would not be inappropriate in Freud's view to talk about 'homosexualities'.

With men, *identification with the mother appeared frequently, the subject loving boys, his own images, as his mother had loved him. Giving up women and running away, he also remained faithful to her. As the father in such cases was often absent or weak, it would appear that the presence of a strong father guaranteed the heterosexual orientation. Not necessarily: in other cases the father was so dominating and demanding that the son assumed the passive attitude towards him and later reproduced it in relation to his other love-objects. Yet another possibility was the reversal of affect: under the demands of upbringing, the hostile and aggressive attitude based on jealousy against a rival (usually an older brother) was repressed and underwent a transformation in which the hated rival became the object of love – but Freud was uncertain whether this development ever resulted in exclusive homosexuality. He regularly added that not everybody under the same circumstances had become homosexual and that some cases would not fit any 'type'.

On the other hand, a remarkable presence of male characteristics was noted in homosexual women, though few cases were actually described. *Dora (a case of hysteria, 1905 [1901]) was called 'gynaecophilic' (but only in retrospect; Freud was convinced she dropped out of analysis because he had not realised she was homosexual), which meant that she assumed the active, masculine attitude towards other women. A much later case of homosexuality in a young woman (1920) was described analogously: she admired instead of letting herself be admired. This change of attitude, in effect a turn of the grammatical voice, indicates (in *Ferenczi's terms) a choice on the subject rather than an *object-choice. The same is implied by 'passive homosexuality' in men.

Freud drew some authority on the topic from his friendship with *Wilhelm Fliess. The recognition that their relationship was essentially love authorised Freud to conclude 'that everyone, even the most normal person, is capable of making a homosexual object-choice, and has done so at some time in his life, and either still adheres to it in his unconscious or else protects himself against it by vigorous counter-attitudes' (1910: 99, n. 2). And whence the urgency to assume these? Freud's invariable answer: from the pressures of social relations.

Not surprisingly after the initial problem with the concept, 'homosexuality' has an elusive status in the psychoanalytical theory of instincts. It is categorically not a special instinct, because the sex of the object is secondary to the constitution of the instinct. Instead, it is an instinctual organisation whose 'overt' or 'manifest' form, its actual practice, is distinguished from its 'latent' form, consisting of the tendencies that could only derive from an unconscious homosexual object-choice.

Again like a sexual instinct, homosexuality was found liable to *sublimation and *repression. Freud bowed to the contribution of manifest homosexuals to civilisation, but he especially praised 'sublimated homosexuality' as the basis of friendship, '*esprit de corps*', etc. In sublimation, the sexual act has been given up and substituted with a non-sexual aim. Repression is a different story: when unsuccessful (and it can never be wholly successful), the repressed fantasy will return 'from without', in the form of a *delusion. Judge Schreber's repressed 'passive homosexual' fantasy returned as his delusion that he was being transformed into a woman by God for His pleasure. The paranoiac contradicts his or her own 'wrong', repudiated love, and at the same time attempts to 'correct the mistake', to restore order. The process may engage considerable intellectual effort and take up elaborate scientific, legal, or religious forms.

Little new has been added to Freud's observations. Ferenczi preferred the etymologically more correct term 'homoerotic' and distinguished object homoerotics from subject homoerotics (transsexuals). *Klein's object relations theory enhanced the view that 'homosexuality' is a primary condition for women, because the mother is the first object; conversely, fixation to the father-object (the penis) is unavoidable not only for the girl but also for the boy who, envying the mother its possession, will at some point wish to take her place with the father.

As a normal but transient stage in sexual development, homosexuality remained an 'aberration', especially when exclusively practised (under Freud's bisexual rule, so was exclusive heterosexuality, but it was left alone 'for practical reasons'). It involved *inhibitions (fear or repulsion of the heterosexual act), *anal fixations (generating *obsessions/compulsions, feeding the 'passive trends' in men), and above all, *autoerotic slavery to *narcissism: 'manifest homosexuals . . . have . . . never emancipated themselves from the binding condition that the object of their choice must possess genitals like their own' (1911: 61).

Theoretically it seemed that homosexuality could be 'removed' under certain circumstances, but this theory has not been confirmed in clinical practice. Freud more than once realised that the ambition to 'cure homosexuality' was overoptimistic, if not oppressive. After all, what was pathological in the sense that it incapacitated the subject was not homosexuality as such but *anxiety and *projections that resulted from repression. The binding condition here was rather that the object of one's choice must *not* possess genitals like one's own, because it was illegal – at best unacceptable, threatening the loss of love, at worst an abomination to be exterminated.

Reinforcing this condition, the attempts to 'cure homosexuality' were unacceptable for *Lacan, who also disregarded the decision made by the Secret Committee of the *IPA in December 1921: arguing it would stigmatise psychoanalysis, should it be practised by known homosexuals who were seen by the general public as perpetrators of a 'repugnant crime', *Jones, who had himself been accused of sexual abuse, demanded they be barred from psychoanalytical ranks. With the support of *Abraham against *Rank, who opposed it vigorously, the motion succeeded and won even the votes of Ferenczi and Freud. *Anna Freud, who developed techniques of 'curing homosexuality', nevertheless campaigned against homosexuals in *training analysis. There was no written resolution, to avoid accusations of discrimination, and the decision has never been revoked. But it has not prevented homosexuals becoming analysts if they remain in the closet.

Freud, S. (1910) *Leonardo da Vinci and a Memory of his Childhood*. S. E. 9. London: Hogarth Press.

Freud, S. (1911) *Psycho-analytic Notes on an Autobiographical Account of a Case of Paranoia (Dementia paranoides)*. S. E. 12. London: Hogarth Press.

B. L.

HORNEY, KAREN (1885–1952) Between 1915, the year of her graduation from medical school, and 1952, the year of her death, Karen Horney wrote some hundred articles and six books. While teaching, supervising and working as a training analyst of the Berlin Psychoanalytic Institute, she wrote in the Freudian paradigm, although she raised pointed questions about Freud's beliefs on feminine psychology. In a series of seminal papers published in 1967 as *Feminine Psychology*, she presented cultural influences as an alternative to biological bases of development, and in the process, questioned the centrality of the *oedipal complex, the role of *penis envy in feminine development, and the origin of *masochism, and introduced such ideas as secondary penis envy, male narcissism, dread of woman, denial of the vagina, and envy of woman's capacity to bear children.

After she emigrated to the United States in 1932, to help Franz Alexander run the Chicago Psychoanalytic Institute, in the 1937 *Neurotic Personality of Our Time*, and the 1939 *New Ways in Psychoanalysis* Horney had become more outspoken in her theory of neurosis. She was strongly influenced by the writings of cultural anthropologists, and by her own observations on the impact of the North American milieu on character development. In her 1945 *Our Inner Conflicts* and her 1950 *Neurosis and Human Growth*, after she had founded the American Institute for Psychoanalysis in New York, Horney elaborated on a theory of the conflicted and split self. Accordingly, the self-structure is an outcome of the child's efforts to cope with the fragmenting human environment – a mixture of constructive and destructive forces – which forcefully impact on the child's inborn qualities (the bases of the real self). The self that gradually develops is a complex interaction of self-idealisations, self-hatreds, and entitlements, all in unconscious conflict with each other. These dynamically interacting aspects form a powerful and tenacious pride-system, striving to achieve a sense of unity, but instead, the pride-system brings about an enormous vertical split in the personality between the real self and the multiple aspects of the neurotic self.

The goal of Horneyan analysis is a fundamental change in these multiple intrapsychic and interpersonal conflicts and splits of the self; a basic shift from self-idealisation to self-realisation. While Horney strongly affirmed the Freudian concept of unconscious process, and therefore the importance of free associations, dreams, and the work with childhood memories; she saw the therapeutic relationship, which is the intersection of transferences and healthy forces of both participants of therapeutic dyad, as the main agent of change. The stance of a wholehearted analytic attitude towards all aspects of the self helps mobilise the constructive forces of the real self, a vigorous ally of the analytic process.

Horney, K. (1999) *The Therapeutic Process: Essays and Lectures*. B. Paris (ed). New Haven, CT: Yale University Press.

Paris, B. (2001) 'Karen Horney: A bibliography of her writings'. *The American Journal of Psychoanalysis* 61.

G. G.

HUMAN NATURE Human nature is a concept referring to the most characteristic features of people (individuals and groups) – their 'species being' – and includes whether or not (and to what extent) they are innately good or evil, whether they are moving progressively toward improvement or degeneration and the limits of hope for the future of humankind. Theories of human nature set out to explain what people are really like, their essence.

Freud described psychoanalysis as a theory of human nature, a method of investigation and a therapy. Psychoanalysis is often treated by historians and practitioners as almost *sui generis*, but for all its originality it is far from that. It takes up positions on age-old questions in philosophy and religion, and it has drawn on and made alliances with various schools of psychology.

Freud has often been called a pessimist, but if he is right about human nature, he is surely a realist, and it behoves us to know about the intermingling of good and evil which constitutes our natures. He said that 'man is a wolf to other men' and alluded to the Hobbesian 'war of all against all'. He considered that human nature is a mixture of positive, life-affirming impulses which he located in the concept of Eros, intermingled with aggressive, destructive and ultimately death-seeking ones which he called the Death wish or *Thanatos. He claimed that all of life and the entire history of civilisation essentially consists of the struggle between Eros and Thanatos. Klein says that the interaction of the life and death instincts governs all of life.

Freud located the origin of morality in an uprising at the dawn of history of the primal horde against the polymorphously perverse and rapacious sexuality of the patriarch. The brothers rose up against him and slew him and declared incest taboo. Freud took this taboo to be the foundation stone for all of morality and civilisation. Note that this means that our decent, forbearing and civilised selves are the result of the inhibition of self-indulgent and self-centred impulses, some of which are aggressive and violent.

Morality is inhibition, and we maintain it by diverting or sublimating aggressive and sexual energies into constructive channels. Keeping these base impulses under control uses up erotic energies and makes us unhappy and often ill. Civilisation and discontent are thereby inextricably linked. Neurosis is the price we pay for civilisation.

Freud was far from believing that our mind is at birth a blank sheet or *tabula rasa*. His conception of human development (extensively enhanced by Abraham) was based on a chronological scheme, the libido theory, which included definite stages linked to erogenous zones – mouth, anus, phallus, and genitals. Sexuality was present at a very early stage; Freud's belief in infantile sexuality was scandalous to some. The crucial developmental process he called the Oedipus complex, which he considered the centrepiece of psychoanalysis and life's most challenging developmental task. It occurred from about three and a half till five or six years of age.

The boy or girl has strong possessive and sexual feelings toward the mother (which in the case of the girl shift to the father) and has to come to terms with the relationship between the parents which, in part, excludes the child but from which he or she benefits. For a strict Freudian it is during this process that the conscience or super-ego is born, while Kleinians believe that the super-ego and guilt feelings are present much earlier and that the Oedipal dynamic has to be re-worked at crisis points throughout life ('Oedipal situation'). Note that we here have a theory of the origin of morality which in its original formulation is at bottom biological and developmental.

Later psychoanalysts, in particular *Fairbairn, *Klein and *Winnicott, de-emphasised the biological and stressed internal objects in the mind, rearranging the priorities of the terms of the theory so that libido is not seen as pleasure-seeking but object-seeking. Libido does not determine object relations; object relations determine libido.

As important as the libido theory and the Oedipus complex are for the psychoanalytic conception of human nature, the concept of the unconscious was even more basic. Many ideas of human nature are rationalistic and their supporters believe that we operate on the basis of reason which is accessible to conscious deliberation. For Freud reason is a small part of the mind. Most of mental life is not directly accessible to consciousness, though it can be glimpsed in various parapraxes (e.g. slips of the tongue, motivated forgetting), and dreams and can be fathomed by following the rule of free association in the psychoanalytic process. Psychoanalysis is unique in the extent to which it has attributed by far the largest part of human motivation to unconscious forces. There are no random irrationalities. We are not plunged from rationality to irrational chaos. Unconscious motivation is highly structured and based on the vicissitudes of the internal objects (parental and other figures) in our inner worlds. According to psychoanalysis, primitive unconscious forces loom very large in the determination of our thoughts and actions. Various figures in the psychoanalytic tradition emphasise this point to varying degrees. Anna Freud and her followers were less inclined to see people as inescapably in the grip of these primitive processes to such a large extent, while Klein and those influenced by her believe that the primitive is never transcended to any considerable degree. The unconscious is always moving back and forth between paranoid-schizoid and depressive positions, with the latter less persecuted and more desirable but still troubled. Many who have wanted to have a dynamic psychology but did not share Freud and his followers' emphasis on the role of aggression in human nature developed gentler views on these matters, for example humanistic psychology. Many within mainstream psychoanalysis have been reluctant or unwilling to place the emphasis on destructiveness, which Freud and Klein placed on the death wish or Thanatos.

Freud was an atheist and was very sceptical indeed about the prospects of utopian social and political philosophies such as socialism and anarchism. He rooted his objections in the theory of human nature developed in clinical and theoretical work in psychoanalysis. Even so, the movement he founded has considerable radical potential and some radical exponents such as Wilhelm Reich and Marcus, but, on the whole, psychoanalytic practitioners and much of psychoanalytic theory have been located within the established order of society.

Freud, S. (1930) *Civilisation and Its Discontents*. S. E. 21. London: Hogarth Press.

Freud, S. (1933) *The Question of a Weltanschauung*. S. E. 22. London: Hogarth Press.

Gay, P. (1988) *Freud: A Life for Our Time*. New York: Norton.

Klein, M. (1946) 'Notes on some schizoid mechanisms' in *The Writings of Melanie Klein*, Vol. 3. London: Hogarth Press.

Rieff, P. [1958] (1994) *Freud: The Mind of the Moralist*. Chicago: University of Chicago Press.

Young, R. (1994) *Mental Space*. London: Process Press.

R. M. Y.

HUNGARY The Hungarian Psychoanalytical Society was founded by Sándor *Ferenczi in 1913. He remained its president until his death in 1933. From 1908 articles on psychoanalysis were accepted both in the medical weekly (*Gyógyászat*), as well as in journals of modern literature (e.g. *Nyugat*). Ferenczi also published books, and gave public lectures in the circles of avant-garde intellectuals. Psychoanalysis became popular among the most progressive thinkers of Budapest's cultural life. By 1919 the Society was twenty members strong, and included Melanie Klein and Ernest Jones, both of them analysed by Ferenczi.

Ferenczi suggested establishing the International Psychoanalytical Society (IPA), in 1910. Budapest organised the Fifth International Congress of the IPA, where Ferenczi was elected President in 1918. Antal Tószegi-Freund offered a huge grant of money to establish a psychoanalytic publishing house, library and an outpatient clinic in Budapest. Because of the high inflation after World War I in Hungary, the library and publishing house was founded in Vienna in 1920.

In 1918 medical students asked that psychoanalysis be added to the medical curriculum. The University Council refused it several times, but in 1919 Ferenczi was named as the first professor of psychoanalysis in the world. Psychoanalysis was given departmental status in the Budapest Medical School and a building for a clinic. The Hungarian psychoanalytic movement could not isolate itself from the turmoil of national and world politics. Since this recognition came in the period of leftist revolution, the rightists, on gaining power, immediately cancelled the Department and Ferenczi's position. Restrictive laws forced by the right-wing dictatorship of Admiral Miklós Horthy, together with the first anti-Jewish political discrimination in twentieth-century Europe caused the first emigration. Many psychoanalysts and students emigrated, including: Sándor Radó, Alice and Michael *Balint, Franz Alexander (Berlin), Sándor Lóránd (New York), Theresa Benedek (Leipzig), and Margaret *Mahler (Vienna). Some of them returned to Hungary in the interwar years and continued their training with Ferenczi (e.g. the Balints). The Hungarian Society recovered. An

Outpatient Polyclinic was founded in 1931. By the 1930s Ferenczi's initiatives became the main thrust of the 'Budapest School': using countertransference, focusing on the early mother-child relationship, dealing with children, and consultation with the parents. István Hollós and Lilli Hajdu used psychoanalysis in psychiatry. Lajos Levy and Michael Balint worked in psychosomatic medicine. There were rich connections between psychoanalysis, and literature and art.

After the passage of anti-Jewish laws in Hungary from 1938, many analysts emigrated to the United States (Géza Róhem, Robert Bak, Sándor Feldmann etc.), Australia (Clara Lázár-Gerõ), or to Great Britain (Michael and Alice Balint). Rado, Alexander, Benedek and Mahler also left Europe and settled in the USA. Many of those who remained in Hungary, became victims of the Holocaust. Vienna, Budapest and Berlin have influenced the development of contemporary psychoanalysis in the USA and in London.

When the Communist Party came to power in 1948, psychoanalysis was proscribed by the Stalinist authorities on ideological grounds; the Society closed its doors in 1949. Some analysts continued their work underground: Endre Almásy, Lilli Hajdu, Imre Hermann, Lucy Liebermann, and Tibor Rajka. In 1975, after almost three decades of clandestine and limited possibilities for training, a Study Group was organised. In 1989 the Hungarian Society once more became a full member of the IPA.

J. Mes.

HYPERCATHEXIS A difficult and abstract term that generally refers to investing an idea with a large quantity of psychic energy. It can be understood more concretely and simply as the direction of a sufficient degree of attention to mental content which then results in its reaching consciousness.

Rapaport, D. (1960) 'The structure of psychoanalytic theory: a systematizing attempt'. *Psychological Issues* 6. Madison, CT: International Universities Press.

See also: attention; cathexis

E. Gil.

HYPNOTISM Freud's interest in the clinical phenomena of hypnotism in the 1880s related to the work of one particular research programme in (ideogenic) hypnotism which maintained that hypnotic effects were consequences of the functioning of complexes of ideas. Such complexes cause symptoms, and their functioning can be altered in the therapeutic relationship. Freud worked on and transformed a number of concepts in this field as he constructed his initial formulations of the conceptual outline of psychonalaysis.

See also: Charcot; negative hallucination

B. B.

HYSTERIA (FREUD) For two millennia hysteria was known as a conduct disorder that mimics diseases of the body, e.g. paralysis, in the absence of any demonstrable disease of the nervous system. Its manifestations were attributed to wanderings of the womb (*hystera*, in Greek) to different parts of the body. The uterine theory was belied by the observation that men can show the same 'paralyses'. Both sexes, explained Freud, suffer from *conversion*, i.e. a transformation of ideas and emotions into bodily 'symptoms'. But symptoms are medical, while hysteria is a social and psychological fact. Freud invented psychoanalysis while treating persons called hysterics. While correctly acknowledging that hysterics mainly suffer from reminiscences, Freud's real discovery is that the hysteric does not suffer from any paralysis, for he/she is an actor impersonating a paralytic. The hysteric is playing a game of charades, or dumb show, for himself/herself and other onlookers, using dramatic gestures as communications instead of making speeches. Hysterics can be partially or fully conscious of the inner desires, motives, and emotions.

Lothane, Z. (1997) 'Freud and the interpersonal'. *International Forum of Psychoanalysis* 6: 175–84.

Z. L.

HYSTERIA (FAIRBAIRN) A critical area of study since *Charcot and Janet, and a central focus of psychoanalytic study since *Breuer and *Freud's 1895 *Studies on Hysteria* described how mental states were converted into physical symptoms with the help of 'somatic compliance'. Fairbairn recognised that a bodily state was substituted for a personal problem so that the individual could ignore the internalised mental conflict. Fairbairn's formulation of hysteria was that excessively exciting and rejecting objects result in a *libidinal ego which is excessively craving and an *antilibidinal ego which excessively persecutory. The resulting excessive ego splitting led to bodily *dissociation. Fairbairn emphasises that hysteria is a defensive technique, which is a reaction to specific outer situations which are essentially traumatic to the individual concerned. Thus it is actual outer trauma which precipitates hysteria.

Fairbairn, W. R. D. [1954] (1994) 'Observations on hysterical states' in D. Scharff and E. Fairbairn Birtles (eds) *From Instinct to Self*, Vol. 1. Northvale, NJ: Jason Aronson.

E. F. B.

HYSTERIA (LACAN) A clinical type within the structure of neurosis characterised by the particular position that is taken up by the subject in the confrontation with *castration and *desire. The hysteric takes the place of the object of desire, in order to veil Imaginary castration. This Imaginary castration nevertheless remains manifest because the hysteric has been constituted in language, which implies a lack-in-being which in turn determines hysterical identification. Her strategy in the face of desire is to keep it unsatisfied. The type of symptomatology that she employs is that of conversion into an expression via the body. In the hysterical pantomime there is a predominance of intrigue and of the presence of the other woman. In this scenario the question ultimately relates to: 'what is a *woman?'

S. Ten.

I

ID One of three agencies present within the structural model of the personality, the 'Id' constitutes the *drive area. It is the place where the somatic drives find their psychic expression in the form of unconscious fantasies. From the *economic point of view, it is the source of psychic *energy. From the *dynamic point of view, it enters into conflict with the *'ego' which is a form of differentiation and by it with external reality and the *'super-ego'.

The structural unconscious belongs to the 'id'. It represents *psychic reality and is distinct from material reality which obeys the principles of the process of primary thought. The aim of psychoanalysis is to integrate parts of the 'id' into the structure of the 'ego'.

The use of the concept differs today in accordance with current thinking trends. Some people tend to reduce it to its biological origins and others, on the contrary, take it to represent a specific form of thought affected by its hallucinatory dimension. Some put the accent on the conflict between internal objects, others on the *object relations of which it is composed. Finally, some tend to deviate its use to the benefit of the concept of the self or to a reducing of the unconscious to language.

D. W.

IDEAL For a child the role of the ego ideal is given to the parents. With the resolution of the Oedipus complex and the establishment of the grade in the ego known as the super-ego, the parents' values are internalised and become the ideal by which the ego is judged. In narcissism, and in early development, the ego takes itself as the ideal (ideal ego). Everything good is ascribed to the self, while everything undesirable is projected onto others. Later, when infantile omnipotence has to submit the case of falling in love, the loved object becomes the ideal; in religion, the deity; and in the positive transference, the analyst.

J. A. Ber.

IDEAL EGO see **EGO IDEAL/IDEAL EGO**

IDEAL OBJECT In Fairbairn, the object to which the *central ego remains consciously attached after the rejecting and exciting internalised objects have been split off and repressed.

D. E. S.

IDEALISATION Freud defined idealisation as a process by which a loved one is aggrandised and overvalued, providing narcissistic value to the subject who feels elevated through the connection with the exalted love object. Melanie Klein emphasised the defensive function of idealisation in protecting the loved object against the subject's destructive impulses. For her, idealisation is one of the schizoid mechanisms, along with *splitting, *projective identification, *introjection and magic omnipotent *denial. The infant splits the object (breast) into an exaggeratedly good breast to defend against the anxiety originating from the persecutory object. Thus, idealisation goes hand in hand with persecutory fears from the bad object. Idealisation may also become instituted as a narcissistic defence, the aim of which is to sustain the wish that one's object can yield unlimited gratification and thereby provide the basis of the illusion of an inexhaustible and ever-bountiful breast.

In the *paranoid-schizoid position, the infant attempts to create this illusion for reasons of self-preservation. Unable to deal with more complicated feelings, the infantile ego uses primitive defences to simplify its world, for instance by maintaining that the good is all within and the bad is outside. Insofar as the infant needs to grow and mature, normal splitting and idealisation are necessary experiences. Alongside its need to believe in its own goodness and love, the infant's belief is in a loving object. If the external caretaking environment can support this ideal state of affairs, its object is also ideal. If this state is punctured because of a breakdown in environmental support, a sense of badness can intrude and by means of the defence of idealisation, these disturbing elements are displaced elsewhere. One reason for this differentiation stems from the infant's need for ideals, which is quite distinct from its need for omnipotence. An ideal object should never be perfect. In the instance of excessive *envy, ideal objects are attacked, leading to the perverse situation where bad objects are idealised and good objects devalued.

A. E. / G. Gor.

IDENTIFICATION (FREUD) Recognising oneself to be similar to another is without doubt the first form of expression of love directed at another. This recognition of *identity is never global, but can be expressed by one or two common characteristics which are judged to be significant. Identification is a form of representation which plays an important part in dreams and more generally in psychopathology. It also plays an important role in the construction of unconscious fantasies.

One can oppose hysterical and narcissistic identifications. The former is characterised by the fantasy of oneself being similar to the love object, or to an object similar to oneself, in the love relationship. Narcissistic identification is characterised by the fantasy that the other has become part of oneself. The object thus internalised no longer exists in external reality. Whilst the hysterical pathology is a good representation of the first form of identification, melancholic pathology well illustrates the second. In the two cases, identification is said to be secondary, in so much as it is at the service of love wishes, possibly tainted with *ambivalence.

Primary identification, in opposition to the two above, is sought for itself. It is present in the very first relationships of the infant with others. It is part of a fusion fantasy.

Numerous clinical forms of identification have been described. Identification with the aggressor is the expression of hate in reaction to the aggression factor. Concepts of projective and introjective identification refer, from a Kleinian point of view, to archaic perceptive processes of external reality, with projection or introjection of internal or external objects. Narcissistic identification is a model of identification by *introjection.

Projective identification leads to recognising in the other the aspects of oneself which have been expelled from the ego and which are now perceived in another.

For Lacan, that which Freud termed identification is an effect of language, that is, the constitution of a subject by the incorporation of signifiers. Different types of otherness correspond to different types of identification, three of which are found in Freud; the otherness of the Father (a mythical identification, according to Lacan, since it precedes any libidinal investment); the otherness of a primary trait of difference (identification with what Freud calls the unary trait – *Einziger Zug* – as the basis of the constitution of ideals); the otherness of the Imaginary other (narcissistic identification founded on the image of the body and on the experience of fellow beings); and the otherness of the object, in so far as the object is the cause of desire (a paradigmatic example of an identification with the *object is the relation of a melancholic subject to the lost object). The subject that psychoanalysis is concerned with is by definition an other and is therefore always taken for an other.

R. R. B. / D. W.

IDENTIFICATION, PRIMARY Primary identification in Freud refers to the mythical identification with the father, and with the overcoming of the state of primary narcissism. The primary, 'pre-oedipal' identification is to be conceived in opposition to the child's later 'turn to the father', and to the identification with the father which marks 'the resolution' of the Oedipus complex. Primary identification is closely related to oral incorporation.

E. B.

IDENTIFICATION WITH THE AGGRESSOR According to Freud, in normal development, the boy resolves Oedipal conflicts by relinquishing incestuous desire for the mother and his rivalrous hostile wishes toward the father. Instead of fighting the father, he 'joins him'. In identifying with, and internalising, the father's attitudes, an internal, potentially hostile and punitive critic – the *super-ego – replaces a formerly external critic.

Anna *Freud, who conceptualised the term as one combining introjection and projection – 'a preliminary phase of super-ego development and an intermediate stage in the development of paranoia' – regards identification with the aggressor as normal as long as it is employed in the ego's efforts to deal with anxiety objects, and as pathological when it is carried over into a person's love life. Identification with the aggressor is a general defence that also comes into play in other situations; it has frequently been reported that those held hostage for a long period of time often completely identify with their captors (the Stockholm syndrome).

See also: aggression; anxiety; defence; Oedipal complex; super-ego

Freud, Anna [1936] (1946) *The Ego and the Mechanisms of Defense*. New York: International Universities Press.

A. W. / M. Eag.

IDENTITY A consciously lived sense of one's self. This partly relies on the process of *identification, whereby one's subjectivity is elaborated in relation to the significant others who cross one's path. Not a concept explicitly found in classical psychoanalytic literature, identity is primarily a matter of social construction and positioning within society. It can also be seen as a more extreme version of identification involved in *projective identification and in *psychosis.

See also: logic; Matte Blanco

J. B.

IDEOGRAM According to Bion, in the non-psychotic personality, an image is formed as a symbol (row C on the *grid). In the psychotic personality, an ideogram is an image formed for the immediate repair of an ego damaged by excessive projective identification.

Bion, W. R. (1963) *Elements of Psychoanalysis*. London: Heinemann. Also in *Seven Servants*. New York: Jason Aronson, 1977.

S. A.

ILLNESS A term used by Freud to designate *neurosis or *psychosis; evidence of the repression of sexual drives. The choice of secondary gain from the symptom characterises the flight into neurosis. The impossibility of repression in psychosis leads the subject to construct substitute solutions, such as *delusion which, while maintaining his social existence, limits it.

J. D. M.

ILLUSION German philosopher Ludwig Feuerbach argued that the concrete sentient individual should be taken as the point of departure for all theorising. He put forward the thesis that *religion – the prototype of all illusion – results from suffering and *projection. When individuals suffer in their material existence, they project wish-fulfilling fantasies into the heavens in an attempt to alleviate that suffering. The consequence of Freud's Feuerbachian position is that religion and – with the notable exception of art – all forms of illusion can be reduced to false consciousness. Later analysts criticised Freud's theory of illusion for its failure to assign any intrinsic value to mythopoetic capacities. *Winnicott and Hans *Loewald, for example, have tried to rethink the entire subject in such a way that illusion is understood as essential to human well-being.

See also: Freud, influences on

J. Whi.

IMAGE According to Lacan, the (mirror) image constitutes a narcissistic ideal and an illusion for the subject. The image (or *imago) can be created when the subject sees itself as a body in a mirror or in the eye of the (m)other thereby constituting itself as a whole in a place where it is not. The image is also an ideal form for the ego of the subject: an *ideal ego.

R. R.

IMAGINARY The Imaginary is one of the three registers to which Lacan relegated all subjective experience, the other two being the *Symbolic and the *Real. It is founded on the constituting role of the *image in regard to the ego. One of Lacan's first papers, 'The *mirror stage', demonstrates how the Imaginary engenders a variety of dual relationships between the ego and its counterpart, identifications which invariably result in *misrecognitions of reality, erotic or aggressive reactions, and other subjective impasses. The analytic experience reintroduces the Symbolic order into the Imaginary identifications of the subject, producing a knotting with the Real of the symptom. In this experience however, the Imaginary mainly functions as a form of *resistance.

R. M. W.

IMAGERY Although Freud had encouraged a stream of visual pictures when he had employed hypnosis, his belief in the supremacy of rational, verbal processes had a profound effect on technique in psychoanalysis. *Ferenczi had asked patients what sort of image was occurring when he noticed various sorts of motor activity. *Fromm suggested asking for the picture of the father in order to get at more unconscious material. He also recommended asking the patient to imagine such events as receiving a phone call that he had died. *Sullivan had observed that people grow up with visual and auditory experiences that influence other experiences. Singer found that during the behavioural technique of systematic desensitisation the critical factor turns out to be the imagery used by the patient, not the hierarchy of frightening situations. Intensely vivid imagery that one cannot control, however, is obviously not helpful. Many interpersonalists have found that images get around defensiveness in a way that words do not because people have not learned so well to censor images. More connections are also made between what has been referred to traditionally as primary and secondary process and, more recently as symbolic and sub-symbolic processes. Asking traumatised patients about sensory recollections helps access memories of experiences patients may avoid consciously.

Levenson, citing the work of Reyher, has described psychoanalysis as not being about words at all. Curtis has described the powerful role of visual images in forming concepts of the ideal self especially since the development and widespread dissemination of photography, film, and television.

See also: body; dissociation; inquiry; interpersonal psychoanalysis; relational psychoanalysis; trauma

Fromm, E. (1955) *The Sane Society*. New York: Rinehart.

Levenson, E. A. (2003) 'On seeing what is said: visual aids to the psychoanalytic process'. *Contemporary Psychoanalysis* 39.

Rehyer, J. (1963) 'Free imagery: an uncovering process'. *Journal of Clinical Psychology* 19.

Singer, J. L. (1974) *Imagery and Daydreaming Methods in Psychotherapy and Behavior Modification*. New York: Academic Press.

Sullivan, H. S. (1956) *Clinical Studies in Psychiatry*. Oxford: Norton.

R. C.

IMAGINATION (JUNG) The meaning and use of images and imagination in *analytical psychology are inextricably bound up with the concept of the *imago, first introduced by Jung in his *Psychology of the Unconscious* of 1919.

Rather than adopt Freud's view of psychic images as representations of instincts (the id) or representations of 'objective' reality (the ego), Jung opted to follow Kant and approach imaging (*Einbildungskraft*) as a primary phenomenon, an autonomous activity of the psyche that constructs our sense of reality. In 1921 Jung wrote: 'The psyche creates reality every day. The only expression I can use for this activity is fantasy . . . Fantasy, therefore, seems to me the clearest expression of the specific activity of the psyche. It is, pre-eminently . . . (a) creative activity'. Psychic images, for Jung, actively participate in constructing the psyche's relation between self and other. Fantasy, he thought, fashions the bridge between the irreconcilable claims of subject and object. Jung's view of the role of images in bridging subject and object is similar to *Winnicott's 'third area' or transitional space, in which inner world fantasy and outer world reality are held together in one 'space' or 'area'. Jung's clinical hermeneutic is based on two levels of interpretation: the subjective and the objective. It is related to his view that psychic images bridge our intrapsychic and interpersonal experiences of reality. To approach the image on the subjective level refers the image to an intrapsychic aspect of the personality, while approaching the image on the objective level refers the image to an intersubjective experience. Therapeutic analysis strives to develop the capacity to successfully hold the tension between these two dimensions in relation to a person's psychic images.

P. K.

IMAGINATION (WINNICOTT) One of the characteristics of Winnicott's formulation of his ideas was his use of vernacular rather than jargon terms to elucidate his themes. While this greatly helped his communication with a wider audience outside psychoanalysis, it sometimes meant that he was in a dilemma when trying to use an ordinary word to convey a sophisticated psychoanalytic concept. Imagination is one such word. He uses it to convey a quality of aliveness in both the activity of the inner world, in the field of relationship and in the subject's expression of himself in work and other cultural activities. It is closely allied to *creativity and associated with the subject's achievement of healthy non-compliant living. Most often it occurs adjectivally, for example, describing 'imaginative mental life' or 'a child imaginatively involved with other people'. It could perhaps be compared with *Rycroft's more elaborate development in his reformulation of a theory of symbolism, where he makes a distinction between primary imagination and fancy. In Winnicott's thinking, imagination is that which powers dreaming, but not daydreaming, that is not fantasying, the latter having a static non-relating quality associated with rigid pattern of dissociation. Imagination is essentially to do with a mental activity which links the subject to his own vital energies and to persons in relationship.

Rycroft, C. (1968) 'Symbolism and its relationship to primary and secondary process' in *Imagination and Reality*. London: Hogarth.

Winnicott, D. W. (1971) 'Dreaming, fantasying and living' in *Playing and Reality*. London: Tavistock.

M. Twy.

IMAGINATION, ACTIVE A synthetic technique developed by Jung to utilise the creative imagination to effect personality change. It is a practical application of the *transcendent function. The process includes: making the ego receptive to unconscious material by inducing a lowered state of consciousness; allowing fantasy images free play; and actively engaging the images either during the initial flow of imagery or upon reflection. Active imagination is not defined by its product, i.e. writing or painting, but by the specific relationship of the ego to the unconscious material. In active imagination the ego must remain ethically and emotionally identical to the waking personality of the imaginer.

Cwik, A. (1995) 'Active imagination: synthesis in analysis' in M. Stein (ed.) *Jungian Analysis*. Chicago and LaSalle: Open Court.

A. Cwik

IMAGO Used in place of *'image' to emphasise that our images, especially of others, are generated subjectively. Originally introduced by Jung the use of this term also draws attention to the often noted fact that the child's images of parents are 'larger than life' and often do not seem to be rooted in reality. Freud adopted the word to describe the unconscious representation of an *object.

R. M. S.

IMPINGEMENT Impingement in Winnicott's thinking refers to anything in the infant's early development which seriously disrupts the infant's sense of 'going-on-being'. The good enough mother's ability to respond empathically to her infant's ego needs is emphasized as crucial to the establishment of ongoing healthy development. In the growth of the central or core self (the *true self) the infant is especially dependent on his mother to shield him from what Winnicott terms as impingements, because these are the cause of great anxiety. An impingement is anything that causes the infant to become a reactor to, rather than a spontaneous discoverer of, the environment. As a discoverer the infant can take on his environment at his own pace and in his own way, so the illusion that he is making his world is supported, and his sense of himself as going-on-being is not impaired. Faulty adaptation to the child induces an experience of impingement and threatens the sense of self which precipitates a withdrawal in an attempt to restore a sense of self. With the failure of good enough environmental provision there is the danger of producing a psychotic distortion of the relationship between the infant and his environment. Where relationships are felt to endanger the sense of self which can only be retrieved by withdrawal and isolation, a process is initiated which involves increasingly defensive organisation against the fear of recurrent impingements by the environment. Winnicott sees such impingements as challenging the infant's right to the illusion of omnipotence at a stage when the infant is not yet able to make a clear distinction between subjective experience and the 'not-me' environment.

Winnicott, D. W. (1958) 'Psychoses and child care' in *Collected Papers, Through Paediatrics to Psychoanalysis*. London: Tavistock.

M. Twy.

IMPOTENCE Persistent or recurrent inability to attain or maintain adequate erection until completion of sexual activity. If not the result of a general medical condition, such as diabetes mellitus, impotence is understood as the ego's avoidance of sexual pleasure. Sexual pleasure has become unconsciously associated with the danger of *castration and/or the dread of the super-ego.

Freud, S. (1926) *Inhibitions, Symptoms and Anxiety*. S. E. 20. London: Hogarth Press.

R. M.

INCEST The sexual involvement of children with their parents or siblings. In his early writings, Freud saw sexual abuse experienced in childhood as the primary cause of later neurosis. Later, he gave up this view, known as the *seduction theory, and posited the universal existence of incestuous fantasies and desires, culminating in the *Oedipus complex.

J. B.

INCEST (JUNG) Psychological incest is understood in *analytical psychology as a regressive fantasy formation which drives toward a return to the source, to the mother ground of pre-differentiated unconscious psychic totality. The positive potential is a dissolving back to the seed level of oneself that leads to rebirth. The negative ranges from being stuck in an infantile state of pre-separation to an adolescent love-death in its ground of origin. This source ground is the unconscious which precedes consciousness, includes consciousness, and continues after consciousness. The incest taboo supports the maturational process of the heroic bearing of the tension of the opposites which are inherent in the original unity of the psyche: they manifest here as the simultaneous pull back to the mother ground versus the maintaining and building of ego boundaries. The closed vessel, the womb, of the analytic container into which one regressively returns corresponds to and facilitates the internal circling of oneself through which the potential is the death of an insufficient adaptation for the sake of a making of self as container, generator, and generated. In the alchemical imagery cited by Jung the vessel of transformation and renewal is named uterus.

Jung, C. G. [1911–12] (1967) *Symbols of Transformation*. Princeton: Princeton University Press.
Jung, C. G. [1913] (1961) 'The theory of psychoanalysis' in *Freud and Psychoanalysis*. Princeton: Princeton University Press.
Jung, C. G. [1946] (1966) 'The psychology of the transference' in *The Practice of Psychotherapy*. Princeton: Princeton University Press.

Neumann, E. (1949). *The Origins and History of Consciousness*. Princeton: Princeton University Press.

L. M.

INCOMPATIBLE IDEAS Freud's earliest theories of *defence are based on the ego's distress at being unable to resolve the incompatibility of certain ideas or representations of the world. The ego, being unable to bear the pain generated by a representation that it finds incompatible with its official version of the world, typically chooses to repress this new version of things. Freud's German term for incompatible (*Unvertraeglich*) and for unbearable (*Unertraeglich*) differ by only one letter; in many other ways, these two terms, the one logical, incompatible – the other expressive of suffering – unbearable, are very close in Freud's early work.

See also: conflict

B. B.

INCORPORATION The primitive prototype of internalisation, based on fantasies of oral ingestion, taking an object into the body. A point of discussion has been whether all identifications are derivations of incorporation fantasies.

See also: identification

Freud, S. (1905) *Three Essays on the Theory of Sexuality*. S. E. 7. London: Hogarth Press.

M. M.

INDIA The historical context of Indian psychoanalysis is inseparable from the life and work of Girindrashekhar Bose. Born in 1886, Bose was the son of the chief minister of a small princely state in Bengal. Though he studied medicine and practised as a physician in Calcutta after graduating in 1910, Bose's intellectual passion was abnormal psychology. He learnt hypnosis and by 1914 he had begun to treat patients suffering from mental disorders by a technique closely akin, as he says, to Freud's original method, presumably the use of hypnosis, suggestion, pressing and questioning to recall memories and encourage associations. He had already developed some of his psychological ideas including the basic elements of his theory of opposite wishes, namely that for every expressed wish there is an opposite wish working in the unconscious, before the first English translations of Freud's writings reached Calcutta, and made a strong impact on the young Bengali doctor's mind.

The founders' meeting of the Indian Psychoanalytic Society took place in 1922 with Bose in the chair. In the same year, Bose wrote to Freud in Vienna. After expressing sentiments of respect and admiration for Freud's work, he informed him of the formation of the Indian society. Freud was pleased that his ideas had spread to such a far-off land and asked Bose to write to *Jones, then president of the *IPA, for membership of that body. Bose did so and the Indian Psychoanalytic Society with Bose as its first president, a position he was to hold till his death in 1953, became a fully-fledged member of the international psychoanalytic community. Although psychoanalysis attracted some academic and intellectual interest in the thirties and forties, mostly in Calcutta, the number of Indian analysts was still fifteen in 1945 when a second training centre, under the leadership of an Italian, Sevadio, was started in Bombay.

Well into the 1940s, the published work of Indian psychoanalysts shows a persisting concern with the illumination of Indian cultural phenomena as well as registering the 'Indian' aspects of their patients' mental life. Mythological allusions to Hindu gods and goddesses like Shiva or Kali regularly crop up in case history reports where the mythology appears to be used by the patient for both defensive and adaptive purposes.

By the 1950s, however, the interest in comparative and cultural aspects of mental life as well as the freshness of the papers written by the pioneering generation of Indian psychoanalysts was lost. Here I can only speculate on the reasons for this total divorce of Indian psychoanalysis from Indian culture and society. Psychoanalysis, in the sense of psychoanalytic concepts and theories which gain a large number of adherents among analysts at a given time and subsequently shape their clinical observations, is not completely independent of the historical situation of the analyst and his patients.

In India, the last forty years have witnessed an ever-increasing pace of modernisation and industrialisation. There has been a phenomenal rise of an urban, educated middle-class to which normally both the Indian analysts and their patients belong. A consequence of these related processes has been the uncritical acceptance by the middle class, itself the child of modernisation, of Western intellectual models with claims to universality. It is perhaps no accident that in Bombay, the most western of Indian cities, both geographically and spiritually, the younger generation of psychoanalysts are adherents of the Kleinian school which, with its focus on the universal aspects of the object – 'good' and 'bad' breasts, 'good' and 'bad' penises and so on – is perhaps the most universalistic of the many relational theories. But even in more traditional Calcutta on the eastern seacoast, any critical engagement with received theory has by now almost disappeared. Far from the intellectual founts of his professional existence, practising in a culture indifferent to psychoanalytic ideas and hostile to its view of the person, the Indian analyst is often tempted to idealise analytic 'gurus' in distant, presumably more receptive lands, and uncritically follow their models in the smallest detail.

S. K.

INDIFFERENCE Freud explored both the question of why we may be interested in some aspects of our reality and also that of why we may have no interest in others. Rather than seeing indifference as a contingent phenomenon, he took it to represent a deliberate reining in of libidinal investment. Freud saw indifference as a precursor to hate. It was the infant's first reaction to the outpouring of stimulation from the outside world; such manoeuvres aim ultimately at the avoidance of pain for the subject. Later in life it may serve as a defense against intense feelings of longing or destructiveness. As a manifestation of depression it suggests the absence of a wish to live.

See also: scotomisation

D. L.

INDIVIDUATION As a scientific term, this was used by *Jung to describe the core concept of his psychological theory. Jung asserted very early in his career that life unfolded in a purposive way but only later named this process 'individuation', first using the term in 1912 to denote separation from the mother and ultimately in 1921 to designate an evolved individuality and the dynamics governing its formation. Jung reconceived commonplace individuality as individualism, a selection of idiosyncratic traits that passes for uniqueness. In contrast, he defined individuation as bringing together all conscious and unconscious contents in their multiple aspects – biological, social, cultural, psychological, and spiritual.

Individuation, as a process, denotes a succession of differentiations and articulations of conscious identity from a timeless background of predispositions of humankind – the *collective unconscious. The *transcendent function mediates between consciousness and the collective unconscious in such a way that the aware individual admits of a larger personality than can be known from conscious attention alone. One-sided attitudes and viewpoints become balanced and *transformed through the integration of *symbols and their particular emotional and behavioural concomitants.

Jung postulates imperatives that every person encounters in the process of individuation. On the worldly side, there are issues of material survival in society, responsibilities of citizenship, and relationships to others. On the inner psychological side, each person must minimally reckon with destructive tendencies – the *shadow; attitudes towards elemental parenting figures – the mother and father *archetypes; and psychological contrasexual identity – *anima/animus. The demands are multitudinous, morally challenging, and threatening to established life patterns, and they mostly require a lifetime of often painful and usually hard introspective work and discipline. Since the unconscious can never be fully known or realised, individuation is never complete. Individuation is an ethical statement about the proper goal of all life: namely, the unfolding of what one was meant to be. The goal of individuation is the actualisation of a whole and unique *Self which is simultaneously like and unlike that of everyone else. The process of individuation can be seen either as natural homeostatic activity at any age, wending consciously or unconsciously towards Self realisation, or as a process more driven by conscious will, often seemingly natural as in moral law, and beneficially facilitated by synthetic analysis.

Individuation invites charges of teleology, top down causation, and vitalism, all of which offend scientific rules of causation. Jung never successfully countered these charges. Ironically enough, it is modern science itself that has been affirming, for the non-linear mathematics of chaos and complexity theory allows for the emergence of original but predictably similar creations wherever complex multiple interactions occur. Hence, the principle of individuation seems part and parcel of all life activity.

Clarke, J. J. (1992) *In Search of Jung*. London: Routledge.

Jung, C. G. [1939] (1968) 'Conscious, unconscious, and individuation' in *The Archetypes and The Collective Unconscious*. Princeton: Princeton University Press.

Nagy, M. (1991) *Philosophical Issues in the Psychology of C. G. Jung*. Albany: State University of New York Press.

D. T.

INFANT OBSERVATION Early observations by Freud and Melanie Klein of babies and young children focused on theoretical implications of their behaviour; *Winnicott described the use of observation in a controlled setting as a diagnostic tool. The value and limitations of behavioural observations as a means of testing theoretical inferences continues to be debated in the context of contemporary interest in the integration of psychoanalysis and child development research. *Bick developed the method of infant observation as a component of psychoanalytic training; it is now an essential part of training in psychoanalysis and psychotherapy throughout the world. The student pays weekly visits of an hour each to a baby in a family setting, and writes detailed notes focusing on his or her own responses as well as on the behaviour of the baby and other family members. The discussion of these notes in a weekly seminar supports the student in learning about emotional development, in encountering powerful primitive feelings and in developing the capacity to use the *countertransference as a source of information. Considering how to maintain the friendly detachment that is an essential aspect of the role of observer, in the absence of guidance from recognised codes of behaviour which apply in clinical settings, can prove of great value in thinking about issues of clinical technique. Apart from its importance in the training of psychotherapists, infant observation is increasingly becoming an area of research in its own right. Questions investigated include the baby's experience *in utero* and the issue of continuity with post-birth development; the implications of work with premature babies for theories of mental development; and the development of the body image. In therapeutic applications of infant observation, the observable benefits of the method are harnessed in the service of early intervention. The *International Journal of Infant Observation and its Applications* serves as a forum for articles concerned with all aspects of infant observation.

See also: dyspraxia

Bick, E. (1964) 'Notes on infant observation in psychoanalytic training'. *International Journal of Psycho-Analysis* 45: 558–66.
Lacroix, M.-B. and Monmayrant, M. (eds) (1995) *Les Liens d'Emerveillement: L'Observation des Nourrissons selon Esther Bick et ses Applications.* Ramonville-Saint-Agne: Eres.
Miller, L., Rustin, M. E., Rustin, M. J. and Shuttleworth, J. (eds) (1989) *Closely Observed Infants.* London: Duckworth.
Negri, R. (1994) *The Newborn in the Intensive Care Unit.* London: Karnac Books.
Piontelli, A. (1992) *From Foetus to Child.* The New Library of Psychoanalysis. London and New York: Tavistock/Routledge.
Reid, S. (ed.) (1997) *Developments in Infant Observation: The Tavistock Model.* London and New York: Routledge.

M. Rho.

INFANTILE AMNESIA see AMNESIA, INFANTILE

INFANTILE SEXUALITY Freud recognised the significance of sexuality early in the child's development. Infantile sexuality was not exclusively located in the genitals. Rather, the child was polymorphously perverse, meaning that the child's sexuality was located in different parts of the body and that their stimulation provided gratification. Freud discussed the various psychosexual stages and their erogenous zones (*oral, *anal, *phallic) as offering sexual satisfaction. The entire surface of the skin was also conceived of as an erotogenic zone. The paired component sexual impulses such as sadism-masochism and voyeurism-exhibitionism are also part of infantile sexuality. All these features in adult life might be thought of as fore *pleasure.

Freud, S. [1924] (1925) *An Autobiographical Study.* S. E. 20. London: Hogarth Press.

D. K. S.

INFINITE A concept suggesting great quantity, first formalised by mathematician Georg Cantor (1845–1918). *Matte Blanco has exploited Cantor's ideas for psychoanalysis in unusual ways. The sequence of counting numbers is clearly infinite, for if we take 1, 2, 3, . . ., n, n + 1, there is always a greater number than the one already reached. Suppose we now correlate or map each number onto its double – we correlate 1 with 2, 2 with 4, 3 with 6, 4 with 8, and so on. Intuitively, the part of the counting numbers consisting of the doubled or even numbers is a smaller part of the whole sequence of numbers which, after all, also include the odd numbers. So common sense tells us there are twice as many numbers as doubles; that is: the part (even numbers) is smaller than the whole (all numbers, odd and even). In set (or class) theory we say two sets are the same size if we can establish a one-one correlation between them and here we can actually do this, for every counting number is mapped one-one on to its double, and conversely. Therefore, in Cantor's theory a part of the counting numbers is equivalent to the whole set of counting numbers. Matte Blanco links this idea to equivalence of whole and *part objects. Surprisingly, Cantor also shows the class of all subclasses of the whole numbers is larger than the (already) infinite class of whole numbers. He therefore shows how there can be 'larger' and 'smaller' infinities.

Charraud, N. (1994) *Infini et Inconscient.* Paris: Anthropos.
Dauben, J. W. (1979) *Georg Cantor: His Mathematics and Philosophy of the Infinite.* Cambridge, MA: Harvard University Press.
Matte Blanco, I. (1975) *The Unconscious as Infinite Sets.* London: Duckworth.

R. M. S.

INFLATION An attitudinal distortion of the ego, manifesting as either a puffed-up, megalomaniacal sense of God-likeness, all-powerfulness, or all-knowingness (positive inflation) or a sense of absolute worthlessness and inferiority (negative inflation). Inflation arises from the ego's mistaken identification with *archetypal images of the *collective unconscious (e.g. the Magician, the Wise Man, the Fool, the *puer aeternus*). Dissolution of this distorted attitude comes about through the ego's separation of personal contents from collective and universal ones. Jung was especially fond of offering Goethe's *Faust* and *Nietzsche's *Zarathustra* as literary/philosophical exemplars of the consequence of dangerous psychic inflation.

Jung, C. G. [1953] (1966) *Two Essays on Analytical Psychology*. Princeton: Princeton University Press.

J. Mar.

INHIBITION A process is inhibited if it is 'switched off' by the operation of some other process. For example, fear can inhibit sexual desire. Inhibition is usually carried out by the *ego or *super-ego; the inhibited process is usually an instinctual impulse. Neuroses are regarded as inhibitions in the development of the libido and thus inhibition can be seen as a *symptom.

See also: compromise formation; neurosis

Freud, S. (1926) *Inhibitions, Symptoms and Anxiety*. S. E. 20. London: Hogarth Press.

K. L.

INNENWELT *Umwelt* is a term used in psychology to designate an individual's subjectively significant surroundings. The *innenwelt* is correspondingly given structure by introjections from this *umwelt*. Lacan finds that the gap represented by the unconscious upsets the correlation between *innenwelt* and *umwelt*, thereby subverting the inner/outer metaphor often used for the psyche.

B. O. D.

INSISTENCE Insistence is the mark of *conflict, or the presence of the opposite idea in the unconscious. In *Hamlet* this knowledge of psychic functioning is expressed in the famous line, 'The lady doth protest too much, methinks'. The *reaction formation observed in obsessive conditions is an insistence on the opposite of what is repressed.

J. A. Ber.

INQUIRY; DETAILED INQUIRY A unique technique of *interpersonal psychoanalysis in which the analyst actively asks questions in order to facilitate the patient's articulation of experience. Whereas the traditional model suggests that once repression is lifted a well-formed thought or experience can be exposed, *Sullivan perceived experiences as often *unformulated (pre-symbolic, non-representational) due to the intensity of anxiety. Inquiry would help the patient mentalise, give representation to these previously diffuse experiences. Asking questions and being curious with the patient was seen by Sullivan as a necessary correction to the formulaic, at times, highly theoretical interpretations he observed in the 1930s and 40s. The focus of inquiry also broadens the analytic investigation to include not simply the patients' representational world of affect and *imagery but also the interpersonal and observable behaviours – attitudes, manner of speech, etc. Though this technique has been criticised as superficial, the inquiry into what appears to be mundane often leads to transferential, conflictual experience. Levenson emphasises that the use of inquiry is an 'indirect approach . . . without any dynamic formulation in mind . . . [unlike] a directed inquiry [which leads] the respondent to some inevitable conclusion . . . The function of a detailed inquiry, then, is not to construct a veridical or instrumentally useful narrative about the patient's life . . . It is to deconstruct the story, locate the omissions and investigate them.'

Cooper, A. (1995) 'The detailed inquiry' in M. Lionells, J. Fiscalini, C. Mann and D. Stern (eds) *Handbook of Interpersonal Psychoanalysis*. Hillsdale, NJ: The Analytic Press.
Evans, F. B. (1996) *Harry Stack Sullivan, Interpersonal theory and psychotherapy*. New York: Routledge.
Levenson, E. (1988) 'The pursuit of the particular'. *Contemporary Psychoanalysis* 24.
Levenson, E. (1996) 'A monopedal presentation of interpersonal psychoanalysis'. *Review of Interpersonal Psychoanalysis*. New York: W. A. White Institute.
Moses, I. (1992) 'The analyst's questions: resistance to asking questions'. *Contemporary Psychoanalysis* 28.
Sullivan, H. (1954) *The Psychiatric Interview*. New York: Norton.

I. M.

INTEGRATION/UNINTEGRATION/DISINTEGRATION In general Winnicott relates the successful formulation of character to the process of integration and sees it as a manifestation of a maturational trend. He stresses that integration includes the concept of *time, and that disorder of character is linked with disorder of ego structure. In terms of the development of the infant ego Winnicott gathers the various trends in maturation under the term integration. As in Freud's theory Winnicott postulates that the ego is originally a body ego but he stresses that healthy development depends on the person of the infant being linked up with bodily functions, and with the skin as a boundary between subjective experience and the outer environment. He uses the term 'personalisation' to denote this process, contrasting this with *'depersonalisation' which denotes a lack of a sense of connectedness between ego and the body. Integration is achievable with holding by the environment, and emerges out of the state of primary* narcissism. Ego-coverage is provided by the good enough mother and such coverage is vital for the integration of the infant ego in the face of what Winnicott describes as unthinkable anxieties. These he classifies as follows: going to pieces; falling for ever; loss of relationship to the infant's own body; and, loss of a sense of orientation. These are recognisable as the components of psychotic anxiety states in adult psychiatric illness, especially in schizophrenia.

Winnicott describes a state of unintegration as a state of relaxation in the infant in which there is no need to integrate, at a point where the mother's ego-coverage and supportive function can be taken for granted. Unintegration refers to unexcited states of being in the infant where he is free from the excitation of need or any *impingement.

Disintegration is delineated by Winnicott as a sophisticated defence, which constitutes an 'active production' on the part of the infant, against unintegration. When there has been a failure of maternal ego support, it is not safe for the infant to allow unintegration for he is liable to be overwhelmed by one or more of the varieties of unthinkable anxiety referred to above. The infant in a state of absolute dependence and failed by the environment in its role as protector from these anxieties constructs the defence of disintegration. This is in itself an extreme manoeuvre but Winnicott sees it as a product of the infant's psyche, separate from the environment and therefore lying within the infant's omnipotent control. In terms of psychoanalytic treatment, he regards this state when present in later life as analysable.

Winnicott, D. W. (1965) 'Ego integration in child development' in *Maturational Processes and the Facilitating Environment*. London: Hogarth Press.

M. Twy.

INTELLECTUALISATION In *ego psychology, this is both a defence mechanism of the ego, averting anxiety caused by instinctual pressure, and an adaptive coping mechanism serving a reality function. Can be understood as a higher-level version of *isolation of affect.

See also: defence

Freud, A. (1966) *The Ego and the Mechanisms of Defense*. New York: International Universities Press.

M. M.

INTENTIONALITY The cardinal principle of phenomenology, the concept of intentionality originated with the Scholastics in the medieval period and was resurrected by Brentano in the nineteenth century which in turn influenced Husserl's conception of phenomenology. Each of the major phenomenological philosophers who were inspired by Husserl differ significantly in their respective conceptions of it. Generally, intentionality represents an alternative to the representational theory of consciousness, which holds that reality cannot be grasped directly because it is only available to the subject through perceptions of reality that are 'represented' in the mind. Husserl countered that consciousness is not 'in' the mind but rather conscious-of-something other than itself (the intentional object), whether the object in question is an actual substance or a figment of imagination, so that the question of the 'realness' of one's perceptions is bracketed. Thus the phenomenological method treats the world neither as a construct of the subject nor as existing independently of the subject, relying instead on the description of phenomena as they are given to consciousness in their immediacy. According to Husserl, phenomenology is not concerned with the scientific study of objects, nor is it a solipsism devoted solely to the subject; rather, it is a science of experience that neither concentrates exclusively on the object or the subject of experience but on the point of contact where being and consciousness meet. Hence consciousness is viewed as intentional because it is directed towards objects that exist in an intentionally constituted world. Put simply, consciousness does not exist without an object of consciousness; thus there is no such thing as empty consciousness or a receptacle of consciousness 'in' which objects may collect. This conception of intentionality is complementary to recent trends in psychoanalysis that emphasise the relational and object-seeking components of experience, but without Husserl's painstaking critique concerning the nature of experience itself.

*Heidegger retains the concept of intentionality in his early work (*Being and Time*) but rejects Husserl's depiction of it as 'object dependent'. Heidegger observes that we do not actually experience ourselves as being strictly conscious 'of' an object because objects already exist in our world before we are conscious of them, so consciousness cannot serve as the foundation for my relationship with the world, as Husserl insists. Rather, my experience is that of being thrown into a situation that overwhelms me with a repertoire of impressions and sensations, none of which can be isolated from the others in the fashion that Husserl's phenomenological method promises. In Heidegger's modification of intentionality, he posits it, not as a vehicle of consciousness, but as my ontological embeddedness in the world with others, characterised by an ever present sense of concern (*Sorge*) and foreboding. In other words, I do not establish a connection with the world by intending objects in it; I am already part and parcel of the world before I endeavour to take stock of it, so my consciousness of objects is always one step behind my engagement with it. This distinction has enormous implications about the role knowledge plays in experience. In Husserl, the task of phenomenology is to examine the objects in my world whereas, for Heidegger, the task is to make myself at home in the world by being with it, so that the question of consciousness itself becomes superfluous. Thus Heidegger's conception of phenomenology (and the role intentionality plays in it) conceives it as a form of therapy, whereas for Husserl it is strictly a mode of investigation whose ultimate purpose is to apprehend reality, a task that Heidegger dismisses as irrelevant to the primacy of being. Heidegger's thesis inspired the various schools of existential analysis that followed in Freud's wake, due to his emphasis on the respective roles of anxiety and equanimity in everyday living, and his project of reclaiming one's selfhood from the relentless forces of social convention, an aspect of his philosophy that distinguishes it from contemporary relational perspectives.

*Sartre both agrees and disagrees with Husserl and Heidegger in his interpretation of intentionality. He agrees with Husserl that intentionality is rooted in consciousness but rejects its 'constituting' function as well as Husserl's claim that consciousness is a product of the ego, problems that Sartre devoted an early work to (*The Transcendence of the Ego*). For Sartre intentionality is a structure of my being in the world and is prior to my capacity to determine my subjective role in it, a position that owes much to Heidegger, though Sartre rejects Heidegger's primacy of being-with-others.

Hence Sartre rejects Husserl's 'ego-centric' version of intentionality as well as Heidegger's 'world-centric' interpretation of it, and posits in their place a conception of intentionality that focuses on my coming-into-awareness of the objects in my world that are disclosed to me by my solitary gaze.

Whereas Heidegger views intentionality as a mode of becoming oneself in the context of being with others, Sartre sees the human predicament in terms of the isolation one feels as a consequence of being rooted in irresolvable conflict with others, an important theme in Sartre's novels.

Like Sartre, Merleau-Ponty combines elements of Husserl's and Heidegger's respective positions, and is perhaps more faithful to them than was Sartre. Unlike Heidegger, who situates human existence in the 'worldliness of the world', Merleau-Ponty locates intentionality in the body. Thus the individual's perspective is located in a spatial orientation that is necessarily unique to each person. Moreover, consciousness is conceived as 'bodily-consciousness', a theme that Merleau-Ponty demonstrates brilliantly in his early work (*Phenomenology of Perception*). Unlike Husserl and Heidegger, who give so much weight to consciousness and being, respectively, Merleau-Ponty reinterprets the conventional understanding of perception by making it not antithetical to rationality, but the source of consciousness and experience alike, fusing the three into one. Like Husserl, Heidegger, and Sartre before him, Merleau-Ponty was intent on solving the mind/body dilemma that was inherited from Descartes; in Merleau-Ponty's case, there is no mind/body split to solve because the mind and body are 'intertwined' and inseparable, a notion that is consistent with certain schools of Buddhism.

These distinctions are necessarily over-simplifications of theses that are both complicated and difficult to explain, but serve to show the central importance that intentionality plays in phenomenology. The inherently technical and philosophical senses of the term should not be confused with the common sense understanding of 'intention' or the psychoanalytic notion of unconscious 'motive' or 'gain.' Intentionality is not a psychological concept of motivation but a philosophical category that addresses my relationship with the world and, hence, others. More recently, the French psychoanalyst, Jacques Lacan, has employed intentionality but in ways that are fundamentally alien to phenomenology. Moreover, the concept of intentionality is complementary to another important phenomenological concept, intersubjectivity, which plays a central role in Husserl's, Heidegger's, Sartre's, and Merleau-Ponty's respective philosophies. The term intersubjectivity has also insinuated its way into contemporary psychoanalytic literature but, again, in a manner that is inconsistent with the way phenomenologists typically employ it.

See also: intersubjectivity; phenomenology/phenomenological method

Mohanty, J. N. (1972) *The Concept of Intentionality*. St Louis: Warren Green, Inc.

Zahavi, D. (2001) *Husserl and Transcendental Intersubjectivity*. Athens, OH: Ohio University Press.

M. G. T.

INTERMEDIATE IDEA An idea which is a link in the chain of associations between the conscious and the unconscious. Intermediate ideas resembling compromises are constructed by use of *condensation, as in *dreams, *slips of the tongue and jokes.

See also: verbal bridge

J. A. Ber.

INTERNAL OBJECT Even though the concept of 'internal objects' was present in Freud's writings, it was Klein who developed it and made it central to her theory of psychic functioning. Klein drew from both Freud's theory of identification in 'Mourning and Melancholia' and from *Abraham's study of the stages of the libido where he describes the incorporation of a part of the object in the anal sadistic stage.

Kleinian theory is both a *drive and an *object relations theory. The concept of 'internal objects' has to be thought of in the context of its interaction with other main hypotheses, such as a theory of early mental functioning which formulates the existence of an ego capable of perceiving anxiety; the development by the ego of primitive defence mechanisms such as *projection and *introjection; and, the hypothesis of *unconscious phantasy and the theory of positions. The ego is present and active from the beginning of life and establishes relations with objects from the first contacts with the external world. Drives (or instincts) are inherently attached to objects, and according to Klein, the workings of the life and death drives include their attachment to objects. The infant projects its own aggression and love prototypically into the mother's breast and introjects a phantastically-distorted picture of the real object upon which it is based.

The concept of 'internal objects' can be described from two different perspectives: as an unconscious phantasy of containing either a friendly or hostile being having an intention and an independent life of its own (this was called by Baranger a 'phenomenological' dimension); and, as playing an integral part in the development of the ego and super-ego, that is, structuring the agencies of the personality (the 'good' breast forms, according to Klein, the core of the ego). The vicissitudes undergone by the internal objects run parallel to what happens to the ego. While in the *paranoid-schizoid position there is a split in the ego and in the object (*part objects, *good and *bad objects), there is a movement towards integration of both the ego and the internal objects in the *depressive position where internalised objects will approximate more closely to reality.

Abraham, K. [1924] (1942) 'A short study of the development of the libido, viewed in the light of mental disorders' in E. Jones (ed.) *Selected Papers of Karl Abraham*. London: Hogarth Press, 418–99.

Baranger, W. (1980) 'Validez del concepto de objeto en la obra de Melanie Klein' in *Aportaciones al Concepto de Objeto en psicoanalisis.* Buenos Aires: Amorrortu.

Bianchedi, E. de et al. (1984) 'Beyond Freudian metapsychology – the metapsychological points of view of the Kleinian school'. *International Journal of Psychoanalysis* 65: 389–98.

Bronstein, C. (2001) 'What are internal objects?' in *Kleinian Theory: A Contemporary Perspective.* London: Whurr.

Freud, S. (1917) *Mourning and Melancholia*. S. E. 14. London: Hogarth Press.

Klein, M. [1935] (1985) 'A contribution to the psychogenesis of manic-depressive states' in *The Writings of Melanie Klein Vol I: Love, Guilt and Reparation and Other Works 1921–1945*. London: Hogarth Press, 262–89.

C. Bro.

INTERNAL OBJECT (FAIRBAIRN) For Fairbairn, the part of the ego formed through identification with an external object. The internal object is part of the ego and is capable of processing and initiating activity.

See also: endopsychic structure; object (Klein)

E. F. B. / D. E. S.

INTERNAL REALITY The subjective experience one perceives as true without, or in defiance of, objective proof from sources such as sense perceptions, commonly accepted fact or agreement from others. Mitchell claims that internal reality does not encompass all inner life, but is limited to phantasy. Later writers appear to use *psychical reality when referring to Freud's ideas and internal reality when elaborating other theories, but this distinction is not consistent. The Jungian, Stein, equated inner reality with the soul.

Klein, M. (1986) *The Selected Works of Melanie Klein*. J. Mitchell (ed.). London: Hogarth Press.
Stein, R. (1998) *The Betrayal of the Soul in Psychotherapy*. Woodstock, CT: Spring Journal Inc.

S. T.

INTERNAL SABOTEUR Fairbairn's original name for the part of the ego attached to the *rejecting object, the self-defeating part of the self.

See also: antilibidinal ego

E. F. B. / D. E. S.

INTERNAL WORLD (FAIRBAIRN) Fairbairn's inner world is the interactive dynamic world of *endopsychic structure which is modelled on interpersonal relationships experienced in external reality. However, the internal world is not a carbon copy of actual experience, but is modified by an infant's limited capacity for understanding, by the biases of previous experience, by the developmental stage concerns at the times of internalisation of experience, and by social influence on the child's understanding. The degree of *splitting and *repression or dissociation depends upon the quality of early experience and the mediating effects of later personal interactions and growth. Through the structures of the inner world, the past is active in the present. But memory is not based primarily on *fantasy, but on lived experience.

See also: dreams

E. F. B. / D. E. S.

INTERNAL WORLD, CLOSED SYSTEM OF (FAIRBAIRN) This refers to an endopsychic situation in which excessive ego-splitting has occurred during development, due to particularly unsatisfying childhood experiences. Therefore constellations of repressed object relationships exist which are excessively rigid and resistant to change, and which the person attempts to keep intact, uninfluenced by external objects. Fairbairn believed that the job of the analyst is to breach the defences of the closed system and to mediate acceptance of outer reality.

Fairbairn, W. R. D [1956] (1994) 'A critical evaluation of certain basic psychoanalysis conceptions' in D. Scharff and E. Fairbairn Birtles (eds) *From Instinct to Self*, Vol. 1. Northvale, NJ: Jason Aronson.
Fairbairn, W. R. D. [1958] (1994) 'The nature and aims of psychoanalytic treatment' in P. Scharff and E. Fairbairn Birtles (eds) *From Instinct to Self*, Vol. 1. Northvale, NJ: Jason Aronson.

E. F. B. / D. E. S.

INTERNATIONAL ASSOCIATION FOR ANALYTICAL PSYCHOLOGY (IAAP) Jung had a decidedly ambivalent attitude towards organisations. As an ambitious young psychiatrist, he was elected the first president of the newly founded International Psychoanalytic Association (IPA) in 1909, a position he held for four years until the breakdown of his relationship with Freud. The only other time he became active in professional organisations was during the 1930s, when he reluctantly took on the presidency of the International Medical Society for Psychotherapy.

Unique to *analytical psychology was the formation of Psychological Clubs. Psychological Clubs allowed analysands to meet one another and to discuss topics of mutual interest. In many cities, these Clubs were the first and often the only Jungian organisation. Jung kept his distance and was never closely involved with the administration of any of the Clubs, including the one in Zurich, but he did lend support by giving lectures and seminars to their members. The first attempt at internationalisation of analytical psychology occurred just prior to World War II, when representatives of all the existing Clubs arranged a meeting in Paris in the spring of 1940 to discuss a confederation. The advent of the war curtailed their efforts. After World War II, interest in Jung's psychology spread and many people began to call themselves Jungians. It was no longer clear who had the permission of Jung to be called a Jungian analyst and who did not. Some of Jung's close associates urged him to consider the formation of an international professional organisation, and thus in 1955 the International Association for Analytical Psychology (IAAP) was founded in Switzerland.

At its inception, the aims of the IAAP were to (1) promote analytical psychology, (2) accredit professional groups and individual members where no group existed, and (3) hold Congresses on a regular basis. The organisational structure called for a president, two vice-presidents, a treasurer, and an honorary secretary, to function together with representatives from elected societies as an executive committee. Each member group is entitled to one delegate for every ten members, and societies with less than ten members send a single delegate to the Delegates Meeting held in conjunction with international Congresses. There they vote on proposals submitted by the executive committee.

The charter groups of the IAAP included Switzerland, England (SAP), New York, San Francisco, Los Angeles, Israel, and the Association of Graduate Analytical Psychologists of the C. G. Jung Institute of Zurich. In order to accredit newly forming professional Jungian groups, minimum standards of training were stipulated, as were accreditation requirements for individual membership where no society existed. Over time these standards have been made more stringent.

The first international Congress was held in Zurich in August 1958. One hundred and twenty members attended, and only analysts were allowed. Jung was present at the opening night reception as well as at the banquet. Many of the first-generation analysts gave lectures at this Congress, and the spirit of the papers followed Jung's thought closely. A report on the Congress appeared in *Time Magazine* (25 August 1958) and showed a picture of Jung with Heinz Westmann of New York. The text underneath the picture stated: 'Naturally, analysts will have to be analysed more and more'. The *Time Magazine* article also discussed the political issues of that first Congress, stating that there were two factions: '1) an orthodox group in favour of strict adherence to Jung's doctrines . . . and 2) a progressive element in favour of a widened approach to man's problems, including the importance of childhood experiences . . .' The article continued: 'Jung refused to commit himself publicly . . . he favoured the more progressive wing, feared that his movement would die if it became too introverted and parochial'. The first president of the IAAP was Robert Moody, a psychiatrist and member of the London society. He died during his presidency, and Franz Riklin, the vice-president from Zurich, took over and assumed the IAAP presidency. The second international Congress also took place in Zurich, in August 1962, four years after the first one. Jung had died in the interim, and the latent tension already present at the first Congress between the London and Zurich groups surfaced. This was the beginning of the split between the Developmental School of London, headed by Michael *Fordham, and the Zurich School, which most other members of the IAAP followed. Fordham and the London analysts were clearly in the minority.

In 1971, the international Congress was for the first time held outside Switzerland, at the Royal College of Physicians in London, and was hosted by the SAP. It was a successful event and shifted the centre of gravity away from Zurich.

Since 1962 the international Congresses have been held triennially and have been located in such cities as Rome, San Francisco, Jerusalem, Berlin, Paris, Chicago, Florence, and Cambridge, England. Specific themes have been chosen for each Congress, and for each there exists a publication of the papers.

Over the years major changes have occurred within the IAAP. In 1980 a newsletter was founded in order to encourage communication among the membership. From modest beginnings, it has become an important historical record and a means of communication among IAAP's far-flung members. The conflict between the Developmental School of London and Zurich has abated as the two sides have integrated aspects of each other. Although many differences of opinion about theory and technique continue to exist, these differences today exist as much within the membership of any given society as they do between societies. It is no longer the case that a society is labelled in a particular theoretical manner. The issue of Jung's relationship to the *Nazis and anti-Semitism has been taken up at IAAP Congresses. After the Congresses in Jerusalem and Berlin, panels on Jung and anti-Semitism were held at the Paris Congress. Since 1989 communications between the IAAP and the former Eastern bloc and Soviet Union, as well as China, have been instituted. From 1992 on several psychotherapists from these areas have been invited as guests to speak at IAAP Congresses, and a new category of membership has been created to include some of these people. The IAAP has played an increasingly important role in the growth of analytical psychology. There are approximately 2500 certified analysts in the world. There were thirty-four Societies in the world as of 2000, most of them with training institutes. Through membership in IAAP, professional analysts are accredited and have their identities in the world as Jungian analysts.

T. B. K.

International Psychoanalytical Association (IPA) The International Psychoanalytical Association is a membership organisation that unites psychoanalysts throughout the world for the purposes of maintaining training, professional and ethical standards and for the exchange and discussion of scientific, scholarly and clinical ideas. Although the IPA is made up of individual members (now in excess of 10,000), membership in the IPA is achieved through graduating from the training institute and becoming a member of one of its component organisations. Component organisations include component societies such as the Paris Psychoanalytical Society, the Israel Psychoanalytic Society and the Buenos Aires Psychoanalytic Association, in thirty countries throughout the world. Some larger countries, for example Brazil, have several component societies. Some component societies have several branches as, for example, the German Psychoanalytical Association and the Canadian Psychoanalytic Society. There is also one regional organisation – the American Psychoanalytic Society – which itself has forty-two component societies.

It was because of this method of appointing members that the IPA needed to establish minimum training standards to which all component organisations are required to subscribe (except for two component societies that had established different training requirements prior to the adoption of the minimum standards). The IPA has no other method, such as admission examinations, to determine whether or not an individual is qualified for membership.

Freud founded the IPA in 1910 to preserve, develop and expand the new science and therapy of the mind that he had created. The constitution of the IPA still preserves this original link to Freud's work in its definition of psychoanalysis in its Constitution and Byelaws: 'The term "psychoanalysis" refers to a theory of personality structure and function and to a specific psychotherapeutic technique. This body of knowledge is based on and derived from the fundamental psychological discoveries made by Sigmund Freud'. Freud developed psychoanalysis in fundamental ways after 1908, when the IPA was founded, by modifying his topographical concept of the unconscious to accommodate unconscious ego functions, by a basic revision of his understanding of the topography and dynamics of anxiety, by a far reaching gender differentiation in his understanding of the *Oedipus complex and by his postulation of a *death instinct. During Freud's lifetime there were members who adhered to Freud's death instinct theory, Melanie *Klein being prominent among them, and those who did not, Anna *Freud being quietly prominent among them. The spirit of self-critical scientific, clinical and scholarly inquiry that informed Freud's own development of psychoanalysis is a spirit that is fundamental to the development of knowledge in any science, humanity or technology. This spirit is especially essential for psychoanalysis because of the moral and methodological limitations required by clinical work in psychoanalysis, clinical work that remains the empirical foundation of psychoanalytic knowledge with the support of extra-clinical and interdisciplinary research.

The IPA does not have a theoretical credo as a condition for membership. Its minimum training standards require only that the curriculum of each training facility should include 'reading and discussion of the writings of Sigmund Freud and of other psychoanalytic literature'. Not a few institute curricula include the study of theories that are at odds with Freud's ideas. American *ego psychology did not take up Freud's theory of a death instinct. *Object relations theories have called into question Freud's theory of the drives. *Self psychology has rejected the primacy of object libidinal conflict in pathogenesis in favour of narcissistic deficit. Not a few IPA members, for example those who espouse *hermeneutics, repudiate Freud's basic premise of psychic determinism. Others have abandoned Freud's scientific epistemology of critical realism for post-modern subjectivism. The IPA was created to preserve and expand Freud's fundamental ideas. But these ideas have not been treated as a credo to which the membership had to subscribe in every detail on pain of being expelled. However, this beneficial absence of orthodoxy is probably less the result of an open spirit of theoretical and clinical inquiry than of a fracturing into multiple competing orthodoxies such as are occasionally found in science but are more often found in philosophy. Moreover, some psychoanalytic groups such as the Jungians and existential analysts are excluded even though their ideas are scarcely less divergent from basic Freudian ideas than some of the schools of thought that remain within the IPA.

The IPA is unique among international scientific organisations in being the primary accrediting and regulatory body for some ten thousand psychoanalysts in thirty countries. However, there is controversy about the minimum training standards. Some hold that their observance should be a condition of membership; others hold that training standards should be decided by component societies. The IPA develops new component societies by means of a sponsoring and supervisory process leading from study group status with at least six IPA members via provisional society status to component society status. Thus far observance of minimum training standards has been a requirement of this process. The unilateral departure from the training standards by established component societies raises a question about the long-term viability of this aspect of the IPA's accrediting function. The procedure the IPA makes available for component societies to apply for a variation from IPA minimum requirements in their training standards has been disregarded. If the IPA abandons minimal training standards in favour of the local autonomy of component societies to set their own standards, the IPA will have difficulty refusing admission to a variety of groups whose applications for membership have been turned down because they refused to accept IPA training standards. In effect, the IPA would have abandoned its accrediting function. More deeply, insofar as the shared professional identity of members depends upon commonly accepted training and professional standards, this development would amount to the loss of a shared professional identity for members of the IPA. The meaning of membership in the IPA could easily have lost its shared psychoanalytic basis.

The recent adoption by the IPA of a minimum code of professional ethics has affirmed the regulatory function of the IPA in relation to its component societies on ethical matters. It has provided the ground, if necessary, for the IPA to discipline a member for ethical reasons. All component societies are now required to have an ethical code that includes the principles of the IPA code and a fair, adequately vigilant means of enforcing it. But if the IPA is unable to establish a minimum training standard, might it not also have difficulty in asserting leadership in the minimum ethical principles that all members must observe? Might component societies not also insist upon autonomy on ethical matters? Perhaps it is less likely because the economic factor does not exert so much influence upon ethical standards as it does on training standards.

The IPA organises biennial congresses on scientific, clinical and applied psychoanalytic topics. In this way, the IPA contributes to the development of psychoanalysis and to the continuing scientific and clinical maturation of its members. The IPA has also engaged in some publishing activities. Some members mistakenly assume that the IPA publishes the *International Journal of Psychoanalysis* but of course it is published by the British Psycho-Analytical Society. A recent attempt by the IPA to participate in the publication of this journal failed. At present there is no market for a new international journal published by the IPA. In reality, the *International Journal of Psychoanalysis* is international in the administrative organisation of its editorial boards, with a board for each of the three IPA regions, and in its editorial policies.

There are three regional organisations which do not have official status within the IPA the European Psychoanalytical Federation (EPF), FEPAL (the federation of Latin American societies) and the North American International Psychoanalytical Association Groups (NAIPAG) a somewhat unbalanced grouping of the American Psychoanalytic Society, the independent US groups and the Canadian Psychoanalytic Society. The EPF and FEPAL have longstanding traditions of sponsoring regional scientific meetings. They have not been involved in the policy and administrative functions of the IPA including accrediting component societies and maintaining training, professional and ethical standards. For some time, these organisations have been growing in prestige because of their homogeneous regional, cultural and, to some extent, linguistic nature.

Within North America there is a powerful precedent for a regional body to take over the policy and administrative functions of the IPA. The American Psychoanalytic Association carries out, in relation to its component societies, all of the regulatory functions of the IPA. If the IPA were to abandon its accrediting and other regulatory functions, it could be a first step towards a fundamental transformation of the IPA in which it would become a coordinating body facilitating interregional communication, cooperation and scientific exchange as the regional bodies took up policy and administrative responsibilities. A division concerning training standards along regional lines could be a catalyst for this development. Regional differences have gradually become substantial. It may be that this development would still satisfy the hopes for an international organisation of psychoanalysis that Freud once had. It would, however, bring to an end the uniqueness of the International Psychoanalytical Association among international scientific organisations. It would probably spell the end of a noble experiment in international scientific collaboration.

T. Han.

INTERPERSONAL PSYCHOANALYSIS A body of thought and mode of practice in psychiatry and psychology embracing fully the important role of unconscious processes as they affect behaviour and mental life, but rejecting the centrality of Freudian concepts such as the Oedipal conflict, penis envy, the reification of psychic structures, sexual and aggressive drives, and the technique of free association. Although there is little agreement among interpersonal psychoanalysts as to theory, there was an open break by all of them with their Freudian colleagues in the 1930s. *Sullivan, one of the founders, argued for sticking to observations regarding what transpires between people and how they live, rather than developing elaborate metapsychologies. Growing out of colloquia designed to bring together social scientists and psychiatrists, the William Alanson White Psychoanalytic Foundation began two training and research institutes in Washington, DC, and New York City, renamed the W. A. White Institute of Psychiatry, Psychoanalysis and Psychology in 1946. Sullivan, *Fromm-Reichmann, Clara Thompson, *Fromm, and David and Janet Rioch are considered to be the founders of interpersonal psychoanalysis, sometimes also referred to as the cultural-interpersonal school, a term that includes *Horney. The White Institute publishes a journal: *Contemporary Psychoanalysis*.

From the beginning, the White Institute trained psychologists as well as psychiatrists, a practice at odds with the institutes of the American Psychoanalytic Association. Excluded from membership in the American Psychoanalytic Association because of the divergence of its points of view and practices, as their ideas spread to other institutes and countries, the interpersonalists began their own international association called the International Federation of Psychoanalytic Societies, which has members from many countries. Exclusion from the American and International Psychoanalytic Associations led for a long time to a lack of acknowledgment of the influence of interpersonal thinking in mainstream psychoanalysis, but also to an underground influence that is only recently being made explicit and recognised.

Sullivan did not see the analysis of transference–*countertransference as the major route to change, although many interpersonalists today might do so, especially in differentiating their mode of therapy from non-psychoanalytic psychotherapies. Instead, Sullivan and other interpersonalists see the psychoanalytic process as one of clarifying what a person is doing with other people, including the therapist, and of demystifying what is happening. Influenced by contemporary ideas in physics, the psychoanalytic situation is viewed as one in which the analyst is a participant-observer. Far from the objective scientist or the 'blank screen' of Freudian analysts, therapists in the interpersonal approach have a *subjectivity of their own interacting with the subjectivity of the patient. As such, the interpersonal model is often referred to as a 'two-person', or even 'three-person' model, with analyst, patient, and the cultural context all as the field of investigation. Levenson, one of the most prolific contemporary contributors to the interpersonal perspective, described the evolution of psychoanalytic theory from the work-machine model, to an information-processing model, to an organismic model today, as is prevalent in biology. From this vantage point, the patient may elicit reactions from the analyst leading to an actual repetition of similar experiences, not only to the patient's perception or fantasy that such experiences are occurring. Such a point of view emphasises what is happening in reality, not only what is happening in the patient's mind. Both analyst and patient must find ways out of the interpersonal entanglements or enactments in which they find themselves, with the analyst taking a backward step from participation to observation, and helping the patient to learn a similar process of reflection upon ongoing interactions. This type of reflection is achieved through *inquiry, as much as through interpretation and empathy.

History-taking is also considered to be an important aspect of treatment. The focus on reality leads interpersonalists to consider actual traumas as requiring different approaches from approaches in classical psychoanalysis designed more to treat fantasies and interpretations of events. Fantasies, however – both daydreams and night dreams – are seen as providing important glimpses into unconscious processes. Sensory processes, such as visual imagery, provide at times more access to emotions processed by the limbic system of the brain than do verbal associations processed through the hippocampus.

Although interpersonalists are very interested in meanings, there is an emphasis on experiencing, not on explanations, as being helpful. New experiences, and how patients are bringing old experiences into the present, are one focus of treatment. Expansion of awareness is another goal. This objective, along with the notion that a reified view of the self is an illusion, has led many interpersonalists since Fromm and Horney to be interested in ancient theories for coping with human suffering, such as Buddhism. With a perspective based more on the social sciences, including *anthropology, than on medicine, psychological difficulties are viewed as problems in living, not as diseases or disorders. Adapting to cultures that have their own limitations is viewed as a major source of human difficulties.

Within any cultural context, anxieties come from threats to security and to cherished beliefs about the self and ways of living, as opposed simply to the impingement of sexual and aggressive impulses unacceptable in Victorian culture. With a view of development drawn largely from *attachment theory and developmental psychology, interpersonalists view anxieties about disintegration, helplessness, and the lack of satisfying relationships as primary experiences to be avoided, not *castration anxiety in its more literal sense. *Penis envy has always been considered to be a cultural issue, not one any more biologically determined than womb envy. The development of *heterosexuality, *homosexuality, and *bisexuality are all considered to be orientations with possible biological and psychological underpinnings, but without one orientation privileged over others. Any experience that threatens an individual's sense of security is not attended to or not spelled out, left *unformulated, and dissociated from one another and/or major ways of experiencing the self. These ideas have now been incorporated into what is referred to as relational psychoanalysis.

See also: chum; culture; dissociation; intersubjectivity; masochism (feminine); modes of experiencing; participant observation; relational psychoanalysis; selective inattention; self-disclosure; self-system

Levenson, E. A. (1972) *The Fallacy of Understanding*. New York: Basic Books.
Lionells, M., Fiscalini, J., Mann, C. H. and Stern, D. B. (eds) (1995) *Handbook of Interpersonal Psychoanalysis*. Hillsdale, NJ: The Analytic Press.

R. C.

INTERPRETATION For Freud interpretation was the main technique for solving psychical symptoms in psychoanalysis. This tool was revealed to him through interpreting dreams, and from there he developed his whole system of interpreting the meaning of the symptoms with their unconscious ingredients. He thought that by interpreting the meaning of the symptom he would reach the unconscious forbidden wish that caused the conflict and the corresponding defensive measures of the ego.

In the analytic process what is important is that the type, mode, depth and timing of interpretation should be finely tuned to the patient's ability to receive it, to the quality of the *transference, and to the position, structure and emotional state of the patient.

Interpretation is an inaccurate translation for Freud's term *deutung*, which really means clarification and explanation. It can also mean a 'pointing out', for example the analyst might say 'That's the first time you have said something positive about your father'. Interpretation therefore, can be directed more to unblocking the fixations of the ego in modes of regression, allowing desire to move freely. Good interpretation is only the last 'nudge' by the analyst while the work is done by the analysand in such a way that he can exclaim with surprise: 'I always knew it but I never thought it!'

Lacan's theory of interpretation was a response to what he saw as the declining effectiveness of classical interpretations in dissolving symptoms. The problem is that the unconscious is a dynamic agency which is changing all the time. It can close itself to interpretations and can become immune to them. So Lacan went in the opposite direction from Symbolic interpretation to encountering the unbearable Real. Interpretation is meant to lead to the construction of phantasy and to its traversing. The way to effective interpretation is not necessarily through words but through the analytic act, like cutting the session. This cut, this silence, leaves an opening that enables the unconscious itself to be the agency of interpretation.

See also: punctuation; traversal of phantasy

R. Gol.

INTERSUBJECTIVE ANALYTIC THIRD Thomas Ogden, building on the work of Bion, Winnicott and André Green has developed a conception of the analytic process that views the analytic relationship as including not only the analyst and the analysand, but also a third co-created unconscious subject of analysis which he terms 'the intersubjective analytic third' or simply 'the analytic third'. The (intersubjective) third subject of analysis stands in dialectical tension with the analyst and analysand as separate individuals with their own distinct subjectivities, histories, personality organisations and so on. Analyst and analysand each participate in the unconscious intersubjective construction (the analytic third), but do so asymmetrically. Specifically, the relationship of the roles of analyst and analysand structures the analytic interaction in a way that strongly privileges the exploration of the unconscious internal object world of the analysand. This is so because most fundamentally the analytic relationship exists for the purpose of helping the analysand make psychological changes that will enable him to live in a more fully human way.

For Ogden, inseparable from the experience of the analytic third in clinical practice is the use of the analyst's reverie experience (including his most ordinary, mundane thoughts, feelings, daydreams, ruminations, sensations and so on) in his effort to gain a sense of the nature of the unconscious co-constructed third subject of analysis. The mutative effect of psychoanalysis from Ogden's perspective depends upon the re-contextualisation in a more verbally mediated, secondary process form of aspects of the analysand's unconscious experience which are given shape in the shared experience of the analytic third.

Ogden, T. H. (1994) 'The analytic third: working with intersubjective clinical facts'. *International Journal of Psycho-Analysis* 75: 3–20.

Ogden, T. H. (1997) 'Reverie and Interpretation'. *Psychoanalytic Quarterly* 66: 567–95.

Ogden, T. H. (1997) *Reverie and Interpretation: Sensing Something Human*. Northvale, NJ: Aronson and London: Karnac Books.

R. S.

INTERSUBJECTIVITY THEORY Developed by collaborators Robert D. Stolorow, George E. Atwood, Bernard Brandchaft, Daphne S. Stolorow, and Donna M. Orange, intersubjectivity theory holds that, both developmentally and in the psychoanalytic situation, psychological phenomena take form within an *intersubjective field constituted by the interacting subjective worlds of child and caregiver or of patient and analyst. The idea of an intersubjective field, along with the concepts of unconscious *organising principle and concrete symbolisation, were applied to illuminate a wide range of clinical issues and problems critical in the practice of psychoanalytic therapy and to a rethinking of the foundational pillars of psychoanalytic theory. The intersubjective perspective has evolved into a broad-based philosophy of psychoanalytic practice termed **contextualism*.

See also: Stolorow

Atwood, G. E. and Stolorow, R. D. (1984) *Structures of Subjectivity: Explorations in Psychoanalytic Phenomenology*. Hillsdale, NJ: The Analytic Press.

Orange, D. M., Atwood, G. E. and Stolorow, R. D. (1997) *Working Intersubjectively: Contextualism in Psychoanalytic Practice*. Hillsdale, NJ: The Analytic Press.

Stolorow, R. D. and Atwood, G. E. (1992) *Contexts of Being: The Intersubjective Foundations of Psychological Life*. Hillsdale, NJ: The Analytic Press.

Stolorow, R. D., Brandchaft, B. and Atwood, G. E. (1987) *Psychoanalytic Treatment: An Intersubjective Approach*. Hillsdale, NJ: The Analytic Press.

R. S.

INTERSUBJECTIVE FIELD An intersubjective field is a dynamic psychological system constituted by reciprocally interacting, differently organised subjective worlds.

See also: intersubjectivity theory

R. S.

INTERSUBJECTIVE SYSTEMS THEORY This theory of intersubjectivity was developed by collaborators (R.) Stolorow, Atwood, Brandchaft, (D.) Stolorow, and Orange. It draws strongly on the philosophers *Heidegger, Husserl and Gadamer. Intersubjectivity theory holds that, both developmentally and in the psychoanalytic situation, psychological phenomena take form within an intersubjective field constituted by the interacting subjective worlds of child and caregiver or of patient and analyst. The idea of an *intersubjective field, along with the concepts of unconscious *organising principle and concrete symbolisation, were applied to illuminate a wide range of clinical issues and problems critical in the practice of psychoanalytic therapy and to a rethinking of the foundational pillars of psychoanalytic theory. The intersubjective perspective has evolved into a broad-based philosophy of psychoanalytic practice termed **contextualism*.

Recognition of intersubjectivity does not entail adherence to or rejection of any specific psychodynamic theory. In fact acceptance of the foundational significance of intersubjectivity enables therapists to employ the various psychodynamic concepts with greater discrimination and effectiveness.

See also: antidote function; concretisation; grandiosity, defensive or expansive; intersubjective field; philosophy, continental; organising principle; unconscious; transference, organising activity of; transference, self-delineating

Atwood, G. E. and Stolorow, R. D. (1984) *Structures of Subjectivity: Explorations in Psychoanalytic Phenomenology*. Hillsdale, NJ: The Analytic Press.

Orange, D. M., Atwood, G. E. and Stolorow, R. D. (1997) *Working Intersubjectively: Contextualism in Psychoanalytic Practice*. Hillsdale, NJ: The Analytic Press.

Stolorow, R. D. and Atwood, G. E. (1992) *Contexts of Being: The Intersubjective Foundations of Psychological Life*. Hillsdale, NJ: The Analytic Press.

Stolorow, R. D., Brandchaft, B. and Atwood, G. E. (1987) *Psychoanalytic Treatment: An Intersubjective Approach*. Hillsdale, NJ: The Analytic Press.

Stolorow, R. D., Atwood, G. E. and Orange, D. M. (2002) *Worlds of Experience: Interweaving Philosophical and Clinical Dimensions in Psychoanalysis*. New York: Basic Books.

R. S.

INTERSUBJECTIVITY (EXISTENTIAL) The field of interaction between the self and the other. Intersubjectivity is a topic that is philosophical in origin and psychoanalytic in its applications. For existential psychoanalysts, intersubjectivity refers variously to the nature of self-other interaction, the quality of human relatedness, and the client-therapist relationship.

The phenomenological-existentialist approach to intersubjectivity was developed chiefly by Husserl, *Heidegger and *Buber. Husserl coined the notion of intersubjectivity to demonstrate how subjects relate to one another. Heidegger rejects Husserl's solipsistic conception of the 'transcendental' ego and redefines the subject as Dasein, a situated mode of being that is enmeshed in a social world. For Buber, the subject is inherently relational and only exists insofar as it swings 'between' two types of relation, the I-It and the I-Thou.

*Sartre's discussion of intersubjectivity in *Being and Nothingness* centres on the direct impact of the other on my experience. Sartre moves beyond Heidegger's ontology to examine the body and the nature of interaction in the concrete social sphere. As delineated in his 'dialectic of the look', the other is an immediate presence that threatens my freedom. In order to recapture my freedom, I seek to subjugate the other. The dialectical nature of this interaction provides the basis for Sartre's discussion of sadism and masochism.

*Binswanger develops a dialogical theory of intersubjectivity in his main work of 1942, *Basic Forms and Knowledge of Human Existence*. He delineates different forms of social existence – singular, plural and dual – which are oriented towards the achievement of loving dialogue with another person. For Binswanger, change and growth are made possible in an I-Thou relationship based on mutuality, openness and directness. He elaborates the dynamic character of self-other interaction in terms of an Hegelian dialectic of separateness and togetherness. It is this essential paradox that provides for the possibility of a shared identity in which individual identity is not only sustained, but also transformed and enhanced in relationship with the other.

Existential psychoanalysts reject the notion of neutrality in order to interact with their patients and engage them. As *Laing maintains, therapists must be willing to enter the client's phenomenal world to the best of their ability. What is therapeutic when it is achieved is 'the moment of real meeting' of two persons. Therein, the self is able to realise its agency when the response from the other imbues its feelings and intentions in a meaningful way. In this way, the I-Thou relation demonstrates that genuine therapeutic work always requires the active involvement of both participants.

See also: intersubjective systems theory

Frie, R. (1997) *Subjectivity and Intersubjectivity in Modern Philosophy and Psychoanalysis: A Study of Sartre, Binswanger, Lacan, and Habermas*. Lanham, MD: Rowman & Littlefield.

R. Fri.

INTERSUBJECTIVITY (GROUP) From an intersubjective perspective human beings do not exist in isolation, but on the contrary, exist in a world with others. Intersubjectivity is a description of the interconnection between human beings. It is a move towards a multi-person psychology. This approach describes the way there is primary relation amongst persons and things in the human world and that it is the interpersonal space between persons from which feelings and meanings emerge. In this context, the subject is mirrored, defined and created.

There is a direct relation between *Foulkes' understanding of the group process and intersubjectivity. Meaning and significance are not seen to reside in each individual group member, but in what happens between them, in the interaction and context. Foulkes views the individual as an artificial abstraction. In his 1948 work he situates the person in his/her social context and later in 1975 refers to the individual as a nodal point in a network of relations. It is the web of relations – as part of the group process – where meanings are forged and moods are evoked. The intersubjective group space takes precedence.

Foulkes' matrix is sometimes synonymous with network; at other times it becomes the basic mould (the womb) in which all individual units are embedded. Whether the matrix is the network of relations or the operational basis for the group process, the matrix exists as an intersubjective process.

Mind is no longer understood as intrapsychic in nature, but becomes a property of the interactive group process. Foulkes argues against a sharp division between inside/outside, suggesting that such a dichotomy is 'philosophically incorrect'. Here he implies an intersubjective account whereby the subject does not exist inside and world outside: since the social penetrates the innermost being of the individual, the subject co-exists with others in a world and inter-psychic activity takes place in between persons in the group.

Cohn, H. W. (1996) 'The philosophy of S. H. Foulkes: existential-phenomenological aspects of group analysis'. *Group Analysis* 29(3): 287–302.
Diamond, N. (1998) *Intersubjectivity: The Fabric of Social Becoming*. London: Routledge.
Diamond, N. (1996) 'Can we speak of internal and external reality?'. *Group Analysis* 29(3): 303–17.
Foulkes, E. (ed.) (1990) *S. H. Foulkes: Selected Papers: Psychoanalysis and Group Analysis*, London: Karnac Books.
Foulkes, S. H. (1948) *Introduction to Group-Analytic Psychotherapy*. Harmondsworth: Penguin.

See also: intersubjectivity (existential)

N. D.

INTERSUBJECTIVITY (LACAN) A relation between a subject and another subject. Some traditions in psychoanalysis have taken this to be a relation between individuals. Lacan however insists that the *subject is the subject of the unconscious who in analysis addresses him- or herself to the *Other, the analyst 'supposed to know', and not to another person.

R. M. B.

INTERSUBJECTIVITY Intersubjectivity designates the continuous and reciprocal subjective interaction of the patient and therapist. The qualities of these interactions are, of course, endlessly varied but proceed without interruption and without pause.

In therapy, patient and analyst assume different roles, but the power of therapy arises from the two interacting subjectivities. Both parties are constantly in multiple, interpenetrating, mutually transforming engagement, largely unconscious. Enactment is the term that best captures the presence of these events.

The concept of intersubjectivity legitimises the sustained importance of the therapist's subjective experience as an originating and shaping force, replacing the traditional view of the neutral therapist with occasional countertransferentially-induced subjective responses.

Recognition of intersubjectivity does not entail adherence to or rejection of any specific psychodynamic theory. In fact acceptance of the foundational significance of intersubjectivity enables therapists to employ the various psychodynamic concepts with greater discrimination and effectiveness.

Natterson, J. (1991) *Beyond Countertransference*. Northvale, NJ: Jason Aronson.

J. Nat.

INTERVENTION An act accomplished by the analyst during the course of a psychoanalysis. It is important to distinguish acts such as questioning, occasional responses to questions, asking the patient to move onto the couch, ending a session, from *interpretation.

R. M. B.

INTRAPSYCHIC FACTORS Internal influences that impinge on an individual's ultimate subjective experience or expressed behaviour. Typically they occur between mental agencies such as the *id, *ego and *super-ego. Intrapsychic factors include drive derivatives emanating from the id as well as the prohibitions, judgments and expectations that are products of the super-ego. Intrapsychic factors also include a host of unpleasant affects like *anxiety, *guilt or *shame. Thinking in terms of mental agencies like the id, ego, etc. helps delineate some of the functional components of the psyche. However, the reification of such abstract concepts or structures can lead to oversimplification, and to the assignment of functions to one agency that are, in fact, shared between agencies.

See also: ego functions, autonomous; structure, psychic

R. T.

INTROJECTION Introjection is the unconscious process of taking inside the self aspects of another. This is particularly likely to occur when an object is lost or has to be given up. In *melancholia the lost object, which is hated as well as loved, is taken inside and the self becomes the recipient of attacks originally meant for the other (the shadow of the object falls upon the ego). At the oedipal level, the parent who is relinquished as a sexual object is taken into the ego, and becomes the basis for the *super-ego. Through introjection, the ego contains, and is built upon, the residues of abandoned object cathexes.

Lacan however makes a firm distinction between introjection and projection, seeing them as representing the ascendancy of two very different registers. Projection relies on a dominance of the *Imaginary, and operates through the assumption of illusions about others, constructed from a template of internal conflict. Introjection however is a taking into oneself of an aspect of what is outside: a process that Lacan takes to be characteristic of the *Symbolic. Just as an organism can acquire internal structure by taking into itself external structure, the construction of human subjectivity is brought about by such an introjection of signifying structure. By introjecting such aspects of the *Other, the organism is transformed into a subject. For Lacan, introjection generates the conditions for the suffering of symptoms, for the pain of existence, and for human bondage.

J. A. Ber. / B. B.

INTUITION The direct and immediate vision or understanding of a reality or a truth, with no intermediate elements. The term derives from the Latin word intuit, derived from *intueri* meaning 'look', and means 'to observe intently'. Various epistemological and philosophical schools have different positions and valuations about intuition and the knowledge it offers.

Bion, who speaks much about intuition and its value, says, in *Attention and Interpretation*, that, for convenience, he will use the term 'intuit' as a parallel in the psychoanalyst's domain, to the physician's use of 'see', 'touch', 'smell' and 'hear'. This is related with his idea that the realisations of *psychical reality cannot be touched, smelled or seen – they are non-sensuous realisations.

*Memory, desire and understanding hinder the intuition of this non-sensorial psychical reality, and since psychoanalysis is not primarily concerned with what is sensorial, nor with what has happened or what will happen, but with what is happening now, analysts should resist the tendency to remember or desire. The evolution of something new is intuited, as when facts which were present previously but had not seen related are felt to cohere. This intuition may then be made public, put into words, for which *alpha function and concepts are necessary. This is the psychoanalyst's position, who has to give *interpretations or make *models or *constructions. It is also the scientist's position in the contexts of discovery and justification as well as that of the creative artist. All are 'mystics' in Bion's use of the term, having an intuition of the evolved aspects of *O and then being capable of publishing them.

Mother's intuition in her relationship with her infant is related to her *reverie, to a mind-to-mind emotional contact, or *'passion' as Bion also calls it when he speaks about the dimensions of the *psychoanalytic object. The analyst's intuition should be maintained in a good state, especially since it is basically frail and exposed to attacks by the patient and also by the analyst himself. Bion suggests that working with the *grid after the sessions is a good way to keep it in a good state.

In his last papers, when Bion began to wonder if there might still be vestiges in the human mind which would suggest a survival of pre-natal functions, he includes 'embryological intuition' amongst these.

See also: prenatal states of mind

Bion, W. R. (1962) *Learning from Experience*. London: Heinemann.

Bion, W. R. (1963) *Elements of Psychoanalysis*. London: Heinemann.

Bion, W. R. (1970) *Attention and Interpretation*. London: Tavistock.

Bion, W. R. (1976) 'Caesura' in *Two Papers: The Grid and Caesura*. Rio de Janeiro: Imago.

E. T. B.

INVARIANCE The unmodified elements in any transformation which allow the recognition of the relationship of the origin and of the T(beta). The concept of invariance is used to illuminate true continuities in mental phenomena versus false continuities brought about with 'memory'. Those elements which are not changed in the process of transformation are invariants. Therefore, invariance is that which allows one to recognise something of the original in the transformed state. Since invariance is not a characteristic of permanence, it must be sought for in transformation.

Bion, W. R. (1965) *Transformations*. London: Karnac Books. Also in *Seven Servants*. New York: Jason Aronson, 1977.

Bion, W. R. (1970) *Attention and Interpretation*. London: Tavistock. Also in *Seven Servants*. New York: Jason Aronson, 1977.

S. A.

IRELAND Psychoanalysis in Northern Ireland and in the Republic of Ireland has developed quite independently.

The founder of psychoanalysis in the Republic of Ireland was Jonathan Hanaghan, an Englishman who arrived in Dublin just before the outbreak of World War II. Analysed by Douglas Brion of the British Psychoanalytic Society, he remained a deeply committed Christian and pacifist and founded the Irish Psychoanalytic Association (IPA). His perspective is neatly summed up in the title of one of his books *Freud and Jesus* and he attracted a number of co-workers, notably three Englishmen: Wilfred Bowell, Rupert Strong, Gordon Fletcher; and four Americans: Dick and John Cameron, Mark Hartman and Mitchell Elliot. It is fair to say that without their Christian perspective the psychoanalytic movement they founded could not have survived in 1950s Ireland dominated as it was by the Catholic Church.

In the early 1980s two new analysts arrived: Father Cormac Gallagher, then a Jesuit who had trained as a Lacanian analyst in Paris; and also Dr Michael Fitzgerald, a child psychiatrist and psychoanalyst trained at the British Society of Psychoanalysis. Soon the Irish Forum for Psychoanalytic Psychotherapy (IFPP) (www.ifpp.org/) was set up with John (now Lord) Alderdice as Chairman and this became a discussion group inviting many speakers from abroad. Gallagher, also a psychologist, set up the first analytic training at St Vincent's Hospital, thus the first training programme was Lacanian. Prominent in this programme were: Olga Cox Cameron, Rik Loose, Patricia McCarthy, Tom McGrath, Maebh Nolan, and

Helen Sheehan. Fitzgerald, with Mary Smith, set up a Child Psychotherapy MSc at St James Hospital of a more eclectic nature.

Most of the Lacanians left the Forum to found the Lacanian Association for Psychoanalytic Psychotherapy in Ireland (APPI) (www.appi.ie/).

Ross Skelton and David Berman, both philosophers at Trinity College Dublin and graduates of the Lacanian training, set up a theoretical psychoanalytic M. Phil in the College. Shortly after this, Ann Murphy, an Irishwoman trained in Canada, returned and acted as a catalyst for Forum members including Mary Pyle, Ellen O'Malley Dunlop, Nessa Childers and Ross Skelton, setting up a more eclectic training. This was achieved in 1997 when a clinical MSc in Psychoanalytic Psychotherapy was founded in Trinity College. Jungian analytic psychology was pioneered by Kate Nowlan of London in the 1980s and developed by Patricia Skar, an American trained in Zurich.

The founding father of psychoanalysis in Northern Ireland was Dr Thomas Freeman, psychoanalyst and psychiatrist. Dr Freeman wrote many papers on the application of Freudian theory to psychotic and other disorders. His work continues today through the N. I. Association of Psychoanalysis (NIASP) (www.bcp.org.uk/). Several psychoanalysts have been trained through the top-up training with the British Institute of Psychoanalysis. In the 1980s a university-based psychoanalytic psychotherapy training course was started by Lord Alderdice and Dr Clare Adams at the Faculty of Medicine at Queen's University Belfast. This produced the first group of psychoanalytic psychotherapists in Northern Ireland, some of whom went on to become psychoanalysts. The course continued the Freudian tradition of Dr Freeman. Jungian psychoanalysis evolved in the early 1990s with the work of Jarlath Benson. Also in the early 1990s therapeutic communities became established with the arrival of the Richmond Fellowship. This organisation is now known as Threshold (www.therapeuticcommunities. org/dir-theshold) and, directed by Ramun Kapoor, took over the psychoanalytic psychotherapy training in the mid-90s when it moved to the School of Psychology at Queen's University Belfast. The theoretical orientation is influenced by the work of Kleinians and post-Kleinians. Two Irishmen distinguished themselves internationally, though based in other countries. J. O. Wisdom was a distinguished Irish academic psychoanalyst from the Republic who made his career in London and Toronto. William Gillespie, a psychoanalyst from Northern Ireland made his distinguished reputation from London.

Alderdice, J. (2002) Introduction to *Terrorism and War: Unconscious Dynamics of Mass Destruction*. London: Karnac Books.

Freeman, T. (1987) *The Psychoanalyst in Psychiatry*. London: Karnac Books.

Hanaghan, J. (1957) *Society, Evolution and Revelation*. Dublin: Runa Press.

Skelton, R. (1983) 'Hanaghan – the founder of psychoanalysis in Ireland'. *The Crane Bag* (17)2.

R. M. S.

ISOLATION A defence mechanism by which the subject isolates an event, thus avoiding its being linked with other experiences which might lead to its discovery. In Freud, isolation usually refers to 'isolation of affect', a defence in which traumatic or emotionally intense events are remembered, but deprived of the feelings originally attached to them. Isolation of affect is a defence used by *obsessionals while repression is the defence of *hysteria.

J. A. Ber. / R. T.

ISRAEL Following pioneering efforts by Eder and Feigenbaum, during a period when young immigrants arrived in Palestine 'with *Das Kapital* under one arm and *Die Traumdeutung* under the other', the Palestine Psychoanalytic Society and Institute were founded in 1933–4. Freud's hope that Eitingon would become a professor at the Hebrew University was frustrated, and Eitingon's energy was directed towards organising what became – after the establishment of the State of Israel in 1948 – the Israel Psychoanalytic Society and Institute.

Gradually a new generation of locally trained analysts took over from the German-speaking founders. International ties evolved, mostly within the International Psychoanalytical Association, which held its 1977 congress in Jerusalem.

The psychoanalytic community was initially predominantly medical (non-medical analysts were admitted ambivalently), quite involved in psychiatry (many institutions were run by analysts) and in education, especially kibbutz education – whose communal ideology involved a utopian interpretation of Freud – and work with immigrant children.

Later on clinical psychologists became the dominant group, and many analysts withdrew from social-institutional involvement, dedicating themselves to a private practice of analysis and therapy, and to teaching in psychotherapy training programs established at the Institute and at several universities. Israeli psychoanalysis has a strong clinical focus, while rarely involved in the arts, humanities or social sciences.

The Freud Chair of the Hebrew University, held by Sandler (1978–83) and other analysts, initiated conferences, interdisciplinary seminars and doctoral theses. Israeli analysts have been active in studying the impact of the holocaust and other traumas.

Initially classical and ego-psychology oriented, Israeli psychoanalysis has diversified, absorbing the competing influences of Klein, Bion, Winnicott, Kohut, and relational-intersubjective trends. As of 2001, the Society had one hundred and twenty members, and was training eighty candidates. Jungians and Lacanians established independent organisations, the Israel Association of Analytical Psychology and the Israel Group of the European School of Psychoanalysis respectively. In 2000, another autonomous organisation was initiated, the Tel Aviv Institute of Contemporary Psychoanalysis.

The structure of training at the Israel Psychoanalytic Institute, modelled after the Berlin Institute, came under heated debate in the 1990s. Many changes were made in policies and rules to reduce authoritarian and infantilising trends, allowing candidates greater individual autonomy and personal expression.

Berman, E. (1988) 'Communal upbringing in the kibbutz: the allure and risks of psychoanalytic utopianism'. *Psychoanalytic Study of the Child* 43: 319–35.

Berman, E. (1998) 'Structure and individuality in psychoanalytic training: the Israeli controversial discussions'. *American Journal of Psychoanalysis* 58: 117–33.

Liban, A. and Goldman, D. (2000) 'Freud comes to Palestine: a study of psychoanalysis in cultural context'. *International Journal of Psycho-Analysis* 81: 893–906.

Moses, R. (1992) 'A short history of psychoanalysis in Palestine and Israel'. *Israel Journal of Psychiatry and Related Sciences* 29: 229–38.

Rolnik, E. (2002) 'From Vienna to Jerusalem: Psychoanalysis in Jewish Palestine' in J. Bunzl and B. Beit-Hallahmi (eds) *Psychoanalysis, Identity and Ideology*. Norwell: Kluwer.

E. Ber.

ITALY Psychoanalysis was introduced in Italy by the psychiatrist Marco Levi Bianchini, who founded the Italian Psychoanalytic Society in 1925. The Society, incremented by Edoardo Weiss, was granted membership by the IPA in 1936; soon afterwards, the Jewish members were persecuted by the fascist dictatorship, some of them left the country to escape anti-Semitism and the Society was compelled to cease its initial activity. In 1946 it was re-organised by Cesare Musatti in Milan, Nicola Perrotti and Emilio Servadio in Rome and Alessandra Tomasi Wolff Stomersee, Princess of Lampedusa, in Palermo. From the initial six analysts, membership slowly increased till the 60s and, since then, has steadily continued to the present number of 640 plus 298 candidates. The members are distributed in ten Centres all over the country and four Training Institutes, two in Rome, one in Milan, one in Bologna. In 1990 uneasiness and conflicts mainly concerning the overly oligarchic organisation of the training functions, arose in one of the centres and then spread all over the SPI, leading to a split into two Societies: the SPI and the AIPsi, which has about forty members.

Italian psychoanalysis has always maintained links with the main foreign schools, being constantly provided with timely, accurate translations of the most important books. Freud's collected works and letters were superbly edited by Cesare Musatti as well as the complete works of the other main authors, from the pioneers to the contemporaries. There are many psychoanalytic reviews; the Rivista Italiana di Psicoanalisi is the official organ of the SPI.

In the last few years SPI has played a greater role in the international debate, participating in IPA (International Psychoanalytic Association) and FEP (European Psychoanalytic Federation) congresses and increasingly contributing to the major psychoanalytic journals.

The main theoretical-clinical orientations and developments of international psychoanalysis have been elaborated and given an original stamp by Italian analysts. Franco Fornari and Eugenio Gaddini contributed creatively to the spread of the post-Kleinian and Winnicottian thought, as well as Francesco Corrao to the post-Bionian development and Ignacio Matte Blanco to the Latin American. There has also been a considerable French influence. In the last years there has been an explosion of interest in US authors too: everything from ego psychology to the most recent authors connected with interpersonal, interactive and intersubjective models has been discussed and criticised by many Italian analysts.

As regards the diffusion of analytic theory in Italy, a number of psychoanalysts have been given chairs in faculties of psychiatry and in the more recently formed faculties of psychology. This development has provided an opportunity to give doctors and psychologists a correct psychoanalytic orientation. Other analysts have devoted themselves to working in psychiatric institutions, either as therapists directly involved in the treatment of patients or as supervisors of psychiatrists, nurses and social workers. Psychoanalysis is now part of the general culture of educated people in Italy. Serious scholars have produced in-depth studies, not only of Freud's work, but also of more recent analytic authors. Creative writers and directors who have undergone analysis have translated their experience into valuable novels, pieces of theatre and films, giving readers and spectators an impressionistic but realistic idea of what analytic treatment is and can achieve.

S. B. / P. G.

J

Jacobson, Edith (Jacobssohn) (1897–1978) Edith Jacobson was born on 10 September 1897 in Haynau, Silesia, to a Jewish family. Like her father and brother she became a medical doctor. After finishing her studies and internships in Jena, Heidelberg and Munich, she moved to Berlin in 1925. While serving residencies at the Oppenheim neurological clinic and Bonhoeffer's psychiatric clinic Charité she began her analysis with Otto *Fenichel and enrolled at the Berlin Psychoanalytic Institute. In 1929, Jacobson was elected member of the German Psychoanalytic Society. She joined Fenichel's Kinderseminar meetings and his Marxist-analytical discussion group, and from 1934 onwards she received Fenichel's secret circular letters (Fenichel 1998). Jacobson decided to stay in Germany in 1933 and was elected training analyst of the German Psychoanalytic Society in 1934. Besides her analytical practice and teaching, she worked for the resistance movement. Jacobson was arrested in October 1935. At the end of 1937, she was granted temporary release from prison for medical treatment and with the help of her friends fled to Prague and then New York. Jacobson became a member of the New York Psychoanalytic Society in 1941. She was elected training analyst of the Institute in 1942 and from 1954 until 1956 served as the Society's president. Jacobson held a position as Visiting Professor of Psychiatry at the Albert Einstein College of Medicine (Montefiore Hospital). On 8 December 1978, Edith Jacobson died in Rochester, New York.

Jacobson's name is linked to American ego-psychology, but her works are also regarded as an independent Freudian object relations position in the United States. Much of her work is devoted to the problem of identifications, super-ego formation and its pathologies, early object relations, the differentiation between self and object representations. Her book *The Self and the Object World* (1964) has been considered the most comprehensive statement about normal development from birth to psychic consolidation at the time. Her name is also most significantly linked to the psychology and treatment of depression and depressive conditions. On this subject she is regarded as the foremost authority in the field of psychoanalysis. Jacobson worked with psychotics and was able to arrive at new conclusions about the relationship between psychotics and the real world. In her work, sociological observations were important; she considered the real trauma significant, and the responses to trauma run as a theme through Jacobson's work.

See also: depression; ego psychology; self

Fenichel, O. (1998) *119 Rundbriefe (1934–1945)*. Vol 1, *Europa* (1934–1938). Vol 2, *Amerika* (1938–1945). E. Mühlleitner, and J. Reichmayr (eds). Frankfurt and Basel: Stroemfeld Verlag.

Jacobson, E. (1937) 'Ways of female super-ego formation and the female castration complex'. *The Psychoanalytic Quarterly* 45: 525–38.

Jacobson, E. (1949) 'Observations on the psychological effects of imprisonment on female political prisoners' in K. R. Eissler (ed.), *Searchlights on Delinquency*. New York: International Universities Press, 341–69.

Jacobson, E. (1964) *The Self and the Object World*. New York: International Universities Press.

Jacobson, E. (1967) *Psychotic Conflict and Reality*. New York: International Universities Press.

Jacobson, E. (1971) *Depression*. New York: International Universities Press.

E. M.

James, William (1842–1910) American psychologist and philosopher. James vigorously denied the existence of an unconscious. He was also suspicious of Freud because of the latter's hostile attitude towards religion. Nevertheless, his *The Principles of Psychology* (1890) is of interest to psychoanalysts, at the very least for his distinctive views on emotion and instinct.

James distinguished between the bodily changes involved in an emotion and the emotion itself. He thought of the bodily changes, and the sensations accompanying them, as arising more-or-less automatically from perceptions of states of affairs, with the emotion proper coming afterwards: 'we are sorry because we cry, angry because we strike, afraid because we tremble', and so forth. He believed that without the initial bodily change, we might – for example – judge a situation to be dangerous, but we would not *feel* fear. Further, he held that humans were able to take control of their emotions even after the bodily changes had commenced. Thus he saw emotions as potential objects of choice and responsibility.

He believed that 'the older writings on instincts are ineffectual wastes of words'. Where they went wrong, in his view, was in treating instincts as somehow involving representations of highly abstract goals such as survival or reproduction. James argued that lower animals clearly have instincts, but they could not possibly have such representations. Freud's tendency to reduce instincts to two fundamental, highly plastic, 'drives' would presumably be subject to this criticism, as Freud clearly thought of these drives as goal-directed. Freud and James would have agreed regarding the importance of instincts in humans, but where Freud saw two fundamental drives, James saw a great number of mechanical, unthinking, highly specific responses. James claimed that the human mind had more instincts than other animals, not less. It was not any plasticity of instincts, but their sheer number, that made humans so flexible in their behaviour.

See also: affect

Deigh, J. (2001) 'Emotions: The Legacy of James and Freud'. *International Journal of Psychoanalysis* 82: 1247–56.

James, W. [1890] (1981) *The Principles of Psychology* (3 vols). in *The Works of William James*. Cambridge, MA: Harvard University Press.

B. Gar.

JAPAN In Japanese psychiatry, psychoanalytic practice was first attempted at Tohoku University by Marui, who had studied at Johns Hopkins University, and his disciple Kosawa, who met Freud in Vienna in 1932. However, the cultural context in Japan at that time did not really welcome it. In the meantime, modern Japanese psychotherapies, apparently stimulated by psychoanalysis, began to grow. In the 1920s, strongly criticising Freud, the psychiatrist Morita invented Morita therapy. In this technique, one confines oneself to bed refraining from any activity, and communicates with the therapist only by a diary. Morita compared his discipline to Zen Buddhism in that it encourages the mind to 'let it be as it is'. Another technique was *Naikan* (introspection) therapy, created by the *Jodo-Shin* Buddhist Yoshimoto: One isolates oneself with a screen in a corner of a room, and reflects on one's past, enumerating what one has done to one's parents and what one owes to them. The therapist comes in every two hours to discuss the recollections.

These Japanese techniques, although they assert their independence from psychoanalysis, are not without similarities to it, in that they emphasise the helplessness of the subject before Nature, and revive the past memories about the significant other, suggesting that Japanese culture had been potentially prepared for psychoanalytical thinking. In fact, as Blowers depicts, Freud himself was delighted and excited to hear a succinct explanation by the psychologist Yabe about how Japanese thinking would be prompt in understanding Freud's idea of death instinct by way of Buddhist tradition, because the ideal of life tending to death had been long familiar to Japanese Buddhists. Thus, the strong influence of Buddhism in Japanese thought since the sixth century might have functioned as both a resistance against and facilitator for the psychoanalytic movement.

Yabe, after being analysed in Berlin, became a certified psychoanalyst and the first to establish a psychoanalytic association in Japan. Kenji Ohtsuki, a literature graduate, collaborated with him, and they published the first volume of their journal *Seishinbunseki* (Psychoanalysis) in 1933. Yabe also led the translation of Freud's work. This movement of literary people might have integrated psychoanalytic thought into traditional Japanese thought to create a new style of thinking, but the Second World War and related military control of public discourse in Japan exerted a devastating effect on its development, although Ohtsuki continued to work even after the war.

On the other hand, psychiatric psychoanalysis survived the war under the shield of medical discipline. Kosawa, who had undergone didactic analysis by Sterba in Vienna and opened a psychoanalytic clinic in Tokyo in the 30s, founded the Japan Psychoanalytic Society (JPS) in 1955, together with a sister organisation, the Japan Psychoanalytic Association (JPA) which was comprised not only of psychiatrists, but also psychologists and educationists. The latter was intended to be an organisation for a propagation of the psychoanalytic trend in psychiatry and clinical psychology, but grew steadily and surpassed the former by far in number of members and in academic activities, and finally instituted a qualification of psychoanalytic psychotherapist for physicians and clinical psychologists in 2000. Meanwhile, the JPS, which, though approved for membership by IPA, had remained a small group, began to reformulate its system for qualification of psychoanalysts around 1993 from a once-a-week basis for didactic analysis to a four-times-a-week basis, hoping for a more authentic psychoanalytic practice in Japan.

The psychoanalytic movement in Japan after the war has been characterised by a massive influx of American ego-psychological psychoanalysis. Already before the war, Kosawa showed a certain divergence from Freudian orthodoxy, in that his method attached less importance to the Oedipal relation than to the emotions of dependence on and hostility towards the mother, with a shift from the technique of free association to one of direct interpretation like that of Rosen. Thereafter, the concept of *Amae* was coined by Doi, who had been trained in the United States. *Amae* is the state of mind of an infinite expectation of unconditional favour from others. Entering the centre of Japanese interpersonal psychology, it popularised a mode of explaining Japanese culture in the light of the maternal relationship. Now it is one of the most popular ideas in the Japanese psychotherapeutic trend that the emotional development of the ego under maternal care should be of utmost importance in therapy. But Doi is in fact a father figure for several members of the JPS, who represent a substantial core for future of the psychoanalytic movement in Japan.

Meanwhile, Kleinian psychoanalysis and object-relations theory were introduced to Japan in the late 70s, by way of psychiatrists and psychologists trained in Britain, and are now being effectively integrated into the activities of the JPA and the JPS. Lacanian psychoanalysis was first introduced by literary people, then by psychiatrists. Although Lacanians in Japan are small in number and they do not have its own psychoanalytical organisation, their influence on Japanese cultural discourse is clear.

Takahashi, T. (1982) 'La psychanalyse au Japon' in R. Jaccard (ed.), *Histoire de la Psychanalyse, Tome 2.* Paris: Hachette.
Okonogi, K. (1995) 'Japan' in P. Kutter (ed.), *Psychoanalysis International, Vol. 2* Stuttgart: Frommann-Holzboog.
Blowers, G. and Yang, H. C. S. (1997) 'Freud's *deshi*: The coming of psychoanalysis to Japan'. *Journal of the History of the Behavioural Sciences* 33(2):115–26.

K. Shi.

Jaspers, Karl (1883-1969) A German psychiatrist who as a research assistant in the Psychiatric Clinic of Heidelberg University between 1908 and 1915 produced seminal work on the methods by which psychiatrists explain disorders, work that ultimately took him into existential philosophy where he became world famous.

Jaspers came to Heidelberg directly from medical school but was chronically ill with bronchitis and therefore could not assume heavy clinical duties. However, as a research assistant for the director of the clinic, Franz Nissl, his skills as an open-minded but critical thinker about psychiatry and its neighbouring disciplines came to the fore. In 1913 he wrote his classical text *General Psychopathology*, based on his experiences that eventually went through seven editions up until 1959.

Jaspers wrote that psychiatry inhabited a middle ground between science, where laws of nature are discerned, and history, where fateful events emerge from human choices and actions. He spoke of 'explanation' (*erklaren*) as the attempt by the psychiatrist to discern nature's laws acting impersonally – through 'causal connections' – to produce mental disorder as in hereditary, neurobiologic, statistically demonstrable mechanisms. He contrasted this method with that of 'understanding' (*verstehen*) that grasped for 'meaningful connections' linking disorder to a conflict between a person's desires and experience – an individual conflict and its mental consequences that the psychiatrist could empathically appreciate.

By differentiating 'explanation' and 'understanding' Jaspers emphasised the epistemological divide that sometimes disrupted psychiatric discourse. However, from each method Jaspers identified crucial contributions to psychiatry even as he emphasised that those contributions were limited by the method from which they were derived. Thus he noted that explanations might slight the personal suffering of an individual whereas interpretations might overlook a neurobiologic process. In essence Jaspers' goal was to show what science cannot know and what psychiatry does not know and cannot claim. As one of the founders of existentialism he thought we could learn from the unsystematic approach of Kierkegaard and *Nietzsche. A theme of Jaspers is the pervasive failure of human aspirations. Failure, he thought, is ultimate but to philosophise is to learn to die and to 'encounter being by means of failure'.

P. McH.

JAFFE, ANIELA (1903–91) Jaffé was born in Berlin and died in Zurich. Fleeing Nazi Germany, Jaffé settled in Switzerland and soon entered the intellectual circle around C. G. Jung. She was the secretarial administrator of the Jung Institut in Zurich from its founding in 1948 until 1955, and then Jung's personal secretary until his death in 1961, all the while maintaining her own analytic practice. Jaffé was one of Jung's closest collaborators and wrote numerous well-regarded texts, most notably *The Myth of Meaning*, but is best remembered for her editing of Jung's autobiography, *Memories, Dreams, Reflections* and of his two volumes of correspondence.

Jaffé A. [1967] Der Mythus vom Sinn Zurich: Rascher. ((1986) *The Myth of Meaning*. Zurich: Daimon.)

Jaffé A. [1967] (1986) *The Myth of Meaning* [*Der Mythus vom Sinn*]. Zurich: Daimon.

R. H.

JEALOUSY A mental uneasiness caused by a suspicion or fear of rivalry and unfaithfulness in love. A belief, suspicion or fear that the good which one desires to gain or keep for oneself has been or may be directed to another person; a resentful feeling towards another on account of a known or suspected rivalry; an apprehension of being displaced in the love or goodwill of someone. Jealousy is usually based on love and aims at the possession of the loved object and the removal of the rival. It pertains to a triangular relationship and therefore presupposes differentiation between objects. It is thought to come from the first experience of sexual rivalry in childhood. It is a reaction of *hate and *aggression to a loss or threat of a loss of a valuable object. For Freud and Klein, jealousy is a primary *affect but they differ in how early they think it appears. A special feature of jealousy is the sense of humiliation owing to the injury it entails to one's self-confidence and sense of security. Freud realised in his own self-analysis that he had a love for his mother and a jealousy of his father and named this the *Oedipus complex.

Klein made a direct link between *envy experienced towards the mother's breast and the development of jealousy. She felt that jealousy was based on the suspicion of an early rivalry with the father, who is accused of having taken away the mother's breast and the mother. For her this rivalry marks the early stages of the direct and negative Oedipus complex. Klein made an important differentiation between envy and jealousy. She felt that envy went back to the subject's relation to one person only and the exclusive relation to the mother; whereas jealousy was based on envy, but involved a relation to at least two people. In both Freud's conception and Klein's a triangular situation can bring up deep feelings of jealous love and hate throughout life. For Lacan, rivalry is the foundation of jealousy, but it is not its only source. There is a triangular relation between the ego, its object, and the (maternal) *Other. Whereas in love, I am that object and 'we' enjoy as One, in hatred, that object is something else, and has to be eliminated. In jealousy, the object is presented by means of the image of an equal, and he or she is the one who enjoys where I was supposed to be.

Klein, M. (1957) 'Envy and Gratitude' in *Envy and Gratitude and Other Works.* London: Hogarth Press.
Freud, S. (1923) *The Infantile Genital Organization.* S. E. 19. London: Hogarth Press.
Riviere, J. (1991) *The Inner World of Joan Riviere: Collected Papers: 1920–1958.* London: Karnac Books.

C. E. / M. V.

JELLIFFE, SMITH ELY (1866–1945) Jelliffe practised in New York City from the 1890s to the 1940s. He was born in Brooklyn and took a bachelor's degree at Brooklyn Polytechnic and in 1889 an MD from the College of Physicians and Surgeons of Columbia University. After an internship and a *Wanderjahr* in Europe, he began as a young physician trying to earn a living wherever he could. He taught pharmacognosy, but his most important career move came in medical journalism – first in general medical journals and then, beginning in 1901, as owner and editor of the *Journal of Nervous and Mental Disease*. Concurrently, he started qualifying himself in neurology and then psychiatry, particularly by studying abroad.

Jelliffe's chief contribution was in familiarising his medical colleagues in the United States with medical publications and advances from Europe. With his close friend William Alanson White, of St Elizabeth's Hospital in Washington, Jelliffe initiated the *Nervous and Mental Disease Monograph Series* (1907) and then, in 1913, the first English-language psychoanalytic periodical, the *Psychoanalytic Review*. That same year, Jelliffe started formally publishing in the field of psychoanalysis.

Jelliffe had an expansive mind as well as a prodigious memory. It took some years for his colleagues to persuade him that he really had to choose between Jung and Freud, but by the mid-1920s, he was a pillar of psychoanalysis in New York and in America. His own contributions were largely speculative, although based on clinical experience. With Georg Groddeck, Jelliffe helped introduce a speculative stage in the development of psychosomatics.

Burnham, J. C. (1983) *Jelliffe: American Psychoanalyst and Physician, and His Correspondence with Sigmund Freud and C. G. Jung,* William McGuire (ed.) Chicago: University of Chicago Press.
Krasner, D. (1990) 'Smith Ely Jelliffe and the Immigration of European Physicians to the United States in the 1930s'. *Transactions and Studies of the College of Physicians of Philadelphia*, 5(12): 49–67.

J. C. B.

JONES, ERNEST (1879–1958) Ernest Jones is an influential figure in the development of psychoanalysis. A Welshman medically trained in London, like Freud he came to psychoanalysis through studying philosophy, neurology, disorders of speech, and psychopathology. He discovered Freud in 1906 and soon began to practice psychoanalysis. Within two years he met Jung, Freud and Ferenczi, impressing Freud with his paper 'Rationalisation in Everyday Life' at the first Psychoanalytical Congress in Salzburg.

In 1908 Jones emigrated to become Associate Professor of Psychiatry at the University of Toronto. He became Assistant Editor of the *Journal of Abnormal Psychology* and in 1911 organised the inaugural meeting of the American Psychoanalytical Association.

When, after brief analysis with Ferenczi, Jones returned to London in 1913, he established the London Psychoanalytical Society amidst conflicting allegiances to Freud and Jung. In 1919 he disbanded it and formed the British Psychoanalytical Society of which he was President from 1919 to 1944. In 1920 he instigated the *International Journal of Psychoanalysis*, in 1924, the Institute of Psychoanalysis and the International Psychoanalytical Library and by 1926 the London Clinic of Psychoanalysis. Between 1927 and 1929 he won recognition for psychoanalysis from the British Medical Association.

As President of the *International Psychoanalytical Association from 1920 to 1924 and from 1932 to 1949, Jones masterminded the resettlement of analysts (including the Freuds) who fled Nazi persecution. He shrewdly managed the ensuing conflict between Melanie Klein, whom he had encouraged to move to London in 1926, and Anna Freud – conflict which led to the *Controversial Discussions. In 1947 he began writing his biography of Freud which was published between 1953 and 1957.

Jones's most significant contributions to psychoanalytic thinking are his work on the theory of symbolism, aphanisis, and female sexuality, together with his exegesis of *Hamlet*.

Brome, V. (1982) *Ernest Jones: Freud's Alter Ego.* London: Caliban Books.

Jones, E. (1959) *Free Associations: Memories of a Psycho-Analyst.* London: Hogarth Press.

K. R.

JOUISSANCE *Jouissance* is Lacan's reformulation of Freud's notion of sexual satisfaction, taking into account that Freud held human sexual life to be characterised by dissatisfaction. This Lacanian concept is closely related to the energistic aspect of Freud's *drive theory. The tension or energy from the erogenous zones seeks release in the form of satisfaction, but that process is inhibited by repression. Some of this energy will indeed be discharged, whilst the rest will be retained and accumulated. There is a third possibility that is not a reality for the human being and that is a complete and full discharge of all the energy. Such a complete satisfaction would annihilate the subject. A partial discharge of energy (a limited form of pleasure) is called phallic *Jouissance* by Lacan. He calls this phallic because this form of satisfaction is limited by language and it is the identification with the phallus as signifier that hooks the subject to language. The remainder of the energy that will be retained in the psyche of the subject is called surplus *Jouissance* (a more to be enjoyed). It is a surplus because it is accumulated, ready to be used, but not actually used. This *Jouissance* is maintained and built up in the erogenous zones. Total satisfaction is called the *Jouissance* of the *Other by Lacan, because the subject supposes that this possibility exists, but always somewhere else. It supposes it indeed elsewhere and of course it does exist in the otherness of death. Besides phallic *Jouissance* and the *Jouissance* of the Other Lacan recognises a third form which he calls feminine *Jouissance*. For Lacan *woman cannot be completely determined by the phallic signifier. His supposition is that an incompleteness or lack in the Symbolic allows the essence of femininity to remain elusive. For this reason, something of her way of enjoying, her *Jouissance*, escapes the limiting grasp of the phallic *signifier. In that sense a woman is divided between ordinary limited (phallic) *Jouissance* and an other (feminine) *Jouissance* she enjoys but about which she cannot speak.

J. P. K.

JUDGEMENT Judgement is part of the mental process aimed at the passage from a real situation to a desired situation, leading from thought to action. The function of judgement is concerned with two sorts of decisions, whether a thing is desirable, and whether it is real, i.e. true or false. The first judgement belongs to the *pleasure principle, and the second to the *reality principle.

V. D.

JUNG, CARL G. (1875–1961) Jung is the founder of *analytical psychology. Born on 26 July 1875 to Johann Paul Jung, a Swiss Reformed pastor, and his wife, Emilie, née Preiswerk, in the Swiss village of Kesswil, he received a classical European education in German-speaking Swiss schools. He studied medicine at the University of Basel from 1896 to 1900. Deeply interested in philosophy and religion as well as science, he read Kant, Schopenhauer, and Nietzsche while a student. These philosophers formed the basis of Jung's thinking and fundamentally influenced him throughout his life. In 1900 he entered a psychiatric residency at the Bürgholzli clinic in Zurich and studied and worked there under the renowned Professor Eugen Bleuler until 1909.

In psychiatry *Bleuler, *Charcot, Janet, and Flournoy were his major reference points. His early publications included a book on schizophrenia and a series of research papers using the Word Association Experiment. In 1903 he married Emma Rauschenbach and eventually became the father of five children – four daughters and a son. Jung began an intense collaborative relationship with Freud in 1907.

Quickly recognising Jung's intellectual gifts and his potential as a charismatic leader, Freud came to designate him his 'crown prince' and heir to the fledgling psychoanalytic movement. Jung was the first President of the *International Psychoanalytic Association, a position he held from 1910 to 1914. He was also the first editor of the early psychoanalytic journal, *Jahrbuch für Psychologische und Psychopathologische Forschungen*, sponsored jointly by Freud and Bleuler. The voluminous correspondence between Jung and Freud was published in 1974 and contains a vivid portrayal of the waxing and waning of the relationship between these two pioneers.

From the beginning, Jung was sceptical about Freud's exclusive emphasis on sexuality in the aetiology of neurosis and psychosis. Later he became strongly attracted to the psychology and philosophy of William James, whom he met in 1909 at Clark University in Wooster, Massachusetts, and whose works agreed more with his own philosophical tendencies. The Freud-Jung relationship broke up in 1913 over personal and theoretical conflicts. From Jung's point of view, the major problems were Freud's emphasis on sexuality and his inordinate need for personal authority in intellectual matters pertaining to psychoanalysis. Freud accused Jung of being mystical. In 1914 Jung founded his own school of *analytical psychology. At the core of it was the view that all human beings share a primordial level of psyche. Jung called this level the *collective unconscious. The contents of the collective unconscious are general patterns of ideation, imagination, and behaviour. The inborn psychological factors that create these universal human patterns he designated *archetypes. Archetypes behave like drives but are represented as images in the psyche and have more a mental than biological quality. Accordingly, instead of the term *libido*, Jung preferred the more general *psychic energy*, which again distanced him from Freud's emphasis on sexuality. Analytical psychology was able to take a positive view of religious experience in a way that psychoanalysis could not, and although Jung did not intend anything mystical in his formulations of the collective unconscious, archetypes, and psychic energy, it was precisely these elements that led Freudians to accuse him of abandoning science for mysticism.

Jung hammered out the bare outlines of his own distinctive psychological theory during the years following his break with Freud. The period 1913–17 was a period of intensive self-analysis, a time that is sometimes mistaken as heavily psychotic rather than what Ellenberger has called a period of 'creative illness', noting that Freud had a similar experience following the death of his father. In these years Jung provisionally published his revision of psychoanalytic theory in the first drafts of what would become, after several editions, *Two Essays in Analytical Psychology*. These essays still provide the best introduction to Jung's approach to psychoanalytic theory and practice. In 1921 he published the major work *Psychological Types*, in which he explored psychodynamic relations between conscious and unconscious and the differences between introverts and extroverts, thinkers and feelers, sensate and intuitive people. He used this theory to understand the differing cognitive styles of Freud, *Adler and himself.

In his writings Jung said little about the details of early childhood development. Perhaps his most important general contribution to the practice of psychoanalysis was the emphasis he placed on the role of the analyst's personality in the treatment of patients and the central importance of genuine interaction between analyst and analysand. He also espoused a more positive view of the unconscious, seeing it as potentially creative and resourceful often beyond the limited perspectives of ego-consciousness. His description of the diversity of innate psychological structures extends the complexity of human thought and behaviour.

Between the World Wars Jung was active teaching at home in Zurich and abroad in England, the United States, and throughout Europe. He also travelled extensively in Africa and India. In the late 1920s he developed a special and abiding interest in Eastern thought and religions. Through his friendship with Richard Wilhelm, the German Sinologist and translator of such works as the *I Ching*, Jung began to see connections between Western psychology and Eastern philosophy. This interest led him to his long-term participation in the Eranos Conferences held every August from 1933 into the 1980s in Ascona, Switzerland.

In 1933 Jung reluctantly accepted the presidency of the International General Medical Society for Psychotherapy, a post that he held until 1940. The story of Jung's politics during this period is complex, and the emotions generated have led easily to oversimplification and splitting. While not a sympathiser, much less a member, of the *Nazi party in Germany, he walked a fine line between neutrality and internationalism on the one side and cooperation with the large German section of this organisation on the other. The frequent accusations that Jung was anti-Semitic and a Nazi sympathiser have been refuted again and again, but with little result. The best discussion to date of this episode in Jung's life is by Thomas Kirsch in *The Jungians*.

Jung's last twenty years bore the fruit of decades of experience with patients and of his vast researches in comparative symbolism. Beset by illness and frail health, he published his most important work on transference (*The Psychology of the Transference*), an interpretation of Western cultural history (*Aion* and *Answer to Job*), a work on psychology and modern physics (*On Synchronicity*), and a summary of his thinking on *individuation (*Mysterium Coniunctionis*). His many friendships bridged religion and science: while collaborating with the Dominican priest, Victor White, on studies of Christian theology, for instance, he was also writing a book with the Nobel Prize-winning physicist, Wolfgang Pauli. Jung's life was filled with honours and accolades (lunch with Winston Churchill during his visit to Zurich after World War II, honorary doctorates from Harvard and Oxford, a literary prize from the city of Zurich) befitting the magnitude of his intellectual achievements.

Ellenberger, H. F. (1970) *The Discovery of the Unconscious*. New York: Basic Books.

Hannah, B. (1977) *Jung, His Life and Work*. Wilmette: Chiron.

Jung, C. G. (1961) *Memories, Dreams, Reflections*. Translated by R. and C. Winston. New York: Vintage Books

Kirsch, T. B. (2000) *The Jungians*. London and Philadelphia: Routledge.

Stein, M. (1998) *Jung's Map of the Soul*. Chicago and LaSalle: Open Court.

Wehr, G. (1987) *Jung, a Biography*. Translated by D. M. Weeks. Boston and London: Shambhala.

M. Ste

JUNG (PRECIS) see ANALYTICAL PSYCHOLOGY

K

Kernberg, Otto (1928–) is Director of the Personality Disorders Institute at the New York Presbyterian Hospital, Westchester Division and Professor of Psychiatry at the Weill Medical College of Cornell University. Dr Kernberg is past-president of the International Psychoanalytic Association. He is also Training and Supervising Analyst of the Columbia University Center of Psychoanalytic Training and Research. In the past, Dr Kernberg served as Director of the C. F. Menninger Memorial Hospital, Supervising and Training Analyst of the Topeka Institute for Psychoanalysis, and Director of the Psychotherapy Research Project of the Menninger Foundation.

His principal contributions to psychoanalysis and dynamic psychiatry include his clarification of the field of personality disorders, the development of a specific psychoanalytic psychotherapy of these conditions, and a new technical psychoanalytic approach to the treatment of the borderline and narcissistic personality disorders. He has also contributed to the development of psychoanalytic object relations theory, and its application as a developmental, diagnostic and therapeutic tool.

The honours he has received include the 1972 Heinz Hartmann Award of the New York Psychoanalytic Institute and Society, and the 1990 Mary S. Sigourney Award for Psychoanalysis. He received the Distinguished Service Award from the American Psychiatric Association in 1995. He was elected Doctor Honoris Causa by the University of Buenos Aires, Argentina, in 1998, and received the Austrian Cross of Honor for Science and Art in 1999.

He is the author of eight books and co-author of nine others: *Psychotherapy and Psychoanalysis: Final Report of the Menninger Foundation's Psychotherapy Research Project*, 1972; *Borderline Conditions and Pathological Narcissism*, 1975; *Object Relations Theory and Clinical Psychoanalysis*, 1976; *Internal World and External Reality: Object Relations Theory Applied*, 1980; *Severe Personality Disorders: Psychotherapeutic Strategies*, 1984; *Aggression in Personality Disorders and Perversion*, 1992; *Ideology, Conflict, and Leadership in Groups and Organizations*, 1998; including, as solo author, *Object Relations, Affects and Transference* (in press), and *Aggressivity, Narcissism and Self-destructiveness* (in press).

R. M. S.

Khan, Masud (1924–89) A one-time leading member of the British Independent group, editor, disciple of Winnicott, author of numerous papers especially on trauma, dreams, sexual deviations and personality disorder, his career ended ignominiously amidst scandals over his chronic transgressions with patients and published anti-Semitic remarks. Born in what is now Pakistan, the youngest son of an elderly father, Khan spuriously claimed to be of patrician stock and would seek such affiliation throughout his life. After completing an MA in English at the University of the Punjab, he moved to London where he trained at the Institute of Psychoanalysis, qualifying in 1950, aged twenty six. In due course he was made a full member (1955) and training analyst (1959) and quickly became involved in the Publications Committee, assuming the editorship of the *International Psychoanalytical Library in* 1969. His grandiosity, arrogance, drinking and extramarital affairs (many with patients) contributed to the failure of his two marriages, souring of relations with colleagues, debarment as a training analyst in 1976 and ultimately to expulsion from the British Society in 1988. He died from cancer, which he had struggled against since the mid-1970s, and the effects of chronic alcoholism.

Despite his notoriety, Khan made serious contributions to the psychoanalytic literature. His concept of 'cumulative trauma' (wherein development is biased through individually slight though cumulatively significant failures in the mother's protective shield role) marked a shift away from a prevalent view of trauma as linked to single pathogenic events. In considering dream psychology, Khan's successive discussions of the 'good dream', 'dream space' and the 'dreaming experience' gradually evolved towards seeing dream (as contrasted with the remembered dream text) as a thing-in-itself within which otherwise inarticulable aspects of the self may be actualisable, a view some have regarded as bordering on mysticism. Finally, in looking at character disorder and perversion, Khan drew on Fairbairn and Winnicott in emphasising environmental failure, splitting processes, alienation and ultimately aggravating omnipotent attempts at self-cure. In perversions, for instance, Khan saw the individual as interspersing an impersonal object, such as a fetish, between his desire and his accomplice, resulting in a transitory and illusory sense of omnipotent self-cure supported by orgasm while more fundamentally exacerbating self-alienation.

Khan, M. M. R. (1974) *The Privacy of the Self.* London: Hogarth Press.

Khan, M. M. R. (1979) *Alienation in Perversions.* London: Hogarth Press.

Khan, M. M. R. (1983) *Hidden Selves.* London: Hogarth Press.

R. W.

KLEIN, MELANIE (1882–1960) Melanie Klein is the founder of a child psychoanalytic theory and technique associated with her name. She was born on 30 March 1882 to Moriz Reizes, a Galician general practitioner and his wife, Libussa Deutsch, in Vienna. Her family, like so many other eastern European Jewish families who harboured assimilationist desires, flocked to major urban centres like Vienna, where they lived a lower middle class existence without any significant social connections. Although educated at the lyceum, Her family could not afford to give her a university education and in 1903, aged twenty-one, she married Arthur Klein, a chemical engineer. By the time their third child was born in 1914, the family's frequent moves and her depressive episodes led her to seek psychoanalytic treatment, which she received from Sándor *Ferenczi in Budapest. He also encouraged her to make systematic observations on young children and she quickly demonstrated a talent for accessing unconscious mental life. As a lay female observer with no university credentials, Klein took what was offered her and worked hard. She began publishing her observations by 1919 and dealt with pedagogical questions, such as how to sexually enlighten young children according to Freudian precepts. After the Great War, when anti-Semitic terrorism erupted in Budapest, she moved to Berlin in 1921, where she continued her work first in supervision and then in analysis with Karl *Abraham. Desirous of finding a talented lay female analyst who could test out his ideas linking early psychosexual fixations and psychosis, Abraham enthusiastically touted Klein's burgeoning skills to Freud in 1924. Abraham's early and unfortunate death in 1925 simultaneously deprived Klein of not only her analyst, but also her mentor and patron, who had defended her work from critics like Franz Alexander and Sándor Radó.

Learning from the work of other pioneers in child analysis, such as Hermine von Hug-Hellmuth, Klein began to experiment with various forms of play as a way to understand the intrapsychic mind of the young child. Regarding play as a form through which the child articulated its associations, she took up this innovation as a way to understand the early unconscious mind. She concentrated her analytic efforts in an area heretofore neglected, namely the young child's subjective relationship to the maternal body, having been struck by the degree to which the child's play behaviour reflected anxiety over maternally-directed aggressive phantasies.

While Klein's analytic work helped her overcome her modest familial origins and dreary marriage, her work could only flourish with the considerable support of powerfully situated patrons like Ferenczi and Abraham. After Abraham's death, she was extracted from her vulnerable position in Berlin by Ernest Jones, who became her new patron and invited her in 1926 to settle, work and teach in London, where she lived for the rest of her life. London proved to be a hospitable place for her child work. One effect of the Great War was to loosen the gendered divisions of labour, so a woman could do a 'man's work'. In the fledgling field of child analysis, females with and without degrees were welcomed into the liberal atmosphere of European psychoanalysis. Once another talented Viennese analyst, Anna Freud, criticised Klein's techniques in print, Jones encouraged Klein and her supporters to defend her evolving position; the ensuing scientific dispute helped establish Klein's reputation as well as that of the British Psycho-Analytical Society as a premier training institute.

Klein regarded herself as a Freudian loyalist and argued that her emerging views were a meaningful 'extension' of his. In her view, there was a basic continuity between the child's play and adult verbal association, essentially arguing that the child was 'minded' long before Sigmund Freud had assumed. She hypothesised that the origins of the *super-ego and *Oedipus complex for example, were rooted in the infant's phantasied experience of the maternal body in the first year of life and universalised these findings by 1932. During the course of the 1930s, there was however an increasingly polarised atmosphere between the London and Vienna schools of child analysis. Klein's work had also come under attack within the British Society, and by the time the Freuds moved to London following the *Anschluß* in 1938, the feud between those loyal to Anna Freud and Melanie Klein could no longer be contained. The ensuing *Controversial Discussions (1941–5) forced both sides to grapple with their theoretical differences while further refining their own views. Against the backdrop of total war and annihilation, Klein became increasingly convinced of the importance of the *death instinct and she is generally credited with urging a more complete analytic understanding of human aggression.

By the end of World War II, a compromise was worked out by the British Society, under which a three-track training system was created: there would be a Klein group, an Anna Freud group and a Middle or Independent group, all existing under the aegis of one training institute.

Although Klein had ended her attempts at a theoretical *rapprochement* with Freud by 1935, when she began to outline her own developmental schema in terms of 'positions,' it wasn't until 1946 that she refined her conception of the child's primitive state of mind with her articulation of the 'paranoid-schizoid' and 'depressive' positions. These fresh perspectives accompanied numerous technical innovations as well, particularly a more existential emphasis on the nature of transference phenomena, where the patient was postulated via the mechanisms of splitting and projective identification, to put his or her primitive experience into the mind set of the analyst. In other words, rather than the classical view of transference, as a displacement from past to present, the Kleinian view was more from 'inside to outside', in the here-and-now of the analytic encounter. It is not surprising that some of Klein's gifted students and analysands, like D. W. *Winnicott and Paula Heimann, began to then consider the impact of primitive patient communications on the countertransference reactions in the analyst, claiming that these phenomena were worthy of analytic consideration.

More importantly, Klein exhorted a new generation of talented analysts to treat, write about and analytically conceptualise the problems of psychotic disorders like schizophrenia. After World War II, a new generation of brilliant pupils emerged: Wilfred Bion, Hanna Segal, Donald Meltzer and Herbert Rosenfeld, all of whom devoted considerable efforts and achieved some measure of success in the analytic treatment of the psychoses. In the last years of her life, Klein continued to make seminal contributions: 'Envy and Gratitude' posited envy as a primary unconscious motivator and she crowned a successful career with the posthumously published *The Narrative of a Child Analysis*, the most extensive account of a child analysis ever published at that time, offering analysts a day-by-day process record of how she worked with a young boy. Her analytic legacy and longevity has been consolidated and extended by the pupils she trained and analysed at the British Psycho-Analytical Society, the Kleinian School now being firmly in the vanguard of international psychoanalysis.

Aguayo, J. (1997) 'Historicizing the origins of Kleinian psychoanalysis: Klein's analytic relationship with Ferenczi, Abraham and Jones, 1914–1927'. *International Journal of Psychoanalysis* 78.

Aguayo, J. (2000) 'Patronage in the dispute over child analysis between Melanie Klein and Anna Freud, 1927–1932'. *International Journal of Psychoanalysis* 81.

Grosskurth, P. (1986) *Melanie Klein: Her World and Her Work*. New York: Knopf.

Segal, H. (1964) *Introduction to the Work of Melanie Klein*. London: Hogarth Press.

J. A.

KLEIN PRECIS In 1921, Klein, as a follower of Freud, remained loyal to him and took the position that the repression of childhood sexuality led to emotional illness and abnormal development, including inhibition in curiosity, creativity and intellectual abilities. However, stimulated and nurtured by her relationships with her two analysts, Sándor *Ferenczi and Karl *Abraham, Klein's Freudian psychoanalysis evolved toward a focus on earlier emotional life, later to be termed pre-genital. This concept broadened to emphasise not only sex but also survival or the drama of life and death. Following the direction of her text reveals a shift from Freud's economic theory to his later emphasis on the life and death instincts as connected with survival. In this context Klein's theory emphasises annihilation anxiety. Sexuality is gradually eclipsed by the function of phantasy as the key concept of Kleinian psychoanalytic discourse. Klein proposed that the drives are never known in a raw form, but are known though the drives and the ideas accompanying them (Freud) and *phantasy (Klein). She proposes that lack of love and difficult external conditions exacerbate the infant's annihilation anxieties, and although she does not delineate a formal definition of the holding and containing parental functions, she lays the ground work for an elaboration of this dimension of mental growth. Klein states that infantile phantasies are shaped and coloured by good and bad experiences.

When the infant is *frustrated or suffering from bodily discomfort (e.g. colic) the signification images of these experiences are of dark and dangerous figures. The *breast is felt to be an enemy, which is attacked, devoured and torn, and produces the narrative of a retaliatory monster in turn eating up the baby's innards causing intense feelings of terror. Similarly, good experiences give rise to positive images of a loving, generous and feeding breast. The infant then feels full of a sense of well-being. By the mid-20s Klein's theories of mental development began to problematise the classical view of libidinal stages and by 1935 she had firmly introduced the notion of positions, with the *paranoid schizoid and *depressive positions being jointly elaborated by the late forties. Klein defines these positions as a group of anxieties and related defences against them.

Much of her description and understanding of critical aspects of these positions are based on her notion of splitting and the projective mechanisms. By the time of her 1946 paper, 'Notes on some schizoid mechanisms', Klein is able to formally elaborate the term projective identification. Many of the processes of the paranoid schizoid position are interconnected to a developing notion of projective identification. She had already grasped aspects and functions of the depressive position in her earlier papers of 1921 and 1928 on mourning and manic depressive states. Klein summarises her thinking about projective identification as the projections of the infant or patient of aspects of the relationship of the infant to good and bad objects. The problematical repercussions stemming from the projection and the identification of the bad *imagoes or *part objects is that these processes install the bad objects inside the ego where they function as a negative presence or an attacking primitive super-ego. The projection and identification with the gratifying part object leads to the introjection of a loving bountiful breast mother that supports love and trust. The two prototypes (good and bad) inside the ego are either split internally or re-projected again, chiefly into the maternal imago. Klein emphasised that projective identification is felt to both rid the infant of emotional pain, by forcing it into an object, and may also protect the good aspects of the self and object by 'giving' them to the other person. Paranoia, claustrophobia, *idealisation and *envy are the result of the manoeuvres brought on by projective identification.

The paranoid schizoid position functions through splitting, projection, omnipotence and hallucinatory gratification. Klein understands the primitive nature of these tactics and their necessity during times of felt or real helplessness. The approach of the depressive position is in part due to maturation processes during the first three months after birth and stimulates integration of the split imagoes and lessens the belief in omnipotence and *hallucination. According to Klein, these changes make entry into the depressive position possible. The differences between internal and external reality are more clearly defined. Regret and the desire to make reparation to what had been the hated, misused object are painfully evoked by the knowledge that the good and bad internal objects are drawn from the same persona. The pain of regret, the loss of omnipotence, the terror of helplessness and the attacks mounted by the old personas that dread growth and loss of control all come together in such a way that the entry into the depressive position may be felt to be catastrophic. Klein links the failure to enter into the new emotional configurations with difficulties in development and also with the onset in later life of mental illness, such as manic depression or even schizophrenia, if the splitting of the *paranoid schizoid position is extreme.

Klein also elaborated a theory of manic defences constructed to avoid the emotional pain of dependency. The infant/patient utilises *projective identification to disavow feelings of vulnerability and takes on the persona of the adult who is felt to have unlimited supplies, power and omnipotent control. Psychological reality is bypassed and the excessive use of *manic defences becomes characterological and robs the subject of the capacity for intimacy, passion and emotional truth. Klein proposes that the stalemate at the entry into the depressive position leaves the subject alienated from deep feelings through the excessive use of the manic defences with accompanying paranoia, negativity and doubt or to put it another way, to remain stuck in an aberrant paranoid schizoid position without the means for introjecting good objects and good mental nourishment.

See especially: internal object; reparation; splitting

See also: bad object; child analysis; death drive gratitude; Klein, Melanie; mother; mother's body (inside); object; Oedipus complex; oral sadism; super-ego; weaning

J. A.

KNOT The metaphor of a knot is present in Lacan's work from 1953. The signifying chain is composed of rings and the *quilting point formed by the *name-of-the-father is a kind of knot binding together rings. The node is inherent in both Symbolic structure and logic. Undoing and tightening knots then becomes part of clinical work.

N. C.

KNOWLEDGE Psychoanalytic knowledge for Lacan is the knowledge of the unconscious unfolding in speech. It supposes a subject who operates through transference which is the re-transcription of traits marking that subject's relation to *jouissance. As a signifying structure, knowledge can never be completed or closed as no body of knowledge can answer for the effects of jouissance.

See also: link

P. D.

KOHUT, HEINZ (1913–81) Kohut was a leading post-Freudian psychoanalyst and the creator of what he called 'psychoanalytic self psychology'. Kohut was born and raised in an upper middle-class, assimilated Jewish family in Vienna, even though he remained conflicted about his own Jewish identity. Kohut's father, Felix who died in 1937 was an accomplished pianist who went into the paper business after four long years of service on the eastern front in World War I. His mother, Else Lampl Kohut who died in 1972, was strong-willed and played the major role in the life of her adored only son, Heinz. When it was time for him to attend school, she hired tutors and kept him at home; later, however, he attended the last year of elementary school and all eight years at the Döblinger Gymnasium from 1924 until 1932. After 1932 Kohut studied medicine at the University of Vienna and graduated in 1938.

For at least two years in his early adolescence, Else Kohut hired a tutor, Ernst Morawetz, who was probably a university student, to spend most afternoons with Heinz and take him to the opera and museums. This tutor, about whom Kohut always spoke with great fondness, gave much meaning to a childhood that was otherwise filled with utter loneliness. It was also a sexualised relationship, Kohut's first love, that he describes in detail but in disguise in his autobiographical case history, *The Two Analyses of Mr. Z.*

Kohut was a highly cultured man with exquisite tastes in music and the arts. He grew up attending opera as much as three times a week and was well acquainted with current trends in literature and painting. He had no special interest in Freud but after his father's death sought psychotherapy in 1937 from a psychologist named Walter Marseilles, who was an expert in the Rorschach test. Later that year Kohut went into analysis with the renowned psychoanalyst and friend of Freud's, August Aichhorn. That analysis – and much else – was to be prematurely terminated as an effect of the *Anschluß*, or takeover, of Austria by Hitler and the Nazis in the spring of 1938. Kohut was appalled at the vulgarity of the Nazis and traumatised by their violence. He was nearly sent to Dachau over the summer, faced great danger during *Kristallnacht* that November, and took his medical exams with new Nazi professors sporting large swastika buttons on their lapels.

In early 1939 Kohut managed to leave Vienna for England, where he stayed for a year, first in a camp for immigrants and then in his uncle's apartment in London, before acquiring his visa for America. He arrived in the United States in March 1940, with $25 in his pocket. Kohut took a bus to Chicago to join his childhood friend, Siegmund Levarie, who had previously arrived and acquired a position at the University.

Further training in medicine took Kohut through residencies in neurology and psychiatry at the University of Chicago during the 1940s. Kohut moved slowly into psychoanalysis. He went through a 'didactic' (and for him painstaking) analysis with Ruth Eissler in the early and mid-1940s and began course work at the Chicago Institute for Psychoanalysis in 1946. He graduated from the Institute in 1950 and immediately joined the faculty. At that point Kohut basically left the university, though he remained a lecturer in psychiatry, and worked full-time for the rest of his life as a clinical psychoanalyst.

Kohut married Elizabeth Meyers in 1948 and had a son, Thomas August, in 1951 (his only child). Kohut's star quickly rose in the 1950s at the Chicago Institute for Psychoanalysis, where he was widely, though sometimes with envy, recognised as its most creative figure. He published a number of important articles in these years on applied psychoanalysis, especially on the psychology of music, but his greatest contribution was an essay on empathy that was first presented in 1956 and published in 1959. In it Kohut argued that the essential way of knowing in psychoanalysis was through empathy, which he defined as vicarious introspection. Anything else was quixotic and false to the tradition. He never wavered from this position, and empathy became the centrepiece of his more general *self psychology.

From 1964 until 1965 Kohut served a term as President of the American Psychoanalytic Association, which marked the culmination of a long and active period of involvement in administrative leadership of psychoanalysis. But from the mid-1960s until his death in 1981, Kohut devoted himself to writing and scholarship. His most important book was the 1971 monograph, *The Analysis of the Self: A Systematic Analysis of the Treatment of the Narcissistic Personality Disorders*. That book had a significant impact on the field by extending Freud's theory of narcissism and introducing what Kohut called the 'self-object transferences' of mirroring and idealisation. A second book in 1977, *The Restoration of the Self*, moved from a focus on narcissism to a discussion of the self, its development and vicissitudes and the 'tension gradient' of what he then called the 'bipolar self', an idea that has not generally endured. In 1978 the first two volumes of his papers, *Search for the Self*, appeared.

Along with his writing, Kohut created a group of devoted followers around him that soon became a national and even international movement in scope. He had conscious ambitions to change the character of psychoanalysis.

Kohut's last decade, however, was a time of personal torment, as the lymphoma he contracted in 1971 caused a steady decline. Kohut kept his cancer a dark secret, known only to his family and one or two close friends. In 1979, he had bypass surgery from which there were complications and a lengthy recovery. In the next few years he had inner ear problems and a bout of pneumonia. By 1981 he was in a state of general decline and died that autumn on 8 October.

Despite his illnesses, Kohut continued to work. By the time of his death his last book, *How Does Analysis Cure?*, was largely complete, although it only appeared in 1984 after being edited by a colleague, Arnold Goldberg, with the assistance of Paul Stepansky. A volume of new and republished essays appeared in 1985, edited by Charles B. Strozier, *Self Psychology and the Humanities*, and in 1990 and 1991 volumes three and four of Kohut's papers, *Search for the Self*, appeared, edited by Paul Ornstein, as well as, in 1994, a selection of Kohut's correspondence, edited by Geoffrey Cocks, *The Curve of Life*.

The essence of Kohut's contributions to psychoanalysis is that he found a way to abandon drive theory but retain a depth psychology focused on the direct and symbolic involvement of the self in the world (what he called *selfobjects). Much else at the level of theory and in the clinic changed. Kohut transformed the way psychoanalysts think about narcissism, about 'objects', about sexuality and sexualisation, about aggression and rage, about dreams, about the relationship between psychoanalysis and the humanities in general, about many of our ethical values, and about the very meaning of the self in human experience.

Because of his murky prose, in some respects Kohut's greatest influence has been indirect, that is, filtered through his impact on the writings of others interested in holistic ideas of the self. He is the pivotal figure for all the competing orientations in self psychology and for what is generally called *intersubjective theory. His work was also critical for the emergence of relational psychoanalysis, constructivism, and postmodernism, although these categories overlap and other thinkers influenced their development. In addition, theologians, philosophers, historians, critics, and humanists have incorporated Kohut's ideas, often without awareness of their source. Feminists with a psychological bent have found in Kohut a perspective on the self that avoids the insidious sexism in most of psychoanalysis. Finally, one might say Kohut has profoundly influenced public discourse in a society obsessed with psychological meanings. The understanding we have of dissociation, for example, from multiple personalities to the ravages of trauma in sexual abuse and war, owes some of its deeper meaning to his work.

Many had flailed at the stout walls of classical psychoanalysis and ego psychology. It took someone from the inside to think through the project from the ground up, discard the debris but recover what remained valuable in its clinical insights. Kohut, for all his own confusions and contradictions, may well have saved psychoanalysis from itself. Kohut's own protean sexuality and identity confusions fitted him uneasily into the world of psychoanalysis as it then existed. Kohut needed to change the theory in order to find a place for himself in it. That project connected with larger themes. Kohut lived out in his life and formulated in his work the core issues surrounding narcissism and the self which were preoccupying contemporary America. He touched its pulse.

Strozier, Charles B. (2001) Heinz Kohut: *The Making of a Psychoanalyst*. New York: Farrar, Straus & Giroux.

C. Str.

Korea During the period of Korea's colonisation by *Japan (1910–45) from where its psychiatric models were derived, one doctor, Sung Hee Kim, trained as an analyst under Kosawa Heisaku. But it was the outbreak of the Korean war, bringing American psychiatrists to Korea and teaching depth psychology, and the return to Korea of a few of the many who had gone to the United States for further training after World War II, which led to psychoanalysis being introduced as a formal system of thought. As with Japan, Koreans have made their psychoanalysis culturally relevant by modifying some of its central tenets. The *Oedipus complex, for example, is understood as being resolved by sublimating incestuous wishes to *hyoa*, the Korean term for filial piety. Prevalent Taoist beliefs about illness being due to an excess of exertion in thought or action has led in some neo-Freudian quarters to 'Taoistic psychotherapy' which emphasises an acceptance rather than a refusal of one's inner conflicts, and transcends them by training the mind towards a more positive outlook.

Not until the 1970s did Korean clinicians seek formal ties with the International Psychoanalytic Association. Cho Doo-Young, trained at Cornell, organised the Korean Psychoanalytic Study Group, which with fifty members has since developed into the Korean Psychoanalytic Study Group and is orthodox Freudian in orientation. Two other organisations, the Korean Academy of Psychotherapy (neo-Freudian and Taoistic with about eighty members) and the Korean Association of Jungian Psychology (with thirty members) are actively pursuing a culturally relevant psychoanalytic practice.

Since the 1980s, psychoanalytic interests in Korea, in line with other parts of the world, have diminished in the wake of a rising interest in biologically based explanations of psychological disturbance. Coupled with the lack of Korean training analysts, this has meant that training has continued in a foreign context where the differences in language and cultural understanding have traditionally (in the West) been viewed as resistance but which might become the wellspring for future developments in cultural psychoanalytic theory.

Fisher, C. P. (1996) 'Panel report: psychoanalysis in the Pacific Rim'. *International Journal of Psychoanalysis* 77: 373–7.
Kim, K. I. (1996) 'Traditional therapeutic issues in psychiatric practice in Korea'. Paper read in a

Transcultural Psychiatry Symposium of the Xth World Congress of Psychiatry, 23–8 August.

G. B.

Kris, Ernst (1900–57) Originally a PhD in art history, Kris became a psychoanalyst in Vienna as a young man and soon became prominent in the field. He was a close associate of Freud in Freud's later years and, together with Anna. *Freud and Hartmann, his literary executor. As such he served as co-editor of Freud's *Collected Psychological Works* (in German) and as editor of *The Origins of Psychoanalysis* (in both German and English). His many articles on the application of psychoanalysis to the study of art are collected in a volume called *Psychoanalytic Explorations in Art*. In 1945 he settled in New York, where he soon became an influential teacher and a training and supervising analyst at the New York Psychoanalytic Institute.

With A. Freud, Hartmann, *Fenichel and other expatriates, Kris pioneered the emphasis on the importance of defence analysis in the USA and co-authored several articles with Hartmann. From its inception until his untimely death, Kris was the director of the Child Study Center at Yale University, the first of its kind in the USA. Kris introduced the concept of regression in the service of the ego to account for the fact that many activities customarily included under the heading of sublimation, e.g. artistic creativity, are accompanied by conscious pleasure, sometimes explicitly sexual in nature; in psychoanalytic terms, by absence of the neutralisation of drive energy supposed to be characteristic of sublimation.

Kris, E. (1951) 'Ego psychology and interpretation in psychoanalytic therapy'. *Psychoanalytic Quarterly* 20: 15–30.
Kris, E. (1953) *The Origins of Psychoanalysis*. New York: Basic Books.
Kris, E. (1955) 'Neutralization and sublimation'. *Psychoanalytic Study of the Child* 10: 30–46.
Kris, E. (1956) 'The personal myth'. *Journal of the American Psychoanalytic Association* 4: 653–81.

C. B.

Kristeva, Julia (1941–) has strongly influenced psychoanalysis, semiotics, philosophy, literary criticism, cultural criticism, and gender studies. Born in Bulgaria, she has lived primarily in Paris since 1966 when she worked with Roland Barthes on her dissertation. In 1967, she joined the *Tel Quel* group, headed by Philippe Sollers, whom she eventually married. Kristeva completed psychoanalytic training in 1979, and started her own practice in Paris while also teaching at the University of Paris VII.

From 1976 to 1999, Kristeva shared a rotating visiting chair of literary semiology at Columbia University with Umberto Eco and Tzvetan Todorov. She is also Executive Secretary of the International Association of Semiology. In April 1997, Julia Kristeva received a *Chevalière de la légion d'honneur* – one of France's highest honours. Her work has been translated into ten languages. Her most recent writings include the three-volume *Le génie féminin: la vie, la folie, les mots* (1999–2002), which examines the lives and works of Arendt, *Klein, and Colette. She is also an accomplished novelist.

Kristeva is well-known for destabilising the symbolic order, thereby putting the subject 'in process' and 'on trial'. As early as 1974 in her dissertation *La révolution du langage poétique*, Kristeva puts the subject '*en procès*' by enriching Bakhtin's idea of 'intertextuality' with psychoanalysis. Her 'semanalysis' – combining semiology with psychoanalysis – facilitates a similar process by reconnecting the body and the drives to language.

S. C.

L

Lacan, Jacques Marie-Emile (1901–81) The most eminent French psychoanalyst and psychoanalytic theorist of the twentieth century, and arguably the most formidably brilliant of Freud's successors. Jacques Lacan is (in) famous as a clinician for his controversial commitment to the 'variable length' clinical session. He is also renowned as a theorist for his idiosyncratic 'return to the meaning of Freud' drawing on contemporary developments in philosophy, linguistics, anthropology, game theory and mathematics, and presented in prose of notorious difficulty. Although Lacan's ideas constantly evolved as he developed them in his famous Paris seminar, his theoretical intervention is grounded in a far-reaching criticism especially of the post-Freudian 'ego psychology' developed by Loewenstein (who analysed Lacan) and Hartmann in the 1940s and 1950s. According to Lacan, the 'Freudian field' (*le champ freudien*) is properly the field of language, and humans are beings who are 'captured and tortured by language'. In order to reground Freudian metapsychology and clinical practice, Lacan proposed three inter-related orders of human experience; the Imaginary, the Symbolic and the Real. Broadly speaking, Lacan's works before 1950, including his famous article 'The Mirror Stage as Formative of the I', focus primarily on the role of the Imaginary in the constitution of subjectivity; the works of Lacan's middle or 'structuralist' period focus on the Symbolic order of language; and Lacan's work after roughly 1960 is increasingly concerned with the Real that eludes symbolisation.

As the title of Catherine Clement's book *The Lives and Legends of Jacques Lacan* suggests, Lacan's private and professional lives are the subject of as much controversy as his theoretical teachings. By all accounts a charismatic character, teacher and womaniser, Lacan was born in Paris on 13 April 1901 to an upper-middle-class Catholic family, the first child of Alfred and Emilie Baudry Lacan. Lacan married twice, having four children. His second wife, Sylvia Makles, was the former wife of author Georges Bataille. Lacan was schooled at the distinguished Jesuit College Stanislas, but by 1916 had embraced atheism and immersed himself in the study of philosophy. In 1919, he commenced medical and psychiatric training at the prestigious *Faculté de Médecine de Paris*, and by 1927 had become the *interne des asiles* at the *Hôpital Sainte-Anne* under the directorship of Clerambault. He studied briefly in Zurich with Jung in 1930, and defended his doctoral thesis *De la Psychose Paranoïaque dans ses Rapports avec la Personnalité* in 1932. In the same year, he was appointed *chef de clinique* at the *Hôpital Sainte-Anne*, and published a translation of Freud's 'Some Neurotic Mechanisms in Jealousy, Paranoia and Homosexuality'. In 1934, Lacan joined the *Société Psychoanalytique de Paris* (SPP), having commenced a training analysis in 1932, and published articles in the *Encyclopédie Française* and the surrealist journal *Le Minotaure* that attested to his increasing conversion to a psychoanalytic viewpoint. In 1936, he first presented the paper on the mirror stage at the Marienbad conference of the International Psychoanalytic Association (IPA) which inaugurated his career as a profoundly original psychoanalytic thinker.

After the second world war, Lacan emerged as the principal theorist in the reconstituted SPP. He was appointed to its committee on psychoanalytic training in 1948, and was influential in the drafting of the SPP's training statutes in 1949. In 1951, Lacan commenced his series of seminars on Freud's texts, which became open to the public in November 1953. It was during this period that the controversy that surrounded all of Lacan's subsequent institutional career began. Lacan headed that part of the SPP that advocated keeping psychoanalytic training open to non-medical practitioners, in opposition to a group headed by Sacha Nacht. The year-long dispute saw resignations from Nacht, and then from Lacan, during which time Lacan replaced Nacht as President of the SPP, but was forced to resign in June of that year after continuing disputes concerning his advocation of 'variable length' analytic sessions. Undaunted, alongside Daniel Lagache, Lacan immediately formed the *Société Française de Psychoanalyse* (SFP). When the SFP applied to the IPA for official affiliation, however, its application was rejected pending a special investigation. In 1955, the SFP was denied membership of the IPA by a committee dominated by Anna *Freud and Heinz *Hartmann. A further application for membership was made in July 1959, and in response to this application the IPA issued the twenty so-called 'Edinburgh demands' of 1961, which all but asked for the direct removal of Lacan and his closest associates from the SFP's training program. On 2 August 1963, the IPA formally demanded Lacan's exclusion from the SFP's list of training analysts, and Lacan was removed by a general vote of the organisation on 19 November 1963. The following day, Lacan announced the cessation of his seminar at the *Hôpital Sainte-Anne*.

At the invitation of the historian Fernand Braunel, and with the help of Marxist philosopher Louis Althusser, Lacan resumed his seminar in January 1964 at the *Ecole Normale Supérieure*. In this forum, the seminar entered into its most illustrious period, becoming something of a cultural event, attended by the leading philosophers, human scientists, and feminists of the day. On 21 June 1964, Lacan formed the *Ecole Française de Psychoanalyse*, later renamed the *Ecole Freudienne de Paris* (EFP). As he stipulated in the published 'Founding Act' of the EFP, the school aimed to institutionalise an alternative to the organisation of the SFP, which Lacan and his followers accused of being excessively hierarchical. One of the central principles of the EFP was the idea that analysts could *authorise themselves* as psychoanalysts though the procedure of *la passe* (the pass). According to this procedure, would-be analysts have to describe their training analysis to three fellow training analysts, who then 'translate' this description to a committee of more senior analysts that approves or rejects the candidate's application, on the basis of this 'translated' redescription. In January 1969, a Lacanian department of psychoanalysis was founded at the controversial *Université de Paris-Vincennes* formed in the light of the May 1968 student revolts. In the same month, the EFP's ratification of Lacan's suggested procedure of the pass saw a number of Lacan's most loyal followers resign from the EFP, on grounds of Lacan's perceived domination of the *Ecole*. The controversy surrounding Lacan increased in 1974 when he intervened in Paris-Vincennes' department of psychoanalysis, appointing his son-in-law Jacques-Alain *Miller as chair, and redirecting the department's curriculum towards a mathematical formalisation of psychoanalytic theory.

In September 1979, the crisis in the EFP came to a head when a contested revision of its by-laws led to Jacques-Alain Miller being elected to the *Ecole*'s Board of Directors. In response to his critics, in January 1980 Lacan unilaterally dissolved the EFP by way of a remarkable '*Lettre de Dissolution*' to its members subsequently published in *Le Monde*. In July 1980, Lacan opened the first congress of his international organisation the *Fondation du Champ Freudien*, in a short address ('Le Séminaire de Caracas'). In this text he announced the organisation of what would – the following year – become the *Ecole de la Cause Freudienne* (ECF), which was to be his final venture in psychoanalytic politics. 'It's up to you to be Lacanians, if you want,' Lacan proclaimed, 'As for me, I am a Freudian.' The autumn of 1980 saw the end of Lacan's seminar, as Lacan increasingly ailed under the effects of age and of abdominal cancer. He died on 9 September 1981 of kidney failure. Lacan's last words are reputed to have been: '*Je suis obstiné . . . je disparais.*'

M. S.

LACAN PRECIS Starting from the premise that the unconscious is structured like a language, Jacques Lacan gave a new orientation to Freudian theory. After his training as a psychiatrist which culminated in an important thesis on paranoid psychosis, Lacan made his entry into psychoanalysis in 1936 with his theory of the *mirror stage. With this theory as its centrepiece, his contributions up to the 1950s located psychoanalysis within what he would later call the register of the *Imaginary. The theory of the mirror stage, a fresh approach to Freud's theory of *narcissism, combines the psychological observation that between the ages of six months and eighteen months, the infant is fascinated by its image in a mirror with the biological fact of its physiological prematurity. The (pre-Oedipal) child greets its specular image with jubilation arising from the anticipation of a bodily unity that contrasts with the immaturity of its motor development. Captivated by the image and identifying with it, the child apprehends it both as its own image and as the image of another. Thus the self (or ego) includes both itself and the other, its counterpart, through an identification with an image of itself as other; the child locates its own image in the (m)other and, conversely, locates the other in the image of its own self.

The mirror stage informs Lacan's view that the ego is the outcome of a series of such *identifications with the other over the course of development. This means that the intersubjective relationship is essentially dyadic, characterised by imaginary identification and alienated in an ambivalent relationship of aggressive rivalry with and erotic attachment to the other. The turning point in Lacan's work came in the early 1950s with the introduction of the distinction between the *Symbolic and the Imaginary. Neither term is employed in its usual sense; 'Imaginary' means based on an image; 'Symbolic' means having to do with language. Lacan's focus shifted from the mirror stage, henceforth taken to typify the Imaginary, onto the Symbolic as the register within which the efficacy of psychoanalytic practice and the explanatory power of psychoanalytic theory are located.

Lacan initially divided the symbolic register into the two dimensions described by Saussure as speech and language. In characteristic fashion, Lacan combines the linguistic concept of speech with *Hegel's master-slave dialectic to yield the claim that speech establishes a social bond or Symbolic pact which overcomes the erotic-aggressive relationship of *ego-to-ego characteristic of the Imaginary. At a more specifically psychoanalytic level, the efficacy of psychoanalytic treatment is also to be understood as located at the level of speech. A neurotic symptom, to take an example, is regarded as an encoded message that has been excluded from the circuit of *discourse and thus can only be communicated in disguised form. By means of the *transference the analyst becomes the addressee of the symptom's hidden message and through interpretation inserts the communication back into discourse. Accordingly, symptoms and other formations of the unconscious (slips of the tongue or pen, bungled actions, memory lapses, jokes and dreams) are regarded as instances of failed communication. Operating solely by means of speech, analysis reestablishes the continuity of the subject's history through retroactively giving meaning to opaque elements of discourse.

Language, the second dimension of the Symbolic, consists of a network of *signifiers that can only be defined diacritically – that is, signifiers or words possess no positive properties but are definable only through their differences. Signifiers (or words as sounds) are, strictly speaking, meaningless. Meaning is not a property of language but the product of speech; it is only produced at the level of the spoken chain of signifiers and unfolds according to a different temporality to that of the signifier; it is anticipated as well as retroactively created.

Intersubjectivity, as the relationship based on the pact or bond between subjects that true speech establishes, is construed as the overcoming of the Imaginary relationship between ego and other that Freud had described in his writings on narcissism and Lacan developed further in his theory of the mirror stage. However, Lacan's work then moved away from the intersubjective dimension of speech onto the more purely formal level of language conceived as a pure network of signifiers located in the locus of the *Other. Henceforth, small other and big Other are contrasted and the Imaginary relationship is regarded as subordinate to the Symbolic relationship of the *subject to the big Other. No simple, single definition of the Other is possible: Lacan characterises it variously as the discourse of the unconscious; as the locus of good faith and the guarantor of truth; as the treasure of signifiers upon which all speech acts must draw. The common element in all Lacan's formulations is that the Other is a third place in discourse, radically external to both speaker and listener or to analysand and analyst.

In urging a 'return to Freud' Lacan contended that the distinction between the Symbolic, as the order of language, and the Imaginary, as characterised by dyadic interpersonal relationships, was already implicit in Freud. Post-Freudian analysis had, Lacan thought, come to concentrate on the Imaginary, and as a result psychoanalytic practice had failed to grasp the fundamental principles of psychoanalysis, which lay in the Symbolic. This made it impossible to distinguish the essentials of analytic practice from its contingent features, resulting in a conservatism that discouraged innovation and ritualised a technique misunderstood by its practitioners.

The introduction of the Symbolic enabled Lacan to distinguish between the ego as constituted by a series of Imaginary identifications and the subject regarded as the result of the effect of language upon the human being. Language subjects the living being to the signifier and the impact of signifiers on the human body can be seen in hysteria. Here, symptoms which make no sense anatomically are organised according to our common 'folk' understanding of the body – clear evidence that language fragments the body according to its own divisions. The Freudian drive is not an instinctual force but possesses a logical grammar, analysed by Freud, from which no separate, biological component can be factored out.

As Symbolic phenomena, both the subject and the Other contain a fundamental *lack. The lack in the subject is a 'want' of being (*manque-à-être*) in the subject which expresses itself as the *desire, distinct from any biological need, for a lost object the subject has never possessed. This lack in the subject – a Symbolic one, which Lacan identifies with *castration, is thus the counterpoise of, and the point of rent or rift in, the plenitude of the Imaginary ego-other relationship exemplified by the pre-Oedipal symbiosis of mother and infant. Desire, now expressed through language, is filtered through and structured by signifiers. Thus unconscious desire is not a 'psychological' phenomenon, for its object is variable, and it lies beyond the pleasure principle and even the subject's interest in his or her own well-being. This is what is meant by Lacan's claim that desire and prohibition, or the (Symbolic) law, are identical. However, this claim also implies that there can be no 'liberation' of desire, if by this is meant the possibility of giving free expression to desire upon the lifting of repression, nor any question of the adaptation or education, but only an ethics, of desire.

The second lack, the lack in the Other, is structural. The battery of signifiers that make up the Other is essentially incomplete, but it contains a key signifier, the *phallus, which both represents and covers over this lack. This lack, which was noted by Freud when he observed that the threat of castration only arises upon recognition of the mother's castration, is the key to Freud's theory of fetishism in which the fetish is a substitute for the woman's 'missing' penis. For Lacan, the lack in the Other is the fundamental trauma that lies at the heart of human sexuality. Lacan's claim that 'man's desire is the desire of the Other' has to be understood in two ways: firstly, as the claim that the subject desires to be desired by the Other, i.e. desires to be the object of the Other's desire, desires to fill the lack in the Other; and secondly, as the claim that the subject's desire is the Other's desire, that its origin lies in the locus of the Other. The function of the father, called the *name-of-the-father (*le nom du père*) to emphasise that its function is Symbolic and that its significance is cultural, is to introduce the law and to subject the human infant to its imperatives. At the same time it organises the sexual being of the subject. The phallus, a signifier distinct from the biological organ, the penis, is the primordial signifier of desire in the Oedipus complex. It is the sole means by which sexual difference is registered in the unconscious; there is no unconscious registration of masculinity or femininity as such, hence no 'sexual rapport', no relationship of natural complementarity, between the sexes. Lacan refers to 'sexuation' to describe, in general terms, the way in which the subject is inscribed within the phallic function.

Freud introduced the concept of the death drive in response to his discovery that the subject 'loves his symptoms more than he loves himself'. Lacan's term *jouissance characterises this hidden satisfaction that the subject derives even from what causes suffering. The Oedipus complex introduces the law that regulates and localises this jouissance through the introduction of the name-of-the-father. Furthermore, while man is inscribed entirely within the phallic function and all his jouissance is subject to the law of the father, there is a supplementary, specifically feminine jouissance which remains outside the law. For Lacan, there are three possible outcomes of the Oedipus complex, three ways in which the division of the subject can be introduced: the neurotic has assumed the law but repressed it; the psychotic has *foreclosed the name-of-the-father; while the pervert has disavowed castration. Normality is not an alternative outcome; for Lacan, in psychoanalysis 'normality' has no other meaning than a successful adaptation to the conditions of existence, and neither psychotic, neurotic nor perverse subjects are excluded from this. Lacan's structural approach enables a distinction to be drawn between a clinical picture and the structure of a subject – between, for example, clinical psychosis and a psychotic subject.

From the mid-1960s the category of the *Real became the focus of Lacan's work. Distinguished from reality, the Real is excluded from the play of signifiers and has no Imaginary dimension. While the Real cannot be symbolised or inscribed within the field of signifiers, it marks the place at which the Symbolic breaks down. It is a point of failure of symbolisation that can never be apprehended in the Symbolic itself, and can only be reconstructed on the basis of the structural distortion it produces in the Symbolic order of the subject. Thus the Real is not some positive entity that transcends the Symbolic; it is an *aporia* or gap internal to the Symbolic itself. It is based on the concept of trauma that Freud initially considered the ultimate origin of all neurotic disorders. However, Lacan opposes developmental approaches in psychoanalysis, maintaining that psychoanalytic theory does not describe the facts of actual development, but a structure which organises and manifests itself within an individual's history without being reducible to its developmental processes. The most striking feature of the evolution in Lacan's thought is that he increasingly formalises and de-psychologises or depersonalises psychoanalytic theory. Whether this will be regarded as what is most valuable in him or as what can best be discarded still hangs in the balance. But what can be said with some certainty is that any rigorous and systematic exploration of the theory and practice of psychoanalysis can no longer avoid the work of Jacques Lacan.

See especially: body; object a; paternal metaphor

See also: alienation; countertransference; demand; desire of the analyst; direction of the treatment; drive; father; fragmented body; hysteria; ego ideal/ideal ego; image; knot; lack; law; loss; lure; masochism; master; matheme; metaphor; metonymy; mother; myth; need; obsessional neurosis; Oedipus complex; part object; partial drive; Pass, the; *passage à l'acte*; passion; perversion; phallus; privation; psychosis; punctuation; reality; recognition; representation; separation; sexual relation; sign; signified; sinthome; speech; structure; subject supposed to know; super-ego; symptom; thing; transitivism; traversal of phantasy; unconscious; variable length session; voice; woman; Zeigarnik

Evans, D. (1996) *An Introductory Dictionary of Lacanian Psychoanalysis*. London: Routledge.
Glowinski, H., Marks, Z. and Murphy, S. (2001) *A Compendium of Lacanian Terms*. London: Free Association Books.
Lacan, J. (1986) *The Seminar, Book VII (1959–1960), The Ethics of Psychoanalysis*. J.-A. Miller (ed.). Translated with notes by D. Porter. New York: Norton.
Lacan, J. (1986) *The Seminar, Book XX (1972–1973), On Feminine Sexuality, the Limits of Love and Knowledge (Encore)*. J.-A. Miller (ed.). Translated with notes by B. Fink. New York: Norton.
Lacan, J. (1993) *The Seminar, Book III (1955–1956), The Psychoses*. J.-A. Miller (ed.). Translated with notes by R. Grigg. New York: Norton.
Lacan, J. (2002) *Ecrits: A Selection*. Translated by B. Fink with H. Fink and R. Grigg. New York: Norton.

R. Gri.

LACK For Lacan, it is lack that situates the subject as a desiring subject. This function inscribes for subjects a whole field in which they are caused to desire by that which is unconsciously experienced as lacking. Lacan devised a matrix of lack as caught up variously with three different objects: the Symbolic *phallus, the Real breast, and the *Imaginary phallus. Lack is invoked and experienced in the corresponding modes of Real *privation, Imaginary frustration and Symbolic castration. The structuring aspect of the subject reveals itself in terms of how the subject resolves wanting-to-be (lack) in the position of the Imaginary phallus and the necessary undergoing of Symbolic castration, an action which is carried out by the real father in the third 'moment' of this Lacanian take on the *Oedipus complex.

G. S.

LAING, R. D. (1927–89) Laing played many roles during his career (psychiatrist, psychoanalyst, philosopher, social critic, author, poet, mystic), and at the peak of his fame and popularity in the 1970s he was the most widely read psychiatrist in the world. Renown of that magnitude is dependent on the happy coincidence of a multitude of factors, including the right message at the most opportune time. This was no doubt true for Laing, when the student unrest of the Vietnam War intersected with his impassioned critique of a society intent on subverting the minds of its youth for unforeseen purposes. His depiction of altered states of consciousness also attracted the interest of the drug culture. Arguably the most controversial psychoanalyst since Freud, Laing's meteoric rise catapulted him into the vanguard of intellectual debate concerning the nature of sanity and madness and the methods typically employed to relieve mental suffering. His emphasis on the family as a source of oppression also aroused debate. His rare ability to make complex ideas accessible inspired a generation of psychology students, intellectuals, and artists to embrace his radical message with such best-selling classics as his 1960 *The Divided Self*, his 1964 *Sanity, Madness and the Family* which was written with Aaron Esterson, the 1967 *The Politics of Experience*, the 1970 *Knots* and his 1971 *Politics of the Family*.

Laing's fame rested on his devastating critique of conventional psychiatric and psychoanalytic practice and his integration of the existentialist perspective into clinical practice. The acknowledged (albeit reluctant) father of 'anti-psychiatry', Laing conceived an alternative to the conventional treatment of psychosis at Kingsley Hall, a therapy centre in London where the participants – therapists and patients alike – lived without clearly defined roles. Though controversial in its day and dismissed by his detractors as a failure, these therapeutic communities continue to flourish, thirty-five years later, under the administration of Laing's umbrella organisation, the Philadelphia Association, now funded by the (British) National Health Service. Laing's legacy remains controversial, and though his light has now dimmed he continues to serve as a beacon to those who challenge conventional treatment mores.

M. G. T.

LALANGUE The concept of lalangue, a soldering of *la* (the) and *langue* (tongue, language), is introduced by Lacan alongside his rethinking of the unconscious as Real: 'the unconscious is the fact that being, by speaking, enjoys'. Lalangue, then, or the Real unconscious, is ultimately the stuff of language, that is to say, the very first signifying material – the talking – exchanged between mother and child.

C. Owe.

LAMELLA Lacan introduces this notion as a mythical organ which represents what we lose as beings who are sexed and thus subject to the cycle of sexual reproduction. What we lose is immortal, indestructible life. The lamella represents life-substance as a bodiless organ of unlimited *jouissance which is no longer accessible to the subject; its only accessible derivatives are the *objects a.

R. Loo.

LANGUAGE From the mid-1950s onwards Lacan develops his thesis of the unconscious as structured like a language. Like language, the unconscious has a formal structure of *signifiers. Freud's discovery of the mechanisms of the unconscious, namely, *condensation and *displacement, is invigorated by Lacan's deployment of *metaphor and *metonymy. These figures of speech which humans use in order to communicate are an attempt to produce meaning, but for Lacan, meaning is a temporary effect of language. In this, Lacan departs radically from Saussure's treatment of the sign. In Saussure there is an arbitrary (yet interdependent) relationship between the signifier and the signified which constitutes the sign, which implies that meaning is the result of convention. Lacan focuses instead on relations between signifiers (basic units of language) alone. The signifiers and their relationships play a crucial role in Lacan's thinking. In fact, the signifier constitutes the subject and this is closely related to his statement that a signifier represents a subject, not for another subject, but for another signifier in the signifying chain. In contrast to this the sign is that which represents something for someone. In the unconscious a chain of signifiers constantly in play proceeds metonymically: meaning residing in the interstices or gaps between signifiers is only determinable retroactively.

See also: linguistics

C. Owe.

LATENCY A period following the resolution of the *Oedipus complex when the child's sexuality goes into a state of quiescence to be revived again at puberty. The latency period (from about five or six to ten or eleven years of age) is a time when, due to the inhibition of sexuality, children become educable and may acquire the skills required by their society.

See also: development

J. A. Ber.

LATENT CONTENT The meaning(s) of a *dream (unconscious thoughts, wishes, fantasies, and allusions to childhood memories) as constructed and interpreted by a psychoanalyst, via the dreamer's *free associations and life *history. The latent content is transformed by the dream-work into the *manifest content.

R. Mol.

LAPLANCHE, JEAN (1924–) Professor Emeritus of Psychoanalysis (Paris VII), Laplanche studied philosophy with Hyppolite, Bachelard and Merleau-Ponty and trained with Lacan. He fought in the Resistance and with Castoriadis and Lefort he founded *Socialisme ou Barbarie* in

1948 as a journal of the anti-Stalinist revolutionary left. He broke with Lacan institutionally and intellectually in 1964 and became a founding member of the *Association Psychanalytique de France*.

His work falls under three headings: archaeology, translation, and the reformulation of seduction. He created critical archaeology of the Freudian conceptual field and the key role of certain lost or marginalised concepts within it: primal fantasy, trauma/seduction, Freud's *Nachträglichkeit* translated in the *SE* as deferred action but by Laplanche as afterwardsness, Freud's *Trieb* or drive translated as instinct in the *SE*. This resulted in two works co-authored with J.-B. Pontalis that have achieved a certain classical status, the essay 'Fantasy and the Origins of Sexuality' (1964) and the great theoretical dictionary *The Language of Psychoanalysis* (1967), translated into fifteen languages, together with his own *Life and Death in Psychoanalysis* (1970).

Closely associated with this archaeological project is his work as a translator of Freud into French. He is the Scientific Director of the translation team responsible for the new twenty-one volume *Oeuvres Complètes de Freud* (1988–).

Growing out of this work of translation and conceptual critique is Laplanche's return to and radical reformulation of Freud's officially abandoned theory of seduction as a cause of neurosis (1895–7) into a general theory of primal seduction, stressing the foundational role of the adult other in all infantile psychic life and sexual development. For Laplanche primal seduction names the fundamental anthropological situation of the human being, in which the ordinary ministrations of childcare implant enigmatic messages in the infant, which are traumatic because compromised by the parenting adults' unconscious fantasy life and sexuality. According to Laplanche, the formation of both the ego and the unconscious is driven by the infant's translation, integration or repression of these exciting adult implantations. A systematic reformulation of classical Freudian metapsychology is being worked out from these premises.

Fletcher, J. (ed.) (2003) *Jean Laplanche and the Theory of Seduction*. New Formations 48, special Laplanche issue.

Laplanche, J. (1987) *New Foundations for Psychoanalysis*. Oxford: Blackwell.

Laplanche, J. (1999) *Essays on Otherness*. London: Routledge.

J. F.

LAW In psychoanalysis the law is a universal principle that regulates sexual enjoyment and relationships between people. For Lacan the most fundamental law is the prohibition of incest that functions between mother and child. This law universalises human desire which results from the lack as a consequence of the mother being prohibited for the child.

See also: name-of-the-father

R. Loo.

LAY ANALYSIS The practice of psychoanalysis by a clinician who is not a medical doctor. Freud believed that medical training could in fact be a hindrance to the techniques of listening specific to the psychoanalytic encounter. Rather than assuming, as did some of his students, that medical qualifications were necessary, he asked instead how psychoanalysis could be saved from the doctors. For Freud 'lay' also had the connotation of 'non-clerical'.

D. L.

LEARNING DISABILITIES Psychotherapeutic work can be carried out with children, adolescents and adults with learning disabilities. The definition of learning disability (previously called mental handicap) is traditionally that of an IQ score of below seventy. Within the category of learning disability, there is a range of severity from profound through moderate to mild. The terminology used in a social context to describe this group of people tends to change over time. Recent years have seen a shift from 'cretin' or 'retard' to 'mental handicap', to the current term, 'learning disability'. The reason for this is that whatever term is used, it eventually becomes a form of verbal abuse. This group of people tend to be overlooked, or looked down on in society, and it is only within the last twenty years that they have been considered as a possible patient group for treatment by psychoanalytic psychotherapy. A recent conceptual differentiation between cognitive IQ and emotional intelligence has been helpful in this respect, and it is now thought to be the case that people with learning disabilities, like the rest of the population, may suffer from emotional difficulties, and in particular, given their social predicament, have very poor self esteem.

Recent evidence, based both on individual clinical cases and on new research in the form of clinical outcome studies, is showing that some children, adolescents and adults with learning disabilities across the range of severity can, following a careful assessment, make good use of long-term individual psychoanalytic psychotherapy or psychodynamic group therapy. Pioneer therapists in this field include Symington and Sinason. The latter has published extensively on the subject, and has introduced into the psychoanalytic literature the concept of 'secondary handicap' whereby emotional factors add another dimension to the original learning disability with the effect of exaggerating the handicap. These defensive exaggerations can be usefully addressed and modified in the psychoanalytic process through the careful study and elucidation by the therapist of the therapeutic relationship with the patient.

Sinason, V. (1992) *Mental Handicap and the Human Condition*. London: Free Books.

L. M.

LEARNING THEORY Learning theory comes from a developmental, rather than a genetic, theoretical perspective and suggests that much of human behaviour is the result of reinforcement and learning experiences rather than being innate (although the presence of certain innate abilities, behaviours and tendencies or traits is recognised). Skinner and others suggested that learning occurs through several mechanisms including punishment, reward, modelling and other forms of operant conditioning and classical conditioning. Pavlov's dogs exemplify classical conditioning; the animals were conditioned to salivate at the sound of a bell that was rung at feeding times and eventually the dogs would salivate to the sound of the bell alone in the absence of food.

In the case of fear acquisition, Rachman provides one of the best examples of the application of learning theory to psychopathology. He suggested that a fear may be modelled by a significant other, may be learned through operant conditioning (learning to avoid dogs because of the pain caused when they bite) or may be learned through education that provokes a fear reaction. However, he also recognised that the theory does not account for all fears, nor does it account for people sometimes fearing objects or animals that are not dangerous or where there is no evolutionary explanation. This exposes the unique selling point and main flaw of learning theory, in that it attempts to explain behaviour in terms of the effects of antecedents and consequences without attention to the mental operations of the organism or the meaning of events. This approach was designed to make the study of behaviour more scientific, but also misses out the vital and most interesting aspect of human beings, that is, thinking and the operations of the mind. Thus, introspection – an important tool for the development of psychoanalytical theories – was regarded as misleading, inaccurate and unscientific by learning theorists.

Skinner, B. F. (1974) *About Behaviourism*. New York: Knopf.

J. W.

LIBIDINAL EGO Fairbairn's term for the split-off part of the self that is attached to the exciting object through affects of unsatisfiable longing and craving. The libidinal ego/exciting object constellation is associated with *desire and hope, even in dire situations. Guntrip wrote extensively about a further repressed libidinal ego that searched for an unreachable part object following states of extreme deprivation of love.

Guntrip, H. (1969) *Schizoid Phenomena, Object Relations and the Self.* New York: International Universities Press.

E. F. B. / D. E. S.

LIBIDO Freud's original libido theory pitted sexual drives (libido), against the ego drives of self-preservation. Later in his dual drive theory, he contrasted libido with aggression (from the *death drive) and he considered that sexual drives and drives of self-preservation were both libidinal. They were together on the side of life, and were opposed by the death drive which works toward the cessation of life. The libido includes everything that energises and binds people together – ties of loyalty, brotherhood and community – while the death drive aims for the total reduction of tension, and the destruction of connections. In most cases the libido is fused with the death drive, and the aggression of the latter provides some of the muscular energy required for performing sexual and other acts. Freud widened the scope of the libido to include family ties, friendship, the positive transference and other affectionate relationships.

J. A. Ber.

LIFE DRIVE/INSTINCT In opposition to the death drive, the life drive consists of all forces which push to maintain life. Sometimes called Eros, the life drive leads us to seek each other's company, make connections, enjoy stimulation, have sex, love, be active, and build ever larger unities. The life drive consists of all the forces which push to maintain life. It includes love of oneself as well as love of others, activity, curiosity, enterprise, interest, self and object preservation, and good will – anything tending to enhance life. It includes non-inhibited sexual drives, inhibited drives and *sublimation, as well as drives of self-preservation. The latter are thus set aside from sexual drives – as opposed to the initial Freudian model which considered the opposition between the sexual drive with the ego drive or self preservation. These two dualisms are not incompatible, but apply to the various pathological levels of organisation.

In contrast to the life drive the death drive allows us to withdraw, take a rest, go to sleep, relax, calm down, enjoy being alone, and ultimately, to completely let go and die.

J. A. Ber. / D. W.

LINGUISTICS AND PSYCHOANALYSIS The use of language is a uniquely human attribute. It was classically seen as a divine gift. However, language is not the property of a single individual; it is learned and used only in a social context. From the beginning, psychoanalysis has been fundamentally concerned with the social aspects of psychic life. Whilst the relationship between the psychic and the social is implicit in Freud's writing, it becomes explicit in the critical theory developed by Derrida and Lorenzer. Language plays a key role in the dialectical development of Freud's theories. In his 1891 paper 'On Aphasia', Freud develops a functional approach to brain function in contrast to the localisation theories of his contemporaries. This early work of Freud's influenced the neuropsychology of Luria and anticipates modern neurobiological concepts.

In the *'Project for a Scientific Psychology' of 1895, Freud postulates the existence of internal psychic 'language signs' and thereby decides to leave the machine metaphor of the psyche and to introduce interactive processes; namely the presence of an environment, which 'misunderstands' the valve-like crying of the child as a message and adequately reacts to it. This is an early nucleus of Freud's typical double metaphor, which embraces bodily and social processes.

In his early work Freud understands the unconscious as a realm of wordless 'thing representations' and their sporadic connection with 'word representations' is seen as the condition of consciousness. Even when Freud formulates his structural theory and describes the unconscious parts of ego functioning, he ascribes language merely to the conscious parts of the ego. Only towards the end of his life does Freud concede that there might also exist linguistically organised ego processes that remain unconscious.

The post-war development of *object relations theory describes inner psychic self and object representations formed in the early dialogue between mother and child. In the interaction between mother (and her fantasies) and child (and his developing fantasy life) a *semiotics of experience takes place. Winnicott's theory of the *transitional object vividly sketches this early semantic and syntactic structuring. At first the mother occupies an illusionary space, as if she were magically controlled by the baby. She emerges at the very moment the baby 'invents' her presence. At a later stage the baby has to experience the failure of this magic, represented by the absence of the mother. It develops the ability to represent the absent mother internally on the basis of the previous experience of magic omnipotence.

Analysing the basic exchange processes between mother and child using the concepts of *projective identification and *container/contained, Bion describes the development of *thinking from *preconceptions to conceptions or thoughts. The implicit assumption of innate object expectations in Bion's theories is not unanimously accepted in psychoanalytic theories of language.

Lacan postulates that 'the unconscious is structured like a language'. Thus the baby experiences itself as fragmented and only when confronted by its physical or psychological image in the *mirror stage does it start to be drawn into the illusion of a unified, yet elusive self. From this moment on this Imaginary unit will be called 'I', a linguistic self-referring cipher for what others might combine in the unit 'you'. From this theoretical viewpoint Lacan thinks that the so-called unconscious is neither an organ nor a non-verbal input into a linguistically organised cognitive apparatus – it is the result of naming. Lacan rejects the notion that there is any means whereby the universe of language might be transcended. Thus all apparently extra-linguistic entities were deemed to be in the realm of the *Imaginary and to have emerged from verbal discourse, particularly the 'I' ('*moi*') of self-perception.

The problem of language acquisition poses an interesting dilemma – even if we had to hear everything we say only once before we said it, we would have to spend half our lives listening. This so-called paradox of learnability indicates that language is an active production and not a reproductive phenomenon. Psychoanalysis can help us to understand this paradox. From birth onwards, the child actively explores its environment. It imitates gestural and vocal stimuli, elaborates them and corrects its imitation again and again. Finally it develops its own language from this imitative action. This process can be described as an 'intrapsychic structuring'. However, psychoanalytic investigation of preverbal structure formation mainly emphasises its interactional aspects such as the mutual fit between the baby's exploration and the caregiver's intuitive empathy, which allows for the development of lasting representations of the self and the other, and thereby permits the development of intra-mental reciprocity and *intentionality.

Stern describes the emerging of the verbal and, later on, the narrative self in the context of interactive affect development in a step-by-step evolution of relatedness. Dore sees the earliest steps of linguistic convention as the result of a secondary mirroring, based upon the primary transformation of spontaneous expression into directed and related responses. Developmental psychology stresses the irreversible modification of experience and interaction caused by the introduction of language.

The theory of *semiotics and the symbol has a key function in psychoanalytic theory. Freud's theory of symbol was based on the etymological and philological orientation of historical linguistics and as a result he had constant difficulties with the problem of attributing fixed unconscious meaning to symbols in an otherwise dynamic system. New developments in structural linguistics and philosophic logic then brought a new definition of the symbol. Since Saussure, symbols have been seen as elements of a system, acquiring meaning not through their denoted objects, but through their place within the system, like the knight in chess, which can be replaced by a wooden cube without losing its function.

These new theories led to an extended definition of the symbol in psychoanalysis whether from the perspective of structural linguistics of Lacan or Lorenzer's critical theory. Lorenzer argues that psychic processes contain a multiplicity of qualitatively different sign-based operations. It is no longer necessary to tie *symbol formation to the *primary process – there might be primary process as well as secondary process aspects to different kinds of symbols. The integration of a psychoanalytic concept of symbolism into a general theory of symbols might risk giving up the connection of some psychoanalytic symbols to specific displaced and repressed contents. On the other hand, it is actually Lorenzer's aim to preserve the specificity of psychoanalytic experience. Therefore, he distinguishes the unconscious symbol as a 'cliché' from conscious symbolic representation. Clichés are symbols that have become unconscious and that are evoked in certain scenic arrangements. In contrast to conscious symbolisation, the unconscious cliché neither allows for reality testing nor for secondary probationary action. It therefore produces invariant, rigid, instinct-like behaviour. The excommunication of the symbol causes its unconscious reproduction in the form of the *repetition compulsion.

A symbolic form can refer to an object only through an intermediate level of 'meaning' or reference, the so-called 'triangle of reference'. As Shapiro points out, Freud's differentiation between *thing representation and *word representation already implies semiotic differentiation and hints at potentially different methods of verbal and non-verbal cognitive representation.

Since the 1960s, linguistic discussion has been shaped by the paradigm of transformational grammar. Chomsky devised his 'Language Acquisition Device', defined as a set of linguistic universals, which enable the child to differentiate linguistic stimuli among themselves and from other stimuli and to execute simple transformations. Chomsky's model is not undisputed, either from the view of grammatical theory or from the perspective of developmental psychology. One of the substantial arguments from a psychological view is the limitations of linguistic phenomena and the exclusion of pragmatic considerations from Chomsky's theory. Generally however, the idea of analysing utterances as transformations of underlying unconscious basic structures has strong parallels with psychoanalysis.

Chomsky opposes his notion of humanity to the views of Skinner. Transformational approaches seem to correspond much more closely with the dynamic metapsychology of psychoanalysis than behaviourism. Nevertheless, there remain some differences. While the transformational point of view employs a minimalist approach to theorising in order to explain the production of well-formed utterances, psychoanalysis always looks for richer and more varied explanations. It cannot wholeheartedly support the notion of innate linguistic structures embodied in Chomsky's 'language acquisition device'. From a classical psychoanalytic view this notion seems too finalistic, as if nature had planned to create human culture.

Psychoanalysis and linguistics often ask the same question: 'what does a linguistic expression change in the world?' On the one hand, only language allows us to lie; it has an alienating effect on the experience of oneself and the experience of being with others. At the same time, language bestows intimacy and relatedness, connecting different subjective worlds in a common symbolic system.

Edelson, M. (1975) *Language and Interpretation in Psycho-analysis*. New Haven, CT and London: Yale University Press.

Edgcumbe, R. M. (1980) 'Toward a developmental line for the acquisition of language'. *The Psychoanalytic Study of the Child* 36: 71–103.

Hamburger, A. (1995) *Entwicklung der Sprache*. Stuttgart: Kohlhammer.

Lacan, J. (1956) 'Fonction et champ de la parole et du language en psychanalyse'. *La Psychanalyse* I: 81–116.

Lorenzer, A. (1970) *Kritik des psychoanalytischen Symbolbegriffs*. Frankfurt: Suhrkamp.

Shapiro, T. (1979) *Clinical Psycholinguistics*. New York: Plenum.

A. H.

LINK A simple definition of this word is one of the loops of which a chain is made; hence, something which connects separate things or objects, a tie. Bion uses this term basically to refer to a mental function, and says so in his 1959 paper 'Attacks on Linking'. He there relates the link to a function, rather than with the objects that subserve the function. Thus, he calls the breast, the penis, and verbal thought a link or linkage function, since they provide the link between two objects.

Having introduced his idea of the link, or of the linkage function that relates objects, he postulates three types of emotional linkages: loving, hating and knowing. He called these relationships the L, H and K links. Placing the K link in the same basic emotional level as the L and H link, he is considering 'learning' as a primary link and not one derived from the other two, as Freud and Klein considered. The prototype of the K link is the relationship between mother and infant, or between the mother's mind (the *container) and the infant's projected feelings (the *contained) plus the container's thinking, linking and understanding functions. This activity then becomes introjected, so that the infant has it as a part of his own thinking, linking, understanding and containing capability. Bion calls this function the *psychoanalytic function of the personality. The containing and understanding function of the mother's mind (the good part object – mother's breast), when introjected, will become the functional nucleus of the ego. This differs from *Klein's idea about the nucleus of the ego, which for her is a more anatomical or morphological concept of the good breast.

The K link is fundamental for learning by and from experience. It is an active link, includes feelings like curiosity and tolerance of doubt, and represents an emotional experience which cannot be conceived in isolation from a relationship. It is related to trying to know the truth, and is painful because of the frustration implicit in the impossibility of really knowing the truth about anything. In a more primitive level of the mind, it can arouse fears of an object opposed to curiosity and knowing.

In the *Oedipus, Babel and Eden myths, Bion finds that the K link is represented in all these stories – aside from their being more classical models for loving and hating relationships. In all of them there are situations related to curiosity and wanting to know, and a god or fate hostile to mankind in its search for knowledge.

Negative Links: Basically, −K, where the emotional factors in K are reversed. The emotion which Bion takes as an important factor is *envy, which precludes a symbiotic relationship and strips and denudes the content and the ontainer of goodness and meaning. *Attacks on linking, especially on the emotional linking function of the parental couple, or of verbal language in the psychoanalytic session, can also be understood as a transformation of a K link into a −K one. The lie is another representative of a −K link. The −L and −K links are also related to the stripping of emotions, resulting in links which are perverse, cruel and sterile.

Commensal, symbiotic and parasitic links or relationships: Using biological analogies for the relationship between the container and the contained, the commensal link is one where two objects share a third one to the advantage of all three. The symbiotic link is one where one depends on the other for mutual advantage. A model for this situation is the mother who derives benefit and achieves mental growth from the maternal experience; the infant likewise abstracts benefit and achieves growth. The parasitic link is one where one depends on the other to produce a third, which is destructive to all three (for example, the lie).

Bion, W. R. (1959) 'Attacks on linking' in *Second Thoughts*. London: Heinemann.
Bion, W. R. (1962) *Learning from Experience*. London: Heinemann.
Bion, W. R. (1963) *Elements of Psychoanalysis*. London: Heinemann.
Bion, W. R. (1970) *Attention and Interpretation*. London: Tavistock.

E. T. B.

LINKING, ATTACKS ON Having established the concept of the *link, Bion describes attacks on the linking function. The linking function can be realised by the breast, the penis, emotional contact, verbal thought, etc. In his paper 'Attacks on Linking' he speaks about the destructive attacks which a patient makes on anything which has the function of linking one object with another. He finds that this phantasied sadistic attack on objects which serve as a link is done by the psychotic part of the personality, and can be observed in severely disturbed patients. In the aforementioned paper, he presents a series of clinical vignettes to show destructive attacks on the linking functions. He concludes that in that state of mind, the patient's psyche contains an *internal object which is opposed to and destructive of all links, and that in this state of mind, emotion is hated.

Bion, W. R. (1957) 'Differentiation of the psychotic from the non-psychotic personalities' in *Second Thoughts*. London: Heinemann.
Bion, W. R. (1959) 'Attacks on linking' in *Second Thoughts*. London: Heinemann.

E. T. B.

LITERATURE AND PSYCHOANALYSIS Psychoanalysis has since its inception borne an intimate relationship to literature. The works of Sophocles, Goethe, Schiller, and Shakespeare provide inspirations for Freud's psychoanalytic enterprise. In turn, psychoanalysis supplies literature with unique interpretative methods. For instance, *Freud pioneers the discussion of Shakespeare's *Hamlet*, *Macbeth*, *Midsummer Night's Dream*, and *King Lear* in terms of latent and manifest contents. He applies his technique of dream interpretation to study Jensen's Gradiva, and his theory of the uncanny to Hoffmann's 'Sandman'. Freud has also produced psychobiography such as 'Dostoevsky and Parricide'. The poet H. D. was Freud's patient. Freud also theorises about artistic creativity. 'Creative Writers and Day-Dreaming' and Lecture 23 of *Introductory Lectures on Psycho-Analysis* associate literary creations with wish fulfilment. Freud has been criticised for concentrating on the psychology of creativity and the psychopathology of artists with little to say about aesthetics and the formal properties of art works.

Psychoanalysts with important contributions to literary criticism include Ernest *Jones, Otto *Rank, and Marie Bonaparte. In 1910 Jones published 'The Oedipus Complex as an Explanation of Hamlet's Mystery'. Rank's 1914 essay 'The Double' elaborates on narcissism and projection by using literary examples from Hoffman, Dostoevsky, Stevenson, Wilde, Maupassant, and Poe. His *Incest Theme in Literature and Legend*, published in 1912, surveys Oedipal dynamics in world literature and mythology. Bonaparte's 1908 study *The Life and Works of Edgar Allan Poe* attempts to infer from biographical and textual details Poe's unconscious wishes and fears. Literary critics assimilating psychoanalytic insights from the 1930s to the 1950s include William Empson, Edmund Wilson, Lionel Trilling, Kenneth Burke, and Leslie Fiedler.

The Swiss psychoanalyst Carl Gustav *Jung regards great literature as an expression of the *archetypes or patterns of psychic energy originating in the collective unconscious. '*Wandlungen und Symbole der Libido*', Jung's first archetypal reading of literary texts, analyses Longfellow's *Hiawatha*. Jung's insight is further developed by Northrop Frye and Leslie Fiedler.

*Ego-psychological aesthetics views artistic activity as bringing the primary process into play at the ego's command. Following the lead of Simon O. Lesser, Norman Holland uses ego psychology to study readers' response to literary texts. Holland, the doyen of reader-response criticism, explains readers' response as the product of a 'transactive' engagement between his/her unconscious and the fantasies that the author has projected in the literary text.

Elizabeth Wright defines *object-relations aesthetics as 'interested in the psychic processes which mediate the relationship between self and world, and the consequences this has for the formal aspects of art'. Melanie *Klein, founder of object relations, has an essay on *Oresteia*.

Among the object-relations theorists, only D. W. *Winnicott has made significant impact on literary thought. Critics influenced by Winnicott look at reader and text as a relationship taking place in a 'transitional' or 'potential space' – a space of trust where knowledge and feeling merge, a space where binary oppositions such as objective/subjective and real/illusory dissolve. Holland believes that 'this way of thinking about the relationship between a reader and a text provides an important dimension to reader-response criticism'. Winnicott also influenced André *Green whose *Tragic Effect* in 1979 discusses the 'potential space' of tragedy as a place for recognition.

Psychoanalysis plays a crucial role in contemporary literary theories such as *Marxism, gender studies, Foucauldianism, deconstruction, cultural studies, and postcolonialism. Traditional psychobiography and characterological studies, however, are generally disfavoured in the age of the 'death of the subject'. (Harold Bloom's tribute to authors is an exception.) Literary attention has been shifted instead to the text.

Despite some *feminists' attack on Freud's patriarchal concepts such as the Oedipus complex and 'penis envy', gender studies has increasingly enlisted the services of revised versions of Freudianism. Exemplary object-relations feminist literary critics include Elizabeth Abel and Marianne Hirsch. Lacanian feminists include Juliet MacCannell, Joan Copjec, and Jacqueline Rose. Psychoanalysis is also important for Judith Butler's writings on queer theory and feminism.

*Lacan frequently makes use of French, English, Irish, and American literature. He performs brilliant readings of 'The Purloined Letter' in 1956, and of *Hamlet* and *Antigone* in 1959. He also discusses Paul Claudel and Joyce. Lacan's impact on the literary profession is evident in the works of Jacqueline Rose, Juliet Flower MacCannell, Ellie Ragland, Slavoj Žižek, Renata Salecl, and Joan Copjec. Rose has performed studies of *Hamlet* and of twentieth-century British and Anglophone literatures. MacCannell has written on the novels of Richardson, Kleist, Stendhal, Duras, Angelou, and Atwood. Ragland has commented on works by Sophocles, Wilde, Wharton, Joyce, and Genet. Žižek has discussed the writings of Cervantes, Shakespeare, Kafka, and Brecht. Salecl has analysed works by Homer, Kafka, Wharton, and O. Henry. Copjec has offered original reading of melodrama.

Examples of Derrida's polemics with psychoanalysis can be found in his 1972 'The Double Session' and the 1981 'Le facteur de la vérité'. The Lacan–Derrida controversy is resumed by many (including Barbara Johnson) in the volume *The Purloined Poe*. Derrida furthers his argument in 'My Chances/Mes

Chances' which focuses on the relationship between literature and psychoanalysis. He critiques psychoanalysis's totalising tendency and compliments literature for being more open to indeterminacy. In similar spirit, Shoshana Felman reads 'literature and psychoanalysis' as a master-slave relationship whereby literature is submitted to the interpretative authority of psychoanalysis. Some post-structuralists go the other extreme and practise what Peter Brooks calls 'imperialism in the reverse' – that is, 'the imperialism that would come from the incursion of literary criticism into psychology in search of mere metaphors'.

Important contemporary psychoanalytic-literary critics outside particular schools include Julia *Kristeva and Peter Brooks. Kristeva draws interesting comparisons and contrasts between literature and psychoanalysis. For Kristeva, poetry, maternity, and psychoanalysis are the three model discourses that challenge identity. Despite this parallel, Kristeva in her 1987 *Soleil Noir* calls psychoanalysis a counterdepressant in contrast to literature which is a mere antidepressant.

Brooks seizes upon Freud's idea of forepleasure as a possibility for considering the erotics of form. He compares reading to transference in which the reader must 'grasp not only what is said but always what the discourse intends, its implications, how it would work on him'. Drawing from Lacan, Brooks holds that the reader should 'refuse the text's demand in order to listen to its desire'.

Felman, S. (ed.) (1977) *Literature and Psychoanalysis*. Baltimore: Johns Hopkins University Press.

Holland, N. (1990) *Holland's Guide to Psychoanalytic Psychology and Literature-and-Psychology*. Oxford: Oxford University Press.

Jung, C. G. (1953–83) *Collected Works*. New York: Pantheon.

Kristeva, J. (1974) *La Révolution du langage poétique*. Paris: Seuil.

Lacan, J. [1956] (1966) 'Seminar on "The Purloined Letter"' in *Ecrits*. Paris: Seuil.

Wright, E. (1984) *Psychoanalytic Criticism: Theory in Practice*. London: Methuen.

S. C.

Little Hans Soubriquet for Herbert Graf (1903–73), who was analytically observed and then analysed by his father, musicologist Max Graf, from 1906 to 1908. During the supervision, Freud saw the child only once. Little Hans is the youngest subject of Freud's five great case histories, the other subjects being *Dora, the *Rat Man, the *Wolf Man, and *Schreber. An oedipal explanation was given to explain Hans's phobia of horses: the birth of his little sister made him wonder about sexuality and the origin of children; he equated the horse with his father who supposedly wanted to castrate him for wanting his mother.

See also: anticathexis/countercathexis; castration

Freud, S. (1909) *Analysis of a Phobia in a Five-Year-Old Boy*. S. E. 10. London: Hogarth Press.

P. M.

Loewald, Hans (1906–93) was born in Colmar, Germany. He studied philosophy with Heidegger before breaking permanently from his mentor during the Nazi era and moving on to study medicine and psychiatry. Loewald emigrated to the United States in 1939, underwent analytic training (and was made a training analyst) in Baltimore and then moved to New Haven to help found the Western New England Institute of Psychoanalysis, remaining there for the rest of his career. Loewald's work is grounded in both his philosophical background and a profound respect for Freud's work. Loewald expanded upon Freud to offer a deepened understanding of pre-Oedipal phases of development and to effect subtle but important modifications of, for example, the understanding of psychic reality, ego development, instincts and drives, and the therapeutic action of psychoanalysis. Loewald identified the internalisation of interaction processes – 'integrative experiences' – between child and mother and between patient and analyst as the building blocks for psychic structure and the medium for therapeutic change.

While built around a sound and clear conceptual framework, Loewald's writing is often evocative and poetical. For example, he compares the unconscious to 'a crowd of ghosts' which, being 'allowed to taste blood' in the here-and-now experience of the transference, are 'laid and led to rest as ancestors'. He viewed the deep, early and non-rational aspects of human experience in a more positive light than did Freud, identifying the mature ego as one for which earlier and more primitive modes of ego-reality integration 'remain alive as dynamic sources of higher organization'. His understanding of internalisation, sublimation, creative processes and religious experience offers illuminating and non-reductive psychoanalytic views of these very fundamental human experiences.

Loewald, H. W. (1978) *Psychoanalysis and the History of the Individual*. New Haven, CT: Yale.
Loewald, H. W. (1980) *Papers on Psychoanalysis*. New Haven, CT: Yale.
Loewald, H. W. (1988) *Sublimation*. New Haven, CT: Yale.
Loewald, H. W. (2000) *The Essential Loewald*. Hagerstown, MD: University Publishing Group.

J. N.

LOGIC AND PSYCHOANALYSIS It might be thought that formal logic could have no connection with the apparent irrationality of unconscious processes. However, Freud knew the formal logic of his day well for he discusses logic in the *Interpretation of Dreams* and often uses strict logical argument in his theorising. His consistent use of logical argument forms part of the Logical Positivist 'shell' with which he protected the new discipline of psychoanalysis.

However in his earlier clinical writings Freud often spoke of catching the 'logical thread' in the patient's material and noted that repression introduces a disconnection into the spatial world of logical threads that traverse human subjectivity. Threads that are unable be followed and material that has been rendered inaccessible, weaken the reasoning abilities of the individual, who is hampered in this way by the effects of the existence of the unconscious. In this sense the neurotic is poor at deductive thinking; undoing some of the effects of repression allows him to gain some access to the consequences of his relations in the field of love.

Psychoanalysis aims to construct pathways that lead into the unconscious. The technique of constructing these pathways is determined by what Freud calls *free association; the pathways themselves Freud calls alternatively 'associative pathways', 'logical connections', or 'logical threads'. Such pathways aim to make their way into regions that would otherwise remain cut off, and Freud's claim is that the successful forging of such pathways re-establishes logical connections between material that had been disconnected by repression. The construction of these logical threads is opposed by *resistance, so Freud proposes a technique of advancing them along peripheries and by detour. The logical connection that they bring about starts to undo the effects of suffering brought about by repression.

The strategy of formal logic can also be detected in Freud's clinical strategy of finding hidden assumptions. However, this approach is as old as Aristotle, who remarked that anyone interpreting dreams should be good at noticing similarities. The unconscious tends to equate things or persons perceived as similar. For example a child may unconsciously experience a sarcastic teacher and their sarcastic father as the same and react to the first as if the first were the second. This phenomenon has been variously called 'paleologic', 'predicate thinking' or 'similarisation'. However Freud was unaware of the emerging discipline of (mathematical) predicate logic.

If we imagine ourselves doing a 'logical X-ray' of how we think and speak about things, we notice that one of the most common formations is ascribing qualities (or predicates) to objects. For example 'John is neurotic', 'Peter is arrogant' and 'six is even' all ascribe a quality to an object. Thus in 'six is even' the object 'six' is given the quality 'is even' or in 'Peter is arrogant' the object 'Peter' is given the quality 'is arrogant'. We can now abstract a part-algebraic expression, 'x is even', called in logic, a 'propositional function'.

In psychoanalysis we are interested in thinking and talking about emotionally charged subjects. *Hegel cites the example of a woman who, watching a man on the scaffold about to be hung, remarks on how handsome he is. Her listeners berate her saying, 'How could a murderer be handsome?!' Clearly they have assumed that he was all bad because a murderer, but Hegel says: 'This is abstract thinking: to see nothing in the murderer except the abstract fact that he is a murderer, and to annul all other human essence in him with this simple quality'. For the masses anyone accused of murder is featureless and identical to anyone else accused of murder. To revert to the language of propositional functions: anyone who fits into the description 'x is a murderer' is the same.

Freud frequently indicates this form of abstract thinking (as does *Marx) especially in his 1909 'Notes upon a case of Obsessional Neurosis'. Rendering this into the language of set theory, as *Matte Blanco does: the individual murderer has been split off into the class of people who are 'all bad'. He regards these classes as infinitely large and to this end draws heavily on Cantor's theory of mathematical *infinity. Matte Blanco also shows how a *part object can be treated as identical to a whole object by exploiting the fact that infinite sets can be shown equivalent to only a part of themselves.

Bion, however uses the notion of propositional functions to show how the infant builds up models of the world. The simple notion is that a 'family' of propositional functions can be seen as a 'world view'. According to his approach models of experience are 'made' by a *depressive process and 'broken' by a *paranoid schizoid one.

Perhaps the best known idea of logic in psychotherapy is Bateson's *double bind. He explains how a young man is caught in a contradictory situation driving him into schizophrenia. As his mother says: 'You know that I love you', she holds out her arms in a most unwelcoming way. Bateson also develops the notion of different (or meta) levels of communication where a patient may classify all messages of a certain type in a highly pathological way.

Bateson and Lacan have both remarked on the 'quantifiers' of predicate logic. The expressions: 'all' and 'some' are found in sentences like: 'All men are mortal' and 'Some numbers are odd'. Bateson notes how the logical quantifier 'some' does not prevail in the unconscious which favours an 'all or nothing' perspective.

Lacan uses quantifiers to characterise sexual difference revolving around phallic function. There are two formulae for the masculine position and two for the feminine position.

The *Real, seen by Lacan as unsymbolisable, can be seen as (logically) impossible: the Real of the trauma is what is impossible to assimilate; the Real of the symptom is what is impossible to bear; the Real of the repressed is what is impossible to say. It is the *Symbolic that gives coordinates to the Real and Lacan invokes Godel's Incompleteness Theorem. Just as Godel's theorem shows that not all arithmetical truths can be captured in formal arithmetic, so not all of the Real can be captured in the Symbolic order. Thus in both psychoanalysis and in mathematics there can be no final guarantee of truth. Truth therefore – in logic as in analysis – is always evasive, and can only be 'half-said'.

Perhaps the greatest difficulty in applying logic within psychoanalysis is that contradictory attitudes coexist whereas in logic, contradictions allow the deduction of absolutely anything thus trivialising the logic. However the more recent 'paraconsistent' logics permit contradiction without allowing host logics to fall into triviality.

See also: rhetoric

Bateson, G. (1972) *Steps to an Ecology of Mind*. New York: Ballatine Books.
Fink, B. (1995) *The Lacanian Subject*. Princeton: Princeton University Press.
Freud, S. (1908) *Notes on a Case of Obsessional Neurosis*. S. E. 10. London: Hogarth Press.
Hegel, G. [1807] (1965) 'Who thinks abstractly?' in W. Kaufmann, *Hegel*. New York: Doubleday & Co.
Skelton, R. (1990) 'Generalisation from Freud to Matte Blanco'. *International Review of Psychoanalysis* 17(4).
Skelton, R. (1995) 'Bion's use of modern logic'. *International Journal of Psychoanalysis* 76(2).
Skelton, R. (1998) 'Matte Blanco, the death drive and possible worlds'. *Journal of Melanie Klein and Object Relations* 16(1).

R. M. S. / B. B. / N. C.

LOGOS Greek word meaning rational principle, structure or order. This term's basic significance in Greek is very broad, and it is Jung's term for the masculine principle. But this meaning is enriched by its historical usage from Heraclitus to Ambrose as the self-actualising rational principle both in the cosmos and the individual. As mediator between God and humanity, it is personified as Hermes/Mercurius and Christ. Jung was also deeply aware of its origin in Sophia, the feminine archetype of divine wisdom. Thus it should not be viewed as exclusively masculine any more than its complementary feminine principle, named for the male god, *Eros, belongs only to women. As the differentiated intelligence it compensates for the blindness of love and teaches the way of *individuation.

E. Beg.

LOOK Sartre uses the look to explain the relation of one consciousness to another. It is through the gaze of the other that I discover that I am not alone in the world and that I have an outside for another consciousness. Sartre's example is a man looking through a keyhole who suddenly hears footsteps. The shift in is from self as subject to self as shameful object for another consciousness. This experience of being gazed upon by another is very different from an experience of relating to the other as a mere body. Existential analysis recognises the developmental importance of the original others who as subjects, rather than drive gratifying objects, see and name me (or misname me or fail to name me). *Object relations theory may implicitly recognise this in its emphasis on the importance of 'mirroring' to early *ego development.

However, Lacan's insistence on the split between the eye and the gaze essentially departs from the Sartrean conflation of seeing and being seen. No mere reciprocal experience of subject to subject exists at the level of the look since Lacan places 'the look' on the side of the Other/object. The subject is caught in wishing to be looked at from the place where he sees the Other. Since this always evades the subject, the look is wholly implicated in the subject's relationship with unconscious desire and Symbolic castration.

Mirvish, A. (1996) 'Sartre and the problem of other (embodied) minds'. *Sartre Studies International 2*.

A. M. / B. C. / H. T.

LOSS Loss is inextricably linked to the concept of *lack, which in turn is linked to the notion of *desire to which it gives rise. Since the human subject is a subject of language and since language is generated out of absence of the thing, as soon as one enters into the world of language one has already entered into the field of loss, initially as loss at the level of pure being.

H. T.

LOVE Psychoanalysis isolates three fundamental elements for consideration. Firstly, love pre-exists the amorous encounter; it is the dream of re-encountering one's lost other half, as well as the myth of completeness that this dream presupposes. Invoked in this is the concept of *narcissism, particularly in the aspect of the libidinal investment of the image of the body. Secondly, it is a movement towards the beloved, because this dream gives direction, shape and focus to the circular movement of the *drive. Lastly, it is a reunion with the loved one – a fleeting arbitrary encounter that nevertheless strengthens the illusion of eternity and inevitability. For Freud, the game between the life and death drives – between construction and destruction – conceptualises the paradoxical role of infatuation.

See also: death drive; life drive; sexual relation

M. V.

LOVE, DEBASEMENT IN In his 'contributions to the psychology of the love life', Freud developed the idea of a basic debasement, *Erniedrigung*, being conceived as the very pre-condition of the masculine enjoyment in man's relation to his love object. The term refers to a splitting, to a doubling of the female figure into the ideal, beloved, adored one, the ideal-mother, and that of the debased, the fallen one: the prostitute. One of the most interesting features of Freud's idea of debasement seems to be the one that sexuality does not tend to satisfaction, and that sexuality itself is anchored in this inner, rather than external, obstacle.

E. B.

LOVE, PARTIAL A concept of Karl *Abraham's which corresponds to a specific moment in his theory of the development of the libido. The concept indicates that wholeness of love is impossible whilst the aim of the lover is still determined by incorporation or ambivalence. Lacan has pointed out that partial love of the object is wrongly confused with the concept of *partial object. This distinction is at play in Lacan's development of the notion of *object relation.

See also: drive, partial

S. Ten.

LOVE RELATIONS Following his early discovery that there is no 'natural' heterosexual relationship between a man and a woman, Freud was led, in the 1920s and 1930s, to propose the existence of a discordance in love relations. This circulates around the different ways in which men and women situate themselves in relation to the Oedipal love ties to the mother. A man tends to take a rather simplistic attitude to love: what he finds attractive in a woman is an allusion to the affectionate love current towards the mother. A woman's attachment to men, however, is based on the more complex and realistic history of her navigation of Oedipal conflicts in love. Where a woman replaces her initial love bond to the mother by an attachment to the father – and thereafter to other men – her original affectionate bond to the mother is replaced by a current of hostility. It is this dissonance between men and women that led Freud to describe the man's love and the woman's love as 'a phase apart', which Lacan later reformulated in terms of 'the non-existence of the sexual relation'.

See also: feminism and psychoanalysis

V. B. / B. B.

LURE Lure is tied to the concepts of ensnarement/deception, but also seduction/attraction. On the one hand it refers to the false trails that the subject lays to deceive the other, on the other it refers to the seductive postures of, for example, the child who aims to captivate the other and occupy the place of the object of desire of this Other.

H. T.

M

MAHLER, MARGARET S. (1897–1985) was a pioneer who early on recognised the importance of the mother-infant relationship for development of the sense of self. Born in the small Hungarian village of Sopron, she attended gymnasium in Budapest, where, through the family of a schoolmate, she met psychoanalysts Sándor Ferenczi and Michael Balint, who sparked in her an early interest in psychoanalysis. She studied medicine, became a paediatrician, and then experienced firsthand the importance of the mother-infant bond: She noticed that severely ill infants whose mothers were allowed to stay with them usually recovered, whereas those who were separated from their mothers often died. This led to her decision to train as a psychoanalyst.

She fled Vienna in 1938 and settled in New York City where she worked as a psychoanalyst with both children and adults. She also taught at the Philadelphia Psychoanalytic Institute, where she had a profound influence on the training of child psychoanalysts. Her research and clinical work continue to be supported and expanded through the Margaret S. Mahler Psychiatric Research Foundation in Philadelphia.

As a child psychoanalyst Mahler worked with severely disturbed, autistic, and psychotic young children who could not develop a sense of self. This led to the study of the normal 'separation-individuation process' which resulted in the formulation of regularly occurring sub-phases: differentiation, practising, rapprochement, and on the way to object constancy.

Mahler and Furer developed a tripartite treatment design simultaneously for work with psychotic and autistic young children and their mothers, who were seen together in intensive treatment. While this treatment design was originally created for mothers with severely disturbed young children, it has since become the standard model of treatment for young children with a variety of attachment disorders.

Mahler's work on the separation-individuation process has become a foundation of psychoanalytic developmental theory.

Bergman, A. and Fahey, M. (1999) *Ours, Yours, Mine: Mutuality and the Emergence of the Separate Self.* New York: Jason Aronson.

Mahler, M. S. (1979) *The Selected Papers of Margaret S. Mahler*, Vols I & II. New York: Jason Aronson.

Mahler, M. S. and Furer, M. (1968) *On Human Symbiosis and the Vicissitudes of Human Individuation.* Madison, CT: International Universities Press.

Mahler, M. S., Pine, F. and Bergman, A. (1975) *The Psychological Birth of the Human Infant: Symbiosis and Individuation.* New York: Basic Books.

A. B.

MAN For Freud, what separated man from other animals was the far greater latitude in the expression of instinctual needs. In animals, instinctual behaviour is innately programmed with little room for variation. In man, sexual and aggressive drives motivate behaviour, but their expression is channelled by social and cultural factors as well as by the strength of the instincts.

J. A. Ber.

MANA PERSONALITY A state of ego consciousness in which there is an over-identification with a sense of extraordinary power or wisdom and a subsequent ego *inflation. As identification with (or possession by) an *archetype (e.g. the Magician, Wise Man, or Hero), it is seen as a precarious state of disequilibrium for the ego. The term derives from the archaic concept of *mana* (power, wisdom or magical ability) believed in some pre-modern cultures to be a gift from a supernatural source. Mana personality can appear as an energised, gifted, or charismatic quality in others who are strong attractors, for example, sports heroes, actors and actresses.

Jung, C. G. [1953] (1966) *Two Essays on Analytical Psychology*. Princeton: Princeton University Press.

J. Mar.

MANDALA Sanskrit for 'circle'. A sacred space existing in many cultures to support meditative visualisations and ritual practice. Mandalas are located in natural or constructed spaces and contain complex geometric elements in a unified schema representing cosmic or psychic reality.

In Buddhism and Hinduism, mandalas initially referred to fixed world-models of divine reality. Later tantric developments fostered the artistic creation of mandalas as two-dimensional blueprints for three-dimensional perfected environments to reflect individual enlightenment.

C. G. Jung understood mandalas as psychological phenomena appearing spontaneously in the dreams and drawings of individuals, expressing the *archetype of wholeness, the *Self, and often compensating for states of disorientation.

See also: model

M. D.

MANIA Joy, exultation, and readiness for action and triumph are described by Freud as the normal equivalents of states of mania which may occur when energy used to work through the emotional suffering caused by the loss of an ambivalently loved and hated object is liberated for other purposes. Freud says, 'The accumulation of *cathexis which . . . after the work of melancholia is finished, becomes free and makes mania possible must be linked with regression of the *libido to *narcissism.'

Freud, S. (1917) *Mourning and Melancholia*. S. E. 14. London: Hogarth Press.

G. Bre.

MANIA (PSYCHIATRY) In common usage, a state of being overly enthused, often in relation to a specific interest, characterised by increased mental and physical activity. In mental health usage, the term similarly refers to the elevated phase of bipolar disorder, also known as manic-depression. A manic episode is characterised by 'a distinct period of abnormally and persistently elevated, expansive, or irritable mood, lasting at least one week (or any duration if hospitalisation is necessary)', and is accompanied by feelings of *grandiosity, decreased sleep, pressured speech, racing thoughts, distractibility, increased goal-directed activity or physical agitation, and an increased participation in pleasurable activities which have a high potential for unpleasant consequences (e.g. excessive spending, unprotected sex). During the manic phase of bipolar disorder, there is a relatively high likelihood of a person injuring or even killing him- or herself; psychopharmacology is considered to be a fundamental component of treatment, in conjunction with non-biological interventions.

See also: depression

American Psychiatric Association (1994) *Diagnostic and Statistical Manual of Mental Disorders* (*DSM-IV*). Fourth edition. Washington, DC: American Psychiatric Association.
Kaplan, H. and Sadock, B. (1998) *Kaplan and Sadock's Synopsis of Psychiatry*. Eighth edition. Baltimore: Williams & Wilkins.

G. Bre.

MANIC DEFENCES For Klein, manic defences constituted a cluster of defences which sought to make a more dependent individual feel superior to the needed object.

The core manic defences – triumph, contempt and control – seek to devalue the object, while avoiding any sense of concern or guilt towards it, concomitantly sidestepping the necessity for any acts of reparation for having damaged the object. As the child navigates its way out of the exclusive sway of the *paranoid-schizoid position, it encounters the separateness and uncontrollability of the needed object. The child can seek to deny its dependency on an object with which it feels rivalry, leading to phantasies which reverse the child-parent relationship. The child can believe that it is the big one, the parent the little one – and in this Gulliveresque world, the child can believe it has become triumphant and acquired power over the parent while projecting its unwanted dependent feelings into the parent.

The more integrated infant on the other hand, can remember and retain love for the good object even while hating it, as is characteristic of ambivalent states. It can mourn the loss of and pine for the good object, as well as facing the task of testing whether its love is as strong as its hate.

G. Gor.

MANIFEST CONTENT The experience of a *dream as remembered by the dreamer. It primarily functions as a disguise which needs to be decoded or translated into significant meaning(s) but also functions to convey meaning in and of itself, especially about childhood traumatic experiences and the dreamer's attitudes toward the disguised meanings.

See also: latent content

Freud, S. (1900) *The Interpretation of Dreams*. S. E. 4, 5. London: Hogarth Press.
Spanjaard, J. (1969) 'The manifest dream content and its significance for the interpretation of dreams'. *International Journal of Psychoanalysis* 50.

R. Mol.

MARX(ISM) Marxism and psychoanalysis both assume that manifest phenomena are explained by underlying realities, the unmasking of which leads to *freedom. Attempts at their synthesis started as early as 1919 with Paul Federn and W. *Reich and persist today.

These attempts have followed two major trends. One is the historicism of Georgy Lukacs, a Marxian philosopher that strongly influenced the Frankfurt School. The second is the linguistic and anthropological structuralism that influenced Jacques Lacan and Louis Althusser. Most endeavours have centred on Freud's theory of repression, ignoring later developments in psychoanalysis.

For the Frankfurt School thinkers Horkheimer, Adorno and Marcuse, a fundamental distortion of human thought happens at the economic foundations of society, in the equalisation *in abstracto* of all objects in the commodity exchange. Pervading all domains of experience this process fosters abstract relationships among people. At the level of thought an invisible mechanics of reification, i.e. of petrification of experience into 'facts', successfully hides their dialectical inter-relatedness and historical evolution, entrapping the individual thinking in a network of abstractions. Knowledge and culture are given unity through a single equalising abstract measure contained for example, in science, logic or mathematics. In their unwitting subjection to this abstract measure men repress their own humanity.

Critical Theory intended to create a self-aware subjectivity of society that would take the place of Lukacs' revolutionary subject, the class-consciousness of the proletariat. It viewed ego, character, personality and identity as dehumanised forms of unfreedom or automatism, 'the reification of real experience', and psychoanalysis as the tool able to deconstruct them and expose the absence of a subject as the empty core of the individual under capitalism.

Similarly *Lacan's psychoanalysis postulates a constitutive fracture, an insoluble foundational antinomy that leaves a lack at the 'centre' of the subject. He has introduced *alienation as a workable psychoanalytical concept and intrinsic part of his developmental theory. Unlike Marx's view of alienation as a historical process rooted in the commodification of labour, Lacan sees it as the result of a transhistorical structural process, intrinsic to society and to individual development. This originated in the fact that all systems of representation including language (which in this view exist outside the historical and economical process), are offered to the child by the *Other (society) and without exception introduce a misrepresentation of the internal reality of desires and of the Imaginary (where 'frozen images' stand for unconscious phantasies) which because of this fact remain beyond complete representation. Inserted in this manner within Symbolic structures that shape all the interactions between self and other, the subject becomes an 'other' to itself, being spoken by language more than speaking his own mind.

The German philosopher Alfred Sohn-Rethel, describes the formation of the commodity as a process of externalisation of unconscious thoughts in which he finds the historical roots of the dissociation between manual and intellectual labour, between the empirical and particular and the abstract and universal. The commodity formation can thus be described within the frame of *object relations theory as the generation of two object relations incompatible in time and space. One is the subjective relation with the object's concrete qualities (or use value) which has to be suspended to give way to another relation with the object as an object for exchange (exchange value), an 'external' object unconsciously invested with the abstract property of exchangeability.

This is strikingly similar to *projective identification and to the formation of a substitute object in extreme trauma: the impossible access to the internal experience of the object is compensated by exchange for an external object bearing formal, external similarities to the lost object which it represents in abstract form.

Likewise in Bion's theory of *thinking the baby needs to objectify his states of mind in the mother in order to be able to know them and internalise stable, abstract versions of himself and/or of his mother. The profound dissociation between the individual as object and the individual as subject seen in cases of extreme trauma is probably due to a fracture between the two arms of this exchange with only the view of self from outside remaining viable.

See also: logic

Bion, W. R. (1967) 'A theory of thinking' in *Second Thoughts*. London: Heinemann.

Kolakowski, L. (1978) *Main Currents of Marxism. 3. The Breakdown*. Oxford and New York: Oxford University Press.

Lacan, J. (1977) *Ecrits: A Selection*. London: Tavistock.

Lukacs, G. (1971) 'Reification and the consciousness of the proletariat' in *History and Class Consciousness*. London: Merlin Press.

Matte Blanco, I. (1988) *Thinking, Feeling and Being*. London and New York: Routledge.

Reyes, A., Reyes, P. and Skelton, R. (1997) 'Traumatised logic: the containing function of unconscious classification in the aftermath of extreme trauma'. *Journal of Melanie Klein and Object Relations* 15(4).

Sohn-Rethel, A. (1978) *Intellectual and Manual Labour. A Critique of Scientific Epistemology*. London: Humanities Press.

A. Rey.

MASCULINITY Masculinity for Freud, meant assuming an active rather than a passive role in sexuality as well as other undertakings. Masculinity is active, *femininity is passive. The passive attitude means being castrated, like a woman, and is therefore energetically avoided. The 'masculine protest', the final resistance in the analysis of men, is the refusal to submit to being cured by the analyst.

See also: active/passive

J. A. Ber.

MASOCHISM Freud described masochism as the experience of pleasure in pain, humiliation or suffering. He describes three different types: sexual, feminine and moral masochism. Sexual masochism occurs when a physically painful situation, like being beaten on the buttocks, is sexualised and becomes a condition for erotic pleasure. Feminine masochism is the pleasure taken in playing the passive role in sexuality and in life, which may include being dominated and humiliated. Moral masochism is the *repetition, presumably pleasurable on some level, of suffering at the hand of fate or of one's super-ego. In his final theory, Freud saw masochism as a manifestation of the death instinct.

For Lacan, the masochist assumes the role of the object, and moves by so doing into a position where his or her subjectivity is annulled. According to Lacan, the violence of the sado-masochistic act is properly a violence that is done to the *subject, rather than to the person. The phantasy described by Freud as 'a child is being beaten' represents the way in which Lacan presents a human being as subject to – beaten by – the law and the elements of the signifying structure. The masochist, in attempting to master this situation (the masochist often tries to lure the sadist so far onto the path of inflicting pain or jouissance that the latter eventually becomes anxious and says 'no!', which implies that the masochist is in control), gains a jouissance which is based on a misunderstanding of the boundaries and cuts introduced by language. We don't utilise language, says Lacan, it utilises us.

J. A. Ber. / J. P. K.

MASOCHISM (FEMININE) In relational psychoanalysis this term generally refers to submission and self-sacrifice, not to physical masochism. Masochism is seen in relational and interpersonal psychoanalysis as a response learned in a variety of situations. It may be a way of attaining a goal that cannot be attained through direct attempts. Self-punishment may be rewarded by another person or may prevent another from inflicting experiences that are even more anxiety-provoking. For Thompson, masochism was seen as a form of adaptation to an unsatisfactory and circumscribed life. According to *Horney, masochism was a neurotic expression of striving toward safety through a merger with a powerful other. Menaker hypothesised that girls may learn to put themselves down to avoid punishment from mothers who want no competition.

Masochistic behavior in women has been considered by Benjamin to stem from a lack of recognition of desires in women by the father. Benjamin suggested that fathers recognised their sons as subjects of desire, but see their daughters often as only objects of desire. Benjamin holds that the father's lack of availability to his daughter leads to increased helplessness and depression. As a result, in adulthood, women often seek, through submission to men, the opportunity of a second chance for ideal love and the recognition of their own desire. The link between the failure of recognition of desire, when it occurs, and masochism in this theory is related to the most common psychiatric problem among both women and men: depression. Experimental research has found support for the idea that people sometimes believe that suffering in the present will lead to better outcomes in the future.

See also: gender; interpersonal psychoanalysis; intersubjectivity; relational psychoanalysis; sadism

Benjamin, J. (1988) *Bonds of Love*. New York: Pantheon Books.

Curtis, R. C. (1989) 'Choosing to suffer or to . . .? Empirical studies and clinical theories of masochism' in R. C. Curtis (ed.) *Self-Defeating Behaviors*. New York: Plenum.

Horney, K. (1939) *New Ways in Psychoanalysis*. New York: Norton.

Menaker, E. (1953) 'Masochism – a defense reaction of the ego'. *Psychoanalytic Quarterly* 22.

Thompson, C. [1942] (1990) 'Cultural pressures in the psychology of women' in C. Zanardi (ed.) *Essential Papers on the Psychology of Women*. New York: New York University Press.

R. C.

MASTER Starting from *Hegel's master-slave dialectic, and with death, the absolute master, on the horizon, the master is called upon and put into question throughout Lacan's work. When Lacan formulated psychoanalysis as a discourse, the position of the master was formulated as the master-signifier in the place of the agent where it appears to instigate the kind of discourse that aims at avoiding castration. In that sense it is possible to say that the discourse of the master is subverted by the discourse of analysis.

R. R. B.

MASTERY, DRIVE FOR see **DRIVE FOR MASTERY**

MASTURBATION To manipulate one's genitals for sexual gratification. During *infantile sexuality, the *erotogenic zones serve as organs of masturbatory activity for the child. Later they become merged with object-love wishful ideas. If renounced in adulthood, and no other mode of sexual satisfaction and/or sublimation intervenes, these unconscious phantasies produce neurotic symptoms.

See also: autoerotic

Freud, S. (1905) *Three Essays on the Theory of Sexuality*. S. E. 7. London: Hogarth Press.
Freud, S. (1908) *Hysterical Phantasies and their Relation to Bisexuality*. S. E. 9. London: Hogarth Press.

R. M.

MATHEMATICS According to Lacan only mathematics is truly able to reach out to and attain what is the *Real. That is why Lacan claims that it is compatible with analytical discourse. In the 1970s Lacan stressed the dependence of the Real on the discourse within which it is grasped. Poetry also gives access to the real of the unconscious, but it can be argued that mathematics is at the very heart of what is poetic.

See also: logic

N. C.

MATHEME Lacan characterised the matheme as an instrument that has the power to formulate and transmit psychoanalysis. This leaves open the question of what exactly a matheme consists of. Was he thinking of the formulae which regularly appear in this teaching, usually composed of a small number of letters (S1, S2, S, a, A)? Or was he rather thinking of the structures which he put forward as non-metaphorical constructions on the torus (doughnut), on the projective plane, or on Cantor's transfinite numbers? He was undoubtedly intending his neologism to be interpreted in a wide sense. In 1973 he pegged the functioning of the matheme to the structure of numbers; elsewhere he took the notion of *doxa* (true opinion) from classical Greek philosophy to make of it a necessary component in the mathematics used in the matheme.

N. C.

MATTE BLANCO, IGNACIO (1908–95) Matte Blanco applied logic and mathematics to the study of the unconscious and the more emotional thinking processes. He also introduced the (mathematical) infinite into psychoanalysis. Born in Santiago (Chile), he graduated in medicine before completing his psychoanalytic training in London and on his return to Santiago in 1944 founded the Chilean Psychoanalytic Society. From 1949 to 1966 he was director of a modern psychiatric clinic and in his daily contact with mental illness, he was struck by the analogy between schizophrenic thought and the manifestations of the unconscious, as delineated by Freud. In 1966 Matte Blanco moved to Italy, where he lived until his death. In 1975 he published his seminal *The Unconscious as Infinite Sets* in which his basic argument is that the unconscious and emotions do not know individuals, but only classes or sets of individuals, as found for example in racial prejudice: 'all Jews/Irish/Blacks are the same!' As a result of what he calls 'symmetrisation' within the class, all elements become identical and interchangeable as well as identical to the entire class, all of whose potential they possess. Remarks such as '*Je suis la France*' are of this nature. Consequently whole and part can be seen as identical – a fact noted by the mathematician Dedekind in his study of infinite sets. Because intensity of emotion is a function of depth, conflict and psychopathology it may be seen as the consequence of frenzied 'infinitisation' – a form of thought which cannot operate within the three-dimensional structures of consciousness. The task of analysis is to liberate a situation or an individual from the infinite attributes implicit in the class. This infinitisation is evident not only in psychosis and in Freud's *primary process thinking but also when we make creative generalisations which are 'insane'. This unaccustomed modality that dissolves difference, transforming every similarity into an identity, is not in itself thinkable, and so can emerge as extreme anxiety. For example, a young woman who yearns for independence becomes extremely anxious when her mother cuts her cat's claws. She experiences herself as a member of the class of all beings, human or animal, whose search for independence is severely punished. The counterpoint to this mode of (symmetric) thought is the establishment of differences in so-called 'asymmetric' thinking in the spirit of the *secondary process. However it is important to see that asymmetric processes are present too in psychosis. In this way, Matte Blanco came to define a third logic which he calls 'bi-logic', a logic for bi-modal reality. This blends two logical strands of thinking: symmetric (dissolving differences) and asymmetric (promoting differences), both of which can be observed in emotional experiencing such as dreaming and also in everyday life. He extended this in 1988, with *Thinking, Feeling and Being* completing a bi-logical revision of the Kleinian theory in general and *projective identification in particular. In this interpretation of Klein the indivisible symmetric mode characterises the deeper emotional strata such as *unconscious phantasy. However his concept of the *death drive is radically different from that of Klein for he sees it as the being pulled beyond aggression into the stillness of absolute symmetry. This mysterious dimension may be manifest as disorganised thought or even in some cases as mystical experience.

See also: infinity; logic; mysticism; time

Bria, P. (1998) 'Infinity in the mind. The biological point of view'. *Journal of Melanie Klein and Object Relations* 16(1).

Ginzburg, A. (1997) 'The bi-logical stratified structure: when cats are panthers'. *Journal of Melanie Klein and Object Relations* 15(4).

Rayner, E. (1995) *Unconscious Logic*. London: Routledge.

A. Gn.

MAY, ROLLO (1909–94) Rollo May was born in 1909 in the tiny midwestern town of Ada, Ohio. He died in Tiburon, California in October of 1994. May was the second of six children of Victorian and traditionally religious parents. In his early twenties, he left America to teach English at a Greek high school in Salonika. While teaching at this school, he suffered what he called a 'nervous exhaustion' and through that trial, found a renewed purpose in life. After spending time painting, travelling, and attending seminars given by *Adler, May returned to America and embarked on a lifelong psychospiritual quest. His work as a minister and his tutelage under the prominent theologian Paul Tillich added immensely to this legacy. His famous 1958 *Existence* with Henri Ellenberger and Ernest Angel, introduced European existential psychoanalysis to the English-speaking world.

From the time of his first book on counselling in 1939, May's psychology of therapy was concerned with the issue of how to see the *human nature that underlies the work of therapy. An 'essentialist' view describes the characteristics of human nature that must be taken into account. For Freud, the sexual instinct was central; for Jung the introversive-extraversive doubleness of human consciousness was decisive. These are the envisioned 'essential elements' in human nature. Science is 'essentialistic' in exactly the sense that matter and energy are the basic substrate of reality. Freud and Jung offered different formulations, but neither moved from a preoccupation with essence to the existence of 'human' being.

With the advent of his classic introduction to *Existence*, May showed that existential, rather than essential, issues have to do with creating a future, a unique openness to an uncharted course not known in the natural world. Existential thought sees human freedom as more than a pocket of indeterminacy; the existential situation is the challenge of deciding one's future. Human 'being', the ontology of human life, forces us to create, whether we see it that way or not. In the face of freedom, human beings shrink from the challenge, from the anxiety of freedom, into the safety of presumed essences. May's psychoanalytic therapy thus attributed human anxiety to the challenges of human freedom. When freedom overwhelms us, we feel bored, lonely, and isolated – each a disguised version of the anxiety of human freedom sighted so vividly by Kierkegaard. Love, will, power, the demonic, the transcending of instinct – these terms outline the challenge which is human existence, which requires tolerating anxiety, sublimating greed, dwelling in love, and eschewing innocence. All of these challenges are fundamentally human, whose rigours we are pleased to call 'psychopathology'. Psychopathology for May is nothing like the disease which afflicts the body; it is the struggle of being human, whose solution is not to be found in a technology of health but rather in a re-orientation to the strenuous exigencies of human freedom.

May's debt to Freud is profound. He sees in Freud's diagnosis of the human being challenges that somehow got muted in the medicalisation of Freud's struggles with human desire and human responsibility. Unlike Freud, May also sees only a limited cure in rationality. Once one has assessed it all, one still needs to find the courage to grasp life's possibilities, in the face of life's necessities, with love and creativity. One of May's favourite books to give to students and patients was Tillich's *The Courage to Be*. The uniqueness of May's legacy is his valuing of paradox. The paradox between freedom and limitation in particular runs through every one of May's major ideas and is central to his approach to therapy. Whenever, in May's view, psychology overemphasised limitation, as with elements of the behavioural and psychoanalytic movements, he reminded colleagues of human possibility; and whenever, in his estimation, psychology overemphasised freedom, as with aspects of the human potential and transpersonal orientations, he recalled people to their frailties. In his theories as with his practice, May upheld the sanctity of human struggle. Without struggle, May emphasised, life becomes hollow; but in its presence, life can become enriched, animated, and purposeful.

May, R. (1950) *The Meaning of Anxiety*. New York: Ronald.

May, R., Ellenberger, H. and Angel, E. (1958) *Existence: A New Dimension in Psychiatry and Psychology*. New York: Basic Books.

May, R. (1969) *Love and Will*. New York: Norton.

May, R. (1972) *Power and Innocence*. New York: Norton.

May, R. (1981) *Freedom and Destiny*. New York: Norton.

E. Kee. / K. S.

MEDICO-LEGAL INTERFACE The medico-legal interface, and specifically the interface between psychiatry and the law, is fraught with conceptual and practical difficulties. In essence the aims of psychiatry are those of welfare and the aim of the law is justice. The two are rarely totally reconcilable. In addition, an adversarial system, whilst it may well be a powerful vehicle for establishing 'facts', does not lend itself to psychiatric or psychological understanding. In practical terms, the two disciplines may meet in productive tension, or even collaboration. Alternatively, they may barely make contact.

A further major difficulty is that the law is founded largely upon cognitive understanding and allows little space for 'emotional thinking'. psychiatry (and psychotherapy), by contrast, emphasise the emotional life (or lack of it) of the client/patient as well as their – intimately entwined – cognitions.

Nevertheless, the medico-legal interface is the territory the forensic psychiatrist inhabits and mostly to reasonably good effect. However, ethical issues are profound and increasingly recognised as problematic. This is especially so in contemporary societies where the demands of the State for more and more statutory 'control' require the clinician to act primarily in the interests of 'public protection.' Forensic psychiatrists in particular, but all clinicians in general, are increasingly expected to disclose hitherto confidential information about patients to the authorities. Clinicians need to battle to maintain a clinical space and not become 'clinical policemen' or 'social hygienists'.

C. C.

MEIER, C. A. (1905–95) A distinguished psychiatrist and Jungian analyst, he was born on 19 April 1905 in Schaffhausen, Switzerland and died in Zurich on 15 November 1995. An encounter with Jung while a schoolboy initiated a change in his life's course from marine biology to psychiatry, and he went on to become Jung's assistant, a founder and first president of the Zurich C. G. Jung Institut in 1948 and Jung's successor as Honorary Professor at the Technical University of Zurich (ETH). He is best remembered as co-founder of the psychiatric *Klinik am Zürichberg* in 1964 and for his many textbooks, in particular *Healing, Dream and Ritual*, which examines ancient incubation and modern psychotherapy.

Meier, C. A. [1949] *Antike Inkubation und moderne Psychotherapie*. Zurich: Rascher. ((1989) *Healing, Dream and Ritual*. Einsiedeln: Daimon)

R. H.

MELANCHOLIA/MELANCHOLY In his very first works between 1895 and 1897, Freud understood melancholia as a form of *depression of variable intensity, linked to a loss of mental energy – he mainly drew on the popular theory of neurasthenia. Two decades later, he integrated the much more psychiatric, Kraepelinian concept of psychotic melancholia, mainly characterised by delusional auto-accusations and severe moral pain, often resulting in suicide attempts. He then differentiated between *mourning, a quasi-normal mechanism in which the subject painfully struggles to admit the loss of the object in spite of his unconscious attachment to it – and melancholia, in which the situation of *loss has not been integrated. Appalled by the object loss, the person incorporates the lost object, identifies himself with it, and consequently attacks himself, whence the auto-accusation symptom. Subsequently, in his second *topography, Freud was to consider that melancholia implied a specific psychic agency capable of fostering self-punitive pangs, the *super-ego, genetically appearing at the same time as the differentiation between the *ego and the *id.

F. S.

MELTZER, DONALD (1922–) has been a key, if controversial figure within post-Kleinian thinking, particularly in proposing a 'concrete' inner world. Born in the USA on 14 August 1922, Meltzer came to psychoanalysis through interests in internal medicine gained during training at Yale and New York University. After practice in St Louis, an initial analysis and participation in the Chicago Institute's satellite study-group, Meltzer came to London where he trained at the Institute of Psychoanalysis (1954–7). Analysed by *Klein (with whom he continued until her death in 1960) and supervised by *Segal and Rosenfeld, Meltzer then completed child analytic training over the next two years. *Bick's supervision during that latter period profoundly impressed him, her influence deepening when he began working with her at the Tavistock Clinic. He resigned from the British Society in 1984.

Meltzer's numerous contributions stem from his early focus on the internal situation, phantasies and curiosity which significantly motivate emotional life. Mapping this internal geography led Meltzer to emphasise the inherent intrusiveness of pathological projective identification, processes he linked with anality and anal masturbation. Intrusive identification is thus an insidious entry into the inside of the internal maternal object, motivated by fear and wishes to control. Having perversely entered the object, the subject becomes prone to identity confusion, 'geographical confusions' and claustrophobic states within what Meltzer terms the claustrum. Inherent in this geography is the notion of a multi-dimensional space, which may be containing or confining, entered intrusively, by consent or invitation, and by concrete or imaginative means. In autism, Meltzer highlighted the two dimensional nature of the subject's internal world wherein contact, as Bick hypothesised, is through adhesive identification. More recently, Meltzer has emphasised the aesthetic dimension, aesthetic conflict emanating from appreciation of the object and respect for its privacy in the face of phantasies of usurpation.

Cassese, S. F. (2002) *Introduction to the Work of Donald Meltzer*. London: Karnac Books.
Meltzer, D. (1988) *The Apprehension of Beauty*. Strathtay: Clunie Press.
Meltzer, D. (1992) *The Claustrum*. Strathtay: Clunie Press.
Meltzer, D. (1994) *Sincerity and Other Works: Collected Papers*. London: Karnac Books.

R. Wil.

MEMORY Memories are stored mental *representations, based on prior experiences, which can be accessed (recalled) to help us negotiate our environments. Memories are connected associatively. For example, if I see a dog on the street, this might remind me of my dog Bailey. This, in turn, might remind me that I need to purchase dog food, which might remind me to stop at the bank to withdraw cash, and so on. The associative links between memories are often held to be idiosyncratic. Reiser believes that memories are usually linked by commonalities in emotion. Memories are not necessarily veridical representations of past experiences. They are often distorted. These distortions are lawful such that the resulting recollections are blends of the actual events, the person's wishes and fears, and his or her current psychological state. Sometimes, memories are so threatening or painful that the person denies him or herself access to them altogether. This is termed *repression. Sometimes, several memories sharing a common theme are combined into a single meta-memory called a *screen memory.

See also: amnesia; distortion

Freud, S. (1900) *The Interpretation of Dreams*. S. E. 4. London: Hogarth Press.
Reiser, M. (1990) *Memory in Mind and Brain*. New York: Basic Books.

J. Wei.

MEMORY WARS This term refers to the so called 'recovered memories' debate. It is the dramatic terminology coined by for the conceptual, theoretical, clinical – and sadly sometimes personal – disputes between those on the one hand who believe in the possible recovery of repressed traumatic memories from earlier life, and those, on the other hand, who deny that such memories can ever be repressed, and therefore 'recovered'.

There are many reasons for the passions and polarisations which this debate has engendered. They include:

Firstly, the concept of repression is under attack: Freud stated that 'the theory of repression is the cornerstone on which the whole structure of psychoanalysis rests'; those in opposition to Freud and psychoanalysis naturally scent 'blood'. According to Fonagy and Target it is a dispute 'just beneath the surface of, (which) the profession of psychotherapy (is) fighting for its life.'

Secondly, individual patients, believing themselves to have been abused, are fighting for acknowledgement of their 'trauma' and therefore for their very identity: likewise, in opposition, the accused are fighting for their innocence and good name.

Thirdly, psychotherapists were originally accused of ignoring child sexual abuse – following Freud's perceived *volte face* from believing all the hysterical and other states of his patients to have been the consequence of actual sexual abuse, to his theory of their having been predominantly related to fantasy. Now, by contrast, some psychotherapists (most obviously recovered memory therapists) are accused of 'inventing' or 'talking up' childhood sexual and other traumatic abuse.

Finally, the issues of recovered memory have become part of socio-political movements, especially in the USA, e.g. 'The study of trauma in sexual and domestic life becomes legitimate only in a context that challenges the subordination of women and children. Advances in the field occur only when they are supported by a political movement powerful enough to legitimate an alliance between investigators and patients and to counteract the ordinary social processes of silencing and "denial"' as noted by Herman in 1992. In Britain two rival groups (The False Memory Society and Accuracy about Abuse) continue to polarise the arguments, proselytise and directly oppose each other.

Actually, as is so often the case, the excessive heat of the debate has obscured the light. On cooler consideration it is true that the psychoanalytic model of 'repression' needs better definition; often Freud uses the term to refer merely to any defensive mechanism which involved 'turning something away, and keeping it at a distance from the conscious'. Equally, those engaged and entrenched in the Memory Wars, and especially Crews himself, as well as some researchers, have used a very concrete model of Freudian repression, as a straw man to be knocked down.

The arguments are complex, and it is certain that no absolute answers exist. Memory is generally less accurate and reliable than each of us likes to believe of ourselves. It distorts with time, and gets mixed up with fantasy in normal subjects. 'Memories' which are claimed for before two and a half or three years are not to be relied upon. Episodic (autobiographical) memories which arise *de novo*, spontaneously – but certainly those 'recovered' during suggestive or hypnotic psychotherapy or counselling – are to be regarded with suspicion. Also, 'procedural' or implicit' memory which is somato-sensorily represented – as in symptoms or reflexes (e.g. of avoidance) – cannot be accurately translated by any means into 'historical' memory. In people with borderline or hysterical personalities who typically exhibit dissociative phenomena the distortions and admixture of fantasy and reality can be especially prominent. The situation is complicated by the fact that these very same people are more likely actually to have been traumatised in earlier life.

'New' memories are most likely to be erroneous, but, on the other hand, patients will often say, for example, that they have 'always known' that they had been abused and have remembered the events, but that they 'put them to the back of (their) mind' – for understandable personal, family and social reasons. These memories are likely to be largely accurate and are to be taken very seriously. Finally, there is no place for therapist 'suggestion' or the use of 'leading' questions where memories of childhood abuse is at issue: the stakes are too high either way.

Crews, F. (1994) 'The revenge of the repressed'. *The New York Review of Books*, 17 November and 1 December.

Herman (1992) *Trauma and Recovery*. New York: Basic Books.
Fonagy, P. and Target, M. (1997) 'Perspectives in the recovered memories debate' in J. Sandler and P. Fonagy (eds) *Recovered Memories of Abuse: True or False?*. London: Karnac Books.
Freud, S. (1914) *On the History of the Psycho-Analytic Movement*. S. E. 14. London: Hogarth Press.
Freud, S. (1915) *Repression*. S. E. 14. London: Hogarth Press.

C. C.

MEMORY, DESIRE AND UNDERSTANDING These three terms are gathered by Bion to put forward his impression that these three ego functions hinder the *intuition of the evolution of the non-sensorial *psychic reality. He calls this reality a 'dream-like reality', which is the stuff of analysis, the psychical *O in the personality.

Bion first spoke about the interference of memory and desire in psychoanalytic practice in his 1967 commentaries about his eight 1950–62 papers published as *Second Thoughts*, and in his 1967 paper 'Notes on Memory and Desire'. He then also included understanding as something which interferes with the contact with the evolved aspects of O (variously described as ultimate reality, absolute truth, thing in itself, *thoughts without a thinker, etc.). His injunction, in these and in all his future papers, books and seminars, is for the analyst to remain without memory, without desire and without understanding in order to allow and aid the intuition of the dream-like psychical reality in evolution. These formulations have often been related to Freud's evenly suspended or freely floating attention, but technically imply much more and are related to a different epistemological and ontological position about the personality and what analysis is about.

Bion considers memory and desire as past and future forms or 'senses' of the same thing. To remain 'without memory' is to leave the mental space open for the reception of something new, something which is not known. What is already known (theories, supervisors' opinions, precise information about the patient) functions as pre-existing contents which belong to the past, and, as such, obstructs contact in the present and the intuition-discovery of something new. He suggests the analyst should tend to be in a mental state so as to feel, in each session, that he has never seen this patient previously. One should always see a patient as if it were the first time one sees him. This of course is not easy, and one has to train and discipline oneself to be in this state of mind while analysing.

'Without desire' is more than the rules of abstinence formulated by Freud. Desires may be considered as the other face of memories, both composed of elements based on sense impressions: memories related to the past and desires with the future. As such, both interfere, as conscious contents, with contact in the present. The desire to cure, the desire for the session to end, the desire a patient should express himself more fluently or speak about something he is not talking about, the desire not to lose the patient for economical, institutional or professional prestige reasons – in fact, any active desire, whether springing from the analyst's drives (his intra-subjective space), from the relationship with the patient (the inter-subjective space) or from the social and institutional one (the trans-subjective space) will interfere with the possibility of a discovery.

'Without understanding' implies a state of uncertainty and lack of knowledge. It excludes the active desire to understand, as well as the active memory of what has already been understood; it requires one to give up for an undetermined period of time, the usual categories of space, time and causality, the source of much understanding in daily life.

These propositions must, however, not be misunderstood (as has often been the case) as a brain washing, a dementalisation or an attack on the ego functions near to the psychotic manoeuvres aimed at avoiding contact with reality. On the contrary, the intention is to establish contact, implying only a partial and temporary suspension of these functions in order to focus better on psychic reality and allow for evolution and development.

Bion suggests that what he has said about the psychoanalytical sessions also applies to the experience of reading psychoanalytic papers written by creative authors. They should be read, and 'forgotten', and thus produce the conditions in which, when one reads them again, they can stimulate the evolution of further development.

Bion, W. R. (1967) *Second Thoughts.* London: Heinemann.

Bion, W. R. (1967) 'Notes on memory and desire'. *The Psychoanalytic Forum* 2(3).

Bion, W. R. (1970) *Attention and Interpretation.* London: Tavistock.

Bion, W. R. (1971) 'The grid' in *Two Papers: The Grid and Caesura.* Rio de Janeiro: Imago.

E. T. B.

MESSIANIC IDEA A revolutionary idea which threatens the structure of the group. The messianic idea has a counterpart, O, for which a thinker is not necessary. When the evolution of a thinker and the evolution of a thought come together, a messianic idea is created. The thought, O, and the thinker can exist in three types of relations to each other: commensal, symbiotic and parasitic.

See also: link

Bion, W. R. (1965) *Transformations.* London: Karnac Books. Also in *Seven Servants.* New York: Jason Aronson, 1977.

Bion, W. R. (1970) *Attention and Interpretation.* London: Tavistock. Also in *Seven Servants.* New York: Jason Aronson, 1977.

S. A.

METAPHOR Metaphor is an effect of a substitution of one signifier for another, a process in which the occulted signifier nevertheless remains in touch with the occulting signifier. It is crucial for the understanding of the structure of repression and its role in the formations of the unconscious, the symptom and the operation of the name-of-the-father: in repression an occluded signifier is forced into the unconscious, the symptom stands in for unconscious material which causes it and the name-of-the-father substitutes for the desire of the mother. It is also the dimension in which the interpretation aims at truth.

P. D.

METAPSYCHOLOGY Following his unpublished attempt at a neuroscientific psychology in 1895, the term 'metapsychology' first appeared in letters to *Fliess of 1896 and 1898: it became a theoretical construction elaborated by Freud throughout his life. His ambition was to formulate a general psychoanalytic theory of the psychic apparatus. Its main ingredients are: the first *topography (*unconscious; *preconscious; *conscious); the second, so-called 'structural' topography (*id; *ego; *super-ego); as well as the *dynamic and *economic dimensions. These ingredients constitute the general or metapsychological theory of the mind.

V. D.

METONYMY The signifying operation which Lacan bases on the Freudian notion of *displacement. Together with that of *condensation (metaphor), it constitutes the unconscious primary processes. Defined as the connection of one signifier to another, it incarnates the logic of desire in its function of attempting to be the desire of the Other. The same logic generates an incessant escape of meaning.

See also: metaphor

R. R. B.

MEXICO Psychoanalysis in Mexico is necessarily a transcultural product. Freud's name first appeared in print here in 1922, in an essay written by the physician José Torres Orozco, who read Freud in German. By 1923 a small amount of Freud's work had been circulated. (At that time Mexico had 15 million inhabitants, 70% illiterate.) However, in 1928 the philosopher Samuel Ramos, who was interested in psychoanalysis, went to Vienna to look for *Adler, though not for Freud.

The first attempts at institutionalisation were made in the fifties; Erich *Fromm and Santiago Ramírez were the pioneers. Fromm was invited to teach in the National University of Mexico in 1951. Ramírez, trained in Argentina, started working in Mexico City in 1958. The first two groups failed in their attempt to start a common movement, each one taking its own way: the orthodox Freudians and the Frommians.

Today it seems that the *Lacanians are the most influential group, followed by the Freudians (divided into different groups). *Klein's influence is slightly perceptible. *Jung has an active disciple in Mexico City. *Bion, *Winnicott, and *Fairbairn are not unknown.

General corruption as well as economic and educational problems negatively affect the qualification and level of achievement of the psychoanalytical movement: the underdevelopment of the nation is due not only to external factors, but also to internal causes.

See also: Boss; Fromm

Bosse, H. (1979) *Diebe, Lügner, Faulenzer*. Frankfurt: Syndikat.

Páramo-Ortega, R. (1992) *Freud in Mexiko*. München: Quintessenz.

Ramírez, S. (1979) *Ajuste de cuentas*. Mexico: Nueva Imagen.

R. P. O.

MILLER, JACQUES-ALAIN (1944–) was an analysand of a member of the *Ecole Freudienne de Paris*, the school of Lacan, founded in 1964 and broken up in 1980 by its founder. He has had a long and distinguished career as an analyst, teacher, editor, writer and administrator. Professor in the Department of Psychoanalysis at the University of Paris-VIII, his weekly lectures have been a companion to the reading of Lacan's work for more than thirty years. His first publication on Lacan was the 'reasoned index of the most important concepts' included in the *Ecrits* in 1966.

He is responsible for Lacan's literary estate and editor of Lacan's *Seminar*. He edited the first seminar in 1973, and has continued ever since. He was the key player in the founding of the *Ecole de la Cause Freudienne* on the eve of Lacan's death in 1981. Ten years later in 1992, he founded the *Association Mondiale de Psychanalyse* (AMP) into which various schools of Lacanian orientation worldwide are integrated. He was its first president, remaining for ten years (1992–2002).

His task as a writer is centred on the most challenging issues of psychoanalytical practice, theory and clinical research. Regarding practice, he has addressed interpretation, setting, ethics, non-standardisation, and principles. Regarding clinical issues, his inquiries on the analytical symptom continue: on this line of investigation, he has put in evidence the main shifts in Lacan's approach of the clinical 'structures'. On the theory of psychoanalytical training as such, his elaborations on the termination of the treatment have been seminal.

Extracts of his *Cours* are regularly published in French in the Lacanian Journals. They are available in Portuguese, English, Italian, German, Danish, and Russian. The complete edition of his *Cours*, published by Paidos in Spanish, has been under way since 1998.

He has recently directed himself to a broader public, addressing psychoanalytical issues for 'enlightened opinion'. Three books have been published so far in two years: *Lettres à l'opinion éclairée*, Seuil, 2002; *Un début dans la vie*, Gallimard, 2002; *Le Neveu de Lacan*, Verdier, 2003.

E. L.

MILIEU THERAPY utilises the social milieu in an environment for therapeutic benefit. It is best understood as an attenuated form of therapeutic community, which uses the reality of living together in a ward, or other institution, to explore the group processes that emerge. Therapeutic community work originated in the military psychiatric hospitals during the second world war, where psychoanalytically orientated psychiatrists such as *Bion and Rickman modified the regime in the wards, allowing the men to take responsibility for aspects of the ward routine, and to talk about their issues in group sessions. Also out of these experiments grew the practice of group psychoanalytic therapy. Most commonly, milieu therapy is carried out in psychiatric wards where the capacity of the residents is impaired, so that they cannot participate fully in a community experience but where some aspects of this can be introduced. For example, a weekly community or ward meeting is arranged to discuss current issues in the ward or a ward chairperson might be elected or appointed to represent the views of patients.

M. Mor.

MIMICRY For Lacan, the infant's mimicking or imitative gestures should not be understood as mere adaptive mechanisms (*qua* some trope of evolutionary psychology or developmentalism) but rather as part of the identificatory apparatus associated with the *mirror stage. As such, it participates in the construction of the *ego. Correspondingly, the mimicry of the baby's behaviour by the mother allows her to function as a specular image.

R. Loo.

MIRROR PHASE STAGE The mirror stage or phase is the key to primary narcissism and the formation of the ego. It lays the ground for subsequent Imaginary identifications. This concept combines the observation that between the ages of six and eighteen months the infant is fascinated by its own image in a mirroring with the biological fact of its physiological prematurity. The infant greets its specular image with jubilation arising from the anticipation of a bodily unity, and contrasting with the immaturity of its motor development. Captivated by the image and identifying with it, the infant apprehends it as its own image and as the image of another. Fundamental to the Mirror stage is that the 'self' and 'other' (counterpart) are constituted through both itself and the Other, its counterpart. The child locates its own image in the other, and conversely locates the other in the image of its own self.

See also: ego; image

R. Gri.

MISRECOGNITION For Lacan, misrecognition (*méconnaissance*) refers to a consciousness of self and of others, which, as a construction of the ego, is based on an image coming from outside, but which nevertheless is experienced as a true self. The root of this systematic *méconnaissance* is alienation based on the recognition of the subject in the field of the Other and as such this recognition is radically misapprehended as oneself.

See also: alienation; aphanisis; recognition

H. T.

MITCHELL, JULIET (1940–) is a British academic and practising psychoanalyst. Her ground-breaking work, *Psychoanalysis and Feminism* in 1974, pioneered the feminist revision of Freudian psychoanalysis. Using Lacan, Mitchell stresses the symbolic nature of the phallus as 'transcendental signifier', thereby ridding Freud of biologism and expressing the potential for change in patriarchal social relations. Her work spawned a new wave of psychoanalytically influenced social and cultural criticism. *Mad Men and Medusas*, 2000, examines the ways that accounts of male hysteria have receded at the expense of feminisations of the 'disease'. Mitchell also introduced her theory of laterality or *sibling which she develops in *Siblings: Sex and Violence*, 2003.

Mitchell, J. (1966) 'Women: the longest revolution'. *New Left Review* 40: 10–30.
Mitchell, J. (1972) *Women's Estate*. London and New York: Penguin.
Mitchell, J. (1974) *Psychoanalysis and Feminism*. London: Allen Lane and Penguin.
Mitchell, J. (2000) *Mad Men and Medusas: Reclaiming Hysteria and the Effects of Sibling Rivalry on the Human Condition*. London: Hamish Hamilton and Penguin.
Mitchell, J. (2003) *Siblings: Sex and Violence*. Cambridge: Polity Press.
Mitchell, J. and Rose, J. (eds) (1982) *Feminine Sexuality: Jacques Lacan and the Ecole Freudienne*. London: Macmillan.
Wright, S. (2001) 'Juliet Mitchell' in A. Elliott and B. Turner (eds) *Profiles in Contemporary Social Theory*. London: Sage.

S. W.

MITCHELL, STEPHEN A. (1946–2000) Stephen Mitchell is considered the leading founder of the relational school of psychoanalysis. Author in 1983 of *Object Relations in Psychoanalysis* with Jay Greenberg, he graduated from the W. A. White Institute in 1977 and was editor of *Psychoanalytic Dialogues*, begun in 1991, and founder of the International Association of Relational Psychoanalysis and Psychotherapy. Greenberg and Mitchell proposed that, beginning with *Sullivan and *Fairbairn, a paradigm change had taken place in psychoanalysis that they called the relational/structure model, in contrast to the drive/structure model preceding it. The relational approach combined ideas about intrapsychic processes from object relations theories and ideas about interactions with others from interpersonal psychoanalysis. The relational umbrella also included self psychological approaches. Constructivist, post-modern, and feminist thinking influenced Mitchell. He viewed sexuality as an important medium in which relational struggles are played out and aggression as the result of pain and frustration.

Mitchell also wrote *Relational Concepts in Psychoanalysis* (1988), *Hope and Dread in Psychoanalysis* (1993), *Freud and Beyond* (1995) with Margaret J. Black, *Autonomy and Influence in Psychoanalysis* (1997), *Relationality: From Attachment to Intersubjectivity* (2000), *Can Love Last?* (2002, posthumously), and edited *Relational Psychoanalysis: The Emergence of a Tradition* (1999) with Lewis Aron.

R. C.

MITWELT A mode of being-in-the-world used by *Heidegger, *Binswanger, and *Boss to refer to the interrelationship of human beings in the world of social relations.

See also: *eigenwelt*; *umwelt*

R. Fri.

MODEL Bion considers model-making part of the equipment available to the psychoanalyst. He felt its use is convenient for several reasons. It has flexibility in contrast with the rigidity of a theory. If the analyst can build appropriate models, he will avoid the temptation to create ad hoc theories. A model helps the analyst to find a correspondence between clinical problems and psychoanalytic theories. It can be easily discarded because it does not have the status of theories. Should it prove useful on different occasions, it can eventually be transformed into a theory. A model is built with elements related to sense experiences and helps to bridge the gap between clinically observed facts and the theories with which the analyst approaches these facts. When an analyst builds a model, he must also be aware of the model used by the patient.

See also: logic

Bion, W. R. (1962) *Learning from Experience*. London: Heinemann.

Bion, W. R. (1963) *Elements of Psychoanalysis*. London: Heinemann.

Bion, W. R. (1992) *Cogitations*. London: Karnac Books.

Skelton, R. (1995) 'Bion's use of modern logic'. *International Journal of Psychoanalysis* 76(2).

L. P. C.

MODEL SCENES Model scenes entail significant communications from the patient about his or her life, and can epitomise a significant traumatic or developmental experience. Lachmann shows how they simultaneously describe a current state of affairs in the analysis, and shape, influence, limit, or enhance the patient's organisation of experience. Model scenes are to be distinguished from *screen memories, which are created by the patient in order to prevent (defend against) the coming into awareness of something regarded as disturbing to know. In contrast, model scenes are created by the analyst and the patient together to depict something previously unknown from a reconception of what is known. The purpose of screen memories is to conceal and obscure; the purpose of model scenes is to give full and complete affective and cognitive representation to obscure repetitive configurations of experience.

Lachmann, F. (2000) *Transforming Aggression: Psychotherapy with the Difficult-to-Treat Patient*. Northvale, NJ: Jason Aronson.

Lachmann, F. M. and Lichtenberg, J. D. (1992) 'Model scenes: implications for psychoanalytic treatment'. *Journal of the American Psychoanalytic Association* 40: 117–37.

H. B.

'MODERN' PSYCHOANALYSIS developed in America as a theory and treatment method for narcissism based on new insights into the role of aggression in personality. It extended Freudian treatment methods to the full range of emotional disorders by exploring the earliest stages of psychic life. At the American Psychiatric Association's annual conference in 1949, Hyman *Spotnitz, a neurologist and psychiatrist, explained the effectiveness of emotional communication in treatment. The analyst was advised to use induced countertransference emotions as the basis for responses to the patient rather than cognitive explanations. In the 1950s, therapists researched the treatment of severe disorders using emotional communications. Colleagues published their findings on the nuclear problems in severe pathologies, how and when the analyst intervenes and how specific emotional responses from the analyst bring about change. Publication of a clinical/research journal, *Modern Psychoanalysis*, began in 1976. In it, modern analysts introduced concepts on narcissism and the use of countertransference, not then in use in the larger psychoanalytic community in America.

Modern drive-based treatment provides a corrective emotional response to patients. Theoreticians asked, 'Can individuals diagnosed with schizophrenia develop a connection to an analyst that will lead to a difference in how they live in the world?' In exploring this question, they learned that later developments in traditional analysis, centred on structural theory and ego development, were a handicap in the analysis of severe pre-verbal pathologies. Moderns found it more useful to respond at the pre-ego level of sensory and somatic experience. Patients responded to non-verbal and verbal communications and were more sensitive to the emotion accompanying the analyst's language. Over-stimulation and under-stimulation during sessions were seen to lead to rigidification of defences.

Techniques for strengthening the protective barrier were necessary to free pathways in the nervous system for new responses. One technique was the use of the patient's contact function to respond 'in kind', thus replacing subjectively determined timing as used in traditional insight-oriented interpretation with what might be called 'demand feeding'.

Following the contact function guards the analyst against overstimulating communications during the narcissistic transference phase and until the patient is ready for teamwork in the treatment.

The modern talking cure emphasises experiences lived and spoken in the analytic room: the here and now of transference, de-emphasising reconstruction of the past. Reports of the world and events and thoughts about them are treated as shadows of the internal world, metaphors for the internal imagery.

Treatment is designed to reach the primary unconscious by utilising an emotional transference which includes pre-language levels. This allows the patient to take back those parts of the self formerly projected.

Meadow, P. W. (1983) 'The Preoedipal Transference'. *Modern Psychoanalysis* 18(2).

Sherman, M. (1999) 'The Trout Reflex'. *Modern Psychoanalysis* 20.

Spotnitz, H. (1969) *Modern Psychoanalysis of the Schizophrenic Patient*. New York: Grune & Stratton.

Spotnitz, H. (1976) *The Preoedipal Conditions*. New York: Jason Aronson.

Spotnitz, H. (1995) 'On emotional communication'. *Modern Psychoanalysis* 20(1).

Spotnitz, H. and Meadow, P. W. (1976) *Treatment of the Narcissistic Neuroses*. New York: Center for Modern Psychoanalytic Studies.

P. Mea.

MODES OF EXPERIENCE (PROTOTAXIC, PARATAXIC, SYNTAXIC) *Sullivan's unique developmental perspective on the child's organisation of experience as shaped by interaction with the environment. Unlike drive/instinct theory, the content of our minds, for Sullivan, originates from the experience of our 'interactions' with the environment in efforts to satisfy (to relax the tensions of) biological and physical needs. Sullivan depicted three developmental modes: the 'prototaxic', the 'parataxic', and the 'syntaxic' which identify the increasing differentiation, elaboration, and organisation of experience. The prototaxic mode includes the infant's immediate, sensory experience of the environment characterised by discrete (e.g. tactile), momentary, unconnected states. It is pre-symbolic, lacking in representation and undifferentiated as to self and other. The infant begins to develop vague prehensions – early perceptions – while transitioning to the parataxic mode that marks the development of cues, signals, signs and symbols. This phase is pre-logical, and is characterised by representation but not causality. This occurs in superstitious thinking in which unrelated events are illogically linked or in myths and dreams that strive to find solutions to life's problems. Parataxic mechanisms are also seen as defensive processes (security operations) such as *selective inattention which strive to reduce anxiety. Emerging toward the end of childhood the 'syntaxic' phase occurs under the sway of socialisation by the establishment of consensually validated language and reasoning.

See also: interpersonal psychoanalysis

Mullahy, P. (1948) *Oedipus, Myth, and Complex: A Review of Psychoanalytic Theory*. New York: Hermitage Press.

Sullivan, H. S. (1953) *The Interpersonal Theory of Psychiatry*. New York: Norton.

I. M.

MOMENT Lacan's approach to time emphasised a logical rather than a chronological structure, considering the unconscious as only *chrono*logically timeless. The reference to moments refers to stable structural points within that logical framework. Changes from moment to moment are 'momentous', abrupt transformations from one discrete point to the next.

See also: time

H. T.

MORAL DEFENCE see **DEFENCE, MORAL**

MOTHER (FREUD) Typically our first relationship is with our mother. Initially it is an *anaclitic relationship, but more is involved than just feeding. It is loving care, tenderness, warmth, physical proximity, availability and watchfulness in the mother who is reading and responding to the cues from her reciprocally involved infant. This dyadic interaction activates both libidinal desires and an attachment system.

See also: father; separation

D. K. S.

MOTHER (KLEIN) In Klein's first exploration of the *Oedipus complex she discovered its early origins. She thought that the infant's relationship to mother began at birth and was determined by the protective influence of the *paranoid-schizoid position, the characteristic strategy of which is to manage the *death instinct. Thus, the unconscious infantile phantasies carry both loving and destructive impulses. For Klein, the early Oedipus complex is an active experience for both male and female children. The girl's phantasies about the need for mother's nurture and care give rise to a maternal *super-ego. The girl, in stressful situations, may be dominated by negative feelings towards mother's body and presence. Phantasies of possession, plundering the fruits of mother's womb, robbery of the internal babies, and attacks on the internal penis, give rise to persecutory phantasies organised as an early persecutory super-ego. Whereas in Freud's Oedipus complex the female child had been seen as deficient, for Klein she is felt to experience a definitive Oedipus complex, which, due to her similarity to mother's situation, intensifies persecutory anxiety.

Klein, M. [(1957)] (1975) *Envy and Gratitude*. London: Hogarth Press. Also in *Love, Guilt and Reparation*. London: Hogarth Press, 1975.

J. V. B.

MOTHER, GOOD-ENOUGH (WINNICOTT) In Winnicott's terms, a mother who provides a degree of care which, although not always immaculately attuned to the needs of her baby, is adequate to protect the baby from *impingement, and thus lays the foundations for subsequent healthy development.

In Winnicott's view, the infant initially individuates from a unit made up of mother-and-baby, and is enabled to do so by means of the sensitivity of an environment, at that time mother in a state of *primary maternal preoccupation. The good-enough mother can respond to the infantile needs of absolute dependency in such a way, and with appropriate timing, so that the infant's continuity of being is not disturbed, impingement does not occur, and the infant is protected from unthinkable anxiety. The processes of *integration as a unit are personalisation, or the sense of whom one is including in the awareness of bodily being; and realisation – the relationship with external reality can occur during this period of absolute *dependence, as can the illusion of infantile omnipotence. With the protection offered by sensitive care, the infant's illusion of omnipotence continues and maturation can occur. Winnicott thought that without the protection offered by the good-enough mother's near perfect care the experience of unthinkable anxiety at this early stage could predispose towards later *psychosis and psychosomatic illness.

As the mother emerges from her primary maternal preoccupation and gradually loses her exquisite adaptation to her baby's needs, the infant becomes increasingly able to fill the deficiencies by means of fantasy. A mother who is misattuned to her baby may respond to him on the basis of her own internal world, disturbing the possibility of a spontaneous relinquishment of omnipotent fantasy. There is then a danger of the infant's response being a compliant one, which lays the foundations for the development of a *false self, in which the infant fails to develop his true potential.

Winnicott's work as a paediatrician allowed him an enormous observational field of mothers and babies. He came increasingly to see that the foundations of psychological development lay in the early relationship between mother and baby, and concentrated on the actual effects of the environment on these earliest stages. Other contributors emphasising the environment include Fairbairn, who also studied the path from dependence towards independence, and who believed that ego-integration was dependent on environmental factors, and that failure affected the splitting of the ego. Kohut's theory has parallels in the area of infantile omnipotence, which he felt was an essential developmental stage.

Fairbairn, R. (1952) *Psychoanalytic Studies of the Personality*. London: Tavistock with Routledge & Kegan Paul.

Winnicott, D. [1945] (1958) 'Primitive emotional development' in *Collected Papers, Through Paediatrics to Psychoanalysis*. London: Tavistock, 145–56.

Winnicott, D. [1949] (1958) 'Mind and its relation to the psyche-soma' in *Collected Papers, Through Paediatrics to Psycho-Analysis*. London: Tavistock, 243–54.

Winnicott, D. [1956] (1958) 'Primary maternal preoccupation' in *Collected Papers, Through Paediatrics to Psycho-Analysis*. London: Tavistock, 300–5.

Winnicott, D. [1960] (1965) 'Ego distortion in terms of true and false self' in *The Maturational Processes and the Facilitating Environment*. London: Hogarth Press and the Institute of Psycho-Analysis, 140–52.

Winnicott, D. [1962] (1965) 'Ego integration in child development' in *The Maturational Processes and the Facilitating Environment*. London: Hogarth Press.

J. Joh.

MOTHER (LACAN) In Lacan's early work, the mother functions as a powerful imago containing the formula for the subject's nostalgic yearnings for harmony, fusion and dependency. By suckling and embracing her child, the mother satisfies the most primitive of desires. She is the primordial Symbolic Other insofar as the child symbolises her presence/absence and her objects. In later writings, it is the Mother's desire that is foregrounded since it mobilises the child's demand to be the object cause of her desire.

C. Owe.

MOTHER'S BODY (INSIDE) Klein believed that a crucial part of the infant's post-natal relationship to mother was its psychic relationship to the inside of her body. The infant finding him or her self thrust into post-natal existence attempts to restore the security and dependability of the umbilical connection through a profound emotional relationship with the breast.

Klein argues that annihilation anxiety, an outcome of the *death drive, intensifies experiences of frustration. She adds that defences against the fear of dying focus around projective identification into mother's insides. In the early days and months of neonatal life phantasies of re-entry into the mother's body, through various points of access, are at their height, these phantasies including those of possession of the interior space and aggressive impulses towards rivals therein: other babies and the father's penis.

Klein, M. [1957] (1975) *Envy and Gratitude*. London: Hogarth Press. Also in *Love, Guilt and Reparation*. London: Hogarth Press, 1975.

J. V. B.

MOTIVATIONAL SYSTEMS Lichtenberg describes five motivational systems: the need for assertion and exploration; the need to regulate physiological arousal and regulation, such as sleep, nutrients, elimination, and tactile stimulation connected with position and movement of the body; the need for *attachment and affiliation; the need for sexual excitement and sensual pleasure and the need to react aversively by antagonism and withdrawal.

Lichtenberg, J. (1989) *Psychoanalysis and Motivation*. Hillsdale, NJ: The Analytic Press.

H. B.

MOURNING The reaction to the loss of a loved one, country, status, ideal, or abstraction. When in mourning, the person withdraws from social activity, experiences sad affect, decreased motivation, lethargy, and disturbances in sleep and/or appetite. Freud distinguished mourning from *melancholia (depression) by showing that depression, although similar in many ways to mourning, additionally manifests a lack in self-regard.

See also: depression

Freud, S. [1915] (1917) *Mourning and Melancholia*. S. E. 14. London: Hogarth Press.

D. K.

MYSTIC An exceptional individual – according to Bion, who contains the messianic idea. The mystic is at-one with O and is both creative and destructive. There is a reciprocal relationship between the mystic and the group to which s/he belongs. The group generally resists the mystic even though it needs him/her to bring about growth, because growth is generally preceded by catastrophic change. The mystic needs the group to contain him/her, even though s/he may feel constrained by it. Bion describes three types of relations that can exist between the mystic and the group: commensal (each exists without affecting the other), symbiotic (mutually beneficial), and parasitic (destructive to both parties).

See also: link

Bion, W. R. (1965) *Transformations*. London: Karnac Books. Also in *Seven Servants*. New York: Jason Aronson, 1977.

Bion, W. R. (1970) *Attention and Interpretation*. London: Tavistock. Also in *Seven Servants*. New York: Jason Aronson, 1977.

S. A.

MYSTICISM AND PSYCHOANALYSIS Psychoanalysis is officially non-mystical or anti-mystical. It sticks pins in mystical bubbles. It understands mystical states as remnants of infantile experience, expressions of primitive drives and structures. Yet – as with so much in life – there are complexities and counter-tendencies. There seem to be mystical aspects to psychoanalysis and there seem to be mystical psychoanalysts, or analysts tinged with spiritual interests. Freud would have viewed this as regressive. He saw religion as a last great hurdle in freeing man's mind for scientific inquiry. Men resort to religion to assuage a sense of helplessness, a heritage of infantile dependency. One wishes for a good outcome of what is a very fragile and rocky existence and beatific promises soothe our fears. On the one hand, mystical states may be related to what Freud (1930) terms 'primary ego-feeling', a sense of all-embracing, limitless I-feeling, including an 'intimate bond between the ego and the world around it'. Here there is an expanded boundary, a sense of infinite inclusion, an 'oceanic feeling'.

On the other hand, Freud, in 1941, notes, 'Mysticism is the obscure self-perception of the realm outside the ego, of the id.' Here the ego is more contracted, separate, 'shrunken', taken aback by what is outside it.

Federn, working with psychosis, picked up on boundary issues in Freud's thought. He was fascinated with the observation that the I contracts and expands, including more or less of the world, body, and mind, in its movements and identifications. The I and not-I keep shifting. Even the I and me-feeling can drop away as consciousness ticks on. Federn portrays the psychotic as one who has difficulty in accepting spatial limitations, especially the fact of having to be where his body is. He portrays a primary boundless consciousness that has to squeeze into a time-space body and world – and not everyone welcomes this challenge or is good at doing it. The psychotic, as Federn portrays him, is not someone who has been embodied and opts out (as Freud seems to suggest) but rather a pre-embodied consciousness opting not to start. Apparently the issue in Freud and Federn is the reaction to pain and attitude toward limitations. Freud depicts a state of shrinking cathexis, withdrawing first from object, then body, then mind, in a series of contractions. Federn depicts a state in which consciousness refuses or is unable to extend itself to body boundaries and social and physical limitations.

It seems for Federn the ego is first and foremost a mental ego and Freud's oral-anal-phallic-genital phases are ways by which the mind gets into the body. It would appear Federn arrived at this position by studying Husserl, for whom the transcendental ego or attitude has a certain privilege. His work with psychosis, and study of Husserl, came together with his incorporation of Freud.

Henry Elkins wonders what world the infant must live in, if the sense of self-and-other emerges prior to awareness of the body. It appears the infant smiles in response to a face and is sensitive to mood before it even knows it has a body. He argues that body-image development can be read in terms of growing eye-hand-mouth coordination, but that self-other awareness, expressed in the smiling response, comes earlier. What must the world of self and other be like, prior to awareness of materiality? Elkin depicts a drama between a sense of self and other which follows contours of mood or spirit. Self may arise in relation to a void or background Other, the latter supporting Self without Self's awareness of being supported. Examples might be the infant Jesus blessing the world on Mary's lap or the cross-legged Buddha facing the Void.

Milner describes a broader, more open focus than the narrower task-oriented, causal, means-end, instrumental, practical orientation – a wide, unfocused sort of attention. She moves between 'sudden moments of intensified perception of the outer world' and 'inarticulate images of the depth mind'. In expressing shifts of awareness that are important to her, she spontaneously blends psychoanalytic and spiritual imagery, traversing body-world-imagination-perception-attention-thinking. For Milner, our body is a very imaginative body indeed.

Matte-Blanco uses logic to distinguish two modes of thinking, one moving towards division, and the other undivided. He attributes asymmetrical thinking to consciousness and symmetrical thinking to the unconscious. The deeper we go into unconscious being, the fewer distinctions there are. We rely on consciousness to create a sense of space-time and awareness that 'I am not you and you are not me'. To unconscious symmetrical thinking, all women may be mother, but in space-time reality, individual women must not be reduced to this. If the deep unconscious is timeless and spaceless, it cannot, by definition, be experienced, since consciousness by definition employs asymmetrical logic that aggressively divides. Yet we incessantly voice intuitions of unity, imprisoning the ungraspable indivisible in some structures we know but are not able to express fully.

Bion's use of mysticism emphasises shattering. He depicts the birth of the psychic universe as a big bang, an explosion into consciousness. It is as if consciousness represents an increment of experiential intensity too much for the organism. Organism explodes into another level, partly too much for it. The theme of excess, a psyche too much for itself or for body, runs through Bion, as does, correlatively, the theme of insufficiency. If we are too much for ourselves, we are, also, not enough.

If Federn is preoccupied with shifting boundaries, Bion seems preoccupied with shifting intensity. We are either more alive or more dead at any time – not only bigger or smaller. And more: Bion conceives of a moment in which we are maximally alive and maximally dead at the same time, a state of maximum/minimum emotion. How do we support such a state if it is real, or is it just a hypothesis, or a hypothesis of something unseen that someday we may notice?

A particular scenario Bion repeats is the difficulty encountered when a mind that has grown up to deal with survival becomes interested in truth for its own sake, e.g. issues of psychic integrity. Is it better to die in or for truth or integrity or live a lie? The death of Socrates is an epiphany.

In Bion's work truth is both nourishing and explosive. The mind cannot grow without it. Yet it can blow one's life away. Truth nourishes. Truth shatters, even kills. We are hungry for truth and truth is dangerous and must be handled with care. The latter is one reason why we have learned to test truth in many ways. We learn to take it in a bit at a time, turn it this way and that, see what it looks like from many angles, develop variable approaches, methods, a sense of context, common sense.

See also: Matte Blanco

Bion, W. R. (1970) *Attention and Interpretation*. London: Tavistock.

Eigen, M. (1998) *The Psychoanalytic Mystic*. London and New York: Free Association Books.

M. Eig.

MYTH (FREUD) Apart from Freud's Oedipal father Freud insisted upon the idea of the primal father, *Urvater*, having been killed and devoured by his sons in the primal tribe, *Urhorde*. The myth of the primal tribe as constitutive of the human civilisation (as opposed to the state of nature) is conceived by Freud either as a real event of the prehistoric age, or as an autonomous phantasy, constitutive of the formation of the human psychic reality (animals have no fathers). Freud refused to decide for either of the two possibilities.

E. B.

MYTH (JUNG) Jung's interest in mythology derives from the fact that it helped him to understand and cure patients, especially those undergoing psychotic episodes, when the ego is overpowered by the collective unconscious. As Jung discovered, these strange contents partake of the same qualities of mythological images of all cultures and times. Also with normal people, whenever Jung found a symbol or a motif in a dream which he could not understand, besides associations produced (or not) by the dreamer, he would search for parallels in mythology. This method is called *amplification, meaning that the image or symbol is not reduced back to some personal aspect. As myths about recurring human conflicts and inner events are everywhere, Jung was able to throw light on his patient's conflicts. When Freud elected the *Oedipus myth as the cornerstone of his theory which his disciples should follow, Jung saw something else that excited him much more: the idea that all the ancient myths are still active in our psyche, finding no reason at all to stay with just one. Different psychological situations would be portrayed by the unconscious drawing from an enormous wealth of possibilities. So knowledge of mythology became a fundamental tool for Jungian analysis. Over the years, Jung came to understand that myths express in their peculiar language the gradual evolution of the soul and the challenges it had to face on the long road towards being recognised by consciousness.

Frey-Rohn, L. (1974) *From Freud to Jung*. New York: G. P. Putnam's Sons.

Jung, C. G. (1965) *Memories, Dreams, Reflections*. New York: Vintage Books.

Jung, C. G. (1991) *Analytical Psychology*. Notes of the seminar given in 1928. Princeton: Princeton University Press.

R. G.

MYTH (BION) Bion proposed using myths to form a picture gallery of verbal elements that can serve as models for different aspects related to emotional experiences that belong to the point of intersection between clinical experience and psychoanalytic theory. This implies using them as *preconception open to unknown facts or to those facts that could not have happened yet, and which the myth acting as a receptive net could help display and illuminate. He wrote in *Elements of Psychoanalysis*, 'The Oedipus myth may be regarded as an instrument that served Freud in his discovery of psychoanalysis and psychoanalysis as an instrument that enabled Freud to discover the Oedipus complex'. To the wellknown Oedipus myth Bion added: the Garden of Eden, the Tower of Babel, the Death of Palinurus, and the burial at the cemetery pit in Ur. He suggested that we free myths from their narrative structure, which is only one form of relating the elements of a constant conjunction and that we use each element in a form analogous to an algebraic unknown. Taking for example the Sphinx, Tiresias and Oedipus, separated from the narrative, he could investigate aspects of −K link, the proscription against truth. This can be found on Bion's *grid, in row C.

Bion, W. R. (1962) *Learning from Experience.* London: Heinemann.
Bion, W. R. (1963) *Elements of Psychoanalysis.* London: Heinemann.
Bion, W. R. (1992) *Cogitations.* London: Karnac Books.

L. P. C.

MYTH (LACAN) A reconsideration by Lacan of the relevance of myth was made possible by his developments of the *Real, *Symbolic and *Imaginary. This effected a return to some of Freud's formulations, in particular, his work on the role of the neurotic's individual myth and a revival of interest in *Totem and Taboo*, the myth of the origin of human social organisation based on the instituting of a law regulating access to *jouissance. All myths deal with birth, death, and sexuality: each of these presents the human subject with a Real to be processed by a knotting of the Real with the Symbolic and the Imaginary.

See also: myth, neurotic's individual

H. T.

MYTH, NEUROTIC'S INDIVIDUAL Lacan derived this idea from Freud's notion of 'the family romances of the neurotics', and related it to Lévi-Strauss's analysis of myths. In interpreting Freud's most famous case study of obsessional neurosis, the *Rat Man Case, Lacan first isolated 'the elementary mytheme' (a specific combination of the father's 'impossible' choice between two women, and of the father's unpaid debt), and then analysed its transformations in the Rat-Man's life, in the actual outbreak of his neurosis, as well as, finally, within the psychoanalytic situation, in the transference on to Freud.

H. T.

N

NAME-OF-THE-FATHER The name-of-the-father, *le nom du père*, is defined as the agency of the law that prohibits incest, enabling the immersion of the infant into the realm of language. Freud's Oedipal, 'normative' paternal figure was redefined by Lacan in the first place as 'the name-of-the-father', with the emphasis on the Symbolic aspect, i.e. on its effect of linguistic determination (the name, the word, the signifier, the letter). Lacan also stressed the notion of 'the paternal metaphor', to be conceived as a function which opposes 'maternal metonymy', which is not being submitted to the operation of displacement, and which also functions as the support of desire. While Freud rarely wrote about 'the *subject', Lacan introduced a conceptual distinction between 'the *ego' as an Imaginary entity formed in 'the *mirror stage', through the Imaginary identification with the child's mirror image, and 'the subject' as an autonomous, distinctive agency, based on the Symbolic identification with the father. Whereas the Imaginary has been conceptualised in the scope of the relationship between the child and the mother, the Symbolic is defined as 'the third dimension', with 'the Symbolic father' as 'the third term', the 'he' who intervenes into this Imaginary, dyadic, narcissistic relationship of the 'I' and the you', and brings the child under 'the law of the father'. The name-of-the-father must be clearly distinguished from the child's actual father of everyday reality.

See also: father

E. B.

NAMING Lacan retained from Freud the central mediating role of the Father (Oedipal/Primal) in the structuring of the psyche. He added the notion that the father is a name or a 'no', which allows the subject to negotiate the mother's desire. In consequence this creates the possibility for the child of receiving a name which will secure its identity. The name of the Father thus serves the primal possibility of naming. In Seminar IX, he shows that this name, contingent to the individual is also primal/necessary; it moves untranslated between actual languages. In his later work Lacan indicates how self-naming becomes possible for the psychotic. This demonstrates how important the inaugural act of naming is for the subject.

G. S.

NAMELESS DREAD A feeling of anxiety or fear stripped of such meaning as it has. The first example Bion gives of such a situation is that of a baby who, feeling that it is dying, *projects this fear into the mother's mind; if the mother cannot accept the projection the infant feels that its feeling is stripped of meaning – including the wish to live – and therefore reintrojects a nameless dread. Later on, discussing the $-K$ situation, he also includes as a factor the baby's *envy and greed of the undisturbed breast and therefore the feeling that the breast removes the good and valuable element in the fear of dying, forcing the worthless residue back into the infant. The infant now contains a nameless dread. The explosive psychotic fear and the sub-thalamic fears could also be dreads without a name or meaning.

Bion, W. R. (1962) 'A theory of thinking' in *Second Thoughts*. London: Heinemann.
Bion, W. R. (1962) *Learning from Experience*. London: Heinemann.
Bion, W. R. (1970) *Attention and Interpretation*. London: Tavistock.
Bion, W. R. (1987) 'Evidence' in *Clinical Seminars and Four Papers*. Abingdon: Fleetwood Press.

E. T. B.

NARCISSISM The term comes from the Greek myth of Narcissus, implying self-love or self-admiration. Late in the nineteenth century, Havelock Ellis used it to refer to a sexual perversion of having erotic feelings toward one's own body. Freud's early conceptualisation was similarly centred on the body. But to Freud narcissism was a part of the self-preservation drive rather than a perversion. As Freud's views (1914) shifted toward a more psychical conceptualisation of narcissism, the *ego rather than the body became the object of narcissistic preoccupation. The more libido is invested in the ego, the less is invested in object and vice-versa. The highest investment of libido in the object is realised when one is in love. In narcissism, much of the libido is withdrawn from the external world and directed toward the ego. Freud introduces a distinction between primary and secondary narcissism. Primary narcissism refers to an 'objectless' psychological state dominated entirely by the internal world with no differentiation between id and ego or self and other. This is thought to be the *initial* internal world of the infant. As the newborn begins to relate to the external world and become aware of the existence of the mother, she enters into the state of secondary narcissism. This line of thinking is more prominent among contemporary psychoanalysts. However, the theoretical emphasis is placed on the personality organisation by

*Kohut or on the self, as the experiencing part of the person. Narcissism is considered adaptive and part of the normal developmental process. Interference with the phase-appropriate narcissism may however lead to pathology. Pathological narcissism revolves around the restoration of self-esteem and defensive attempts at healing the psychic wounds caused by a sense of shame or humiliation. The narcissist's self-absorption is nothing but a strategic method of coping with psychic injuries to the self. Withdrawal from others is viewed as a defensive strategy for protecting the self against further shame and humiliation. Thus what was once considered as self-love is now being perceived as self-hate. Self-love and object-love are no longer considered to be mutually exclusive. Object-love requires self-love as a prerequisite.

For Lacan, narcissism is a structuring of libidinal investment that is both necessary and constitutive for the construction of *subjectivity. Freud distinguishes between two forms of narcissism: primary and secondary. Primary narcissism is defined as the primordial investment of libido into the ego; secondary narcissism refers to the return to the ego of object libidinal investment. For Lacan it represents a logic of the structuring of the subject, namely a libidinal mechanism which takes the ego as object. Essentially the constitution of the ego through the identification with the specular image in the *mirror stage is Lacan's reworking of Freud's concept.

See also: autoerotic; dual relation; imaginary; self-psychology

Freud, S. (1914) *On Narcissism: An Introduction*. S. E. 14. London: Hogarth Press.
Kernberg, O. (1975) *Borderline Conditions and Pathological Narcissism*. New York: Jason Aronson.
Kohut, H. (1971) *The Analysis of the Self*. New York: International Universities Press.

S. Mov. / A. I.

NARCISSISTIC NEUROSES Freud made a distinction between *transference neurosis* and *narcissistic neurosis*. Freud did not feel that the usual psychoanalytic method was effective in the treatment of narcissistic neuroses. Analysis of *transference and *resistance is the core of the psychoanalytic method. The nature of transference in narcissistic neuroses is quite different than that which develops in transference neuroses. The ordinary technique of interpretation does not influence this type of patient to relinquish their resistance. Their resistance, as Freud put it, is 'unconquerable'. Treating cases of narcissistic neuroses like transference neuroses, the analyst quickly comes to 'a wall that brings him/her to stop'.

Freud, S. (1916) *Introductory Lectures on Psychoanalysis*. S. E. 16. London: Hogarth Press.

S. Mov.

NARCISSISTIC OBJECT-CHOICE Narcissistic object-choice occurs when one chooses a love object on the basis of a similarity to oneself rather than on the model of a prior attachment relationship to *either* parent, termed by Freud an *anaclitic object-choice. Freud uses this concept to explain phenomena ranging from parental love for children to homosexual object-choice.

See also: ego /ideal ego ideal narcissism;

A. R.

NARCISSISTIC RAGE Self psychology distinguishes between the anger felt by an intact self when blocked from its goals, and the narcissistic rage of a weakened self toward selfobjects experienced as depriving, threatening, damaging, shaming or humiliating. Chronic narcissistic rage refers to the persistence of the fury, either as a painful memory or in a latent state, even long after the event or person who inspired it has gone. It may lie within the self as a paranoid organisation, and may flare up long after the traumatising experience, either toward the perceived perpetrator of the injury or as a *displacement. Kohut also described an acute narcissistic rage, which arises in response to a sudden injury to the sense of self, and which may be a restorative self-organiser. In these instances, the particular stress is likely neither consonant with the individual's specific self-vulnerabilities nor does it significantly repeat the experience of early trauma.

Kohut, H. (1972) 'Thoughts on narcissism and narcissistic rage'. *The Psychoanalytic Study of the Child* 27: 360–400.

H. B.

NAZIS AND PSYCHOANALYSIS In 1933 psychoanalysis in Germany faced extinction by the Nazi regime. The Nazis condemned psychoanalysis as a 'Jewish science' and books by *Freud were burned by Nazi mobs. In 1935 Jewish members of the Berlin Psychoanalytic Institute and the German Psychoanalytic Society were forced to resign. This move was approved by Freud and *Jones, president of the *International Psychoanalytic Association, as a means of preserving the practice of psychoanalysis in Germany. *Jung, president of the International General Medical Society for Psychotherapy from 1933 to 1940, exercised through word and deed controversial and ambiguous influence on psychoanalysis in Germany and Europe during this period.

In 1936 the psychoanalytic institute and society became part of the German Institute for Psychological Research and Psychotherapy under psychotherapist Matthias Heinrich Göring, a cousin of Nazi leader Hermann Göring. The new institute, housed first in the old psychoanalytic institute, represented an attempt by various schools of psychotherapy in Germany to protect and advance the discipline within the new order. Nazi bureaucrats saw the institute and the allied German General Medical Society for Psychotherapy as a means of eliminating an independent psychoanalytic presence in Germany and of mobilising the expertise of psychotherapists in service to the regime. 'Göring Institute' psychoanalysts Carl Müller-Braunschweig, Felix Boehm, Werner Kemper, and 'neo-analyst' *Schultz-Hencke argued protectively and ambitiously for the practical utility of psychoanalysis in strengthening human performance, a view somewhat in line with neo-Freudian concepts of social adjustment and productivity. In 1938, however, the German Psychoanalytic Society was abolished, becoming 'Work Group A' of Göring's institute, while the Nazi annexation of Austria that same year destroyed the Vienna Psychoanalytic Institute and Press.

The history of psychoanalysis between 1933 and 1945 was largely repressed in Germany for almost forty years after the war, even though – or especially because – there were distinct continuities of psychoanalytic personnel and practice after 1945 in both post-war German states. In West Germany, a split psychoanalytic movement had two versions of the history. The German Psychoanalytic Society (e.g. Dührssen) took the position that psychoanalysis had been 'saved' by a few during the Nazi regime, while the German Psychoanalytic Union argued that it had been 'destroyed'. Younger generations of West German psychoanalysts, spurred by the historical work of Cocks, have since documented the more complicated and problematic history of the field under Nazism.

Brecht, K., Friedrich, V., Hermanns, L., Kaminer, I. and Juelich, D. (eds) (1985) *'Hier geht das Leben auf eine sehr merkwürdige Weise weiter . . .'*. Hamburg: Verlag Michael Kellner.

Cocks, G. (1985) *Psychotherapy in the Third Reich*. New York and Oxford: Oxford University Press. Rev. edn New Brunswick and London: Transaction Publishers, 1997.

Dührssen, A. (1994) *Ein Jahrhundert Psychoanalytische Bewegung in Deutschland*. Göttingen: Vandenhoeck & Ruprecht.

Goggin, J. and Goggin, E. (2000) *Death of a 'Jewish Science'*. Lafayette: Purdue University Press.

Lockot, R. (1985) *Erinnern und Durcharbeiten*. Frankfurt: Fischer Verlag.
Lockot, R. (1994) *Die Reinigung der Psychoanalyse*. Tübingen: edition diskord.

G. C.

NEED Lacan argues that, as a driving force, need is to be distinguished from demand and desire, even though the latter also derive their pressure from a lack. The source of need is a physiological lack at the level of the organism. It has an identifiable object (such as food or drink) which temporarily fulfils need in order to keep the organism alive.

See also: demand; deprivation; desire; frustration

R. Loo.

NEED FOR PUNISHMENT An internal force borne of conflict between *ego and *super-ego, one byproduct of which is *guilt, which impels an individual to seek humiliating or painful situations, the attainment of which paradoxically produces enjoyment or pleasure.

See also: masochism

Freud, S. (1924) *The Economic Problem of Masochism*. S. E. 19. London: Hogarth Press.

A. S.

NEGATION Negation may be the first approach to the contents of the unconscious. When in the course of association, the patient declares that something is not true, it may be an acknowledgement that such an idea exists. In ordinary conversation remarks like, 'I don't want to hurt your feelings', may reveal an unconscious wish. According to Freud, there are not any no's in the unconscious.

Lacan considers Freud's term as the main neurotic way of dealing with the return of repressed material from the unconscious. He distinguishes between negation as the mechanism of the neurotic, *disavowal as the mechanism of the pervert and *foreclosure as the mechanism of the psychotic. Thus the way one deals with psychical content that is threatening and anxiety-provoking is of diagnostic importance.

See also: denial

A. Ber / R. Gol.

NEGATIVE CAPABILITY AND THE LANGUAGE OF ACHIEVEMENT The last chapter of *Attention and Interpretation* is called 'Prelude To or Substitute For Achievement', and begins with a quotation from Keats by which Bion introduces the idea of negative capability as the ability of a person who is 'capable of being in uncertainties, mysteries, doubts, without any irritable reaching after facts and reasons'. Bion thought this negative capability was akin to the discipline of eschewing *memory, desire and understanding that analysts need for being in at-one-ment. This capability is linked to the concept of a language of achievement. This language has an unsaturated quality that promotes transformations in evolution towards achievement. It is the language of artistic or scientific creations and it has the capacity of traversing *caesuras of time and space. It can be expressed by a thought or by an action, and in both cases it is a prelude to a change that means evolution. It has a quality of endurance that goes beyond the time or the culture in which it emerges. Bion contrasts language of achievement with language of substitution, which is used as a substitute for action and not as a prelude to it. The latter arises from inhibition, due to a combination of envy and greed toward growth-stimulating objects.

Bion, W. R. (1970) *Attention and Interpretation*. London: Heinemann.
Keats, J. (1952) *Letters*. London: Oxford University Press.

L. P. C.

NEGATIVE HALLUCINATION Freud's interest in Bernheim's work in the 1880s focused particularly on the phenomenon of negative hallucination. A negative hallucination is the opposite of a positive hallucination. A person subject to a positive hallucination perceives things that are not there; a person subject to a negative hallucination fails to perceive things that are there. Throughout his life, Freud maintained positive hallucination to be an index of psychosis, and negative hallucination to be a characteristic of neurotic and normal states of consciousness. Someone subject to a neurosis regularly fails to perceive aspects of their love relations with others.

A person can have suggested to them in a hypnotic trance that they will, subsequently to the trance state being lifted, fail to perceive certain aspects of the world around them. Testing of such people in a post-hypnotic state shows that these objects and relations really are absent from the field of their conscious perceptions. However, other tests show that a person avoids objects that they cannot perceive in this state. The vivid and forceful nature of these results led Freud to the conclusion that a person in this state has perceptions that cannot become conscious, and knowledge that cannot become conscious. Freud's further proposal that repression brings about a situation of negative hallucination allowed him to situate such results quite outside of the field of hypnotism, and to construct the central notion of psychoanalysis – that of the unconscious.

See also: false connection; scotomisation

B. B.

NEGATIVE OEDIPUS COMPLEX The child's desire for the parent of the same sex and murderous jealousy of the parent of the opposite sex. Freely used by Klein, it is for Freud one aspect of Oedipality in general. Its dominance and persistence as later *homosexuality has been interpreted as a regressive defence against *castration anxiety or *penis envy by those psychoanalysts who have wished to take the positive Oedipal path as a norm.

J. B.

NEGATIVE THERAPEUTIC REACTION Freud uses this term to designate the *resistance of the patient to the curing of their symptom. Initially he located the reasons for this negative reaction to treatment in psychic conflict, invoking amongst other things gain from sickness, fixation of the libido, and negative transference. On a deeper level, Freud indicated the existence of a trans-psychological principle in the 'sentiment of unconscious guilt'. In relation to this guilt, one would say that the patient tries to maintain a certain quantity of suffering. This masochistic position Freud connected to the *death drive. What follows from this is a re-examination of the therapeutic aims of psychoanalytic technique for Freud, now forced to take account of a paradox – that the patient really does not want his own well being.

S. Cot.

NETHERLANDS The history of psychoanalysis in the Netherlands can be divided into four distinct phases: the establishment of the Dutch Association for Psychoanalysis and the emergence of internal problems (1917–37), the unification and the Occupation period (1938–45), the blossoming period and the two associations (1946–77), and state interference and the movement towards integration (1978–present). From about 1905 there was a growing interest among psychiatrists in psychoanalysis. Contact was made with Freud and two Dutch psychiatrists became members of the Viennese association in 1911. At the same time others had contact with Jung in Zurich. Academic interest culminated in Jelgersma's Provost's Speech in Leiden in 1914 which was the first official recognition of psychoanalysis in Europe. Thirteen people from this group founded the Dutch Association for Psychoanalysis in 1917. This was the seventh branch of the International Psychoanalytical Association (IPA).

The ensuing years saw disagreements about lay analysis, the tripartite training model and compulsory training analysis. When four experienced Jewish psychoanalysts emigrated to the Netherlands in 1933, conflicts ensued and the president founded a second association. This split was abandoned in 1938. In the same year, Lampl de Groot and her husband returned to the Netherlands from Vienna. They joined the others who were involved in training on Viennese principles. In 1940 the Netherlands was occupied by the Germans. In solidarity with the Jewish members, non-Jewish members also gave up their membership. Training continued underground and in 1945 the Association was reinstated.

Old resentments and differences of opinions led to a new split in 1947. Westerman Holstijn and van der Hoop, active members from the pre-war period, established the Dutch Psychoanalytic Association. Initially many were members of both associations, but relations deteriorated and for a period of about thirty years there was barely any contact between the two groups.

Meanwhile psychoanalysis flourished with the rise of ego-psychology and there was great scientific and clinical activity. The number of members and patients increased and professors in psychiatry and psychology were almost all trained in psychoanalysis. There were IPA conferences in Amsterdam in 1951 and 1965 and Van der Leeuw was president and Montessori secretary of the IPA from 1965 to 1969. In 1966, with the help of the Hampstead Clinic, training in child analysis commenced. In 1946 an Institute for training was established in Amsterdam by the Association and, much later, one in Utrecht. In 1977 a new attempt at unification between the two societies was made, but failed.

At the end of the seventies and beginning of the eighties there was greater interference by the government, partly as a result of public financing of the Institutes and analysis and partly as a result of a reorganisation of the mental health sector. This led to the virtual disappearance of private practices and a request for shorter treatments. The newly appointed professors were focused upon behavioural therapies and sciences and attacked analysis, as did society as a whole. As a result of these problems and difficulties experienced by the new generation in resolving the conflicts of the past, new attempts were made to collaborate. Both Institutes founded a new society for psychoanalytical psychotherapy in 1979 and actions were agreed by three parties, and were more based upon theories comparable to the Independent tradition in England. In 1993 there was another IPA conference in Amsterdam and in 1995 there was an amalgamation between the two Institutes. In 2001 the association became an IPA component society, which paved the way for a further integration which needs to be further formalised in the future.

A. Stu.

Neumann, Erich (1905–60) Born in Berlin in 1905, he trained first in philosophy and then in medicine before going to study analytical psychology with C. G. *Jung. With the rise of Nazism in Germany, he settled in Tel Aviv in 1934 where he remained until his death in 1960. He is best known for his contribution to developmental theory. Neumann claimed that the growth of the child's *ego consciousness paralleled the evolution of human consciousness and used mythology, history of religion and ethology to illustrate his theory in *The Origins and History of Consciousness*. According to Neumann, the early mother-infant bond is characterised by a state of psychic union or *participation mystique* symbolised by the mythological image of the snake swallowing its own tail. Gradually the infant begins to experience the caregiver in her *archetypal form, as Neumann discussed in his masterwork, *The Great Mother*, initially as all-nurturing but eventually as undermining. The child's urge for separation inevitably leads to a conflict, symbolised as the 'dragon fight' in which the ego consciousness, under the influence of the 'hero myth', seeks to free itself from the regressive pull of the negative mother. In his unfinished study, *The Child*, published posthumously, he extended his conception through adolescence. He also provided the key metaphor for how the psyche operates in terms of an *ego-self axis. Neumann was fascinated with creativity, culture and moral sense. He wrote analyses of the sculptures of Henry Moore and Mozart's *Die Zauberflöte* among others. Returning to Europe after the holocaust, he presented his controversial ideas concerning morality and ethics in the work *Depth Psychology and the Search for a New Ethic*. He returned annually for the Eranos Conferences in Ascona, Switzerland. His most lyrical work is an interpretation of the tale of Amor and Psyche, in which he illustrates the stages of feminine development. Erich Neumann died in 1960 at the height of his powers, aged fifty-five.

Neumann, E. (1954) *The Origins and History of Consciousness*. Princeton: Princeton University Press.

Neumann, E. [1963] (1990) *The Child*. Boston: Shambhala.

Neumann, E. (1971) *Amor and Psyche*. Princeton: Princeton University Press.

H. A.

NEURASTHENIA Nervous weakness, fatigue, with various aches and pains; the classical 'civilised' disease. Freud first attributed it to exhaustion caused by excessive masturbation, different from anxiety, which is caused by sexual deprivation. Today we see it as related to depression, it and anxiety being the basic emotions of unpleasure, signals of interpersonal problems.

Z. L.

NEUROPSYCHOANALYSIS A branch of neuropsychology, the science that deals with the relationship between behaviour and the mind on the one hand, and the nervous system, especially the brain, on the other. In light of the definition of psychoanalysis as the scientific study of the unconscious mind, the discipline of neuropsychoanalysis studies the relationship between behaviour and the unconscious mind, and the brain systems that process information at a nonconscious level. The early origins of neuropsychoanalysis are embedded in the early roots of psychoanalysis; indeed they are the roots of psychoanalysis. The sources of both are found in Freud's early career as a researcher during 'the golden age of neurology,' a period of twenty years in which he produced over a hundred neuroscientific works.

It is commonly accepted that *Charcot and *Breuer significantly influenced Freud's major contribution to science – the exploration of the central role of the dynamic unconscious in everyday life. Yet it is not appreciated that both of these authors also contributed to neurology, Charcot in studies of face recognition disorders, and Breuer in work on the brain vagal system. But perhaps the most significant influence on Freud was the great English neurologist John Hughlings Jackson. Jackson conceived the human mind in terms of a hierarchical series of functional levels, with 'higher,' voluntary functions overlaying and 'keeping down' the more involuntary, 'lower' ones. And in contrast to Broca's discovery that left hemisphere lesions often result in linguistic loss, Jackson's studies indicated that the right hemisphere supports emotional speech and mediates preverbal mentation and automatic emotional functions which are subsequently arranged in words in the left hemisphere into a propositional form. Freud subsequently incorporated the latter ideas into his model of *primary process, and Jackson's hierarchical construct appeared in both his topographic model of stratified conscious, preconscious, and unconscious systems, and his structural model of a *super-ego and *ego, which sit astride the *id.

Thus Freud turned to the foundations of modern neurology, the scientific study of the brain, as a primary source for many of his groundbreaking hypotheses about the mind. In 1895 Freud attempted to utilise what was then known about neurobiology to begin to construct a set of regulatory principles for psychological processes and a neuropsychological model of brain function. In *Psychology for Neurologists*, later renamed **Project for a Scientific Psychology*, Freud used an approach grounded in clinical neurology, neuroanatomy, and neuropsychology in order to 'furnish a psychology which shall be a natural science'. This short essay sets forth, for the first time, a number of elemental constructs that would literally serve as the foundation, the bedrock of psychoanalytic theory. In this remarkable document Freud introduces the concepts of primary and *secondary processes; the principles of *pleasure-unpleasure, constancy, and reality testing; the concepts of *cathexis and *identification; the theories of psychical *regression and *hallucination; the systems of *perception, *memory, unconscious and preconscious psychic activity; and the *wish-fulfilment theory of dreams. It also contains the seeds of Freud's developmental theory and a neurophysiological model of *affect generation.

The *Project* was never published in his lifetime, as in his subsequent development of psychoanalytic theory Freud attempted to expunge the neurophysiological and biological roots of his psychological model. Despite this, it is now thought that the ideas generated in this work, many of which were incorporated into the seventh chapter of *The Interpretation of Dreams*, represent the source pool from which he later developed the major concepts of his psychoanalytic model. And yet, according to Sulloway in his *Freud, Biologist of the Mind: Beyond the Psychoanalytic Legend*, Freud 'never abandoned the assumption that psychoanalysis would someday come to terms with the neurophysiological side of mental activity'.

Forty years after Freud's death, in the 1970s, spurred by the split brain research of the time, psychoanalysis again became interested in the data generated by neurology. In a collaborative work, Karl Pribram, a pioneer of modern neuroscience, and the psychoanalyst Merton Gill revisited Freud's *Project*, and concluded that its concrete neurobiological hypotheses were testable. They suggested that the obscure concepts of psychoanalytic metapsychology, especially Freud's germinal hypotheses concerning the regulatory structures and dynamics that underlie the mechanisms of affect, motivation, attention, and consciousness, could be illuminated by modern neurobiology. Although the major theoreticians of this time (*Kernberg, *Kohut, *Mahler, *Bowlby) all included speculations about the nature of inner psychic structure, the time was not yet right for a rapprochement between neurology and psychoanalysis.

In 1984 Reiser continued to call for a convergence of psychoanalysis and neurobiology. But it was during the 1990s, one hundred years after the *Project* and the centennial of the birth of psychoanalysis, that neuropsychoanalysis experienced an intense revitalisation. At the beginning of the decade Levin published a volume offering ideas on the neurobiological underpinnings of dreaming, nonverbal communication, and transference, as well as a hierarchical developmental model, and Miller offered chapters on hysteria, dreams, and Freudian slips. In 1994 Schore published *Affect Regulation and the Origin of the Self*, exploring the neurobiological underpinnings of developmental and clinical psychoanalysis. In parallel, throughout this 'decade of the brain', the investigative tools of neuroscience were greatly expanded – advances in neuro-imaging technologies greatly enhanced the study of brain/mind/body functions. And developmental psychology and emotion research were now producing research that was directly relevant to psychoanalysis.

In a 1997 issue of the *Journal of the American Psychoanalytic Association* Solms applied a neuropsychoanalytic perspective to the problem of consciousness, and Schore proposed that a rapprochement between neurobiology and psychoanalysis was finally at hand. By the end of the decade, the journal *Neuro-Psychoanalysis* appeared, with a dual editorial board of neuroscientists and psychoanalysts. Special issues were devoted to such themes as Freud's theory of affect, the neuropsychology of sleep, the unconscious homunculus, and a cognitive neuroscience perspective of confabulation. Contemporary neuropsychoanalysis is thus currently focusing on the essential problems that were defined at the dawn of psychoanalysis, including affect, motivation, attention, and consciousness.

Furthermore, developmental neuropsychoanalysis, the study of the early structural development of the human unconscious mind, is now inquiring into how object relational experiences, embedded in the affective transactions of the mother-infant *attachment relationship, are registered in the deep unconscious, and how they influence the development of the systems which dynamically process unconscious information for the rest of the life span. Knowledge of these developmental events offers us a chance to more deeply understand not just the contents of the dynamic unconscious, but its origin, structure, and dynamics. Other current themes in this area include the role of the right brain as the neurobiological substratum of Freud's dynamic unconscious; the enduring effects of early relational trauma on the development of the right brain intrapsychic structure and the aetiology of psychopathogenesis, the elaboration of psychoneurobiological models of defensive projective identification and dissociation; the neuropsychoanalysis of intersubjective processes within the therapeutic alliance; and the mechanism of right brain to right brain affective transactions in transference-countertransference communications.

These trends indicate that current knowledge in neuropsychoanalysis must impact not only theoretical but clinical psychoanalysis. Watt now describes the critical importance of recent work on neurodevelopment as 'the great frontier in neuroscience where all of our theories will be subject to the most acid of acid tests. And many of them I suspect will be found wanting'. And in a recent overview volume, Kernberg concludes that 'neurobiology and psychoanalysis are really two basic sciences, that are not in competition with each other, but should complement each other'.

The rapid advances in neuropsychoanalysis suggest that we now know enough about psychic structure that any theory can no longer only address psychological functions. Rather it must be psychoneurobiological, consonant with what neuroscience is now informing us about internal structure as it exists in nature. As in its beginnings, neuropsychoanalysis, which currently serves as a critical two-way interdisciplinary link to the other sciences, can potentially enrich both neurology, the study of the brain, and psychoanalysis, the study of the unconscious mind.

Levin, F. M. (1991) *Mapping the Mind*. Hillsdale, NJ: The Analytic Press.

Miller, L. (1991) *Freud's Brain: Neuropsychodynamic Foundations of Psychoanalysis*. New York: Guilford.

Pribram, K. H. and Gill, M. M. (1976) *Freud's 'Project' Re-assessed*. New York: Basic Books.

Reiser, M. (1984) *Mind, Brain, Body: Toward a Convergence of Psychoanalysis and Neurobiology*. New York: Basic Books.

Schore, A. N. (1997) 'A century after Freud's project: is a rapprochement between psychoanalysis and neurobiology at hand?'. *Journal of the American Psychoanalytic Association* 45.

Schore, A. N. (1999) 'The right brain, the right mind, and psychoanalysis'. *Neuro-Psychoanalysis* web site: www.neuro-psa.com/ schore.htm.

Solms, M. (1997) 'What is consciousness?'. *Journal of the American Psychoanalytic Association* 45.

Watt, D. (2000) 'The dialogue between psychoanalysis and neuroscience: alienation and reparation'. *Neuro-Psychoanalysis* 2.

A. Sch.

NEUROSIS A neurosis is the result of a conflict between an unacceptable infantile wish and an immature ego. Because the ego cannot handle the conflict in a more mature way, the idea is repressed into the unconscious where it continues to exert a force and to press for discharge. The struggle between the impulse and the ego may take place invisibly for a long time, only manifesting itself in the expenditure of energy not available for other activities. However, when a neurosis occurs, the repressed or otherwise isolated idea breaks through in distorted form as a symptom, compulsive act, or inhibition. The central component in the neuroses is the positive *Oedipus complex – the desire for *incest with the parent of the opposite sex, or in the case of the negative Oedipus complex, with the same sex parent. Hostile feelings for the other parent are also involved. In hysteria, the sexual wish is repressed and may return in the form of a somatic conversion (hysterical paralysis) or in some phobia that prevents the forbidden sexual act from occurring. The symptom represents both a defence against, and a gratification of, repressed sexual or hostile wishes. In the obsessional neurosis, the patient regresses to the anal level where the major defences are not repression but the disconnecting of an idea from its feeling, reaction formation, doubt, and the imposition of rites and rituals aimed at preventing hostile acts. What Freud called the 'transference neuroses' were the conditions treatable by psychoanalysis. The neurotic patient was capable of forming a relationship with the analyst (called the transference) which could be utilised in effecting a cure. The neuroses were basically the hysterias (including phobias) and obsessions. Other disorders (paranoia, schizophrenia, mania, melancholia) were sometimes referred to as 'narcissistic neuroses', but were not considered treatable by Freud because they did not form useable transferences to the analyst.

In Lacanian psychoanalysis, neurosis is one of the three fundamental ways in which a subject can relate to the Symbolic structure of language (the Other), alongside psychosis and perversion. As such, neurosis is not diagnosed on the basis of a clearly delineated set of symptoms or a specific pattern of pathological behaviours, but with reference to speech and transference. Neurotic speech is characterised by uncertainty, hesitation and a profound discordance between knowledge and truth. Neurotic subjects continuously feel that their words either say more than they want them to convey or that they do not adequately capture the true nature of a particular experience. They believe, yet without being entirely sure, that their knowledge of themselves fails to unravel the obscure, unknown truth which continues to hamper their existence. At the same time they also believe, yet with an equal degree of uncertainty, that this truth will be revealed by the analyst, which they therefore perceive as a *subject-supposed-to-know. For Lacan, the attribution of the supposed-subject-of-knowing to the analyst is the defining criterion for the neurotic transference and it constitutes in itself a factor the significance of which needs to be resolved at the end of the analytic treatment. This does not imply that Lacan ever argued that psychoanalysis is able to relieve the structure of neurosis altogether. At best, it can only effect a transformation of the painful human dramas into the more ordinary miseries of everyday life.

See also: neurosis, actual

J. A. Ber. / D. N.

NEUROSIS, ACTUAL Undischarged sexual tensions manifest in symptoms of *anxiety, irritability, *excitation and hypersensitivity to external stimuli. Freud thought the aetiology of this nosological condition to be purely physical and contemporary as contrasted with the psychoneuroses whose origins are psychical and derive from the repressed sexual events of childhood. *Fenichel classified the condition as a 'dammed up state' and the direct symptoms of psychical *conflict. Gediman postulated actual neurosis as a state of mounting sexual, aggressive, and other psychic tensions cutting across all conditions and not as a separate diagnostic entity.

See also: neurosis; symptom; trauma

Fenichel, O. (1945) *The Psychoanalytic Theory of Neurosis*. New York: Norton.
Freud, S. (1898) *Sexuality in the Aetiology of the Neuroses* S. E. 3. London: Hogarth Press.
Gediman, H. K. (1984) 'Actual neurosis and psychoneurosis'. *International Journal of Psycho-Analysis* 65:191–202.

H. G.

NEUROSIS, CHOICE OF This term refers to the processes and causes that determine a person's choice of the different kinds of neuroses. Most women, for example, choose the hysterical mode, most men the obsessional mode. These are like different dialects of the same language. 'Choice' in this sense means choice of position regarding the conflict between the sexual drive, the demands of reality and the *super-ego. The choice is mostly unconscious but nevertheless it implies responsibility for one's position in the face of his or her drive satisfaction.

See also: hysteria; obsessional neurosis

R. Gol.

NEUTRALITY The defining characteristic of the analytic attitude meant to ensure the avoidance of any type of suggestion or deliberate influence on the patient. Anna *Freud aptly defined neutrality as the analyst's remaining equidistant from *id, *ego, and *super-ego. Total neutrality is thought to be a worthy goal, but one impossible to fulfil.

See also: abstinence

Laplanche, J. and Pontalis, J.-B. (1973) *The Language of Psychoanalysis*. New York: Norton.

A. E.

NIETZSCHE, FRIEDRICH WILHELM (1844–1900) Nietzsche, building on Schopenhauer, developed basic conceptual foundations for depth psychology and psychoanalysis. He was born on 15 October 1844 in Röcken, a village in Prussian Saxony, and grew up in Naumberg. Insanity overtook Nietzsche in January of 1889, probably due to his contraction of syphilis earlier in his life. After his breakdown, his fame as a philosopher soared and his influence on the intellectual and cultural life within and beyond Europe grew rapidly. He died on 25 August 1900 in Weimar.

Nietzsche was an exceptionally prominent figure in Freud's Vienna of the 1870s, and Freud's university friends were deeply involved with his writings. During late 1883 and early 1884, one of Freud's closest friends met with Nietzsche a number of times and wrote extensively to Freud about these meetings.

Nietzsche explored the notion of repression, writing in the *Genealogy of Morals* that 'forgetting is no mere *vis inertiae*; it is rather an active and in the strictest sense positive faculty of repression' (more accurately, inhibition). Discussing unconscious mental processes, Nietzsche wrote in *Daybreak* of an unconscious 'conflict of motives' and that 'we are accustomed to exclude all these unconscious processes from the accounting'. Regarding the understanding of an action, Nietzsche wrote in *Beyond Good and Evil* that what is ' "conscious", still belongs to its surface and skin – which, like every skin, betrays something but conceals even more the intention is merely a sign and symptom that still requires interpretation'. Nietzsche also explored the vicissitudes (including sublimation) of drives, especially the will to power and aggression. He wrote in the *Genealogy* of aggression turned against the self as the origin of the 'bad conscience' that provided one of the ancient and fundamental substrata of civilisation and culture.

Freud insisted that his development of psychoanalysis was uninfluenced by Schopenhauer and Nietzsche, although he acknowledged their 'intuitive' insights into dynamic unconscious mental processes. In addition to Nietzsche's influence on Freud, he was a major influence on other early analysts, including Rank, *Adler, and *Jung, and later on existentially oriented psychotherapists such as *Jaspers, *Binswanger, Rollo *May and Yalom. Recent advocates of hermeneutic or perspectivist approaches to knowledge in the therapeutic relationship can trace their origins to Nietzsche through Gadamer.

Golomb, J., Santaniello, W., and Lehrer, R. (eds) (1999) *Nietzsche and Depth Psychology*. Albany: State University of New York Press.

Hollingdale, R. J. (1999) *Nietzsche: The Man and His Philosophy*. Revised edition. New York: Cambridge University Press.

Lehrer, R. (1995) *Nietzsche's Presence in Freud's Life and Thought*. Albany: State University of New York Press.

R. Leh

NORMALITY A concept associated with the medical model within which Freud and his followers addressed behavioural phenomena as 'symptoms', thus defining 'normality' as the absence of symptoms; also with the ego psychological model within which a value is placed on successful *adaptation to internal and external reality, including social norms.

Dimen, M. (2001) 'Perversion is us? eight notes'. *Psychoanalytic Dialogues* 11(6): 825–60.

N. A.

NORWAY The first reference in Norway to psychoanalysis was in 1905, in a textbook of psychiatry by Professor Ragnar Vogt who referred to the 'psycho-cathartic method of Freud'. In the twenties, Harald Schjelderup and others who were trained in central Europe practised psychoanalysis in Norway. Psychoanalysis was established as a clinical discipline during the thirties, sometimes meeting heavy opposition from the medical and clerical establishment. On the public scene, psychoanalysis was well received and discussed both theoretically (the Freud-Marx debate) and at the practical-political level in, for example, the journal *Sexual Information*. Pioneers included Hjørdis Simonsen, Trygve Braatøy, Ola Raknes and Nic Waal.

In 1934 a Norwegian-Danish Society was established with Schjelderup, then University Professor of Psychology, as President. The thirties was marked by two forceful personalities spending some years in Oslo, *Fenichel from 1933 until 1935 and *Reich from 1934 till 1939. Reich's works on character-analysis strongly influenced Norwegian psychoanalysis.

During the German occupation the psychoanalytic society was dissolved to avoid Nazi interference. Many members were active in the resistance movement. Schjelderup, who was resistance leader at the university, and others were sent to concentration camps, where some were killed.

The society was re-established in 1947 but was not accepted by the IPA authorities. For different reasons, perhaps the shadow of Reich, the Norwegians did not receive study group status until 1971 and became a component society of the IPA in 1975.

The Norwegian Psychoanalytic Institute was established in 1967 with Peter Andreas Holter as prime mover: psychoanalytic education, research and lecturing are its main tasks.

At the beginning of the twenty-first century the Society has about sixty-five members and about twenty-five candidates in training. There is an active child-analytic group and a group working with psychoanalytic research. The main trend is an object-relational approach with an emphasis on analysis of character.

The Scandinavian Psychoanalytic Review is published in collaboration with the other Nordic societies, which also arrange a psychoanalytic congress biannually.

Alnæs, R. (1980) 'The development of psychoanalysis in Norway'. *The Scandinavian Psychoanalytic Review* 3: 55–101.

Alnæs, R. (1994) 'Psychoanalysis in Norway. History, training, treatment, research.' *Nordic Journal of Psychiatry* 48(32).
Hansen, F. and Varvin, S. (1995) 'Norway (Psychoanalysis)' in P. Kutter (ed.) *Psychoanalysis. A Guide to Psychoanalysis Throughout the World*, Vol. 2. Stuttgart-Bad Cannstatt: Frommann-Holzboog.

A. Z. / S. V.

NOTHINGNESS Existential philosophy and psychology recognise the radical contingency of human existence, the fact that, as *Sartre says, I have no essence other than that which I create through my actions and that according to *Heidegger I am bound for death or non-being. I am not a 'thing' – I am 'no-thing'. For Sartre, nothingness permeates human existence as the nihilating consciousness (freedom) through which we constitute the world; it is because I am aware that I am *not* the objects of my consciousness that I am able to be conscious *of* those objects. For example, it is my awareness that I am *not* this table or that I am *not* you that makes me aware of the table or of you. Because of nihilation, change is possible in existential analysis. Sartre describes radical change or reorientation in a person's project of being as a moment of 'double nothingness'. I am no longer what I was, and I am no longer what I was about to become. Patients on the verge of major life shifts often report a feeling of 'standing over the abyss' or 'losing the ground beneath my feet'.

Sartre, J.-P. [1943] (1956) *Being and Nothingness: An Essay on Phenomenological Ontology*. Translated by Hazel E. Barnes. New York: Philosophical Library.

A. M. / B. C.

NUMINOSITY A word that derives from the Latin *numen*, 'nod', it signifies a binding and sacred form of promise from the divine life-soul situated in the head. By extension it came to mean spirit, manifested in both gods and humans. Rudolf Otto – whose 1917 book, *The Idea of the Holy*, much influenced Jung – saw it as the central characteristic of Divinity. For Jung it is the approach to the numinous that is the real therapy, bringing release from the curse of pathology. The numinous may be experienced in *archetypal dreams, visions, *synchronicities or wherever the Wholly Other breaks through into the limited world of everyday consciousness, transcending personal neurosis.

E. Beg.

O

O Bion uses this term to stand for Ultimate Reality or Absolute Truth which is unknown and unknowable. However, an analyst, by suspending memory and desire, can be at-one with O and can consequently know evolutions of O. This is the analyst's primary task. Becoming O stands for the total experience, the openness to that which is unknown and unknowable. It is a state in which unconscious preconceptions and saturated elements do not interfere with experiencing emotional reality. O is the origin of any transformation, the realisation, the thing-in-itself.

Bion, W. R. (1965) *Transformations*. London: Karnac Books. Also in *Seven Servants*. New York: Jason Aronson, 1977.
Bion, W. R. (1970) *Attention and Interpretation*. London: Tavistock. Also in *Seven Servants*. New York: Jason Aronson, 1977.

S. A.

OBJECT (FREUD) Freud defined the object as 'the thing by which or through which the drive is able to attain its aim'. As the definition suggests, for Freud, the primary psychological significance of the object lies in its role in gratification of one's needs and drives, that is, in providing pleasure. Early in *development, we respond to part objects (e.g. the breast), and only later are we capable of responding to the whole object (e.g. the mother). Freud clearly implied in his writings that were objects not necessary for need and drive satisfaction, we would never develop an interest in, or even a conception of, objects. This idea, as well as the radical distinction Freud made between drive and object, was disputed by *Klein, who believed that they were inextricably linked from the very beginning of life. Freud's conception of the primary pleasure-producing function of the object was sharply rejected by *Fairbairn, who argued that we are inherently object-seeking creatures. Klein's and Fairbairn's reconceptualisation of the role of the object in psychic life constitutes the foundation for British *object relations theory. It is important to note that many concepts and formulations in psychoanalysis that include the term object – e.g. object relations, internalised object – refer not, or not only, to the actual external objects, but to an internal mental *representation of the object.

Fairbairn, W. R. D. (1952) *Psychoanalytic Studies of the Personality*. London: Tavistock.
Freud, S. (1905) *Three Essays on the Theory of Sexuality*. S. E. 7. London: Hogarth Press.

M. Eag.

OBJECT (LACAN) see **PART OBJECT (LACAN)**

OBJECT (FAIRBAIRN) (ACCEPTING/REJECTING) The term Fairbairn first used to describe the satisfying aspect of the introjected primary caretaker, an object that could be retained in relative consciousness by the central organisation. He later called this structure the *ideal object. The rejecting object is Fairbairn's first term for the libidinally *bad object, which was too painful to be borne in consciousness and was therefore split off and repressed, thus forming the basis for two internal *bad objects: the *rejecting object and the *exciting object.

See also: endopsychic structure; internal object

Fairbairn, W. R. D. [1944] (1952) 'Endopsychic structure considered in terms of object relationships' + Addendum (1951) in *Psychoanalytic Studies of the Personality*. London: Routledge. Pbk 1994.

E. F. B. / D. E. S.

OBJECT (KLEIN) INTERNAL OBJECT Even though the concept of 'internal objects' was present in Freud's writings, it was Klein who developed it and made it central to her theory of psychic functioning. Klein drew from both Freud's theory of identification in 'Mourning and Melancholia' and from *Abraham's study of the stages of the libido where he describes the incorporation of a part of the object in the anal sadistic stage.

Kleinian theory is both a *drive and an *object relations theory. The concept of 'internal objects' has to be thought of in the context of its interaction with other main hypotheses, such as a theory of early mental functioning which formulates the existence of an ego capable of perceiving anxiety; the development by the ego of primitive defence mechanisms such as *projection and *introjection; and, the hypothesis of *unconscious phantasy and the theory of positions. The ego is present and active from the beginning of life and establishes relations with objects from the first contacts with the external world. Drives (or instincts) are inherently attached to objects, and according to Klein, the workings of the life and death drives include their attachment to objects. The infant projects its own aggression and love prototypically into the mother's breast and introjects a phantastically-distorted picture of the real object upon which it is based.

The concept of 'internal objects' can be described from two different perspectives: as an unconscious phantasy of containing either a friendly or hostile being having an intention and an independent life of its own (this was called by Baranger a 'phenomenological' dimension); and, as playing an integral part in the development of the ego and super-ego, that is, structuring the agencies of the personality (the 'good' breast forms, according to Klein the core of the ego). The vicissitudes undergone by the internal objects run parallel to what happens to the ego. While in the *paranoid-schizoid position there is a split in the ego and in the object *part objects, *good and *bad objects), there is a movement towards integration of both the ego and the internal objects in the *depressive position where internalised objects will approximate more closely to reality.

Abraham, K. [1924] (1942) 'A short study of the development of the libido, viewed in the light of mental disorders' in Ernest Jones (ed.) *Selected Papers of Karl Abraham*. London: Hogarth Press, 418–99.

Baranger, W. (1980) 'Validez del concepto de objeto en la obra de Melanie Klein' in *Aportaciones al Concepto de Objeto en psicoanalisis*. Buenos Aires: Amorrortu.

Bianchedi, E. de et al. (1984) 'Beyond Freudian metapsychology – the metapsychological points of view of the Kleinian school' *International Journal of Psychoanalysis* 65: 389–98.

Bronstein C. (2001) 'What are internal objects?' in *Kleinian Theory: A Contemporary Perspective*. London: Whurr.

Freud, S. [1915] (1917) *Mourning and Melancholia*. S. E. 14. London: Hogarth Press.

Klein, M. (1935) 'A contribution to the psychogenesis of manic-depressive states' in *The Writings of Melanie Klein Vol I: Love, Guilt and Reparation and Other Works 1921–1945*. London: Hogarth Press, 1985, 262–89.

C. B.

OBJECT (LACAN) see **PART OBJECT (LACAN)**

OBJECT A see **PART OBJECT (LACAN)**

OBJECT CHOICE The selection of an object (person), considered, in part, to be determined by unconscious motives. The term is often reserved for love-objects. The choice of the person is subdivided into choosing a person who is like oneself or possessing qualities one wishes s/he had (*narcissistic object-choice), or choosing a person from whom one can passively receive gratification of needs for nurturance or protection (*anaclitic choice).

See also: cathexis

C. P.

OBJECT RELATION Object relations are the structures that govern and determine the outline of a person's relations to others. Normal and neurotic object relations are brought into being, according to Freud, as a result of an early experience of *frustration, where a retraction of promise in the field of love leads to a regressive reorganisation of the early form of these relations. The dissatisfaction experienced by the child leads it to prefer a simplified relation to the other, a relation based on *phantasy. Frustration is thus a crucial experience which leads the human subject to refuse the complexity of relations of love, and to choose a flight into an over-simplified form of relation to the other person, where phantasies are preferred, as long as the individual is 'uncertain whether reality will offer them anything better'.

B. B.

OBJECT RELATIONS THEORY (GENERAL) Object relations theory is a form of psychoanalytic theory from Britain drawing principally from and integrating the work of *Fairbairn, *Klein, *Winnicott, *Bion, *Guntrip, *Balint, Sutherland, *Bowlby, and more recent contributions from Kleinians such as Britton and Steiner, as well as British Independent analysts such as Bollas. In psychoanalysis an *object is usually taken to be a person or part of a person, represented in the internal world or *psychical reality. Taught in the US since the 1970s, and amplified by *Kernberg, *Grotstein, Ogden and Scharff and Scharff, object relations theory has moved psychoanalysis away from its basis in instinct-based *ego psychology. Object relations theory holds that the infant has instincts or drives, of course, but they are not the thing-in-itself that motivates the growing child. The drives simply secure survival and *attachment while the human period of dependency is successfully negotiated with the help of loving caretakers. The instincts or drives are given meaning in the context of these emotionally nurturing relationships. In object relations theory, the infant is motivated primarily by the need to be in a relationship, and the drives simply serve that purpose. Without a mother, the infant dies. Infants build the personality and the sense of self from the various meaningful interactions that they have with their mothers (or other primary caretakers) who meet their needs for nurture and security, and with the other family members with whom they move through the life cycle.

An internal model of relationships is built up inside the self. This determines the way the person thinks and feels and perceives the world. It acts as a blueprint for future relationships. The inner world is built in childhood, continues to be modified through adolescence and adulthood, and affects choice of marital partner, child-rearing techniques, and attitudes to work, sex and play.

The inner constellation of parts of the self can be inferred from current ways of relating. Most important for the therapist, the inner constellation can be changed by registering the occurrence of patterns of behaviour in the here-and-now of therapy, connecting them to perceptions and expectations based on past experience, and modifying them by interpretation of the patterns re-created in the transference-countertransference dimension of the therapeutic relationship. Object relations theory supports a flexible therapeutic stance applied to individual, couple, family, and group therapy. It is worth mentioning that although *Kohut's *selfobjects are not strictly 'objects' in our sense, there is a definite relationship between the concept of selfobjects and objects in the object relations tradition. The self psychology concept is elaborated, but also more limited: the object is there to serve the self for better and worse, but the selfobject doesn't seem to have any dynamic 'life of its own'. On the other hand, in object relations, for example in Winnicott, the mother, who is the model for an internal object, also has a subjective life. So object relations has the crucial dimension of including relationship between two subjects, even in the mind of the individual. When the internal object becomes only a selfobject, that represents a breakdown of the normal mutuality of subjective relationships, even in the mind of the single individual.

Object relations theory is not only applicable in clinical situations. It has given rise to a teaching method called the Affective Learning Model. The patterns of the internal object relationships are expressed in the group dynamic of a seminar as participants react emotionally to psychologically profound material while studying together to understand and apply the concepts. So the seminar group for discussing the concepts is at the same time a 'laboratory' for studying the theory and therapeutic application of object relations in real time. Object relations also forms the basis for understanding and consulting to institutions. Relationships and their experience in groups are central to the function of all institutions, and the same theory that contributes to individual and group therapy, augmented by principles of large group and multi-subgroup function, allows a trained consultant to apply object relations theory to a wide variety of institutional situations.

Greenberg, J. R. and Mitchell, S. (1983) *Object Relations in Psychoanalytic Theory*. Cambridge, MA and London: Harvard University Press.

Scharff, J. S. and Scharff, D. E. (2000) *Tuning the Therapeutic Instrument: The Affective Learning of Psychotherapy*. Northvale, NJ: Jason Aronson.

D. E. S.

OBJECT RELATIONS THEORY (EXISTENTIAL CRITIQUE) For existential analysts influenced by Sartre, what the object relations theorists refer to as the object is really the other as subject. Sartre comments on the ubiquitous subject-object alternation in human relationships. It is through the other's *look, which reveals to me the other as subject, that I become aware of my object side. This is important to development because the child appropriates the kind of object she becomes in the eyes of the parent as part of her *ego or self as object, a phenomenon object relations theorists refer to as mirroring. If the child is treated as a mere object, like a table or chair, rather than as a human being with agency, then neurosis or worse may occur, as Sartre says happened to *Flaubert or as *Laing notes occurred for a patient with *ontological insecurity about his status as a person. Sartre further notes that support for the child's developing personhood is given in the form of 'valorisation' or permission to develop fully as a person. Precisely because she experiences herself as object without substantiality, the neurotic is drawn into the project to be her own foundation, secure from lack. However, this desire to be an ultimate object or God exacerbates fear of a lack of substantiality, leading the individual to strive all the harder – whether hysterically or obsessively – to become his own foundation. The therapist's task is to support but also challenge the patient to accept that human reality is temporal, and that authentic relations demand a subject-subject model that avoids objectifying all roles, one's own and others.

Mirvish, A. 'Sartre, psychoanalysis and neurosis'. *Bulletin de philosophie de langue française* 4: 2–3.
Sartre, J.-P. (1992) *Notebooks for an Ethics*. Translated by D. Pellauer. Chicago and London: University of Chicago Press.

A. M. / B. C.

OBJECT RELATIONS (LACAN CRITIQUE) Lacan, like Freud, stresses the importance of *frustration for the construction of object relations. The subject's first relations to others are based, he claims, on the experience of the lack of an object. He criticises and develops the arguments introduced by *Jones, in distinguishing frustration, *privation and *castration – this latter formulated as a loss of the most cherished love attachment. He then indicates how it is frustration – read as a retraction of promise in the field of desire – rather than privation that is at play in the descriptions that Winnicott gives of the construction of a transitional space. On the one hand Lacan situates object relations in the Imaginary, the result of 'Imaginary passion'. If object relations theory tends to identify objects as actual parts of the body, or even as others, Lacan emphasises the status of objects insofar as they are given in signifying material. Furthermore, where object relations theorists presume that there is an encounter with the object, Lacan claims that there is a renewed encounter with a lack of object. Lacan's notion of the object (object a) has it as fundamental to the functioning of the Symbolic: given the interdependence of the three registers – the Real, the Symbolic and the Imaginary – he can also say that object relations indicate something of the subject's relation to the Real.

See also: lack

B. O. D.

OBJECT RELATIONS THEORY (GROUP) Object relations theory is about people's innermost fantasies about relationships. It is concerned with the earliest life experiences, namely, those in infancy and toddlerhood, that occurred with those who are psychologically significant in a person's emotional development. These experiences left imprints in the mind, namely, schemata about relationships. Those constitute templates which then influence subsequent relationships, and in people with psychopathology, to an untoward degree. In a group, particularly an analytic one, these fantasies will be re-enacted. Group analysis aims to modify such aberrant interactions that take place on the stage of the mind by modifying them in the living group in a particular way, such that they are replaced with realistic and adaptive ones.

The object relations perspective, as Kibel shows, has enriched group analysis, as concepts from the former have been woven into the latter.

Analogies of the relation between the infant and mother have been brought to bear on the understanding of both the group member and the group-as-an-entity. Just as the mother tolerates and contains the primitive affects, i.e. the chaotic, undisciplined emotions, of the developing child, so has the group been seen by James and others as a *'holding' environment for each member's untoward thoughts and attitudes. This has enriched the concept of the group matrix. Just as infants and toddlers use a blanket or some treasured object to take the earliest steps toward separating from mother and becoming an individual, so has the analytic group been seen as a place to try out new ways of being. The way in which group members influence one another and induce reactions in each other has been better understood by employing the notion of *projective identification, a pivotal concept in object relations theory that describes the way infants and toddlers induce reactions in their caregivers. Scheidlinger shows how this has enriched the concept of scapegoating. Early relationships that are playful have been said to be the prototype for experiencing oneself in a new way in group analysis and then internalising the therapeutic experience to correct maladaptive aspects of personality. This has broadened the concept of the mirroring process.

Object relations theory has not transformed the practice of group analysis, but has enriched the understanding of its process and its therapeutic value. The theory has helped clinicians appreciate both the group member's role and the dynamics of treatment.

James, C. (1984) 'Bion's "containing" and Winnicott's "holding" in the context of the group matrix'. *International Journal of Group Psychotherapy* 34: 201–13.

Kibel, H. D. (1992) 'The clinical application of object relations theory' in R. H. Klein, H. S. Bernard and D. L. Singer (eds) *Handbook of Contemporary Group Psychotherapy: Contributions from Object Relations, Self-Psychology, and Social Systems Theories.* Madison, CT: International Universities Press, 144–76.

Kibel, H. D. (1993) 'Object relation theory and group psychotherapy' in H. I. Kaplan and B. J. Sadock (eds) *Comprehensive Group Psychotherapy*. Third edition. Baltimore: Williams & Wilkins, 165–76.

Kosseff, J. W. (1991) 'Anchoring the self through the group: congruences, play and the potential for change' in S. Tuttman (ed.) *Psychoanalytic Group Theory and Therapy: Essays in Honor of Saul Scheidlinger.* Madison, CT: International Universities Press, 78–108.

Scheidlinger, S. (1982) 'On scapegoating in group psychotherapy'. *International Journal of Group Psychotherapy* 32: 131–43.

Schermer, V. L. (2000) 'Contributions of object relations theory and self-psychology to relational psychology and group psychotherapy'. *International Journal of Group Psychotherapy* 50: 199–217.

H. K.

OBSESSIONAL NEUROSIS Freud defined neurosis as the negative of perversion, and, further, obsessional neurosis as 'a dialect of *hysteria'. The central features of this neurosis are those of obsessive thoughts (and acts), submitted to the compulsion to repeat, and articulated in close relation with the characteristic obsessional inability to decide. Obsessional doubt, procrastination, and the viewing of the subject's life as an eternal approach to death, combine with de-sexualisation and idealisation of the mother to bring about the specific clinical picture of obsessional neurosis.

Lacan introduced the notion of 'the individual myth of the neurotic'. In interpreting Freud's most famous case study of obsessional neurosis, the *Rat Man, Lacan first isolated 'the elementary mytheme' (a specific combination of the father's 'impossible' choice between two women, and of the father's unpaid debt), and then analysed its transformations in the Rat Man's life, in the actual outbreak of his neurosis, as well as, finally, within the psychoanalytic situation, in the *transference on to Freud.

See also: guilt

E. B.

OBSESSIVE COMPULSIVE DISORDER Obsessive compulsive disorder is defined in the *DSM-IV* as the presence of either obsessions or compulsions (or both). Obsessions are defined as recurrent and persistent thoughts, impulses or images that are experienced as intrusive and inappropriate and that cause marked anxiety or distress. They are not simply excessive worries about life's problems; the person attempts to ignore, suppress or neutralise them in some way and they recognise that they are a product of their own mind and are excessive or unreasonable. Compulsions are repetitive behaviours (e.g. handwashing, ordering, checking) or mental acts (e.g. praying, counting, repeating words silently) that the person feels driven to perform in response to an obsession, or according to rules that must be applied rigidly. These behaviours are aimed at reducing distress or preventing some dreaded event or situation; however, they are not connected in a realistic way with what they are designed to neutralise or prevent, or are clearly excessive.

The ego-alien nature of this disorder makes the problem particularly distressing for sufferers and their families. As with other anxiety disorders, for example phobias, avoidance is a key component in the maintenance of the disorder. The function of the compulsions is to avoid the distress, discomfort or anxiety provoked by the obsession. For example, the obsession with cleanliness provoked by an unrealistic fear of dirt or contamination, may result in lengthy cleaning and washing procedures which are carried out in a fastidious and time-consuming way (only to be repeated from scratch if incorrectly performed or contamination occurs partway through). The cleaning procedures and rituals would be classified as compulsive behaviours, which are then routinely reinforced when the anxiety or discomfort drops following the completion of the compulsive act.

Treatment through cognitive behavioural strategies targets feelings of responsibility and may challenge these directly through paradox, or behavioural experiments. *Behavioural therapy uses exposure (to the distress caused by obsessions) with response (compulsive behaviours and rituals) prevention. Eventually the person may be said to be treated when they learn that habituation to the distress occurs without the need to act on their compulsions.

Often the obsessive thoughts that are be defended against by compulsions concern violent fears of catastrophe. This links to the psychoanalytic view regarding obsessional and rigid thinking as a defence against violence and destructiveness. Obsessive compulsive disorder is not to be confused with obsessional personality traits which include tendencies to be rigid and rule-based, to be preoccupied with orderliness and perfectionism and are present from early adulthood.

American Psychiatric Association (1994) *Diagnostic and Statistical Manual of Mental Disorders (DSM-IV)*. Fourth edition. Washington, DC: American Psychiatric Association.

J. W.

OCCULTISM, THE OCCULT The attempt to control natural processes by secret and magical procedures, or a belief in the possibility of such control. Evidence of beliefs that thoughts or spiritual beings exist in space with no discernible physical body has existed since the dawn of history. Freud thought of occult phenomena as the actual existence of psychical forces beyond the familiar experience with human and animal minds. It troubled Freud greatly that the discovery of thought transference in psychoanalysis became associated with occult phenomena because he could not deny or explain all such psychical phenomena. Throughout his life, Freud showed an exquisite oscillation between scepticism and belief in telepathy, fearing that it could deprive psychoanalysis of its scientific reputation while also harbouring a favourable prejudice towards it. By the time of his final words on the subject in 1933, he had come to believe that open discussion would not endanger the scientific outlook of psychoanalysis. Indeed, he once stated that if he were to live his life over, he would devote it to psychical research rather than to psychoanalysis. Although Freud denied ever making a statement of this nature (a letter of his validates his statement), it shows how deeply influenced he was by the occult.

In 1880, the Society for Psychical Research was formed by distinguished scientists of the time to investigate the evidence of the occult. In 1911, Freud was made a Corresponding Member of the Society for Psychical Research. In 1915, he was made an Honorary Fellow of the American Society for Psychical Research, and in 1923, he received a similar honour from the Greek Society for Psychical Research. These honours were presumably expressions of hope that psychoanalysis would prove able to shed light on the obscure problems of occultism.

Freud's first paper on the subject, 'A Premonitory Dream Fulfilled', dated 10 November 1899, was found after his death and published two years later. His last published mention of telepathy is found in 'Dreams and Occultism' in the 1932 *New Introductory Lectures*, in which he notes the secret language which so easily grows up between two people who are closely connected, as an example of thought transference. Freud's collaboration with Jung and Ferenczi, and his experiments with his daughter, Anna, also evidence his intense interest in telepathy. Freud was impressed that the first published papers of both Jung and Ferenczi were on the psychological implications of the occult; they however were far more immersed in such ideas than Freud. It is important to note that, for psychoanalysis, what fell under the shadow of occultism was precisely the experience of unconscious communication between patient and analyst. Freud noted the remarkable capacity of the unconscious of one human being to react on that of another without passing through consciousness. Having a close emotional relationship facilitates such transmission, and particularly when a thought is moving from primary into secondary process. Dreams were initially considered to carry prophetic information but Freud took great pains to explain away this idea as it was unscientific. The state of sleep was thought to facilitate telepathic receptivity but the content of dreams was not believed to be specific to actual future events.

*Fenichel, *Ferenczi, Burlingham and *Deutsch were some of the more prominent analysts who agreed with Freud that the capacity for thought transference originates in the early mother-infant relationship of non-verbal communication. Experiences of the uncanny were often explained as projections of this early period including the sense of oceanic feeling. On several occasions Freud specifically defined telepathy as communication between people spatially distant or without the use of words or signs. He constantly moved from examples in which transmission is from a distance to examples where individuals are in one another's presence. Psychoanalysts, physicists and biologists seriously study today, non-local thought transmission, or unconscious communication. Mayer has summarised this work.

The evolution of clinical psychoanalysis has witnessed an embracing of the importance of unconscious communication, particularly in the work of Bion, and subsequently by proponents of the intersubjective. The more recent writings of Ogden, Bollas, and Casement, to mention but a few, are particularly relevant to thought transmission or unconscious communication. Countertransference is no longer a concept referring to an impediment derived from the analyst's unanalysed unconscious life, but is a clinically useful concept referring to unconscious communication between analyst and analysand (just as Theodore Reik had noted many years ago). Although Freud was strongly admonished by Ernest Jones not to express his views of the occult in public, unconscious communication as an important aspect of psychoanalysis is no longer connected with occultism.

Bion, W. R. (1965) *Transformations: Change from Learning to Growth*. New York: Basic Books.

Freud, S. (1922) *Dreams and Telepathy*. S. E. 18. London: Hogarth Press.

Freud, S. (1925) *The Occult Significance of Dreams* S. E. 19. London: Hogarth Press.
Freud, S. (1932) *Dreams and Occultism*. S. E. 22. London: Hogarth Press.
Mayer, E. L. (1996) 'Subjectivity and intersubjectivity of clinical facts'. *International Journal of Psychoanalysis* 77: 709–37.
Roustang, F. (1983) *Psychoanalysis Never Lets Go*. Baltimore and London: Johns Hopkins University Press.

C. Mor.

Oedipus complex (Freud) According to Freud, *infantile sexuality reaches its peak in the formation of the Oedipus complex at age three to five. For the boy, a positive Oedipus complex is characterised by sexual (incestuous) impulses toward mother and hostile and rivalrous impulses toward father. Because of our inherent bisexuality, one can find a negative Oedipus complex in which the above attitudes towards parents are reversed. Early on, Freud believed that the situation was entirely analogous for the girl, that is, sexual (incestuous) wishes toward father and hostile rivalrous feelings toward mother. In his later writings, influenced by the recognition that the mother is also the girl's first love object, he formulated a more complex scenario that included the following elements: resentment and turning away from the mother, *penis envy and the desire for a baby with father as a symbolic compensation for the absence of a penis. This convoluted scenario suggests that Freud was thinking primarily of the boy when he formulated the concept of the Oedipus complex.

According to Freud, the Oedipus complex is the nucleus of neuroses; how one resolves Oedipal conflicts has a great influence in the final shape of the individual's erotic life. For the boy, an adequate resolution includes renunciation of incestuous wishes toward mother (and eventually finding one's own love object outside the family); identification with the father, thus consolidating the boy's gender identity, and the *introjection of father's authority which constitutes the nucleus of the *super-ego. An analogous process, not as clearly spelled out by Freud, constitutes resolution of the Oedipus complex for the girl. It includes identification with the mother, a shift from the sexual emphasis on the clitoris to the vagina (symbolically suggesting acceptance of a lack of penis) and desire for the baby. Freud's views regarding the psychological development of women have come under serious questioning.

From a clinical point of view, the most salient expressions of an inadequate resolution of Oedipal conflict include inability to find a love object outside the family and an inability to combine sexual desire and love.

See also: homosexuality; impotence; incest

Freud, S. (1923) *The Ego and the Id*. S. E. 19. London: Hogarth Press.
Freud, S. (1925) *Some Psychical Consequences of the Anatomical Distinction between the Sexes*. S. E. 19. London: Hogarth Press.

M. Eag.

Oedipus complex (Klein) The Oedipus complex – maternal according to Klein – sets in during the earliest days of post-natal life. Since this is a time when the early oral-sadistic and anal-sadistic stages are active, they become connected with the Oedipus tendencies, and are directed toward the objects around which the Oedipus complex develops – the parents. The infant's hatred for the same sex parent as its rival for the opposite sex parent is coloured with the hate, aggression and phantasies derived from the oral-sadistic and anal-sadistic fixations. Later, Klein added that the primitive Oedipal configuration began with intermittent flashes of awareness that mother and baby are two, stimulating the possibility of three and hence the familiar triangularity inherent in that and related situations.

See also: symbol formation

Klein, M. (1927) 'Criminal tendencies in normal children'. *British Journal of Medical Psychology* 7. Also In *Love, Guilt and Reparation*. London: Hogarth Press, 1975.
Klein, M. (1928) 'Early stages of the Oedipus conflict'. *International Journal of Psycho-Analysis* 9. Also in *Love, Guilt and Reparation*. London: Hogarth Press, 1975.
Klein, M. (1945) 'The Oedipus complex in the light of early anxieties'. *International Journal of Psycho-Analysis* 26. Also in *Love, Guilt and Reparation*. London: Hogarth Press, 1975.

S. A.

Oedipus complex (Fairbairn) Fairbairn held a modified view of the *Oedipus complex based on the vicissitudes of early relationships. He thought that the parents' early attempt to kill the child in the Oedipus myth was a model of the *rejecting and persecuting object relationship which begins the process of internal *splitting which can eventuate in Oedipal rivalry and aggression to one parent and excited longing for the other. The very young child has *ambivalent relationships with each parent, and during the Oedipal phase the complexity of dealing with two ambivalent relationships is resolved by making one parent the object of libidinal attachment and the other the object of antilibidinal attachment. This split is usually accomplished along gender lines. In this way, the child fashions the mental Oedipal situation through its own initiative. Fairbairn describes no theoretical difference between male and female Oedipal development.

E. F. B. / D. E. S.

Oedipus complex (self psychology) Self psychologists do not regard the Oedipal situation as necessarily occupying a crucial psychological position in development or in pathogenesis. While they recognise the validity and significance of Oedipal conflicts, they do not regard their presence as evidence of psychopathology. In effect, they regard the Oedipus as significantly entailing selfobject relatedness that may have normal or pathological dimensions. Kohut embodied these two dimensions of relatedness in his distinction between an *Oedipal stage* and an *Oedipal complex*. An *Oedipal stage* develops in consequence of interactions between the child's natural strivings in triangular situations and the parents' more or less optimal responsiveness to them. As Tolpin puts it, the expression of the child's naive sexuality, affectionateness and assertiveness go together from the start and his experience of hurt, anger and jealousy are to some extent inevitable in consequence of his sense of rejection of his claims for exclusive love and commitment. However, if appropriate soothing and ongoing confirmation of the child adequately counteract disappointment and injury, the degree of his expectation of himself and of his selfobject world becomes modified and his self is thus strengthened to meet further disappointments in life. An Oedipal complex arises from interactions between the child's strivings and the parents' inadequate or inappropriate responses to them. If the parents react to the Oedipal child as wanting actual sexual relations or as offering serious competition to the parent, the child may become overstimulated, anxious, conflicted and confused. If, then, he is 'rejected', or 'accepted' in ways with which he cannot cope, he may become overwhelmed by shame and guilt, and may experience a sense of inadequacy as well a fear of his own strength and that of the parent. In such a situation, not only are the seeds of the polymorphic neurotic disturbances of the Oedipal phase sown but also the sense of self is always significantly affected. Self psychologists refer, then, to 'Oedipal self pathology'.

Bacal, H. and Newman, K. (1990) *Theories of Object Relations: Bridges to Self Psychology*. New York: Columbia University Press.
Tolpin, M. (1988) 'The Psychology of Women' (unpublished).

H. B.

OEDIPUS COMPLEX (LACAN) At the start of his teaching, Lacan devoted himself to a structural, transhistorical and transcultural reading of the Oedipus complex and its associated *castration complex. In his account, which goes under the name of the *paternal metaphor, the signifier of the *name-of-the-father substitutes itself for that of the desire of the mother, and interposes itself symbolically between the mother and the child. The child passes from the position of being the phallus of the mother, to that of having the phallus or not, and gains access in this way to phallic signification, the effect of *metaphor. This is Lacan's linguistic account of what is usually referred to as triangulation. Where there is *foreclosure of the name-of-the-father, the metaphor is unable to be constituted, and the subject, not having the phallus, is exposed to psychosis. Later, Lacan moved towards an investigation of what lies beyond the Oedipus, constructing a domain which detaches psychoanalysis from the residue of religious attachment, which is implicitly referred to with Lacan's concept of the name-of-the-father. Lacan constituted this going-beyond through his invention of the *object a, which he then gave the key position of the irreducible Real of jouissance.

J. C. R.

ONTOLOGICAL INSECURITY A term coined by R. D. Laing to depict the core anxiety of those suffering from psychotic states of disintegration. Laing makes a distinction between the 'ontologically secure' person who feels real, alive, and whole and who encounters the day-to-day challenges of living from a centrally firm sense of his and the other's reality, with the 'ontologically insecure' person who feels more unreal than real, more dead than alive and who is so precariously differentiated from the world that his identity and autonomy are always in question. This way of characterising the psychotic individual is rooted in a rigorous *phenomenological description of that person's experience of self rather than an inventory of psychological symptom formation. Following Heidegger's emphasis on the ontological aspect of a person's Being instead of narrow psychological and/or biological factors, Laing's conception of ontological insecurity serves as a way to understand the nature of psychotic anxiety, a manifestation of the individual's fragile sense of existence.

Laing, R. D. (1969) *Self and Others*. Revised edition. New York: Pantheon.

M. G. T.

OPTIMAL FRUSTRATION see **TRANSMUTING INTERNALISATION**

OPTIMAL PROVISION Denotes a way of working psychoanalytically that replaces the rule of abstinence, which Lindon, who introduced the term, regards as detrimental to the efficacy of the analytic process. Optimal provision is, for him, any provision that, by meeting a developmental longing, facilitates the uncovering, illuminating, and transforming of the subjective experiences of the patient.

See also: optimal responsiveness

Lindon, J. (1994) 'Gratification and provision in psychoanalysis: should we get rid of "the rule of abstinence"?'. *Psychoanalytic Dialogues* 4: 549–82.

H. B.

OPTIMAL RESPONSIVENESS Bacal uses optimal responsiveness to refer to the *diversity* of verbal and non-verbal responses that are therapeutically effective when working with the specific psychological needs of a particular patient.

See also: optimal provision; specificity theory

Bacal, H. A. (1985) 'Optimal responsiveness and the therapeutic process' in A. Goldberg (ed.) *Progress in Self Psychology*, Vol. 1, 202–26.
Bacal, H. A. (1990) 'The elements of a corrective selfobject experience'. *Psychoanalytic Inquiry* 10: 347–72.

Bacal, H. A. (ed.) (1998) *Optimal Responsiveness: How Therapists Heal their Patients*. New York: Jason Aronson, 141–70.

H. B.

ORAL ATTITUDE Fairbairn held that the child's first reciprocal relationship is largely conducted through an attitude of incorporation, which becomes a model for mental activity that uses the mouth as its primary organ of bodily expression. The oral stage exists because the child is psychically structured to incorporate experience, not because of the infant's physically determined focus on sucking and taking in. For Fairbairn, the oral attitude is primarily a way of relating to objects by incorporating or expelling them. Later, a second stage of biting, attacking, and division into *accepted and *rejected objects occurs. *Suttie offers an alternative view stressing the importance of the larynx in tonal communication between mother and child.

Suttie, I. D. [1935] (1988) *The Origins of Love and Hate*. Intro. Dorothy Heard. London: Free Association Books.

E. F. B. / D. E. S.

ORAL DEPENDENCE The oral phase, the first of Freud's five psychosexual stages, is marked by the importance of feeding and the connection of the infant to the caregiver, a relationship Freud never fully appreciated. Major aspects of orality – the mouth as a source of sensual gratification and the infant's dependence on the caregiver for physical and psychological survival – persist in adult behaviour. Eating, drinking, passivity, dependence, obedience, helplessness, and discomfort in being alone are vestiges of the oral phase. Considerable empirical evidence attests to the validity of this concept.

J. Mas.

ORAL SADISM Oral sadism is a concept of *Abraham's, who split Freud's oral stage into erotic-dependent and sadistic (sometimes called *cannibalistic) components. Abraham believed that orality contains both erotic-dependent and aggressive aspects (i.e. biting, sarcasm, harping criticism). The difficulty in distinguishing between various forms of aggression has limited the utility of this concept.

J. Mas.

ORAL-SADISTIC IMPULSES For Klein, there is always an interaction between oral-libidinal and oral-sadistic impulses corresponding to the fusion between life and death instincts. Essentially linked to vigorous introjective processes, oral sadism is bound up with the emergence of greed, which intensifies whenever there are internal or external privations. Any increase in greed strengthens feelings of frustration and in turn aggressive impulses. Whenever innate aggression in a child is strong, persecutory anxiety, frustration and greed are easily aroused which, in turn, contributes to the child's difficulty in tolerating privation and in dealing with anxiety. This may become the cause of the earliest feeding inhibitions as well as a root of later anorexic and bulimic pathology.

Klein, M. (1952) 'Some theoretical conclusions regarding the emotional life of the infant'. *Developments in Psycho-Analysis* with P. Heimann, S. Isaacs, and J. Riviere. London: Hogarth Press. Also in *Envy and Gratitude*. London: Hogarth Press, 1975.

S. A.

ORGANISING PRINCIPLE Recurrent patterns of intersubjective transaction within the child-caregiver system result in the establishment of organising principles that unconsciously pattern subsequent experiences. From an intersubjective perspective, psychoanalytic therapy seeks to investigate and illuminate pre-established organising principles and establish the possibility of alternative ones.

See also: intersubjectivity theory

R. S.

OTHER As a concept the Other acquires its function and meaning within psychoanalytic theory in Lacan's work of the 1950s. In that period he opposes the other (person), as someone recognisable or as someone more or less equal to oneself, to the Other, as the Symbolic field in which every person is constituted as a speaking subject with a desire. The Other is an order that is situated beyond the subject but which nevertheless allows for the possibility of a social bond or a relationship with the other. The Other is the locus of language that is necessary to provide the message with its articulated meaning.

R. L.

OTHER SCENE/STAGE Freud cites this hypothesis of Fechner several times: 'the stage on which the dream takes place in the soul is a different one from that of waking life'. From this follows the necessity of decoding the operations that are specific to it: the primary processes of *displacement and *condensation, which presuppose the unconscious.

F. R.

OTHER-CENTRED LISTENING Fosshage has proposed that the analyst adopt a dual listening perspective. He suggests that the analyst should vary his stance between the empathic vantage point advocated by Kohut and a point that he calls 'other-centred', as this will provide a more comprehensive grasp of the patient's experience.

See also: empathic vantage point of observation

Fosshage, J. (1998) 'Optimal responsiveness and listening/experiencing perspectives' in H. Bacal (ed.) *Optimal Responsiveness: How Therapists Heal their Patients*. New York: Jason Aronson, 117–39.

H. B.

OUTCOME STUDIES (ADULT) Studies of psychoanalytic outcomes date back to 1917. They can be divided into four research 'generations', marked by increasing methodological and technological sophistication. What I call 'first-generation' research covers the half-century from 1917 to 1968. It consists of enumerations of cases from the Treatment Centres of the pioneering psychoanalytic institutions – reported by Fenichel from Berlin and Alexander from Chicago in 1937, all summarised by Knight in 1941 together with additional cases from the Menninger Clinic, a total of 952 patients. There were also individual series from Coriat in Boston in 1917, Hyman and Kessel in New York in 1933, a massive collation of 3,000 termination questionnaires by 800 analysts of the American Psychoanalytic Association in 1967, and finally, another clinic series, from the Southern California Institute, by Feldman in 1968. The benefit rate across these studies was approximately 60% for those designated as neurotic, 80% for the psychosomatic, and only 25% for the psychotic. The pitfalls of these 'first-generation' studies are clear; judgments of improvement were made by the (inevitably biased) therapist; there was a lack of specified criteria at almost every step; and the studies were all retrospective, with all the potential for contaminated judgments and *post hoc ergo propter hoc* reasoning.

'Second-generation' studies attempted to address these issues, including the introduction of prospective inquiry and the fashioning of predictions to be tested by subsequent assessment. They began in the 1950s in America. Six landmark projects from this second generation comprised three group-aggregated studies of clinic cases from the Boston, the Columbia and the New York Institutes, and three individually focused studies in New York, San Francisco and Chicago. Currently there are many second-generation studies elsewhere in the world. Three large current European projects are: 1) the Anna Freud Centre review by Fonagy and Target of 765 cases treated over a four-decade span; 2) the

German Psychoanalytical Association Study of Leuzinger-Bohleber involving 190 patients drawn from cooperating DPV members; and, 3) the European multi-centre study of psychoanalytic treatment involving analysts from Holland, Finland, Norway, Sweden and Italy.

The three earlier American group-aggregated studies had comparable structures. The Boston Institute research (Knapp et al., Sashin et al.) reported on 283 patients rated for suitability for analysis, with only fair predictions to judgements of analysability at the one-year mark, and with no effective predictions to outcomes from the patients' characteristics as judged initially. A major reason is that patients selected by clinic committees are carefully screened, with obviously unsuitable cases already rejected. This narrowed variability in the accepted cases makes differential prediction inherently less reliable. The Columbia project (Weber et al.) consisted of a much larger sample (1,585 cases, 40% in psychoanalysis and 60% in psychotherapy). Criteria for therapeutic benefit were established distinct from criteria for a therapeutic process. The most striking finding was that across every category of patient, therapeutic benefit always exceeded the measures of an analytic process. An equally striking finding was that the outcomes, in terms of both therapeutic benefit and analysability, were only marginally predictable from the initial evaluation. What the New York Study (Erie and Goldberg) of 242 patients added, was that the majority were private patients treated by experienced analysts; outcomes from these experienced analysts were completely comparable to those with clinic patients treated by candidates.

The individually focused American studies were initiated by Pfeffer at the New York Institute and comprised patients who had completed Treatment Centre analyses, and agreed to follow-up interviews by a 'follow-up analyst' who had not conducted the treatment. The interviews were weekly, 'analytic' in character, and up to seven in number before the participants agreed upon a natural close. The chief finding consisted of the rapid reactivation of characteristic analytic transferences, including transitory symptoms, as if to the original treating analyst, with subsequent rapid subsidence, and in a manner that indicated new ways of conflict management achieved in the analysis. Neurotic conflicts were not obliterated by analysis but rather were better mastered, with more adequate solutions. Two other research groups (in San Francisco and Chicago) replicated and confirmed this sequence, now called 'the Pfeffer phenomenon'.

A shared characteristic of these second-generation studies was the failure to segregate outcomes from the stability of results at subsequent follow-up. What I call 'third-generation' studies are formal therapy projects that attempt both to assess outcomes across a significant array of cases and to examine the processes through which these outcomes have been reached via the intensive study of each case. They thus combine the methodological approaches of the group, aggregated, and the individually focused studies, and additionally, they have separated outcomes at termination from functioning at follow-up.

Major exemplars of third-generation studies are the newer Boston Institute studies of Kantrowitz et al., and the thirty-year-long Psychotherapy Research Project of the Menninger Foundation, of which Wallerstein was Principal Investigator. Major findings of the Boston Studies (of twenty-two analytic cases) were again that therapeutic benefit was consistently in excess of what could be accounted for by the evocation and resolution of the transference neurosis, and that outcomes could not be predicted from the predictor variables. A surprise finding was that one predictor variable, the quality of the 'therapist-patient match', was demonstrated at follow-up to be significantly related to outcome, with facilitating matches linked to good outcomes, and impeding matches to poor outcomes.

The Menninger project was the most ambitious research program ever carried out. It followed the treatment careers and life careers of forty-two patients from their initial evaluations, through the entire span of their treatments, and then at a several-year follow-up point (reaching 100% of the sample), with open-ended follow-up after that, up to twenty-four years post-treatment. There were three treatment groups: psychoanalysis, expressive analytic therapy, and supportive analytic therapy. The aim was to study both what changes actually took place (the outcome question) and how these changes came about, through the interactions of variables in the patient, in the therapist and therapy, and in the patient's life situation (the process question).

The conclusions can be summarised as follows. All the treatments, even the most purely psychoanalytic, were consistently modified, incorporating supportive techniques, and these supportive techniques accounted for more of the changes than had been predicted; and the supportive therapies often brought about the kinds of structural changes that had been presumed to be achievable only through expressive-analytic conflict resolution. This was clearly counter to the common conviction that the kinds of changes achieved (structural change or just 'behavioural change') were tightly linked to the intervention mode, expressive-analytic, or supportive-'ego strengthening', by which they were brought about. Another major finding was that the more psychoanalytic treatments often achieved less than initially predicted, while the more supportive treatments often achieved more, so that the results in psychoanalysis and in varying mixes of expressive-supportive psychotherapies tended to converge, rather than diverge. Because of greater conceptual and methodological complexity, research into the processes of change in psychoanalytic therapies – investigation of the how question – has been more recent and has not yet undergone generational transformation. Since it usually entails detailed focus on moment-to-moment interactions, process research has only been feasible on a significant scale since the development of suitable technology, audio and video recording, and high-speed computer searches. This has led to the recent explosive proliferation of psychoanalytic process research, mainly in the United States and Germany. Great impetus came from a workshop of American and German researchers held in Ulm, Germany, in 1985. The proceedings of the conference were published in a 1988 monograph, *Psychoanalytic Process Research Strategies* (Dahl et al.). The problem in process research has been that each group has developed its own concepts and measures, and has employed these on its own database of recorded sessions. The Ulm conference was an effort to compare findings from the disparate studies, in a search for elements of congruence, in accord with a principle of congruence in the representation of the *patient's* conflicts, the *treatment* undergone, and the assessment of *outcome*, dubbed PTO congruence.

To properly test this principle, researchers would need to deploy their concepts and measures on a common data base. It would then be possible to determine the convergence of the concepts and instruments elaborated separately to this point, and also to determine the degree of imbrication of process and outcome studies – the degree to which PTO Congruence can be realised. It is this program of coordinated study of a shared data base that is the design of a Collaborative Analytic Multisite Program (CAMP) organised by Wallerstein under the auspices of the American Psychoanalytic Association. CAMP has been meeting for the entire decade of the nineties and considerable cross-group work has taken place, but the inability to secure the substantial necessary funding has till now precluded the full implementation of the programme. Nonetheless, Wallerstein's is the major direction of psychotherapy research at this turn of the millennium; it is what I call the 'fourth-generation' of therapy research. This fourth generation holds the possibilities for truly accelerating breakthroughs, methodological and substantive.

Wallerstein, R. (2000) 'The Generations of Psychotherapy Research: An Overview'. www.psychomedia.it/spr-it/artdoc/waller02.htm.

R. W.

OUTCOME STUDIES (CHILD PSYCHOTHERAPY) In the early 1990s, there was still relatively little outcome research into psychoanalytic psychotherapy with children and adolescents. In 1991 Barnett and others wrote an important review article in which they considered forty-three studies. Many were methodologically flawed, so that it was not possible to draw firm conclusions about outcome or effectiveness although many did report improvement in the young people concerned. Trowell, reviewing studies on individual and group psychotherapy, considered that there were specific issues and difficulties in evaluating outcome with children and adolescents. Co-morbidity was one such issue, since most children and young people do not present with pure disorders. Another issue involved criteria for judging effectiveness: should this rest on improvement in well-being; on perceived adjustment at home, at school or in the community; or on self-report?

Since then, more robust studies have been reported. Foremost among these is the large retrospective study undertaken at the Anna Freud Clinic in London. Children ranged in age from three to eighteen years; 75% were seen four to five times weekly, the remainder once or twice weekly; the average duration of treatment was two years, and the number of cases considered was 763. Emotionally disordered children in treatment for at least six months improved. Phobic and anxious children did particularly well, whereas depressed children and those with obsessive-compulsive disorder did less well. High frequency treatment helped more severely disturbed children. Children with disruptive behaviour did less well and terminated early.

Lush, Boston and Grainger reviewed fostered or adopted children treated at the Tavistock Clinic in London. They showed that these severely deprived children could make good use of therapy. However, although fifty-one cases were referred for treatment, only thirty-eight took up the offer. The remaining cases were used as a comparison group. The therapist rated change, as did schools and outside social workers; there was also an external clinical rater. Compared to the outside agencies and the independent rater, more therapists rated improvement as less and stated that more therapy was needed. This finding has important implications for future research methods.

Currently, outcome studies are being actively undertaken and planned in a number of centres. At the Tavistock Clinic, Long and Trowell presented a study of the response to therapy of sexually abused girls, in which girls between six and fourteen years were randomly allocated to brief individual or group psychotherapy. Overall, these girls were very troubled, with high levels of depression and post-traumatic stress disorder. The co-morbidity was particularly high, and yet across the whole sample, the girls improved in terms of psychiatric disorders. Post-traumatic stress disorder responded more, and was less at follow-up, with individual therapy. The process of the individual therapy was also studied: it was found that working with the negative transference was particularly helpful, and that the girls experience the losses and disruptions they had suffered as being more troubling than the abuse itself. The work with the girls' parents and the work of supervisors of individual therapy have also been written up, with important lessons for clinicians and researchers.

Barnett, R. J., Doherty, J. P. and Fronmett, S. M. (1991) 'Special article: a review of child psychotherapy research since 1963'. *Journal of the American Academy of Child and Adolescent Psychiatry* 3: 1–14.

Fonagy, P. and Target, M. (1994) 'The efficacy of psychoanalysis for children with emotional disorders'.

Journal of the American Academy of Child and Adolescent Psychiatry 33: 361–71.
Long, J. and Trowell, J. (2001) 'Individual brief psychotherapy with sexually abused girls'. *Psychoanalytic Psychotherapy* 15: 39–59.
Lush, D., Boston, M. and Grainger, E. (1991) 'Evaluation of psychoanalytic psychotherapy with children: therapists' assessments and predictions'. *Psychoanalytic Psychotherapy* 5: 191–234.
Rushton, A. and Miles, G. (1999) 'A study of support services for current carers of sexually abused girls'. *Clinical Child Psychology and Psychiatry* 5.
Trowell, J. (1994) 'Individual and group psychotherapy' in M. Rutter, E. Taylor and L. Hersov (eds) *Child and Adolescent Psychiatry*. Oxford: Blackwell.

J. Tro.

OVERDETERMINATION Used in subtly different ways in Freud's writings. At times, the term is used interchangeably with multiple determination to mean that in order for a given event (e.g. a symptom or a particular dream content) to occur, multiple determinants must converge. The implication here is that each determinant by itself is necessary, but not sufficient, to bring about the event. At other times, the term is used to suggest that several motives and causes, each of which is separately sufficient to produce a given effect, converge to generate the event. At still other times, it refers to the multiple meanings of a given content as, for example, one sees in the operation of *condensation in dreams.

Following Freud, Lacan holds that all formations of the unconscious are necessarily over-determined. That is, to be admitted as such these formations, being compromise formations, must be constituted by at least a double meaning. Being structured like a language, these formations exhibit all of its characteristics including multiple, nodal and intersecting meanings.

M. Eag. / H. T.

P–Q

PAIN The avoidance of pain was the basis for the development of the complex human psyche. According to Freud, pleasure was nothing more than the perceived reduction of unpleasure (or pain). The psyche developed as a mechanism for reducing pain. Physical pain (like any other sensation) could become sexualised as in masochism, and evolve into mental pain in moral masochism.

See also: pleasure principle

J. A. Ber.

PARADOX Paradoxes are seemingly absurd or contradictory statements and were often used by Winnicott to draw attention to his understanding of the complexity of human development. They are presented in a way that calls upon the reader to explore both Winnicott's proposals and the reader's own responses to them. His interest in and use of paradox is often seen as playful, and as evidence of Winnicott's interest in play and *playing. Examples are his 1952 remark: 'There's no such thing as a baby' – the implication being that a baby cannot survive alone, and to be complete the study of a baby must also include a parallel study of its environment.

'It is a joy to be hidden, and disaster not to be found' – a 1963 statement emphasising that in order to be able to *communicate with others there must be an individuality which he conceived of as being an isolate, a permanently non-communicating core. Another is the title of his 1958 paper 'The Capacity to be Alone' – which he describes as arising out of the infant's developing ability to play in the presence of another.

In an important paper of 1949: 'Mind and the Psyche-Soma', he takes his own stance on the mind-body problem, studying a 1946 paradox from Jones: 'mind does not really exist as an entity', and develops his theory of mind as 'a special case of the functioning of the *psyche-soma'.

Jones, E. (1946) 'A valedictory address'. *International Journal of Psychoanalysis* 27.

Winnicott, D. W. (1949) 'Mind and its relation to the psyche-soma'. *British Journal of Medical Psychology* 27, 1954, and in *Collected Papers: Through Paediatrics to Psychoanalysis*. London: Tavistock, 1958.

Winnicott, D. W. [1952] (1958) 'Anxiety associated with insecurity' in *Collected Papers; Through Paediatrics to Psychoanalysis*. London: Tavistock.

Winnicott, D. W. [1963] (1965) 'Communicating and not communicating leading to a study of certain opposites' in *The Maturational Processes and the Facilitating Environment*. London: Hogarth Press.

Winnicott, D. W. [1958] (1965) 'The capacity to be alone' in *The Maturational Processes and the Facilitating Environment*. London: Hogarth Press.

J. Joh.

PARANOIA According to Freud, paranoia, which he viewed as a psychosis that had 'close affinity to dementia praecox', 'regularly arises in an attempt to fend off excessively strong homosexual impulses'. In his most extensive discussion of a case of paranoia, the 1911 *Schreber case, Freud writes that the longed-for person (of the same sex), becomes the persecutor and 'the content of the wishful fantasy became the content of the persecution'. The 'I love him' becomes transformed into 'I hate him' which, in turn, becomes transformed into 'he hates (persecutes) me'. Thus, one can see that projection of internal feelings on to external others is a key mechanism in paranoia. Other aspects of paranoia include fixation at a narcissistic level of object choice – one chooses an object anatomically similar to oneself. Freud viewed paranoia as one of the 'narcissistic neuroses' not amenable to psychoanalytic treatment.

For Lacan, paranoia is the basic model for psychosis. Starting with the Aimée case in his medical thesis of 1932, a case of erotomania which Lacan diagnosed as a self-punishing paranoia, and continuing with his account of the Papin sisters, Lacan determined a central function at play in the operations of paranoia. In paranoia the Imaginary dialectic which is initiated in the mirror stage is allowed to progress to its end point of destruction of the 'other-like-oneself', as the double in the mirror, without any limitation by the Symbolic dimension. By 1955, in his seminar on psychosis, Lacan had come to formulate these themes within the context of his elaboration of Freud's notion of foreclosure (*Verwerfung*) as the mechanism generative of psychosis.

See also: projection

Freud, S. (1911) *Psycho-analytic Notes on an Autobiographical Account of a Case of Paranoia (Dementia Paranoides)*. S. E. 12. London: Hogarth Press.

Lothane, Z. (1992) *In Defense of Schreber. Soul Murder in Psychiatry*. Hillsdale, NJ: The Analytic Press.

M. Eag. / D. Cre.

PARANOID SCHIZOID POSITION Klein formulated the paranoid schizoid position as a group of related anxieties, defences and object relations which commence from the very beginning of life. By using the term 'position' Klein sought to convey that this exists as a dynamic organising and relational configuration within the mind, rather than as a strict developmental phase, as conceived by classical Freudian theory, the linearity of which Klein had previously critiqued. Certain features are characteristic of thinking in the paranoid schizoid position and are particularly dominant in the infant between birth and three months of age. During this period destructive impulses and persecutory anxiety (deriving from both internal and external sources) are at their height. The working of the death instinct within gives rise to fear of annihilation, which is the primary cause of persecutory anxiety. The first external anxiety situation can be found in the experience of birth. The pain of birth and the loss of the intrauterine state are felt by the infant as an attack by hostile forces. In the infant's destructive phantasies, the breast is bitten, torn up, devoured, and annihilated, actions which the infant fears will result in retaliation in kind. As urethral and anal sadistic impulses gain strength, the infant fears poisonous and explosive attacks from the breast as well.

The details of infantile sadistic phantasies determine the subjective experience of the phobic content of internal and external persecutors, primarily of the retaliating (bad) breast. Since the phantasied attacks on the object are fundamentally influenced by greed, the fear of the object's greed is an essential element in persecutory anxiety. The infant feels the bad breast will devour it in the same greedy way as he or she desires to devour it. In these circumstances, the frustrating bad object is felt to be a terrifying persecutor, and the good object is turned into an 'ideal' object as a counterphobic ally and as an object which should fulfil greedy desire for unlimited, immediate and everlasting gratification. The stronger the infant's persecutory anxiety, the greater the need to increase the power of the all-gratifying perfect and inexhaustible object.

The coexistence of persecutory anxiety and the desire for unlimited gratification contribute to the infant's feeling that both an ideal breast and a dangerous devouring breast exist, which are largely kept apart from each other in the infant's mind. *Splitting, *omnipotence, *idealisation, *denial, and control of internal and external objects, typically through *projective identification, are dominant at this stage. While in some ways these defences impede the path of integration, they are essential for the whole development of the ego, for they relieve the infant's anxieties again and again and importantly aid differentiation of (for example) good from bad. This temporary security is achieved predominantly by the persecutory object being kept apart from the good one. The presence in the mind of the good object enables the ego to maintain at times a feeling of protection against the persecuting object because it is believed to have replaced it (as in *wish-fulfilling hallucinations).

Klein, M. (1946) 'Notes on some schizoid mechanisms'. *International Journal of Psychoanalysis* 27. Also in *Envy and Gratitude*. London: Hogarth Press, 1975.

Klein, M. (1952) 'Some theoretical conclusions regarding the emotional life of the infant' in *Developments in Psycho-Analysis* with P. Heimann, S. Isaacs and J. Riviere. London: Hogarth Press. Also in *Envy and Gratitude*. London: Hogarth Press, 1975.

J. A.

PARAPHILIAS Disorders of sexual preference, mainly described in men, and characterised by recurrent, intense sexually arousing fantasies, urges or behaviours (*philia*, the love of; *para*, the beyond or irregular) which lead to clinically significant distress or impairment in social, occupational, or other areas of functioning. They include exhibitionism (exposure of genitals to a stranger), *fetishism (use of non-living objects – the *fetish), frotteurism (touching and rubbing against a non-consenting person), paedophilia (sexual activity with a prepubescent child), sexual *masochism (receiving humiliation or suffering), sexual sadism (inflicting humiliation or suffering), transvestic fetishism (cross-dressing) and voyeurism (observing unsuspecting individuals who are naked, disrobing or engaging in sexual activity). Less frequently encountered paraphilias include telephone scatologia (obscene phone calls), necrophilia (corpses), partialism (exclusive focus on part of body), zoophilia (animals), coprophilia (faeces), klismaphilia (enemas), and urophilia (urine). Once called sexual deviations or perversions, paraphilias are defined by the social and moral climate of the time. Thus, homosexuality, which previously was considered a disorder of sexual preference, is no longer considered to be so as a result of social and cultural pressures, and fellatio and anal intercourse are no longer illegal in heterosexual relationships. In 1919 in 'A child is being beaten', Freud saw perversions as defending against the castration anxiety aroused by oedipal wishes, and against attacks from the super-ego with its oedipal origins. Thus, perversions were viewed as a defence against instinctual derivatives. Disavowal, splitting of the ego, aggression, regression, and sadistic control of the object have all been posited as perverse defences. The older psychoanalytic literature overwhelmingly ascribes many cases of perversions to maternal overstimulation and absent and distant fathers – a view reactivated by *Lacan's wordplay on *père-version*. Some modern psychoanalytic thinking, for example Steiner, has reclaimed the term *perversion, concentrating on its phenomenology rather than rigid categories. Parsons reports a shift in psychoanalytic literature since Freud to a view that perversions are a defence against object relatedness. He argues that a common unifying feature is the blocking of normal intimacy, so that the disorder is a compromise between total isolation and a mutual adult genital relationship. In the sado-masochistic dynamic common to all paraphilias, obvious or not, the relationship is to a part, rather than a whole object but this may be the only way an individual can achieve any form of intimacy at all.

American Psychiatric Association (1994) *Diagnostic and Statistical Manual of Mental Disorders (DSM-IV)*. Fourth edition. Washington, DC: American Psychiatric Association.

Parsons, M. (2000) 'Sexuality and perversion a hundred years on: discovering what Freud discovered'. *International Journal of Psychoanalysis* 81: 37–49.

Steiner, J. (1993) *Psychic Retreats*. New Library of Psychoanalysis. London: Routledge.

J. W.

PARAPHRENIA Freud used the term as synonymous with Kraepelin's dementia praecox, and *Bleuler's schizophrenia. Paraphrenics, according to Freud, are characterised by 1) a turning away of libido from the external world; 2) megalomania, which results from the fact that the libido that has been drawn from the external world is then directed to the ego. Paraphrenics, thus, suffer from extreme *narcissism.

Freud, S. (1914) *On Narcissism: An Introduction*. S. E. 14. London: Hogarth Press.

M. Eag.

PARAPRAXIS Literally, faulty action, also called failed action and lapsus, or the famous 'Freudian *slip', such as going to the wrong address, speaking the wrong name, or making a wrong statement. Such 'mistakes', Freud explained, were not mere accidents but determined and meaningful acts due to unconscious desires, motives, and conflicts.

Z. L.

PARENT-INFANT PSYCHOTHERAPY A form of treatment used to help resolve difficulties arising between parents and infants. These may manifest as disorders relating to sleeping, eating, etc., but are understood as often arising from some distortion within the relationship between the parents and their infant.

Although the approach can be seen as having its roots in the mother-baby consultations described by *Winnicott in 'The observation of infants in a set situation', the seminal paper for this kind of work is that of Fraiberg and her colleagues called 'Ghosts in the nursery: a psychoanalytic approach to the problems of impaired infant-mother relationships'. In that paper she introduced the concept of the ghosts that may haunt the nursery: that is, the way in which parents may see their infants not as individuals in their own right but rather through the distorting lens of their own early childhood experiences. She also suggested that when this takes a pathological form it can only be relieved by enabling the parents to remember those childhood experiences with the appropriate feelings.

Fraiberg's ideas have been widely adopted and strongly inform the brief therapy models subsequently developed by Cramer and colleagues in Geneva and at the Tavistock Clinic, London although these programmes do not necessarily target the very deprived client group that Fraiberg described.

A cardinal principle of this kind of therapy is that it addresses the relationship between parents and infant rather than any single member of the family. The infant's presence in the consultation is seen as a powerful factor, in part as a prompt to the parents' associations but also because it allows the therapist to observe the relationship at first hand. Indeed, the technique of *infant observation has had a powerful influence on this approach. In practice most interventions rely heavily on detailed observation of the transactions between parent and infant. Sometimes this involves encouraging the parents to observe their children more closely (as in the Watch Wait and Wonder technique described by Muir), or it may involve close observation of the parent-infant interaction by the therapist to identify what Cramer has called 'symptomatic interactive sequences' that highlight the key conflict in the relationship. Less common is the use of the observation method as a therapeutic intervention in itself.

Fraiberg's paper can be seen as having inaugurated the discipline of infant mental health as a specific field, and since its appearance there have been major developments including the establishment of the World Association for Infant Mental Health, with its own dedicated journal. Most of the work in this area continues to be primarily psychoanalytic in orientation but with considerable, and increasing, contributions now being made from *attachment theory. The contributions of developmentalists such as Stern and Trevarthen have been very influential as also, increasingly, the work of researchers such as Schore looking at early brain development. This latter work has tended to emphasise the importance of early influences on development affecting the actual structure of the infant brain, and thereby reinforce the case for early intervention.

The great strength of parent-infant psychotherapy is that it has the potential to reverse pathological developments before they have become entrenched and more fully internalised. This should obviate the need for more lengthy treatments at a later stage. The appeal of this approach has led to the establishment of a number of training programmes dedicated to parent-infant work, mostly dominated by a psychoanalytic paradigm and many of them making use of some form of infant observation as a key part of the training.

Cramer, B. (1995) 'Short-term dynamic psychotherapy for infants and their parents'. *Child and Adolescent Psychiatric Clinics of North America* 4(3): 649–60.

Daws, D. (1989) *Through the Night*. London: Free Association Books.

Fraiberg, S., Adelson, E. and Shapiro, V. [1975] (1980) 'Ghosts in the nursery: a psychoanalytic approach to the problems of impaired infant-mother relationships' in S. Fraiberg (ed.) *Clinical Studies in Infant Mental Health*. London: Tavistock.

Muir, E. (1992) 'Watching, waiting, and wondering: applying psychoanalytic principles to mother-infant intervention'. *Infant Mental Health Journal* 13(4): 319–28.

Schore, A. N. (1994) *Affect Regulation and the Origin of the Self*. Hillsdale, NJ: Erlbaum.

Stern, D. (1995) *The Motherhood Constellation*. New York: Basic Books.

P. B.

PART OBJECT (KLEIN) Klein believed that the infant's first experiences of feeding and of the mother's presence initiate a particular type of object relationship to her. She postulated that both oral-libidinal and oral-sadistic impulses are directed from the beginning of life not toward the mother *per se* (a whole object) but rather toward the mother's breast (a part-object) and the functions that are associated with it.

Klein, M. (1952) 'Some theoretical conclusions regarding the emotional life of the infant' in

Developments in Psycho-Analysis with P. Heimann, S. Isaacs and J. Riviere. London: Hogarth Press. Also in *Envy and Gratitude*. London: Hogarth Press, 1975 (111).

S. A.

PART OBJECT (LACAN): OBJECT A Lacan called the object 'object a' or 'little object a'. He related it at first to the Imaginary other, later he considered it to be a leftover from the signifying operation. As such it became the complement of the barred subject, the counterpart of its lack-in-being. It is the lost object and it functions as the vector of desire, as support for the phantasy. Its prototype is found in Freud's (pregenital) objects (breast, faeces), separated parts of the body which form a series that is ordered by castration or separating out. Lacan adds to these Freudian objects two more: the *look and the *voice. Contrary to the usual trend in formulating the object, he elevates the object a to a powerful position, namely as the actual cause of desire rather than as something that will merely satisfy desire. The object a bears on the ultimate part of the subject; it is the soul of his or her phantasy, the incarnation of his or her look, the receptor of his or her being. Approaching his place as object in the desire of the *Other opens up to the subject in analytical treatment a transition to the position of analyst. The object is without an image and beyond the signifier, inscribing the Real into the heart of the analytical discourse.

See also: partial object; subject

G. Waj.

PARTIAL DRIVE A concept on the border between the organic and the psychical. It is a psychic representation of an organic impulse. It is neither instinctual nor innate, and it responds to a constant stimulation which is produced by the excitation of an erogenous zone. It searches for satisfaction by means of a contingent object.

Partial (or component) drives are unified by *forms of organisation of the drive. The Anglo-Saxon literature tends to distinguish drives according to their *source, rather than according to the forms of organisation that are found in Freud's work. Freud takes orality to be a form of organisation determined by the drive's having an *aim which is a cannibalistic incorporation of the object. Anality is a form of organisation that is ambivalent in terms of taking in or expelling the object, and the phallic function is a form of organisation that recognises loss and the subsequent retrieval that can take place in relation to the object.

S. Ten. / B. B.

PARTIAL LOVE see **LOVE, PARTIAL**

PARTIAL OBJECT (LACAN) For Lacan every object is partial not in relation to a totality but in relation to the drives involved: oral, anal, invocative, scopic. These four drives build their circuit around four objects which are by definition partial ones (the breast, excrement, the voice, and the gaze). These objects cause desire and the division of the subject.

See also: drive; drive, partial

D. Bas.

PARTICIPANT OBSERVATION Participant observation is a term used by *Sullivan to characterise the analyst as both an observer and a participant in the analytic process. This view challenges the notion of classical analysis where the analyst is to be a blank screen, a neutral object which serves as a template for the patient's projections. By defining the task of the analyst as being that of an observer and a participant, Sullivan describes psychoanalysis in terms of a two-person psychology where analyst and analyst actively interact with one another. The analyst cannot avoid having an impact on the analytic process and any given analytic understanding is therefore co-constructed by analyst and patient. The analytic experience needs to be a dyadic process where analyst and patient study the interpersonal processes which characterise their interaction collaboratively.

Interpersonal psychoanalysts have gradually expanded the concept of participant observation to include not only data from the patient's narrative and from the interactive process, but also from their own *countertransference experiences varies. *Fromm for instance criticised Sullivan for not going far enough in stressing the analyst's participatory role in the analytic work and thought of the analyst as an 'observant participant'. Other interpersonalists tend to be less specific in terms of articulating and explicating their countertransference reactions to the patient. But regardless of whether the emphasis is on the analyst as a participant observer or as an observing participant, viewing the analytic venture as a shared exploration of the process between analysis and analyst puts analyst and analyst and on a level playing field. It acknowledges that each is affected by the other and that interpretive truths or understandings derive from consensus, with interpretive authority shared by analyst and analysis.

Fiscalini, J. (1995) 'Transference and countertransference as interpersonal phenomena' in M. Lionells, J. Fiscalini, C. H. Mann and D. B. Stern (eds) *Handbook of Interpersonal Psychoanalysis.* Hillsdale, NJ: The Analytic Press.

Fromm, E., Suzuki, D. T. and DeMartino, R. (1960) *Zen Buddhism and Psychoanalysis.* New York: Harper & Row.

Sullivan, H. S. (1949) 'The theory of anxiety and the nature of psychotherapy'. *Psychiatry* 12.

C. M.

PARTICIPATION MYSTIQUE A term *Jung adopted from anthropologist Levy-Bruhl referring to a primitive mentality in which subjective perception is experienced as intermingled with the objective world: one is unable to distinguish oneself consciously from the objects of one's awareness, intertwining self and world in a single fabric. Jung used this term clinically to refer to transferential experiences in which one partner exerts an almost magical or absolute influence over the other to the point of felt identity. Dissolved through withdrawing *projection and establishing a conscious integrity of the *ego, participation mystique has often been compared with *projective identification in object relations theory.

J. Mar.

PASS, THE The Pass, invented by Lacan in 1967, represents a procedure to recognise a grade of analyst within the psychoanalytic institution, namely those who are able to testify to crucial problems concerning the end of analysis. It also provides a means to examine and clarify the subjective effects of analysis viewed as an experience of truth via the testimony of those who have concluded (rather than terminated) an analysis. Finally it seeks to address the question of what a didactic analysis is, in terms of demonstrating the presence of the desire of the analyst. In practical terms the person doing The Pass describes their experience of analysis to two others who act as witnesses, and who, in turn, transmit this experience to a Cartel of the Pass, which judges the transmitted experience. While some Lacanian groups endorse and have built on this procedure (e.g. The Pass to enter the School) others have been critical of its effects, and have ultimately rejected this procedure.

A. R.

PASSAGE A L'ACTE Lacan proposed a structural distinction between *acting out and *passage à l'acte*. While the former implies that the subject 'acts out' because he or she is subjected to a puzzling question incarnated by *object a, the latter is described as an attempted solution, a flight from the scene of *phantasy, which aims at a final solution, a 'new being'. Lacan discussed the suicide attempt in Freud's famous case of a young homosexual girl, Dora, and considered both this, and Dora's slapping of Herr K's face when he told her that 'his wife doesn't count for him', as examples of *passage à l'acte*.

F. S.

PASSION Psychoanalytic experience discovers in passion not only its triggering by the image of the object of desire, but also its linguistic foundations. In order to define this more precisely, Lacan chose to use this term to recuperate the meaning of the Freudian term 'affect', thereby freeing it from traditional biological readings. Affect is not an expression of the fluctuations of a vital energy, but rather the translation into the Imaginary of the body of the way in which one is affected by the words of the Other. Although these signifying marks may be codified by culture, they remain, within the framework of subjective experience, dependent upon the unique way in which each of us mobilises the drive in speech.

See also: affect; drive; jouissance; other; real

M. V.

PATERNAL METAPHOR The Freudian Oedipus myth is insufficient to account for the function of the father in an unconscious that is 'structured like a language'. Lacan therefore utilised Saussure's formula for linguistic metaphor in order to accentuate the effect of the father as name, or as a prohibition, a 'no' (*le non[m] du père*), on the desire of the mother, henceforth correlated with the phallus. The paternal metaphor is the substitute of the name-of-the-father for the desire of the mother.

J. D. M.

PATHOLOGICAL ACCOMMODATION According to Brandchaft and *intersubjectivity theory, when the psychological organisation of the parent cannot sufficiently accommodate to the changing, phase-specific needs of the developing child, then the more malleable and vulnerable psychological structure of the child will accommodate to the archaic needs of the parent, in order to maintain the needed tie at whatever cost to authentic self experience. A template forms, largely beyond the corrective influence of reflective self-awareness and/or relational experience, and continues to shape the conditions which the child perceives as promoting safety or danger. It predetermines what the child expects and believes is required of it, positively and negatively, in ensuing relational encounters including that with the analyst. The ever-present threat of self-endangerment and unbearable pain as a consequence of the loss of connectedness constitutes a major source of resistance to analysis and to fundamental change in general. This requires systematic *working through of contextual determinants, developmentally and with respect to their inevitable replications in analysis, that continue to support, maintain and restore the pathological structures.

Atwood, G. and Stolorow, R. (1984) *Structures of Subjectivity: Explorations in Psychoanalytic Phenomenology*. Hillsdale, NJ: The Analytic Press.

R. S.

PENIS ENVY The desire for a penis expressed by a girl. Seen as a motivating factor in the development of *femininity, whereby the little girl notices that like her mother, she lacks a penis, and wishes she had one. This serves the dual purpose of enabling her to turn her desire away from the mother, whom she blames for allowing her to be relegated to the category of castrated beings (in the girl's phantasy), and of facilitating an orientation towards her father, and beyond him, towards men, as symbolically able to provide her with a penis substitute, i.e. a child.

J. B.

PERCEPTION In early Freud the registration of currently present external or internal stimuli by the psychic apparatus. In metapsychological terms, consciousness is a function of the agency of perception-consciousness. In topographical terms, perception-consciousness is peripheral to the preconscious and the unconscious. In his 1895 model, Freud attributed perception and consciousness to two different systems of neurons.

Perception transforms sensory messages into mental representations of external reality. It is neither passive nor completely reflective of reality. The environment is actively scanned for desired and/or anxiety-arousing objects. Unconscious bias and defence can creep into this process.

Lacan emphasises the primacy of perception as a form of being in the world prior to consciousness and subjectivity. The perceptual process is governed by the pleasure principle and tends towards hallucinated wish fulfilment, the failure of which establishes, via ego inhibition, the reality principle. The structuring of this experience is brought about on the basis of the signifying chain, which for Lacan is fundamental to understanding the nature of hallucination.

See also: attention; conscious; preconscious; psychic apparatus; unconscious

Freud, S. (1923) *The Ego and the Id*. S. E. 19. London: Hogarth Press.

J. Wei. / E. K. / A. R.

PERSONA From the Latin, meaning 'mask'. Social adaptation and role expectation require the development of provisional identities to present to the world, e.g. parent to child, employer to employee, official to private citizen. *Jung's concept of the persona acknowledges that different social contexts oblige different responses. Learning to employ a provisional identity, or persona, appropriate to a given situation is a function of socialisation and maturation. An individual who believes he or she is only the persona will suffer a loss of identity when that provisional role is ended. An individual too identified with the persona is said to be *inflated, and his or her unconscious will react in compensatory ways through the *shadow.

J. Hol.

PERSONALITY see **CHARACTER**

PERU The first reference to psychoanalysis in Peru is found in a thesis submitted in 1914. The following year the psychiatrist Honorio Delgado published an article on the new discipline in the major newspaper of the time and in 1919 he published the first book on the subject in Spanish. Freud mentioned Delgado in his works and his articles were published in the main psychoanalytic journals. Paradoxically, in 1927, at a time when he started to become critical of the movement, he was appointed member of the British Psychoanalytical Society, took part in the Innsbruck Congress and visited Freud for the second time in Semmering.

In the 1920s, psychoanalysis was included in courses of psychiatry and cultural magazines published translations of texts by Freud and articles by Peruvian academics on the subject. One of them devoted an entire issue to Freud and psychoanalysis in 1926. José Carlos Mariátegui, Peru's most outstanding thinker of the twentieth century and founder of the Communist Party in Peru, devoted an article and a chapter of one of his works to psychoanalysis, and in 1929, one year before his early death, he published a literary essay clearly inspired by psychoanalysis.

By the early 1930s, Delgado was no longer an exponent but had become an overt detractor of psychoanalysis and a major obstacle for the expansion of the psychoanalytic movement. Interest in the discipline practically disappeared and was not to reappear until the 1950s, promoted by Carlos Alberto Seguín. As director of the first psychiatric service in a general hospital in Latin America he had a marked influence: 90% of the members of the Peruvian Psychoanalytic Society who began in psychiatry had been his students.

1969 saw the return to Peru of Saúl Peña, trained in England, who initiated a period of active work in clinical and university circles, to be consolidated with the return of Carlos Crisanto in 1973 and Max Hernández in 1974, both also trained in the British Society. The Peruvian Psychoanalytic Society (SPP) was recognised as a Component Society of the IPA in 1987, and currently has forty-six members. Training at the Peruvian Institute is plural in nature, with influence from a variety of schools (British, American, Argentinean, French and Frankfurt), disseminated by Peruvian psychoanalysts trained abroad and by foreigners linked to the SPP.

The SPP has organised and sponsored numerous psychoanalytical congresses and successful international and interdisciplinary events which have enhanced the presence of psychoanalysis in society. Some of Peru's most outstanding psychoanalysts include Max Hernández, an influential Peruvian intellectual figure, whose contributions to psychoanalysis have been internationally recognised with the Sigourney prize; Saúl Peña, SPP Honorary President and former president of the Latin American Psychoanalytic Federation; César Rodríguez Rabanal, advisor to Peru's president, with major contributions to work with marginalised and dispossessed populations; Moisés Lemlij, currently a candidate for the presidency of the IPA; and Álvaro Rey de Castro, current IPA vice-president.

Besides the SPP, there are various psychoanalytic institutions in Peru, both in the clinical area and in the application of psychoanalysis to the arts, education, social sciences and humanities. The most prestigious private university offers a Master's degree in Theoretical Studies in Psychoanalysis. A large number of books have been published; and the Peruvian Psychoanalytic Library and the SIDEA Publishing Fund, both directed by Moisés Lemlij, have published more than forty of them over the last ten years. The SPP publishes an annual journal.

M. L.

PERVERSION Deviations from the normal aims or objects of the sexual drive were described as perversions by Freud. Deviations from the normal in terms of object choice included animals, children, and *fetishes. Deviations from the norm in terms of the aims of the drive included stopping at some intermediate stage (component drive) instead of going on to genital intercourse. It included fellatio, sadomasochism, voyeurism and exhibitionism. For *homosexuals who had attained the genital level but who chose a same sex partner, Freud suggested the term 'inversion'.

For Lacan perversion is defined by a particular clinical structure rather than by the presence of any particular sexual behaviour. He distinguished it from other clinical structures by the exclusive and fundamental operation in it of *disavowal. This disavowal of the mother's castration means that while the pervert knows about castration he denies it. Rather than symbolise the lack in the Other, the pervert identifies with the object, the Symbolic phallus, which would complete or mask her loss, the Imaginary object of her desire. At the level of the drive, the perverse subject devotes his activity to assuming the position of the instrument of the Other's enjoyment.

See also: paraphrenia

J. A. Ber. / H. T.

PFISTER, OSKAR (1873–1956) Oskar Pfister fits none of the stereotypes associated with Freud's loyal followers. As a Swiss pastor in Zurich he profoundly disagreed with Freud's most famous stated outlook on religion. In response to *The Future of an Illusion* Pfister published in 1928 a piece of comparable length: *The Illusion of a Future*. Pfister, also differing from Freud on art and morality, found Freud's approach to ethics, philosophy, as well (implicitly) as the practice of psychotherapy to be inadequate. Pfister's essay appeared first in Freud's journal *Imago*, and was an unusual sign of Freud's willingness to tolerate disagreement within his movement.

When the pre-World War I difficulties between Jung and Freud broke out, Pfister was exceptional as a Swiss in not resigning along with Jung. Freud must have appreciated this sign of Pfister's loyalty. Following World War I Pfister and Dr Emil Oberholzer started a new Swiss Society for Psychoanalysis which was affiliated with the International Psychoanalytic Association. After Freud published *The Question of Lay Analysis* Oberholzer left to found an exclusively medical group; once again Pfister stuck with Freud's side, and Oberholzer's Swiss Medical Society for Psychoanalysis did not survive World War II.

The 1963 edition of the letters (1909–39) between Freud and Pfister has, like all such early collections of Freud's correspondences, been severely cut, and someday a new volume of the complete exchanges may be undertaken. Until then it is necessary to be tentative about the relationship between Freud and Pfister. It will be particularly interesting to be able to read what they wrote each other about clinical cases. We know, for example, that Pfister sent one American patient to Freud whom Freud diagnosed as schizophrenic yet Freud treated him in analysis for a number of years; that patient was also seen by some famous European psychiatrists, and ended his days living in a private mental hospital outside Boston. We also know that in addition to what Pfister had to say on the subject of religion, he was prolific as a populariser of psychoanalysis, specialising in the implications of Freud's work for early education.

By now psychoanalysis has had a transforming impact on what clergymen know about human psychology, and Pfister has to be credited with having taken a leading role in legitimising this whole area. Whatever eighteenth-century Enlightenment prejudices against priests Freud may have had, he could somehow make an exception when it came to Pfister. Pfister's critique of *The Future of an Illusion* is not well enough known, even though by now many of our contemporary psychoanalytic thinkers would be inclined to take a favourable view of the innovations that Pfister was attempting to make then. While Freud thought he was overturning many of the most central features to Western ethics, Pfister was trying to show how psychoanalysis could be used to breathe new life into some of the oldest values in Christian thought. Freud's willingness to maintain his tie to Pfister shows a different side to Freud's convictions as expressed in *The Future of an Illusion*. And the debate over religion between Freud and Pfister retains its vitality today.

Freud, S. (1963) *Psychoanalysis and Faith: Dialogues with the Reverend Oskar Pfister.* New York: Basic Books.

P. R.

PHALLUS To be distinguished from the penis as a real biological organ, although this latter serves as a vehicle for presenting an image of what Real the Symbolic is lacking. The phallus is initially conceived as a purely Imaginary object, the third player in the supposed dual relation between child and mother, where it is imagined she goes, namely that what she desires beyond the child. The phallus is, therefore, what the child strives to become. This position must be renounced by the child in order to attain a place in the *Symbolic, the register which is made possible only by the lack of an object, represented by the notion of castration. This passage from Imaginary to Symbolic is co-extensive with the passage from identity to sexed identity. Thus, by renouncing the Imaginary phallus, the Symbolic phallus can be had. Being the phallus is given up, and having the phallus is made possible, at least now and again. From this Symbolic phallus is derived the notion of the phallus as the signifier without a signified, the idea of a unique signifier that orders and generates meaning, the signified which is the whole of signification itself. The psychoses bear witness to this, where 'being the phallus' allows one access to the whole truth, to certainty, grandiosity and omnipotence.

H. T.

PHALLUS, PRIMACY OF THE Freud introduced the notion of the primacy of the phallus in 1923. His problem was to give an account of how boys and girls come to assume a psychic position in relation to their physiological sex. The phallic organisation dominates the final phase of *infantile sexuality, and its primacy consists in its retrospectively reorganising the child's previous understanding of itself and its relations to others. It is brought about by the assumption that there is a single sexual organ – common to men and women – and that there can be either restitution or recompense for its loss or threatened loss. This phallic form of organisation is threatened, according to Freud, in different ways in girls and boys. *Castration threats operate on the boy with the force of logic; conflict between castration and phallic functioning in the girl appears earlier, is more intricate, and is formulated more in terms of compensation.

V. B. / B. B.

PHANTASY (FREUD) In Freud's first writings, this term mostly refers to daydreaming activities in hysterical patients, with a combination of erotic and ambitious contents leading to acute symptomatology (especially hysterical fits, surges of anxiety) or enduring symptoms. Some phantasies are described as utterly conscious and others as unconscious and forbidden; *phantasierung* is typically connected to family *myths (Lacanian) and Oedipal contents and plays a paramount role in the representation of the various versions of sexuality at each stage (*oral, *anal, phallic). These, to some extent, imply fears of retaliation or punishment (especially castration threats) leading to repression and symptom-formation. In his 1911 'Two Principles of Mental Functioning', Freud distinguished between a primary principle remaining closely determined by sexual phantasies whereas the secondary is submitted to the *reality principle and the acceptance of frustration. As he elaborated his second topography, Freud became more sensitive to the masochistic content of unconscious phantasies, suggesting in 'A child is being beaten' that a significant proportion of these fantasies had such contents, the enduring fascination with which may be explained in view of Freud's later death drive. Whereas his first elaborations on phantasies hardly distinguished them from the structure of dream contents and the splitting of the subject between several dream-characters, his later research insisted on the way phantasies connect the subject with a traumatic object related with the *death drive.

See also: imagination

F. S.

PHANTASY, UNCONSCIOUS (KLEIN) Klein expanded Freud's concept of fantasy into what she thought was the primary content of unconscious mental processes. Unconscious phantasies (the 'ph' spelling denoting their unconsciousness) are the mental representation of libidinal and destructive impulses or instincts and they accompany gratification as well as frustration. They also become elaborated into defences, as well as into wish-fulfilling thoughts. Unconscious phantasies are present in rudimentary form from birth onwards, being active in the mind before language has developed. The earliest phantasies spring from bodily impulses and are interwoven with bodily sensations and affects. These sensations are experienced as part of a relationship to an object which, in phantasy, carries an intentionality to produce this sensation. Through projective and introjective mechanisms a phantasised internal world peopled by internal objects is constructed. The concept of unconscious phantasy became a central scientific topic of the Controversial Discussions at the British Society when it was most clearly described by Susan Isaacs as 'the mental corollary, the psychic representative of instinct'. Unconscious phantasies exert a continuous influence throughout life, though they are always inferred rather than observed as such.

Hinshelwood, R. D. (1989) *A Dictionary of Kleinian Thought*. London: Free Association Books.
Isaacs, S. [1948] (1989) 'The nature and function of phantasy' in J. Riviere (ed.) *Developments in Psychoanalysis*. London: Karnac Books, 67–121.
King, P. and Steiner, R. (eds) (1991) *The Freud/Klein Controversies, 1941–1945*. London: Routledge.
Segal, H. (1997) 'Phantasy and reality' in J. Steiner (ed.) *Psychoanalysis, Literature and War*. The New Library of Psychoanalysis. London and New York: Routledge.
Spillius, E. B. (2001) 'Freud and Klein on the concept of phantasy' in C. Bronstein (ed.) *Kleinian Theory: A Contemporary Perspective*. London: Whurr.

C. Bro.

PHANTASY (LACAN) Lacan theorised phantasy as a singular structure present in the subject and not as a form of daydream. It is obtained as a residue at the end of an analysis and functions as a fundamental axiom, setting in place the presuppositions underlying a person's relations to others. There are three dimensions to the term. Lacan emphasises its Imaginary aspect in which it functions as an obstacle to the *Symbolic. Under this aspect, phantasy concerns Imaginary scenes which leave the ego exultant. The Symbolic dimension appears when the phantasy can be (fully) represented by a phrase (which according to Freud is always possible). However, the fundamental dimension of the phantasy is the *Real. Phantasy brings into relation two heterogeneous elements: the symbolically constituted subject and (desire of) the *object a. This latter acquires a Real value as the impossible primordially lost object of *jouissance. Grasping the real function of the phantasy requires a logical conversion which determines the end of analysis.

S. Ten.

PHANTASY SELFOBJECTS AND PHANTASY SELFOBJECT RELATIONSHIPS What self psychologists call selfobject 'transference' is not *transference in the traditional psychoanalytic sense but the patient's experience of the analyst as someone with whom a different or even new relationship might unfold or is already unfolding. Elaborations in phantasy – both consciously and unconsciously – of images of significant others variously contribute to their being experienced as selfobjects, and these images become integral components of selfobject relationships to varying degrees. The term 'phantasy selfobject', introduced by Bacal, designates the phantasy of the other as a sustaining figure. Phantasy selfobject relationships can become survival tools for some people when an adequate selfobject milieu has been unavailable, in particular, when they have been chronically exposed to significant trauma or deprivation. In such situations, the capacity of the child – and then the patient – for creative illusion (see *Winnicott), will be more significant in determining selfobject experience than the *optimal responsiveness of caretakers. The phantasy component of the selfobject is similar to the exercise of an idealising capacity but is based to a minimal degree on idealisable aspects of the object. The experience of a selfobject relationship with the analyst that is determined predominantly by phantasy will be especially susceptible to disruption. While the analyst's setting, responses, and personal characteristics undoubtedly trigger phantasy selfobject experiences, they are essentially the patient's constructions, and he uses them in an attempt to fashion a self-sustaining *selfobject relationship with the analyst. It is important that the analyst accept this state of affairs as long as the patient needs it, rather than interpreting it as a *defence.

See also: curative fantasy

Bacal, H. A. (1981) 'Notes on some therapeutic challenges in the analysis of severely regressed patients'. *Psychoanalytic Inquiry* 1: 29–56 (see esp. 36).
Bacal, H. A. (1985) 'Optimal responsiveness and the therapeutic process' in *Optimal Responsiveness: How*

Therapists Heal Their Patients. New York: Jason Aronson, 3–34.
Bacal, H. A. (1990) 'The elements of a corrective selfobject experience'. *Psychoanalytic Inquiry* 3: 347–72 (see esp. 366–9).
Bacal, H. A. (1994) 'The selfobject relationship in psychoanalytic treatment' in A. Goldberg (ed.) *A Decade of Progress: Progress in Self Psychology* 10. Hillsdale, NJ: The Analytic Press, 21–30.
Bacal, H. A. and Newman, K. M. (1990) *Theories of Object Relations: Bridges to Self Psychology.* New York: Columbia University Press.
Winnicott, D. W. (1951) 'Transitional objects and transitional phenomena' in *Collected Papers.* London: Tavistock, 229–42.

H. B.

PHENOMENOLOGY/PHENOMENOLOGICAL METHOD Although previously employed by *Hegel, it was Husserl's adoption of this term around 1900 that propelled it into becoming the designation of a philosophical school. As envisioned by Husserl, phenomenology is a method of philosophical inquiry that rejects the rationalist bias that has dominated Western thought since Plato in favour of a method of reflective attentiveness that discloses the individual's 'lived experience'. Loosely rooted in a sceptic device called *epoché*, Husserl's method entails the suspension of judgment while relying on the intuitive grasp of knowledge, free of presuppositions and intellectualisation. Sometimes depicted as the 'science of experience', the phenomenological method is rooted in *intentionality, an idea developed from Brentano who taught both Husserl and Freud. Intentionality represents an alternative to the representational theory of consciousness which holds that reality cannot be grasped directly because it is available through perceptions of reality that are 'represented' in the mind. Husserl countered that consciousness is not 'in' the 'mind' but rather conscious 'of' something other than itself (the intentional object), whether the object is a substance or a figment of imagination. Hence the phenomenological method relies on the description of phenomena as they are 'given' to consciousness, in their immediacy.

*Heidegger modified Husserl's conception of phenomenology because of (what he perceived as) Husserl's subjectivist tendencies. Whereas Husserl conceived of human beings as having been constituted by states of consciousness, Heidegger countered that consciousness is peripheral to the primacy of one's existence, that is, Being which cannot be reduced to one's consciousness of it. From this angle, one's state of mind is an 'effect' rather than a determinant of existence, including those aspects of existence that one is not conscious of. By shifting the centre of gravity from consciousness (psychology) to existence (ontology), Heidegger altered the subsequent direction of phenomenology, making it at once both personal and mysterious. One of the consequences of Heidegger's modification of Husserl's conception of phenomenology was its increased relevance to psychoanalysis. Whereas Husserl gave priority to a depiction of consciousness that was fundamentally alien to the psychoanalytic conception of the unconscious, Heidegger offered a way to conceptualise experience that could accommodate those aspects of one's existence that lie on the periphery of sentient awareness.

*Sartre, who subtitled his major philosophical work, *Being and Nothingness*, a 'phenomenological ontology', returns to an emphasis on consciousness but discards the 'transcendental' ego of Husserl. *Epoché*, for Sartre, is an impossibility because consciousness can never divorce itself from the world of which it is conscious. Nonetheless, Sartre does propose that something approximating 'pure reflection', or the simple presence of consciousness reflecting to the consciousness reflected on, is possible and indeed may be a precondition for change in existential analysis. Sartre's term in his later philosophy for experiences on the periphery of awareness, which may be opaque and blind and yet nonetheless intentional, is *le vécu* or lived experience. This is as close as he came to the Freudian unconscious.

Natanson, M. (1973) *Edmund Husserl: Philosopher of Infinite Tasks*. Evanston, Il: Northwestern University Press.

Safranski, R. (1998) *Martin Heidegger: Between Good and Evil*. Cambridge, MA: Harvard University Press.

M. G. T.

PHILOSOPHY (ANALYTIC) Many central issues in psychoanalytic theory have been tirelessly examined in philosophy since the time of Plato: the nature of the mind, thought, meaning, the self and personal identity; the relations between mind and body, reason and passion, thought and emotion; the explanation of irrationality; our knowledge of the external world, including other minds. Despite his dismissive remarks about it, Freud staked out a number of areas in philosophy. Hence Freud may himself be considered a philosopher; indeed he was a student of Franz Brentano at the University of Vienna, as well as a reader of *Schopenhauer and *Nietzsche.

There is, then, a wide border shared by the two disciplines. A number of philosophers in this century who are sympathetic to psychoanalysis have attempted to illumine old philosophic problems in the new light of psychoanalysis, or to mark out areas of study that only a combined understanding of philosophy and psychoanalysis might suggest, or to study psychoanalytic theses with philosophic rigour, or to reflect on the kind of self-knowledge that psychoanalytic therapy affords. Other philosophers have challenged Freud's claim that psychoanalysis is a science, or questioned its interpretive methods. Clearly there is neither room to discuss all these issues, nor any of them with the carefulness they deserve. I will attempt a brief and broad overview of those issues that circle around common themes: mind and body, reason and passion, thought and emotion, irrationality, the self, considering at the end the question of psychoanalysis as science.

Plato, Descartes, and Kant to name a few canonical philosophers, saw the mind, or reason – Plato's word is *nous* – as essentially timeless, incorruptible, immortal. Only in this earthly existence, which each of these philosophers contrasted with an existence of a categorically different sort, are mind and matter, mind and body, linked. In the view of Descartes, a view limned in some of Plato's dialogues as well, this mind-body link is what accounts for error. Passions, or emotions, originate with the body, and are in part responsible for both error and lapses of rationality.

There has been a consensus in philosophy for at least a century that Descartes was wrong in holding mind and body to be two different substances. Some philosophers, like some contemporary psychoanalysts, maintain one or another species of reductionism, according to which mental states are considered to be spin-offs from bodily or neurological states. Other philosophers maintain what might be called a dual language position: mind and body are not two distinct substances; indeed mind is not a thing or a substance at all. The only 'things' in the universe are material. Nevertheless the mentalistic or *intentionalist language of belief, desire, intention, emotion, and so on, is indispensable in our descriptions and explanations of human behaviour, and irreducible to a purely physicalist language.

What is the relation between emotion and thought? Clearly some such relation exists in the typical case. Sophie feels guilty because she believes she is responsible for her daughter's death; the *Rat Man, in Freud's case history, is afraid because he believes his parents can read his murderous thoughts. But is the thought somehow tacked on to an emotion that is essentially independent of it? Where philosophic tradition had considered emotions independent of reason and thought, philosophers now generally hold that most emotions are constituted partially from cognitive components (see for example *affect).

The position of psychoanalysis on the mind-body question has always been ambiguous, for which the concept of the unconscious is largely responsible. Psychoanalysts often defend it on this very count. They urge the prevalence of what Freud called primary process thinking, an aspect of the unconscious lacking the very characteristics which, according to many philosophers, are constitutive of thought. Philosophers may then press the question: what is it, then, that makes *primary process a kind of thought? The issue is not whether creatures with minds are not also creatures with bodies; nor whether mental states are functions of brain states. It is rather the question of reducibility I raised earlier. Freud calls instinct something on the border between body and mind. But what sort of a border is this? Phantasies, considered the earliest mental states, picture incorporation of the mother's breast, or the expulsion of the baby's own bad feelings into the mother, and so on, as in the writings of Melanie *Klein. But do phantasies have, or do they not, an irreducibly mental component? And if so, how is the theory to capture this? Often Freud describes reason as a veil which covers unconscious, namely irrational, or rather, a-rational, instinctual strivings. Yet at the same time his own interpretations of unconscious thought processes typically discover beliefs. This is a position in accord with some contemporary philosophical work on irrationality. Irrational thought is not a-rational, as are bodily states, this work maintains; it is rather rationality gone wrong. For instance, we might view weakness of the will, the phenomenon of doing something inconsistent with one's own view of what is best for one to do, not as the victory of passion over reason, or of a rational conscious mind over an essentially a-rational unconscious mind, but as some kind of a failure of integration between two essentially rational mental structures.

The ambiguity on the mind-body question colours Freud's thinking about the emotions. Freud followed philosophical tradition in dividing reason from passion. His official view was that 'affects and emotions correspond to processes of discharge'. It was the failure of psychoanalysis to confront this assumption squarely that was responsible for what it itself regarded for a long time as the lack of a coherent theory of the emotions. Recent work has gone a long way towards providing such a theory. Perhaps the first step was taken by *Bowlby, who called *affects 'evaluative states'. Another step was taken by infant-watchers, like Daniel Stern and Robert Emde, who view emotions as part of a developing mental array occurring in the mother-child relationship repertoire.

It is tempting to think of Freud's *structural theory of the mind as analogous to Plato's myth about the three parts of the soul. Plato gives the soul a tri-partite structure: reason is a charioteer, trying to control the two horses of will and passion. The well-ordered soul, like the well-ordered state, is one in which these elements are in the right proportion to each other: reason ascendant over a submissive will and an even more subservient passion. But the comparison is misleading. Id, ego, and super-ego are not at all counter-parts to Plato's reason, passion, will; furthermore, Plato sees the three parts as distinct, while Freud sees them as structures of enduring mental representations, schemas, habits of perception and of thought that overlap. The id is the reservoir of instincts. By definition it is unconscious. But the unconscious reaches into the ego, which grows out of it. Similarly the super-ego grows out of the id via the *Oedipal complex and its precursors, and it is fired by the instinctual id.

Personal identity and the nature of the self did not become philosophical perplexities until the eighteenth century. Descartes had claimed that each of us knows for certain that he exists as a unitary, enduring, mental substance. John Locke argued on the contrary that we can in no way intuit or experience such a substance. Nevertheless, he continued, we must assume its existence if we are to explain the coherence of mental states that personal identity, one's remaining in some important sense the same person over time, presumes. Hume mined the sceptical vein that Locke had struck, arguing that we can experience no such thing as the self, a continuous entity, identical from one moment and one thought to the next. The unity of the self comes up only implicitly in psychoanalytic theory with the ideas of repression and *intrapsychic realities; repression presumes a unitary mind: a censor who is in touch with both unconscious and conscious elements, with both ego-syntonic aims and aims that are not. Intrapsychic *conflict similarly presumes a unity, no matter how complicated. Freud's idea of splits in the ego suggested rather that what we call a self might sometimes be more accurately thought of as several selves. This position has been more or less explicitly argued by psychoanalysts who favour the idea of *dissociation over that of *repression.

The certainty that Descartes claimed for self-knowledge contrasted with his arguments against the possibility of certain knowledge about any aspect of the external world. I can know for certain of my own existence as a mind; I can also know for certain what it is I am thinking. But whether there is something in the external world that corresponds to my thought must always be in doubt. A strong movement in contemporary philosophy argues against Cartesian scepticism of this sort. It contends that knowledge of the external world, and therefore of some other minds, and of one's own existence, is inextricable from each other. Objectivity, *intersubjectivity, and *subjectivity, necessarily arise together. But on this issue there is by no means a philosophical consensus. Much psychoanalytic theory reflects this division. Beginning with Freud, the sceptical Cartesian view that the only thing one can ever know, be in touch with, is one's own inner world, prevailed, but to some extent that is changing. *Object relations has been ambiguous on this point: are the object relations in question entirely inner representations, or are they also real relations with real people in a real external world? The question has clinical implications in the importance that clinical theory assigns to the real world, and to attempts, however uncertain the results must be, to reconstruct a real historical past.

Debate among philosophers, and psychoanalysts as well, about the scientific status of psychoanalysis has centred on the following positions: psychoanalysis is a science like any other; it is in principle a science like any other, but it is a very bad science; it is a specifically *hermeneutic science which attempts to interpret meanings, to investigate the reasons for actions, rather than to discover causes; its peculiar value as a science lies in the way it combines hermeneutic and causal reasoning. Some debate on this issue might be resolved, as many think it in effect has been, through careful attention to the nature of our reasoning about causes and about reasons.

This last debate brings us back to the mind-body question. Are reasons themselves a kind of cause? Are all causes necessarily physical in nature? Can interpretations of behaviour in terms of a person's reasons be reduced, in principle, to explanations that relate strictly physical classes of events? It is clear, I hope, from these brief remarks, that psychoanalytic disputes are not entirely empirical in nature, to be resolved through more and better empirical study. Rather they are also disputes on philosophical, or conceptual matters: what can we say about the mind, thinking, emotion, our knowledge of other minds, that is coherent, that is, consistent with and illuminating of, other positions we maintain and which are important to our conceptual scheme?

See also: neuropsychoanalysis; philosophy, continental; science

Cavell, M. (1993) *The Psychoanalytic Mind – From Freud to Philosophy.* Cambridge, MA and London: Harvard University Press.

Grunbaum, A. (1984) *The Foundations of Psychoanalysis, A Critique.* Berkeley: University of California Press.

Ricoeur, P. (1970) *Freud and Philosophy, an Essay on Interpretation.* New Haven, CT: Yale University Press.

Shevrin, H. et al. (1996) *Conscious and Unconscious Processes: Psychodynamic, Cognitive, and Neurophysiological Convergences.* New York: Guilford.

Westen, D. (1999) 'The scientific status of unconscious processes: is Freud really dead?'. *Journal of the American Psychoanalytic Association* 47(4).
Wollheim, R. (1984) *The Thread of Life.* Cambridge, MA: Harvard University Press.

M. C.

PHILOSOPHY, CONTINENTAL The relationship between psychoanalysis and philosophy has long been tenuous. Freud's interest in establishing the validity of his explanations as natural science led him to distinguish sharply between psychoanalysis and the human sciences (*Geisteswissenschaften*). He especially separated the findings of psychoanalysis from conclusions of a similar nature in philosophy. Freud recognised the way in which the notion of irrationalism developed in the work of the German philosophers *Schopenhauer and *Nietzsche coincided with the theory of psychoanalysis, yet made the dubious claim not to have read either. And when Freud's philosophically inclined colleague, *Binswanger, questioned the psychoanalytic conception of the unconscious, Freud asked accusingly, 'Has the philosophical devil got you in his claws?' Freud's project of creating a natural science while maintaining a bulwark against what he referred to as 'speculative metaphysics' of philosophy had a lasting effect on the discipline of classical psychoanalysis.

In contrast to classical psychoanalysis, revisionist approaches are less wedded to a natural scientific paradigm. This has allowed for the inclusion of the human sciences – especially the continental philosophical tradition – in the conceptualisation of theory and technique. *Existential-phenomenological and *Lacanian traditions in Europe, and interpersonal, *relational, *intersubjective psychoanalysis in North America, have either reformulated or altogether rejected key aspects of Freud's *metapsychology, including the tripartite theory of mind, the notion of instinctual energy and drives, the unconscious, and classical analytic technique, particularly neutrality and objectivity. In order to fashion new conceptions of the mind, body, and interaction, they have drawn on the work of continental philosophers, particularly existential, phenomenological, hermeneutic and postmodern thinkers.

The interest shown by revisionist psychoanalysts in continental philosophy has until recently not extended to analytical philosophy. In fact, analytical philosophy has historically been rather cool towards psychoanalysis, often demonstrating the same antipathy towards Freud that it has shown for modern continental philosophers. Conversely, continental philosophers and literary theorists have written at length about psychoanalysis, and have applied its methods to the realms of social theory, politics, history, feminism, textual analysis and many other fields.

The interaction between continental philosophy and psychoanalysis is not fortuitous. Both developed out of a European intellectual tradition of asking questions about *human nature that have direct relevance for clinical practice. Thus continental philosophers might ask: How can we achieve insight into the way we live our lives? How can we understand the nature of human love and intimacy? What is the role of the body in my experience and perception of the world around me? How can we account for the multifaceted, often opposing tendencies, of human interaction? And how is the human being, or subject, situated in a world or shared understandings?

Continental philosophers reject the traditional Cartesian conception of the subject as isolated and closed in on itself. Descartes' famous dictum 'I think, therefore I am' makes it difficult to account for the reality of other minds. In its place, continental philosophers seek to formulate a conception of the subject and subjectivity that is true to our lived experience. They elucidate the implicit connections between the self and other within the context of intersubjectivity. They pay particular attention to prereflective and somatic experience, and consider the ways in which we are always and inevitably enmeshed in social contexts. Not by chance, revisionist psychoanalysts embrace these same changes, broadening for inclusion in analysis experiences that were similarly excluded from classical Freudian consideration.

A brief history of the application of continental philosophy to psychoanalysis will help the reader appreciate the connections between the two disciplines. I will begin with the work of the Swiss psychiatrist and psychoanalyst, Binswanger, since he was the first to attempt an integration, as early as the 1920s. Binswanger was representative of a tradition of European intellectuals which freely combined philosophical ideas with clinical insights. Although an early colleague of Freud's, Binswanger became dissatisfied with the deterministic and causal nature of Freud's theories. By drawing on philosophy, he sought to provide a new theoretical basis for psychoanalysis that would overcome Freud's reliance on psychic determinism and became known as *daseinsanalysis.

Rather than view the mind in terms of the tension between *id, *ego and *super-ego, Binswanger turned to Husserl's theory of phenomenology in an attempt to account for the 'visual reality' rather than intrapsychic structure of the mentally ill person. Similarly, *Heidegger's philosophical analysis of human existence in *Being and Time* provided a radically different perspective from the internal drive theory of psychoanalysis. In contrast to Freud's intrapsychic structures, Heidegger argues that the human being, or *Dasein, is neither autonomous nor self-contained but exists as being-in-the-world. From this perspective, human behaviour can only be understood within the context in which it develops. For the psychoanalyst, according to Binswanger, it is the way in which the individuals structure their world that provides an insight into how they experience themselves and their environment.

In order to overcome the problem of the isolated Cartesian mind, Binswanger turned to the philosophy of *Hegel. Rather than stress the notion of intrapsychic structure, Binswanger was interested in showing that self-consciousness and self-understanding is dependent upon the Other, in an interpersonal process that Hegel referred to as mutual recognition. In order to conceptualise the interaction between analyst and analysand, Binswanger turned to *Buber's philosophy of dialogue. Binswanger was particularly interested in the way in which Buber's conception of the I-Thou relation related to clinical interaction. According to Buber, the I-Thou relation is characterised by mutuality, openness, and immediacy. For Binswanger, change and growth were made possible through the emergence of an I-Thou relationship in the clinical setting. Here was a new form of interaction and technique, which owed little to classical psychoanalytic emphasis on neutrality and the notion of the psychoanalyst as a blank screen.

In France, the early work of *Lacan and Foucault was indebted to Binswanger. Lacan drew first on phenomenology and then structuralism in order to reformulate Freudian psychoanalysis from the perspective of language. In the early phase of his work, he drew on the interactions of self and other described by Hegel, Kojeve and *Sartre, and on Heidegger's formulations of being and time. The inclusion of structural linguistics was achieved by turning to the work of the anthropologist Lévi-Strauss and the linguist Saussure. In the process, Lacan developed a school of psychoanalysis that takes as its starting point the role of language in the formulation of subjectivity and the unconscious. Likewise, Foucault's first published work in 1954 was a discussion of Binswanger's approach to dream analysis, and in a wider sense, an elaboration of the philosophical and historical basis of Freudian psychoanalysis and psychiatry.

The impact on psychoanalysis of Sartre's philosophy cannot be underestimated. His critique of the unconscious revealed the potential flaws of a deterministic theory of mind, grounded in a conception of instinctual energy. For Sartre, Freud's notion of repression was ultimately a self-contradictory idea, because the so-called conscious mind has to know what to repress in order to be able to do its work. In the process, Sartre sought to give greater credence to the role of agency, and less to the notion of causality in human behaviour. His notion of 'prereflective' or implicit consciousness kept the experiencing individual at the centre of analytic consideration, while making room for understanding divisions in consciousness that are an object of psychoanalytic investigation.

Sartre's primary influence was on the work of the British psychiatrist, Laing. Although trained as a mainstream psychoanalyst, Laing turned to Hegel, Heidegger, Buber, and particularly Sartre in order to elaborate the divided nature of human experience and to fashion a theory of analytic interaction that stressed reciprocity over distance and neutrality. A further important influence of existential-phenomenological philosophy on mainstream psychoanalysis was the work of Hans *Loewald, who was a student of Heidegger's before moving to the United States, and wrote about themes of a philosophical nature. Roy Schaefer's later attempt to develop a new 'action language' in psychoanalysis similarly draws on the philosophical discussions of the problem of agency.

The essential rejection of Freud's drive theory in existential-phenomenological and Lacanian psychoanalysis made necessary the reformulation of bodily experience. The clinical work of the Swiss psychiatrist, Medard *Boss, illuminates the role of the body in the context of psychosomatic illness. Like Binswanger, Boss formulates an embodied subject akin to the philosophy of Maurice Merleau-Ponty, which challenges the traditional division between mind and body. Merleau-Ponty's formulation of the body-subject takes as its focus the lived experience of the patient and provides the basis for an embodied psychoanalysis that seeks to overcome the traditional psychoanalytic distinction between intellect and soma.

The development of revisionist psychoanalytic perspectives also has direct links to the work of 'critical theory', which seeks to examine the interconnections between the psyche and society. Erich *Fromm, a pioneer in critical theory and psychoanalysis at the Frankfurt School, was a founder of interpersonal psychoanalysis. Other critical theorists, including Herbert Marcuse and Theodore Adorno, sought to use psychoanalytic theory as a bridge between the sociological and psychological analysis of society. The critical theorist and philosopher, Jürgen Habermas, has introduced the Freudian unconscious as a pivotal concept for analysing the repression of the subject's needs and desires from public and political life. According to Habermas' influential reading of Freud, consciousness contains the discourses of the public sphere, while the unconscious contains those needs and desires that are prevented or denied full articulation in society.

For many contemporary revisionist psychoanalysts, continental philosophy, particularly hermeneutics and postmodernism, provides a way of countering the modernist essentialism and epistemology of classical psychoanalysis. For interpersonal, *relational, and *intersubjective psychoanalysis, the reliance on the analytic neutrality and objectivity that defined classical psychoanalysis has given way to an analytic relationship based on mutuality, in which traditional assumptions about authority and reason yield to ambiguity and uncertainty. In place of foundational concepts such as objectivity and truth, these revisionist perspectives emphasise constructivism or perspectivism. And in contrast to the materialistic, nonrelational entity that characterises the so-called modernist self, the postmodernist psychoanalyst sees the self as generated and maintained by the relational, linguistic, and cultural contexts in which it is embedded.

In developing their postmodern views on psychoanalytic theory and treatment, revisionist psychoanalysts draw on a variety of sources. The work of Hegel, Binswanger, Buber and even Habermas is cited in the conceptualisation of mutuality and the refashioning of classical technique. The philosophy of Heidegger and Gaudier is used in the development of a hermeneutic perspective on clinical experience. By drawing on Gaudier, revisionist psychoanalysts suggest that it is the historical matrix in which we are embedded that provides the ground for all interpretation and understanding. The work of Foucault and Derrida provides a perspective on the deconstruction of the subject through the dislocating forces of history, language, and society. Of course, the challenge for postmodernist psychoanalysis is to retain a conception of the subject, however minimal, as the locus of understanding and change in the clinical setting.

Inclusion of bodily experiencing in subjective life is central to the work of *relational analysts, who draw on Merleau-Ponty. In a larger sense, the entire project of relational psychoanalysis is motivated by the optimism of encountering alterity, and draws inspiration from the work of Levinas. His ideas are also used to develop the ethical dimension of psychoanalysis that is often lacking in discussions of postmodernism. Finally, the theme of *intersubjectivity, which has a long history in continental philosophy, has become a key tenet of contemporary psychoanalysis. In contrast to classical psychoanalysis, intersubjectivity theory seeks to overcome the traditional distinctions between inner and outer experience by drawing on the work of a variety of intersubjective philosophers to argue that all experience is thoroughly contextualised and always dependent upon interactions between self and other.

Foucault, M. [1954] (1993) 'Dream, imagination and existence' in K. Hoeller (ed.) *Dream and Existence*. Atlantic Highlands, NJ: Humanities Press, 31–78.
Frie, R. (1997) *Subjectivity and Intersubjectivity in Modern Philosophy and Psychoanalysis: A Study of Sartre, Binswanger, Lacan, and Habermas*. Lanham, MD: Rowman & Littlefield.
Frie, R. and Reis, B. (2001) 'Understanding intersubjectivity: psychoanalytic formulations and their philosophical underpinnings'. *Contemporary Psychoanalysis* 37: 297–327.
Habermas, J. (1972) *Knowledge and Human Interests*. London: Heinemann.
May, R., Angel, E. and Ellenberger, H. (eds) (1958) *Existence: A New Dimension in Psychiatry and Psychology*. New York: Basic Books.
Theunissen, M. (1984) *The Other*. Translated by C. McCann. Cambridge, MA: MIT Press.

R. Fri.

PHOBIA (FREUD) A phobia is a fear of a particular object or situation which is linked with anxiety and is the object of avoidance strategies. Freud discussed the significance of phobia in his Little Hans case history and gave it the status of the main symptom of 'anxiety hysteria', as opposed to conversion hysteria and obsessive neurosis. Lacan, in his commentary on the case, stresses that Hans's phobia is a fixed signifier, open to multiple and changing significations during his cure. The function of castration is to make up for the failure of the real father as an agent of castration who institutes a separation from the mother. He opposed phobia as 'prevented desire' to hysteria as 'unsatisfied desire', and to obsessive neurosis as 'impossible desire'. Later, he maintained that Hans's phobia embodied his *jouissance, experienced as alien and rejected.

M. Eyd.

PHOBIAS A phobia is defined in the *DSM-IV* as a marked and persistent fear that is excessive or unreasonable, cued by the presence or anticipation of a specific object or situation (e.g. flying, heights, animals, receiving an injection, seeing blood). The individual suffering from the phobia generally realises that the fear is irrational but feels unable to cope with the anxiety and discomfort elicited by the feared object or situation (stimulus). Typically this results in avoidance of the feared stimulus, and a fear response (intense anxiety or distress) if the stimulus is encountered. Panic attacks involving (adrenaline-induced) extreme physical symptoms or anxiety (racing heart, sweating, trembling, shortness of breath, chest pain, nausea, feelings of choking, dizziness, derealisation or depersonalisation) and fear of going mad or losing control may or may not be present. Panic attacks are often associated with agoraphobia (fear of open spaces) but may be present as part of a panic disorder with no particular identified stimulus, or in conjunction with another phobia.

The only phobias with an atypical response are needle phobia and blood injury phobia where the initial anxiety response or increased heart rate, blood pressure, etc. may often be quickly followed by a dramatic drop in blood pressure and heart rate frequently resulting in loss of consciousness. This vasovagal response makes disphasic behavioural therapy (exposure with response prevention) – often the treatment of choice for specific phobias – rather difficult because the patient quickly passes out when exposure is attempted. The novel approach to treatment in such cases involves treating the patient in the supine position with their legs elevated to prevent loss of consciousness, thus allowing treatment to progress.

Learning theory suggests that phobias develop from childhood through association of the phobic stimulus with fear, a process referred to as 'conditioning' by Rachman. The psychoanalytic perspective suggests that fear acquisition results from the phobic stimulus which symbolically represents something that is feared unconsciously.

American Psychiatric Association (1994) *Diagnostic and Statistical Manual of Mental Disorders* (*DSM-IV*). Fourth edition. Washington, DC: American Psychiatric Association.

J. W.

PHOBIC TECHNIQUE see **TRANSITIONAL TECHNIQUES**

PICTURE A Lacanian conception of a picture necessitates the distinction between the eye as the instrument of perception and the gaze as both object of desire and as an eye that is fuelled by desire. As a creation a picture is the visual demonstration of the gaze of the artist and for the spectator a picture functions as a pacifier of the desire of the gaze.

R. L.

PLAY AND PLAYING Experiences that were passively endured by children may be actively inflicted on others in play in an effort to achieve mastery. Dreams, jokes, and creative endeavours take advantage of word play in order to express unconscious meaning. Later clinicians have considered the play of children to be equivalent to the free associations of older patients.

*Winnicott places play in a direct relationship with the creative process, seeing its origin in the interaction between the feeding infant and his mother. Following this, the use of gestures, words, toys and playthings constitute the language of play. Play is seen as vital to the developmental process and as a medium for development, where the expression of the self in play marks the beginning of creative living. An important stage in this development is the child's selection of a particular toy or other object – it may be a piece of sheet or blanket or a soft toy – as having particular significance, to be taken with the child and sought at times when the child needs comfort. This *transitional object constitutes an original contribution by Winnicott to psychoanalytic theory, for the significance of this phenomenon, commonly recognised by parents and children, forms a central theme of his thought. The child's 'work' in the course of his development is in his play. Winnicott thought that play, to be truly an expression of the child's development, is an activity of the ego and only minimally invested with libidinal or aggressive energy. The presence of either impulse to excess interferes with play, and may interfere with the expression of the *true self. Winnicott stresses the importance of play between mother and child as the prototype for all future (potential) fruitful interactions. What he does not include is the role of the *father in play, which is a striking omission in that fathers are likely even in infancy to play with their children and to contribute substantially to a child's increasing capacity for symbolisation, a capacity which among other things begins to link the child to the outside world.

Winnicott, D. W. (1971) 'Playing, a theoretical statement and playing: creative activity and the search for the self' in *Playing and Reality*. London: Hogarth Press.

J. A. Ber. / M. Twy.

PLEASURE As a source of happiness, pleasure is the aim of the *pleasure principle which is to maintain the psychic apparatus at its lowest level of tension. Lacan distinguishes it from *jouissance, which moves beyond the pleasure principle in order to reach the lost object and brings pain with pleasure.

R. M. B.

PLEASURE PRINCIPLE The pleasure principle is the guiding principle by which human life is conducted and the reason for the acquisition of a mental apparatus. The aim of the pleasure principle is to reduce tension by the shortest route possible. To reduce the unpleasure of hunger, the infant hallucinates a breast. When the fantasied breast does not reduce tension as satisfactorily as the real breast, the infant begins to adopt the *reality principle, which is a more indirect, but ultimately a more effective method for satisfying the demands of the pleasure principle. The pleasure principle was so basic to Freud's understanding of how human beings operate that he was baffled by his patients' repetitions of situations that had never given any pleasure nor were ever likely to do so. In 1920 he developed a new theory to describe what seemed to be the failure of the pleasure principle. He determined that there was a tendency to repeat the past (the *repetition compulsion) which overrode the pleasure principle. He saw it as an expression of a *'death drive' whose aim was to repeat the past, to return living matter to the inanimate state, and to eliminate the tension of life. The death drive was thus the ultimate servant of the pleasure principle.

J. A. Ber.

POLAND Before World War II the centres for psychoanalysis in Poland were Warsaw, Cracow and Lvov. Hitler's Nazism followed by Stalinism caused the disappearance of psychoanalysis in Poland as a method of treatment and as a philosophy officially taught at universities. Poland has a number of distinguished analysts, notably Bychowski and Maurycy Bronstein, as well as renowned psychoanalysts associated with European psychoanalysis such as Hélène *Deutsch, and Maria Sokolnicka who was responsible for introducing psychoanalysis into France.

The years from 1965 to 1990 saw a renaissance of psychoanalysis in Poland stemming from two sources, Budapest and Prague. Jan Malewski (in Heidelberg from 1975) trained with Imre Hermann in Budapest and later founded the Centre for Group Psychotherapy in Rasztow near Warsaw, while developing individual psychoanalysis through private practice. Zbigniew Sokolik, trained in Prague, also established a private practice. In 1989, Katarzyna Walewska and Elzbieta Bohomolec became *IPA members at the IPA congress in Rome. The development of Polish psychoanalysis in recent years is largely based on the activities of London with *Segal of the British Society, Paris with Lebovici of the Paris Psychoanalytical Society, Heidelberg with Malewski and Canzler, Berlin with Kuchenbuch and others.

The strongest trend of psychoanalysis in Poland is associated with the IPA. With headquarters in Warsaw, the *Polskie Towarzystwo Psychoanalityczne* (Polish Study Group – Sponsoring Committee in IPA) consisting of psychologists, psychiatrists and physicians, has twenty-two members in 2002, six of whom are full members of the IPA, and is presided over by Wojciech Hanbowski. The Study Group trains future IPA members. The *Lacanian trend in psychoanalysis has centres in Cracow and Warsaw. As a science, psychoanalysis is taught at the psychology and philosophy departments of the Warsaw, Wroclaw and Bialystok universities.

*Jungian analytical psychology is promoted by the Polish Analytical Psychology Society in

Warsaw, which bases its practices on the London Jungian group. Warsaw is also the site of the Rasztow Institute for Group Psychoanalysis associated with EGATIN. There are four groups of analytical psychotherapy associated with EFPP: Warsaw, Lodz, Cracow and Gdansk.

The two major annual events in Polish psychoanalysis are the International Psychoanalytical Conference held each May since 1999 by the Study Group, and the Institute of Psychoanalysis (IPP) Days held in February, organised since 1990 by Walewska at Warsaw University.

Currently the following journals are produced in Poland: *Dialogi* quarterly published by IPP (since 1996); *Swiat Psychoanalizy* published by the Psychoanalysis Workshop, Department of Pedagogy and Psychology, Bialystok University; and *Albo albo* (psychological and cultural issues).

Wroclaw is home to the Society for Psychoanalytic Studies, presided over by R. Saciuk.

E. F. / R. F.

POLITICS AND PSYCHOANALYSIS Clinical thinking has a key utility for the study of politics. To the extent that each person has in him or her something of the manipulating politician, and everyone has to play roles that events assign, then politics is an inherent aspect of the psychology of everyday life.

Although the collaborative book by Freud and William C. Bullitt on Woodrow Wilson did not get published until 1967, the joint work initially took place in the late 1920s and was completed in the early 1930s. Bullitt thought that political considerations mandated that the book go into cold storage. Although it may never prove possible fully to establish the extent of Freud's contribution to this study, his handwritten Introduction states that 'for the analytic part we are both equally responsible'. According to Anna Freud, her father gave the ideas to Bullitt but the manner of application and the style were Bullitt's own. Freud and Bullitt both shared an intense dislike of Wilson, and this partisanship of theirs underlay the unfortunate lack of detachment in the text itself. The book, for example, claimed to have uncovered 'the neurosis which controlled' Wilson's life, and also described Wilson near his death as 'very close to psychosis'. What got omitted were Wilson's achievements, as a great teacher, a legislative and administrative leader, and a moulder of world opinion. Equally damaging to the Freud-Bullitt text was the lack of proper research into the social context in which Wilson grew up. When using the earliest psychoanalytic propositions, or at least 'applying' them reductively, there is always the danger that no one will end up looking good under such a biased microscope. So the Freud-Bullitt work became the hidden ancestor to many subsequent uses of psychoanalysis for partisan purposes.

On the other hand, the American Walter Lippmann (1889–1974) deserves the credit for being one of the first students of politics to appreciate the genuine potential of psychoanalytic thinking. In his 1922 book *Public Opinion* he noted the significance of individual character as well as the vagaries of any concept of selfhood. In general Lippmann was attracted by psychoanalysis's attention to irrationality, and he introduced an unforgettable contrast between the complexities of the outside world and the distortions inherent in our need for 'pictures' in our heads. This antithesis between, on the one hand, the immense social environment in which we live and, on the other, our ability to perceive it only indirectly, has continued to haunt democratic thinkers. Not only do our leaders acquire fictitious personalities, but also symbols often govern political behaviour. People can respond as powerfully to fictions as to realities, and often help create the pseudo-environment to which they later react. Lippmann was writing in a relativistic spirit that emphasised the significance of the subjective psychological dimension.

Censorship poses a special threat for a functioning democracy; news from a distant psychological world can be arranged to suit practical ideological purposes. Lippmann was therefore troubled by the distinct limits he perceived to the possibility for the circulation of ideas and the difficulties in the path of genuine tolerance. Limited time and attention, combined with the impact of our different social circumstances and modern means of communication, mean that each of us is necessarily far less open and responsive than we usually choose to think. Lippmann thereby established for political thought the role of stereotypes in the making of public opinion.

Harold Lasswell's *Psychopathology and Politics* (1930) was the first book by a professional political scientist devoted to the implications of depth psychology. He was more impressed by the observational methods implicit in the psychoanalytic approach than by any specific theoretical formulation that then existed. Lasswell was interested in the potential usefulness of the files of hospitalised patients, and was perhaps most notably influenced by the example of Harry Stack *Sullivan. Lasswell was remarkably emancipated from the sectarianism that has beset the history of psychoanalysis. Accordingly he was respectful toward Adler and Jung, as well as Rank, and heavily influenced by the ideas of Ferenczi and Horney.

Lasswell reported that the case histories in *Psychopathology and Politics* made him sound disreputable in the mainstream political science of his day, but they still read convincingly. Even though the passage of time means that they may seem simplistic today, they can still serve as an introduction. One of the hardest parts of the psychoanalytic framework to communicate to outsiders is the spirit of the clinical give-and-take, and Lasswell was intelligent enough to have penned concrete portraits whose artistry belied his commitment to science. In subsequent publications he became explicit about the origins of specifically political talent arising from problems of maintaining self-esteem.

To generalise, Freud's shattering of rationalistic presuppositions probably had the greatest effect on subsequent political thinking. When he demonstrated the degree to which the child lives within the adult, and the extent to which psychological insecurities prevent us from ruling ourselves, he was challenging many democratic hopes. But his thought leads in multiple ideological directions, and can be read as the liberal tradition turning on itself in self-inquiry. In my view psychoanalysis retains liberationist as well as conservative strands, and is itself neither inherently left-wing nor right-wing; the Marxist Frankfurt school of critical sociology (including Erich Fromm, Theodor Adorno, and Herbert Marcuse) made their own idiosyncratic use of psychoanalytic theories. As long as we appreciate that Freud's doctrines can be both emancipatory as well as disillusioning, simultaneously containing thought for multiple strands of different ideologies, we are less likely to reduce his heritage to any simple set of convenient slogans.

Freud, S. and Bullitt, W. C. (1967) *Thomas Woodrow Wilson*. Boston, MA: Houghton Mifflin.

Lasswell, H. D. (1930) *Psychopathology and Politics*. Chicago: University of Chicago.

Lippmann, W. (1922) *Public Opinion*. New York: Macmillan.

P. R.

PORTUGAL Egas Moniz was the first to introduce Freud's theories and therapeutic procedures into Portugal. Between 1915 and 1928, Moniz, who was later to become famous as a 1949 Nobel Prize winner in Medicine and Physiology, lectured and published papers in which he showed a wonderful understanding of psychoanalysis (childhood sexuality, repression, the origin of neuroses). Moniz was well prepared to receive psychoanalysis because of early interest in sex physiology and pathology which led him to publish his treatise *Sex Life* (which had nineteen editions between 1901 and 1933 – an unprecedented success for a scientific book in Portugal).

On an historical note, the eighteenth-century Portuguese scientist, Abbe Faria, can be mentioned in the pre-history of psychoanalysis. He was a full-time hypnotist and, as is now known, hypnotists such as Mesmer, by experimenting with hysterical patients prepared the ground for Freud's discoveries. Among the hypnotists Faria was the first to discard the theory of magnetic fluid, putting in its place a psychological influence. This is made clear in his book *De la cause du sommeil lucide*. Faria, outside the circle of specialists, is better known through Alexander Dumas' novel, *The Count of Monte Cristo* (where his nationality is changed from Portuguese to Italian). He was also mentioned by Chateaubriand in his *Memoires d'outre-tombe.* After Moniz, psychoanalysis came of age around 1950 when two Portuguese neuro-psychiatrists (F. Alvim and P. Luzes) went to Geneva for training in Saussure's group, another (J. Santos) going to Paris, for the same purpose. Together with three Spanish analysts, they became founders of the Luso-Spanish Psychoanalytical Society, later to split giving rise to an actual Portuguese Psychoanalytical Society. This component Society of the IPA developed along the main lines of psychoanalysis in Europe (classic Freudian, Kleinian, and Bionian). These orientations have had a tendency to become gradually integrated and the growth of the PPS has steadily progressed.

Ellenberger, H. F. (1970) *The Discovery of the Unconscious.* New York: Basic Books.
Vale, M. A. M., Santos, O. S., Alvim, F. and Luzes, P. (1979) 'Recently discovered letters by Freud to a correspondent'. *International Review of Psycho-Analysis.*

P. Luz.

POST TRAUMATIC STRESS DISORDER (PTSD) An anxiety disorder typically occurring after exposure to a major trauma involving actual or threatened death, either as victim or witness. There are three major groups of symptoms. Firstly, an intrusive re-experiencing of events as if being there again (flashbacks), and recurrent dreams of the event. Secondly, avoidance of anything associated with the trauma in order to numb the memory as well as feelings of estrangement and irritability. Thirdly, subjects are easily startled and prone to insomnia and anger.

In his 1923 paper 'Beyond the Pleasure Principle' Freud described how the psychic shield protecting the mind can be overwhelmed, leading to a tendency, both to re-experience, and avoid, events. His ideas have been developed by Horowitz and incorporated into a cognitive model. Psychoanalysis has been accused of neglecting the importance of trauma, (somewhat linked to the fierce debate around the *seduction theory), but there have been important contributions from two psychoanalysts: Lifton who has a combination of classical psychoanalytic, ego psychology and existentialist concepts and Garland who uses the Kleinian concepts of projective identification, containment and impairment of symbolisation. There has been much argument and research regarding the importance of stressful events versus individual psychology. This has brought increasing interest in how a victimised child can be vulnerable in adulthood, as well as those with *borderline personality disorder. Sandler and others describe a process of traumatisation where the traumatic event brings about an internal adaptation which may or may not be pathological. With regard to treatment, recent research of psychic defensive structures has shown that immediate de-briefing at the time of an accident does not help and indeed may precipitate traumatisation.

Post traumatic stress disorder has occupied an even longer place in the justice system, for example in criminal law it has been used to explain a person's offence. An example is a soldier charged with grievous bodily harm who is said to have been suffering from a post traumatic condition. In civil cases it has been increasingly cited with regard to compensation claims, not only after major accidents such as an aeroplane crash, but also medico-legal accidents and increasingly minor incidents. This has caused some disquiet amongst both lawyers and doctors as there is a potential for misuse of the diagnosis.

Garland, C. (1991) 'External disasters and the internal world: an approach to psychotherapeutic understanding of survivors' in J. Holmes (ed.) *Psychotherapy in Psychiatric Practice*. New York: Churchill Livingstone, 507–32.
Horowitz, M. J. (1986) *Stress Response Syndromes*. Second edition. Northvale, NJ: Aaronson.
Lifton, R. J. (1993) 'From Hiroshima to the Nazi doctors: an evolution of psychoformative approaches to understanding traumatic stress syndromes' in J. P. Wilson and B. Rafael (eds) *International Handbook of Traumatic Stress Syndromes*. New York: Plenum, 11–23.
Sandler, J., Dreher, A. U. and Drews, S. (1991) 'An approach to conceptual research in psychoanalysis illustrated by a consideration of psychic trauma'. *International Review of Psycho-Analysis* 18: 133–41.

C. V.

PRECONCEPTION A state of expectation in which the mind is prepared to receive a restricted range of phenomena. A preconception can be thought but cannot be known. When a preconception meets with a realisation (sense impression) it brings into being a conception.

Bion, W. R. (1962) *Learning from Experience*. London: Heinemann. Also in *Seven Servants*. New York: Jason Aronson, 1977.
Bion, W. R. (1963) *Elements of Psychoanalysis*. London: Heinemann. Also in *Seven Servants*. New York: Jason Aronson, 1977.
Bion, W. R. (1965) *Transformations*. London: Karnac Books. Also in *Seven Servants*. New York: Jason Aronson, 1977.

S. A.

PREAMBIVALENT OBJECT Fairbairn's term for the first internal object that represents the relationship in the early *oral stage in which the infant's psyche has not yet split apart love and hate for the mother.

E. F. B. / D. E. S.

PRECONSCIOUS Mental contents which are potentially but not currently conscious are preconscious. An example is the name of your high school which is typically not in awareness but easily becomes so when attention is focused upon it. This is in contrast to dynamically unconscious contents whose awareness is actively resisted. Originally, Freud saw the preconscious as part of a mental system (conscious system). Later he saw it as a quality of mental life, having no systematic meaning.

The preconscious is not as such a concept in Lacanian theory. The kernel of the Lacanian unconscious belongs to the *Real, thus resembling Freud's unconscious. The productions or formations of this unconscious belong to the *Imaginary and the *Symbolic, and in that sense they relate to both Freud's preconscious and dynamic unconscious.

See also: Rapaport

Freud, S. (1915) *The Unconscious*. S. E. 14. London: Hogarth Press.
Rapaport, D. (1960) 'The structure of psychoanalytic theory'. *Psychological Issues* 2(2).

J. Wei. / D. B.

PRENATAL STATES OF MIND In Bion's essay on the *caesura he asks if it is possible for psychoanalysts to think that there may still be in the human being vestiges which would suggest the survival in the mind of embryonic intrauterine functioning. He asks: 'Is there any part of the human mind which still betrays signs of an 'embryological' intuition either visual or auditory?' In 1961 Bion took up the hypothesis of the proto-mental system where the physical and mental remain undifferentiated, expanding it with the conjecture of an embryological or prenatal emotional/mental functioning which is closer to neurophysiology than to psychology. He suggests that such primitive experiences as the ones of intrauterine life can somehow find expression in the child or in the adult. He asks whether during intra-uterine life the first stages of what, after birth, will be called fear, hate, and so on develop.

The usefulness of making conjectures about a continuity between pre-natal and post-natal functioning is that it allows us to widen the field of clinical observation and understanding of certain manifestations, seeing them as traces of the first stages of emotional development. Certain expressions on a bodily level, like an intense blush or an extreme pallor, for instance, might be understood as vestiges of intense 'thalamic or sub-thalamic' fears of pre-natal life. Thinking about the first stages of fear as thalamic fears might help to understand certain bodily manifestations, which we observe in today's child or adult patient as vestiges of pre-natal emotions in intra-uterine life.

Bion, W. R. (1961) *Experience in Groups*. London: Tavistock.

Bion, W. R. (1977) *Two Papers: The Grid and Caesura*. Rio de Janeiro: Imago.

Bion, W. R. (1979) *A Memoir of the Future: Book Three*. Strathtay: Clunie Press.

Bion, W. R. (1987) *Clinical Seminars and Four Papers*. Oxford: Fleetwood Press.

S. A.

PREOEDIPAL The sexuality and character traits belonging to the earliest years. Each psychosexual stage (autoerotic, oral, anal, phallic) provides a possible point of fixation for sexual deviation or character pathology. In terms of the ability to relate, the progression is from narcissism to investment in others; and from indifference and hatred to love. Freud believed many of the preoedipal disorders. i.e. schizophrenia and paranoia, could not be influenced by psychoanalysis because such patients either lacked an interest in the analyst or could only feel hatred for him.

For Lacan, this 'phase' consisting of the triangular figuring of mother, child and Imaginary phallus is the first 'moment' of the Oedipus complex and has the function of the realisation of lack. Wishing to please the mother, identifying himself as the *phallus, the Imaginary object of his mother's desire, the child realises his own lack, since he cannot completely satisfy her, and the mother's lack, since her desire lies beyond him.

J. A. Ber. / D. O.

PRESENCE In existential psychology, a quality of profound attention that serves three chief functions: the illumination of clients' (and therapists') experiential worlds; the creation of a sense of therapeutic safety or what Craig terms 'sanctuary'; and, the deepening of clients' capacities to constructively act upon their discoveries. Through illuminating clients' and therapists' worlds, presence highlights both the obstacles and opportunities to understand those worlds. In turn, such understanding leads to a sense of accompaniment, support, and trust – a sense of safety – within which delicate problems can be addressed. Finally, presence deepens clients' connection with their inmost strivings, and with their capacity to sort through and constructively respond to those strivings. For May and Bugental, presence is the key condition of therapeutic facilitation. Presence brings therapeutic relationships alive, and it challenges clients to find aliveness in themselves. For *Jaspers, presence is a single 'decisive moment', a key opportunity for therapeutic understanding. For *Binswanger, presence is akin to therapeutic rapport, which awakens the client's 'divine spark'. For *Heidegger, finally, presence is intimately associated with **Dasein* or 'being there', both to oneself and the world. In short, presence is an attitude of – immediate, kinesthetic, affective, and profound – attention, and it is the ground and eventual goal of diverse existential practices.

Bugental, J. F. T. (1978) *Psychotherapy and Process: The Fundamentals of an Existential-Humanistic Approach*. Reading, MA: Addison-Wesley.

Craig, P. E. (1986) 'Sanctuary and presence: an existential view of the therapist's contribution'. *The Humanistic Psychologist* 14 (1): 22–8.

Heidegger, M. (1962) *Being and Time*. New York: Harper & Row.
May, R. (1983) *The Discovery of Being: Writing in Existential Psychology*. New York: Norton.
Schneider, K. J. and May, R. (1995) *The Psychology of Existence: An Integrative, Clinical Perspective*. New York: McGraw-Hill.

K. Sch.

PRESSURE OF THE DRIVE The mental apparatus is created by the pressure of the drives to achieve satisfaction. Pathology results when the drive level is higher than the ego can manage. Drive pressure may increase to unmanageable levels during adolescence, parturition, or involution.

J. A. Ber.

PRIMAL FANTASY Universal fantasies (e.g. *primal scene, *castration, *seduction, *family romance) that Freud considered to be transmitted through phylogenetic inheritance and that constitute the fantasy organisation of human beings regardless of their personal experiences. Primal fantasies demonstrate the ways humans imaginatively seek answers to central enigmas in life.

LaPlanche, J. and Pontalis, J. B. (1964) 'Fantasme originaire, fantasme des origins, origins de fantasme'. *Les Temps Modernes* 215: 1833–63.

D. K.

PRIMAL SCENE The scene of sexual intercourse between adults – usually one's parents – that a child either witnesses or fantasises about. Lack of clarity in the literature surrounds its traumatogenic potential, its connection to the *Oedipus complex, its fantasy vs reality aspects, and the multiple and shifting identifications involved.

See also: primal fantasy

Knafo, D. and Feiner, K. (1966) 'The primal scene: variations on the theme'. *Journal of the American Psychoanalytic Association* 44(2): 263–72.

D. K.

PRIMARY AND SECONDARY GAIN Unconsciously motivated advantages accruing from a physical or emotional symptom or illness. In each case these benefits can be internal or external. Primary gain is thought to be tied directly to the initial formation of the symptom, i.e. as a relief from anxiety. Examples of secondary gain: financial remuneration; increased attention from loved ones.

S. Saw.

PRIMARY MATERNAL PREOCCUPATION The heightened state of sensitivity towards her baby developed by a normal woman towards the end of pregnancy and for a few weeks after the birth of her child.

In Winnicott's developmental scheme, a mother's role is to provide exquisite sensitivity at the start. Only after a time can she begin to frustrate the baby gradually, the reason being that with maturation the baby develops a strong enough ego to survive each succeeding frustration. This gradual failure of maternal sensitivity, is described as 'good-enough' mothering.

Winnicott described the 'ordinary devoted mother' in 1949. Later he used the phrase 'primary maternal preoccupation' to describe the psychological state of a normal mother's absorption in and sensitivity to her baby around childbirth as a 'normal illness'. He emphasised that this state provides a setting for the infant's developmental tendencies to begin their process, and described its development gradually towards the end of pregnancy and persistence for a few weeks after the birth. It is this state which allows the mother to respond delicately and with extreme sensitivity to the infant's needs at the beginning of life, thus allowing complete *dependence, and protecting the baby from *impingements, such as overwhelming frustration, which is experienced and responded to by the baby as a threat of annihilation, or unthinkable anxiety.

If there is failure of this sensitivity then the experience of impingement can interrupt the infant's experience of 'going on being', and threaten ego-development, feeling real and the sense of self, which risks development of a *false self.

Winnicott, D. W. [1949] (1957) 'The ordinary devoted mother and her baby'. *Nine Broadcast Talks*, published later in *The Child and the Family*. London: Tavistock.

Winnicott, D. W. [1956] (1958) 'Primary maternal preoccupation' in *Collected Papers: Through Paediatrics to Psychoanalysis*. London: Tavistock.

J. Joh.

PRIMARY PROCESS Metapsychologically, primitive, drive-dominated ideation using unbound (free) psychic energy in *condensation and *displacement. Freud also described its observable forms in *dream work, joke work, psychotic speech, etc., precisely enough for clinical and even research use. It is a form of thought dominated by wish fulfilment, association, dreams, slips and jokes as well as creativity. It shows little concern for the strictures of logic or reality. Primary processes are ruled by the pleasure principle and their aim is to cathect *representations of objects of satisfaction.

See also: pleasure principle; unconscious

Holt, R. R. (2003) *Primary Process Thinking: Theory, Measurement, and Research*. Madison, CT: International Universities Press.

R. Hol. / E. K.

PRIMARY REPRESSION see **REPRESSION**

PRINCIPLE OF CONSTANCY The earliest and most fundamental of Freud's metapsychological assumptions; it states that a basic function of the nervous system (or mental apparatus) is 'to keep the quantity of *excitation present in it as low as possible or at least to keep it constant'. It does so through adequate discharge, usually a motor reaction. One can understand the principle of constancy as an expression of the assumption that the nervous system tends toward homeostasis.

See also: trauma

Freud, S. (1920) *Beyond the Pleasure Principle*. S. E. 18. London: Hogarth Press.

M. Eag.

PRISTINE UNITARY EGO According to Fairbairn, a pristine unitary (unsplit) ego exists from birth. Under the pressure of post-uterine life *splitting of the ego and the development of *endopsychic structure occurs. In the endopsychic structure, the *central ego represents the residual core of the original unsplit, unrepressed ego, which comes to be associated with the *ideal object and is in direct communication with external reality. The central ego employs aggression to repress the *libidinal and *antilibidinal egos and their objects. Its role as mediator between *outer and *inner reality is central to development.

E. F. B. / D. E. S.

PRIVATION Lacan noted that 'frustration' in Freud is traditionally taken to mean deprivation of the object of a drive or wish. Furthermore, Freud's term indicates a taking away, or retraction of promise, in the field of love, and is central to his account of the child's falling under the sway of phantasy in relation to others.

Lacan, in 1956–7, opposed (Real) privation to (Imaginary) *frustration and (Symbolic) *castration, as three modes of lack of an object. The Real privation of a symbolic object refers in particular to the female castration complex (mother separating from child as Imaginary phallus via Symbolic father). Here the privation of the phallus is Real, but the object is

Symbolic because it refers to and operates on a signifier of difference between the sexes.

M. Eyd.

Project for a Scientific Psychology In the spring of 1895 Freud began the long and ambitious essay known to us as the 'Project for a Scientific Psychology'. In a letter of 25 May 1895 to *Fliess, his friend and principal scientific correspondent at the time, Freud wrote, 'I am vexed by two intentions: to discover what form the theory of psychical functioning will take if a quantitative line of approach, a kind of economics of nervous force, is introduced into it, and, secondly, to extract from psychopathology a yield for normal psychology'. Although the Project failed in its enormous mission, many aspects of this elaborately dense and highly speculative treatise, which attempted essentially to explain not only neurosis but all psychological processes on the basis of neurophysiology, foreshadowed key concepts of psychoanalytic theory.

Perhaps most importantly it appears that just such a feverish and massive intellectual effort – the Project was written, at intervals, in a matter of weeks – directed at the very border of soma and psyche, was required for Freud to transcend the relatively exclusive neuroanatomy emphasis of his time in order to develop the kind of scientific psychology embodied by psychoanalysis.

Because of its scope, density and complexity an adequate synopsis of the Project is virtually impossible. Furthermore, the reader must bear in mind that Freud never published the work during his lifetime; it appeared in 1950 as an appendix to a volume of his letters charting the origins of psychoanalysis, and we have Fliess to thank for its preservation.

The Project, like Caesar's Gaul, is divided into three parts: (1) a general plan, (2) psychopathology, and (3) representation of normal psychical functions. Freud was much concerned with quantitative notions of physical energy and postulated the existence of a complicated system of 'material' neurones whose characteristics of charge and permeability were made to account for a staggering diversity of mental phenomena, such as the basis of cognition, perception, consciousness, thought and reality, sleep, dreams, trauma, and the experience of satisfaction. A blurring of the physical and psychical seems, in retrospect, inevitable and in the end even the most committed reader is hard-pressed to follow Freud's differentiation.

Nonetheless, a variety of ideas now considered integral to psychoanalysis is present in embryo. They include: (1) a principle of constancy and inertia, (2) the distinction between primary and secondary processes, (3) thought as experimental action, (4) the presence of stimulus barriers, (5) *wish-fulfilment (6) differences between unconscious and preconscious, and (7) the mechanism of repression, among others. Its most powerful legacy, to this author's mind, finds expression in the much-neglected economic viewpoint of psychoanalysis, where notions of psychic energies, *cathexes and their transformations are indispensable to an understanding of the human mind in normality and pathology.

The Project, inasmuch as it demanded theoretical abstraction of the highest order, also served as a template for Freud's justly famous seventh chapter of the *Interpretation of Dreams* and all subsequent metapsychological excursions.

In summary, the value of the Project lies not so much in the science it espoused, but in the critical role it played in Freud's journey, both inward and outward, towards the discovery of psychoanalysis. As a waystation of genius which occupied Freud during a fascinating period of rich intellectual and emotional tumult, the Project has yet to be adequately investigated.

See also: neuropsychoanalysis

Freud, S. [1895] (1950) *Project for a Scientific Psychology*. S. E. 1. London: Hogarth Press.

Jones, E. (1953) *The Life and Work of Sigmund Freud*, Vol. I. New York: Basic Books.

Pribram, K. H. and Gill, M. M. (1976) *Freud's 'Project' Reassessed.* New York: Basic Books.
Wollheim, R. (1991) *Freud.* London: Fontana Press

E. G.

PROJECTION A mental operation by which feelings and desires that a subject rejects or refuses to recognise are treated as if they emanate from within another individual. It is a defensive operation in that the subject is able to disavow unacceptable affects and wishes. Projection figures prominently in, for example, racist attitudes, where disavowed ideas are attached to some hated group; in *paranoia, where self criticism is experienced as reproach from others, and in *phobias, where some internal danger is felt to be emanating from an external source, which can then be avoided to produce a greater sense of safety.

See also: defence

Klein, M., Heimann, P., Isaacs, S. and Riviere, J. (1989) *Developments in Psychoanalysis.* London: Karnac Books.

A. E.

PROJECTIVE IDENTIFICATION (KLEIN) Although Freud wrote extensively about projection as early as 1895, he only implied projective identification in 'On Narcissism' and 'Mourning and Melancholia'. The first use of the term projective identification comes from Klein. The origins of the concept in her writings go back to at least 1930, at which point she had described what she regarded as the ego's earliest defence mechanism, a violent expulsive mechanism directed against the subject's own sadism and the attacked and retaliatory object. Her definitive statement on the concept came in her 1946 paper on schizoid mechanisms and the term itself was introduced on that paper's republication in 1952. The term projective identification was meant to describe an unconscious defensive process in which there is a phantasy involving splitting off parts of the self and projecting them onto (or as she saw it, into) another person. Klein primarily saw the motivation for projective identification as an aggressive defensive one, that is, for the purposes of ridding oneself of unwanted parts of the self and/or exerting omnipotent control over the object. Bion subsequently postulated an additional communicative or investigative motive to the mechanism of projective identification, thus broadening the concept from one allied to schizoid pathology to include (and indeed be foundational of) normal functioning.

Klein believed that projective identification is bound up with developmental processes arising during the first three or four months of life when splitting is at its height and persecutory anxiety predominates. In her later works Klein suggested envy was a major motivator of projective identification, particularly as a means of intrusively entering the object and spoiling its desirable contents.

Freud, S. (1914) *On Narcissism: An Introduction.* S. E. 14. London: Hograth Press, 67–102.
Freud, S. (1917) *Mourning and Melancholia.* S. E. 14. London: Hograth Press, 237–60.
Klein, M. (1946) 'Notes on some schizoid mechanisms'. *International Journal of Psycho-Analysis* 27. Also in *Envy and Gratitude.* London: Hogarth Press, 1975 (111).
Klein, M. (1955) 'On identification' in *New Directions in Psycho-Analysis.* London: Tavistock. Also in *Love, Guilt and Reparation Gratitude.* London: Hogarth Press, 1975 (1).

S. A.

PROJECTIVE IDENTIFICATION (BION) This mechanism, defined by Klein as an omnipotent phantasy of the baby, infant, young child or adult, was extended by Bion in various ways. He introduces the idea of 'realistic' projective identification, which is not only an omnipotent phantasy but also a realistic projection which produces effects in the receptor's mind (be it the mother, any other member of a family, a couple, a friend, a group member, the analyst, etc.). It is often so in cases of severely disturbed patients.

He then holds that this realistic projective identification is a primitive and non-verbal form of communication. The first normal situation where this occurs is between the infant's projections of *beta elements and mother's *containing mind with her function of *reverie plus her *alpha function. The receptor of these realistic projective identifications (again, the mother, a group member, the analyst . . .) may be able to think about them and then act accordingly, react by re-projecting them or act them out instead of thinking about them.

Another extension of the concept is related to the contents. Bion holds that not only objects and/or parts of the self can be split off, projected, and identified with the object into which they have been projected, as Klein proposes, but also that mental functions (consciousness, attention, judgment, perceptions, etc.) can be fragmented, split off, projected and sometimes identified with an object.

In his last papers he holds that the unborn baby could also use the mechanism of projective identification in order to free himself of his as yet undeveloped mental functions.

Bion, W. R. (1956) 'Development of schizophrenic thought' in *Second Thoughts.* London: Heinemann.

Bion, W. R. (1962) 'A theory of thinking' in *Second Thoughts.* London: Heinemann.

Bion, W. R. (1962) *Learning from Experience.* London: Heinemann.

Bion, W. R. (1975) 'Caesura' in *Two Papers: The Grid and Caesura.* Brazil: Imago Editora.

E. T. B.

PS-D Bion's own version of Klein's P(aranoid), S(chizoid), and D(epressive) positions; the hyphen suggests an oscillating relationship between them. When an analyst suspends memory and desire and does not cling to what is already known, he or she will necessarily come in contact with a kind of anxiety analogous to Melanie Klein's paranoid-schizoid position. For this state, Bion coins the term 'patience' to describe a non-pathological state which is associated with suffering and tolerance of frustration. Bion felt that during an analysis the analyst needs patience to be maintained until a selected fact emerges and a pattern evolves. He felt that at that point, the analyst will enter into a state akin to Klein's depressive position. For this, he uses the term 'security' with its association of safety and diminished anxiety. He considered the experience of oscillation between 'patience' and 'security' to be an indication that valuable work is being achieved.

Bion, W. R. (1963) *Elements of Psychoanalysis.* London: Heinemann. Also in *Seven Servants.* New York: Jason Aronson, 1977.

Bion, W. R. (1965) *Transformations.* London: Karnac Books. Also in *Seven Servants.* New York: Jason Aronson, 1977.

Bion, W. R. (1970) *Attention and Interpretation.* London: Tavistock. Also in *Seven Servants.* New York: Jason Aronson, 1977.

S. A.

PSYCHE-SOMA Term used by Winnicott to describe the healthy functioning and interrelationship of mind-in-body, or 'psyche indwelling in the soma' in his description of the early development of the individual.

According to Winnicott, the infantile ego is unintegrated at the beginning; elements of the ego come together and normally enter a relationship with each other in those circumstances when the infant is being cared for by an environment-mother in that state of *primary maternal preoccupation that allows exquisite adaptation (*holding) to her baby's needs. This care permits the baby the experience of 'going on being', and the elements of psyche and soma can emerge. Psyche and soma then develop an interrelationship, 'psyche indwelling in soma' and in health the mind develops as a special function of the psyche-soma. Psychosomatic disorders in later life are thus seen as following failure of the environment to provide the adequate consistent care in which the innate maturational tendency can operate.

See also: integration

Winnicott, D. W. [1949] (1958) 'Mind and its relation to the psyche-soma' in *Collected Papers: Through Paediatrics to Psychoanalysis*. London: Tavistock.
Winnicott, D. W. [1956] (1958) 'Primary maternal preoccupation' in *Collected Papers: Through Paediatrics to Psychoanalysis*. London: Tavistock.
Winnicott, D. W. [1964] (1966) 'Psychosomatic disorder'. *International Journal of Psycho-Analysis* 47: 510.

J. Joh.

PSYCHIATRY AND PSYCHOANALYSIS See aggression; amnesia; behavioural therapy; borderline personality disorder; boundaries and boundary violations; character disorder/personality disorder; de Clerambault's syndrome; delinquency; depersonalisation; electroconvulsive therapy (ECT); epilepsy; evidence-based medicine and evaluation; forensic psychiatry; learning theory; medico-legal interface; milieu therapy; memory; memory wars; obsessive compulsive disorder; paraphilias; phobias; psychopath; punishment; suicide

---

PSYCHIC APPARATUS Whenever Freud started to theorise the unconscious, he reached out for spatial representations. The psychic apparatus is the mode of representation of psychic reality: in Freud's 'first topography', the represented space is conceived through the articulation of consciousness, the unconscious, and the preconscious (being placed in between the two extremities of the apparatus, those of 'perception'/'hallucination' and 'motricity'). In the 'second topography' the space is constructed through the attributes of the ego, the id, and the super-ego. For Freud, the psychical apparatus had the value of 'a model', or 'a fiction'. He constantly compared the psychical apparatus with optical apparatus: the microscope, the telescope, the photographic apparatus (and in his later work with 'the magical writing-pad', the *Wunderblock*). The stress is put on, precisely, the realm of 'the virtual', and therefore its nature is not to be reduced to anatomy. The psychic apparatus is conceived in terms of the idea of energy transformation, and on that of the distribution of libidinal energy among the distinctive parts, spaces, and instances of the apparatus. Its principal task is defined as obeying the rule of 'the pleasure principle', or 'the principle of constancy'.

Lacan considered this approach to be constitutive of a series of metaphors for the subject, from which he later extracted a *topology in which the *subject is no longer the subject of a description, but rather the effect of a cut.

E. B. / R. R. B.

PSYCHICAL REALITY According to Freud, whatever in the subject's psyche that presents a consistency and resistance comparable to the material world. After Freud gave up the theory that actual trauma and seduction caused neurosis he postulated phantasy as the cause of neurosis. Phantasies have psychical – as contrasted with material – reality. Psychical reality appears to originate at a developmental stage when the child experiences an equivalence between the internal and external worlds. The analyst gains access to unconscious psychical reality by bracketing out factual details. In listening to a patient talking about her parents, for example, the analyst centres not so much on facts but more on how parents were perceived – 'my father was kind but in a strange way I felt he didn't like me'. This form of bracketing is sometimes called 'analytic decentred listening'. The psychical reality of her parents for this woman will be revealed by how she speaks of them as well as the facts about them. More exactly, it is her reaction to the facts about them that is important – her perception of, for example, father's absence or mother's protectiveness.

See also: internal reality; intersubjectivity

R. M. S.

PSYCHIC STRUCTURE see **STRUCTURE, PSYCHIC**

PSYCHOANALYTIC FUNCTION OF THE PERSONALITY A mental function which allows self-containment and self-knowledge. In his theory of functions, and speaking of the K link, Bion holds that the human being, from a very early age, acquires and develops – if things go well – this function in his mind. A factor of it is *alpha function.

Bion, W. R. (1962) *Learning from Experience.* London: Heinemann.

E. T. B.

PSYCHOANALYTIC OBJECT The psychoanalytic object is Bion's designation for the evolution of emotional experience during the psychoanalytic session. It designates the focus of the analysand's maximum unconscious anxiety. An interpretation must illuminate a psychoanalytic object which at the time of interpretation contains the domains of sense, *myth and *passion. Bion proposes that psychoanalytic elements and the objects derived from them have these three dimensions.

Bion, W. R. (1965) *Elements of Psychoanalysis.* London: Heinemann.

S. A.

PSYCHOID Jung uses the term psychoid as an adjective to designate those phenomena that establish boundary conditions around the notion of the psyche proper, most notably instinctual behaviour at one end of a continuum and irreducible spiritual phenomena at the other. The term psychoid originated with the philosopher and biologist Driesch (1867–1941) who used the term in a vitalistic sense to designate the fundamental guiding force or entelechy in action. Jung's superior at the Burghölzli Hospital, *Bleuler (1857–1939), adopted the term to refer to reflex actions of interest to psychology but not commonly associated with the psyche. Jung rejected both of these uses, although he remained closer to Bleuler. In his discussion of psychoid phenomena, Jung insisted that the psyche proper was in principle under the control of the will. Psychoid phenomena, on the other hand, were not under the control of the will, but neither were they entirely automatic. Thus digestion would not be considered psychoid in nature but instinctual behaviour would be. As such, the psychoid defines a sub-category of unconscious phenomena, specifically those unconscious psychic elements that are incapable of becoming conscious. Some dimensions of spiritual experience share these qualities with the biologically-based instincts as do the archetypes of the *collective unconscious.

Jung, C. G. [1946] (1960) 'On the nature of the psyche' in *The Structure and Dynamics of the Psyche.* Princeton: Princeton University Press.

G. H.

PSYCHOLOGICAL TYPES The roots of *Jung's theory of different types of consciousness lay in his experimental observations of psychiatric patients at the Burghölzli Clinic. He noted that when he administered the word association protocol, some subjects' reactions took on a markedly objective, impersonal tone whilst others insisted on subjectively evaluating the test experience throughout, in a strongly feeling toned manner. In 1913, Jung noted the extraverted tendency of the hysterics whom he found to be more suited to Freud's approach to treatment than the more introverted schizophrenics, whose preoccupation with inner images had led them to withdraw their libido from outer objects. His classic work, *Psychological Types*, elaborated the basis for his belief that psychotherapy should be tailored to these individual differences. By then extraversion and introversion had come to be called 'attitudes' of the ego, and four 'functions' of consciousness were recognised: 'sensation' – which tells us that a thing is there; 'thinking' – which gives it a name;

'feeling' – which evaluates it; and, 'intuition' – which estimates its possibilities. Jung called sensation and intuition 'irrational functions' in that they operated unbidden as pure perception, rather than being deployed by the ego, like thinking and feeling, through rational judgment.

Jung had thus established three axial dimensions – extraversion/introversion, thinking/feeling, and intuition/sensation – by which to assess human consciousness. In his book he noted many earlier attempts within the human sciences to solve the type problem, such as William *James's division of people into tough-minded and tender-minded and *Nietzsche's distinction between the Apollonian and the Dionysian dispositions toward art and life. Jung was less concerned, however, than his predecessors with typing people and more interested in typing the varieties of consciousness called forth in the course of building up the ego's standpoint. Jung's system of typology is therefore his ego-psychology, in which an ego's capacity is revealed through identifying its most developed function of consciousness. This superior function is always extraverted or introverted, and can also be either rational or irrational. Jung further postulates that, in any given individual, the auxiliary function will be different in every respect from the superior function. A person with introverted thinking as the superior function will therefore have as his or her accompanying, auxiliary function a type of consciousness that is both irrational and extraverted – either extraverted intuition or extraverted sensation. Using Jung's typology, eight superior functions are possible (introverted feeling, introverted thinking, introverted sensation, introverted intuition, extraverted feeling, extraverted thinking, extraverted sensation, extraverted intuition), and each of these superiors can be accompanied by either of two auxiliaries. Thus it follows that there are sixteen potential type combinations in all. The identification of these sixteen type profiles (often confusingly referred to as the sixteen types) has been largely left to the Myers-Briggs Type Indicator (MBTI), a paper and pencil self-report of forced-choice preferences in basic life situations. In the US, the widespread use of this instrument by teachers and vocational counsellors has led to the formation of an Association for Psychological Type based in Kansas City and a Center for the Application of Psychological Type in Gainesville, Florida. The Murphy-Meisgeier test has been used to establish the types in children, raising the question as to whether the disposition to develop a certain profile is innate. Jung seemed to imply that it is, although he admitted the possibility of falsification of type due to family and cultural influences and noted that one's type tends to change in the course of *individuation. Jungian analysts have developed the Gray-Wheelwrights Type Survey and the Singer-Loomis Inventory of Personality (SLIP), the latter being the first such test to measure the eight functions independently of each other. Among other Jungians who have emphasised type, *von Franz has delineated the 'inferior function' associated with each of the different superior functions. Beebe has extended her observations to describe how all of the individual's eight functions express themselves in their different positions, including, alongside the superior, auxiliary, and inferior, the tertiary and the four functions in shadow.

Harris, A. S. (1996) *Living with Paradox*. Pacific Grove, CA: Brooks/Cole.

Jung, C. G. [1921] (1971) *Psychological Types*. Princeton: Princeton University Press.

J. Bee.

PSYCHOLOGY, CLINICAL A branch of psychology that takes as its subject matter the broad area of abnormal behaviour. This may include a consideration of what in psychoanalytic terms would be referred to as psychopathology.

Clinical psychology as a discipline and profession has its roots in a wide array of theoretical traditions. Its early origins lie in the experimental psychology tradition established by Wundt and his colleagues at the University of Leipzig towards the end of the nineteenth century. Since then psychoanalytic, analytic, behavioural, cognitive behavioural, humanistic and systemic theories have all left their mark on the discipline. More recently, critical psychology, community psychology, organisational psychology and a host of social theories have been added to the repertoire of conceptualisations available to practitioners to inform their formulations of client problems and possible interventions. This eclecticism is both a strength and a weakness. As a discipline it is vulnerable to the charge of being too easily swayed by fashionable theories within academic psychology. It also gives rise to a fractured body of professionals who may have widely differing and at times incompatible loyalties to various theoretical orientations. In its favour is the expectation that through professional training the practitioner will be equipped with generic competencies to deliver treatments across a number of modalities without necessarily being a specialist of any one in particular. This allows clinical psychologists to address a very wide range of problems from a number of perspectives, and to do so on the basis of research evidence as to the efficacy of particular treatments for particular problems.

The strong conceptual and philosophical links with an empirical tradition within general psychology has given rise to a 'scientist practitioner' model of clinical practice. This model of education, training and professional practice is usually attributed to the Boulder Conference on Graduate Education in 1949. The model emphasises a conceptual structure to each piece of clinical work that requires the objective measurement of identified presenting problems; hypothesis generation as to the predisposing, precipitating and maintaining factors; the testing of an hypothesis through a specific and clearly delineated intervention; and re-testing of the identified problem to measure efficacy. The implicit model of what constitutes scientific practice, what constitutes evidence and ultimately knowledge, differs fundamentally from that used to underpin the intellectual rigour of psychoanalytic inquiry. It is significant that qualitative research methods have only recently begun to have any credibility outside of the margins of clinical psychology.

While the more recent editions of the *Diagnostic and Statistical Manual of Mental Disorders* (DSM) have been accepted as a common language with psychiatry in the USA, Canada and many developing nations, this has been strongly resisted within the United Kingdom. This resistance has been in favour of a focus on problem behaviours, or symptoms, rather than a syndromal approach. This is partly an attempt to avoid the stigmatisation of a diagnostic label, but also allows the redefinition of identified problems in a discipline specific language. It has been argued that the only aspect of the professional role of the clinical psychologist that is unique is the administering and interpretation of psychometric tests, literally the measurement of psychological attributes. This can range from the measurement of intelligence, to neuropsychological functioning, symptoms of disorder and personality. The use of projective testing is a stark illustration of how different clinical psychology traditions can be in different settings. Where psychoanalytic ideas are accepted as a mainstream part of the corpus of knowledge practitioners can draw on, projective testing (for example, the use of the Rorschach inkblots, or the Thematic Apperception Test or TAT) is a significant part of clinical psychology training, in the USA for example. Where this is not the case, such as in the UK, training in the administration and interpretation of projective tests is actively discouraged as they are viewed as unscientific.

The psychological treatments or interventions employed by clinical psychologists differ from psychoanalytic approaches in a number of ways. They are typically short term, pragmatic in their focus, and targeted at specific identified and quantified problem behaviours or thoughts. There is an emphasis on actively maintaining a positive *transference, even if the working alliance is not viewed in these terms, and actively avoiding the negative transference. Regression and dependency could also be seen as *negative therapeutic reactions. There has also been a tendency to minimise or deny altogether the influence of the therapeutic relationship on progress and outcome of treatment, instead choosing to focus on technique and a dose response model. It is worth noting however that many clinical psychologists challenge this orthodoxy within the profession, and that there is a strong tradition of training in psychotherapy or psychoanalysis after qualifying as a clinical psychologist.

Frosh, S. (1989) *Minding the Gap: Psychoanalysis and Psychology*. London: Sage.
Roth, A. and Fonagy, P. (1996) *What Works for Whom? A Critical Review of Psychotherapy Research*. New York: Guilford.

C. V.

PSYCHOPATH Psychopaths are those who are violent, delinquent, manipulative and/or uncaring. Other synonyms include 'dissocial' or 'antisocial personality'. Psychopathic personality has similarities with the *borderline personality, both displaying disorders of interpersonal functioning with impulsive behaviour but, whereas the violence of the borderline is expressed towards the self, with self-harm, self-mutilation and drug use, the violence of the psychopath is directed towards the other. This violence may be catathymic, explosive and impulsive. It may be expressed as part of a particular lifestyle – for example in a member of a bank-robbing criminal gang; or it may be the more psychological and perverse violence seen in sex offending. It is associated with male gender and its prevalence in the general population is thought to be about 4%.

The fact that some psychopathic characteristics can also be observed and described in very successful and creative people lead to the notion of the creative psychopath. Another way of explaining this is that, like other personality descriptions psychopathy is best understood as a trait which we all exhibit to some degree, and the so-called psychopaths are merely those at one end of a spectrum. Unlike borderline personality, psychopathy seems not to have had much attention from psychodynamic writers. Meloy proposes a model of disordered attachments in childhood leading to the characteristic lack of empathy exhibited by psychopaths. Others have explored the meaning of other symptoms such as violence and murderousness.

Cleckley argued that psychopathy was a sort of 'moral insanity' in those who, to all other intents and purposes, were psychologically well. In the last three decades, Hare and other criminologists have used these concepts to devise an effective and predictive measure of the degree of psychopathy, the Psychopathy Checklist (PCLR). As well as a high score accurately predicting dangerousness, the PCLR distinguishes two types of psychopathy, namely 'interpersonal psychopaths', characterised by shallow affect, callousness and an enjoyment of duping people, and those who are more physically violent. The former may be more dangerous because of their ability to feign progress in psychological treatments.

Effective treatment is an area causing much debate. There is some tentative evidence that the therapeutic community/*milieu therapy model shows the most hopeful way forward, although there has been a suggestion that psychotherapeutic treatment can worsen the disorder.

Cleckley, H. (1941) *The Mask of Sanity*. St Louis: Mosby.
Hare, R. C. (1985) *The Psychopathy Check List*. Vancouver: University of British Columbia.
Meloy, J. R. (1992) *Violent Attachments*. Northvale, NJ: Jason Aronson.

M. Mor.

PSYCHOSIS Freud compares the mechanisms of *neurosis and psychosis in the following terms: in both there is a withdrawal of investment, or object-*cathexis, from objects in the world. In the case of neurosis, the cathexis withdrawn from objects in the world is invested in fantasised objects in the neurotic's internal world. In the case of psychosis the withdrawn cathexis is invested in the *ego. This takes place at the expense of all object-cathexis, even in fantasy, and the turning of libido upon the ego accounts for symptoms such as hypochondria and megalomania. The delusional system, the most striking feature of psychosis, arises in a second stage. Freud characterises the construction of a delusional system as an attempt at recovery, in which the subject re-establishes a new, often very intense, relation with the people and things in the world by way of his or her delusions.

For Lacan, in psychosis *jouissance is not curtailed by the framework of language (or field of the Other) and is consequently experienced as invasive. In paranoia, the subject localises invasive jouissance in the field of the Other; in schizophrenia, jouissance returns to the body, as manifested in the primary symptoms of hypochondria, body delusions and body phenomena. This is consistent with Freud's theory of schizophrenia as a regression to auto-erotism.

Psychosis, together with neurosis and perversion, is one of the main differentiations of structural organisation made by Lacan. When triggered, it is characterised by language disorders or by symptoms such as delusion and hallucination. These troubles indicate the return in the Real of signifiers which have not been signified because of the foreclosure of the Name of the Father. The onset of psychosis is linked to an encounter with a signifier which represents the 'one father' which is not included in the Symbolic structure. Before the onset, psychosis is characterised by abnormal indices which can be established during preliminary analytical sessions and which lead to a more prudent attitude towards the subject entering the analytical process.

D. Cre. / M. Eyd. / R. Gri.

PSYCHOSIS (CHILDHOOD) Psychotic states of mind in children arise in response to mental pain beyond the endurance of the immature ego of the child. If such states repeatedly overwhelm ways of dealing with mental pain which are more in touch with reality, the development of the personality is profoundly affected and the child can become trapped in a disturbed way of apprehending experiences, and, in consequence, in disturbed object-relationships which make him unavailable to benefit from nurture. Both emotional and intellectual functioning are massively damaged by the depletion and distortion of the *projective and *introjective processes on which the growth of mind depends.

Primitive emotional experience which overwhelms ego functioning leads to mental states characterised by atrophy or failure in the development of symbolic capacities, including the development of communicative language, concrete thinking and confusional states, withdrawal into a private world, manic unregulated discharge of emotion through physical behaviours, and persistent thought disorder.

The defences against unmanageable mental pain to which the child resorts often unfortunately cut him off from the external understanding and support which is the primary resource for modifying his emotional experience. These defences include efforts to evacuate the unbearable distress and to force it into other people by *projective identification. This mechanism underlies the persistent screaming, violent and abusive attacks on the body of self and others, and the use of language to disturb and confuse rather than communicate. Much of the bizarre behaviour of children in the grip of psychotic anxieties seems to represent either their desperate efforts to gain relief from inner torment through externalising the threat to their inner sense of self, or their retreat to idiosyncratic activities through which they feel they can gain protection because their magical belief systems endow a particular object or action with the power to ward off imagined dangers.

Developments in psychoanalytic theory have made childhood psychosis available to understanding and therapeutic intervention. *Klein's interest in early disturbance was the origin of therapists' efforts to reach children imprisoned in mad inner worlds. Other significant psychoanalytic writers in this field include *Meltzer, *Tustin and Alvarez, and, in the *Lacanian tradition, Mannoni. Strong traditions of therapeutic work with psychotic children have developed in those countries influenced by Kleinian or Lacanian thinking.

Psychoanalytic understanding of such severely disturbed children has been profoundly influenced by *Bion's concept of containment and his investigation of the origins of thought in maternal reverie and alpha function. Clinical technique has remained broadly classical within the framework of child psychoanalysis. The therapist aims to contain and transform the child's distress by providing a reliable treatment setting, by using careful observation to gather and understand the transference and counter transference phenomena, and by describing the child's unfolding inner world in ways which can introduce meaning and differentiation of emotional experience and lessen the chaos and the saturation by painful emotion which have been dominant. Such work depends on establishing a relationship of trust with the child's family and providing support for parents in coping with the immense disturbance of everyday life entailed by the presence of a psychotic child in the family. Families have often turned themselves into hospital-like settings to accommodate the extreme terror of the child, and, in consequence, lost much of their own sustaining sense of connection with a wider world. However, it is now widely acknowledged that childhood psychosis often springs from a multi-generational disturbance, and in such cases intensive work with the parents alongside the child's therapy is needed.

Psychiatric approaches to childhood psychosis tend to focus on organic features and to favour pharmacological and environmental treatments, paying little attention to the potential effective contribution from psychoanalytic psychotherapy. However, there are pockets of significant dialogue and inter-disciplinary cooperation. The recognition of the role of traumatic experience in the aetiology of childhood psychosis, particularly the link to emotional, sexual and severe physical abuse at the hands of parental figures, has given rise to increased interest in psychotherapeutic help being provided for such children.

The overlap between *learning disability and psychiatric disorder is another area where child psychotherapy and child psychiatry meet. The psychoanalytic understanding of early childhood *autism has undoubtedly made it possible to treat some autistic children psychotherapeutically. The greater cognitive sophistication of post-Bion psychoanalytic theory also opens up treatment potential for other learning disabilities.

The non-autistic, more schizophrenic forms of childhood psychosis, characterised less by failure of development and more by perversity, hatred and disconnection from reality, are the most disturbing to encounter, partly because they challenge modern tendencies to idealise childhood. The increasing use of 'forensic' approaches to serious mental illness in children when it is manifested in violent behaviour present a similar challenge to psychoanalytic thinkers whose perspective is needed to influence public policy on the treatment of these troubled children.

Clinical research in the treatment of psychotic children is well represented in recent publications. The psychotherapy such children require is necessarily long-term and this does not match the current desire for brief interventions, and practitioners need to be well-trained and well-supported. However, intervention in childhood may not only transform the life chances of the individual child and the day-to-day experiences of those around him at home and at school, but also save the community the long-term burden of the care of a mentally ill adult.

Bion, W. R. (1962) *Learning from Experience.* London: Heinemann.

Klein, M. [1932] (1975) 'The psycho-analysis of Children' and other papers, in *The Writings of Melanie Klein,* Vols 1 and 2. London: Hogarth Press.

Mannoni, M. (1973) *The Child, his 'Illness' and the Others.* London: Tavistock.

Meltzer, D. (1986) *Studies in Extended Metapsychology.* Strathtay: Clunie Press.

Rustin, M., Rhode, M., Dubinsky, A. and Dubinsky, H. (eds) (1997) *Psychotic States in Children*. London: Duckworth/Tavistock.
Tustin, F. (1972) *Autism and Childhood Psychosis*. London: Hogarth Press. Reprinted London: Karnac Books, 1995.

M. R.

PUBERTY The reawakening of sexual feelings and interests following the *latency period is marked by the physical maturation of the sexual organs. In girls, the menstrual cycle begins, and in boys ejaculation occurs.

J. A. Ber.

PUNCTUATION Punctuation of the analysand's speech functions as a Lacanian analytic tool of intervention, in particular where it heralds the suspension of a session. The kind of technique which varies the length of the session recognises that the timing of the session should neither be arbitrary, nor fixed at fifty minutes, since this misses the opportunity for the problematising of meaning within the subject's discourse.

C. Owe.

PUNISHMENT The fear of punishment, especially of *castration, motivates renunciation and defences against sexual and aggressive satisfaction. Corporal punishment which arouses intense sensations may be sexualised and enjoyed in *masochism. In moral masochism the individual is punished by the super-ego. *Guilt may inspire the need for punishment and the *negative therapeutic reaction.

J. A. Ber.

PUNISHMENT, NEED FOR see **NEED FOR PUNISHMENT**

PURPOSIVE IDEA Even when our thoughts are carried along by a seemingly meaningless and purposeless stream of ideas, it can be shown, Freud maintained, that these are unconscious purposive ideas that determine the course of our associations. One can see that without this assumption, it would make little sense to interpret patients' *free associations and their associations to dreams. The concept is related to such concepts as *Aufgabe*, set and determining tendency, formulated in early experimental and theoretical psychology.

See also: chance

Freud, S. (1900) *The Interpretation of Dreams*. S. E. 5. London: Hogarth Press.

M. Eag.

PUSH-TO-THE-WOMAN This phrase, coined after a popular French idiom (a wine or a person is said to be *'pousse-au-crime'* when their flavour is an invitation to violent passion) implies a criticism of Freud's hypothesis that paranoia is determined by repressed homosexual fixations. Instead, Lacan suggests that homosexual delusions in psychotic individuals are determined by the movement from a pre-psychotic position in which the subjects limit themselves to a fundamental identification with the mother's *phallus, to another position in which this identification is no longer possible. Lacan suggests that one extreme solution is transsexualism.

R. Loo.

QUILTING POINT Lacan took this expression from upholstery in order to indicate the point where a signifier halts the constant sliding of the signifying chain. Using this he explains the relation between diachrony and synchrony, and the effect of meaning as the result of the *metaphoric function of the signifier (selection or substitution) which temporarily 'quilts' the *metonymic movement of the signifying chain. In this way it is possible to give an account of interpretation as a signifying activity.

See also: subject

R. R. B.

R

RACKER, HEINRICH (1910–61) Racker was born in Poland in July 1910 and died of cancer in Buenos Aires in January 1961.

In 1914 the family moved to Vienna, where Racker studied philosophy and music, graduating in 1935. He started to train in 1936 and began his analysis with Hans Lampl-de Groot, which lasted until the 1938 *Anschluss*.

He left Austria and arrived in Buenos Aires in 1939. He first had analysis with Garma and, from 1942, with Langer.

Racker's most outstanding contribution was his discovery (simultaneously with Heinmann) of countertransference as a technical instrument. His first paper on this topic was presented in 1948 and his main contributions were published in 1957 as 'The meanings and uses of countertransference.' In this paper he distinguishes direct and indirect countertransference, concordant and complementary countertransference and countertransference thoughts and countertransference positions.

His work resulted in a seminal book, *Estudios sobre técnica psicoanalítica* (1960), which substantially changed the paradigm of the psychoanalytic process.

Racker also wrote about music, art, jealousy, and Freud's life (*Psicoanálisis del espíritu*, 1957), as well as on psychopathological stratification and ethics.

He died young but he left behind a vast and widely acknowledged psychoanalytic legacy.

Racker, H. (1968) *Transference and Countertransference*. London: Karnac Books.

R. H. E.

RANGELL, LEO A leading proponent of ego psychology, he was born in Brooklyn, New York, in 1913. He began his career, like Freud, as a neurologist and from there moved to psychiatry as a means of practising psychoanalysis. His first supervising analyst was Margaret Mahler with whom he co-wrote what is probably the only psychoanalytic paper ever written on the diagnosis and treatment of Tourette's syndrome as a psychosomatic condition. During World War II Rangell met and arranged to be analysed by Otto Fenichel but was denied this opportunity when Fenichel died prematurely in 1946. Fenichel's classic *The Psychoanalytic Theory of Neurosis* (1950) was described by Rangell as a psychoanalytic bible which continuously shaped his own theorising. Rangell's inaugural membership paper (1950) 'The Analysis of a Doll Phobia' is still read in most training institutes as an authoritative study of a phobia. It contains many parallels with Freud's 'Little Hans' case.

For most of his career Rangell played a central role in the local, national and international organisation and institutions of psychoanalysis. He has twice been President of both the American and the International Psychoanalytic Associations. One commentator has characterised his theoretical contributions as 'a fusion of science and politics'. Partially due to an early catalytic experience in Los Angeles, where he witnessed a hostile bifurcation within rival factions of psychoanalysis resulting in analysts and friends going over to either side of two emergent LA institutions, Rangell developed his lifelong interest in the 'psychology of splits'. He found a further source of insight into individual and group dynamics in the lead up to the political climate of the Nixon era culminating in the Watergate Scandal. The resulting 'national crisis' provided the material for a psychoanalytic study in one of his well regarded books (1980). Here, he identifies ambition, power and opportunism as 'three horsemen of the syndrome of the compromise of [unconscious] integrity'. When in balance, he considers this triad as psychologically healthy constituting normal adaptations in any given social milieu. But when 'hypertrophied and malignant' there is often an ensuing individual and group pathology – 'In conflicts between the ego and the id, I postulated, seen more in the individual, the id is compromised and neuroses develop, whereas in conflicts between ego and super-ego, more visible in group life, the super-ego is the system compromised, and problems of integrity result.'

Rangell penned over 450 articles and seven books of psychoanalytic literature. Approaching the age of ninety he wrote his autobiography *My Life in Theory* (2004) which is for the most part a privileged, and needless to say 'insider's' view of the personalities, events and dynamics within psychoanalysis. Beginning in the twenties it presents a decade-by-decade focus right up to the present on the vicissitudes of his subject. Currently the Honorary President of the International Psychoanalytic Association, Dr Rangell resides in Los Angeles, California.

Rangell, L. (1980) *Mind of Watergate: An Exploration of the Compromise of Integrity*. New York: Norton.

Rangell, L. (2004) *My Life in Theory*. Fred Busch (ed.). New York: Other Press.

S. Byr.

Rank, Otto (1884–1939) Pioneer of client-centred, experiential, 'here-and-now' and existential therapies. Next to Freud, Rank was the most prolific author during the first two decades of the movement. Freud invited Rank to be Secretary and, later, Vice-President of the Vienna Psychoanalytic Society; co-editor of the two leading journals, *Internationale Zeitschrift für Psychoanalyse* and *Imago*; director of Freud's *Verlag*; and member of the Secret Committee.

In 1923 *Ferenczi and Rank published *The Development of Psychoanalysis*, which criticised the classical technique of the 'unnatural elimination of all human factors in the analysis'. In 1924 Rank published *The Trauma of Birth*, exploring how art, myth, religion, philosophy and therapy were illuminated by separation anxiety in the 'phase before the development of the Oedipus complex'. After some hesitation, Freud distanced himself from both books, signalling to *Abraham and *Jones that Ferenczi and Rank were perilously close to anti-Oedipal heresy. In May 1926, with no friends left in the inner circle, Rank resigned from the movement, moving to Paris where he became an analyst for artists such as Henry Miller and Anaïs Nin. Travelling frequently to America, Rank lectured at universities such as Harvard, Yale, Stanford and Pennsylvania on object-relational, experiential and 'here-and-now' psychotherapy, art and the creative will, and 'neurosis as a failure in creativity'. Rollo *May credited Rank as the most important precursor of existential therapy. 'I became infected with Rankian ideas,' said Carl Rogers. Paul Goodman, co-founder with Fritz Perls of Gestalt therapy, described Rank's ideas on art and creativity as 'beyond praise'.

Lieberman, E. J. (1985) *Acts of Will: The Life and Work of Otto Rank*. New York: The Free Press.

Menaker, E. (1981) *Otto Rank: A Rediscovered Legacy*. New York: Columbia University Press.

Rank, O. (1996) *A Psychology of Difference: The American Lectures*. R. Kramer (ed.). Princeton: Princeton University Press.

R. K.

Rapaport, David (1911–60) was born in Budapest and studied mathematics and physics at the University of Budapest, receiving his PhD in psychology from the Royal Hungarian University. His doctoral thesis was on the history of the concept of association from Bacon to Kant. He came to the United States in 1938 and after working briefly at Mount Sinai Hospital in New York and Osawatomie State Hospital in Kansas, he moved to the Menninger Clinic in 1940. After a period of time, he became chief psychologist and head of research at Menninger. In 1948, Rapaport moved to the Austen Riggs Center in Stockbridge, Massachusetts where he remained until his death.

Rapaport's place in psychoanalysis rests on his role as a systematiser of psychoanalytic theory, particularly *ego psychology; as well as (along with Schafer and Gill) work on psychological assessment from an ego psychological point of view. Rapaport, Gill, and Schafer's 1945 to 1946 *Diagnostic Psychological Testing* was virtually a bible among students and practitioners engaged in psychodynamically oriented psychological assessment. As Gill notes, 'Rapaport's central goal was to make psychoanalysis a general psychology', a goal he shared with *Hartmann. Along with Hartmann, Rapaport's writings represent the most articulate and systematic formulation of ego psychology found in the psychoanalytic literature.

Rapaport's main theoretical interests lay in clarifying the nature of ego functions, including thinking and memory and, based on the work of Hartmann, the concept of ego autonomy. One of his original theoretical contributions was the idea that ego autonomy consists not only in the ability to delay in the face of instinctual promptings, but also in reaction to external stimulation. He further suggested that the presence of external stimulation serves to enhance autonomy of the ego from instinctual drives and conversely, that the presence of instinctual drives serves autonomy from external stimulation and protects one from social enslavement.

A description of Rapaport's ideas do not capture his personal qualities of intellectual brilliance, encyclopaedic knowledge, humour, extraordinarily high standards, generosity, intensity, and charisma. As Gill writes, 'It was not possible to know him well without being profoundly influenced'.

Gill, M. M. (1967) 'In memoriam: David Rapaport, 1911–1960' in M. M. Gill (ed.) *The Collected Papers of David Rapaport*. New York: Basic Books.

M. Eag.

RAT MAN Soubriquet for Ernst Lanzer (1878–1919), the *obsessional patient whom Freud analysed for several months spanning 1907–08. The patient's great obsessive fear stemmed from imagining that both his girlfriend and his father were being tortured by rats trying to eat their way into the anus. In the flare-up of dramatic symptomology, Lanzer fantasied that rats were symbolised by a host of objects and activities, ranging from gambling and marriage to children and faeces. The case history of the Rat Man is the only complete *and* successful analysis that Freud published.

Freud, S. (1909) 'Notes upon a case of obsessional neurosis'. S. E. 10. London: Hogarth Press.
Mahony, P. (1987) *Freud and the Rat Man*. New Haven, CT: Yale University Press.

P. M.

RATIONALISATION The process of giving reasons for an action or state of mind which also conceal its true motivation. A person suffering from persecution feelings may rationalise this by claiming that he must be a very important person to be so persecuted. Another form of rationalisation is compared to the *secondary revision of a dream where the dream is reconfigured to satisfy the vanity of the dreamer. This is how the unthinkable is rendered both palatable and coherent. Bion hints that reason in the child begins with blaming rationalisations which develop to responsible reasoning.

See also: defence; intellectualisation; logic

Bion, W. R. (1963) *Elements of Psychoanalysis*. London: Maresfield.
Freud, S. (1900) *The Interpretation of Dreams*. S. E. 4. London: Hogarth Press.
Freud, S. (1953) *A Special Type of Choice of Object Made by Men*. S. E. 11. London: Hogarth Press.
Jones, E. (1923) 'Rationalisation in everyday life'. *Papers on Psychoanalysis*. London: Maresfield.

R. M. S.

REACTION FORMATION Refers to the exaggerated and compulsive character of a positive feeling or behaviour (e.g. affection, solicitude) which, by its very exaggeration and compulsivity betrays its very opposite (e.g. hostility, hatred). Freud viewed certain strong expressions of morality, shame and disgust as reaction formations and believed that reaction formation was an especially characteristic defence of obsessional neuroses.

See also: anticathexis/countercathexis; defence; obsessional neuroses

M. Eag.

REAL One of Lacan's three registers, the Real was initially subordinated to the Symbolic and Imaginary organisation of human reality, but has emerged as the crucial term for an understanding of the clinic. Resisting symbolisation, and thus integration into the psychical system, it is essentially traumatic and inscribes itself in the order of the 'impossible'. Lacan defined three periods of the Real in his teaching: the real as that which 'always returns to the same place' (trauma, repetition compulsion, death drive); the Real grasped by 'logic' as an impasse in formalisation (letter, topology, sexual non-rapport); and as the ultimate irreducibility of the symptom as the subject's most fundamental relation to language.

See also: borromean knot; sinthome

P. D.

REALITY The 'reality principle' succeeds and modifies the pleasure principle. The immediate, even hallucinatory, satisfaction sought by the pleasure principle is replaced by a regulatory function that, in the interest of greater pleasure overall, is capable of both deferring satisfaction and pursuing it indirectly. This function is connected with that of 'reality testing', a process that enables the subject to distinguish a *perception from a hallucinated wish-fulfilment. Finally, Freud introduced the expression *psychical reality to refer to the causal efficacy of fantasy. For Lacan reality is the result of the interplay between the *Real, the *Imaginary and the *Symbolic, and coexistent with the coming into being of the subject. The Real resists meaning and is expressed for instance via the *drive and *trauma; the Imaginary implies the fixidity of meaning and interpretation; whilst the Symbolic permits the shifting of meaning through the chain of signifiers.

See also: ego function

R. Gri. / I. De. G.

REALITY TESTING An ego function of evaluating the relationship between one's self and its surroundings, and determining whether or to what extent a given mental content derives from inner phantasy or a *perception of the external world.

See also: reality

Freud, S. (1911) *Two Principles of Mental Functioning*. S. E. 12. London: Hogarth Press.

A. Ste.

RECOGNITION Lacan used this concept in an Hegelian sense, namely, as the desire to be recognised by the other (as desiring). Furthermore, recognition is intimately linked with, and is indeed the cause of, misrecognition. This latter refers to conscious constructions made by an ego which have their foundation in the *Other; a fact that is not recognised by the ego. The root of this systematic misrecognition is the denial of a more fundamental recognition that the ego is essentially an alienated construction.

H. T.

REGISTER The three registers – the *Real, the *Symbolic and the *Imaginary – make up the conceptual apparatus required to work with the experience of the human subject in the light of Freud's discovery of the unconscious and its effects. The interdependence of the three registers was later 'supported' by Lacan through his use of the apparatus of the *Borromean knot.

B. O. D.

REGRESSION A reversion to a level of functioning that was characteristic of an earlier stage of one's development. Regression can occur with regard to: 1) The types of satisfactions one predominantly seeks: libidinal regression to the *oral or *anal stage away from a more *phallic or *oedipal orientation; 2) The ways in which one relates to others. Regression of object-relatedness entails potential loss of ego boundaries, intensified dependency, or a tendency to view oneself as lacking the requisite abilities that others are seen as possessing to cope with the environment; 3) The overall ability to function, particularly the way in which one copes with danger: employment of more primitive defences such as *splitting and *projection; exhibiting primitive forms of functioning such as regression from *secondary process thinking to *primary process thinking; losing developmentally acquired control over one's body (loss of sphincter control); or 4) With regard to the quality of *super-ego functioning, regression leads to the person's being exposed to a harsher level of judgment and punishment.

Regression can also lead to a defusion. Regression is also a *defence mechanism that is triggered by the development of strong affects that signal the ego to set in motion defences that help avert a traumatic situation. The developmental point that regression leads back to is determined by a process known as *fixation. Regression can be adaptive, as when it occurs in the service of the ego when regression is a temporary and reversible losing of structures, which facilitates creativity. Regression in the service of the ego is an essential element in psychoanalytic treatment.

For Lacan regression appears in analytic work in the form of the return of primary *signifiers, which are mediated by the subject's *demands as supported by the analyst, not in order to frustrate the subject, but rather to make present the signifiers to which the subject's frustration has been tied.

See also: fusion/defusion

R. M. W. / R. T.

REICH, WILHELM (1887–1957) Wilhelm Reich was a pioneer of psychoanalysis who made important contributions to libido theory in the 1927 *The Function of the Orgasm*, and to clinical technique in his 1933 *Character Analysis*. He was discovered anew by the student movement of 1968 as the prophet of the 'sexual revolution'. Born 24 March 1897 in Dobrzanica in Galicia, he grew up in the eastern part of the Austro-Hungarian Empire near Jurinetz (today Ukraine) on the estate of his parents, assimilated Jews. His father Leon Reich died in 1914 of tuberculosis (as did Reich's younger brother Robert in 1926); his mother Cecilia, née Roniger, committed suicide in 1909. Reich reached the rank of lieutenant in the First World War and then studied medicine. In 1920 he joined the Psychoanalytic Society of Vienna and there began a brilliant career. In 1922 he was working in the *Ambulatorium*; in 1924 he took over the *Technical Seminar*. Beginning in 1927 he was politically active, first as a Social Democrat in Vienna and in 1930 as a member of the Communist Party in Berlin. He championed the unity of psychoanalysis and Marxism and thereby ran into increasing conflict with Freud and with the Communist Party. When Hitler came to power Reich left Berlin for Vienna and then Copenhagen and Oslo. In exile in 1933 he published *The Mass Psychology of Fascism* where he analysed the ideological beliefs of those who join the parties of authoritarian regimes; that publication caused his expulsion from the Stalinist-organised Communist Party. Because Reich in his efforts against fascism also brought psychoanalysis into play he was also recognised as a danger to the continued existence of the German Psychoanalytic Society under Hitler. For that reason he was expelled from that society in a secret meeting in the summer of 1933. The leadership of the International Psychoanalytic Association confirmed that decision in 1934 by asserting the incompatibility of Reich's point of view with Freudian psychoanalysis. At this time Reich conceived vegetotherapy, which his student Alexander Lowen later developed into bioenergetics. Reich emigrated to the United States in 1939 and there continued the experiments with which he sought to prove the existence of a new form of energy: 'orgone' energy. In the end he fell victim to the very mysticism he had criticised in others in a political context. He was found to be in contempt of court following an injunction against the sale of his 'orgone accumulators' which were claimed to help in the cure of cancer; and sentenced to two years in prison. There he died on 3 November 1957 (in Lewisburg, Pennsylvania) of heart failure.

Boadella, D. (1973) *Wilhelm Reich. The Evolution of his Work*. London: Vision Press.

Fallend, K. and Nitzschke, B. (eds) (1997) *Der 'Fall' Wilhelm Reich. Beiträge zum Verhältnis von Psychoanalyse und Politik*. Frankfurt: Suhrkamp. Giessen: Psychosozial Verlag 2002 (new edition).

Reich, W. (1988) *Passion of Youth. An Autobiography 1897–1922*. New York: Farrar, Straus & Giroux.

Reich, W. (1994) *Beyond Psychology. Letters and Journals 1934–1939*. Introduction by M. Boyd Higgins (ed.). New York: Farrar, Straus & Giroux.

Reich, W. (1999) *American Odyssey. Letters and Journals 1940–1947*. M. Boyd Higgins (ed.). New York: Farrar, Straus & Giroux.

Sharaf, M. (1983) *Fury on Earth. A Biography of Wilhelm Reich*. New York: Farrar, Straus & Giroux.

B. N. (translated by Channing Bates)

REJECTED / REJECTING OBJECT Fairbairn's first term for the libidinally bad object, which was too painful to be borne in consciousness and was therefore split off and repressed, thus forming the basis for two internal bad objects: the *rejecting object and the *exciting object. 'Rejecting object' was Fairbairn's term for the internalised rejecting and/or persecuting aspects of the primary caretaker or mother, the *antilibidinal object. This is one of the two bad objects.

See also: endopsychic structure; internal object

Fairbairn, W. R. D. [1944] (1952) 'Endopsychic structure considered in terms of object relationships' + Addendum (1951) in *Psychoanalytic Studies of the Personality*. London: Routledge. Pbk 1994.

E. F. B. / D. E. S.

RELATION Although Lacan in general uses this term to indicate mathematical structuring, the term can also refer to the relation of a subject to his or her counterpart. The term generally used for this more particular usage has been *object relation. In Lacan it is a concept internal to the conception of *transference and implies both a libidinal mechanism and a grammar of the drives. It is necessary to bear in mind that the adequate object does not exist, and that there is no pre-determined harmony in the subject-object relation.

A. I.

RELATIONAL PSYCHOANALYSIS branches off from drive and ego analysis on two tracks. One leads away from instinct theory via an emphasis on object relations. The other is methodological, moving from an interpretive stance towards an interpersonal negotiating and sharing. The latter overlaps with an existential analysis that emphasises approaching and being with the other.

The term relational was used by Greenberg and *Mitchell to refer to a model of psychoanalysis intended to bridge the conceptualisations of British object-relations theorists on one side and of interpersonal relations on the other. Not limited to external interpersonal or social relations, the term was also meant to include internal relations among various self-states, conceptualised as the *self-system, and later as multiple selves.

Thus relational theory substitutes the concept of objects or persons for those of instincts, drives and defences as the fundamental units of analytic thought. It is not that relational persons do not have drives and defences, but that interactions between persons are the basic medium in which psychological work takes place.

Relational analysis developed by characterising those interactions. This is one reason *countertransference attains a great prominence in relational work. Analysts and patients are both objects in the therapeutic milieu. The voice of reason illuminating and controlling instincts is replaced by a more level, less authoritative clinical field in which neither party is privileged.

New importance is also given to selfhood. The self is not a significant unit in much analytic theorising; it is more likely to be seen as a fantasy of the ego. Relationally, object, person, and selfhood are difficult to distinguish, and for all the relational doubts about the solidity of selfhood (*Sullivan remarked that we may all be different in different relationships), it is the central interactive agent and is often thought to arise out of the interactive processes. (That it cannot completely result from such processes is suggested by temperamental and genetic considerations.) An overarching role for selfhood has been proclaimed by self-psychologists, but a way of working dominated by mirroring and idealising, as in *self-psychology, is in danger of losing those parts of the self which one cannot empathise with or admire. Relationalists believe that much more of the patient can be admitted to clinical understanding by means of dialogue and negotiation.

The nature of selfhood has been illuminated by theorists close to relational thinking. Bromberg's idea of 'standing in the spaces' is particularly notable. This refers to an ideal state of being able to observe all aspects of oneself without needing to *dissociate or repress (or for that matter act on) any. Bromberg also suggests that this openness to oneself is critical to being open to others, and therefore to treatment. In turn, 'standing in the spaces' is contrasted to a more familiar concept of the ideal self, integration. Integration suggests a more or less harmonious coordination of all self elements. But the inevitable conflicts within psychic functioning, so central to the concept of psychodynamics, cannot be altogether resolved. Furthermore, the dilemmas of everyday life, for example, how much to attend to self or to others, make the goal of inner harmony unrealistic.

Still closer to the heart of relational theory is the problem of objectivity. Traditional analysis founds its objectivity in reason and observation on one model of experimental science. The relational perspective takes a typically postmodern position in which objectivity is seen as the disguise that power often wears, with truth functions to one side. Relationalism attempts to avoid the resulting descent into subjectivity by invoking consensus, along the lines of Habermas' work, which is carried forward by Hoffman and others. But here, of course, power may also be operating.

Perhaps the most compelling claim relational theory makes is epistemological, that there are no one-person observations; there are only two-or-more-person fields. Freud himself was acutely conscious of the effects of suggestibility on analytic data and some of the detached, neutral, anonymous stance of traditional analysis was an effort to offset it. Relational workers are skeptical of this effort and seek an approach to objectivity by acknowledging mutual influences and then trying to correct or account for those effects. A comparison has often been made to particle physics in which observer effects are also prominent and may not be escapable.

The second track is still more methodological and technical. For example, the relational arguments against the primacy of interpretation and clarification rest not only on their critique of the truth value of one-person statements, but as much on the impact of any such statements on the clinical relationship. The content of interpretation may be less the source of resistances than the fact of one person interpreting the experience of another. Certainly, parental *transferences can hardly be the sole result of patients' psychopathology when the interpreter is taking the perennially authoritative position.

Since some elements of interpreting and clarifying are impossible to exclude from human discourse, relationalists do their best to keep those elements modest and tentative. There is sometimes an effort to avoid cognitive formulations altogether so as to deal largely with affects, as by empathic statements. Here the approach to existential work is still closer. Countertransferential possibilities may also be kept foremost. Patients may even wonder who is being treated. But the objective is clear, to open the work for free discourse.

Free discourse replaces free association as the clinical ideal. The fundamental rule, to say whatever comes to mind, recedes and respectful listening and exchanging come forward. Because there is inevitably conflict between free and respectful speaking, some loss occurs at either end of the continuum.

As suggested, relational analysis blurs the sharp distinction between analyst and patient. And because the difficulties in the way of progress may lie not only in the analyst but in the available understanding of human interactions, a common observation gains prominence: analysts may learn as much in some analyses as the patients do, or more. Obviously, the old reliance on analysts' own analyses is less to be trusted. Moreover, when Bromberg's ideal of the clinician being open to all human manifestations and not surprised by any is taken seriously, no one can be expected to have completed an analytic education. While such a conclusion of relational thought may seem forbidding, it is in keeping with a consumer *culture that threatens increasingly to question offerings of any kind. Happily it opens to analysts and therapists a lifetime of continued growth.

Relational psychoanalysis became institutionalised with the publication of the early, independent work of Mitchell (1988); the establishment of the relational track of the New York University Post-Doctoral Program in Psychotherapy in Psychoanalysis, the first training program designed to teach relational analysts; the establishment of the journal *Psychoanalytic Dialogues*; and the inauguration of the International Association for Relational Psychoanalysis and Psychotherapy, with the proliferation of relational theory beyond the United States. Mitchell and Aron (1999) edited the first collection of papers on relational analysis.

See also: body; gender; inquiry; interpersonal psychoanalysis; intersubjectivity; masochism (feminine); object relations theory; participant observation; sexuality; unformulated experience

Bromberg, P. M. (1998) *Standing in the Spaces*. Hillsdale, NJ: The Analytic Press.

Curtis, R. C. and Hirsch, I. (2003) 'Relational Approaches to Psychoanalysis' in A. S. Gurman and S. B. Messer (eds) *Essential Psychotherapies*. New York: Guilford, 69–106.

Greenberg, I. and Mitchell, S. A. (1983) *Object Relations in Psychoanalytic Theory*. Cambridge, MA: Harvard University Press.

Habermas, J. (1990) *Moral Consciousness and Communicative Action*. Cambridge, MA: MIT Press.

Mitchell, S. A. and Aron, L. (1999) *Relational Psychoanalysis: The Emergence of a Tradition*. Hillsdale, NJ: The Analytic Press.

L. H.

RELATIONISM Relationism branches off from conventional instinct and ego analysis on two tracks: from instinct theory by means of an emphasis on *object relations: and from *ego psychology on a more purely methodological basis, moving from an interpretive stand towards an interpersonal negotiating and sharing. The latter overlaps with an *existential analysis that emphasises approaching and being with the other.

Relational theory substitutes the concepts of objects or persons for those of instincts, drives and defences as the fundamental units of analytic thought. It is not that relational persons do not have drives and defences, but that interactions between persons are the basic medium in which psychological work takes place. This is where analyst and patient are.

Relational analysis developed by characterising those interactions. This is one reason *countertransference has attained a great prominence in relational work. Analysts and patients are equally objects in the therapeutic milieu. The voice of reason illuminating and controlling instincts is replaced by a more level, less authoritative clinical field in which no party is privileged.

New importance is also given to selfhood. The self is not a significant unit in much analytic theorising; it is more likely to be seen as a fantasy of the ego. Relationally, object, person, and selfhood are difficult to distinguish, and for all the relational doubts about the solidity of selfhood (*Sullivan remarked that we may all be different in different relationships), it is the central interactive agent and is often thought to arise out of the interactive processes. (That it cannot completely result from such processes is suggested by temperamental and genetic considerations.) An overarching role for selfhood has been proclaimed by *self-psychologists, but a way of working dominated by mirroring and *idealising, as in self-psychology, is in danger of losing those parts of the self which one cannot empathise with or admire. Relationists believe that much more of the patient can be admitted to clinical understanding by means of dialogue and negotiation.

The nature of selfhood has been illuminated by theorists close to relational thinking. Most notable is Bromberg's idea of 'standing in the spaces'. This refers to an ideal state of being able to observe all aspects of oneself without needing to dissociate or repress (or for that matter act on) any. Bromberg also suggests that this openness to oneself is critical to being open to others, and therefore to treatment. In turn, 'standing in the spaces' is contrasted with a more familiar concept of the ideal self, integration. Integration suggests a more or less harmonious coordination of all self elements. But the inevitable conflicts within psychic functioning, so central to the concept of psychodynamics, cannot be altogether resolved. Furthermore, the dilemmas of everyday life, for example, how much to attend to self or to others, make the goal of inner harmony unrealistic.

Still closer to the heart of relational theory is the problem of objectivity. Traditional analysis found its objectivity in reason and observation, based on one model of experimental science. The relational perspective takes a typically postmodern position in which objectivity is seen as the disguise that power often wears, with truth functions to one side. Relationism attempts to avoid the resulting descent into subjectivity by invoking consensus, along the lines of Habermas' work. But here, of course, disguised structures of power may also be operating.

Perhaps the most compelling claim relational theory makes is epistemological, that there are no one-person observations; there are only two-or-more-person fields. Freud himself was acutely conscious of the effects of suggestibility on analytic data and some of the detached, neutral, anonymous stance of traditional analysis was an effort to offset it. Relational workers detach themselves from this effort and seek an approach to objectivity by acknowledging mutual influences and then trying to correct or account for those effects. A comparison has often been made to particle physics in which observer effects are also prominent and may not be escapable.

The second track is still more methodological and technical. For example, the relational arguments against the primacy of interpretation and clarification rest not only on their critique of the truth value of one-person statements, but as much on the impact of any such statements on the clinical relationship. The content of interpretation may be less the source of resistances than the fact of one person interpreting the experience of another. Certainly, parental transferences can hardly be the sole result of patients' psychopathology when the interpreter is taking a constantly authoritative position.

Since some elements of interpreting and clarifying are impossible to exclude from human discourse, relationists do their best to keep those elements modest and tentative. There is sometimes an effort to avoid cognitive formulations altogether so as to deal largely with affects, as by empathic statements. Here the approach to existential work is still closer. Countertransferential possibilities may also be kept foremost. Patients may even wonder who is being treated. But the objective is clear – to open the work for free discourse.

Free discourse replaces free association as the clinical ideal. The fundamental rule, to say whatever comes to mind, recedes and respectful listening and exchanging come forward. Because there is inevitably conflict between free and respectful speaking, some loss occurs at either end.

As suggested, relational analysis blurs the sharp distinction between analyst and patient. And because the difficulties in the way of progress may lie not only in the analyst but in the available understanding of human interactions, a common observation gains prominence: analysts may learn as much in some analyses as the patients do, or more. Obviously, the old reliance on analysts' own analyses is less to be trusted. Moreover, when Bromberg's ideal of the clinician being open to all human manifestations and not surprised by any is taken seriously, no one can be expected to have completed an analytic education. While such a conclusion may seem forbidding, it is in keeping with a consumer culture that threatens increasingly to question offerings of whatever kind. Happily it opens to analysts and therapists a lifetime of continued growth.

Bromberg, P. M. (1998) *Standing in the Spaces*. Hillsdale, NJ: The Analytic Press.

Greenberg, I. and Mitchell, S. A. (1983) *Object Relations in Psychoanalytic Theory*. Cambridge, MA: Harvard University Press.

Habermas, J. (1990) *Moral Consciousness and Communicative Action*. Cambridge, MA: MIT Press.

L. H.

RELIGION, PSYCHOANALYSIS AND Development of the interface between psychoanalysis and religion has moved from Freud's agnostic and antireligious stance to more open and challenging explorations of the meaning of human religious experience. The history of this engagement is one of constant struggle to find the common ground of dialogue while remaining respectful and tolerant of the disciplinary constraints and commitments of both sides.

Freud's reflections on religion began with his view of religion as comparable to *obsessional neurosis, in 1907 and his phylogenetic fantasies expounded by 1913 in *Totem and Taboo*, postulating existence of a primal horde in which murder of the father-leader leads to worship of a totem-god as his substitute. More definitive formulations in his 1927 *The Future of an Illusion* and the 1939 *Moses and Monotheism* declared religion to be a form of *illusion, or even mass *delusion, based on infantile desires for a powerful and loving God to protect vulnerable humans from the forces of death and fate. His longtime friend and follower, the Lutheran pastor Oskar *Pfister, criticised Freud's approach. Pfister regarded identifying certain forms of religious behaviour with obsessional neurosis as emphasising pathologically tinged aspects of religious belief and practice that did not represent the full range of religious experience and reflection. Even before Freud's death, analytic thinking about religion began to diverge. *Jung, for example, developed his approach to the mythic, numinous, mystical and esoteric aspects of religion. While Freud's view saw religious beliefs as forms of illusory *wish-fulfilment, Jung regarded spiritual entities, such as God, as psychic realities whose existence can only be established by psychic means. Jung never clarified this distinction between *psychic reality and actual existence – he was only concerned with 'psychic truth'. Freud could dispense with God, but for Jung God was a necessary and inevitable psychic fact although he was not concerned with questions of God's actual existence.

Subsequently, along quite independent lines, *Erikson broke decisively with Freud's orientation to religion, not only in his genial broadening of the scope of analytic concepts regarding personality development and the formation of *identity, but particularly in his interpretations of Luther and Gandhi. Erikson connected profoundly spiritual aspects of human experience with fundamental infantile roots and dynamics without entertaining the reductionistic fallacy that had plagued earlier efforts.

At this juncture, Winnicott provided a fresh orientation to analytic thinking about religion by way of his analysis of religious belief as transitional phenomenon. He focused on the interaction between mother and child in the earliest stages of life, particularly on the child's first apprehension of the real world. A critical step was formation of a *transitional object, referring to the child's emotional attachment to some external real object, often a doll or teddy bear, serving as a substitute for the mother, facilitating gradual separation from her. This transitional object became the child's first not-me possession and provided a transition from complete *subjectivity to dawning objectivity. The essential quality of the transitional object was that it existed objectively outside the child but at the same time was invested with subjective meaning. Winnicott called this an area of illusion that was neither exclusively subjective nor objective, but both. He argued, for example, that in feeding at the breast when the infant's need is responded to optimally by the mother, the infant's experience of the appearance of the breast in conjunction with his need was equivalent to his subjectively creating the breast his need required. At the same time, the breast pre-existed his need and was independent of it. Thus, the breast was simultaneously a subjective creation and an objective reality.

Winnicott extended this analysis to *transitional phenomena, referring to cultural experiences including capacity for play and forms of symbolic expression such as religion and religious beliefs. The emphasis on religion as 'illusion' diverges radically from Freud's understanding. For Freud, illusions were essentially *wish-fulfilments regardless of their connection with reality but without a connection with reality they were regarded as delusional. For Freud religious beliefs were delusions, whereas in contrast, Winnicott's illusion is both necessary developmentally as a bridge between infantile self-absorption and involvement in reality, and an essential component of human experience corresponding to profound human needs for symbolic, artistic, and religious meaning and involvement. Transitional experience and illusion were essential for satisfying higher human needs for creatively seeking and finding meaning and self-expression in human existence.

Winnicott's analysis of transitional experience opened the way to more fruitful dialogue between psychoanalysis and religious thinking. Winnicott made it possible to understand that the subject-object split could be surpassed and supplanted by a way of understanding religious phenomena that declined this dichotomy. Like the transitional object of the child, religious objects could be regarded as transitional, and therefore as neither subjective nor objective. The ecstatic experience of the 'presence of God' need not be regarded as merely subjective and hallucinatory, but might remain open to objective, even existential, reference. These insights found further elaboration in Rizzuto's 1979 analysis of the God-representation as a form of transitional experience and Meissner's 1984 and 1990 formulation of transitional conceptualisation as constituting a distinct realm of discourse within which the disparate approaches of psychoanalysis and religious and theological conceptualisation could find common ground. For example, the concept of God can be given a full psychoanalytic rendering and understanding in terms of the formation and implications of the God-representation analogous to the transference model without negating or contradicting the full spectrum of theological conviction and argument regarding the actual existence of God or necessarily reducing the intelligibility of the concept to limited analytic terms.

Erikson, E. H. [1958] (1962) *Young Man Luther: A Study in Psychoanalysis and History*. New York: Norton.

Meissner, S. J., W. W. (1984) *Psychoanalysis and Religious Experience*. New Haven, CT: Yale University Press.

Meissner, S. J., W. W. (1990) 'The role of transitional conceptualization in religious thought' in J. H. Smith and S. A. Handelman (eds) *Psychoanalysis and Religion*. Baltimore: Johns Hopkins University Press.

Rizzuto, A.-M. (1979) *The Birth of the Living God*. Chicago: University of Chicago Press.

Winnicott, D. W. (1971) 'Transitional objects and transitional phenomena' in *Playing and Reality*. New York: Basic Books.

W. Mei.

REMEMBERING Within the psychoanalytic setting, remembering and giving voice to constellations of events, relationships and emotional states known from the past elaborates their meanings and connects those experiences to the structures, needs and beliefs shaping the present. When conscious memory is blocked through repression, trauma, or because what is remembered is a non-verbal imprint of crucial, repeated early interactions, unconscious remembering in the form of *symptoms, enactments or other distorted expressions, occurs.

Lacan distinguishes memory, the machine-like functioning of the *Symbolic order, from remembering, which is a retroactive registering whereby the subject's history is produced. Recollection in analysis recalls the signifiers inscribed by the function of remembering.

See also: hysteria; repetition compulsion; repression

Freud, S. (1914) *Remembering, Repeating and Working-Through*. S. E. 12. London: Hogarth Press.

Winnicott, D. W. (1974) 'Fear of breakdown'. *International Review of Psycho-Analysis* 1: 103–7.

J. Kup. / B. O. D.

REPARATION For Klein, side by side with the destructive impulses in the unconscious both of the small child and the adult, there exists a profound urge to help and to restore loved people who in phantasy have been damaged or destroyed. In the *depressive position the urge to restore the internal and external objects is linked with strong feelings of loss, responsibility, *guilt, and concern for them. In phantasy we re-create and enjoy the wished-for love and goodness of our parents. Reparation is also a way of dealing with the sufferings and grievances of the past (e.g. frustrations due to weaning, etc.). We personally benefit from the sacrifices we make for others when 'making reparation' because of our capacity for identification with others. This capacity is a fundamental element in love and in all human relationships.

In normal development, persecutory and depressive anxieties are mitigated by the cycles of projection and introjection of good experiences, leading to the development of security and integration (and hence the capacity for genuine reparation). However, when good experiences are not adequately internalised, the child cannot sufficiently trust in their own reparative and constructive feelings. Manic reparation, which involves omnipotence and denial (in addition to obsessional mechanisms) is resorted to. In manic reparation, the desire to control the objects and to triumph over them enters so strongly into the act of reparation, that the 'benign' circle of genuine reparation is broken.

Klein, M. (1937) 'Love, guilt and reparation' in *Love, Hate and Reparation* with Joan Riviere. London: Hogarth Press (I). Also in *Love, Guilt and Reparation*. New York: Free Press (I), 1975.

Klein, M. (1940) 'Mourning and its relation to manic-depressive states'. *International Journal of*

Psychoanalysis 21. Also in *Love, Guilt and Reparation and Other Works 1921–1945*. London: Hogarth Press, 1985.

J. A.

REPETITION Repetition phenomena are at the core of psychoanalysis. Due to resistance, a patient repeats symptoms (some of which, like obsessional rituals, are themselves repetitive in character) and inhibitions, instead of *remembering. Function of repetition is commonly understood as ego-attempts at mastery of tension. As the *transference, too, can be seen as a lived-out repetition (transference repetition), which expresses the indestructibility of unconscious fantasies, the handling of it, according to Freud is 'the main instrument . . . for curbing the patient's *repetition compulsion and for turning it into a motive for remembering.'

In Lacan's early work repetition was equated with Symbolic repetition and coincided with Freud's pleasure principle. From 1964 onwards however, Lacan no longer envisaged the *signifier as the object of repetition and thereafter defined it as the ever-failing integration of a traumatic encounter with the *Real. It operates as such 'beyond' the pleasure principle and within the network of signifiers.

See also: automatism; death drive; working through

Freud, S. (1914) *Remembering, Repeating and Working-Through*. S. E. 12 London: Hogarth Press.
Freud, S. (1920) *Beyond the Pleasure Principle*. S. E. 18. London: Hogarth Press.

A. W. / D. B.

REPETITION COMPULSION AND THE DREAD TO REPEAT For *self psychology, the possibility of repeating old, painful experiences or behaviour patterns is accompanied by a sense of dread because patients fear that they will be responded to in ways that would again prove traumatic and also, that they will respond to the analyst in the old ways. Since *selfobject transferences contain the possibility for new experiences in the analysis, the dread of repeating expresses the hope for a new beginning.

Freud, S. (1920) *Beyond the Pleasure Principle*. S. E. 18. London: Hogarth Press.
Ornstein, A. (1974) 'The dread to repeat and the new beginning'. *The Annual of Psychoanalysis* 2: 231–48.
Ornstein, A. (1991) 'The dread to repeat: comments on the working through process in psychoanalysis'. *Journal of the American Psychoanalytic Association* 39: 377–98.

H. B.

REPRESENTABILITY, CONSIDERATIONS OF The dream that is experienced in consciousness during sleep is the result of the transformation of an underlying thought. The process of transformation Freud claims has only three component elements: condensation, displacement, and 'considerations' of representability, or putting onto the stage. The underlying dream-thought is not immediately representable in a dramatic form. The dramatisation of a version of this latent script is what produces the figurations present in the experience of the dream.

B. B.

REPRESENTATION An inner impressionistic image or *imago of oneself (self-representation) or of others (object representations). A representation is not a memory as such, in that it does not serve as a registration of a particular interactional event. Nor does it closely approximate misleading aspects of reality as memories attempt to do. Instead, it combines a wide variety of impressions one has of one's objects and the interactions one has had with those objects, coloured by one's fantasies. An internal image of one's own self that takes into consideration multiple aspects of the self and one's interactions with others is created. A mental representation is a theoretical construct that is inferred from the observable workings of an individual's mind. Mental representations, which may be conscious or unconscious, are acquired through experience, and are considered to be a substructure of the ego. Self and object representations do not start out as separate entities because the mental distinction between self and non-self is initially blurred. As infants interact with their objects, good and bad internal objects (mental representations) are formed that correspond roughly to their internal experience of the interactions they have with need-satisfying (*part object) aspects of their objects. As development progresses, the whole object becomes appreciated above and beyond its capacity to satisfy one's needs. At this point one has developed the capacity to maintain a stable object representation regardless of the state of one's needs (pressing or satiated). It is here that what has been referred to as 'object constancy' is achieved.

*Lacan shows that Freud borrowed the term 'representation' (*Vorstellung*) from philosophy, to mean, broadly speaking, the elements within the mind from which a world of experience is constructed. Lacan introduced the importance of the *signifier for the unconscious and used this term rather than representation. One can relate Freud's *word-presentation to Lacan's *signifier and Freud's *thing-presentation to Lacan's *signified. Using the notion of the signifier Lacan emphasises the determining character of the *Symbolic in the unconscious, the symptoms, parapraxes, etc., over the *Imaginary.

In a more general psychological context, representations are similar to the concept of internal working model (IWM) in *attachment theory describing a process through which significant external events lead to the establishment of mental products (e.g. thoughts and images) that express important dimensions of these significant experiences. Freud's detailed consideration of the processes of representation in dreams have been elaborated by the formulations of Sandler and Rosenblatt. In developmental psychology, Piaget and Werner described developmental sequences leading to different levels in the organisation of mental representations that are congruent with aspects of psychoanalytic theory as Blatt has shown. The content and structural organisation of these mental schemas are most often established in interpersonal transactions throughout life, beginning with the earliest experiences of the infant in the caring relationship with the mother. The development of representations (cognitive-affective schemas) of the self in interaction with the significant other, unfolds in a natural, well-defined epigenetic sequence that begins with a representation of the actions of the significant other; to concrete and global representations of the external manifest properties of the caregiver; to iconic representations that are based on significant part properties or functions of the object; to representations, beginning in adolescence, that are more conceptual and symbolic. The developmental level of the representation indicates the level of an individual's psychological development as well as qualities of the relationship with the object in which these representations were established.

Blatt, S. H. (1974) 'Levels of object representation in anaclitic and introjective depression'. *Psychoanalytic Study of the Child* 24: 107–57.

Sandler, J. and Rosenblatt, B. (1962) 'The concept of the representational world'. *Psychoanalytic Study of the Child* 17.

R. T. / S. J. B. / M. Eyd.

REPRESSED, RETURN OF THE Material may break through the *repression barrier as *symptoms, conversions, or a sensation of the *uncanny, when drive pressure increases as in adolescence, or when the ego control is weakened, through fatigue, physical illness, or sleep. Dreams are the 'royal road to the unconscious' because during sleep, repressed wishes get past the *censorship.

J. A. Ber.

REPRESSION One of the earliest psychoanalytic concepts, defined as the banishment of an unacceptable mental content (e.g. a wish, an idea) from consciousness. Freud viewed repression as the 'cornerstone' of psychoanalysis. As an ego defence, its primary function is to ward off the anxiety that one would consciously experience were the forbidden mental contents that are repressed to reach consciousness. Hence, one would expect, and as one can readily observe clinically, that when repression (and other defences) fail, and there is a '*return of the repressed', the anxiety and other dysphoric affects hitherto held in check by repression erupt. Repressed wishes and ideas can be expressed in disguised form in dreams, slips and neurotic symptoms.

See also: conflict; defence

Eagle, M. (2000) 'Repression'. Parts I and II. *Psychoanalytic Review* 87 (1 and 2): 1–38; 161–89.
Freud, S. (1915) *Repression*. S. E. 14. London: Hogarth Press.

M. Eag.

REPRESSION, PRIMARY Primary repression is at the origin of the first unconscious formations – the core of the unconscious. It is close to the concepts of 'primary' *defence and *fixation. These primary unconscious thoughts are formed via *anticathexis – not cathexis – linked as they are to the very early experiences of excessive degrees of excitation. As late as 1926 Freud admitted that very little was known about this process. But it derives logically from the theory of repression that states that repression is caused both by superior psychological agencies, and by an attraction by already unconscious content. The formation of the latter required a special concept: 'primary' repression.

V. D.

REPRESSION (FAIRBAIRN) Repression is the process of burying from consciousness experiences associated with painful affect. Repression is always paired with *splitting of the ego. Together they shape dynamic mental structure. In Fairbairn, primary repression is carried out by the *central ego, and occurs because of infantile *anxiety and the ego's inability to contain *ambivalence. Secondary repression occurs when the *antilibidinal ego directs a hostile attack on the *libidinal ego and the *exciting object to further repress them. In current thought, secondary repression can also be carried out by an attack by the libidinal ego to further repress the antilibidinal ego, that is when a person uses an excessive goodness of personality to hide aggression from the self.

E. F. B.

REPRESENTABILITY The dream that is experienced in consciousness during sleep is the result of the transformation of an underlying thought. The process of transformation Freud claims has only three component elements: condensation, displacement, and 'considerations' of representability, or putting onto the stage. The underlying dream-thought is a linguistic entity, or text, and is not immediately representable in a dramatic form. The dramatisation of a version of this latent script is what produces the figurations present in the experience of the dream.

B. B.

REPUDIATION OF FEMININITY In Freud's usage, repudiation – *Verwerfung* – has several meanings: a fairly loose sense of refusal (in repression); a form of conscious judgment of condemnation; and a rejection of the incompatible idea together with its affect.

In relation to femininity, Freud postulates that in the course of normal psycho-sexual development, the girl reluctantly renounces the aim of having a penis, adopts a feminine attitude towards her father, and replaces her wish for a penis with a desire to have a baby. In some cases, this 'regular development towards femininity' is thwarted by the repudiation of femininity, a 'masculinity complex'. This pattern – a reaction to 'female castration' and *penis envy – is characterised by the woman's insistence on being like a man, and includes such behaviour and processes as continued emphasis on 'clitoridal activity', unconscious identification with the phallic mother, or father and, in extreme form, homosexual choice.

According to *Horney, 'the flight from womanhood' – a mode of defence that secures the subject from the libidinal wishes in connection with the father – though bringing about a sense of inferiority, is still a gain for the ego, as it can tolerate it more easily than the sense of guilt associated with the feminine attitude. Horney places the topic of female psychosexual development in a broader social context, a useful position for authors who have since criticised and revised Freud's account.

See also: castration

Freud, S. (1925) *Some Psychical Consequences of the Anatomical Distinction between the Sexes*. S. E. 19. London: Hogarth Press.
Horney, K. (1926) 'The flight from womanhood'. *The International Journal of Psychoanalysis* 7: 324–9.

A. W. / M. Eag.

RESISTANCE Anything that impedes the work of analysis, or that prevents the analsyand from gaining access to his or her unconscious. It is particularly apparent as an impediment that interferes with the subject's ability to associate freely or even prevents associations altogether. It is never absent from the *transference. For Lacan resistance is mainly due to Imaginary obstacles to the (*Symbolic) revelation of the unconscious. This is why Lacan writes that resistance is that of the analyst, as far as he or she engages him- or herself in an Imaginary relation with his patient in an *ego to ego relation. Another source of resistance comes from the *jouissance included in the symptom.

See also: analytic relation

M. Eyd. / R. Gri.

REVERIE Reverie can be defined as the maternal state of immersion with the infant in which the mother detoxifies and digests her infant's projections by the use of her *alpha-function. Bion used this term to designate the mother's capacity to receive the infant's *projective identification of intolerable emotions and return them detoxified, enabling the infant to introject them as part of his personality in a tolerable form. The infant, being in himself unable to make use of the sense data, has to evacuate his emotions into the mother, relying on her to convert them into a form suitable for employment as alpha-elements (thoughts). If the projection is not accepted, the infant feels that its feeling is being stripped of meaning. He therefore reintrojects not an emotion made tolerable but a nameless dread. In 'A Theory of Thinking' Bion also defines reverie as the 'physiological source of supply of the infant's needs for love and understanding. If the feeding mother cannot allow reverie or if reverie is allowed but is not associated with love for the child or its father, this fact will be communicated to the infant even though incomprehensible to the infant'. The tasks that the breakdown in the mother's reverie leave unfinished are imposed on the rudimentary consciousness of the infant. This can lead to the establishment of a 'projective identification – rejecting object'. That means that instead of an understanding object the infant has a wilfully misunderstanding object with which he becomes identified.

Bion, W. R. (1962) 'A theory of thinking'. *International Journal of Psycho-Analysis* 53. Also in *Second Thoughts*. London: Heinemann, 1967.
Bion, W. R. (1962) *Learning from Experience*. London: Heinemann.

L. P. C.

REVERSAL INTO THE OPPOSITE Certain drives seem to exist in pairs of opposites. Freud used sadism and masochism, and voyeurism and exhibitionism to illustrate how the aim of a drive gets reversed from active (torturing, looking) to passive (being tortured, being looked at). Turning against the self may defend against the active expression of the wish and may also signify a passive or narcissistic preference.

J. A. Ber.

REVERSIBLE PERSPECTIVE A model for a type of disagreement between patient and analyst. This is not about an ordinary difference of opinion, in which the difference is overt and concerns the facts. In reversible perspective, which is a feature of the psychotic personality, the difference is hidden. Both patient and analyst seem to agree on the facts. However, on further investigation, it becomes clear that it is a false agreement. The facts are considered obvious to both, interpretations are accepted, but the basic premises are rejected and others deliberately and silently substituted. The conflict is kept out of the discussion because it is confined to a domain which is regarded as insignificant. The nature of the falsity lies in the implication that the premises are of the kind that leads one person to see two faces when s/he might with equal propriety have seen a vase (as in binocular vision).

Bion, W. R. (1963) *Elements of Psychoanalysis*. London: Heinemann. Also in *Seven Servants*. New York: Jason Aronson, 1977.

S. A.

RHETORIC AND PSYCHOANALYSIS Rhetoric, or the art of persuasion, has always held a central position in human experience – in the telling of a story or dream or even in the singing of a song, rhetoric is present. The storyteller tries to make the listener feel what it was like to be actually experiencing the events of the story. Most of the time that we are speaking (to ourselves or to others) we are trying to persuade and so our everyday experience is saturated in the so-called 'figures' of rhetoric such as simile or metaphor.

In Freud's writings we find many references to the figures and tropes of rhetoric; he mentions: personification, antithesis, metathesis, metaphor, simile, alliteration and many others. The persuasive or rhetorical function of speech he called 'indirect' speech. Here is an illustration of his, using a joke: Two particularly villainous citizens managed to get elected to the council in which they quickly rose to the rank of having their portraits hung in the Town Hall. A local journalist looking at the two remarked: 'But where is our Saviour?' The joke is, of course, that Jesus was crucified between two thieves and this is an indirect reference to the villainous activities of the two councillors. In terms of rhetoric the journalist has used the figure of allusion to make an anti-social comment in a concealed and persuasive way.

*Sharpe fastened on to this interest of Freud in her 1937 *Dream Analysis*. She thinks that, just as in poetry and novels there is an attempt to communicate private experience to another person, so also the dreamer, through telling their dream, tries to communicate atmospheric experience to the listener. More subtly perhaps, the dream is an unconscious communication to the dreamer when awake.

Sharpe claims that the laws of poetic diction, evolved by the critics from great poetry and the laws of dream formation as discovered by Freud, spring from the same unconscious sources and have many mechanisms in common. The figures of speech used to construct poetry are analogous to the dreamwork in constructing the dream.

As Freud says in the *Interpretation of Dreams* the relation of similarity or simile is greatly favoured by the dreamwork. The role of simile in speech can easily be linked to *logic in 'predicate thinking'. All psychoanalysts are familiar with this phenomenon though perhaps not under that name. Its essence can be captured in a remark by Aristotle to the effect that all good dream interpreters have a good ear and eye for similarities.

In predicate thought two objects can be equated in virtue of some similarity; this is the basis of classical symbolism. Here is an example: a hospitalised patient saw sex, cigar boxes and women as identical. It emerged eventually that he thought that as the cigar box was encircled by the tax band, the head of Jesus was encircled by a halo and finally that a woman was encircled by the sexual glance of a man, he consequently equated all three. Here is a more subtle example of what is called 'predicate thought':

> Mother to son: 'Nettles will sting you.'
> Son: 'And do they make honey?'

To return to the hospital patient, the point was however that, since the man in question regarded sex, cigar boxes and Jesus as identical, he was engaged in the process of *metaphor making.

Let us pass to the question of metaphor, which Sharpe regards as a compressed simile. For example, take the simile: 'The plough turns up the land as the ship furrows the sea'. By omitting the word 'as', we get the metaphor: 'The ship ploughs the sea'. Thus a simile says, this is like this, while a metaphor identifies two knowns. It is worth noting that *Lacan's notion of metaphor differs significantly from Sharpe's. He stresses the tension between the two parts of a simile that form metaphor. This might explain why metaphor is even more powerful than simile in creating emotional impact, and indeed it is one of the best known and frequently employed figures of speech. Now that we have dealt with simile and metaphor, let us move on to *metonymy, which means literally 'change of name'. This change of name however is usually underpinned by referring to the part of the whole object. For example the expression: 'The White House denies that . . .' is clearly a way of saying indirectly that the President has made or sanctioned a denial. This metonymy serves the purpose of increasing the emotional impact of the political statement.

Sharpe refers to other figures of speech such as onomatopoeia, parallel, antithesis, *repetition and so on, but these need not detain us here, for the principal figures of speech are simile, metaphor and metonymy. We can now proceed to her general thesis about language, namely that we learn language phonetically before we know meanings. Further, in the case of words which acquire second meanings, it is the earlier meaning that dominates in the unconscious. Thus she interprets a client's forgetting of the word for 'nails' (for timber) as due to the fact that the sound 'nails' is learnt, first of all, in connection with fingernails and that this earlier meaning is implicit in the later meaning. Her point is this, fingernails are associated with scratching and hurting and that these associations remain in place with the sound 'nails' even when it is used with the later acquired meaning of 'nails for hammering into wood'. The fact that many modern words have a more primitive childhood meaning offers enormous opportunities for interpretation or subversion of received meanings. This idea and the central preoccupation with puns in the patient's speech was to fascinate Lacan. In fact in his work we constantly encounter the feeling that language, so far from being something that humans use, is something that uses us.

Of all the rhetorical figures Lacan gives pride of place to metonymy (which he equates to *displacement) and metaphor (equated with *condensation) for he assumes a central dynamic 'need to persuade' in man centred on metaphor and metonymy.

Lacan's adjustment of Freud moves the emphasis from images to sounds, from sight to hearing, and therefore towards the listening of the analyst. This enables him to provide a simple model of spoken language. In the session, the patient free associates as well as he can, and produces a flow of words and pauses. We can regard this as the horizontal axis – a kind of endless metonymy, one word after another. From time to time, a pun or metaphor will move the analyst and he may point this out, bringing into existence a depth to the associations. We can regard this as the vertical axis. This is the simple co-ordinate model of language that Lacan uses. For example a patient could say: 'in my dream someone stood up' but the analyst may pick up on the pun 'stood up' and say: 'stood up?' This may have a resonance for the patient which who had recently been stood up on a date.

This example brings out an important point, namely that the pun is a metaphor in the sense that two distinct meanings are 'condensed' in the same sounds while the difference in meanings is preserved. This is a good time to introduce Lacan's use of what he calls the 'signifier'. Basically free association uses words and all words are signifiers in that they mean something or other, but there are also signifiers that are not words. Where the client is free associating, there will be many things going on in the session which are not words. For example the patient's tone, physical movements, sighs, holding of the breath, etc. This means that we need a more general concept other than words to 'bear meaning' and this, for Lacan, is the signifier. Lacanians make much of the fact that, for them, signifiers do not bear meaning but what this means in practice is that signifiers do not bear fixed meanings. Here are simple examples: a sigh, thumbs up, waving goodbye, making eyes, the numeral 6, a signpost; the list is endless. Thus in one stroke he achieves a generalised concept of a language, for a signifier does all that words do and more besides. This means of course that what is 'going on' in a session is a flow of signifiers, not necessarily words.

The reason why Lacan makes such strenuous efforts on behalf of the centrality of language is, I believe, bound up with an idea from the linguist Emil Benveniste to the effect that human subjectivity is brought into existence by the operation of learning a language in childhood. Since he emphasises the *subject at the expense of the mere *ego, and subjectivity is the product of language, the subject must exist or insist in the network of signifiers.

Aristotle (1984) *Rhetoric*. Translated by H. Lawson-Tancred. London: Penguin.

Benveniste, E. (1971) *Problems in General Linguistics*. Oxford, OH: University of Miami Press.

Sharpe, E. (1937) *Dream Analysis*. London: Hogarth Press.

Skelton, R. (1990) 'Generalisation from Freud to Matte Blanco'. *International Review of Psychoanalysis* 17: 471–4.

Skelton, R. (1995) 'Is the unconscious structured like a language?'. *International Forum of Psychoanalysis* 4 (Stockholm).

R. M. S.

Russia The history of psychoanalysis in Russia can be divided into several periods. The first period began in 1904 with Ossipow's Russian translation of an article by Freud on the interpretation of dreams. Ossipow was a psychiatrist trained in Germany and Switzerland in psychoanalysis and in 1908 collected a group of interested students in Moscow. He was to meet Freud in 1910 in Vienna. Later the journal *Psychotherapy* was founded, which published Russian psychoanalytical papers by Russian as well as foreign authors. Moishe Wulff, an analyst trained in Berlin, returned to Russia in 1909. Another interested physician was Drosnès (who brought the *Wolf Man to Freud). Sabina Spielrein had been in analysis with Jung in 1906. In 1911 the Moscow Psychoanalytical Society was established with Ossipow as president. This first period was ended by the Great War in 1914.

The second period – 1921 to 1927 – was a flourishing time for psychoanalysis in Russia. After the Bolshevik revolution many intellectuals left the country; others, like Sabina Spielrein and Tatjana Rosenthal, returned to Russia. Rosenthal was trained in psychoanalysis in Zurich. Psychoanalysis became popular and enjoyed official support in the expectation of educating 'new people'. In 1922 the Russian Psychoanalytical Society was founded by fourteen founders, some of them top functionaries of the Ministry of Education. The most influential among them was Otto Schmidt, a scientist, politician and publisher. His wife, Vera Schmidt, became the head of the Psychoanalytical

Kindergarten, which was opened in Moscow in 1921. In the Kazan there was also a Psychoanalytical Circle with Alexander Luria as head. Both the Society and the Circle applied in 1922 for membership in the IPA. The decision was postponed; Luria came to Moscow as the scientific secretary of the Society. In 1923 the State Psychoanalytical Institute was founded by the same group (Luria, Ermakov, Schmidt); the Kindergarten became a part of it. New interests and discussions involving the young members took place – 'The synthesis of Freudism and Marxism on the base of the Pavlovian theory of conditioned reflexes' was written by Luria and his friend N. Vigotsky in 1925. Psychoanalysis became more and more involved in political discussions about the raising of new generations. This period of time seems to be closely connected with the rise and fall of Trotsky who was interested in psychoanalysis. His friend Joffe was a patient of Adler in Vienna, but he spoke sceptically about the theories of sexuality. The Institute was founded at the peak of Trotsky's power and was closed after his defeat in 1925. In 1927, the year of Trotsky's death, the collapse of the Russian Psychoanalytical Society came: Wulff emigrated, Luria retired. In 1926 the new science of paedology replaced psychoanalysis. Paedology boomed around 1930 and many analysts found refuge in its material, before it was officially replaced by paedagogics. There is little information about development in later years. The official critics of psychoanalysis became more and more ideological until in the sixties the opening to western ideas started and the official Pavlovian 'nervism' theory lost influence.

More recently there has been a wide interest in psychoanalysis and its applications and now seems to be omnipresent in public life. Many groups offer study and training but there is no training analyst in Russia accepted by the *IPA. Enthusiastic young analysts travel to other countries for training; foreign analysts offer seminars and lectures for interested psychotherapists in Russia.

E. F. / R. F.

Rycroft, Charles F. (1914–98) Rycroft became an important influence in the British Psychoanalytical Society as soon he qualified as an Associate Member in 1949. He held several offices in the Society and played an important role in the discussion of new ideas, but after 1956 he gradually withdrew and built an international reputation writing about psychoanalysis for the general public. He was in private practice from 1948 until a few weeks before his death. Rycroft is best known for his highly praised *Critical Dictionary of Psychoanalysis* published in 1968.

His clinical papers in *Imagination and Reality* chart the development of his divergence from classical theory. His paper on symbolism acknowledges a debt to *Jones's 1916 paper but contradicts it in favour of the idea of symbolism as a general capacity of mind. *Anxiety and Neurosis* offers biological explanations of emotions without the death instinct; Rycroft drew attention to the adaptive nature of anxiety, in such innate responses as the startle reflex or a baby's cry. In *The Innocence of Dreams* he rejected Freud's theory of dreams as wish-fulfilling, establishing his own idea of dreams as sleeping thoughts. Primary and secondary processes are seen as complementary modes of thinking, and dreams are messages to oneself concerned with biological destiny. Freud's idea that sexuality in dreams is 'something else besides' becomes a category error.

Rycroft's last two books, *Psychoanalysis and Beyond* and *Viewpoints*, contain essays on psychoanalytic and literary subjects which display his vast erudition and an incomparable prose style.

Rycroft, C. F. (1968) *Imagination and Reality*. London: Hogarth Press.

Rycroft, C. F. (1968) *Anxiety and Neurosis*. London: Allen Lane.

Rycroft, C. F. (1972) *A Critical Dictionary of Psychoanalysis* (rev.). London: Penguin.

Rycroft, C. F. (1979) *The Innocence of Dreams*. London: Hogarth Press.

Rycroft, C. F. (1985) *Psychoanalysis and Beyond.* London: Chatto Tigerstripe.
Rycroft, C. F. (1991) *Viewpoints.* London: Hogarth Press.

M. A.

S

SADNESS Since the object is always lost for Lacan, *lack and maladjustment are unavoidable. They appear as loss and as guilt when experienced as if they were separated from the circuit of *desire. Sadness is related to the presence of *jouissance in the body which is experienced as suffering because it is excluded from the realm of subjective signification.

M. V.

SADO-MASOCHISM The sexologists of Freud's time, such as Krafft-Ebing and Havelock Ellis, had integrated together the sexual enjoyment of sadism and masochism and Freud initially followed them in this. For Freud, sadism was a component sexual instinct in which pleasure was achieved by controlling, hurting or humiliating the object. It was inevitably paired with masochism in which the aim was to suffer pain or humiliation at the hands of the object. As the organism matured, this component instinct came under the primacy of genital sexuality toward which it made its contribution in the form of foreplay. As a perversion sadomasochism became an aim in itself. Originally, Freud saw sadism, which made its appearance during the anal phase, as the primary expression of the drive, while masochism was considered a vicissitude in which the self was substituted for the object. However, when Freud developed his dual drive theory in 1920, he gave primacy to masochism as an expression of the *death instinct, which must be turned outward in order for the person to survive. Freud had given primacy to masochistic enjoyment, in its dependency on the love of the father. Lacan takes up this point of view, in maintaining that sadism is only the denegation of masochism.

J. A. Ber. / S. Cot.

SANDLER, JOSEPH (1927–98) was born in Cape Town in 1927. He received his first degree in psychology from the University of Cape Town when just eighteen, his Masters at nineteen. He came to England to pursue his Doctoral studies with Sir Cyril Burt at University College and worked as a clinical psychologist at the Maudsley Hospital. He obtained his PhD at the age of twenty-three and immediately began medical training at University College Hospital. He became a qualified analyst of the British Psycho-Analytical Society in 1952 at the age of twenty-five. He was the youngest Editor of the *British Journal of Medical Psychology*, a post he held from 1956 to 1962 and from 1968 to 1974. In 1957 he was elected Fellow of both the Institute of Statisticians and of the British Psychological Society. He became Chairman of the Society's Medical Section in 1952.

Sandler was a pioneer in bringing psychoanalysis to academia. He taught at the Middlesex Hospital and the Institute of Psychiatry. In 1968 he was appointed Chair of Psychoanalysis Applied to Medicine at Leiden University. He was Founder and Director of the Sigmund Freud Centre at the Hebrew University in Jerusalem, where he was the first to hold the Sigmund Freud Professorship, between 1979 and 1984. He returned to England in 1984, and became the first incumbent of the Freud Memorial Chair in Psychoanalysis at University College London, and then Emeritus Professor when he retired in 1992. At both universities he established special units for graduate work in psychoanalytic research and education. He was Editor of the *International Journal of Psycho-Analysis* from 1969 to 1978, and Founding Editor of the *International Review of Psycho-Analysis.* He was elected President of the International Psychoanalytic Association in 1989 and served a successful four-year term.

Sandler's contribution to psychoanalysis was immense. He was the intellectual leader of the London Contemporary Freudian tradition which represented a viable alternative approach to the Kleinian and Winnicottian (Independent) schools in British psychoanalysis during his lifetime. He was unique in British psychoanalysis in basing his theoretical advances both in clinical work and in systematic conceptual research. His research work began as Research Psychologist at the Tavistock Clinic, but his most important early contribution was a major initiative to clarify psychoanalytic ideas at the Hampstead Clinic under Anna Freud and Dorothy Burlingham, now the Anna Freud Centre. Based on the systematic study of case records Sandler's group refined a slew of psychoanalytic ideas from the concepts of internalisation to uses of the term transference. His ten papers on basic psychoanalytic clinical concepts, in the *British Journal of Psychiatry*, and his twelve papers on frames of reference in psychoanalytic psychology in the *British Journal of Medical Psychology*, all with Alex Holder and Chris Dare, defined the field for psychiatrists and psychologists interested in psychoanalytic ideas. The most important products of this work are his systematic reformulations of classical psychoanalytic ideas, rooted in nineteenth-century biology, into a language of human relationships. In a highly productive collaboration with his wife, Anne-Marie Sandler, Joseph Sandler arrived at a unique integration of drive theory and object relations theory using the construct of the 'representational world' and a focus on affect as the organiser and driver of internal adaptation. Mechanistic notions such as defences could be restated as modifications of self and other representations driven by unconscious motives. The relationships of patient and analyst could be understood as enactments of internalised role relationships where the actual other could be subtly 'nudged' to play the role of an actual or real internal figure and thus create an interpersonal environment that was familiar and thus experienced as 'safe' by the patient.

P. F.

SANDPLAY A non-verbal form of psychotherapy based on the psychological theories of C. G. Jung, sandplay is a powerful technique that facilitates the psyche's natural capacity for healing. Over the past several decades, sandplay has become widely recognised as an effective tool in both long term and brief therapy with children and adults. Developed by Dora M. Kalff, a Swiss analyst, sandplay helps the individual create a concrete manifestation of the inner imaginal world using sand, water and miniature objects. This symbolic play serves the process of *individuation as it bridges between *ego consciousness and the unconscious, making possible access to the creative imagination, ultimately revealing and leading to an expression of the *Self.

Mitchell, R. R. and Friedman, H. (1994) *Sandplay: Past, Present, and Future*. London: Routledge.

H. F.

SARTRE, JEAN-PAUL (1905–80) An existential philosopher, playwright, novelist and political activist/polemicist, Sartre for many personified French letters for over forty years. Born in south-central France, he graduated from the *Ecole Normal Supérieure* in 1929. There he met his lifelong companion, Simone de Beauvoir, one of the pioneers of feminism and women's psychology. Before World War II, he studied Husserl and *Heidegger in Berlin. Later he served in the French army and was a member of the resistance. In 1964 he declined the Nobel Prize for Literature.

Always interested in psychological subjects, Sartre published *Transcendence of the Ego; The Emotions: Outline of a Theory* and *The Psychology of Imagination* between 1937 and 1940. In 1943, he published his early major philosophical work, *Being and Nothingness*, which contains a section on *existential psychoanalysis. Existential analytic biographies of Baudelaire and Genet followed. His 1963 *The Words* is an existential analytic examination of his own childhood. Sartre's interest in psychoanalysis continued to the end of his life, when he was still working on his unfinished biography of *Flaubert. *The Freud Scenario*, a screenplay written for John Huston, was posthumously published in 1984.

For Sartre, Freud the phenomenologist was to be congratulated while Freud the metapsychologist was mistaken. The phenomena which Freud explained as unconscious, Sartre re-examined as resulting from divided consciousness and 'bad faith' or lying to oneself about the nature of existence. Sartre disagreed with the mechanical and deterministic underpinnings of Freud's psychology and proposed instead that human beings are radically free within particular situations. For Sartre, human beings are free not because we have a *self but because we are a *presence to self. The Sartrean *ego is not a psychic structure, but a product of reflective consciousness and the objectifying *'looks' of others, especially the early others in a person's life. Because we are not identical to the ego or self thus constituted, we may change. The purpose of existential psychoanalysis is to discover the fundamental project (or way of projecting oneself from the past toward the future) that defines a person's way of being in the world. For Sartre as for Buber, the reciprocal nature of the analytic relationship is emphasised over the idea of the analyst as neutral projection screen.

B. C.

SATISFACTION Satisfaction is obtained when a *drive achieves its aim. Reduction of drive tension is felt as pleasure. Attempts to reproduce experiences of drive satisfaction start the processes of hallucinatory wish-fulfilment, reality testing, thought, and purposeful activity. The mental apparatus develops out of the ever-continuing need for drive satisfaction.

J. A. Ber.

SCAPEGOAT, GROUP A deviant role in a group occupied by a person who does not conform to group norms and values. Used by others who attempt to rid themselves of unwanted or feared and unwanted self-representations through projective identification. Coming to terms with the scapegoat means facing the darker side of oneself while overcoming the regressive elements in the group.

Beck, A., Eng, A. and Broussard, J. (1989) 'The evolution of leadership during group development'. *Group* 13 (3 & 4): 155–64.

Scheidlinger, S. (1982) 'On scapegoating in group psychotherapy'. *International Journal of Group Psychotherapy* 32(2): 131–43.

M. P.

SCENE, OTHER Lacan's deployment of the term follows Freud's naming of the locus of the unconscious after Fechner's *eine anderer Schauplatz*: another scene. This 'scene' marks out a territory of the Imaginary and Symbolic, which like a theatre stage, frames the subject's fantasy. The *'*passage à l'acte*' as an escaping from, or toppling off the stage, is a moment of (sometimes irrevocable) departure from the scene.

C. Owe.

SCHAFER, ROY Training and supervising analyst at Columbia University Centre for Psychoanalytic Training and Research and former Vice President of the International Psychoanalytic Association. He was the first Freud Memorial Professor at University College London.

Elaborating upon the seminal ideas he put forward in *Aspects of Internalization* (1968), his *A New Language for Psychoanalysis* (1976) attempted to provide an innovational contribution to metapsychology which he regards as best understood as a 'language for action'. It was designed to replace what he considered outmoded classical metapsychological conceptions borrowed from physics (forces, energy); chemistry (sublimation, neutralisation); and evolutionary biology (drive, adaptation). In its place

Schafer proposes that we follow Wittgenstein's approach that language is a set of rules 'for saying things of the sort that constitute or communicate a version of reality or a world'. Schafer deems this project as much a philosophical enterprise as it is a psychoanalytic one. While it is readily acknowledged by many analysts that metapsychology is often gratuitously dense and involved, few have endorsed his 'psychoanalysis without psychodynamics'. For a review of metapsychology as action language see Macay (1991).

Schafer (1997) is among the few American psychoanalysts who have given serious consideration to the work of Melanie Klein and her followers.

Macay, N. (1991) '*Motivation and Explanation*: an essay in Freud's philosophy of science'. *International Review of Psychoanalysis* 18(1).
Schafer, R. (1968) *Aspects of Internalization.* New York: International Universities Press.
Schafer, R. (1973) 'Action: its place in psychoanalytic interpretations and theory'. *Annual of Psychoanalysis* 1: 159–96.
Schafer, R. (1976) *A New Language for Psychoanalysis.* New Haven, CT: Yale University Press.
Schafer, R. (1997) *The Contemporary Kleinians of London.* Madison, CT: International Universities Press.

S. Byr.

SCHEMAS In Lacan's *Ecrits* there are four graphs, called schemas, which are ordered in relation to their clinical pertinence. For instance, the schema-L of intersubjective dialectic gives prominence to the way in which the Imaginary functions as an obstacle to the apprehension of the Symbolic and to the realisation of the subject. The whole of the Lacanian orientation to clinical work is condensed in many of these schemas.

N. C.

SCHIZOID PERSONALITY/PROCESSES A style of personality and disorder described by Fairbairn, characterised by excessive splitting and living an interior life with impoverished external relationships. Such characters are introverted, dampen affect and are drawn to intellectualisation. Schizoid states are characterised by a sense of futility. The deeply schizoid person lives in the interior world with a withdrawal from external impingement. This development results from excessive *splitting of the ego, hence greater investment in *internal reality, a diminished *central ego, and a marked aversion to participation in events and relationships in external reality. Excessive schizoid responses are most prominent in infants whose mothers alternate excessive excitement and rejection, or in cases of trauma. The affect most characteristic of schizoid persons is futility. Contrary to received wisdom, Fairbairn believed that, with understanding, schizoid patients were capable of insight and recovery. *Guntrip elaborated on the universality of schizoid phenomena, and a regressed libidinal ego that is characteristic of the most entrenched schizoid personalities. Schizoid processes are ubiquitous in early development and involve *splitting of objects and of the ego into internal objects and subegos. Fairbairn identified these processes as fundamental to the organisation of mind into the basic *endopsychic structure. Excessive use of schizoid mechanisms involves excessive compartmentalisation of inner experience.

Fairbairn, W. R. D. [1940] (1952) 'Schizoid factors in the personality' in *Psychoanalytic Studies of the Personality*. London: Routledge.
Guntrip, H. (1969) *Schizoid Phenomena, Object Relation and the Self.* New York: International Universities Press.

E. F. B. / D. E. S.

SCHOPENHAUER, ARTHUR (1788–1860) Schopenhauer was a German philosopher who wrote widely about metaphysics, ethics and aesthetics among other topics. Schopenhauer saw himself as the true inheritor of Kant's (1724–1804) philosophical views, which he extended and modified in various ways. Schopenhauer published his only major work, *The World as Will and Representation*, while still in his twenties, and never departed from its doctrines.

In *The World as Will and Representation*, Schopenhauer argues that the world can be regarded from two fundamental perspectives. On the one hand, the world is a representation – that is, we cannot go beyond our representations of the external world in our attempts to know it. Alternatively, we may consider the world as will. Schopenhauer believes that the will underlies and animates everything that we would call the objective world. We may have some direct knowledge of the will because our own volition is a limited manifestation of the same will that underlies everything.

Although we have limited knowledge of the will through our own volition, according to Schopenhauer the will is largely unconscious. It is in his treatment of the will as unconscious that Schopenhauer's thought contains a large number of parallels with Freud's thought.

The will manifests itself most notably in sexual desire. Like Freud, Schopenhauer believed that the pervasive influence of the sexual instinct goes largely unnoticed. Like Freud, Schopenhauer argued that consciousness is fragmentary. Thus, if mental life has coherent psychological causes, these causes must be unconscious. Schopenhauer's speculations on the aetiology of psychosis (made after visits to asylums) also anticipates Freud's theory of *neurosis. Indeed, it contains both the notions of *repression and *resistance, and views defence-mechanisms essentially as unconscious techniques developed to cope with trauma. He added to these insights a theory of *dreams, and an emphasis on the technique of *association for bringing unconscious thoughts to consciousness and thereby depriving them of their influence.

Freud claimed that he only read Schopenhauer late in life, and after he had already independently arrived at some of the same conclusions. Schopenhauer's dominance of the intellectual culture in which Freud came to maturity makes Freud's claim somewhat unlikely.

Ellenberger, H. (1970) *The Discovery of the Unconscious*. New York: Basic Books.

Kaiser-Al-Safti, M. K. (1987) *Der Nachdenker: Die Entstehung der Metapsychologie Freuds in ihrer Abhaengigkeit von Schopenhauer and Freud*. Bonn: Bouvier Verlag Herbert Grundmann.

Schopenhauer, A. [1819 and 1844] (1969) *The World as Will and Representation: Volumes I and II*. Translated by E. F. J. Payne. New York: Dover Publications.

Young, C. and Brook, A. (1994) 'Schopenhauer and Freud'. *International Journal of Psychoanalysis* 75.

A. Bro. / C. Y.

Schreber The only main subject in Freud's five great case histories whom he never saw in person. Relying on the *Memories of my Nervous Illness* written by the eminent jurist, Dr Daniel Schreber (1842–1911), Freud underlined that the core conflict in male paranoia is a homosexual wish fantasy of loving a man. Key defences in that psychodynamic are reversal and projection; as a result, the male paranoiac transforms the declaration 'I love him' into its opposite, 'I hate him', which is further transformed into the projection, 'I hate him because he persecutes me'.

Freud, S. (1911) *Psychoanalytic Notes on an Autobiographical Account of a Case of Paranoia (Dementia Paranoides)*. S. E. 12. London: Hogarth Press.

P. M.

Schultz-Hencke, Harald (1892–1953) Psychoanalyst, physician and founder of a neo-analytical theory. He received psychoanalytical education at the Berlin Institute and a training analysis with Radó. Together with *Fenichel he founded the *Kinderseminar*. Giving up the essentials of psychoanalysis, he was barred in

1929 from teaching at the Institute. Although he was not a Nazi, his teachings fitted better with the prevailing ideology which enabled him to attract disciples. In 1945, together with Kemper he founded a neoanalytical teaching institute and supported by the health service even acquired an ambulance. A confrontation at the 1949 IPA Congress with Müller-Braunschweig led to a split in the society and the provisional recognition of his *Deutsche Psychoanalytische Gesellschaft* (DPG) as an IPA member.

Lockot, R. (1985) 'Erinnern und Durcharbeiten' in *Zur Geschichte der Psychoanalyse und Psychotherapie in Nationalsozialismus*. Frankfurt: Fischer Taschenbuck Verlag.

R. Loc.

SCIENCE AND PSYCHOANALYSIS There seems to be a consensus among practising psychoanalysts that, as a discipline psychoanalysis has much more in common with the *descriptive* methods of biology, *ethology, palaeontology and the social sciences or even economics than with the methods of the 'exact' sciences, physics, chemistry or astronomy. However, most harsh critics of 'psychoanalysis as science', notably the philosophers of science Popper and Grünbaum, take physics as their paradigm. This has the unfortunate effect of cutting mind out of nature and also emotion, subjectivity, and bodily knowing along with it. That Freud's papers should be read in the original in no way pushes psychoanalysis away from science and towards the humanities where original texts are prized for their continuing fertility. As Lakatos has shown, even so-called 'pure' sciences such as mathematics can be effectively shown to be historical in character.

The scientific tradition taking physics as its model started with Pythagoras who had been able to tie numbers to the physical world. This in turn led to Descartes and Galileo's view that the only real truths we knew about the physical world had to be mathematical. Such an approach, relying heavily on the isolation of quantifiable variables and the conducting of experiments, has led to very successful technological exploitation of the uniformities and probabilities in nature. It has therefore had an overwhelming if undue weight on the idea of what science is and should be. These successes have infused the 'hard' sciences with a certainty verging on religious fervour – an attitude called 'scientism'.

The other outlook, the descriptive one issuing from Aristotle as a biologist, relies not on number but on observation, collection and descriptions of specimens, of exemplars and on the recognition of forms and of their unfolding in nature as processes. Such an approach does not allow the tracking of well-behaved variables and most often makes no pretence at numerical precisions. These descriptive methods dominate *ethology and the so-called 'human' sciences and it is surely noteworthy that economics, despite being a highly mathematised human science, is nevertheless descriptive and therefore excluded by Nagel from the hallowed realms of science.

The most influential criticisms of psychoanalysis as science come from the 'hard' sciences camp. Popper excludes psychoanalysis (as well as *Marx's and *Darwin's theories) from science on the grounds that we cannot specify the conditions under which we would give up the theory. He claims that if the hypotheses of astronomy are falsified they can then be given up as mistaken notions. *Contra* Popper, Grünbaum believes that Freud's theory can be falsified and cites his claims about repressed homosexuality in paranoia. Grünbaum (while rejecting the validity of dreams as wish fulfilment) thinks that the evidence of cures is important to validate the claims of psychoanalysis. However within the hard sciences paradigm this raises difficulties about the subjectivity of the analyst and how it influences the patient. According to this view the analyst can inadvertently make suggestions and propagandise the patient. It is not easy to see how *outcome studies could fulfil his request to exclude what Grünbaum sees as extraneous factors in treatment, given that the very *person* of the analyst should, in his view, not enter into play. Grünbaum's simplistic causal vision presumes that symptoms are caused by early psychological environment in the same way as smoking causes lung cancer.

Where does Darwin fit in, or Freud whom Jones fittingly called the 'Darwin of the mind'? Popper admits he finds no clear manner in which Darwin's theory can be falsified. It gave rise to ethology which has established the uncomfortable fact that what we feel and think about human relationships is based on what we share with the apes. Along with Darwin who revealed the invisible histories of species, Freud too emphasises the continuities of our basic psychic structures with our animal belongings, and he saw each clinical psychoanalytic process as partaking of the nature of a scientific endeavour – which he obviously saw in observational terms for both analysand and analyst.

The psychoanalytic session can be seen as an unfolding evidential field of the psychic processes of analysand and analyst. This permits attempts at description and access to hitherto unconscious emotional and relational assumptions or 'theories'. It is of interest that the German word *Deutung* rendered in English as 'interpretation' has in the German language more the sense of clarification by way of a 'pointing to', either with the finger or with the eye. Thus Freud's own word has a definitely ostensive flavour. As Ahumada points out, the analyst's 'interpretation' can thus be seen as offering a counterexample to the patient's unconscious theory of his world, mainly as it happens to be enacted at the time. The analytic process then allows the analyst to clarify unconscious assumptions or theories and to help in rediscovering and helping re-draw basic assumptions, often by the use of counterexamples opening the way to ostensiveness and psychic growth.

See also: anti-Freud literature; linguistics

Ahumada, J. L. [1994] (2000) 'What is a clinical fact? Clinical psychoanalysis as inductive method' in *The Logics of the Mind. A Clinical View.* London: Karnac Books.

Grünbaum, A. (1993) *Validation in the Clinical Theory of Psychoanalysis.* Madison, CT: International Universities Press.

Lakatos, I. (1976) *Proofs and Refutations. The Logic of Mathematical Discovery.* Cambridge: Cambridge University Press.

Nagel, E. (1961) *The Structure of Science. Problems in the Logic of Scientific Explanation.* New York: Harcourt, Brace and World.

Popper, K. [1963] (1991) *Conjectures and Refutations. The Growth of Scientific Knowledge.* London: Routledge.

J. Ahu.

SCOPOPHILIA The pleasure in looking, originally at the genitals, may be sublimated in the direction of art and intellectual curiosity. It may also become a perversion if, instead of being preparatory to the normal sexual aim, it supplants it. It is related to voyeurism and (by reversal) to exhibitionism.

J. A. Ber.

SCOTOMISATION A defence mechanism in which the subject seems unable to perceive certain aspects of his environment, including himself, especially those aspects giving rise to anxiety or emotional conflict.

See also: negative hallucination

S. Byr.

SCREEN MEMORY A seemingly fortuitous memory of an apparently insignificant event, it 'screens' (and, through the process of free association, ultimately reveals) something of great importance in the psychic life of the individual.

See also: amnesia; defence; denial; repression

J. A. Ber.

Searles, Harold F. (1918–) pioneered countertransference in treating psychotic and borderline patients. His lively papers set a model for self-honesty, giving generations of mental health practitioners an inside view of intensive analytically-informed treatment of psychosis. Born and raised in Hancock, New York, in the bucolic Catskill Mountains, he received his medical training at Harvard. From 1949 to 1964, he worked at Chestnut Lodge in Rockville, Maryland during the Dexter Bullard Sr and Frieda *Fromm-Reichmann era. He was the most prolific of its distinguished staff. He was a Training and Supervising Analyst at the Washington Psychoanalytic Institute and was President of its Society from 1969 to 1971. He was a Clinical Professor of Psychiatry at Georgetown and a Consultant in Psychiatry for NIMH. His popular patient-interview demonstrations remain pivotal events for many psychiatrists.

Langs, R. and Searles, H. (1980) *Intrapsychic and Interpersonal Dimensions of Treatment*. New York: Jason Aronson.

Searles, H. (1960) *The Nonhuman Environment*. New York: International Universities Press.

Searles, H. (1965) *Collected Papers on Schizophrenia and Related Subjects*. New York: International Universities Press.

Searles, H. (1979) *Countertransference and Related Subjects*. New York: International Universities Press.

Searles, H. (1986) *My Work with Borderline Patients*. Northvale, NJ: Jason Aronson.

A. L. S.

SECONDARY PROCESS A mental process that takes place under inhibition by the ego. In the (primary) thought process the immediate satisfactions of the pleasure principle are given free reign. In the secondary process they are inhibited in favour of the delayed rewards provided by rational thought and *conscious action. From the point of view of Freud's first topography, secondary processes are *preconscious or conscious. In economic-dynamic terms, they involve the circulation of weak *cathexes, as a result of *binding. The essential aim of all secondary processes is stable thought processes.

Descriptively, it is an ideal type of conscious, logical, realistic, adaptive thought, with affect held to signal quantities, said to develop gradually overlaying *primary process during adolescence. Phylogenetically, Freud thought it a late achievement of civilisation, helping delay and control instinctual impulses.

Holt, R. R. (2003) *Primary Process Thinking: Theory, Measurement, and Research*. Madison, CT: International Universities Press.

R. Hol. / E. K.

SECONDARY REPRESSION see **REPRESSION**

SECONDARY REVISION Reflects the operation of the dream censor in the formation of the reported *dream. However, unlike other aspects of the censor, its function is not a disguise of latent thoughts, but rather the provision of interpolations and additions that fill gaps in the dream-structure and render the dream less absurd and more intelligible. In a sense, it results in a version of the dream that is already interpreted by the dreamer; secondary revision turns a night dream into an intelligible *daydream.

See also: rationalisation

Freud, S. (1900) *The Interpretation of Dreams*. S. E. 5. London: Hogarth Press.

M. Eag.

SEDUCTION Influenced by the theory of the traumatic origin of hysteria, as well as his belief in the sexual origins of hysteria, early in his writings Freud proposed that his hysterical patients were subjected to the trauma of seduction early in their childhood. He then rejected this idea and concluded instead that hysterical patients created to fantasies of seduction. This then led to a broad examination of the role of *infantile sexuality in mental life. It should be noted that Freud did not deny that actual seduction could occur in some cases.

Freud, S. (1914) *On the History of the Psychoanalytic Movement*. London: Hogarth Press.

M. Eag.

SEGAL, HANNA MARIA (née Poznanska) has been the leading contemporary exponent of Kleinian ideas, as well as making outstanding contributions in her own right. Born in Poland on 20 August 1918, she studied medicine in Warsaw, Paris and Edinburgh where she met *Fairbairn. Encouraged by him, she trained at the Institute of Psychoanalysis in London, qualifying in December 1946. Analysed by Klein and supervised by Heimann and Riviere during that training, Segal then qualified in child analysis, supervised this time by Heimann, *Bick and *Klein.

Having read 'A psycho-analytical approach to aesthetics' in 1947, Segal followed this two years later with her membership paper 'Some aspects of the analysis of a schizophrenic'. Here she introduced seminal ideas on *symbol formation, which she related to thought disorder and concretisation. Concomitantly, she emphasised the technical need for focusing firmly on the analysis of leading anxieties as well as eschewing strengthening defences. This paper pioneered, alongside Rosenfeld and later *Bion, post-Kleinian work with psychosis. Since her appointment as a training analyst in 1952, Segal has championed psychoanalysis internationally, fulfilling among other roles those of President of the British Psychoanalytical Society (1977–80; 1981–2), Vice-President of the IPA (1976–81; 1990–3) and the Visiting Freud Memorial Professor at University College London (1977–8).

While Segal highlights her own specialism simply as 'psychoanalysis', certain underlying themes may be observed in her work. John Steiner suggests a core focus is on the dynamic balance between the capacity to tolerate reality (frustration) versus surrendering to omnipotent phantasy, the vicissitudes of which hinge on the flux between the life and death instincts. Bell adopts a slightly different vertex, emphasising the subtleties of depressive position phenomena and particularly phantasy in Segal's concerns. Such exegesis reinforces Segal's root emphasis on the role of representational processes within the mind and culture, ideas perhaps best expressed in her work on symbol formation and *symbolic equation.

In her later work Segal has highlighted the dangers of omnipotent thinking associated with societal disavowal of the danger of nuclear war and its inherent risk of species annihilation. Segal co-founded Psychoanalysts for the Prevention of Nuclear War in 1983 and International Psychoanalysts Against Nuclear Weapons in 1985, organisations which extend the purchase of reason and the life instinct beyond the consulting room.

Bell, D. (1997) *Reason and Passion: A Celebration of the Work of Hanna Segal*. London: Duckworth.

Segal, H. (1981) *The Work of Hanna Segal: A Kleinian Approach to Clinical Practice*. Northvale, NJ: Jason Aronson.

Segal, H. (1997) *Psychoanalysis, Literature and War: Papers 1972–1995*. Introduction by J. Steiner (ed.). London: Routledge.

R. Wil.

SELECTED FACT A selected fact is an emotion or an idea that gives coherence to what is dispersed and introduces order into disorder. The name of the element that appears to link together elements not hitherto seen to be connected is used to particularise the selected fact. The constant conjunction is formed from multiple selected facts from which only one is used to nominate the constant conjunction. Its significance is epistemological, and the relationship between the selected facts must not be assumed to be logical. This term was used by the mathematician, Poincare, who thought that the facts science selects as valuable are those that harmonise and give coherence to known facts that were previously scattered and seemingly foreign to each other.

Bion, W. R. (1962) *Learning from Experience*. London: Heinemann.
Bion, W. R. (1992) *Cogitations*. London: Karnac Books.

L. P. C.

SELECTIVE INATTENTION Experiences are kept out of awareness in order to avoid the anxiety that comes from threats to the *self-system. Attention is selective by its very nature. By avoiding attention to anything that would bring the anxiety-provoking material closer to consciousness, the self-system is maintained. According to *Sullivan, selective inattention preserves the separation of dissociated experiences. This process is not an active exclusion of experience from awareness. Instead, the experience never enters conscious awareness in the first place. Without attention, ideas can not be spelled out nor formulated. Much of what is ordinarily said to be repressed is merely *unformulated. Selective inattention and dissociation are the primary mechanisms of defense, then, in interpersonal theory. The concepts of selective inattention and dissociation provide a bridge from the dynamic unconscious of psychoanalysis to the cognitive unconscious of psychology. Selective inattention is not entirely a cognitive process, however. One simply does not know what one does not wish to know. Therefore, the process is intrinsically related to motivation. The normal processes of perception, attention, recognition of familiar schemas, and the regulation of stimulation are applied to the problems of living. Adaptive processes have a maladaptive effect when protecting the narcissistic fiction of the self. According to Curtis, all perception, attention, and memory are motivated by their very nature in service of major motivations such as survival and survival of the meaning system, that is the theories of self, others, the world, and causality.

Mullahy, P. (1945) 'A theory of interpersonal relations and the evolution of personality' in H. S. Sullivan (ed.) *Conceptions of Modern Psychiatry*. New York: Norton, 239–94.
Sullivan, H. S. (1953) *The Interpersonal Theory of Psychiatry*. New York: Norton.
Sullivan, H. S. (1954) *The Psychiatric Interview*. New York: Norton.

R. C.

SELF (FAIRBAIRN) For Fairbairn, the self is a complex construct of the person as an organised system, capable of consciousness, subjective experience and action. Fairbairn moved psychoanalytic theory from an instinct theory to a theory of the self derived from Aristotle and *Hegel, which formed the basis of the Scottish philosophical position, within which the person exists in varying relationships within a total social, linguistic and cultural environment. For Hegel self-consciousness is the defining characteristic of humans. In Fairbairn, as in Hegel, human development is a process of positive enhancement of potential. In a similar vein to *Lacan's 'silence in the encounter', lack of relating symbolises lost opportunity. *Kohut elaborated on the vicissitudes of the self focusing on the self's use of the object, but omitting any emphasis on the reciprocity of relationship, that is, the object's use of the self. Hegel also described how specific content and affect are embedded within individual experience of objects. Fairbairn's theory is compatible with modern European philosophers such as Marcuse, Foucault, *Heidegger and MacIntyre who rely on theories of relativity and interpersonal relationships. Fairbairn's biographer, Sutherland, has elaborated on the 'autonomous self', the person as a self-organising system that seeks further potential throughout life.

Fairbairn Birtles, E. (1998) 'Developing Connections: Fairbairn's Philosophic Contribution' in *Fairbairn Then and Now*. Hillsdale, NJ: The Analytic Press.

Skolnick, N., Scharff, D. and Fairbairn Birtles, E. (2002) 'Why is Fairbairn relevant today: a modernist/postmodernist view' in F. Pereira and D. Scharff (eds) *Fairbairn and Relational Theory Today*. London and New York: Karnac Books.

Sutherland, J. D. (1994) 'The autonomous self' in J. S. Scharff (ed.) *The Autonomous Self: The Work of John D. Sutherland*. Northvale, NJ: Jason Aronson, 303–30.

E. F. B. / D. E. S.

SELF (JUNG) The pivotal centre of Jung's model of the psyche. Like his other key contributions, the self is one that he experienced first and later incorporated into his theoretical framework. Jung's encounter with the self occurred during the years 1916–18 in the difficult time that followed his break with Freud in 1913. In the course of these two years he had direct experience of what he came to see as the bedrock of psychological wholeness, that which both keeps the psyche from falling apart at times of great stress but also transcends and goes beyond the psyche.

Jung fully elaborated his notions of the self in his book *Aion*, which represents the collective aspect of the *individuation process. Jung means by this the coming into being of the individual as an integrated and unified whole person distinct from other people. This process belongs to what he called the second-half of life, which starts around thirty-five years of age. In the first-half of life, the individual's task is the development of the *ego and *persona, which are needed in order to relate to the outer world. The self manifests gradually throughout a person's life, but it is the task of the second-half of life for it to emerge fully into consciousness.

Aion starts with simple definitions of the ego and the self, and Jung warns of the twin dangers of the former being assimilated by the latter and of the latter by the former. The word 'Aion' denotes a historical period of time, and in the book Jung explores psychological development related to different signs in the Zodiac. For instance, the period from 0 to 2000 CE is the time of the sign of the fishes – the first thousand years being the time of Christ and the second thousand the time of the Anti-Christ. The symbols of the self are different at different historical epochs and, like everything in life, symbols have their day.

Jung says that the self is a true *complexio oppositorum* and has a paradoxical character. It is both the totality of psyche and also the agent in its manifestation as the *archetypal urge to co-ordinate, relativise and mediate the tension of opposites. To quote Jung, the self 'is the real organising principle of the unconscious'.

As Jung's personal encounter with the unifying power of the self occurred in mid-life, he went on to theorise that others experience this in the same phase of life. *Analytical psychologists since Jung have disputed this claim about the self. The London Jungian analyst, *Fordham, revised Jung's theory of the self in many ways. In contrast to Jung, Fordham stated in 1985 that there is a unified 'primary self' at the beginning of life, which combines the totality of conscious and unconscious systems. Therefore, according to Fordham, integrating processes – what Jung called individuation – were active in the psyche from the start, in contrast to Jung's theory that this started in the second-half of life. Through a dynamic process of disintegration and reintegration from this primary state of integration, the infant interacts with objects in the outer world.

Similarly, Fordham turned away from an exclusive emphasis on the integrating function of the self and became interested instead in what he called part-selves, each felt equally to be the individual's self. This is echoed in *Hillman's work, which is critical of Jung's monistic approach in seeing the unifying power of the self as superior to the polytheism of the psyche with all its *complexes and archetypes.

Fordham, M. (1985) *Explorations into the Self*. London: Academic Press.

Hillman, J. (1971) 'Psychology: monotheistic or polytheistic'. *Spring* 1971.
Jung, C. G. (1951) *Aion*. Princeton: Princeton University Press.

A. D. E. C.

SELF (SARTRE) Existential analysts do not see the self as a fixed entity. For Sartre, there are three forms of the self: the self as subject, the self as object and the self as aim or value. The self as subject (*conscience (de) soi de l'objet*) is not a 'this' but a certain flavour of selfness that pervades my awareness of objects. The self as object or ego (*conscience (de) soi de soi*) is my reflective characterisation of my actions, qualities and states. The self as aim or value is my self-in-the-making, my future-directed project of being which may be changed in a moment of radical world reorientation. Cannon believes that certain confusions in object relations theory and self psychology might be avoided by grounding the self in existential metapsychology.

B. C.

SELF-ANALYSIS Process first explicated in Freud's letters to Fliess – 'The chief patient I am concerned with is myself.' Initially an analysis of Freud's own *dreams, considered to be at the core of the invention of the psychoanalytic method. Seen as complementary to the psychoanalytic treatment proper (a continual demand for the patient's self-reflection), self-analysis is also considered to be a form of *resistance, as it bypasses the *transference. Its essential incompleteness, already recognised by Freud, makes the training analysis, i.e. analysis by another person, the basis of psychoanalytic education.

See also: free association

Anzieu, D. (1959) *L'auto-analyse*. Paris: P. U. F.
Freud, S. [1892–99] (1950) *Extracts from the Fliess Papers*. S. E. 1. London: Hogarth Press.
Freud, S. (1914) *On the History of Psychoanalytic Movement*. S. E. 14. London: Hogarth Press.

A. W.

SELF-DISCLOSURE This is a technical innovation where the analyst uses his own affective experience of the analysis to move the analysis forward. This is in sharp contrast to Freud's notion that the analyst must be a neutral mirror so that the patient can project her or his reactions and feelings on the analyst without being contaminated by the analyst's personality. Interpersonalists do not believe that the analyst can be totally anonymous to the patient since the analyst discloses himself or herself unintentionally or intentionally all the time, even by silences.

Self-disclosure has become readily accepted among interpersonalists as a way to make use of countertransference affects and reactions. There are vast differences, however, among practitioners in terms of how they put personal disclosure to use. Issacharoff and Greenberg are particularly cautious, underlining the potential dangers implicit in the use of disclosure. Greenberg, as a rule of thumb, will analyse a given interaction between himself and his patient before deciding to self-disclose. Issacharoff warns that the analyst will interfere with the ability to identify projections or distortions used by the patient to resolve his conflicts.

While Issacharoff advocates judicious use of *countertransference, other interpersonalists argue that a more expressive use of self-disclosure is clinically important. By making the analytic experience closer to real life, it highlights how the patient can have an impact on the analyst and how that impact can be explicated in all its complexity and interpersonal consequences. Wolstein objects to the blank screen notion because it prevents genuine collaborative inquiry into the process between analyst and patient.

Despite the increasing acceptance of self-disclosure as a fundamental aspect of the analytic venture, most analysts continue to stress its potential pitfalls and caution against unthinking and unanalysed self-disclosure as potentially disruptive to treatment particularly since it may simply serve to gratify the analyst's narcissism and therefore not be helpful to the patient.

Moses, I. and McGarty, M. (1995) 'Anonymity, self-disclosure, and expressive uses of the analyst's experience' in M. Lionells, J. Fiscalini, C. M. Mann, and D. B. Stern (eds) *Handbook of Interpersonal Psychoanalysis*. Hillsdale, NJ: The Analytic Press.

C. M.

SELF-PRESERVATIVE DRIVES see **LIFE DRIVE**

SELF PSYCHOLOGY PRECIS Self psychology is a theory and a method within psychoanalysis introduced by *Kohut. Perhaps its most critical feature is the use of *empathy through vicarious introspection as the most crucial factor of psychoanalytic methodology. In the effort to improve the effectiveness of psychoanalytic treatment of patients with narcissistic personality disorders, Kohut, listening carefully from their vantage point, learned that the essence of their struggle was not the need to control aggressive or sexual drives, but to receive responses that would evoke, maintain, or enhance their sense of self. Kohut found that this need was expressed in the treatment by an experience that that he conceptualised as *selfobject transference. This experience was an attempt to satisfy thwarted developmental needs for 'mirroring', 'idealising', and 'alterego' experiences. When the analyst is experienced as meeting such a need, he or she is a *selfobject. During the past twenty-five years, since Kohut formally introduced self psychology, the breadth of disorders of the *self to which the theory is usefully applied has extended well beyond that of *narcissistic personality disorders.

Unlike Freudian theory, self psychology does not use a model in which the primary motivation is to reduce drive tension and does not view the *Oedipal conflict as central in human motivation or pathology. The theory essentially holds that maintaining, restoring or enhancing the continuity and vigour of the self are primary human psychological motivators and that *selfobject relationships are essential to achieving this. The method consists of the employment of sustained empathic attentiveness to the patient's experience of selfobject needs and to the associated anxieties and conflicts associated with their expression, along with responsiveness that promotes the cohesion, strength, and vitality of the self.

The consistent maintenance of an empathic stance in relation to the patient's subjectivity has had significant effects on psychoanalytic practice. Two, in particular, stand out:

Firstly, because the self psychologist is tuned more sharply to how it feels to be the subject rather than the target of the patient's needs and demands, there is a less adversarial quality to the therapeutic process than one that is informed by more traditional analytic perspectives.

Secondly, there is reconceptualisation of 'narcissistic needs' as selfobject needs. Kohut accorded recognition to the legitimacy of phase-appropriate selfobject needs throughout all phases of development.

As a result, self psychologists could, in practice, abandon the expectation that psychological maturation would entail a decreasing interest in the needs of one's self. The patient's expectation that the analyst be responsive to selfobject needs constitutes a selfobject relationship. The analyst's therapeutic responsiveness to disruptions of the selfobject relationship enables its repair along with the opportunity to work through analogous early relational disappointments. The maintenance and restoration of the selfobject relationship following its disruption have come to be regarded as central therapeutic factors by most self psychologists.

This process leads to the development of a more cohesive and vitalised self and the increased capacity to make effective and appropriate use of selfobjects.

See also: corrective selfobject relationship; empathic vantage point; intersubjective systems theory; intersubjectivity; motivational systems; optimal responsiveness; phantasy selfobjects and phantasy relationships; self, disorders of the; self-regulation and interactive regulation; selfobject relationship; transference, forward and trailing edge

Goldberg, A. (ed.) *Progress in Self Psychology*. An annual bound volume of articles. New York: Guilford and The Analytic Press.
Kohut, H. (1971) *The Analysis of the Self.* New York: International Universities Press.
Kohut, H. (1977) *The Restoration of the Self.* New York: International Universities Press.
Ornstein, P. H. (ed.) (1991) *The Search for the Self, Selected Writings of Heinz Kohut*. 1950–1981 in 4 vols. New York: International Universities Press.
Schwaber, E. (1979) 'On the "Self" within the matrix of analytic theory – some clinical reflections and reconsiderations'. *International Journal of Psychoanalysis* 60.

H. B.

SELF-REGULATION AND INTERACTIVE REGULATION Self- and mutual regulations refer to the interaction patterns that underlie the organisation of experience in infancy as well as in subsequent development. In infants, self-regulation refers to the capacity to regulate arousal: to activate arousal to maintain alertness and engagement with the world, and to dampen arousal in the face of overstimulation; and, to calm or soothe oneself or to put oneself to sleep. Self-touching, looking away, and restricting the range of facial expressiveness are examples of infant self-regulation strategies during face-to-face play. In adults, self-regulation includes symbolic elaborations, fantasies, identifications, and defences. In infancy as well as adulthood, self-regulation is a critical component of the capacity to pay attention and to engage with the partner.

Mutual regulation means that each partner's behaviour affects, that is, can be predicted by, that of the other. Beebe and Lachmann prefer the term 'interactive regulation' since it is less likely to imply a positive or desirable interaction. The processes of self- and interactive regulations are basic to therapeutic and developmental transformations.

Beebe, B. and Lachmann, F. M. (1988) 'The contributions of mother-infant mutual influence to the origins of self and object representations'. *Psychoanalytic Psychology* 5.

F. L.

SELF-SYSTEM Contemporary thinking in interpersonal and relational psychoanalysis follows the thinking of *Sullivan (1964) that the feeling of an inner core to the self is nothing more than a narcissistically invested fiction, albeit a useful one. Instead of trying to determine the structure of the self, that is, the characteristics of an individual's id, ego, and super-ego, Sullivan thought the focus should be upon what is going on interpersonally. He believed that every human being had as many personalities as he had interpersonal relations – what he called 'me–you' patterns, predating current writing on the multiplicity of the self.

Sullivan, influenced by ideas of information processing, conceived of the self-system in ways similar to the notion of schemas, modified by processes similar to what Piaget described as assimilation and accommodation. Anxiety-provoking experiences produce more resistance to change, leading to selective inattention to experiences inconsistent with prior cognitive-emotional schemas. For Sullivan, personality is the entire functioning of a person. The 'self' refers to the organisation of experience within the personality and is largely a composite of internalised experiences with others. Anxiety-free experiences as an infant with the caretaker, usually the mother, lead to the experience of the 'good me', whereas anxiety-filled experiences lead to the 'bad me'. Some experiences, however, are so traumatic that they can not be integrated at all. These experiences Sullivan refers to as the 'not me' and are experienced as dread or horror. Sullivan's view of the personality was criticised by Greenberg and Mitchell and others for failing to have a fully developed theory of intrapsychic processes, leading to the recommendation of supplementing interpersonal theory with ideas from object relations theories into an overarching *relational psychoanalysis.

See also: dissociation; selective inattention

Greenberg, J. and Mitchell, S. A. (1983) *Object Relations in Psychoanalytic Theory*. Cambridge, MA: Harvard University Press.

Sullivan, H. S. (1953) *The Interpersonal Theory of Psychiatry*. New York: Norton.

Sullivan, H. S. (1964) *The Fusion of Psychiatry and Social Science*. New York: Norton.

R. C.

SELF, BIPOLAR Kohut gave the bipolar self a two-part definition: developmental and clinical.

Developmentally, under optimum circumstances the archaic mirroring needs of the infant are gradually transmuted into reliable self-esteem, effective self-esteem regulation and stable capacity for the pursuit of goals and purposes. Kohut called the end of this development the structure of self-assertive ambition – one pole of the bipolar self. Similarly, archaic needs to idealise will under optimum circumstances establish capacities for self-soothing and self-calming as well as for successful affect-regulation. Kohut called the end of this development the pole of internalised values and ideals – the other pole of the bipolar self. A tension arc exists along which stretch an individual's talents and skills are pushed and pulled between these two poles.

Clinically, the deficits in self-assertiveness mobilise a mirror-transference. Its successful working through brings about the transformation of these mirroring needs into mature self-esteem. Deficits in self-soothing, self-calming and affect-regulation mobilise an idealising transference, whose successful working through will ultimately lead to acquisition of the missing self-regulating capacities.

The term 'bipolar self' has fallen into disuse among most self psychologists, despite its accurate description of developmental and clinical phenomena, perhaps because it has been mistakenly viewed as a fixed, abstract metapsychological structure.

Kohut, H. (1977) *The Restoration of the Self.* New York: International Universities Press.

Wolf, E. (1988) *Treating the Self.* New York: Guilford.

P. O.

SELF COHESION The experience of being in a state of well-being derives from the cohesion of one's self. The primary aim of self psychological treatment is the strengthening of the weakened self, rendering it less vulnerable to experiences of *selfobject failure and less inclined to marshal self-defeating defences that make it difficult to use available selfobjects.

See also: self fragmentation

H. B.

SELF, DISORDERS OF THE Also referred to as self- or selfobject disorders. Described by Wolf as disorders associated with damage to the self's structural integrity and strength, as a result of faulty selfobject responsiveness. In the following conditions, the cohesion, vigour and harmony of the self are thus variously impaired:

**Psychosis* – permanent or prolonged serious damage to the self with no defensive organisation covering the defect. Antecedent biological factors operate in conjunction with psychologically self damaging determinants.

**Borderline states* – prolonged serious damage to the self; experiential and behavioural manifestations of the defect are covered by complex defences.

**Narcissistic (behaviour) disorders* – damage to the self is significant but less so than in the preceding conditions. Symptoms reflect the attempt to force others to provide selfobject experiences through behavioural manoeuvres in interpersonal relationships or to seek perceptions of restored selfobject functioning through addictive, perverse or delinquent behaviour sometimes referred to as 'antidote function'.

**Narcissistic personality disorders* – the injury sustained by the self is also significant but more easily reparable through appropriate psychoanalytic treatment. Symptoms represent tensions associated with the weakening or even break-up of the self and their associated subjective manifestations (such as hypochondria, depression, hypersensitivity to slights, and lack of zest).

Some self psychologists regard only the narcissistic behaviour disorders and the narcissistic personality disorders as analysable, while others regard the possibility of effective psychoanalytic treatment as residing in the capacities and limitations of the particular dyad.

See also: specificity theory

Kohut, H. and Wolf, E. (1978) 'The disorders of the self and their treatment: an outline'. *International Journal of Psychoanalysis* 59: 413–25.
Wolf, E. (1988) *Treating the Self.* New York: Guilford.

H. B.

SELF FRAGMENTATION A weakened self lies at the core of all disorders of the self. Diminished cohesion of the self is associated with faulty or deficient selfobject experience. Fragmentations tend to occur along the fault lines where a particular individual's self-structure is vulnerable. The fragmentation may be experienced as decreased self-esteem, emptiness or depression, and may vary from mild anxious discomfort to panic and fear of imminent death or dissolution. Fragmentation may also manifest as narcissistic rage. When the vulnerable self is narcissistically injured, perhaps by an unempathic interpretation, the patient may react with rage, as if the analyst was attacking the integrity of the patient's self.

Kohut, H. (1977) *The Restoration of the Self.* New York: International Universities Press.

H. B.

SELF STATE DREAMS Kohut distinguished between dreams whose *manifest content express drive wishes and their attempted solutions; and dreams that aim to bind the tension of traumatic states. Kohut termed dreams of the second type 'self-state dreams'. These dreams do not yield further unconscious meaning through associations; the essential meaning of the dream may be understood from the manifest content. Self-state dreams are appropriately interpreted from the perspective of the patient's vulnerabilities. While Kohut recognised these two kinds of dreams and that mixed dreams occur in which archaic self states and drive conflict are portrayed, Tolpin's view is that insofar as the data of psychoanalytic observation is subjected to scrutiny on the basis of the essential significance of selfobject relationships, all dream material as well as the patient's associations, may be meaningfully understood in terms of selfobject relations.

Kohut, H. (1977) *The Restoration of the Self.* New York: International Universities Press, 109.
Tolpin, P. (1983) 'Self psychology and the interpretation of dreams' in A. Goldberg (ed.) *The Future of Psychoanalysis.* New York: International Universities Press, 255–71.

H. B.

SELFOBJECT The pivotal concept of self psychology. Denotes a sense of oneself in relation to the other that is needed for the sustenance, vitalisation, or enhancement of the self. A selfobject is neither self nor object, but the subjective aspect of a self-sustaining function performed by a relationship of self to objects who by their presence or activity evoke and maintain the experience of selfhood. The selfobject experience, the *selfobject transference, as well as the *selfobject relationship, are variously co-created by patient and analyst. For the various kinds of selfobjects generally identified by self psychologists see selfobject transference.

See also: object relations theory; phantasy

Bacal, H. (1991) 'Notes on the relationship between object relations theory and self psychology' in A. Goldberg (ed.) *The Evolution of Self Psychology: Progress in Self Psychology*, Vol. 7. Hillsdale, NJ: The Analytic Press, 36–44.
Lichtenberg, J. (1991) 'What is a selfobject?'. *Psychoanalytic Dialogues* 1: 455–79.
Wolf, E. (1988) *Treating the Self*. New York: Guilford.

H. B.

SELFOBJECT, BAD Ostensibly, the term, 'bad selfobject' is self-contradictory if the term *'selfobject' is defined as an experience that evokes or vitalises the sense of self. Yet, self psychologists regularly refer to selfobject failure or empathic failure, indicating a recognition that the patient does not always experience the selfobject as totally 'good'. Bacal and Newman have introduced the term 'bad selfobject' to denote a selfobject that is experienced as relatively bad, and to redress the emphasis in self psychology on self-depletion by recognising the fact that patients also suffer from self-distortion. They regard the term bad selfobject as analogous to, but more useful than, the term 'hostile introject' in *object relations theory – a term that has always referred to the internalised *bad object. The concept 'bad selfobject' denotes the internal experience of the original selfobject following its having proved, at critical developmental junctures, to have failed in some traumatic way, yet remaining as an *exciting object, a concept pioneered by *Fairbairn. In self psychological language, we are talking about a selfobject that stimulates one's need for responsiveness but fails to meet it adequately. The internalised experience of this failure – in effect, the memory of the bad selfobject – will become activated whenever a current psychic event paralleling earlier needs for its functions are awakened. Gehrie and Herzog use the term 'negative selfobject' to emphasise that a failed selfobject not only leaves the child with a deficiency of positive selfobject experience, but also with a reservoir of negative selfobject experience around which the self may be organised.

Bacal, H. A. (1995) 'The essence of Kohut's work and the progress of self psychology'. *Psychoanalytic Dialogues* 5(3): 353–66.
Fairbairn, W. R. D. (1944) 'Endopsychic structure considered in terms of object relationships' in *Psychoanalytic Studies of the Personality*. Boston, MA: Routledge & Kegan Paul, 82–136.
Gehrie, M. J. (1996) 'Empathy in a broader perspective: a technical approach to the consequences of the negative selfobject in early character formation'. *Progress in Self Psychology* 12: 159–79.
Herzog, B. (1998) 'Compliance, dewance and the development of relational templates'. Presented at the 21st Annual International Conference on the Psychology of the Self, San Diego, CA.

H. B.

SELFOBJECT FAILURE Synonymous with self-selfobject disruption and 'empathic failure'. The experience of the other's out-of-tuneness with one's selfobject needs, or the experience of the rupture of an ongoing selfobject relationship.

See also: selfobject, bad

H. B.

SELFOBJECT RELATIONSHIP One may distinguish between a selfobject experience that occurs in relation to another and a selfobject relationship, insofar as the latter also connotes a mutuality or relatively stable sense of the other's availability as a selfobject. There is a bond with the analyst at the centre of which is the expectation that the analyst will be with the analysand in the way he or she needs the analyst to be.

Bacal, H. A. (1994) 'The selfobject relationship in psychoanalytic treatment' in A. Goldberg (ed.) *A Decade of Progress: Progress in Self Psychology*, Vol. 10. Hillsdale, NJ: The Analytic Press, 21–30.

H. B.

SEMIOTICS The field of semiotics is much broader than linguistics and includes all the data of the psychoanalytic process. As the study of signs, semiotics provides a set of tools that integrates the dichotomies psychoanalysts often make between thoughts and feelings, mind and body, internal and external, verbal and nonverbal, and 'one-body' vs 'two-body' psychology.

The term 'semiotics' comes from the Greek word for sign. The Stoics distinguished three aspects of the sign: the signifier, meaning, and object of the sign. The Latin tradition, from Augustine ('On the Teacher') through the Scholastics (especially John Poinsot) further elaborated natural and verbal signs as well as outward and inward signs. Thomas Sebeok subsequently differentiated natural signs into endosemiotic signs, pertaining to intra-corporeal and cellular processes, and zoosemiotic signs, referring to signs used by animals, especially in predator/prey relations as well as in courting rituals. His further delineation of anthroposemiotic signs in human life draws on the work of the American philosopher Charles Sanders Peirce (1839–1914).

The French tradition, including Lacan, draws on the 'semiology' of Ferdinand de Saussure (1857–1913) who distinguished speech from language, where language is a system of *signs, with a sign being composed of a *signifier and *signified, each of which is constituted through reciprocal differentiation from all the other elements in the system. In most linguistic signs the link between signifier and signified is arbitrary, a function of convention, and this 'unmotivated' aspect of the signifier frees it from any fixed meaning, facilitating thereby the process of condensation and displacement which sustains unconscious forms of thought. The signifier, moreover, can take any material form – visual images in a dream (constituting, as Freud termed it, a rebus), or olfactory, tactile and auditory traces signifying the history of one's desire.

Peirce elaborated a triadic vision of the sign, in effect by distinguishing within the signified two distinct aspects: the sign's object and what he called the sign's interpretant. The sign's interpretant brings new knowledge of its object; it does so by producing specific effects on the receiver of the sign, and these effects can be unconscious as well as conscious. Peirce described three types of interpretant: feeling, dynamic, and logical. The feeling interpretant of a sign is the affect aroused in the sign's receiver; this is often the first clue in the analyst's experience that something yet unnamed has entered the analytic discourse. The second type, the dynamic interpretant, is the effect of the sign exhibited in what we term an enactment, when the feeling interpretant has not been identified and instead we are moved into an action that stages the meaning of the sign. The third type of interpretant, the logical or conceptual interpretant, enables us to link feelings to actions in relation to the signs that generated them – in other words, what we call 'interpretation'.

Peirce's clinical utility is best seen in the delineation of the three types of signs (the icon, the index, and the symbol), each carrying out a specific function in clinical practice. Icons relate to their objects through resemblance, as when facial mirroring conveys to a patient the recognition of a counterpart and thereby may restore a sense of coherence. Empathy is a form of 'enacted iconicity', for iconic effects are central to the development of emerging subjectivity. Icons are transitional signs, marking the border between the *real and the *imaginary and promoting this transition. They are sought by patients caught at this border, whose 'icon-seeking' behaviour constitutes Kohut's mirror transference.

The index is related to its object through contiguity: 'I' indicates the speaker in the act of addressing 'you' the hearer. The index is both a sign of separation, establishing a place for the subject in transmitting who I am as I am here, as well a as a sign of conjoined presence. Indexical speech establishes limits, context, and relationship. Symbols are signs related to their objects by convention – as noted above with reference to Saussure's signifier. During psychotic states when everything bears meaning for the patient, the fundamental semiotic derailment consists of treating indexes (rustling leaves) as if they were symbols (related by convention to their objects) addressing the patient rather than as signs of the contiguous/causal activity of the wind.

Colapietro, V. M. (1989) *Peirce's Approach to the Self: A Semiotic Perspective on Human Subjectivity*. Albany: State University of New York Press.

Colapietro, V. M. (1993) *Glossary of Semiotics*. New York: Paragon House.

Deely, J. (1990) *Basics of Semiotics*. Bloomington and Indianapolis: Indiana University Press.

Jøhansen, J. D. (1993) *Dialogic Semiosis: An Essay on Signs and Meaning*. Bloomington and Indianapolis: Indiana University Press.

Muller, J. P. (1996) *Beyond the Psychoanalytic Dyad: Developmental Semiotics in Freud, Peirce, and Lacan*. New York: Routledge.

Muller, J. P. with Brent, J. (ed.) (2000) *Peirce, Semiotics, and Psychoanalysis*. Baltimore: Johns Hopkins University Press.

J. P. M.

SEPARATION The second process in the coming into being of the *subject which follows *alienation. It is based on a confrontation with the lack in the *Other, which affords a degree of separation from the Other, from the signifying chain and its effects. Separation makes possible a choice of a desire of one's own for the subject.

I. De. G.

SEPARATION ANXIETY According to Fairbairn anxiety concerned actual and emotional separation from the mother or primary caretaker; separation anxiety is the basis for an active feature of the war neuroses expressed as the compulsion to return home. Separation anxiety has been elaborated in *attachment theory by Bowlby.

Bowlby, J. (1969, 1973, 1980) *Attachment and Loss*, 3 vols. New York: Basic Books.

E. F. B. / D. E. S.

SEXUAL DIFFERENCE The division between the sexes does not depend on anatomical difference but on the inscription of a speaking being in the positioning of the sexes. This sexual partitioning results from its relation to the phallic function, in so far as it incarnates the connection of *jouissance with *castration.

S. Ten.

SEXUAL RELATION Freud saw all relations as essentially sexual – seemingly non-sexual relations were sublimated or displaced expressions of sexuality. The attachments of children to their parents, of group members to each other, were attenuated or disguised forms of sexual relations.

Lacan's position in respect of sexual difference is condensed into the statement '*il n'y a pas de rapport sexuel*' – there is no relation between the sexes. This aims to subvert any notion of a natural instinctual relationship, impossible because the positions of man and woman are arrived at through the defile of signifiers. Any notion of reciprocity between the sexes is equally undermined since within the signifying network (through which all subjects pass) only one signifier, the phallus, governs the relation between the sexes. This results in asymmetry in how *castration is viewed as between male and female. (So for both sexes there is only one Other sex, the *woman.) Finally, the real sexual relation does not take place between a man and a woman but between a subject and a drive. Relations between men and woman can never be harmonious since the drive does not recognise the other as subject.

J. A. Ber. / H. T.

SEXUALISATION Kohut's view of sexualisation is that it is an indication of a structural deficit. From a selfobject point of view, it would be claimed that a necessary relationship to a sustaining other is lacking. This view is confirmed when it is found that sexualisation is dissipated by the establishment of a selfobject transference. Sexualisation is revealed as a strategy that functions to aid in the maintenance of psychic equilibrium. It brings pleasure. It is used to obliterate painful affects. It can serve to stem further regression. It can allow for the establishment of a relationship that, although it may be considered infantile, is a further aid to develop self cohesion. With all of the psychological gain from sexualisation, it is often resistant to analytic intervention without the development and working through of one or another selfobject transference.

Goldberg, A. (1995) *The Problem of Perversion*. New Haven, CT: Yale University Press, 29–45, 64–79.
Kohut, H. (1977). *The Restoration of the Self*. New York: International Universities Press, 217–18; 272–3.

A. I. G.

SEXUALITY Freud included many of the activities of infants and children (thumb sucking, swinging, toileting) in what he considered sexual. The erotogenic zones of infancy were the basis for fixations that prevented the acquisition of mature (genital) sexuality. Perversions were satisfactions restricted to component drives involving the oral cavity, lips, anus or other zones replacing the genital. The need to deny the absence of the penis in women led to fetishism in which an item representing the woman's penis is required to attain sexual satisfaction. The choice of a sexual object of the same sex (homosexuality) was called 'inversion' by Freud and was related by him to the narcissistic requirement that the sexual object be like the self. The repression of sexuality was responsible for the development of the neuroses and the unconscious wishes present in dreams, slips of the tongue, jokes, creative endeavours, and symptoms were almost always of a sexual nature.

Although sexuality is conventionally located in genital functioning, sexual experience yields pleasures exceeding, and therefore inexplicable by, mere need-satisfaction. A drive in classical theory, in *relationism, sexuality becomes (like *attachment) a relation. In Freud's one-person psychology, sexuality starts off merged with *aggression, from which it then diverges; as opposites, they later morph into other polarities – love and hate, *life and *death instincts. *Mitchell indicates that relationism (two-person psychoanalysis) situates sexuality in relationship as a derivative of *attachment, which is deemed primary by *Winnicott. In a third point of view that combines elements of both one- and two-person psychologies, some contemporary theorists like *Kristeva and *Laplanche locate the origins of sexuality in the transmission to the infant of the maternal unconscious. Given the paradoxical linkage of sexuality, aggression, and attachment, our lexicon of pleasure should include *Lacan's *jouissance, which is generally read as orgasm in all its ineffability but better construed as a kind of enjoyment so intense as to be nearly indistinguishable from pain. Notably, contemporary views of sexuality no longer regard reproductive heterosexuality as the criterion of mental health or apex of development: rather, everyone, gay and straight, bisexual and transsexual, male and female and transgender, is invited to desire's poignant banquet, with all of its sweets and all of its sours.

See also: gender

Dimen, M. (2003) *Sexuality, Intimacy, and Power*. Hillsdale, NJ: The Analytic Press.
Kristeva, J. (1983) *Tales of Love*. Translated by L. S. Roudiez. New York: Columbia University Press.

Laplanche, J. (1976) *Life and Death in Psychoanalysis*. Translated by J. Mehlman. Annapolis, MD: Johns Hopkins University Press.
Laplanche, J. and Pontalis, J.-B. [1967] (1973) *The Language of Psycho-Analysis*. Translated by D. N. Smith. New York: Norton.
Winnicott, D. W. (1953) 'Transitional objects and transitional phenomena'. *International Journal of Psycho-Analysis* 34: 89–97.

J. A. Ber. / M. Dim.

SEXUALLY ABUSED CHILDREN (PSYCHOTHERAPY WITH) For all sexually abused children a fundamental rule has been broken. The natural role of an adult as guardian and protector has been abandoned, the stronger has exploited and damaged the weaker and the child has lost unequivocal faith in the existence of an adult world which is by and large benign and favourable to development. An important task of the therapist is to give the child an experience where important rules and boundaries are maintained and respected. This extends into the basic parameters of the setting including finding an approach to intimacy in all its forms. The notion of intimacy is contaminated by sexuality, and communication feels concrete. Sexual abuse can result in an 'annihilation of the symbolic', such that ordinary symbolic play or thinking becomes filled with sexual connotation or is seriously impaired. Enactment in the room of early patterns of relating and abusive modes of communication is prevalent. These include not only enactments of the abusive object relationships but also pre-existing deprivation particularly in early maternal containment which very often underpins the abuse. A major task of the therapy is to help move the level of communication from the concrete towards the symbolic. Suitable words and language to use with children has to be found to describe play and behaviour as well as to recognise and bear feelings projected into the therapist and felt by them in the countertransference. It is sometimes impossible and undesirable for the therapist to name and speak to the *countertransference in the session. The emotional experiences arising from lack of early maternal containment prior to the abuse, especially the more primitive ones of disintegration, withdrawal and fragmentation, have to be processed first and a decision made as to whether the child has a space in their mind to receive them back, or whether an experience of the therapist bearing and containing them is all that can be managed.

Supervision of this type of work is essential since, in the absence of adequately functioning parental figures (often including external ones), the supervision process provides some essential parental functions to support the therapeutic process. A focus on memory is essential in order to avoid everything being seen in the light of the abuse, and the children have to be helped not to base their core identity on being abused children. Similarly, the abusers were not just abusers, and all the ambivalent and complicit feelings and emotions aroused by them have to worked through. Reassurance that the abuse is not the child's fault does not take account of the unconscious triumphant and rivalrous oedipal phantasies often underlying the abuse and giving rise to guilt and shame.

Alvarez, A. (1992) 'Child sexual abuse: the need to remember and the need to forget' in *Live Company*. London: Routledge.
Emanuel, R., Miller, L. and Rustin, M. (2002) 'Supervision of sexually abused girls'. *Clinical Child Psychology and Psychiatry* 7.
Gluckman, C. (1987) 'Incest in psychic reality'. *Journal of Child Psychotherapy* 13: 109–23.
McCarthy, B. (1982) 'Incest and psychotherapy'. *Irish Journal of Psychotherapy* 1: 11–16.
Trowell, J. and Kolvin, I. (1999) 'Lessons from a psychotherapy outcome study with sexually abused girls'. *Clinical Child Psychology and Psychiatry* 4: 79–90.

R. E.

SHADOW The shadow represents largely unconscious contents of the personality with which one has no intention of identifying or of which one is afraid. Often the contents of the shadow are identified in such experiences as anger or sexuality, which may feel destabilising to the ego or the culture and therefore are repressed. But just as easily, creativity or spontaneity may also be repressed. There are four modalities of the experience of the shadow contents: they remain unconscious; they are projected onto others; one identifies with them; or, one assimilates them into a richer sense of personality. The collective shadow contains the repressed values of an entire culture.

J. Hol.

SHAME Unlike *guilt which is felt when an external 'moral' rule is not kept, shame occurs when we fail to live up to a personal ideal. Shame is closer to the body than guilt as seen for example in blushing. *Rycroft suggests that shame occurs in schizoid persons who overvalue or 'fancy' themselves while knowing that others do not share their high opinion of themselves.

Rycroft, C. (1968) *Anxiety and Neurosis*. London: Allen Lane, Penguin.

R. M. S.

SHARPE, ELLA FREEMAN (1875–1947) Ella Sharpe was born near Cambridge, England. She studied literature, drama and poetry at Nottingham University and worked as a teacher until her early forties. Her interest in psychoanalysis developed from her love of literature and her teaching work with young people. She was analysed in Berlin by Sachs and became a member of the British Psycho-Analytical Society in 1921. She was an active member of that society as a teacher, supervisor and as a training analyst. She was involved in the Controversial Discussions and was a member of the Middle or Independent Group. Her seminal 1937 *Dream Analysis* showed, decades before Lacan, that the figures of speech in our spoken language such as *metaphor and *metonymy have marked similarities to the *dream work. Her *Collected Papers* include writings on creativity, symbolism, aesthetics and papers on literary interpretation, notably Shakespeare. However her major contribution was in the area of psychoanalytic technique and practice.

Whelan, M. (2000) *Mistress of her own Thoughts – Ella Freeman Sharpe and the Practice of Psychoanalysis*. London: Rebus Press.

M. W.

SIBLING A person's brother or sister. Whilst psychoanalysis has tended to emphasise intergenerational conflict (in particular, in Freud's analysis of the Oedipal dynamic), recent theorists have stressed the need to seek out laterality, or siblings, as an alternative. Juliet *Mitchell's *Mad Men and Medusas* questions the prominence of the Oedipus complex in Freud and the castration complex 'returned to' by Lacan, for psychoanalytic accounts of hysteria, and presents siblings, or more generally, laterality as an alternative to the exclusive theory and practice of the vertical model. She argues that it is from lateral relations – so widely acknowledged as critical in anthropological theories of affinity – that the human subject is thrust back onto the parents who thus become the mother and father of the *Oedipus and *castration complexes. In *Siblings: Sex and Violence* Mitchell draws siblings into visibility from within a range of psychoanalytic, literary, mythic and filmic accounts. The psychic means through which siblings are negotiated are of crucial importance, not only in themselves, but for all lateral relationships: the *splitting of the ego and object, identification and projection, and the simultaneous reversal of love and hate, followed by the transformation of narcissism into object-love and murderousness into an objective hatred for what is wrong or evil in the self and the other. Siblings also point to the importance of laterality for understanding the interpenetration of violence, power and non-reproductive sexuality. Lastly, sibling trauma instigates the construction of gender, the 'equal but different' forged within sameness, offering a challenge to hierarchical views of gender difference.

Mitchell, J. (2000) *Mad Men and Medusas: Reclaiming Hysteria and the Effects of Sibling Rivalry on the Human Condition*. London: Hamish Hamilton, Penguin.

Mitchell, J. (2003) *Siblings: Sex and Violence*. Cambridge: Polity Press.

S. W.

SIGN In his earlier theory, Lacan, following Saussure, recognised that the sign as a basic element of *language is made up of a *signifier and a *signified. However, he differed from Saussure in the sense that according to Lacan, the signifier has primacy over the signified. Subsequently Lacan moved further away from Saussure by proposing that the basic element of language is not the sign but the signifier. From Seminar XX onward he returned to the concept of the sign. While the signifier is defined as 'that which represents the subject for another signifier', the sign is defined as 'something that represents something for someone'. While signification or the signified is created retroactively from the difference between signifiers, the sign is more directly tied up with the *Real and as such it can represent a particular state of affairs or change for a subject in terms of his or her *jouissance economy. A sign, for example, can be a sign of love in the transference or it can be a sign that something has changed in the transference relationship.

R. Gol.

SIGNIFIED Together with the *signifier the signified constitutes the sign, as conceived by Saussure. Lacan, however, underlines that there is no fixed relation between the two as Saussure supposes in his formulation of the sign. On the contrary, the signified only acquires its 'content' from its connection with different signifiers. So for Lacan the signified is an effect of meaning which comes about via the combination of signifiers.

R. R.

SIGNIFIER Signifier, a concept which Lacan borrows from Saussure, is an element or unit from a signifying system (such as a spoken or written word) which is arbitrarily connected to a *signified. Together with the signified, the signifier constitutes the *sign as conceived by Saussure. For Lacan, the signifier mostly concerns spoken language, as it shows itself in the cure. The focus of the cure is not the meaning of the word, but the relation between different signifiers, even though such a relation sometimes creates a specific meaning. In so far as the unconscious is structured like a language, the analyst can thus discern specific words phonetically and allow the analysand, the *subject, to work with these signifiers, creating room for new unconscious material. In this way, a signifier represents the subject (of the unconscious) for another signifier, which implies that the subject is only present in the interval between two signifiers, whilst the analyst supposes that their existence presumes a subject connecting them.

See also: aphanisis; symbolic

R. R.

SINTHOME The sinthome is the result of Lacan's gradual rethinking of the 'symptom'. Towards the end of his work Lacan poses the sinthome as an indecipherable aspect of the subject's management of his or her jouissance. As such, the sinthome is a radically particular way by which the subject enjoys. Whilst unanalysable per se, the point at which the subject can identify with the sinthome is relevant to the end of an analysis.

R. Loo.

SLEEP DISORDERS (IN CHILDREN) Sleep problems in infants and children consist principally in difficulty in falling asleep, or in night-waking, or both. The International Classification of Sleep Disorders defines three major categories: dysomnias, parasomnias and sleep disorders associated with medical/psychiatric conditions. Children's problems come mainly within the category of dysomnia.

Newborn infants sleep for two-thirds of the twenty-four hours, but any period of sleep is no longer than about three and a half hours. Within the first month of life, wake-state organisation begins to adapt, or entrain, to the light-dark cycle, and to social cues. Although babies begin to sleep for long periods, brief night-waking is universal, as in adults, and video recordings show most babies waking once or twice in the night. Whether this is a problem depends on the infant's ability or not to return to sleep. As Sadeh and Anders show, 95% of new infants cry (signal) on waking and require a parental response, but by one year 60 to 70% are able to self-soothe without waking their parents.

Difficulty in sleeping may connect with the infant's own sensitivity or with their relationship with their parents. Similarly, Hopkins reminds us that persistent crying is a function of a relationship as well as of the baby's endowment. Guedeney and Kreisler show a connection between sleep problems in the first eighteen months of life and traumatic events, maternal depression, and maternal anxiety during pregnancy. Intergenerational influences are depicted in Fraiberg's *Ghosts in the Nursery*. Daws points out that parents of such children often have separation problems and have suffered bereavement or serious losses.

Joyce McDougall describes parents who cannot manage psychic separation as the guardians of their children's sleep, echoing Freud's theory that dreams are the guardian of sleep.

Paret shows that frequency of sleep disturbances rises again in the second half of the first year. She reminds us of Anna Freud's theory of transitory difficulties due to the external and internal stresses of this developmental period. Margaret Mahler discusses separation/individuation and the anxiety produced by the baby's new ability to move away from the mother. The excitement of the discovery of crawling and walking may also mean that a baby finds it hard to relax into sleep.

Security and attachment link to sleep. Daniel Stern says: 'Others regulate the infant's experience of somatic state . . . namely the gratifications of hunger and the shift from wakeful fatigue to sleep. In all such regulations a dramatic shift in neurophysiological states is involved'. Thus the quality of an attachment relationship through physical mediation affects the baby's ability to sleep.

Feeding and sleeping are closely linked and the setting up of satisfying feeding rhythms between mother and baby leads to similar regulated sleep patterns. Daws notes that weaning can raise separation issues which may also lead to sleep problems.

Winnicott's idea of transitional objects shows how these can allow babies to start to feel separate from parents. 'There may emerge some thing or some phenomenon – perhaps a bundle of wool or the corner of a blanket or eiderdown or a word or a tune or a mannerism that becomes vitally important to the infant for use at the time of going to sleep, and as a defence against anxiety, especially anxiety of the depressive type'.

Klein suggested that the toys a small child takes to bed could represent the super-ego, to ensure the child does not disturb the parents. Thus, as children grow older, sleep disturbances may represent the conflict between impulses and relationships, in this case Oedipal ones. Mixed feelings about being toilet trained can have the same effect.

With older children attachment issues may still prevail, as well as stresses from their developing lives and individual anxieties. Nightmares are frequent in children, and are an opportunity to express and work out the conflicts and anxieties of waking life. Hartmann asks, 'are your nightmares dreams?' and uses the accounts of these to differentiate them from night terrors which are not remembered. Night terrors may occur when there is stress, or unacknowledged hostility in the family.

Children in abusive, unsafe situations will naturally need to remain vigilant and be unable to sleep well. M.-S. Moore says that anxious and depressed individuals psychically perceive themselves to be in danger and thus cannot fall deeply asleep. In such anxiety-related sleep dysfunction there is an alteration in both physiological sleep states and in dream function (with reduced deepest Stage 4 and REM sleep).

Daws suggests that brief *parent-infant psychotherapy for sleep problems, linking parents' experiences with their fears about their infants, may be effective. The same principle means that family work is usually indicated for older children, with some also needing individual psychoanalytic therapy in their own right.

American Sleep Disorders Association (1990) *The International Classification of Sleep Disorders – Diagnostic & Coding Manual.* Kansas City: Allen Press.

Daws, D. (1989) *Through the Night: Helping Parents and Sleepless Infants.* London: Free Association Books. Reprinted 1993.

Guedeney, A. and Kreisler, L. (1987) 'Sleep disorders in the first eighteen months of life: hypothesis on the role of mother-child emotional exchanges'. *Infant Mental Health Journal* 8: 307–18.

Hopkins, J. (1994) 'Therapeutic interventions in infancy: two contrasting cases of persistent crying'. *Psychoanalytic Psychotherapy* 8: 141–52.

Moore, M.-S. (1989) 'Disturbed attachment in children: a factor in sleep disturbance: altered dream production and immune system dysfunction'. *Journal of Child Psychotherapy* 15: 49–111.

Sadeh, A. and Anders, T. F. (1993) 'Sleep disorders' in C. H. Zeanah (ed.) *Handbook of Infant Mental Health.* New York: Guilford, 305–16.

D. D.

SLIP see **PARAPRAXIS**

SOCIAL CHARACTER Applying Freud's dynamic understanding of character to society and by understanding human beings primarily as social beings *Fromm developed from 1930 onwards the concept of social character to describe the psychic matrix common to the members of a societal group. In contrast to the individual character, social character is defined as 'the nucleus of the character structure, which is shared by most members of the same culture'. Its function is to substitute the lost instinctual equipment and 'to mould and channel human energy within a given society for the purpose of the continued functioning of this society'

The name introduced by Fromm thus describes the core aspects of character that members of a particular culture share in common. Fromm derived this concept from Marx's assertion that 'relative drives' can be distinguished from 'constant' drives in that the former are molded by the particular characteristics of a society as determined by the means of production, social stratification, and social communication. Fromm codified this particular theory of drives in order to explain how primary human motivations are linked to the fundamental economic realities of a society via ideas and ideals. He believed that 'the libidinal structure' of a society was the way in which economics influenced individuals' mental manifestations and that these mental manifestations, or thoughts, were in turn capable of altering the politico-economic basis of a particular culture.

To fully appreciate the concept of social character, it is necessary to understand that 'society' was for Fromm defined by objective conditions ranging from climate and geography, all the way to technology, levels of economic development, and political systems of organisation. Thus, the fact that there is no single society, as such, makes it necessary to include the interaction of social factors and the individual psyche in any comprehensive explanation of human character.

Fromm went on to propose that certain social character formations correspond to the western industrial society of the twentieth century. The most commonly mentioned one is the 'marketing orientation', usually referred to as the marketing personality. This character orientation was seen as a product of the economic supply and demand characteristics of that society which trigger a perpetual process of internal self-valuation, that is triggered by one's perceived acceptability to others, and to the society at large. Thus, alienation versus conformity became one of Fromm's principal ways of understanding the dilemma of being human in the twentieth century.

See also: culture

Fromm, E. (1941) *Escape from Freedom*. New York: Avon Books.
Funk, R. (1982) *Erich Fromm: The Courage to be Human*. New York: The Continuum Company.

R. F. / E. M. W.

SOMATISATION The study of interrelationships among biological, psychological, and social factors in health, illness, and disease. This study is not confined to a specific type or category of medical disorders, but rather is a research and clinical approach to all bodily illnesses, including those with structural tissue changes and those with functional changes only. The psychosomatic approach contrasts with the traditional biomedical approach which separates mental from somatic phenomena and seeks single causal explanations of bodily symptoms.

The origins of psychosomatics can be traced to the Greco-Roman era when philosophers wrote about the inseparability of psyche and soma and the need for physicians to consider emotions as well as physical factors in the study and treatment of disease. However, the term 'psycho-somatic' did not appear in the medical literature until 1818, when the German psychiatrist Heinroth used it in a discussion of insomnia. It is likely that the term was coined a few years earlier by the English poet Coleridge, who referred to his 'Psycho-somatic Ology [or science]' in a fragmentary essay on the emotions. In the twentieth century the hyphen in the term was removed.

Psychosomatics began to emerge as an organised medical discipline in America and Germany during the first third of the twentieth century. This development was prompted by psychoanalysis, even though Freud encouraged his followers to refrain from trespassing into the problem of organic disease. Perhaps to ensure the survival of psychoanalysis as a science that had boundaries and could exist alongside other disciplines, Freud established a distance from the physical body and limited psychoanalysis to psychological disorders. During the 1920s and 1930s, however, several psychoanalysts and analytically-oriented physicians began to apply psychoanalytic principles to the understanding and treatment of organic illnesses. They violated Freud's prohibition either by assimilating organic illnesses into the model of *conversion hysteria, thereby giving symbolic meaning to all somatic symptoms, or by linking organic illnesses with the actual neuroses, which Freud considered somatic in origin and without psychological meaning.

The pioneers in Europe were Groddeck and Stekel, who advanced a psychogenic model of disease by extending the concepts of conversion and symbolisation to a wide array of somatic symptoms. Their ideas were elaborated further in the United States during the 1940s and 1950s by Deutsch and Sperling, who emphasised the symbolic expression of pregenital conflicts by way of organic disease. Alexander, however, adopted Freud's distinction between actual neuroses and psychoneuroses, and argued against the symptoms of somatic diseases having primary symbolic meaning. With colleagues at the Chicago Institute of Psychoanalysis, he investigated a small group of seven diseases (later referred to as the 'classic' psychosomatic diseases) and found them to be associated with specific unconscious conflicts. Alexander attributed the symptoms of these diseases to the effect of physiological changes that accompany repressed emotions associated with conflicts. Moreover, he advocated a multifactor model, which included biological vulnerabilities and specific life situations to activate the conflicts.

During the 1950s and 1960s, several psychoanalysts shifted the focus of investigation from unconscious conflicts to the life setting in which people fall ill. Engel and Schmale observed that the onset or exacerbation of disease is associated frequently with a recent separation or loss of an important relationship, which evokes the depressive affects of helplessness and hopelessness and a conservation-withdrawal physiological response. This psychobiological complex was thought to initiate other biological changes that might lead to disease if the necessary constitutional and/or environmental factors are also present. Engel and others observed also that many physically ill patients manifest developmental arrests and remain excessively dependent on symbiotic relationships to compensate for certain ego deficits. The nature of these deficits was not fully explored, but it seemed that the excessive dependency rendered such patients more vulnerable to illness relapses or remissions in response to the vicissitudes of their interpersonal relationships. Despite these observations, Engel and Schmale failed to integrate their formulations with the psychoanalytic theories of object relations that were emerging at the time as alternatives to Freud's drive theory. Nonetheless, their research helped shift psychosomatic theory from its earlier one-person, conflict-defence models to models that encompass the regulatory functions of human relationships.

During the next two decades, research in developmental psychobiology revealed that mothers play an important role in the emotional development of their child, and in regulating certain physiological functions during infancy. These findings provided new ways of understanding how deficits in psychobiological functioning might be acquired. This research also supported the views of *Winnicott, who stressed that the integration of psyche and soma is determined by the mother's emotional attunement and physical handling of her infant, and that a not-good-enough holding environment leads to a tendency to somatic disorders. Winnicott retained the hyphen in 'psycho-somatic' to signify a split in the patient's personality that involves dissociation between psyche and soma. Developmental research also provided an impetus for integrating self psychology and attachment theory into the field of psychosomatics.

Another important psychoanalytic contribution to psychosomatics during the 1970s was the formulation of the alexithymia construct, which was based on clinical observations that many somatically ill patients have difficulty identifying and describing feelings. Advances in emotion theory and in the psychoanalytic theory of symbolisation suggest that the association between alexithymia and somatic disorders is due to a failure to link subsymbolic emotional representations with symbolic representations, in particular with images and words. Bucci proposes that without regulation by connections to symbolic representations, activated emotions are likely to result in prolonged and repetitive states of physiological arousal, which can potentially lead to a variety of somatic disorders, the specific nature of which is determined by constitutional and other vulnerability factors. This conceptualisation is consistent with McDougall's proposal in *Theaters of the Body* that organic illness is related to primitive pre-neurotic pathology that has failed to achieve mental representation.

As psychosomatics evolved, it became an interdisciplinary endeavour that generated more complex models of illness and disease. Weiner and Taylor proposed psychobiological dysregulation models, which incorporate a psychoanalytic understanding of object relations and the development of the self, as well as emotion theory and findings from developmental biology and the biomedical sciences. Derived from general systems theory, these models view the psyche as one component within a hierarchical arrangement of reciprocally regulating subsystems. A transition from health to illness or disease is likely to occur when there are perturbations in one or more of the feedback loops, which lead to changes over time in the rhythmic functioning of one or more of the subsystems. By resolving conflicts and repairing psychological deficits, psychoanalytic therapy attempts to enhance the regulatory functions of the psyche and thereby reduce the impact on the body of perturbations arising in any of the subsystems.

Bucci, W. 'Symptoms and symbols: a multiple code theory of somatisation'. *Psychoanalytic Inquiry* 17: 151–72.

Engel, G. L. and Schmale, A. H. (1967) 'Psychoanalytic theory of somatic disorder: conversion, specificity and the disease onset situation'. *Journal of the American Psychoanalytic Association* 15: 344–65.

Greco, M. (1998) *Illness as a Work of Thought. A Foucauldian Perspective on Psychosomatics*. London: Routledge.

Taylor, G. J. (1987) *Psychosomatic Medicine and Contemporary Psychoanalysis.* Madison, CT: International Universities Press.

Taylor, G. J., Bagby, R. M. and Parker, J. D. A. (1997) *Disorders of Affect Regulation: Alexithymia in Medical and Psychiatric Illness*. Cambridge: Cambridge University Press.

G. T.

SOURCE OF DRIVE According to Freud, a drive can be characterised by the pressure or demand it exerts, its aim (satisfaction), its object (the thing permitting satisfaction), and its source. The latter refers to the 'somatic process which occurs in an organ or part of the body'. An investigation of the sources of instinct, Freud believed, lies outside of scope of psychology. From a psychological perspective, we have knowledge of drives only through their aims.

Freud, S. (1915) *Instincts and their Vicissitudes*. S. E. 14. London: Hogarth Press.

C. S.

SPAIN From 1956, professionals trained in different countries started to organise the *Sociedad Luso-Española de Psicoanálisis*. The foundational germ of the Society was constituted by Bofill, Folch and Corominas in Barcelona; Portillo, Rallo, Ruiz and Zamora in Madrid, and Luzes and Alwin in Portugal. In 1959, at the International Congress of the IPA held in Copenhagen, this Society was recognised as a member of the IPA. Later, it was divided into the *Sociedad Española de Psicoanálisis* (SEP), based in Barcelona, *Asociación Psicoanalítica de Madrid* (APM) and the *Sociedade Portuguese de Psicanálise*.

The SEP and the APM share similar criteria for the training of candidates, which takes place, basically, in accordance with the triad 'personal analysis, supervision and seminaries'. In other aspects they differ as to orientation. Didactic members of Barcelona have spent long periods in London to continue their training with members of the British Psycho-Analytical Society, which has resulted in a strong Kleinian and Bionian influence in the SEP. In the last few years the dawning of a strong interest in new tendencies, such as intersubjectivism, interaction theory, two-person psychology, the patient-analyst relationship in the 'here and now', etc., can be observed. The SEP has an extension in Sevilla, the *Grupo de Andalucia*. In the APM diverse orientations coexist: Kleinian, ego psychology, the theory of object relationships, and the most strictly Freudian and the Lacanian. Some of its foundational members received their analysis in Paris. The APM has a Training Institute in Valencia and the *Centro Psicoanalítico del Norte* in Bilbao.

There are three journals of psychoanalysis published in Spain. The SEP publishes the *Revista Catalana de Psicoanàlisi* and *Temas de Psicoanálisis*. The APM publishes the *Revista de Psicoanálisis*.

Since 1989, the APM, the SEP and the *Sociedade Portuguese de Psicanálise* have celebrated the *Congreso Ibérico de Psicoanálisis* biannually. Congresses of Romance Language Psychoanalysts, of Francophone Psychoanalysts and of the European Federation of Psychoanalysis have taken place. The IPA's

International Congress of Psychoanalysis has taken place twice in Spain, in 1983 in Madrid, and in 1997 in Barcelona. Terttu Eskelinen and José Cruz have both held the office of Vice-President of the IPA.

Twelve university lecturers and professors in Spain are members of the SEP or the APM. A large number of psychoanalysts work in psychiatric hospitals and centres for mental health. Furthermore, a large group of psychoanalysts, who belong to South American Societies which are members of the IPA, are active in Spain.

J. Cod.

SPECIFICITY THEORY Specificity theory, introduced by Bacal, has as one of its central hypotheses that the benefit of any experience is dependent on a particular therapeutic constellation at a given moment in time. This constellation constitutes the capacities and limitations of the participants involved for therapeutic relating.

Specificity theory recognises the infinite possibilities of interaction in the therapeutic dyad or pair, a dyad which is acknowledged to be a dynamic, actively changing system. It assumes that the patient's experience will be subject to often unpredictable changes in the patient-therapist relationship, encouraging therapists to continually modify their efforts and choose what they feel is the best of the numerous possible variations in relating. The analyst must therefore be aware of fluctuations in the therapeutic relationship, in order to offer responses that may achieve the best possible therapeutic result at that time. This requires that the analyst be aware of his own, as well as the patient's experience from moment to moment. This enables the analyst to appreciate the particular complexity of the patient's experience that is activated and respond to it in the most effective way that he or she can. Specificity theory holds that all interventions in the treatment setting are potentially beneficial, with the proviso that they not interfere with the therapist's professional functioning or exceed either the therapist's or the patient's personal tolerance. While this theory has been developed within the context of self psychology it is, in principle, applicable to any psychoanalytic perspective that is intrinsically relational.

See also: optimal responsiveness

Bacal, H. A. (1985) 'Optimal responsiveness and the therapeutic process' in A. Goldberg (ed.) *Progress in Self Psychology*, Vol. 1. Hillsdale, NJ: The Analytic Press, 202–26.

Bacal, H. A. (ed.) (1998) *Optimal Responsiveness: How Therapists Heal their Patients*. New York: Jason Aronson, 141–70.

H. B.

SPEECH Speech is the dimension in which analysis unfolds. It presupposes a relation between two people: the one who speaks and the other who listens and responds. Between these two positions is the Symbolic field of language. In articulating this field the subject manifests its division in the difference between what it wants to say and what is said. Speech either resolves itself in a signification supported by the ego, or aims beyond the code to the Other in its pure signifying dimension where it links up with the structure of the unconscious. All speech calls for a reply and it is in returning the subject's message to him in an inverted form that the subject is able to testify to the cause of its division.

P. D.

SPLITTING OF EGO According to Freud, manifested by persons who consciously know some fact but behave as though they had not noticed it or didn't believe it, especially cases of fetishism where a person knows that women don't possess a penis but unconsciously denies this. *Splitting of objects figures in Klein's early work, but in 1946 she speaks of splitting of the ego as the source of the *super-ego.

Klein, M. (1946) 'Notes on some schizoid mechanisms' in *Envy and Gratitude*. London: Hogarth Press.

E. Gil.

SPLITTING OF THE OBJECT (KLEIN) Klein thought of splitting (of the object) as one of the main schizoid mechanisms employed by the infant to divide the object into good and bad. This process of separation resulted from the intolerability of experiencing bad aspects inherent within a needed good object. Klein thought that splitting of the object was always accompanied by a corresponding splitting of the ego.

Splitting was necessitated by the need to separate out good experiences from anxiety-provoking bad ones. In order to identify with good experiences and objects, the infant creates phantasies of a life-preserving object separate from phantasies of deadly forces. The infant can thus be supported by loving experiences and objects against the frustrations of reality which stimulate its hatred. In phantasy, the infant attempts to securely preserve its love and its loving objects against the adverse forces of impinging reality.

Klein also links splitting to idealisation in the egocentric world of the infant, who attempts to protect a sense of goodness by removing it from any quality of badness. When these forces are modulated by development and benign parental response, there will be a predominance of good reality experiences over bad ones. The infantile ego gradually comes to accept a belief in the strength of both its loving objects over its persecuting bad ones and of its own life forces over deadly ones. Such developments set the stage for living in the *depressive position, in which the splitting processes are lessened due to the strength of the ego. If *envy is excessive in the *paranoid-schizoid position, normal splitting cannot be attained because of extreme splitting or fragmenting attacks on the goodness and badness of the objects. Movement towards the depressive position is then severely impeded because of the predominance and reinforcement of destructiveness.

G. Gor.

SPLITTING, 'ENFORCED' (BION) A split between material and psychical satisfaction. This mechanism arises as a kind of 'solution' of a conflict between the need of the infant to survive and the fear of violent emotions stimulated by the contact with the nurturing object. Strong fear of emotions can inhibit the infant's impulse to obtain sustenance. If fear of death through starvation compels the infant to resume feeding, this is done but at the price of developing an enforced splitting. This state originates in a need to be rid of the emotional complications of awareness of life and a relationship with live objects. Steps are taken to destroy awareness of all feelings. This splitting differs from the one carried out to prevent depression and also from the one impelled by sadistic impulses. Its object and effect are to enable the infant to obtain material comforts without acknowledging the existence of a live object on which these benefits depend. The need for love, understanding, and mental development is split off and transformed into the search for material comforts.

Bion, W. R. (1962) *Learning from Experience*. London: Heinemann.

L. P. C.

SPLITTING (SELF PSYCHOLOGY) The psyche is often illustrated in a pictorial fashion, and splitting is one way to present such a picture. If the split is horizontal, it is used to demonstrate a division between upper and lower. If the split is vertical, it is to show a side-by-side separation. The first of these – the horizontal – represents *repression. The second – the vertical – may be considered to represent *disavowal. A horizontal split, the repression barrier, divides *unconscious material from *preconscious contents, while the vertical split essentially divides material that is more or less available to consciousness. While most readers are familiar with Freud's ideas about repression and the forces that maintain it, the idea of a vertical split is somewhat less well known. In the vertical split, which is sustained by disavowal, the self retains a sense of pseudo self-esteem (even grandiosity) by maintaining a merger-bond with the other that entails an adaptation to the other's archaic selfobject requirements (a situation that is not dissimilar to Winnicott's *false-self organisation and Brandchaft's *pathological accommodation). To the extent that this situation is disavowed, self experience may be that of isolation, depression and emptiness, as there is no support for the assertion of one's own selfobject needs.

In the horizontal split, Kohut initially referred to 'unfulfilled archaic narcissistic demands' of the self as lying below a repression barrier and later, to unfulfilled selfobject needs of an incompletely organised nuclear self, the expression of which he regarded as 'healthy grandiosity'. The latter could be compared with the emergence of Winnicott's *true self.

See also: defensive or expansive grandiosity,

Kohut, H. (1971) *The Analysis of the Self.* New York: International Universities Press.
Kohut, H. (1977) *The Restoration of the Self.* New York: International Universities Press.
Winnicott, D. W. (1960) 'Ego distortion in terms of true and false self' in *The Maturational Processes and the Facilitating Environment.* London: Hogarth Press, 56–63.

H. B.

SPONTANEITY Term used by Winnicott to describe authentic action, personal impulsiveness or an expression of the *true self. Winnicott addresses spontaneity when discussing many areas of psychic life and development. He sees the ordinary acquisition of life skills, where learning control is important, as a relinquishment of some spontaneity in favour of *compliance, while encouraging the maintenance of a degree of personal impulse. When compliance, as a result of maternal inability to respond to the infant's spontaneous gesture, becomes a way of life, formation of a *false self occurs, and the true self, together with its spontaneity, becomes hidden.

He discusses the importance of spontaneity in relation to *playing, and to drawing and the *squiggle game. He sees it as lost in the antisocial and the deprived child, again due to environmental failure. In his writing about *aggression, he states that spontaneity becomes aggression when opposition is experienced by the young infant.

Winnicott, D. W. [1950] (1984) 'The deprived child and how he can be compensated for loss of family life' in *Deprivation and Delinquency.* London: Tavistock.
Winnicott, D. W. [1950] (1958) 'Aggression in relation to emotional development' in *Collected Papers: Through Paediatrics to Psychoanalysis.* London: Tavistock.
Winnicott, D. W. [1958] (1965) 'The first year of life: modern views on the emotional development' in *The Family and Individual Development.* London: Tavistock.
Winnicott, D. W. [1960] (1965) 'Ego-distortion in terms of true and false self' in *The Maturational Processes and the Facilitating Environment.* London: Hogarth Press.

J. Joh.

SPOTNITZ, HYMAN (1908–) Hyman Spotnitz, an American psychiatrist, addressing the American Psychiatric Association in 1949, introduced the notion that psychotics could be treated psychoanalytically if, in the dialogue, cognitive interpretations were replaced by emotional communications that joined the patient's way of perceiving himself and his world. In the 1950s he explained his theory of technique in a series of lectures given at the Polystuyvesant Clinic in New York City. The institution named this series, 'Lectures on Modern Psychoanalysis'. Modern psychoanalysis was built on Freud's work, specifically his understanding of the unconscious, transference, resistance and repetition. It viewed schizophrenia as a pathological mode of psychic insulation used to cope with destructive internal emotional states and overstimulation from the environment. In 1971 a training institute was founded to train candidates in Dr Spotnitz's approach. In 1973, the Boston Graduate School of Psychoanalysis was founded as part of a movement to create psychoanalysis as a separate profession freed from its roots in America as a subspecialty of medicine.

Modern techniques, used to provide a corrective emotional experience, are now taught in institutes in California, Massachusetts, New York, New Jersey and Vermont. Modern techniques were designed to release blocked-off core longings hidden behind the stone wall of narcissism by narcissistic defences. Success in treatment is not equated with the disappearance of specific symptoms or with an adjustment to external standards. Finding the way to bring patients into touch with their deep desires in the transference interaction is the challenge.

In 1976, under the editorship of Phyllis W. Meadows, a scientific journal began publication. The journal and the institutes were interested in extending psychoanalytic treatment to the full range of emotional pathologies including the perversions and the psychoses. The journal accepts papers for publication on treatment interventions.

P. Mea.

SQUIGGLE GAME Technique used by Winnicott in communicating with children, allowing the skilled therapist access to what is unconsciously or preconsciously preoccupying the child.

First described in 1953, and elaborated in 1964 and 1968, Winnicott's technique for the initial interview with a child was to invite the child to *play a game. Drawing materials would be to hand, and if the child agreed, Winnicott drew a random line – a squiggle – on the paper. The child might then comment, and then add to the drawing, allowing further comments, by him or herself, before drawing another, fresh line for Winnicott to elaborate upon. This beginning, when successful, allowed for the child to communicate imaginatively, and for Winnicott to demonstrate to the child his own interest in the internal world, thus encouraging the child in a mutual exploration of his or her thoughts, dreams, nightmares, and so on. Winnicott had reservations about publishing the technique, as he was concerned lest it be formalised into a routine that he felt could become meaningless. He did eventually devote one book to child consultations largely illustrated by the use of the 'squiggle game'. Since then, other workers, notably Brafman, have taken up the technique.

Brafman, A. H. (2001) *Working with Children and Parents*. London: Karnac Books.

Winnicott, D. W. [1953] (1958) 'Symptom tolerance in paediatrics' in *Collected Papers: Through Paediatrics to Psychoanalysis*. London: Tavistock.

Winnicott, D. W. [1964, 1968] (1989) 'The Squiggle Game' in *Psychoanalytic Explorations*. London: Karnac Books.

Winnicott, D. W. (1971) *Therapeutic Consultations in Child Psychiatry*. London: Hogarth Press.

J. Joh.

STAGE/PHASE An innate sequence of psychosexual phases – oral, anal, phallic, and genital – is dependent on the maturation of the corresponding erotogenic zone. Each stage contributes something to the development of the ego which moves by stages from narcissism to object relatedness.

J. A. Ber.

STAGES OF LIFE Jung's idea about the stages of life depends on his concept of an internal *self that both lures and propels one through the process of psychic development he terms *individuation. Acting like a gyroscope, the self regulates psychological balance as the human psyche expands in a widening spiral throughout life. Prenatal unconsciousness gives way – in infancy – to islands of consciousness which, as they cohere, create knowledge and memory, or *ego-consciousness. Puberty brings psychic birth, as separation from the parental ethos prompts emergence of dualities, the problem of conflicting impulses necessitates choice between unconscious instinct and the further development of a self in social context through work and relationship. From youth until mid-life, aspects of the self are chosen which further the development of the ego through an increasingly consolidating sense of identity in the world. Relinquished inclinations and dormant characteristics often return at mid-life when ego-identity lacks a sense of fullness and meaning. The search for missing aspects of the self creates turmoil at this time, yet if one's attention can be modified from exclusively external considerations and turns toward self-reflection, culture may be furthered beyond the mere natural replacement of earlier interests, the eternal round of 'getting and spending'. Entering the afternoon of life invites ego-consciousness to begin a rapprochement to the realm of the not-conscious, which one previously supposedly had left at birth. If enough significance has been gained in the first half of life, one may – with satisfaction and curiosity – turn attention toward the next life passage, death. While unwilling to make a claim for life after death, Jung's conviction as to the psychic reality of archetypal patterns allowed him to argue for aligning oneself with this line of inquiry, one expressed in images and symbols throughout religious history. The second half of life, then, properly has death as its goal. Psychological health depends on one's continuing ability to attach ego to the self's unknown purposes.

J. J.

Stolorow, Robert D. (1942–) Born 4 November 1942 in Pontiac, Michigan, Robert D. Stolorow is one of the originators of the *intersubjective perspective in psychoanalysis. Influenced by the personological research methods he encountered during his doctoral studies at Harvard University in the late 1960s, Stolorow and collaborator George Atwood in the early and mid-1970s conducted a series of psychobiological studies of the personal, subjective origins of the theories of Freud, Jung, Reich, and Rank, culminating in the 1979 book, *Faces in a Cloud*. In this book, Stolorow and Atwood concluded that what psychoanalysis needed was a theory of subjectivity itself, a depth psychology of personal experience. Drawing from the heritage of structuralism, Continental phenomenology, and philosophical hermeneutics, their proposals for such a framework have come to be known as *intersubjectivity theory. Its basic premise is that, both developmentally and in the psychoanalytic situation, psychological phenomena take form at the interface of reciprocally interacting, differently organised subjective worlds. Stolorow and his collaborators' perspective has evolved into a sweeping methodological and epistemological stance calling for a radical contextualisation of all aspects of psychoanalytic thought.

Stolorow, R. D. and Atwood, G. E. (1979) *Faces in a Cloud: Subjectivity in Personality Theory.* Northvale, NJ: Jason Aronson.

R. M. S.

Structure, psychic In ego psychology, a stable, enduring organisation that results from the linking of simple mental elements into a complex unity. For instance the elements within each particular structure of the tripartite model of id, ego and super-ego are interrelated on the basis of function. However, other mental elements that can be thought to constitute structure are groupings of thoughts, beliefs, fantasies, mental representations, behavioural patterns, etc. Such structures are on the basis of observable manifestations of an individual's functioning. The functions and contents of psychic structures can be inborn, such as the *autonomous ego functions of *ego psychology; or acquired as adaptations to the environment; or as *compromise formations in response to intrapsychic *conflict. Maturing inborn structures and developmentally acquired structures replace more primitive levels of organisation, leading to the structuralisation of the mental apparatus. During this process, structures that exhibit higher levels of complexity replace more primitive ones. The fact that psychic structures are slow to change lends stability to the overall functioning of the mental apparatus. But this slowness to change also accounts for length of time to bring structural change during psychoanalytic treatment. There is general agreement that meaningful psychological change (as opposed to transient and superficial change) is brought about by *transference cure – that is, change which is not merely the result of the analysand's wish to please the analyst.

In Lacan there are three levels or temporal phases in the elaboration of structural apparatus. Firstly, the narcissistic, Imaginary structure of the *mirror phase. Secondly, that of the unconscious structured like a language. Here, unlike his inspiration Lévi-Strauss, he considered the subject's relation to structure as central to the dialectic of *desire. Finally, from aspects of the above, Lacan developed topological and mathematico-logical models, whose points of perceptual and rational singularity open onto a clinically significant *Real.

See also: logic; mathematics

R. T. / G. S.

SUBGROUPS, FUNCTIONAL In systems-centred group psychotherapy, survival, development and transformation of the group and its members are assumed to be a product of the process of the discrimination and integration. Systems-centred group psychotherapy deliberately encourages discrimination and integration of information through functional subgrouping. Functional subgroups are formed either explicitly or implicitly.

Explicit functional subgrouping is the method used to contain and explore conflicts by encouraging members to subgroup explicitly around similarities, discover the differences in the apparently similar within each subgroup, recognise similarities in the apparent differences between subgroups and to integrate both the similarities and differences into the group-as-a-whole in a transformative process which makes the unconscious conscious.

Implicit subgrouping is making functional the subgroups that are implicit in the group process already in order to facilitate integration in the group-as-a-whole. For example: a group is watching two of its members fight. The first part of the intervention brings the group's attention to the fact that the members who are fighting over their differences are in the same sub-group – a 'fight' subgroup (discriminating the similarities in the apparently different). This is almost always a surprise. The second intervention points out that the apparently uninvolved group are in fact playing the role of supporting the fight by watching. This makes explicit the group's two implicit subgroups. Having made explicit the two different subgroups, the third intervention introduces a similarity into their apparent difference by asking them to discover what function they are playing for the group-as-a-whole: 'Does the group have a sense of what is the purpose of encouraging a fight at this moment?'

Agazarian, Y. M. (1997) *Systems-centered Therapy for Groups.* New York: Guilford.

Y. A.

SUBJECT The discovery of unconscious desire reveals that the subject represented in speech is neither reducible to the ego nor to the grammatical form of the I. According to Lacan the subject is a result of language and its existence can be deduced from effects in the field of language. Lacan's formula, 'a signifier represents a subject for another signifier', affirms the subject's subordination to the signifying structure which represents it in speech and determines its existence in language. The subject has no positive determination or being, cannot appear in what is said, but exists only through the differential articulation of the signifying chain. It is not equivalent to the structure which determines it, but is the effect of a lack-in-being which creates a want-to-be that leads to the subject posing the question of its existence in the field of the Other. The subject is constituted in two moments: the first moment marks the subject's *alienation in the metonymy of the chain of signifiers representing the demand by the Other on the subject. The second affords the subject a degree of *separation from the Other, because the confrontation with this lack in the Other results in the subject having to accept a lack within him or herself, that is to say, the Other is lacking signifiers which could complete the subject and this constitutes the *object a as cause of desire for the subject.

P. D.

SUBJECT SUPPOSED TO KNOW The subject supposed to know is Lacan's account of the operative principle of *transference. Love is at the centre of psychoanalysis. One learns there in so far as one is a lover, and Lacan, like Socrates, claims to know something about love: that love loves knowledge. The one that you suppose to know is loved. The patient's supposing that you know the truth is the Freudian artifice that delivers a power of *suggestion to the place of the analyst. If the analyst avoids these foundations of his power, he is ignorant. If it is something he is complicit with, he is a rascal. If he pretends to actually know, he is an imposter. It is in not using this power that the analyst allows the development of the transference.

G. W.

SUBJECTIVITY The subjective experience of the individual person which can never be reduced to objectivity. Existential psychoanalysts seek to understand, demonstrate, and articulate the fundamental connections that exist between our individual subjectivities and the world in which we live. In this pursuit, they draw on the work of existential-phenomenological philosophers. Husserl introduces the notion of *intersubjectivity to demonstrate the connection between individual subjects. *Buber uses the notion of the I-Thou relation to show that the individual self can never be understood outside of the context of relationship to another person, a Thou. *Heidegger introduces the notion of being-in-the-world to demonstrate that the human being, or *Dasein, achieves conscious awareness through its interactions with the world. Merleau-Ponty develops the notion of the body-subject to show that individual subjectivity always exists and develops in a bodily context. For existential psychoanalysts, therefore, the task is to elaborate and explore the ways in which the individual subjectivity of the client exists within a bodily, social, and environmental context. Fostering understanding of one's own subjective experience is seen as essential to the therapeutic process.

R. Fri.

SUBJECTIVITY, SUBORDINATED The analyst's subjectivity is a continuously active and influential component of the co-created therapeutic process. While it may be characterised as subordinated subjectivity, it is nonetheless crucial. From the perspective of love, the therapeutic process may be regarded as an engagement of the subjectivities of both patient and analyst addressing the problematic of love, resulting in the enhanced actualisation of love and self in both parties.

See also: intersubjectivity

Natterson, J. (1991) *Beyond Countertransference.* Northvale, NJ: Jason Aronson.

J. Nat.

SUBLIMATION Occurs when desires are diverted towards new, non-sexual and socially valued aims. The main types of activity described by Freud as sublimated are artistic creation and intellectual inquiry. Freud contrasted sublimation with *idealisation, which has to do with altering the perception and value of a particular object.

Freud saw sublimation as a satisfaction without *repression – a change of object for the drive. Lacan claims that in sublimation the object of desire is seen anew, elevated to the level of *'the thing' (*das Ding*), that is, to the level of the extimate point beyond language and the law of *signifiers. Sublimation therefore is transgression. What is crucial here is that this process does not concern the subject, only the object. For instance, in courtly love, the loving subject always maintains a distance from the ultimate object, an object that is deliberately maintained beyond the reach of the subject's desire. When the subject takes the place of the thing, Lacan speaks of *perversion, which he frequently illustrates with quotations from the Marquis de Sade.

See also: compromise formation; defence; extimacy

Freud, S. (1916) *Introductory Lectures on Psycho-Analysis*. S. E. 15–16. London: Hogarth Press.
Freud, S. (1930) *Civilization and its Discontents*. S. E. 21. London: Hogarth Press.

K. L.

SUBSTITUTE FORMATION When the wishful impulses that originate in response to pressure from the drives are repressed, they may find substitute outlets in *symptoms, *phobias, *somatic conversions, *obsessions or *sublimations. Substitute formations bind the anxiety that might otherwise arise from the conflict between impulse and prohibition.

J. A. Ber.

SUGGESTION Freud equated the power of the *transference with the analyst's ability to influence the patient through suggestion. However, he noted that in psychoanalysis, suggestion is employed to get the patient to engage in analytic work, rather than being used as the method of cure, as was the case with hypnotic suggestion.

Lacan's entire teaching is aimed at clearly distinguishing psychoanalytic practice from the use of (hypnotic) suggestion, basing this distinction on the following grounds: clinically, a suggestive interpretation obstructs desire and favours *identification; epistemologically, it nourishes the sense rather than the Real of non-sense; and ethically, it constitutes an abuse of power.

J. A. Ber. / R. M. W.

SUICIDE The act of killing oneself. It remains a major cause of death among all age groups, being the third most common cause of death in those aged fifteen to thirty-four. Suicide has proved difficult to investigate reliably because of historical and theological taboos, but twentieth-century research methods have allowed better identification of associations and risk factors. More common in men of all age groups, it is known to be associated with increased rates of unemployment, divorce, homicide and alcohol abuse. Other known associations include: season – most common in spring; social class – higher in lowest groups; occupation – most common amongst lawyers, doctors and bar owners; religious belief – a protective factor; age – increased incidence; and, imprisonment – greatly increased risk.

In both deliberate self-injury, a related behaviour, and completed suicide, it can be difficult to determine the intention behind the act, and the absence of international standardised criteria for the reporting, defining and measuring such behaviour, with a historical tendency to under-report, has led to difficulty comparing rates over time and between countries. Suicide is a recognised potential consequence of psychiatric conditions such as depression and schizophrenia, and it is strongly associated with alcohol and drug misuse, personality disorder, epilepsy, and chronic physical illness.

As Cole has said it can also follow none of the above, requiring greater consideration of the role of hopelessness, whether sudden or chronic. Methods of suicide vary, but males tend to choose more violent methods, including hanging or exhaust poisoning, while females are more likely to opt for overdosing with drugs. Although genetic and neurochemical factors have been implicated, and major risk factors are known, detection and prevention have remained difficult, not least because the intent to commit suicide is not a static phenomenon.

Durkheim provided an early typology, which retains value in understanding suicidal behaviour – his anomic, egoistic and altruistic suicides emphasise the social context of the behaviour. Others, such as Boldt, have argued that social meaning is an integral part of the behaviour, which cannot be understood or prevented if the individual stands alone. Suicide is not a unitary phenomenon, motivation can be ambiguous, multiple and complex, and the psychological processes involved are impossible to assemble in retrospect. Despite this, prevention remains at the top of the political agenda, if somewhat elusive.

Boldt, M. (1987) 'Defining suicide: implications for suicide behaviour and for suicide prevention'. *Crisis*: 3–13.
Cole, D. A. (1980) 'Hopelessness, social desirability, depression and parasuicide in two college samples'. *Journal of Consulting Clinical Psychology* 56: 131–6.
Durkheim, E. (1951) *Suicide: A Study in Sociology*. New York: The Free Press.

A. F.

SULLIVAN, HARRY STACK (1892–1949) H. S. Sullivan was a pioneer student of the social, relational sources of personality development that today constitute the main interest not only of interpersonal psychoanalysis but of two other principal psychoanalytic schools, object relations and self psychology. Relational concepts can also be expected increasingly to enter neuroscience as evidence for the social construction of the human brain accumulates.

Sullivan did not see patient and observer as separate and contended that the site of psychiatric observation was not the patient alone but the field of patient and observer together; psychological observation is inevitably participant observation. Thus the importance of countertransference has come to rival that of transference in both analytic treatment and research. It is widely accepted that sound classification of diseases depend on the stabilisation of interview protocols. Sullivan's intuitions also gave rise to such means of normalising the interpersonal field as the counterprojection of paranoid developments.

Sullivan's largest divergence from Freud was to place security needs on a par with instinctual and sexual drives, including the needs for sleep and relaxation. He also gave self-formation a larger place than Freud, who made selfhood a fantasy formation of the ego.

H. S. Perry, Sullivan's biographer and literary executor, has provided a moving account of his early years in an impoverished county of upper New York. He attended medical school in Chicago, came under the influence of William Alanson White at St Elizabeth's Hospital in Washington, DC, and began his formal research on relational aspects of schizophrenia at Sheppard and Enoch Pratt Hospital in Towson, Maryland, in 1923, linking his work with that of sociologists, anthropologists and linguists. The last years of his life were devoted to clinical practice and the founding of institutions: the Washington School of Psychiatry in Washington, DC, the William Alanson White Institute in New York, and the journal *Psychiatry*, devoted to interpersonal studies. He began to apply his concepts to the understanding and alleviation of such social ills as racism and war, becoming active in the World Health Organization, and died in Paris while participating in the United

Nations Educational, Scientific and Cultural Organization.

Eisenberg, L. (1995) 'The social construction of the human brain'. *American Journal of Psychiatry* 152: 1563–75.
Havens, L. (1976) *Participant Observation*. New York: Jason Aronson.
Perry, H. S. (1982) *Psychiatrist of America*. Cambridge, MA: The Belknap Press.

L. H.

SUPER-EGO (FREUD) Along with the id and ego, one of the basic components of Freud's structural model. Super-ego is the product of an internalisation of, and *identification with, parent and parental authority, including prohibition and values associated with such authorities. Insofar as parental authority reflects the broader social context, the super-ego can be seen as the indirect product of the internalisation of society's demands and values. The formation of the super-ego betokens the developmental move from having one's behaviour entirely governed by external authority, to its regulation by internal authority, that is, one's conscience. An evidence of the operation of the super-ego in psychic life, in particular the tension between ego and super-ego, is the experience of *guilt and the need for punishment. Freud referred to the super-ego as the heir to the Oedipus complex (at least in the male), because the boy's relinquishment of incestuous and rivalrous wishes and their replacement by identification with the father, marks the emergence of the super-ego. Freud remarked that, in healthy development, the super-ego operates less and less as a strict and harsh father confronting a child, and becomes more and more depersonified. This suggests the transformation from a harsh and primitive – in Fairbairn's terms – internalised object, to a more reasonable set of internalised values. Other aspects of the super-ego that should be mentioned include its role as the instigator of repression and other ego defences; its central role in certain forms of *masochism and 'obsessional types'; and, particularly in its punitive function, its close link to *aggression.

See also: ego-ideal

Freud, S. (1923) *The Ego and the Id*. S. E. 19. London: Hogarth Press.

M. Eag.

SUPER-EGO (FAIRBAIRN) Fairbairn describes the super-ego as a group of mental functions undertaken by a group of mental structures, *the ideal object, the *antilibidinal ego and the *rejecting object operating in varying permutations. He believed that the differing modes of action of these components of the ego accounted for the differing directions and degrees of severity of the super-ego, as well as its status as repressed but also acting to repress aspects of the psyche.

Fairbairn, W. R. D. [1929] (1994) 'What is the super-ego?' and 'Is the super-ego repressed?' in E. Fairbairn Birtles and D. Scharff (eds) *From Instinct to Self*, Vol. II. Northvale, NJ: Jason Aronson.
Fairbairn, W. R. D. [1963] (1994) 'Synopsis' in D. Scharff and E. Fairbairn Birtles (eds) *From Instinct to Self*, Vol. I. Northvale, NJ: Jason Aronson.

E. F. B. / D. E. S.

SUPER-EGO (KLEIN) Klein departs somewhat from Freud's mature conception of the super-ego. In *New Introductory Lectures*, Freud described the super-ego as a part of the ego which, as a result of the ego splitting itself, comes to 'stand over' against the other part. He described it as a largely unconscious structure consisting of certain aspects of imagos derived from introjected parental figures. Klein agreed with this view but differed with Freud when she claimed that introjection, which she saw as leading to the super-ego, occurred from birth. She believed that the early introjection of the good and bad breast is the foundation of the super-ego and influences the development of the Oedipus complex. This conception of super-ego formation is in contrast to Freud's explicit statements that the identifications with the parents are the heir of the Oedipus complex and only succeed if the Oedipus complex is overcome. She saw a sense of guilt as the product of super-ego formation, and described how, in its primitive incarnation (unmoderated by benign oedipal experience), the super-ego may be particularly harsh and omnipotent.

Freud, S. (1933) *New Introductory Lectures on Psycho-Analysis*, S. E. 22. London: Hogarth Press.
Klein, M. (1928) 'Early stages of the Oedipus conflict'. *International Journal of Psycho-Analysis* 9. Also in *Love, Guilt and Reparation*. London: Hogarth Press, 1975 (1).
Klein, M. (1958) 'On the development of mental functioning'. *International Journal of Psycho-Analysis* 29. Also in *Envy and Gratitude*. London: Hogarth Press, 1975 (111).

S. A.

SUPER-EGO (BION) A misunderstanding (−K) internal part-object which shows itself as a superior object asserting its superiority by finding fault with everything and making envious assertions of moral superiority without any morals. Its most important characteristic is its hatred and attacks of any new development in the personality. As to the resemblance between the *super-ego and conscience, Bion's super-ego retains the power to arouse guilt, but a guilt which is meaningless. Bion also considers this 'super' ego as one of the *invariants in *transformations in hallucinosis.

Bion, W. R. (1962) *Learning from Experience*. London: Heinemann.
Bion, W. R. (1965) *Transformations*. London: Heinemann.

E. T. B.

SUPER-EGO (LACAN) An essential paradox pertains to Lacan's dual conception of the super-ego. The first of these conceptions, coinciding with that of Freud, is that of the super-ego as the psychical agency whose function, under the dominance of the pleasure principle, is to consolidate the claims of civilisation through the issuance of prohibitive injunctions against *jouissance*. Lacan's second and inverse conception of the super-ego is that of the imperative of *jouissance* epitomised by the commandment: Enjoy! The super-ego thus is the agency of the introjection of the law, impelling the subject to reinstate the *jouissance* that had been lost by way of Symbolic castration, and thereby propelling the subject beyond the pleasure principle and the Symbolic order.

SURPLUS JOUISSANCE This concept is related to the concept of *object a, which is, according to Lacan, the cause and compass of human desire. These two terms express that 'little something' in the body of the loved one, a dimple, a slight squint, that makes them special, as well as the enjoyment provided there. This enjoyment is the result of an exchange of a supposed primordial total **jouissance* for one limited by the phallic function; in this sense Lacan's notion is analogous to that of surplus value in Marx. The presence of this 'little something' that insists from within the object of desire and that hints at something more, is responsible for surplus *jouissance*.

M. V.

SUTTIE, IAN D. (1888–1935) *The Origins of Love and Hate*, Ian D. Suttie's major work, was published in 1935, shortly after his death at the age of forty-six. The ideas formulated in this book represent a fundamental break with Freudian theory. Central to Suttie's thesis is the concept of an innate human need for companionship. This is the infant's only protection and gives rise to parental and fellowship 'love'. Companionship was thought to be genetically independent of sexual need. For Suttie, emotional expression was not an outpouring for its own sake, but an overture that demands a response from others. In its absence lies the source of all anxiety and rage, and behind the anxiety, the dread of separation.

Suttie's line of thought had important implications for therapy. He advocated that a 'fellowship of suffering' or basic companionship be established between patient and therapist. Influenced by Ferenczi, he believed that love was the effective healing agent in psychotherapy – the love being understood as the therapist's 'feeling interest responsiveness'.

Suttie was critical of too great an emphasis on therapeutic technique, and thought that psychoanalysis had institutionalised a taboo on tenderness.

Suttie's re-orientation and supplementation on psychoanalytic theory anticipated the work of Fairbairn, Winnicott, Guntrip and, in particular, Bowlby.

A. Har.

SWEDEN Freud wrote *On the History of the Psychoanalytical Movement* in 1914. Nine years later, in 1923, he felt it necessary to append the following footnote: 'At the present time the Scandinavian countries are still the least receptive.'

In Sweden, psychoanalysis was introduced in an ambiguous way. The two main pioneers, Emanuel af Geijerstam and Poul Bjerre, were united in a common ambivalent attitude towards it. Geijerstam, a conscientious scientist and psychotherapist, felt a kinship with Alfred Adler and Carl Gustav Jung. He had written about Freud as early as 1902, but after 1916, he consistently pointed out that so-called 'anagogue analysis' must be regarded as an improvement on Freud's method.

Poul Bjerre, who introduced Lou-Andreas Salomé to Freud, met the latter in 1910. The following year, he presented a selection of Freud's ideas to the Swedish Society of Physicians, and in 1924 he translated and published some of Freud's articles. Already after their first meeting, Bjerre was preoccupied with the notion that his own ideas were more important than those of Freud. He believed that Freud's allegedly mechanistic views interfered with the latter's capability to understand the significance of so-called psychosynthesis. Thus, during the first three decades of the twentieth century, two physicians, who were both – in spite of otherwise decisive differences – incapable of or unwilling to embrace Freud's theory as a whole, introduced Freud in Sweden.

There were additional sources of opposition to Freud. In the Society of Physicians, the influential psychiatrists Bror Gadelius (1862–1938) and Olof Kinberg (1873–1960) set the tone in the end of the 1920s and the beginning of the 1930s.

In the second half of the 1920s, psychoanalysis was also discussed in *Clarté*, a socialist literary journal that was part of the international Clarté movement. Here, impassioned with the idea that psychoanalysis could be an element of radical political theory and an instrument of social change, various intellectual advocates of psychoanalysis published their contributions.

In literary circles, an interest in psychoanalysis was reflected in the 1930s in a new journal, *Spektrum*. Not only modernist poetry and prose were published there, but also translations of works of psychoanalytic writers such as Anna Freud, Erich Fromm, and Wilhelm Reich. One of the editors was Pehr Henrik Törngren, who also published psychoanalytic contributions of his own. During this period, parts of *The Interpretation of Dreams* and the complete *The Future of an Illusion* and *Civilisation and its Discontents* were translated into Swedish.

In August 1931, a group of Scandinavian clinicians that were interested in psychoanalysis met to discuss the establishment of a psychoanalytic society. Two groups were formed. Alfhild Tamm (1876–1959), who was Sweden's first female psychiatrist and, from 1926, a member of the Psychoanalytic Society in Vienna, became chairperson of the Finnish-Swedish Psychoanalytical Society. In the spirit of enlightenment, Tamm fought prejudice about masturbation. However, her relative isolation and lack of support appears to have prevented her from developing a forceful Swedish branch of psychoanalysis.

In 1934, the teacher Hanna Bratt founded a psychotherapeutic Clinic for children under the name of *Ericastiftelsen* (The Erica Foundation). Eventually, a psychoanalytically-oriented training program was offered to child psychiatrists and psychologists who wished to learn psychotherapy for children. The Tavistock clinic in London was a source of inspiration. An early leader was Gunnar Nycander, who was trained in the Swedish-Finnish Institute. Another psychoanalyst, Gösta Harding, trained in Stockholm, headed the Erica Foundation from 1945. Harding's successors have all been psychoanalysts trained within the IPA.

In the early thirties, psychoanalysts trained in Central Europe, particularly in Vienna, started arriving in the Scandinavian countries. Ludwig Jekels, a pupil of Freud's, stayed in Stockholm for almost three years. He experienced his stay as wearing and difficult, and it was with a sense of defeat that he left Sweden. During the same period, Scandinavians travelled to Vienna, Berlin, and Zurich to be in analysis with August Aichhorn, Hélène Deutsch, Paul Federn, Eduard Hitschmann and Oskar Pfister.

While the Scandinavian psychoanalysts were educating and organising themselves according to the norms of the International Psychoanalytic Association after 1926, alternative psychotherapeutic organisations were established in the Scandinavian countries. These organisations tended to reject certain basic psychoanalytic tenets, such as the theories of infantile sexuality and dreams. In 1932, the Nordic Psychoanalytical Association (*Nordisk psykoanalytisk samfund*) was founded in Norway. In Denmark a society called The Psychoanalytical Association (*Psykoanalytisk samfund*) was established in 1933. Bjerre was involved in the foundation of both these associations.

In the wake of the rise of Nazism and the outbreak of World War II, the Dutch psychoanalyst René de Monchy came to Sweden, settling in Stockholm. A key person in Dutch psychoanalysis, and one who had had personal contact with Freud, de Monchy played a dominating role during his eight years in Sweden. He was the analyst of Ola Andersson as well as of the Hungarian psychologist Lajos Szekely. The latter had arrived in Sweden as a Jewish refugee. Szekely, who had started his analytic training in Holland, completed it in Sweden. During five decades he played an important role for Swedish physicians and psychologists in psychoanalytic training. He published articles on creativity and on the unconscious, in English, French, German, Hungarian, and Swedish.

Historically, relatively few Swedish contributions to psychoanalytic thought have had an international impact. An outstanding exception is Ola Andersson's doctoral dissertation from 1962, *Studies in the Prehistory of Psychoanalysis*. Andersson uncovered the historical and philosophical context of the development of Freud's ideas up till 1896, that is, up to the point where psychoanalysis started to take form as an independent discipline. He demonstrated Herbart's influence on Freud, and he also carried out original research leading to the verification of the true identity of Freud's patient, Emmy von N.

Since the late 1960s, the membership of the Swedish Psychoanalytic Society has grown steadily; the current number of members is approximately 170. In 1982 and 1986, the respective presidents of the Swedish Psychoanalytical Society, Bo Larsson and Birgitta Ejve, asked the International Psychoanalytic Association to provide consulting visits. The background of this request was a sense of a deadlock in the society's organisation and of a diminished creativity within it. The consultations resulted in a strengthening of the society's democratic organisation as well as in a more open intellectual climate. One aspect of this development was also an increased openness towards the public.

The orientation of the Swedish Psychoanalytical Society has been mainstream

Freudian since the beginning, with a growing influence of contemporary Kleinian thought in recent years. In the late 1970s, a group of Swedish psychoanalysts invited Herbert Rosenfeld of London to lead clinical seminars in Stockholm, which inspired a wave of interest in Kleinian thought among Swedish psychoanalysts.

In 1988, Lars Sjögren and Ludvig Igra – the latter a member of the non-IPA Swedish Society for Holistic Psychoanalysis and Psychotherapy as well as of the Swedish Psychoanalytical Society – translated and published a selection of texts by Melanie Klein. Sjögren subsequently published a biography of Freud. Together with Clarence Crafoord and Bengt Warren (the latter a member of the Holistic Society), in 1996 Sjögren launched the largest psychoanalytic publication project in Sweden yet, an authorised and carefully edited translation of Freud's collected works, published by *Natur och Kultur*.

The Holistic Society has sought ideological support in the work of neo-Freudians such as Erich Fromm, Frieda Fromm-Reichmann, and Harry Stack Sullivan. Until his death in 1976, Harold Kelman of New York was an important figure for the Holistic Society in Stockholm. The society, founded in 1968, joined the non-IPA, International Federation of Psychoanalytic Societies in 1972. In recent years it has gradually oriented itself towards the British object-relations schools, Klein, Bion, and then, in the manner of a swinging pendulum, back towards Freud. After a period of collaboration in scientific matters with the Swedish Psychoanalytical Society, the Holistic Society has applied to the International Psychoanalytic Association for membership on behalf of its seventy-five members, and has subsequently been accepted as a provisional society under the name of *Svenska psykoanalytiska sällskapet* (the Swedish Psychoanalytical Association) within the IPA, with membership effective as from 2001.

The translation into Swedish of French structuralist philosophers and social thinkers triggered an interest in Jacques Lacan and French psychoanalysis among people in various university departments within the humanities. However, only a small part of Lacan's own writings have been translated. A selection of his *Ecrits* was edited by Iréne Matthis and published in 1989. In her widely read books, Matthis, a member of the Swedish Psychoanalytical Society, has combined psychoanalysis with semiotics. She has also recently defended a psychoanalytic dissertation called *The Thinking Body*. Jörgen Reeder, a member of the Holistic Society, is another writer in the Lacanian tradition.

During the 1970s and 1980s, psychoanalysts from the USA and Latin America worked in Gothenburg for short periods of time, offering training in psychoanalytically oriented psychotherapy. In 1974, the Gothenburg Psychotherapy Institute was founded by Angel and Dora Fiasché, who had previously worked with, among others, Leon Grinberg and Enrique Pichon Rivière. Like the Holistic Society, the Gothenburg institute officially has a pragmatic, socialist orientation. It has approximately a hundred members.

At the turn of the twentieth century and the beginning of the twenty-first, a consistent and almost complete Swedish translation of Freud's text is under way – though not without resistance. The strength and endurance of psychoanalysis in the past, in a culture that has often seemed to reject it and its followers, is a paradox that one might find cheering in light of Freud's downhearted reflection in 1923 about psychoanalysis in Scandinavia.

P. M. J.

SWITZERLAND The Swiss were 'psychoanalysts of the first hour' as Hans Walser wrote in 1976. In the nineteenth century there were progressive innovations in Swiss psychiatry and August Forel (1848–1931), Professor of Psychiatry in Zurich, who had had contact with Sigmund *Freud, postulated a dynamic psychology. Eugen Bleuler (1857–1939), who created the concept of schizophrenia, and Adolf Meyer (1866–1950) both studied with Forel and were able to acquire on this basis a first-hand understanding of psychoanalysis. Eugen Bleuler drew the attention of his new assistant physician Carl Gustav *Jung to Freud's *Interpretation of Dreams* shortly after it was published in 1900. Swiss psychiatry gave rise to psychodynamic psychiatry, which spread worldwide. A considerable number of physicians from abroad, such as Karl Abraham, Hermann Nunberg, H. W. van Ophuysen, Sabina Spielrein, Otto Gross, Max Eitingon and Abraham Arden Brill found their way to Freud by working in Eugen Bleuler's University Psychiatric Clinic, Burghölzli, in Zurich and went on to become world-renowned psychoanalysts. The institutionalisation of psychoanalysis began in 1907 with the formation of the Society of Freudian Studies in Zurich; in 1919 the Swiss Psychoanalytical Society was founded.

Interest in the emerging subject of psychoanalysis was not limited to German-speaking areas of the country; in Francophone Switzerland, at the University of Geneva, Théodore Flournoy (1854–1920) and Edouard Claparède (1873–1940) prepared the ground for a positive response. However, after the special reception that was given to psychoanalysis several Swiss analysts went their own way, developing an increasing ambivalence towards Freud. Carl Gustav Jung (1875–1961) founded the school of analytical psychology. Ludwig Binswanger (1881–1966) and Medard Boss (1903–90) applied the principles of existential phenomenology, in particular those formulated by Martin Heidegger, to psychotherapy and created existential analysis – *Daseinsanalyse*. In Zurich Leopold Szondi (1893–1986) founded a third school of depth psychology, Schicksalsanalyse (Fate analysis).

There are several outstanding historical figures in Swiss psychoanalysis. The Zurich pastor Oskar Pfister (1873–1956) published over 170 titles and had an important exchange of letters with Sigmund Freud. Hermann Rorschach (1884–1922) was a psychoanalyst before achieving world renown with his projective test. Rudolf Brun (1885–1965) developed bio-psychological views, summarised in his well-known work, *Allgemeine Neurosenlehre* in 1942. Heinrich Meng (1887–1972) made significant contributions in the field of psycho-hygiene. Hans Zulliger (1893–1965) was one of the founders of psychoanalytic education and child analysis. He published two modified Rorschach tests, the Behn-Rorschach-Test and the Z-Test for group investigations. Raymond de Saussure (1894–1971), from Geneva, son of the linguistician Ferdinand de Saussure, was involved in the founding of the Swiss Psychoanalytical Society in 1919 and in 1927/28 in the founding of the Psychoanalytical Society in Paris. He was the main architect and organiser of psychoanalysis in Francophone Switzerland and worked alongside Charles Odier (1886–1954) and Henri Flournoy (1886–1955). Marguerite A. Sechehaye (1887–1964) and later Gaetano Benedetti became known for their publications about psychoanalytic therapeutic work with schizophrenics. Germaine Guex (1904–84) published *La névrose d'bandon*, one of the first books about psychoanalytic work with borderline patients. With Paul Parin and Goldy Parin-Matthèy, Fritz Morgenthaler (1919–84) carried out some original ethno-psychoanalytical investigations with the Dogon in Mali, the Agni in Ivory Coast and the Iatmul in Papua New Guinea. Fritz Meerwein (1922–89) became known for his psychoanalytic research in the field of psychosomatics and psycho-oncology, and Jacques Berna (1911–2000) was one of the first pioneers of child analysis.

Moser, A. (1992) 'Switzerland' in P. Kutter (ed.) *Psychoanalysis International*, Vol. 1. Stuttgart-Bad Cannstatt: Frommann-Holzboog.

Walser, H. H. (1976) Psychoanalyse in der Schweiz in D. Eicke (ed.) *Psychologie des Jahrhunderts*. Bd. I I. Zurich: Kindler.

A. Mos.

SYMBOL (JUNG) Plutarch's use of the word *symbolon* to denote any outward expression of a hidden meaning comes very close to that of Jung, for whom the symbol is the best possible way of expressing something relatively unknown. He saw Freud's theory of symbolism, based on predictable and fixed equivalences, as nothing more than signs or symptoms. His 1912 book, *Symbols of Transformation*, marked his break with Freud and emphasised the teleological as opposed to the causal nature of the symbol. Symbols emerge from the personal or collective unconscious naturally and spontaneously in dreams, and in interpreting these it is essential to establish the dreamer's own associations to each content. If correctly understood, the content will carry an emotional charge and become a living symbol, part of the individual's private myth. Symbols are experienced not only in dreams but also in the events of everyday life, especially in *synchronicities. The main function of the symbol is to transform *energy and reconcile opposites within the psyche, thus bringing about a change of attitude. When psychic energy is blocked, as in depression, the resultant inactivity on the conscious level stimulates symbol-making activity in the unconscious, pointing the way to new goals so that life can flow on.

Religious symbols, which are the self-revelation of archetypal forces from the collective unconscious capable of giving meaning to whole societies and eras, often occur in similar forms throughout the world. Jung demonstrated that collective religious symbols for God are indistinguishable from individual symbols of the self.

In the final volume of his *Collected Works*, 'The Symbolic Life', Jung indicates what this might imply. It is to go 'on the Quest' without any fixed objectives, paying attention to what the soul is saying in the symbols it transmits. There is no other guidance or certainty.

E. Beg.

SYMBOL FORMATION (KLEIN) As soon as the infant turns his/her interest towards objects other than the mother's breast, desires (both libidinal and aggressive) and anxieties are also transferred from the first and unique object to other objects. New interests develop which become substitutes for the relation to the primary object. This primary object, however, is not only the external but also the internalised good breast, and this deflection of the emotions and creative feelings which become related to the external world is bound up with projective processes. In all of these processes, the function of symbol formation and phantasy activity is of great significance. When depressive anxiety arises, the ego feels driven to project, deflect, and distribute emotions and desires, as well as guilt and the urge to make reparation onto new objects and interests. These processes, in Klein's view, are a mainspring for sublimations throughout life.

Her theory is based on the assumption that the early stages of the Oedipus conflict take place during a phase of development which is inaugurated by oral sadism (with which urethral, muscular and anal sadism associate themselves) and terminate when the ascendancy of anal sadism comes to an end.

The child's sadistic attacks have as their object both the mother and the father, who are in phantasy bitten, torn, cut or stamped to bits. The attacks give rise to anxiety lest the child should be punished by the united parents, viewed as a nightmarishly terrifying combined parental figure, and this anxiety becomes internalised via oral-sadistic introjection of the objects. The installation of the harsh primitive super-ego convinces the infant that their loving and passionate feeling is innately bad and perhaps inextricably confused with destructiveness.

In her earlier work Klein concluded that symbolism is the foundation of all sublimation and talents, since it is by way of *symbolic equations that things, activities and interests become the subject of libidinal phantasies. Later she added that side-by-side with the libidinal interest, it is the anxiety arising in the early oedipal stage which sets going the mechanism of identification. This anxiety contributes to equating the attacked objects with other initially less persecutory things. These in their turn become objects of anxiety, and so the child is impelled constantly to make other and newer equations, which form the basis for an interest in new objects and in symbolism. Thus, not only does symbolism come to be the foundation of all phantasy and sublimation, but more than that, it is the basis of the subject's relation to the outside world and to reality in general.

In *psychosis the ego's excessive and premature defence against sadism inhibits the establishing of a relation to reality and the development of phantasy life. The further sadistic appropriation and exploration of the mother's body and of its substitutes in the outside world are brought to a standstill, and this causes the more or less complete suspension of symbolic relations to objects.

Klein, M. (1923) 'Early analysis'. *Imago* 9. Also in *Love, Guilt and Reparation*. London: Hogarth Press, 1975 (1).

Klein, M. (1930) 'The importance of symbol formation in the development of the ego'. *International Journal of Psychoanalysis* 11. Also in *Love, Guilt and Reparation*. London: Hogarth Press, 1975 (111).

Klein, M. (1952) 'Some theoretical conclusions regarding the emotional life of the infant' in *Developments in Psycho-Analysis* with P. Heimann, S. Isaacs, and J. Riviere. London: Hogarth. Also in *Envy and Gratitude*. London: Hogarth Press, 1975 (111).

S. A.

SYMBOLIC, THE The Symbolic, *Imaginary and *Real are the three heterogenous registers or orders to which Lacan relegated all subjective experience. The Symbolic consists of the structures through which language orders, regulates and pre-structures human relationships for any subject, determining the subject as its effect. The Symbolic functions through a chaining of differential elements of language called *signifiers, exemplified by the basic pair S1 and S2 which relate to each other (rather than to an external reference), and to a Real unsymbolisable void within the Symbolic by relations of metaphor, metonymy, and temporal retroaction.

R. M. W.

SYMBOLIC EQUATION Freud uses this term to indicate the different responses of the young girl and the boy in confronting conflicts in oedipal love. Where the boy experiences only the 'logical shock' of *castration, the girl responds to the threat of loss of primary love by moving 'along the line of a symbolic equation'. The equation might be 'penis = baby', or 'opening and shutting door = parent's legs'. Ferenczi took up the term from the German child-psychologist Ernst Meumann, and introduced the term into psychoanalysis. Melanie *Klein developed the term in her construction of a theory of symbol formation. It was further developed by *Segal to describe primitive modes of object association and symbolisation, that in pathological states imply concretisation of thought processes. In a number of early works, particularly 'The importance of symbol-formation in the development of the ego' of 1930, Klein suggests that as primary objects become affectively saturated, substitutes are developed through identification that may be used more freely, although as these in turn become objects of anxiety new symbolic equations are required. Klein argues that such symbolism is the basis of internal and external relatedness.

Drawing on this, Segal emphasises that, as well as anxiety about one's objects fuelling symbol-formation, the differentiation between ego and object (as well as between the paranoid-schizoid and depressive positions) is reflected in that between the symbol and the object symbolised, the signifier and the signified. Stressing the triadic relation between the symbol, the thing-in-itself that is symbolised and the person within whose mind the one represents the other, Segal is able to distinguish between mature triadic symbol-formation characteristic of the depressive position (as well as of sublimation) and more primitive variants within the paranoid-schizoid position (and in symptom formation) where there is a failure to adequately differentiate the symbol and object symbolised, underlying which is an active conflation of ego and object. The latter process Segal terms a 'symbolic equation', which concept she uses to clarify the concrete thinking common to the psychoses.

While initially conceptualised in terms of *projective identification, Segal later described symbolic equation with reference to Bion's concepts of normal and pathological projective identification, container-contained, and the transformation of beta into alpha elements. Finally, Segal sees the attainment of triangular oedipal relations as linked with the development of mental space within which symbol-formation germinates, the disruption of such 'thinking' space in its nascent stages predisposing the infant to later thought disorder, psychopathology and further symbolic equations.

Ferenczi, S. (1916). 'The Ontogenesis of Symbols' in R. Badger (ed.) *Six in Psychoanalysis*. Boston, MA: Gorham Press.

Segal, H. [1957] (1981) 'Notes on symbol formation' in *The Work of Hanna Segal: A Kleinian Approach to Clinical Practice*. Northvale, NJ: Jason Aronson, 49–65.

B. B. / R. Wil.

SYMBOLISATION Meaning making, as in art and creativity. In cognitive theory, the linking of a symbolic vehicle (a word or gesture) to a referent. In psychoanalytic theory part of the *representational process where one item of experience is linked to another in distinct spheres of the mind where one represents the other. There are levels of symbolisation: incipient, discursive, and the symbolisation of dynamic conflicts. Psychoanalytic process rests on the creation of symbolising space in the interpretation of transference. Its absence may mark the cessation of analytic work, be it in the form of desymbolisation or *symbolic equation, which involves a breakdown of the linking process.

Freedman, N. and Russell, J. (2003) 'Symbolization of the analytic discourse'. *Psychoanalysis and Contemporary Thought* 26 (1): 39–88.

Loewald, H. (1988) *Sublimation*. New Haven, CT: Yale University Press.

Ogden, T. (1986) *Matrix of the Mind*. Northvale, NJ: Jason Aronson.

Segal, H. (1957) 'Notes on symbol formation'. *International Journal of Psychoanalysis* 38: 391–7.

Werner, H. and Kaplan, B. (1963) *Symbol Formation*. New York: John Wiley.

N. F.

SYMPTOMS/SYMPTOM FORMATION For *ego psychology, neurotic symptoms result when the ego fails in its attempts to keep repressed drives, wishes, fantasies, memories or affects from emerging into consciousness. The threatened emergence of repressed material triggers signal *anxiety, which results in the ego's redoubling its defensive efforts to keep such material repressed. If such efforts are successful, a traumatic state is avoided via a compromise formation, which allows disguised, partial satisfaction of the repressed wish. The *primary gain of neurotic symptoms lies in their achievement of at least partial gratification of the drive. Symptoms may remain circumscribed, or they may become characteristic of the way in which the individual experiences certain situations – *character neurosis. Inhibitions that restrict ego functioning, for example mobility, constitute neurosis only if they are a disguised expression of repressed drives.

For Lacan in the period of the 1950s when he strongly emphasises the Symbolic, the symptom is the expression of language, a metaphor, a part of the fundamental structural dimension. During the process of the psychoanalytic work interpretation tries to reach this Symbolic dimension through the signifier. Later, the symptom will also include the part of pleasure attached to it, already described by Freud and formulated by Lacan as *jouissance. This dimension is not included in the signifier, but in the Real. One of the main goals of the psychoanalytic act in the last part of Lacan's teaching is to demonstrate by means of the *borromean knot the way in which the symptom is linked to the Real as well as to the Imaginary and the Symbolic.

D. Cre. / R. T.

SYNCHRONICITY Jung used the term synchronicity for 'meaningful coincidence' when there is an acausal, meaningful connection between a psychic state and an objective external event. Synchronicities usually occur in relation to an *archetype. They are observed in paranormal events such as pre-cognitive dreams and in analytic work when a patient's unconscious is strongly constellated. Examination of synchronistic events can reveal or *amplify archetypal constellations and offer a deep level of significance and meaning to the individual. Jung's classic example involved the unusual appearance of a gold-green scarab beetle while a female patient was telling Jung her dream of being given a golden scarab beetle, an Egyptian *symbol of the archetype of rebirth. The synchronicity at that crucial moment in a difficult case helped the patient break through her over-rational *animus and intellectual defences, which proved to be a turning point in the analysis. Experiences with synchronicity and acausal natural phenomena like radioactive decay led Jung and the physicist Wolfgang Pauli to hypothesise a four-dimensional universe consisting of the space-time continuum, energy, causality, and synchronicity.

Jung, C. G. [1952](1969) 'Synchronicity: an acausal connecting principle' in *Collected Works*, Vol. 8. Princeton: Princeton University Press.

D. M.

T

TAUSK, VICTOR (1879–1919) Tausk was born in Slovakia, but grew up in Croatia. He started attending the University of Vienna in 1897, where he was trained in law. He married in 1900, and two sons were born in Croatia. In 1905 Tausk and his wife separated; Tausk had been dissatisfied with the law as a profession, and tried translating, poetry and play-writing, as he struggled at journalism. After a short depression and then a spontaneous recovery, Tausk turned to Freud and psychoanalysis. Tausk went to medical school in 1908, and began attending meetings of the Vienna Psychoanalytic Society (1909); he specialised in psychiatry, and his most original clinical achievements were to be his studies of schizophrenia and manic-depression. In 1912, when Lou Andreas-Salomé entered Freud's circle, she considered Tausk 'the most prominently outstanding' among Freud's adherents; they had a brief romance.

Freud was unhappy with Tausk's independent spirit, and the way Tausk could lock his original mind onto the same intellectual problems that were bothering Freud himself. Tausk was loyal to Freud throughout the difficulties Freud had with Adler and Jung. Tausk became the first in Vienna to give lectures on psychoanalysis for the lay public. He represented a broadening of the therapeutic interests of psychoanalysis; Tausk first originated the concepts of both 'ego boundaries' and 'identity'.

After having completed his medical studies, Tausk was called up for military service (1915). Following his contributions during the war, Tausk requested a personal psychoanalysis with Freud. Freud refused Tausk, fearing that if he took Tausk into analysis the problems between them would worsen. Freud instead recommended that Tausk go into analysis with a psychiatrist some years younger than himself, a newcomer to Freud's circle: Hélène Deutsch. Freud had taken her into analysis with him a few months earlier. Freud told her that it made an 'uncanny' impression on him to have Tausk at the Society, where he could take an idea of Freud's and develop it before Freud had finished with it. Freud complained that Tausk would not merely receive ideas, but would come to believe they were his alone. Any struggle with

Tausk over priorities was extremely disagreeable to Freud.

Even though it seemed an offence to be referred to someone so junior, Tausk went into analysis with Deutsch. He then talked with her almost entirely about Freud, grieving over Freud's attitude toward him. Tausk felt that he had some ideas before Freud himself did, but that Freud would not acknowledge them. Having heard complaints and accusations from both sides, Deutsch thought there was reality to what both felt. Near the end of March 1919, after three months, Freud explained to Deutsch that Tausk had become an interference with her own analysis; Freud asked her to choose between terminating Tausk's analysis and discontinuing her own analysis with Freud. She unhesitatingly communicated Freud's stand to Tausk, and Tausk's treatment with her ended.

Tausk had been unsuccessful in firmly establishing a relationship with a woman. The precipitating cause of Tausk's suicide on 3 July 1919 was his being unable to go through with an intended marriage. Freud wrote the official psychoanalytic obituary, which blamed Tausk's death on the war. In private Freud did not allow himself to grieve. The inner circle of analysts was shocked at Tausk's suicide, readily believing that if Freud dropped someone it could lead to self-extinction.

Roazen, P. (1969) *Brother Animal*. New York: Knopf.

P. R.

TELEOLOGY From the Greek term *telos* (goal, end, purpose), teleology refers to the approach that emphasises purposes and goals rather than causes. Teleology was central to C. G. Jung's approach to interpretation. Characteristically he wrote in 'The Soul and Death': 'Life is teleology *par excellence*; it is the intrinsic striving towards a goal, and the living organism is a system of directed aims which seek to fulfil themselves. The end of every process is its goal.' Most aspects of his theory are closely connected with his teleological perspective. In differentiating his psychology from that of Freud, Jung claimed that the Freudian approach was 'causal-reductive', whereas his own was more 'teleological'. By this, he meant that Freud's attention to early childhood amounted to a reduction of the current conflict to its past causes. In contrast, Jung argued that in order to have a fuller understanding of one's predicament, one also needs to consider goals and ultimate purpose. Occasionally, Jung seems to have been ambivalent about adopting the full implications of teleology: 'I use the word 'final' rather than 'teleological' in order to avoid the misunderstanding that attaches to the common conception of teleology, namely that it contains the idea of an anticipated end or goal, he wrote in 'On Psychic Energy'. However he was aware that, inevitably, final causes postulate a foreknowledge of some kind and that it is certainly not a knowledge that is connected with the *ego, and hence not a conscious knowledge as we know it, but rather a self-subsistent 'unconscious' knowledge. Jung adopted a teleological approach to his understanding of *dreams (as having a 'purposive meaning', of *development (as a gradual differentiation from the collective and impersonal realms to the uniquely personal one), of *neurosis (neurosis is teleologically oriented), and ultimately, of *individuation, as the fulfilment of the teleological purpose of the individual. The spiritual overtones of Jung's work can also be understood in terms of teleology, i.e. the ultimate meaning and purpose of life.

See also: energy; temporality

Jung, C. G. [1934] (1969) 'The soul and death' in *Collected Works*, Vol. 8. Princeton: Princeton University Press.
Jung, C. G. [1928] (1969) 'On psychic energy' in *Collected Works*, Vol. 8. Princeton: Princeton University Press.
Jung, C. G. [1952] (1969) 'Synchronicity: an acausal connecting principle' in *Collected Works*, Vol. 8. Princeton: Princeton University Press.

Jung, C. G. [1928] (1966) 'The relations between the ego and the unconscious' in *Collected Works*, Vol. 7. Princeton: Princeton University Press.

Jung, C. G. [1943] (1966) 'On the psychology of the unconscious' in *Collected Works*, Vol. 7. Princeton: Princeton University Press.

R. P.

TEMPORALITY A term brought to prominence by Husserl and developed by *Heidegger with his publication of *Being and Time* in 1927. The *phenomenological study of temporality is a departure from the conventional scientific approach, that is 'clock time', that measures it in relation to the movement of heavenly bodies around the sun. Heidegger revolutionised the conventional conception of Being by proposing that it can be understood only in reference to temporality. Virtually all phenomenological philosophers (including Husserl, Sartre, and Merleau-Ponty, among others) have shown intense interest in the nature of human (or 'lived') time as it is experienced, in the everyday sense. Whereas psychoanalysts are usually preoccupied with the impact of the past-on-the-present, Heidegger (and existential analysts generally) is more inclined to emphasise the impact of the future. In Heidegger's view, the constant weight of the future serves as the ontological source of human anxiety, epitomised by our anxiety about death. Minkowski published an important work in 1970, *Lived Time*, on the role that one's experience of time plays in the aetiology of psychopathology.

See also: teleology; time

M. G. T.

TERMINATION/END OF ANALYSIS Freud differentiated the actual termination of a period of analytic work from the question of the end of analysis. This end or aim goes beyond questions of therapeutic effect, and envisages the lifting of repression, and the laying out of the structure of the unconscious. Effectively this aim is not without problems: a part of repression – primary repression – will never be analysed, and similarly a residue of the drive will remain for ever incomprehensible, and will always constitute a source of disharmony for the subject. In other words, even at the end of analysis, the subject will not be transparent to themselves. Freud, towards the end of his life, responded to what he perceived as the typical lengthening of the duration of an analysis by giving an account of what he saw as the reasons for this asymptotic, 'interminable', aspect of analytical work. He claimed that a common factor in both men and women brings about this impasse in analytical work, an impasse indicative of a conflict – and moreover of an irreconcilable conflict – between the subject and their sexual being. The form that this 'rock of castration' takes in both men and women he called 'the *repudiation of femininity'.

S. Cot.

THANATOS Freud's perhaps most controversial idea, intended to explain human destructiveness; rejected by most contemporary analysts. Freud argues that all living things contain a catabolic force, which strives to get rid of vital tensions and return to a condition of stasis. Freud maintains that in humans this tendency operates as an inward form of destructiveness directed towards the self – primary masochism – which is later deflected towards the external world. The idea of the death drive had been present *in nuce* since Freud's earliest theory, when he postulated the constancy hypothesis and argued that the purpose of the psychic apparatus is to reduce tension. 'Attacks on linking' are one place where we might identify the work of the death drive in the clinical situation. Bringing together critical ideas and feelings in analysis can involve considerable anxiety. Patients therefore oppose the analyst's attempts to make connections between dissociated elements in their psychic lives. If not a death drive *per se*, attacks on linking are manifestations of an anti-therapeutic force at work in a person's psyche.

See also: Eros; life drive

Bion, R. (1959) 'Attacks on linking'. *International Journal of Psychoanalysis* 40.
Freud, S. (1920) *Beyond the Pleasure Principle.* S. E. 18. London: Hogarth Press.

J. Whi.

THING, THE For Lacan the Thing (*das Ding*) is the product of an action which is governed by language. The Thing is the absolute *Other of the *subject; it is lost through the introduction of language and it is therefore the lost object that is to be refound. According to Lacan it is that something in the subject which causes him or her to speak. The lost *Mother occupies its place: an empty place around which are constructed human endeavours such as science, art, and religion.

G. W.

THING-PRESENTATION The 'thing-presentation' is the *cathexis of an affective idea, wish or memory which may be unconscious. In order to be made conscious it must be linked to the *word-presentations corresponding to it. When the thing-presentation and the word-presentation are connected to each other, consciousness is possible.

J. A. Ber.

THINKING, THEORY OF Bion's theory of thinking was first explicitly presented in his 1962 paper 'A theory of thinking', but his previous clinical work with severely disturbed or psychotic patients with thought disorders (presented in the papers re-published in his 1967 book *Second Thoughts*) had given him the basis for a general theory of thinking. In his 1962 paper, which was then be expanded in his book *Learning from Experience* and in *Elements of Psychoanalysis*, he holds that thoughts exist before the capability of thinking and that thinking has to be called into existence to deal with thoughts. These thoughts, or problems to be solved, are preconceptions mated with a negative realisation, a frustration. The first model is that of an infant's expectation of a breast and the realisation that no breast is available for satisfaction.

The infant is born with innate *preconceptions, or empty, *a priori* thoughts which may or may not mate with a realisation. When they mate, a conception develops; if not, the infant may tolerate, modify or evade the frustration – perhaps by hallucinating the object, or using *projective identification. If he can tolerate the frustration, or modify it, he will do this by creating ideograms or symbols (alpha elements). Before the distressed baby can create symbols, his (as yet non-mentalised) feelings and perceptions, like things-in-themselves, are evacuated as *beta elements. If a receptive containing mind (mother's or father's with *reverie) can realistically receive these feelings, understand them and transform them into things to be thought about, the infant will introject the combined pair (*container-contained) and eventually acquire his own *alpha function. What Bion calls the 'psychotic' baby will, due to its excessive greed and envy, or mother's incapability to contain the realistic projective identifications, will probably have thought disturbances and be incapable of learning from experience.

If things go well, thoughts will evolve genetically and in growing levels of abstraction, from beta elements to alpha elements, to unconscious thinking, dream thoughts, dreams and myths, then conceptions, concepts, scientific deductive systems and algebraic calculi. This can be seen in the vertical axis of Bion's *grid. They can be used in a number of ways, as he proposes in the horizontal axis of that same grid. His theory of thinking includes (in his first papers and books) the Kantian concept of noumena and phenomena, and in his later papers and books, also the Platonic conceptions of ideal objects and forms.

Bion, W. R. (1962) *Learning from Experience.* London: Heinemann.

Bion, W. R. (1962) 'A theory of thinking' in *Second Thoughts*. London: Heinemann.
Bion, W. R. (1963) *Elements of Psychoanalysis*. London: Heinemann.
Bion, W. R. (1965) *Transformations*. London: Heinemann.

E. T. B.

THOUGHTS WITHOUT A THINKER Bion places thoughts epistemologically prior to thinking and postulates that an apparatus for thinking has to be developed in order to deal with thoughts. When a preconception meets with a frustration it becomes a thought. If the capacity to tolerate frustration is inadequate (or, Bion later adds, there is either the absence of an adequate container, or the presence of an anti-container), the psyche will evade it, and rather than thinking emerging, projective identification will be resorted to excessively. Thoughts will be experienced as bad objects and will exist without an apparatus available for thinking them.

Bion, W. R. (1962) *Learning from Experience*. London: Heinemann. Also in *Seven Servants*. New York: Jason Aronson, 1977.
Bion, W. R. (1963) *Elements of Psychoanalysis*. London: Heinemann. Also in *Seven Servants*. New York: Jason Aronson, 1977.
Bion, W. R. (1970) *Attention and Interpretation*. London: Tavistock. Also in *Seven Servants*. New York: Jason Aronson, 1977.

S. A.

TIME AND PSYCHOANALYSIS Time may be defined in two broad ways: as subjective experience, what is known as psychological or absolute time; and as objective, clock, calendar or mathematical time.

Time in the experiential sense is the unifying element of consciousness, a process that ascribes unity to the perception of the self in a world of constant change. Time provides a sense of identity to the experience of discontinuous emotional states and to the perception of discontinuity in change.

The experience or sense of time, and later the perception of time as an attribute of objective reality, is a function of consciousness. As Freud said in 1915: 'The processes of the system Ucs. [unconscious] are timeless; i.e. they are not ordered temporally, are not altered by the passage of time; they have no reference to time at all. Reference to time is bound up, once again, with the work of the system Cs.'

Time as a conscious, subjective phenomenon exists in two ways: as a sense of duration, and as tense or perspective. Time as duration is a sense or feeling. The sense or feeling of duration is based on the ability to experience one's self and the world of internal objects as continuous, as flowing together, synchronously, simultaneously, harmoniously; or apart, disjointedly, incongruously, out of step with each other, fast or slowly, or as slowly as to be hardly noticeable. The sense of time as duration is more elementary, developing before that of time as future, past, or present. In fact, time as perspective is derived from the sense of duration and as such it is more conceptual than intuitive or feeling-like. The feeling of duration and, in general, the consciousness of the world as time-bound, creates the experience of before and after, which results in the notion that all things and experiences have a past and a future, a beginning and an end point, a notion that in turn becomes converted into institutional in essence notions such as growth, progress, generation, conservation, decay and death.

The development of the experience of time as perspective is intimately related to the development of affects and conscience – the *superego. By warning the *ego of the dangerous consequences of instinctual wishes, the superego assists in the development of the ability to anticipate the future; and by condemning the ego's failure to resist such wishes, it assists in the development of the sense of an irrevocable past. The sense of time as either duration or tense varies according to the affective state of the individual, reflecting the relative state of adequacy of his ego or the integrity of his self. To the extent that the ego can perceive the noxious influence – in essence, the ego's own inadequacy – as something that is still in the future, only potential and therefore avoidable, the experience tends to be that of fear or anxiety; while perceiving itself as inadequate in relation to a noxious event in the past, the ego assessing reality as irrevocable, the experience is that of sadness or depression. Like anxiety and depression, other affects, painful as well as pleasurable, can be placed into a cognitive relation involving the ego's self-assessed adequacy and its position along the continuum of subjective time.

Psychoanalytic theory holds that, inasmuch as dreams are dominated by the unconscious, they are not bound by the constraints of time. According to Freud, in dreams, 'there is a complete lack of sense of time'. But as is the case with the unconscious itself, the timelessness of dreams is only relative. Both the experience and the abstract notion of time may be present in a dream, even though often in disguise. And when the notion of time is explicitly present, it means something different from what its manifest content seems to indicate.

*Free association, the basic technique of psychoanalysis, and the use of the couch with the analyst out of the patient's sight, enhance the sense of timelessness that prevails in the unconscious. In the here and now of the analytic situation the patient's mind moves backward and forward on a fantastic voyage into the past or the future or into a time vacuum that can make him so anxious as to declare that there is nothing to say, that nothing comes to mind. This sense of timelessness is enhanced by the open-endedness of the analytic process. On the other hand, the precision, consistency of duration and regularity of the analytic sessions enhance the ego boundaries of a vulnerable psychic organisation. The analyst's strict adherence to the boundaries of time conveys a sense of responsibility and purpose, playing a positive role in the relationship. By being regular and predictable, the duration of each session becomes a routine that the patient takes for granted so much so that he soon surrenders its control to the analyst.

'Psychoanalysis is always a matter of long periods of time; of half a year or whole years – of longer periods than the patient expects,' Freud wrote in 1913, at the height of his analytic career. By current standards, however, Freud and the early analysts did not keep their patients in analysis for very long. With a shift of emphasis from oedipal to preoedipal problems and character pathology, the length of analysis has become much longer.

*Transference, the resurgence of feeling and fantasies from early object relations in the analytic situation and their projection on the person of the analyst, is a time-bound phenomenon. *Arlow compared transference to depersonalisation and the experience of deja vu. Transference, so far as the patient's experience is concerned, has much in common with the dream, where the sense of time is that of the present. In interpreting the transferential relationship, past experiences can be seen to converge into the actual experience of a more or less advanced therapeutic relationship – an *intersubjective relationship. The sense of time during a session can vary, being experienced as either fast or slow, according to the vicissitudes of transference. The sense of time may be disturbed for the analyst as well, indicating the presence of countertransference.

In Freud's time no one talked about the presence of covert, unconscious or unintended wishes of patient and analyst toward each other in the here-and-now of the analytic situation, what Gill has named 'transference enactment'. Nevertheless, to the extent that the patient's or the analyst's wishes or intentions are grounded in unconscious memories or fantasies of early life, the interplay between past and present functions in the same way as that involved in the traditional view of transference and *countertransference. Elements of the analytic situation, such as the open-endedness of its overall duration and the frequency and the fixed time of its sessions, conditioned as they are by the concept of time, contribute to the development of transference and its various manifestations, including those of transference and enactment.

Arlow, J. A. (1966) 'Depersonalization and derealization' in R. M. Loewenstein et al. (eds) *Psychoanalysis – A General Psychology*. New York: International Universities Press.
Freud, S. (1900) *The Interpretation of Dreams*. S. E. 5 London: Hogarth Press.
Freud, S. (1913) *Observations and Examples from Analytic Practice*. S. E. 13. London: Hogarth Press.
Freud, S. (1915) *The Unconscious*. S. E. 14. London: Hogarth Press.
Gill, M. (1984) 'Psychoanalysis and psychotherapy: a revision'. *International Review of Psychoanalysis*, 11: 161–79.
Hartocollis, P. (1972) 'Time and the dream'. *Journal of the American Psychoanalytic Association* 28: 861–77.
Schafer, R. (1983) *The Analytic Attitude*. New York: Basic Books.

P. H.

TOPOGRAPHY The question of the unconscious (or *other scene), is set up by Freud in terms that are map-like or topographic. The so-called first topography divides the mind into *conscious, *preconscious and *unconscious. The second topography sees the mind as *id, *ego and *super-ego. These topographies can be seen as topological in the mathematical sense, in that they organise *representations according to relations of nearness, and their registration in files, in strata, and in sequences has nothing to do, he claims, with cerebral localisation. This is equally true of the lobes that he uses in his second topography to distinguish the ego from the id.

N. C.

TOPOLOGY The theory of topological structure tries to give a formulation of very great generality to the notion of space. An element of such a space can be a memory or a phrase – each located within its appropriate spatial structure. So the classical spaces studied by physicists are more special – and less subtle – than these general spaces. Boundaries, limits or other processes, that settle a neighbourhood structure within a space, determine these general topologies. The spatiality of such a topology is not affected by continuous processes of stretching and relaxation; but it is altered by cuts or tears. The extent of Lacan's development of topology is very wide. It ranges from the idea of the necessity of a new transcendental aesthetic, more appropriate for the reality of the subject of psychoanalysis than that underpinned by euclidian geometry, to the work involved in the setting up of the formulae of 'Lacanian algebra'. The Mobius strip, for example, can be introduced to represent the subject of the unconscious (S) as a writing surface with only one edge, where you can move continuously from a surface to its other side. Such a representation resolves many of the paradoxes of Freud's first topography, for instance, the problem of double inscription, or the situating of the unconscious between perception and consciousness. When this Mobius strip is completed by sticking to its single edge the corresponding single edge of a disc – representing the object a – it becomes a non-spherical closed surface whose interior is continuously connected to its exterior and which cannot exist in three-dimensional space, requiring an extra dimension for its construction. This surface is the projective plane, and it is able to show that in the structure of the phantasy (Sa) 'the reciprocity between the subject and the object is complete'. A figuration can be found for this surface in euclidian three-dimensional space, but only through the illegitimate introduction of a line of self-intersection.

N. C.

TORTURE The deliberate infliction of physical and psychological pain to terrorise individuals, and beyond them groups and entire populations. Nightmares and the inability to feel or enjoy, chronic recurrent depressive states and somatisation prevail. Intrusion from past experiences that are felt to have the same immediacy as present ones (re-experiencing instead of remembering) and a blurring of the boundaries between past, present and future are characteristic. The mind presents itself as if any differentiated structures such as a central agency like the ego, or the capacity for memory have been erased or flattened, making it impossible, in extreme cases, to discern constitutional factors or previous personality.

One feature that helps to distinguish victims of such extreme man-made horror from sufferers of more ordinary traumas is the stability in time of their psychic state. Another is their peculiar relation to their children to whom they can silently pass on the unconscious horror/grief to which they have been unable to give form. The dependent child is 'trusted' because he or she is controllable and is often the victim's only object available for the purpose of emotional exchange. A child can thus become the recipient of multiple silent projections, effectively functioning as a universal, substitute object.

A climate of ambiguity also seems to be an important ingredient of the terrifying environment used by the torturers aimed at dismantling the mind of the victim as well as of the social climate of the nation where terror prevails as a form of social control.

An important issue in therapy is the permeability between the therapeutic space (in a restricted sense) and the social space that surrounds it. It is the function of the therapist to regulate this permeability, bearing in mind that ways must be found to deal with a patient where the boundaries between an internal space and the external social space have disappeared. In such cases the patient's self (or its fragments) often need to be tracked in external reality. Transferential work needs to be postponed, analytic neutrality greatly modified, and conceptual tools to deal with this abolition of spatial differences need to be found.

Groups of similar cultural background and/or of similar experiences are indispensable supports for the victim particularly if, as is frequently the case, the therapy happens in exile. Literary and artistic elaboration of the experience can be of crucial importance.

As well offering therapeutic possibilities, psychoanalytic ideas have been used to discern the social contexts that make torture possible, to identify the characteristics of the perpetrators, to understand torture itself as a dynamic process, and to analyse the short and long term effects on both victims and perpetrators. Extreme trauma is one of the dominant concerns of psychoanalysis at the turn of this century just as hysteria was in the previous one.

Reyes, A., Reyes, P. and Skelton, R. (1997) 'Traumatised logic: the containing function of unconscious classification in the aftermath of extreme trauma'. *Journal of Melanie Klein and Object Relations* 15(4).

Staub, E. (1990) 'The psychology and culture of torture and torturers' in P. Suedfield (ed.) *Psychology and Torture*. New York: Hemisphere Publishing.

A. Rey.

TOXIN In a Lacanian sense a toxin can be anything that is detrimental to the subject and is therefore an inevitable aspect of existence. Nevertheless its presence requires that the subject remain at a distance from it. Toxins are typically those aspects of the body that were not symbolised but can also be for instance the suggestive words in a hypnotic relationship.

R. Loo.

TRADITION What is omitted or changed in the written record may be preserved intact in tradition. Freud posits that the survival of a tradition is based on inherited memory rather than on transmission by communication. The *Oedipus and *castration complexes and the reactions they inspire are made intelligible by their connection with the experience of earlier generations.

J. A. Ber.

TRAINING Psychoanalytic training is modelled on seminars conducted by Freud in Vienna as psychoanalysis developed. Psychoanalytic institutes may be 'free-standing' (not academia-affiliated) or university-based. Training is comprised of coursework in psychoanalytic theory and practice, personal analysis, and 'control analysis' (clinical supervision).

Roazen, P. (1976) *Freud and his Followers*. New York: Knopf.

M. M.

TRANSCENDENT FUNCTION A natural psychological process that rises out of, unites, and thus transcends the opposition of conscious and unconscious viewpoints that exist in compensatory relationship to each other and that we experience as conflict. Jung understood this process as the way conflict gets resolved and suggests ways we can enhance it by our conscious cooperation. We then arrive at a solution that feels creative and novel, which includes each of the two former opposites, yet surpasses them. Such solutions feel like a blessing from God, Jung says.

Jung, C. G. [1916] (1960) 'The transcendent function' in *Collected Works*, Vol. 8. Princeton: Princeton University Press.
Ulnae, A. B. (1996) *The Functioning Transcendent*. Wilmette, IL: Chiron.

A. U.

TRANSFERENCE A central concept in the psychoanalytic theory of treatment, transference refers to the patient's transfer of feelings, wishes and reactions experienced toward an important figure from his or her childhood (usually a parental figure) onto the analyst. But it should be noted that transference is a universal phenomenon that occurs in many spheres of life in which one's reactions to a current person (e.g. boss, spouse) are reminiscent of early patterns. The patient's transference can be positive or negative. Freud viewed positive transference as a critical motive for the patient's collaboration. It can be understood as both a *resistance (the patient repeats rather than remembers) and hence, an obstacle to the analysis; and as of an indispensable value to the analysis. One reason for the latter is that insofar as they refer to feelings and reactions in the here and now, they are more likely to posses an emotional immediacy and thus more likely to carry emotional conviction. Unlike the traditional views of a 'blank screen' analyst, in contemporary views the patient's transference reactions are understood as, at least to some degree, elicited by cues emitted by the analyst.

See also: transference neurosis

Freud, S. [1938] (1940) *An Outline of Psychoanalysis*. S. E. 23. London: Hogarth Press.
Gill, M. M. (1982) *The Analysis of Transference*, Vol. 1. Madison, CT: International Universities Press.
Strachey, J. (1934) 'The nature of the therapeutic action of psychoanalysis'. *International Journal of Psychoanalysis* 15: 127–50.

M. Eag.

TRANSFERENCE (FAIRBAIRN) The imposing of a state of mind from the inner world of the patient onto the analyst. In Fairbairn's view, real relationships occur in external reality and are susceptible to change. Relationships emanating from the closed system of the world of inner reality are manifested in the *external world in the transference when the patient behaves as though the analyst actually is an object within the inner closed system.

Fairbairn, W. R. D. [1952 and 1958] (1994) 'Theoretical and experimental aspects of psychoanalysis' and 'The nature and aims of psychoanalytic treatment' in David Scharff and E. Fairbairn Birtles (eds) *From Instinct to Self*, Vol. I. Northvale, NJ: Jason Aronson.

E. F. B.

TRANSFERENCE (JUNG) A term denoting attribution to the analyst via projection of subjective unconscious emotions, ideas, and motivations; sometimes it connotes the total analytic relationship. *Jung was the first to recognise the multi-layered and far-reaching nature of projection, which may be generated by unconscious perceptions of objective, here and now reality, as well by images of important figures from the past. They also arise *sui generis* from the totality of the psyche, the *self. The latter were of special importance to Jung, who realised that transferences are packed with vitalising affect and images that hint at unrealised potential for growth.

Interpreting transference only in terms of the personal past misses its most important function. Therefore, a Jungian always asks, 'To what end?' as well as, 'From where?' *Libido, for Jung, not only constituted instinctual drives (Freud), and was not only *object-oriented (Fairbairn, Klein), but was self-oriented, meaning that libido urged psychological growth toward wholeness in a process he termed individuation. To test this hypothesis Jung studied ancient alchemical texts, which he saw as an imaginative testament to the alchemists' projection onto matter of their unconscious impulse toward psychological development. For a few contemporary Jungian analysts the processes of alchemical transformation are a living guide to individuation as it transpires in the analytic relationship. Most Jungian analysts, while valuing the alchemical metaphor, see little value in transposing its operations onto the analytic process, and in the spirit of Jung's investigations, look for other evidence – both in the wider culture and in the immediacy of the therapeutic encounter – to substantiate his theories.

See also: countertransference

Jung, C. G. [1946] (1954) 'Psychology of the Transference' in *Collected Works*, Vol. 16. Princeton: Princeton University Press.

J. K.

TRANSFERENCE (LACAN) Lacan's theory of transference is what distinguishes the Lacanian clinical approach. It is axiomatic that treatment is driven by transference, rather than being driven by a therapeutic alliance holding between the analyst's 'good', 'well-adjusted' ego and the healthy part of the analysand's ego. For Lacan, transference is the relation between analysand and analyst that holds between the subject and the Other, a consequence of the analysand's belief in the *subject supposed to know, that the analyst can yield the knowledge which concerns the subject. This precious little nugget is imputed to the analyst as *object a (*objet petit a*), object-cause of desire. This field of the Symbolic register is the proper terrain of transference and interpretation and psychoanalytic work proceeds along this unconscious Symbolic axis as opposed to the axis of the Imaginary *ego to ego relation, even if this latter is always present and having effects.

See also: resistance

H. T.

TRANSFERENCE (RELATIONISM) Originally conceptualised by Freud as a reliving of infantile experience in particular, the concept of transference has been broadened by for example, Wolstein, to include all feelings, fantasies, attitudes, perceptions, defensive operations and expectancies toward a person in the present which do not entirely befit that person. That is, transference refers to a repetition of reactions originating with significant caretakers, unconsciously lived-out with figures of the present.

The psychoanalytic situation is an ideal laboratory or playground for the stimulation of the patient's essential inner world to seek repetition and reliving. The analyst's relative reserve and ambiguity encourages the emergence of all aspects of the patient's subjectivity, including the unconscious wish to repeat and to relive the essential aspects of internalised relational configurations. *Gill has clarified the contributions of many contemporary post-Freudian theorists by extending the meaning of transference to include the analyst's unconscious participation in living-out with the patient the latter's key relationships of the past. This has expanded the field of analytic *inquiry to attempts at understanding the patient through examination of dyadic interaction, the transference–*countertransference matrix, beyond examination of the patient *in vacuo*. Because of the affective immediacy and inherent anxiety in emphasising here-and-now relatedness, most current analysts agree with Freud's original observation that analysis of transference is the hardest part of analysis, and all too often avoided.

See also: interpersonal psychoanalysis; relational psychoanalysis

Freud, S. [1912] (1957) *The Dynamics of Transference*. S. E. 12. London: Hogarth Press, 97–108.
Gill, M. (1982) *The Analysis of Transference*. New York: International Universities Press.
Levenson, E. (1972) *The Fallacy of Understanding*. New York: Basic Books.
Wolstein, B. (1964) *Transference*. New York: Grune and Stratton.

I. H.

TRANSFERENCE NEUROSIS The idea that in analysis the patient's neurotic conflicts are relived in relation to the analyst. According to Freud, by replacing the patient's ordinary neurosis with the 'transference-neurosis', the patient can then be cured by the therapeutic work. Not all, or even many, contemporary analysts accept the distinction between transference and transference neurosis nor do they believe that the development of a full blown transference neurosis is necessary before cure can be achieved. The term 'transference neurosis' should not be confused with 'transference neuroses', the term Freud used to refer to conditions – e.g. obsessional neuroses, hysteria – where, in contrast to psychosis, a transference can develop.

Freud, S. (1914) *Remembering, Repeating and Working-through*. S. E. 12. London: Hogarth Press.
Greenson, R. R. (1964) *The Technique and Practice of Psychoanalysis*. New York: International Universities Press.

M. Eag.

TRANSFERENCE SELFOBJECT Defined by Wolf, in his *Treating the Self*, as the displacement onto the analyst of the analysand's needs for a responsive selfobject matrix, derived in part from remobilised and regressively altered editions of archaic infantile selfobject needs, in part from current age- and phase-appropriate selfobject needs, and in part from selfobject needs mobilised in response to the analyst and the analytic situation. Stolorow and Atwood distinguish between the 'selfobject' dimension and the 'repetitive' dimension of the transference. The repetitive dimension of the transference refers to the patient's fearful expectation of a repetition of early experiences of developmental trauma in relation to the analyst. The selfobject dimension refers to a longing for selfobject experiences from the analyst that were missing or deficient during the patient's formative years. This formulation of selfobject transference invites the question as to whether it is always a 'transference', or the (selfobject) organisation of a new experience. A number of selfobject transferences have been described. It was Kohut who initially described these in the following terms:

Merger transference – the organisation of an identity with the selfobject of early life by extending the self to include the analyst. The merger transference may include the expectation that the analyst's attunement be so in sync with the patient that he should apprehend him without any words being spoken.

Twinship, or alterego, transference – the organisation of experience that acknowledges a bond of sameness between patient and analyst. Kohut initially saw the alterego transference as part of the mirror transference, but later identified it as distinct. The alterego transference serves a basic human need: the need to have one's humanness, one's kinship or sameness with others of the species, quietly acknowledged. (See also Kohut's 1984, *How Does Analysis Cure?*)

Mirror transference – in Kohut's 1987 formulation is an expression of the fact that others are experienced and needed in the sense of being *agents for self-confirmation*, for self-approval. Kohut initially used the term generically to include merger transference, alterego transference and the mirror transference itself, all in distinction to the idealising transference. He then appreciated that in the development of the mirror transference we see that, from merger to twinship to the mirror transference, there is obviously an increasing recognition cognitively that the other person is really another person.

Idealising transference – connotes a need for, and an experience of, uniting with someone one looks up to – a calm, strong and wise other who is felt to lend inspiration, strength and stability to the sense of self. It may emerge as a more or less undisguised admiration of the analyst, or by defences against this experience, such as ongoing and bitter depreciation of the analyst (see Wolf, *Treating the Self*).

Adversarial, or antagonistic transference – another form of transference was independently identified by Lachmann and Wolf. For Wolf it implies the need for, and experience of, the other as supportive and respectful while simultaneously engaged with him in competitive, or antagonistic interaction. Lachmann indicates that the readiness of the patient to risk competition leads to the possibility of deriving a selfobject experience, a sense of vitality, vigour, cohesion and positive self regard through an adversarial relationship.

Basch, M. F. (1988) *Understanding Psychotherapy*. New York: Basic Books, 142.
Kohut, H. [1972] (1996) *The Chicago Institute Lectures*. P. Tolpin and M. Tolpin (eds). Hillsdale, NJ: The Analytic Press, 34.
Kohut, H. (1984) *How Does Analysis Cure?* Chicago: University of Chicago Press, 194–201.
Kohut, H. (1987) *The Kohut Seminars*. M. Elson (ed.). New York: Norton, 64.
Lachmann, F. (2000) *Transforming Aggression: Psychotherapy with the Difficult-to-Treat Patient*. Northvale, NJ: Jason Aronson, Chapter 3.
Stolorow, R. and Atwood, G. (1992) *Contexts of Being*. Hillsdale, NJ: The Analytic Press, 24.
Wolf, E. (1978) 'On the developmental line of selfobject relations' in A. Goldberg (ed.) *Advances in Self Psychology*. New York: International Universities Press, 125–6.
Wolf, E. (1988) *Treating the Self*. New York: Guilford, 187.

H. B.

TRANSFERENCE, CREATIVITY OF A creative individual may need to experience a connection with a selfobject while engaged in demanding creative tasks. The nature of this selfobject 'transference' is perhaps most commonly an idealisation, but it also takes the form of a mirroring or twinship selfobject experience. Freud's connection to Fliess during his writing of *The Interpretation of Dreams* would be an example of a mixture of a mirroring and idealising transference of creativity.

Kohut, H. (1971) *The Analysis of the Self*. New York: International Universities Press, 316–17.
Kohut, H. (1977) *The Restoration of the Self*. New York: International Universities Press, 46n.

H. B.

TRANSFERENCE, FORWARD AND TRAILING EDGE The concept that there are 'trailing edge' and 'forward edge' transferences denotes two developmentally distinct intrapsychic configurations mobilised in the psychoanalytic situation. The trailing edge of the transference is an unconscious repetition of the patient's core childhood disorder – re-experienced, lived out, and remembered in the alive present with the analyst. This dimension of the pathology of self-selfobject experience and the disorder of the self corresponds to what Freud described as a 'new edition' of the nuclear childhood disorder, a replacement of the original neurosis with an 'artificial illness' re-experienced with the analyst. The forward edge of the transference consists of a revival of the remaining health of the childhood nuclear self, a new edition of the normality of childhood development which was derailed, and now re-experienced, strengthened, and integrated with the analyst. (Freud described an 'unobjectionable positive transference' necessary for successful treatment, but did not discover the depths of remobilised healthy strivings which are especially important to treatment and cure.) Until recognised and welcomed, the forward dimension of the self usually appears as mere 'tendrils' or 'bits' of once normal childhood motivations and strivings. When recognised, accepted, and responded to, the patient's strivings and hopes for the various kinds of selfobject experiences (mirroring, idealising, twinship, self-delineating, adversarial, etc.) restore the intrapsychic climate which normally constitutes, maintains, and restores the self.

M. T.

TRANSFERENCE, ORGANISING ACTIVITY OF From an intersubjective perspective, transference is redefined as unconscious *organising activity. The patient assimilates the analytic relationship according to the principles that unconsciously organise his or her subjective life. This conception invites analytic attention both to the analyst's contribution to the patient's transference experience and to the recurring meanings into which the analyst's contribution is assimilated by the patient. Transference is seen as having two broad dimensions. In the developmental dimension, the patient longs for missing or lost development-enhancing experiences. In the repetitive dimension, the patient fears or experiences a repetition of early developmental trauma. These dimensions oscillate between the background and foreground of the patient's experience in concert with the meanings of specific happenings within the therapeutic intersubjective field.

See also: intersubjectivity theory

R. S.

TRANSFERENCE, SELF-DELINEATING When the analyst's attunement serves to articulate, crystallise, consolidate, and validate a patient's emotional experience, *intersubjectivity theory terms this relational configuration a self-delineating selfobject transference.

R. S.

TRANSFORMATION (JUNG) In confronting the depths of his psyche Jung tells us that he realised that the 'unconscious is a process and that the psyche is transformed or developed by the relationship of the ego to the contents of the unconscious'. Throughout our life-long development, according to Jung, we undergo continuous cycles of conscious progression followed by regressions, returning to earlier phases of development where dream imagery and symbolic meaning predominate. Regression, as Jung sees it, is not an undesirable setback and should be understood (especially in clinical contexts) as a vital part of the psychological growing process. At each 'turn' of these cycles, the opportunity afforded is part of the intrinsically self-regulatory function of the psyche. Frustration of what Jung considers a drive for wholeness – aiming to reconcile opposing internal tensions – leads to increasing degrees of neurosis and/or psychosis proportionate to the degree and nature of that frustration.

Transformations may be individual or collective. The process of transformation does not imply, as is often believed, transmogrification. Although every transformation involves symbolic death and rebirth of part of the individual (or collective), some measure of a relatively stable ego-continuity is necessary to register and assimilate the particulars of the concomitant transformations (similar to ego conflict-free-zones of ego psychology). If such stable ego-continuity were not assumed the psyche of the individual would face a kind of Heraclitan psychical paradox, which Jung suggests would lead to psychosis or total amnesia. The discovery of transformation led Jung to formulate an even more central feature of his psychology, namely, the process of individuation.

In Jung's view, the process of inner transformation is symbolically revealed in the traditions of religious ceremony, alchemy, and ancient ritual practices. For example, the symbolism of the mass is held by Jung to reveal an instance of our use of externalising inner transitions and alterations of the psyche – in this respect consider the meaning behind the symbolism of transubstantiation. In projecting inner psychic change into highly symbolic ceremonies, we can discover and control the importunate and benevolent 'dictates' of the unconscious facilitating greater emotional fulfilment.

Externalisation though symbolism allows the ego to achieve greater consciousness and acceptance of inner transformations. Also by concretising inner psychical processes by the use of physical symbols (chalices, the host-bread), the anxiety aroused by transformations can be warded off.

In his scholarly, creative studies and elaborations of the alchemical process Jung refers to one of two interrelated aims, namely, to transform 'base matter into spirit'. It is noteworthy that this notion is remarkably similar to Bion's theory of alpha-function. There is arguably an 'alchemical' trope in Bion's claim that beta-elements (bodily/emotional experiences) are modified and thereby transformed into alpha elements (purely mentalised categories). Furthermore, central to Bion's work is the concept of internal reconfiguration aptly entitled in one of his great epistemological works, *Transformations* (1965). The late Michael Fordham noted some – though not all – of the parallels between Bion's and Jung's ideas on psychic processes. He also experimented with the idea that *projective identification and Jung's theory of transformations were closely linked notions.

S. Byr.

TRANSFORMATIONS A transformation is a change in form. Bion, as a psychoanalyst, was interested in changes in forms in the mind. Bion saw psychoanalytic theories as groups of transformations. He uses the example of a painter who transforms a landscape (the realisation) into a painting (the representation) as an analogy to the work of a psychoanalyst who transforms the facts of an analytic experience (the realisation) into an interpretation (the representation). Bion borrows the terms rigid motion transformations and projective transformations from geometry. Rigid motion transformations in the mind imply little deformation. The invariants are easily observed (e.g. thoughts or emotions into words). In rigid motion transformations, the intention of the transformation is to reveal further dimensions of the emotional experience.

Projective transformations imply a change of size or location (e.g. a map). Bion used the term to describe a type of mental transformation in which one of the significant characteristics is massive *projective identification. There is a confusion between the patient and the analyst. Projective transformations are an outcome of the patient's attempt to avoid a deepening of an emotional experience. In the analytic situation, an attack is delivered against analytic potency by means of *splitting which in turn splits the patient. The essential feature experienced by the analyst is the stimulation and frustration of hope, and work that is fruitless except in that it discredits the analytic work. Bion also describes this as an instance of parasitism. The patient draws on the love, benevolence, and indulgence of the host to extract his/her knowledge and power which then enables him/her to poison the association and destroy the care on which s/he depends for his/her existence.

Transformations in hallucinosis refer to a mental process in which emotional experiences which have begun to be transformed into alpha elements then undergo a reversal of that process. The *alpha elements are then degraded and cannibalised back to a primitive state, similar to *beta elements, which are then evacuated by a reversal of the function of the sense organs and taken back again as new perceptions. The end product of this process can be a *hallucination.

See also: link; O

Bion, W. R. (1963) *Elements of Psychoanalysis*. London: Heinemann. Also in *Seven Servants*. New York: Jason Aronson, 1977.

Bion, W. R. (1965) *Transformations*. London: Karnac Books. Also in *Seven Servants*. New York: Jason Aronson, 1977.

Bion, W. R. (1970) *Attention and Interpretation*. London: Tavistock. Also in *Seven Servants*. New York: Jason Aronson, 1977.

S. A.

TRANSITIONAL OBJECTS AND TRANSITIONAL PHENOMENA Transitional objects are a small child's 'special' objects, for example a particular blanket or teddy bear, which become important to and almost inseparable from the infant. Transitional phenomena exist between the inner subjective world and the capacity to perceive objectively, and are the root of creative living. Sometimes described as Winnicott's most important contribution, the concepts arise from his study of the infant's developing capacity to discover and adapt to reality, first addressed in 1945.

Transitional objects have their origin in that phase of early development when the infant reaches the stage of distinguishing inner and outer reality. Being both 'me' and 'not-me', they facilitate the transition from the omnipotence of the tiny baby for whom external objects have not yet separated out, to the capacity to relate to 'objectively perceived' objects. The transitional object may be seen as contributing to the infant's autonomy, for it is under his control, in a way that his mother is not, and he can dictate how it is used. It can be thrown away and retrieved allowing the infant to exercise an agency in relation to it which he is powerless to exercise in relation to adults in his world. Transitional space, also referred to as the intermediate area, or third area, is the space that develops between the inner and outer worlds, and is contributed to by both. Winnicott states that creativity has its origins here.

Describing common patterns of infancy in which a very young baby finds a thumb to suck, and may stroke his own face, gather a piece of material to suck or stroke, Winnicott assumed the existence of fantasy and used the term 'transitional' for these phenomena. Later both the activity and the object may become necessary when the baby is going to sleep, or is anxious. Babies may discover a particular object, or a sound, or piece of behaviour, and this becomes important and recognised to be so, since it represents a needed continuity of experience. It becomes the first 'not-me' possession, symbolic of a part-object, but neither the baby nor that object. Winnicott listed the special qualities of the relationship with the object, which must survive; must, from the baby's point of view, come from neither without nor within; and will lose its significance, neither forgotten or mourned, when a wider cultural field has come into being. In early infancy the *'good-enough mother' allows the baby the illusion of unity and omnipotence, in which the infant 'creates' the breast.

Subsequent disillusion necessary to permit awareness of outside reality must be given to the infant in such a way that the infant's creativity survives the passage to the recognition of objective reality.

Winnicott compared this with the therapeutic situation, where the worlds of the patient and analyst overlap, echoing *Freud's concept of the analytic playground. Winnicott takes this thinking further in his 1971 'The Use of an Object and Relating Through Identification', in which he charts a further stage of change from that of 'object-relating', when the object, while separate, is felt to be still under the omnipotent control of the infant, to that of 'object-usage', when the object is allowed reality and autonomy. Related subjects include: *fetishistic objects; Milner's concept of illusion of unity within a framework; *Tustin's autistic object; *Kohut's *selfobject; Bollas' transformational object; *Fairbairn's thinking on the transitional stage/quasi-independence.

Winnicott, D. W. [1951] (1953) 'Transitional objects and transitional phenomena'. *International Journal of Psycho-Analysis* 34. Also in *Collected Papers, Through Paediatrics to Psychoanalysis*. London: Tavistock, 1958.

Winnicott, D. W. [1945] (1958) 'Primitive emotional development' in *Collected Papers, Through Paediatrics to Psychoanalysis*. London: Tavistock.

Winnicott, D. W. (1971) 'The use of an object and relating through identifications' in *Playing and Reality*. London: Tavistock.

J. Joh.

TRANSITIONAL TECHNIQUES For Fairbairn certain *defensive strategies developed during the transition from infantile *dependence to mature dependence, leading to specific attitudes towards internal objects. Anxiety is handled by varying psychic techniques. Thus, the hysterical technique treats the good object as external and the bad as internal; the obsessional technique treats both the good object and the bad object as internal: the paranoid technique treats the good as internal and the bad as external; and the phobic technique treats both good and bad as external. With progress to more mature dependence, the individual can give up these techniques and relate to an integrated object.

E. F. B. / D. E. S.

TRANSITIVISM The phenomenon whereby one young child can hit another of similar age and then cry as if he himself had been hit. This illustrates the effect of the *mirror phase in the formation of the 'I': I is an other – the ego and other are confused. The alienation, aggression and the suffering to which this gives rise is evident in this example.

H. T.

TRANSLATIONS OF FREUD Linguistically, Freud is one of the greatest prose writers and one of the greatest rhetoricians in German literature. The nature of the German language and Freud's distinctive use of it chiefly inform the polemical discussion over extant and ideal translations of Freud's works.

Historically, most attention has been given to the English translation in what is commonly called the *Standard Edition*; Strachey is usually referred to as its sole translator, although he had assistants. Strachey's translation of Freud's analytic works was a monumental achievement. Yet *Bettelheim and others have criticised Strachey's translation for its impersonal and abstract qualities. Giving short shrift to the humanistic quality of Freud's prose and overemphasising its scientific character, Strachey's translation has less appeal to the reader's emotional response and turns him aside from embarking on his own voyage of self-discovery.

A comparative sampling will illustrate what Strachey does with the emotional resonance, object relations, and vividness in the original German text. Strachey's neologisms *cathexis and *parapraxis do not render respectively the everyday evocativeness of '*anlehnung*' (a leaning on) and '*fehlleistung*' (faulty achievement).

Whereas Freud will underscore a commonness between the analyst and the patient by describing them with the same qualifier, Strachey will use different qualifiers, thus subtly undermining the commonness. Then again, Strachey's rendition of 'the patient' neutralises the personal closeness of Freud's 'my patient' or 'our patient' (in the latter instance, the 'our' may not just be an editorial plural but Freud's having his audience contextually identify with him. Strachey's toning down of Freud's vividness sometimes has deeper implications: for example, whereas in the original German, Freud records nearly all the dreams in the present tense, Strachey typically translates them into the past tense, thus flying even in the face of Freud's explicit theoretical stance that the latent dream is in the optative mood and the dream work changes that thought-material into the present indicative tense.

The 1995 publication of the *Konkordanz* to Freud's works has a potentially twofold value for his translators. First of all, a comparison of the *Konkordanz* with the 1980 English *Concordance* to Freud's works is valuable in pointing up the difference between the two languages. The *Konkordanz* occupies strikingly more shelf space than its English, due in large measure to the highly inflectional nature of the German language and its prominence of lexical compounds, all of which necessitates many more separate lexical entries for the German language. The following lists of index words with contrasting frequencies warn the translator away from any naive overexpectation of correspondences: father (2182), *Vater* (1680); God (620), *Gott* (372); super-ego (375), *Überich* (220); libido (1038), *Libido* (777).

Secondly, the German computerised *Konkordanz* offers the possibility in the third millennium to identify Freud's macrolinguistic DNA, i.e. to detect his phonetic, morphological, and syntactic patterns, some of which may be relatively stable and others of which may vary according to the changes in his ageing, purpose, subject matter, audience, and use of literary genre. The future will reveal the newborn struggles of translators in their attempt to convey Freud's linguistic DNA.

Finally, on a related score, one should note that Freud was not only one of the historically pre-eminent theoreticians of translation but that he himself also translated a number of works.

Bettelheim, B. (1983) *Freud and Man's Soul*. New York: Knopf.

Bourguignon, A., Cotet, P., Laplanche, J. and Robert, F. (1989) *Traduire Freud*. Paris: Presses Universitaires de France.

Mahony, P. (1987) *Freud as a Writer*. Second edition. New Haven, CT: Yale University Press.

Mahony, P (1996) 'Book review of Guttman et al. *The Concordance to the Standard Edition of the Complete Psychological Works of Sigmund Freud*. Boston: G. K. Hall, 6 vols'. *International Journal of Psycho-Analysis* 7(7).

Ornston, D. (ed.) (1989) *Translating Freud*. New Haven, CT: Yale University Press.

P. M.

TRANSMISSION Symbolisation, including the production of *knowledge, devitalises *jouissance, according to Lacan. Hence, in analysis, knowledge, which is the object of transmission there, produces a loss of jouissance as an effect. This paradox is tied to the fact that the production of knowledge and the transformation of the jouissance economy of the *subject constitute one and the same operation. Lacan referred to this operation as having an ascetic effect.

R. R. B.

TRANSMUTING INTERNALISATION According to Kohut, the process whereby new self structure is built. Through pressure generated by manageable, non-traumatic optimal frustration, functions formerly experienced as being provided through interactions with the analyst as selfobject are internalised and taken over by the patient's self. Kohut, in his early writings, advocated that the analyst conduct the analysis according to the principle of optimal frustration, though it is doubtful that he practised in this way himself. The validity of the process of optimal frustration/transmuting internalisation for psychological structure formation has been seriously challenged by a number of psychoanalysts, such as Bacal, who has introduced the concept of *optimal responsiveness; Terman, who emphasises participation and who offers the concept of a dialogue of construction; Lindon, who describes optimal provision; Socarides and Stolorow who state that the central curative element may be formed in the selfobject transference bond itself; and Stolorow, Brandchaft and Atwood, who claim that the notion of optimal frustration is incompatible with an empathic-introspective psychology of the self.

Bacal, H. A. (ed.) (1998) *Optimal Responsiveness: How Therapists Heal their Patients*. New York: Jason Aronson, 60–74.

Kohut, H. (1971) *The Analysis of the Self*. New York: International Universities Press.

Kohut, H. (1977) *The Restoration of the Self*. New York: International Universities Press.

Lindon, J. (1994) 'Gratification and provision in psychoanalysis: should we get rid of "The rule of abstinence"?' *Psychoanalytic Dialogues* 4: 549–82.

Socarides, D. and Stolorow, R. (1984/5) 'Affects and selfobjects'. *Annual of Psychoanalysis* 12/13: 105–19.

Stolorow, R. D., Brandchaft, B. and Atwood, G. E. (1987) *Psychoanalytic Treatment: An Intersubjective Approach*. Hillsdale, NJ: The Analytic Press.

Terman, D. (1998) 'Optimal responsiveness and a new view of structuralization' in Bacal (1998) above.

H. B.

TRAUMA IN CHILDREN In trauma the whole psychic organisation is affected by violent shock and an experience akin to physical wounding. *Freud, in 1922, suggested that a breach of the protective psychic shield in either a single, very violent event or an accumulation of excitations constitutes trauma. He originally related trauma to the experience of *sexual abuse in childhood and then came to the conclusion that stories of seduction were, in fact, *unconscious phantasies. Since the late 1970s actual physical and sexual abuse has been widely recognised as much more common than had previously been believed. More recently, emotional abuse has been recognised as equally traumatic and severe deprivation is also recognised as traumatic for the victim. Threat of spontaneous abortion and difficulties during pregnancy, premature and complicated births and acute or chronic illness in infancy are now understood to have *post-traumatic *sequelae* which can delay or alter the normal development of children.

Transgenerational transmission of trauma is seen by Main as linked with disorganised attachment patterns in parents who appear as fleetingly terrified of or terrifying to their children. Following *Bion's development of *Klein's concept of *projective identification, it is accepted that uncontained projections of extreme anxiety, hostility or fear from parents into vulnerable children is itself traumatic; parents need to be containers of the children's projections of unbearable mental states, unbearable until ego-formation has proceeded sufficiently for the internalisation of the parental containing function. When this is reversed, undigested parental experience threatens the entire psyche of the child. Examples might include those whose parents have themselves been traumatised through war, famine, violence or loss and have become psychically unavailable to their children.

Perry and others describe the impact on children's neurological development of trauma and severe deprivation. They found that neural synapses had become 'superhighways' rather than tiny tracks in the brain, leading to symptoms of hypervigilance and states of dissociation as traumatised children sought to protect themselves from further trauma. Dissociation is the only defence in traumatised babies or young children who are unable to use the fight-flight mechanism available to older individuals. Psychoanalytic treatment of traumatised children appears to normalise synaptic formation in addition to changing the internal structure of the mind, and dissociative states become less frequent. The particular age and stage of development of the child at the time of the trauma is highly significant. Babies and very young children may manifest pervasive *developmental delay or *autistic-like features. They may develop emotionally determined learning difficulties because they cannot concentrate, may appear hyperactive or have specific difficulties with symbol formation. Learning to read or to grasp basic mathematical concepts may be particularly problematic, and some children cannot play imaginatively or create stories. Hypervigilance may be such that what appears to be a lack of concentration may, in fact, be a far-flung use of vision or hearing on the watch for danger, for example sudden sounds or movements. The freeze-response of *dissociation is common but may be fleeting and not easily detectable. Physical coordination may also be affected. The effects of post-traumatic anxiety may be confused with neurological deficit or damage. The containment offered in child psychotherapy and in parallel work with parents can help to distinguish the two.

Children and adolescents may 'identify with the aggressor' in behaving cruelly or coldly, or in maltreating animals or other children. There is danger, particularly in adolescence, of deriving sexual excitement from sadism. *Post traumatic stress disorder in children differs from its manifestation in adults. Children may play out traumatic situations in a way similar to adults' flashbacks. Children may experience great trauma from police investigations or sudden removal from an abusive family, for example, so that rescuers are experienced as abusers. Similarly, medical interventions may be experienced as attacks rather than treatment. Klauber shows that there is always the threat of a widening gulf developing between traumatised parents and traumatised child. The most vulnerable psyches are most likely to develop post-traumatic stress. Previous fault-lines in the personality, as described by Garland, can become exacerbated so that previously quite well-functioning parents become incapacitated. Psychotherapy is seen as helping children and young people to work through the trauma. Alvarez stresses the need for abused children to be helped to think as well as remember, in a safe and hopeful relationship with a therapist who can distinguish between deed and phantasy, action and metaphor. She also stresses the importance of being able to forget the abuse in order to learn how to play 'innocently' before being able to work on the trauma. Parents, traumatised themselves by trauma to their children, may become less available to their children and need support for themselves.

Alvarez, A. (1992) 'Child sexual abuse: the need to remember and the need to forget' in *Live Company*. London and New York: Routledge.

Garland, C. (1991) 'External disasters and the internal world: an approach to understanding survivors' in J. Holmes (ed.) *Handbook of Psychiatric Psychotherapy*. Edinburgh: Churchill Livingstone.

Klauber, T. (1998) 'The significance of trauma in work with parents of severely disturbed children, and its implication for work with parents in general'. *Journal of Child Psychotherapy* 26: 85–107.

Main, M. and Hesse, E. (1990) 'Parents' unresolved traumatic experiences are related to infant disorganized attachment status: is frightened and/or frightening parental behaviour the linking mechanism?' in M. Greenberg, D. Cicchetti and M. Cummings (eds) *Attachment in the Pre-School Years*. Chicago: University of Chicago Press.

Perry, B. D., Pollard, R., Blakley, T., Baker, W. and Vigilante, D. (1995) 'Childhood trauma, the neurobiology of adaptation and "use-dependent" development of the brain: how "states" become "traits".' *Infant Mental Health Journal* 16: 271–91.

T. C.

TRAUMA, DEVELOPMENTAL According to *intersubjectivity theory, pathogenic developmental trauma occurs in an intersubjective context where painful feelings, produced by injurious events, meet with massive malatunement.

R. S.

TRAVERSAL OF PHANTASY This phrase was coined by Lacan in 1964 to specify what should be the aim of the analytic cure. It was inspired by Heidegger's 'Being-unto-death' (as a mental attitude allowing the discrimination between superficial Beings and essential Being) and was contrasted to Bálint's theory of the end of the cure through the retrieval of 'primary love'. Lacan deemed that the aim of the cure should also bring about a maximum difference between ideals and the object cause of desire; accordingly the essence of the transference, i.e. the 'subject supposed to know', should collapse. In doing so, the frame of fantasy which controls the functioning of drives is put into question (hence the proposal of the *pass as testimony of what happens when a subject has managed to reach the final term of this process). This concept of the end of the cure is intrinsically tied to the idea that *object a (the Lacanian version of the *transitional object) as cause of desire is the last term of the subject's consistency; for this reason, when Lacan came to formulate his later theory of the 'Real-Symbolic-Imaginary', which differentiated between three types of jouissance (whereas the object a primarily implied only one), he preferred to envisage the end of the cure in terms of a hard-fought 'identification with the symptom', which is constructed at the end of analysis.

F. S.

TRISTITIA According to Lacan, this concept was originally derived from ancient and medieval theology in which *tristitia de bono divino*, the despair concerning the goodness of God, was called a capital sin. It was first implicitly applied by Lacan to account for the mechanism involved in an unconscious decision which causes depression and melancholia. Initially, manic-depressive disorders were said to be determined by the rejection of *object a, the object of desire. Later, tristitia was described as what determines the 'rejection of the unconscious'.

F. S.

TRUE SELF These concepts have a particular meaning within Winnicott's view of early development. The true self is described by Winnicott as the 'inherited potential' of the child which comprises the core of his personality. When supported by the facilitating environment provided by good-enough mothering the true self's continuing development can be established. Such good-enough mothering will include consistent and coherent responsiveness to the infant's sensory motor needs and attunement to the infant's emotional expression of himself. In essence the expression of the true self is the continual development of the subject's idiom through which he can live his life imaginatively and creatively. In Winnicott's view the true self is never fully knowable even to the subject himself; part of it remains utterly private. In some ways this is a difficult concept because its range seems to include a physical biological element alongside a hard-to-define psychic entity.

See also: false self

Winnicott, D. W. (1965) 'True and false self' in *The Maturational Processes and the Facilitating Environment*. London: Hogarth Press.

M. Twy.

TRUTH Freud's interpretations and constructions attempted to arrive at the truth of repressed memories and events implicated in the patient's illness. However, he cautioned that informing patients of truths before they were ready was *wild psychoanalysis and constituted a danger to the patient's equilibrium. Psychic truth rather than reality prevails in the unconscious.

Bion uses the symbol O to stand for Absolute Truth which can never be known. A lie is a falsification in someone who has perceived the truth. The true thought does not require a thinker but the lie and the thinker are inseparable. Bion distinguishes two kinds of lies – conscious and denuding formulations (Lies) over and against defensive strategies (lies). Falsity, on the other hand, refers to the fact that we can never know Absolute Truth, only an approximation of it. In that sense, everything is a falsity.

For Lacan truth enters the domain of psychoanalysis as the revelation of the position of the subject when he or she faces his or her unconscious desire. This confrontation encounters a limit when approaching the *Real, which presents itself not as a subjective position confronting desire, but rather as a demand of the drive. Hence, truth can only ever be 'half-said'.

J. A. Ber. / S. A. / R. R. B.

TURNING AGAINST THE SELF Drives may seek satisfaction through the subject's own self or body. In sadism and masochism the instinct of aggression remains the same, but the object of the aggression alternates between the self and the other. In depression, the self is attacked instead of some hated object.

J. A. Ber.

TUSTIN, FRANCES (1913–94) Frances Tustin was the first child psychotherapist to make a contribution to psychoanalytic theory. Four books and numerous papers, published over a time-span of thirty years beginning in the 1960s, document her pioneering investigations into childhood *autism and psychosis. They have inspired generations of psychoanalysts and psychotherapists, as well as being welcomed by parents who found her style of writing highly accessible and responded to her empathetic and compassionate attitude.

In 1966, Tustin first described the experience of the 'black hole', which she considered characteristic of childhood autism. Her patient John, who recovered sufficiently after analysis to go to public school, enacted vividly his experience of discovering that the mother's breast was not part of his mouth, which he felt instead was 'broken' and contained 'the black hole with the nasty prick'. Tustin believed that bodily separateness from the mother had been experienced traumatically by children with autism at a stage in development when they were not able to cope with it. In her first books, she followed the theoretical position of Winnicott and Mahler, whose descriptions of psychotic and autistic phenomena she recognised as fitting her own cases, and proposed a stage of normal primary autism to which autistic children had regressed. By the time of her last book, *The Protective Shell in Children and Adults*, which was published in 1990, she had revised her views in the light of evidence from child development research. From then onwards she held that autism was always an aberrant condition, associated with a mother-child relationship that was at first unduly close and undifferentiated. The traumatic awareness of bodily separateness then overwhelmed an infant whose mother, for whatever reason, was insufficiently able to help with processing the experience. The result was what Tustin called an 'agony of consciousness', in which the child suffered terrors of annihilation as well as extreme anxieties concerning bodily integrity, such as falling forever, spilling out, liquefying, burning, freezing and so on. She suggested that children with autism protected themselves against these terrors by turning away from human relationships and feelings to the comfort provided by sensations. These could be hard sensations engendered by autistic objects, which provided the child with an illusory sense of strength, or soft, soothing sensation 'shapes'; both could be derived from the child's own body as well as from external objects. In Tustin's view, uninformed interference with these protective devices could be extremely dangerous, since they served to ward off catastrophic experiences. The child could however be encouraged to give them up gradually within a therapeutic framework which was safe enough so that the traumatic experiences could be worked over in the infantile transference.

Tustin had striking therapeutic success with a number of cases of childhood autism. Organicists tended to dispute that these children could have been autistic in the first place, although they had been referred by Mildred Creak, a child psychiatrist with internationally acclaimed expertise in childhood psychosis. Tustin was in fact careful never to claim that the aetiology of autism was purely psychodynamic; only that any brain defects in her patients could not be detected with the tools available. She thought of autism as a psychobiological protective device, in keeping with the fundamental problems of existence and identity that were at issue. A similar lack of partisanship was evident in her use of concepts from *Winnicott and *Jung in addition to those deriving from her Kleinian training and her analysis with *Bion. Her contributions have opened up fresh approaches to the investigation of the development of the mind and its relation to the body, as well as of the sense of identity and of the primordial terrors which may underlie neurotic difficulties.

Mitrani, T. and Mitrani, J. (eds) (1997) *Encounters with Autistic States: A Memorial Tribute to Frances Tustin*. Northvale, NJ: Jason Aronson.

Spensley, S. (1995) *Frances Tustin*. Makers of Modern Psychotherapy. London and New York: Routledge.

Tustin, F. (1990) *The Protective Shell in Children and Adults*. London: Karnac Books.

Tustin, F. (1994) 'The perpetuation of an error'. *Journal of Child Psychotherapy* 20: 3–23.

M. Rho.

U

UBERWELT This term refers to the act of transcending the world of mundane experience. It is used by *Binswanger to refer to the experience of love and nonverbal communication with another person and transcends the world of individual, private experience.

See also: *eigenwelt; mitwelt; umwelt*

R. Fri.

ULTIMATE CONCERNS The term derives from *Jaspers' idea of ultimate or boundary situations, which Jaspers defines as those situations in life which cannot be dealt with by relying on the type of rational knowledge used to solve problems in everyday life and requiring a radical change in attitude and one's way of thinking. One can choose either an optimistic or a pessimistic attitude toward boundary situations such as the inevitability of struggle and suffering, guilt, and death. Boundary situations can provoke hopelessness and despair or can awaken one to the urgency of living authentically without self-deception.

Tillich similarly writes in *The Courage to Be* of three great anxieties which face modern human beings: anxiety of death, of guilt and of meaninglessness – each to be understood as an expression of fear of non-being. He argues that we must accept the inevitability of these threats to our existence since it is in the act of acceptance of that which is beyond us, and over which we have no mastery, that we confront our anxiety and relinquish our fear.

Yalom utilises the notion of ultimate concerns to distinguish between those basic conflicts deriving from instinctual strivings which are centre-stage in traditional psychoanalysis and those in existential-phenomenological work which have their roots in the client's confrontation with the givens of existence. He believes it is possible to identify four specific ultimate concerns: death, freedom, isolation, and meaninglessness. He observes that ultimate concerns may emerge from the ground of our everyday lives during a process of reflection such as that afforded by therapy or as a result of existential crisis, such as a confrontation with one's own death, or the collapse of some important part of the meaning-giving structure of our lives.

Van Deurzen criticises Yalom for replacing the complexity and paradox of **umwelt*, **eigenwelt*, **mitwelt* and **uberwelt* of **daseinsanalysis* – the physical, personal, social, and spiritual dimensions in which we engage with life – with one-dimensional anxiety-provoking mechanisms, not dissimilar to drives in psychoanalytic theory. In the absence of a clear connection between these concerns and the understanding of what it means to be human which is to be found in the work of existential philosophers, the door is opened for a medical cure for these anxieties and symptoms, rather than a deeper understanding on the part of the client of the inevitable difficulty and challenge in living. The result may be that clients learn ways of dealing with the anxiety associated with ultimate concerns, rather than the wisdom and fortitude to engage creatively with them as inevitabilities.

Tillich, P. (1952) *The Courage to Be*. New Haven, CT: Yale University Press.
Van Deurzen, E. (1997) *Everyday Mysteries, Existential Dimensions of Psychotherapy*. London: Routledge.
Yalom, I. (1980) *Existential Psychotherapy*. New York: Basic Books.

S. P.

UMWELT A mode of being-in-the-world used by Binswanger to refer to the natural environment within which a person exists. It includes biological drives and needs that are outside of our self-awareness. According to Binswanger, the three modes (*umwelt*, **mitwelt* and **eigenwelt*) together constitute a person's world-design – the general context of meaning within which a person exists – and should not be seen as separate.

R. Fri.

UNBEARABLE There are many representations of the world that the ego would prefer to ignore. When it finds such a representation sufficiently unbearable, the ego prefers to hide it away. Freud's earliest theories of repression are based on this inability of the ego to apply reason to a conflict that it finds intolerable. In these early formulations, Freud takes the conflict to be particularly acute in the domain of sexual love, so that this theme of unbearable conflict represents his original version of the structure of the *Oedipus complex.

B. B.

UNCANNY The weird or eerie sensation that accompanies a perception that seems to contradict belief in scientific reality or in the laws of nature. Freud related the experience of the 'uncanny' to the re-arousal of ideas that had been repressed or surmounted. Thus the belief in ghosts, in magic, in animism, in the omnipotence of thoughts, or in the repressed ideas connected with the Oedipus complex may arouse uncanny feelings when revived. He notes that in German, the words for what is homely and familiar, and for what is uncanny and unfamiliar converge so that eventually what is uncanny is something that is familiar. It is the return of the repressed.

J. A. Ber.

UNCONSCIOUS The use of the term as an adjective results from the idea that thought in itself is unconscious. This is one of the foundations of scientific psychology. Psychoanalysis uses it widely to describe the way in which certain thoughts are forgotten or repressed and which continue to have an influence on the psychic life of the individual. The processes which regulate unconscious psychic life and the mechanisms which prevent access to the conscious are the main objective of psychoanalytic clinics. As a substantive, and from a descriptive point of view, the term 'unconscious' can be applied to elements of psychic life which the conscious cannot spontaneously access. However, from a structural point of view, the unconscious system proper is in opposition to the pre-conscious system in that the mental contents of the latter can be accessible to the conscious by an effort of *attention. The unconscious system is radically inaccessible to the conscious. The pre-conscious can only construct an indirect representation. The unconscious itself obeys with the law of the primary process. One can distinguish a secondary unconscious of which the contents come from a repression mechanism (a process of which the paradigm is infantile amnesia) and a primary unconscious, more problematic and more discussed, which prefigures all repression – the 'unrepressed' unconscious.

The structure of the unconscious system remains problematical. Its links with fantasies, its origin in drive, and the place held by linguistic structures have given cause to various theoretical constructions. However, the unconscious, in the psychoanalytical sense of the term, retains radical specificity compared with other approaches, particularly the unconscious in the cognitive sense of the term (syntax or sub-personal level) versus semantic or personal level or in neurobiology.

D. W.

UNCONSCIOUS, COLLECTIVE (JUNG) The collective unconscious, as conceived by Jung, is that area of personality that contains the *archetypes and instincts. It is the phylogenic region of psyche that contains general propensities of modes of action and reaction. As such, it is the deepest substratum of mind and constitutes the psychic heritage of the human race. The collective unconscious is differentiated from the personal unconscious by the fact that the contents of the former have never been in the conscious sphere. The personal unconscious is located above the collective unconscious and shapes its contents through archetypal processes. For this reason the collective unconscious is sometimes called the objective psyche in order to differentiate it from the more individualistic contents of the personal unconscious.

Empirical evidence for the collective unconscious is found through the comparative study of religions, myths and fairytales. Analogous patterns and images can be discerned that are not explainable by other means, i.e. migration among disparate populations. These omnipresent motifs can be identified in various cultures, ethnic groups and civilisations existing throughout time. Similarly, the study of dreams will also reveal recurrent universal themes and symbols.

One can never have direct access to the collective unconscious but only experience its effects indirectly. The collective unconscious contains elements and forces that create typical patterns of human behaviour and experience both of the lowest-common-dominator and of the highest value. The former constitute behavioural patterns in which the person can become repetitive and compulsive while the latter may lead to powerful experiences filled with *numinosity. Since Jung posited that the drive to *individuation was also instinctive in man, the goal becomes one of increasing differentiation from the collective, both inner and outer. The concept of the collective unconscious becomes a heuristic device that allows one to use the technique of *amplification in order to help the ego distinguish the non-personal from the lived personal history. With maturity, i.e. an increased emotional separation from personal *complexes, the individual may come to place his or her seemingly insurmountable difficulties into a larger perspective which encompasses the universal human dilemma.

Jung, C. G. (1960) 'The structure and dynamics of the psyche' in *Collected Works*, Vol. 8. Princeton: Princeton University Press.

A. Cwi.

UNCONSCIOUS PHANTASY (KLEIN) Klein expanded Freud's concept of fantasy into what she thought was the primary content of unconscious mental processes. Unconscious phantasies (the 'ph' spelling denoting their unconsciousness) are the mental representation of libidinal and destructive impulses or instincts and they accompany gratification as well as frustration. They also become elaborated into defences, as well as into wish-fulfilling thoughts. Unconscious phantasies are present in rudimentary form from birth onwards, being active in the mind before language has developed. The earliest phantasies spring from bodily impulses and are interwoven with bodily sensations and affects. These sensations are experienced as part of a relationship to an object which, in phantasy, carries an intentionality to produce this sensation. Through projective and introjective mechanisms a phantasised internal world peopled by internal objects is constructed. The concept of unconscious phantasy became a central scientific topic of the Controversial Discussions at the British Society when it was most clearly described by Susan Isaacs as 'the mental corollary, the psychic representative of instinct'. Unconscious phantasies exert a continuous influence throughout life, though they are always inferred rather than observed as such.

Hinshelwood, R. D. (1989) *A Dictionary of Kleinian Thought*. London: Free Association Books.
Isaacs, S. [1948] (1952 and 1989) 'The nature and function of phantasy' in J. Riviere. (ed.) *Developments in Psychoanalysis*. London: Karnac Books, 67–121.
King, P. and Steiner, R. (eds) (1991) *The Freud/Klein Controversies, 1941–1945*. London: Routledge.
Segal, H. (1997) 'Phantasy and reality' in J. Steiner (ed.) *Psychoanalysis, Literature and War*. The New Library of Psychoanalysis. London and New York: Routledge.
Spillius, E. B. (2001) 'Freud and Klein on the Concept of Phantasy' in C. Bronstein (ed.), *Kleinian Theory: A Contemporary Perspective*. London: Whurr.

C. Bro.

UNCONSCIOUSNESS, (INTERSUBJECTIVITY ACCOUNT) *Intersubjectivity theory distinguishes three realms of unconsciousness, each developing in formative intersubjective contexts: (1) the prereflective unconscious – the organising principles that unconsciously pattern a person's experiences; (2) the dynamic unconscious – emotional experiences that were denied articulation because they were perceived to threaten needed ties; and (3) the unvalidated unconscious – emotional experiences that could not be articulated because they never evoked validating attunement from caregivers.

R. S.

UNCONSCIOUS (LACAN) For Lacan, the unconscious is structured like a language. He writes in *Ecrits*, 'What the psychoanalytic experience discovers in the unconscious is the whole structure of language'. This maxim of his, and its exegesis, is repeated in one way or another in his work from the 1950s onwards. He says that the unconscious knows something, but this knowledge is neither primitive nor instinctual, it is rather a knowledge of the elements of the signifier, that is to say, a knowledge of the most basic unit(s) of language. As such, the unconscious in its formations follows the laws of the *signifier. In the dream for instance, the twin laws of the signifier (*metaphor and *metonymy) are understood to serve the Freudian functions of condensation and displacement. The unconscious is immanent in the effects of the signifier upon the subject. The formations of the unconscious (dreams, parapraxes, symptoms, jokes, etc.) are the resulting products of the return of the signifier which was repressed. Indeed, Lacan's linguistic approach to the unconscious allows him to describe the ways in which the unconscious gets written down in a variety of forms on/in the subject: on the body of the hysteric, in the hysterical symptoms, which, like language, reveals itself through the properties of inscription and translation; in childhood memories; in the semantic evolution of the subject; and, in the legends, myths and stories which form the unconscious lexicon of the subject. This invigorated linguistics of the unconscious affords an understanding of desire as that which motivates the repetition of the signifier in spite of resistances, as that which insists upon enunciation, and always as that which is addressed to the Other.

C. Owe.

UNCONSCIOUS, SOCIAL Introduced by *Fromm and developed in group analysis by *Foulkes and his colleagues, the concept of the social unconscious is similar to the 'cultural unconscious', sometimes used in the United States, and to contemporary versions of the Jungian concept of the *collective unconscious. Whereas the 'collective' unconscious is said to be species-based and, therefore, universal, the social unconscious refers to the constraints on personal and social identity of social, cultural and communicational arrangements, of which people may be unaware, because they are not perceived (not known), but if perceived, not acknowledged (denied), and if acknowledged, not taken as problematic (given), and if taken as problematic, not considered with an optimal degree of detachment and objectivity. The sociological concept of constraint implies both restraint and facilitation, that is, from the beginning of life the person is always both individual and social. Not merely a matter of the *preconscious, the constraints of the social unconscious may be as unconscious as those of the biologically based non-conscious and the dynamic unconscious. Just as the dynamic unconscious is structured according to primary process, symbolisation and symbolic equations, the social unconscious manifests patterns and regularities. For example, gender identity is a function of the body, the family structure, the cultural norms of a society and its classes and ethnic groups, and structured opportunities for males and females to reach their goals. The social unconscious is relevant to the study of normality and health as well as abnormality and disease, and is manifest in persons, families and groups, as well as in society itself. Based on projective and introjective identification and other forms of externalisation and internalisation, especially in connection with child rearing, the constraints of the social unconscious are recursive from one generation to the next.

Foulkes, S. H. (1964) *Therapeutic Group Analysis*. London: Allen & Unwin.

Fromm, E. [1930] (1984) *The Working Class in Weimar Germany: A Psychological and Sociological Study*. Translated by Barbara Weinberger. Cambridge, MA: Harvard University Press.

Hopper, E. (2002) 'The social unconscious in clinical work' in *The Social Unconscious: Selected Papers*. London: Jessica Kingsley.

Ormay, T. (guest editor) (2001) 'The social unconscious'. Special Issue of *Group Analysis* 34: 1, 5–8.

Person, E. S. (1991) 'Romantic love: at the intersection of the psyche and the cultural unconscious'. *Journal of the American Psychiatric Association* 39: 383–411.

E. H.

UNDOING A compulsion particularly characteristic of *obsessional process. According to Freud, it seeks to void the reality of a previous thought or deed by opposing another act or thought. More generally, undoing is a defence mechanism that attempts to prevent the consequences, inner or external, of an action, or transform or hide the thought behind it, particularly a hostile or destructive one; it may also include undoing of one's success in the world, or of an advance in psychoanalysis, thus maintaining a familiar equilibrium threatened by emotional development or change.

Freud, S. (1909) *Notes upon an Obsessional Neurosis*. S. E. 10. London: Hogarth Press.

J. Kup.

UNFORMULATED EXPERIENCE A way of conceiving reflective consciousness and what it means for mental life to be unconscious, inspired by the early, suggestive 1940 work of Sullivan but articulated only much later Stern. In this constructivist, hermeneutic frame of reference, unconscious contents are potential experience that must still be given form. Experience attains articulated shape only as it becomes conscious, and the form it takes is only partially predetermined. Experience becomes conscious by being articulated in verbal language. It is language that makes it possible to shape, know (consciously), and reflect.

This is a contextual and relational account of the mind: the particular experience eventually articulated is a joint function of the pre-existing structure of unformulated experience and the nature of the current interpersonal field. Each interpersonal field tends to facilitate the formulation of certain kinds of experiences and to discourage the articulation of others.

The theory of unformulated experience implies a new notion of the *defences, one different than the *repression hypothesis that is often taken for granted. If experience remains to be given shape, then we defend not by keeping fully formed unconscious contents from entering awareness, but by shutting down the curiosity that would allow the formulation of the unformulated. This unconscious refusal to formulate experience (synonymous to the insistence on maintaining experience in an unformulated state) is defined in this frame of reference as *dissociation.

Critics, such as Fourcher, argue that the theory of unformulated experience fails to consider the substantive or absolute *unconscious – i.e. highly structured unconscious contents that remain unconscious no matter what. Unformulated experience, these critics suggest, is an unconscious that exists only relative to language, and that detracts from the traditional power of the unconscious in psychoanalytic theory.

See also: hermeneutics

Fourcher, L. A. (1992) 'Interpreting the relative and absolute unconscious'. *Psychoanalytic Dialogues* 3.

Stern, D. B. (1997) *Unformulated Experience: From Dissociation to Imagination in Psychoanalysis*. Hillsdale, NJ: The Analytic Press.

Sullivan, H. S. (1940) *Conceptions of Modern Psychiatry*. New York: Norton.

D. B. S.

United States of America Freud's psychoanalysis has influenced the popular and professional culture of the United States, a nation Freud came to denigrate, more profoundly than that of any other country. There were unique reasons for Freud's early favourable reception. Americans faced concurrent crises in psychiatry and in social attitudes toward sexuality in the first two decades of the last century.

The psychiatric crisis resulted from a decline in recovery rates in public mental hospitals from about 40% to 60% in the 1870s to 15% to 35% by 1910. A few younger pragmatic physicians and psychologists believed that existing somatic methods and theories of heredity had failed to successfully explain or treat nervous and mental illness. They had absorbed the French psychopathology of Alfred Binet and Pierre Janet which explored psychological factors while Freud and his followers offered new and hopeful methods of interpreting and treating the symptoms of neurotic and possibly psychotic patients.

American psychiatry was more open to these novelties than its counterparts in Europe. New psychiatric clinics and research institutions were created beginning with the New York Psychiatric Institute in 1895. Its director, Adolf Meyer (1866–1950), an immigrant Swiss psychiatrist, believed that life experience was more important than heredity. Under his influence these new institutions became centres of change in psychiatric theory and treatment, including interest in psychoanalysis.

The second major factor in Freud's favourable reception was a rebellion against what protesting intellectuals, including a number of physicians, regarded as the overly severe and hypocritical restraints of religiously based sexual morality. This prescribed purity of thought, lifelong monogamous marriage and a relatively asexual view of women. A revolt against these views was underway in the 1890s with studies of sexuality and childhood, and became part of intellectual modernism after the turn of the century. Finally psychoanalytic ideas were widely disseminated through a closer interaction between professional and popular culture than obtained in most other western nations. Inspired by Mary Baker Eddy's Christian Science, a growing public expressed interest in the psychological treatment of illness including nervous and mental disorders, and consequently, in psychoanalysis with its intriguing theories of dreams, sex and the unconscious.

Because of Freud's own enthusiasms and ambiguities, as well as native optimism, some of his first American interpreters tended to make him more sanguine about treatment as well as less iconoclastic about sexuality, stressing his theory of sublimation. Most emphasised the dangers of repressing sexual thoughts and feelings, and a few radical popularisers argued that neurosis was the price of failing to fulfil sexual drives. From the outset, the psychiatric and sexual views of the psychoanalysts aroused heated opposition which abated in the 1950s but resumed in the 1980 and 1990s.

American psychoanalysis, which must be viewed as a social movement, evolved in three major periods: the first, from 1909 to 1945 witnessed the creation of a new psychoanalytic profession and a receptive public. The second, from 1945 to 1970 included the domination of academic psychiatry, considerable influence in the social sciences and humanities, and expansive popularisation. Finally, the third period from 1970 to the present, suggests a slow but unmistakable decline in prestige particularly in psychiatry.

A small intellectual and professional advance guard were attracted to Freud's new and startling theories which he presented to Americans in a beguilingly simplified version at Clark University in 1909. Many at first lumped together the theories of Freud and his erstwhile disciples Alfred Adler and Carl Jung in popular and professional writing. Such eclecticism marked the early American Psychoanalytic Association founded in 1911. But orthodoxy marked the more closely organised New York Psychoanalytic Society founded that same year. Freud's disciple, the psychiatrist A. A. Brill, an immigrant from Austria-Hungary, organised the latter and presented a relatively accurate version of Freud's ideas in his own work and in his sometimes clumsy translations of Freud's major writings. But to Freud's dismay, Brill insisted that psychoanalysis was a medical profession and a discipline of scientific psychiatry, a model that characterised organised American psychoanalysis into the 1980s.

World War I brought greater acceptance of psychoanalysis, as a method of understanding shell-shocked soldiers. After the war with the founding of training institutes in Berlin, Vienna, and London, psychoanalysis became an organised profession. A number of Americans went for treatment or training to Freud or the new Institutes and returned as zealous missionaries for his cause.

From 1920 to 1945 psychoanalysis began to influence social work, progressive education and child rearing, and to Freud's growing irritation, was vulgarly simplified and popularised. The first American psychoanalytic institutes were founded in New York in 1931 and later in Boston, Baltimore, Washington, DC, Los Angeles and other major cities. Psychoanalysts and others created psychosomatic medicine, an apparently promising approach to the understanding of illnesses whose origins then were obscure: peptic ulcer, asthma, ulcerative colitis and hypertension. Followers of Harry Stack Sullivan in Washington, DC and New York developed interpersonal psychiatry, an approach to mental illness that combined psychoanalysis with an emphasis on social relationships. All these factors, the professionalisation of psychoanalysis, its medical and psychiatric applications as well as growing publicity, set the stage for its truly extraordinary influence from the end of World War II in 1945 until 1970.

European refugee psychoanalysts, many of them highly gifted, who immigrated to the United States to escape Hitler in the 1930s and 1940s, played a decisive role in these developments. They dominated the new American institutes and stamped the American movement with their particular kinds of orthodoxy or dissent. For example, Kurt Eissler, later director of the Freud archives, sharply defined the parameters of orthodox psychoanalytic treatment. Otto Fenichel codified psychoanalysis in the first widely used American text, *The Psychoanalytic Theory of Neurosis*. Heinz Hartmann, Freud's last trainee, created a Viennese-American ego psychology, which attempted to make psychoanalysis a 'general psychology' emphasising innate modalities of adaptation. Other European immigrants advanced revisionist ideas in both theory and therapy and several became allied with Sullivan's group. Independently, Franz *Alexander sought to make psychoanalysis a 'corrective emotional experience,' through manipulations of transference and length of treatment. More radically, Karen *Horney in several popular books argued that cultural and social factors and a basic conflict between innate insecurity and the need for affection, rather than the vicissitudes of sexuality and the Oedipus complex, caused the neuroses. She sharply rejected Freud's theories of female development, including penis envy. Resulting disagreements over what should be taught to analytic candidates led to organisational splits within the psychoanalytic movement in the late 1930s and 1940s. The American Academy of Psychoanalysis was founded in 1956 to provide a forum for the revisionists.

During World War II, major psychiatric services in the Army, the Navy and the Air Force were headed by physicians who had trained as psychoanalysts or were sympathetic to its approach. Although the use of sodium pentothol probably was rare in the military, it received wide publicity because of its inherently dramatic nature: lost battlefield experiences could be relived in what seemed a stunning proof of Freud's theories of trauma and catharsis. A number of young psychiatrists in the armed services became acquainted with psychoanalytic conceptions. After the war, the largest centre for training psychiatrists was the psychoanalytically-oriented program directed by Karl Menninger and his associates in Topeka, Kansas. Psychoanalytic institutes were flooded with candidates and psychoanalysts headed Departments of Psychiatry at prestigious medical schools.

The war had created a cadre of psychologists who not only administered psychological tests but also functioned as psychotherapists. Social workers, beginning in the later 1920s, were also taking on a therapeutic role; the major models for both psychologists and social workers were psychoanalytic. However, the American Psychoanalytic Association, with some exceptions for research academics, restricted membership to physicians. As a result, psychologists and social workers sought and received unofficial psychoanalytic training but it was not until 1987 that non-physicians were fully accepted by the American Psychoanalytic Association. By then psychologists had extensive training programs of their own and their organisations exceeded in numbers the membership of the American Psychoanalytic Association.

Beginning as early as 1912, but chiefly after World War II, psychoanalysis influenced major figures in the social sciences and humanities: Talcott Parsons in sociology; Clyde Kluckhohn in anthropology; Frederick Crews and Lionel Trilling in literary criticism, to name but a few. The psychoanalyst Erik Erikson emphasised early interaction between the child and the social environment, the sense of identity and the life cycle. He applied these conceptions to historical movements in widely read biographies of Luther and Gandhi. American fiction, popular and serious, reflected psychoanalytic influence in writers such as Philip Roth and Saul Bellow. Dr Benjamin Spock provided psychoanalytic advice to parents in his best selling *Baby and Child Care*. In magazines and popular books, celebrities recounted their experiences on the couch, which to this day remains the standard cartoon symbol of psychotherapy.

Journalists had been publicising psychoanalysis since Freud lectured at Clark University and by 1912 psychoanalysis had become a topic in newspapers and magazines, including the *New York Times*. The trend grew from the 1920s on. By 1939, the year Freud died a refugee in England, he had become a popular symbol of courageous resistance to Nazism. After the war, the journalistic accounts of psychoanalysis multiplied and its movie career flourished. The Hollywood director Alfred Hitchcock's *Spellbound*, was produced with the advice of a prominent Los Angeles psychoanalyst. By the centennial of Freud's birth in 1956 a journalist could attribute cultural reforms, such as treating instead of punishing juvenile delinquents, to the influence of Freud and his disciples.

But this image changed during the counter-cultural revolution of the 1960s, provoked by American military intervention in Vietnam and by the feminist and gay liberation movements. Feminists saw Freud as a Victorian *pater familias*, the author of theories that denigrated women. Both movements as well as some social radicals condemned Freud and psychoanalysis as part of a psychiatric establishment bent on enforcing conformity, although there were also influential radical psychoanalytic philosophers such as Herbert Marcuse and Norman O. Brown.

The decline of psychoanalysis began with critical examination of its theories of psychosomatic illness. After World War II, as medicine insisted on controlled studies for the confirmation of hypotheses, psychoanalysis was judged accordingly. Behaviourist critics such as Hans Eysenck argued that psychoanalytic psychotherapy was no more effective than a placebo. Behaviourists elaborated their own techniques of therapy. More recently hybrid psychoanalytic and behavioural approaches have developed, such as cognitive behaviour therapy or interpersonal therapy, each with standardised treatment manuals. Psychoanalysts have been collecting statistics on outcomes since the 1920s but have been unable to agree on definitions of psychoanalysis. Nevertheless success rates for systematic studies of large groups of patients in psychoanalytic therapy have ranged between 60% and 90%. Controlled studies have confirmed the efficacy of short-term psychotherapy; including cognitive behavioural and psychodynamic therapy, but to date there have been no comparisons of long-term psychoanalysis with non-analytic therapies. The most elaborate, systematic American study carried out under Robert Wallerstein at the Menninger Foundation concluded that both psychoanalysis and supportive psychotherapy were effective for 62.5% of its sample of forty-two sicker than usual patients, some of them followed for nearly thirty years. However, the study did not include an untreated control group. But controlled outcome studies have their own limitations, among them, artificiality and difficulties of recruiting untreated subjects for a lengthy period. Arguing that long-term psychotherapy, including psychoanalysis, had not been proven cost effective, insurance companies and managed care programs curtailed payments, and reduced sharply the number of sessions covered.

In addition to the relative failures of psychosomatic medicine, the attacks of behaviourists, the problems of outcome studies, new psychological therapies and managed care, the decisive factor in the decline was the rise of a renewed somatic psychiatry, always a strong undercurrent in America, particularly with the introduction of shock therapies in the 1930s. The discovery of anti-psychotic medications in the early 1950s created perhaps the first successful pharmacological treatment for symptoms of the psychoses, and with the development later of other drugs such as Prozac, symptoms of the neuroses. These developments were accompanied by new knowledge of the brain and nervous system and a renewed search for the genetic and somatic origins of nervous and mental disorder. The very pragmatism that had inspired the first American physicians to turn to Freud's theories was now deployed against their successors.

The post-modernist critique of positivist science, and the insistence of some European intellectuals, notably Paul Ricoeur and Jürgen Habermas, that psychoanalysis was essentially a humanistic, interpretive enterprise rather than a 'science' opened Americans to new psychoanalytic viewpoints, previously marginalised. These included British object relations theorists such as the neo-Kleinians, French Lacanians and proponents of the intersubjectivity of the analytic process. This last view was distant indeed from Freud's own sureness about the scientific and objective nature of his discoveries.

Psychoanalysis still provides an influential model for psychotherapy; its internal disputes have been muted in the toleration of a wide variety of viewpoints and conscientious, sophisticated efforts to study process and outcome have been undertaken. Increasingly psychoanalysts are non-physicians and more women than men are entering the profession. Despite recent attacks, Freud and psychoanalysis remain a powerful influence in American cultural life, particularly in the humanities. Freud's lasting contributions remain the importance of early childhood and family relationships, and sexuality; the widespread use of psychotherapy; unconscious motives of sexuality and aggression; the personal significance of dreams and symptoms; the therapeutic venting of uncensored thoughts and feelings; and the formation of theories applicable to the humanities and social sciences.

Burnham, J. C. (1958) *Psychoanalysis and American Medicine 1914–1918*. New York: International Universities Press.

Galatzer-Levy, R., Bachrach, H. and Waldron, S. (2000) *Does Psychoanalysis Work?* New Haven, CT: Yale University Press.

Hale, N. G. Jr (1995) *Freud and the Americans*, Vol. 1: *The Beginnings of Psychoanalysis in the United States 1876–1917*; Vol. 2: *The Rise and Crisis of Psychoanalysis 1917–1985*. New York: Oxford University Press.

Mitchell, S. A. (1988) *Relational Psychoanalysis*. Cambridge, MA: Harvard University Press.

N. G. H.

URUGUAY Dr. Rafael Pérez Pastorini was the founding father of psychoanalysis in Uruguay. His decision to study psychoanalysis and to be analysed himself in Buenos Aires was inspired by the visit of Dr López Ibor in the 1940s. His analyst was Dr Pichón Riviere until his early death in 1948.

Rodolfo Agorio and Gilberto Koolhas continued their predecessors' studies, forming a group with Juan Carlos Rey and Héctor Garbarino y Laura Achard who also went to Buenos Aires for analysis and supervisions.

In 1954 Willy and Madeleine Baranger, from Buenos Aires, settled in Montevideo, becoming training analysts and supervisors. The following analysts joined the group: Mercedes Freire de Garbarino, Marta Nieto, Luis Enrique Prego, Vida Maberino de Prego, Sélika Acevedo de Mendilaharzu and Carlos Mendilaharzu. They are regarded as our founding analysts.

In 1957 during the twentieth IPA Congress in Paris, the Uruguayan Psychoanalytic Association (APU) was recognised as a study group and in 1961 during the twenty-second International Congress in Edinburgh it was recognised as an association. It is also part of the FEPAL (Latin America Psychoanalytic Federation).

The *Uruguayan Journal of Psychoanalysis* has been published since 1956. The papers published are written by both Uruguayan and foreign authors that are thought to be of interest.

At the time of writing the APU has forty-six full members and fifty associate members. In the Institute there are twenty-eight candidates who have finished the Seminars and twenty-eight who are still attending them. The APU accepts medical doctors and psychologists who have been analysed by a training analyst and accepted by the Admittance Committee which depends on the Training Committee.

Freud's writings are regarded as basic to the Seminars but different authors are also studied, including Melanie Klein, Lacan, Bion, Winnicott, and various Argentinean and Uruguayan authors. This reflects their theoretical and technical pluralism.

Besides the Institute's activities there is much important scientific activity in general meetings, different departments (groups that study and discuss adolescence, research, children, couples and families, psychosis), meetings with APU members and with members outside the APU who have similar interests, and national and regional congresses.

In 1992 the Exchange Centre was founded with the aim of establishing a link with the community providing psychoanalytic-oriented counselling, courses and supervisions in

Montevideo and other local cities, and also in relation to educational and cultural areas. Psychoanalytic assistance is available for people with low incomes who otherwise could not obtain psychoanalytic treatment.

The APU has a web page whose address is: http//www.apuruguay.com/ where more information can be obtained.

There are also other groups interested in psychoanalysis which have been in existence for several years, but do not belong to the IPA.

G. Bou.

USE OF THE OBJECT Winnicott makes a distinction between object relating and object usage in a formulation developed late on in his thinking. Winnicott takes for granted object relating at this stage as a phenomenon of the subject. Object usage, however, enjoins an examination of the nature of the subject's object as it exists in reality, not as a series of projections. He relates object usage to *transitional objects and transitional phenomena reiterating the essential *paradox and with emphasis on the necessity for the paradox to be accepted. The infant is allowed to create the object, but the object existed to be created and to become a cathected object. The capacity to use an object is developed, not being inborn, and concerns the operation of the reality principle. It depends for its development on the subject's placing of the object outside the area of the subject's omnipotent control; it entails the subject's recognition of the object as existing as an entity in its own right. In Winnicott's view the object can now be destroyed in unconscious fantasy, since it can be seen to survive in reality, and consequently the subject can start to live in a world of real objects. What remains essential in the mother/infant dyad as well as the analyst/patient couple is the survival of the mother, or analyst, and that there is no retaliation in the face of this destructiveness in unconscious fantasy, but rather a recognition of the nature of the actual impulse to destroy and its developmental importance. Winnicott sees a distinction here between his theory and more orthodox theories of aggression. Orthodox theory sees aggression as reactive to an encounter with reality – for example, frustration, whereas he postulates that 'it is the destructive drive which creates the quality of externality'. The cycle of destruction of the object in fantasy and its survival 'strengthens the feeling tone and contributes to object constancy'.

Winnicott, D. W. (1971) 'The use of an object' in *Playing and Reality*. London: Tavistock.

H. T. R.

V

VARIABLE LENGTH SESSION Lacan introduced a form of analytical technique whereby the analyst varies the length of the session. The aim is to end the session with the accentuation of an important element of the work. In this he is drawing on the working of a *Zeigarnik effect, which ensures that the breaking of the session allows the material to be better remembered, both in subsequent sessions and between them. More than this, he holds breaking effects of this kind to be evocative of early loves; the incomplete and broken love relations of childhood are brought into the material of the session by such a technique. This breaking effect thereby automatically generates a transference within which interpretation can bring about a shift.

B. B.

VENEZUELA The psychoanalytic movement in Venezuela formally began in 1965 with the establishment of the first Psychoanalytic Study Group recognised by the International Psychoanalytical Association (IPA). In 1978 the School of the Freudian Field (*Escuela del Campo Freudiano*), a Lacanian school, was established. Finally in 1980 a Jungian study group, the Centre for Jungian Studies (*El Centro de Estudios Junguianos*), was started; and subsequently a training program for Jungian analysts, the Venezuelan School of Depth Psychology (*Escuela Venezolana de Psicologia Profunda*), was initiated.

By 2001 Venezuela, had three different types of psychoanalytic training – Freudian, Lacanian and Jungian – and two societies affiliated with the International Association of Psychoanalysis (IPA): the Venezuelan Association of Psychoanalysis (*Asociacion Venezolana de Psicoanalisis*) with about eighty full members; and the Caracas Psychoanalytic Society (*Sociedad Psicoanalitica de Caracas*) with about sixty full members. Both bodies offer psychoanalytic training in accordance with the standards of the IPA. With training programs based primarily on the work of Sigmund Freud and secondarily on Kleinian teachings they nonetheless study a variety of theoretical views, considering them in an ecumenical spirit. The School of the Freudian Field, having about twenty full members, and affiliated with the World Psychoanalytic Association bases its work primarily on the teachings of Jacques Lacan and Jacques-Alain Miller. The Jungian School has about fifteen full members offering training in accordance with the standards of the International Association of Analytical Psychology (IAAP), but its official affiliation is still pending at the time of writing. Its work is based on that of Carl Gustav Jung, other Jungians and the post-Jungians. All schools provide training to medical doctors, psychiatrists, psychologists, and other professionals with appropriate university degrees.

Each school has endured its share of political turmoil. The Jungian School suffered an early split that postponed the establishment of its training program until 1980. The Venezuelan Association of Psychoanalysis split in 1989 giving birth to the newer Psychoanalytic Society of Caracas. The School of the Freudian Field underwent a recent split of its own.

Psychoanalytic services in Venezuela have always been paid for privately and been conducted in the context of private practices. There is not and never has been, a state-run health program that could pay for psychoanalytic services in Venezuela. Psychoanalytic practice has always been well accepted as a private practice profession with hospital affiliations. Although the demand for psychoanalytic services has suffered recent decline, there continues to be an ongoing demand for psychoanalytic training.

All the three schools of psychoanalysis enjoy strong and well-established connections with the various universities, university hospitals and their post-graduate training programs in psychiatry and clinical psychology. Open conferences and public presentations as well as in-house (members only) theoretical and clinical activities have been a hallmark of all of the schools. Sometimes the different schools organise joint conferences and members of one school often attend and participate, through invitation, in the meetings and conferences of other schools. Thus, even in conflict the dialogue continues.

R. L.

VERBAL BRIDGE In *free association, words provide connections, or verbal bridges to other words and ideas. Similarity in sound, condensation, metaphor and symbolisation provide the material for the verbal bridges used in the construction of puns, jokes, dreams and slips of the tongue.

See also: wit

J. A. Ber.

VOICE Lacan establishes a connection between the object voice from Freud's bipolar perversion of sadism and masochism. Lacan presents de Sade as a formal completion of Kant's philosophical ethics. Lacan shows both that sadism and masochism have different dynamics, and that they are positioned in their mutual orientation around the enunciation of the Law, through a voice of command, which is both implacable and intractable. Whereas sadism endeavours through its command to enforce the logic of a universal law of jouissance, beyond the good, masochism, through its particular subversion of the voice of the Law, elicits a yield of surplus enjoyment, through the economy of the perverse contract.

G. S.

VON FRANZ, MARIE-LOUISE (1916–99) Born in Munich in 1916, she was taken to Switzerland as a child, where she became a citizen and lived the rest of her life. She first met Jung as a young woman, and that meeting eventually convinced her that 'psychological reality was the real reality'.

She received her doctorate in classical philology and began working with Jung in 1934 when he needed someone to translate Greek and Latin for his research. He called her *diese kleine Genie* (this little genius) and used her brilliant talents extensively, especially in his research on alchemy.

Her voluminous publications include her pioneering work on the psychological interpretation of fairy tales. She wrote *Aurora Consurgens* and co-authored (with Emma Jung) *The Grail Legend*. She also edited *Man and his Symbols*. In 1969, at the annual Jung Memorial Lecture at the Zurich Institute, she spoke on 'C. G. Jung and the Problems of our Time'. In 1972 she was the presenter at the twenty-fifth anniversary of the Jung Institute. Her expertise in interpreting dreams resulted in a series of films, *The Way of the Dream*, which she saw as a major part of her legacy to future generations. Her classes at the Jung Institute were always overflowing, which was a tribute to her brilliance and phenomenal insights into the working of the psyche.

Her desire to remain close to Jung resulted in the construction of her 'Tower' on a hill above Bollingen. When asked to describe what appealed most to her about Jung, she said, 'his universality, his flexibility, his broadmindedness'. In 1946 she took up residence in Kusnacht with her colleague Barbara Hannah, where she remained until her death on 17 February 1999. She remained true to Jung's fundamental concepts of analytical psychology and defended them brilliantly and vigorously. She probably touched more lives and influenced more people through her classes, books, and films, than any other of Jung's colleagues.

D. L. F.

W–Z

WALLERSTEIN, ROBERT S. (1921–) has had a long and impressive career as psychoanalyst, psychoanalytic researcher and educator, prolific author and long-time administrator. He is Emeritus Professor, and former Chair, of the Department of Psychiatry at the University of California at San Francisco (UCSF) School of Medicine, and Emeritus Training and Supervising Analyst at the San Francisco Psychoanalytic Institute. He is also a past President of the American Psychoanalytic Association (1971–2), and a past President of the International Psychoanalytical Association (1985–9).

He was Associate Director, and then Director, of Research at the Menninger Foundation in Topeka, Kansas (1954–66), and there, together with colleagues, he created the landmark Psychotherapy Research Project of the Menninger Foundation, the most ambitious and comprehensive study of psychoanalytic processes and outcomes ever carried out, covering a thirty-year span from the midfifties to the mid-eighties. He was Chief of Psychiatry at Mt Zion Hospital in San Francisco (1966–78), before becoming Chair of the Department of Psychiatry at UCSF. He has been twice a Fellow at the Center for Advanced Study in the Behavioral Sciences at Stanford, California (1964–5, 1981–2), and also a Fellow at the Rockefeller Foundation Study Center at Bellagio, Lake Como, Italy (1992). In 1991 he received the Mary S. Sigoumey Award for outstanding contributions to psychoanalysis.

He has been on the Editorial Boards of twenty-one professional journals, and has over 325 professional publications (starting in 1946), including being author, co-author, or editor of twenty books and monographs. He has been Chair of the Research Scientist Career Development Committee of the National Institute of Mental Health (1966–70), Chair of the Committee on Research of the Group for the Advancement of Psychiatry (1958–66), and a Fellow of the Center for Advanced Psychoanalytic Studies in Princeton (1964–76).

R. M. S.

WAR Freud postulated a death drive, whose aim is to return life to an earlier, inanimate state. In healthy development the death instinct is turned outward, and aggression is directed against others. Innate aggression makes war almost inevitable. The influence of civilisation and reason are mitigating factors.

J. A. Ber.

WEANING For Klein, while progress in integration and the corresponding synthetic processes in relation to the object give rise to depressive feelings, these feelings are further intensified by the experience of early weaning. During the process of being weaned, both persecutory and depressive anxieties strongly affect the relation to the mother and food. An interaction of internal and external factors determines the success or failure in working though the *depressive position. Much depends on how far the good breast has already been established internally, on the relationship between mother and child, and consequently how far love for the mother can be maintained in spite of deprivations. Fundamental attitudes toward *frustration and grievance largely determine the infant's capacity to accept substitutes for the primary object. The anxiety about the loss of the *good object comes to a head during periods of weaning. The mother's loving attention helps the infant work through depressive feelings. Ideally, the infant is weaned not only from the mother's breast but also to other sources of gratification and satisfaction which are needed for building up a full, rich and happy life. Success at this stage allows experiences of weaning, loss and mourning later in the life cycle to be more easily navigated.

Klein, M. (1952) 'On observing the behaviour of young infants' in *Developments in Psycho-Analysis* with P. Heimann, S. Isaacs and J. Rivière. London: Hogarth Press. Also in *Envy and Gratitude*. London: Hogarth Press, 1975 (111).

S. A.

WELTANSCHAUUNG Freud argued that psychoanalysis did not have its own *Weltanschauung* (worldview), for it was a *science. However, two different meanings of the concept of the scientific *Weltanschauung* can be identified in Freud's thinking. At times, it is identified with the mechanistic worldview of positivism. But there is also a broader conception of science offered by Freud, which can be traced to the distinction between *logos* and *mythos* (reason and myth). Conceived in this way, science consists in the critique of illusion, idolatry and prejudice. A scientific ethos – a truth ethic – may be a better reference: there can be little doubt not only that psychoanalysis partakes of that ethos, but that it has made a major contribution to its advancement.

J. Whi.

WHEELWRIGHT, JOSEPH BALCH (1906–99) Wheelwright was born in Boston, Massachusetts to an old New England family. He dropped out of Harvard after three years and moved to Santa Barbara with Jane Hollister, whom he married in 1927. They travelled to China and Russia and ended up in Zurich where they both went into analysis with Jung in 1932. Wheelwright graduated from St Bartholomew Medical School in London in 1938 and returned to San Francisco in 1939.

'Jo' was cofounder of the Society of Jungian Analysts of Northern California, and in 1941 he was a founding faculty member of the

Langley-Porter Neuropsychiatric Institute, where he taught a seminar on Jung's psychology to the psychiatric residents for thirty years. He was most interested in the subject of psychological types, and along with Jane and Horace Gray, he devised the Gray-Wheelwright Type Survey, which has been used extensively by universities and businesses to assess psychological type. Today other psychological type tests have become more popular, and the Gray-Wheelwright test is not used as much.

In the 1950s, Wheelwright became the only American Jungian to be accepted by the Freudian establishment, being made a member of the prestigious Group for the Advancement of Psychiatry (GAP). He was the chair of the Student Health Committee and edited a book entitled *Sex and the College Student*, published in 1967.

Wheelwright was active in international Jungian politics, and he became the third president of the *International Association for Analytical Psychology (IAAP) in 1965, serving until 1971. He established policies that still hold today. In 1989 he retired to a ranch outside Santa Barbara; he died ten years later.

T. B. K.

WHITMONT, EDWARD C. (1921–98) Whitmont was born in Vienna, he received his medical degree in 1936 and fled Nazism in 1938 for New York, where he practised individual and group therapy until his death in 1998. He practised homeopathy in the 1940s, studied *analytical psychology in the 1950s with *Harding, and was a founder of New York's Jung Institute. In *The Symbolic Quest* (1969), he integrated *archetypal and personal factors, which he also applied to dream interpretation (*Dreams, A Portal to the Source*, with S. B. Perera). In *Psyche and Soma* he pursued the interface between psyche and soma in psychology, homeopathy, and the sciences. Unusually for a Jungian, he emphasised that some aspects of the archetypal dimension were more accessible in groups than in individual therapy.

Whitmont, E. C. (1964) 'Group therapy and analytical psychology'. *Journal of Analytical Psychology* 9 (1).

G. K.

WILD PSYCHOANALYSIS The 'wild' practice of analysis by those not trained for it: on one hand, they do not grasp the scope and subtleties of psychosexuality; on the other hand, they ignore aspects of technique dealing with timing, resistance, and transference.

Freud, S. (1910) *'Wild' Psychoanalysis*. S. E. 11. London: Hogarth Press.

P. M.

WINNICOTT, DONALD WOODS (1896–1971) Winnicott was born in Plymouth, Devon and died in 1971 in London. Donald Winnicott was the youngest child of a prosperous, nonconformist, middle-class family, living in Plymouth, Devon, where the family business was situated. He had two older sisters. It seems likely that his mother suffered from depression, and he possibly saw little of his busy father who was extremely active in local politics, serving two terms as Lord Mayor of Plymouth and receiving a knighthood. Following attendance as a boarder at the Leys School in Cambridge, where he was excited by Darwin's ideas and the theory of natural selection, Donald Winnicott proceeded to Cambridge University in 1914 to read biology, intending later to go to London to train in medicine. At school, away from his rather strict family background, he seems to have found freedom and developed his natural playfulness as well as an interest in art and music; however World War I, which cost him several friends, overshadowed his university education. He served as surgeon-probationer in a destroyer towards the end of the War.

On demobilisation he went to London to further his medical studies at St Bartholomew's Hospital, and by 1919 he had read *The Interpretation of Dreams*, beginning his fascination with the ideas of *Freud. Winnicott qualified in medicine in 1920; in 1923 he was married for the first time, to Alice Taylor; he gained posts as a specialist in paediatrics at Paddington Green and in Hackney, where he remained for forty years seeing an estimated sixty thousand mother/baby couples; he established his own private practice, and also began his personal analysis with James Strachey, an analysis that lasted ten years and introduced him to the work of Melanie *Klein. Winnicott's mother was to die during that analysis, in 1925.

He trained in psychoanalysis from 1927 to 1934, during which time he published his first book, *Clinical Notes on Disorders of Childhood*, which emphasises his sensitivity to the emotional aspects of ill-health in children alongside careful descriptions of the physical examination and diagnosis of the sick child. Having entered a second analysis in 1933 with Joan Riviere that was to last five years, by 1935 Winnicott had trained in child analysis in supervision with Melanie Klein, and by 1940 he was not only a respected member of the medical establishment but also a Training Analyst in the British Psycho-Analytical Society. This 'foot in both camps', being both paediatrician and psychoanalyst, allowed him to write and broadcast widely on matters to do with the welfare of children and families; his information and ideas proved useful to parents as well as health professionals.

In 1939, together with John *Bowlby and Emmanuel Miller, he warned publicly of the dangers of the Government's evacuation policy, foreseeing that the difficulties of children separated from home would require serious psychological help and management. Working with these damaged, often delinquent children introduced Donald Winnicott to Clare Britton, a social worker who later became his second wife.

Between 1941 and 1945, the dispute known as the Controversial Discussions developed in the British Psycho-Analytical Society. Donald Winnicott, although trained by Klein, wished to supplement her theories about the earliest instinctual conflicts, developing his own ideas about environmental influences at the beginning of life, particularly the quality of early care. He also valued Anna* Freud's ideas. Winnicott aligned himself with neither side, and remained independent, although he was seen as identified with the 'Middle Group' of British psychoanalysts.

In 1948, shortly after his father's death, Winnicott suffered his first heart attack, and in 1949 separated and was divorced from his wife, Alice, who suffered from serious psychological difficulties and had needed much psychoanalytic treatment during the marriage. He married Clare Britton in 1951; she then trained as a psychoanalyst. This marriage appears to have stimulated Winnicott's writing endeavours further, and it was during this period that he produced by far the bulk of his publications, including six books before his death, and enough papers to fill twelve more posthumously.

Winnicott was Physician-in-Charge of the Child Department of the London Clinic of Psycho-Analysis for twenty-five years, President of the British Psycho-Analytical Society twice, from 1956 to 1959, and from 1965 to 1968, and sat on many of the Society's Committees. He initiated the Society's series of Public Lectures. Internationally he chaired the International Psychoanalytic Association's investigation of the clinical practices of *Lacan. He was instrumental in setting up the Finnish Psychoanalytic Society and received their honorary membership.

In the British paediatric world, he was President of the Paediatric Section of the Royal Society of Medicine and of the Association for Child Psychology and Psychiatry. He was also Chairman of the Medical Section of the British Psychological Society. He won the James Spence Medal for Paediatrics in 1968.

Donald Winnicott died in January 1971, asleep after watching a TV film. His own description of himself, given to a child psychiatric conference in 1970 shortly before his death, includes the following: 'Among other things was always the fact that I am rather an ordinary person, neurotic along the English inhibited pattern, at one time being inordinately shy, and not quite so tall as I intended to be, which I have always felt to be a major fault. I spent the first two decades of my life half-drowned in a perpetual sense of guilt, from which psychoanalysis rescued me, except that I can never escape from the sense that I ought not to have escaped the death that eclipsed the careers of so many of my friends in the '14–'18 War.'

Kahr, B. (1999) *D. W. Winnicott, A Biographical Portrait*. London: Karnac Books.
Phillips, A. (1988) *Winnicott*. London: Fontana Press.

J. Joh.

WINNICOTT PRECIS Winnicott's contribution to psychoanalytic theory is closely enmeshed with his thorough knowledge and great imaginative sympathy with the world of ordinary mothers and their children. Broadly speaking he views the psychoanalytic dyad of analyst and patient as reflecting the mother/infant dyad especially in its early phases. Terms such as *primary maternal preoccupation, 'the ordinary *good-enough mother', 'environmental provision', *holding, testify to the significance he gave to aspects of normal development which nevertheless connected to important analytic ideas. His theory is essentially a *developmental one; he stands within the broad stream of object-relations theorists but unlike some, for example, *Fairbairn, he did not abandon the concept of the drives. He said, 'If you want to have a really interesting personality, you have to link up with the drives'. This he would connect with the subject's capacity for *creativity in living, in relationships and in work, intellectual endeavour and artistic expressiveness.

In terms of infant development Winnicott attributes primary importance to the way a mother presents herself, as the environment in which the infant first experiences extra-uterine life. How she does this, and how by the various techniques he describes in extensive elaboration of his ideas, determines in his view the degree to which the foundations of the child's (and ultimately the adult's) healthy psychic and somatic development depend. The mother's task is essentially to present herself and the word in comprehensible doses to the infant, bearing in mind Winnicott's idea that she allows to the infant the *illusion that he is creating the world as he goes, and that *disillusion is only to be introduced as and when the infant can tolerate it.

This process is then applied to the psychoanalytic situation, especially where Winnicott describes and explains his work in the clinical setting with a particular type of patient, that is, when he recognised a disturbance as having its origins in very early traumatic experience. The interplay between his work as a paediatrician and as a psychoanalyst gave to his theory-building a unique breadth. Allied to this was the extraordinary intuitive capacity he possessed to get to the heart of things quickly, especially in his consultations with children which led to his being able to make substantial interventions in child cases where analysis would not have been either available or indeed appropriate. What both the ordinary good-enough mother and the psychoanalyst are conceptualised as doing is facilitating in the child or patient the emergence of a self available for fulfilling imaginative living. Winnicott uses the concept of the self in ways that differ from other more usual psychoanalytic usage, sometimes with idiosyncratic force but on occasions stretching such usage to the point of obscurity, bordering on the mystifying. For example, 'At the centre of each person is an incommunicado element, and this is sacred and most worthy of preservation.' While this may be notice to parent and analyst to respect the privacy of the core of the child's/patient's personality, it sits uneasily in the analytic setting where interpretation and understanding are the medium for the encounter. In Winnicott's theory the infant self begins as potential and is constituted firstly through the mother's recognition of the infant's *spontaneous gesture, and secondly through the mother's survival of the infant's aggression in reality and also in unconscious fantasy.

In understanding disturbance in adult patients Winnicott saw the individual's symptomatology as not only representing evidence of instinctual conflict, but also as a developmental achievement, manifesting the processes and structures which held the history of those failures in environmental provision which had interrupted healthy development.

Essentially Winnicott postulates a two-body psychology and his main study is of ego-relatedness. While retaining a theory of instincts, he stressed that instincts are an important fuel for ego-relatedness. He did not accept Klein's *death instinct as he thought the love/hate concept was not comprehensive enough to encompass the elaborate interplay of fantasy and affect in relation to the object. His own views on *aggression developed over time; he saw motility in the infant, for example, as a precursor of aggression. He postulated rather an innate developmental energy that contained an aggressive quality and could be used to describe intra-uterine movements, hand-grasping, then biting – but this is seen rather as contributing to self-realisation. He is eventually addressing the process whereby aggression, seen as 'more evidence of life', is fused with the infant's capacity for object relating. In other words, like many other psychoanalytic theorists, he faces the question of how aggressive and libidinal or erotic impulses towards the object are brought into relationship. It is clear that he sees an interdependence between 'aggressive potential' and 'erotic life'. Where aggression in its potential becomes destructiveness, it is because aggression has been dissociated from a relationship with an object.

Winnicott paid particular attention to the terrors in infancy which lie at the heart of the infant's absolute *dependence and he describes in accounts of work with both children and adults how these states may present in the consulting room. The terror of annihilation is mentioned in this context, not as a manifestation of the death instinct, but rather as a response to a failure in the holding environment.

See also: antisocial tendency; anxiety; breakdown; communication; compliance; concern; delinquency; deprived children; false self impingement; integration/unintegration/disintegration; paradox; play and playing; psyche-soma; transitional phenomena; true self

Phillips, A. (1988) *Winnicott*. London: Fontana Press.
Kohon, G. (ed.) (1999) 'The intuition of the negative in playing and reality' in *The Dead Mother. The Work of André Green*. London: Routledge.

J. Joh.

WISH FULFILMENT A psychological process in which a wish seems to the imagination to have been realised. Freud proposed that products of the unconscious, *dreams, symptoms, and especially fantasies, are all wish fulfilments wherein the wish is to be found expressed in a more or less disguised form.

See also: compromise formation

Freud, S. (1900) *Interpretations of Dreams*. S. E. 4–5. London: Hogarth Press.

K. L.

WIT Freud observes that the gift of wit is possessed by some as a means of obtaining pleasure. In contrast to dream-work, which is essentially a private affair, wit is intrinsically a social activity. Wit-work follows the dream-work in its use of condensation and displacement. It also echoes the incomprehensible rebus-like narrative of *manifest content in its use of the comic device of absurdity. For defensive purposes manifest content must be censored. For wit to be successful on the other hand it must have the condition of intelligibility, however idiosyncratic or novel that intelligibility may be.

While both wit and dream function to produce pleasure, the dream does so by expressing a wish fulfilled whereas employment of wit obtains pleasure though 'developed play'.

S. Byr.

WOLF MAN Soubriquet for the Russian-born Serguï Pankejeff (1886–1979), whom Freud first analysed from February 1910 to July 1914. Freud concluded that his patient had a severe obsessional neurosis. The case history, concentrating on the patient's childhood and adolescence, is known for its elaboration of oral and anal psychosexuality, the analysis of a dream about wolves, the reconstruction of a related primal scene, its deferred traumatic effect, and the imposition by Freud of a terminating date for the analysis. The chronically ill Pankejeff, now considered a borderline, was reanalysed by Freud in 1919–20, and afterwards by others.

Freud, S. (1918) *From the History of an Infantile Neurosis*. S. E. 17. London: Hogarth Press.
Mahony, P. (1984) *The Cries of the Wolf Man*. New York: International Universities Press.

P. M.

WOLF, ALEXANDER Alexander Wolf began therapy groups in New York in 1938. Wolf asserted the primacy of the individual over the group, both in society and in psychotherapy. He vigorously opposed group-centred methods; his aim was to sponsor the individual growth of each group member's creative ego. His approach has been termed psychoanalysis of the individual *within* the group as contrasted to the *Bion/Tavistock approach of psychoanalysis of the group and that *of* *Foulkes, psychoanalysis *by* the group. Wolf encouraged frank disclosure of group members' associations, and vigorous analysis of transference and resistance. He advocated 'alternate' sessions, which are scheduled meetings of patients without the presence of the therapist. This reinforces peer relationships in the absence of the parental authority as represented by the therapist, and ensures continuity of meetings when the therapist is away. Wolf vigorously opposed 'group-as-a-whole' approaches, stating that they foster deafness to differences, pseudo-cohesion and submit the individual to the tyranny of the prevailing group process.

Wolf is the outstanding pioneer of psychoanalytic approaches to groups in North America. His opposition to group process as intrinsic to group therapy is now a minority position in contemporary psychoanalytic group therapy.

Wolf, A. (1999) 'The foundation of psychodynamic group therapy: the fallacy of the group as a whole' in S. de Schill and S. Libovici (eds) *The Challenge of Psychoanalysis and Psychotherapy*. London: Jessica Kingsley.
Wolf, A. and Kutash, I. L. (eds) (1990) *Group Therapists' Handbook*. New York: Columbia University Press.

M. P.

WOLFF, ANTONIA (1889–1953) Antonia (Toni) Wolff began analysis with C. G. Jung in 1910, at twenty-one, following the death of her father. Her later and ongoing association and collaboration with Jung lasted until her death in 1953. She became an analyst, an important person in Jung's life and a pivotal figure in the group that studied and worked with Jung in formulating *analytical psychology.

Her 1934 paper 'Structural Forms of the Feminine Psyche' was a pioneering work, giving birth to the conceptual terms hetaira, amazon, and medial woman, thus expanding and clarifying Jung's study of masculine and feminine psychology.

S. Sho.

WOMAN Lacan states that Woman – as distinct from *a* woman – does not exist. The psychic apparatus lacks the signifier which could name the Woman, since the only signifier which is inscribed here in relation to sexual difference is the *phallus. Since therefore the universal woman cannot exist, she is a problem, if not a symptom, for every man or woman. The bar that Lacan puts across the term (Woman) expresses the division of woman in her confrontation with *jouissance.

S. Ten.

WORD For Lacan, the word creates a world which is fundamentally without guarantee because there is no intrinsic connection between a word and what it signifies. It is through this aspect of language that the material support of speech imposes itself in psychoanalysis as the agency of the *signifier.

P. D.

WORD-PRESENTATION The 'word' is the unit of the function of speech which acquires its meaning by being linked to particular memories, events, emotions and 'things'. In schizophrenia the word-presentations are retained, but their connections to the affect-laden experiences to which they refer are lost.

J. A. Ber.

WORKING THROUGH The process whereby psychical problems, conflicts, and losses are run through in different psychical systems, and new configurations of the initial material are reached. Freud introduced the term in opposition to repetition, suggesting that the working through of material was an alternative to blindly repeating patterns of behaviour. Indeed, for Freud, working through was the single variable that ultimately distinguished psychoanalysis from other treatments that relied on suggestion for their effects. Little studied in psychoanalytic literature, it has often been compared to the work of *mourning, although Freud's singling out of working through as specific to psychoanalysis would seem to block any outright equation of the two processes.

D. L.

WRITING For Lacan one effect of the functioning of language is writing. However, the difference between writing and speaking is important insofar as the latter bears more direct witness to the effects of the unconscious.

B. O. D.

ZEIGARNIK Bluma Zeigarnik, a researcher working with Kurt Lewin in the 1920s, discovered that interrupted tasks are remembered significantly better than ones that are allowed to be completed. The importance of this effect for psychoanalysis has been investigated by Heinz *Hartmann, by Daniel Lagache, and by Jacques *Lacan. One of the aims of psychoanalysis is to augment memory, and this effect indicates that introducing a break into the sessions can achieve this. Lacan's technique of varying the length of the session aims to produce such a Zeigarnik effect: as a result more material will be remembered in the following sessions, and more will be worked on between sessions as well.

See also: interpretation; punctuation

B. B.

Contributors

A. A.	Anne Alvarez	Tavistock Clinic, London, UK
A. B.	Anni R. Bergman	New York University, USA
A. Bro.	Andrew Brook	Carleton University, Ottawa, Canada
A. C.	Audrey Cantlie	University of London, UK
A. Cwi.	August Cwik	C. G. Jung Institute of Chicago, USA
A. D. E. C.	Ann D. E. Casement	Association of Jungian Analysts, London UK
A. D. M.	Alain de Mijolla	Psychoanalytical Society of Paris, France
A. E.	Anne Erreich	New York University, USA
A. F.	Andrew Forrester	University of London, UK
A. Gin.	Allesandra Ginzberg	Psychoanalytic Institute of Rome, Italy
A. H.	Andreas Hamburger	University of Kassel, Germany
A. Har.	Alan Harrow	Scottish Institute of Human Relations, UK
A. Hay.	André Haynal	Institute of Contemporary Psychoanalysis, Los Angeles, USA
A. Hir.	Albrecht Hirschmüller	University of Tübingen, Germany
A. I.	Amelia Imbriano	John F. Kennedy University, Buenos Aires Argentina
A. I. G.	Arnold I. Goldberg	Rush University Medical School, Chicago, USA
A. J.	Anis Janmohamed	Claybrook Centre, Charing Cross Hospital, London, UK
A. L. S.	Ann Louise Silver	Washington School of Psychiatry, USA
A. M.	Adrian Mirvish	California State University, USA
A. Mos.	Alexander Moser	Zurich Psychoanalytic Society, Switzerland
Ann. M.	Annett Moses	University of Tübingen, Germany
A. O.	Anna Ornstein	Harvard University, USA
A. P.	Arthur Pomponio	National Psychological Association for Psychoanalysis, New York, USA
A. Pro.	Alan Prodgers	Red House Psychotherapy Service, UK
A. R.	Alan Rowan	Middlesex University, UK
A. Rey.	Alejandro Reyes	Lincoln Centre and Clinic for Psychotherapy, London, UK
A. S.	Andrea Sabbadini	British Institute of Psychoanalysis, UK
A. Sch.	Allan E. Schore	University of California, USA
A. Ste.	Alexander Stein	National Psychological Association for Psychoanalysis, New York, USA
A. Stev.	Anthony Stevens	Independent Group of Analytical Psychologists, Corfu, Greece
A. Stu.	Antonius Stufkens	Nederlands Psychoanalytisch Genootschap, Netherlands
A. U.	Ann Ulanov	C. G. Jung Center of New York, USA
A. W.	Aleksandra Wagner	National Psychological Association for Psychoanalysis, New York, USA

A. Z.	Anders Zachrisson	Private Practice, Oslo, Norway
B. A.	Bernard Apfelbaum	Berkeley Sex Therapy Group, USA
B. B.	Bernard Burgoyne	Middlesex University, UK
B. C.	Betty Cannon	Colorado School of Mines, USA
B. E.	Barbara Eisold	Institute of Contemporary Psychoanalysis, New York
B. G.	Brian Garvey	Trinity College, Dublin, Ireland
B. L.	Bogdan Lešnik	University of Ljubljana, Slovenia
B. N.	Bernd Nitzschke	Institute for Psychoanalysis and Psychotherapy, Düsseldorf, Germany
B. O. D.	Barry O'Donnell	D. B. S. School of Arts, Dublin, Ireland
C. B.	Charles Brenner	State University of New York, USA
C. Bro.	Catalina Bronstein	British Institute of Psychoanalysis, UK
C. C.	Christopher Cordess	University of Sheffield, UK
C. E.	Carolyn Ellman	Institute for Psychoanalytic Training and Research, New York, USA
C. Eiz.	Claudio Eizirik	Federal University of South Rio Grande, Brazil
C. E. N.	Carla Elliott-Neely	Washington, DC Psychoanalytic Institute, USA
C. H.	Charles Hanley	University of Toronto, Canada
C. M.	Carola Mann	William Alanson White Institute, New York, USA
C. Mor.	Carole Morgan	The Los Angeles Institute and Society for Psychoanalytic Studies, USA
C. N.	Chantal Nyssen	Author, Paris, France
C. Owe.	Carol Owens	Association for Psychoanalysis and Psychotherapy in Ireland, Ireland
C. P.	Craig Piers	Williams College, New York, USA
C. S.	Charlotte Schwartz	New York University, USA
C. Str.	Charles Strozier	City University of New York, USA
C. V.	Cleo van Velsen	Forensic Services of the East London and City Mental Health Trust, UK
C. Y.	Christopher Young	Cornell University, USA
D. B.	David Blomme	Ghent University, Belgium
D. Bro.	Dennis Brown	The Group-Analytic Practice, UK
D. Bur.	Daniel Burston	C. G. Jung Analysts' Training Program of Pittsburgh, USA
D. C.	Donald Carveth	York University, Toronto, Canada
D. Cre.	Didier Cremniter	Service d'Aide Médicale Urgente, Paris, France
D. D.	Dilys Daws	Tavistock Clinic, London, UK
D. E. S.	David E. Scharff	International Institute of Object Relations Therapy, Chevy Chase, USA
D. J.	Dorothy Judd	Private Practice, London, UK
D. K.	Danielle Knafo	Long Island University, USA
D. K. S.	Doris K. Silverman	New York University, USA
D. L.	Darian Leader	Centre for Freudian Analysis and Research, London, UK
D. L. F.	Dean L. Frantz	Friends of Jung, Fort Wayne, USA
D. M.	Dennis Merritt	The Integral Psychology Center, Madison, Wisconsin, USA

D. N.	Dany Nobus	Brunel University, UK
D. O.	Derek Owens	St John's University, New York, USA
D. Sed.	David Sedgwick	North Carolina Society of Jungian Analysts, Charlottesville, VA, USA
D. St.	Donnell Stern	William Alanson White Institute, New York, USA
D. S. W.	Dorothy Stock Whitaker	University of York, UK
D. T.	David Tresan	C. G. Jung Institute of San Francisco, USA
D. W.	Daniel Widlöcher	Pierre et Marie Curie University, Paris, France
D. Wol.	David Wolitsky	New York University, USA
E. B.	Eva Bahovic	University of Ljubljana, Slovenia
E. Beg.	Ean Begg	Independent Group of Analytical Psychologists, Glasgow, UK
E. Ber.	Emmanuel Berman	University of Haifa, Israel
E. C.	Eric Craig	Pacifica Graduate Institute, California, USA
E. F.	Eugenia Fischer	German Psychoanalytical Society, Frankfurt, Germany
E. F. B.	E. Fairbairn Birtles	Author, Edinburgh, UK
E. G.	Emanuel Garcia	Philadelphia Association for Psychoanalysis, USA
E. Gil.	Eric Gillet	Private Practice, Kentfield, California, USA
E. H.	Earl Hopper	Private Practice, London, UK
E. K.	Eduardo Keegan	University of Buenos Aires, Argentina
E. Kee.	Ernest Keen	Bucknell University, USA
E. L.	Eric Laurent	University of Paris, VIII, France
E. M.	Elke Mühlleitner	Humboldt University, Berlin, Germany
E. M. W.	E. Martin Walker	CUNY
E. O.	Eileen Orford	Child Psychotherapy Trust, UK
E. R.	Esa Roos	Helsinki Institute of Psychoanalysis, Finland
E. S.	Elizabeth Singer	National Psychological Association Psychoanalysis, New York, USA
E. T. B.	Elizabeth Tabak de Bianchedi	Psychoanalytic Association of Buenos Aires, Argentina
F. L.	Frank Lachmann	Institute for the Psychoanalytic Study of Subjectivity, New York, USA
F. R.	Francois Regnault	University of Paris, VIII, France
F. S.	Francois Sauvignat	University of Rennes, II, France
G. A.	Gwen Adshead	West London Mental Health NHS Trust, UK
G. B.	Geoffrey H. Blowers	University of Hong Kong, China
G. Bou.	Graciela Bouza de Suaya	Committee on Women and Psychoanalysis, Uruguay
G. Boul.	Ghislaine Boulanger	Columbia University, New York, USA
G. Bre.	Grant Brenner	Mount Sinai School of Medicine, New York, USA
G. C.	Geoffrey Cocks	Albion College, Chicago, USA
G. G.	Giselle Galdi	Association for the Advancement of Psychoanalysis, New York, USA
G. Gor.	Gregory Gorski	The Psychoanalytic Center of California, USA
G. H.	George Hogenson	The C. G. Jung Institute of Chicago, USA
G. K.	Georgette Kelley	C. G. Jung Institute of New York, USA

G. S.	Gerry Sullivan	Centre for Freudian Analysis and Research, London, UK
G. S. F.	Gilda Sabsay Foks	Argentine Psychoanalytic Association, Argentina
G. S. M.	G. S. Medina	Colombian Psychoanalytic Society, Colombia
G. T.	Graeme J. Taylor	University of Toronto, Canada
G. W.	Gerhard Wilke	Institute of Group Analysis, UK
G. Waj.	Gerard Wajcman	University of Paris, VIII, France
G. Wil.	Gianna Williams	Tavistock Clinic, London, UK
H. A.	Henry Abramovitch	Tel Aviv University, Israel
H. B.	Howard Bacal	International Association for Psychoanalytic Self Psychology, California, USA
H. C.	Hamish Canham	Tavistock Clinic, London, UK
H. D.	Helene Dubinsky	Tavistock Clinic, London, UK
H. E. B.	Hazel E. Barnes	University of Colorado, USA
H. F.	Harriet Friedman	New York Center for Jungian Studies, USA
H. G.	Helen Gediman	New York Freudian Society, USA
H. Gor.	Haim Gordon	Ben-Gurion University of the Negev, Israel
H. K.	Howard Kibel	New York Medical College, USA
H. O.	Haya Oakley	College of Psychoanalysts, London, UK
H. P.	Henning Paikin	Danish Psychoanalytical Society, Denmark
H. T.	Helena Texier	Private Practice, Dublin, Ireland
H. T. R.	Helen Taylor Robinson	University College London, UK
H. T. S.	Henry T. Stein	The Alfred Adler Institute of Northwestern Washington, USA
H. W.	Herbert Will	Private Practice, Munich, Germany
H. W. C	Hans W. Cohn	Society for Existential Analysis, London, UK
I. De. G.	Iris de Groote	Ghent University, Belgium
I. H.	Irwin Hirsch	New York University, USA
I. M.	Ira Moses	William Alanson White Institute, New York, USA
J. A.	Joseph Aguayo	Psychoanalytic Center of California, USA
J. A. Ber.	June A. Bernstein	Centre for Modern Psychoanalytic Studies, New York, USA
J. A. D.	Jacques Delaunoy	Belgian Society of Psychoanalysis, Belgium
J. Ahu.	Jorge Ahumada	Psychoanalytic Association of Buenos Aires, Argentina
Jan. W.	Jan Wiener	Thorpe Coombe Hospital, London, UK
J. Ast.	James Astor	Tavistock Clinic, London, UK
J. B.	Julia Barossa	Middlesex University, UK
J. Bro.	Jason Brown	New York University, USA
J. Bee.	John Beebe	Private Practice, San Francisco, USA
J. C.	Joseph Cambray	Harvard Medical School and Center for Psychoanalytic Studies, USA
J. C. B.	John C. Burnham	Ohio State University, USA
J. Cod.	Joan Coderch	Spanish Society of Psychoanalysis, Barcelona, Spain
J. C. R.	Jean-Claude Razavet	Ecole de la Cause freudienne, Paris, France
J. D.	Jody Davies	Soka University, USA

J. D. M.	Jean-Daniel Matet	Institut du Champ freudien, Section Clinique de Paris - Ile de France, France
J. F.	John Fletcher	University of Warwick, UK
J. F. M.	Juliet F. MacCannell	University of California, Irvine, USA
J. G.	Joanne Greenberg	Colorado School of Mines, USA
J. H.	Jeremy Hazell	British Association of Psychotherapists, Cardiff, UK
J. Hol.	James Hollis	Private Practice, Houston, USA
J. Hop.	Juliet Hopkins	Tavistock Clinic, London, UK
J. J.	Julia Jewett	Chicago Society of Jungian Analysts, USA
J. Joh.	Jennifer Johns	British Psychoanalytical Society, UK
J. K.	Jean Kirsch	C. G. Jung Institute of San Francisco, USA
J. Kup.	Jane Kupersmidt	National Psychological Association for Psychoanalysis, New York, USA
J. Kwa.	Jay Kwawer	William Alanson White Institute, New York, USA
J. M.	Jeanne Magagna	Great Ormond Street Hospital for Children, UK
J. Mar.	Jan Marlan	Inter-regional Society of Jungian Analysts, Pittsburgh, USA
J. Mas.	Joseph Masling	State University of New York, Buffalo, USA
J. Mes.	Judit Mészáros	Private Practice, Budapest, Hungary
J. Mil.	Jon Mills	Adler School of Graduate Studies, Toronto, Canada
J. Mit.	Juliet Mitchell	Jesus College, Cambridge, UK
J. N.	Jennifer Nields	Yale University, USA
J. Nat.	Joseph Natterson	Southern California Psychoanalytic Institute, USA
J. P. K.	Jean Pierre Klotz	Institut du Champ freudien, Section Clinique de Paris-Saint-Denis, France
J. P. M.	John P. Muller	Austen Riggs Center, USA
J. R.	Johannes Reichmayr	Sigmund-Freud-University, Vienna, Austria
J. Rob.	Jeff Roberts	The Group-Analytic Practice, UK
J. S.	June Singer	Jung Institute of San Francisco, USA
J. S. G.	James S. Grotstein	Los Angeles Psychoanalytic Institute, USA
J. T.	Judith Trowell	Tavistock Clinic, London, UK
J. Ts.	John Tsiantis	Athens University Medical School, Greece
J. V.	Judith E. Vida	Institute of Contemporary Psychoanalysis, Los Angeles, USA
J. V. B.	Jane van Buren	Psychoanalytic Center of California, USA
J. W.	Julian Walker	Fromeside Clinic, Bristol, UK
J. W. B.	Jason W. Brown	New York Medical Center, USA
J. Wei.	Joel Weinberger	Adelphi University, New York, USA
J. Whi.	Joel Whitebook	Columbia University, New York, USA
K. H.	Kirsty Hall	Middlesex University, UK
K. L.	Kenneth N. Levy	Pennsylvania State University, USA
K. Lib.	Katrien Libbrecht	Psychiatrische Centrum Sleidinge, Belgium
K. P.	Karl Peltzer	University of the North, South Africa

K. R.	Ken Robinson	Private Practice, UK
K. S.	Kirk Schneider	Existential-Humanistic Institute, California, USA
K. Shi.	Kazushige Shingu	Kyoto University, Japan
L. A.	Lewis Aron	New York University, USA
L. B. R.	Lucille B. Ritvo	Yale University, USA
L. H.	Leston Havens	Harvard Medical School, USA
L. M.	Lynda Miller	Tavistock Clinic, London, UK
L. Mor.	Laurel Morris	Private Practice, Southport, Australia
L. P. C.	Lia Pistiner de Cortinas	Psychoanalytical Association of Buenos Aires, Argentina
L. R.	Leland Roloff	Northwestern University, Seattle, USA
L. R. S.	Luis Rodrigues de la Sierra	British Psychoanalytical Society, UK
M. A.	Margaret Arden	Private Practice, London, UK
M. B.	Miquel Bassols	Institut du Champ freudien, Section Clinique de Paris-Saint-Denis, Barcelona, Spain
M. Bos.	Mary Boston	Tavistock Clinic, London, UK
M. C.	Marcia Cavell	University of California, Berkeley, USA
M. D.	Mary Dougherty	C. G. Jung Institute of Chicago, USA
M. Dim.	Muriel Dimen	New York University, USA
M. D. K.	Marc de Kesel	Ghent University, Belgium
M. Eag.	Morris Eagle	Adelphi University, New York, USA
M. Eig.	Michael Eigen	New York University, USA
M. Eyd.	Marcel Eydoux	Association Mondiale de Psychanalyse, Quimper, France
M. F.	Michael Fitzgerald	Trinity College, Dublin, Ireland
M. F. E.	Mark F. Ettin	Private Practice, Princeton and East Brunswick, New Jersey, USA
M. G.	Mario Gomberoff	Chilean Psychoanalytic Society, Chile
M. G. F.	M. Gerald Fromm	Austen Riggs Center, USA
M. G. T.	M. Guy Thompson	Psychoanalytic Institute of Northern California, USA
M. H.	M. Haber	Belgian Psychoanalytical Society, Belgium
Mich. M.	Michael Moran	University of Colorado, USA
M. K.	Maurice Krasnow	C. G. Jung Institute of New York, USA
M. L.	Moisés Lemlij	Psychoanalytic Society of Peru, Peru
M. M.	Merle Molofsky	Columbia University, USA
M. Mor.	Mark Morris	Kneesworth Hospital, Cambridge, UK
M. N.	Morris Nitsun	The Group-Analytic Practice, UK
M. P.	Malcolm Pines	Institute of Group Analysis, UK
M. R.	Margaret Rustin	Tavistock Clinic, London, UK
M. Rho.	Maria Rhode	Tavistock Clinic, London, UK
M. S.	Matthew Sharpe	Melbourne School of Continental Philosophy, Australia
M. Sch.	Michael Schröter	German Psychoanalytic Society, Berlin, Germany
M. Ste.	Murray Stein	International School for Analytical Psychology, Zurich, Switzerland
M. T.	Marian Tolpin	Institute for Psychoanalysis, Chicago, USA

M. Twy.	Mary Twyman	University College London, UK
M. V.	Marcus Vieira	Federal University of Rio de Janeiro, Brazil
M. W.	Maurice Whelan	Private Practice, Sydney, Australia
N. A.	Neil Altman	New York University, USA
N. C.	Nathalie Charraud	University of Rennes, France
N. D.	Nicola Diamond	Regents College, UK
N. F.	Norbert Freedman	State University of New York, USA
N. G. H.	Nathan G. Hale	University of California, Riverside, USA
N. Q. C.	Nancy Qualls-Corbett	C. G. Jung Institute, Zurich, Switzerland
N. S.	Nina Sutton	Journalist, Paris, France
P. B.	Paul Singleton Barrows	United Bristol Healthcare (NHS) Trust, UK
P. C.	Paul Cooper	Institute for Expressive Analysis, New York, USA
P. D.	Philip Dravers	University of Oxford, UK
P. F.	Peter Fonagy	University College London, UK
P. G.	Paola Golinelli	Italian Psychoanalytic Society, Padova, Italy
P. H.	Peter Hartocollis	Hellenic Psychoanalytical Society, Athens, Greece
P. K.	Paul Kugler	Inter-Regional Society of Jungian Analysts, East Aurora, New York, USA
P. L.	Paul Lippmann	William Alanson White Institute, New York, USA
P. Lom.	Peter Lomas	Private Practice, Oxford, UK
P. Luz.	Pedro Luz	Portuguese Society of Psychoanalysis, Portugal
P. M.	Patrick Mahoney	University of Montreal, Canada
P. McH.	Paul McHugh	Johns Hopkins University, USA
P. Mea.	Phyllis Meadows	Boston Graduate School of Psychoanalysis, USA
P. Mig.	Paolo Migone	Italian Psychoanalytic Society, Italy
P. M. J.	Per Magnus Johansson	University of Gothenburg, Sweden
P. O.	Paul Ornstein	Harvard University, USA
P. R.	Paul Roazen	University of Toronto, Canada
P. V.	Paul Verhaeghe	Ghent University, Belgium
R. C.	Rebecca C. Curtis	Adelphi University, New York, USA
R. C. W.	Ray C. Walker	Eastern Carolina University School of Medicine, USA
R. D.	Ronald Doctor	California State University, Northridge, USA
R. E.	Ricky Emanuel	Royal Free Hospital, London, UK
R. F.	René Fischer	German Psychoanalytical Society, Frankfurt, Germany
R. Fri.	Roger Frie	Columbia University College of Physicians and Surgeons, New York, USA
R. Fun.	Rainer Funk	Literary Executor of Erich Fromm and psychoanalyst in private practice, Tübingen, Germany
R. G.	Roberto Gambini	Private Practice, Sao Paulo, Brazil
R. Gol.	Ruth Golan	New Lacanian School, Israel
R. Gri.	Russell Grigg	Deakin University, Australia
R. H.	Robert Hinshaw	C. G. Jung Institute, Zurich, Switzerland
R. H. E.	R. Horacio Etchegoyen	Psychoanalytic Association of Buenos Aires, Argentina

R. Hol.	Robert Holt	New York University, USA
R. K.	Robert Kramer	American University, Washington, DC, USA
R. Kra.	Rainer Krause	Saarland University, Germany
R. L.	Rómulo Lander	Caracas Psychoanalytic Society, Venezuela
R. Leh.	Ronald Lehrer	Touro College, New York, USA
R. Loc.	Regine Lockot	Private Practice, Berlin, Germany
R. Loo.	Rik Loose	D. B. S. School of Arts, Dublin, Ireland
R. M.	Robert Mendelsohn	Adelphi University, Garden City, New York, USA
R. M. B.	Reine-Marie Bergeron	Private Practice, Montreal, Canada
R. Mol.	Robert Mollinger	New Jersey Institute for Training in Psychoanalysis, USA
R. M. S.	Ross Murray Skelton	Trinity College, Dublin, Ireland
R. M. W.	Rivka M. Warshawsky	Centre for Freud Lacan Studies, Tel Aviv, Israel
R. M. Y.	Robert M. Young	University of Sheffield, UK
R. P.	Renos Papadoupoulos	University of Essex, UK
R. P. O.	Raul Páramo-Ortega	Círculo Psicoanalítico Mexicano Guadalajara, Mexico
R. R.	René Rasmussen	Private Practice, Copenhagen, Denmark
R. R. B.	Romildo do Rego Barros	Brazilian School of Psychoanalysis, Rio de Janeiro, Brazil
R. S.	Robert Stolorow	Institute for the Psychoanalytic Study of Subjectivity, Los Angeles, USA
R. T.	Richard Tuch	University of California, Los Angeles, USA
R. T. M.	R. T. Martin	University of Queensland, Australia
R. W.	Robert Wallerstein	San Francisco Psychoanalytic Institute, USA
R. Wil.	Roger Willoughby	University of Essex, UK
S. A.	Shelley Alhanati	Institute of Imaginal Studies, Petaluma, California, USA
S. Bol.	Stefano Bolognini	Italian Society of Psychoanalysis, Italy
S. Byr.	Stephen Byrne	Trinity College, Dublin, Ireland
S. C.	Sinkwan Cheng	University of California, Irvine, USA
S. Cot.	Serge Cottet	University of Paris, VIII, France
S. E.	Steven Ellman	City University of New York, USA
S. J.	Steven Joseph	C. G. Jung Institute of San Francisco, USA
S. J. B.	Sidney J. Blatt	Yale University, USA
S. K.	Sudhir Kakar	Vikram Sarabhai Foundation, New Delhi, India
S. Kar.	Sigmund Karterud	University of Oslo, Norway
S. M.	Stanton Marlan	Duquesne University, USA
S. Mov.	Siamak Movahedi	Boston Graduate School of Psychoanalysis, USA
S. Mik.	Sherine Mikhail	Chase Farm Hospital, Middlesex, UK
S. P.	Simon du Plock	Regent's College, London, UK
S. R.	Susan Reid	Tavistock Clinic, London, UK
S. S.	Sonu Shamdasani	University College London, UK
S. Saw.	Susan Sawyer	National Psychological Association for Psychoanalysis, New York, USA
S. Sho.	Susanne Short	Jungian Psychoanalytic Association, New York, USA

S. T.	Stephanie Teitelbaum	Institute for Expressive Analysis, New York, USA
S. Ten.	Silvia Tendlarz	Private Practice, Buenos Aires, Argentina
S. V.	Sverre Varvin	Norwegian Psychoanalytic Society, Oslo, Norway
S. W.	Sarah Wright	University of Hull, UK
T. B. K.	Thomas B. Kirsch	Stanford University, USA
T. C.	Trudy Clauber	Tavistock Clinic, London, UK
T. G.	Toby Gelfrand	University of Ottawa, Canada
T. H.	Theresa Howard	Institute of Group Analysis, UK
T. Han.	Thomas Hanley	Toronto Institute of Psychoanalysis, Canada
T. J. J.	Theodore J. Jacobs	New York Psychoanalytic Institute, USA
T. K.	Thomas Kohler	Psychologisches Institut III Hamburg, Germany
T. O.	Thomas Ogden	San Francisco Psychoanalytic Institute, USA
U. M.	Ulrike May	Private Practice, Berlin, Germany
V. B.	Vivien Bar	Centre for Freudian Analysis and Research, London, UK
V. D.	Vincent Dachy	Centre for Freudian Analysis and Research, London, UK
V. G.	Virginia Goldner	Ackerman Institute for the Family, New York, USA
V. P.	Vincente Palomera	Institut del Camp Freudiá, Barcelona, Spain
V. V.	Véronique Voruz	University of Leicester, UK
W. M.	William McGrath	University of Rochester, USA
W. Mei.	William Meissner	Boston College, USA
W. Mer.	Wolfgang Mertens	University of Munich, Germany
W. R.	William J. Richardson	Boston College, USA
W. S.	Warren Steinberg	C. G. Jung Institute of New York, USA
Y. A.	Yvonne Agazarian	Systems-Centered Training & Research Institute, Philadelphia, USA
Z. L.	Zvi Lothane	Mount Sinai School of Medicine, New York, USA

Index

NOTE: Page references in **bold type** refer to main encyclopaedia entries.

Abel, Elizabeth, 289
Aberastury, Arminda, 33
Abraham, Hilda, 3
Abraham, Karl, **3–4**, 6, 7, 20, 118, 130, 168, 172, 182, 190, 221, 223, 241, 267, 268, 269, 294, 332, 333, 342, 389, 450
abreaction, **4**, 69
absence, **4**, 29, 76, 162, 173, 174, 192, 293, 297, 314, 339, 427
abstinence, **5**, 183, 306, 341
abstraction, 58, 94, 197, 315, 457
accepting object, **5**, 158, 193, **332**
act, **5**
acting out, **5**, 51, 353
activity, 5, 91, 92, 105, 106, 129, 145, 162, 174, 213, 219, 220, 298, 313, 404
Adams, Clare, 255
adaptation, **5**, 6, 101, 103, 138, 160, 232, 313, 330, 372, 482
addiction, **6–7**, 28, 143
ADHD *see* Attention Deficit Hyperactivity Disorder (ADHD)
adhesive identity, 53–4
Adler, Alfred, 7–8, 15, 36, 181, 265, 301, 308, 330, 407, 481
adolescents, 70, 82–3, 84
  groups, **198–9**
  identity formation, 145
Adorno, Theodor, 175, 297, 366, 371
aesthetics, 35, 289, 304
affect, **8–10**, 39, 68, 138, 204
Agazarian, Yvonne, 199–200, 206
aggression, **15–16**, 28, 105, 106, 107, 115, 127, 128, 129, 142, 183, 261, 284, 342
  displacement of, 123–4
Agorio, Rodolfo, 484
Ahumada, J. L., 414
Aichhorn, August, 43, 75, 271, 448
Ainsworth, Mary, 38, 66
Alcibiades, 14
Alderdice, Lord John, 254, 255
Alexander, Franz, 96, 190, 191, 222, 224, 343, 433, 482
alienation, **18**, 50, 61, 75, 117, 125, 129, 134, 137, 159, 187, 267, 270, 277, 287, 297, 309, 391, 426, 433, 442, 469
Almásy, Endre, 225
alpha elements, **18**, 19, 52, 94, 197, 207
alpha function, 18, **19**, 51, 58, 59, 253
altered states of consciousness, 280
Althusser, Louis, 276, 297
Alvarez, A., 63–4, 386, 472
Alvim, F., 372
Amae, **19**, 260
ambivalence, **20**, 21, 60, 113, 228
Ambrose, 293
American Sign Language (ASL), 149–50
amnesia, **20**, 218
anal fixation, 4, **21**, 144, 170, 221
anal-sadistic phase, 4, **21**
analysand, destitution of the, 117
analysis
  contract, **21**
  end of, **141**, **456**
analyst, 57, 94, 149, 249, 252, 265, 331, 343
  desire of the, 14–15, **117**, 133, **306–7**
  direction of the treatment, **123**
  fundamental rule, **188**
  the Pass, 276, **353**
  as subject supposed to know, 123, **442**
analyst-patient relationship, 5, 40, 151, 159, 172, 222, 249, **306–7**
  and boundaries, **65**
  expressive relating, **154**
  see also countertransference; transference
analytic philosophy, **361–3**
analytic relation, **22**
analytic third, **22**
  intersubjective, **249**
analytical psychology, **22–3**, , 31–2, 131, 243
  classical (Zurich) school, 22, 23, 243, 244
  developmental (London) school, 23, 243, 244
  group psychotherapy, 56, 58, 199, **208–9**
Anders, T. F., 431
Andersson, Ola, 448
Angel, Ernest, 301, 449
anima/animus, **23–4**, 235
animal studies, 39, **149–51**
Anna O, 24, 69
annihilation anxiety, 47, 269
anorexia nervosa, 130, 342
Anthony, E. J., 199
anthropology, **26–8**, 144, 147–8, 167, 248
antilibidinal ego, **28**, 158, 226
antisocial behaviour, **28–9**, 79, 110–11
anxiety, 9, **29–31**, 38–9, 110, 135, 182, 212, 216, 231, 253
Anzieu, Didier, 177, 200
archetypes, 17, 22, 24, **31–2**, 90, 98, 126, 128, 143, 217, 218, 235, 237, 264, 289
Arendt, Hannah, 274
Aristotle, 69, 157, 164, 291, 404, 413, 417
Arlow, Jacob A., **33–4**, 68, 459
Aron, L., 395
art, **34–6**, 101, 274
  psychology of, 157
as if personality, **36**, 62, 118
Asperger, Hans, 36–7
Asperger's syndrome, **36–7**, 45
assumptions, basic, **48–9**, 199, 200, 208
at-one-ment, **37**, 59, 322
attachment, 9, 21, **37–40**, 39, 66, 87, 115, 149, 163, 248, 426
Attention Deficit Hyperactivity Disorder (ADHD), **40–1**, 83
Atwood, George E., 249, 250, 440, 464, 471
Aubry, Jenny, 177
Augustine, Saint, 425
Aulagnier, Piera, 177
authenticity, 30, **44**, 154, 216
autism, **45–6**, 60, 121, 129, 172
autoerotism, 4, **46**, 67–8, 81, 221
autonomous ego function, **134**, 135, 137–8, 142

Bacal, Howard, 97, 98, 341, 359, 424, 436, 470
bad objects, **47**, 152, 158, **192–3**, 227, 270
Bak, Robert, 225
Balint (née Székely-Kovács), Alice, 48, 167, 190, 224, 225
Balint, Michael, 35, **48**, 53, 143, 167, 190, 198, 224, 225, 295, 333, 472
Baranger, Madeleine, 33, 67, 484
Baranger, Willy, 33, 67, 241, 332, 484
Barnett, R. J., 346
Barrows, P., 85
Barthes, Roland, 274
basic assumption mentality, **48–9**, 199, 200, 208
Bateson, G., 125, 292
Bauer, Ida *see* Dora

Beckett, Samuel, 56
Beebe, B., 119, 382, 421
behaviourism, **49–50**, 149, 283, 286, 337, 483
Behn-Eschenburg, Hans, 64
being-in-the-world, 55, 104, **139**, 209, 216
Bellow, Saul, 482
Benedek, Therese, 167, 190, 224, 225
Benedetti, Gaetano, 450
Benjamin, J., 189, 299
Benkert, Karoly Maria, 219
Benson, Jarlath, 255
Berdyaev, N. A., 152
Berelowitz, M., 62
Berman, David, 255
Berna, Jacques, 450
Bernfeld, Siegfried, 190
Bernheim, Hippolythe, 323
beta elements, 18, **51**, 52, 58, 197, 207
beta screen, **51–2**, 59
Bettelheim, Bruno, 45, **52**, 469
Bianchini, Marco Levi, 256
Bick, Esther, **53–4**, 83, 235, 304, 416
Binet, Alfred, 480
Bini, Lucio, 139
Binswanger, Hilde, 153
Binswanger, Ludwig, **54–5**, 64, 69, 99, 104–5, 139, 152, 153, 251, 310, 330, 364, 365, 374, 450, 475, 476
Bion, Wilfred Ruprecht, 18, 19, 26, 46, **55–60**, 72, 83, 94, 98, 121, 151, 195, 198, 205, 206, 249, 268, 298, 309, 315, 319, 322, 333, 338, 416, 453, 475
  alpha function, **18–19**, 467
  on arrogance, **34**
  on at-one-ment, **37**, 59, 322
  on basic assumption mentality, **48**, 199, 200, 208
  on caesura, **72**
  on container-contained, 82, **94–5**, 219, 386
  on emotional experience, **140–1**
  on 'enforced' splitting, **437**
  on evolution, **151**
  and Foulkes, 202
  on the grid, 58, 59, **197**, 229, 254
  ideogram, **229**
  on intuition, **253–4**
  on the link, **287–8**
  on maternal reverie, **403**
  on model-making, **310**
  on mysticism, 316–17
  on myth, **317–18**
  on O, 37, 57, 59, 140, 151, 254, **331**, 473
  on prenatal states of mind, **373–4**
  on projective identification, **378–9**
  on propositional functions, 292
  on PS-D, **379**
  on psychoanalytic function of the personality, **381**
  on psychoanalytic object, **381**
  on reason, 390
  on the super ego, **446**
  theory of thinking, 58, 197, 285, **457–8**
  on transformation, **467–8**
bipolar self, 272, **422**
Birksted-Breen, D., 130
bisexuality, 24, **60**, 161–2, 171–2
bizarre objects, 58, **60**
Bjerre, Poul, 447, 448
Björk, Stig, 170
Bleuler, Eugen, 3, 31, 43, 55, **60**, 64, 264, 350, 381, 449–50
Blowers, G., 259
body, 238, 240, **433–5**
  fragmented, **176**, 278
  imaginary, 61
  relationism, **61**
body image, **61**, 121
Boehm, Felix, 3, 191, 321
Bohomolec, Elzbieta, 369
Boldt, M., 444
Bollas, Christopher, 333, 338, 469
Bonaparte, Marie, 11, 50, 162, 176, 183, 196, 288
bonobo, 149, 150
Borch-Jacobson, M., 70
borderline pathology, **63–4**, 122, 198
borderline personality disorder, **61–2**, 79, 80
Borecki, I., 103
Bose, Girindrashekhar, 233
Boss, Medard, 55, **64–5**, 105, 153, 310, 366, 450
Boston, M., 85, 115, 346
bound energy, 142, **178**
boundaries, **65**, 99, 475
Bouvet, Maurice, 177
Bowell, Wilfred, 254
Bowlby, John, 9, 38–9, 53, **65–6**, 149, 194, 195, 326, 333, 362, 426, 447, 490
Boyd, Robert, 209
Braatøy, Trygve, 330
Brafman, A. H., 439
brain disorders, 114, 139, **144**, 175, 326
Brandchaft, Bernard, 249, 354, 438, 471
Bratt, Hanna, 448
Braunel, Fernand, 276
breast, 29, 47, **67–8**, 144, 193, 227, 261, 269, 280, 314
Brenman-Pick, Irma, 13–14
Brenman-Gibson, Margaret, 192
Brenner, Charles, 33, **68**
Brentano, Franz, 185, 239, 360, 361
Breuer, Josef, 20, 24, 29, **68–70**, 103, 166, 168, 180, 185, 226, 325
Bridger, H., 175, 206
brief psychotherapy, 17–18, **70**, 83
Brierley, Marjorie, 95, 96
Briggs, A., 53
Brill, Abraham Arden, 450, 481
Brion, Douglas, 254
Britton, Clare, 490
Britton, R., 333
Bromberg, P. M., 394, 395, 396, 397
Bronstein, Maurycy, 369
Brooks, Peter, 290
Brown, D. G., 49
Brown, Norman O., 483
Brun, Rudolf, 450
Brunswick, Ruth Mack, **70–1**, 162, 183
Buber, Martin, 18, 55, **71**, 152, 203, 251, 365, 366, 410, 442
Bucci, W., 434
Buddhism, 16–17, **71–2**, 240, 248, 259
Bugental, J. F. T., 152, 374
Bühler, Charlotte, 53
bulimia nervosa, 130, 342
Bullard, Sr, Dexter, 415
Bullitt, William C., 183, 370
Burckhardt, Jacob, 32
Burke, Kenneth, 289
Burke, Mark, 66
Burlingham, Dorothy, 179, 338, 409
Burrow, Trigant, 175, 199, 204
Burt, Sir Cyril, 408
Busch, F., 134, 136
Butler, Judith, 189, 289
Bychowski, Gustav, 369

caesura, 59, **72**, 94
Cameron, Dick, 254
Cameron, Donald, 41
Cameron, John, 254
Cameron, Olga Cox, 254
Campbell, D., 111
Camus, Albert, 152
cannibalism, 20, **74–5**, 342
Cannon, B., 152–3, 419
Cantor, Georg, 236, 292, 300
Canzler, Peter, 369
Cárcamo, C., 32
care, children in, **84–5**
caregiver-child relationship, 37–40, 66, 120, 149, 194
Carmona, Manuel A., 85
Carpelan, Henrik, 170
Cartesian dualism, 104, 117, 155, 210, 240, 362–3, 364–5
Caruso, Igor A., 44, **75–6**
castration, 4, 6–7, 66, **76**, 90, 101, 123, 162–3, 164, 168, 173, 188, 212, 218, 226, 232, 278, 280
cathartic technique, 69, 180–1
cathexis, 54, **77**, 131
censorship, **77**, 124, 188, 370–1
central ego, 126, **132**, 142, 158, 227
Cerletti, Ugo, 139
chaos theory, **78**, 142, 235
  groups **78–9**

character, **79**, 186–7, 238; *see also* personality; social character
Charcot, Jean Baptiste, 69, **80–1**, 96, 124, 180, 185, 226, 264, 325
Charcot, Jean-Martin, 176
Chavafambira, John, 12
Chentrier, Theodore, 73
Cheshire, N., 110
Chethnik, M., 63
child analysis, **81**, 172, 179, 182
child development, 118–19, 157, 172, 235
child psychotherapy, **82–3**, 194, 267–70
  outcome studies **346**
Childers, Nessa, 255
children
  attachment, 37–40
  borderline psychosis, 63–4
  in care, **84–5**
  developmental delay, **121**, 129
  groups, **198–9**
  psychosis, 52, 121, **385–6**
  sexually abused, 155, 157, 181, 232, **428**
  trauma in, **471–2**
chimpanzee studies, 149–50
Cho Doo-Young, 273
Chodorow, Nancy, 163, 189
Chomsky, Noam, 150, 286
civilisation, **87**, 101, 131, 140, 183, 222–3
Cixous, Hélène, 164
Claparède, Edouard, 450
Clarkin, J., 122
Clavreul, Jean, 177
Cleckley, H., 384
Clement, Catherine, 275
clichés, 286
clinical psychology, 151, **382–4**
Cocks, G., 272, 321
cognitive behavioural therapy, 49, 114
cognitive development, 121
cognitive neuroscience, 127
cognitive psychology, 66
cognitive science, 40
cohort studies, 151
Cole, D. A., 444
Coleridge, Samuel Taylor, 433
Colette, 274
collective unconscious, 21, 31–2, 90, 128, 208, 209, 234, 237, 264
Collomb, Henri, 12
communication, 9, **89**, 149–50, 175
  double bind, **125**, 292
  see also non-verbal communication
complex, **89–90**, 93, 126
complexity theory, groups, **78–9**, 235
compliance, **90–1**, 226
compromise formation, 68, **91**, 92, 97, 120, 172
condensation, **92**, 241, 281
conditioning, 50, 283
conflict, 79, **92**, 106, 121, 131, 134–5, 137–8, 181, 237
confounding variables, 151
Connell, Ernest, 156
conscience, 134, 147, 223
consciousness, **93–4**, 126
  representational theory of, 239
  see also altered states of consciousness; false consciousness
constructivism, 272
contact barrier, 19, 58, **94**
container-contained model, 34, 53, 58, 59, 77, 82, **94–5**, 207, 285, 287
contextualism, **95**, 250
Controversial Discussions, 81, **95–6**, 157, 179, 194, 263, 268, 429
conversion, 9, **96**, 189, 225
Cooper, A., 42
Copjec, Joan, 164, 289
Corrao, Francesco, 257
corrective emotional experience, 18, 96, **96–7**, 201
countertransference, 22, 26–8, 33, 48, 83, **97–100**, 109, 148, 166, 225, 235, 247, 268
couple therapy, 195
Couve, Cyril, 14
Crafoord, Clarence, 449
Craig, P. E., 374
Cramer, B., 351
Crapanzano, Vincent, 12
Creak, Mildred, 474
creativity, 24, 34–6, **100–1**, 113, 128, 169, 230, 231, 274, 288
  of transference **465**
Crespo, Pizarro, 32
Crews, Frederick, 24, 305, 482
criminal behaviour, 110–11
Crisanto, Carlos, 356
critical theory, 284–5
Cruz, José, 436
cultural anthropology, 27, 222
Cultural School of psychoanalysis, 101
cultural studies, 27, 101, 145, 147–8, 289
cultural-interpersonal school *see* interpersonal psychoanalysis
culture, **101**, 148, 202
culture and personality research, 148
Curtis, Rebecca, 230, 417

Dai, Bingham, 86
Dare, Chris, 409
Darwin, Charles, 8, **103–4**, 150–1, 180, 185, 413, 414, 489
Darwinism, 66, 68, 75, 166
Dasein, 30, 64, 75, **104**, 143, 156, 216, 251, 442
Daseinsanalyse, 54–5, 65, **104–5**, 450
David, Fakhry, 14
Daws, D., 431, 432
de Beauvoir, Simone, 152, 188, 409
de Clerambault, Gatain, 107
de la Sierra, Rodríguez, 6
De Maré, Patrick, 175, 202–4
De Martino, R., 72
de Monchy, René, 448
de Quincey, Thomas, 6
death, 75, 84, **105**
death drive, 15, 16, 29, **105–7**, 127, 132, 144, 284
death instinct, 47, **106**, 245, 268
deconstruction, 133, 154, 289
Dedekind, J. W. R., 301
defence, **107–9**, 111, 173, 214, 233
  and resistance, 89, **109**
defence analysis, **108**, 135, 274
defensive strategies, 24, 63, 108, **109–10**, 137, 142, 148, 153–4, 201, 255
Delgado, Honorio, 355
delinquency, 28–9, **110–11**
delusion, **111**, 140, 220, 229
demand, **111**, 116, 190
dementia praecox see schizophrenia
denial, 84, **112**, 122
dependence, 28, 48, 101, **112–13**, 121, 136, 218–19, 270
depersonalisation, **113**, 238
depression, 4, 9, 21, **113–15**, 114, 234
depressive position, 92, **115**, 213, 241, 268, 269, 270
depth psychology, 22, 44, 80, 191, 272
Derrida, Jacques, 284, 289–90, 367
Descartes, René, 361, 362–3, 364, 413; *see also* Cartesian dualism
desensitisation, 50, 230
desire, 14–15, **116–17**, 127, 174, 215, 226, 253, 278, 284, 293
  of the analyst, 14–15, **117**, 133, **306–7**
desmolysis, 190
determinism, psychic, 78, **117**, 178, 245
Deutsch, Hélène, 3, 36, 62, **117–18**, 162, 175, 182, 190, 338, 369, 433, 448, 454–5
development, **118–21**, 170–1
developmental delay, **121**, 129
developmental psychology, 248, 286
developmental psychopathology, 179
developmental tasks (Erikson), 145
Devereux, Georges, 148
Diagnostic and Statistical Manual of Mental Disorders (*DSM IV*), 87, 122, 367, 383
dialectic, **122**, 215, 251
dialogue, 203, 208, 209, 251
Diatkine, René, 177
Dilthey, Wilhelm, 217
Dinnerstein, D., 189
disavowal, 122, **123**
discourse, **123**, 174, 277

displacement, 108, **123–4**, 281, 321
dissociation, 24, 61, 87, **124**, 226, 242, 273
Doi, T., 19, 260
Doktor, Ronnie, 14
Dolto, Françoise, 176
Dora, 15, **125**, 181, 220, 290, 353–4
Dore, J., 285–6
Dosuzkov, B., 102, 103
dream thoughts, **18**, 19
dream-work, 18, 19, 92, 127, 144
dreams, 17, 22, **125–7**, 166, 168, 181, 188, 197, 223, 288
 censorship and, 77, 124
 and daydreams, **105**
 day's residue, **105**
 interpretation of, 248
Drever, James, 127
Driesch, H. A. E., 381
drive, **127–9**, 164, 179, 294
 aim inhibited, **16**
 form of organisation of the, 20, **173–4**
 for mastery, **129**
 source of, **435**
drives, fusion of the, **188**
Drosnès, L., 406
DSM IV see Diagnostic and Statistical Manual of Mental Disorders (DSM IV)
dual drive theory, 139, 142, 218
Dugautiez, Maurice, 50, 51
Dührssen, Annemarie, 191, 321
Durkheim, Emile, 26, 444
dynamic approaches, 142, 226
dyspraxia, 121, **129**

early childhood experience, 66, 148, 179
Eco, Umberto, 274
economic point of view, 131, 226
ECT *see* electroconvulsive therapy (ECT)
Eddy, Mary Baker, 480
Eder, M. D., 255
Edinger, Edward F., **131**, 137
ego, 5, 26, 103, 106, **131–9**, 160, 226, 233, 241, 253, 277, 287, 293
 and the body, 61, 138, 238
 consciousness, 17, 23
 pristine unitary, **376**
 and self, **137**
 splitting of the, **436**
 and subject, 132, 278
 see also integration; self; splitting
ego function
 autonomous, **134**, 135, 137–8, 142
 change of, **133–4**
ego ideal, **134**, 204, 218, 226
ego psychology, 6, 33, 35, 46–7, 106, 129, 131, 132, **134–7**, 137–8, 142, 144, 160, 194, 245
 and defence, 107, **108**
 intellectualisation in, **238**
ego strength and weakness, 135, **137–8**, 142, 213
ego to ego (Lacan), **138**, 218, 277
ego training in action, groups, **138**, 210
Ehrenzweig, A., 35
Eigenwelt see being-in-the-world
Einstein, Albert, 157
Eissler, Kurt, 481
Eissler, Ruth, 18, 271
Eitingon, Max, 3, **139**, 190, 255–6, 450
Ejve, Birgitta, 448
Ekstein, R., 63
electroconvulsive therapy (ECT), 114, **139**
Elias, Norbert, **140**, 175
Elkins, Henry, 316
Ellenberger, H. F., 24–5, 264, 301
Elliot, Mitchell, 254
Ellis, Havelock, 41, 319, 408
Emanuel, R., 40
Emde, Robert, 119, 362
Emmy von N., 69, 448
emotional development, 119, 120, 121, 235
emotional experience, **140–1**, 287
emotional intelligence, 283
empathy, **141**, 159, 183, 272
Empirikos, 196
Empson, William, 289
endopsychic structure, 124, 132, **141–2**, 158–9, 213, 242
energy, 90, 131, **142–3**, 226
 free/bound 142, **178**
 neutral 129, 142
Engel, G. L., 434
Enlightenment, 184
environment, 66, **143**
envy, 94, 106, 113, 138, **143–4**, 193, 215, 227, 261, 269, 270, 287
epilepsy, 139, **144**, 171
Erikson, Erik H., **144–5**, 191, 398, 482
Eros, 87, 139, **145–6**, 222–3, 284, 293; *see also* life drive/instinct
Eskelinen, Terttu, 436
Esterson, Aaron, 280
Etchegoyen, R. Horacio, **146**
ethics, 145, **146–7**, 246
ethnopsychoanalysis, 12, 26–8, **147–9**
ethology, 8, 66, **149–51**
evolutionary psychology, 32, 127, 195
excitation, 91, 103, **152**
exciting object, 28, 47, 121, 126, **152**, 158, 159, 284
existence, **152**, 216
existential analysis, 143, 239–40, 245, 293
existential anxiety, 30, 153
existential guilt, 45, 71
existential psychoanalysis, 64–5, 71, 104–5, 133, **152–4**, 171, 178, 251
existentialism, 18, 71, 195, 216, 261, 365–6
experience, 27–8, 154, 158, 239, 248
 modes of, **312**
 unformulated, 24, 237, **479–80**
 see also early childhood experience; emotional experience
experimental psychology, 38
Expressionism, 169
extraversion, 264, 381–2
Eysenck, H. J., 25, 49, 483
Ezriel, Henry, **155**, 175, 199, 205

facticity, 45, 75, **156**, 216
Fairbairn, W. R. D., 47, 96, 124, **156–60**, 198, 213, 223, 310, 314, 333
 on aggression, 15, **16**
 on antilibidinal ego, **28**
 on anxiety, **29**
 on bad object, **47**
 on death drive, **107**
 on dependence, **112–13**
 on developmental stages, **121**
 on dreams, **125–6**
 on drive, **127–8**
 on ego, **132**
 on endopsychic structure, **141–2**
 on the exciting object, **152**, 424
 on external object, **154–5**
 on fantasy, **161**
 on genital attitude, **189**, 190
 on good object, **193**
 on hysteria, **226**
 on ideal object, **227**
 on incorporation, 342
 on internal object, **242**
 on internal saboteur, **242**
 on the internal world, **242**
 on moral defence, 47, **109**
 on the object, **332**
 on the Oedipus complex, **340**
 on preambivalent object, **373**
 on pristine unitary ego, **376**
 on rejected/rejecting object, **393**
 on repression, **402**
 on schizoid personality/process, **411**
 on the self, **417**
 on separation anxiety, **426**
 on the super-ego, **445**
 on transference, **462**
 transitional techniques, **469**
false connection, 124, **160**
false consciousness, 229
false memories, 155
false persona, 90–1
false self, **160–1**
family experience, corrective emotional, **96–7**
family romance, **161**
family therapy, 195
Fanon, Frantz, 11

fantasy, **161**, 230, 248
curative, **102**
primal, **375**
traversing of the fundamental, 141, **472–3**
Faria, Abbe, 371–2
father, 45, 76, 134, **161**, 220, 228, 354; *see also* name-of-the-father
Fausto-Sterling, A., 189
Fechner, G. T., 68, 343, 410
Federn, Paul, 165, 169, 297, 315–16, 448
Feelan, Herbert, 206
Feigenbaum, Dorian, 255
Feldman, Michael, 14, 343
Feldmann, Sándor, 225
Felman, Shoshana, 290
female sexuality, 125, 163, 182
feminine jouissance, 263, 279
feminine principle, 145, 219–20, 293
feminine psychology, 117–18, 221–2
femininity, 23–4, 36, **161–2**, 163, 192, 263
repudiation of, **402–3**
feminism, 125, **162–4**, 289
Fenichel, Otto, 64, 102, 103, **165**, 169, 170, 190, 214, 257, 274, 328, 330, 338, 343, 388, 412, 481
Ferenczi, Sándor, 18, 29, 35, 117, **165–7**, 183, 220, 221, 224, 230, 262, 267, 269, 295, 338, 389, 447, 452
fetish, 123, **167–8**, 267, 278
Feuerbach, Ludwig, 185, 229
Fiasché, Angel, 449
Fiasché, Dora, 449
Fichte, Johann Gottlieb, 215
Fiedler, Leslie, 289
field research, 147, 148
Fitzgerald, Michael, 254
Fiumara, R., 209
Flaubert, Gustave, 133, **171**, 335, 410
Fletcher, Gordon, 254
Fliess, Robert, 172, 190
Fliess, Wilhelm, 130, **171–2**, 181, 220, 307, 377, 419, 465
flooding, 49–50
Flournoy, Henri, 450
Flournoy, Théodore, 264, 450
focal conflict theory, groups, **200–1**
Fonagy, Peter, 62, 66, 195, 305, 343
Fordham, Michael, 23, **172**, 243, 418, 467
foreclosure, 111, 122, **173**, 214
of the name-of-the-father, 7, 173, 279
Forel, August, 449, 450
forensic psychiatry, **173**
formal logic, 291
Fornari, Franco, 257
Fosshage, J., 98, 343
Foucault, Michel, 289, 365, 367, 417
Foulkes, Sigmund Heinrich, 26, 138, 140, **174–6**, 190, 195, 199, 202, 205, 206, 208, 210, 478, 493
on group matrix, **206–7**, 251–2
Fourcher, L. A., 480
fragmented body, **176**, 201–2
Fraiberg, S., 350–1
Frances, A., 62
Frankfurt School, 140, 175, 186, 210, 215, 371
Frankl, Viktor, 71, 152
free association, 90, 136, 146, 168, **178**, 205, 223, 291
freedom, 117, 153–4
existential, 45, **178**
Freeman, Thomas, 255
Freire de Garbarino, Mercedes, 484
Freud, Anna, 6, 63, 73, 102, 118–19, 134, 144, 162, **178–9**, 182, 190, 214, 223, 228, 245, 274, 276, 338, 370, 409
on curing homosexuality, 221
on neutrality, **329**
see also Controversial Discussions
Freud, Jakob, 180, 184
Freud, Sigmund, 24, 25, 42–3, 64, 102, 152, 178, **180–4**, 321
and Abraham, 3
on affect, 8, **9–10**
and aggression, 15, 16
on amnesia, 20
on anorexia, 130
on anxiety, **29**, 30, 135–6
on art, 101
on association, 37
on beating, 49
on binding, 54
and Breuer, 69
and Brunswick, 71
and Bullitt, 370
on caesura, 72
on cannibalism, **74–5**
on castration, 76
and Charcot, 80, 81
on childhood, 81–2
on civilisation, **87**, 131, 222–3
on the comic, 88
on complex, 89–90, 93
on component, 91
on condensation, **92**
on consciousness, **93**
on contact barrier, 94
on conversion, **96**
correspondence with Fliess, 171–2, 181, 377, 419, 465
on criminality, 110
critical literature on, **24–5**
and Darwin, 103–4
on death drive, **105–6**
on defence, **107**
on delusion, 111
on depression, **113–14**
on distortion, **124–5**
on doubt, **125**
on dreams, 19, **125–6**
on drives, 20, **127**, **129**, 139, 142, 435
on the ego, **131–2**, 134
on energy, **142**
on ethics in psychoanalysis, **146–7**
on the father, **161**
on female sexuality, 125, 182
on femininity, **161–2**
and Ferenczi, 166, 167, 183
on fetish, 167
on fort-da, **174**
on free association, **178**
on groups, **198**
on guilt, **212**
on hallucination, **213**
on hypnotism, **225**
on hysteria, **225–6**
on idealisation, **227**
on identification, **227–8**
on identification with the aggressor, **228**
on illness, **229**
on imagery, **230**
influences on, **184–5**
on interpretation, **248–9**
Irma dream, 145
on jealousy, 261
and Jones, 262
and Jung, 181–2, 264, 323, 357, 418, 451
and Kris, 274
on language, 284–5
letters to Binswanger, 55, 99
libido theory, **284**
on literature, 288
on logic, 291
on masculinity, **298**
on masochism, **298–9**
on melancholia, **303**
on the mother, **313**
on mourning, **315**
on myth, **317**
on the object, **331–2**
on occult phenomena, **337–8**
on the Oedipus complex, **339**
on paranoia, **348**
on perception, **354–5**
on perversion, 350, **356**
and Pfister, 356–7, 450
on the phallus, **358**
on phantasy, **358**
and philosophy, **361–7**
on phobia, **367**
on pleasure principle, **369**
on the preconscious, **373**
on preoedipal disorders, **374**
on primal fantasy, **375**
on primary process, 362, **376**
on principle of constancy, **376**
Project for a Scientific Psychology, 325–6, **377**
on psychic apparatus, **380**
on psychical reality, 47, **380**

on psychoanalysis, 66, 117, 222–3
on psychosis, **384–5**
and Rank, 389
on reaction formation, **390–1**
on reality, 124, **391**
on religion, 315, 357, **397**
on repetition, **400**
on representation, **401**
on repression, 305, **402**, 476
on repudiation of femininity, **402–3**
on rhetoric, **404**
on sadism and masochism, 408
on secondary process, **415**
seduction theory, 181, 232, **415–16**
on sexual difference, 162–3
on the sexual relation, **426**
on sexuality, **427**
on splitting of ego, **436**
on sublimation, **443**
on suggestion, **443**
on the superego, **445**
on the symbolic equation, **452**
and Tausk, 454–5
on termination of analysis, **456**
on Thanatos, **456**
on time, **458–9**
topography, **460**
on transference, **462**, 464
on transformation, 400
translations of his work, 194, **469–70**
on trauma in children, **471**
on truth, **473**
on the uncanny, **476**
Weltanschauung, **488**
wish fulfilment, **492**
on wit, **492**
on working through, **494**
friendship, 86–7, 220
Fromm, Erich, 101–2, 152, 175, **186–7**, 190, 208, 230, 247, 308, 353, 366, 371, 449
on social character, **432–3**
on the social unconscious, **478–9**
Fromm-Reichmann, Frieda, 101, 152, 175, 186, **187**, 190, 247, 415, 449
frustration, 15, 16, 76, 107, 138, **188**, 269, 280, 376
Frye, Northrop, 289
Fuchs *see* Foulkes, Sigmund Heinrich
full speech, 138, **188**
Furer, M., 295
fusion of life and death drives, 105, **188**, 228

Gadamer, Hans-Georg, 250, 330
Gaddini, Eugenio, 257
Gadelius, Bror, 447
Galileo Galilei, 413
Gallagher, Cormac, 254
Garbarino y Laura Achard, Héctor, 484
Garland, C., 372, 472
Garma, Angel, 32, 190, 388
Garma, Elizabeth, 33
Gaudier, H., 366–7
Gay, P., 184
gaze, 153, 240, 293; *see also* look
Gediman, H. K., 328
Gedo, J., 35–6
Geertz, C., 26, 27
Gefühl see affect
Gehrie, M. J., 424
Geijerstam, Emanuel af, 447
Geleerd, E., 63
gender, 162, 163, **188–9**
gender identity, 49, 60
gender studies, 289
genetic reconstruction, 159
genital sexuality, 171, **189–90**
genital stage, 4
George, Princess, 183, 184
Geroe, Clara, 42
Gestalt psychology, 23, 175, 199, 207, 389
giftedness, 145
Gill, Merton, 6, **191–2**, 326, 389, 390, 459, 463–4
Gillespie, Sadie, 13
Gillespie, William, 73, 255
Glasser, Mervyn, 14
Glover, Edward, 3, 6, 15, 34, 95, 96, 194
Glover, James, 194
Gödel, Kurt, 292
Goethe, Johann Wolfgang von, 68, 237, 288
Goldberg, A., 35, 344
Goldstein, Kurt, 175, 210
good objects, **192–3**, 270
Goodall, Jane, 150
Goodman, Paul, 389
Goodsitt, A., 130
Göring, Matthias Heinrich, 190, 321
Graf, Herbert *see* Little Hans
Grainger, E., 346
Granoff, Wladimir, 177
graph of desire, **116–17**, 174
gratification, 138, 170
Gray, Horace, 489
Gray, Jane, 489
Gray, P., 134, 136
Gray-Wheelwright Type Survey, 489
Green, André, 33, 67, 177, **196**, 249, 289
Greenacre, P., 168, 219
Greenberg, Jay, 310, 393, 419, 421–2
grid, 58, 59, **197**, 229, 254
Grinberg, Leon, 33, 449
Groddeck, Georg, 117, 167, 190, **197–8**, 262, 433
Gross, Otto, 450
Grosz, George, 164
Grotjahn, M., 96
Grotstein, James S., **198**, 333
group analysis, 92, 140, 174–6, 199, 204
group cohesion, **200**, 208
group culture, 48–9
group dynamics, 155, 201
group intersubjectivity, **251–2**
group matrix, 199, **206–7**, 252
group mentality *see* basic assumption mentality
group psychotherapy, 56, 58, 199, **207–9**
analytical psychology, **208–9**
children, 83
existential, **209–10**
history, **204–6**
self-psychology, **210–11**
group self, **211**
group therapist function, **211**
group therapy, 96, 195
group-as-a-whole, **199–200**, 493
groups, **198–211**
anti-group processes, 25–6
chaos and complexity theory, **78–9**
container-contained, 95
dreamwork with, 127
ego training in action, **138**
focal conflict theory, **200–1**
functional subgroups, **441**
large, **201–3**
leaderless group project, 56
median, **203–4**
object relations theory, **335–6**
Grünbaum, A., 24, 413–14
Guedeney, A., 431
Guex, Germaine, 450
Guggenbühl-Craig, Adolf, **211–12**
guilt, 4, 17, 71, 91–2, 134, 202, **212–13**, 253, 322; *see also* existential guilt
Guntrip, Harry, 132, **213**, 284, 333, 411, 447

Haag, G., 121
Haas, Ladislav, 103
Habermas, Jürgen, 366, 394, 483
Hadfield, J. A., 56
Hajdu, Lilli, 225
Haley, J., 125
hallucination, 19, 31, 140, 160, **213–14**
negative, **323**
Hanaghan, Jonathan, 254
Hanbowski, Wojciech, 369
Hannah, Barbara, **214**, 487
Hannibal, 185
Harding, Gösta, 448
Harding, M. Esther, 131, **214**, 489
Hare, Robert C., 80, 384
Harris, J. R., 87
Hartman, Mark, 254
Hartmann, Heinz, 46, 134, 135, **214–15**, 274, 275, 276, 390, 431, 481, 494
Hartocollis, P., 196

hate, 98–9, 106, 202, 203–4, **215**, 228, 261
Hayman, Anne, 13
Hegel, G. W. F., 18, 49, 122, 157, 159, **215**, 251, 292, 360, 365, 366, 417
  master-slave dialectic, 277, 300, 391
Heidegger, Martin, 18, **216**, 310, 331, 341, 360, 374, 409, 417, 450, 472
  on anxiety and fear, 30
  on authenticity, 44–5
  on being-in-the-world, 55, 104, 209, 216
  on care, **75**, 216
  on Dasein, 30, 64, 75, **104**, 143, 156, 216, 251, 365, 442
  on facticity, **156**
  influence of, 55, 64–5, 143, 152, 153, 154, 178, 217, 239, 250, 251, 290
  on temporality, **456**
Heilbrun, Erich, 11
Heimann, Paula, 56, 99, 100, 268, 416
Heinroth, J. A. C., 433
Heisaku, Kosawa, 273
Heisenberg, Werner, 100
helplessness, 29, **216**
Henderson, Joseph Lewis, 23, **217**
Henry, G., 85
Heraclitus, 141, 216, 293
Herbart, Johann Friedrich, 448
Hermann, Imre, 225, 369
hermaphroditism, 219
hermeneutics, **217**, 245
Hernández, Max, 356
Herzog, B., 424
Hesnard, Angélo, 176
heterosexuality, 24, **218**
Hillman, James, 23, **218**, 418
Hinduism, 16, 233
Hirsch, Marianne, 289
Hirschfeld, Magnus, 219
history, **218**, 248
Hitchcock, Alfred, 168, 169, 482
Hitschmann, Eduard, 175, 169, 448
Hobson, R. F., 45, 209
Hoffman, Ernest, 50
Hoffman, E. T. A., 288
Hoffman, Irwin, 192, 394
Holder, Alex, 409
holding, 113, **218–19**
Holland, Norman, 289
Hollister, Jane, 488
Hollós, István, 225
Holmes, J., 147
Holstijn, Westerman, 324
Holt, Robert R., 192
Holter, Peter Andreas, 330
hominidae, 149
homosexuality, 24, 172, **219–21**
Hopkins, J., 431
Hopper, E., 49, 208
Horkheimer, Max, 175, 297
Horney, Karen, 3, 64, 117, 118, 162, 163, 182, 186, 190, 205, **221–2**, 247, 248, 299, 371, 403, 482
Horowitz, M. J., 372
Horthy, Miklós, 48, 224
Horwitz, L., 155
Hug-Hellmuth, Hermine von, 267
human nature, 26–8, **222–4**
humanistic psychology, 23, 186–7, 195, 224
Hume, David, 26, 362
Husserl, Edmund, 55, 143, 152, 216, 239, 240, 250, 251, 316, 360, 365, 409, 442, 456
hypnotism, 69, 80, 81, 166, **225**, 233
hysteria, 28, 49, 69, 80, 96, 157, 159, 172, 180, 185, **225–6**, 228, 255, 278

I *see* ego; self
I-It relationship, 71, 251
I-Thou philosophy, 55, 71, 251
IAAP *see* International Association of Analytical Psychology (IAAP)
Ibor, López, 484
ICD 10 *see International Classification of Diseases of the World Health Organisation* (ICD 10)
ICES *see* International Classification of Epileptic Seizures (ICES)
id, 197–8, 214, **226**, 253
ideal ego, **134**, 227, 229
ideal object, 132, 158, 159, 193, **227**; *see also* accepting object
idealisation, 89, **227**, 270, 272
Idealism, German, 215
identification, 19, 36, 49, 204, **227–8**, 229, 277
  with the aggressor, **228**
  and gender identity, 60, 220
  primary, 9–10, 219, **228**
  see also projective identification
identity, 124, 137, 145, 227, **228–9**
Ignotus (a.k.a. Hugo Veigelsberg), 166
Igra, Ludvig, 449
Ikonen, Pentti, 170
Illing, H. A., 208
illusion, 124, **229**
image, 75, **229**
imagery, 8, **230**
Imaginary, the, 22, 61, 64, 112, 129, **229**, 253, 275, 277, 285
imagination, 126, 218, **230–1**
imago, 229, 230, **231**, 270, 400
inauthenticity, 44–5
incest, 101, 150, 223, **232**, 282
Incompleteness Theorem, 292
individual
  as a cultural construction, 26, 27
  and social, 27, 28
individual development, 145
individual differences, 38–9, 120
individual psychology, 7
individuation, 17, 22, 119, 126, 141, **234–5**, 265, 293
infant observation, 53, **235**
infantile amnesia, 218
infantile autism, 45
infantile dependence, 112–13, 121, 313
infantile omnipotence, 101, 227, 232, 238, 313, 314
infantile psychosis, 52
infantile sexuality, 25, 41, 46, 146, 150, 163, 223, **236**
infants
  development, 119–20
  thinking, 58
  see also mother-infant relationship
infinite, 59, 95, **236**, 292
inflation, 21, **236–7**
information processing theory, 142
inhibition, 221, 223, **237**
initiation, 101, 217
innate ideas, 27–8
inquiry, **237**, 248
instinct, 22, 194
instinctive factors (Jung), 128
instinctual tendencies, 127–8
integration, 218–19, **238**, 291
intellectualisation, 21, **238**
intentionality, **239–40**, 285
interactive model, 159
intergenerational ethics, 145
internal object, 47, 106, 144, 158–9, 193, 223, **241**, **242**, 288, **332–3**, 373
internal saboteur, 28, 158, **242**
internal working model (IWM), 38, 401
internal world, 155, **242**
internalisation, transmuting, **470–1**
International Association of Analytical Psychology (IAAP), **242–4**
International Classification of Diseases of the World Health Organisation (ICD 10), 87
International Classification of Epileptic Seizures (ICES), 144
International Psychoanalytical Association (IPA), 3, 22, 43, 166, 181, 224, 242, **244–7**
interpersonal psychoanalysis, 101–2, 114, 167, 237, **247–8**
interpretation, 20–1, 126, 144, 157, 159, 217, **248–9**, 252, 414
intersubjective analytic third, 22, **249**
intersubjective systems theory, 95, **250**
intersubjectivity, 55, 71, 123, 240, **252**, 277–8, 367
  existential, **251–2**

group, **251–2**
origins of, 150
intersubjectivity theory, 28, 92, 193, 215, **249–50**, 272, 440
of unconsciousness, **478**
intertextuality, 274
intrapsychic conflict, **92**, 122
intrapsychic factors, 167, **253**
introjection, 132, 166, 175, 219, 228, **253**
introspection, 259, 272, 283
introversion, 264, 381–2
IPA *see* International Psychoanalytical Association (IPA)
IQ (intelligence quotient), 283
Irigaray, Luce, 162, 164
Irma dream (Freud), 145
Isaacs, S. B., 95, 161, 358, 478
isolation, 108, 215, 238, 240, 255, **255**
Issacharoff, A., 419

Jackson, John Hughlings, 325
Jacobson, Edith, 190, **257–8**
Jaffé, Aniela, **261**
James, C., 336
James, William, **258–9**, 264, 382
Janet, Pierre, 24–5, 69, 80, 96, 124, 226, 264, 480
Jaspers, Karl, 143, 152, **260–1**, 330, 374, 475
jealousy, 138, 215, **261–2**
Jekels, Ludwig, 169, 448
Jelliffe, Smith Ely, **262**
Joffe, Max, 13, 144, 407
Joffe, Wally, 13
Johnson, Barbara, 289
Jokipaltio, Leena-Maija, 170
Jones, Ernest, 11, 29, 31, 42, 50, 64, 70, 73, 96, 157, 182, 194, 221, 224, 233, **262–3**, 268, 288, 321, 338, 407
biography of Freud, 24, 25, 41, 184, 263
on Ferenczi, 167, 183
jouissance, 6–7, 61, 116, 123, 161, 164, **263**, 271, 279; *see also* feminine jouissance; surplus jouissance
Judd, D., 84
Jung, Carl G., 22, 41, 55, 64, 190, 214, 217, 243, **263–5**, 296, 321, 324, 330, 338, 450, 481, 487, 493
on the active imagination, **231**
on alchemy, 17
on amplification, 20–1
on anima/animus, 23–4
and Bleuler, 60
on the collective unconscious, **477**
on complex, **90**
on consciousness, **93**, 126
on countertransference, **97–8**
on defences of the self, **109**
on dreams, **125–6**
on drive, **128**
on ego, **132**
on ego-self axis, **137**
on energy, **142–3**
on Eros, **145–6**
and Freud, 181–2, 264, 323, 357, 418, 451
on group psychotherapy, **208–9**
on imagination, **230–1**
on incest, **232**
on individuation, 141, **234–5**
and Jaffé, 261
on literature, 289
on myth, **317**
on participation mystique, **353**
on the persona, **355**
on the psyche as part of nature, 26–8
on psychoid, **381**
on psychological types, **381–2**
on religion, **397–8**
on the self, **418**
on stages of life, **439–40**
on the symbol, **451**
on synchronicity, **454**
teleology, **455**
on transcendent function, **462**
on transference, **463**
on transformation, **466–7**
see also analytical psychology
Jurjevich, R., 25

Kalff, Dora M., 409
Kane, B., 84
Kanner, L., 45
Kano, T., 150
Kant, Immanuel, 32, 55, 59, 147, 230, 264, 361, 389, 411, 457, 486
Kapoor, Ramun, 255
Keats, John, 59
Keen, E., 154
Kelman, Harold, 449
Kemper, Werner, 321, 413
Kernberg, Otto, 15, 62, 67, 86, 122, **266**, 326, 327, 333
Khan, Masud, **266–7**
Kibel, H. D., 335
Kierkegaard, Søren, 18, 30, 152, 261, 302
Kinberg, Olof, 447
King, Pearl, 170
Kirsch, James, 127
Kirsch, Thomas, 265
Klauber, T., 472
Klein Bottle, 93
Klein, George, 192
Klein, Melanie, 29, 53, 92, 121, 161, 162, 182, 190, 219, 224, 245, **267–70**, 303, 362, 431
on aggression, 15, 16
on art, 101
on autism, 45
child analysis, **81**
on childhood psychosis, **385–6**
on the death instinct, **106**, 127, 223
on denial, 112
on eating disorders, 130
on the ego, **132**, 287
on envy, 143–4, 261
on good and bad objects, 47, **192–3**
on guilt, **212–13**
on homosexuality, 221
on idealisation 227
infant observation, 235
on infantile dependence, 113
on infantile sexuality, 163
on the internal object, 241, **332–3**
on literature, 289
on manic defences, 296–7
on the mother, **313**
on the mother's body, **314**
on the Oedipus complex, **339**
on paranoid schizoid position, **348–9**, 379
on part object, **351**
on projective identification, 82, **378**
on reparation, **399**
on splitting of the ego, **436**
on splitting of the object, **437**
on the superego, **445–6**
on symbol formation, **451–2**
on unconscious phantasy, 358, **477–8**
on weaning, **488**
see also Controversial Discussions
Kluckhohn, Clyde, 482
knot, 64, 161, **270**
knowledge, 59, 77, 239, **271**
Koch, Adelheid, 66
Kofman, Sarah, 162
Köhler, T., 25
Kohut, Heinz, 18, 19, 35, 73, 98, 109, 122, **271–3**, 314, 320, 321, 334, 343, 417, 425, 438, 469
on the bipolar self, 272, **422**
on empathy, **141**
on group self, **211**
on the Oedipus complex, **340**
on self state dreams, **423**
on selfobject transferences, 464–5
on sexualisation, **427**
on transmuting internalisation, **470**
see also self psychology
koinonia, 202, 204
Kojève, Alexandre, 215, 365
Koolhas, Gilberto, 484
Kosawa, K., 16–17, 259, 260
Kouretas, N., 195, 196
Kraepelin, Emil, 350
Krafft-Ebing, Richard, 166, 408
Kreisler, L., 431

Kretschmer, Ernst, 190
Kris, Ernst, 35, 134, 214, **274**
Kristeva, Julia, **274**, 290, 427
Kubler, G., 34
Kučera, O., 103
Kulovesi, Yrjö, 169
Kusama, Yayoi, 34–5

L-schema *see* schema-L
labelling, 88
Lacan, Jacques, 4, 5, 14, 176–7, 195, **274–80**, 297, 299, 308, 336, 365, 494
on addiction, 6
on affect, 9, **10**
on aggressivity, 16
on alienation, 18
on analysis, 22, 122, 123, 218, 417, 485
on anxiety, 30
on automatism, 46
on the beautiful soul, 49
on the body, **61**
on capitation, 75
on castration, 76
on cause, 77
on combinatorial structure, 88
on comedy, 88–9
on complex, **90**
on compulsion, 91
on condensation, 92
on consciousness, **93–4**
on countertransference, **99**
on death, 105
on defence, **108–9**
on delusion, 111
on denegation, **112**
and Derrida, 289–90
on desire, 14–15, **116–17**, 127, 174, 215, 226, 253, 278, 284, 293
on destitution, **117**
on diagnosis, **122**
on discourse, **123**, 174, 300
on displacement, 123–4
on distortion, 124
on division, **125**
on dreams, **125–6**
on drive, **128–9**
on the dual relation, **129**
on the ego, 26, **132–3**, 160
on ego to ego, **138**
on the ego-ideal, 134
on elementary phenomenon, **140**
on equivocation, **144**
on ethics, 147
on extimacy, **155**
on the father, **161**
on fetish, 168
on foreclosure, **173**
on formalisation, **174**
on formation of the unconscious, **174**
on the fragmented body, **176**
on frustration, **188**
on the gaze, 153, 293
on guilt, 212
on hallucination, **214**
on homosexuality, 221, 387
on hysteria, **226**
on identification, 228
on the Imaginary, 22, 61, 64, 112, 129, **229**, 253, 275, 277, 285
on intentionality, 240
on interpretation, 249
on intersubjectivity, **252**
on jealousy, 261
on jouissance, **263**, 427
on the knot, 64, **270**
on lack, 4, 50, 116, 117, 174, 188, 214, 278, **280**, 293
on language, 15, 95, 105, 152, **281**, 285
on law, **282**
on literature, 289
on matheme, 300
on metaphor and metonymy, **307**, 405–6
on the mirror stage, 18, 61, 132–3, 153, 176, 229, 276–7, 285, **309**
on misrecognition, **309**
on the mother, **314**
on myth, **318**
on name-of-the-father, 7, 161, 173, 270, 278–9, **318–19**
on narcissism, 320
on object relations, **335**
on the Oedipus complex, **341**
on the Other, 22, 31, 61, 64, 111, 116–17, 123, 133, 190, 252, 253, 263, 277–8, 278, 293, **343**
on the other scene, **410**
on paranoia, **348**
on part object, **351**
on partial object, **351**
on the Pass, **353**
on *passage à l'acte*, **353–4**
on paternal metaphor, **354**
on perception, 355
on perversion, 350, **356**
on phantasy, **359**
on phobia, **367**
on pleasure, **369**
on preoedipal phase, **374**
on privation, **376**
on the psyche, 143, 441
on psychosis, **385**
on quantifiers in predicate logic, 292
on quilting point, **387**
on the Real, 22, 51, 61, 64, 108, 112, 123, 174, 275, 279, 292, **391**
on reality, **391**
on recognition, **391**
on register, **391–2**
on regression, **392**
on relation, **393**
on remembering, **399**
on repetition, **400**
on representation, **401**
on resistance, **403**
on sadism and masochism, 408
on sadness, **408**
on schemas, 22, 138, **411**
on sexual development, 190
on sexual difference, 426
on the sign, **430**
on the signified and signifier, 117, **430**
on the sinthome, **430**
on the subject, **441–2**
on the subject supposed to know, **442**
on sublimation, **443**
on suggestion, **443**
on the super-ego, **446**
on surplus jouissance, **446**
on the Symbolic, 22, 47, 61, 64, 112, 174, 253, 275, 277, 278, 292, **452**, 453
on the thing, **457**
on time, 312
topology, 380, **460**
on transference, **463**
on traversal of phantasy, **472–3**
on tristitia, **473**
on truth, 473–4
on the unconscious, 95, **478**
on voice, **486**
on woman, **493–4**
on the word, **494**
Lacanian feminism, 162, 164
Lachmann, F., 311, 421, 465
lack, 4, 50, 116, 117, 174, 188, 214, 278, **280**, 293
Laforgue, René, 11, 176
Lagache, Daniel, 176, 275, 494
Laing, R. D., 71, 125, 152, 154, 195, 251, **280–1**, 335, 341, 366
Lakatos, Imre, 413
Lamarckism, 32, 103–4
Lampl-De Groot, Hans, 324, 388
Lampl-De Groot, Jeanne, 190
Langer, Marie, 32, 33, 388
language, 123, 274, 275, 277, 278, **281**, **404–6**
acquisition of, 120, 121, 149–50, 285
alienation in, 125
animals learning, 149–50
aphasia, 31
castration by, 164
and existence, 152
and identification, 228
Lacan on, 15, 95, 105, 152, **281**, 285
as *logos*, 216
and the subject, 122
and thought, 150
and unconscious, 95, 276
see also linguistics

Language Acquisition Device, 286
Lanzer, Ernst *see* Rat Man
Laplanche, Jean, 177, **281–2**, 427
Larsson, Bo, 448
Lasswell, Harold, 371
latency, 81, **281**
latent content, 126, **281**, 288
law, 122, 278–9, **282**
Lawrence, W. G., 49
lay analysis, 139, 167, 182, **282**
Lázár-Gero, Clara, 225
Leach, E., 27
leadership, 205–6, 210
learnability, paradox of, 285
learning, 287
learning disabilities, 121, **282–3**
learning theory, 50, **283**
Lebon, Gustav, 204
Lebovici, Serge, 177, 369
Lechat, Fernand, 50, 51
Lechat-Ledoux, Mme, 50
Leclaire, Serge, 33, 177
Leicester model *see* Tavistock model
Lemlij, Moisés, 356
Leonard, L. S., 153
Lesche, Carl, 170
Lesser, Simon O., 289
Leuba, John, 50
Levenson, E., 102, 230, 237, 247
Lévi-Strauss, C., 27, 150, 318, 365, 441
Levin, F. M., 326
Levinas, Emmanuel, 367
Levy, Lajos, 225
Lévy-Bruhl, Lucien, 353
Lewin, Kurt, 205–6
liberalism, 184–5
libidinal ego, 28, 158, 226, **284**
libido, 15, 142, 162, 179, **284**
  absence of, 105
  adhesiveness of the, 171
  development of, 4, 81–2, 294
libido theory, 3, 118, 144, 223
Lichtenberg, J. D., 128, 314–15
Liebermann, Lucy, 199, 225
life drive/instinct, 105, 106, 127, 128, 129, 193, **284**
Lifton, R. J., 372
Lindley, R., 147
Lindon, J., 341, 470
linguistics, 150, **284–7**, 286, 425–6, 430
link, 59, **287–8**
linking, attacks on, 287, **288**
Lins, Jose, 67
Lippmann, Walter, 370–1
literary criticism, 288–9
Little Hans, 24, 29, **290**, 367
Locke, John, 26, 362
Loewald, Hans, 152, 229, **290–1**, 366
Loewenstein, Rudolf, 176, 275
logic, 174, 286, **291–3**
Logos, 145–6, **293**
logotherapy, 152
Long, J., 346
look, **293**; *see also* gaze
Loose, Rik, 254
Lóránd, Sándor, 167, 224
Lorenz, K., 149
Lorenzer, A., 284, 286
loss, 114, **293**
love, 111, 116, 145–6, 187, 193, 215, **294**
  debasement in, **294**
  partial, **294**
Lowen, Alexander, 393
Lubbe, T., 63
Lukacs, Georg, 297
Lumière brothers, 168
Luria, Alexander, 284, 407
Lush, D., 346
Luzes, P., 372, 435

Macay, N., 411
MacCannell, Juliet, 164, 289
McCarthy, Patricia, 254
McDougall, Joyce, 177, 431, 434
McGrath, Tom, 254
MacIntyre, Alasdair, 417
MacLeod, Alastair, 73
Magagna, J., 53, 54
Mahler, Margaret S., 45–6, 119, 167, 224, 225, **295**, 388, 431, 474
Main, Mary, 66, 471
Main, T. F., 175, 206
Malan, D. H., 155
male sexuality, 129
Malewski, Jan, 369
manic depressive disorders, 4, 6, 270
manifest content, 281, 288, **297**
Mannheim, Karl, 140
Mannoni, Maud, 121, 177, 386
Mannoni, Octave, 11, 177
Marcel, Gabriel, 152
Marcuse, Herbert, 297, 366, 371, 417, 483
Mariátegui, José Carlos, 355
Marseilles, Walter, 271
Martins, Mario, 66
Marty, Pierre, 177
Marui, Kiyoyasu, 259
Marx, Karl, 18, 186, 215, 292, 297–8, **297–8**, 413, 432, 446
Marxism, 75, 165, 171, 183, 289, **297–8**, 392
masculine principle, 145–6, 219–20, 293
masculinity, 23–4, 164, **298**
Maslow, Abraham, 8
masochism, 15, 118, 127, 222, 236, 251, **298–9**, 408
Mason, Albert, 198
mass psychology, 204
mastery, **129**, 133, 142
maternal body, 267, 268, **314**
maternal reverie, 34, 58, 94–5, 254
maternity, 163
matheme, 64, 174, **300**
matrix, 199, **206–7**, 210, 252
Matte Blanco, Ignacio, 85, 236, 257, 292, **300–1**, 316
Matthis, Iréne, 449
May, Rollo, 104, 152, **301–2**, 330, 374, 389
Mayer, E. L., 338
Meadows, Phyllis W., 439
meaning, 281, 286
meaning therapy, 152
medical approach, 18, 87, 330
medical practice, and psychoanalysis, 41
medicine, evidence-based, **151**
medico-legal interface, 173, **302–3**
Meerwein, Fritz, 450
Meier, C. A., **303**
Meissner, W. W., 398
melancholia, 9, 113, 253, **303**
Meloy, J. R., 384
Meltzer, Donald, 46, 53–4, 146, 268, **303–4**, 386
memory, 20, 230, 253, **304**
  desire and understanding, **306–7**
  loss of *see* amnesia
  repressed *see* abreaction
  screen, 20, 168, **414**
memory wars, 20, **304–5**
men, and homosexuality, 220
Menaker, E., 299
Mendilaharzu, Sélika Acevedo de, 484
Meng, Heinrich, 190, 450
Menninger, Karl, 482
mental disorders, classification of, **87–8**, 173
Menzies Lyth, I., 84
Merleau-Ponty, Maurice, 152, 240, 366, 367, 442
Mesmer, Franz Anton, 372
meta-analysis, 151
metaphor, 76, 92, 174, 281, **307**, 354, 405
metapsychology, 5, 6, 15, 33, 131, 132, 176, 182, **307**, 326
metonymy, 124, 174, 281, **307**
Metz, C., 168
Meumann, Ernst, 452
Meyer, Adolf, 450, 480
military psychiatry, 56, 182, 206
Miller, Emmanuel, 490
Miller, Jacques-Alain, 177, 276, **308**
Miller, L., 326
Milner, B. A., 35, 316, 469
mind, cybernetic model of the, 159
Minkowski, Hermann, 456
mirror stage, 18, 61, 132–3, 153, 176, 229, 276–7, 285, **309**
mirroring, 89, 138, 272, 285–6, 293
misrecognition of reality, 229, **309**
Mitchell, Juliet, 162, 164, 241–2, **309–10**, 427, 429
Mitchell, Stephen A., **310**, 393, 395, 421–2

Mitscherlich, Alexander, 191
Money, John, 188–9
Money-Kyrle, Roger, 99, 149–50
Moniz, Egas, 371
Moody, Robert, 243
Moore, M.-S., 432
moral defence, 47, **109**, 157
moral therapy, 81
morality, 147, 223
Morawetz, Ernst, 271
Morgenthaler, Fritz, 148
Morita therapy, 259
mother, **313–14**
  desire to kill, 16–17
  good-enough, 124, 231, **313–14**
  primary maternal preoccupation, **375–6**
  see also breast; maternity
mother-child relationship, 66, 71, 167, 225
mother-infant relationship, 53, 111, 158–9, 161, 194
  compliance in, 90–1
  depressive position, 115
  and development, 119
  non-verbal communication, 89
mothering, 117, 118, 182, **315**
mourning, 66, 114, 149, **315**
Muir, E., 351
Müller-Braunschweig, Carl, 321, 413
Müller-Braunschweig, Hans, 191
Mulvey, L., 169
Murphy, Ann, 255
Musatti, Cesare, 256, 257
Myers-Briggs Type Indicator (MBTI), 382
myths, 17, 31, 34, 59, 195, 218, 287, **317–18**, 336

Nacht, Sacha, 176, 177, 275
Nagel, Ernest, 413
naikan therapy, 259
name-of-the-father, 7, 161, 173, 270, 278–9, **318–19**
naming, 285, **319**
narcissism, 4, 15, 35, 61, 79, 80, 127, 133, 134, 139, 147, 226, 272, 277, 294, **319–21**
  in homosexuality, 221
narcissistic identification, 228, 238
narcissistic libido, 19
narcissistic neurosis, 113, 122, **320**
narrative self, 285
Nathan, Tobie, 148
Navarro, Fernando Allende, 85
Nazism, 52, 71, 176, 179, 183, 187, 190–1, 216, 219, 244, 265, 271, **321**
need, 111, 116, 158–9, **322**
Needham, R., 27
negation, 112, **322**
negative capability, 59, **322**
negative therapeutic reaction, 29, 53, 109, **323**

Nelson, Marie, 12
Neumann, Erich, 23, 137, **324–5**
neurasthenia, 29, **325**
neuropathology, 81, 327
neuropsychoanalysis, 120, **325–7**
neuroscience, 33, 150
neurosis, 77, 87, 106, 112, 122, 155, 171, 181, 222, 223, 229, 318, **327–9**
neutrality, 183, **329**
Nieto, Marta, 484
Nietzsche, Friedrich Wilhelm, 151, 152, 197, 237, 261, 264, **329–30**, 361, 364, 382
nirvana, 16, 71–2
Nissl, Franz, 260
Nitsun, M., 25–6, 202
Nolan, Maebh, 254
non-verbal communication, 83, 89, 150, 338
normality, 148, **330**
Northfield experiment, 206
noumena, 59
Nousiainen, Tapio, 170
Nowlan, Kate, 255
nuclear conflicts, 200–1
nucleus, 90, 287
Nunberg, Hermann, 175, 450
Nycander, Gunnar, 448

O (ultimate reality), 37, 57, 59, 140, 151, 254, **331**
Oberholzer, Emil, 357
Obholzer, Anton, 14
object, **331–3**
  attitudes towards the, 219–20
  splitting of the, **437**
  use of the, **485**
  see also accepting object; bad objects; exciting object; external object; good objects; ideal object; internal object; part object; rejecting object; transitional objects
object choice, 21, 220, **333**
  narcissistic, **320**
object a (Lacan), 30, 64, 77, 116, 164, 174; *see also* part object
object relations, 4, 48, 126, 138, 166, 179, 188, 218, 285, **333**
  feminism, 162, 163
  Lacan critique, **335**
object relations theory, 19, 38, 156, 157, 172, 206, 241, 245, 293, **333–6**
  existential critique, **334–5**
  group, **335–6**
objectivity, 100, 147, 148
observation, 82–3, 118, 129, 197, 247
  empathic vantage point of, **141**
  see also infant observation; participant observation
obsessional neurosis, 9, 21, 91, 125, 212, 318, **336**

Odier, Charles, 450
Oedipus complex, 17, 49, 66, 76, 82, 90, 161, 183, 218, 221–2, 223, 232, 245, 261, 279, 280, **339–41**, 429
  negative, 220, **323**
Oedipus myth, 59, 287
offenders, with mental disorders, 173
Ogden, Thomas, 22, 333, 338, 249
Ohtsuki, Kenji, 259
O'Malley Dunlop, Ellen, 255
ontogenesis, 31
open systems, 159, 207, 210
Oppolzer, Theodor, 68
opposite wishes, theory of, 141, 233
oral attitude, 189, **342**
oral eroticism, 6
oral fixation, 170
oral phase 4, 67–8, **342**
oral sadism, 4, 16, **342**
Orange, Donna M., 249
Orford, E., 41
Ornstein, Paul and Anna, 102
Orozco, José Torres, 308
Ortiguez, Edmond, 12
O'Shaughnessy, Edna, 13
Ossipow, N. J., 102, 406
Other, the, 22, 31, 61, 64, 123, 133, 252, 253, 263, 277–8, 293, **343**
  response to demand of, 111, 116–17, 190
Otto, Rudolf, 331
overdetermination, 144, **347**

Pankejeff, Serguï *see* Wolf Man
Pappenheim, Bertha *see* Anna O
paranoia, 79, 138, 172, 215, 270, **348**
paranoid-schizoid position, 47, 59, 81, 192, 212, 227, 241, 268, 269, 270, **348–9**, **379**
parapraxis, 90, 146, 181, 223, **350**
Paret, I., 431
Parin, Paul, 148, 450
Parin-Matthèy, Goldy, 148, 450
Parkin, Alan, 73
Parsons, Talcott, 482
part object, 171, 236, 270, 292, **351–2**
partial drive, 74, 91, 128–9, 173–4, 190, **352**
participant observation, 100, 247, **352–3**
passage à l'acte, 5, **353**
passivity, **5**, 91, 92, 162, 216, 219, 220, 221, 298, 299, 404
Pastorini, Rafael Pérez, 484
Paton, H. J., 55
patriarchy, 162, 164, 223, 289
Pauli, Wolfgang, 32, 265, 454
Payne, Sylvia, 56, 96, 194
PDD *see* Pervasive Developmental Delay (PDD)
Peirce, Charles Sanders, 174, 425
Peña, Saúl, 356
penis, 66, 76, 162

penis envy, 24, 143, 162–3, 222, **354**
Perls, Fritz, 11, 389
Perrier, François, 177
Perrotti, Nicola, 256
Perry, B. D., 40, 471
Perry, H. S., 444
personality
  development, 8
  as if, **36**, 62, 118
  psychoanalytic function of the, 58–9, 287, **381**
  see also character
personality disorder, **79–80**, 266, 272; *see also* borderline personality disorder; borderline psychosis
Pervasive Developmental Delay (PDD), 121
perversion, 6, 15, 76, 122, 279, **356**, 443
Pfeffer, Arnold, 344
Pfister, Oskar, **356–7**, 397, 448, 450
phallocentrism, 89, 162–3, 164, 358
phallus, 4, 76, 190, 263, 278–9, 280, **358**
phantasy, 47, 49, 105, 123, 161, 269, **358–9**
  traversal of, **472–3**
  unconscious, **477–8**
phenomenology, 55, 64, 75, 104, 143, 153, 178, 195, 209, 215, 217, 239–40, **360–1**, 365
Philippson, Ludwig, 184
philosopher's stone, 17
philosophy, **361–7**
phobia, 29, 290, **367–8**
phylogenesis, 31
Piaget, Jean, 401, 421
Pichon-Rivière, Enrique, 449
Pine, F., 63
Pines, Malcolm, 13
Plato, 14, 216, 361, 362
play, 101, 120, 145, 159, 174, 267, **368**, 439
pleasure, 123, 236, **369**
pleasure principle, 72, 263, **369**
Plutarch, 451
Poincaré, J. Henri, 416–17
Poinsot, John, 425
politics, **370–1**
Pontalis, Jean-Bertrand, 177, 282
Popper, Karl, 24, 413, 414
postcolonialism, 289
postmodernism, 35, 154, 167, 272, 366–7, 483–4
poststructuralism, 163–4, 290
potentiality, 186–7
Pozzi, M., 40
Prados, Miguel, 73
Pratt, Joseph, 205
preconception, 94, 197, 285, **373**
predicate logic, 291–2
Prego, Luis Enrique, 484
Prego, Vida Maberino de, 484
preoedipal stage, 4, 71, 290, **374**
presence, 143, **374**
Press, Sydney, 14
Pribram, Karl, 326
primal scene, 20, 110, **375**
primary identification, **228**
primary process, 37, 107, 123, 178, 286, **376**
privation, 28, 76, 188, 280, **376–7**
process psychology, 215
projection, 108, 132, 166, 168, 219, 229, **378**
projective identification, 19, 51, 54, 58–9, 82, 109, 111, 112, 228, 229, 269–70, 285, **378–9**
  and maternal reverie, 94–5
  and splitting, 56–7, 378
propositional functions, 292
psyche, 15, 26–8, 47, 143, 230
  and the Self, 17, 31
  splits in the, 166
  structure of the, **440–1**
psyche-soma, **379–80**, 434
psychiatry, 151, 187, 225, **380**
  classification in, **87–8**
  depression in, **114**
  see also forensic psychiatry; military psychiatry
psychic energy, 77, 128, 133, 143, 166, 264
psychical reality, 47, 57, 111, 143, 155, 161, 226, 242, 253, **380**
psychical research, 337–8
psychoanalysis
  compared with anthropology, 26–8
  ethics in, **146–7**, 246
  film portrayals of the profession, 168
  IPA definition of,244–5
  methodology, 8, 151
  'modern', **311–12**
  as the talking cure, 122, 181
psychoanalytic feminism, 189
psychoanalytic object, 59, 254, **381**
psychobiography, 144, 145, 288, 289
psychodynamic approach, 114, 129
psychogenesis, 140
psychoneurosis, 121, 122
psychopathology, 6, 118, 154, 169, 181, 283, 327
psychopathy, 80, **384**
Psychopathy Checklist (PCLR), 384
psychopharmacology, 121
psychosis, 3, 58, 60, 87, 112, 122, 173, 198, 214, 229, **384–6**
psychosomatics, 17–18, 197–8, 225, **433–5**, 483
psychosynthesis, 23
punishment, 212, 322, **387**
Pyle, Mary, 255
Pythagoras, 413

queer theory, 289
quilting point, 270, **387**

Rabanal, César Rodríguez, 356
Rachman, S., 283, 368
Racker, Heinrich, 33, 67, 98, 100, 146, **388**
Radó, Sándor, 6, 165, 183, 190, 224, 412
Ragland, Ellie, 289
Rajka, Tibor, 225
Raknes, Ola, 330
Ramirez, Santiago, 308
Ramos, Samuel, 308
randomisation, 151
Rangell, Leo A., **388–9**
Rank, Otto, 29, 35, 43, 71, 117, 166, 182, 221, 288, 330, **389**
Rapaport, David, 5, 6, 93, 134, 170, 192, **389–90**
Rascovsky, A., 32, 33
Rascovsky, M., 32
Rat Man (Ernst Lanzer), 290, 336, 361, **390**
reaction formation, 24, 108, 237, **390–1**
reader-response criticism, 289
Real, the, 22, 51, 61, 64, 108, 112, 123, 174, 275, 279, 292, **391**
reality
  internal, **241–2**
  and language, 152
  misrecognition of, 229, **309**
  psychical *see* psychical reality
  testing, 138
  ultimate *see* O (ultimate reality)
reality principle, 124, 155, 263, **391**
reason, 184–5, 223, 293, 390
Rechardt, Eero, 170
Redl, Fritz, 205
Reeder, Jörgen, 449
reflection, 128, 133, 153, 248
Régis, E., 176
regression, 21, 48, 108, 111, 142, 171, 213, 274, **392**
rehabilitative psychoanalysis, 198
Reich, Anni, 103, 190
Reich, Wilhelm, 64, 134, 169, 183, 190, 224, 297, 330, **392–3**
Reik, Theodor, 11, 190, 338
Reiser, M., 304, 326
rejected/rejecting object, 28, 47, 121, 126, 158, 159, 242, 332, **393**
relational psychoanalysis, 24, 35–6, 61, 165–7, 272, 367, **393–5**
relationism, **395–7**
  body, **61**
  and countertransference, **100**
  and transference, 100, **463–4**
religion, 229, **397–9**
reparation, 92, 101, **399**
repetition compulsion, 46, 106, 218, 286, **400**
representation, 54, **400–1**, 412
repressed, return of the, 112, 158, 322, **401**

repression, 24–5, 76, 107, 108, 124, 160, 218, 220, 242, 255, 291, **402**
resistance, 5, 135, 136, 144, 153, 229, 291, **403**
  and defence, 108, **109**
reverie, maternal, 34, 58, 94–5, 254, **403**
Rey, Carlos, 484
Rey de Castro, Alvaro, 356
Rhode, M., 130
Rice, E., 184
Rickman, John, 56, 195, 206, 309
Ricoeur, Paul, 152, 217, 483
Rieff, P., 147
Riklin, Jr, Franz, 211, 243
Rioch, David, 101, 200, 247
Rioch, Janet, 101, 247
Rioch, Margaret, 210
Ritalin, 40
Rittmeister, John, 191
Rivers, W. H. R., 156
Riviere, Joan, 95, 162, 490
Rivière, Pichon, 32, 33, 484
Rizzuto, A.-M., 398
Roazen, Paul, 146
Robertson, J., 84
Rogers, Carl, 389
Roheim, Gezá, 148, 190, 225
Roman Catholicism, 184–5, 254
Rorschach, Hermann, 450
Rorschach test, 271
Rose, G., 35, 36
Rose, Jacqueline, 289
Rosenfeld, Herbert, 6, 15, 268, 304, 416, 449
Rosenfeld, S. Kut, 63
Rosenthal, Tatjana, 406
Roth, Philip, 482
Rustin, M., 85
Rycroft, Charles F., 231, **407**, 429

saboteur, internal, 28, 158, **242**
Sachs, Hans, 48, 64, 186, 190, 429
Sachs, Wulf, 11–12, 13
Saciuk, R., 370
Sade, Marquis de, 147, 443, 486
Sadeh, A., 431
sadism, 127, 129, 251, 288, 408
sado-masochism, 15, 236, **408**
Salecl, Renata, 289
Salomé, Lou-Andreas, 162, 447, 454
Sandler, Anne-Marie, 10, 409
Sandler, Joseph, 10, 13, 42, 256, 372, **408–9**
Santos, J., 372
Sartre, Jean-Paul, 18, 152, 153, 216, 360, 365–6, **409–10**
  on anxiety, 30
  on authenticity, 45
  on bad faith, 45, 143, 410
  on ego, **133**
  on existence, 178
  on facticity, 156
  on Flaubert, **171**, 335, 410
  on Freud, 410
  on gaze, 293, 410
  on intentionality, 240
  on intersubjectivity, 251
  on nothingness, **331**
  on the self, **419**
  on situation, 143
  on subject-object, 334–5
Saussure, Ferdinand de, 150, 174, 277, 281, 286, 354, 365, 425, 426, 430
Saussure, Raymond de, 450
scapegoat, 195, 201, **410**
Schafer, Roy, 152, 192, 366, 389, **410–11**
Scharff, D. E., 333
Scharff, J. S., 333
Scheidlinger, S., 199, 336
schema-L, 22, 138, **411**
Scherer, K., 8
Scheunert, Gerhard, 191
Schilder, Paul, 113, 175, 205
Schiller, Friedrich von, 288
schizoid process, 158, **411**
schizophrenia, 3, 60, 140, 173, 187, 198, 238, 268, 270, 292
Schjelderup, Harald, 330
Schmale, A. H., 434
Schmidt, Otto, 406
Schmidt, Vera, 406
Scholastics, 239, 425
Schopenhauer, Arthur, 16, 264, 329, 361, 364, **411–12**
Schore, A. N., 128, 326, 351
Schreber, Daniel, 220, 290, **412**
Schultz-Hencke, Harald, 190, 191, 321, **412–13**
Schur, Max, 71, 184
science, 43, 66, 117, **413–14**
Scott, Clifford, 73
screen memory, 20, 168, **414**
Searles, Harold F., 98, 100, **415**
Sebeok, Thomas, 425
Sechehaye, Marguerite A., 450
secondary process, 54, 178, **415**
seduction theory, 181, 232, 294, **415–16**
Segal, Hanna Maria, 35, 212, 268, 304, 369, **416**, 452–3
Seguín, Carlos Alberto, 355
selected fact, 59, 83, **416–17**
self, 235, 394–5, **417–19**
  bipolar, 272, **422**
  defences of the (Jung, Carl G.), **109**
  disorders of the, **422–3**
  and ego (Jung, Carl G.), 23, 132, 137, **418**
  false, **160–1**
  fragmentation, **423**
  group, **211**
  and psyche, 17, 31
  split, 222
  true, 213, 231, **473**
  turning against the, **474**
self psychology, 73, 89, 109, 245, 271–3, **420–1**
  and countertransference, **98**
  curative fantasy, **102**
  defence and resistance, **109**
  group psychotherapy, **210–11**
  Oedipus complex, **340**, 420
  splitting, **437–8**
self-deception, 152, 153, 154, 215
self-system, 87, **421–2**
selfobject, 11, 28, 89, 98, 102, 131, 272, **423–5**
  transference, **464–5**
selfobject relationship, 109, 420, **424**
  corrective, **97**
  phantasy, **359**
semanalysis, 274
semiotics, 285, 286, **425–6**
separation, 46, 75, 76, 119, 149, 194, **426**
separation anxiety, 29, 66, 182, 213, **426**
Servadio, Emilio, 233, 256
sexology, 166
sexual abuse, 155, 157, 181, 232, **428**
sexual difference, 162–4, 279, 292, **426**
sexual drive, 67–8, 127, 173–4
sexual excitation, 146, 167–8
sexual identity, 82
sexual intercourse, 105, 123, 150
sexual inversion, 220
sexual relation, 294, **426–7**
sexuality, **8**, 128, 155, 166, 172, 278, 294, **427**; *see also* female sexuality; genital sexuality; infantile sexuality; male sexuality
sexuation, 90, 174, 279
shadow, 212, 235, **428–9**
Shakespeare, William, 288
shame, 134, 253, **429**
Shapiro, T., 286
Sharpe, Ella Freeman, 95, 96, 404–5, **429**
Sheehan, Helen, 254
Shevrin, H., 93
Shore, A., 40–1
sign, 150, 281, 425–6, **430**
signal anxiety, 30–1, 92, 108, 137
signified, 174, **430**
signifier, 18, 88, 111, 117, 123, 124, 150, 164, 174, 190, 214, 277, 278, 281, 406, **430**
Silberer, Herbert, 188
Simenauer, Erich, 11
Simmel, Ernst, 190
Simonsen, Hjordis, 330
Sinason, V., 283
Singer, J. L., 230
sinthome, 64, **430**
situation, 52, 143, 160, 186

Sjögren, Lars, 449
Skar, Patricia, 255
Skelton, Ross, 255
skin phenomena, 53–4, 83, 236
Skinner, B. F., 49, 283, 286
Skynner, Robin, 195
Smit, Elmore, 14
Smith, Mary, 254
Socarides, D., 470
social character, 186, **432–3**
social psychology, 205
field theory 100
social unconscious, 208, **478–9**
socialisation, 101, 138
sociogenesis, 140
Socrates, 8, 14
Sohn-Rethel, Alfred, 298
Sokolik, Zbigniew, 369
Sokolnicka, Maria, 369
Sollers, Philippe, 274
Solms, Karen, 14
Solms, Mark, 13, 14, 195, 326
Sonn, Leslie, 14
Sophocles, 175, 288
soul, 146, 242
beautiful, **49**
specificity theory, 97, **436**
speech, 111, 122, 123, 188, 277, **436**
in animals, 149–50
see also full speech
Sperling, M., 433
Spielrein, Sabine, 162, 406, 450
Spitz, René A., 119, 191
splitting, 56, 60, 112, 125, 142, 166, 167–8, 193, 219, 227, 242, 269
of the ego, **436**
'enforced', **437**
of the object, **437**
self psychology, **437–8**
Spock, Benjamin, 482
Spotnitz, Hyman, 311, **438–9**
Sprince, M., 63
Sroufe, Alan, 39
Stamm, J., 113
statistical methods, 151
Stein, Sam, 14
Stekel, Wilhelm, 181, 433
Sterba, Richard, 11, 52, 259
Stern, Daniel, 9, 62, 285, 351, 362, 431, 479
Sternbach, Oscar, 105
Stockholm syndrome, 228
Stokes, Adrian, 35
Stoller, Robert, 35, 189
Stolorow, Daphne S., 249
Stolorow, Robert D., 249, **440**, 464, 470, 471
Strachey, James, 91, 110, 194, 469–70, 490
Strong, Rupert, 254
structuralism, 27, 33, 286
Stuchliks, J., 102
subject, 31, 64, 228, 252, 253, 274, 289, **441–2**
and ego, 132, 278
and language, 117, 122, 125, 281
subjectivity, 43, 100, 141, 145, 161, 189, 195, 247, 275, **442**
sublimation, 34, 45, 100–1, 134, 220, 274, 284, **443**
suicide, **443–4**
Sullivan, Harry Stack, 55, 86, 100, 101, 167, 186, 205, 230, 237, 247, 310, 312, 371, 394, **444–5**, 449, 479, 481
on participant observation, **351–2**
on selective inattention, 417
on the self-system, **421–2**
Sulloway, F. J., 25, 326
Sung Hee Kim, 273
superego, 60, 92, 94, 106, 134, 144, 159, 162, 163, 171, 212, 223, 226, 232, 253, **445–6**
surplus jouissance, 263, **446**
Surrealism, 169, 176
Sutherland, J. D., 333, 417
Suttie, Ian D., 342, **446–7**
Suzuki, D., 72
Swoboda, Hermann, 172
symbolic equation, **452–3**
Symbolic, the, 22, 47, 61, 64, 112, 174, 253, 275, 277, 278, 292, **452**
symbolisation, 96, 250, **453**
symbols, 126, 143, 212, 234, 286, **451–2**
formation, **451–2**
Symington, J., 53, 283
symptoms, 4, **453–4**
synapses, 94, 156
synchronicity, 98, **454**
systems theory, 66, 199
intersubjective, **250**
Szasz, Thomas, 35
Szekely, Lajos, 448
Székely-Kovács, Alice, 48
Szondi, Leopold, 450
Szur, R., 85, 115

t-group movement, 205
taboos, 101, 150, 223, 232
Tähkä, Veikko, 170
Tamm, Alfhild, 169, 447–8
Taoism, 273
Target, M., 305, 343
Tarnopolsky, A., 62
Tausk, Victor, **454–5**
Tavistock model, 56, 200, 210–11
Taylor, G. J., 434
T(beta), 254
technique, 95–6, 141, 144, 146, 166, 235, 237, 485
teleology, 69, 235, **455**
Terman, D., 470
textual analysis, 168–9
TFP *see* transference focused psychotherapy (TFP)
Thanatos, 222–3, 224, **456**; *see also* death drive
Thenon, Jorge, 32
therapeutic community, 175, 206, 280
thing, 4, 59, 77, **457**
thing representation, 286, **457**
thinking, Bion's theory of, 58, 197, 285, **457**
Thoma, H., 110
Thompson, Clara, 101, 167, 247, 299
Thompson, M. G., 153, 154
Thomson, P. G., 98
Thornton, E., 25
thoughts, 150, **458**
thrownness, 143, 156, 216
Tillich, Paul, 152, 301, 302, 475
time, 238, 312, **456**, **458–60**
Todorov, Tzvetan, 274
Tolpin, M., 340
Tolpin, P., 423
topography, 94, 245, **460**
topology, 95, **460**
Törngren, Pehr Henrik, 447
Tószegi-Freund, Antal, 224
training, 82, 97, 139, 166–7, 221, 235
standards (IPA), 244–6
transcendent function, 143, 231, 234, **462**
transference, 17, 22, 48, 81, 83, 100, 109, 113, 123, 126, 148, 153, 155, 159, 183, 208, 218, 219, 265, 268, 277, **462–6**
creativity of, **465**
forward and trailing edge, **465–6**
organising activity of, **466**
see also countertransference
transference focused psychotherapy (TFP), 122
transference neurosis, **464**
transference selfobject, **464–5**
transformation, 59, 76–7, 234, 254, **466–8**
transformational grammar, 286
transitional objects, 168, 285, 398, **468–9**
transitional space, 35, 130, 230, 289
transitional techniques, 121, **469**
transitivism, 138, **469**
trauma, 20, 40–1, 66, 81, 167, 171, 182, 266–7, 279, **471–2**
Trevarthen, C., 45, 351
Trilling, Lionel, 289, 482
Tripet, Lise, 12
Trotsky, Leon, 407
Trotter, Wilfred, 56
Trowell, J., 346
true self, 213, 231, **473**
Turo, J. K., 110
Turquet, P., 49, 202
Tustin, Frances, 46, 386, 469, **474–5**

umwelt, 143, 237, **476**
Unamuno, Miguel de, 152

uncanny, 155, 169, 288, **476**
unconscious, 10, 54, 90, 124, 126, 162, 215, 223–4, 291, **476–9**
  formation of the, **174**
  interpretation of the, 43, 248
  intersubjective account, **478**
  and language, 20, 95, 226, 276, 285
  see also collective unconscious; social unconscious
unconscious processes, 148, 247–8
understanding, 253, 260, **306–7**
undoing, 108, **479**
Usandivaras, R. J., 209

vagina, 163, 189, 222
Valabrega, Jean-Paul, 177
van der Hoop, J. H., 324
Van der Leeuw, P. J., 324
Van Deurzen, E., 475
van Ophuijsen, Johann H. W., 11, 450
Verwerfung see foreclosure
victimisation, 118, 173
Vigotsky, N., 407
vision, binocular, **54**
Vogt, Ragnar, 330
Von Franz, Marie-Louise, 23, 382, **487**
von Gebsattel, V. E., 64, 75

Waal, Nic, 330
Walewska, Katarzyna, 369
Wallerstein, J., 63
Wallerstein, Robert, 344, 345, 483, **487–8**
Walrond-Skinner, S., 217
Walser, Hans, 449
Warnock, M., 178
Warren, Bengt, 449
Waters, Everet, 39
Watson, J. B., 49
Watt, D., 327
Weber, Alfred, 140
Weiner, H., 434
Weininger, Otto, 172
Weiss, Edoardo, 256
Westmann, Heinz, 243
Wheelwright, Joseph Balch, **488–9**
Whitaker, D. S., 199
White, Victor, 265
White, William Alanson, 262
Whitmont, Edward C., **489**
Widigier, T. A., 62
Wilder, Thornton, 217
Wilhelm, Richard, 265
Wilke, G., 202
Williams, A., 111
Williams, G., 130
Wilson, Edmund, 289
Wilson, L., 110
Wilson, Woodrow, 370
Windholz, Emanuel, 102, 103
Winn, Roy, 41, 42
Winnicott, Donald Woods, 16, 28, 105, 121, 162, 170, 194, 213, 223, 249, 268, 285, 289, 333, 474, **489–92**
  on antisocial behaviour, 110–11
  on attachment, 427
  on breakdown, 67
  capacity to be alone, 124
  on character formulation, 238
  on communication, 89
  on compliance, 90–1
  on concern, 91–2
  on countertransference, **98–9**
  on creativity, 100–1
  on dependence, **112–13**
  on eating disorders, 130
  on the false self, **160–1**, 313, 438
  on the good enough mother, **313–14**, 334
  on holding, **218–19**
  on illusion, 229
  on imagination, **231**
  on impingement, **231–2**, 313
  on infant observation, 235, 350
  on object use, **485**
  on paradox, **347**
  on play, **368**, 439
  on primary maternal preoccupation, 313, **375–6**
  on psyche-soma, **379–80**, 434
  on religion, 398
  on spontaneity, **438**
  on transitional objects, 431, **468–9**
  transitional space, 35, 230, 335
  on true self, **473**
Wisdom, J. O., 255
wish fulfilment, 213, 229, 288, **492**
Wittels, Fritz, 180
Wittenberg, Isca, 14
Wittgenstein, Ludwig, 411
Wittkower, Eric, 73
Wolf, Alexander, **493**
Wolf, E., 98, 109, 205, 422–3, 464–5
Wolf Man, 71, 110, 290, **493**
Wolfe, Toni, 208
Wolff, Antonia, **493**
Wolff Stomersee, Alessandra Tomasi, 256
Wolstein, B., 102, 419, 463
women
  and borderline personality disorder, 62, 80
  conflict between eroticism and motherliness, 118
  Freud on, 161–2, 182
  gynaecophilic, 220
  and homosexuality, 221
  Lacan on, **493–4**
  male dread of, 222
Woolf, Virginia, 162
word representation, 286, **494**
Wright, Elizabeth, 289
Wulff, Moishe, 406, 407
Wundt, Wilhelm, 382

Yabe, Y., 259
Yalom, I. D., 152, 200, 209–10, 330, 475
Yeomans, F. E., 122
Yerushalmi, Y. H., 184
Yoshimoto, I., 259

Zavitsianos, George, 196
Zeigarnik effect, 485, **494**
Zen Buddhism, 72, 259
Zinkin, L., 209
Žižek, Slavoj, 289
Zulliger, Hans, 450
Zurich School of psychoanalysis, 22, 23, 243, 244